Macmillan
Encyclopedia of
Architects

Editorial board

Macmillan
Encyclopedia of

Architects

ADOLF K. PLACZEK, *editor in chief*

Volume 4

THE FREE PRESS
a division of Macmillan Publishing Co., Inc.
New York

COLLIER MACMILLAN PUBLISHERS
LONDON

THE FREE PRESS
A Division of Macmillan Publishing Co., Inc.
866 Third Avenue, New York, N. Y. 10022

Collier Macmillan Canada, Inc.

Library of Congress Catalog Card Number: 82-17256

Printed in the United States of America

printing number

1 2 3 4 5 6 7 8 9 10

Library of Congress Cataloging in Publication Data
Main entry under title:

Macmillan encyclopedia of architects.

    Includes bibliographies and indexes.
      1. Architects—Biography.   I. Placzek, Adolf K.
II. Title: Encyclopedia of architects.
NA40.M25   1982   720′.92′2 [B]   82-17256
ISBN 0-02-925000-5 (set)

SCHMIDT, CLARENCE

Clarence Schmidt (1897–?) built a seven-story, thirty-five-room complex of haphazardly added boxlike units that climb the slope of a mountain near Woodstock, New York. Both the interior, wired with colored lights, and the surrounding exterior "garden" include shrines and grottoes filled with found and natural objects wrapped in aluminum foil that is covered with tarred string and studded with mirrors.

JANET KAPLAN

WORKS

*Late 1930s–1967, Journey's End; *1964–1967, House of Mirrors; *1968–1971, Mark II; Woodstock, N.Y.

BIBLIOGRAPHY

BLASDEL, GREGG, and LIPKE, BILL 1974 "Clarence Schmidt: Toward Journey's End." Pages 42–51 in Walker Art Center, *Naives and Visionaries*. New York: Dutton.
CARDINAL, ROGER 1972 Pages 65–68 in *Outsider Art*. New York: Praeger.
KAPROW, ALLEN 1966 Pages 170–172 in *Assemblage, Environments & Happenings*. New York: Abrams.

S

CONTINUED

SCHMIDT, HANS

Hans Schmidt (1893–1972) was the most important theoretician of modern architecture in Switzerland; his writings are marked by his Marxist attitude.

Schmidt studied architecture in Zurich. In Rotterdam, Netherlands, he met MART STAM, with whom he edited the magazine *ABC* (1924–1928). In 1928, he settled in Basel, where he had an office with PAUL ARTARIA from 1925 to 1930. Their architecture reflects his idea that building is not architecture but technology and therefore a matter of necessity.

As a result of his political views Schmidt joined ERNST MAY and others to work in the Soviet Union from 1930 to 1937. The architectural debates there caused him to turn to classicism which was, however, closer to his earlier architecture than it may seem: "Behind the question of architecture there is always the question of classicism as the idea of logical architecture," he wrote after he returned to Basel.

In 1956, Schmidt was called to East Berlin to work at the Deutsche Bauakademie; in 1970 he returned again to Basel.

MARTIN STEINMANN

WORKS

1924, House Im Schlipf; 1927, House (with Paul

Artaria) Wenkenhalde; 1928, House (with Artaria) Sandreuterweg; Riehen, Switzerland. 1928, Schorenmatten Estate (with Artaria); 1929, House for Single Women (with Artaria); Basel, Switzerland. 1929–1932, Neubühl Estate (with Artaria, RUDOLF STEIGER, CARL HUBACHER, MAX ERNST HAEFELI, WERNER MOSER, EMIL ROTH), Zurich. 1935–1936, Apartment Buildings, Orsk, Russia. 1943–1946, Infection Hospital, Basel, Switzerland. 1946–1947, Haselrain Estate, Riehen, Switzerland. 1951, Apartment Building, Basel, Switzerland.

BIBLIOGRAPHY

"Hans Schmidt: 1893–1972." 1972 *Werk* 59, no. 10:548–562.

ROSSI, ALDO 1974 *Hans Schmidt: Contributi all'architettura 1924–1964.* Italian translation of Hans Schmidt, *Beiträge zur Architektur* (1965) with an introduction by Rossi. Milan: Angeli.

SCHMIDT, HANS 1965 *Beiträge zur Architektur: 1924–1964.* Edited with an introduction by Bruno Flierl. Berlin: Bauwesen.

SCHMIDT, HANS 1970 *Gestaltung und umgestaltung der Stadt.* Berlin: Bauwesen.

SCHMIDT, HANS, and BLATTER, HANS 1943 *Schweizerische Regional- und Landesplanung.* Zurich.

VÉRY, FRANÇOIS 1972 "Hans Schmidt et la construction de la ville socialiste d'Orsk." *VH lol* 7–8:147–155.

SCHMIDT, GARDEN, and MARTIN

The Chicago partnership of Schmidt, Garden, and Martin consisted of Richard Ernest Schmidt (1865–1958), Hugh Mackie Gordon Garden (1873–1961), and Edgar Martin (1875–1951). Schmidt, who was trained at the Massachusetts Institute of Technology, began independent practice in 1887, hiring Garden as head designer in 1895. Garden had worked for various architects, including Henry Ives Cobb, Howard Van Doren Shaw, and FRANK LLOYD WRIGHT. Garden frequently exhibited in the Chicago Architectural Club annuals of the 1890s. His buildings designed before World War I often bear innovative ornament comparable to that of LOUIS H. SULLIVAN and other Chicago school greats. Martin, an architect and structural engineer, was with the firm until 1926 when he became a partner in Pond, Pond, Martin, and Lloyd. Schmidt, Garden, and Martin specialized in industrial, commercial, and hospital work. Their successors, Schmidt, Garden, and Erickson continue to specialize in health care and educational facilities under design director Peter Pran.

JOHN ZUKOWSKY

WORKS

1896, Joseph Theurer House; 1898, Montgomery Ward and Company Office Tower (later altered); 1902, Albert F. Madlener House; 1902, Schoenhofen Brewery Building; 1904, Chapen and Gore Building; 1905, Chicago Athletic Association Annex; 1906, Montgomery Ward and Company Warehouses; 1906, Michael Reese Hospital; 1910, Chandler Apartments; 1911, Dwight Building; 1913, Cook County Hospital; *1913, Underwriter's Laboratories (addition); 1917, Mergenthaler Linotype Building; 1919, Ambassador Hotel; Chicago.

BIBLIOGRAPHY

A collection of 2,593 drawings by Schmidt, Garden, and Martin can be found at the Burnham Library of Architecture, Art Institute of Chicago.

BROOKS, H. ALLEN 1972 *The Prairie School: Frank Lloyd Wright and His Midwest Contemporaries.* University of Toronto Press.

DAVID, ARTHUR C. 1904 "The Architecture of Ideas." *Architectural Record* 15:361–384.

GARDEN, HUGH M. G. 1908 "Modern Garden Architecture in Germany." *Architectural Review* 15:81–86.

GARDEN, HUGH M. G. (1939)1966 "The Chicago School." *Prairie School Review* 3, no. 1:1922.

GREENGARD, BERNARD C. 1966 "Hugh M. G. Garden." *Prairie School Review* 3, no. 1:5–18.

HERBERT, WILLIAM 1908 "An American Architecture." *Architectural Record* 23:111–122.

HORNSBY, JOHN ALLAN, and SCHMIDT, RICHARD ERNEST 1914 *Modern Hospital.* Philadelphia and London: Saunders.

PEISCH, MARK L. 1964 *The Chicago School of Architecture: Early Followers of Sullivan and Wright.* New York and Toronto: Random House.

SCHMIDT, RICHARD ERNEST 1930 "The Rise and Growth of Hospitals." Pages 103–113 in Arthur Woltersdorf (editor), *Living Architecture.* Chicago: Kroch.

STURGIS, RUSSELL 1905a "The Schoenhofen Brewery." *Architectural Record* 17, Mar.:201-207.

STURGIS, RUSSELL 1905b "The Madlener House in Chicago." *Architectural Record* 17, Jun.:491–498.

WESTFALL, CARROLL W. 1980 "Manners Matter." *Inland Architect* 24, no. 3:19–23.

SCHMITTHENNER, PAUL

Paul Schmitthenner (1884–1972) was born in Alsace, studied at the Technische Hochschule in Karlsruhe, and in 1909 became director of the Municipal Building Administration in Kolmar, Germany. In 1912, he was appointed chief housing architect by the Reich ministry of the interior, and designed and built, from 1914 to 1917, the innovative and influential *Gartenstadt Staaken* in Berlin under the auspices of the ministry. Staaken consisted of groups of row houses and community facilities carried out in south German and other rural styles, arranged in squares and villagelike streets; it was directly influenced by RICHARD RIEMER-SCHMID's plan for Dresden-Hellerau and less directly by the urban design ideas of THEODOR FISCHER and CAMILLO SITTE.

Staaken brought Schmitthenner fame and helped to secure his appointment to a professorship at Stuttgart in 1918, as a younger colleague of PAUL BONATZ. During the Weimar Republic, Schmitthenner's commissions were few, and he rapidly became one of the leading opponents of the modern movement. As a teacher at Stuttgart and later as a lecturer for the Nazi party, Schmitthenner was an attractive figure to many young architects: personally approachable and outgoing, a talented speaker and gifted storyteller, Schmitthenner argued persuasively that the revolution of 1918 had caused the decline of the best traditions of German architecture and had spawned instead the decadent internationalism of the Bauhaus, the Weissenhof housing development in Stuttgart, and the modern movement in the arts in general.

One of the earliest recruits to Alfred Rosenberg's Nazi organization for artists and architects, the Kampfbund für deutsche Kultur, Schmitthenner enjoyed a brief prominence in Germany after Hitler came to power. He replaced HANS POELZIG as director of the important United Schools of Architecture, Painting and the Applied Arts in Berlin, and he was given the direction of a Nazi housing development in Stuttgart. As Rosenberg's influence in Nazi cultural policy waned, so did Schmitthenner's, and after 1935, he returned to relative obscurity in Stuttgart.

BARBARA MILLER LANE

WORKS

1914–1917, Reichsgartenstadt Staaken, Berlin. 1920–1930, Annette Kolb House; 1920–1930, Rene Schickele House; Badenweiler, Germany. 1920–1930, Wertheimer House; 1922, Werner & Pfleiderer Company Factory; 1922, Paul Schmitthenner House; 1922–1923, Richard Kahn House; 1924, Haus des Deutschtums; 1933–1934, Housing Development (Kochenhof); 1950–1953, Dresdner Bank Buildings; Stuttgart, Germany. 1954, Dresdner Bank, Heilbronn, Germany. 1955, Bayerische Staatsbank (reconstruction); 1956, Frankonia Insurance Company Administrative Offices, Bogenhausen; Munich. 1957, Town Hall, Hechingen, Germany.

BIBLIOGRAPHY

Arbeiten von Paul Schmitthenner: Gebautes und Ungebautes. 1941 Munich: Callwey.
AULER, J. 1973 "Das sanfte Gesetz: Zum Lebenswerk Paul Schmitthenners." *Bauwelt* 64:580–585.
LANE, BARBARA MILLER 1968 *Architecture and Politics in Germany, 1918–1945.* Cambridge, Mass.: Harvard University Press.
PETSCH, JOACHIM 1976 *Baukunst und Stadtplanung im Dritten Reich.* Munich: Hanser.
SCHMITTHENNER, PAUL 1917 *Die Gardenstadt Staaken.* Berlin: Wasmuth.
SCHMITTHENNER, PAUL 1933 *Die 25 Einfamilienhäuser der Holzsiedlung am Kochenhof.* Stuttgart: Hoffmann.
SCHMITTHENNER, PAUL 1933 "Tradition und neues Bauen." *Deutsche Kultur-Wacht* 2, Heft 17:11–12. Text of speech given for Kampfbund in 1931.
SCHMITTHENNER, PAUL 1934 *Die Baukunst im neuen Reich.* Munich: Callwey.
SCHMITTHENNER, PAUL (1932)1940 *Baugestaltung: Das Deutsche Wohnhaus.* Stuttgart: Wittwer.

SCHMUZER FAMILY

The influential south German Schmuzer family of Wessobrunn were stuccoists and architects from the sixteenth through the eighteenth centuries. Most famous of the architects were Johann (1642–1701) and his son, Joseph (1683–1752), who built ecclesiastical structures. Johann's huge Benedictine Monastery at Wessobrunn (begun 1680) shows the church embedded in an axial baroque plan composed of a series of rectangular courtyards. The exteriors were reticent, but the interiors were exuberantly stuccoed. Johann's centralizing pilgrimage church in Vilgertshofen (1686–1692) broke new ground in its use of a Greek-cross plan, encircling galleries, and double altar. Joseph built the Heiligkreuz-Kirche, Donauwörth (1717–1722), on a wall-pier scheme, and at Saint Anton, Partenkirchen (1735–1736), he exploited a unique site and used the indigenous tradition of open porches on pilgrimage churches.

BEVERLY HEISNER

WORKS

JOHANN SCHMUZER

1670–1676, Maria Heimsuchung. Pilgrimage Church, Ilgen near Schongau, Germany. 1673–1678, Saint Koloman Pilgrimage Church, Germany. 1680 and later, Benedictine Abbey, Wessobrunn, Germany. 1681–1683, Church of Unsere liebe Frau am Berg, Füssen, Germany. 1682–1685, Parish Church, Nesselwang, Germany. 1686–1692, Schmerzhaften Muttergottes Pilgrimage Church, Vilgertshofen, Germany. 1686–1694, Parish Church, Ziemetshausen, Germany. 1699–1701, City Hall, Landsberg, Germany.

JOSEPH SCHMUZER

1717–1722, Benedictine Monastery Church of Heiligkreuz, Donauwörth, Germany. (A)1726–1727, Saint Leonard-im-Forst Pilgrimage Church, Germany. 1729–1733, Parish Church, Garmisch, Germany. 1733–1735, Parish Church (nave), Gablingen, Germany. (A)1735–1736, Saint Anton Pilgrimage Church, Partenkirchen, Germany. 1735–1742, Parish Church, Oberammergau, Germany. 1736–1740, Parish Church, Mittenwald, Germany.

BIBLIOGRAPHY

DISCHINGER, GABRIELE   1977   *Johann und Joseph Schmuzer*. Sigmaringen, Germany: Thorbecke.

HAUTTMANN, MAX   1921   *Geschichte der kirchlichen Baukunst in Bayern, Schwaben und Franken: 1550–1780*. Munich: Schmidt.

HITCHCOCK, H. R.   1966   "The Schmuzers and the Rococo Transformation of Medieval Churches in Bavaria." *Art Bulletin* 48, no. 2:159–176.

SCHOCH, HANS

Hans Schoch (1550?–1631) was a German architect born in Strasbourg and contemporary of JACOB WOLFF THE YOUNGER. In his best known work, the Friedrichsbau of the Schloss of Heidelberg (1601–1607), Schoch paved the way for the baroque in Franconia. Schoch designed closely knit and heavily molded structures which were richly ornamented.

JEANINE CLEMENTS STAGE

WORKS

1582–1585, Neuer Bau; 1586, Grosse Metzig; Strassbourg, Germany. 1601–1607, Friedrichsbau, Schloss Heidelberg, Germany.

BIBLIOGRAPHY

HEMPEL, E.   (1965)1977   *Baroque Art and Architecture in Central Europe*. New York: Viking.

SCHOFFER, NICOLAS

Nicolas Schoffer (1912–), whose name is also spelled Miklós Schöffer, is a leading proponent of kinetic art. He is not only a painter and sculptor, but also a constructor. He is an innovator of modern sculpture, with his plastic constructions producing moving, projected lights and concrete music sounds.

Schoffer, who was born in Kalocsa, Hungary, started out as a painter, studying at the School of Arts in Budapest. In 1937, he went to France, and in 1939, he became a student at the Ecole des Beaux-Arts in Paris. After working in Expressionist and Surrealist modes, he began to be engaged more intensively in kinetic art in 1950 under the influence of LÁSZLÓ MOHOLY-NAGY. Five years later, in 1955, his space construction made of 42.5 meter long steel tubes was erected in France. His "spatio-dynamic" sculptures and constructions visualize the moving, vibrating surroundings of urban life.

JUDITH KOÓS

BIBLIOGRAPHY

HABASQUE, GUY, and CASSOU, JEAN   1963   *Nicholas Schoeffer*. Neuchâtel, Switzerland: Wittenborn.

SCHOLANDER, FREDRIK WILHELM

Fredrik Wilhelm Scholander (1816–1881) was the most prominent Swedish architect during the third quarter of the nineteenth century. Educated at the Royal Academy of Arts in Stockholm (1831–1836), he made a grand tour (1841–1846) and worked for a time in the studio of LOUIS HIPPOLYTE LEBAS in Paris. Professor of architecture at the Royal Academy of Arts since 1848, leading architect of the National Board of Public Building, and architect of King Karl XV (for whom he decorated the royal castles), he dominated the architectural scene until HELGO ZETTERVALL took over. Most of his buildings have suffered from later alterations, but his masterpiece, the Stockholm Synagogue (1867–1870), is extremely well preserved being also from an international point of view an outstanding example of the picturesque eclecticism of the period.

Scholander had a versatile genius, being dedicated also to art and to literature.

ANDERS ÅMAN

WORKS

1850–1854, Warodellska House, Stockholm. 1859–1860, Wasa Monument in Utmeland, Mora, Dalecarlia, Sweden. 1860–1863, Royal Institute of Technology; 1865, Ulriksdals Slottskapell; Stockholm. 1867–1869, High School (Katedralskolan), Uppsala, Sweden. 1867–1870, Synagogue, Stockholm.

BIBLIOGRAPHY

GRANDIEN, BO   1979   *Drömmen om renässansen: Fredrik Wilhelm Scholander som arkitekt och mångfrestare*. Stockholm: Nordiska museet. An English summary is on pages 441–457.

SCHOLER, FRIEDRICH

Friedrich Eugen Scholer (1874–?), born in Sydney, Australia, studied at the Technische Hochschule in Munich (1897–1989). For most of his career, he was the partner of PAUL BONATZ. Although Scholer influenced matters of structure and aesthetics, Bonatz secured the commissions and approved each design. They are famous for the train station in Stuttgart (1911–1928), constructed on rock-faced ashlar and brick.

JAMES WARD

WORKS

1910–1912, Library, Tübingen University, Germany. 1910–1914, School, Rottwell, Germany. 1911–1914, City Hall (with Paul Bonatz), Hannover, Germany. 1911–1928, Train Station (with Bonatz), Stuttgart, Germany. 1920, Urban Development, Cologne, Germany. 1925, Hornschuch House, Mainleus-Kulmbach, Germany. 1926–1928, Buildings, Nekarkanal, Germany. 1929–1931, Graf Zeppelin Hotel, Stuttgart, Germany.

BIBLIOGRAPHY

BONATZ, PAUL 1928 "Der Bahnhof in Stuttgart und andere Arbeiten der Architekten Paul Bonatz und F. E. Scholer." *Wasmuths Monatshefte für Baukunst* 12:145–152.
HEGEMANN, WERNER 1928 "Nachwort über die Arbeiten von Bonatz und Scholer und Renaissance des Mittelalters?" *Wasmuths Monatshefte für Baukunst* 12:153–166.
HEGEMANN, WERNER 1931 "Paul Bonatz und seine Schüler." *Wasmuths Monatshefte für Baukunst* 15:337–343.
Moderne Bauformen 1913 12:593–599. Plates of buildings.
Paul Bonatz: Ein Gedenkbuch Technische Hochschule, Stuttgart. 1957 Stuttgart, Germany: Deutsche Verlagsanstalt.
PLATZ, GUSTAV A. 1927 *Die Baukunst der neuesten Zeit.* Berlin: Propyläen.
"Der Wettbewerb zur Erlengen von Entwürfen für das Empfangsgebäude des neuen Hauptbahnhofes in Stuttgart." *Deutsche Bauzeitung* 45:456–459.

SCHÖNTHAL, OTTO

Otto Schönthal (1878–1961) was born and died in Vienna. As a pupil and collaborator of OTTO WAGNER, he was a Secessionist from the very outset. The ornamentation of the Villa Vojczik in Vienna (1902) is in the early Secessionist style, colorful and lush. Schönthal was connected with Emil Hoppe and also for a while with Marcel Kammerer. For the trotting-race course (Trabrennbahn; 1912) which he built in the Vienna Prater, he used a slim reinforced concrete construction.

SOKRATIS DIMITRIOU

WORKS

1902, Villa Vojczik; 1912, Trotting-race course, Vienna.

BIBLIOGRAPHY

GRAF, OTTO ANTONIA 1969 *Die vergessene Wagnerschule.* Vienna: Jugend & Volk.
HOPE; ÉMIL, and SCHÖNTHAL, OTTO 1931 *Projekte und ausgeführte Bauten.* Vienna: Elbemühl.
POZZETTO, MARCO 1979 *La scuola di Wagner: 1894–1912.* Trieste, Italy: Comune di Trieste.

SCHULTZ, ROBERT WEIR

Robert Weir Schultz (1860–1951), who in 1915 changed his name to R. W. S. Weir, was an Arts and Crafts architect much involved with the revival of Byzantine architecture in the late nineteenth century. Schultz was born in Scotland and articled to ROBERT ROWAND ANDERSON in Edinburgh. In 1884, he entered the office of R. NORMAN SHAW, where he met his lifelong friend, WILLIAM RICHARD LETHABY. Schultz also worked in the office of Ernest George (see GEORGE AND PETO). In 1887, Schultz won the Royal Academy's Gold Medal and went on an extended tour of Greece and the Near East. In 1891, Schultz set up in practice in London. Most of his first jobs were for his important patron, the third marquess of Bute. Schultz maintained a large and successful country house practice before 1914, working in a variety of styles.

GAVIN STAMP

WORKS

1892–1900, Saint John's Lodge (alterations and *two new chapels), Regent's Park, London. 1892–1908, House of Falkland (alterations), Fife, Scotland. 1895–1905, Dumfries House (alterations), Ayrshire, Scotland. 1897–1898, Scoulag Lodge; 1897–1900, Wester Kames Tower (reconstruction); Bute, Scotland. 1899, West Green House, Hartley Witney, Hampshire, England. 1899–1900, Church of Saint Michael and All Angels, Woolmer Green, Hertfordshire, England. 1899–1901, Inholmes, Harley Wintney, Hampshire, England. 1900–1901, Scalers Hill, Cogham, Kent. 1901–1902, The Croft, Hartley Wintney; 1901–1905, Tylney Hall (additions and outbuildings); Hampshire, England. 1902, Braeside, Cobham, Surrey, England. 1902–1905, Pickenham Hall, Swaffham, Norfolk, England. 1903–1905, South African War Memorial, Aldershot, Hampshire, England. 1903–1908, Old Place of Mochrum (alterations), Wigtownshire, Scotland. 1903–1912, The Barn (extension of old barn as Schultz's house), Harley Wintney, Hampshire, England. 1904–1905, How Green House, Hever, Kent. 1904–1907, Archbishop's Chapel, Greenhill Gardens, Edinburgh. *1904–1907, University Settlement, Cardiff, Wales. 1904–1912, Holloway Sanatorium (new buildings), Virginia Water, Surrey, England. 1905, Village Hall, Shorne, Kent, England. 1906–1913, Cathedral Church of All Saints, Khartoum. 1907–1909, Children's Homes and School, Chalfont Saint Peter, Buckinghamshire, England. 1907–1910, Knockenhair, Dunbar, East Lothian, Scotland. 1909–1912, Saint Ann's Hospital, Canford Cliffs, Bournemouth, Hampshire, England. 1910–1912, Lowood, Cramong Bridge, near Edinburgh. 1910–1915, Saint Andrew's Chapel, Westminster Cathedral, London. 1911, Holly Brake, Tilmore Gardens, Petersfield, Hampshire, England. 1911–1914, Cottesbrooke Hall (reconstruction), near Northampton, England. 1911–1914, The Haye, Monk Sherborne, Hampshire, England. 1913–1915, Mausoleum, South Mimms, Middlesex, England. 1914–1918, Housing, Gretna Green, Dumfriesshire, Scotland.

BIBLIOGRAPHY

OTTEWILL, DAVID 1979 "Robert Weir Schultz (1860–1951): An Arts and Crafts Architect." *Architectural History* 22:88–116.

OTTEWILL, DAVID n.d. "Robert Weir Schultz, Architect, (1860–1951)." Unpublished Ph.D. dissertation, Courtauld Institute, London.

SCHULTZ, ROBERT WEIR 1897 "Byzantine Art." *Architectural Review* 1:192–199, 248–255.

SCHULTZ, ROBERT WEIR 1909 "Reason in Building." Pages 1–40 in R. Raffles Davison (editor), *The Arts Connected with Building.* London: Batsford.

SCHULTZ, ROBERT WEIR 1938 *William Richard Lethaby.* London.

SCHULTZ, ROBERT WEIR, and BARNSLEY, SIDNEY H. 1901 *The Monastery of St. Luke of Stirls in Phocis.* London: Macmillan.

STAMP, GAVIN 1981 *Robert Weir Schultz and His Work for the Marquesses of Bute.* Mount Stuart, Scotland: Privately printed.

SCHULTZE-NAUMBURG, PAUL

Paul Schultze-Naumburg (1869–1949) was a German architect and theoretician whose writings and ideas were used by the Nazis in the early 1930s to attack International style architects and particularly those of the Bauhaus.

Although Schultze-Naumburg first established himself as a Progressive architect, designing large country estates in simplified historicist styles, he spent most of his time after World War I developing his racist theories of architecture in books and magazine articles. In books such as *The ABC of Building* (1926), *Art and Race* (1928), and *The Face of the German House* (1928), he tried to show how architecture and the arts express racial identity and how German architecture was degenerating due to foreign racial influences. In 1930 and 1931, in a series of articles and well-publicized lectures for the Kampfbund für deutsche Kultur, a Nazi cultural organ, Schultze-Naumburg established himself as one of the country's most prominent critics of the "new" architecture of Walter Gropius and the Bauhaus.

When the Nazis gained partial control of the Thuringian provincial government in 1930, Schultze-Naumburg was appointed director of the United Institutes for Art Instruction, the Weimar school that had been the Bauhaus before Gropius moved his institution to Dessau in 1925. During his brief one-year tenure as director, Schultze-Naumburg fired all teachers associated with the Bauhaus and removed paintings of Paul Klee, Wassily Kandinsky, and "eastern or otherwise racially inferior" artists.

Despite Schultze-Naumburg's strong credentials as a Nazi theorist, party infighting prevented him from receiving any important building commissions after Hitler took power in 1933.

CLIFF PEARSON

BIBLIOGRAPHY

HINZ, BERTHOLD 1979 *Art in the Third Reich.* New York: Pantheon.

LANE, BARBARA MILLER 1968 *Architecture and Politics in Germany: 1918–1945.* Cambridge, Mass.: Harvard University Press.

SCHULTZE-NAUMBURG, PAUL 1902–1917 *Kulturarbeiten.* Munich: Callwey.

SCHULTZE-NAUMBURG, PAUL 1927 *Das ABC des Bauens.* Stuttgart, Germany: Franck'sche Verlagshandlung.

SCHULTZE-NAUMBURG, PAUL (1928)1938 *Kunst und Rasse.* 3d ed. Munich: Lehmann.

SCHULTZE-NAUMBURG, PAUL 1929 *Das Gesicht des deutschen Hauses.* Munich: Callwey.

SCHULTZE-NAUMBURG, PAUL 1940 *Bauten Schultze-Naumburg.* With an introduction by Rudolf Pfister. Weimar, Germany: Duncker.

SCHULZE, PAUL

Paul Schulze (1827/1828–1897) was born in Breslau, the capital of Prussian Silesia (now Wroclaw, Poland). After receiving his art training in Berlin and Vienna, he arrived in Boston in 1849, where he designed buildings for Harvard College, Cambridge, Massachusetts. In 1858, Schulze settled in New York and practiced with Charles Gildemeister (1860), Paul F. Schoen (1866–1875), and William G. Steinmetz (1875–1876). In 1877, Schulze moved to Washington, where, in partnership with Adolph Cluss (1878–1889), he designed and supervised the construction of several major government buildings. Schulze submitted designs to the major competitions, and he worked predominantly in the *Rundbogenstil* and Second Empire style. In the 1850s, he published a lithographic series of designs for funerary monuments. In 1861, he assisted with the illustrations of Henry Hudson Holly's *Country Seats* (1863). He was founder and president of the Palette Club, a New York art association of the 1870s. Schulze died in California, where he resided with his son, Henry A. Schulze, a prominent San Francisco architect.

JOY M. KESTENBAUM

WORKS

*1855–1858, Appleton Chapel; 1857–1858, Boylston Hall; Harvard College, Cambridge, Mass. *1868–1875,

United States Post Office (with Paul F. Schoen and Committee of Architects; remodeled by ALFRED B. MULLETT); *1870–1871, German Uptown Savings Bank (with Schoen); *1871, Eleventh Ward Savings Bank (with Schoen); *1873–1874, Kurtz Building (with Schoen); New York. 1878–1881, Model Hall, Old Patent Office (now National Portrait Gallery; with Adolph Cluss); 1879–1881, Arts and Industries Building (with Cluss), National Museum; *1883–1884, The Portland Flats (with Cluss); *1886–1888, United States Army Medical Museum and Library (with Cluss); Washington.

BIBLIOGRAPHY

CAMBRIDGE HISTORICAL COMMISSION 1973 *Survey of Architectural History in Cambridge, Report Four: Old Cambridge.* Mass.: The commission.

CLUSS, ADOLPH n.d. "Paul Schulze." Unpublished manuscript, American Institute of Architects, Washington.

FRANCIS, DENNIS STEADMAN 1980 *Architects in Practice, New York City, 1840–1900.* New York: Committee for the Preservation of Architectural Records.

HITCHCOCK, H. R. (1936)1975 *The Architecture of H. H. Richardson and His Times.* Cambridge, Mass.: M.I.T. Press.

"Obituary" 1897 *American Architect and Building News* 55, no. 1101:42.

SCHULZE, PAUL (1856)1860 *Original Designs in Monumental Art.* 4th ed. Boston: The author. Schulze published four different editions under slightly varying titles.

SCHUMACHER, FRITZ

Born in Bremen, Germany, but raised in New York where his father served as the German Consul General, Fritz Schumacher (1869–1947) was educated in Munich and trained in the offices of GABRIEL VON SEIDL in Munich and HUGO LICHT in Leipzig. Seidl's regionalism influenced Schumacher's numerous houses built during his professorship in Dresden (1899–1909), where he also organized the third German Arts and Crafts Exhibition in 1906. A founding member of the Deutscher Werkbund in 1907, Schumacher pursued his theories of architectural reform in innumerable polemical writings and public buildings. As chief city architect in Hamburg from 1909 until his forced retirement in 1933, he forged a personal but characteristically unpretentious municipal style of architecture based on the North German brick tradition. His style shifted considerably after World War I. Abandoning picturesque compositions dominated by high-pitched tile roofs and evocations of Hanseatic buildings in favor of rectilinear, flat-roofed compositions with considerable use of steel, he gave his Hamburg work a unified image through consistent materials and meticulous attention to detail. In contrast to the brick Expressionism of his Hamburg contemporary FRITZ HÖGER, Schumacher's buildings have a calm sobriety in their monumental simplicity and straightforward structural expression.

From his Hamburg Stadtpark (1910–1924), designed even before he arrived in Hamburg, Schumacher viewed comprehensive planning embracing social as well as aesthetic issues as central to his task. It was, however, only in 1914 that he succeeded in establishing a City Planning Office providing him the necessary legal tools and controls. The replanning of Cologne, directed on a leave of absence from his Hamburg post during 1920–1923, was the testing ground for the large-scale planning projects, especially housing developments, that dominated his late career. Already in his 1917 book, *Die Kleinwohnung* (The small apartment), he argued that the efficient planning of small housing units for mass production was the principal challenge facing architects. A pioneer in the German movement for regional planning, Schumacher was instrumental in the creation of Greater Hamburg in 1937.

BARRY BERGDOLL

BIBLIOGRAPHY

ARCHITEKTEN UND INGENIEUR-VEREIN, HAMBURG 1929 *Hamburg und seine Bauten: 1918–1929.* Hamburg, Germany: Boysen & Maasch.

BOSSOM, ALFRED C. 1927 "German Municipal Architecture, Illustrating the Work of Fritz Schumacher." *American Architect* 132:709–714.

FISCHER, MANFRED F. 1977 *Fritz Schumacher: Das Hamburger Stadtbild und die Denkmalpflege.* Hamburg, Germany: Christians.

HAENEL, ERICH 1902–1903 "Fritz Schumacher." *Dekorative Kunst* 11:281–300.

KALLMORGEN, WERNER (editor) 1969 *Schumacher und Hamburg: Eine fachliche Dokumentation zu seinem 100. Geburtstag.* Hamburg, Germany: Hans Christian.

LANGMAACK, GERHARD 1964 "Fritz Schumacher." *Vorträge und Aufsätze* 12:4–29.

NEUNDÖRFER, LUDWIG 1948 "Fritz Schumacher." *Die Neue Stadt* 2:53–58.

OCKERT, ERWIN 1950 *Fritz Schumacher: Sein Schaffen als Städtebauer und Landesplaner.* Tübingen, Germany: Wasmuth.

ROSNER, ROLF 1980 "Fritz Schumacher's Hamburg." *Architectural Review* 167:166–169.

SCHAEFER, KARL 1919–1921 *Hamburger Staatsbauten von Fritz Schumacher.* 2 vols. Berlin: Zirkel Architekturverlag.

SCHUMACHER, FRITZ 1897 *Im Kampfe um die Kunst: Beiträge zu architektonischen Zeitfragen.* Strasbourg, France: Heitz.

SCHUMACHER, FRITZ (1898)1902 *Leon Battista Alberti und seine Bauten.* 2d ed. Berlin: Spemann.

SCHUMACHER, FRITZ 1907 *Streifzüge eines Architekten: Gesammelte Aufsätze.* Jena, Germany: Diederichs.

SCHUMACHER, FRITZ c.1910 *Probleme der Grossstadt.* Leipzig: Seemann.

SCHUMACHER, FRITZ 1916a *Ausblicke für die kunsttechnische Zukunft unseres Volkes.* Weimar, Germany.

SCHUMACHER, FRITZ (1916b)1949 *Grundlagen für das Studium der Baukunst.* 2d ed. Munich: Rinn. Originally published with the title, *Grundlagen der Baukunst: Studien zum Beruf des Architekten.*

SCHUMACHER, FRITZ (1917a)1919 *Die Kleinwohnung: Studien zur Wohnungsfrage.* 2d ed. Leipzig: Quelle & Meyer.

SCHUMACHER, FRITZ 1917b *Das Wesen des neuzeitlichen Backsteinbaues.* Munich: Callwey.

SCHUMACHER, FRITZ 1919 *Hamburgs Wohnungspolitik von 1818 bis 1919: Ein Beitrag zur Psychologie der Gross-Stadt.* Hamburg, Germany: Friederichsen.

SCHUMACHER, FRITZ 1920a *Kulturpolitik: Neue Streifzüge eines Architekten.* Jena, Germany: Diederichs.

SCHUMACHER, FRITZ 1920b *Wie das Kunstwerk Hamburg nach dem grossen Brande entstand.* Berlin: Curtius.

SCHUMACHER, FRITZ 1923a *Das Entstehen einer Grossstadt-Strasse "Der Mönckebergerstrassen-Durchbruch.* 2d ed. Brunswick, Germany: Westerman.

SCHUMACHER, FRITZ 1923b *Köln: Entwicklungsfragen einer Grosstadt.* Cologne, Germany: Saaleckverlag.

SCHUMACHER, FRITZ 1926 *Das bauliche Gestalten.* Leipzig.

SCHUMACHER, FRITZ 1928a *Die bauliche Zukunft der Hamburgischen Universität.* Hamburg, Germany.

SCHUMACHER, FRITZ 1928b *Plastik im Freien.* Hamburg, Germany: Oberschulbehörde.

SCHUMACHER, FRITZ 1929 *Zeitfragen der Architektur.* Jena, Germany: Diederichs.

SCHUMACHER, FRITZ 1932a *Das Werden einer Wohnstadt: Bilder vom neuen Hamburg.* Hamburg, Germany: Westermann.

SCHUMACHER, FRITZ 1932b *Wesen und Organisation der Landesplanung im Hamburgisch-Preussischen Planungsgebiet.* Hamburg, Germany: Boysen & Maasch.

SCHUMACHER, FRITZ (1935a)1955 *Strömungen in deutscher Baukunst seit 1800.* Cologne, Germany.

SCHUMACHER, FRITZ 1935b *Stufen des Lebens: Erinnerungen eines Baumeisters.* Stuttgart, Germany: Deutsche Verlags-Anstalt.

SCHUMACHER, FRITZ 1937 *Begleitmusik des Lebens: Ausgewählte Gedichte.* Stuttgart, Germany: Deutsche Verlags-Anstalt.

SCHUMACHER, FRITZ 1938 *Der Geist der Baukunst.* Stuttgart, Germany: Deutsche Verlags-Anstalt.

SCHUMACHER, FRITZ 1940 *Probleme der Grossstadt.* Leipzig: Seemann.

SCHUMACHER, FRITZ 1941 *Lesebuch für Baumeister.* Berlin: Henssel.

SCHUMACHER, FRITZ 1942 *Die Sprache der Kunst.* Stuttgart, Germany: Deutsche Verlags-Anstalt.

SCHUMACHER, FRITZ 1944 *Selbstgespräche: Erinnerungen und Betrachtungen.* Hamburg, Germany: Springer.

SCHUMACHER, FRITZ 1945 *Zum Wiederaufbau Hamburgs.* Hamburg, Germany: Trautmann.

SCHWARZ, RUDOLF

Rudolf Schwarz (1897–1961), a major figure in the development of modern church architecture, was born in Strasbourg, then part of Germany, in 1897. His interest in the search, so common after World War II, for those "sacred" forms which best express the Catholic liturgy, was aroused before he entered the Berlin Academy of Arts in 1919. Study there under the Expressionist architect HANS POELZIG reinforced this interest. After graduating from the academy in 1923, he spent a half year with the liturgically minded Roman Catholic youth group at the Castle Rothenfels on the Main, led by Romano Guardini. In 1928 Schwarz simplified and furnished several rooms in the castle to promote intimate groupings for worship.

He had already taught for two years (1925–1927) at the Arts and Crafts School in Offenbach, whose faculty included, until 1926, the respected church architect DOMINIKUS BÖHM. Their only joint project was, significantly, the prize-winning competition design for the Church of Our Lady of Peace in Frankfurt (1926–1927), unfortunately too far ahead of official taste to be executed. But its overall concept was embodied by Schwarz in his revolutionary Corpus Christi Church, Aachen (1928–1930), a pure white box in which the only distinction between the congregation's space and that surrounding the black altar block is a monumental flight of steps.

From 1927, Schwarz was director of the Arts and Crafts School in Aachen, until it was closed by the Nazi government in 1934. During the rest of the 1930s, government restrictions on church building severely limited his work, done in collaboration with his pupil, Johannes Krahn. However, in 1938 appeared the most influential of his many publications, *Vom Bau der Kirche* (*The Church Incarnate* [1958]). In richly poetic imagery, Schwarz described, by means of six archetypal plans, the mystical symbolism of various interrelationships of structure and people, whom he considered constitutive building materials of the church.

He engaged in regional planning in the Saarland during World War II, was city planner of Cologne from 1946 to 1952, and taught city planning at the State Academy of Art in Düsseldorf from 1952 until his death. Nevertheless Schwarz achieved his greatest renown after the war as a church architect.

He created elemental, sheltering enclosures which order the people in clearly defined masses around the altar, the pulpit, and the font. His trabeated ferroconcrete framing is strongly expressed; the intervals in the frame are filled in with brick, stone or glass. Three churches can serve as examples. Saint Anna, Düren (1951–1956), often cited as his masterpiece, has its altar in the bend of an L-shaped plan. Sheer red sandstone walls enfold the outer faces, in dialogue with glass walls in the inner angle, above a low diagonal connecting hall. At Saint Michael, Frankfurt (1953–1954), altar and font occupy opposite ends of an elongated ellipse enveloped by high brick walls relieved only by a band of glass block under the flat ceiling. In the square Holy Family Church, Oberhausen (1956–1958), four thin columns define the central altar space and turn the roof into a baldachin over the entire congregation.

Sudden death ended Schwarz's career in 1961. His last churches were completed by his wife of ten years, the architect Maria Lang Schwarz, and his pupils.

HOWARD V. NIEBLING

WORKS

1928, Castle Rothenfels am Main (renovation), Germany. 1928–1930, Corpus Christi Church (with Hans Schwippert), Aachen, Germany. 1932–1933, Saint Albert Chapel (with Johannes Krahn), Leversbach, Germany. 1942–1952, Assumption of Mary Church (with Karl Wimmenauer), Wesel, Germany. 1943–1951, Romanesque Church (reconstruction; with Rudolf Steinbach), Johannisberg, Germany. 1947–1954, Mechtern Church (with Maria Schwarz); 1949–1959, Gürzenich Festival Hall (reconstruction; with Karl Band); 1950–1952, All Saints Anglican Church (with Josef Bernard); Cologne, Germany. 1951–1954, Saint Albert Church, Andernach, Germany. 1951–1956, Saint Anna Church (with Schwarz), Düren, Germany. 1951–1957, Wallraf-Richartz-Museum (reconstruction; with Bernard), Cologne, Germany. 1952–1953, Saint Anna Church (with Wimmenauer), Duisburg, Germany. 1952–1954, Church of Mary the Queen (with Wimmenauer), Frechen, Germany. 1952–1954, Saint Joseph Church (with Bernard); 1952–1955, Church of Our Lady (reconstruction and enlargement; with Schwarz); Cologne, Germany. 1952–1957, Holy Cross Church (with Bernard), Bottrop, Germany. 1953–1954, Saint Michael Church (with Schwarz), Frankfurt. 1954–1957, Saint Andrew Church (with Wimmenauer), Essen, Germany. 1956–1958, Holy Family Church (with Bernard and Herbert Herrmann), Oberhausen, Germany. 1956–1959, Saint Anthony Church (with Helmut Gutmann, Günther Kleinjohann, and Schwarz); 1957, Saint Francis Church (with Gutmann and Schwarz); Essen, Germany. 1957–1962, Saint Theresa Church (with Gutmann and Schwarz), Linz, Austria. 1957–1963, Saint Florian Church (with Hubert Friedl and Schwarz), Vienna. 1958–1959, Saint Pius Church (with Kurt Faber), Wuppertal, Germany. 1958–1960, Saint Gertrude Church (with Herrmann), Aschaffenburg, Germany. 1959, Church of Mary the Queen (with Friedl and Schwarz), Saarbrücken, Germany. 1959–1961, Saint Boniface Church (executed by Schwarz, Erwin Drese, and Paul Altgassen; not completed until 1964), Aachen, Germany. 1960–1961, Saint Pius Church (executed by Schwarz; not completed until 1962), Hausen, Germany. 1960–1961, Saint Boniface Church (executed by Schwarz and Werner Strohl; not completed until 1964), Wetzlar, Germany. 1960–1961, Saint Ludger Church (executed by Schwarz; not completed until 1965), Wuppertal, Germany.

BIBLIOGRAPHY

BERNHARD, RUDOLF 1972 "In Memoriam Rudolf Schwarz." *Das Münster* 25:22–26.
DEBUYST, D. FRÉDÉRIC 1973 "Vers une réévaluation des 'Classiques.'" *L'Architecture d'Aujourd'hui* 168, July–Aug.:48–50. An English summary is given in the supplementary pages.
HAMMOND, PETER (editor) 1962 *Towards a Church Architecture.* London: Architectural Press.
SCHWARZ, MARIA, and CONRADS, ULRICH 1979 *Rudolf Schwarz, Wegweisung der Technik und andere Schriften zum neuen Bauen 1921–1961.* Wiesbaden, Germany: Vieweg.
SCHWARZ, RUDOLF 1958 *The Church Incarnate.* Translated by Cynthia Harris. Chicago: Regnery.
SCHWARZ, RUDOLF 1960 *Kirchenbau; Welt vor der Schwelle.* Heidelberg, Germany: F. H. Kerle Verlag.
SMITH, G. E. KIDDER 1964 *The New Churches of Europe.* New York: Holt.

SCHWARZMANN, HERMANN J.

Hermann J. Schwarzmann (1846–1891) was a German-American who made a spectacular record in Philadelphia when in his twenties. He was apparently self-taught in civil engineering and architecture. He served as assistant engineer for the Fairmount Park, Philadelphia (1869). His plan for the park (1871) was chosen over that of FREDERICK LAW OLMSTED and CALVERT VAUX. Appointed chief engineer and architect-in-chief for the Centennial International Exhibition, he created the grounds for the Centennial in 1876 and designed thirty-four of its buildings, including the two permanent buildings, Memorial Hall (Art Gallery) and Horticultural Hall.

JOHN MAASS

WORKS

1871, Fairmount Park, Philadelphia. 1873, Philadelphia Zoological Garden. *1874–1876, Horticultural Hall; 1874–1876, Memorial Hall (Art Gallery); *1875–1876, German Pavilion; *1875–1876, Judges Pavilion; *1875–1876, Pennsylvania Building; *1875–1876, Woman's Building; *1876, Art Annex; *1876, Photographic Hall; Centennial Exhibition, Philadelphia.

*c.1880, Koster and Bial Music Hall; *1881, Lieder-kranz Club House; 1882, Mercantile Exchange Building; New York.

BIBLIOGRAPHY

MAASS, JOHN 1973 *The Glorious Enterprise: The Centennial Exhibition of 1876, and H. J. Schwarzmann, architect-in-chief.* Watkins Glen, N.Y.: American Life Foundation.
SCHWARZMANN, HERMANN J. 1877–1879 "Exhibition Grounds and Permanent Buildings," Volume I, pages 281–305 in United States Centennial Commission *International Exhibition 1876: Report of the Director General.* Philadelphia: Lippincott.

SCHWECHTEN, FRANZ

Franz Heinrich Schwechten (1841–1924) was born in Cologne, Germany, where he was a student of JULIUS RASCHDORF. In Berlin, he studied at the Bauakademie and also received training from FRIEDRICH AUGUST STÜLER and WALTER GROPIUS. After he acquired further practical experience in collaboration with Hermann Pflaume in Cologne, Schwechten traveled to Italy on the Schinkel Prize in 1868. Upon his return to Berlin in 1869, he established a private architectural practice, was appointed chief architect of the Berlin Railroad Company in 1871, and became director of an atelier at the Prussian Academy of Art in 1902. During his eleven-year tenure with the Railroad Company, Schwechten was responsible for the Anhalter Bahnhof in Berlin (1875–1880), the first major work of his career and an important monument in Berlin's architectural history. The influence of KARL FRIEDRICH SCHINKEL was manifest in the polychromatic brick and terra-cotta Bahnhof, which displayed coherent organization and a rare success in the integration of masonry elements with the metal structure of the shed roof. Under the patronage and influence of Emperor Wilhelm II, Schwechten's later work evinces a preference for a more stark and severe Romanesque mode as seen in the Kaiser-Wilhelm-Gedächtniskirche (1891–1895) in Berlin and the Kaiserschloss (1905–1910) in Posen, Poland. Schwechten died in Berlin after an exceptionally long and productive career.

SHELLEY SMITH KELLAM

WORKS

1875–1880, Anhalter Railroad Station (fragment remains), Berlin. 1875–1880, Railroad Station, Dessau, Germany. 1875–1880, Railroad Station, Wittenberg, Germany. 1880–1882, Military Academy; 1886, Industrial Building; 1887–1889, Gratweilsche Beer Hall; 1888–1890, AEG Factory (façade), Wedding; 1891–1895, Kaiser-Wilhelm Gedächtniskirche (fragment remains); 1892, Saint Simeon's Church; 1892–1893, Loeser Industrial Building; 1893–1895, Church of the Apostle Paul; Berlin. 1898–1899, Kaiser-Wilhelm Tower, Grünewald, Germany. 1899, Power Station, Municipal Electric Company, Moabit; 1905–1906, Savings Bank, Teltow; Berlin. 1905–1909, Church of the Redeemer, Essen, Germany. 1905–1910, Kaiserschloss; 1905–1910, Posener Landschaft Buildings; Posen, Poland. 1908–1911, Hohenzollern Bridge, Cologne, Germany. 1911–1915, Germany Church, Rome. 1912, Potsdam House, Berlin. n.d., Concert Hall, Dessau, Germany. n.d., Genezareth Church, Berlin. n.d., Rhine Bridge, Mainz, Germany. n.d., Royal Tomb, Dessau, Germany. n.d., South Bridge, Cologne, Germany. n.d., War College, Potsdam, Germany.

BIBLIOGRAPHY

"Die Erlöserkirche in Essen-Ruhr." 1918 *Neudeutsche Bauzeitung* 14:127–132, 137–141.
"'Haus Potsdam' in Berlin." 1912 *Deutsche Bauzeitung* 46, no. 47:421–426.
"Die Kaiser-Wilhelm-Gedächtniskirche in Berlin." 1901 *Blätter für Architektur und Kunsthandwerk* 14:plates 99–103.
POSENER, JULIUS 1979 *Berlin auf dem Wege zu einer neuen Architektur: Das Zeitalter Wilhelms II.* Munich: Prestel.
SARRAZIN, OTTO, and SCHULTZE, FRIEDRICH 1910 "Das neue Residenzschloss in Posen." *Zentralblatt der Bauverwaltung* 30, no. 6g:453–458.
"Tote." 1924 *Deutsche Bauzeitung* 58:427–428.

SCHWEINFURTH, A. C.

Born in Auburn, New York, Albert Cicero Schweinfurth (1864–1900) was the son of a designer of architectural ornament. His brothers Charles, Julius, and Henry also became architects. Trained in the office of PEABODY AND STEARNS (1881–1884), he worked for A. PAGE BROWN in New York until 1888. Two years later, after unsuccessful attempts at independent practice in New York and Denver, he rejoined Brown, then in San Francisco, as chief draftsman. Schweinfurth worked on his own between 1895 and 1898, when he departed for two years of travel in Europe. He died of typhoid fever shortly after his return. Schweinfurth played a formative role in developing a regional mode of expression inspired by California's Hispanic legacy.

RICHARD W. LONGSTRETH

WORKS

*1895–1896, Hearst House (Hacienda del Pozzo de Verona), Pleasanton, Calif. 1896–1897, Bradford House, San Francisco. 1896–1897, Moody House, Berkeley. *1897–1898, Examiner Building, San Francisco. 1898, First Unitarian Church, Berkeley.

BIBLIOGRAPHY

ANDERSEN, TIMOTHY J. ET AL. (editors) 1974 *California Design 1910: Pasadena Center, October 15–December 1, 1974.* Pasadena: California Design Publications.

"The Later Work of A. C. Schweinfurth, Architect." 1902 *Architectural Review* New Series 4:76–81.

LUMMIS, CHARLES F. 1904 "The Greatest California Patio House." *Country Life in America* 6:533–540.

"Obituary of A. C. Schweinfurth." 1900 *American Architect and Building News* 70:22.

WOODBRIDGE, SALLY (editor) 1976 *Bay Area Houses.* New York: Oxford University Press.

SCHWEINFURTH, CHARLES FREDERICK

Charles F. Schweinfurth (1856–1919) opened his Cleveland practice in 1883 after studying with an unknown New York architect (1874) and then serving as supervising architect of the U.S. Treasury Department (1875–1881). He designed at first mainly in Richardsonian (see H. H. RICHARDSON) Romanesque, later turning to late English Gothic, particularly for his collegiate work.

GWEN W. STEEGE

WORKS

*1883, Sylvester T. Everett House; 1887–1890, Calvary Presbyterian Church; 1894, Charles F. Schweinfurth House; 1896, Backus Law School, Case Western Reserve University; 1901–1907, Trinity Episcopal Cathedral; 1902, Haydn Hall, Flora Stone Mather College, Case Western Reserve University; 1907–1910, Samuel Mather House; Cleveland, Ohio.

BIBLIOGRAPHY

CAMPEN, RICHARD N. 1971 *Architecture of the Western Reserve: 1800–1900.* Cleveland, Ohio: Press of Case Western Reserve University.

FRARY, I. T. 1917 "The Rebuilding of Longwood, Residence of John L. Severance, Esq. Cleveland, Ohio." *Architectural Record* 41:483–503.

HUBBELL, BENJAMIN S. "Obituary—Charles F. Schweinfurth." *American Institute of Architects Journal* 8:139–140.

JENKINS, CHARLES E. 1897 "A Review of the Works of Charles Frederick Schweinfurth." *Architectural Reviewer* 1:81–115.

WODEHOUSE, LAWRENCE 1976 *American Architects from the Civil War to the First World War.* Detroit, Mich.: Gale.

SCHWEITZER, HEINRICH

Heinrich Schweitzer (1871–?), a German architect born in Stuttgart, studied at the Technische Hochschulen in Stuttgart and Munich. He worked for FRIEDRICH VON THIERSCH in Munich and ALFRED MESSEL in Berlin before establishing an independent practice in Berlin. His main works were the Admiralspalast (1913), the Wertheim Department Store extension (1913), a workers' housing project (1918), and the modernization of the Allianz Office Building (1928).

RON WIEDENHOEFT

WORKS

1913, Admiralspalast; 1913, Wertheim Department Store (extension); 1928, Allianz Offices (renovation); Berlin.

SCHWEIZER, O. E.

German architect, city planner, and educator, Otto Ernst Schweizer (1890–1966) was born in Schramberg in the Black Forest of Germany. He studied architecture in Stuttgart and Munich and assisted THEODOR FISCHER in Munich. He became building director of Nuremberg (1925), where his designs for the planetarium, the municipal stadium complex, and a public hospital (1925–1927) brought him wide recognition.

Professor of architecture in Karlsruhe from 1930, Schweizer published his design principles in 1935 as *Grundlagen des architektonischen Schaffens.* Following World War II, he contributed to the rebuilding effort through publications and competition designs for German cities, for example, Giessen (1947), Mannheim (1950), Bonn (1951), and Rheinhausen (1954). In the late 1950s, Schweizer summarized his life's work in the book *Die architektonische Grossform.*

RON WIEDENHOEFT

BIBLIOGRAPHY

BIER, JUSTUS 1929 *Otto Ernst Schweizer.* Berlin: Hübsch.

DÖCKER, RICHARD 1960 "Zum 70. Geburtstage Otto Ernst Schweizers." *Baukunst und Werkform* 13:346–347.

SCHWEIZER, OTTO ERNST 1935 *Über die Grundlagen des architektonischen Schaffens.* Stuttgart, Germany: Hoffman.

SCHWEIZER, OTTO ERNST 1957 *Die architektonische Grossform: Gebautes und Gedachtes.* Karlsruhe, Germany: Braun.

TSCHIRA, ARNOLD ET AL. 1950 *Otto Ernst Schweizer und seine Schule.* Ravensburg, Germany: Maier.

SCHWITTERS, KURT

Kurt Schwitters (1887–1948) was born in Hannover, Germany, and trained in Dresden as an academic artist. In 1917, he began to create collages constructed from street rubbish. He labeled these constructions *Merz,* a term which he subsequently applied to his efforts in other media. Schwitters's life-work was his *Merzbau* (1923–1932), a fantastic structure which eventually filled his house. Totally nonfunctional in form and purpose, *Merzbau* stressed notions of enclosure and irrational space and reflected Schwitters's knowledge of Expressionist and Constructivist architecture. Schwitters fled the Nazis in 1937 and began new *Merz* structures in Norway and then England. His *Merzbarn* in Ambleside (1947–1948) survived his death.

ERIKA ESAU

WORKS

*1923–1932, Merzbau, Hannover, Germany. *1937–1940, Merzbau, Lysaker, Norway. 1947–1948, Merzbarn, Ambleside, England.

BIBLIOGRAPHY

ELDERFIELD, JOHN   1971   "Early Work of Kurt Schwitters." *Artforum* 10:54–67.
ELDERFIELD, JOHN   1977   "On a Merz-Gesamtkunstwerk." *Art International* 21:19–26.
SCHMALENBACH, WERNER   (1967)1970   *Kurt Schwitters.* New York: Abrams. Originally published in German.
STEINITZ, KATE T.   1968   *Kurt Schwitters: A Portrait from Life.* Berkeley: University of California Press.

SCOTT, ADRIAN GILBERT

Adrian Gilbert Scott (1882–1963) was the youngest child of GEORGE GILBERT SCOTT, JR., and, along with his brother, GILES GILBERT SCOTT, was articled to TEMPLE MOORE. Before 1914, Scott assisted his elder brother on such jobs as No. 129 Grosvenor Road, London. After securing the commission for Cairo Cathedral (1918–1938), Scott developed an independent practice, principally of work for the Roman Catholic Church, but he remained closely dependent upon his brother's work for inspiration. Scott's reduced design of 1953 for EDWIN LUTYENS's Roman Catholic Cathedral mercifully remained unexecuted.

GAVIN STAMP

WORKS

1907, Cottages, Bushey; 1907, Greystanes (with Giles Gilbert Scott), Mill Hill; Hertfordshire, England. *1918–1938, All Saints' Anglican Cathedral, Cairo. 1923, Mount Saint Mary's College Chapel, Spinkhill, Derbyshire, England. 1928, Church of Christ the King, Wimbledon Park, Surrey, England. 1928, Roman Catholic Church of the Holy Name (tower), Manchester, England. 1929–1931, Concert Hall, Mayfield Convent,

Sussex, England. 1930, Shepherd's Well (Adrian Gilbert Scott's House), Frognal, Hampstead, London. 1931, Saint Joseph's Roman Catholic Church, Wealdstone, Middlesex, England. 1931–1934, Farnborough Hill Convent Chapel, Hampshire, England. 1937, Saint James's Church, Vancouver. c.1939–1943, Christ Church, Port Sudan. 1951–1953, Roman Catholic Church of Saints Joseph and Mary, Lansbury, Poplar, London. 1951–1957, Roman Catholic Church of Saint Oswald, Old Swan, Liverpool, England. 1953–1961; Saint Leonard's Parish Church, Sussex, England. 1957, Roman Catholic Church of Our Lady of Victories, Kensington, London. 1959, Roman Catholic Church of Our Lady and Saint Rose of Lima, Birmingham, England. 1958–?, New Church, The Friars, Aylesford, Kent, England.

BIBLIOGRAPHY

"Obituary—Adrian Gilbert Scott." 1963 *Journal of the Royal Institute of British Architects* 70:298.
"Scott, Adrian Gilbert." 1972 Volume 6, page 1012 in *Who Was Who: 1961–1970.* London: Black.

SCOTT, GEORGE GILBERT

George Gilbert Scott (1811–1878) was indeed an "eminent" Victorian, a central figure in the architectural profession whose 850 known works include many important buildings. In financial terms, Scott was a successful practitioner who left a large estate to his sons, two of whom were architects themselves. Something of Scott's stature is revealed in the fact that as his large funeral cortège moved slowly across London, it was joined by Queen Victoria's coach as it proceeded to an unofficial "state" funeral in Westminster Abbey.

George Gilbert Scott was born in rural Gawcott, Buckinghamshire, the third son of the village incumbent, Reverend Thomas Scott. Scott grew up in a family with strong religious ties; his paternal grandfather was Thomas "Bible" Scott, whose commentary on the Bible remained well regarded in clerical circles for generations. Scott's mother's family had strong connections to John Wesley.

Scott's father had a fancy for planning buildings and designed his own parsonage in Gawcott in 1808. Scott's boyhood village was old-fashioned and isolated, and the Scott family was generally shunned for being too evangelical, an interesting background for an architect who grew up claiming to represent the Broad Church of the masses within the established Church of England. Scott received an education highlighted by the twice weekly visits of a Mr. Jones, a drawing master from Buckingham who encouraged Scott's interest in the medium. Scott took pleasure in sketching the Perpendicular churches in the nearby villages of

Buckinghamshire. In 1826, Scott's uncle, Samuel King, a Cambridge-educated incumbent in Latimers offered to tutor the young Scott in mathematics and mechanics. Scott then went to live with his aunt and uncle for a year and there saw his first books on architecture.

Scott's uncle searched London architectural practices for an architect who shared the family's evangelical views. In 1827, it was decided to article Scott to James Edmeston, a man, as Scott wrote in his autobiography, more known as a poet than as an architect. Scott worked and lived with Edmeston, supplementing his articles with drawing classes at the Furnival's Inn studio of George Maddox. In the Edmeston office, Scott met his future partner, WILLIAM BONYTHON MOFFATT. At the end of his articles in 1831, Scott went to work for the builders Peto and Grissell who were working at the time on Hungerford Market designed by CHARLES FOWLER. Scott had already met Samuel Morton Peto of this partnership in his drawing classes with Mr. Maddox.

Scott became friendly with a young architect with evangelical religious views, Sampson Kempthorne, and through him met HENRY ROBERTS who was then building Fishmongers' Hall in London. Scott assisted Roberts at Fishmongers' Hall until early in 1834. While with Roberts, Scott took on his first private commission, a house for his father in Wappenham in the accepted red brick Georgian of its day. In 1834, Scott took chambers next to Kempthorne and began looking for work in the new building boom brought about by Edwin Chadwick's Poor Law Amendment Act of 1834. Scott's sojourn with Kempthorne was ended prematurely by the death of his father which forced Scott to begin his professional career as he now needed to support himself fully.

Scott set himself up in practice in 1835 actively attempting to win commissions for Poor Law buildings in the district where his family had clerical connections. As he worked with Moffatt on Poor House designs, a loose association between the two men was formed in 1835 which provided for both the sharing of commissions and retention of individual commissions. By 1838, the relationship became a partnership which lasted until 1846. Scott and Moffatt designed more than fifty workhouses which was about 15 percent of the total number of Poor Law institutions built in those years.

In 1838, Scott's career began to change. He built his first church in Flaunden, Buckinghamshire. That same year, Scott married his cousin Caroline Oldrid of Boston, England. While working near Latimers and Flaunden, Scott must have met EDWARD BLORE who was in Latimers from 1832 to 1835 and again later in the decade. It would seem that Blore and Samuel King were closely connected as the commission for Latimers church and mansion went to Blore. Despite Scott's loss of work in Latimers or perhaps because of it, Blore seemed to exercise a bit of behind-the-scenes promotion for Scott in the 1840s. At every important turn in Scott's career in this decade, Blore seemed to be there just before Scott received his big opportunity. It was Blore who assessed the competitors for the building of a new church of Saint Giles in Camberwell in 1841 which Scott and Moffatt won. In 1843, Blore, working at Worsley Hall, seems to have arranged for Scott to do a church, Saint Mark, for the same client, Lord Francis Egerton, later earl of Ellesmere. In 1847, Scott received his first important position as restoration architect to a major medieval cathedral, that at Ely. Here, he succeeded Blore who must have also recommended Scott as his successor at Peterborough and Westminster Abbey.

Following the church at Flaunden, Scott received a commission for the church of Saint Nicholas, Lincoln (1839–1840), probably through the good offices of his father-in-law in Lincolnshire. In 1840, Scott was asked by friends of his late father to compete for the design of the Martyrs' Memorial at Oxford which he won and built in 1841–1842, basing his design on the Eleanor Crosses he had admired and carefully sketched as a young man. At about the same time, Scott and Moffatt designed and built ten churches in the Norman and early English styles, simple in execution with repetition of details from one church to another. Scott, whose first house was in a Georgian manner, wrote extensively in his later life about his youthful and lifelong love of Gothic buildings. Yet, from his Poor Law institution and domestic work of the 1830s it is clear that he was working in a manner common to many others in the profession at the time. By the 1840s, the wave of Poor Law institution building had ended, having been replaced by a growing interest in new churches.

Scott and Moffatt's first major commission was that for Saint Giles, Camberwell, in 1841. During that same year, Scott read the *Dublin Review* article by A. W. N. PUGIN, stating Pugin's position on parish church building. As Scott was making a career as a parish church architect and Pugin was a recognized leader in the profession, Scott tested the waters by speaking to Pugin and Benjamin Webb and reading the approved Anglican publication, *The Ecclesiologist*. In 1842, Scott jumped aboard the bandwagon by joining the Cambridge Camden Society despite his strong evangelical background. Scott became a regular contributor to *The Ecclesiologist* with his church designs which

*Scott.
Saint Giles.
Camberwell, England.
1841–1843*

conformed to the mandates of the Society. Scott's relationship to the Camden group was disrupted, however, when he began to build a church for the Lutherans in Hamburg, Germany.

Scott's career took on international importance in 1844 when he was convinced to enter a competition to rebuild the Nikolaikirche in Hamburg. English Gothic Revival architects were held in such high international regard that an English architect was given to believe he might succeed in the competition. Therefore, despite his only previous visit to the Continent—a two-day holiday in Calais—Scott journeyed to Hamburg and entered the competition. Scott and Moffatt came in third, but through the pressures of ERNEST FRIEDRICH ZWIRNER, Scott was given the job. With such clear success, Scott was aware that he could now gain far more work than his partner could bring to the office. Further, Moffatt had become too extravagant and had begun to join speculators in the railroad mania of the mid-1840s. In 1845, Scott, through his wife, informed Moffatt that the partnership was ended.

Although the Hamburg church had ended Scott's courtship with the members of the High Church, Scott saw that he could now develop a practice within the broad middle range of the church and went on, as he noted himself, to repre-

*Scott.
Albert Memorial.
London.
1863–1872*

sent the broad mass of the church. The later years of the 1840s saw Scott enhancing his church building career while solidifying his work as a church restorer. At the same time, Scott saw architects in the forefront of the profession taking up an interest in Continental Gothic, replacing the insularity of earlier decades. Scott journeyed to France and then, with BENJAMIN FERREY, to Venice in 1851 where they both made numerous sketches.

In 1856, Scott entered a public competition for the War and Foreign Office. Scott's design, one of the few that was not classical, strongly resembled the venerable Cloth Hall at Ypres, a favorite source for Victorian architects, and the inspiration for DEANE AND WOODWARD's Oxford Museum as well as for Scott's unbuilt but victorious design for the Hamburg Rathaus competition of 1854–1855. The results of the competition combined with changes in government produced one of the most famous episodes in the battle of the styles of the nineteenth century. In the classical style demanded by Lord Palmerston, Scott built the edifice that is now the Foreign Office. The building, finished only in the 1870s, represents Scott's rare departure from the Gothic of his maturity, but it is a departure that reveals Scott's early training in the Georgian and classical styles.

In 1861, Queen Victoria's husband, Albert, died of typhoid fever. A committee was formed to erect a national tribute to the late prince, and six architects were invited to submit designs. Scott's entry drawn by his son, GEORGE GILBERT SCOTT, JR., was selected, chosen, it was rumored, by Victoria's daughter, the Princess Royal. Scott's gilded ciborium for Hyde Park was unpopular from the beginning; it was judged to be expensive and not functional. Critics further noted that Scott's final design was quite close to another Albert Memorial, that in Manchester, by Thomas Worthington of 1862–1863. Despite the complaints, the work was begun in 1864 and finished in 1872 at the enormous cost of £150,000. For his secular metal shrine, Scott was knighted by Queen Victoria.

As construction of the vast base of the Albert Memorial proceeded in 1866, Scott entered, and this time lost, a major London competition, that for the new Law Courts. Scott's plan was well received by the judges, but his design was not popular. The commission was given to Scott's one-time assistant, GEORGE E. STREET.

Although he may have had a disappointment at the Law Courts, Scott won a major victory at the Midland Hotel, Saint Pancras Station, London, where his design of 1865 won in what may have been a weighted competition. Surely, the fact that he gave them a very expensive, elaborate hotel above the stated requirements would seem to indicate some compliance on the part of the director of the railroad. The hotel is based on continental sources which Scott had employed earlier, such as Ypres and the library at Louvain, and is in keeping with his earlier work such as Kelham Hall, Nottinghamshire, and the town hall at Preston, and even his rejected first design for the Foreign Office. With the Midland Hotel, Scott had the opportunity to leave a large building in his eclectic Gothic Revival style on the London skyline.

By the 1870s, Scott was aging. He had been giving lectures on Gothic architecture at the Royal Academy Schools and was a professor there from 1868 to 1873. His increasing scholarliness can be seen in his work, which began to turn more and more to restoration rather than to new design. In his late years, his list of works in progress is a list of England's most prominent medieval buildings. Working with his second son, JOHN OLDRID SCOTT, he still had much work, but he had fallen behind the advanced line in practice led by such figures as R. NORMAN SHAW, JOHN JAMES STEVENSON, and his son, George Gilbert Scott, Jr.

During the four decades of Scott's practice, his office had grown to become one of the largest in London. Many important architects who trained in the Scott office remembered the sight of Scott dashing in and out of the office racing to a conference with clients for new buildings. Scott's office, in its size and sense of being fertile training ground, compares well to the office of McKIM, MEAD, AND WHITE in New York.

Scott should have been happy in his last years—knighted, wealthy, with a monumental hotel gazing across London, working on the major cathedrals of England, but he was not. The growing antirestoration movement focused on Scott as a source of their complaint. The Society for the Protection of Ancient Buildings was founded in 1877 by WILLIAM MORRIS after the announcement that Scott would begin work on Tewkesbury Abbey. Scott, sadly, seems to have had a lifelong penchant for attracting criticism. His first church commission, the privately financed parish church for his uncle in Flaunden of 1838, inspired an outraged letter to *The Builder* (1844, vol. 2, p. 156), complaining that the new church would cause the destruction of the old church with its picturesque appearance.

The career of Scott demands attention first of all because of the sheer number of buildings he and his office produced. Rarely an innovator, Scott was always second to implement advances in style and technique and as such was an important channel in the dissemination of these advances to a much wider public.

MOSETTE GLASER BRODERICK

Scott.
Saint Pancras Station.
London.
1868–1874

WORKS

1835, Old Windsor Workhouse (now a hospital), Berkshire, England. 1837, Workhouse (now Saint Edmund's Hospital), Northampton, England. 1840, Great Dunmow Workhouse, Essex, England. 1840–1842, Martyrs' Memorial, Oxford. 1841–1842, Christ Church, Turnham Green, Middlesex, England. 1841–1843, Infant Orphan Asylum, Wanstead, Essex, England. 1841–1843, Saint Giles, Camberwell, England. 1842–1845, Reading Gaol, Berkshire, England. 1844–1846, Saint Mark, Worsley, Lancashire, England. *1844–?, Nikolaikirche, Hamburg, Germany. 1845–1846, Saint John the Baptist, West Meon, Hampshire, England. 1846–?, Saint John's (later rebuilt), Newfoundland. 1847–1848, Saint Andrew, Bradfield, Berkshire, England. 1852–1854, Houses, Broad Sanctuary, Westminster, London. 1853–1858, Saint George, Doncaster; 1856–1859, All Souls Haley Hill, Halifax; Yorkshire, England. 1856–1859, Exeter College and Chapel, Oxford. 1857, Literary Institute, Sandback, Cheshire, England. 1858–1862, Kelham Hall, Nottinghamshire, England. 1859, Walton Hall, Warwickshire, England. 1861–1862, Hafodunos House, Denbigh, England. *1862, Town Hall, Preston, Lancashire, England. 1862–1873, Government Offices, Whitehall, London. 1863–1869, Saint John's College Chapel, Cambridge. 1863–1872, Albert Memorial, London. 1864–1868, Infirmary, Leeds, England. *1866, Brill's Baths, Brighton, England. 1867–?, Glasgow University, Scotland. 1868–1874, Saint Pancras Station; 1869–1872, Saint Mary Abbots, Kensington; London. 1874–1879, Anglican Cathedral, Edinburgh.

BIBLIOGRAPHY

BAYLEY, STEPHEN   1981   *The Albert Memorial: The*

Monument in Its Social and Architectural Context. London: Scolar.

BRIGGS, MARTIN S. 1908 "Sir Gilbert Scott, R.A." *Architectural Review* 24:92–100, 147–152, 180–185, 290–295.

BURY, SHIRLEY (editor) 1971 *Victorian Church Art.* London: H.M. Stationery Office. Catalogue of an exhibition at the Victoria and Albert Museum.

CLARKE, B. F. L. 1958 *Anglican Cathedrals Outside the British Isles.* London: S.P.C.K.

CLARKE, B. F. L. 1966 *Parish Churches of London.* London: Batsford.

COLE, DAVID 1950 "Some Early Works of Scott." *Architectural Association Journal* 66:98–108.

COLE, DAVID 1980 *The Work of Sir Gilbert Scott.* London: Architectural Press.

GIROUARD, MARK (1971)1979 *The Victorian Country House.* Rev. ed. New Haven: Yale University Press.

HITCHCOCK, H. R. (1954)1972 *Early Victorian Architecture in Britain.* Reprint. New York: Da Capo.

JACKSON, THOMAS GRAHAM 1950 *Recollections.* Edited by Basil Jackson. London: Oxford University Press.

PHYSICK, JOHN, and DARBY, MICHAEL 1973 *Marble Halls.* London: H.M. Stationery Office. Catalogue of an exhibition at the Victoria and Albert Museum.

PORT, M. H. 1961 *Six Hundred New Churches.* London: S.P.C.K.

PORT, M. H. 1968 "The New Law Courts Competition: 1866–67." *Architectural History* 11:75–93.

SCOTT, GEORGE GILBERT 1850 *A Plea for the Faithful Restoration of Our Ancient Churches.* London: Parker.

SCOTT, GEORGE GILBERT 1857 *Remarks on Secular and Domestic Architecture, Present and Future.* London: Murray.

SCOTT, GEORGE GILBERT 1860s *Design for the New Law Courts.* London: Day.

SCOTT, GEORGE GILBERT (1861)1863 *Gleanings from Westminster Abbey.* 2d ed., rev. Oxford University Press.

SCOTT, GEORGE GILBERT 1879a *Lectures on the Rise and Development of Medieval Architecture.* London: Murray.

SCOTT, GEORGE GILBERT (1879b)1977 *Personal and Professional Recollections.* Reprint. New York: Da Capo.

STAMP, GAVIN 1976 "Sir Gilbert Scott's Recollections." *Architectural History* 19:54–73.

STREET, A. E. (1888)1972 *Memoir of George Edmund Street.* Reprint. New York: Blom.

VICTORIA AND ALBERT MUSEUM 1978 *Sir Gilbert Scott (1811–78): Architect of the Gothic Revival.* London: The museum.

SCOTT, GEORGE GILBERT JR.

George Gilbert Scott, Jr. (1839–1897) is less well-known than either his father, GEORGE GILBERT SCOTT, or his son, GILES GILBERT SCOTT, but was recognized as one of the most talented and influential church architects of his generation. Along with JOHN D. SEDDING, Scott challenged the mid-Victorian orthodoxy in the Gothic Revival, which maintained the supremacy of the thirteenth century, and dared admire Perpendicular Gothic. With his friend and relative, GEORGE F. BODLEY, Scott rejected continental precedents and the High Victorian aesthetic. He designed churches in a refined, English Late Gothic manner and his secular buildings in Queen Anne and free classical styles.

Articled to his father in 1857–1860, he entered Cambridge University and began his independent practice in 1863, eventually becoming a fellow of Jesus College. Unlike his brother, JOHN OLDRID SCOTT, Scott reacted against his father's style and methods. His restorations were sensitive; at Pembroke College, for example, Cambridge (1879–1883), he respected CHRISTOPHER WREN's work. Scott's reputation and influence rested upon his principal work, Saint Agnes's, Kensington, London (1874–1891). In 1880, Scott became a Roman Catholic. In 1884, he was declared to be of unsound mind; after several times being confined in lunatic asylums, Scott died in the Midland Hotel, Saint Pancras Station, London. Several of his buildings were completed by his pupil TEMPLE MOORE.

GAVIN STAMP

WORKS

1868–1870, Peterhouse Hall and Combination Room, Cambridge. *c.1868–1874, Garboldisham Manor, Norfolk, England. 1873–1876, Saint Mark's Vicarage, Leamington Spa, England. *1874–1891, Church, School, and Vicarage of Saint Agnes, Kensington, London. 1875–1876, Woolton Hill Vicarage, Hampshire, England. 1876–1877, Houses, Park Street, Hull, England. 1876–1878, Pevensey Vicarage, Sussex, England. 1876–1879, Saint Mark's Church, Leamington Spa, England. *1877–1892, All Hallows' Church, Southwark, London. 1878–1879, Great Bedwyn Vicarage, Wiltshire, England. 1879–1882, Church of Saint Mary Magdalene, Eastmoors, Yorkshire, England. 1879–1883, Pembroke College (new hostel and extension of chapel), Cambridge. 1880–1882, Saint John's College (new building), Oxford. 1881–1897, Roman Catholic Church (now Cathedral) of Saint John the Baptist (completed in 1910 by John Oldrid Scott), Norwich, England.

BIBLIOGRAPHY

MILLARD, WALTER 1898–1899 "Notes on Some Works of the Late Geo. Gilbert Scott, M.A., F.S.A." *Architectural Review* 5:58, 67, 124–132.

"Obituary." 1897 *The Builder* 62:531.

SCOTT, G. G., JR. 1880 "On Modern Town Churches." *Building World* 4:411–414; 5:11–14, 51–54.

SCOTT, G. G., JR. 1881a *An Essay on the History of English Church Architecture prior to the Separation of England from the Roman Obedience.* London: Simpkin.

SCOTT, G. G., JR. 1881b "The True Work of the

Architect." *British Architect* 15:1–2.
STAMP, GAVIN 1978 "George Gilbert Scott, Junior, Architect: 1839–1897." Unpublished Ph.D. thesis, Cambridge University.

SCOTT, GILES GILBERT

Giles Gilbert Scott (1880–1960), one of the leading British architects of the twentieth century, occupied an important and influential position in the interwar years. Although he had been trained in the tradition of the Gothic Revival and had won fame by winning the competition for Liverpool Cathedral at the age of twenty-two, Scott was keen to design new and large types of modern buildings which in the 1920s and 1930s included university libraries and electric power stations. In the conflict of the 1930s between traditionalists and modernists, Scott occupied an important middle position, respected by both parties and believing in the necessity of compromise and in the idea of a true modern architecture being developed by evolution.

Scott's early work was influenced by that of his father, GEORGE GILBERT SCOTT, JR., to whose pupil, TEMPLE MOORE, he was articled. In 1903, Scott won the second round of the second competition for Liverpool Cathedral. At first associated with GEORGE F. BODLEY until the latter's death in 1907, Scott was occupied with this commission for the rest of his life and modified the original design in response to new and original ideas about the interpretation of the Gothic style. In this and in his many other churches Scott's Gothic became increasingly monumental and touched by a feeling for the sublime by the concentration of ornament, at the same time that he showed great skill in the handling of natural lighting. In several churches of the 1920s, Scott used the Romanesque style.

After World War I, Scott received several secular commissions, including university libraries in Oxford (1935–1946) and Cambridge (1930–1934). In these, and especially in his external treatment of the controversial Battersea Power Station (1930–1934) in London, Scott was strongly influenced by American architecture and adopted a modernist treatment. Scott made extensive use of reinforced concrete construction and was anxious to tackle new types of industrial design. He was responsible for the 1924 and 1935 models of the General Post Office telephone kiosk and designed the new Waterloo Bridge (1934–1945) in London. However, Scott had reservations about the external exposure of concrete and about the abandonment of tradition; he was uninfluenced by the International style.

World War II produced the commissions for rebuilding the House of Commons (1944–1951) and Coventry Cathedral, although Scott resigned from the latter in 1947. After 1945, he found himself working in an increasingly unsympathetic climate, and his style and methods were rejected by a younger generation.

Scott was knighted in 1924 and was president of the Royal Institute of British Architects in 1933–1935. After his death, his practice was continued by his son Richard Gilbert Scott.

GAVIN STAMP

WORKS

1903–1960, Liverpool Anglican Cathedral (not completed until 1980), England. 1905–1906, Roman Catholic Church of the Annunciation, Bournemouth, England. 1909–1912, Roman Catholic Church of Saint Maughold, Ramsay, Isle-of-Man, England. 1909–1935, Roman Catholic Church of Saint Joseph, Sheringham, Norfolk, England. 1913–1915, 129 Grosvenor Road (with Adrian Gilbert Scott; altered), London. 1913–1916, Anglican Church of Saint Paul, Stonycroft, Liverpool, England. 1913–1916, Roman Catholic Church of Our Lady, Northfleet, England. 1917–1939, Downside Abbey (nave of church and new buildings), Somerset, England. 1922–1927, Charterhouse School Chapel, Godalming, England. 1922–1954, Memorial Court, Clare College, Cambridge. 1922–1960, Ampleforth Abbey and College (new church and new buildings), Yorkshire, England. 1924–1925, Chester House, Clarendon Place, London. 1927–1956, Roman Catholic Church of Our Lady and Saint Alphege, Bath, England. 1927–1959, Roman Catholic Church of Saint Michael, Ashford, England. 1928–1929, Anglican Church of Saint Francis, Terriers, High Wycombe, England. 1928–1929, Longwall Quad, Magdalen College, Oxford. 1929–1931, Whitelands College, Putney; 1930–1932, Anglican Church of Saint Alban, Golders Green; 1930–1934, Battersea Power Station (with Halliday and Agate); London. 1930–1934, Cambridge University Library. 1931–1932, Anglican Church of Saint Andrew, Luton, England. 1931–1932, Lady Margaret Hall (chapel and new building), Oxford. 1931–1951, Roman Catholic Cathedral, Oban, Scotland. 1933–1951, Guinness Brewery (with Alexander Gibb and partners), Park Royal; 1934–1945, Waterloo Bridge (with Rendel, Palmer & Tritton); London. 1935–1946, New Bodleian Library, Oxford. 1935–1951, Electricity House, Bristol, England. 1944–1951, House of Commons (rebuilding; with A. G. Scott), London. 1947–1948, Rye House Power Station (incomplete), Hertfordshire, England. 1947–1960, Bankside Power Station; 1950–1954, Guildhall (restoration and new building), City of London. 1954–1959, Roman Catholic Carmelite Church, Kensington; London.

BIBLIOGRAPHY

REILLY, C. H. 1931 *Representative British Architects of Today*. London.

"Obituary." 1960 *Journal of the Royal Institute of British Architects* Series 3 67:193–194.

SCOTT, GILES GILBERT 1933 "The Inaugural Address." *Journal of the Royal Institute of British Architects* Series 3 41:5–14.

STAMP, GAVIN 1979 "Giles Gilbert Scott and the Problem of Modernism." *Architectural Design* 69, nos. 10–11:72–83.

STAMP, GAVIN, and HARTE, GLYNN BOYD 1979 *Temples of Power.* London: Cygnet.

SCOTT, JOHN

Born in Haumoana, New Zealand, John Scott (1924–) studied architecture at Auckland University. His work in New Zealand includes some notable Catholic churches, houses and community buildings, occasionally with Maori inflexions but always with a strong structural bias. In 1969, he traveled to Japan as a Churchill Fellow. He was in partnership with L. J. J. Hoogerbrug from 1965 to 1972.

JOHN STACPOOLE

WORKS

1954, Saint John's College Chapel, Hastings, New Zealand. 1959, Saint Patrick's School for Girls, Napier, New Zealand. 1960, Church of Our Lady of Lourdes, Havelock North, New Zealand. 1962, Fortuna Chapel, Karori, New Zealand. 1963, Seamen's Institute, Napier, New Zealand. 1964, Maori Battalion Memorial, Palmerston North, New Zealand. 1966–1967, Saint Augustine's School, Wanguni, New Zealand. 1967, Pattison House, Waipawa, New Zealand. 1970, Urewera Park Headquarters, Waikaremoana, New Zealand. 1972, Saint Mary's Church, Taradale, New Zealand. 1974, Flaxmere Village, Hastings, New Zealand. 1974–1978, Raratonga Hotel (with Ivan Mercep), Cook Islands. 1976, Saint Canice's Church, Westport, New Zealand. 1977, Macphail House; 1979, Rowe House; Havelock North, New Zealand.

BIBLIOGRAPHY

DALZELL, J. 1977 "John Scott, Architect." *Designscape* 92:23–30.

SCOTT, J. 1964 "Maori Battalion Memorial." *Te Ao Hou* June: 32–33.

SCOTT, J. 1965 "Futuna Chapel." *Architect's Journal* 142: Dec.: 391–394.

SCOTT, J., and FAN, M. C. 1973 "Of Woodsheds, Houses and People." *Islands Quarterly* 2, no. 3:289–302.

SCOTT, JOHN OLDRID

John Oldrid Scott (1841–1913) was the second son of GEORGE GILBERT SCOTT and heir to his father's architectural practice. Born in London, John Oldrid was educated at Bradfield College and entered his father's office in 1860. Although he remained an assistant to and occasional collaborator with his father, Scott did some work on his own and with his brother GEORGE GILBERT SCOTT, JUNIOR. Following the death of his father in 1878, Scott continued and wound down his father's late-life specialty of church alteration and restoration.

MOSETTE GLASER BRODERICK

WORKS

1869, Saint John the Baptist, Hythe, England. 1870, Saint Mary, Speldhurst, Kent, England. 1874–1872, Saint Sophia, Moscow Road, London. 1875–1913, Saint Mary, Slough, Buckinghamshire, England. 1876, Saint Paul, New Cross Road, Manchester, England. 1890–1891, Bradfield College Chapel, Berkshire, England.

BIBLIOGRAPHY

COLE, DAVID 1980 *The Work of Sir Gilbert Scott.* London.

"Obituary." 1913 *The Builder* 104:143, 650–651.

"Obituary." 1913 *Building News* 104:773–774.

ROYAL INSTITUTE OF BRITISH ARCHITECTS DRAWINGS COLLECTION n.d. "The Work of the Scott Family." London: The institute. Forthcoming publication.

SCOTT, MICHAEL

Michael Scott (1905–), born in Louth, has been a doyen of the Modern movement in Ireland since the 1930s. He was one of the first to introduce WALTER GROPIUS's style, as seen typically in Scott House, Sandycove (1938). Less dogmatic and more whimsical—in the LE CORBUSIER or Festival of Britain style—is the Central Bus Station, Dublin (1950–1953). With Ronald Tallon and Robin Walker, he was responsible for major public buildings. Since the Radio Telefis Eireann Studios (1959–1961), he has designed in a distinctly Miesian (see LUDWIG MIES VAN DER ROHE) style.

RODERICK O'DONNELL

WORKS

1937, County Hospital, Port Laoise, Ireland. 1938, Scott House, Sandycove, Dublin. 1940, Ritz Cinema, Athlone, County Westmeath, Ireland. 1950–1953, Central Bus Station; 1959–1961, Radio Telefis Eireann Studios (with Ronald Tallon); Dublin. 1967–1970, Carroll's Cigarette Factory (with Tallon), Dundalk, County Louth, Ireland. 1968–1972, Bank of Ireland Headquarters (with Tallon), Baggot Street; *1979, Altar and Cross for Papal Mass (only the cross is extant; with Tallon), Phoenix Park; Dublin.

BIBLIOGRAPHY

NATIONAL GALLERY OF IRELAND, DUBLIN 1975 Numbers 95–97, 100–106, 108–109 in *The Architecture of Ireland in Drawings and Paintings*. Dublin: The gallery. Exhibition catalogue.

ROYAL COLLEGE OF ART, LONDON 1980 Pages 21–22, 34–35, 39, 40, 46 in *Traditions and Directions: The Evolution of Irish Architecture*. London: The college. Exhibition catalogue.

SCOTT, THOMAS SEATON

Thomas Seaton Scott (1826–1895) emigrated to Canada from England in the mid-1850s and established a modest private practice in Montreal. As a designer, Scott is best known for his work in the Gothic style which included a number of small Anglican churches and the extension to the West Block of the Parliament Buildings in Ottawa (1874–1877). In 1871, Scott assumed national prominence when he was appointed first chief architect of the Department of Public Works, a post he held until 1881. Although it was primarily an administrative position, Scott directed the federal government's large post-Confederation building program which produced some of Canada's finest examples of public buildings in the Second Empire style.

JANET WRIGHT

WORKS

1857–1859, Christ Church Cathedral (with Frank Wills), Montreal. 1860, Saint John's Anglican Church, Prescott; 1863, Ballymena, Maitland; Ontario. 1868, Saint Bartholomew's Church, Ottawa. 1869, Trinity Church, Cornwall, Ontario. 1871, Saint Luke's Church, Waterloo, Quebec. 1874–1877, Parliament Buildings Mackenzie Tower and extension to the West Block), Ottawa. 1887–1888, Bonaventure Station, Montreal.

BIBLIOGRAPHY

CAMERON, CHRISTINA, and WRIGHT, JANET 1980 "Second Empire Style in Canadian Architecture." *Canadian Historic Sites: Occasional Papers in Archaeology and History* no.24:13–14.

WRIGHT, JANET 1977 "Thomas Seaton Scott: Architect and Administrator." Unpublished manuscript, Canadian Inventory of Historic Building, Parks Canada, Ottawa. Paper read before the Society for the Study of Architecture in Canada, May 24, 1977.

SCOTT, CHESTERTON, and SHEPHERD

The practice of Elizabeth Scott (1898–1972), Maurice Chesterton (1883–1962), and John Chiene Shepherd (1896–) lasted only from 1928 to 1939 and was chiefly noted for one building, the Shakespeare Memorial Theatre, won in competition by Elizabeth Scott. She was the granddaughter of GEORGE GILBERT SCOTT and was trained at the Architectural Association, London (1919–1924). She was working for Chesterton when she won the competition in 1928, and for its construction went into partnership with him and Shepherd. The theater, constructed in brick in a functionally expressive Dutch style, was a remarkably radical statement for its time in England.

MARGARET RICHARDSON

WORKS

1928–1932, Royal Shakespeare Memorial Theatre, Stratford-on-Avon, Warwickshire, England. 1933 Doctor's House and Surgery, Morden, Surrey, England. 1935, House, Gidea Park, Essex, England. 1936, Homer Farm School for Infants, Henley-on-Thames; 1937, House, Fludger's Wood; 1938, Houses, Stoke Row, Henley-on-Thames; Oxfordshire, England. 1938, Newnham College (extensions), Cambridge. 1938, Restaurant; 1938, Royal Shakespeare Memorial Theatre; Stratford-on-Avon, Warwickshire, England. 1941, Elementary School, Northallerton, Yorkshire, England.

BIBLIOGRAPHY

"Obituary." 1972 *Architect's Journal* 156, no. 28:68.
"Obituary." 1972 *Building* 272, no. 6736:55.
"Obituary." 1972 *The Times,* June 24, p. 169.

SEARLES, MICHAEL

Michael Searles (1750–1813) was apprenticed in his father's profession of surveying and became surveyor of the Rolls Estate in South London. He expanded his role into architect for the estate and for others, principally designing small shops and houses. Gloucester Circus (1790–1792), Surrey Square (1794–1795), and Princes Place (1788–1790) were innovative in using colonnades to link a crescent of semidetached villas. The Paragon (1790–1791) and Clare House (c.1793) are noted for originality in the interior composition. The evidence of Searles's work and draftsmanship reveal that his talent exceeded his available opportunities.

RICHARD LORCH

WORKS

1784, 1791, Surrey Place; c.1787, Marlborough House (now 317 Kennington Road); 1788–1790, Princes Place (now 114–135 Kennington Park Road); 1789–1790, Southwark Paragon; 1790–1791, Paragon, Blackheath, Greenwich; 1790–1792, Gloucester Circus, Greenwich; London. c.1793, Clare House, East Malling, Kent, England. 1794–1795, Surrey Square; 1795–1800, Rolls Estate Office (now 155 Kent Road); London. 1802, Reigate Priory (alterations to the west front façade), Surrey, England. 1805, Kent Street Inn (now Tabard Street); 1812–1813, Walworth Chapel; London.

BIBLIOGRAPHY

MARTIN, A. R.   1949   "Letter." *Country Life* 106: 1149–1150.
NARES, GORDON   1949   "Clare House." *Country Life* 106:826–829, 898–901.
SUMMERSON, JOHN   (1962)1970   *Georgian London: An Architectural Study.* New York: Praeger.

SEARS, WILLARD

See CUMMINGS and SEARS.

SEDDING, JOHN D.

According to Niklaus Pevsner, John Dando Sedding (1838–1891) was "perhaps the most original church architect of the late Gothic Revivalist school" (Pevsner, [1936] 1960, p. 26). He was born in Eton, England, and in 1858 entered the office of GEORGE E. STREET. He practiced first (1863) at Penzance, Cornwall, with his brother Edmund, and then in Bristol after the latter's death in 1868. In 1874, he established his office in London and in 1876 he became influenced by JOHN RUSKIN. Sedding's office in the 1880s was the nurturing ground for a generation of architects who became the leaders of the Arts and Crafts movement. His Holy Trinity Church, Sloane Street, London (1888–1890), a showcase of fine craftwork and decoration, was his last and most mature work. He was a prolific designer of church metalwork, and textiles and wallpapers. Late in life he became interested in garden design. He died in Winsford, Somerset, where he had been engaged in restoration work.

BETTY ELZEA

WORKS

1871, Saint Clement's Church, Boscombe, Hampshire, England. 1887–1888, Church of the Holy Redeemer, Clerkenwell; 1888–1890, Holy Trinity Church, Sloane Street; London.

BIBLIOGRAPHY

NAYLOR, GILLIAN   1971   *The Arts and Crafts Movement.* London: Studio Vista.
PEVSNER, NIKOLAUS   (1936)1974   *Pioneers of Modern Design.* Rev. ed. Harmondsworth, England: Penguin. Quotation in the text is from the 1960 edition.
SEDDING, J. D.   1893   *Art and Handicraft.* London: Kegan Paul.
SEDDING, J. D.   1891   *Garden-craft Old and New.* London: Kegan Paul.
WILSON, HENRY ET AL.   1892   *A Memorial to the Late J. D. Sedding.* London: Batsford.

SEDDON, J. P.

Mainly an ecclesiastical architect and designer practicing in England and Wales, John Pollard Seddon (1827–1906) worked principally in a vigorous Gothic style. He was in partnership with John Pritchard of Llandaff from 1852 to 1862 and with John Coates Carter of Cardiff from 1884 to 1904, though from 1857 he had his own office in London.

J. E. HESELTINE

WORKS

c.1856–1862, Ettington Park, Warwickshire, England. c.1858, Beckford Hall (alterations and additions), Gloucestershire, England. 1859–1872, Chapel (restoration); 1861–1864 (and later), School Buildings; Christ's College, Brecon, Wales. 1864, Castle House Hotel, Aberystwyth, Cardigan, Wales. c.1868–1878, Church of Saint James, Great Yarmouth, England. 1869–1872, University College of Wales, Aberystwyth. 1874–1875, Church of Saint Peter, Ayot-Saint-Peter; c.1874–1885, Church of Saint Catherine (rebuilding), Hoarwithy; Herefordshire, England. c.1880–1885, Houses, Hotels, and Bungalows, Birchington-on-Sea, Kent, England. 1886, University College of Wales (rebuilding), Aberystwyth.

BIBLIOGRAPHY

"Contemporary British Architects."   1890   *Building News* 58:115–116.
DARBY, MICHAEL   1981   *A Catalogue of Drawings by John Pollard Seddon.* London: H.M. Stationery Office. Forthcoming publication.
"Obituary."   1906   *The Builder* 90:150, 176–177.
"Obituary."   1906   *Building News* 90:203.
"Obituary."   1906   *Journal of the Royal Institute of British Architects* 13:194, 221.

SEDILLE, PAUL

Born in Paris, the son of an architect, Paul Sedille (1836–1900) entered the Ecole des Beaux-Arts in 1857, the pupil of J. F. J. B. Guénepin. Although Sedille later turned to painting, he remained a stylish designer and architect, concerned with domestic architecture. He was in charge of the arrangement of the exhibits at the international exposition of 1889.

R. D. MIDDLETON

WORKS

1864, Apartment Block, 55 Boulevard Malesherbes; 1866, Hôtel Boulevard Haussmann (with C. J. Sedille); 1869–1870, Apartment Block, 19 Boulevard Magental; 1877, Hôtel Sédille, 28 Boulevard Malesherbes; *1877, Porte des Beaux-Arts (partly re-erected, 4 rue de la Pierre Levée), Exposition Universelle 1878; *1877, Usine Creusot Pavilion (a small part of this was re-erected in 1880 and survives at the Plaine des Riaux, Le Creusot, Saône et Loire, France), Exposition Universelle; 1878; before 1882, Villa Dietz-Monnin, 82 rue Lafontaine, Auteuil; 1882–1885, Magasins du Printemps (first stage), Boulevard Haussman; Paris. 1883, Château de Boisrond, Bussy-le-Repos, near Villeneuve-sur-Yonne, France. 1885–1886, Villa, rue d'Erlanger, Auteuil; 1886–1887, Hôtel Amedi Lacarière, 11 rue Vernet; 1887–1888, Apartment Block, 13 rue Vernet; 1887–1888, Théâtre du Palais Royal (foyer and redecoration), 40 rue de Montpensier; 1891, House and Workshops, 10 rue Collange, Levallois-Perret; 1892–1893, House and Photographic Studio, 105 Avenue de Neuilly; Paris. 1893–?, Pilgrimage Church of Jeanne d'Arc, Bois Chenu, Dorémy la Pucelle, Haute Marne, France. 1900, Société Centrale des Architectes (main doorway; with André Allar), 8 rue Danton; n.d., Apartment Block, 14 rue Le Peletier; Paris. n.d., Château de Presles, (extensive restoration; redecoration and outbuildings), Ferté-Alais, Seine et Oise, France. n.d., Hôtel, 58 rue de Lisbonne, Paris. n.d., Schneider Monument, Le Creusot, Sâone et Loire, France. n.d., Villa at Montretout, near Marseille, Bouches du Rhône, France. n.d., Villa Sédille, Chatenay, France.

BIBLIOGRAPHY

ETIENNE, LUCIEN 1900 "La vie et les oeuvres de Paul Sédille." L'Architecture 13:305–308, 313–315.

LE NORMAND, ANTOINETTE 1979 "Une bonbonnière d'artiste." Monuments historiques 102:66–68.

LUCAS, CHARLES 1899–1900 "Nécrologie: Paul Sédille." Construction Moderne 1899–1900:179–180.

SÉDILLE, PAUL 1873 "Salon de 1873: Exposition des oeuvres d'architecture." Bulletin Mensuel de la Société Centrale des Architectes 1873:135–155.

SÉDILLE, PAUL 1875 "Monuments, musées et paysages de l'Espagne." Bulletin Mensuel de la Sociéte Centrale des Architectes 1875:97–112.

SÉDILLE, PAUL 1882 Villa rue La Fontaine, 82, à Auteuil. Paris: Morel.

SÉDILLE, PAUL 1884 "La céramique monumentale." L'Architecture 1894.

SÉDILLE, PAUL 1885 Grands Magasins du Printemps à Paris. Paris: Morel.

SÉDILLE, PAUL (1886)1890 L'Architecture moderne en Angleterre. Paris: Librairie des Bibliophiles. Extracts were also published in L'Architecture 1891:185–190.

SÉDILLE, PAUL (1887)1888 "Etude sur la renaissance de la polychromie monumentale en France." L'Architecture 1:13–16, 37–40, 97–99.

SÉDILLE, PAUL (1884)1890 L'Architecture moderne à Vienne. Paris: Librairie des Imprimeries Réunies.

SÉDILLE, PAUL, and LUCAS, CHARLES 1881 Etude sur quelques monuments portugais, d'apres des notes de M. le C.te da Silva. Paris: Imprimerie nationale.

SULLY-PRUDHOMME, RENÉ FRANÇOIS ARMAND 1901 "Paul Sédille." Revue de l'art ancien et moderne 9:77–84, 149–160.

SEGAL, WALTER

Walter Segal (1907–) was born in Ascona, Switzerland, of parents who had come originally from Rumania. His father was an Expressionist painter, and he was brought up in a liberal and utopian artists commune receiving his early education from his parents and their friends. Only at the age of thirteen, he says, did he discover the real world. His early experiences left him with a vigorous independence of mind, a determination to find his own way in everything, and a profound distrust of artistic and religious cults. Perhaps in reaction to his father's artistic aspirations, his own work has always been downright practical, though often ingenious. He can be very tolerant of flights of fancy in others, but he has always kept himself strictly to the task in hand, and most of his work is on a small scale and domestic. He speaks enthusiastically about the spirit of adventure which motivates him, but his architecture is adventurous not so much in a spatial or formal sense as in the way it is put together.

Segal's relationships with bureaucracy and institutions have always been stormy, and it is hardly surprising that he attended no less than three architectural schools, at Delft, Berlin, and Zurich. While in Berlin, he made the acquaintance of the avant-garde and became firm friends with BRUNO TAUT.

After qualifying as an architect and undertaking a couple of small jobs, Segal traveled for a couple of years engaged in archeological research. His studies brought him to England where he married and set up practice. He soon established himself as a colorful figure on the London architectural scene, writing, teaching, and building. Many of his works of the 1940s and 1950s were published, but it was in the 1960s and 1970s that he made his most original contribution to British architecture. It started with a temporary house that he built in 1964 for the amazingly low price of £850. This was of timber frame construction with a flat roof without excavated foundations. Materials were used uncut wherever possible, fitting into a tartan grid based on manufactured sizes. Segal went on to develop and refine his building system in a series of private houses, but it reached its climax with a daring experiment in social housing for the London borough of Lewisham, where tenants built their own houses, the borough providing site and materials.

PETER BLUNDELL-JONES

WORKS

1932, Casa Piccolo, Ascona, Switzerland. 1933, House, Terreno, Palma, Majorca, Spain. 1945, Block of Flats, Leigham Court Road, Streatham; 1950, Housing Estate, Saint Anne's Close, Highgate; London. 1961, House, Rugby Road, Twickenham, Middlesex, England. 1966, Block of Flats, Cat Hill, East Barnet, London. 1970, Timber House, Main Street, Yelling, Huntingdonshire, England. 1971, House, Ballycummisk, County Cork, Ireland. 1977, Two-story House, Mill Hill; 1977–1980, Lewisham Self-Build Housing Association; London.

BIBLIOGRAPHY

MCKEAN, JOHN MAULE 1976a "Walter Segal: Pioneer." *Building Design* 286, Feb. 20:10–14; 287, Feb. 27:18–19.
MCKEAN, JOHN MAULE 1976b "Walter Segal." *Architectural Design* 46:288–295.
SEGAL, WALTER 1974 "Meeting Gropius Again." *Architects' Journal* 159, no. 7:298–300.
SEGAL, WALTER 1977 "Timber Framed Housing." *Journal of the Royal Institute of British Architects* 84:284–295.

SEGUIN, MARC

A French engineer born in Annonay (Ardeche), Marc Séguin (1786–1875) was the son of a fabric manufacturer and the nephew of the aeronaut J. Montgolfier. Known for building more than eighty suspended bridges in France, Spain, and Italy, he was a genius in mechanics. With little academic education, he apprenticed in Paris with his uncle and with Leroux until 1810, then worked with his father. His own experimentation with cable resistance led him, in 1823, to span the Rhône between Tain and Tournon with the first suspended bridge using iron wires instead of chains or ropes as in the United States and England. He invented a tubular steam boiler used in industry and for railway engines and built railways under his own company together with his four younger brothers. His discoveries extended to molecular physics, mechanics, astronomy, and social theories.

MARC DILET

WORKS

1824, Tournon Bridge over the Rhône, France. 1836, Railway between Paris and Versailles, France.

BIBLIOGRAPHY

SÉGUIN, MARC 1824 *Des Ponts en fil de fer*. Paris: Bachelier.
SÉGUIN, MARC 1826 *Mémoire sur le chemin de fer de St.-Etienne à Lyon*. Paris: Didot.
SÉGUIN, MARC 1828 *Mémoire sur la navigation à la vapeur*. Paris: Bachelier.
SÉGUIN, MARC 1839 *De l'Influence des chemins de fer et de l'art de les tracer et de les construire*. Brussels: Société Typographique Belge.
SÉGUIN, MARC 1857 *Mémoire sur l'origine et la propagation de la force*. Paris: Bachelier.

SEHEULT, FRANÇOIS LEONARD

François Leonard Seheult (1771–1840), whose name is also spelled Scheult or Schuelt, was born in Nantes, France, the son of a contractor. He studied in Paris at the Académie (1786–1789), a pupil of A. F. Peyre (see PEYRE FAMILY), and traveled to Italy, where he measured a number of small villas and farmsteads, the basis of his future designs. Seheult was not an innovator. He worked at Nantes in the wake of MATHURIN CRUCY. His son, Saint Félix (1793–1858), was also an architect.

R. D. MIDDLETON.

WORKS

1810, Château de Montis, Haute Goulaine; 1824, Hôtel Seheult, 8 rue de l'Héronnière, Nantes; n.d., Hôtel, 8 rue Lafayette, Nantes; n.d., Hôtel, 22 rue Copernic, Nantes; Loire Atlantique, France.

BIBLIOGRAPHY

LEVOT, P. 1857 Volume 2, pages 834–844 in *Biographie Bretonne: Recueil de notices sur tous les bretons qui se sont fait un nom*. Paris: Dumoulin.
MELLINET, CAMILLE *Annales de la société académique de Nantes et de la Loire Inférieure* 13:363–365.
SCHUELT, F. L. (1821)1840 *Recueil d'architecture dessinée et mesurée en Italie*. 2d ed. Paris: Bance.

SEIDL, GABRIEL VON

Descended from a family of Munich bakers, Gabriel von Seidl (1848–1913) rose to a position of extraordinary prominence among German architects. His influence can be observed in the work of KARL HOCHEDER, FRIEDRICH VON THIERSCH, THEODOR FISCHER, and Gabriel's brother, Emanuel Seidl.

Widely traveled and well-read, Seidl absorbed the intellectual influences of his time and expressed them in his eclectic architecture. His building style alternated among the German Renaissance revival, the neobaroque, and an asymmetrical and massive neo-Romanesque. All his buildings, however, were known for their sound construction, fine workmanship, and careful planning. Seidl was knighted and received many official honors.

BARBARA MILLER LANE

WORKS

1879–1880, Deutsches Haus; 1879–1880, Seidl House; 1880?, Sedlmayr House; 1881–1882, Arzberger-Keller; 1886, Franziskaner-Keller; 1887–1889, Villa Kaulbach; 1887–1891, Villa Lenbach; 1887–1892, Sankt-Anna-Pfarkirche; Munich. 1888?, Sedlmayr House, Berlin. 1888–1889, Erhard House; 1889–1891, Onuphriushaus Store and Offices; Munich. 1891?, Town Hall (remodeling), Ingolstadt, Germany. 1893–1894, Bauerngirgl; 1893–1900, Künstlerhaus; 1894–1900, Bavarian National Museum; 1897–1899, Palais Berchem; 1899, Stadler House; Munich. c.1900, Museum, Speyer, Germany. 1900–1902, Karlstor-Rondell Store and Offices; 1901–1902, Palais Klopfer; 1901–1903, Sankt-Rupertus-Kirche; 1903–1905, Ruffinihäuser Store and Offices; 1904–1906, Korpshaus Germania; 1906–1913, Deutsches Museum (not completed until 1925); 1907–1908, Maria-Thalkirche (extension); Munich. 1910–1913?, City Hall (reconstruction and remodeling, with addition), Bremen, Germany. 1911–1912, Drey House; 1911–1913, Freundlich House; Munich.

BIBLIOGRAPHY

BEENKEN, HERMANN 1944 *Das neunzehnte Jahrhundert in der deutschen Kunst.* Munich: Bruckmann.
BÖSSL, HANS 1966 *Gabriel von Seidl.* Munich: Verlag des Historischen Vereins von Oberbayern.
Deutsche Bauzeitung 1902 34:444–494, 497–500, 537–538, 541.
DÖRING, O. 1924 *Zwei Münchener Baukünstler: Gabriel von Seidl, Georg von Hauberrisser.* Munich: Allgemeine Vereinigung für christliche Kunst.
FISCHER, THEODOR 1913 "Gabriel von Seidl." *Zentralblatt der Bauverwaltung* 33:233–235.
GROESCHEL, JULIUS 1900 "Der Neubau des Nationalmuseums in München." *Zentralblatt der Bauverwaltung* 20:539–543.
KARLINGER, HANS 1937 *München und die deutsche Kunst des neunzehnten Jahrhunderts.* Munich: Knorr & Hirth.
"Das neue Rathaus in Bremen." 1913 *Zentralblatt der Bauverwaltung* 33:141–146, 153–156.
SCHMAEDEL, JOSEPH VON 1914–1915 "Gabriel von Seidl." *Wasmuths Monatshefte für Baukunst und Städtebau* 1:31–41.
"Das Sedlmayrsche Haus in Berlin." 1885 *Zentralblatt der Bauverwaltung* 5:440–441.

the Brazilian OSCAR NIEMEYER. He eventually moved to Australia, in 1948. His first ten buildings had a direct and immediate influence on Australian architecture and attracted world attention. They began with the R. Seidler House and included the immaculate Rose House (1949–1954). All of his architecture is reduced to the most essential, effective statement.

In the 1960s, his designs continued to explore the rationale of mid-twentieth century functionalism which he learned in North America. In 1969, he began to explore the baroque character of a curved line in plan in an attempt to break from the box. Coupled with a love for structural clarity, his architecture in the 1970s brought curved forms and structure together. This blend is exemplified in parts of the Trade Groups Offices (PIER LUIGI NERVI was structural consultant) in 1970 and wholly in the Australian Embassy in Paris (with Nervi and Breuer) completed in 1979.

DONALD LESLIE JOHNSON

WORKS

1949–1954, Rose House, Turramurra; 1950–1951, Sussman House, Kurrajong Heights; New South Wales, Australia. 1961, Lend Lease House Office Building; 1961–1967, Australia Square; Sydney. 1963, Block of Flats, Diamond Bay, New South Wales, Australia. 1964–1968, N. S. W. Government Stores, Alexandria, Australia. 1966–1967, Seidler House, Killara, New South Wales, Australia. 1970–1974, Trade Groups Offices, Canberra. 1971–1973, Seidler's Office, Milsons Point; 1971–1975, M. L. C. Centre; Sydney. 1977–1978, Australian Embassy, Paris.

BIBLIOGRAPHY

BLAKE, PETER 1973 *Architecture for the New World: The Work of Harry Seidler.* Sydney: Horowitz; New York: Wittenborn; Stuttgart, Germany: Kraemar. Includes an excellent bibliography.
BLAKE, PETER 1979 *Harry Seidler, Australian Embassy.* Sydney: Horowitz; New York: Wittenborn; Stuttgart, Germany: Kraemar.
BOYD, ROBIN 1952 *Australia's Home.* Melbourne University Press.
JOHNSON, DONALD LESLIE 1980 *Australian Architecture 1901–51: Sources of Modernism.* Sydney University Press.
SEIDLER, HARRY 1954 *Houses, Interiors and Projects.* Sydney: Associated General Publications.
SEIDLER, HARRY 1963 *Harry Seidler, 1955/63.* Sydney: Horowitz; New York: Wittenborn; Stuttgart, Germany: Kraemar.

SEIDLER, HARRY

Vienna-born, English- and Canadian-trained, Harry Seidler (1923–) completed postgraduate study at the Harvard Graduate School of Design before working with MARCEL BREUER and, briefly,

SELLARS, JAMES

James Sellars (1843–1888) practiced in Glasgow, from 1872 in partnership with Campbell Douglas, an ex-assistant of JOHN DOBSON. Under Douglas's supervision, he designed public and commercial buildings first in ALEXANDER THOMSON Grecian infused with French features, and in a free Renaissance manner thereafter. His churches were usually early French Gothic, his mansions Scots baronial or R. NORMAN SHAW Tudor, and his Glasgow Exhibition Buildings (1887–1888) Saracenic.

DAVID M. WALKER.

WORKS

*1873, Saint Enoch's Free Church, Argyle Street; 1873–1877, Saint Andrew's Halls (now part of Mitchell Library), Berkeley Street; Glasgow. *1874, Keil House, Campbeltown, Argyllshire, Scotland. 1877, Free Church (now Saint John's) Bonnygate, Fife, Scotland. *1877–1878, City of Glasgow Bank (completed as Mann Byars Building); 1878, Finnieston (later Kelvingrove) Church, Derby Street; 1879–1880, Glasgow Herald Building; Glasgow. 1880–1881, Town Hall and Municipal Buildings, Ayr, Scotland. *1882–1883, Mugdock New Castle, Stirlingshire, Scotland. 1883–1885, Wylie & Lochhead's (now Fraser's) Department Store, Glasgow. *1885–1886, Saint Andrew's Church, Drumsheugh, Edinburgh. *1887–1888, Glasgow International Exhibition Buildings.

BIBLIOGRAPHY

GOMME, ANDOR, and WALKER, DAVID 1968 *The Architecture of Glasgow.* London: Lund Humphries.
KEPPIE, JOHN 1888 "The Late James Sellars, Architect, Glasgow." *Scottish Art Review* 1:191–193.
WALKER, DAVID M. 1967a "James Sellars, Architect, Glasgow, 1843–1888." *Scottish Art Review* 9, no. 1:16–19.
WALKER, DAVID M. 1967b "James Sellars, Architect: Work in Glasgow 1880–1888." *Scottish Art Review* 9, no. 2:21–24.

SELLERS, J. H.

J. Henry Sellers (1861–1954) was born in Manchester, England. Working as an informal partner of Edgar Wood, he designed three striking buildings in Lancashire between 1904 and 1920. Thinking of himself as a rationalist, he applied symmetrical plans and flat roof structures of reinforced concrete to buildings of residual Gothic or classical detail. His buildings after 1910 were more traditional.

RODERICK O'DONNELL

WORKS

1906–1907, Dronsfields's Offices, King Street, Oldham, Lancashire, England. 1908–1910, Durnford Street School; 1908–1910, Elm Street School; Middelton, Manchester, England.

BIBLIOGRAPHY

ARCHER, JOHN 1975 "Edgar Wood and J. Henry Sellers: A Decade of Partnership and Experiment." Pages 372–384 in Alastair Service (editor), *Edwardian Architecture and Its Origins.* London: Architectural Press.
TREUHERZ, JULIAN (editor) 1975 *Partnership in Style: Edgar Wood and J. Henry Sellers.* Manchester, England: City Art Gallery. Exhibition catalogue.

SELMERSHEIM, TONY

Tony Selmersheim (1872–?) was a French interior designer who worked in a restrained Art Nouveau style during the 1890s, and later changed to a modern style that featured pared-down pastiches of traditional classical furniture styles. His career as a designer was successful because he modified any influential trend he adopted, be it Art Nouveau, Art Deco, or Bauhaus functionalism, with the forms of traditional furniture design.

JAMES WARD

BIBLIOGRAPHY

Art et Décoration 1923–1935 44:161–184; 47:177–228; 64:201–224.
GÜNTHER, SONJA 1971 *Interieurs um 1900.* Munich: W. Fink.
JOURDAIN, FRANTZ 1904 "Tony Selmersheim." *Art et Décoration* 16:189–198.
JULLIAN, PHILLIPPE 1974 *The Triumph of Art Nouveau.* New York: Larousse.
MADSEN, STEPHAN TSCHUDI (1956)1975 *Sources of Art Nouveau.* Translated by Ragna Christopherson. New York: Da Capo.
MASINI, LARA VINCA 1976 *Art Nouveau.* Florence: Martelli.
OLMER, PIERRE 1927 *La Renaissance du Mobilier Français (1890–1920).* Paris: Vanoest.
RUSSELL, FRANK (editor) 1979 *Art Nouveau Architecture.* New York: Rizzoli.
SAUNIER, CHARLES 1914 "Concours pour un Cabinet de Président du Conseil Municipal de Paris." *Art et Décoration* 35:89–96.
SOULIER, GUSTAVE 1900 "Charles Plumet et Tony Selmersheim." *Art et Décoration* 7:11–21.

SELVA, GIOVANNI ANTONIO

Giovanni Antonio Selva (1751–1819) was born in Venice, Italy, and practiced almost exclusively in the Veneto. Selva admired the architecture of ANDREA PALLADIO, MICHELE SANMICHELI, and JACAPO SANSOVINO, but the principal influences upon his architecture were his master, TOMMASO TEMANZA, the rigorist theories of FRANCESCO MILIZIA, and the neoclassicist sculptor Antonio

Canova, his longtime friend. Selva was extremely well-traveled and well-read. As a young man, he traveled throughout Italy with Canova to look at antiquities. He also visited England, Austria, France, Holland, and Constantinople, and translated into Italian various works by Sir WILLIAM CHAMBERS and VINCENZO SCAMOZZI. Selva is best known for his design for the Teatro La Fenice in Venice (1790–1792) and his rebuilding of the Duomo at Cologna Veneta (1806–1817), where he came closest to achieving the Roman grandeur he so often sought. Selva taught at the Accademia in Venice and was the master of many, including GIUSEPPE JAPPELLI, perhaps the most original of the next generation of north Italian architects.

ELIZABETH GREENE

WORKS

1782–1783, Palazzo Pisani (restoration), Padua, Italy. 1782–1784, Villa Manfrin, Treviso, Italy. 1784, Palazzo Mangilli-Valmarana (restoration); 1790–1792, Teatro della Fenice; 1794, Palazzo Manin (restoration); Venice, Italy. 1796, Palazzo Dotti, Padua, Italy. 1798–1801, Teatro Nuovo, Trieste, Italy. 1806–1817, Duomo (rebuilding), Cologna Veneta, Italy. 1807–1810, Public gardens; 1815–1819, Chiesa del Santissimo Nome di Gesù (not completed until 1834); Venice, Italy.

BIBLIOGRAPHY

BASSI, ELENA 1936 *Giannantonio Selva: Architetto veneziano.* Padua, Italy: CEDAM.

MEEKS, CARROLL L. V. 1966 *Architecture in Italy: 1750–1914.* New Haven: Yale University Press.

MEZZANOTTE, GIANNI (1966)1975 *Architettura neoclassica in Lombardia.* Naples: Edizione Scientifiche Italiane.

MILIZIA, FRANCESCO (1781)1785 *Memorie degli architetti antichi e moderni.* 4th ed. Bassano, Italy: Remondini.

SELVA, GIOVANNI ANTONIO 1814 *Sulla voluta ionica.* Padua, Italy.

SEMPER, GOTTFRIED

Gottfried Semper (1803–1879) was the most admired architect in Germany for the generation, after KARL FRIEDRICH SCHINKEL, and his major book, the two-volume *Der Stil in den technischen und tektonischen Künsten oder praktische Aesthetik* (Style in the Industrial and Structural Arts, or Practical Aesthetics, 1860–1863), shows Semper to have been one of the most prescient theorists of the nineteenth century. His writings are not affected by the occasional parochialism of, for example, EUGÈNE EMMANUEL VIOLLET-LE-DUC, A. W. N. PUGIN, or WILLIAM MORRIS. He was in every sense of the word a European. He received his training in Germany and France, made a three-year study tour to Italy and Greece, and worked as an architect and teacher in Germany, England, Switzerland, and Austria. His influence reached into the twentieth century and can be found among such a wide-ranging group of architects as BERNARD R. MAYBECK, OTTO WAGNER, H. P. BERLAGE, WALTER GROPIUS, and BRUNO TAUT. For Central European architects, Semper assumed the kind of position Viollet-le-Duc had in Western Europe. His writings were also well known to such American architects as JOHN W. ROOT and LOUIS H. SULLIVAN.

The subtlety of Semper's thought, together with the convolutions of his German, has made his theory the subject of severe misrepresentation. A clear understanding of his concepts is further obstructed by the fact that *Der Stil* is incomplete. Semper had planned to write a third volume which, presumably, would have clarified and synthesized the content of the first two. Thus, the full and coherent development of his ideas must often be surmised from earlier essays and form suggestions made in the prolegomena to *Der Stil*. Four standard incorrect classifications have emerged: (1) to see him as a utilitarian materialist; (2) to see him as a Darwinian evolutionist; (3) to see his analysis of architectural archetypes as examples of "first origins"; and (4) to use his general theory as a handbook for building.

Semper was born in Hamburg and studied law and mathematics at the University of Göttingen from 1823 to 1825. In 1825, after he decided to become an architect, he studied in Munich with FRIEDRICH VON GÄRTNER. In 1826, he fled to France after fighting a duel. There, he worked under FRANZ CHRISTIAN GAU and JACQUES IGNACE HITTORFF. From 1830 until 1833, he traveled to southern France, Italy, and Greece. In 1834, Semper became the director of the Bauschule of the Royal Academy in Dresden, a post which he had received on the recommendation of Schinkel. While there, he designed, among other things, the Opera (1838–1841) and the Picture Gallery (1847–1854), whose wing completed the fourth open side of the baroque Zwinger and thus formed a group with one of Dresden's most important buildings.

Semper's participation in the 1849 revolution in Dresden may serve as a clue to his interpretation of architecture. In 1849, he was engaged in several royal commissions. Thus, when he joined the side of the republican revolutionaires—among them was his friend Richard Wagner—he had much to lose. When the royalists were victorious, he had to flee the country. He lived for a time in Paris and even considered emigrating to America, but then

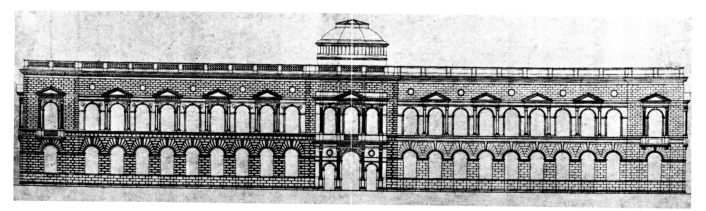

Semper.
Picture Gallery.
Dresden, Germany.
1847–1854 (completed later
by Kruger and Hänel)

he received an invitation from London to participate in the design of the Great Exposition of 1851. Subsequently, he taught at the School for Practical Art at Marlborough House. In 1855, he accepted a professorship at the Polytechnical School in Zurich, becoming its director later that same year. Between 1869 and 1876, he was involved in the supervision of several Vienna Ringstrasse projects, the most important of which was his design with KARL VON HASENAUER of the Museum of Art History and the Museum of Natural History (1872–1881), creating a forum for the Neue Hofburg. Semper died in Rome.

It is against a background of strongly held political beliefs that his convictions about architecture become comprehensible. Beginning with one of his earliest essays (1834) about the use of color in ancient architecture to his last essay (1869) about architectural styles, Semper insists that style be seen as a reflection of sociopolitical conditions. He often compared, for instance, the formalized processional route of Egyptian temples with the nonaxial, open approach to Greek temples. The former is taken as an example of a rigid, priestly class and a stratified society, the latter as an example of a democratically structured people. His greatest admiration was always reserved for Greek architecture, not because he thought it was sublime, but because he thought he could accept its social implications. At the same time, he expressed his distaste for the Gothic and baroque styles because to him they exuded church hierarchy and aristocratic authority respectively.

During his exile, at the outset of which he had few commissions, he began to concern himself with more general, theoretical problems. In 1851, in an essay called Die Vier Elemente der Baukunst, he made his first attempt to classify systematically all architectural forms as a kind of typology of architecture. The initial inspiration for this had been Georges Cuvier's exhibit of animal skeletons at the Jardin des Plantes in Paris, which he had seen during his student days there. The multitude of skeletons, exhibited in no particular order

(Cuvier believed in a fixist not an evolutionary theory), produced in Semper the desire to find the underlying similarities and relationships, to produce some coherence in what appeared to be random creations of nature. In the same way, he believed, human artifacts, especially architecture, seem to present a chaotic picture, but one in which some order might be found. He sought in architecture the kind of synthetic unity Goethe had assumed existed in nature. Semper's quest for archetypal built form is analogous to Goethe's search for the archetypal plant. This direction was perhaps indicated by Schinkel, who had included references to Goethe's *Urpflanze* in the didactic ornament of his Berlin Bauschule. In an essay on a system of comparative styles of 1853, Semper wrote that he wanted to establish a taxonomy comparable to Alexander von Humboldt's *Der Kosmos,* which, like Goethe's work in the natural sciences, is a unifying study of the physical universe. Idealism for Semper, as for Goethe and Humboldt, was tempered by a degree of pragmatism. For instance, before he published the ideas (at the time still controversial) on the use of color in classical architecture, Semper visited ancient sites, had scaffoldings erected to check out remains of color, and had them analyzed by a chemist. His approach borrowed from that tradition of the natural sciences which was not simply interested in cataloguing the random phenomena of nature but which sought rational constructs that would at once synthesize and explain an apparently meaningless multiplicity of forms.

Semper divided all built form into four types in his 1851 essay. The hearth is the first element, the communal prerequisite for architecture. It represents for him the basic social nucleus, the gathering point for family and tribe and, as such, the germ of civilization. The hearth is the central element around which the other three group themselves to provide the more traditional architectural concept of shelter, for both man and hearth. The second element is the substructure, or platform, used to raise the hearth off the damp ground. The third element is the roof to protect the fire against rain. The roof is treated as a unit together with the framework on which it rests. The fourth and last element is the enclosure to keep out wind and cold. The latter, Semper saw as a generally non-loadbearing filler made of hides, textiles, wattle, and so on, placed between the posts supporting the roof.

What is exceptional in Semper's schema of classification is that he begins with a nonarchitectural element—the fire—an element without spatial dimension but one which bestows social significance on the site. The other three elements follow in logical sequence from the first. His postulation of the hearth as the generator of substructure, roof, and enclosure leads him to a further unusual categorization. The roof with its supporting posts is read as a continuous unit, and the fourth element, enclosure, represents the final (nonstructural) step in dividing outside from inside. (The Indian tepee and wigwam might be considered succinct examples of a continuous frame and roof covered by a thin enclosure.) Semper does not use the more readily perceivable elements—at least in Western architecture—of wall and roof nor does he choose to follow conventional nineteenth-century construction methods which would have presumed a wall-roof sequence and which would not have allowed him to see the enclosure as a nonloadbearing zone. Semper found his system confirmed in a Caribbean cottage shown at the Great Exposition in London. It had a hearth elevated on a platform, poles supporting a roof, and woven mats suspended between the poles. This suggests that Semper's four elements describe primitive building not architecture; he himself stressed this point. In a more evolved architecture, according to Semper, these four elements became integrated so that they could no longer be read as separate categories. And although the four elements were categories more explicit in primitive building, Semper did not attempt to imply a chronological sequence. He was too aware of the complexity of human history to assume that he was describing the "first" building. His was not the naïve positivism of James Fergusson, for example, who assumed an inexorable progress from simplicity to complexity. Semper knew that primitive forms can coexist with more evolved forms (the Caribbean cottage, though transplanted, was as much a part of a living tradition as the Crystal Palace in which it was housed), and that periods of high civilization can be succeeded by a regression to primitivism. His categories must therefore be interpreted as archetypal concepts not chronological data.

He believed that these four elements are subject to transformations, separately or together. While one element may undergo extended technical development, another one may persist only in symbolic form. Since his schema is not time-specific, it cannot be attacked by pointing to building types that do not seem to be covered by his categories. For instance, the Dogon house or the Eskimo igloo do not have frameworks supporting a roof nor do they treat enclosure as a discrete entity. Although Semper did not deal with these particular examples, one could answer for him that they are actually proof of his insistence on reading roof and support as a continuous unit. That the roof and its support have in these cases also absorbed the fourth element, enclosure, could be understood as a transformation to accommodate extremes of climate. Further, we know that the Dogon house reflects aspects of Muslim architecture. The Dogon house is, then, a case in which an apparently primitive building retains echoes of a high culture in which the four elements had presumably been integrated. Of course, Semper's whole system is a construct, and its "correctness" depends only on the workability of its model of architectural transformations. In this regard, it is no different from any specific law man has invented to understand the workings of nature. Semper himself borrowed some of his terminology from natural science, particularly his notion of vestigial form in architecture. He believed, for example, that the church altar was a relic of the place used for burnt offerings, hence ultimately of the sacred hearth.

Through his exposure to the advanced state of industrialization in England, Semper became aware of a general breakdown of normal evolutionary processes of all artifacts, as stated in his *Wissenschaft, Industrie und Kunst* (1852). However, he believed that no corrections could be undertaken until these processes were understood, and to understand and clarify them was the goal of *Der Stil*. In *Der Stil*, he turned to a study of industrial arts as the prerequisite for the comprehension of architectural processes of change. For he now supposed that the industrial arts constituted more basic types than his four architectural elements. He linked his four elements of architecture with four categories of industrial arts: the production of ceramics and metallurgy are related to the hearth (because they require heat), industrial arts of stone are linked to masonry and the substructure, woodwork with the frame and roof, and textiles with the enclosure. In *Der Stil*, Semper also gave his categories a new sequence. One would expect metallurgy and ceramics first and textiles last. Instead he began with textiles and continued with ceramics, carpentry, masonry, concluding with metal-

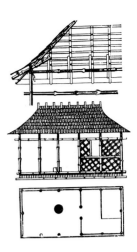

Semper.
Caribbean Hut of the Great
Exposition from Der Stil.
1860–1863

lurgy. In placing them in this particular order which runs from soft to increasingly harder materials, he gives the impression that he has shifted from his former social-ordering principle to one in which materials and their properties dominate the schema. However, the hearth is still referred to as "the oldest symbol of society," and in his introduction to the specific discussion of materials, he wrote concerning the "Classification of Industrial Arts" that his new categories were to be treated inclusively not exclusively. On the other hand, there might be ceramic objects such as tiles, certain terra cottas, or any ceramics used primarily as thin coverings that might be more appropriately discussed under textiles. His categories are really functional ones; materials do not seem to be used in a purely materialistic sense.

A further evidence of his desire to see artifacts grouped by function not materials was his criticism of existing museums in his essay on a comparative system of styles of 1853. Semper thought that little could be learned by comparing a piece of metal armor with a metal vase. In his opinion, it would have been much more revealing to compare a metal vase with a glass vase. In the same essay, he defined style as a functional notation: $Y = F(x,y,z, . . .)$, where Y is the artifact, F is the function of the object, and x,y,z, . . . are the theoretically infinite number of components that interact in the production of Y. Semper saw in this formula the confluence of a stable and of a variable set of influences. Function is posited as a constant element; the shape of a drinking vessel, no matter what its material, would primarily be determined by its function to contain a liquid. Influences that are variable—the coefficients x,y,z, . . .—he subdivided into the following three classes: (1) materials and techniques; (2) local and ethnological influences such as religion, politics, climate, or the specific site; and (3) personal influences such as those of the artist and the patron. It is clear from Semper's formulation of style that function has a more tangible effect on design than materials or the artist's idiosyncrasies, the latter being only subcategories of an infinite number of variable coefficients.

Despite the comparative precision of this aspect of Semper's ideas, by the turn of the century he was already radically misunderstood. He was generally seen in the light of the prevailing materialist and Darwinian attitudes. Indeed, if *Der Stil* is scanned rapidly, its chapter headings, organized by materials (textiles, ceramics, carpentry, masonry, and metallurgy), might suggest just such a reading, a misrepresentation avoidable only if Semper's introductory remarks in his prolegomena are taken seriously. Alois Riegl, the Viennese art historian, as early as 1893 in his *Stilfragen* (Questions of Style), found it necessary to defend Semper against overly materialistic interpretations. He wrote that those purporting to be followers of Semper had as little in common with Semper as Darwinism with Darwin.

Architects, too, were beginning to superimpose their own predilections upon Semper's theoretical framework. Otto Wagner, for example, in his *Die Baukunst unserer Zeit* (1894), although paying tribute to Semper, went on to point out what he saw as his shortcoming: "Semper did not have the courage, like Darwin, to complete his theories upwards and downwards and he made do with a symbolism of construction instead of designating construction itself as the germ cell of building." Semper's theory was, of course, something more than the symbolic utilitarianism Wagner cited. It also dealt with religious, social, and political function. To Wagner, for whom every architectural form ultimately derived from construction, this point was lost. Similarly, Semper's "failure" to adopt a Darwinian model of evolution is quite consistent within the context of his intentions. He, in fact, was familiar with Darwin's work (*Origin of the Species* was published in 1859) and apparently read it with interest. However, by 1859

Semper.
Polytechnikum.
Zurich.
1858–1864

Semper had already written most of his essays, and the bulk of *Der Stil* (certainly its basic conception) must have been completed by the time he read Darwin. The only direct reference Semper made to Darwin is in one of his late essays, *Über Baustile* (About Architectural Styles) of 1869, in which he stated unequivocally that Darwin's theory of natural selection, particularly the axiom that nature makes no leaps, is not transferable to the creation and development of artifacts, be they crafts or architecture.

H. P. Berlage, who had studied at the Federal Institute of Technology in Zurich, often referred to Semper's theory as practical aesthetics, a usage intended by Semper but one difficult to carry out since the last volume of *Der Stil* (the one which would have dealt with architecture) was never completed. Like Wagner, Berlage believed construction to be the generator of architecture. In his *Gedanken über Stil in der Baukunst* (1905), he named Semper and Viollet-le-Duc in one breath as theoreticians he intended to follow. Berlage's desire to see these two figures' ideas as being of a piece is an indication of Berlage's constructivist vision. To Berlage, the most urgent question for architects was to evolve a new style. To do this, he suggested turning to prototypes in nature. Just as the hide of animals never seems to conceal their skeletal structure, so, he believed, a building should always reveal its construction. Berlage's literal analogy with animals reflects quite closely Viollet's conviction that "forms not determined by structure should be spurned." It does not, however, conform with Semper's stylistic principles. Semper's Caribbean hut may have revealed structure, but it was seen by Semper as an example of building not architecture. It was an archetype used to describe the evolution of architectural elements, but it was not proposed as a model to be followed by contemporary architects. In a more highly developed architecture, Semper believed, the separate architectural elements become fused and integrated and no longer reveal construction in a direct way. In fact, in his introduction to *Der Stil*, Semper wrote that his conception of basic forms and their origins has nothing in common with the materialistic understanding of building in which architecture is "nothing more than evolved construction, an illustration and illumination of statics and mechanics, pure revelation of material as it were."

It is essentially Wagner's and Berlage's view of Semper which has come down to us. It was passed on, for instance, in more or less this form by Franz Boas, the German anthropologist, who established anthropology as a serious endeavor in America and who trained a whole generation of American an-

thropologists. Even in recent Semper studies, his place vis-à-vis Darwinism is not made clear. Leopold Ettlinger, for example, in his essay "On Science, Industry, and Art" (1964), after acknowledging that Semper did not transfer Darwin's method fully to the arts, added that "he firmly believed that the principle of *Evolution*—in the strict scientific sense of the term—could be applied to the arts and to architecture." Ettlinger substantiated his depiction of Semper as an evolutionist by referring to the latter's interest in Cuvier. Cuvier, however, had been a defender of "fixism" and had nothing in common with evolutionary concepts. Further, there is not now, and never was, a principle of evolution in a "strict scientific sense." The nineteenth century produced a variety of competing scientific theories. Even today, when Darwin's version is the generally accepted one, new definitions and revisions of his theory are being put forward. The concept of evolution itself is continually undergoing an evolution also, and it is, therefore, not very meaningful to speak of evolution in a "strict scientific sense."

Joseph Rykwert, in his recent book, *On Adam's House in Paradise* (1973), in contrast to Ettlinger, is careful not to portray Semper as a materialist Darwinist. He does, however, believe that Semper in *Der Stil* is describing the origins of architecture rather than conceptual archetypes. Because Semper dealt first with textiles, Rykwert suggests that for Semper the first artifact was a knot, that the origin of the house coincided with weaving, and that the first house was a tent. But in his introduction to the chapters on textiles, Semper stated that even the oldest and apparently the most primitive cul-

Semper.
Museum of Natural
    History.
Vienna.
1872–1879 (with
    Hasenauer; not completed
    until 1881)

tures would probably turn out to have been a vestige of a yet earlier higher culture. He found the attempt to fix origins in time, therefore, a thankless task. In the same way, he wrote that he could not determine which one of the various crafts came first in time. The reason he commenced with textile crafts is that it appeared to him, from all available evidence, that textiles bore the origin of many ornamental types and symbols found in other crafts. He referred to textiles as *Urkunst,* a basic art form which seems to have provided typological models but not necessarily a prototype which was first in time.

A different sort of illustration of the still prevailing misconception of Semper is the current historical view of his relation to the Chicago school. Architects working in Chicago in the 1880s and 1890s were without doubt exposed to his writings. In 1880, the *American Architect,* as part of its obituary of Semper, recommended *Der Stil* to its readers and gave a bibliography of several essays by Semper published in various foreign periodicals. This advice seemed to have been effective, for in the late 1880s, a more general interest in Semper can be documented. In 1887, the *Inland Architect* published a discussion held by the Illinois State Association of Architects in which Louis Sullivan and John Root had participated and in which the German-born Frederick Baumann quoted from Semper's essay *Über Baustile.* John Root, with the help of Fritz Wagner, edited and translated this particular essay; it appeared in serialized form in the *Inland Architect* (1889–1890). DANKMAR ADLER, Sullivan's German-born partner, apparently was fond of reciting quotations from Semper. The evidence that Sullivan was familiar with Semper's ideas is, therefore, quite substantial.

Although most historians of this period of American architectural history acknowledge Semper's influence, none has traced specific aspects of Sullivan's ideas to those of Semper. It would appear that Sullivan's eurythmic organization of a building into a clearly perceivable and forthrightly readable *Gestalt* (an organization of the exterior that expresses symbolic functions more clearly than structural-mechanical ones) can be associated with concepts found in Semper's prolegomena to *Der Stil.* Sullivan's ornamental emphasis of a building's entrance and termination is also comparable to Semper's analysis of the design principles found in a Greek hydria, discussed in Semper's essay "Keramisches" (On Pottery) of 1852–1855. Semper wrote that the ornament must emphasize the characteristics of each part as well as its relation to the whole object and the surrounding environment. In both the foot and the neck of the hydria Semper saw conflicting directional forces at work.

The foot is the receiver of the belly which seems to press down on it but, at the same time, it rests on the ground and holds up the vessel. The counterforces run upward and downward, and this, Semper found, was usually expressed by vertically arranged vegetable ornament. The ornamentation of the neck, he wrote, is informed by the action of filling and pouring out liquid. The opposing forces here also move upward and downward and this is signified by ornament similar to that used on the foot. The hydria's belly, which Semper saw as a container in complete hydrostatic balance, is a neutral zone without directional forces, usually reserved for pictorial representations. Elsewhere, Semper showed how this type of an analysis can be transposed to form an understanding of architectural *Gestalt.* A comparable dynamic interpretation of ornament would have allowed Sullivan to see the entrance, where the greatest activity between inside and outside occurs, similar to the neck of Semper's hydria. The hydria's neutral belly can be associated with Sullivan's conception of office floors, which, in his essay "The Tall Office Building Artistically Considered" of 1896, he described as being all identical and therefore a kind of neutral zone between the perceptually active basement and entrance and the forcefully stated termination at the cornice level which helps to set the building off from its general background and also helps to make it readable in terms of Semper's principles regarding a visual field.

FRANK LLOYD WRIGHT, who worked in Sullivan's office in the late 1880s and early 1890s, could also have been familiar with Semper. In Wright's work, one might point to his ceremonial emphasis of the fireplace, which often, as in his Willits and Robie Houses, seems to generate the plan itself. It is clear, though, that Wright's personal belief in the importance of the family has much to do with this particular organization of the house. However, Semper's description of the hearth as the most elementary social nucleus of a building would have reinforced Wright's own attitudes.

In a discussion of the general relationship of Semper to the Chicago school architects one might also investigate the origin of the term "curtain wall" as it was used to describe the thin envelopes of Chicago skyscrapers. By extension, Wright's sources for the "textile" blocks of his California houses might be explored further and compared with the textile effects of the Coonley House titles, a device used by Wright long before he turned to the more literally "woven" effect of the hollow concrete blocks. This may perhaps have been an adaptation of Semper's fourth architectural element, that of a thin, fabriclike enclosure. Semper himself would not have advocated such an application of what he regarded as an archetypal element, although the attempt to use Semper's theories as a handbook would be rather typical of his influence on architects. In any case, Semper's relationship with the Chicago school is obviously a rich one and bears further investigation. Yet, most historians have reduced, rather than expanded, our understanding of this connection.

Donald Drew Egbert, in his essay on "The Idea of Organic Expression and American Architecture" (1956), explained Semper's importance for America by referring to him as if he were a Darwinian evolutionist.

Semper conceived art to be a special process of development . . . and thus of evolution. For this reason he dealt especially with the principles of style in their adaptation to new inventions. He investigated structure from a genetic point of view, and explained it as derived from the specific nature of the material, from the nature of tools and the methods of construction and also from the nature of the use to which the structure is to be put.

Semper's symbolic functionalism is submerged in Egbert's primarily materialistic explication.

Similarly, Albert Bush-Brown in his *Louis Sullivan* (1960) quoted from Semper out of context to show how his ideas are supposedly Darwinian. Carl W. Condit in the *Chicago School of Architecture* (1964) completely sealed Semper's fate as a Darwinian: "The organic theory of architecture that was rising in Germany under the influence of Darwinism came to be known originally through Root's translation . . . of Gottfried Semper's 'Development of Architectural Style'." It seems that none of these authors checked Semper's essay to see whether he did, in fact, propose a Darwinian model of evolution.

Further proof, if more were needed, that Semper was not a materialist or a Darwinian, is his so-called *Stoffwechseltheorie* (untranslatable; literally "theory of change in materials") and his interest in linguistics as a potential model for the evolution of man-made forms. The *Stoffwechseltheorie* describes his conviction that formal patterns have been taken from one medium and reused in another, sometimes with slight changes, sometimes with strong symbolic transformation. For example, patterns devised for textiles may reappear first as wall ornament on a textile enclosure. If buildings which had such textile enclosures become more permanent, the wall may be done in masonry but the same ornament which had been used for the textile enclosure may be used on the masonry wall. Or, if swags of garlands were used in sacred buildings, references may be made to these in a later development as painted garlands. Whereas the original pattern may have been affected by its

medium, in its subsequent transformations the material on which it occurs is no longer of primary significance. This aspect of Semper's theory accounts for the traditionalism that prevailed before our own age in the usage of forms. Semper dealt with form that evolves slowly and gradually and goes through traceable transformations comparable to the processes of change in language. This gradual process of change allowed for the conservation of symbolic language, a process Semper found usurped by industrialization. Industry's ability to produce many forms out of many materials meant that symbolic content could be transferred from one artifact to another that is functionally quite different, thereby rendering it meaningless. For Semper, a constant barrage of neologisms in designed form, just as in language would defeat the central purpose of any communication to be understood.

Semper was interested in comparative linguistics; he had high hopes for its usefulness in tracing the origin of forms. A word through its stem can reveal its original meaning and place of origin even after many transformations. In the same way, Semper wanted to find in the names of architectural parts evidence of their origin. He gave as an example the German words *Mauer* and *Wand.* Both mean "wall," but the secondary meaning of *Mauer* is "battlement," and *Wand* can also mean "screen." Semper saw evidence in these words for his division of architectural elements into the substructure and its relation to masonry and the enclosure and its derivation from a thin skin. *Wand* he thought of as being related to the word *Gewand* ("dress"). Modern etymology actually relates *Wand* more directly to the verb *winden* ("to braid"), and gives the original meaning of *Wand* as having been "wickerwork" or "wattling." However, this still supports Semper's theory of the primitive wall as filler.

Semper's *Stoffwechseltheorie,* together with his etymological approach, was confirmed in more recent scholarship by Karl Lehmann. Lehmann traced the image of the dome as a symbol of heaven to temporary Greek canopies embroidered with stars. The symbolic function of such canopies is supported by their name, *uraniscus.* Or, one might consider the term reredos, usually a synonym for retable, a structure forming the back of an altar. The secondary meaning of reredos, however, refers to the back of an open hearth or fireplace, a relationship that bears out Semper's connection of hearth and altar.

Semper stated in *Der Stil* that established meaning and symbols in architecture may not be ignored or willfully altered without loss of context. He continued:

Semper.
Burgtheater.
Vienna.
1873 (executed by
* Hasenauer 1874–1878)*

The observing public and the majority of active architects follow these traditions rather unconsciously. But the same advantage, which comparative linguistics and the study of archetypal relationships give the rhetorician, will accrue to that architect who recognizes the oldest symbols of his language in their original meaning. . . . I also believe that the time is not far off when the study of linguistics and that which is concerned with forms in art will enter a reciprocal relationship. From such a relationship the most curious mutual discoveries in both fields must emerge.

Semper, then, although influenced by taxonomic studies in the field of natural science, was not strictly a materialist nor was he strictly a utilitarian functionalist. Materialism for him stood in a reciprocal relationship with idealism, and utilitarian functionalism with symbolic functionalism. His discussion of evolution is not linear or progressivist nor does it deal with first origins; rather, he deals with the complex transformations of archetypes comparable to the changes in language—another artifact in which no clear progression from simplicity to complexity exists. Semper probably shied away from adopting a Darwinian model because in the evolution of nature there is no return to old forms—it is unlikely that there will be another age of dinosaurs—but in artistic change, a return to older forms is indeed possible as is a complete coexistence of old and new forms. Semper did not see human history and the creation of crafts and architecture as a simple progression. The more conceptual models of Goethe and Humboldt, also devised for the study of natural science, were clearly more directly applicable to his own endeavors.

Considering the frequency with which Semper's analysis of archetypal form in architecture was adopted as a handbook for building by later architects, one wonders whether for Semper himself the theory was discrete from his architecture and whether some relationship exists between these two areas. Why do Renaissance forms predominate in his designs when he had reserved his highest admiration for the Greek style? The answer would seem to be that Renaissance buildings provided more suitable functional prototypes for the multistory building types of the nineteenth century. Why were baroque and Gothic forms used in his buildings when he had disdained them in his writing? A Gothic style, for example, was chosen for his project of a town hall for Zurich. It would appear that although he had little use for church Gothic (even though he did admire individual Gothic churches), when the building types in question could properly refer to the bourgeois town halls of the later Middle Ages, he was willing to use this style. He could accept the Gothic when it sprang from a nonhierarchic context. In a similar vein, one might ask why Semper used baroque forms for his museums in Vienna, a style he had rejected along with the Gothic in his writings. Here we come to the conclusion that the museums first of all are, in fact, a royal commission and are extensions of baroque settings. This style was perhaps used simply for the sake of continuity (a continuity much admired by CAMILLO SITTE who had seen in these projects coherent principles of city planning that stood in sharp contrast with, for example, most of the other projects along the Ringstrasse in Vienna, in which each is treated as a separate monument). A secondary meaning of the baroque style may possibly be revealed by the building type of these projects, namely, museums. They may be seen as people's palaces. Museums are not just public buildings of any sort. They provide intellectual and artistic instruction, a function which in the nineteenth century would certainly have been regarded as being higher than other types of public buildings, such as railway stations. Perhaps for this reason also, the "aristocratic" baroque style may have seemed appropriate.

One of the problems the nineteenth-century architect faced was the emergence of new building types which had no clear precedent in older architecture. Often, the solution was to choose that style or building type from the past which seemed functionally the most correct, without, however, attempting to transfer the symbolic aspects of the prototypes. Thus, for his designs of a railroad station and a stock market, Semper alluded to the forms of Roman baths—good prototypes for large halls containing a variety of utilitarian spaces. For a laundry ship, a type without clear genealogy, Semper devised a magnificent Pompeian wall decoration. Its linear and billowing flat panels were perhaps meant to suggest laundry on a line, but in essence a Pompeian style in this context was no more appropriate than several other styles would have been. Together with the problems created by new building types, there were often quick shifts in the kind of commissions Semper received—from royal patronage to bourgeois patronage, from an old order to a new order—and such ambiguities could not always be resolved.

ROSEMARIE HAAG BLETTER

WORKS

*1838–1841, Opera; 1847–1854, Picture Gallery (completed later by Bernard Kruger and K. M. Hänel); Dresden, Germany. 1858–1864, Polytechnikum, Zurich. 1871–1878, New Opera (executed by Manfred Semper), Dresden, Germany. 1872–1879, Museum of Art History (with Karl Hasenauer; not completed until 1881); 1872–1879, Museum of Natural History (with Hasenauer; not completed until 1881); 1873, Burgtheater (executed by Hasenauer in 1874–1878); Vienna.

BIBLIOGRAPHY

ETTLINGER, LEOPOLD D. 1937 *Gottfried Semper und die Antike.* Bleicherode, Harz, Germany: Nieft.
ETTLINGER, LEOPOLD D. 1964 "On Science, Industry and Art." *Architectural Review* 136:57–60.
FRÖHLICH, MARTIN 1974 *Gottfried Semper: Zeichnerischer Nachlass an der ETH Zürich, Kritischer Katalog.* Basel: Birkhäuser.
Gottfried Semper 1803–1879—Baumeister zwischen Revolution und Historismus. 1979 Munich: Callwey.
Gottfried Semper und die Mitte des 19. Jahrhunderts. 1976 Zurich and Basel: Birkhäuser.
ILLINOIS STATE ASSOCIATION OF ARCHITECTS 1887 "Discussion." *Inland Architect and News Record* 9, no. 3:26.
J. T. C. 1880 "Gottfried Semper." *American Architect and Building News* 7, no. 214:33–47; 7, no. 215:43–44.
QUITZSCH, HEINZ 1962 *Die aesthetischen Anschauungen Gottfried Sempers.* Berlin: Akademie.
RYKWERT, JOSEPH 1973 *On Adam's House in Paradise.* New York: Museum of Modern Art.
SEMPER, GOTTFRIED 1851 *Die Vier Elemente der Baukunst; Ein Beitrag zur vergleichenden Baukunde.* Braunschweig, Germany: Vieweg.
SEMPER, GOTTFRIED (1852)1966 *Wissenschaft, Industrie und Kunst.* Edited by Hans M. Wingler. Berlin, and Mainz, Germany: Kupferg.
SEMPER, GOTTFRIED 1860–1863 *Der Stil in den technischen und tektonischen Künsten oder praktische Aesthetik—Ein Handbuch für Techniker, Künstler und Kunstfreunde,* 2 vols. Munich: Bruckmann.
SEMPER, GOTTFRIED 1884 *Kleine Schriften von Gottfried Semper.* Edited by Manfred Semper and Hans Semper. Berlin, and Stuttgart, Germany: Spemann.
SEMPER, GOTTFRIED 1890 "Development of Architectural Style." Edited and translated by John W. Root. *Inland Architect and News Record* 14, no. 7:76–78; 14, no. 8: 92–94, 15, no. 1:5–6; 15, no. 2:32–33.

SENMUT

Biographical data about Senmut or Senenmut can be derived from inscriptions on several of his numerous statues, oil jars from the tombs of his parents, from his own tomb, and from more than sixty figures and inscriptions behind the doors of Queen Hatshepsut's temple at Deir el Bahari (1520 B.C.).

Senmut's career is intimately linked with the reign of Queen Hatshepsut (1503–1482 B.C.) who was crowned as "king" in the second regnal year of Thutmose III (1504–1450 B.C.), her nephew, a young boy whom she waived aside to govern alone. Senmut enjoyed the exceptional favor of the queen, and even became the tutor of her daughter Nefrure, until regnal year 16 (1486 B.C.). He boasted to be "the greatest of the great in the entire land" (Hayes, 1973, vol. 2, p. 318). On the statues inscribed during the joint reign Senmut associates himself with the "two kings," stating that he is the "confident" of Hatshepsut and the "trusted one" of Thutmose III, who "executed their eternal monuments and remained in favor with them each day" (statuette M.M.A. 48.149.7). Of the seven titles describing Senmut on the back pillar of the statuette, he gave preeminence to "overseer of the Fields of Amun" (inscribed below the left hand) and "overseer of the Works of Amun" (below the right hand) (Hayes, 1957, pp. 78–90).

The drama that led to Senmut's fall from

Hatshepsut's grace in 1486 B.C. has not been clarified. Perhaps the premature death of Nefrure was one of the reasons. It was once thought that Senmut was expelled for his secret carving of the panels behind the doors in Hatshepsut's temple and excavation of his second tomb on the north edge of the temple. Queen Hatshepsut had work on his tomb stopped and the panels in her temple erased. However, Senmut's plan was obviously to keep this activity unobtrusive, though not secret. His claim that it was carried out with Hatshepsut's permission is supported by an inscription on the two largest panels on the reveals of the doorway leading into the northwest hall of offerings, where Hatshepsut's permission is described specifically as "a favor of the king's bounty which was extended to this servant in letting his name be established on every wall." The sixty panels (21 x 25 to 46 x 165 cm.) carved on the reveals normally hidden behind the door valves represent Senmut kneeling and standing, both hands upraised praying for the "life, prosperity and health" of Hatshepsut. The Viceroy of Nubia, Nehy, carved similar panels in the temple of Hatshepsut and Thutmose III at Buhen. Senmut's excessive adulation for Hatshepsut was also expressed in numerous statues representing him kneeling, proffering a cartouche containing a rebuslike writing of her name. Yet Hatshepsut alone was responsible for the destruction of Senmut's work and not Thutmose III when he became sole king, because Hatshepsut's

name was left untouched. Senmut seems even to have been honored, probably posthumously, since his statuette stood in an accessible place in Thutmose's temple Djeser-akhet at Deir el Bahari. This was perhaps a reminiscence of the king's early youth, when he and Nefrure were cherished by Senmut. Both names appear together on Senmut's statue (Lesko, pp. 113–118).

Work. The mortuary temple of Hatshepsut at Deir el Bahari (Western Thebes) is the most sophisticated achievement of Egyptian architecture, its terraced porticoes blending with the horizontal ledges and vertical clefts of the mountain cirque behind them. There is no definite proof that Senmut was its architect, other than Hatshepsut's permission to carve his panels on "every wall." Building inscriptions on shards (ostraca) also mention the names of the high priest Hapuseneb, chancellor Nehesi, the overseer of the Treasury Djehuti, and the overseer of the Granaries Minmose. Their names with the inscription "Ma't-ka-Re" (Hatshepsut) appear on blocks built into the valley temple and causeway.

The name "the great temple of millions of years, the temple of Amun Djeserdjeserw ('Holy of Holies') at its wonderful place of the first time" refers to a primeval hill. The location was chosen on account of the valley cliff and the proximity of the hallowed temple of Mentuhotep II (south corner of the cirque) and its Valley Feast. The stepped profile of Mentuhotep's temple, reminiscent of the

Senmut.
Plan of the Temple of Queen Hatshepsut.
Deir el Bahari, Egypt.
1520 B.C.

Senmut.
Temple of Queen Hatshepsut.
Deir el Bahari, Egypt.
1520 B.C.

pyramidal peak dominating the mountain above it, might have influenced the terraced design in Hatshepsut's temple, which, however, blended fully with the sacred mountain. Apart from being the best example of imperial Thutmoside style the temple was the first prototype endowed with the three sanctuaries typical of all mortuary temples of the New Kingdom at Thebes: Amun (Lord of Thebes) flanked to the north by the open court dedicated to Re Horakhty (sunrise god of Lower Egypt at Heliopolis) and to the south by a shrine to the father of Thutmose I.

The construction required fifteen years (regnal years 7 to 20–22). Only a few remains of the valley temple stand at the lower end of the causeway, leading up to the main temple: a street 37 meters broad bordered by limestone walls passing under a gateway and, at 520 meters from the forecourt, a way station for the sacred bark in the shape of a peripteral chapel with Osiride pillars, preceded on its eastern façade by trees. The causeway proceeded, flanked at 10 meter intervals by 50 pairs of female sphinxes in painted sandstone, to the entrance, probably a pylon and two persea trees. The sphinx alley continued with 7–10 pairs of sphinxes to the foot of a ramp flanked by two T-shaped basins of papyrus for ritual papyrus harvesting and fowl hunting. The walled forecourt is nearly rectangular. Along the cliff edge, beyond its north wall, were houses for priests and workmen, bathing basins, and embalming workshops. Along the rear side (west) of the court runs a portico subdivided in two aisles by a ramp rising along the axis of the court. The parapets of the ramp were protected at their lower end by a lion in relief, and at the upper end by a lion statue. The portico consists of an inner row of polygonal columns and an outer row of hybrid supports shaped as pillars combined with engaged columns on their inner face to conform to the polygonal columns. The portico thus shows along the court a row of pillars carved each with the *serekh* representing the entrance façade of the palace, topped by the royal falcon—a motif repeated along the south side of the terrace. A colossal Osiride pillar stood on either side of the portico. In the northern aisle of the portico are relief scenes of fowling and hunting in the papyrus thickets, and in the southern aisle a unique representation of the transport of obelisks. An inscription by Senmut at Aswan (where granite was quarried) records that he initiated work on "the two great obelisks" of "the God's Wife and King's Great Wife, . . . Hatshepsut" for the festival of "Million-of-Years." The obelisks that were then quarried by the treasurer Djehuty measured (together) 108 cubits, and were "sheathed in their entirety in gold" (Hayes, 1973, vol. 2, p. 330). The

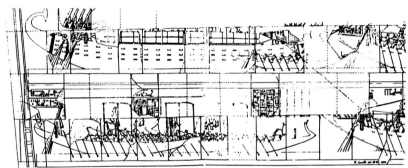

two obelisks were lashed between baulks and anchored butt to butt on to sleds on a barge probably 100 meters long and 33 meters wide, towed by 27 ships in 3 rows manned by 864 oarsmen, and led by 3 pilot boats, accompanied by 3 vessels on which rites were performed. The wall scenes depict the unloading of the obelisks at Thebes and their erection, probably east of Amun's temple. Confusion arises as a second pair of smaller obelisks was freed from the quarry in 7 months (regnal year 15) by Senmut's colleague Steward Amenhotep and readied for transportation in year 16, perhaps erected between pylons IV and V at Karnak.

The middle square court at the top of the first ramp contains a rear portico of two rows of fluted columns in the two aisles that flank a second ramp, and along its north side an unfinished portico of beautiful fluted columns, defined as proto-Doric by J. F. Champollion. On either parapet of the ramp a giant serpent coils its scaly body. On the rear wall of the north aisle scenes represent a pseudohistorical narrative of the theogamy (divine marriage) of Amun and the queen mother Ahmose—a device to assert Hatshepsut's right to kingship. On the south wall scenes record the trade expedition sent in regnal year 9 to Punt

Senmut.
Wall sculpture, Temple of Queen Hatshepsut.
Deir el Bahari, Egypt.
1520 B.C.

Senmut.
Wall scene depicting the transport of Hatshepsut's obelisk, Temple of Queen Hatshepsut.
Deir el Bahari, Egypt.
1520 B.C.

Senmut.
Details from Temple of
Queen Hatshepsut.
Deir el Bahari, Egypt.
1520 B.C.

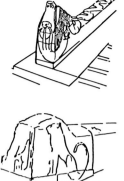
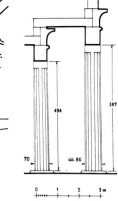

(Somaliland) with 5 seagoing ships to bring not only exotic products such as incense, leopard hides, ivory, ebony, but also such living items as giraffes, panthers, baboons, and myrrh trees. The formal style of the relief is enlivened by realistic topical detail such as the portrayal of the deformed Iti (wife of Parahu, the ruler of Punt), the huts built on piles, palm trees arranged in a decorative group of three, and typical species of Red Sea fish. In addition, shrines dedicated to Anubis (north) and Hathor (south) stand at either end of the west side of the court. The latter, on a T-shaped plan with two transverse columned halls, was enlarged with three rows of Hathoric columns and pillars. This sanctuary, roofed with a catenary vault, probably contained a statue of the sacred cow of the goddess (marble head find), similar to that in the shrine built by Thutmose III (regnal year 45) southeast of his temple and dedicated to Hathor, "Lady of the West Mountain in Djeser-akhet."

The façade of the upper terrace features a front portico consisting of 24 colossal Osiride pillars (5.5 meters tall), flanked on either side (north and south) with a still larger colossus. The granite doorway in the center of the rear wall of the portico was flanked by a granite colossus of Hatshepsut. The hypostyle hall beyond had four rows of columns on the north, west, and south, but only two on the east, leaving a small hypaethral area in the middle (Dabrowski, pp. 101–104). This was the offering place before the sanctuary of the bark, as proved by the four colossal pairs of kneeling statues and probably twelve more smaller ones between the columns, and by the Osiride statues of Hatshepsut in the ten niches of the west wall. To the south are a small magazine for vestments and unguents (southwest), a central large apartment for the funerary cult, and a temple–palace (southeast) with its "appearance window"—prototype to such temple–palaces in later mortuary temples. On the north are the chapel of Thutmose I and Anubis Imiut, and the open court of Re Horakhty containing the monumental altar accessible from a

west stairway. The main sanctuary of Amun, axial and carved deep into the mountain, consists of a room for the bark of Amun when on visit from Karnak, and beyond it a room for his statue. The corbel vault is surmounted by a gabled relieving chamber. A window opened in the east wall to the statue room. At the four corners of the bark room were Osiride statues of Hatshepsut, and around the bark, four basins for milk in which the torches were put out after the night vigil.

In addition to the outstanding monumentality of the mortuary temple Senmut displayed originality in the design of Hatshepsut's tomb and in his own second tomb, which was similar to it. A succession of sloping passages lead 46 meters below ground level to a third unfinished chamber. The first chamber has an astronomical ceiling, the first of the New Kingdom, with representations of the decàns and twelve months.

Senmut made an extensive use of architectural statuary, with colossal Osiride pillars and numerous sphinxes of granite and sandstone. The Thutmoside facial type established in this statuary of Hatshepsut is reflected in his own statues, which represents him kneeling proffering the rebus-like name of the queen, or as a geometrized block-statue where modelling concentrates on the two faces, his own and that of Nefrure embracing, emerging from the cubical block.

ALEXANDER BADAWY

WORK

1520 B.C., Temple of Queen Hatshepsut, Deir el Bahari, Egypt.

BIBLIOGRAPHY

ARNOLD, D. 1975 "Deir el-Bahari III." *Lexikon der Ägyptologie* 1:1017–1022.

DABROWSKI, L. 1970 "The Main Hypostyle Hall of the Temple of Hatshepsut at Deir El-Bahari." *Journal of Egyptian Archaeology* 56:101–104.

HAYES, W. C. 1957 "Varia from the Time of Hatshepsut." *Mitteilungen des Deutschen Archäologischen Instituts, Abteilung Kairo* 15:78–90.

HAYES, W. C. 1973 Volume 2, part 1, pages 318–330 in *Cambridge Ancient History*. Cambridge University Press.

LESKO, S. 1967 "The Senmut Problem." *Journal of the American Research Center in Egypt* 6:113–118.

NAVILLE, EDOUARD 1895–1908 *The Temple of Deir el Bahari*. 6 parts. London: Offices of the Egypt Exploration Fund.

WERBROUCK, M. 1949 *Le temple d'Hatshepsout à Deir el Bahari*. Brussels: Editiones de la Fondation égyptologique reine-Elisabeth.

WINLOCK, H. E. 1942 *Excavations at Deir el Bahari, 1911–1931*. New York: Macmillan.

SEREGNI, VINCENZO

Born in Milan, Italy, Vincenzo di Bonardo Seregni (1509?–1594) was an important practitioner of that city's decorative mannerist architectural style as developed by GALEAZZO ALESSI and PELLEGRINO TIBALDI. From 1547 to 1562 and again, briefly, some five years later, he served as chief architect of the Milan Cathedral. Although involved in several religious commissions, Seregni specialized primarily in secular architecture.

CHARLES RANDALL MACK

WORKS

1537–1558, Mausoleum of Giovanni del Conte, San Lorenzo; 1553–?, San Vittore al Corpo with associated second Cloister and Monastic Buildings (renovation; with others); Milan. 1556–1566, Sanctuary of the Madonna dei Miracoli, Saronno, Italy. 1559–1564, Grand Cloister at San Sempliciano; 1561–1564, Collegio dei Giureconsulti (initial phases); *1565–?, Palazzo di Pio IV dei Medici; 1570, San Giovanni in Conca (renovation); c.1580, Church and Cloister of Santa Radegonda; *1589, Cloister, Santa Maria della Vittoria; *1589, San Apollinare; Milan. n.d., Monastery of San Ambrogio, Voghera, Italy. n.d., San Magno, Legnano, Italy.

BIBLIOGRAPHY

ANNONI, AMBROGIO 1936 "Vincenzo Seregni." Volume 21, pages 429–430 in *Enciclopedia Italiana*. Rome: Istituto della Enciclopedia Italiana.

BARONI, COSTANTINO 1934 *Gli Edifici di Vincenzo Seregni nella Piazza dei Mercanti a Milani*. Milan: Perrella.

BELTRAMI, LUCA 1889 "Palazzo di Pio IV in Milano." *Archivo storico dell'arte*. 2:57–65.

HOFFMANN, HANS 1934 "Die Entwicklung der Architektur Mailands von 1550–1650: Der Ausgang der Hochrenaissance." *Wiener Jahrbuch für Kunstgeschichte* 23:66–69.

MEZZANOTTE, PAOLO 1914 "La Casa dei Medici di Nosiggia e il Palazzo di Pio IV in Milano." *Rassegna d'arte* 14:138–144.

VENTURI, ADOLFO (1940)1967 *Storia dell'arte italiana: Architettura del Cinquecento*. Reprint. Nendeln, Germany: Kraus.

SERLIO, SEBASTIANO

Sebastiano Serlio (1475–1555) was one of the most important architectural theoreticians active in Europe during the Renaissance. He wrote *L'architettura,* published posthumously in 1584, one of the first architectural treatises in a modern language that was printed with illustrations in sixteenth-century Europe. The treatise was composed of seven books, six of which had been published earlier. The first installment, *Regole generale di architettura sopra le cinque maniere de gli edifice cioe Thoscano, Dorico, Ionico, Corinthio, et Composito* (1537), outlines the later books. Serlio's treatise was revolutionary, since before his time the only architectural treatises published with illustrations were the Latin editions of VITRUVIUS's *De architectura.* Serlio's treatise was the first devoted to problems of the modern practicing architect.

Documentation of Serlio's life is very scant and little is known of his activity as a practicing architect since only two of his buildings are extant. Serlio was born on September 6, 1475, in Bologna, the son of a painter, Bartolomeo Serlio. He was trained as a painter like other Renaissance architects, including MICHELANGELO, RAPHAEL, and LEONARDO DA VINCI. At first active in Pesaro between 1511 and 1514, he went to Rome where he worked in the Vatican workshop under DONATO BRAMANTE, Raphael, and BALDASSARE PERUZZI, whom he acknowledged as his principal teacher of the fundamentals of architecture.

After the sack of Rome by Charles V's armies in 1527, Serlio went to Venice, where he is documented by April 1, 1528. Since he had decided to devote his life to the publication of his treatise, Venice was the logical choice. It was the leading city in Italy for the printing of books. In Venice, Serlio also worked as a freelance architect and painter. In 1534, he participated with Fortunio Spira, Titian and JACOPO SANSOVINO in a debate on the proportions of the church of San Francesco della Vigna. Serlio probably also designed buildings in the vicinity of Venice, such as the Villa at Cricoli (1537–1538) of Giangiorgio Trissino. In 1539, Serlio submitted a design with MICHELE SANMICHELI and Giulio Romano in the famous competition for the renovation of the basilica at Vicenza which was won by ANDREA PALLADIO. Serlio's project illustrated in Book 4 (folio 24) is extremely close to Palladio's final solution. Serlio

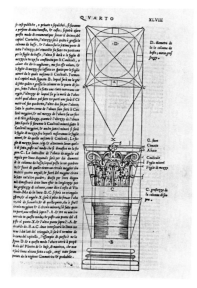

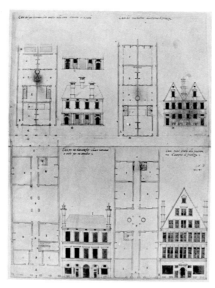

Serlio.
Corinthian Capital from Book IV, On the Roman Orders.

Serlio.
Houses for Artisans and Merchants from Book VI, On Domestic Architecture.

contributed at this time to Torello Sarayna's book *On The Antiquities of Verona, De origine et amplitudine civitatis Veronae* (1540), since his portrait forms a frontispiece for the book.

His main occupation remained, however, the publication of his treatise. He finally found a permanent patron in King Francis I of France, who paid for the publication of *Delle antiquita: Il terzo libro nel quale a descrivano le antiquita di Rome e le altre che sono in Italia e sopra Italia* (1540). *Della antiquita* is extremely important because it provides information on Serlio's early years in Rome and includes illustrations of buildings and projects by Bramante, Raphael, and Peruzzi.

In the fall of 1541, Serlio left for France, where on December 27, 1541, he was appointed consultant for the architecture and decoration of the castle Fontainebleau and for the king's other castles. While at Fontainebleau, Serlio published *De metrie et De perspective: Il primo (secondo) libro d'architettura* (1545). These were followed by *Quinto libro d'architettura nel quale se tratta de diverse forme de tempii* (1547), which contains information about Serlio's training in the Vatican workshop. He also began *Il settimo libro d'architettura nel quale si tratta di molti accidenti,* which was published posthumously in 1575. This book, primarily on domestic architecture, discusses such practical problems as building homes on irregular sites and includes plans for remodeling medieval dwellings. The final book in the treatise, *Libre extraordinaire de architecture,* appeared in 1551.

Of these books, the most important is the one on domestic architecture. Composed in two stages, the first version, dedicated to Francis I, was written mainly at Fontainebleau between 1542 and 1547. The second version was written between 1547 and 1550 in Lyons, where Serlio lived after the death of Francis I. This book contains four types of country

houses and five types of urban dwellings arranged according to a social hierarchy that ranged from houses of the poor to those of the king. Each housing type showed variations according to French and Italian usage. Serlio was one of the first architectural theoreticians to consider medieval and Roman traditions equally valid in contract to the prevalent humanistic theory of LEON BATTISTA ALBERTI. Serlio also rejected Alberti's use of Pythagorean harmonic proportions because they were not easily adaptable to different climatic conditions.

While Serlio was at Fontainebleau, he produced designs for several buildings, many of which are illustrated in the manuscripts of Books 6 and 7 of his treatise: the Grotte des Pins, the Salle du Bal (1541–1547) at the Castle (1541–1548) itself, the Grande Ferrare (1541–1548), a house of Ippolito d'Este, papal legate to France, in the town of Fontainebleau, the castle of Ancy-le-Franc (1541–1550) for Antoine de Clermont-Tonnerre in Burgundy, and a Stock Exchange (1541–1547) and Merchants Square (1541–1547) in Lyons, military camps for Francis I in Piedmont and Flanders, and a castle in the south of France (1541–1548). The Grotte des Pins was not executed according to Serlio's plans. The Stock Exchange and Merchants Square in Lyons and the Grande Ferrare at Fontainebleau were destroyed. Only the Salle du Bal and the Castle of Ancy-le-Franc are still extant. The Salle du Bal, located at the south side of the Cour de l'Ovale at the castle of Fontainebleau, was begun in 1541 by GILLES LEBRETON, and completed by PHILIBERT DELORME in 1548 after Serlio's departure from Fontainebleau. The Salle du Bal shows the influence of Raphael's loggia of the Villa Madama. The castle of Ancy-le-Franc, with its rectangular inner courtyard and square corner towers, shows the influence of the villa of Poggioreale built by Giuliano da Maiano (see MAIANO FAMILY) in Naples.

In 1550, Serlio in Lyons met Jacopo Strada, a Mantuan antiquarian and art dealer for the Fugger Family, Duke Albert V of Bavaria, and Maximilian II of Austria. According to Strada's introduction to Book 7, he bought Serlio's unpublished manuscripts and was responsible for their publication after the architect's death. Although the exact date of Serlio's death is unknown, he probably died at Fontainebleau between 1553 and 1555.

Serlio had a far-reaching influence in spite of the small number of his completed buildings. His published books and copies of his unpublished manuscripts circulated amongst contemporary and later architects. Serlio's centrally planned villas and town houses had an influence on the subsequent

designs of Andrea Palladio. His treatise, the first one addressed specifically to the problems of the modern architect, with its clearly presented visual models, and specific information on methods of construction, was a forerunner of Andrea Palladio's *Four Books of Architecture* (1570). Serlio's system of rational planning influenced not only Italian architects such as Palladio, but also later seventeenth and eighteenth century French architects such as CLAUDE PERRAULT and CLAUDE NICOLAS LEDOUX. In fact, the designs of Serlio's domestic buildings for the poor and middle classes had the greatest influence on his successors and are part of our architectural heritage.

M. N. ROSENFELD

WORKS

*1537–1538, Villa Trissino (remodeling), Cricoli, Vicenza, Italy. *1541–1547, Merchants Square; *1541–1547, Stock Exchange; Lyons, France. 1541–1547, Salle du Bal (completed by Philibert Delorme in 1548), Fontainebleau, France. *1541–1548, Castle, Rosmarino, France. *1541–1548, Grand Ferrare, Fontainebleau, France. 1541–1550, Castle of Ancy-le-France, Burgundy, France.

BIBLIOGRAPHY

BOLOGNINI AMORINI, ANTONIO 1823 *Elogio di Sebastiano Serlio: Architetto Bolognese.* Bologna, Italy: Nobili.
CHARVET, LEON 1869 *Sebastiano Serlio, 1475–1554.* Lyons, France: Mendet.
DINSMOOR, WILLIAM B. 1942 "The Literary Remains of Sebastiano Serlio." *Art Bulletin* 24:55–91, 115–155.
PUPPI, LIONELLO 1971 "Un letterato in villa: Giangiorgio Trissino a Cricoli." *Arte Veneta* 25:72–91.
ROSCI, MARCO 1967 *Il sesto Libro delle habitatione di tutti le gradi degli huomini.* Milan.
ROSENFELD, MYRA NAN 1978 *Sebastiano Serlio: On Domestic Architecture.* New York and Cambridge: Cambridge University Press.
SERLIO, SEBASTIANO 1537 *Regole generale di architettura sopra le cinque maniere de gli edifice cioe Thoscano, Dorico, Ionico, Corinthio, et Comporito.* Venice: Marcolini. Book 4 in Serlio (1584).
SERLIO, SEBASTIANO 1540 *Delle antiquita: Il terzo libro nel quale e descrivano le antiquita de Rome e le altre che sono in Italie e sopra Italia.* Venice: Sessa. Book 3 in Serlio (1584).
SERLIO, SEBASTIANO 1545 *De geometrie et De perspective: Il primo (secondo) libro d'architettura.* Paris: Barbé. Books 1 and 2 in Serlio (1584).
SERLIO, SEBASTIANO 1547 *Quinto libro d'architettura nel quale se tratta de diverse forme de tempii.* Paris: Vascosan. Book 5 in Serlio (1584).
SERLIO, SEBASTIANO 1551 *Libre extraordinaire de architecture.* Lyons: Tournes. Book 6 in Serlio (1584).
SERLIO, SEBASTIANO 1575 *Il settimo libro d'architectura nel quale si tratta di molti accidenti.* Frankfurt: Wecheli. Book 7 in Serlio (1584). Published posthumously.
SERLIO, SEBASTIANO 1584 *Libro primo (-settimo) d'architettura.* Venice: Franceschi. Includes titles listed above under Serlio 1537, 1540, 1545, 1547, 1551, and 1575. Published posthumously.

Serlio.
Salle du Bal.
Fontainebleau, France.
1541–1547 (completed by Delorme in 1548)

Serlio.
Castle of Ancy-le-France.
Burgundy, France.
1541–1550

SERRURIER-BOVY, GUSTAVE

Born and trained in Liège, Belgium, Gustave Serrurier-Bovy (1858–1910) never became a practicing architect. Instead, he devoted his talents to the design, manufacture, and marketing of his own line of furniture, which may be categorized as Art Nouveau in style. Serrurier-Bovy was influenced by WILLIAM MORRIS, the Darmstadt School, and Belgian vernacular furniture. In addition to individual pieces and suites of furniture, Serrurier-Bovy designed complete architectural interiors.

ALFRED WILLIS

WORKS

1897, Chatham House (interior), Paris. *1897, Imports Room (interior), Colonial Exposition, Tervueren, Belgium. *1900, Le Pavillon bleu Restaurant (interior), Universal Exposition, Paris.

BIBLIOGRAPHY

Borsi, Franco 1977 *Bruxelles 1900.* New York: Rizzoli.

Brooklyn Museum 1890 *Belgian Art: 1880–1914.* New York: The museum.

Madsen, Stephen Tschudi (1956)1976 *Sources of Art Nouveau.* Reprint. New York: Da Capo.

Puttemans, Pierre (1974)1976 *Modern Architecture in Belgium.* Translated by Mette Willert. Brussels: Vokaer.

Russell, Frank (editor) 1979 *Art Nouveau Architecture.* New York: Rizzoli.

Van de Voort, Jan 1956 "De Bouwkunst en de Kunstnijverheid in België van 1900 tot 1950." Volume 3, part 13 in H. E. Van Gelder and J. Duverger (editors), *Kunstgeschiedenis der Nederlanden.* Utrecht: De Haan.

Watelet, J. G. 1974 *Gustave Serrurier-Bovy: Architecte et décorateur, 1858–1910.* Brussels: Académie Royale des Beaux-Arts.

SERT, JOSEP LLUIS

When Josep Lluis (José Luis) Sert (1902–) retired from Harvard University in 1969, Walter Gropius wrote in flowering praise of the professional life of "my friend of forty years":

As the far-sighted organizer of CIAM who was able to keep the zealous celebrities of its membership in line for fruitful pioneer work.

As a cultural leader of broad international scope, befriended by the best architects, painters and sculptors, a champion of collaboration between the arts.

As an avant-gardist demanding and teaching the integration of our whole environment.

As a great architect.

Prototypes of your own creative work grace Europe, the Middle East and South America, and you have greatly enriched the skyline along the Charles River for Harvard and Boston University.

You have united the Mediterranean spirit with that of the New World, giving the age-old patio idea of the dwelling a new meaning.

In all your activities you have kept a truly human concern predominant.

This measure Sert had achieved in the forty years following his graduation in 1929 from the Escuela Superior de Arquitectura in Barcelona, the city of his birth. He had worked for a year in Paris with Le Corbusier and Pierre Jeanneret, and in 1930 he returned to Barcelona where he opened his own practice. Sert organized the first group of architects in Barcelona affiliated with the CIAM (Congrès Internationaux d'Architecture Moderne); the group encouraged teamwork and was concerned with the role of architects in city planning. Sert's first association with CIAM had been in the Second Congress in Frankfurt in 1929 where Walter Gropius and Alvar Aalto and others gathered to discuss the subject "Dwellings for the Lower Income Class." Sert returned to Paris in 1937 and there designed the Spanish Pavilion for the 1937 World's Fair for which Pablo Picasso painted the "Guernica," Juan Miro contributed a painting, and Alexander Calder designed a "quicksilver fountain." Sert moved to the United States in 1939. From 1941 to 1958, he was associated with Paul Lester Wiener and Paul Schulz as Town Planning Associates. In Cuba, the Associates were involved in city planning for Havana and designed a palace for President Fulgencio Batista. Plans were prepared for Tumaco, Medellin, Cali, and Bogota in Colombia; Chimbote and Lima in Peru; and Brasil Motor City, near Rio de Janeiro. They were also consulted in the design of an industrial community in Sidney, New York. Sert was a consultant for the Ministry of Housing in Caracas, Venezuela. He served on the Planning Committee of the Citizens' Housing and Planning Council of New York. From 1944 to 1945 he was professor of city planning at Yale University.

Sert was president of CIAM from 1947 to 1956. In 1953, recommended by Walter Gropius, he was appointed dean of the faculty of the graduate school of design and chairman and professor of architecture at Harvard University. Sert established the Urban Design Program at Harvard, the first formal professional degree program in this field in the United States. In 1955, Sert opened his own office in Cambridge, Massachusetts, and in 1958 entered into partnership with Huson Jackson and Ronald Gourley, with Joseph Zalewski, associate; in 1963, the firm became Sert, Jackson, and Associates and as such designed several private homes, office buildings, and university buildings. In 1957, Sert was appointed consultant on Harvard University's planning, development, and design committee; he was also commissioned to design several major structures for the university. In June of 1969, Sert reached retirement age and, other than a year as professor of architecture at the University of Virginia, has since devoted himself to the practice of architecture.

Sert is one of the few architects who has had a truly close relationship with modern painters and sculptors. Members of Sert's family were artists and Sert himself was closely associated with many artists. He saw a unique relationship existing between art and buildings: either external or internal to a building, a work of art can be an integral part of the construction and focus of that building. Another of Sert's contributions to architecture was his adaptation and furthering of the principles of the patio house.

In 1981, Sert was awarded the Gold Medal of the American Institute of Architects, a substantiation of Gropius's accolade some dozen years earlier.

REGINALD R. ISAACS

WORKS

1931, Apartment House, Calle Muntaner; 1933, Master Plan (with others); 1934, Casa Bloc (low-rent apartments; with others), Paseo Torras y Bages; Barcelona, Spain. 1937, Spanish Pavilion (with Luis Lacasa), World's Fair, Paris. 1945, Motor City Plan, Brazil. 1948, Plan for Chimbote, Peru. 1949, Plan for Medellin, Colombia. 1951, Plan for Bogotá (with Le Corbusier). 1955, Studio for Joan Miró, Palma, Majorca. 1955, Presidential Palace, Havana. 1955, United States Embassy, Baghdad. 1958, Center for the Study of World Religions; 1958, Health and Administration Center; Harvard University, Cambridge, Mass. 1958, New England Gas and Electric Association Headquarters, Boston. 1959, Museum of Contemporary Art (with others), Saint Paul de Vence, France. 1960, Boston University Buildings (with others). 1966, Martin Luther King Elementary School, Cambridge, Mass. 1969, Carmelite Convent, Carmel de la Paix, Cluny, France. 1970, Undergraduate Science Center, Harvard University, Cambridge, Mass. 1972, Center for the Study of Contemporary Art (with others); 1974, Les Escales Park Housing (with others); 1977, Cultural Center and Offices; Barcelona, Spain.

BIBLIOGRAPHY

BASTLUND, KNUD 1967 *José Luis Sert.* Zurich: Editions d'Architectura.
BORRÀS, MARIA LLUISA (editor) (1974)1975 *Sert: Mediterranean Architecture.* Translated from the Spanish by Kenneth Lyons. Boston: New York Graphic Society.
DEAN, ANDREA O. 1977 "The Urbane and Varied Buildings of Sert, Jackson and Associates." *Journal of the American Institute of Architects* 66, May:50–58.
FREIXA, JAUME 1979 *Josep Ll. Sert.* Barcelona, Spain: Gili.
SERT, JOSEP LLUIS 1972 "Sert: Obras y proyectos 1929–1973." *Cuardenos de Arquitectura y urbanismo* 93: entire issue.
SERT, JOSEP LLUIS 1944 "The Human Scale in City Planning." In Paul Zucker (editor), *New Architecture and City Planning.* New York: Philosophical Library.
SERT, JOSEP LLUIS 1954 "The Changing Philosophy of Architecture." *Architectural Record* 116:181.
SERT, JOSEP LLUIS 1957 "The Architect and the City." In H. Warren Dunham (editor), *The City in Mid-century.* Detroit, Mich.: Wayne State University Press.

SERT, JOSEP LLUIS ET AL. 1942 *Can Our Cities Survive?* Cambridge, Mass.: Harvard University Press.
SERT, JOSEP LLUIS, and SWEENEY, JAMES J. (1960)1970 *Antonio Gaudi.* Reprint. New York: Praeger.
SERT, JOSEP LLUIS, and TYRWHITT, JAQUELINE (editors) 1957 *The Shape of the Cities.* Cambridge, Mass.
SERT, JOSEP LLUIS; TYRWHITT, JAQUELINE; and ROGERS, E. M. (editors) 1952 *The Heart of the City.* London: Lund Humphries.

Sert.
Peabody Terrace Married Student Housing, Harvard University. Cambridge, Massachusetts. 1963–1965

SERVANDONI, GIOVANNI NICOLANO GERONIMO

Born in Florence, the son of a coachman from Lyons, Giovanni Nicolano Geronimo Servandoni (1695–1766) studied painting in Rome with Gian Paolo Panini and architecture under Giuseppe Ignazio Rossi. In 1724, he established himself in Paris and was appointed *premier peintre décorateur* to the Académie Royale de Musique, a post he held for eighteen years. He was an adventurous and exuberant designer of décors, fêtes, and fireworks displays, and worked in this capacity in Paris and throughout Europe—London (1749), Dresden (1755), Brussels (1759), Vienna (1760), Stuttgart (1762) and Lisbon—but he was also renowned as a painter of ruin scenes, being admitted to the Académie de Peinture in 1731 and exhibiting with some regularity at the Salon from 1737 onward.

His fame rests on his design for the west front of the Church of Saint Sulpice, which he won in competition in 1732, taking up a design submitted in 1726 by GILLES MARIE OPPENORD, and which he developed during the course of construction to produce a colonnaded architecture of a grandeur and severity that his contemporaries, Louis Petit de Bachaumont, JACQUES FRANÇOIS BLONDEL, and Marie Joseph Peyre (see PEYRE FAMILY) among them, regarded as a reversion to Greek antiquity, the beginning of a new style. His chief pupils were CHARLES DE WAILLY and JEAN FRANÇOIS CHALGRIN.

R. D. MIDDLETON

WORKS

1733–1777, Saint Sulpice (west front; south tower revised and completed by Oudot de Maclaurin in 1749, the north tower redesigned and completed by J. F. T. Chalgrin in 1777; *high altar, *organ loft, and *Chapelle de la Vierge); *1738, Salle des Machines (fully refurbished and decorated), Palais des Tuileries; *1738, Temple à la grecque, Pont Neuf; *1738, Hôtel d'Auvergne (staircase), rue de l'Université; Paris. 1738, Saint Bruno des Chartreux (high altar and baldacchino; revised in execution, 1742–1745, by J. G. Soufflot), Lyons, France. 1739–1742, Cathedral (high altar and baldacchino) Sens; 1742, Church at Coulanges-la-Vineuse (rebuilding); Yonne, France. *1749, Saint James's Park (decorations to celebrate the peace of Aix-la-Chapelle), London. *1753–?, Saint Sulpice Seminary at Vaugirard, near Paris. *1754, Triumphal Arch (erected for the laying of the foundation stone of Saint Sulpice); 1754–1757, Hôtel Servandoni (the first stage of a square designed in front of the church), 6 Place Saint Sulpice; Paris. *n.d., Brandenburgh House Gallery, Hammersmith, Middlesex, England. *n.d., Fountain, Cloister of Sainte-Croix de la Bretonnerie; *n.d., La Maison de l'Enfant Jésus (entrance doorway), Barrière de Vaugirard; Paris. *n.d., Temple and Ice House, Maréchel de Richelieu Château Park, Gennevilliers, Seine, France.

BIBLIOGRAPHY

BLONDEL, JACQUES FRANÇOIS 1740 Description des Festes Données par la Ville de Paris à l'Occasion du Mariage de Madame Louise-Elizabeth de France, & de Dom Philippe, Infant & Grand Amiral d'Espagne les vingt-neuvième & trentième Août mil sept cent trent-neuf. Paris: Le Mercier.
CHARVET, ETIENNE LÉON GABRIEL 1899 Lyon artistique. Architectes: Notices biographiques et bibliographiques. Lyon: Bernoux & Cumin.
HAUTECOEUR, LOUIS 1952 Volume 4 in Histoire de l'architecture classique en France. Paris: Picard.
MIDDLETON, R. D. 1962 "The Abbé de Cordemoy and the Graeco-Gothic Ideal: A Prelude to Romantic Classicism." Journal of the Warburg and Courtauld Institutes 25, nos. 3–4:278–320.
PALISSOT DE MONTENOY, CHARLES, and FRANQUE, FRANÇOIS (1767)1860–1861 "Servandoni, architecte." Revue universelle des Arts 12:115–118.

SEVERUS and CELER

The architects of Nero's remarkable palace in Rome, Severus and Celer (first century) are known through a large, existing fragment of the palace and sparse references to them and their work in ancient literature. Nero chose them as his architect–engineers for two huge projects; none of their other work is identifiable. One project was a canal (c.60s), begun but never finished, intended to run nearly three hundred kilometers through difficult country from Lake Avernus, beside the north shore of the Bay of Naples, all the way up to the Tiber. The other was the Domus Aurea or Golden House (64–68), a palace-villa set down in the heart of Rome after the Great Fire of the summer of 64. Remains of that vast undertaking (which, unlike the overambitious canal project, was largely completed) show that Severus and Celer turned their backs on traditional architecture of the kind prescribed by VITRUVIUS and, with great confidence and originality, created highly sophisticated combinations of interior spaces. Nero's sincere if flamboyant interest in the arts, and his rejection of much from the past that he found stultifying, seem to have led him to choose these modernists. The result, which can still be seen in a surviving wing of the palace, was a radically new, interiorized and nontrabeated architecture, one with an all but limitless future.

Their names appear only in the Annals of the Roman historian Tacitus, who after describing the fire and its effects, says that

. . . Nero turned to account the ruins . . . by building a palace, the marvels of which were not to consist so much of gems and gold . . . as in fields and lakes and the air of solitude given by wooded ground alternating with clear tracts and open landscapes. The architects and engineers were Severus and Celer . . . They had undertaken to sink a navigable canal running from Lake Avernus to the mouths of the Tiber . . . (15.42).

He also describes the difficulties the canal project faced, speaks of the public works the government put in hand after the fire, and gives a précis of a new, postfire set of building regulations, a kind of building code. Tacitus also refers to the ingenuity and courage of Severus and Celer and, given his anti-imperial convictions, that ranks as high praise. Suetonius, in his chapter on Nero in his Lives of the Twelve Caesars, briefly mentions the public works (16.1), and gives a famous description of the Domus Aurea, with its ingenious mechanical devices, factitious rusticity, and baths with both fresh and sea water (31). What chiefly impressed contemporaries was the amount of land the palace covered—there was a lake where the Colosseum now stands, as well as far-flung pastures and woods—but today it is the surviving architectural evidence of the palace wing that matters most.

Approximately one hundred rooms have been cleared in an area some 60 by 200 meters; an unknown portion of the wing has been lost. The fabric is of concrete, with thin brick facing on the

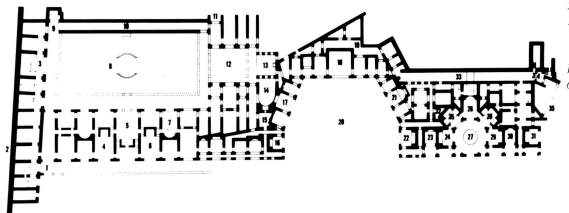

walls and piers. Apparently the Orders were used only in courtyards and along the façade from which one looked out over the lake mentioned above. Concrete had by then been brought to a high state of technical development and had long been used in utilitarian structures, baths, and, more recently, in fairly large public and residential buildings; its fire-resistant qualities surely recommended it to Severus and Celer. But their chief contribution to architectural art was the way they shaped space, going in this well beyond the limits of previous experiments to create entirely new kinds of architectural volumes and effects. That this was done in the emperor's palace, the center of fashion and influence, gave this novel architecture great prestige.

At what may originally have been the center of the wing is an octagonal hall or atrium, shorn of its marbles and mosaics, a centralized space with spatial dependencies extending radially out from it. Of this ingenious, complicated ensemble J. B. Ward-Perkins (1956) claimed that "it is hardly an exaggeration to say that the whole subsequent history of European architectural thought hangs upon this historic event." The octagon, a pavilion-like structure, is formed by angled piers supporting a dome that modulates, as it rises, to a more or less spherical shape, its uppermost zone pierced by a broad oculus. Past five of the openings between the piers are the radially extended, subordinate volumes, lower than the central pavilion and cleverly lit. The whole is a cagelike composition of nearly minimal solids that shows a remarkably clear understanding of the potentials of concrete construction. The lighting effects are impressive, and the possible symbolic implications of them and of the encompassing canopy of the central space have not been lost on modern observers.

Architecture was a major profession in the Roman world, but few architects' names have survived. Perhaps there were others as talented and original as Severus and Celer. But the Domus Aurea wing, when set against the many classical

buildings available for comparison, shows beyond doubt that they deserve the high rank given them by historians. Under the sponsorship of an autocrat defiant of tradition their creativity blossomed. No previous building approached the technical and artistic solutions found in the Domus Aurea octagon. Though the disaster of the fire, Nero's megalomania, and certain concepts explored by their predecessors all help to explain Severus and Celer's achievement, it was their genuine originality that pushed them beyond established solutions to produce a masterful, definitive statement about the revolutionary new architecture of vaulted space.

WILLIAM L. MacDONALD

WORKS

64–68, Domus Aurea of Nero; c.60s, Avernus-Tiber Canal (aborted); Rome.

BIBLIOGRAPHY

English translations of the ancient texts can be found in the volumes of the Loeb Classical Library series, published by Harvard University Press and Heinemann.

BOËTHIUS, AXEL 1960 Chapter 3 in *The Golden House of Nero: Some Aspects of Roman Architecture.* Ann Arbor: University of Michigan Press.

MACDONALD, WILLIAM L. 1965 Volume 1, chapters 2 and 6 in *The Architecture of the Roman Empire.* New Haven: Yale University Press.

PLINY THE ELDER, *Natural History,* Book XIV, chapter 3.

SUETONIUS, *Lives of the Twelve Caesars,* Book VI, sections 16 and 31.

TACITUS, *Annals,* sections 38–43.

WARD-PERKINS, J. B. 1956 "Nero's Golden House." *Antiquity* 30:209–219.

SHARON, ARYEH

Aryeh Sharon (1902–), an Israeli architect, graduated from the Bauhaus in 1929 and worked for HANNES MEYER in Berlin from 1929 to 1931. He has been practicing architecture and city planning in Tel Aviv since 1932, and has been instrumental in shaping the modern architecture of Israel.

Sharon's Bauhaus education, especially the functionalist aproach of Hannes Meyer, is often reflected in his architectural works, particularly the early ones. Sharon has worked extensively on the planning of Jerusalem, attempting to create an organic correlation between the Old City and the new Jerusalem. He has also been concerned with the planning of medical centers and hospitals in the developing countries.

MEHRANGIZ NIKOU SEXTON

WORKS

1934–1939, Cooperative Housing, Tel Aviv. 1952–1955, Beilinson General Hospital (with Ora Fardis and Benjamin Idelson), Peta Tikvah, Israel. 1961, Ezra Nashim Mental Hospital (with Idelson), Jerusalem. 1963–1977, Buildings (with others), Ife University, Nigeria. 1971, Convalescent Home, Tiberias, Israel.

BIBLIOGRAPHY

HERBERT, GILBERT 1980 "Sharon Arieh." Pages 742–745 in *Contemporary Architects.* New York: St. Martin's.

SHARON, ARIEH 1968 *Hospitals in Israel and Developing Countries.* Tel Aviv.

SHARON, ARIEH 1970 "Planning for Hospitals and Medical Centers for Developing Countries." *World Congress of Engineers and Architects* 2, no. 1:251–257.

SHARON, ARIEH 1974 "Planning Jerusalem: The Old City and Its Environs." *Ekistics* 38, no. 228:368–376.

SHARON, ARIEH; BRUTZKUS, D. A.; and SHARON, E. 1973 *Planning Jerusalem: The Old City and Its Environs.* Jerusalem: Weidenfeld & Nicolson.

SHAW, JOHN I

John Shaw (1776–1832) trained with George Gwilt the elder and opened his own London office in 1798. He was successful as a designer of picturesque cottages and country houses. In the area of civic building, Shaw was appointed architect and surveyor of Christ's Hospital, London, in 1816 and was later employed by the Phoenix Assurance Company.

BRIAN LUKACHER

WORKS

1804, Putney Hill; 1818, Rooksnest; Surrey, England. 1820–1832, Christ's Hospital, London.

SHAW, JOHN II

John Shaw (1803–1870) was a pupil of his father, JOHN SHAW I, and assumed his father's position as architect to Christ's Hospital in London in 1832. Working in the Tudor Gothic and "Wren Revival" styles, Shaw was also surveyor to Eton College and was employed by the Church Building Commissioners of London. Like his father, he was a property appraiser and was designated an official referee under the Metropolitan Buildings Act of 1844.

BRIAN LUKACHER

WORKS

1837–1838, Holy Trinity Church, London. 1844–1846, Weston's Yard, Eton College, Buckinghamshire, England. 1853–1855, London and Provincial Law and Life Assurance Office.

SHAW, R. NORMAN

The most representative and versatile of British domestic architects in the late Victorian period, Richard Norman Shaw (1831–1912) owes his fame not to any lasting innovation in the architectural vocabulary but to his power of deploying and combining existing styles and of solving specific problems with unfailing conviction, ease, charm, and originality.

Norman Shaw (as he is generally known) was born in Edinburgh. His mother was Scottish; his father, an Irish Protestant, died in 1833 leaving the family impoverished. Little is known of his upbringing. In 1845, the family moved to London, where after a period with an unknown architect Shaw was articled in 1849 to WILLIAM BURN, then the leading country house designer of the "Scottish school." Here he met W. EDEN NESFIELD, the closest friend of his early years and his future partner. Together they were drawn to A. W. N. PUGIN and the ecclesiological wing of the emerging Gothic Revival, which was little favored in Burn's office. Attending the Royal Academy's evening classes in architecture, Shaw won prizes in 1852 and 1853, followed in 1854 by the Travelling

Studentship. This enabled him to tour Europe (chiefly France and Germany) in 1854–1856. The drawings which Shaw subsequently published in *Architectural Sketches from the Continent* (1858) are Gothic and ecclesiastical in the main. Having worked for ANTHONY SALVIN in 1856–1858, Shaw acted from 1859–1862 (following PHILIP S. WEBB) as chief clerk to the great Gothic Revivalist GEORGE EDMUND STREET who, he sometimes claimed, taught him all that was worth learning about architecture.

Shaw's practice started in 1862 with a smattering of small domestic and commercial jobs. A year later Nesfield and he took a London office together, which they shared until 1876. The arrangement was of convenience and friendship only, even if for a short period (1866–1869) a partnership formally existed. The two influenced each other greatly and helped each other out, but their works remained separate. After Shaw's marriage to Agnes Wood in 1867 he gradually drifted apart from Nesfield, less for architectural than for personal reasons.

Some of Shaw's early designs, such as Holy Trinity Church, Bingley, Yorkshire (1866–1868), continue the advanced Gothic idiom he had acquired under Street, and to Gothic he remained generally faithful in his later ecclesiastical work. But the most significant part of his oeuvre in this first phase was the series of picturesque domestic buildings in the "Old English" style which Nesfield and he developed in the 1860s. This style combined the sober and rational approach architects like Street and WILLIAM BUTTERFIELD adopted for their secular buildings with borrowings from vernacular English architecture of the sixteenth and seventeenth centuries. In this Nesfield and Shaw were preceded by GEORGE DEVEY and others, but their houses are more refined and better articulated than what had gone before. To Shaw particularly belongs the responsi-

bility for first transferring this style from small cottages and lodges to full country houses. The first important examples were Glen Andred (1866–1868) and Leyswood (1868–1869), both near Groombridge in Sussex. Leyswood in particular became well known through Shaw's spectacular perspective drawings of it, exhibited at the Royal Academy in 1870. They were quickly illustrated in the *Building News,* which regularly published Shaw's drawings of his houses in the 1870s and so made him well known not just in England but in the United States, where his perspectives briefly affected the direction of the Shingle style.

At home Shaw was elected first an associate (1872) and then a full member (1877) of the Royal Academy, which he increasingly championed (in opposition to the Royal Institute of British Architects) as the right body for encouraging architecture. During the 1870s, the middle-sized country house, commissioned almost invariably by commercial or industrial clients, was his chief preoccupation. The detail of the smaller examples is predominantly Old English, but the Tudor dress of some of the larger stone-built houses (for instance, Adcote [1876–1880], Cragside [1870–1884], Flete [1878–1883] and Dawpool [1882–1886]) is a reminder that Shaw's work also continues the domestic traditions of Burn and Salvin. From 1873, Shaw also contributed to the Queen Anne revival in London with a set of brick townhouses that outdo their country cousins in originality. Of these, the many well-windowed studio houses built for Shaw's painter friends along with his own home in Hampstead (1875–1876) and a series on the Chelsea Embankment (1875–1877) now enjoy the greatest approbation. His contributions to the planned suburb of Bedford Park, London, where he designed a church, a club, an inn and stores, and several types of small middle class houses (1877–1880) are also highly valued today. All Shaw's houses, whether in city, country, or

Shaw.
Glen Andred.
Near Groombridge, Sussex,
*   England.*
1866–1868

Shaw.
Dawpool.
Cheshire, England.
1882–1886

suburb, are exceptional in their planning, combining practicality and ingenuity with great verve and unusual picturesque effects. At a time when the stricter architectural ideologues distrusted hidden ironwork as "dishonest," Shaw did not hesitate to use girders in his sections to liberate the plan from constraints. But his plans are never free or organic in the later sense of these terms.

After 1880, Shaw grew disillusioned with Gothic principles, and the direction of his practice changed. Perhaps partly because of the agricultural depression in Britain, he built fewer new country houses but adapted and altered more older ones. This too encouraged his growing sympathy for formal classicism, particularly of the English and French seventeenth-century varieties. At the same time, following illness in 1879–1881, he reduced his workload, published less, and allowed a freer hand in detail work to his assistants, of whom the most distinguished was WILLIAM RICHARD LETHABY, his chief clerk between 1879 and 1889. This new approach gathered force in reticent buildings like Barings Bank, London (1880–1881), and Bolney House, London (1883–1885) and came to a head in the cool, "Wrennaissance" 170 Queen's Gate, London (1888–1890), and its vast rural corollary, the French-classical Bryanston (1889–1894). But Shaw's increasing thoughtfulness in the 1880s was not primarily a matter of style. At his All Saints Church, Leek, Staffordshire (1885–1887), the stylistic innovations of GEORGE F. BODLEY and GEORGE GILBERT SCOTT, JR. are distilled by virtue of structural originalities into a composition of great and original power; at New Scotland Yard, London (1887–1890; 1901–1907),

Shaw's one complete public building, designed as the headquarters of the Metropolitan Police, the showmanship of style gives place to an austere yet colorful expression.

Shaw retired from practice in 1896, at which time he was widely recognized as England's leading architect. Afterward, he continued to intervene in architectural matters at all levels, having in 1892 somewhat broken through his earlier public diffidence by coediting (with THOMAS G. JACKSON) *Architecture: A Profession or an Art,* a book of polemical essays attacking those who sought the compulsory registration of architects. His last designs, many of them done in collaboration with others, were as bold as ever in planning and structure. Two commercial buildings in Liverpool, the White Star Offices (1895–1898) and Parr's Bank (1898–1901), have forceful plans, and his final work, Portland House, London (1907–1908) was built of reinforced concrete behind its conventionally classical façade. During his retirement Shaw contributed enthusiastically to civic improvements in London, his largest task being to supply elevations for the controversial rebuilding of the Regent Street Quadrant (1905–1908). Despite the vigor of his classic designs, only a small portion was built, owing to the opposition of the tenants. In 1912 Shaw resigned from the project and he died in November of that year.

"A most delightful and gifted man, a bold constructor with a turn for invention, and a clear, quick, and able draughtsman," is Lethaby's characterization of Norman Shaw (p. 75). Shaw's biographer Reginald Blomfield summed him up as "a cool clear-headed Scot, of first-rate ability, with immense power of concentration, with no string instincts for poetry" (p. 13). He was in fact an empirical architect, motivated by tasks to be mastered and skills to be learned rather than by social or artistic ideals. Shaw was as much at home pioneering a system of concrete construction or perfecting a new type of house drainage as he was designing furniture or (in his later years) new cases for the many old clocks he collected in his home. Courteous, gentle, and witty, Shaw exercised influence through his personality as well as through his architecture. Many who later distinguished themselves passed through his office, including, besides Lethaby, Sydney Barnsley, Gerald Horsley, MERVYN MACARTNEY, ERNEST NEWTON, E. S. Prior, and R. Weir Schultz. The pervasive influence of Shaw's many styles and his gentlemanly approach toward practice touched all English architects of the Arts and Crafts movement, most strongly of all perhaps his admirer and spiritual successor, EDWIN LUTYENS.

ANDREW SAINT

WORKS

1866–1868, Glen Andred, near Groombridge, Sussex, England. *1866–1868, Holy Trinity Church, Bingley, Yorkshire, England. *1868–1869, Leyswood, near Groombridge, Sussex, England. 1870–1884, Cragside, Rothbury, Northumberland, England. 1874–1876, Convent of Bethany, Hampshire, England. 1875–1876, 6 Ellerdale Road; 1875–1877, Cheyne House and Swan House; London. 1876–1880, Adcote, Shropshire, England. 1877–1880, Bedford Park, London. 1878–1883, Flete, Devonshire, England. 1879–1886, Albert Hall Mansions, Kensington Gore; *1880–1881, Barings Bank; London. *1882–1886, Dawpool, Cheshire, England. 1881–1883, Alliance Assurance Offices; *1883–1885, Bolney House; London. 1885–1887, All Saints' Church, Leek, Staffordshire, England. 1887–1890, 1901–1907, New Scotland Yard; 1888–1890, 170 Queen's Gate; London. 1889–1894, Bryanston, Dorset, England. 1895–1898, White Star Offices; 1898–1901, Parr's Bank; Liverpool, England. 1907–1908, Portland House, London.

BIBLIOGRAPHY

BLOMFIELD, REGINALD T. 1940 *Richard Norman Shaw R.A., Architect 1831–1912.* London: Batsford.

LETHABY, W. R. 1935 *Philip Webb and His Work.* London: Oxford University Press.

PEVSNER, NIKOLAUS (1941)1963 "Richard Norman Shaw." Pages 235–246 in Peter Ferriday (editor), *Victorian Architecture.* London: Jonathan Cape.

SAINT, ANDREW 1975 "Norman Shaw's Letters: A Selection." *Architectural History* 18:60–85.

SAINT, ANDREW 1976 *Richard Norman Shaw.* London: Yale University Press.

SHAW, R. NORMAN 1858 *Architectural Sketches from the Continent.* London: Day.

SHAW, R. NORMAN, and JACKSON, T. G. (editors) 1892 *Architecture: A Profession or an Art; Thirteen Short Essays on the Qualifications and Training of Architects.* London: John Murray.

SHCHUKO, VLADIMIR A.

Vladimir Alekseevich Shchuko (1878–1939) is best known for his continuous participation (1931–1939) in the much heralded competition for the Palace of the Soviets in Moscow. His winning project (in partnership with B. M. IOFAN and V. G. Gelfreikh) was hailed as the model of socialist realism, the official Soviet style inaugurated in the 1930s.

Shchuko (born in Berlin, but reared in Tombovsk, Russia) exemplifies a generation of Russian architects shaped by tradition and nineteenth-century eclecticism, interested in new ideas and fashions, and amenable to clients' taste and desire. Typically, he studied (1896–1904) first art, then architecture, at the Academy of Art in St. Peters-burg, traveling annually (1901–1907) to expand his knowledge of the Russian and European architectural heritage.

Shchuko's architectural works were strongly affected by his numerous theater set designs (exceeding forty productions) as evident in his Russian pavilions for the Rome and Turin (Italy) International Exhibitions (1910–1911) and the Propylaea to the Smolnyi Institute (1923) in Leningrad. (The building itself is by GIACOMO QUARENGHI.) His outstanding Theater of Rostov-on-Don, Russia (1930–1936) illustrates Shchuko's dashing mastery of Russian constructivism when it pervaded the theater and architecture. As official taste changed, Shchuko continuously redesigned the façades of Moscow's Lenin Library (1927–1938) and of the Palace of the Soviets (1932–1939) until the architecture of socialist realism finally emerged not long before he died.

MILKA T. BLIZNAKOV

WORKS

1909–1910, Twin Apartment Buildings, St. Petersburg, Russia. *1910–1911, Russian Pavilion, International Exhibition, Rome. *1910–1911, Russian Pavilion, International Exhibition, Turin, Italy. 1913–1927, Town Hall (now the Palace of Labor), Kiev, Russia. 1922–1923, Restaurant and Pavilion of Foreign Affairs (with V. G. Gelfreikh), First All-Russian Exposition for Agriculture and Home Industries, Moscow. 1923–1925, Propylaea (with Gelfreikh), Smolnyi Institute; 1925, Lenin's Monument (with Gelfreikh and S. A. Evseev), Finland Railroad Terminal; Leningrad. 1927–1938, Lenin's Library (with Gelfreikh), Moscow. 1930–1936, Theater Maxim Gorky (with Gelfreikh), Rostov-on-Don, Russia. 1937–1939, Main Pavilion (with Yu. V. Shchuko and Gelfreikh), All-Union Agricultural Exposition; Moscow.

BIBLIOGRAPHY

AFANASIEV, K. N. (editor) 1963–1970 *Iz istorii Sovetskoi arkhitektury.* 2 vols. Moscow: Akademiya Nauk SSSR.

BARKHIN, M. G. (editor) 1975 Volume 1, pages 255–279 in *Mastera sovetskoi arkhitektury ob arkhitekture.* Moscow: Iskusstvo.

KAUFMAN, S. A. 1946 *Vladimir Alekseevich Shchuko.* Moscow: Akademiya Arkhitektury SSSR.

KOPP, ANATOLE (1967)1970 *Town and Revolution: Soviet Architecture and City Planning, 1917–1935.* Translated by Thomas Burton. New York: Braziller.

KOPP, ANATOLE 1978 *L'architecture de la période Stalinienne.* Grenoble, France: Press Universitaires.

LIZON, PETER 1971 "The Palace of the Soviets: Change in Direction of Soviet Architecture." Unpublished Ph.D. dissertation, University of Pennsylvania, Philadelphia.

SHCHUKO, V. A. 1935 "Tvorcheskii otchet." *Arkhitektura SSSR* 6:16–21.

SHCHUKO, V. A., and GELFREIKH, V. G. 1936a

"Rostovskii teatr im. Gorkogo." *Arkhitektura SSSR*
1:30–39.

SHCHUKO, V. A., and GELFREIKH, V. G.   1936*b*
"Glavnyi pavilon na Vsesoyuznoi selskokhozyaist-
venoi vystavke 1937 g. v Moskve." *Arkhitektura SSSR*
7:36–37.

SHCHUSEV, ALEKSEI V.

Aleksei Viktorovich Shchusev (1873–1949), artist
by inclination, archeologist, restorer, and architectural historian by avocation, architect, urban designer, and planner by profession, was the most
honored exponent of Socialist Realism in the Soviet Union.

Born in Kishinev (Russia), Shchusev demonstrated early his artistic talents, receiving stipends
for education at St. Petersburg's Academy of Art
(1891–1897), for travel in Russia (1894) and
abroad (1897–1898), and for brief art studies at the
Académie Julien in Paris. He established his practice in St. Petersburg, restoring and designing
churches in medieval Russian decor.

In his first major projects—the Russian pavilion at the International Exposition (1913–1914)
in Venice, Italy, and the Kazan Railroad Terminal
(1912–1948) in Moscow, Shchusev freely combined Russian vernacular forms and abundant decoration to dress up present technological needs.
This revealed his lasting commitment to developing a uniquely Russian national architecture and
ensured him the patronage of the Czarist and the
ensuing Soviet regimes.

For the resumption of Kazan Terminal's construction after the Bolshevik Revolution,
Shchusev transferred to Moscow. There, he presided over Moscow's Architectural Association
(1922–1926), directed the Tretyakov Gallery
(1923–1926), taught at the Higher State Art and
Technical Studios (1918–1924), and headed (with
IVAN V. ZHOLTOVSKY) the Architectural Studio of
Mossovet (1918–1921), the urban design studio
"New Moscow" (1921–1923), and the Architectural Studio 2. Under the avant-garde ideas of Russian Constructivism, Shchusev temporarily abandoned his ornate style for simple modern forms,
beginning with the well-known Mausoleum of
Lenin (1924, 1929–1930) in Moscow, and using
them throughout all his 1920s projects.

Following governmental guidelines, Shchusev
reverted in 1930 to integrating again elements
from the architectural heritage of diverse times and
peoples in the Soviet Union. His flowery neo-
national style was justified by Socialist Realism's
slogan: "Socialist in content and national in
form." His pompous buildings spread from Moscow to Tashkent (Uzbek S.S.R.). A prolific designer and writer, Shchusev died at the pinnacle of
his career, honored with medals, four Stalin
Awards, a museum in Kishinev dedicated to him,
and the Museum of Architecture in Moscow
named after him.

MILKA T. BLIZNAKOV

WORKS

1908–1912, Church-Museum, Natalevka, Russia.
1908–1912, Troitskiy Cathedral, Pochaevskaya Monastery, Russia. *1913–1914, Russian Pavilion, 11th International Exhibition, Venice, Italy. 1912–1915, 1918–
1926, 1930–1948, Kazan Railroad Terminal; 1918–1923,
Master Plan for Moscow (with I. V. Zholtovsky);
*1924, Lenin's Temporary Mausoleum and Lenin's First
Mausoleum; Moscow. 1925–1927, Master Plan for
Tuapse (with Leonid A. Vesnin [see VESNIN FAMILY]
and A. C. Mukhin), Russia. 1926–1927, Master Plan for
Smolensk, Russia. 1927–1928, Sanatorium, Matsesta,
Russia. 1928–1930, Narkomzem (now the Ministry of
Agriculture); 1929–1930, Lenin's Permanent Mauso-
leum; 1930–1934, Military-Transportation Academy;
1930–1935, Hotel Moskva (with L. I. Savel'ev and
O. A. Stapran); Moscow. 1933–1938, Institute Marx-
Engels-Lenin, Tbilisi, Georgian Soviet Socialist Repub-
lic. 1933–1947, Alisher Navoi Theater, Tashkent,
Uzbek Soviet Socialist Republic. 1935–1939, Institute
for Genetics to the Academy of Science of the Union of
Soviet Socialist Republics; 1946–1948, Administrative
Building, Dzerzhinskii Square; 1948–1951, Komsomol-
skaya Subway Station; Moscow.

BIBLIOGRAPHY

AFANAS'EV, K.   1967   "Zodchiy A. V. Shchusev."
Arkhitektura SSSR 8:29–35.

DRUZHININIA-GEORGIEVSKAYA, E. V., and KORNFEL'
D YA. A.   1955   *Zodchiy A. V. Shchusev.* Moscow:
Akademiya nauk SSSR.

KOPP, ANATOLE   1978   *L'architecture de la période
Stalinienne.* Grenoble, France: Presses Universitaires.

NOVIKOV, I.   1953   "Traditsii natsional'nogo
zodehestva v tvorchestve A. V. Shchuseva." *Arkhitektura SSSR* 5:15–21.

SHCHUSEV, ALEKSEI V.   1905   "Restavratsiya i
raskopka fundamentov tserkvi sv. Vasiliya v
Ovruche." *Starye gody* 11:132–133.

SHCHUSEV, ALEKSEI V.   1924*a*   "Moskva
budushchego." *Krasnaya Niva* 17:414–418.

SHCHUSEV, ALEKSEI V.   1924*b*   "Zadacha sovremennoy
arkhitektury." *Stroitel'naya promyshlennost* 12:760–
762.

SHCHUSEV, ALEKSEI V.   1927   "Proekt gostnitsy v
Matseste." *Sovremennaya arkhitektura* 3:98–99.

SHCHUSEV, ALEKSEI V.   1934   "K voprosu o monumental'nom iskusstve." *Iskusstvo* 4:2–20.

SHCHUSEV, ALEKSEI V.   1935   "Gostnitsa 'Moskva.'"
Stroitel'stvo Moskvy 17–18:3–8.

SHCHUSEV, ALEKSEI V.   1938   "Proekt Glavnogo
zdaniya Akademii nayk SSSR v Moskve." *Vestnik AN
SSSR* 7–8:6–19.

SHCHUSEV, ALEKSEI V.   1940   *Arkhitektura i stroitel'stvo*

Instituta Marksa-Engelsa-Lenina v Tbilisi. Moscow: Vsesoyuznaya Akademiya arkhitektury.

SHCHUSEV, ALEKSEI V. and LAVROV, V. A.   1946 "General'nyy plan Novgoroda." *Arkhitektura i stroitel'stvo* 5:3–10.

SOKOLOV, N. B.   1952   *A. V. Shchusev.* Moscow: Gos. izd. literatury po stroitel'stvu i arkhitekture.

STARR, S. FREDERIC   1978   *Melnikov: Solo Architect in a Mass Society.* N.J.: Princeton University Press.

SHEKHTEL, FEDOR

Fedor (Franz) Osipovich Shekhtel (1859–1926), was the leading Moscow architect in the decades before World War I, was a masterful exponent of Art Nouveau and the first in Russia to realize the spatial possibilities of iron, glass, and reinforced concrete technology. President of the Moscow Architectural Society (1908–1922), he was closely associated with the new wealthy merchants of Moscow; in the private mansions and commercial buildings that he built for them he shaped decisively the new skyline of the formerly medieval city. Widely imitated by contemporaries, his innovative structures formed a foundation on which the Constructivists of the 1920s, such as Alexander and Leonid Vesnin (see VESNIN FAMILY), would build.

Shekhtel came to Moscow from the Volga river town of Saratov in the mid-1870s, working as an illustrator and theater designer before turning exclusively to architecture. His theatrical approach to space continued to be reflected in the settings he designed for the imperial coronation ceremonies in 1896, the Russian Pavilion at the International Exposition in Glasgow (1901), and his interiors for Konstantin Stanislavsky's new Moscow Art Theater (1902). He taught composition at the Stroganov School of Applied Art (from 1896) and at the postrevolutionary Higher Artistic and Technical Workshops until his death. He designed all his own interiors often working with the leading painters, sculptors, and ceramicists of The World of Art movement. He organized "The New Style" exposition in Moscow in 1902–1903, in which the works of JOSEPH MARIA OLBRICH and CHARLES RENNIE MACKINTOSH were introduced to Russia.

Even within the historical vocabulary of his neo-Gothic mansions for the Morozov family in the 1890s and the neo-Russian pavilion in Glasgow (1901) and Yaroslavsky Railway Station (1902), Shekhtel created a new language for Moscow. He exploited the possibilities of the medieval styles to produce a dynamic perspective of flexible, expanding interior space. Developed to its fullest in the Ryabushinsky Mansion (1900–1902) and the Derozhinsky Mansion (1901–1902), both in Moscow, where the sculptural masses of the buildings, as geometrical volumes, are set carefully into a harmonious surrounding space. The exquisitely detailed interiors owe much to the Vienna Secession and the Glasgow school. His offices, banks, hotels, printing houses, apartment houses, and movie theaters between 1900 and 1912 evolved a language of elegant and laconic austerity accented by the rhythm of large windows, undecorated glazed tile façades, and simple geometrical repetition of forms, somewhat reminiscent of the Chicago school. When the St. Petersburg fashion for neoclassicism began to show its influence in Moscow, Shekhtel designed a house for himself (1910) in which modernism was partially translated back into a traditional vocabulary of columns and frieze; the building remained nevertheless essentially a variation on the asymmetrical Art Nouveau volumes of a decade earlier.

After the Revolution of 1917, Shekhtel designed the Turkestan Pavilion for the first Soviet Agricultural Exposition (Moscow, 1923) and worked on designs for hydroelectric stations, a crematorium, factories, and a Lenin Mausoleum. Illness and political chaos had already ended his career before he died. His buildings were rejected in the Stalin era, and only in the late 1970s were some efforts at restoration begun.

LINDA GERSTEIN

WORKS

1893, Morozova House; 1896, Shekhtel House; 1898–1899, Kuznetsov Store; 1900–1902, Ryabushinsky Mansion; 1901, Boyarsky Dvor Hotel; Moscow. 1901, Russian Pavilion, Glasgow, Scotland. 1901–1902, Derozhinsky Mansion; 1902, Moscow Art Theater; 1902, Yaroslavsky Railway Station; 1902–1904, Stroganov School Apartment House; 1903, Ryabushinsky Bank; 1907, "Utro Rossii" Printing Press; Moscow. 1907, Patrikeev Villa, Khimki, Russia. 1909, Moscow Merchants' Society Building; 1910, Shekhtel House; 1912, Art Movie Theater; 1923, Turkestan Pavilion, Soviety Agricultural Exposition; Moscow.

BIBLIOGRAPHY

BORISOVA, ELENA A., and KAZHDAN, TATIANA P.   1971   *Russakaya arkhitektura Kontsa XIX—nachala XX veka.* Moscow: Nauka.

KIRICHENKO, ERGENIIA I.   1975   *Fedor Shekhtel.* Moscow: Stroiizdat.

KIRICHENKO, ERGENIIA I.   1977   *Moskva na rubezhe stoletii.* Moscow: Stroiizdat.

KIRICHENKO, ERGENIIA I.   1978   *Russkaya arkhitektura 1830–1910—kh godov.* Moscow: Iskusstvo.

SHEKHTEL, FEDOR   1975   "Architecture and Its Relationship to Painting and Sculpture." Volume 1 in *Masters of Soviet Architecture About Architecture.* Moscow.

SHENSTONE, WILLIAM

An English poet and amateur landscape designer, William Shenstone (1714–1763) created at The Leasowes, Warwickshire (begun in 1743), a highly influential contribution to the development of the English landscape garden. The circuit walk through the belts of trees surrounding his farm, past a Gothic ruin and cascade, provided a series of continuously unfolding and precisely framed vistas near and far. Garden seats with poetic inscriptions provided rest, prescribed viewpoints, and evoked literary associations. For Shenstone a garden tour was as much a meditative as a sensuous event.

RICHARD O. SWAIN

BIBLIOGRAPHY

HUNT, JOHN DIXON, and WILLIS, PETER (editors) (1975)1976 *The Genius of the Place: The English Landscape Garden, 1620–1820.* New York: Harper.

MALINS, EDWARD G. 1966 *English Landscaping and Literature, 1660–1840.* London: Oxford University Press.

SHENSTONE, WILLIAM (1765)1980 *Unconnected Thoughts on Gardening.* Reprint. New York: Garland.

SIRÉN, OSVALD 1950 *China and Gardens of Europe of the Eighteenth Century.* New York: Ronald Press.

SHEPHEARD, PETER FAULKNER

As a youth, Peter Faulkner Shepheard (1913–) was dissuaded from becoming a biologist by the need to specialize. In architecture, he has avoided overspecialization, preferring the design of buildings in a full landscape to abstract design. He has by nature ignored the boundaries erected between the disciplines of architecture, landscape architecture, and planning. He received a fine grounding in planning under PATRICK ABERCROMBIE on the Greater London Plan (1943–1944), and under WILLIAM GRAHAM HOLFORD on Stevenage New Town (1944–1947). He formed an architectural partnership with Derek Bridgwater, which was later joined by Gabriel Epstein and Peter Hunt, but which has always been kept a small working unit. The firm was one of the first to recognize the social problems of high-rise housing—some of which it had designed in the 1950s—and thereafter they began to stress high-density yet medium-rise developments, convincing some clients to give up ideas of high-rise. In 1971, Shepheard accepted the deanship of the University of Pennsylvania, where he helped to promote undergraduate courses in environmental design, which brought together related design disciplines previously separated.

BRIAN HANSON

WORKS

1950–1953, Housing, New Street, Lansbury, Poplar, London. 1957–1960, Scraptoft Hall Teacher Training College, Leicester, England. 1960–1963, London Zoo (Cattle and Zebra Houses, landscaping), Regent's Park, London. 1962–1965, University of Liverpool (Student's Union), England. 1964–1971, Lancaster University (Master Plan and buildings), Lancastershire, England. 1968, University of Keele (Sports Center), England. 1971–1975, Université Catholique de Louvain (DaVinci Building, with R. Thirion), Louvain-la-Neuve, Belgium. 1974, University of Ghana (library), Accra. 1975, Housing, Gough Walk, Tower Hamlets, London. 1976, University of Lancaster, Flyde College (site development), Lancastershire, England. 1978, University of Warwick (Social Sciences Building), Coventry, England. 1980, Wapping Sports Center, London. 1980, Open University (buildings), Walton, Milton Keynes, Bedfordshire, England.

BIBLIOGRAPHY

EPSTEIN, GABRIEL 1974 "That Little Bit Extra." *Journal of the Royal Institute of British Architects* 81, no. 11:14–19.

"Getting it all Together." 1980 *Building* 238:37–39.

MALTZ, BOB 1977 "Philadelphia: Penn's City at a Glance." *Building Design* 352:2.

SHEPHEARD, PETER FAULKNER 1953 *Modern Gardens.* London: Architectural Press.

SHEPHEARD, PETER FAULKNER 1969 *Gardens.* London: Macdonald.

SHEPHERD, EDWARD

Edward Shepherd (?–1747) was a speculative builder and architect, important for work in Mayfair and for the developments he carried out in the West End of London for the duke of Chandos and for Sir Richard Grosvenor. In 1735, with his own money, he built Shepherd's Market in Mayfair on the site of the old fairground. This building had two levels, the lower filled with butchers' shops, the upper floor a theater that was used at the time the fair was open. Little he built survives now but during his life he was widely known in the London building world.

DAVID CAST

WORKS

1724–1728, Cavendish Square; 1730, Houses, Grosvenor Square (north side); 1735, Shepherd's Market, Mayfair; 1736–1737, 71 South Audely Street; London.

BIBLIOGRAPHY

COLLINS BAKER, C. H., and COLLINS BAKER,

MURIEL I. 1949 *The Life and Circumstances of James Brydges, Duke of Chandos.* Oxford: Clarendon.
SUMMERSON, JOHN (1945)1978 *Georgian London.* 3d ed., rev. Cambridge, Mass.: M.I.T. Press.

SHEPLEY, RUTAN, and COOLIDGE

George Foster Shepley (1860–1903), Charles Hercules Rutan (1851–1914), and Charles Allerton Coolidge (1858–1936), all members in the office of H. H. RICHARDSON, entered into partnership with each other following their predecessor's death in 1886. Completing Richardson's unfinished work, the firm of Shepley, Rutan, and Coolidge went on to become one of the most successful architectural offices in the United States, and although it did not exploit Richardson's name, the reputation and esteem which it had inherited contributed greatly to its popularity.

The greatest demand for the firm's work came in the fields of commercial and institutional building. One of its first commissions was for the campus of Stanford University (1892) in Palo Alto, California. Two years later, Shepley, Rutan, and Coolidge completed perhaps their most acclaimed structures of the period. The Ames Building (1892) in Boston was the tallest building in the city at the time of its construction and is still the second highest wall-bearing structure in America.

Despite the accolade with which it was received, however, the façade of the Ames Building, articulated in a seemingly arbitrary division of stories, differed little from those of most tall office buildings at the turn of the century and reflected what had become an almost standardized solution to the problem of the skyscraper. In the 1890s, like many firms, Shepley, Rutan, and Coolidge were beginning to adopt the stylistic formulas of MCKIM, MEAD, AND WHITE, the leading architects of the period, rather than continuing in the Richardsonian tradition at which they were more accomplished. For the most part, Shepley, Rutan, and Coolidge's best work is their earliest in the 1880s which retains Richardson's clean yet not overbearing usage of the Romanesque, combined with symmetry and moderate detailing. Examples include the Public Library in New Orleans (1887), the Springfield Railroad Station (1889), Massachusetts, and the Lionberger Warehouse in St. Louis, Missouri (1887), a sort of scaled-down Marshall Field Store. Later designs, such as the Chicago Public Library (1893) and the Art Institute of Chicago (1897) reflect a strong Renaissance and classical influence made popular by McKim, Mead, and White.

Shepley, Rutan, and Coolidge.
Stanford University.
Palo Alto, California.
1892

Both educated at the Massachusetts Institute of Technology, George Shepley, who joined Richardson's office in 1882, and Charles Coolidge, who joined a year later, had been responsible as draftsmen for Richardson's last buildings, while Charles Rutan had been chief engineer for the master since 1880. But unlike the over-all supervision which Richardson exercised over his staff, responsibilities in the new firm were pretty much equally divided among the three partners with each one overseeing their own particular area of expertise. Consequently, this lack of consistent leadership resulted in a great hodgepodge of buildings and styles. Any individuality which the firm retained following Richardson's death was further dissipated as Shepley, Rutan, and Coolidge opened branch offices in St. Louis and Chicago.

The firm's Stanford University complex in Palo Alto, California, for example, stands as a series of solidly neo-Romanesque buildings based on an alternating rhythm of arches; but two years later, another set of university buildings, Conant and Perkins Halls at Harvard (1894), resemble eighteenth-century Georgian structures common in the surrounding area. In the Boston Chamber of Commerce (1892), there is even a confused mixture of two styles in a single building—Romanesque window arches capped by Gothic pediments.

Following the death of George Shepley in 1903, the firm continued to design until Rutan's death in 1914. Subsequently, Charles Coolidge formed the office of Coolidge, Shepley (George Shepley's son), Bulfinch, and Abbott.

PETER L. DONHAUSER

WORKS

1887, Lionberger Warehouse, St. Louis, Mo. 1887, Public Library, New Orleans, La. 1889, Railroad Station,

Springfield, Mass. 1892, Ames Building; 1892, Chamber of Commerce; Boston. 1892, Shadyside Presbyterian Church, Pittsburgh. 1892, Stanford University, Palo Alto, Calif. 1893, Chicago Public Library. 1894, Conant Hall; 1895, Perkins Hall; Harvard University, Cambridge, Mass. 1897, Chicago Art Institute. 1897, New England Building, Cleveland, Ohio. 1899, South Terminal Station, Boston. *1900, United States Building, Paris Exposition. 1902, Chapel, Vassar College, Poughkeepsie, N.Y. 1903, Government Hospital for the Insane, Washington. 1903, John Hay Library, Brown University, Providence, R.I. 1903–1907, Medical School; 1907, Langdell Hall; Harvard University, Cambridge, Mass. 1911–1913, First Congregational Church, Fall River, Mass. 1913–1914, Gore, Smith, and Standish Halls, Harvard University, Cambridge, Mass.

BIBLIOGRAPHY

HITCHCOCK, H. R.   1975   *The Architecture of H. H. Richardson and His Times.* Cambridge, Mass.: M.I.T. Press.

SHEPLEY, RUTAN, and COOLIDGE   1887   "The Lionberger Warehouse." *American Architect and Building News* 21:246.

SHEPLEY, RUTAN, and COOLIDGE   1891   "The Buildings of Leland Stanford, Jr. University." *Inland Architect and News Record* 17.

SHEPLEY, RUTAN, and COOLIDGE   1897   "The Chicago Public Library." *American Architect and Building News* 58:67.

SHEPLEY, RUTAN, and COOLIDGE   1899   "South Terminal Station." *American Architect and Building News* 65:95.

STURGIS, RUSSELL   1895–1896   "Shepley, Rutan and Coolidge." *Architectural Record Supplement* 3:special issue.

SHEPPARD and ROBSON

Richard W. Sheppard (1910–) and Geoffrey Robson, two English architects, started their partnership in the late 1950s. They have specialized in school design and institutional buildings for which they use conventional materials and modern technology in the most economical way. Their most interesting building is Churchill College, Cambridge (1959) with a number of small and medium sized courts arranged around the towering concrete-vaulted hall.

FARHAD NIROUMAND-RAD

WORKS

1958–1962, Digby Hall, Leicester University, England. 1959, Churchill College, Cambridge. 1959, T. P. Riley County Secondary School, Blokwick, Wolsall, England. 1959–1961, School of Navigation, Southampton, England. 1960, Science and Mathematics Building, King's College, New Castle, England. 1960, Student Hostel, Prince's Garden, London. 1960–1963, Midland Training College, Walsall, England. 1961, Grammar School, West Bronwick, England. 1961, School, Wallingford, England. 1963, Hall of Residence, Imperial College, London. 1964, Teachers' Training College, Walsall, England.

BIBLIOGRAPHY

"Canteen in the North of England." 1944 *Architectural Review* 96:34–37.

"College at Pershore." 1955 *Architectural Review* 118:301–303.

"Developments in Post-war Housing in 1944." 1945 *Architect's Journal* 101:54–57.

"Hostel at Wye College, Kent." 1950 *Architect's Journal* 111:160–167.

"House at Storrington." 1954 *Architectural Review* 116:293–294.

"School of Navigation, Warsash," 1962 *Architectural Review* 131:239–248.

"University Buildings." 1960 *Architectural Review* 127:11–19.

SHIMIZU, KISUKE

Born in Iba-machi, Toyama Prefecture, Japan, and trained as a carpenter, Kisuke Shimizu II (1815–1881) came to Edo (now Tokyo) and married Shimizu's daughter to succeed the family. He worked frequently in Yokohama where he learned Western building styles. He designed and built a number of notable buildings. Through his friendship with Eiichi Shibusawa who was then a notable financier, he was able to organize his work group into a modern company. It is now called the Shimizu Construction Co. Ltd., one of the five biggest contractors in Japan. He created a peculiar, eclectic style by mixing both Japanese tradition and Western architectural elements. His buildings were considered the symbols of a civilized era and were frequently depicted in wood-block prints.

HIROSHI YAMAGUCHI

WORKS

*1868, Tsukiji Hotel; *1872, Number One National Bank (formerly Mitsui-gumi House); *1874, Kawase-Bank Mitsui-gumi; Tokyo.

BIBLIOGRAPHY

KOSHINO, TAKESHI   1979   *Nihon-no Kenchiku: Meiji, Taisho, Showa.* Tokyo: Sansei-dō.

SHINOHARA, KAZUO

Born in Shizuoka Prefecture, Japan, Kazuo Shinohara (1925–) graduated from the Tokyo School of Physics in 1947, then studied mathematics at

Tohoku University. He became an assistant professor at Tokyo Medical College, but later he entered the Tokyo Institute of Technology to pursue a career as an architect. Graduating in 1953, he remained at the Tokyo Institute to teach architectural design. He took his doctorate in 1967; the title of his dissertation was "Space Composition of Japanese Architecture."

Besides being an educator, Shinohara is known as an excellent designer with much influence and popularity among the younger generation. Most of his works are houses, whose structure and plan are simple in composition, based on traditional Japanese architecture. Many of his early works are timber houses, but in recent works he has preferred to use reinforced concrete construction, with a part of the building frame exposed to the interior space as an important factor in the design.

TAKASHI HASEGAWA

WORKS

1954, House, Kugayama; 1960, Karakasa House; 1965, House in White; Tokyo. 1969, Cubic Forest, Kawasaki, Kanagawa Prefecture, Japan. 1975, House, Uehara; 1978, House, Crooked Road; Tokyo.

BIBLIOGRAPHY

SHINOHARA, KAZUO 1971 *Jūroku no jūtaku to kenchikuron.* Tokyo: Bijutsu Shuppan-sha.
SHINOHARA, KAZUO 1976 *11 Houses and Architectural Theory.* Tokyo: Bijutsu Shuppan-sha.

SHIRAI, SEIICHI

Born in Kyoto, Japan, Seiichi Shirai (1905–) studied architecture at the Kyoto Polytechnic Institute. Going to Germany for further education, he stayed in Berlin and Heidelberg, where he studied mostly philosophy; he was particularly interested in the thought of Karl Jaspers. At the same time, he had a keen interest in Gothic architecture, for which he traveled around Europe. Returning to Japan, he began his career as an architect in 1935 and designed several timber houses that gave the impression of being influenced by medieval architecture. After World War II, his designs drew attention because he rejected the influence of modernism, which was dominant among Japanese architects, and created traditional shapes and spaces in his works. The characteristic features of his designs are seen most prominently in the series of buildings for the Shinwa Bank (1966–1969), for which he was awarded a prize from the Architectural Institute of Japan as well as many other prizes. His fondness for European medieval architecture and his admiration of the dynamism of

space in baroque architecture are expressed in all his designs.

TAKASHI HASEGAWA

WORKS

*1942, Shimanaka Villa, Nagano, Japan. 1955, Matsuida Town Office, Gunma Prefecture, Japan. 1958, Zenshōji Temple, Tokyo. 1966–1969, Shinwa Bank Headquarters; 1975, Shinwa Bank (Kaishokan); Sasebo, Nagasaki Prefecture, Japan.

BIBLIOGRAPHY

The Architecture of Seiichi Shirai. 1974 Tokyo.
Kaishokan. 1978 Tokyo.

*Shinohara.
House in white.
Tokyo.
1975*

*Shirai.
Shinwa Bank.
Sasebo, Nagasaki
    Prefecture, Japan.
1975*

SHOOSMITH, A. G.

Arthur Gordon Shoosmith (1888–1974), perhaps the most brilliant British architect working in India under the influence of EDWIN LUTYENS, built little, but Saint Martin's Church (1928–1931) is one of the most original and powerful church designs of the twentieth century. Born in Russia, he studied at the Royal Academy Schools. In 1920 Shoosmith became Lutyens's representative in New Delhi, where he designed the Garrison Church (1928), a brick building fusing Lutyens's "elemental mode" with the early twentieth-century industrial aesthetic and interest in the monumental and the sublime. Shoosmith returned to England in 1931, but he never succeeded in establishing himself in independent practice.

GAVIN STAMP

WORKS

1928, Garrison Church; 1928–1931, Saint Martin's Church; 1930–1931, Lady Hardinge Serai; New Delhi.

BIBLIOGRAPHY

SHOOSMITH, A. G. 1931 "The Design of New Delhi." *Indian State Railways Magazine* 4, no. 5:423.
SHOOSMITH, A. G. 1938 "Present-day Architecture in India." *The Nineteenth Century and After* 123:204–213.
STAMP, GAVIN 1976 "Indian Summer." *Architectural Review* 159:365–372.

SHREVE, LAMB, and HARMON

Best known for their Empire State Building in New York (the tallest building in the world when completed), Shreve, Lamb, and Harmon produced a distinct body of corporate, commercial, and institutional architecture in Art Deco and then functionalist styles. Richmond Harold Shreve (1877–1946) and William Frederick Lamb (1883–1952), after working in the office of CARRÈRE AND HASTINGS as early as 1906, began a partnership with their old firm in 1920, dropping the Carrère and Hastings names in 1924.

An early commission for the independent Shreve and Lamb was the General Motors Building in New York (1925–1927), which brought them into contact with John J. Raskob. When Raskob became involved with the Empire State Building in 1928, Shreve and Lamb were retained; Arthur Loomis Harmon (1878–1958) became a partner during the final designs in 1929. The Empire State Building operation was completely industrial; Lamb proudly stated that "hand work was done away with," and the efficient construction scheduling was widely noted at the time, although the actual design was generally ignored.

Later work essentially followed the conservative stone and stainless steel or aluminum detailing of the Empire State, and their Brill Building (1933–1934) and Hunter College (1939–1940) were basically plain boxes, deriving interest from the overall form and metal details. After 1943 the firm was reorganized as Shreve, Lamb, and Harmon Associates, under which name it is still operating today. Within the firm, Shreve was often associated with production and Lamb and Harmon are usually mentioned as designers. Harmon was prominent in New York City architecture before his association with the firm, especially for his Shelton Towers Hotel (1923–1924), an influential example of setback design.

CHRISTOPHER S. GRAY

WORKS

1925–1927, General Motors Building (Shreve and Lamb only); 1928–1931, Empire State Building; 1929–1931, 500 Fifth Avenue; 1933–1934, Brill Brothers Store; 1939–1940, Hunter College (with WALLACE K. HARRISON and ANDRÉ FOULIHOUX); 1948–1950, Mutual Life Insurance Building; New York.

SHRYOCK, GIDEON

Gideon Shryock (1802–1880) introduced the Greek Revival to the Kentucky region, which has produced some of the most remarkable buildings of the geometric phase of Federal architecture in the United States. In place of low, symmetrical, multiple-pavilion layouts, polygonal, circular, and elliptical forms, long masonry arcades, and the use of arched and Palladian openings, the tide turned toward Hellenic classicism, establishing a new ideal of compact, cubic momumentality, featuring colossal-order porticoes and authentic architectural details.

Shryock was born in Lexington, Kentucky, and educated at the Lancastrian Academy. At twenty-one he went to Philadelphia to work and study under WILLIAM STRICKLAND for a year. In 1827 he won the competition for the new Kentucky State House, constructing the first Greek Revival edifice west of the Allegheny Mountains. Inspired by the Temple of Athena at Priena, Ionia, the imperial staircase in a circular well under the dome is among the foremost engineering masterpieces in America. Shryock returned to Lexington in 1830 and built Morrison College (1830–1833), having a hexastyle Doric portico set in a complex composition of rectangular severity. In 1835 he moved to Louisville to build the Jefferson County courthouse, which, had it followed his design, would have been his most impressive work; but disintegrating masonry and bureaucratic vicissitudes prompted curtailments.

CLAY LANCASTER

WORKS

1827–1829, Kentucky State House, Frankfort. *1830–1833, Morrison College, Transylvania University, Lexington, Ky. 1832–1833, Franklin County Courthouse (alterations); 1835, Orlando Brown House; Frankfort, Ky. 1835–1842, Jefferson County Courthouse (completed by others in 1860; much changed); *1838, Louisville Medical Institute; Louisville, Ky.

BIBLIOGRAPHY

ANDREWS, ALFRED 1945 "Gideon Shryock—Kentucky Architect." *Antiques* July:33–37.
BELL, THEODORE 1880 "Obituary of Gideon Shryock." *The Courier-Journal* (Louisville) 22 June:4.
FIELDS, ELIZABETH SHRYOCK 1934 "Gideon Shryock, His Life and His Work." Unpublished paper written for and now in the archives of the Filson Club, Louisville, Ky.
LANCASTER, CLAY 1943 "Gideon Shryock and John McMurtry, Architect and Builder of Kentucky." *Art Quarterly* 6:257–275.
NEWCOMB, REXFORD 1928 "Gideon Shryock: Pioneer Greek Revivalist of the Middlewest." *Register of the Kentucky State Historical Society* Sept.:221–235.
PRICE, CAROLINE 1943 "The Louisville Buildings of Gideon Shryock." Unpublished senior thesis, University of Louisville, Ky.
"State House of Kentucky." 1833 *Atkinson's Casket* Dec.:553.
THOMAS, SAMUEL W. 1967 "The Jefferson County Courthouse: Designed and Built between 1835 and 1842 by the City Architect, Gideon Shryock." *Louisville Bar Association Bulletin* Spring:6–9.

SHUJĀᶜ B. QĀSIM AL-IṢFAHĀNĪ

Ḥājjī Shujāᶜ b. Qāsim al-Isfahānī was an Iranian architect who restored three buildings during the reign of the Safavid shah, Sulaymān I, in the last third of the seventeenth century. His earliest work is a door added in 1667 to the south side of the west court of the Shah Mosque in Iṣfahān; it is signed the work (ᶜamal) of Shujāᶜ, son of the master (ustād) Qāsim, the builder (al-bannā') of Iṣfahān. He evidently moved from Iṣfahān to Mashhad, for his two other signed works are found there a decade later. In 1676 the muṣallā (prayer ground) of Mashhad was refaced with tiles, and Ḥājjī Shujāᶜ's signature, the work of Ḥājjī Shujāᶜ of Iṣfahān, appears twice, once at the end of a dedicatory poem in Persian with a chronogram equivalent to 1676 and again in a small tile in the mihrab also dated 1676. Soon afterward, he participated in

the restorations of the mosque of Gawhar Shād in Mashhad; a tile at the base of the left minaret is signed the work of Ḥājjī Shujāᶜ, builder (al-bannā') of Iṣfahān in 1677.

SHEILA S. BLAIR

BIBLIOGRAPHY

MAYER, L. A. 1956 Page 120 in *Islamic Architects and Their Works*. Geneva: Kundig.

SHUTE, JOHN

John Shute (?–1563) was the author of the first English treatise on architecture, *The First and Chief Groundes of Architecture* (1563). The title page describes him as a "Paynter and Archytecte," but the book is his only certain work, and almost all of the little that is known of him has been gleaned from it. In it he describes how the book was the outcome of his being sent (1550) to Italy to study architecture by the duke of Northumberland, one of a group of influential members of the court of Edward VI who tried to promote a classical style of architecture in England at this time. The book is now very rare (less than a dozen copies are known, all of the first edition, apart from two of an edition of 1587), and the extent of its influence is uncertain. It did, however, introduce many architectural terms to the English language; indeed, the very words architect and architecture make their first recorded appearance in it. Essentially, it is a treatise on the orders, compiled rather laboriously from sources such as VITRUVIUS and SEBASTIANO SERLIO, but there are some personal observations on what Shute had seen in Italy, and the illustrations, perhaps Shute's own work, are striking and original.

IAN CHILVERS

BIBLIOGRAPHY

GENT, LUCY 1981 *Picture and Poetry 1560–1620: Relations between Literature and the Visual Arts in the English Renaissance*. Lexington Spa, England: James Hall.
HIND, A. M. 1952 "The Tudor Period." Part 1 in *Engraving in England in the Sixteenth and Seventeenth Centuries*. Cambridge University Press.
LEES-MILNE, JAMES 1951 *Tudor Renaissance*. London: B. T. Batsford.
PAPWORTH, WYATT 1878 "John Shute, 1563." *The Builder* 36:826–828.
POLLARD, A. W., and REDGRAVE, G. R. (editors) (1926)1976 *A Short-Title Catalogue of Books Printed in England: 1475–1640*. London: The Bibliographical Society.
SHUTE, JOHN (1563)1912 *The First and Chief Groundes of Architecture. . . . A Facsimile of the First Edition with an Introduction by Lawrence Weaver*. London: Country Life. The Gregg Press, London, has also

published a facsimile of the treatise.

SIMPSON, W. DOUGLAS 1944 "Dudley Castle: The Renaissance Buildings." *Archaeological Journal* 101:119–125. An unconvincing attempt to credit Shute with work at Dudley and elsewhere.

SUMMERSON, JOHN (1953)1977 *Architecture in Britain: 1530 to 1830.* 6th ed., rev. Harmondsworth, England: Penguin.

WITTKOWER, RUDOLF 1974 *Palladio and English Palladianism.* London: Thames & Hudson.

SHUTZE, PHILIP TRAMMELL

Philip Trammell Shutze (1890–) was born in Columbia, Georgia, and attended the Georgia Institute of Technology (1912) and the School of Architecture, Columbia University (1913). In 1915, he won the Prix de Rome and remained in Italy to 1920. On returning home, he worked for F. Burrall Hoffman, Jr., and Mott B. Schmidt in New York and, in 1923, he joined the firm of Hentz, Reid, and Adler. He became a partner in 1926 in Hentz, Adler and Shutze, changed in 1944 to Shutze, Armistead and Adler, from 1945 to 1950 Shutze and Armistead, then Shutze alone to 1960.

HENRY HOPE REED

WORKS

1921–1922, Calhoun-Thornwell House; 1926–1928, Swan House; 1929, Citizen's and Southern National Bank Main Office; 1929–1930, Glenn Memorial Church, Emory University; 1930, English-Chambers House; Atlanta, Ga. 1930, William C. Potter House; 1930, Francis Wetherbottom House; Albany, Ga. 1931, Horgan–Curtis House, Macon, Ga. 1931–1932, Hebrew Benevolent Congregation Temple; 1940, Fulton County Medical Society; 1940, Glenn Memorial Church (Sunday school and chapel), Emory University; 1945, Whitehead Memorial Annex, Emory University Hospital; Atlanta, Ga. 1947–1948, Julian Hightower House, Thomaston, Ga. 1954, Charles Daniel House, Greenville, S.C.

BIBLIOGRAPHY

REED, HENRY HOPE 1977 "America's Greatest Living Classical Architect: Philip Trammell Shutze of Atlanta." Volume 4, pages 5–44 in *Classical America.* New York: Classical America.

SIBOUR, JULES HENRI DE

A designer of institutional, government, commercial, and residential buildings, Jules Henri de Sibour (1872–1938) worked in periods of both economic optimism and blight. Although he remained active during the Depression on such government commissions as the Administrative Head-

quarters of the United States Service Bureau (1934), he is primarily recognized for his luxurious private residences and apartments of the era preceding the 1929 stock market crash.

Sibour's background eminently suited him for the architectural profession, deemed "genteel" by late nineteenth-century minds. Born in Paris to a French diplomat and his American wife, Sibour traced his lineage to Louis IX. His education, however, was American. He graduated from Yale University in 1896 and began a formal study of architecture at the Ecole des Beaux-Arts in Paris two years later. Returning to New York, he entered a partnership with BRUCE PRICE which became Sibour's alone upon Price's death in 1903. Although he had worked in Washington for several years, it was not until 1909 that he closed the New York office and based his firm in the capital city, where he remained until his death.

Responding to a socioeconomic climate defined by individual wealth and prestige, Sibour's architecture emphasized luxury within the context of the Beaux-Arts tradition. His work on three projects, the Charles Moore Mansion (1906–1907; now the Canadian Chancery), the investment firm with which Moore was associated (1906–1907), and the Chevy Chase Country Club (1910), to which both Moore and Sibour belonged, illustrates the degree to which his architecture symbolically unified an individual's personal, business, and social life.

When a population influx mandated multifamily dwellings, Sibour answered with scaled-down palatial apartments such as those at 1785 Massachusetts Avenue (1915–1917), which featured refrigerated tap water and electric washing machines.

JAN SCHALL

WORKS

1906–1907, Charles Moore House; 1910, Chevy Chase Country Club; 1915–1917, 1785 Massachusetts Avenue Apartments; 1922, Hamilton House Hotel; 1922, Lee House Apartment Hotel; 1934, Administrative Headquarters of the U.S. Public Service Bureau, Washington.

BIBLIOGRAPHY

ALDER, GALE SHIPMAN 1979 "1785: Architect and Image Maker Jules Henri de Sibour." *Historic Preservation* 31:12–13.

"Obituary." 1938 *New York Times* Nov. 6, p. 49.

SICCARDSBURGH, AUGUST SICCARD VON

See VAN DER NÜLL and SICCARDSBURGH.

SILOE, DIEGO DE

Diego de Siloe (c.1495–1563) was the greatest architect of the Renaissance style known as the Plateresque in Spain. To the historian José de Sigüenza, writing at the end of the sixteenth century, Siloe inaugurated classicism in Spain. Francesco de Hollanda called Siloe one of the four "eagles" of the new art. Siloe was a brilliant sculptor as well as an architect and, in both arts, his style was influential throughout Castile and southern Spain.

Siloe was the son of an important French sculptor, Gil de Siloe, who settled in Burgos. Diego was born there and must have been trained first by his father, but his style was formed in Italy. In 1517, Siloe was in Italy in the company of another important sculptor, Bartolemé Ordóñez, with whom he collaborated on sculpture in the Caraccioli Chapel in San Giovanni a Carbonara in Naples. By 1519, Siloe was back in Burgos where he executed a number of important commissions in the cathedral there: the tomb of Bishop Luis de Acuña in the Chapel of Saint Anne (1519); the altarpiece for that chapel (1522); the altarpiece for the Chapel of the Constable (finished in 1523 in collaboration with Felipe Bigarny; gilded and painted by Leon Picardo); and the Escalera Dorada (1519–1523). These works reveal Siloe's mastery of the Florentine sculptural tradition, in particular his knowledge of works by JACOPO SANSOVINO and MICHELANGELO, but they also show Siloe's emerging talent for architecture which, as far as is known, he had not practiced in Italy.

The Escalera Dorado is a symmetrical interior staircase connecting the Porta de la Coroneria with the floor of the cathedral. A central ramp leads to a landing where two ramps diverge on either side of a central portal and lead to landings where two flights return to a central balcony on the upper level. The composition is similar to Michelangelo's later staircase for the vestibule of the Laurentian Library in Florence (designed 1555–1558) but Wethy has shown that Siloe's design was based upon DONATO BRAMANTE's staircases in the Cortile del Belvedere (begun 1505). Siloe's staircase is a tour-de-force of grotteschi decoration beautifully carved in low and high relief and covering all available surfaces with animal and vegetable ornament of classical inspiration. The vocabulary of this rich surface ornament derives from contemporary Italian decoration: RAPHAEL's decoration of the Vatican Loggie and Michelangelo's lower register of the Tomb of Julius II which Siloe must have known; but Siloe's grotteschi are more active and expressive. Siloe's staircase is unique in its combination of a novel spatial motif with lavish decoration in a composition of monumental authority.

In April 1528, Siloe was summoned to Granada, and his career changed dramatically. Henceforth he was primarily an architect although he continued to be an important sculptor. Burgos had been an important center of sculpture in Castile but when Siloe arrived in Granada, it was the center of the most experimental and Italianate architecture in Spain. PEDRO MACHUCHA was planning the palace for the Emperor Charles V in the gardens of the Alhambra (from 1524) and Jacopo Fiorentino "El Indaco" had built part of the Church of San Jerónimo (1523–1526) in a bold Italianate manner. Siloe arrived to take up the work at San Jerónimo after Jacopo's death in 1526 and he completed the sanctuary (1528–1543). Chueca (1953) believes that Jacopo's style strongly influenced him but Siloe's genius must already have been evident for, by June 1528, Siloe had been placed in charge of the works at the cathedral.

The cathedral was the city's largest building program and one of the most ambitious projects in Spain. It was on the site of the old mosque, next to the Royal Chapel which had been built by ENRIQUE EGAS. It had been planned in 1521 by Egas in the Gothic style but these plans were revised by Egas in 1528. Shortly after, Egas was dismissed and Siloe designed the cathedral anew, using Egas's foundations and part of the extant construction of the chevet. Rosenthal (1962) has shown that Siloe was not hampered by Egas's designs. He presented a new plan in the Renaissance or Roman style—as it was called. From 1528 to 1532, a wooden model of the whole church was prepared; but Siloe's design was so innovatory that he was obliged to go to Toledo in 1529 to defend it to the emperor who was concerned that it might contrast too much with the Gothic of the adjacent Royal Chapel. Siloe's scheme was approved, however, and construction began on 15 March 1529. The chevet was

Siloe.
Cathedral.
Burgos, Spain.
1519–1523

Siloe.
Escalera Dorado, Cathedral.
Burgos, Spain.
1519–1523

Siloe.
Cathedral.
Granada, Spain.
1528–1563 (not completed
until the seventeenth
century)

the first part to be built and the only part nearly complete in Siloe's lifetime. Rosenthal has determined from documentation that the center chapel of the ambulatory was vaulted by 1540; the triumphal arch of the rotunda was complete by 1552; the sanctuary and ambulatory chapels were finished by 1557. In 1558, the dome was completed, and by 1561, the cathedral could be consecrated. Work on other parts of the church proceeded more slowly: four piers framing the choir were laid in 1555, determining the design of the nave piers. The Ecce Homo portal (1531), San Jerónimo portal (1532), and the lower part of the Portal of Pardon (1536) were complete and the foundations for the triple recessed openings of the main façade had been laid before Siloe's death in 1563. Later architects seem to have followed Siloe's plans where possible. Lazaro de Velasco used them for his project for the main façade in 1577, but the actual façade was designed by ALONSO CANO in the 1660s. The main vaults of the nave and aisles (c.1582–1614) do not follow Siloe's plans.

Siloe.
Colegio Fonseca
(courtyard).
Salamanca, Spain.
1529–1534

The Cathedral of Granada is a five-aisled basilica whose chevet is treated as a rotunda surrounded by an ambulatory and chapels. The conception, as Rosenthal argued, is a Renaissance one derived from Christian antiquity—specifically from the rotunda of the Holy Sepulchre in Jerusalem—and from contemporary Italian centralized church plans. The central rotunda may have been chosen in response to the mortuary program of the church since Charles V had chosen to be buried in front of the main altar. This was not realized, however, and Philip II's monastery of the Escorial became the burial place of the Spanish Hapsburgs.

Siloe's classicism is brilliantly original. The main order of the interior of the cathedral is a rich Corinthian with a frieze decorated with relief sculpture; but the fluted columns are clustered to form compound piers raised high on pedestals; above them, in the transepts and nave, a tall upper order of pilasters, also on pedestals and, in the sanctuary, an order of engaged columns and pilasters rise to the vaults and dome. The result is a classically structured verticality which is fundamentally un-Italian, as if Siloe had rethought the essential qualities of a Gothic cathedral in classical terms. The interior of the cathedral was intended to be stuccoed and painted white with touches of gold in the sanctuary and Siloe planned the pavement in patterns of black and white corresponding to the major elements of the plan, but the effect is not austere. Siloe's ornament is rich and sculptural and the decorative patterns of the architecture, whether in the vaults, cornices, or in surface reliefs, are boldly articulated.

The freedom of Siloe's classicism and his preference for ornamental display are characteristic of the style known as the Plateresque. But no other architect of the period achieved Siloe's mastery of scale and his organic unity. The lower zone of the Portal of Pardon (1536) combines heraldic and figural relief sculpture, grotteschi decoration (in the frieze, pilasters, and arches), and freestanding columns and arches in a spacious and judiciously scaled architectural whole.

Siloe's mastery of scale and the integration of abstract and figural motifs is evident in his other works. In 1529, Siloe was in Castile and provided designs for the college founded by the archbishop of Toledo, Alonso de Fonseca, in Salamanca. The design history of the Colegio Fonseca or Colegio de los Irlandeses is complex. The portal is often attributed to ALONSO DE COVARRUBIAS as well as to Siloe whose style it more closely resembles; but the courtyard is accepted as Siloe's work (1529–1534). Siloe used arches on slim piers decorated with engaged fluted composite columns on the lower gallery. Above, the arches are lowered on piers with engaged baluster columns. The roof is marked with candelabra over each support. In the *Medidas del Romano,* published in Toledo in 1526 and dedicated to Siloe's patron, Fonseca, Diego da Sagredo had raised the baluster to the status of another order. Siloe's elegant courtyard is a confirmation of its suitability.

While he was master of the works in Granada, Siloe was routinely invited to criticize the plans of other building projects and to submit plans of his own. In 1530, he entered designs for the Capilla de los Reyes Nuevos in the Cathedral of Toledo, later executed by Alonso de Covarrubias. In 1534, the Cathedral of Seville requested his advice on the designs of the sacristies and chapter room (finished in 1543). In 1536, he prepared plans for Francisco de los Cobos for the church of San Salvador in Ubeda (Jaen), later built by ANDRÉS DE VANDELVIRA with a rotunda based on Siloe's design for Granada. Siloe also provided plans for the Cathedral at Guadix in 1541 and may have been involved in the Cathedral of Málaga at the same period. In 1549, he designed the Church at Iznalloz, which was built by Juan de Maeda from 1566–1574 but was left unfinished.

Siloe influenced a whole generation of architects in Andalucia and southern Spain. Among his pupils were Juan de Maeda who succeeded him at the Cathedral of Granada from 1563 until his death in 1576. His son Asencio de Maeda was also trained in the Granada workshop. In 1577, Juan de Orea and Lazaro de Velasco, the son of Jacopo Fiorentino El Indaco, competed for the position of master of the works at Granada and both were indebted to Siloe's style. Siloe's influence is an important factor in the architecture of Andrés de Vandelvira whose designs at Ubeda and for the Cathedral of Jaen follow Grenadine solutions.

CATHERINE WILKINSON

WORKS

1519, Tomb of Bishop Luis de Acuña, Chapel of Saint Anne; 1519–1523, Escalera Dorado, Cathedral; 1522, Chapel of Saint Anne (altarpiece); 1523, Chapel of the Constable (with Felipe Bigarny), Cathedral; Burgos, Spain. 1528–1543, San Jerónimo (completion of work begun by Jacopo Fiorentino "El Indaco" in 1523–1526); 1528–1563, Cathedral (not completed until the seventeenth century); Granada, Spain. 1529–1534, Colegio Fonseca (courtyard), Salamanca, Spain. c.1563, Church (executed by Juan de Maeda in 1566–1574), Iznalloz, Spain.

BIBLIOGRAPHY

CHUECA GOITIA, FERNANDO 1953 *Arquitectura del Siglo XVI, Ars Hispaniae XI.* Madrid: Plus Ultra.
GÓMEZ-MORENO, MANUEL 1941 *Las Águilas del Renacimiento Español: Bartolomé Ordóñez, Diego Silóee,*
Pedro Machucha, Alonso Berruguete: 1517–1558. Madrid: Uguina.
GÓMEZ-MORENO, MANUEL 1967 *Provincia de Salamanca.* 2 vols. Madrid: Dirección General de Bellas Artes, Ministerio de Educación y Ciencia.
KUBLER, GEORGE, and SORIA, MARTIN 1959 *Art and Architecture in Spain and Portugal and Their American Dominions: 1500–1800.* Baltimore: Penguin.
LLAGUNO Y AMIROLA, EUGENIO, and CEAN-BERMÚDEZ, AGUSTÍN 1977 Volume 1 in *Noticias de los Arquitectos y Arquitectura de España desde su restauración.* Genoa, Italy, and Madrid: Turner.
ROSENTHAL, EARL E. 1961 *The Cathedral of Granada.* N.J.: Princeton University Press.

SILSBEE, J. LYMAN

Joseph Lyman Silsbee (1845–1913), perhaps best known as the first employer of FRANK LLOYD WRIGHT, was born in Salem, Massachusetts, and educated at Harvard University and the Massachusetts Institute of Technology. He set up practice in Syracuse, New York, in 1872, remaining there about ten years before moving to Chicago. During that period, he also had an office in Buffalo, New York. In Chicago, he established a partnership with Edward A. Kent, a draftsman in his Syracuse office, who returned east probably in 1884.

Little is known about Silsbee's work in New York State, but his work in Chicago can be categorized into several overlapping stylistic periods. During his first few years in Chicago, his designs were based on the styles made popular by the Centennial Exposition of 1876 in Philadelphia. From 1884 to 1886, Silsbee used the Queen Anne style in brick or stone for a number of residences in Illinois and back in New York State. He began experimenting with the Shingle style in 1885, at first combining its contained shapes with Queen Anne elements. From 1887 to 1892, the Richardsonian (see H. H. RICHARDSON) Romanesque style often characterized his designs. In the Chicago Telephone Company Building of 1887, he included Queen Anne ornament, but later he depended solely on the heavy masonry for articulation. Numerous works from 1888 to 1892 made use of Colonial Revival motifs, while retaining the asymmetry and containing forms of the Shingle style.

Silsbee.
Judge Egbert Jamieson House.
Lake View, Illinois.
1888

An example is the Judge Egbert Jamieson House of 1888 in Lake View, Illinois, with its dark sweeping shingles and classical columns supporting the porch roof. Works after 1892 became increasingly eclectic and exotic with combinations of elements from many styles.

ELSA GILBERTSON

WORKS

1883, Milwaukee Club Clubhouse, Wisc. 1884, Potter Palmer House (interior remodeling); Chicago. 1885, All Souls' Society Church; *1885, James E. Taylor House; Chicago. 1885, Unity Chapel, Spring Green, Wisc. 1886, Episcopal Church, Antrim, Pa. *1887, Chicago Telephone Company Building. 1887, Hotel, Quincy, Ill. 1888, Church, Rockford, Ill. 1888, Frederick Greeley House, Winnetka, Ill. 1888, Judge Egbert Jamieson House, Lake View, Ill. 1888, Stablehouse; 1888, Joseph Lyman Silsbee House; Chicago. 1889, Arthur Orr House, Evanston, Ill. 1890, Kirkland School; 1890, Lincoln Park Palm House and Conservatory; 1891, H. N. May House; *1891, North Dakota State Building, World's Columbian Exposition; *1891, West Virginia State Building, World's Columbian Exposition; 1892, Calumet Electric Railway Company Power House; 1892, Hagenbeck Geological Arena Building; Chicago. 1893, Henry D. Barber House, Polo, Ill. 1895, J. F. Palmer House, Riverside, Ill. 1896, Highland Park Animal House, Pittsburgh. 1897, Garfield Park Grandstand, Chicago.

BIBLIOGRAPHY

"Design for the Club-house of the Milwaukee Club, Milwaukee, Wis." 1883 *American Architect and Building News* 14, Sept. 22:138, plate 404.
HASBROUCK, WILBERT R. 1970 "The Earliest Work of Frank Lloyd Wright." *Prairie School Review* 7, no. 4:14–16.
"Residence for Egbert Jamieson." 1896 *Inland Architect* 24, Jan.:plate, plan.
"Residence of J. L. Silsbee, Edgewater, Chicago." 1890 *Inland Architect* 16, Nov.:plate.
"Residence for Judge Jamieson, Lake View, Illinois." 1899 *Inland Architect* 13, May:plate.
SORELL, SUSAN KARR 1970a "Silsbee: The Evolution of a Personal Architectural Style." *Prairie School Review* 7, no. 4:5–13.
SORELL, SUSAN KARR 1970b "A Catalog of Work by J. L. Silsbee." *Prairie School Review* 7, no. 4:17–21.
"Stable Building, Edgewater, Illinois." 1891 *Inland Architect* 16, Jan.:plate.

SILVANI, GHERARDO

Gherardo Silvani (1579–1675) was born in Florence, Italy, and studied both sculpture and architecture under Ludovico Cardi da Cigoli, GIOVANNI BATTISTA CACCINI, and BERNARDO BUONTALENTI, to whom he was related through his wife. He began his artistic career as a sculptural and architectural assistant to Caccini, working with that master at the Church of Santissima Annunziata in Florence, where his refurbished Chapel of San Sebastiano (1606–1607) presents an almost fifteenth-century appearance with a vault supported by four corner columns. His architectural decoration (1611) in the Salviati Chapel in the Church of Santa Croce, Florence, is regarded as one of the best demonstrations of the classical style of the late Renaissance. The façade (1616) of the sacristy in Santa Maria Novella, Florence, which has been attributed to him, shows a plasticity obviously influenced by the architecture of MICHELANGELO, while his remodeled interior (1625–1630) for the Church of San Simone, Florence, indicates an appreciation for the manner of BARTOLOMMEO AMMANNATI. The Nuns' Cloister (1628–?) at the Church of San Frediano in Castello, Florence, represents Florentine postclassical architecture at its best and is one of the most important pieces of seventeenth-century monastic architecture in the city.

The classicizing manner of Buontalenti may be noted in Silvani's sacristy (1633–1648) in the Church of San Gaetano, Florence; his treatment of the interior of the church, executed during the same period, reveals a richly decorative approach with an almost medieval use of incrustation. Silvani had been at work on San Gaetano since 1628, when he had taken over the project from MATTEO NIGETTI. Silvani's solution for the front of the church, completed in 1649, produced the most significant baroque façade in Florence. Compositionally, the design is reminiscent of Buontalenti's façade for Santa Trinità, Florence, executed at the end of the sixteenth century. The general scheme may be due in part to Nigetti or to an even earlier proposal made in 1604 by GIOVANNI DE' MEDICI. For the façade of San Gaetano, Silvani used a two-tiered arrangement. The lower story is divided into three bays separated by pilasters. The door frames contained in each of these units are flanked by heavy columns; a massive gable tops the central portal, while sculpturally decorated tabernacles are placed above the side doors. In the upper story, a central bay containing a large round window is tied to the two side bays of the lower story by volutes. Throughout, there is a plastic quality which is clearly baroque, yet the architect manages to retain his personal allegiance to the more sober tradition of Florentine classicism. In this project, as well as in others, Silvani was assisted by his son Pier Francesco.

Like other prominent Florentine architects of his time, Silvani submitted (1636) a model for the façade of Florence Cathedral. His proposal, although classicizing, did strive at harmony with the rest of the Gothic building. The Oratory of San Agostino (1640–?) represents one of Silvani's major architectural achievements. The overall design is an adaptation of the Gesù in Rome but is reconciled in many of its features with the architectural taste of Florence.

CHARLES RANDALL MACK

WORKS

1603?, San Pier Gattolini (presbytery); 1606–1607, Chapel of San Sebastiano (assisted in renovation), Santissima Annunziata; 1611, Salviati Chapel (renovation), Santa Croce; 16ll, Santa Margherita de' Ricci (arcade in front); 1612, Second Tribune Chapel, Santissima Annunziata; *1612–1615, Choir Chapel (renovation), San Pier Maggiore; Florence. 1615, Palazzo Inghirami (completion), Volterra, Italy. 1616?, Santa Maria Novella (entrance façade of sacristy); *1616, Santa Maria Novella (portal to cemetery) 1620, Palazzo Panciatichi-Ximenez; 1620–1621, Calderini Chapel (renovation), Santa Croce; 1623, Palazzo Covoni; 1625–1630, San Simone (remodeling of choir and nave walls); 1626–1632, Palazzo Albizzi (renovation); 1628–1649, San Gaetano (completion of façade); 1630?, Gianfigliazzi Chapel, (renovation), Santa Trinità; c.1630–?, Cloister, San Bernardo; c.1630–?, Nuns' Cloister, San Frediano in Cestello; c.1630–?, Cloister, Santa Maria Maddalena dei Pazzi; 1630–1648, Cloister (east façade) San Gaetano; 1633–1648, San Gaetano (interior and sacristy; 1634, Palazzo Marucelli-Fenzi; c.1635, San Carlo Borromeo (enlargement), Via San Agostino, and associated Cloister; 1636, San Apollinare (renovation); Florence. 1638, Cathedral (renovation of presbytery), Prato, Italy. 1640, Cloister and Monastic Buildings (rebuilding), Santa Margherita de' Ricci; 1640–?, Oratory (completion), San Agostino; c.1647, Second Cloister, (renovation), Santa Maria degli Angeli; c.1660, San Jacopo Soprarno (bell tower); n.d., Palazzo Aldobrandini-Borghesi; n.d., Palazzo Corsini (remodeling), Via Maggio; n.d., Palazzo Guadagni–San Clemente; n.d., Palazzo Guicciardini (completion); *n.d., Santa Lucia di Camporeggi (restoration); n.d., Palazzo Salviati (remodeling), Via de' Serragli; n.d., Palazzo Strozzi-Giaconi; Florence, n.d., Villa Ugolino, San Martino a Strada, Italy.

BIBLIOGRAPHY

BUCCI, MARIO 1971–1973 *Palazzi di Firenze*. 4 vols. Florence: Vallecchi.
GOLZIO, VINCENZO 1936 "Gherardo Silvani." Volume 31, page 786 in *Enciclopedia Italiana*. Rome: Istituto della Enciclopedia Italiana.
LINNENKAMP, ROLF 1958 "Una inedita vita di Gherardo Silvani." *Rivista de arte* 33:73–114.
PAATZ, WALTER, and PAATZ, ELISABETH 1940–1954 *Die Kirchen von Florenz*. 6 vols. Frankfurt, West Germany: Klostermann.
VENTURI, ADOLFO (1939)1967 *Storia dell'arte italiana: Architettura del Cinquecento*. Reprint. Nendeln, Germany: Kraus.

Silvani.
San Gaetano.
Florence.
1628–1649

SIMONETTI, MICHELANGELO

In 1772, Michelangelo Simonetti (1724–1781) became *architetto camerale* at the Vatican where he worked on the transformation of the Vatican museum and the Pio Clementino museum with Visconti and with Camporese the elder (see CAMPORESE FAMILY). He was a member of the Accademia di San Luca from 1778 and of "I Virtuosi del Pantheon" from 1769.

His preference for unplastered brick, perfect in shape and color, started the pursuit for precise construction in Rome. A traditional conformist (Lavagnino, 1956), he was also the Roman architect who corresponded most closely to GIUSEPPE PIERMARINI in Milan (Meeks, 1966). His buildings reveal an aulic sense of space and deliberately emulate antique forms, even in their structural and construction systems.

MARTHA POLLAK

WORKS

1772–1773, Casino of Innocent VIII (works); 1773, Octagonal Cortile (round hall); 1776, Sala della Biga (with Giuseppe Camporese); (A)n.d., Belvedere Court (portico); (A)n.d., Gallery of Chandeliers, Hall of Muses; (A)n.d., Museum (entry hall and double ramp; with Camporese the Elder); Vatican, Rome.

BIBLIOGRAPHY

LAVAGNINO, EMILIO 1956 Volume 1, pages 44–49 in *L'arte moderna dai neoclassici ai contemporanei*. Turin,

Italy: Union tipografico editrice.

Meeks, Carroll L. V. *Italian Architecture: 1750–1914.* New Haven: Yale University Press.

SIMONS, RALPH

Ralph Simons (flourished 1584–1604) was a master mason, active mainly in Cambridge, England. For some of the buildings associated with him Simons may have been only the contractor, but he is known to have made a model for the hall at Trinity College, and his drawings for his work at Saint John's College are preserved in the college library. He was a conservative and uninspired designer, but is significant as a leading example of "one of those artificers who were gradually creating the professional role of architect" (Summerson, 1977). An inscription on a portrait of Simons at Emmanuel College describes him as "the most skilled architect of his age."

IAN CHILVERS

WORKS

1584–1586, Emmanuel College (Simons's work now forms part of New Court); 1596–1598, Sidney Sussex College (with Gilbert Wigge; Simons's work is now Hall Court); 1598–1602, Saint John's College (Second Court; with Wigge); 1604–1605, Trinity College (hall); Cambridge.

BIBLIOGRAPHY

Airs, Malcolm 1975 *The Making of the English Country House: 1500–1640.* London: Architectural Press.

Oswald, Arthur 1959 "The London Charterhouse Restored—III." *Country Life* 126:538–541. Simons made designs for the charterhouse that were not used.

Pevsner, Nikolaus (1954)1970 *The Buildings of England: Cambridgeshire.* 2d ed. Harmondsworth, England: Penguin.

Royal Commission on Historical Monuments, England 1959 *An Inventory of the Historical Monuments in the City of Cambridge.* 2 vols. London: H.M. Stationery Office.

Salway, Peter 1960 "A College Hall Restored: Repairs and Discoveries at Sidney Sussex, Cambridge." *Country Life* 127:380–383.

Summerson, John (1953)1977 *Architecture in Britain: 1530–1830.* 6th ed. Harmondsworth, England: Penguin.

Willis, Robert, and Clark, J. W. 1886 *The Architectural History of the University of Cambridge.* 4 vols. Cambridge University Press.

SIMPSON, ARCHIBALD

Archibald Simpson (1790–1847), a prominent architect of early nineteenth-century Scotland, studied briefly with ROBERT LUGAR. After a journey to Italy, Simpson opened his practice in 1813 in his hometown of Aberdeen, a thriving city then in need of capable builders. Designing in both the Greek and Gothic Revival styles, Simpson executed ambitious public commissions and many country houses.

BRIAN LUKACHER

WORKS

1814–1815, Castle Forbes; 1816–1817, Saint Andrew's Episcopal Church; 1820–1822, County Assembly Rooms; 1835, Linton House; Aberdeenshire, Scotland.

SINAN

If there are artists who portray in their work the whole spectrum of a period style, Sinan (?–1588), the celebrated master of Ottoman architecture, is one of the rarest. In the introduction to Sinan's deed of trust, the scribe who prepared the document presents him in the flowered style of the time as "the eye of the illustrious engineers, the ornament of the great founders, the master of the learned men of his time, the Euclid of his century and of all times, the architect of the Sultan, the teacher to the empire." His fame, which was already established in his lifetime, lives on with undiminished vigor.

A very long life in the service of the great sultans during the mightiest period of the Ottoman Empire—the sixteenth century—confers upon him the unique status of founder and pre-eminent representative of classical Ottoman architecture and an incommensurable authority for following generations. Through the sheer number and size of his buildings, he became one of the legendary figures of Ottoman culture. In a sense, an understanding of his art gains an insight into the nature of the Anatolian-Turkish synthesis.

Sinan is the only Muslim architect who received some recognition by Westerners. However, he remains a little-known artist to the world at large, in the same way that the Turkish architecture of the Ottoman period remains an underevaluated and little-known architectural style.

There exist a great number of written sources for Sinan's life and work. There are several complete and incomplete autobiographical manuscripts, the registers or account books for his buildings, the deed of trust founded personally by him, numerous documents of canonical courts and *wakfs,* records of the Council of State (*Divan*) from the period when he was the chief architect of the court, as well as contemporary and subsequent historical works which record relevant information. These are extremely valuable sources not only for the reconstruction of his life, but also for an evaluation of the building activities of his time. In addition to this wealth of documents, a great number of well-preserved, dated, and still used monuments bear witness to his talent and creativity.

The main sources for Sinan's life are the so-called autobiographical manuscripts, which have never been critically studied. Only two could possibly be accepted as complete: *Tuḥfat al-Mi' mârîn* (A Book on Architecture) and *Risale-i Taẕkirat al-Abniya* (Memoirs of Buildings). The first seems to have been written in Sinan's lifetime during the reign of Murad III (1575–1595). It includes Sinan's remarks on architecture and construction, which do not appear in other manuscripts, and a list of his buildings.

The second manuscript, written by Sinan's friend, the poet and painter (*Nakkaṣ*) Saî Mustafa Çelebi, contains a biography and a list of buildings. Some inconsistencies exist in this manuscript, and the list of monuments seems more pedantic than professional. Instead of giving the mosque complexes with their components as in the first manuscript, it classifies buildings by typologies. Nevertheless, it is the source used most frequently by scholars. The lists of buildings are not identical in both manuscripts, but for Sinan's life and main endeavors, both contain the same information (Meriç, 1965).

In addition, Sinan's deed of trust gives information about his family and worldly possessions (Konyali, 1948). From the records of the Council of State, it is possible to follow his responsibilities for public buildings, and a long sustained search through the Imperial Archives would probably establish a chronology of his activities.

Finally, the account books for his buildings supply basic information for the organization of building sites, work schedules, materials, workers, artisans, and the construction processes. The important registers for the mosque of Süleymaniye, offer extraordinary insight into the building practices of the time (Barkan, 1972–1979).

Biography. According to the *Taẕkirat al-Abniya,* Sinan, the son of Abdülmennan, was recruited for the Janizary corps during the reign of the late Sultan Selim Han (Selim I). He participated in the campaigns of Rhodes (1521), Belgrade (1523), Mohács (1526), Germany (1529–1532), and in the campaigns and conquests of Corfu and Puglia (1537) and Moldavia (1538). In August 1538, he was ordered to build a bridge over the Pruth River in Moldavia for the advancing army. After the completion of this work, in which he displayed his competence as an engineer, he was appointed chief architect of the sultan's court.

Although tradition holds that Sinan lived more than a century, the dates of his recruitment indicate that he was probably born at the turn of the century. Once an inhabitant of the village of Ağırnas near Kayseri (then in Karaman province), he was possibly apprenticed in the carpenter's craft. As he relates in *Taẕkirat,* his training in the pre-Janizary and Janizary corps gave him the opportunity to develop this talent.

In later periods of the Ottoman administration, there was a department of court architects as well as a preparatory school for architects. Since chief architects were usually selected from the architects educated at this school and since Sinan, whose career as chief architect covers half a century, came to his post from the ranks of the army, the department and the school were probably developed, if not founded, during his lifetime.

Thus, Sinan, like many other grandees of the Ottoman state, was a true representative and product of the Ottoman sociopolitical system which in its structure amalgamated several races and creeds. The organizational character of the Ottoman state made the Anatolian peasant boy a high officer in the service of the Ottoman sultans. His life story brings out the peculiar structure of the Ottoman Empire which, disregarding constraints, availed itself of all the possibilities of human resources and put them at the service of a single raison d'être, the survival of the Ottoman house, exploiting all existential factors for a single-minded synthesis.

In the administrative framework of the Ottoman state, Sinan's position was that of minister of public works. His responsibilities included construction of every nature—mosques, palaces, fortifications, aqueducts and water works, roads and bridges—control over the building market and building materials, and supervision of constructions in the cities, where he shared responsibility with local officials.

As in a big modern firm, everything produced in his office went under the name of Sinan, so that many of the secondary buildings in the provinces may have been built by his assistants. A case in point is the mosque of Murad III at Manisa, where two of Sinan's assistant architects, Mahmut and Mehmet, were sent to execute the work at the place, but the building is listed among Sinan's works. Some buildings mentioned in the lists were built in distant provinces and in distinctive styles. As Sinan spent only a few weeks in these cities and at a time when he was not yet chief architect, his role might therefore have been limited to suggesting the preliminary concept. The extant written documents positively indicate the existence of plans and models of these buildings, but none have been found.

The list of buildings in *Tazkirat al-Abniya* contains eighty-four mosques, fifty-two small mosques, fifty-seven madrasahs, seven Koran schools, twenty-two mausolea, seventeen public kitchens, three hospitals, six aqueducts, eight bridges, twenty caravansaries, thirty-five palaces, eight granaries and storehouses, and forty-eight baths, quite a large number of which are preserved. Those buildings bearing the names of the sultans in Istanbul and Edirne and the important foundations of the grand viziers there and in adjacent cities have the mark of Sinan; the others have less claim to his direct control and authorship.

After a long and glorious career, Sinan died during the reign of Murad III apparently still at his post (Altinay, 1930). Before his death, he requested to be buried near the mosque of Süleymaniye (1550–1557), possibly his most cherished endeavor, although he defined Selimiye (1569–1575) as his most mature work.

Background. The sixteenth century was the apogee of the Ottoman Empire; its political might, economical resources, and cultural creativity were at their zenith. Sinan's career spans the most glorious half of this century (1538–1588). It is not mere chance that his fame corresponds to the reigns of Süleyman the Magnificent and his two successors, though it was good fortune that his robust health and long life were equal to his genius.

In order to understand the task of the architect and the resources at his disposal, one should recall that the sultans in Istanbul reigned over an area as large as that of the Roman Empire at its peak. The entire eastern Mediterranean was practically under Turkish control. Istanbul itself was the greatest city of Europe in size and population. In Sinan's time when Paris had a population of about one hundred fifty thousand, Rome less than sixty thousand, and London around two hundred thousand, the estimated population of Istanbul was approaching five hundred thousand. The resources provided by the state to the chief architect were of amazing dimensions, as witnessed by the great complex of Süleymaniye which was completed in only seven years through the employment of fifteen hundred to two thousand workers per day and on certain occasions up to twenty-eight hundred as we see in the construction accounts published by Barkan (1972–1979, vol. 1, p. 160). Sultan Selim II could afford to spend the largest part of the revenue from the conquest of Cyprus for the construction of his complex at Edirne. In technology, the arts, and literature, Ottoman society was equally creative. Obviously, Sinan's work was not an isolated phenomenon. Yet, his unique performance was of such quality and longevity that he was further distinguished as the foremost representative of the creative exuberance of his epoch. His greatness lies not only in the shapes expressing those vast possibilities offered to him in the opportune historical circumstances, but also in the fact that this precious legacy has been preserved until now.

Sinan's work. Author of some of the most renowned monuments of Muslim architecture and creator of the classical Ottoman style, Sinan is important in the history of architecture because of his contribution to the development of monumental domed buildings. From Central Asia to Europe, in many architectural traditions, the dome had been the fundamental structural and symbolic device for more than a thousand years. Sinan's contribution to its historical development was his ingenious and possibly exhaustive experimentation with square, hexagonal, and octagonal domed baldachins within a rectangular enclosure. As a result, he created a variety of structurally expressive domed spaces and, eventually, realized some conceptually perfect forms. In all of his experiments, the rectangular outer enclosure was a traditional and functional constant, a pragmatic choice for liturgical purposes. If he never fancied playing with the basic functional arrangement of the mosque, this in no way implies a lack of imagination but rather a disposition of mind of his time that was functionalist or structuralist.

A rather steady line of domed monuments from the late fourteenth to the sixteenth centuries paved the way for Sinan. In the structural schemes of such mosques as Üçşerefeli at Edirne (1438–1447) and those of Mehmet the Conqueror (1467–1479) and Beyazıt II (1501–1506), both in Istanbul, all the essential themes of domed space had come into being: a central dome flanked by half-domes and smaller domes, an interior space developed longitudinally or transversally, and a perceptible development toward the centralized scheme. Totally centralized schemes were even found in the provinces, such as in the mosque of Fatih Paşa in Diyarbakır. The outer configurations of these pre-Sinan mosques also share a common trait of less emphasis on decorative aspects and more exploration of the spatial and volumetric qualities, qualities brought to their logical culmination and maturity in Sinan's work.

The consistent efforts of Sinan seem to have been concentrated on the formal perfection of structurally sound domed buildings. His approach to this design problem was experimental. It cannot be compared with that of LEONARDO DA VINCI and DONATO BRAMANTE for whom experimenting with the possible variations of geometrical forms was of a theoretical nature and who were much less concerned with the structural feasibility of their schemes. Sinan's engineering and practical background did not allow him to play with forms of two dimensions. Herein probably lies the main trait of his architecture. His was a down-to-earth attitude, also to be found in other aspects of Ottoman culture. Nevertheless, he was creative enough to run the entire gamut of centrally planned square, hexagonal and octagonal structural space schemes in mosques of various sizes.

For more than a decade after he had become chief architect, Sinan designed variations on the theme of the square baldachin. His first imperial commission, the Sehzade Mosque and adjoining complex at Istanbul (1543–1548), marks the beginning of his spatial experiments with the square baldachin as well as the beginning of the classical period of Ottoman architecture. The mosque was built in the center of a social complex composed of a madrasah, a Koran school, a hospice, a public kitchen, a bakery, and the mausoleum of Şehzade Mehmet. Theoretically, the plan of the mosque is a variation of the old cross-in-square scheme but the system of vaulting had some recent prototypes. In Byzantine as well as Western architectural styles, the cross arms were usually covered with barrel vaults and, in terms of dimensions, the domes of Byzantine cross-in-square examples are rather small. A central dome buttressed by half-domes on its four sides did not find much favor with Christian architects, possibly because the symbolism of the cross was too strong. Thus, in the history of dome-covered space with ambulatory, the spatial arrangement as well as the outer configuration of Şehzade Mosque was an important statement. A highly developed and more unified space composition than its Christian predecessors, it had a much more elaborate design than its simpler Turkish forerunners.

The modular planning, which was quite common in earlier buildings, also appears in Şehzade. The mosque plan is composed of two main squares corresponding to the *Sahn* (the interior of the mosque) and the courtyard. The square of the courtyard is divided into twenty-five units, nine of which constitute the open central space of the courtyard. The same division is employed in the *Sahn*. Here the main dome covers the central nine units while the exterior arcades constitute the surrounding sixteen units. However, the use of modular planning in Şehzade is more sophisticated than a simple application of geometry. With Şehzade, Sinan radically changed the physiognomy of mosque façades. He introduced the exterior arcade placed between the buttresses and, with a novel placement of windows in the upper registers, was able to produce an impression of lightness that changed the massive character of earlier mosques.

All the façade elements were also sensibly used to accentuate the structural centrality of the building. Thus, not only the use of external arcades but also the externalization of the design as a whole in comparison with former periods bears significance. Arcades had been in use in Muslim architecture since the seventh century, yet except for a building such as Kubbat as-Sakhra, which has an east Roman scheme, their function was restricted to interiors of buildings or courtyards. Aside from some Indian buildings, Muslim architects preferred sober massive exteriors which contrasted, forcefully, with the airiness of their interior design. The role Sinan assigned to arcades in the outer configuration of Şehzade is one of the identification marks of the Mediterranean spirit and signals the rise of a new period of design.

That Sinan regarded the mosque of Şehzade as his "sampler" is confirmed by the fact that in Şehzade we can distinguish some formal statements or themes characteristic of his whole work. Although summarizing the previous development of Ottoman architecture, they also establish a new style. The structural and unambiguous expression of the dome, the subtle use of modularization, the direct relationship between outer and inner configuration, and externalization of the interior system were to stand as the bases of his later practice and the work of his followers.

Another variation of the domed square is found in the Mihrimah Mosque (or Iskele Mosque) at Üsküdar, Istanbul (?–1547/1548). The laterally developed space is covered by a central dome flanked by three half-domes, a variation of the destroyed mosque of Mehmet II the Conqueror. The outer form of the mosque remains stern and somewhat archaic. A second mosque of Sultan Mihrimah, again at Istanbul (?–1565?), is a more direct expression of the square baldachin. It exhibits a monumentality which medium-sized mosques seldom, if ever, achieved. At the center of a moderately sized complex composed of a madrasah, an arcade for shops, a bath, a Koran school, and a mausoleum, the mosque is a simple rectangular prayer hall covered at the center by a dome 20 meters in diameter and, over each side aisle, by three small domes in a row. This play between the dimensions of the domes and the articulation of the supporting structure in order to coax them into a coherent plastic and spatial totality was the basic design explored by Sinan; despite its apparent simplicity, Mihrimah is a striking solution. The great unified mass of the supporting base rises with majesty above the surrounding cluster of small domes which form a proper visual base for it. The corners of the cubic enclosure are emphasized by four octagonal pillarlike buttresses topped with domes. Through this simple formal device, Sinan obtained a subtle continuity of contours. By perceptibly raising the extrados of the great arches above the horizontal cornices of the walls, he integrated the dome with the supporting elements. In addition to the simple but grandiose plasticity of its exterior, the fenestration of the filling walls provide a superb illumination of the interior, where the great dome contrasts with the luminous curtain of the enclosing walls, creating a unique example of spatial single-mindedness.

The age-old scheme of a central dome on a square base flanked by two half-domes was adopted again in the Süleymaniye Mosque (1550–1557) in Istanbul. It is one of the most renowned of the great sultan mosques, not only for its size or the great social complex conjoining it, or its place in the physiognomy of the capital city, but also as a symbol of the most glorious epoch in Turkish history. Moreover, it is one of the most controversial buildings in Ottoman architecture because of its structural kinship with Hagia Sophia. A great central dome set between two half-domes which make up the vaulting system of the central nave of the Hagia Sophia had been employed in the mosque of Beyazıt II before Sinan. But Beyazıt Mosque was also a logical step in the development of Ottoman architecture, a coherent development in the geometric modularization of space, which started with the early fifteenth-century mosques at Bursa. In Süleymaniye, Sinan's departure from the absolute rationality of the centralized plan of Şehzade to this structural anomaly can be explained only by the prestige of Hagia Sophia. The extraordinary visual and spatial quality of the great church was a constant challenge for Turkish architects. Even after his experience with totally centralized buildings, Sinan was tempted to reinterpret the sixth-century scheme with the vocabulary of the sixteenth century. This whole process of influence gains significance if it is viewed as one stage in the parallel development of the domed building tradition which, in the West, started with Roman examples and climaxed with Saint Peter and in Turkey, again on a Roman background, passed through Hagia Sophia and reached Sinan after incorporating Islamic components.

A short comparison of the Hagia Sophia with Süleymaniye is in order. The architects of Justinian were not much concerned either with the asymmetrical buttressing of the dome or with the instability of the flat dome, since their basic problem was to cover a pre-established type of plan, namely the basilica. Hagia Sophia has been acclaimed as one of the finest interior spaces ever created and praised for the boldness of its construction, but never for the rationality of its structure. Sinan worked to rationalize the old scheme. The lateral buttressing of the central dome, unsolved in the prototype, here was handled with a structurally and plastically mature solution through a careful subdivision of thrusts. The number and the size of the supporting elements were determined by their function in the vaulting scheme of the prayer hall. The side aisles were covered by an alternating sequence of domes of two different dimensions. Furthermore, the lateral buttress system was integrated into the east and west walls with the addition of outer and inner galleries in the lower register.

In Süleymaniye, there is no emphasized separation between the central nave and the aisles, contrasting with Hagia Sophia where the screen created by the double arcades of the aisles and the galleries is one of the sources of the central nave. Whereas in Hagia Sophia the space vanishes into the darker boundaries of the aisles, in Süleymaniye, the outer enclosure is clearly perceived. The so-called immaterialization of the Justinianic church is replaced in Süleymaniye by a complete perceptibility of space; mysticism is replaced by rationalism. The exterior configuration of Hagia Sophia is like an imposing but unhewn sculpture. Süleymaniye, with its minarets integrated into the design of its silhouette, gracefully brings together the mosque and the courtyard. Lacking the massive buttresses of Hagia Sophia, it is incomparably superior to its prototype.

In Süleymaniye, Sinan also broke the simple geometrization of the Beyazıt II Mosque through a conscious use of variations of rhythmical elements in the interior as well as on the exterior, bringing forth a more sophisticated quality of design, lacking in its predecessor. In its total subordination of decoration to structural form, Süleymaniye further underscores its distinctive personality. Nevertheless, since Sinan's age also produced great masters in the fields of calligraphy, stained glass, and the art of ceramics, some of the best examples of classical Turkish architectural decoration can be found in Süleymaniye. They bestow the finishing Islamic touch to its design.

To this day, the mosque of Süleyman the Magnificent has stood as the ultimate physical symbol of the great age of the Ottoman Empire. For Sinan's structural experiments, however, it proved to be a dead end. The importance of the Süleymaniye complex does not, needless to say, lie only in the mosque. The layout of the buildings and their individual architecture are also masterfully designed. This, the largest complex in Ottoman history, was arranged on the lower terrace of the grounds of the first palace of Mehmet the Conqueror. Occupying an area of approximately 300 by

300 meters along its diagonals, it dominates the Golden Horn. It is composed of a large hospital with its medical school, two madrasahs for lower grades, two madrasahs for higher education, a Koran school, a school of Tradition (*Hadis*), a large public kitchen, a caravansary composed of a hospice and stables, a bath, and many shops. In the garden of the mosque, the monumental mausoleum of Süleyman and that of his wife Hürrem Sultan were built. Service buildings and monumental gateways completed the program which was arranged around inner and outer courtyards and inner streets.

The slope of the terrain and the irregularities of the plot were challenges to which Sinan responded with the resourcefulness of a virtuoso. This can readily be seen in the two northern madrasahs overlooking the Golden Horn, unique by the disposition of their rooms around stepped courtyards, in his organization of several levels, and in his variations on the usual types of buildings. Among the remaining buildings of the complex, the mausoleum of Süleyman I deserves special mention. It is an octagonal building with detached columns on the interior and roofed with a double-shell dome. It is surrounded by an outer arcade overhung by large eaves. It is legitimate to consider this plan as a reworking of the plan of the mausoleum of Dioletian at Spalato (Split, Yugoslavia), which is also an octagon with inner detached columns and outer colonnade. In spite of their similarity as geometrical schemes, the architecture of Süleyman's tomb is of a radically different composition. Its proportions, its fenestration and interior illumination, and its decoration produce an effect of lightness that contrasts sharply with the massive enclosure of the Roman building.

If this reminiscence is evidence of a Mediterranean Roman strain in the classical period of Ottoman architecture, it also stands as proof of the vitality of the interpretations of the Ottoman architect who did not imitate slavishly. This is entirely understandable when we recall that the Turk, unlike the Italian, never viewed the Roman world as a spiritual forebear; he only inherited its material products.

Sinan's experiments with hexagonal schemes started with the uncompleted mosque of Sinan Paşa, Beşiktaş, Istanbul (?–1555?). In this first experiment, he closely imitated the old scheme of Uçşerefeli Mosque at Edirne but in the contemporary mosque of Kara Ahmet Paşa (completed after 1555), the hexagonal baldachin is underlined by detached columns coupled with supporting piers, receiving a treatment overtly similar to that of the contemporary mausoleum of Süleyman the Magnificent. The side aisles, here reduced to narrow

Sinan.
Süleymaniye Complex.
Istanbul.
1550–1557

ancillary spaces, are drawn into the central space by reason of their half-domes. The final solution for space based on the structure of a hexagonal baldachin was reached in the Sokollu Mosque at Kadırga, Istanbul, completed in 1571. Built on rather difficult terrain, the mosque, with its courtyard surrounded by a porticoed madrasah and adjacent convent, is masterfully arranged. The dome, buttressed and integrated with the four half-domes rising from the sides of the hexagon, covers a single space for which both the supported and the supporting elements harmoniously complete the continuous enclosure. The solution is of extreme simplicity and elegance. This small masterpiece is one of the finest examples of Sinan's art, not only for the clarity of its concept but also for the subdued beauty of its decoration (Kuban, 1963).

Sinan's last group of volumetric experiments was based on the octagonal scheme, culminating in his magnum opus, the Mosque of Selimiye at Edirne. This last group may be regarded as a return to the roots since it consists basically of variations on the theme of the dome on squinches, the age-old form of Persian and Islamic architectures. In a sense, the octagonal baldachin is inherent in squinch-domed space. It is conducive to a visual, if not structural, underscoring of an octagonal base by the simple device of vertical articulation of the supporting walls at the squinch corners. As a matter of fact, some of the early examples of the octagonal scheme have this articulation (Kuban, 1958; Batur, 1967).

The Mosque of Sokollu at Lüleburgaz (?–1567), noteworthy for its monumental configuration despite its modest size; the Mosque of Ibrahim Paşa at Istanbul (?–1551); and that of Rüstem Paşa at Istanbul (?–1561?) may have served as preliminary approaches to Selimiye's design. The Rüstem Paşa Mosque, renowned for its tile decoration, is in the commercial quarter of Istanbul, on the Golden Horn. Sinan elevated the prayer hall and courtyard above the ground floor, thus separating them from the noisy transactions of the surroundings. The mosque plan is similar to that of Mihrimah at Edirnekapı, a central space flanked by less elevated side aisles, but here, with the adoption of squinches as transition elements and of two supporting piers on either side, the impression of an octagonal volumetry is obtained, paving the way for Selimiye's design.

The great mosque of Selimiye at Edirne, built between 1569 and 1575 for Sultan Selim II, is the pinnacle, as Sinan himself agreed, of a long pursuit for the ideal solution of domed space. The octagonal baldachin seems to be the most proper form to overcome the duality between the dome and its support. It is clearly more consonant with the desire to create a structure in which the dominance of the central dome will not be subject to the dimensional weight of other architectural elements. In addition, a central space with deambulatory is not congenial to the function and spirit of a Muslim. Even in this wholly centralized scheme, Sinan did not emphasize circumambulating secondary spaces, which makes his selection even more appropriate. By unifying all secondary spaces under the spell of the big dome and by reducing the size of supports, Sinan obtained the maximum dimensional effect from a single dome. The primitive power of the Pantheon has been refined here by the technical mastery and elegance of the sixteenth century.

On the interior, the transparent enclosure walls, united with the airy system of counterforts, meet the enclosed space without effort and produce that expression of space wherein the oppres-

sive nature of massive enclosure walls has been overcome and light moves freely over the articulated surfaces. The overwhelming plasticity of the exterior design of Selimiye, the acme of Sinan's style, is an admirable recapitulation of his formal researches. In this configuration, all the elements of the composition are masterly bonded into the pyramidal mass as so many pieces of a three-dimensional mosaic. The enclosure walls of the lower register are defined by a multirhythmical gallery level. The bases of the minarets, the buttresses, the arcade system, and the recessed terminal arches pierced by windows compose a singularly expressive façade. The transition to the dome is underscored by the gentle tectonic movement of the enclosing walls toward it, a stepped vertical movement that unfolds into the horizontal movement of polygonal spires around the dome. The dome loses its identity as a simple hemisphere; the terminating contour becomes a logical extension of the momentum of continuity created by the surrounding towers. The four symmetrical minarets of Selimiye strongly emphasize the centrality of the design.

The tectonic aspects were always accented in classical Ottoman architecture. In the hands of Sinan, the controlled ascending movement of the general mass and the careful use of vertical elements neutralize the leveling effect of horizontals. Yet, there is no neglect of the tectonic character. The subtlety which he maintained in handling architectural elements may be regarded as the hallmark of his style.

The symbolism of Selimiye is evident on several levels. Its architectural concept is the expression of a rationalism attained by sixteenth-century Ottoman art, which impresses upon us the fact that this concept so congenial to the sketches of

Sinan.
Selimiye Complex.
Edirne, Turkey.
1569–1575

Sinan.
Axonometric perspective of
the Selimiye Complex.
Edirne, Turkey.
1569–1575

Leonardo could have come from a cultural ambiance which partook in some ways of the prevailing spirit of the Mediterranean world. It remains, nevertheless, Islamic and non-European, for despite Sinan's masterful manipulations, it stands linked to the primordial dome on squinches and expresses the spiritual kinship between the Ottoman and the earlier styles of Perso-Turkish cultures.

Selimiye's design urges speculation on the working of Sinan's architectural imagination. Since he had the opportunity to see and possibly study the great octagonal mausoleum of Sultan Oljaitu Khodabandah Khan at Sultanıya in Adharbaijan during the campaign of Iraq in 1534, it seems safe to suggest that this great monument could have served as a stimulus for Selimiye's octagonal scheme.

Other works. Among the 460 buildings attributed to Sinan in *Tazkirat al-Abniya,* 321 are in Istanbul, with the rest scattered throughout the empire. Although the list does not include his numerous engineering works executed while he was in the army, it does mention some of the works he completed before becoming the chief architect of the court, some of which are of quite doubtful attribution. Numerically, mosques form a large proporton of Sinan's production: *Tazkirat* lists eighty-four large and fifty-two small mosques. In Istanbul alone, there are ten such socioreligious complexes built by Sinan. Many of these—Zal Mahmut Paşa (1560?–1565?) at Eyüp, Atik Valide (?–1583) and Şemsi Ahmet Paşa (?–1580) at Üsküdar—are remarkable examples of layout.

Apart from the series of square, hexagonal, and octagonal schemes which evolved toward simplic-ity and unity, two other groups of mosques should be mentioned. The first significant group seems to be the collective creation of the office of Sinan. Built mostly in the provinces, these mosques essentially follow the plan of the mosque of Hadım Ibrahim Paşa at Istanbul: a single squinch dome with lateral buttresses taken inside the building; the ancillary spaces thus obtained are integrated into the main prayer room. The mosque of Canbolat at Kilis (?–1553), the mosque of Behram Paşa at Diyarbakır (?–1572), and the mosque of Kurşunlu or Ahmet Paşa at Kayseri (?–1581) were built on this scheme, but with local variations applied most probably by Sinan's assistants. Similar mosques were built in other cities following Sinan's designs.

Another group of mosques consists of those that do not belong to any specific type, but that express the preferences of their founders or a new experiment of the architect. The mosque of the great Admiral Piyale Paşa at Istanbul (?–1573) is a case in point. It has a curious plan, unique in Ottoman architecture. The transversal prayer hall is covered by six equal domes, and on its two sides there are vaulted galleries above which great arches give light to the interior. This hall is surrounded by a complicated system of arcades on its three sides, the function of which is not clear. In the mosque of Kılıç Ali Paşa, another great admiral, at Istanbul (?–1580), Sinan repeats, this time more closely, the scheme of Hagia Sophia. The building has vaulted side galleries and a longitudinal central nave. It is quite possible that Kılıç Ali Paşa, an Italian convert, had a personal desire to have as his mosque a replica of Hagia Sophia.

Sinan.
Selimiye Complex.
Edirne, Turkey.
1569–1575

Sinan.
Aerial perspective of the
    Selimiye Complex.
Edirne, Turkey.
1569–1575

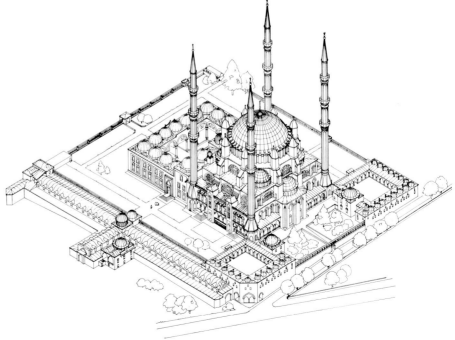

In addition to those of a socioreligious nature, Sinan erected a great many building complexes of large size for commercial purposes. The Sokollu at Lüleburgaz, Selim II at Payas, or Lala Mustafa Paşa at Ilgın and imposing caravansaries such as the Rüstem Paşa (?–1560?) at Edirne are among the best examples of this type of building.

Except that of Sokollu at Lüleburgaz, the masjids of these complexes are mostly unpretentious, single-domed halls. But other buildings, such as travelers' quarters, stables, baths, and streets of shops (arasta), offer all facilities for large caravans. Sinan's mastery of ingenious combinations and picturesque groupings is eminently illustrated in these complexes, now desolate.

Sinan's talent for plastic form found expression in some of his tomb buildings. Although removed from the great Perso-Turkish tomb tradition of Central Asia and Iran and mostly of common types, tombs such as those for Şehzade Mehmet and Hüsrev Paşa display a fine sensitivity in their undulating and articulated surfaces and use of color. The tombs of the sultans under whom he served as chief architect, on the other hand, have greater sophistication on their interiors. Like the mausoleum of Süleyman I described above, the mausoleum of Selim II (?–1577) in Istanbul is also a more researched space conception. An octagonal baldachin is placed inside a square enclosure, and the corners are marked by small half-domes. A comparison with the Mausoleum of Süleyman the Magnificent immediately reveals the architect's capacity for variation and novelty.

Most of the forty-eight baths mentioned are connected with mosques or mosque complexes. So well-suited for spatial play and fanciful decoration and with so many exquisite examples from the fifteenth century, baths did not seem to arouse any particular interest and care in Sinan's designs. The great double bath of Ayasofya or Haseki (?–1553) in Istanbul and that of Sokollu at Edirne reveal only strong volumetric articulation and elementary geometrical forms.

The most ill-fated among his buildings were the palaces and large mansions, most of which have been destroyed. Of the close to thirty-five palaces of the Ottoman grandees mentioned in Taz-kirat, only a small portion of the Palace of Ibrahim Paşa at Istanbul and a small kiosk of Siyavuş Paşa near Istanbul are intact today; they are inadequate for making an evaluation of his secular architecture. Though his reconstruction of the palace of Topkapı during the reign of Murat III was apparently extensive, we cannot properly single out his contribution, for it has since undergone remodeling and redecoration. The great kitchen complex at the palace of Topkapı is the only untouched part of Sinan's reconstruction; despite its functional character, it is an impressive piece of architecture.

Sinan's purely functional buildings or, in a sense, his works of civil engineering, are always mentioned among his major works by Ottoman historians. The aqueduct of Maglova near Istanbul, completed in 1563 to replenish the water supply of Istanbul during the reign of Süleyman I, is worthy of being considered as a great piece of architecture, especially on account of its remarkable and original shape.

Sinan's approach to architectural form. To a sixteenth-century architect, architecture and engineering were nearly synonymous. Sinan's long training as a master carpenter, bridge builder, and military engineer make him comparable to such architects as FILIPPO BRUNELLESCHI with his artisan and engineering background. His emphasis on the problems of foundations, the dimensioning of the great piers and arches, and the challenge of the dimensions of the great dome of Hagia Sophia reveal his preoccupation with the structural aspects of his buildings. Sinan's style brought to traditional mosque architecture the spatial and plastic integrity of design, manifest in the conceptual continuity between the whole and the parts that is lacking in previous periods. In the Ottoman domains, Sinan represents the advent and culmination of the regional synthesis.

The style that reached its mature expression in Sinan's work has the following trait: in interiors, the impression of a definite enclosure is total. The visual dispersal of the boundaries of perceived space in multipillared mosques, in Hagia Sophia, or in baroque churches is not to be found. Sinan was always indifferent to the intrigues of spatial complexity, for he sought, above all, structural clarity. Another distinct characteristic of his style may be defined as a correspondence in mass between the supporting and supported elements: the relationship of the vaulting to the supporting walls and pillars is not determined, as in the Gothic style, by a unified system of continuous architectural elements, but is conceived in its totality. Although the system of domes covering the space does determine the corresponding support system, this is not expressed by an accentuated geometric display of architectural elements which is basic in the geometrization of a Renaissance building. Accordingly, the plastic articulation of the wall mass and the frontality derived from it do not exist in his style. The concept of interior space in the great mosques is based on the duality between the dome and the rectangular prayer hall. The use of the dome as the measure-giving unit and the supporting base as a mass continuum was the central design principle for Sinan and for the Ottoman architects in general.

If reduced to its basic lines, the outer configuration of Sinan's buildings can correctly be called an architecture of mass. Consequently, the relationship between the planes and the openings constitute the single mechanism for expressing his general architectural concept. Thus, the orchestration of various parts into the unity of the contours and the rhythm of the openings are the key marks of his exteriors. That he reached an organic plasticity from the simple geometrical scheme of his buildings is the touch of architectural genius.

Sinan also succeeded in dissolving the basic cubistic image of the earlier periods of Muslim architecture. A more differentiated texturing composed of more elements is evident in his buildings. As his audacity as a designer increased as he moved in this direction, he became more and more experienced in dealing with this variety.

Variation is a key word for Sinan's art, and it is clearly observed in his detailing of façades. Characteristically, Sinan used a series of moldings or colored stripes or linear decorative motifs to contour the windows and doors and to delineate the roof line. These elements weave a geometric pattern of linear movement and create an impression of continuity of contours. Horizontal cornices emphasizing the tectonics of the building are also quite conspicuous. The manipulation of linear elements on the surfaces, the conscious use of delicate moldings to frame the surfaces, and the arches to integrate them into the rhythm of the whole were his most cherished devices. This pursuit of continuity also contributed to the plastic integrity of his designs. Sinan was a master of fenestration. In his hands, the window became a most compliant element of design, entering into various shapes and dimensions on a single wall surface. It became the constituent element of rhythm and modulation that produced the impression of unusual strength on the south façade of the Mosque of Mihrimah or on the side façades of Selimiye at Edirne; in the mosque of Azapkapı at Istanbul, it supplied an exquisite chiaroscuro texture to the wall surfaces.

Sinan's dealing with gateways is not consistent. Whereas he greatly emphasized the great portal-building of the Süleymaniye courtyard, the role of gates in Selimiye was extremely limited. One hardly remembers his gateways in the totality of his buildings. Decoration has a secondary place at best. It is concentrated mostly on specific points, such as the Kibla Wall, the Sultan's loggia, or the window spandrels. The already developed decorative schemes and the emphasis given to certain decorative techniques were apparently satisfactory to his mind; there is scarcely an innovation in the decoration of his buildings. In more general terms, his striving toward a unified spatial and volumetric form on the one hand and toward variety of elements and texture on the other are the dialectical extremes of his style and they are combined in his vision of plastic totality.

Sinan's greatness as an architect lies essentially in his analytical and exploring mind and in his superior taste for total form. But was there a philosophical foundation for his approach to design? Was he, as the most renowned of Turkish architects, representative of a certain theoretical approach to the relationship of man and his artifacts? Might we discern traces of a world view reflected in his buildings as we do in regard to the masters of the Renaissance? Since this aspect of Ottoman or Muslim architecture has been little studied, our first recourse should be to the manuscript written during the reign of Murad III, *Tuhfat al-Mimarin,* at the beginning of which the unknown writer says, in the master's words, that architecture is the work of civilization—literally, that man builds because he has a predisposition for civilized life. In order to demonstrate the importance of the building art, he refers to the difficult construction of the Hagia Sophia, the collapse of its dome, and its subsequent reconstruction as the complexity of a developed social life. The significance given to buildings such as Hagia Sophia, Süleymaniye, and Selimiye, the aqueducts, and the great bridges in the autobiographical manuscripts and related historical texts indicates that great monuments of architecture and engineering were viewed as symbols of the magnificence of the sultan and, therefore, the state, and were level markers of the height of civilization attained during his time.

Sinan was aware of the importance of his contribution and prepared his autobiography for readers of succeeding generations. Although his submission to Allah and to the house of Osman was absolute, he was nevertheless assured of recognition for his individual importance as an architect on two accounts: the architect as the creator of the civilized environment and the architect as witness to a glorious epoch. We cannot infer more than this from his autobiography.

The main quality manifest in Sinan's design and planning, also discernible in the preceding period, is a distinct urge for simplicity and rationalization. But this is not equivalent to saying that this rationalism was the outcome of the prevailing spirit of that period, for sixteenth-century Ottoman culture had left behind the rationalist period of medieval Muslim philosophy. Nor can we suggest that the neo-Hellenism of late Byzantine philosophy, which later played a certain role in Renaissance thought, bore any influence on sixteenth-century Ottoman culture. The dominant philosophy was dogmatic Islam, which rejected rationalism as such. Thus, any similarities that might be found may be explained by a spontaneous coinciding of totally different approaches, theoretical on the Renaissance side, practical on the Turkish side; exploitation of the inherent possibilities of a particular structural system on the part of Sinan and the mathematical speculations of the Renaissance masters. Sinan is the product of a certain culture formed on the frontiers of two distinct areas, Islamic and European, and he represents the former.

DOĞAN KUBAN

WORKS

?–1536, Hüsrev Mosque, Aleppo, Syria. ?–1538/1539, Haseki Complex (imaret added in 1540); ?–1541, Harettin Mausoleum; ?–1542, Hüsrev Mausoleum; 1534–1548, Sehzade Complex; ?–1546, Hayrettin Bath; Istanbul. ?–1547/1548, Mihrimah Complex, Üsküdar, Turkey. ?–1550, Rüstem School; 1550–1557, Haseki Mausoleum; 1550–1557, Süleymaniye Complex; ?–1551, Ibrahim Complex; Istanbul. ?–1551, Iskender Mosque, Diyarbakir, Turkey. ?–1551, Zal Mahmut Mausoleum, Istanbul. ?–1552, Gözleve Complex, Crimea, Russia. ?–1553, Haseki Bath; ?–1555, Kara Ahmet Mausoleum; ?–1555?, Sinan Complex; Istanbul. ?–1555, Süleyman Complex, Damascus, Syria. Completed after 1555, Kara Ahmet Complex; 1560?–1565?, Zal Mahmut Complex; Istanbul. ?–1560, Rüstem Caravansary, Edirne, Turkey. ?–1561?, Rüstem Complex, Istanbul. 1561–1565, Ali Complex, Babaeski, Turkey. ?–1563, Maglova Aqueduct; ?–1565, Mihrimah Complex; Istanbul. ?–1566/1567, Büyükçekmece Bridge, Turkey. After 1566, Selim Complex, Karaptnar, Turkey. ?–1567, Sokollu Mehmet Complex, Lüleburgaz, Turkey. ?–1568, Ali Caravansary; 1569–1575, Selimiye Complex; Edirne, Turkey. ?–1570, Iskender Complex; ?–1571, Sokollu Mehmet Complex; Kadirga, Turkey. 1572–1579, Pertev Mosque, Izuit, Turkey. ?–1572, Behram Mosque, Diyarbakir, Turkey. ?–1572, Pertev Mausoleum; ?–1573, Piyale Complex; ?–1577, Selim II Mausoleum; ?–1577/1578, Sokollu Mehmet Mosque, Azapkapi; ?–1579, Sokollu Mehmet Mausoleum; ?–1580, Kiliç Ali Complex; ?–1580, Şemsi Ahmet Complex; Istanbul. 1583–1586, Kurat Complex, Manisa, Turkey. ?–1583, Atik Valide Complex, Üsküdar, Turkey. 1584–1588, Nişanci Mehmet Complex; ?–1584/1585, Kadiasker Ivaz Mosque; ?–1584/1585, Mesih Mosque; ?–1589, Molla Çelebi Complex; Istanbul. n.d., Ali Complex; n.d., Defterdar Mustafa Çelebi Mosque; Edirne, Turkey. n.d., Ferhat Mosque, Bolu, Turkey. n.d., Gözlüce Aqueduct, Istanbul. n.d., Haseki Imaret, Edirne, Turkey. n.d., Ibrahim Palace (reconstruction), Istanbul. n.d., Mehmet Bath, Edirne, Turkey. n.d., Mehmet Bath, Istanbul. n.d., Mehmet Bridge, Sarajevo, Yugoslavia. n.d., Mehmet Palace; n.d., Rüstem Caravansary; Istanbul. n.d., Mustafa Caravansary, Ilgin, Turkey. n.d., Piyale Mausoleum, Istanbul. n.d., Rüstem Caravansary, Ereğli, Turkey. n.d., Rüstem Caravansary, Galata, Turkey. n.d., Rüstem Complex, Tekirdağ, Turkey. n.d., Sokollu Mehmet Complex, Payas, Turkey. n.d., Sokollu Mehmet Complex, Sarajevo, Yugoslavia. n.d., Topkapi Palace (kitchens and reconstruction), Istanbul. n.d., Valide Caravansary, Üsküdar, Turkey.

BIBLIOGRAPHY

ALTĬNAY, AHMET REFIK 1930 "Mimar Sinan, Hazine-i evrak vesikalarına nazaran." *Tarihi Osmani Encumeni Mecmuası* 1930, no. 5:1–29.

ALTĬNAY, AHMET REFIK 1931 *Mimar Sinan.* Istanbul: Kanaat Kütüphanesini.

ALTĬNAY, AHMET REFIK 1932 *Türk Mimarları.* Istanbul: Hilmi Kitaphanesi.

ALTĬNAY, AHMET REFIK 1935 *On altıncı Asırda Istanbul Hayatı.* Istanbul: Devlet basinevi.

ARSEVEN, CELAL E. 1939 *L'art Turc, depuis son origine juscu'à nos jours.* Istanbul: Devlet basĭnevi.

ASLANAPA, OKTAY 1949 *Edirne'de Osmanlĭ Devri Abideleri.* Istanbul: Uçler basĭnevi.

ASLANAPA, OKTAY 1966 "Sinan maddesi." *Islâm Ansiklopedisi* 108:655–661.

ASLANAPA, OKTAY 1971 *Turkish Art and Architecture.* London and New York: Praeger.

AYVERDI, E. H. 1955 "Hüsrev Pasa Türbesi." *Istanbul Enstitüsü Dergisi* 1:31–38.

BABINGER, FRANZ 1914 "Die türkische Renaissance, Bemerkungen zum Schaffen des grossen türkischen Baumeisters Sinan." *Beiträge zur Kenntnis des Orients* 11:67–88.

BABINGER, FRANZ 1914 "Sinan." Volume 4, pages 428–432 in *Encyclopedia of Islam.* London: Luzac.

BARKAN, Ö. L. 1960 "Türk Yapı ve Yapı Malzemesi Tarihi icin Kaynaklar." *Istanbul Üniversitesi Iktisat Fakültsei Mecmuasi* 17:3–26.

BARKAN, Ö. L. 1972–1979 *Süleymaniye Insaat Defterleri.* 2 vols. Istanbul.

BATUR, A. S. BATUR 1967 "Sinan's Ait Yapıların Listesi." *Mimarlık* 5, no. 49:35–39.

BATUR, A. S. BATUR 1967 "Sinan Bibliyografyası." *Mimarlık* 5, no. 49:40–44.

BILGE, AYGEN 1969 "Mimar Sinan Hakkında Araştırmalar." *Mimarlık* 7, no. 67:17–34.

BILGE, AYGEN 1972–1973 "Mimar Sinan Hakkında Araştırmalar, II." *Sanat Tarihi Yiliği* 5:141–174.

BOZKURT, ORHAN 1952 *Koca Sinan'ın Köprüleri, XVI, Asır Osmanlı Medeniyeti Icinde Sinan, Köprülerin Mimari Bakımından Tetkiki, Silüet ve Abide Kıymetleri.* Istanbul: Pulhan Matbassi.

CHARLES, MARTIN A. 1930 "Hagia Sophia and the Great Imperial Mosques." *Art Bulletin* 12:321–344.

CORBETT, SPENCER 1953 "Sinan: Architect in Chief to Suleiman the Magnificent." *The Architectural Review* 113:290–297.

DAĞDEVIREN, ARIF 1968 *Edirne'de Sinan ve Selimiyesi.* Istanbul: Özdemir Basinevi.

DANISMEND, I. H. 1947–1961 Volumes 2 and 3 in *İzahlı Osmanlı Tarihi Kronolojisi*. Istanbul: Türkiye Yayınevi.

DIEZ, E. 1946 *Türk Şanati, Başlang icindan Günümüze Kadar*. Istanbul: Istanbul Üniversitesi Edebiyat Fakültesi.

DIEZ. E. 1953 "Der Baumeister Sinan und sein Werk." *Atlantis* 25:183–184.

EGLI, ERNST (1954)1976 *Sinan, der Baumeister osmanischer Glanzzeit*. Reprint. Stuttgart, Germany: Rentsch.

ERDENEN, O. 1966 "Osmanlı Devri Mimarları, Yardımcıları ve Teşkilâtları." *Mimarlık* 27:15–18.

EYICE, SENAVI 1965 "Sultaniye-Karapınara Dâir." *Istanbul Üniversitesi Edebiyat Fakültesi tarih dergisi* 15, no. 20:117–140.

GABRIEL, ALBERT 1926 "Les Mosquées de Constantinople." *Revue Syria* 1926:370, 374–379, 387–389, 404.

GABRIEL, ALBERT 1936 "Le Maître architecte Sinan." *La Turquie Kemaliste* 16:2–13.

GABRIEL, ALBERT 1939 "Sainte Sophie, source d'inspiration de la mosquée Suleymaniye." In *Résumé des rapports et communications*. Paris: Comité d'organisation du congrès international des études byzantines.

GIURA, G. 1937 "Il maestro dell'architettura Turcka: Sinan." *Rassegne Italiana* July:539–548.

GLUCK, H. 1926 "Neues zur Sinan-Forschung. Die bisherige Forschung über Sinan." *Orientalische Literatur-Zeitung* 1926:854–858.

GOODWIN, GODFREY A. 1971 *A History of Ottoman Architecture*. Baltimore: Johns Hopkins University Press.

GURLITT, CORNELIUS 1907–1912 *Baukunst Konstantinopels*. Berlin: Wasmuth.

GURLITT, CORNELIUS 1910–1911 "Die Bauten Adrianopels." *Orientalisches Archiv* 1:55–60.

HOAG, JOHN D. 1977 *Islamic Architecture*. New York: Abrams.

JACOB, GEORGE (editor) 1920 Volumes 4 and 5 in *Deutsche Übersetzungen türkischer Urkunden*. Germany: University of Kiel.

KOÇU, AHMED BUCEND 1940 *Mimar Sinan*. Istanbul: Türkiye Yayinevi.

KONYALI, IBRAHIM HAKKI 1948 *Mimar Koca Sinan*. Istanbul: Nihat Topçubaşi.

KONYALI, IBRAHIM HAKKI 1950 *Mimar Koca Sinan'ın Eserleri*. Istanbul: Ülkü Basimevi.

KUBAN, DOĞAN 1958 *Osmanli Dini Mimarisinde İç Mekân Teşekkülü Rönesansla Bir Mukayese*. Istanbul.

KUBAN, DOĞAN 1961 "Atik Valide Camii." *Mimarlık ve Sanat* no. 1:33–36; no. 2:59–63.

KUBAN, DOĞAN 1963 "Les Mosquées à coupole à hexagonale." *Beiträge zur Kunstgeschicts Asiens, In Memoriam E. Diez*. Edited by Oktay Aslanapa. Istanbul: Baha Matbaasi.

KUBAN, DOĞAN 1967 "Mimar Sinan ve Turk Mimarisinin Klâsik Çağı." *Mimarlık* 5, no. 49:13–34.

KUBAN, DOĞAN 1968 "An Ottoman Building Complex of the Sixteenth Century: The Sokollu Mosque and Its Dependencies in Istanbul." *Ars Orientalis* 7:19–39.

KUBAN, DOĞAN 1971 "Sinan'ın Sanati." *Türkiyemiz* no. 3/2:2–3.

MARTINY, G. 1936 "Piyale Pascha Moschee." *Ars Islamica* 3:157–171.

MAYER, LEO A. 1956 *Islamic Architects and Their Work*. Geneva: Kundig.

MERIÇ, RIFKI MELÛL 1938 "Mimar Sinan." *Ülkü Mecmuası* 63:195–206.

MERIÇ, RIFKI MELÛL 1965 *Mimar Sinan, Hayatı, Eseri I: Mimar Sinan'ın Hayatı'na Eserlerine Dair Metinler*. Ankara: Türk Tarih Kurumu Basımevi.

ÖGEL, SEMRA 1972 *Der Kuppelraum in der türkischen Architektur*. Istanbul: Nederlands Historisch-Archaeologisch Instituut in het Nabije Oosten.

ÖZTUNA, Y. 1966 "Mimar Sinan'ın Hatıraları." *Hayat Tarih Mecmuası* 5:4–11; 6:42–51; 7:49–55.

PAPAZOĞLU, A. N. 1938 "Sinan ho architekton." *Epeteris Hetaireias Byzantinon Spoudon* 14:443–460.

RIFAT, OSMAN n.d. "Mimar Koca Sinan ibn Abdulmennan." *Millî Mecmua* 7, no. 83:1335–1346.

SÖZEN, METIN 1975 *Türk Mismarisinin Gelişimi ve Mimar Sinan*. Istanbul: Türkiye Iş Bankasi.

STRATTON, A. 1972 *Sinan*. New York: Scribner.

TUNCAY, RAUF 1969 "Edirne'de Selimiye Camii." *Belgelerle Türk Tarihi dergisi sayi* 23:3–12.

ÜLGEN, A. S. 1942a "Pertev Mehmet Paşanin Eserleri Hakkında Mimarî Izahat." *Vakıflar Dergisi* 2:241–243.

ÜLGEN, A. S. 1942b "Topkapı'da Ahmet Paşa Heyeti." *Vakıflar Dergisi* 2:169–172.

ÜLGEN, A. S. 1952 "Rüstem Paşa Heyeti." *Mimarlık Dergisi* 9, nos. 1–2:23–28.

VOGT-GÖKNIL, ULYA 1953 *Türkische Moscheen*. Zurich: Origo.

VOGT-GÖKNIL, ULYA 1966 *Living Architecture: Ottoman*. New York: Grosset & Dunlop.

SINATRA, VINCENZO

Vincenzo Sinatra (1707?–?) worked as a stone cutter, a *capomaestro,* a tax estimator, and an architect in the city of Noto in southeastern Sicily. He began his career as an architect in the 1740s working on projects alone or in conjunction with a colleague. From all indications, he seems to have been a reliable builder but just how proficient he was as a designer and an architect is still an unresolved question. In 1745, just as he was becoming recognized as an architect, Sinatra married ROSARIO GAGLIARDI's sister, thereby strengthening his relationship with the man who was most certainly his master.

Sinatra has left a single autographed design, a poorly drawn map, which gives little indication that he was a talented designer. Yet, his name has been linked to many of the buildings of Noto and of its valley. He was certainly the architect of Noto's city hall, begun in the 1740s, which although Italian in elevation, is based on French prototypes. The other buildings attributed to him indicate that he borrowed liberally from his mentor, Gagliardi, but he infused his work with a more classical interpretation of baroque elements and, paradoxically, with touches of rococo ornament.

STEPHEN TOBRINER

WORKS

1742–1776, City Hall; 1747, Monastery of Montevergine (portions); 1750, San Francesco all'Immacolata; 1751, San Francesco di Paola; 1753, Oratory of San Filippo Neri (repairs); 1765–1768, San Nicolò (with others); 1766, Crociferi Fathers House (portions); Noto, Italy.

BIBLIOGRAPHY

BOTTARI, STEFANO 1958 "Contributi alla conoscenza dell'architettura del Settecento in Sicilia." *Palladio* New Series 8:69–77.
TOBRINER, STEPHEN 1982 *The Genesis of Noto: An Eighteenth Century Sicilian City.* London: Zwemmer; Berkeley: University of California Press.

SIRÉN, HEIKKI, and SIRÉN, KAIJA

Heikki Sirén (1918–) received a diploma in architecture at the Polytechnic Institute, Helsinki, where he studied with his father, JOHAN SIRÉN. Throughout his career, Heikki Sirén has often collaborated with his wife, Kaija Sirén (1920–) who also received a diploma in architecture from the Polytechnic Institute, Helsinki. The two, who were married in 1944, have won many awards.

The Siréns' architecture shows both an interest in traditional Finnish building materials and a straightforward expression of function that is the legacy of ALVAR AALTO and LUDWIG MIES VAN DER ROHE, respectively. Although the Siréns did not take up Johan Sirén's style, the latter's neoclassicism with its clarity of structure must have provided a point of departure for the young Siréns' rationalist style.

One of the Siréns' most interesting works is Tech Town, the residential complex for the Polytechnic Institute at Otaniemi, Finland (1950–1973). An early European example of the American campus, Otaniemi's plan was laid out by Alvar Aalto, who took first prize in the competition of 1949 in which Heikki Siren and AARNE ERVI had taken second. Assisted by Martti Melakari, the Siréns elected to carry out Aalto's triple tower complexes. Independently, Sirén designed the Tech Town Sauna (1951), the Restaurant Servin Mökki (1952), and the outstanding chapel at Otaniemi (1957). Like Aalto's brick and wood

structures nestled into the trees, these buildings are placed into the landscape gracefully but with force. His use of logs for the sauna and exposed pine trusses and metal fasteners in the restaurant give these buildings a rugged, woodsy quality that is both reflective of the Finnish landscape and, especially because of the emphasis on the means of construction, fitting for an Institute of Technology. In the chapel, the restraint of the other buildings is carried to an extreme of delicacy, and the influence of Mies van der Rohe is evident, as it is later in the Parish Center, Kankaanpää (1967).

Buildings by the two Siréns include industrial complexes, residences, and schools. Of these, the Kallio Municipal Offices, Helsinki, a ring-shaped structure with a circular building inside, is perhaps the most spectacular. In the Brucknerhaus in Linz, Austria (1974), the Siréns used circular shapes in a complex composition, yet achieved the balance of the simpler Otaniemi Chapel on a dramatic scale. The Brucknerhaus, which overlooks the Danube, has been called "one of the last examples of Scandinavian classicism which was united in the thirties with functionalism" (Friedrich Achleitner, quoted in Bruun & Popovits 1977, p. 195). Whether the Brucknerhaus is the last or a recent example of Scandinavian classicism remains to be seen; still, the Siréns' work demonstrates how vital is the ability to join foreign influence with native tradition in Scandinavia.

JUDITH S. HULL

WORKS

1950–1973, Tech Town (with Alvar Aalto and Martti Melakari); 1951, Tech Town Sauna, Otaniemi; 1952, Servin Mökki Restaurant, Otaniemi; 1951–1960, House, Lauttasaari; 1956, Apartment House, Otalaakso, Otaniemi; 1957, Chapel, Otaniemi; Helsinki. 1961, Church, Orivesi, Finland. 1965, Kallio Municipal Offices, Helsinki. 1965, Prefabricated Row Houses (Heikki Siren, with Kaarlo Rautkari and Kauko Rastas), Tapionsolu, Tapiola, Helsinki. 1966–1969, Villa, Lingonsö Island, Barösund Archipelago, Finland. 1970, La Pierrefitte Housing Project, Boussy Saint-Antoine, Val d'Yerres, Paris. 1967–1970, Parish Center and Town Hall, Kankaanpää, Finland. 1970, Lautasaari Coeducational School, Helsinki. 1974, Bruckner Concert Hall, Linz, Austria.

BIBLIOGRAPHY

BORRÀS, MARIA LLUISA 1967 *Arquitectura Finlandesa en Otaniemi: Alvar Aalto, Heikki Sirén, Reima Pietilä.* Barcelona, Spain: Ediciones Poligrafa.
BRUUN, ERIK, and POPOVITS, SARA (editors) (1977)1978 *Kaija and Heikki Sirén: Architects.* Introduction by Jurgen Joedicke. 2d ed. Stuttgart, Germany: Kramer.
DUOMATO, LAMIA 1980 *Heikki and Kaija Sirén: Finnish Design Team.* Monticello, Ill.: Vance.

SIRÉN, JOHAN

Johan Sigfrid Sirén (1889–1961) was born at Ylihärmä, Finland, and studied at the Polytechnic Institute, Helsinki. During the 1920s, he traveled and studied abroad. Noted as a leader of neoclassicism, Sirén was responsible for the Parliament Building and the extension of JOHANN CARL LUDWIG ENGEL's 1810 University Building, both in Helsinki. Even after World War II, Sirén's work retained a classical tendency, as may be seen in his restoration of bombed buildings of Helsinki University and the enlargement of its festival hall. In the Bank of Finland, Vaasa (1943–1952), Sirén used simplified classical detail and maintained classical proportions and allusions to traditional Scandinavian architecture. In 1931, Sirén was appointed professor at the Technical Institute in Helsinki, where he influenced several generations of modern Finnish architects, including his son and daughter-in-law, Heikki and Kaija Sirén (see SIRÉN AND SIRÉN), whose rationalism may be the logical culmination of their father's classicism.

JUDITH S. HULL

WORKS

1931, Helsinki University (enlargement); 1931, Parliament Building, Helsinki. 1943–1952, Bank of Finland, Vaasa. 1944–c.1950, Helsinki University (enlargement of Festival Hall and restoration of old section); *1944–1950, Technical Institute (chemistry laboratory); Helsinki.

BIBLIOGRAPHY

EKELUND, HILDING 1959 "J. S. Sirén, 70 vuotta 27.5.1959." *Arkkitehti-Arkitekten* 39, no. 8:113.
MEISSNER, CARL 1938 "Finnland II: Tradition und Neuschaffen im Werk J. S. Siréns." *Monatshefte für Baukunst und Städtebau* 22, no. 1:33–40.

SITTE, CAMILLO

Considered a pivotal figure in the development of the town planning profession, Camillo Sitte's (1843–1903) influence rests almost entirely on a slender, copiously illustrated volume, *Der Städtebau nach seinen künstlerischen Grundsätzen* (1899). He had few opportunities actually to carry out any of his architectural or planning schemes. Wide ranging in his intellectual and artistic interests, the social and cultural ambience of Vienna influenced his life and thought. The recent Sittesque revival—one of the reactions against the absoluteness of the International style—makes it appropriate to question the rigidity of any modern planning.

Among important architects strongly influenced by Sitte, either directly or indirectly, were Karl Henrici, THEODOR FISCHER, RAYMOND UNWIN, JOSEPH MARIA OLBRICH, BRUNO TAUT, WERNER HEGEMANN, ELIEL SAARINEN, and in his youth, LE CORBUSIER.

Born in Vienna, the son of an architect, Sitte attended the Piaristen school on the Piaristenplatz which was typical of the enclosed squares he later so admired. His friends remained important to him throughout his life; many of them achieved prominence among the cultural elite of Vienna. One friend, Hans Richter, who was to become concertmaster for Richard Wagner, introduced Sitte to GOTTFRIED SEMPER, the contemporary architect Sitte most admired.

Upon finishing school in 1863, Sitte entered the atelier of the architect HEINRICH VON FERSTEL at the Wiener Polytechnisches Institut (now Technische Hochschule). While apprenticed to Fersel, Sitte attended courses in archeology and art history at the University of Vienna taught by Rudolf Eitelberger von Edelberg. It is evident that he sought a broad education that combined the academic with practical experience in the arts. He was also an accomplished cellist and throughout his life was seriously involved with music.

At the end of his university studies, (1868/1869) he traveled—sketchbook in hand—to Italy and Germany. In later years, he journeyed repeatedly in Italy and Germany, as well as in France, Greece, Asia Minor, Constantinople, and Egypt.

From an early age on, he had assisted his father, and thus became familiar in practical ways with polychromatic interior decoration, the integration of arts and crafts into total architectural design, and the restoration work that relied on traditional workmanship. In 1873 his father was given the task of expanding the monastery of the Mechitarists, and Sitte received his first independent architectural commission, the design of their church, the Mechitaristenkirche (1873–1874), in German Renaissance style.

In 1875, on the recommendation of Eitelberger Sitte was offered the directorship of the newly founded State School of Applied Arts in Salzburg. Over his father's objections, he accepted the position. Sitte devoted himself with enthusiasm to his work as an art educator. He organized the school, lectured on arts and crafts, and published numerous articles on related subjects, many of these appearing in the periodical *Salzburger Gewerbeblatt*, which he founded in 1877. Sitte's relationship to the English influence in Austria and Germany remains to be explored; it is known that he admired WILLIAM MORRIS, and certain similarities exist between Morris's Red House and Sitte's home at the State School of Applied Arts in Vienna. In 1883, he was asked to become the director of the school and to supervise its move to a new building on the Schellinggasse, which also contained an apartment for himself.

Upon his return to Vienna in 1883, Sitte's attention was on architecture and city planning. It has been suggested that his interest in planning derived from his teacher Eitelberger, who had lectured and published on the subject (1858/1859), but, more likely the building of the Ringstrasse was the immediate stimulus. The urban transformation of Vienna initiated by Emperor Franz Joseph's decree of December 20, 1857, to raze the fortifications that enclosed the old city, had been watched avidly in Austria and abroad. The great variety of entries in the competitions for the layout of the Ringstrasse and the monumental buildings along its majestic sweep were the subjects of intense debate. It is not surprising, then, that Sitte's interests were kindled, and that he began to publish articles on city planning. Significant among these are three pieces about Semper's ideas on town planning which Sitte apparently wrote for his friend Victor K. Schembera, who published them in the *Neues Wiener Tagblatt* in January 1885.

The appearance of *Der Städtebau nach seinen künstlerischen Grundsätzen* was, however, unanticipated. The instantaneous success of this book was a surprise. Within a month of publication in May 1889, a second edition was called for, a third followed in 1901, a fourth in 1909, and by 1972 a seventh was published. *Der Städtebau* was translated into French in 1902, Russian in 1925, Spanish in 1926, English in 1945 and 1965, and Italian in 1953. Free of jargon and reading easily in spite of certain repetitiveness, the book is often poetic, as Sitte addressed himself to the concerned citizen as much as to the professional and the bureaucrat. He assailed the mechanical manner in which the gridiron plan and straight streets of even width were imposed in the laying out of new sections without regard for terrain or existing road patterns, and how old towns were ruthlessly and destructively modernized in the name of improved sanitation and traffic circulation. Alarmed about the lack of aesthetic consideration in modern city plans, Sitte set out to analyze the pattern of squares and streets, and the placement and context of buildings and monuments, in the unspoiled preindustrial towns that charmed him in his travels. "The basic idea of this book is to go to school with Nature and the old masters also in matters of townplanning," he wrote in the preface to the 1901 edition. "Nature" here is an inner force or an organic consistency, thus the man-made environment is compared to a living organism in an almost Jugendstil metaphor. Sitte's references to "old masters" should not be interpreted strictly in terms of historical periods or styles, but rather in terms of anonymous, timeless assemblage in older towns of what would now be "vernacular" or "folk."

In the very heyday of eclecticism, when the buildings along the Ringstrasse vied with each other in their historicism, Sitte had the courage to disregard specific styles. His aim was to discover universal principles in planning, a timeless vocabulary that could be relevant to both contemporary and future situations. His reverence for the past has often been misinterpreted, and he has been unjustly considered a medievalist and hopeless romantic unable to face the realities of the industrial metropolis. Sitte himself states quite clearly:

Modern living as well as modern building techniques no longer permit the faithful imitation of old townscapes, a fact which we cannot overlook without falling prey to barren fantasies. The exemplary creations of the old masters must remain alive with us in some other way than through slavish copying; only if we can determine in what the essentials of these creations consist, and if we can apply these meaningfully to modern conditions, will it be possible to harvest a new and flourishing crop from the apparently sterile soil. ([1889]1965, p. 111).

He has been classed as an "archaist" and contrasted with his contemporary OTTO WAGNER, whose influence and prominence in Vienna as the champion of modern large-scale planning far surpassed that of Sitte. It is quite possible, however, that even Wagner did not entirely escape Sitte's influence, as his close associate Olbrich attended the State School of Applied Arts in Vienna (1882–1886). Olbrich probably attended Sitte's classes in architectural history and freehand drawing, and shared the musical interests of the Sittes' social gatherings. Olbrich's own works and drawings reveal much that is Sittesque.

The appearance of *Der Städtebau* transformed the author's life, as he became the hero of the architectural wing of the planning profession. Invitations to lecture and to serve as juror proliferated. As shown in his articles, Sitte's interest in city planning broadened to include extra-artistic matters and many of his writings discuss local issues, but in Viennese official circles his counsel went unheeded.

"Grosstadt-Grün," two articles on greenery in the modern city written in 1900 for a Hamburg periodical, were added as an appendix to the later editions of *Der Städtebau*. He also intended to publish a second volume dealing with socioeconomic aspects, under the title "Der Städtebau nach seinen wirtschaftlichen Grundsätzen." He died before the first number of his magazine *Der Städtebau* appeared in January 1904, the earliest city planning periodical. Founded by Sitte and Theodor Goecke, it was a "Monthly journal for the artistic development of cities according to their economic, hygienic, and social principles." The prologue to its first issue was written almost entirely by Sitte and reflects his later ideas about the building of cities. This influential architectural periodical continued publication under Goecke's editorship until he died in 1919; briefly suspended during 1923/1924, it became part of *Wasmuths Monatshefte* from 1930 until 1942 when publication ceased.

Sitte's actual buildings and projects for urban layouts have been overshadowed by his theoretical contributions. Besides the Mechitaristen Church, only a few other completed buildings are known: the *Jagdschloss* (hunting lodge) for Prince Colloredo-Mansfeld (1891), for which Sitte provided not only working drawings but actually crafted life-size models of details, and the complex in Oderfurth-Přivoz (1894–1899). In the latter case, Sitte had the opportunity to situate his buildings in a city extension he also designed.

His city planning projects were for extensions to small or middlesized towns. Generally considered the most significant of these is his plan of 1894 for the subdivision of land surrounding the old city of Olmütz. It leaves intact the historic city core, situated on a plateau, and subdivides the surrounding sloping land into long narrow blocks of residential buildings with continuous interior gardens. The use of this block form (200 meters by 40 meters) was to prevent interior build-up. A greenbelt, 150 meters in width, separates a residential area of single villas (cottages) from an industrial area to the southwest along the railroad. The comprehensive plan for the city of Laibach (1895), after its partial destruction by an earthquake, uses the remaining landmark buildings as orientation or focal points for new road extensions. Another of his plans is for an extension of Marienberg in Silesia (1903), in which a church, also his design, is situated on a terraced plaza with steps and green areas connecting various levels. This plan was published after his death in *Der Städtebau*. In 1896 Sitte designed a small resort town at Marienthal, Austria, next to an artificial lake to be created by a proposed dam which, however, was not built. Sitte's plan includes a hotel with terraces and landing pier, also a park and playground facing the lake, a harbor and residential areas for vacation homes, shops, and a community center. Sitte's plans actually show a preference for straight streets, combined, however, with a sensitivity to irregular terrain and existing property lines. This is in marked contrast to some of his followers, like Henrici, who tended to use sinuous streets with continuous façades for a picturesque effect. The matter of straight versus curved or crooked streets obsessed German planning for decades.

A truly visionary project, that was not to serve any practical purpose but was to incorporate Sitte's life philosophy, remained purely conceptual. Called the "Holländer-Turm," revealing ties to Richard Wagner, it was to have the shape of a lofty tower symbolizing a striving for perfection in all the arts in an all-encompassing harmonious creativity: a *Gesamtkunstwerk*.

CHRISTIANE C. COLLINS

WORKS

1873–1874, Mechitaristenkirche, Vienna. 1887, Parish Church, Temesvár, Hungary. 1891, Hunting Lodge, near Zbirow, Bohemia, Czechoslovakia. 1894–1899, Marienkirche, Townhall, and Parish House, Oderfurth-Přivoz, Ostrava, Czechoslovakia.

BIBLIOGRAPHY

Berichte zur Raumforschung und Raumplanung. 1968 12, no. 4. Entire issue dedicated to Camillo Sitte.
COLLINS, GEORGE R., and COLLINS, CHRISTIANE C. 1965 *Camillo Sitte and the Birth of Modern City Planning.* New York: Random House. Includes an extensive bibliography.
FEHL, GERHARD 1980 "Stadtbaukunst contra Stadtplanung: Zur Auseinandersetzung Camillo Sittes mit Reinhard Baumeister." *Stadtbauwelt* 65:451–461.
HEGEMANN, WERNER, and PEETS, ELBERT (1922)1972 *The American Vitruvius: An Architect's Handbook of Civil Art.* Reprint. New York: Blom.
SCHORSKE, CARL E. 1980 "The Ringstrasse, Its Critics, and the Birth of Urban Modernism." Chapter 2, pages 24–115 in *Fin-de-Siècle Vienna: Politics and Culture.* New York: Knopf.
SITTE, CAMILLO (1889)1965 *City Planning According to Artistic Principles.* Translated by George R. Collins and Christiane C. Collins. New York: Random House; London: Phaidon. Originally published in German.

SKIDMORE, OWINGS, and MERRILL

When John O. Merrill (1896–1975), born in St. Paul, Minnesota, joined the partnership of Louis Skidmore (1897–1962), born in Lawrenceburg, Indiana, and Nathaniel A. Owings (1903–), born in Indianapolis, Indiana, in 1939, Skidmore, Owings, and Merrill (SOM) embarked upon a program of development that would lead by 1950 to the firm's becoming the principal exponent of a characteristically American team approach to architectural design. SOM's achievement is due in large part to its commitment to the objectives and principles articulated by the founding partners.

According to Owing's autobiography, the firm would strive toward insuring the recognition of and respect for the architect and enlarging his role and responsibilities in the design process. On a more idealistic level and fully consistent with their commitment to design only in the modern mode, the firm embraced the belief that architecture could improve the quality of human life. The firm was organized and expanded on the model of a large business enterprise, enabling it to render complete architectural, engineering, planning, interior and environmental design, and project management services within a single frame. The medieval builders guild system, with its ideal of cooperation and anonymity, provided the model for the team approach. As the means to insuring consistency and integrity in design, the constitution of the core group of each team—an administrative partner, a design partner, project manager, senior designers, and technical personnel—remains constant on any given project. The team approach to design was formally recognized in 1962 when SOM received an award from the American Institute of Architects for excellence in design, the first such award for an architectural firm. A 1950 show at the Museum of Modern Art constituted the first exhibition by that museum of the work of a firm rather than an individual architect.

On the assumption that the degree of recognition and respect accorded to a firm relates proportionally to the volume of work handled, SOM has continually expanded its geographic facilities as well as the services offered. Major offices include

Chicago (1936), New York (1936), San Francisco (1946), Portland, Oregon (1951), Washington, (1967), Boston (1971), and Denver (1977). At present, thirty-five general partners, ninety-three associate partners, and 212 associates constitute the management organization.

Notwithstanding the large-scale commissions undertaken by the firm prior to 1950, including the Terrace-Plaza Hotel in Cincinnati, the Brooklyn Veterans' Administration Hospital, the Manufacturers Hanover Trust Building in New York, and the planning and execution of Oak Ridge, Tennessee, SOM's reputation was secured with the design of Lever House (1952), New York. The significance of the Oak Ridge project (a new town commissioned by the United States Government [1942–1946]) must not be underestimated; not only did it establish a government connection, but it required that SOM's work force be expanded, hence laying the groundwork for the firm's ability to execute large-scale commissions. By 1949, William Brown, GORDON BUNSHAFT, Robert Cutler, and J. Walter Severinghaus (all of whom later would become the core group of the New York office), William Hartman, and WALTER NETSCH had become full partners.

One of the first structures to present a new technical and aesthetic concept for the design of tall curtain wall business buildings, Lever House demonstrates SOM's commitment to excellence in detail and to the principles of the International style. In order to provide for public space and to accommodate zoning laws that in part had determined the set-back profiles of earlier skyscrapers, the building was restricted to only a portion of its site. The concept was quickly formularized by both SOM and other firms, and it initiated a line of development for SOM that included the Chase Manhattan (1960), Harris Trust (1975), Union Carbide (1960), and Inland Steel (1958) Buildings. In all of these, the steel structural members are located outside the slab's curtain walls. In addition, although SOM had been recognized for its organization, Lever House (1952) established the firm's, and specifically Gordon Bunshaft's, reputation in design.

Even in the early years, the firm's commitment to experiment with structure and design and its refusal simply to invoke its own well-tested formulae became apparent in the Banque Lambert Building (Brussels [1965]), the John Hancock Building (New Orleans [1960–1962]), and the Hartford Building (Chicago [1971]). In these, reinforced concrete takes the place of the steel exterior skeleton. The scale of the buildings undertaken by SOM demands exploration of the relation between structure and engineering—a major preoccupation

Skidmore, Owings, and Merrill.
Lever House.
New York.
1952

Skidmore, Owings, and Merrill.
Chase Manhattan Bank.
New York.
1961

of the firm generally and specifically of its structural engineers including Fazlur Khan and Myron Goldsmith. Exemplary are the John Hancock Center in Chicago (1970), a multi-use building whose structure is conceived as a rigid, rectangular tube with trussed walls carrying all principal stresses and floor slabs providing secondary lateral stability (a concept first investigated in the less successful Alcoa Building of 1968); the fifty-two-story One Shell Plaza, Houston, technically a tube within a tube; and the 110-story Sears Tower, Chicago, whose structure consists of a cluster of framed tubes of varying heights, each of which has its own structural integrity.

A concern with preserving the formal integrity of the free-standing building is the key to SOM's site planning. For example, the Hirshhorn Museum and Sculpture Garden (1974) clarifies the north/south axis of the east/west oriented mall in Washington, and the siting of the Lyndon Baines Johnson Library (1971) at the University of Texas, Austin, enhances its monumentality.

While consistency in the quality of technical detail and innovation may be the hallmark of the firm, regional and individual variations are evident and since the 1960s have not been minimized. (Previously, in keeping with the medieval ideal of anonymity, individual responsibility for design was not acknowledged publicly.) In Chicago, Netsch employs highly efficient structural and geometric systems as the means for generating plans. The New York office, on the other hand, while engaged in structural experimentation, is noted for innovative interpretations of standard problems.

SUSAN STRAUSS

WORKS

1942–1946, Atom City, Oak Ridge, Tenn. 1949–1950, Brooklyn Veterans' Administration Hospital, N.Y. 1949–1950, Lake Meadows, Chicago. 1949–1950, Terrace Plaza Hotel, Cincinnati, Ohio. 1952, Lever House, Park Avenue, New York. 1952–1955, United States Navy Postgraduate School, Monterey, Calif. 1954, Manufacturer's Hanover Trust, Fifth Avenue, New York. 1955, Hilton Hotel, Istanbul, Turkey. 1957, Connecticut General Life Insurance Company Building, Bloomfield, Conn. 1957, United States Navy Service School, Great Lakes, Ill. 1958, Inland Steel Company Headquarters, Chicago. 1959, Crown Zellerbach Corporate Headquarters; 1959, John Hancock Mutual Life Insurance Company Building; San Francisco. 1960, PepsiCo Incorporated World Headquarters; 1960, Union Carbide Building; Park Avenue, New York. 1960–1962, John Hancock Building, New Orleans, La. 1961, Chase Manhattan Bank, New York. 1962, Solar Telescope, Kitt Peak, Ariz. 1962, United States Air Force Academy, Colorado Springs. 1963, Beinecke Rare Book and Manuscript Library, Yale University, New Haven. 1965, Banque Lambert Building, Brussels. 1965, Brunswick Building; 1965, Civic Center; 1965, Equitable Life Assurance Society of the United States Building; Chicago. 1965, Library and Museum; 1965, Vivian Beaumont Theater; Lincoln Center, New York. 1965, Mauna Kea Beach Hotel, Hawaii. 1965, University of Illinois at Chicago Circle. 1966, Life Sciences Building, Illinois Institute of Technology, Chicago. 1967, Hartford Fire Insurance Building, San Francisco. 1967, Marine Midland Bank, New York. 1968, Alcoa Building, Golden Gate Center; 1968, Bank of America Headquarters; San Francisco. 1968, Boots Pure Drug Headquarters, Nottingham, England. 1970, John Hancock Center; 1971, Hartford Fire Insurance Company Building; Chicago. 1971, Lyndon Baines Johnson Library, University of Texas, Austin. 1971, One Shell Plaza Offices, Houston, Tex. 1971, Sid W. Richardson Hall, University of Texas,

Skidmore, Owings, and Merrill.
Banque Lambert Building.
Brussels.
1965

Skidmore, Owings, and Merrill.
Sears Tower.
Chicago.
1974

Austin. 1973, W. R. Grace Building, Avenue of the Americas, New York. 1974, Hirshhorn Museum and Sculpture Garden, Washington. 1974, Philip Morris Factory, Richmond, Va. 1974, Sears Tower; 1975, Harris Trust and Savings Bank; Chicago. 1977, Khaneh Center, Teheran. 1978, New World Center, Hong Kong. 1979, National City Bank, Cleveland, Ohio. 1980, Arab International Bank, Cairo. 1980, International Museum of Photography, George Eastman House, Rochester, N.Y. 1982, Haj Terminal, King Abdul Aziz International Airport, Jeddah.

BIBLIOGRAPHY

"Architecture is Alive and Well." 1977 *Architectural Review* 162:231–236.

"The Architects from 'Skid's' Row." 1968 *Fortune* Jan.:139–140, 210–211, 215.

"Atom City: Oak Ridge, Tennessee." 1946 *The Builder* 170:404–408.

"$2 Billion Worth of Design by Conference." 1954 *Business Week* Dec. 4:96–104.

BLAKE, PETER 1959 "SOM Puts the Bones Outside the Skin." *Architectural Forum* 120:92–95.

BOYLE, MICHAEL 1977 "Architectural Practice in America 1865–1965: Ideal and Reality." Pages 309–344 in Spiro Kostof (editor) *The Architect: Chapters in the History of the Profession.* New York: Oxford University Press.

"Campus Design by Function, Not by Discipline." 1961 *Architectural Record* 130:12–13.

"Chicago's Multi-use Giant." 1967 *Architectural Record* 141, no. 1:137–144.

"Cincinnati Offices Adopt the Chicago Window." 1978 *Architectural Record* 163:41.

DANZ, ERNST 1962 *The Architecture of Skidmore, Owings & Merrill: 1950–1962.* New York: Praeger.

"Down to Earth Tower." 1968 *Architectural Forum* 128, no. 3:36–45.

DREXLER, ARTHUR, and MENGES, AXEL 1974 *The Architecture of Skidmore, Owings & Merrill: 1963–1973.* New York: Architectural Book Publishing Company.

FISCHER, ROBERT 1972 "Optimizing the Structure of the Skyscraper." *Architectural Record* 152:97–104.

GIEDION, SIGFRIED 1957 "The Experiment of SOM." *Bauen und Wohnen* 12:113–117.

"The Gleaming of Buffalo Brass." 1976 *Interiors* 136, no. 4:80–83.

"A Handsome Library in a Resort Town Designed to Lure the Sun-loving Public Indoors." 1978 *Architectural Record* 164:96-98.

"Hilton's Newest Hotel." 1955 *Architectural Forum* 103:120–127.

"The Hospital in the City: NYU's Giant Medical Center." 1964 *Architectural Forum* 120:92–95.

"In Praise of a Monument to Lyndon B. Johnson." 1971 *Architectural Record* 150:113–120.

"Lever House Complete." 1952 *Architectural Forum* 96:69, 110–111.

"Lever House, New York: Glass and Steel Walls." 1952 *Architectural Record* 111:130–135.

"Manufacturer's Hanover Builds a Conversation Place on Fifth Avenue." 1954 *Architectural Record* 116:149–156.

"Mecca Academe." 1979 *Architectural Review* 165: 5–7.

"A New Art Gallery for the Capitol Mall, Washington, D.C." 1967 *Architectural Record* 142:112–115.

"Olympic Tower." 1975 *Progressive Architecture* 56:44–47.

OWINGS, NATHANIEL ALEXANDER 1973 *The Spaces in Between: An Architect's Journey.* Boston: Houghton Mifflin.

"Pilgrimage Bank." 1977 *Progressive Architecture* 58, no. 9:70–73.

"Rare Book and Manuscript Library, Yale University, New Haven, Conn., USA." 1961 *Architectural Design* 31, no. 2:85.

"Skidmore, Owings & Merrill: The Mandala Collaborative." 1979 *Progressive Architecture* 60:108–109.

"SOM's Hirschhorn Museum." 1975 *Architectural Review* 157:119–120.

"SOM,s New Tower in Jeddah." 1979 *Architectural Record* 165:102–106.

"SOM Stacks Three Atriums in Chicago Office Building." 1978 *Architectural Record* 163:41.

"Tower with a Front Yard." 1957 *Architectural Forum* 106:110–115.

"Two Developments by Gerald Hines, One from SOM San Francisco for Houston . . . Another from SOM Chicago for Minneapolis." 1978 *Architectural Record* 163:42.

WOODWARD, CHRISTOPHER 1970 *Skidmore, Owings & Merrill.* New York: Simon & Schuster.

SKOPAS

Skopas, a famous Greek sculptor and architect of the Temple of Athena Alea at Tegea (360 B.C.), was active c.375–330 B.C.. He was a son of the sculptor Aristandros of Paros.

According to Pausanias 8.45.4–5,

The ancient sanctuary of Athena Alea was made for the Tegeans by Aleos. Later on the Tegeans set up for the goddess a large temple, worth seeing. The sanctuary was utterly destroyed by a fire [394 B.C.]. . . . The present temple is far superior to all other temples in the Peloponnesos on many grounds, especially for its size and splendor. Its first order of columns is Doric, and the next is Corinthian; also, within the temple, too, stand columns of the Ionic order. The architect, I learned, was Skopas the Parian, who made statues in many places of ancient Greece, and some besides in Ionia and Caria.

Pausanias (8.47.1) also reports that Skopas made the cult images of Asklepios and Hygeia flanking the archaic statue of Athena. Although he does not record the name of the sculptor responsible for the pedimental and acroterial sculptures, their style is identical with that of Skopas's other works. Hence, it is assumed by all writers that

Skopas was the designing architect–sculptor at Tegea.

Built c.360 B.C. of local Doliana marble, it was the first marble temple in the Peloponnesos. Its chief model was IKTINOS's temple at Bassai. Again, the temple is Doric and many features of both plans are related as was the location of the sculptured metopes above the porches. Especially notable was its interior, whose lateral walls were articulated by an engaged Corinthian order defined by pilasters at the corners, creating a setting for the cult images which, as at Bassai, occupied virtually the entire width of the cella. Conceivably, a shorter engaged Ionic order stood on the Corinthian order.

At Tegea, Skopas gave definitive form to the Corinthian capital which, henceforth, throughout antiquity, would follow its essential organization and continue its emphasis on naturalistic, leafy forms in both the acanthus leaves at the base and the luxuriant sheaths of stalks whence tendrils uncurled to support the upper member of the capital. The sculptor's eye had reshaped this new architectural form originally designed by Iktinos.

There is abundant evidence to attribute to Skopas, again as designing architect–sculptor, another highly original and richly sculptured building, the Propylon leading into an open-air precinct in the Sanctuary of the Great Gods in Samothrace. Dated c.340 B.C. and donated by Philip II of Macedon, the novel features of both the architecture and the sculpture of the Propylon proved of major influence in the later history of Greek architecture and sculpture.

PHYLLIS WILLIAMS LEHMANN

WORKS

c.360 B.C., Temple of Athena Alea, Tegea, Greece. (A)c.340 B.C., Propylon to the Temenos, Sanctuary of the Great Gods, Samothrace, Greece.

BIBLIOGRAPHY

Translations of the classical texts can be found in the Loeb Classical Library series published by Harvard University Press, Cambridge, Mass., and Heinemann, London.

ARIAS, PAOLO ENRICO 1952 *Skopas.* Rome: L'Erma di Bretschneider.
ARIAS, PAOLO ENRICO 1966 "Skopas." Volume 7, pages 364–369, in *Enciclopedia dell'arte antica, classica e orientale.* Rome: Istituto della Enciclopedia Italiana.
ASHMOLE, BERNARD 1967 "Skopas." Volume 13, columns 57–62, in *Encyclopedia of World Art.* New York, Toronto, and London: McGraw.
BERVE, HELMUT, and GRUBEN, GOTTFRIED 1963 Pages 354–357 in *Greek Temples, Theatres and Shrines.* New York: Abrams. Photographs by Max Hirmer.
DINSMOOR, W. B., Sr. (1950)1975 *The Architecture of Ancient Greece: An Account of its Historic Development.* Reprint. London: Batsford. Originally published as a third edition of W. J. Anderson and R. P. Spiers, *The Architecture of Ancient Greece and Rome.* London: Batsford.
DUGAS, CHARLES ET AL. 1924 *Le Sanctuaire d'Aléa Athéna à Tégée au IVe siècle.* Paris: Geuthner.
LEHMANN, PHYLLIS WILLIAMS 1973 *Skopas in Samothrace.* Northampton, Mass.: Smith College.
LEHMANN, PHYLLIS WILLIAMS, and SPITTLE, DENYS 1981 *The Temenos.* Volume 5 in *Samothrace.* N.J.: Princeton University Press.
PAUSANIAS, *Description of Greece,* 3.18.8, 8.45, 4–5, 47.1.
PLINY, *Naturalis historia,* 36.5.25.
STEWART, ANDREW 1977 *Skopas of Paros.* Park Ridge, N.J.: Noyes.

SLADE, J. MORGAN

When he died unexpectedly at thirty, Jarvis Morgan Slade (1852–1882) had designed numerous commercial buildings in lower Manhattan, especially in the Soho district. Most had façades of cast iron. His Ruskinian (see JOHN RUSKIN) Victorian Gothic store at 8 Thomas Street is an official landmark. Slade launched his practice in 1873 after working for Beaux-Arts-trained Edward H. Kendall.

MARGOT GAYLE

WORKS

1874, 489 Broome Street (iron front); 1875, 8 Thomas Street (brick and iron); 1876, 147 Wooster Street (stone and iron); 1881, 88 Franklin Street (iron front); 1882, 654 Broadway (iron front); 1882, 45 Green Street (iron front); 1882, 109 Prince Street (iron front); 1882, 42 Wooster Street (brick and iron); *n.d., 685 Broadway; *n.d., Central Real Estate Association, Leonard Street; New York.

BIBLIOGRAPHY

GAYLE, MARGOT, and GILLON, EDMUND V. 1974 *Cast Iron Architecture in New York: A Photographic Survey.* New York: Dover.
"The Late Mr. J. Morgan Slade." 1882 *New York Times* Dec. 6, p. 5.
NEW YORK CITY LANDMARKS PRESERVATION COMMISSION 1973 *SOHO Cast Iron Historic District: The Designation Report.* New York: The commission.

SLOAN, SAMUEL

Samuel Sloan (1815–1884), "Architect of Philadelphia," was born in Beaver Dam, Pennsylvania, in the first year of "The Age of Jackson." He was an archetypical man of the time—brash, opportunistic, inventive, a quick learner and a driving worker who was hungry for success and who had, throughout his life, an abiding belief in America's destiny. He was descended from Presbyterian Irish with a tradition of carpentering and cabinetmaking, to which trades he was apprenticed. He came to Philadelphia in 1836 and began work, as a journeyman carpenter, on JOHN HAVILAND's Eastern State Penitentiary. Two years later at the new Department for the Insane of the Pennsylvania Hospital he was foreman carpenter under the architect Issac Holden. When Holden returned to England in 1838, before the building was completed, Sloan became superintendent of work and was responsible for the building's completion in 1841.

While the Department for the Insane was under construction Sloan married Mary Pennell, of an old Quaker family, and was befriended by another Quaker, young Dr. Thomas S. Kirkbride, who was America's foremost alienist and hospital consultant in the mid-nineteenth century. Kirkbride, who had followed Sloan's work at the Department for the Insane, encouraged him to become an architect and remained for the rest of his life Sloan's most constant patron. Because of Kirkbride, Sloan received thirty-two commissions for hospitals for the insane which made him an international authority on their design.

Sloan's architectural practice opened in 1849, and was an immediate success. In May of that year he won—over THOMAS U. WALTER—a competition for the public buildings of Media, Pennsylvania. The following spring Andrew M. Eastwick, millionaire industrialist of Philadelphia, chose him to design a luxurious suburban villa, "Bartram Hall" (1851), which was so to the taste of the city's mercantile aristocracy that Sloan became their favorite architect for the next decade. For them he executed residences, churches, and commercial buildings; and through them he received commissions for public buildings, schools, and charitable foundations. He also became in that decade, one of the favored church architects of the Baptist and Presbyterian denominations.

Sloan's first book, *The Model Architect* (1852–1853), initiated a series of seven works, appearing over the next eighteen years, which made Sloan one of the leading authors of architectural books in the country, and brought to him clients from every state in the union. By late summer of that year, when the first of the Kirkbride hospitals was directed to his office, Sloan had more work than he could manage and entered into partnership with John S. Stewart. For the next six years Sloan & Stewart was among the most active firms in Philadelphia, for they became the chosen architects of the city's speculative builders. As a result, Sloan was largely responsible for the early townscape of West Philadelphia and much of the commercial façade of Center City. The partnership continued until the panic of 1857–1858, when it was amicably dissolved for lack of work.

Philadelphia's economy, and Sloan's practice, had begun to revive by 1860, but in that year a political scandal incident to the competition for a new City Hall raised doubts as to his professional ethics. He never lived down the animosity this engendered, despite forming a new partnership with ADDISON HUTTON (1864–1868), and becoming a Fellow of the reorganized American Institute of Architects (1868). One of his few successes after the hiatus of the Civil War was publication of *The Architectural Review and American Builder's Journal,* which Sloan edited between 1868 and 1870. This was the first periodical in the United States exclusively devoted to architecture. He also won second prize in both Philadelphia Centennial competitions, but such recognition was exceptional, for his practice in Pennsylvania steadily declined after 1870. Outside of Pennsylva-

nia, however, particularly in the reconstruction South, Sloan retained his prominence and received numerous commissions. When practice in Philadelphia became unprofitable Sloan moved his office to Raleigh, North Carolina. He had been there a year, supervising construction of the Western State Asylum (1875–1884) in Morganton, North Carolina, when he suffered a stroke and died, on July 18, 1884.

Ironically, Sloan died just as a truly "American Architecture," for which he had called all of his life, was beginning to appear. In planning Sloan was a "functionalist" long before that word was coined, but his visual vocabulary contained too many debased cliches from a century of revivalism. As a consequence his many contributions to the development of American architecture were quickly forgotten or attributed to other men.

HAROLD N. COOLEDGE, JR.

WORKS

1851, Bartram Hall, West Philadelphia, Pa. 1851–1866, Eighteen Public Schools, Philadelphia. 1852, Alabama Insane Hospital (now Bryce Hospital), Tuscaloosa. 1853, Masonic Temple, Philadelphia. 1854–1861, Longwood Villa, Natchez, Miss. 1855, Bennett and Co. Store (Tower Hall); 1856, Joseph Harrison, Jr., Town Mansion; Philadelphia. 1856–1859, Department for Males, Pennsylvania Hospital for the Insane, West Philadelphia, Pa. 1866, Horticultural Hall, Philadelphia. 1875–1884, Western State Hospital for the Insane, Morgantown, N.C.

BIBLIOGRAPHY

EDMUNDS, FRANKLIN DAVENPORT (1745–1845)1913–1933 *The Public School Buildings of the City of Philadelphia.* 7 vols. Philadelphia: Privately printed.

COOLEDGE, HAROLD N., JR. 1960 "A Sloan Check List." *Journal of the Society of Architectural Historians.* 19, Mar.:34–38.

COOLEDGE, HAROLD N., JR. 1964 "Samuel Sloan and the 'Philadelphia Plan.'" *Journal of the Society of Architectural Historians* 23, Oct.:151–154.

GLEASON, F. (editor) 1854 "The Eastwick Villa." Volume 5 in *Gleason's Drawing Room Companion.* Boston: Gleason.

HERSEY, GEORGE L. 1959 "Godey's Choice," *Journal of the Society of Architectural Historians* 28, Oct.:104–111.

KIRKBRIDE, THOMAS S. (1854)1880 *On the Construction, Organization, and General Arrangements of Hospitals for the Insane.* Philadelphia: Lippincott.

The Presbyterian Church in Philadelphia. 1895 Philadelphia: Allen, Lane & Scott.

SLOAN, SAMUEL (1852–1853)1873 *The Model Architect: A Series of Original Designs for Cottages, Villas, Suburban Residences, etc.* 4th ed. Philadelphia: Lippincott.

SLOAN, SAMUEL (1859a)1867 *City and Suburban Architecture: Containing Numerous Designs and Details for Public Edifices, Private Residences and Mercantile Buildings . . .* 2d ed. Philadelphia: Lippincott.

SLOAN, SAMUEL (1859b)1873 *Sloan's Constructive Architecture: A Guide to the Practical Builder and Mechanic, in Which is Contained a Series of Designs for Domes, Roofs and Spires . . .* 3d ed. Philadelphia: Lippincott.

SLOAN, SAMUEL (1861a)1870 *Sloan's Homestead Architecture, Containing Forty Designs for Villas, Cottages, and Farm Houses, With Essays on Style, Construction, Landscape Gardening, Furniture, etc.* 3d ed. Philadelphia: Lippincott.

SLOAN, SAMUEL (1861b)1868 *American Houses, A Variety of Designs for Rural Buildings.* 2d ed. Philadelphia: Baird.

SLOAN, SAMUEL 1873 *Description of Design and Drawings for the Proposed Centennial Buildings, To be Erected in Fairmount Park . . .* Philadelphia: King & Baird.

SLOAN, SAMUEL 1868 *Specifications of the Worksmanship and Materials to be Used in the Erection and Construction of the Western State Asylum for the Insane: at Morganton, Burke Country, North Carolina.* Philadelphia: Lippincott.

SLOAN, SAMUEL, and LUKENS, CHARLES J. (editors) 1868–1870 *The Architectural Review and American Builder's Journal.*

WEBSTER, RICHARD J. (editor) 1976 *Philadelphia Preserved: Catalog of the Historic American Building Survey.* Philadelphia: Temple University Press.

WHITWELL, WILLIAM L. 1975 *The Heritage of Longwood.* Jackson: University Press of Mississippi.

YARNELL, ELIZABETH BIDDLE 1974 *Addison Hutton: Quaker Architect, 1834–1916.* Philadelphia: Art Alliance Press.

SMARANDESCU, PAUL

Paul Smarandescu (1881–1945) graduated from the School of Architecture in Bucharest in 1903 and went on to study at the Ecole des Beaux-Arts, from which he graduated in 1906. His architecture expresses his personal view of Rumanian traditional architecture. He designed many residences, sanatoriums, hotels, and banks and restored old architectural monuments.

CONSTANTIN MARIN MARINESCU

WORKS

1913, Hotel Casino, Busteni, Rumania. 1926–1930, Informatia Bucarestiuli Headquarters, Bucharest. 1929–1930, Hotel Park, Sinaia, Rumania. 1931, Urban Renewal, University Square; 1931, Urban Renewal, Victoria Plaza; 1932–1933, Ministry of Electric Power; 1934–1935, Apartment Building, 27 Boulevard Magheru; 1942, Urban Renewal, Palace; Bucharest.

BIBLIOGRAPHY

IONESCU, GRIGORE 1965 Volume 2 in *Istoria Arhitecturii in Romania.* Bucharest: Editura Academiei Republicii Romañe.

IONESCU, GRIGORE 1969 *Arhitectura in Romania: Perioda anilor 1944-1969.* Bucharest: Editura Academiei Republicii Socialiste Romańia.

IONESCU, GRIGORE 1972 "Saptezeci si cinci de ani de la infiintarea invatamintului de arhitectura din Romania." *Arhitectura* 20:35-42.

MAMBRIANI, ALBERTO 1969 *L'Architettura Moderna nei Paesi Balcanici.* Bologna, Italy: Capelli.

PATRULIUS, RADU 1973-1974 "Contributii Romanesti in Arhitectura Anilor '30." *Arhitectura* 21, no. 6:44-52; 22, no. 1: 53-59.

SASARMAN, GHEORGHE 1972 "Inceputurile gindirii teoretice in arhitectura românešca (1860-1916)." *Arhitectura* 20, no. 6:44-46.

SMEATON, JOHN

John Smeaton (1724-1792) was the foremost British civil engineer of the eighteenth century in the days before JOHN RENNIE and THOMAS TELFORD. He did much to establish professional standards and was the leading member of the Society of Civil Engineers founded in 1771.

Smeaton was born in Austhorpe, near Leeds, where his father was an attorney. Though he embarked on legal studies in his father's office and then in London, he soon dropped them and became, for a time, a scientific instrument maker. He also frequented meetings of the Royal Society and contributed papers describing his own researches, notably on the power of wind and water to turn mills. He was elected a fellow in 1753. By then his interest was turning more to engineering. The following year he made a study tour of harbors, canals, and mills in the Netherlands.

On the recommendation of the president of the Royal Society, Smeaton undertook the rebuilding of the Eddystone Lighthouse (1756-1759) near Plymouth, England, a formidable task on account of the extreme exposure of the Eddystone rocks. He completed it in exemplary manner, using dovetailed or keyed blocks of stone throughout to resist the wave action and personally devising and supervising every detail of the construction. He later wrote a full account of it, including a description of his experiments to determine a suitable hydraulic mortar mix.

Until ill health forced him to curtail his activities, Smeaton produced large numbers of reports and designs for mills, canals, drainage schemes, harbors, and bridges. Four major bridges were built to his designs, three in Scotland and one in England. All were of stone arch construction with multiple spans and with circular rings of masonry ornamenting the spandrels above the intermediate piers. His chief immediate successor was his pupil and assistant William Jessop, but his influence on later generations was much wider through the posthumous publication of his collected reports.

ROWLAND MAINSTONE

WORKS

1756-1759, Eddystone Lighthouse (rebuilding; upper part re-erected on Plymouth Hoe in 1882), near Plymouth, England. 1763-1766, Colstream Bridge, Scotland. 1777-1780, Hexham Bridge (rebuilt to same design after foundations were flooded in 1782), England.

BIBLIOGRAPHY

SKEMPTON, A. W. (editor) n.d. *The Works of John Smeaton.* Forthcoming publication.

SMILES, SAMUEL (1861)1968 Volume 2 in *Lives of the Engineers.* Reprint. Newton Abbot, England: David & Charles.

SMEATON, JOHN (1791)1813 *A Narrative of the Building . . . of the Eddystone Lighthouse.* Reprint. London: Longmans.

SMEATON, JOHN (1797)1837 *Reports of the Late John Smeaton, FRS.* 2d ed. 2 vols. London: Taylor.

SMIRKE, ROBERT

Robert Smirke (1780-1867) is generally remembered as a Greek Revivalist, the architect of the British Museum (1823-1846). But his reputation as the most successful architect of the Regency period was due to his proven ability as businessman and builder rather than to his popularity as a stylist. His father, Robert Smirke Sr., was a talented artist and a prominent figure in the Royal Academy. Through him, he was able to build up a set of powerful patrons—notably the Earl of Lonsdale, Earl Bathurst, and Sir Robert Peel—and an influential architectural clientele. Smirke, a Tory architect, wore a political label in much the same way as JAMES GIBBS and HENRY HOLLAND. His patrons were almost exclusively Tory at a time when the Whigs were in the political wilderness. His rise to fame was therefore astonishingly swift. A few unhappy months in the office of Sir JOHN SOANE; training in the Royal Academy Schools, with private coaching from GEORGE DANCE THE YOUNGER; five years travel in France, Italy, Greece, and Germany; and the young architect was ready to set up practice in 1805. The next year he secured his first important commission, Lowther Castle, Westmorland (1806-1811). Three years later his revolutionary Covent Garden Theatre (1808-1810) was the talk of fashionable London. He thus made his name with one design, like JAMES WYATT with the Pantheon. And in 1815 he reached the top of the profession when he joined JOHN NASH and Soane as one of the three government architects attached to the Office of Works. Nash and Soane were already in their sixties; Smirke was only thirty-four. He became an associate of the Royal Academy in 1808, a member in 1811, and treasurer in 1820. A knighthood followed naturally in 1832, and the Gold Medal of the Royal Institute of British Architects in 1853. He retired from practice in 1845, and from the academy in 1859.

In sheer bulk, Smirke's practice more than matched up to those of Nash, Soane or any of the Wyatts. Apart from a series of unexecuted designs, he worked on more than twenty churches, more than fifty public buildings, and more than sixty private houses. It was even rumored that he turned down jobs worth less than £10 thousand. Influence made him architect to the Royal Mint in 1807. An expanding reputation made him surveyor to the Inner Temple (1819) and the Duchy of Lancaster (1820). And in the 1830s he united the functions of architect, surveyor, and planner as architect to the London Bridge Approaches. His office was large and efficient, and his pupils included WILLIAM BURN, C. R. COCKERELL, LEWIS VULLIAMY, and his younger brother SYDNEY SMIRKE. When he died in 1867, he left £90,000.

Besides being a fashionable stylist and an establishment architect *par excellence,* Smirke was a pioneer of cast-iron and concrete construction at a time when the functions of architect and engineer were not readily distinguishable. He seems to have been the first architect to rationalize the various eighteenth-century systems of estimating, measuring, and cost accounting; and the first to employ a new type of assistant, the quantity surveyor. He became an arbiter in all matters of professional conduct. And he was called in so often to rescue a building in a state of *rigor mortis* that he came to be known as "the Dr. Baillie of architects." At Millbank Penitentiary, London (1817–1822), he was the first to employ concrete foundations, mixed in measured quantities, and used for load-bearing purposes. The idea was partly JOHN RENNIE's; in any case lime concrete had already been used independently in France. But Smirke must be credited as the first British architect to demonstrate the effectiveness of the new technique on a large scale. He repeated his performance, with still greater *éclat,* at the London Custom House (1825–1827). He was probably also the first to use load-bearing cast-iron beams in British domestic (as opposed to industrial) architecture. At Cirencester Park, Gloucestershire (1810–1811)—during a wartime timber shortage—he rebuilt the garden front, using 30-foot cast-iron girders, instead of the customary oak beams. In the King's Library of the British Museum, thirteen years later, the girders were up to fifty feet in length.

According to T. L. DONALDSON, Smirke could please "men whom it was proverbially impossible to please." Certainly Lonsdale found him "ingenious, modest and gentlemanly in his manners." The extent of his patrons' confidence can be measured in two types of public building which Smirke made very much his own: the London clubhouse and the provincial court. Apart from his castellated scheme for Carlisle (1810–1812) and his Ionic design at Gloucester (1814–1816), all Smirke's county courts are very similar in plan. Dignified and economical, his work at Hereford (1815–1817) and Perth (1816–1819) is gravely Doric, at Shrewsbury (1836–1837) perfunctorily Italianate, at Lincoln (1823–1830) cheaply Gothic, and at Maidstone (1824–1828) plainly astylar. But at Bristol (1824–1827) he came near to achieving the kind of richness which is often christened *néo-grec.* As for the London clubs, neither CHARLES BARRY, Nash, nor DECIMUS BURTON deserves to be remembered as the architect of London's clubland so much as Smirke and his younger brother. The astylar reticence and functional planning of Robert's United Services Club (1817) started a fashion that was copied elsewhere, and which he elaborated with equal success at the Union Club and Royal College of Physicians (1822–1825; now Canada House) in Trafalgar Square; and at the Carlton Club (1833–1836) and the Oxford and Cambridge Club (1836–1837), both in Pall Mall.

Smirke's Gothic Revival castles, notably Lowther (1806–1811), Eastnor (1812–1815), and Kinfauns (1820–1822), should really be judged as a series of scenic devices. Lowther, for example, had two separate façades, one monastic, the other baronial. This emphasis on pictorial values makes questions of authenticity or accuracy largely irrelevant. Indeed, the essence of Lowther's "majestic pile . . . the stately walls, the pinnacles, the broad embattled brow," admired by Wordsworth and Southey, lay in the striking manipulation of architectural masses, the superb scenic qualities that now make it peculiarly suitable as a derelict folly. His tentative essays in Tudoresque and Jacobethan, such as Wilton Castle, Yorkshire (c.1810), or Drayton Manor, Staffordshire (1831–1835), were soon to be eclipsed by JEFFRY WYATVILLE and Barry. Smirke's Gothic detailing often lacks conviction. What Charles Lamb called "Gothicisings and Smirkefyings" at the Inner Temple (1816–1838) were poor examples of a poor period: Picturesque Gothic without the justification of a Picturesque setting. The fact that his schemes for rebuilding Windsor Castle (1823–1824) and the Houses of Parliament (1834–1835) were never executed can hardly be regarded as a matter for regret.

Smirke's medievalizing was therefore seldom

Smirke.
Covent Garden Theatre.
London.
1808–1810

more than a profitable blind alley. His Grecian designs, on the other hand, form an integral part of the neoclassical revolution. Brought up by Dance in the JACQUES-FRANÇOIS BLONDEL—MARC-ANTOINE LAUGIER tradition, he believed the architect had a twofold function: to rediscover pure classical forms and to adapt them to new circumstances. Of course, both functions pulled in opposite directions. That was the crux of the neoclassical dilemma: the battle between archeology and invention. Smirke recognized the problem, even if he failed to solve it. Antibaroque and anti-Palladian, his most significant designs assume a disparate, geometrical form consonant with the ethos of the Picturesque. "Rectangular shapes," he wrote, "are the component materials of every modern work." A. W. N. PUGIN called it "the New Square Style of Mr. Smirke." Unfortunately Smirke was too prolific to live up to his own ideals. The promise of

Covent Garden Theatre was not fulfilled. In its emphasis on geometrical forms, its juxtaposition of blocks independently conceived, its almost cubic simplicity, Covent Garden embodied that transition from baroque coherence to Picturesque disparity which lay at the heart of neoclassicism. As a young man, Smirke stood in the vanguard of the new international style. But it was the paraphernalia of revivalism rather than the compositional possibilities of the new idiom which won immediate recognition. And Smirke spent the remainder of his career catering for the market he had helped to create. Four of his country houses—Kinmount, Dumfriesshire (1812), Whittingham, Haddingtonshire (1818), Luton Hoo, Bedfordshire (c.1816–1842), and Normanby Park, Lincolnshire (1821)—go some way toward creating what might almost be described as a Greco-cubic style. Contemporaries sometimes simply called it "modern." But in most cases decoration from the Ilissus temple, the Theseion or the Erechtheion is merely grafted on to Georgian stock. The British Museum was a triumphant performance, a magnificent essay in the adaptation and integration of antique forms. But his Commissioners' churches are dull. And in general Smirke's enormous influence channelled the Greek Revival away from the geometrical abstraction he learnt from Dance and Soane and into the arid wastes of copyism. His architecture of understatement was too easily multiplied. Nevertheless, Smirke's position in the hierarchy of English classicists is secure. In 1846 his greatest pupil, C. R. Cockerell, wrote to him: "My dear maestro . . . you are . . . truly the grandfather of all my productions."

J. MORDAUNT CROOK

WORKS

*1806–1811, Lowther Castle, Westmorland, England. *1808–1810, Covent Garden Theatre; 1809–1811, Royal Mint (additions); London. c.1810, Wilton Castle, Yorkshire, England. 1810–1811, Cirencester Park (additions), Gloucestershire, England. 1810–1812, County Courts, Carlisle, England. 1812, Kinmount, Dumfriesshire, Scotland. 1812–1815, Eastnor Castle, Herefordshire, England. 1812–1816, Eden Bridge, Carlisle, England. 1814–1816, Shire Hall, Gloucester, England. 1815–1817, Shire Hall, Hereford, England. 1816–1819, County Buildings and Jail, Perth, Scotland. 1816–1819, Landsdowne House (additions); 1816–1838, Inner Temple (additions); London. c.1816–1842, Luton Hoo (additions; since altered), Bedfordshire, England. 1817, United Services Club (later rebuilt), London. 1817, Wellington Testimonial, Dublin. 1817–1822, Millbank Penitentiary (additions), London. c.1818, Armley House, Yorkshire, England. 1818, Whittingham House, Haddingtonshire, Scotland. 1820–1822, Kinfauns Castle, Perthshire, Scotland. *1821, Eden Hall, Cumberland, England. 1821, Normanby Park, Lincoln-

Smirke.
British Museum.
London.
1823–1846

shire, England. 1821–1822, Saint George, Bristol, England. 1822–1824, Saint Anne; *1822–1824, Saint James; London. 1822–1825, Saint Philip, Salford, England. 1822–1825, Union Club and Royal College of Physicians; 1823–1824, Saint Mary; *1823–1829, General Post Office; London. 1823–1830, County Courts, Lincoln, England. 1823–1846, British Museum, London. 1824, Edmond Castle, Cumberland, England. 1824–1827, Council House, Bristol, England. 1824–1827, Temple Church (restoration), London. 1824–1828, County Courts, Maidstone, England. 1825–1827, Custom House (rebuilding), London. 1828, Erskine House, Renfrewshire, Scotland. 1829–1835, King's College; London. 1829–1835, Somerset House (completion of river front); 1829–1839, London Bridge Approaches; London. 1830–1832, York Minster (restoration), England. 1831–1832, All Saints, Nottinghamshire, England. *1831–1835, Drayton Manor, Staffordshire, England. 1833–1836, Carlton Club (later rebuilt); 1834–1837, Temporary Houses of Parliament; 1836–1837, Oxford and Cambridge Club (with Sydney Smirke); London. *1836–1837, Shire Hall, Shrewsbury, England.

BIBLIOGRAPHY

CROOK, J. MORDAUNT 1965–1966 "Sir Robert Smirke: A Pioneer of Concrete Construction." *Transactions of the Newcomen Society* 38:5–22.
CROOK, J. MORDAUNT 1967 "Sir Robert Smirke: A Centenary Florilegium." *Architectural Review* 142:208–210.
CROOK, J. MORDAUNT 1972 *The British Museum.* London: Penguin; New York: Praeger.
CROOK, J. MORDAUNT, and PORT, M. H. 1973 Volume 6 of *The History of the King's Works.* London: H. M. Stationery Office.

SMIRKE, SYDNEY

Sydney Smirke (1798–1877) was the youngest brother of ROBERT SMIRKE, and he owed much of his professional success to family influence and inherited Tory patronage. He was, however, a scholarly architect in both Renaissance and Gothic styles: his restoration of York Minster (1840–1845) was executed with learning and restraint; and his three London clubhouses mark the triumph of Victorian Renaissance over Regency neoclassicism. His contributions to the housing of London's retail trade (Oxford Street Pantheon, 1833–1834; Exeter Change, Strand, 1843–1844) were novel solutions to novel problems, and his great domed Reading Room (1854–1857) at the British Museum, London, remains one of the outstanding mid-Victorian achievements in the field of cast-iron construction. Smirke was professor of architecture at the Royal Academy from 1861 to 1865.

J. MORDAUNT CROOK

WORKS

*1833–1834, Oxford Street Pantheon (reconstruction); 1835–1838, Oxford and Cambridge Club (with Robert Smirke); 1838–1846, Bedlam Hospital (extension); London. 1840–1845, York Minster (restoration), England. *1843–1844, Exeter Change, Strand; 1843–1845, Conservative Club (with GEORGE BASEVI); *1845–1856, Carlton Club; London. 1854–1856, Brookwood Cemetery, Woking, England. 1854–1857, Round Reading Room, British Museum; 1859–1874, Burlington House (Royal Academy; additions); London.

BIBLIOGRAPHY

CROOK, J. MORDAUNT (1976)1977 "Sydney Smirke: The Architecture of Compromise." Pages 50–65 in Jane Fawcett (editor), *Seven Victorian Architects.* University Park: Pennsylvania State University Press.

SMITH, CHLOETHIEL WOODARD

Chloethiel Woodard Smith (1910–) was born in Peoria, Illinois, and earned degrees in architecture and city planning at the University of Oregon and the University of Washington. She served as chief of research and planning for the Federal Housing Administration before establishing her own general practice firm in 1945.

EUGENIE L. BIRCH

WORKS

1955–1975, Chestnut Lodge Mental Hospital, Rockville, Md. 1959, American Embassy Chancery and Residence, Asunción. 1962, Washington Channel Waterfront Master Plan. 1964, Harcourt, Brace and World Store and Executive Offices, New York. 1968, Capitol Park Urban Community, Washington. 1968, La Clede Town, St. Louis, Mo.

BIBLIOGRAPHY

TORRE, SUSANA (editor) 1977 *Women in American Architecture: A Historic and Contemporary Perspective.* New York: Whitney Library of Design.

SMITH, FRANCIS

Francis Smith (1672–1738), the leading master builder of midland England in the earlier eighteenth century, was born in Staffordshire. He moved to Warwick in 1697, where, with his brother William, he rebuilt the parish church to the designs of William Wilson. Later he worked for THOMAS ARCHER and JAMES GIBBS, whose influence is keenly felt in Smith's country houses as he moves from the rather gauche baroque grandeur of Stoneleigh Abbey (1714–1726), through the Archeresque exuberance of Chicheley Hall

(1719–1721), to the assured Palladianism of Sutton Scarsdale (1724). Smith's churches are built to a plain sub-Wrennish formula; his one civic building—the refined Palladian courthouse at Warwick (1725) is reminiscent of MICHELE SANMICHELI's Palazzo Canossa. "Smith of Warwick" had a reputation for economy and reliability—hence his extensive employment: more than sixty houses and other buildings can be confidently attributed to him. His son William continued the practice.

ANDOR GOMME

WORKS

c.1695–1700, Umberslade Hall, Warwickshire, England. 1708–1710, Clifton Campville Hall, Staffordshire, England. 1714–1726, Stoneleigh Abbey; 1716, Newbold Revel Hall; Warwickshire, England. 1719–1721, Chicheley Hall, Buckinghamshire. 1719–1726, Saint Modwen's Church, Burton-upon-Trent, Staffordshire, England. *1720–1733, Capesthorne Hall, Cheshire, England. c.1720–1724, Saint Peter-at-Arches Church, Lincoln, England. 1720–1731, Ditchley House (with James Gibbs), Oxfordshire, England. 1723–1726, Ombersley Court, Worcestershire, England. 1724, Sutton Scarsdale, Derbyshire, England. 1724–1726, Temple Balsall Hospital, Warwickshire, England. 1725–1726, Sibson Church, Leicestershire, England. 1725, Courthouse, Warwickshire, England. 1726, Davenport Hall; 1727–1729, Kinlet Hall; 1730, Mawley Hall; 1731, Berwick House; 1735–1736, Brogyntyn; Shropshire, England.

BIBLIOGRAPHY

COLVIN, H. M. 1972–1973 "Francis Smith of Warwick 1672–1738." *Warwickshire History* 2, no. 2:3–13.
DOWNES, KERRY 1966 *English Baroque Architecture.* London: Zwemmer.
GOMME, ANDOR 1981 "The Genesis of Sutton Scarsdale." *Architectural History* 24. Forthcoming article.
HUSSEY, CHRISTOPHER (1955)1965 *English Country Houses: Early Georgian, 1715–1760.* 2d ed. London: Country Life.
LEE-MILNE, JAMES 1970 *English Country Houses: Baroque, 1685–1715.* London: Hamlyn.

SMITH, GEORGE

An accomplished civic architect, predominantly in the Greek style, George Smith (1783–1869), born in Aldenham, England, was articled (1797–1802) to ROBERT F. BRETTINGHAM and was clerk to JAMES WYATT, DANIEL ASHER ALEXANDER, and Charles Beazley. He exhibited at the Royal Academy (1801–1849) and also worked as a surveyor.

R. WINDSOR LISCOMBE

WORKS

1810?, Colney Lodge, Hertfordshire, England. 1819–1822, Mitcham Church (reconstruction), Surrey, England. *1820–1826, The Royal Exchange (rebuilt entrance front and tower); *1822, Whittington's Almshouses, Highgate; *1823–1824, Saint Paul's School, Saint Paul's Churchyard; 1825, York Square, Stepney; *1827–1828, The Corn Exchange (with ARTHUR BOWYER CLAYTON), Mark Lane; *1829–1832, Mercers' School, College Hill; London. 1829–1833, Courthouse and Town Hall, Saint Albans, Hertfordshire, England. 1838, Saint Thomas's Church (with W. Barnes), Stepney; 1840, Saint George's Wesleyan Chapel, Stepney; *1841–1844, London Bridge Railway Station (with HENRY ROBERTS); *1842–1843, Gresham College, Basinghall Street; London. 1848–1849, Newlands, Copthorne, Sussex, England.

BIBLIOGRAPHY

DARLEY, GILLIAN 1978 "York Square Rehabilitation." *Architect's Journal* 168:678.
STRATTON, ARTHUR 1917 "The Royal Exchange, London." *Architectural Review* 42:26–29, 45–50.

SMITH, GEORGE WASHINGTON

A fascination with images of the past was an essential concern of American domestic architecture of the 1920s, and one of its principal exponents was the California architect George Washington Smith (1876–1930). His national reputation was based upon his designs for upper middle class suburban villas in the Spanish, Mediterranean, Islamic, and medieval modes. Born in East Liberty, Pennsylvania, his early education was at the Lawrenceville Scientific School. In 1894, he entered the School of Architecture at Harvard University, but because of family financial difficulties he was unable to complete his degree. After leaving Harvard, he entered the Philadelphia architectural firm of Newman, Woodman, and Harris as a draftsman. In 1912, he and his wife went to France where he studied painting. At the onset of World War I, he returned to the United States, and in 1916 he built his first house in Montecito, California. In 1919, he established his architectural office in Montecito, and between 1919 and 1930 he received numerous commissions for suburban and country villas in and around Santa Barbara, in the Los Angeles area, south of San Francisco, and elsewhere.

DAVID GEBHARD

WORKS

1916, G. W. Smith (Heberton) House; 1920, Parshall House; 1921, Wright House; Montecito, Calif. 1922–1924, Lobero Theater, Santa Barbara, Calif. 1922, Steedman House, Montecito, Calif. 1922, Daily News Building, Santa Barbara, Calif. 1922, Stewart House; 1923, Wagner House; 1924, Robinson House; Montecito,

Calif. 1924, Vincent House, Pebble Beach, Calif. 1924–1925, Roman Catholic Church, Ajo, Ariz. 1925, Jackling House, Woodside, Calif. 1925–1926, Bryce House, Hope Ranch, Calif. 1925, Kern House, Beverly Hills, Calif. 1926–1927, Heller House, Atherton, Calif. 1926–1928, Maverick House, San Antonio, Tex. 1927–1928, Johnson House, Montecito, Calif. 1928–1929, Cheney House, Fisher's Island, N.Y. 1929–1930, Culley House, Montecito, Calif.

BIBLIOGRAPHY

Boyd, John Taylor 1930 "Houses Showing a Distinguished Simplicity." *Arts and Decoration* 33 no. 6:57–60, 112.

Gebhard, David 1964 *George Washington Smith, 1876–1930: The Spanish Colonial Revival in California.* Santa Barbara: University of California.

Gebhard, David 1980 "George Washington Smith." Pages 88–111 in Wayne McCall, Herbe Andree, Noel Young, and David Gebhard, *Santa Barbara Architecture, from Spanish Colonial to Modern.* Santa Barbara, Calif.: Capra.

Morrow, Irving F. 1922 "Architecture with a Personality." *Architect and Engineer* 71 no. 3:47–87.

Morrow, Irving F. 1924 "A Dialogue Which Touches Upon Mr. Smith's Architecture." *Architect and Engineer* 78 no. 1:53–97.

Newcomb, Rexford 1922 "Some Spanish Residences in Southern California by George Washington Smith, Architect." *Western Architect* 31 no. 5:58–61.

SMITH, IVOR

Born in Leigh-on-Sea, Essex, England, Ivor Smith (1926–) attended the Bartlett School of Architecture, University of London (1943–1945); Cambridge University School of Architecture (1948–1950); and the Architectural Association School, London (1950–1952). He became senior architect in the City Architect's Department, Sheffield, Yorkshire (1952–1961). Since 1966, he has practiced with Cailey Hutton. Smith has also taught extensively.

Smith had the gift to explain in plain language the functional principles underlying the architectural organization of his buildings—how the bedrooms faced east catching the morning sun, how the living room faced south capturing the afternoon sun. Smith's work has expanded to meet the changing critical demands and now bespeaks an urban context. He has grown weary of functionalism and now advocates a porous, loose-fitting, more accountable architecture.

Christopher Fawcett

WORKS

1961, Park Hill Neighbourhood Development, Sheffield, England. 1966, Housing, Heston Grange, Middlesex, England. 1967, Two Houses and Studio, Ewelme, Oxford. 1969, Old People's and Family Housing, Dibleys, Blewbury, Berkshire, England. 1970, Suburban Housing, Rushey Mead, Leicester, England. 1971, King Street (stage 1 of redevelopment), Cambridge. 1977, Greenleys Activity Centre, Milton Keynes, Buckinghamshire, England. 1977, King Street (stage 2 of redevelopment), Cambridge. 1977, Somerville College (alterations and additions), Oxford. 1977, SSM Priory, Willen, Buckinghamshire, England. 1979, Old People's Housing, Saint Peter's Vicarage, Poole, Dorset, England. 1981, Housing (five-hundred dwellings), Exwick Farm, Exeter, Devon, England.

BIBLIOGRAPHY

Smith, Ivor 1966 "Louisiana Museum of Modern Art." *Journal of the Royal Institute of British Architects* 73, no. 5:214–221.

Smith, Ivor 1967 "Architect's Approach to Architecture." *Journal of the Royal Institute of British Architects* 74, no. 7:271–280.

Smith, Ivor 1975–1976 "Architecture—A Celebration." *New Universities Quarterly* 30:470–489.

SMITH, JAMES

James Smith (c.1645–1731) was a leading figure in Scottish architecture at the end of the seventeenth century and played a part, as yet not clearly defined, in the genesis of British Palladianism. Like so many Scottish architects, he was the son of a master mason and eventually followed the same trade himself. But originally he "was bred to the Church," and was educated abroad, perhaps as a candidate for the Catholic priesthood. He certainly traveled on the continent as a young man and in particular visited Italy. By 1679 he was established in Edinburgh, where he married the daughter of Robert Mylne (see Robert Mylne and Family), master mason to the Scottish Crown. He was also in touch with William Bruce, the leading Scottish architect of his day, and in 1683 succeeded Bruce as surveyor or overseer of the royal works in Scotland.

As surveyor of the royal works in Scotland Smith's chief responsibility was the maintenance of Holyroodhouse, where in 1688 he fitted up the former abbey church as a Chapel Royal for King James II. He is best known, however, as a designer of country houses in the classical style recently introduced into Scotland by Bruce. Of these the most important were Hamilton Palace (1693–701); Melville House (1697–1700), Yester House (c.1700–1715), and Dalkeith House (1702–1710). Although these are handsome buildings with pedimented or pilastered façades, they are scarcely Palladian and it is only in his surviving drawings that Smith's precocious interest in the architecture of ANDREA PALLADIO can be demonstrated. There is evidence that these drawings passed into the possession of COLEN CAMPBELL, the leading publicist of English Palladianism, and reason to think that Campbell may have been in contact with Smith at the outset of his career as an architect. Certainly Smith's Palladian drawings appear to antedate any comparable designs by Campbell or any other British architect of the eighteenth century.

H. M. COLVIN

WORKS

*1688, Chapel Royal, Holyroodhouse; 1688–1690, Canongate Church; Edinburgh. c.1690, Whitehall (now Newhailes) House, Midlothian, Scotland. *1693–1701, Hamilton Palace, Lanarkshire, Scotland. 1697–1700, Melville House, Fife, Scotland. c.1700–1715, Yester House, East Lothian, Scotland. 1702–1710, Dalkeith House, Midlothian, Scotland.

BIBLIOGRAPHY

COLVIN, H. M. 1974 "A Scottish Origin for English Palladianism?" *Architectural History* 17:5–13.

SMITH, JAMES KELLUM

Born in Towanda, Pennsylvania, James Kellum Smith (1893–1963) received a B.A. from Amherst College in 1915 and an M.S. from the University of Pennsylvania in 1919. He won the John Stewardson Fellowship in 1919 and the Prix de Rome in 1920, traveling in Europe until 1924. Upon his return, he entered the firm of McKim, Mead, AND White in 1924, becoming a partner in 1929. He was the last surviving partner of the firm before his death.

STEVEN MCLEOD BEDFORD

WORKS

1931, City Hall, Schenectady, N.Y. 1935, United States Army Infantry School, Fort Benning, Ga. 1939, Kirby Theatre, Amherst College, Mass. 1948–1954, Dormitory Groups, University of Connecticut, Storrs. 1948–1962, American Military Cemetery, Florence, Italy.

BIBLIOGRAPHY

BEDFORD, STEVEN, and NEVINS, DEBORAH 1980 *Between Tradition and Modernism.* New York: National Academy of Design.
KOYL, G. S. (editor) 1955 *American Architects Directory.* Washington: American Institute of Architects.

SMITH, ROBERT

Robert Smith (1722–1777) was a designer and constructor of buildings. He was the leading pro-fessional in Philadelphia when it was the metropolis of Colonial America. Smith's designs were executed as far away as Virginia and Rhode Island. In the line of engineering he made plans for a bridge over the troublesome Schuylkill (not built) and the underwater defenses of the Delaware River (executed, and with great effect).

Born in Dalkeith Parish, Lothian, Scotland, the son of a baker, Smith was probably recruited by WILLIAM ADAM while working at Dalkeith Park. In any case, he appeared in Philadelphia by early 1749 as a full-fledged journeyman house carpenter with an aptitude for design. Almost immediately successful, he built up a large practice which included most of the public buildings and many of the great mansions of the city.

At the time of his death, Smith was engaged in erecting an army barracks in Billingsport, New Jersey.

CHARLES E. PETERSON

BIBLIOGRAPHY

GARVAN, BEATRICE 1976 "Robert Smith, 1722–1777." Pages 31–32 in *Philadelphia: Three Centuries of American Art.* The Philadelphia Museum.
JACKSON, JOSEPH 1923 Pages 66–69 in *Early Philadelphia Architects and Engineers.* Philadelphia.
PETERSON, CHARLES E. 1953 "Notes on Robert Smith, Architect of Carpenter's Hall." *Transactions of the American Philosophical Society* 43, part 1:119–123.
PETERSON, CHARLES E. 1981 "The Building of Christ Church, Philadelphia." In *University Hospital Antiques Show.* Philadelphia: The hospital.

SMITH, ROBERT

British-born Robert Smith (1787–1873), colonel with the Bengal Engineers, arrived in India in 1805. While in Calcutta, he built a lighthouse at Kedgeree (1808) and some buildings at Diamond Harbour (1808). In 1816, he was sent to Penang where he built Saint George's Church (1816–1819), a classical edifice. During the 1820s at Delhi, he designed the Doab Canal (1823–1830) and Saint James's Church (1828–1835). His own house there (1823?) on the Delhi Wall was much admired. Upon returning to England in 1831, he lived at Bideford and later in Italy. His houses Redcliffe (1853–1865?) at Paignton, Devon, and Château Smith (1858–?) at Nice, France, are important examples of Indian Gothic inspired by his restoration of Mogul monuments in Delhi.

RAYMOND HEAD

WORKS

*1808, Diamond Harbour (buildings); *1808, Lighthouse, Kedgeree; Calcutta. 1816–1819, Saint George's

Church, Penang, Malaysia. 1823?, Robert Smith House; 1823–1830, Doab Canal; Delhi, India. 1827?, The Abbey, Mussoorie, India. 1828–1835, Saint James's Church, Delhi, India. 1853–1865?, Redcliffe House, Paignton, Devon, England. 1858–? Château Smith, Nice, France.

BIBLIOGRAPHY

ARCHER, MILDRED 1969 *British Drawings in the India Office Library.* 2 vols. London: H. M. Stationery Office.

ARCHER, MILDRED 1972 "An Artist Engineer— Colonel Robert Smith in India (1805–1830)." *The Connoisseur* 179, Feb.:79–88.

HEAD, RAYMOND 1981 "Colonel Robert Smith C.B.: Artist, Architect and Engineer." *Country Life* May 21 & 28.

NILSSON, STEN 1968 *European Architecture in India, 1750–1850.* London: Faber.

SMITHMEYER and PELZ

John L. Smithmeyer (1832–1908) and Paul Johannes Pelz (1841–1918) began an architectural partnership in Washington, D.C., in 1873, entering a Renaissance-style design for the new Library of Congress building and winning the first prize from among a national field of competitors. Winning again when the competition was reopened in 1874, they were chosen over H. H. RICHARDSON, WILLIAM A. POTTER, THOMAS U. WALTER, and Edward Clark, architect of the Capitol.

After twelve more years of work by the firm, including alternative designs, Congress in 1886 authorized the new Library, but in 1888 it dismissed Smithmeyer and made Pelz architect with Gen. Thomas L. Casey of the U.S. Army Engineers in charge of constructing a somewhat modified "$6,000,000" version of Smithmeyer and Pelz's plan of 1886. Pelz was dismissed in 1892 and replaced by the general's son, Edward Pearce Casey, who was primarily responsible for modifications to the dome and the interior decoration of a building substantially completed in 1897.

Smithmeyer and Pelz took their case to court, enlisting the support of the American Institute of Architects in subsequent attempts to win both recognition and full payment for almost twenty years of work on the Library, their most important commission. Although its central plan was criticized as outdated at a time when large libraries were organizing their collections within specialized departments, the overall design and details of the Library of Congress were the subject of critical approval and popular admiration. Its ambitious program of sculptural and painted enrichment set a precedent followed, but never again matched, in federal buildings during the next forty years.

Smithmeyer, a native of Austria who came to this country at an early age, was the business partner of the firm, with few original designs to his credit. After serving an apprenticeship in Chicago in the 1850s, he began practice in Indianapolis, working on the old Courthouse in South Bend, Indiana, before coming to Washington, D.C., where by 1873 he had risen to the position of superintendent of public buildings in the Southern states in the office of the U.S. Supervising Architect. His partnership with Pelz remained under the name of John L Smithmeyer & Co. until after 1876, securing commissions for the new buildings at Georgetown College(1876–1881); the U.S. Soldiers Home Library (1877–1882); the Federal Army and Navy Hospital (1884) in Hot Springs, Arkansas; and the Carnegie Library and Music Hall (1887) in Allegheny, Pennsylvania. Unsuccessful in his costly attempts to win reimbursement for a building in which he apparently contemplated suicide in 1899 and without a substantial practice of his own, Smithmeyer died, destitute and embittered, in 1908.

Pelz, whose name appears on most of the firm's drawings, was clearly its principal designer. Born in Silesia (Prussia) and educated in Germany, he came to New York in 1858. The following year, he became an apprentice in the office of DETLEF LIENAU, where his associates were HENRY J. HARDENBERGH and HENRY VAN BRUNT, whom he succeeded as chief draftsman in 1864. After almost seven years with Lienau, Pelz briefly worked for HENRY FERNBACH in New York before joining the firm of Grant and Pierce in Washington, D.C., in 1867. Soon thereafter, he entered the service of the U.S. Lighthouse Board, where he remained until 1873, designing many lighthouses on the American sea and lake coasts, including those at Bodie Island, North Carolina, and Spectacle Reef, Lake Huron, Michigan. In 1873, Pelz accompanied Col. George H. Elliott on a tour of European lighthouses and illustrated a report on American lighthouses which won the Diploma of Honor at the World's Fair in Vienna.

During his trip, Pelz studied library architecture in Europe and the British Isles in preparation for the Library of Congress competition. Except for occasional essays in the American Colonial Revival, Pelz's designs relied largely on the vocabularies of Renaissance and medieval architecture in Germany, France, and Italy. The characteristics of his native land, however, remained ever present in his architectural composition and employment of materials and details.

In addition to projects undertaken in association with Smithmeyer, such as the Library of Congress and Georgetown College Buildings, Pelz individually executed a number of works. Besides the U.S. Government Hospital (1884) at Hot Springs, Arkansas, he designed the Georgetown College Medical School and the administration building of the University of Virginia's Clinic Hospital. Of his many houses in the Washington area, most notable were those for Senator Stephen Benton Elkins (1892, 1896), Senator Joseph Benson Foraker (1897), and Captain Frederick A. Miller (1900–1901). Pelz also designed several large houses in Charleston, South Carolina. Other executed works include Washington's Trinity Methodist Episcopal Church (n.d.), Grace Memorial Church (n.d.), the Aula Christi (1901) of the Chatauqua, New York, Assembly, Washington's McGill Building (1891), the Chamberlin Hotel (1890–1893) at Old Point Comfort, Virginia, and the Machinery Palace (1903) at the Louisiana Purchase Exposition (with the St. Louis firm of Widmann, Walsh, and Boisselier).

Among Pelz's ambitious but unsuccessful projects were designs for a Memorial Bridge (1886, 1896) across the Potomac in Washington, a National Gallery of History and Art, a palatial Executive Mansion (1898–1901) to take the place of the White House, and a Supreme Court building (1911) to parallel that of the Library of Congress. Failing eyesight forced the end of his active career in 1913.

C. FORD PEATROSS

WORKS

SMITHMEYER AND PELZ

1873–1892, Library of Congress; 1876–1881, Georgetown College (additions); *1877–1882, U.S. Soldiers Home Library; Washington. 1884, U.S. Army and Navy Hospital, Hot Springs, Ark. 1887, Carnegie Library and Music Hall, Allegheny, Pa.

PAUL J. PELZ

*1890–1893, Chamberlin Hotel, Old Point Comfort, Va. 1891, McGill Building; *1892, 1896, Stephen B. Elkins House; *1897, Joseph B. Foraker House; 1900–1901, Frederick A. Miller House; Washington. 1901, Aula Christi, Chautauqua, N.Y. *1903, Machinery Palace, Louisiana Purchase Exposition, St. Louis, Mo. n.d., Grace Memorial Church; *n.d., Trinity Methodist Episcopal Church; Washington.

BIBLIOGRAPHY

COLE, JOHN Y. 1972a "The Main Building of the Library of Congress, A Chronology: 1871–1965." Quarterly Journal of the Library of Congress 29, Oct.:267–269.
COLE, JOHN Y. 1972b "Smithmeyer & Pelz: Embattled Architects of the Library of Congress." Quarterly Journal of the Library of Congress 29, Oct.:282–307.
GOODE, JAMES M. 1979 Capital Losses: A Cultural History of Washington's Destroyed Buildings. Washington: Smithsonian Institution Press.
HAMLIN, TALBOT F. 1943 "Pelz, Paul Johannes." Volume 14, pages 411–412 in Dictionary of American Biography. New York: Scribner's.
HARDY, GEORGE 1972 "Georgetown University's Healy Building." Journal of the Society of Architectural Historians 31, Oct.:208–216.
HILKER, HELEN-ANNE 1980 Ten First Street, Southeast: Congress Builds a Library, 1886–1897. Washington: Library of Congress.
HOPKINS, ARCHIBALD 1906 "Smithmeyer and Pelz vs. the United States." American Architect and Building News 90, July 28:27–29.
SMALL, HERBERT (1897)1901 Handbook of the New Library of Congress. 2d ed. Boston: Curtis & Cameron.
SMITHMEYER, JOHN L. 1883 Suggestions on Library Architecture, American and Foreign, with an Examination of Mr. Wm. F. Poole's Scheme for Library Buildings. Washington: Gibson.
SMITHMEYER, JOHN L. 1906 History of the Construction of the Library of Congress. Washington: Beresford.

SMITHSON, ALISON, and SMITHSON, PETER

Alison Smithson (1928–) and Peter Smithson (1923–), who married in 1949 and established a partnership in 1950, were among the major contributors of ideas to British architecture in the 1950s and 1960s. With their Secondary School, Hunstanton, Norfolk (1954), they led a younger generation of architects toward a style which became known as Brutalism, although their work does not display all its characteristics. The Hunstanton School was notable for its Miesian (see LUDWIG MIES VAN DER ROHE) purity of structure, while their Economist Building, Saint James's Street, London (1964), set a fashion for vigorously modeled surfaces as an antidote to the then prevailing flatness and emphasized a concern for the activities of people in relation to the building.

The Smithsons have been equally influential through their books, articles, exhibitions, and lectures in which they have developed an architectural ideology based on the founding fathers of modernism but applicable to current circumstances. They have preserved their zealous enthusiasm of the 1950s for bringing art and life together and have struck a balance between didacticism and reflection. They have emphasized the quality of integrity in architecture, even at the expense of more superficial attractions, but have always shown an interest in architectural history, attending the Royal Academy School of Architecture under ALBERT E. RICHARDSON after receiving their main training at Durham University. They have always insisted on the relationship between architecture and society, rejecting EDWIN LUTYENS, for instance, as an irresponsible picture maker. Having attracted a considerable following in architectural schools in the last twenty-five years, they now seem rather isolated in the wake of recent architectural events.

ALAN POWERS

WORKS

1949–1954, Hunstanton Secondary Modern School, Norfolk, England. 1956, Sanders Garage, Bark Place, London. 1957, Watford House, Devereux Drive, Watford, Hertfordshire, England. 1960, Caro House, Frognal, Hampstead; 1961, Iraqi House, Piccadilly; 1963, Occupational Health Unit, Park Royal Hospital; 1964, Economist Building, Saint James's Street; London. 1970, Garden Building, Saint Hilda's College, Oxford. 1972, Robin Hood Gardens (housing), Robin Hood Lane, London.

BIBLIOGRAPHY

"Alison and Peter Smithson: Gentle Cultural Accommodation." 1975 *L'Architecture d'Aujourd'hui* 177:4–13.
MCKEAN, JOHN MAULE 1977 "The Smithsons: A Profile." *Building Design* 345:22–24.
SMITHSON, ALISON 1973 "Ruminations on Founder's Court." *Architectural Design* 43:524–529.
SMITHSON, ALISON 1974 "How to Recognize and Read Mat-building." *Architectural Design* 44:573–590.
SMITHSON, ALISON (editor) (1965)1968 *Team 10 Primer.* 2d ed. Cambridge, Mass.: M.I.T. Press.
SMITHSON, PETER 1971 "Simple Thoughts on Repetition." *Architectural Design* 41:479–481.
SMITHSON, PETER 1973 "Collective Design: Initiators and Successors." *Architectural Design* 43:621–623.
SMITHSON, PETER 1974 "The Free University and the Language of Modern Architecture." *Domus* 534:1–8.
SMITHSON, PETER 1976 "Oxford and Cambridge: Walks." *Architectural Design* 46:342–354.
SMITHSON, PETER 1978 "Charles Eames." *Journal of the Royal Institute of British Architects* 85, no. 11:438.
SMITHSON, ALISON, and SMITHSON, PETER (1960)1967 *Urban Structuring.* Rev. ed. London: Studio Vista; New York: Reinhold. Originally published with the title *Uppercase.*
SMITHSON, ALISON, and SMITHSON, PETER 1975 *Bibliography of the Work of Alison and Peter Smithson.* London: The authors.
SMITHSON, ALISON, and SMITHSON, PETER 1976 "Alvar Aalto." *Arkkitehti* 73, nos. 7–8:special issue.
SMITHSON, ALISON, and SMITHSON, PETER 1981 *The Heroic Age of Modern Architecture.* New York: Rizzoli.

SMYTHSON, ROBERT

Robert Smythson (c.1535–1614) was the outstanding English architect of the sixteenth century, indeed the only English architect of his period who has a strong personal artistic identity. However, even though the quality and originality of his work proclaim him as "one of the great geniuses of English architecture" (Summerson, 1953), comparatively little is known of the details of his career. The inscription on his tombstone, which says he died aged seventy-nine, is the only evidence for his birthdate, and nothing is known of his background.

He is first documented in 1568 at Longleat, where he worked as principal mason for Sir John Thynne. The building history of Longleat is extremely complex, and Smythson's share in the de-

Smythson.
Wollaton Hall.
Nottinghamshire, England.
1580–1588

sign of the present structure is uncertain; Thynne, who had a passionate interest in architecture, may himself have had a hand in it. Whatever Smythson's creative role at Longleat, several characteristic features of his later work seem to develop from it, so it can fairly be said to have played a crucial part in the formation of his style. Longleat is remarkable (among much else) for its almost complete symmetry about both axes, its "extroversion" (it is emphatically outward-looking rather than arranged around a court) and for the huge area of wall space occupied by windows, and these features, all novelties in English domestic architecture, reoccur in Smythson's first independent building, Wollaton Hall. Whereas Longleat, however, is serene in aspect and chaste in detailing, Wollaton is overwhelmingly dramatic and is decorated with very lavish, Flemish-inspired ornamentation. Wollaton also goes beyond Longleat in the concentration of its planning, dispensing with a court altogether and having a central hall that rises majestically above the rest of the building. Smythson drew on a variety of models for Wollaton, particularly illustrations in foreign architectural treatises, but he handled his sources with such vitality that the result is not a pastiche, but a creation of magnificent originality.

Smythson settled in Wollaton village and is buried in the church there. He is not strictly documented as the architect of any subsequent building, but his tombstone says that as well as the house at Wollaton, he built "divers others of great account," and there is evidence to connect him with a series of outstanding houses, mainly in the Midlands and fairly close to Wollaton. The evidence is mainly stylistic, "bold grouping, deep recession, soaring height, evocative silhouette" being the characteristics that Girouard (1966) considers hallmarks of a Smythson house, but there are also similarities between some of the buidings and surviving drawings by Smythson. Family connections between several of the patrons for whom the houses were built further increase the likelihood of links with Smythson. In the case of the best-known of these houses, Hardwick Hall, the accumulated evidence indicates with near certainty that Smythson was the designer. Celebrated for its enormous areas of window ("Hardwick Hall, more glass than wall" in the local adage), it has some of the compositional grandeur of Wollaton, but in its restrained detail and air of effortless dignity it seems to look back to Longleat. Like them, it ranks among the great masterpieces of English architecture.

Robert's son, John Smythson (?–1634), followed his father's profession. He is first recorded in 1588 working as a mason at Wollaton, and later he seems to have practiced estate management. His work as a designer was not extensive, but includes one celebrated building, Bolsover Castle, Derbyshire, on which he worked from about 1612 until his death. Described by Summerson (1953) as a "unique, eccentric, and extraordinarily attractive building," it is more massive and consciously medieval in appearance than any of Robert's houses and stands at the beginning of the tradition of the romantic "sham-castle." John is buried at Bolsover Church, as is his son Huntingdon (?–1648). Huntingdon's epitaph (where the family name is spelled "Smithson," as had become more common by this time) refers to his "skill in architecture," and although he is not certainly known to have designed anything, he was very probably responsible for some of the later work at Bolsover.

The Royal Institute of British Architects in London has a large collection of drawings by Robert and John Smythson, with a few perhaps by Huntingdon and his son, another John Smythson (1640–1717), an obscure figure who seems to have done some architectural work. The drawings by the two senior members of the family, which include ones made on visits to London by Robert in 1609 and by John in 1618–1619, rank in documentary importance alongside those by JOHN THORPE.

IAN CHILVERS

WORKS

1572–1580, Longleat (completion); 1576–1578, Wardour Old Castle (remodeling); Wiltshire, England. 1580–1588, Wollaton Hall, Nottinghamshire, England. (A)1583, Barlborough Hall, Derbyshire, England. *(A)c.1585, Heath Old Hall, Yorkshire, England. *c.1585 Worksop Manor, Nottinghamshire, England. 1590–1597, Hardwick Hall, Derbyshire, England. (A)1593–1600, Doddington Hall, Lincolnshire, England. 1597, Welbeck Abbey (wing; later remodeled as the Oxford Wing), Nottinghamshire, England. 1601–1610, Burton Agnes Hall, Yorkshire, England. (A)c.1602, Chastleton House, Oxfordshire, England. (A)c.1610, Wootton Lodge, Staffordshire, England. (A)c.1611, Fountains Hall, Yorkshire, England.

BIBLIOGRAPHY

AIRS, MALCOLM 1975 *The Making of the English Country House 1500–1640.* London: Architectural Press.
GIROUARD, MARK 1962 "The Smythson Collection of the Royal Institute of British Architects." *Architectural History* 5:21–184.
GIROUARD, MARK 1966 *Robert Smythson and the Architecture of the Elizabethan Era.* London: Country Life.
LEES-MILNE, JAMES 1951 *Tudor Renaissance.* London: Batsford.
SUMMERSON, JOHN (1953)1977 *Architecture in Britain 1530–1830.* 6th ed. Harmondsworth, England: Penguin.

SNEYERS, LEON

Born in Brussels and trained there under PAUL HANKAR, Léon Sneyers (1877–1949) came under the influence of the Viennese school of decorative arts through his participation in the 1902 Turin exposition. In the years before World War I, he emerged as Belgium's most active and accomplished exponent of the Viennese Secessionist style in architecture, interior decoration, and graphic design. His later architecture, while influenced by the International style, was generally of an Art Deco character.

ALFRED WILLIS

WORKS

1900, House, 6 rue de Nancy, Brussels. *1905, Congo Pavilion (and other facilities), Liège Exhibition, Belgium, *1906, Belgian Pavilion, Milan Triennale. *1906, Coppet House, Brussels. *1906–1907, Belgian Pavilion, Venice Biennale, Italy. 1907, Waxweiler House, Brussels. 1913, Pavilion of Higher Education in the Sciences and Letters, International Exhibition, Ghent, Belgium.

BIBLIOGRAPHY

BORSI, FRANCO 1977 *Bruxelles 1900.* New York: Rizzoli.

CULOT, MAURICE 1976 "Léon Sneyers (1977–1949) ou la Sécession importée." *AAM Bulletin* no. 9:11–16.

CULOT, MAURICE, and TERLINDEN, FRANÇOIS 1969 *Antoine Pompe et l'effort moderne en Belgique: 1890–1940.* Brussels: Musée d'Ixelles.

RUSSELL, FRANK (editor) 1979 *Art Nouveau Architecture.* New York: Rizzoli.

SCHMITZ, MARCEL 1937 *L'architecture moderne en Belgique.* Brussels: Editions de la Connaissance.

VAN DE WINKEL, M. 1975 "Architecture et symbolisme en Belgique vers 1900." *Annales, XLIIIᵉ Congrès de la Fédération des Cercles d'Archéologie et d'Histoire de Belgique.* Sint-Niklaas, Belgium: RINDA.

VAN KUYCK, H. 1955 *Modern Belgian Architecture.* 3d ed. New York: Belgian Government Information Center.

SNOOK, JOHN BUTLER

John Butler Snook (1815–1901) was born in London and came to New York as a child. Lacking formal architectural training, he served an apprenticeship in his father's carpentry business. In the mid-1840s, Snook established an architectural partnership with Joseph Trench which lasted until 1857. Their most significant project was the A. T. Stewart's Department Store (1845–1846), New York, the first luxury dry goods store in America, designed in the Anglo-Italianate Palazzo style. Snook's most notable clients were the Lorillard and Vanderbilt families, for whom he designed the original Grand Central Station (1869–1871), New York, and the William H. Vanderbilt Residences (1879–1882), New York.

SANDRA E. GILBERT

WORKS

1845–1846, A. T. Stewart Department Store (with Joseph Trench); 1847–1848, Odd Fellows Hall; *1849–1850, Niblo's Garden; *1850–1852, Metropolitan Hotel; *1864–1865, Hoffman House Hotel; *1867, Saint John's Park Freight Depot; *1869–1871, Grand Central Station (train shed attributed to Isaac C. Buckhout); *1879–1882, William Henry Vanderbilt Houses (constructional consultant); *1880–1890, All Angel's Episcopal Church; New York.

BIBLIOGRAPHY

The John B. Snook Architectural Collection is in the Map and Print Room of the New York Historical Society.

"Obituary of John B. Snook." 1901 *American Architect and Building News* 74, Nov.:9:41.

NEW YORK LANDMARKS PRESERVATION COMMISSION 1973 *Soho-Cast Iron Historic District; Designation Report.* New York: The commission.

ROSEBROCK, ELLEN FLETCHER 1975 "John B. Snook and Meyer's Hotel, 116–119 South Street." *South Street Seaport Reporter* 9, Spring:14.

SMITH, MARY ANN CLEGG 1974a "The Commercial Architecture of John Butler Snook." Unpublished Ph.D. dissertation, The Pennsylvania State University, University Park.

SMITH, MARY ANN CLEGG 1974b "John Snook and the Design for A. T. Stewart's Store." *New York Historical Society Quarterly* 58:18–33.

SOANE, JOHN

John Soane (1753–1837)—the letter *e* was a later addition—was the last of the four sons and three daughters of a Berkshire builder and his wife Martha who had previously lived for several years in the parish of Basildon. The future architect always maintained a noticeable reticence about his childhood, but it is known that by 1761 the family had moved to Reading where the father rented a house from Timothy Tyrrell. Here, young John was sent to William Baker's Academy where in due course he developed the "natural inclination to the study of Architecture" which, allied to a facility in drawing, encouraged him to make this his future career. When he was fifteen, he obtained through a family acquaintance, James Peacock, a recommendation to GEORGE DANCE THE YOUNGER, then architect to the City of London, into whose office he was taken as a junior assistant.

Two years later, finding that Dance's work was

almost entirely concerned with official City buildings, Soane sought permission to move to the office of HENRY HOLLAND whose growing practice provided the varied town and country house work in which his interest then lay. There is no doubt, however, that the period spent with Dance was to have a lasting influence in the development of Soane's own style, and the two men remained lifelong friends. The seven years in Holland's office, on the other hand, gave Soane practical experience in costing and building work generally, and provided time for him to attend the lectures then being given by the Royal Academy's professor of architecture, Thomas Sandby. In 1772, he entered the Academy's annual competition with a drawing of the Banqueting House, Whitehall, which won him a silver medal. In 1776, he again entered the competition and this time was given the gold medal for his design for a Triumphal Bridge. Shortly afterward, through the good offices of the Academy's Treasurer, WILLIAM CHAMBERS, Soane was awarded King George III's traveling studentship which enabled him to set out for Italy. Before leaving, however, he put together a small octavo book of designs for garden buildings which was published in 1778, but which some years later he attempted to suppress.

Leaving London on March 18, 1778, in the company of a fellow student, ROBERT F. BRETTINGHAM, Soane arrived in Rome on May 2 and at once set to work on measuring and drawing the city's more important buildings. Later on, he was to make various expeditions to Naples, Florence, Sicily, Venice, Verona, Mantua, and Parma, submitting to the Academy of the latter city a design for a triumphal bridge for which he was made an honorary member of that institution. He also sent home a design for a British senate house which was included in the Royal Academy exhibition of 1779.

Soane's two years in Italy were important not only in providing a first-hand knowledge of antique and Renaissance architecture, but also in affording introductions to several influential Englishmen then making the Grand Tour who were later to become clients. Less happy in its outcome was his patronage by the capricious Lord Hervey, bishop of Derry, whose blandishments raised Soane's expectations of employment at Downhill, the bishop's home in Ireland. Unwisely cutting short his studies in the summer of 1780, Soane left Italy and traveled to Downhill where he spent a month measuring and planning, only to find that the bishop had changed his mind. His dismissal meant that he returned to London with empty pockets and for several months was dependent on trivial jobs found for him by his old master George

Dance. This mortifying experience, which might have been shrugged off by a more resilient character, left a permanent scar on Soane's inherently nervous disposition and doubtless increased the moments of irritability and ill-founded suspicion as to the intentions of others to which he remained prone throughout his life.

News of his plight brought commissions from some of the men whom he had met in Rome, notably Thomas Pitt, later Lord Camelford, who required alterations to a house at Petersham, Surrey, and Philip Yorke (later Lord Hardwicke), who first employed Soane to refurbish two London houses and later obtained designs for lodges and a rustic dairy at Hamels Park (1781–1783), Hertfordshire. Additions to a house at Walthamstow, Essex, a shop front for premises in Southwark, London, and the redecoration of Number 148 Piccadilly, London, gained him a reputation for competence which led to his first official undertaking, a small bridge built over the river Wensum in 1783 for the City of Norwich, Norfolk. Also from Norfolk came Soane's first commission for an entirely new house, Letton Hall, designed for B. Gordon Dillingham in June of that year. From these stemmed a number of other works for East Anglian clients, notably Saxlingham Rectory (1784–1787), Norfolk; Tendring Hall, Suffolk (1784–1786); a Music Room (1784–1785) at Earsham Park, Suffolk; and two gateways with lodges for Langley Park, Norfolk.

The Royal Academy Exhibition in the spring of 1784 included five entries under the name of "John Soane architect"—the first recorded occasion on which he added an *e* at the end of his name. Early in that year he had begun the courtship of Elizabeth Smith, niece of the wealthy city builder George Wyatt, whom Soane had first met when working for George Dance. They were married at Christ Church Southwark on August 11, and returned to the apartment at 53 Margaret Street which Soane had rented since 1782. In the next two years, his practice widened considerably and he was remodeling houses as far apart as Mulgrave Castle, Yorkshire; Piercefield, Monmouthshire; Chillington Hall, Staffordshire; and Holwood (Kent), where his alteration of a library, staircase, and other works for William Pitt, then prime minister, was to prove significant for his future career.

In general, Soane's house designs in these early years reflect the pattern of simplicity in elevation and compactness in planning already set by Henry Holland and JAMES WYATT. Only in the Hamels Dairy with its "primitive" porch, in the top-lit picture gallery for William Beckford at Fonthill, Wiltshire, and in the oil jars poised on the stable block at Lees Court are there hints of the latent individuality which Soane deemed it wiser to keep in check until the turn of events from 1788 onward released him from a respectful deference to his clients' wishes. Early in 1788, he arranged for the publication of a volume entitled *Plans, Elevations and Sections of Buildings Erected in the Counties of Norfolk, Suffolk, etc.* This consisted of engraved plates accompanied by the briefest of captions. Writing did not come easily to Soane, and although some twenty years later he took considerable trouble in preparing the written lectures which, as professor of architecture, he was to deliver annually to students at the Royal Academy, the result proved a somewhat superficial outline of the history of his subject. The *Lectures,* no more than the *Plans* of 1788, throw little light on the development of his own highly idiosyncratic style which was to emerge soon after 1788. On September 27 of that year, ROBERT TAYLOR died, leaving vacant the post of architect to the Bank of England. Soane at once applied and, with the support of William Pitt, proved successful although he competed against such established figures as James Wyatt, Henry Holland, and SAMUEL PEPYS COCKERELL. This prestigious office brought him a salary of £200 a year and was also to prove valuable for the contacts it afforded with potential City clients. There was further good fortune early in 1790 when Soane and his wife inherited a considerable legacy on the death of her uncle George Wyatt. This wealth enabled Soane to build the first of his houses in Lincoln's Inn Fields and to begin collecting works of art. Even more significant was that the combination of financial independence and professional opportunity allowed the architect's latent powers to emerge in that highly individualistic approach to design which became known as the Soane style. It consisted of certain basic themes which, expanded or contracted, embellished or pared to a minimum, were to reappear in his work for nearly forty years.

The most characteristic of these themes was the domed ceiling with segmental arches resting on four piers and usually, but not always, lit by a glazed lantern or oculus. Although owing much to George Dance's Council Chamber at Guildhall, built in 1777, its eventual emergence in the Bank of England Stock Offices showed an entirely original, even eccentric, adaptation of classical forms. The second theme was related to the first but in it the dome and lantern were replaced by a splayed cross vault springing from the four piers. This idea, too, had already been used by George Dance in his ballroom ceiling at Cranbury, Hampshire, where Soane would have seen it on a visit in 1781, shortly after its completion. Originally, however, it almost certainly derived from a plate in P. S.

Bartoli's *Gli Antichi Sepolcri ovvero Mausolei Romani* of 1768, a book of which Soane acquired a copy and in which he found the inspiration for many of his details. A third theme in his repertoire was the tribune or open well, rising through two floors, guarded at first floor level by a rail or balustrade and receiving light from a glazed lantern in the roof. Here, the source was doubtless Henry Holland's octagonal vestibule at Carlton House. A fourth theme is to be found in Soane's use of "primitivism," distilled from the theories of MARC-ANTOINE LAUGIER. A fleeting early example appeared in the dairy at Hamels Park, but in its later manifestations Soane transformed such simple rustic features as bark-covered tree trunks into columns or pilasters of flint or brick, with a narrow band cut away below the abacus to form a retracted necking. In the entablature associated with these features he frequently introduced two bricks set on edge, representing his own version of triglyphs. While this idiosyncratic interpretation was at first reserved for smaller buildings such as lodges and gateways, it appeared in a larger version for the stable block at Betchworth Castle, Surrey, in 1798, and ultimately played an important part in his conception of the Dulwich College picture gallery and mausoleum (London) of 1811.

Since it was to be the precursor of the later halls at the Bank and of several derivatives elsewhere, Soane's first Stock Office of 1792 was of major significance and for many months was the subject of deliberation. It stemmed from his main task in the year following his appointment as architect to the Bank of England to survey and report on the state of Taylor's banking halls, built for security reasons with windowless walls and lit by glazed lanterns over timber-framed roofs. The survey revealed that the roofs were now defective, the worst being that over the Bank Stock Office. For this, Soane was instructed to design a new roof and lantern to be placed over the existing walls. He submitted drawings on 24 November, 1791, but

Soane.
Dulwich College (picture gallery, mausoleum).
London.
1811–1814

Soane.
Stock Office, Bank of
*   England.*
London.
1791–1792

Soane.
Bank of England.
London.
1788–1833

from a number of surviving rough sketches it is evident that he had for some time been convinced that total rebuilding of the Office was the only right course. It is also clear that he had discussed the problem with his friend George Dance who, thirteen years before, had built a new Council Chamber at Guildhall on a site which necessitated top or clearstory lighting. The sketches show that Soane's first idea, deriving from the Basilica of Constantine in Rome, was for a rectangular hall of three vaulted bays, lit from a clearstory of glazed lunettes in its side walls. This, however, was finally replaced by a design which owed little to the basilica and a great deal to Dance's Council Chamber, with its central dome springing from four massive piers and lit by a vertically glazed lantern over an oculus. This central space was now dominant, the vaulted flanking bays being reduced in size and lit by lunettes high up in the side walls. As a fire precaution, light-weight, hollow clay cones were introduced for the construction of both dome and vaults. Probably Soane expressed his doubts about only replacing the roofs and lanterns when submitting his drawings at the November meeting of the Building Committee, for on December 6 he laid before the members seven drawings for rebuilding the whole office.

If the adopted design was heavily indebted to Dance's Council Chamber, it was equally unmistakably a product of Soane's originality in the detailing. Although essentially classical, it employed no recognized order, the piers being faced with vertical flutes over which short strips of incised fret denote token capitals. Thus began the program of rebuilding which, as the older offices became decrepit and more land was acquired, gradually covered the whole island site between Threadneedle Street and Lothbury, Princes Stret, and Bartholomew Lane.

In view of Soane's financial independence and the amount of work demanded by the Bank, it is surprising that in 1792 he should have undertaken a clerkship in the Office of Works with responsibility for Whitehall, Westminster, and Saint James's. This he relinquished two years later only to take an appointment as deputy surveyor of woods and forests, entailing supervision of some indifferent buildings in the royal parks but providing opportunities for designing a remarkable brick and flint lodge in his primitive style for Cumberland Gate, Hyde Park (London), and a pair of similar lodges and a gateway at Bagshot, Surrey, for the duke of Clarence (later King William IV). Soane resigned the post in 1799. In 1806, he was appointed professor of architecture at the Royal Academy in succession to George Dance and began the onerous preparation of the lectures which, with two short breaks, he continued to give to the students for twenty-seven years from 1809 onward. Following the death of SAMUEL WYATT in 1807, Soane succeeded him as clerk of the works at Chelsea Hospital, in which capacity he designed several additional buildings of which the stable block and secretary's office are notable survivors. In 1815, when there was a rearrangement in the Office of Works after the death of James Wyatt, he was appointed as one of the three attached architects with responsibility for the palaces in Whitehall, Westminster, Richmond Park, Kew Gardens, and Hampton Court, holding this post until its abolition in 1832.

It is evident that Soane found working for

Soane.
Tyringham Hall.
Buckinghamshire, England.
1793–c.1800

Soane.
Tyringham Hall.
Buckinghamshire, England.
1793–c.1800

committees or departments less trying to his nervous temperament than working for unpredictable private clients, and from about 1800 the number of the latter diminished rapidly. For certain old friends and a handful of new ones he continued to produce designs, including a new banking house for William Praed in Fleet Street, London; alterations to Port Eliot, Cornwall, for Lord Eliot (a brother-in-law of William Pitt); a library and vestibule for the marquis of Buckingham at Stowe, Buckinghamshire; the Dulwich Picture Gallery and Mausoleum, London, in accordance with the will of Sir Francis Bourgeois; the rebuilding of Wotton, Buckinghamshire, after a fire, again for the marquis of Buckingham; and a new house for Purney Sillitoe at Pellwall, Staffordshire.

The 1820s were largely occupied with official work in Westminster, beginning with a new Royal Entrance and staircase leading to a gallery and anteroom (1822–1827) in which his favorite themes appeared on a monumental scale with embellishments in the way of recumbent consoles, ball-beading, and reeded moldings buttoned down with plaster rosettes. Much of this work disappeared in the burning of the Houses of Parliament in 1834. Even more expressive of his ingenuity, however, were the new Law Courts (1822–1825) which he designed early in the same decade for an awkward site between the existing Stone Building and the buttresses of Westminster Hall. The seven Courts emerged as an amalgam in which the walls were essentially classical while above them glazed lanterns rose from weirdly attenuated domes without supporting piers, appearing more like Gothic canopies hanging in space.

In April 1829, when he was seventy-five, Soane was directed to design a new repository for the national archives, to be known as the State Paper Office in Saint James's Park. Externally, it proved to be unlike any of his previous works, and its astylar, rusticated façades, bracketed eaves, and

massive doorway clearly derived from GIACOMO BAROZZI DA VIGNOLA's Villa Farnese at Caprarola. He had seen this during his student days in Italy, and later he described it in his Royal Academy lectures as a building which "can never be sufficiently admired or too much studied." In spite of criticism from an interfering Member of Parliament, who wished to have pilasters incorporated, Soane's design was adopted and was more or less complete in 1831. The fact that CHARLES BARRY and CHARLES R. COCKERELL were soon to exploit the Italian villa theme in several of their works has overshadowed the originality of Soane's building, which stood for scarcely three decades and was soon forgotten after its demolition to make way for the new Foreign and India Offices. At the time of its design, however, it was a striking innovation and a fitting conclusion to Soane's long years of service in the Office of Works. With the accession of his early patron as William IV this was recognized by the bestowing of a knighthood on him in September 1831.

Two years later, failing eyesight forced Soane's resignation as architect to the Bank of England, but his interest in the profession remained as keen as ever. He was a generous donor to the Institute (later Royal Institute) of British Architects at its inception in 1834, and he endowed a fund to help distressed architects and their dependents. He died on 20 January 1837 at the age of eighty-three and was buried beneath the monument which he had designed for his wife in the burial ground of Saint Giles-in-the-Fields (now Saint Pancras Gardens). It is, however, his house in Lincoln's Inn Fields (1812–1813) that remains as his most telling memorial, embodying in miniature much of his architectural philosophy and enshrining the treasures which he had collected and cherished over the years, as well as his own drawings and those of other illustrious architects.

Unlike several of his near contemporaries such

Soane.
National Debt Redemption
Office.
London.
1818–1819

as Holland, Dance, and JOHN NASH, Soane took no part in town planning, and in general he regarded the speculative laying out of urban streets and terraces as "abominable and fatal to the advancement of architecture." The influence of his annual Royal Academy lectures is difficult to evaluate, but there is no doubt as to the thorough understanding of classical architecture which he instilled in the many draftsmen and pupils taken into his office from 1784. Among the most notable of these was JOSEPH MICHAEL GANDY, an assistant from 1798 who proved particularly successful in interpreting Soane's ideas and who was responsible for several of the large watercolors sent in the latter's name to the annual exhibitions of the Royal Academy. In GEORGE BASEVI, a pupil for six years from 1810, Soane saw much of the promise which he had hoped to find in his own sons. George Bailey, who entered the office as a pupil in 1806, remained as a valued assistant until Soane's death when, under the terms of the latter's will, he became the first curator of the Soane Museum.

If in his own country Soane had few imitators, on the international scene he had none, and although at first sight some of the works of KARL FRIEDRICH SCHINKEL suggest a link, this is entirely fortuitous and can be accounted for by their common interest in neoclassical theory.

The Soane style certainly did not lack criticism. As early as 1796 Joseph Farington recorded in his *Diary* a remark that "Soane's architecture at the Bank was . . . affected and contemptible." A vicious attack appeared in *Knight's Quarterly Magazine* for January-April 1824 under the heading of "The Sixth or Boeotian Order of Architecture," but the most painful episode for Soane was some ten years earlier when two articles appeared in *The Champion* for 10 and 24 September, 1815, reviewing the arts in general and architecture in particular. In these, his work was ridiculed by an anonymous writer who proved on inquiry to be his son George. The resulting estrangement from George, coupled with the death of his wife in November 1815, led to a long period of loneliness during which he sought consolation in his work and his ever growing collection.

In the spate of rebuilding which took place in the second half of the nineteenth century, much of Soane's City work was destroyed. The Bank of England, however, survived until 1922 when everything within the encircling wall was rebuilt. To appreciate the most impressive survivors of his genius and originality, it is now necessary to look for such examples as the stables and offices at the Royal Hospital, Chelsea, his own villa on Ealing Green, or the now restored Art Gallery and Mausoleum at Dulwich.

DOROTHY STROUD

WORKS

1781–1783, Hamels (alterations, lodges and dairys), Hertfordshire, England. 1783–1784, Blackfriars Bridge, Norwich; 1783–1785, Burnham Westgate Hall; 1783–1789, Letton Hall; 1784ff., Langley Park (lodges and gateways); 1784–1785, Earsham Hall (music room); Norfolk, England. *1784–1786, Tendring Hall, Suffolk, England. 1784–1787, Saxlingham Rectory, Norfolk, England. 1785–1786, Blundeston, Suffolk, England. 1785–1788, Shotesham Park, Norfolk, England. 1785–1789, Chillington Hall, Staffordshire, England. 1785–1793, Piercefield (in ruins), Monmouthshire, England. *1786–1787, Fonthill House (picture gallery); 1788, Wardour Castle (addition to chapel); Wiltshire, England. 1788–1798, Bentley Priory, Middlesex, England. 1788–1833, Bank of England (interior altered), London. 1789, Sydney Lodge, Hamble, Hampshire, England. *1789–1794, County Goal, Norwich, Norfolk, England. 1791–1793, Wimpole Hall (alterations and additions), Cambridgeshire, England. 1792, Caius College (Hall remodeled), Cambridge, England. *1792–1795, Buckingham House, 91 Pall Mall, London. 1793–c.1800, Tyringham Hall, Buckinghamshire, England. *1797, Cumberland (gate and lodge), Hyde Park,

Soane.
13 Lincoln's Inn Fields
(now Sir John Soane's
Museum).
London.
1812–1813

London. 1798–1799, Betchworth Castle (additions; dairy and stables), Surrey, England. 1799–1804, Aynho Park, Northamptonshire, England. 1800–1802, Albury Park, Surrey, England. 1800–1803, Pitzhanger Manor, Ealing, Middlesex, England. 1802, Bramley Church (Brocas Chapel), Hampshire, England. 1804, Simeon Obelisk, Market Place, Reading, Berkshire, England. 1804–1806, Port Eliot, Cornwall, England. 1805–1806, Stowe House (Gothic library and alterations) Buckinghamshire, England. *1807–1810, New Bank Buildings, Princes Street, Lothbury, London. 1809–1811, Moggerhanger, Bedfordshire, England. 1809–1817, Royal Hospital (infirmary, Secretary's Office, stables), Chelsea; 1811–1814, Dulwich College (picture gallery, mausoleum); 1812–1813, 13 Lincoln's Inn Fields; *1818–1819, National Debt Redemption Office, Old Jewry; London. 1821–1822, Wotton House (reconstruction), Buckinghamshire, England. *1822–1825, Law Courts, Westminster; *1822–1827, Parliament (House of Lords Royal Entrance, gallery, library, committee rooms), Westminster; London. 1822–1828, Pellwall House, Staffordshire, England. 1823–1824, Insolvent Debtor's Court, Portugal Street; 1823–1824, Saint Peter's Church, Walworth; 1824–1826, Board of Trade and Privy Council Office, Whitehall; 1826–1827, Holy Trinity Church, Marylebone; 1826–1828, Saint John's Church, Bethnal Green; *1828, Freemason's Hall (council chamber), Great Queen Street; 1829–1833, Banqueting House (restoration); Whitehall; *1830–1834, State Paper Office, Westminster; London.

BIBLIOGRAPHY

BOLTON, ARTHUR (editor) 1927 *The Portrait of Sir John Soane.* London: Sir John Soane's Museum.
BOLTON, ARTHUR (editor) 1929 *The Lectures on Architecture, by Sir John Soane.* London: Sir John Soane's Museum.
STROUD, DOROTHY 1961 *The Architecture of Sir John Soane.* London: Studio.
STROUD, DOROTHY 1982 *Sir John Soane, Architect.* London: Faber.
SUMMERSON, JOHN 1952 *Sir John Soane, 1753–1837.* London: Art & Technics.

SOAVE, FELICE

Felice Soave (1749–1803), son of the architect and painter Raffael Angelo Soave, studied in Genoa and Parma, Italy, but his major activity was in Milan, where he taught geometry, mechanics, and design. In 1791, he was named head architect of Milan Cathedral. He continued the construction of Carlo Buzzi's facade, since his own design was never adopted. His executed work was largely domestic, including the Casa Anguissola and others in Milan.

GARY M. RADKE

WORK

n.d., Casa Anguissola, Milan.

SOCOLESCU, TOMA T.

Toma T. Socolescu (1883–1960) graduated from the School of Architecture in Bucharest in 1911. Initially, his designs, mostly for country houses, were traditional, but in the 1930s, he turned to a modern Rumanian style, characterized by a clear space organization. His buildings in reinforced concrete, in contrast to those in the West, have a human, warm character.

CONSTANTIN MARIN MARINESCU

WORKS

1935, Lyceum, Cimpina, Rumania. 1935, Lyceum; 1935, Saint John's Cathedral (tower); 1943, Central Market; Ploieşti, Rumania.

BIBLIOGRAPHY

IONESCU, GRIGORE 1965 Volume 2 in *Istoria Arhitecturii in Romania.* Bucharest: Editura Academiei Republicii Romañe.
IONESCU, GRIGORE 1969 *Arhitectura in Romania; Perioda anilor 1944–1969.* Bucharest: Editura Academiei Republicii Socialiste Româñia.
IONESCU, GRIGORE 1972 "Saptezeci si cinci de ani de la infiintarea invatamintului de arhitectura din Romania." *Arhitectura* 20:35–42.
MAMBRIANI, ALBERTO 1969 *L'Architettura Moderna nei Paesi Balcanici.* Bologna, Italy: Capelli.
PATRULIUS, RADU 1973–1974 "Contributii Romanesti in Arhitectura Anilor '30." *Arhitectura* 21, no. 6:44–52; 22, no. 1:53–59.
SASARMAN, GHEORGHE 1972 "Inceputurile gindirii teoretice in arhitectura româneasča (1860–1916)." *Arhitectura* 20, no. 6:44–46.

SOHIER, HECTOR

As both an architect and a stonemason, Hector Sohier seems to have been responsible for the design and execution of numerous edifices in the French city of Caen, in spite of the fact that very little actual documentation exists on Sohier and only one building can be certainly attributed to him. According to contemporary records, by 1555 Sohier had been named court architect and head mason for the city of Caen and the entire Normandy region. Thus, it seems likely that he either supervised or at least played some role in the execution of structures built at that time in and around Caen.

In all probability, what merited Sohier's appointment to this position was his work on the chevet at the Church of Saint-Pierre de Caen between 1521 and 1538. Though essentially derived from Gothic structural tenets, the choir also reflects Italian Renaissance decorative motifs. For example, buttress piers are treated as pilasters; pinnacles are topped with vaselike fixtures and resemble candelabras; and everywhere the façade is adorned with Renaissance grotesque ornamentation. The interior decoration is no less elaborate with various sculptural reliefs and statues depicting mythological and pagan as well as Christian figures.

Because of its resemblance to Saint-Pierre, the north apse of the Church of Saint-Saveur (c.1536) in Caen is also attributed to Sohier. In addition, the Château de Lasson just outside Caen uses a number of Renaissance devices with unmistakably Gothic motifs in the manner of Saint-Pierre. Specifically, the most notable aspect of this building is its buttresslike structure—adorned with grotesque imagery—that sets off one wing of the castle abutting from another.

Other buildings in Caen attributed to Sohier on the basis of their similarity to various parts of Saint-Pierre include the Hôtel Ecoville (c.1538), an addition to the Hôtel Mondrainville, and the apse at the Church of Notre Dame de Froide Rue.

PETER L. DONHAUSER

WORK

(A)1521–1538, Church of Saint-Pierre (chevet), Caen, France.

BIBLIOGRAPHY

HAUTECOEUR, LOUIS (1948)1965 Volume 1 in *Histoire de l'Architecture Classique en France.* Paris: Picard.
VACHON, MARIUS 1910 *La Renaissance Française.* Paris: Flammarion.

SOISSONS, LOUIS DE

Louis Emmanuel Jean Guy de Savoie-Carignan de Soissons (1890–1962) was noted for his public housing and town planning in England, particularly at Welwyn Garden City, Hertfordshire (1920–1960). Born in Montreal, Canada, he studied at Royal Academy Schools and at the Ecole des Beaux-Arts in Paris. He worked in partnership at various times with G. GREY WORNUM and others in London.

LORRAINE WELLING LANMON

WORKS

1914, Houses, Bagshot, Surrey, England. 1920–1960, Domestic and Public Buildings, Welwyn Garden City, Hertfordshire, England. 1928–1929, Earl Haig Memorial Homes, Meadow Head, Sheffield, England. 1932–1933, Broom Park and Huxhams Cross Houses, Dartington Hall; 1935–1936, Cliff Park Houses, Paignton Estate; 1936–1937, Churston Estate Houses; 1936–1937, Dittisham Estate Houses, River Dart; Devon, England.

1938, Saint James's Priory Estate, Exeter, England. 1962, Saint James Place Maisonettes (not completed until 1963), London.

BIBLIOGRAPHY

There are numerous entries regarding individual buildings at Welwyn Garden City designed by Louis de Soissons in Architect and Building News *from 1927 to 1960.*
"The Architect and Housing by the Speculative Builder—VI: Some Estates in Devon, Architect, Louis de Soissons," 1936 *Journal of the Royal Institute of British Architects* Series 3 43:975–984.
CHAMBERS, GEORGE 1929 "The Larkhall Estate." *Architectural Review* 66, July:7–16.
CHATTERTON, FREDERICK (editor) 1923 *Who's Who in Architecture.* London: Architectural Press.
"The Late Louis de Soissons." 1962 *Architect and Building News* 222:442.
"Tenements, Wilcove Place, St. Marylebone, N.W. 1." 1934 *Journal of the Royal Institute of British Architects* Series 3 41:1016–1020.
WARE, DORA 1967 *A Short Dictionary of British Architects.* London: Allen.
"Working-Class Flats at Kennington for the Duchy of Cornwall Estate, Architect: Louis de Soissons, F.R.I.B.A., S.A.D.G." *Architect and Building News* 135:34–38.

SOLERI, PAOLO

Paolo Soleri (1919–) was born in Turin, Italy. In 1946, he received a Ph.D. from the Torino Politecnico, and shortly afterward, he moved to the United States where he was apprenticed to FRANK LLOYD WRIGHT from 1947 to 1949. Soleri is one of the best-known utopian planners of the twentieth century. He is a steadfast proponent of the megaplan, and his schemes have provoked great controversy. In the 1960s, Soleri developed the idea of "arcology," which engages the mutual relationship of ecology and architecture. As an alternative to the horizontal growth of most American cities and suburbs, he has proposed arcologies of self-contained, vertical, and comprehensive environments. Soleri's city buildings consist of layers that combine living, working, and the natural environments into a condensed superorganism. Soleri's prototypes for human habitation are supported by a complex philosophical position which relates these mega-cities to the entire evolutionary process. The arcologies generate a population implosion to create the rich interconnections and interdependencies of density.

Soleri lives in Scottsdale, Arizona. Nearby is the building site for Arcosanti, an arcology for 3,000 using only ten acres surrounded by an 860-acre greenbelt. The fifteen-story prototype is also a study center where Soleri conducts experimental workshops for students and professionals who help sustain the ongoing project.

More recently, Soleri has been developing concepts for arcologies that turn with the sun and have bases such as mining, timbering, and the performing arts.

PATRICIA C. PHILLIPS

WORKS

1951–1952, Artistica Ceramica, Solimene, Italy. 1956, Earth House, Cosanti Foundation, Ariz. 1969–, Arcosanti, Cordes Junction, Mayer, Ariz.

BIBLIOGRAPHY

Paolo Soleri: Architectural Drawings. 1981 New York: Susan Caldwell. Exhibition catalogue.
SKY, ALISON, and STONE, MICHELLE 1976 *Unbuilt America.* New York: McGraw-Hill.
SOLERI, PAOLO 1969 *Arcology: The City in the Image of Man.* Cambridge, Mass.: M.I.T. Press.
SOLERI, PAOLO 1971 *The Sketchbooks of Paolo Soleri.* Cambridge, Mass.: M.I.T. Press.

SOLER Y MARCH, ALEJANDRO

Alejandro Soler y March (1874–1949) was born in Barcelona, Spain. He was professor and director of the School of Architecture of Barcelona from 1931 to 1939. He restored the façade of the Cathedral of Manresa (1918–1921) and wrote "The sarcophagus of Saint Eulalia" in *Arquitectura i Urbanisme* (1934), and "Gaudí at the Seu de Manera," in *Ciutat* (1926).

JUAN BASSEGODA NONELL
*Translated from Spanish by
Judith E. Meighan*

WORKS

1906–1909, Casa H. Pons, 19 Rbla. de Cataluña; 1907, Convento de Los Angeles en Pedralbes; Barcelona, Spain. 1908, Iglesia de La Bauma, Spain. 1909–, Iglesia de Arucas, Grand Canary Island, Spain. 1912, Casa Abadal, Manresa, Spain. 1912, Monumento al P. Claret, Sallent, Spain. 1918–1921, Cathedral (restored façade), Manresa, Spain.

BIBLIOGRAPHY

CIRICI PELLICER, ALEJANDRO 1951 *El Arte modernista catalán.* Barcelona, Spain: Ayrrá.
RÀFOLS, JOSÉ F. 1949 *Modernismo y modernistas.* Barcelona, Spain: Destino.

SOMMARUGA, GIUSEPPE

Giuseppe Sommaruga (1867–1917) was born to a family of decorators and artisans in Milan. He at-

Sommaruga. Palazzo Castiglione. Milan. 1901–1903

tended classes at the Brera Academy in Milan where he was exposed to the ideas of CAMILLO BOITO and LUCA BELTRAMI.

In 1890, he entered the National Parliament Building competition in Rome with LUIGI BROGGI. Following a series of modest commissions in Milan and Rome in the 1890s, he was commissioned in 1900 to design a large palazzo in Milan. His patron, Ermenegildo Castiglione, like many of Sommaruga's clients, was an engineer and member of the urban industrial middle class of northern Italy. In preparation for this task, Castiglione and Sommaruga traveled extensively in Europe studying contemporary architecture. The Palazzo Castiglione was constructed between 1901 and 1903. It is one of the major monuments of the Italian *stile liberty* and contains most of the chief characteristics of Sommaruga's personal style: asymmetrical accents contrasting with but not detracting from the overall impression of classical solidity and symmetry, the enrichment of surface through the juxtaposition of textures, and the animation of the whole through exuberant figural and vegetal ornamentation. The scandalous nude female figures flanking the main entrance (executed by Ernesto Bazzaro) were removed soon after the completion of the building. A great stairhall serves as the focal point of the interior.

In 1903, Sommaruga won the competition for the design of the Italian pavilion at the International Exposition in St. Louis, Missouri. The pompous monumentalism of the pavilion is typical of Sommaruga's designs for civic commissions and contrasts with the livelier sense of ornament and massing in his private commissions.

The exotic nature of Sommaruga's sources, his strong sense of massing, and his unabashed zest for ornament influenced a number of Lombard architects, including GIULIO ARATA, ALFREDO CAMPANINI, and ANTONIO SANT'ELIA.

DENNIS DOORDAN

WORKS

1897, Palazzine Aletti, Rome. 1901–1903, Palazzo Castiglione, Milan. *1903–1904, Italian Pavilion, St. Louis World's Fair, Mo. 1906, Villa Comi; 1906, Villa Salmoiraghi; Milan. 1906–1907, Villa Faccanoni; 1907, Faccanoni Mausoleum; Sarnico, Italy. 1908–1912, Hotel Tre Croci, Campo di Fiori, Italy. 1913, Villa Romeo, Milan.

BIBLIOGRAPHY

MONNERET DE VILLARD, UGO (editor) 1908 L'Architettura di Giuseppe Sommaruga. Milan: Preiss & Bestetti.
NICOLETTI, MANFREDI 1978 L'Architettura Liberty in Italia. Bari, Italy: Laterza.
PEVSNER, NICOLAUS, and RICHARDS, J. M. (editors) 1973 The Anti-Rationalists. London: Architectural Press.

SONCK, LARS ELIEL

Along with the internationally famous ELIEL SAARINEN, Lars Eliel Sonck (1870–1956) was the pre-eminent Finnish architect of the early twentieth century who gave Finnish architecture the robust, indigenous qualities that made the "golden age of Finnish art" a distinctive variation of the *Jugendstil*. He achieved this distinction through the skillful integration of contemporary international styles and national idioms. For example, Sonck's familiarity with international domestic architecture and the Karelian wooden buildings of eastern Finland, then regarded as the cradle of Finnish culture, are successfuly combined in his early wooden villas, a type which he used throughout his career, albeit later in simplified form.

Sonck may be best known for his imposing commercial structures in Helsinki as well as several large churches. In 1894, his last year at the Polytechnic Institute, Helsinki, he won the competition for Saint Michael's Turku, a major commission based in part on German ecclesiastical architecture and brickwork which Sonck studied in Germany. Saint Michael's makes an interesting comparison with his early masterpiece, The Cathedral of Saint John's (1902–1907), Tampere. Although Finland is usually associated with timber building, in western Finland there is stone building, a tradition with which Sonck was familiar because he had lived in the Åland Islands from childhood and attended the prestigious Åbo Academy in Turku as a boy. However, the use of rough-faced stone at Saint John's is of international inspiration, although the granite is from Finnish quarries, was laid according to Sonck's design (irregular surface level of stones, large and small stones contrasting, and small voussoirs, quoins, and courses set against the rough-faced body), and incorporated Sonck's intriguing sculptural detail.

This use of stone and sculpture appears again on the Telephone Building (1905), Helsinki, a large, picturesquely conceived building planned around a courtyard. The Stock Exchange Building (1911), Helsinki, and the Mortgage Society Building (1908), Helsinki, are two monumental stone buildings in which the smooth granite blocks and symmetry of the plan reflect the general trend toward classicism. The impact of modernism on Sonck's later work is particularly evident in his outstanding late work, Mikael Agricola Church (1935), Helsinki, with its smooth, undecorated brick surfaces.

As for town planning, Sonck was critical of the existing planning of Helsinki and of the grid plan in general. He preferred the city planning principles of CAMILLO SITTE and began a series of articles in 1898 that reflected the Austrian's ideas. In these articles, Sonck also made suggestions for planning Eira, a residential area of southern Helsinki where he also built the picturesque Eira Hospital (1905); in 1908, he submitted a plan, incorporating his idea of plots with independent houses and small gardens, which was carried out. In addition to other town planning schemes, Sonck laid out Kulosaari (1907–1909), a suburb of Helsinki, and drew up influential plans for the Töölö district of Helsinki (1903) that were used in modified form.

JUDITH S. HULL

WORKS

1894, Saint Michael's, Turku, Finland. 1895, Lasses Villa, Bartsgårda, Finström; 1896, Villa Skogshyddan, Mariehamn; Åland Islands, Finland. 1902–1907, Saint John's Cathedral, Tampere, Finland. 1903, Town Plan (with Gustaf Nystrom), Töölö District, Helsinki. 1904, Villa Ainola, Järvenpää, Finland. 1905, Eira Hospital; 1905, Telephone Building; 1907–1909, Town Plan, Kulosaari; 1908, Mortgage Society Building; 1908, Town Plan (with Armas Lindgren and Bertel Jung), Eira District; 1909–1912, Kallio Church; 1911, Stock Exchange Building; Helsinki, Finland. *1913–1923, Villa Brakeudd, Hirsala, Kirkkonummi, Finland. 1915, Fire Station, Kulosaari, Helsinki. 1927, Mariehamn Church, Åland Islands, Finland. 1935, Mikael Agricola Church (with Arvo Muroma), Helsinki. 1939, Town Hall, Mariehamn, Åland Islands, Finland.

BIBLIOGRAPHY

SONCK, LARS 1897 "Till frågan om restaurering af Åbo Domkyrka." Finsk Tidskrift Jan.:22–28.
SONCK, LARS 1898 "Modern Vandalism: Helsingfors Stadsplan." Finsk Tidskrift 1898:262–287.
SONCK, LARS 1900 "Några reflexioner (rörande Helsingfors stadsplan)." Tekniska Föreningens i Finland Förhandlingar no. 1:28–30.

SONCK, LARS 1902 "Maamiehen koti I." *Rakentaja* 1:5.

SONCK, LARS 1904*a* "En arkitektonisk fråga, behandlad på kyrkostämma i Åbo." *Arkitekten* 2:17–20.

SONCK, LARS 1904*b* "På orätt spår." *Arkitekten* 8:83–84.

SONCK, LARS 1909 "Huru det bygges i Helsingfors." *Argus* no. 7:66–67.

SONCK, LARS 1915 "En segsliten kyrkobyggnadsfråga: Platsen för Borgå nya kyrka." *Arkitekten* 2:19–23.

TREIB, EDWARD MARC 1971 "Lars Sonck: From the Roots." *Journal of the Society of Architectural Historians* 30 no. 3:228–237.

SORBY, THOMAS CHARLES

Born in Chevet, Yorkshire, England, Thomas Charles Sorby (1836–1924) was articled in London to Charles Reeves and succeeded him briefly in 1867 as surveyor of county courts and surveyor to the Metropolitan London Police. Returning to private practice, he designed several residences in the Old English manner. In 1883, Sorby emigrated to Canada and found work in Montreal with the Canadian Pacific Railway, producing designs for stations and hotels. He moved to British Columbia with the railway in 1886 and designed several of Vancouver's early office buildings. He completed his career in Victoria with private residences in the Queen Anne style.

HAROLD KALMAN

WORKS

1864, Town Hall, Bromley, Kent, England. *1865–1868, Wyggeston's Hospital, Leicester, England. *1866–1867, Saint Michael and All Angels, Sheffield, England. 1868, Clerkenwell Police Station, London. 1868, Courthouse, Barnsley; 1868, Courthouse, Halifax; Yorkshire, England. 1870, Whitehill, Luton, Bedfordshire, England. 1878, New Grange, Pirton, Hertfordshire, England. 1883, Canadian Pacific Railway Station, Peterborough, Ontario. *1883, Canadian Pacific Railway Station, Port Arthur, Ontario. *1885–1886, Glacier House, British Columbia. *1886–1887, Hotel Vancouver; *1887, Harry Abbott House; 1889, Bank of British Columbia; Vancouver, British Columbia. 1890, The Laurels; 1898, Weiler Building; Victoria, British Columbia.

BIBLIOGRAPHY

KALMAN, HAROLD 1978 *Exploring Vancouver 2.* Vancouver: University of British Columbia Press.

LINSTRUM, DEREK 1978 *West Yorkshire: Architects and Architecture.* London: Lund Humphries. Includes a list of Sorby's buildings in that county prepared by Kalman.

"Obituary." 1924 *Victoria Daily Times* Nov. 17, p. 18.

SEGGER, MARTIN, and FRANKLIN, DOUGLAS 1979 *Victoria: A Primer for Regional History in Architecture.* Watkins Glen, N.Y.: American Life Foundation.

SORBY, THOMAS C. 1901 "Domestic Architecture in England During the Middle Ages." *American Architect* 72:6–7, 52–53, 76–78.

SORDO MADALENO, JUAN

Juan Sordo Madaleno (1916–) has designed and constructed an enormous quantity of important works in Mexico City and in Acapulco, Mexico, noted both for economy and for his organizational talents for clients of the national bourgeoisie. In his works, there is a preoccupation with clarity, a well-understood funtionalism in the structural solution, and a magnificent aesthetic sense, certainly in materials and dimensions.

Prominent in his numerous works are his solutions for office buildings, private homes, and various religious chapels to integrate them into the surrounding architectural complexes.

Sordo Madeleno has been professor of architectural design at the National University of Mexico. Recently, he completed one of the largest banking complexes in the country.

SALVADOR PINOCELLY
Translated from Spanish by Judith E. Meighan

SØRENSON, CARL THEODORE

The Danish landscape architect Carl Theodore Sørenson (1892–1979) trained under the landscape architect E. Erstad-Jørgensens and went into independent practice in 1922. Appointed lecturer at the Royal Art Academy in 1940, he later became professor there (1954–1963). He was city gardener at Gentofte, Sjaelland, a suburb of Copenhagen (1959–1963), and was noted for the architectonic quality of his landscapes; he worked in collaboration with leading Danish architects.

JUDITH S. HULL

WORKS

1932, University of Aarhus (landscaping; with KAY FISKER, POVL STEGMAN, and C. F. MØLLER), Denmark. 1935, Storgaarden Apartments (landscaping; with POVL BAUMANN and Knud Hansen); 1939, Klokkergaarden Apartments (landscaping; with Baumann and Hansen); Copenhagen. 1962, Nygaardsparken Apartments (landscaping), Brønbyøster, near Copenhagen.

BIBLIOGRAPHY

"C. Th. Sørenson." 1979 Page 1060 in *Kraks Bla Bog 1979.* Copenhagen: Krak.

SØRENSON, C. TH. 1931 *Parkpolitik i Sogn og Købstad.* Copenhagen: Gyldendal.

SØRENSON, C. TH. 1939 *Om Haver.* Copenhagen: Emil Wiene.

SØRENSON, C. TH. 1959 *Europas Havekunst.* Copenhagen.

SØRENSON, C. TH. 1963 *Origins of Garden Art.* Copenhagen: Arkitektens Forlag.

SØRENSON, C. TH. 1975 *Haver: Tanker og Arbejder.* Copenhagen: Ejlers.

SORIA, GIOVANNI BATTISTA

Born in Rome, Giovanni Battista Soria (1581–1651) studied with the woodcarver and architectural draftsman GIOVANNI BATTISTA MONTANO. As a young man, he traveled in central Italy and Sicily, assisting in the construction of some buildings. In Rome, he was employed as a worker in wood (*falegname*), and documents show his considerable production on behalf of the Borghese family, at the Palazzo Borghese and other properties (1614–1626), the Cappella Paolina at Santa Maria Maggiore (1614–1615), and elsewhere. He also worked at St. Peter's in this capacity, beginning in 1618. After the death of his teacher in 1621, Soria saw to the publication of Montano's drawings, editing the *Scielta di varij tempietti antichi* (Rome, 1624, dedicated to Cardinal Borghese, with a preface written by Soria) and other works. It was only in the mid-1620s, when he was about forty-five years old, that Soria emerged as an architect, with the patronage of Cardinal Scipione Borghese.

Soria.
San Gregorio Magno.
Rome.
1629–1633

Soria's works show that he was aware of recent developments in Roman architecture but that, in spite of the patronage of the prominent Borghese and Barberini families and the friendship of PIETRO BERRETTINI DA CORTONA, he remained conservative. His first work, the façade of Santa Maria della Vittoria (1625–1627, paid for by Scipione Borghese), must be compared to its neighbor, Santa Susanna, CARLO MADERNO's masterpiece of 1603. Soria accepted the same two-story basilica format but rejected Maderno's clarity of composition, vigor, and hierarchical plasticity in favor of a flat and restrained composition. Some detailed forms clearly refer to Maderno's work, but the inert scroll-buttresses to the sides of the second story betray the absence of Maderno's vital vision. The façade of San Crisogono (1626), Cardinal Borghese's titular church, shows a simple one story portico, set before the basilical body of the church. Soria modernized this traditional type by making it more substantial, framing the central five-bay colonnade with broad mural bays; but the classical forms (characteristically more austere than at Santa Maria della Vittoria), the restraint, and the careful composition speak rather of the late sixteenth century than of more recent Roman architecture. In the façade of San Gregorio Magno (1629–1633), Soria presents his most complex synthesis of Roman types, bringing together the façade of two stories equal in width, its center bays topped by a pediment corresponding to the nave within, as in the late sixteenth-century Church of San Luigi dei Francesi; the two-story façade with open portico below and windows above, as at San Sebastiano fuori le mura (1612); and the dynamic development of this second type in GIOVANNI LORENZO BERNINI's façade of Santa Bibiana (1624). Yet, the difficult composition, forcefulness, and almost primitive classical forms of Bernini's design are eschewed in favor of a calm and regular composition of familiar elements. Soria's façade for San Carlo ai Catinari (1635–1638) also depends on the established type of San Luigi dei Francesi, and here the contrast with the almost exactly contemporary work of his friend Pietro da Cortona at Santi Luca e Martina is most telling. Cortona completely reinterprets the type, while for Soria it is enough to make slight adjustments and revisions. In the façade and portico of Santa Caterina da Siena (1638–1640), Soria resumes the theme of San Gregorio, with its three arched openings, but the subdued dynamism of San Gregorio is entirely suppressed. Santa Caterina's uniformity of emphasis, narrowness, and single large triangular pediment call to mind its near-contemporary and neighbor, Santi Domenico e Sisto.

As Soria stepped back from the plasticity, originality, and forcefulness of his Roman contemporaries, so too he avoided the implications of the works of Montano which he edited in the 1620s. Whereas FRANCESCO BORROMINI and others seem to have welcomed the variety and spatial complexity of Montano's sometimes fantastic view of antiquity, Soria consistently maintained the prudent forms and compositions of late sixteenth-century architecture.

During the years of his architectural activity, Soria continued to work as a woodcarver, sometimes taking on projects of architectural scope. After the death of his earlier patron Scipione Borghese in 1633, he worked for the Barberini family, always as *falegname* rather than as architect, at various places in Rome and outside the city. His work in the new south wing of the Palazzo Barberini, executed between 1633 and 1638, included the magnificent colonnaded wood fittings for the library; in 1639, he provided woodwork for the Barberini Theater, newly built to the north of the palace.

PATRICIA WADDY

WORKS

1625–1627, Santa Maria della Vittoria (façade); 1626, San Crisogono (restoration and façade); 1629–1633, San Gregorio Magno (façade and atrium); Rome. 1630, Cathedral (nave), Monte Compatri, Italy. 1633–1635, Library, Palazzo Barberini; 1635–1638, San Carlo ai Catinari (façade); 1638–1640, Santa Caterina da Siena (façade and portico); Rome.

BIBLIOGRAPHY

For additional information on Giovanni Battista Soria, see the Barberini Archives in the Biblioteca Apostolica Vaticana, and the Borghese Archives in the Archivio Segreto Vaticano, both in Vatican City.

APOLLONJ GHETTI, BRUNO M. 1966 *S. Crisogono.* Rome: Marietti.

BAGLIONE, GIOVANNI (1642)1935 *Le vite de' pittori, scultori ed architetti.* Rome: Calzone.

HIBBARD, HOWARD 1962 *The Architecture of the Palazzo Borghese.* American Academy in Rome.

HIBBARD, HOWARD 1971 *Carlo Maderno and Roman Architecture: 1580–1630.* University Park: Pennsylvania State University Press.

MATTHIAE, GUGLIELMO 1938 "Giovan Battista Soria Architetto Romano." *Capitolium* 13:412–420.

ORTOLANI, SERGIO 1927 *San Carlo a' Catinari.* Rome: Treves.

PASCOLI, LIONE (1736)1933 *Vite de' Pittori, scultori, ed architetti moderni.* Reprint. Rome: Calzone.

POLLAK, OSKAR 1928–1931 *Die Kunsttätigkeit unter Urban VIII.* Vienna: Filser.

ZANDER, GIUSEPPE 1958–1962 "Le invenzioni architettoniche di Giovanni Battista Montano Milanese (1534–1621)." *Quaderni dell'Istituto di Storia dell'-Architettura* 30:1–21; 49–50:1–32.

SORIA Y MATA, ARTURO

Arturo Soria y Mata (1844–1920) invented modern linear planning in the 1880s. He was not an engineer, as he has often been called, but rather a scientifically educated inventor, a radical republican politician (1866–1873), an administrative official in Puerto Rico and Cuba in the early 1870s and late 1880s, and the founder of one of Madrid's first tramways which he ran for about ten years in the 1870s and 1880s.

As Soria envisaged it, a linear city is formed and grows along an artery of transportation and transmission of people, goods, and services. In ancient times, there have been natural linear road-towns, formed like caravansaries, and there are the "natural," disastrously congested "ribbon" developments and exploding metropolises of recent times. Soria's desire was to avoid unhealthy urban congestion by simple linear connectors between cities that would redistribute the urban population and industry in parallel superblocks, allowing residents easy access to the healthy flanking countryside. In 1892, Soria founded the Companía Madrileña de Urbanización which undertook to establish a fifty-five-kilometer railroad/trolley line around Madrid. In 1894, he celebrated the inauguration of the first house in what was to become La Ciudad Lineal of Madrid, a five-kilometer portion of his project, which, through his tree-planting of the meseta on annual Arbor Day, became an attractive suburban garden-city. Its green swath with cottage-scale buildings was particularly visible from the air until it recently was swallowed up into Greater Madrid and overbuilt. The Ciudad Lineal antedated Letchworth in England as the first garden-city plan, and for many years Soria's theory rivaled that of EBENEZER HOWARD, largely through the efforts of the Frenchman GEORGES BENOIT-LÉVY who lobbied internationally for linear planning and, indirectly, caused it to play an important role in Soviet planning of the 1920s.

In 1897, Soria began to publish the magazine *La Ciudad Lineal* which continued until 1932, and from 1902 when it began to call itself the "Revista de urbanización, ingenería, higiene, y agricultura" was essentially the first periodical ever devoted to city planning. Soria and his associate Hilarión González del Castillo produced many articles and booklets publicizing linear planning and took part in numerous early city planning congresses. They gained adherents such as the English Linear City Association, and especially Chile, itself a linear country, where the engineer and housing reformer Carlos Carvajal almost brought about several linear settlements. In India, Captain J. W. Petavel of England, an exponent of decentralization through

Soria y Mata.
La Ciudad Lineal.
Madrid.
1892–1894

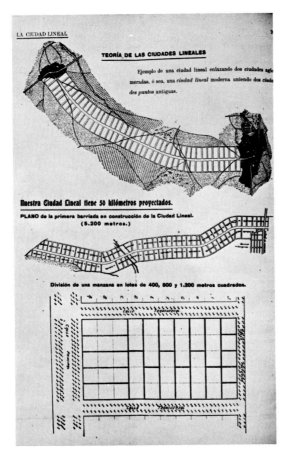

high-speed locomotion, proposed linear colonies. By the 1930s, the Ciudad Lineal idea, which had come about largely through the tracked mass transit of the late nineteenth century, became car and bus oriented and gained many adherents, including Henry Ford, FRANK LLOYD WRIGHT, and LE CORBUSIER as well as the Soviets. In an outburst of visionary planning in the 1960s, there appeared more linear schemes than any time before, taking a variety of forms. These ranged from single-axis plans to production line arrangements similar to factory assembly lines and compound forms generally associated with branching "neighborhood" plans, to huge regional triangular and hexagonal networks, and monumental linear megastructures.

GEORGE R. COLLINS

WORK

1892–1894, La Ciudad Lineal, Madrid.

BIBLIOGRAPHY

COLLINS, GEORGE R. 1970 "Linear Planning and its Bibliography." *Newsletter of the Urban History Group* 29:1–12. Includes a representative selection of writings on linear planning.
COLLINS, GEORGE R.; FLORES LOPEZ, CARLOS; and SORIA Y PUIG, ARTURO 1968 *Arturo Soria y La Cuidad Lineal.* Madrid: Revista de Occidente. Includes an almost complete bibliography of writings by Arturo Soria y Mata, his son, Arturo Soria y

Hernández, the Compañía Madrileña de Urbanización, Hilarión González del Castillo, George Benoit-Lévy and others on the Ciudad Lineal de Madrid.

SOSTRATOS OF KNODOS

Sostratos of Knodos (flourished c.280–250 B.C.) designed the greatest lighthouse of the ancient world—one of its seven wonders—the Pharos of Alexandria (c.270 B.C.). The base was about 100-feet square, tapering up for about 200 feet to a platform from which an octagonal section rose to a second platform, from which, in turn, the final cylindrical section reached to some 440 feet above the ground. Ramps and stairs on the interior gave access to the beacon at the summit. The Pharos stood until c.1375, when the last remains were destroyed by an earthquake.

B. M. BOYLE

WORK

*c.270 B.C., Pharos, Alexandria, Egypt.

BIBLIOGRAPHY

English translation of the ancient texts can be found in the volumes of the Loeb Classical Library series, published by Harvard University Press and Heinemann.
DINSMOOR, WILLIAM B. (1902)1975 *The Architecture of Ancient Greece.* Reprint of 1950 ed. New York: Norton. Originally published with the title *The Architecture of Ancient Greece and Rome.*
LAWRENCE, ARNOLD W. (1957)1975 *Greek Architecture.* Harmondsworth, England: Penguin.
PLINY, *Historia naturalis,* Book 36.83.

SOSTRES, JOSEP MARIA

Josep Maria Sostres (1915–) was the theoretical leader of *Grupo R,* founded in 1952 by a small circle of architects in Barcelona to recover the threads of the Modern movement lost under the Franco regime. He also was a founder member of *Amigos de Gaudí* which gave ANTONIO GAUDÍ Y CORNET worldwide recognition. These twin activities make Sostres an unusual precursor of the historical awareness of the 1960s and 1970s. His theoretical work has been complemented by a small output of buildings, four of which form the cornerstones of modern architecture in Catalonia: Agustí House (1953–1955) in Sitges, with its Aaltonian (see ALVAR AALTO) liberation of the cube; the M.M.I. House (1955–1958) in Barcelona with its reminder of the elegant values of rationalism; the Hotel Maria Victoria Puigcerda (1956–1957); and the El Noticiero Universal Newspaper Building

(1963–1965) in Barcelona which introduced the notion of "background" architecture without concessions to historicism. Sostres now holds the chair of history at the Barcelona School of Architecture.

DAVID MACKAY

WORKS

1953–1955, Agustí House, Sitges, Spain. 1955–1958, M.M.I. House, Ciudad Diagonal, Barcelona, Spain. 1956–1957, Hotel Maria Victoria, Puigcerdà, Gerona, Spain. 1963–1965, El Noticiero Universal Newspaper Building, Barcelona, Spain.

BIBLIOGRAPHY

MACKAY, DAVID 1980 "Sostres Maluquer, Josep Maria." Pages 764–765 in Muriel Emanuel (editor), *Contemporary Architects.* New York: St. Martin's.

SOTA MARTINEZ, ALEJANDRO DE LA

Alejandro de la Sota Martinez (1913–) was born in Pontevedra, Spain. He received his architectural degree in 1941. His work is one of the strongest examples of clarity and intuition among the Spanish architects of his generation. Together with JOSÉ ANTONIO CODERCH Y DE SENTMENAT, he represents the most rigorous conceptual position of the postwar period in Spain. His position of advanced individuality has earned him both the admiration of his many students and a generally cool attitude from his fellow architects.

Several stages can be distinguished in his work. The first phase which lasted until approximately 1957 is characterized by a populist poetry with surrealist nuances whose best examples are the township of Esquivel, Sevilla, and the village of Fuencarrel "B" in Madrid. From 1957 to 1962, he attempted to achieve in his works a rigorous refinement of the rationalist language. From the purity of the Civil Government building of Tarragona (1957) to the Gymnasium of the Maravillas School (1962) in Madrid, he progressively broke with the orthodoxy of the Modern movement.

The third phase which still continues is characterized by a formal independence and utopian proposals that are truly disconcerting and difficult to classify. In this phase, he moved from a Brutalist interpretation toward a certain humble architecture devoid of ideological connotations. De la Sota seems to probe the very limits of his architecture. Precise and ordered, imprecise and ambiguous, elementary and subtle at the same time, it explores the contradictions of the complex culture of modern-day Spain.

In 1979–1980, he designed Iberia Airlines branch offices in Kuwait, Rio de Janeiro, Munich, Geneva, Moscow, Frankfurt, and Madrid.

MIGUEL ANGEL BALDELLOU
Translated from Spanish by
Judith E. Meighan

WORKS

1950, Mision Biologica, Pontevedra, Spain. 1954, Treasury Delegation, Tarragona, Spain. 1956, Treasury Delegation, La Coruña, Spain. 1957, Civil Government Building, Tarragona, Spain. 1962, Gymnasium, Maravillas School, Madrid. 1964, House, Mar Menor, Murcia, Spain. 1966, Sports Pavilion, Pontevedra, Spain. 1973, Savings Building, Madrid. 1979–1980, Iberia Airlines Branch Offices, Kuwait, Rio de Janeiro, Munich, Geneva, Moscow, Frankfurt, Madrid.

BIBLIOGRAPHY

BALDELLOU, MIGUEL ANGEL n.d. "La arquitectura de Alejandro de la Sota." *Hogar y Arquitectura* 115.
BENEVOLO, LEONARDO (1963)1971 *History of Modern Architecture.* Cambridge, Mass.: M.I.T.
DOMENECH GIRBAU, LUIS 1968 *Arquitectura española contemporánea.* Barcelona, Spain: Blume.
FLORES LOPEZ, CARLOS 1961 *Arquitectura española contemporánea.* Madrid: Aguilar.
FLORES LOPEZ, CARLOS, and AMANN, EDUARDO 1967 *Guía de la arquitectura de Madrid.* Madrid: Artes Gráficas Ibarra.

SOUFFLOT, JACQUES-GABRIEL

Jacques-Gabriel Soufflot (1713–1780) was one of the most important architectural personalities of the eighteenth century, both a predecessor of doctrinaire neoclassicism and independent of those visionary tendencies which led to so-called "Revolutionary" architecture. A practical architect, he conquered the tasteful reign of the rococo in France and redirected architectural practice to an interest in the architectonic and in technical problems. Together with CHARLES DE WAILLY and (see PEYRE FAMILY) he belongs to that generation which established new standards in both ecclesiastical and secular architecture, as well as in theater design, an especially future-striving building type. More than any of his contemporaries Soufflot was in a position which enabled him not only to take up the newest archeological impulses (especially from Paestum), but also to integrate a thorough knowledge and appreciation of the French classical tradition in architecture since JACQUES FRANÇOIS BLONDEL and CLAUDE PERRAULT with ancient and modern Italian architectural tradition. These most diverse traditions meet in Soufflot's major work, the church of Sainte-Geneviève in Paris (1755–1780), which in its turn joined the ranks of the greatest modern ecclesiastical buildings: St. Peter's in Rome and Saint Paul's in London.

Soufflot was born on July 22, 1713, in Irancy near Auxerre and was able to travel to Rome for study as early as c.1731. He is known to have been in Rome by spring 1733 at the very latest. At the end of 1734 he was in the French Academy at Rome, having been taken up by Wleughel; he remained attached to this institution until his return to France in 1738. His first Roman stay coincided with the last flourishing of Roman-Papal building activity, including the great workshops of the façades of San Giovanni in Laterano and Santa Maria Maggiore as well as the Trevi Fountain. These are recognizably indebted to the heritage of the great Roman Seicento architectural tradition and clearly reveal the direct progeny of CARLO FONTANA and FILIPPO JUVARRA, with the limits and richness of a calibrated architecture, indebted to architectonic elements rather than to a decorative style. Soufflot's first years in Rome also coincided with the Accademia di San Luca's awarding of prizes and election to membership of LUIGI VANVITELLI and BERNARDO ANTONIO VITTONE (April 1713), whose taut architectural language is comparable with Soufflot's work in Lyon. Also comparable—as they are typical of the period—are the content and results of Soufflot's earliest Roman studies, which include studies of GIOVANNI LORENZO BERNINI's Monument to Mathilde di Canossa (1633–1637), drawings of San Andrea della Valle, San Ignazio and San Carlo al Corso—which was later exhibited and discussed in the Academy of Lyon (1739)—and finally his intense involvement with St. Peter's.

After his return from Rome, Soufflot began in Lyons that practical activity which he would sustain throughout his life. His work was in part facilitated by contacts he had secured in Rome. In Lyon he created his first significant architectural works: the Hôtel-Dieu (Hospital) (1739–1748), the Loge des Changes (1748–1750), and the theater (1753–1756). He had scarcely arrived in the city when he was elected in 1738 to the Academy of Lyon, where in succeeding years he presented papers on Proportions, Taste and Rules, and Gothic architecture as well as reported his Italian experiences inclusive of his measurements of Roman churches up to St. Peter's and Bernini's colonnade. After returning from his second Italy Journey in 1751, Soufflot, renewed, introduced the most up-to-date discoveries, including the first reports from Herculaneum and from the "archaeological front." These pronouncements displayed his equal command of architectural tradition and theory, and revealed him, already in 1744, as an opponent of fashion ("la nouveauté, enfant monstreux"

[novelty, a monstrous child]) and as a rationalist advocate of solid knowledge and rules. They showed him nonetheless to be open to the new and the newest experiences. Thanks to his close contacts with his younger colleagues, whose services he could always procure, Soufflot was also aware of the innovations among the circle of French "pensionnaires" in Rome in the 1740s and 1750s. Dumont, Bellicard and Petitot were his most reliable contacts in this group.

Apart from several private commissions, Soufflot was occupied at first in Lyon primarily with the Hôtel-Dieu, where he had to work with the preceeding project of Le Bon (1732) for new buildings along the Rhone. After 1736 even greater opportunities for expansion presented themselves. In 1739–1741 Soufflot designed the extensive new sections, including the central pavilion and the flanking avant-corps. The corner stone was laid in 1741 and the mid-section was completed in 1748. In 1747 Soufflot exhibited drawings of his project in the Académie Royale in Paris, followed by functional plans in 1749. The project was engraved by Sellier, Poulleau, and Blondel, and was a substantial impetus for Soufflot's subsequent career. It probably also fostered his contact with Madame de Pompadour, who choose him to accompany de Vandières on his Italian tour. This was to be especially consequential for Soufflot.

While the long river façade of the Hôtel-Dieu is, ultimately, more or less, another variation on the elevation of Perrault's Louvre colonnade, relying also on the motive of oval oculi ornamented with garlands, the middle portion, on the other hand, displays for the first time in a major architectural work the new Louis XVI style. Although the multiple enframements of the attic windows and their placement within a linear skeleton of moldings still recall Italian and Piedmontese models; the garlands, lion's heads, drapery and meander-like decorative forms suggest however—despite the use of the Ionic order—the imminent "goût grec" [Greek taste], with which the young pensionnaires were experimenting at this time, especially in drawings and in decorative arts.

Soufflot's second principle work of his early Lyon period, the Loge des Changes, which he designed from 1747 on (but did not execute himself, does not display such progressive elements. In the use of the orders it reveals antique characteristics indeed, while the treatment of the corners displays an Italian flexibility. Specifically Roman stylistic motives are quoted here, as in the design of the clock in particular. At the beginning of 1750, as Soufflot undertook a second Italian trip, he had already a rich architectural *oeuvre* behind him, which included also works for Cardinal de Tencin (renovation of the Archepiscopal Palace (1747–1749) among other works) and other ecclesiastical buildings. Ever vigilant in his attention to the newest trend, Lyon's own contribution to Soufflot's concrete experience should not be undervalued. Lying near to Italy (and especially to Piedmont), the city witnessed also a fertile architectural development in interior organization and arrangements. The wealth of types of Lyon architecture and the diversity of commissions Soufflot was offered there provided an ideal introduction for his later work.

In many respects Soufflot's journey to Italy in the antourage of M. de Vandières, the later Marquis de Marigny, together with the Abbé Le Blanc and Cochin, represented an especially propitious experience. This event of 1750, which linked Soufflot with the most influential architectural patron and the most important critic, is often and quite correctly seen as the pronouncement of the official shift in taste in favor of the "Louis Seize" and furthermore as the beginning of that fertile involvement with the Greek Doric order in architecture. In fact the visit to Paestum—even if Dumont's print appeared only much later in 1764—and also that to Herculaneum were most important. The latter aroused in addition the discussion over the form of theaters to which Dumont, Soufflot, as well as Cochin made important contributions. Soufflot's return to Rome was crowned by his election to the Accademia di San Luca. His meeting with the future minister and Marquis de Marigny guaranteed him a career in Paris.

However, before he was called to Paris by Marigny in 1755, Soufflot had the opportunity to add a further influential design to his Lyon *oeuvre,* with the milestone building of his Lyon Theater. He presented the plans to the Lyon Academy in 1753, the ground stone was laid in 1754, and the theater already opened in 1756. The theater offered a decisive impetus to the subsequent development and independence of the free-standing theater type, in its integration of stage and auditorium as a single mass, which certainly found, general recognition by the time of the Odeon in Paris [see Peyre and De Wailly] at the very latest.

In 1755 Marigny provided Soufflot with the commission of his career, one which occupied him until his death: the building of the church to the Parisian patron saint Sainte-Geneviève. Various activities, some involving city planning, were still to tie him to Lyon. Soufflot also assumed a wealth of new duties in Paris. For Marigny himself he designed and built a suburban house (1769) in the newly developing Champs-Elysées neighborhood, with whose planning Soufflot was involved exten-

sively. Similar neo-Palladian elements were integrated in Marigny's country estate at Ménars, begun in 1765, where Soufflot's designs—including the temple, garden, and grotto—illustrate the new fashion for "Rustica". Also through Marigny's continuing agency, Soufflot was considered for substantial city planning commissions in Paris including even the "dégagement," or clearing, of the square before Perrault's Louvre collonnade. In that flurry of Royal Square building in France's provincial cities, Soufflot also worked on those in Reims and Lyon. Finally, among his duties in his position as "Contrôleur des Bâtiments," he was occupied from 1756 with the sacristy of Notre-Dame Cathedral.

All of these diverse works, however, were subordinate to the one great commission, which gave him the opportunity after his early Roman studies of religious architecture, to compete with and to improve upon St. Peter's. The work was protracted, and not yet complete at Soufflot's death, resulting later in debates of fundamental significance concerning concrete questions of a technical sort in such a large-scale architectural endeavor. The foundations were begun in 1757. The crypt was completed in 1763, so that the festive groundstone laying ceremony could be held in 1764. Between 1765 and 1770 the walls and portico were executed, in 1772 the portico was roofed, while already in 1776, in removing the scaffolding from the portico, the first sinking was discovered. This discovery intensified the debate already begun in 1770 with Patte over the limits of architectural genius.

The undisputed kernel of the design is the maximal typology of (the effort to develop to its fullest) a cross-shaped plan with a dome on a drum and a columnar portico. From the beginning, the effect of a Latin cross plan—with its long entry sequence—was skillfully combined with the ideal symmetricality of the Greek cross type. Also from the beginning on, an indisputable significance was accorded to the free-standing columns and colonnades, which hark back to an earlier discussion of sacred architecture beginning at least with Cordemoy and to its subsequent impact on French ecclesiastical design. Striking, in any case, are the richly-treated corinthian columns, of an unprecedented monumentality. Especially noteworthy also are the projects for the crypt, in which already in the late 1750s the first effects of the discovery of the Greek Doric order at Paestum are reflected. The façade composition is also effective; its temple-front embodies the Vitruvian type and is evocative of the Pantheon's monumentality. The "corner strengthening" of the hexastyle portico with side columns which continue the inner order of the portico at the same time as they produce a façadelike closure in the side elevations, was a traditional solution of columnar composition since FRANÇOIS MANSART's Eglise des Minimes. Also on the interior, the colonnades—in the spirit of the Pantheon portico and of Perrault's Vitruvian interpretation—are primarily the starting point for the vaulting system set on transverse ribs and intersecting arches rising above the columns. Thus the bold system of great vaulted compartments is carried on a "supporting scaffold" of piers dissolved into columns. With this ingenious combination of vaulted and domed architecture, the most honored symbol of sacred design since the Renaissance, with the modern conception of a "Greek" trabeated architecture, Soufflot's building represents the first large-scale and consequential realization of a French ideal of ecclesiastical architecture. Doubts and lacks modified this ideal condition to a certain extent so that even in the drum of the dome, the free-standing colonnade is compromised in its purity by strengthening members. Nonetheless Soufflot's extremely noteworthy achievement lies precisely in the constructional aspect, a solution engendered by the ideal combination of two architectural systems never before coupled. In eighteenth-century Europe such daring is to be found otherwise only in the work of JOHANN BALTHAUSER NEUMANN. On the other hand it should also be recalled that reliable calculations of statics—made possible by the infinitesimal calculus—was only little by little made available during the second half of the century. Thus Soufflot's achievement appears in proper perspective only with the hindsight of the later polemic over Sainte-Geneviève, with JEAN BAPTISTE RONDELET and his follower the vaulting specialist EMILIAND MARIE GAUTHEY. Since FILIPPO BRUNELLESCHI and since St. Peter's the quest for a "maximal architecture" was always a problem of technical mastery as well. CHRISTOPHER WREN, the creator of Saint Paul's, was an experienced mathematician and scientist and in the 1740s St. Peter's—as a result of suspected dangerous junctures in the structure—was of great interest to the "matematici" Polenis, Boscovich', Lesueurs, and Jacquiers. In this context Soufflot's measurements of St. Peter's and those of his friend and adviser Dumont take on a significance which exceeds the artistic and typological moments of the relationship of Sainte-Geneviève to St. Peter's and returns to the fundamental problem of architectural mastery in a "super project".

Along with this undeniable priority of the technical, the planning of Sainte-Geneviève reveals also Soufflot's endeavor to realize the then modern style, which in the executed work is reflected in the rich protoneoclassical architectural ornament. The first project after 1755 employed on the interior of the dome's drum that first "classicist" Louis Seize wall articulation, which seems a modernization of the rear wall of Perrault's east Louvre façade and which was first programmatically applied by ENNEMONDO ALESSANDRO PETITOT DI LIONE in his decorations for the Chinea [Festival] of 1749 in Rome. Soufflot linked, even later, the modern stylistic formulation with Petitot—as well as with the other "Romans". It was a style propagated as the official modern style at this time in the Academy of Parma by Soufflot's protegé Petitot.

The second phase of planning, after 1764, projected a double-shelled dome, in which Soufflot was inspired by another Roman academy project, that of his friend Dumont, whose 1746 "Temple of the Arts" had been engraved in the meantime. However, in execution all these "fashionable" elements disappeared from the design in favor of a variation of the proven elements of a classical domed structure. Such a procedure was characteristic of Soufflot, who, although he over and over again rejected the fashionable, responded nonetheless to the new possibilities of stylistic developments. He maintained, however, as his chief interest, built architecture and its concommitent constructional and technical problems, in contrast to the stylistic formers of eighteenth-century French architecture from the "Piranésiens" to the painter-architect ETIENNE LOUIS BOULLÉE. That is the more profound reason why it fell to Soufflot, the architect most fortunate in career and patronage, to create in Sainte-Geneviève an epoch-making masterpiece, which as an emblem of the Revolution experienced an imposed change of meaning from the church of the City of Paris to the French Panthéon.

WERNER OECHSLIN
*Translated from German by
Barry Bergdoll*

WORKS

After 1738, Hôtel Lacrox-Laval (planning and construction?); 1739–1748, Hôtel Dieu (extension building with Rhone wings and pavilion; not completed until later); after 1742, Eglise des Chartreux (high altar and ciborium; after a design by Giovanni Nicolano Servandoni); 1747–1749, Archepiscopal Palace (renovation); 1748–1750, Loge des Changes; 1751–1752, Perachon House; *1753–1756, Theater; Lyon, France. 1755–1780, Sainte-Geneviève (now the Panthéon; not completed until later by others); 1756–1760, Notre Dame Cathedral (sacristy); Paris. 1765 and later, Marquis de Marigny House (including garden pavilions), Ménars, France. 1769 and later, Marquis de Marigny House, Roule, Paris. c.1774, Bertin Estate (nymphaeum), Chatou, France.

BIBLIOGRAPHY

BRAHAM, A. 1971 "Drawings for Soufflot's Sainte-Geneviève." *Burlington Magazine* 1971:592ff.

BRAHAM, A. 1980 *The Architecture of the French Enlightenment.* London: Berkeley.

MIDDLETON, R. D. 1962 "The Abbe of Cordemoy and the Graeco-Gothic Ideal." *Journal of the Warburg and Courtald Institutes* 1962:178ff.

MONDAIN-MONVALE, J. 1918 *Soufflot, sa vie, son oeuvre, son esthetique.* Paris.

PETZET, M. 1961 *Soufflots Sainte-Geneviève und der französiche Kirchenbau des XVIII. Jahrhunderts.* Berlin.

Soufflot et son temps. 1980 Paris: Caisse Nationale des Monuments Historiques et des Sites. Exhibition catalogue.

TERNOIS, D., and PEREZ, F. 1982 *L'Oeuvre de Soufflot à Lyon.* Lyon, France: Presses Universitaires de France.

SOUFFLOT LE ROMAIN, FRANÇOIS

A cousin of JACQUES GERMAIN SOUFFLOT, François Soufflot Le Romain (?–1802) was a *pensionnaire* in Rome in 1761. Upon his return to Paris, he obtained the title of inspector of works at the Church of Sainte Geneviève. In 1785, he built the Hôtel de Montholon, 21 Boulevard Montmartre, and the Maison d'Epinay in Sceaux. He also built the stairway of the Priory of Saint Martin des Champs (1786) and designed a portal for the Cathedral of Sens. He was also the architect of the pavilion at 32 rue des Bois in Bagnolet.

GÉRARD ROUSSET-CHARNY
Translated from French by
Richard Cleary

BIBLIOGRAPHY

CHARTRAIRE, EUGÈNE (1921)1963 *La cathédrale de Sens.* 4th ed., rev. Paris: Laurens.

SOUTHCOTT, JOHN T.

John Thomas Southcott (1853–1939), was born in St. John's, Newfoundland, the son of one of the colony's principal contractors. Completing an apprenticeship in the family firm he went to Exeter, England, to study architecture with W. R. Best. Returning to Newfoundland about 1877, he brought with him the Second Empire style. In St. John's and for the Anglo-American Cable Company at Heart's Content, his father and uncle built a large number of houses to his designs. The concave-curved mansard roofs of these houses were the hallmark of St. John's architecture at the end of the nineteenth century and, in a simpler fashion, are found on Newfoundland outport houses of the same period.

After the 1892 fire, St. John's was rebuilt almost entirely in the Second Empire style but the major buildings—the institutions, the commercial premises and the mansions—tended to be of the Queen Anne style and the work of other, newer architects. Having served for a time as a municipal councillor, Southcott served briefly (in 1898) as Newfoundland's Superintendent of Public Works. In 1909 financial difficulties drove him to Vancouver with his family where, while he still called himself an architect, he appears to have built only two houses before his death in 1939.

SHANE O'DEA

WORKS

c.1880, Park Place Houses, St. John's, Newfoundland. 1882, Senior Staff Houses, Heart's Content, Newfoundland. c.1886, Rothwell Houses, St. John's, Newfoundland.

SPADA, VIRGILIO

Virgilio Spada (1596–1662) was not a professional architect but an intelligent amateur with a good sense of design and an administrative flair that allowed him to leave his mark on most of the major papal projects of mid-seventeenth-century Rome. He was the son of Paolo Spada, a minor nobleman and amateur builder from Brisighella in the Romagna, and it was in his father's service that he gained his early architectural experience as the overseer of minor projects such as the Casino di San Pancrazio (1620–1622), a project for a Villa Spada at Zattaglia (1620–1622), the convent of Santa Francesca Romana at Brisighella (1615–1632), and a project for the Cistercian monastery of San Bernardino at Brisighella (1628). He submitted a project in 1619–1621 for a monumental fountain in Faenza, which was not executed according to his design. His early education was the kind of general education expected of a nobleman, including mathematics, military science, astronomy, horsemanship, and eventually theology, after his decision to enter the priesthood and join the Roman Oratory of San Filippo Neri in 1622. He quickly rose to prominent administrative positions within the Oratory and exerted a decisive influence over the planning of the new residence to be built next to Santa Maria in Vallicella, at first working in close collaboration with PAOLO MARUSCELLI, the Oratorians' architect between 1622 and 1636, and after 1637 with FRANCESCO BORROMINI, who introduced many changes into the design and gave the oratory its famous curved façade. Spada continued to oversee buildings connected with his family, in particular the façade and high altar of the Church of San Paolo Maggiore in Bologna (1634–1636), working in close collaboration with Ercole Fichi and GIOVANNI LORENZO BERNINI. In 1654–1655, Virgilio and Bernardino Spada jointly planned the Spada Chapel in San Girolamo della Carita, where a strain of Neapolitan polychromy enlivens what is basically an ancestor gallery based on the brothers' genealogical researches.

In 1644, Spada was appointed to a position in the administration of Pope Innocent X (1644–1655), whom he served as unofficial adviser in architecture and architectural finance, particularly on: the rebuilding of the Lateran basilica under Francesco Borromini in 1644–1650, the investigation into structural defects caused by Bernini's campanile on the façade of St. Peter's in 1645, the design of the Palazzo Pamphilj in Piazza Navona by GIROLAMO RAINALDI and Borromini in 1646, the plan to demolish the so-called *spina* of the Vatican *borgo* in 1651, and the building of the New Prisons on the Via Giulia by ANTONIO DEL GRANDE in 1652–1653. He retained his position under Pope Alexander VII (1655–1667), relinquishing it only a few months before his death. Although he built nothing himself, he advised his older brother, Cardinal Bernardino Spada, on the alterations to the family palace, the Palazzo Spada-Capodiferro, carried out particularly under Maruscelli and Borromini in 1633–1652. Furthermore, the rebuilding of the Piazza dell'Orologio in Rome can be considered something of a personal monument, since he supervised the building of Borromini's Torre dell'Orologio over his own apartment in 1647–1650 and the rebuilding of the adjacent Palazzo del Banco di Santo Spirito in 1661–1662 (later purchased by his heir and finished as the Palazzo Spada a Monte Giordano).

Aside from his contribution as an administrator, Spada's originality can best be seen in his many architectural writings, particularly unpublished critiques and erudite projects in which a vivid and innovative language of architectural criticism is developed. The most interesting of these are a project for a Pamphilj villa of 1644–1645, based on astronomy and references to antiquity and described as a study in applied mathematics, and the long text known as the *Opus Architectonicum* (1725), which Spada coauthored in 1647 with Borromini.

JOSEPH CONNORS

BIBLIOGRAPHY

BORROMINI, FRANCESCO, and SPADA, VIRGILIO (1725)1972 *Opus Architectonicum*. Reprint. London: Gregg.

CONNORS, JOSEPH 1980 *Borromini and the Roman Oratory: Style and Society*. Cambridge, Mass.: M.I.T. Press.
EHRLE, FRANCESCO 1928 "Dalle carte e dai disegni di Birgilio Spada (d.1662) (Codd. Vaticani lat. 11257 e 11258)." *Atti della Pontificia Accademia Romana di Archeologia* Series 3 2:1–98.
HEIMBÜRGER RAVALLI, MINNA 1977 *Architettura, scultura e arti minori nel barocco italiano. Richerche nell'Archivio Spada*. Florence: Olschki.
INCISA DELLA ROCCHETTA, GIOVANNI 1959 "Una relazione del padre Virgilio Spada." *Archivio della Società Romana di Storia Patria* 82:25–78.
INCISA DELLA ROCCHETTA, GIOVANNI 1967 "Un dialogo del P. Virgilio Spada sulla fabbrica dei Filippini." *Archivio della Società Romana di Storia Patria* 90:165–211.
NEPPI, LIONELLO 1975 *Palazzo Spada*. Rome: Editalia.
THELEN, HEINRICH 1967 *Francesco Borromini: Mostra di disegni e documenti vaticani*. Vatican City: Vatican Library.

SPECCHI, ALESSANDRO

Although his efforts are little appreciated by the present-day visitor to Rome, only a handful of architects had a greater influence on the shape of parts of the city than Alessandro Specchi (1668–1729). Two of his designs, for the Port of the Ripetta and for the Spanish Steps (in which his design was taken over by FRANCESCO DE' SANCTIS) provided key examples of late baroque urban architecture. In addition, his engravings of the city of Rome are a crucial record of many of the sites—ancient, Renaissance, and baroque.

Specchi was born in Rome and trained in the studio of CARLO FONTANA. His main works of civil architecture were the palaces De Carolis (1716–1722), now the Bank of Rome, and Pichini (1710), both in Rome. Specchi's major work, however, was the Port of the Ripetta (begun 1703), a docking area that he built for Pope Clement XI. This zone had been a muddy and irregular landing site on the flood-prone Tiber. Through the construction of an oval piazza and a series of curving, wavelike steps, Specchi managed to define a new focus for the area and to suggest a dynamic relation between river and shoreline that in form evokes the great architectural works of the high baroque. Most important, as Tod Marder (1980) has shown, the construction of a stable landing site available for docking and unloading no matter the height of the Tiber enabled the Roman government to ensure a steadier flow of food into the city.

Although Specchi was a pupil of Fontana, his architectural manner looks more to the vigorous manner of FRANCESCO BORROMINI than to the rather tame classicism of his teacher. One of

Specchi's major disappointments was his failure to win the competition for the staircase of the Trinità dei Monti, the so-called Spanish Steps. Wolfgang Lotz (1969) has shown, however, that the design ultimately adopted by the architect of the Steps, Francesco de' Sanctis, was probably determined by the project of Specchi.

Specchi was appointed architect to the Camera Capitolina in 1719 and architect to St. Peter's in 1721.

NICHOLAS ADAMS

WORKS

*1703–1705, Port of the Ripetta (with Niccolò del Guidice); 1710, Palazzo Pichini; 1716–1722, Palazzo De Carolis; 1721–1724, Pontifical Stables; Rome.

BIBLIOGRAPHY

ASHBY, THOMAS, and WELSH, STEPHEN 1927 "Alessandro Specchi." *Town Planning Review* 12, no. 4:237–248.
DE ROSSI, DOMENICO (editor) 1702? *Studio d'architettura civile.* With engravings by Alessandro Specchi. Augsburg, Germany: Krausen.
FALDA, GIOVANNI BATTISTA (1665)1699 *Il nuovo teatro delle fabriche et edificii in perspectiva di Roma moderna.* With engravings by Alessandro Specchi. Rome: Rossi.
FONTANA, CARLO 1694 *Templum Vaticanum et ipsius origo.* 2 vols. With engravings by Alessandro Specchi. Rome: Buagni.
LOTZ, WOLFGANG 1969 "Die Spanische Treppe: Architektur als Mittel der Diplomatie." *Römisches Jahrbuch für Kunstgeschichte* 12:39–94.
MARDER, TOD 1980 "The Porta di Ripetta in Rome." *Journal of the Society of Architectural Historians* 39, no. 1:28–56.

SPEER, ALBERT

Born in Mannheim in southwest Germany, Albert Speer (1905–1981) received his architectural training in Karlsruhe, Munich, and Berlin, studying with HERMANN BILLING, GERMAN BESTELMEYER, and HEINRICH TESSENOW. Tessenow employed him in his Berlin office (1927–1929) and made him his assistant at the Charlottenburg Technische Hochschule (1929–1932), unusual honors for such a young man. But when, at the start of the Depression, Speer tried to establish his own practice, architectural commissions were few. Seeking an understanding of the deepening economic and political crisis, Speer joined the Nazi party and, like many of his generation, was soon mesmerized by the personality of Adolf Hitler. Hitler, in turn, was attracted by Speer's youth, engaging personality, malleability, ambition, and willingness

to build at "the American tempo" (Speer, 1969, p. 107). After the death of PAUL LUDWIG TROOST in 1934, Speer became Hitler's principal architect and personal confidant, winning many public offices and official commissions.

Although Hitler's and Speer's architectural tastes differed, Hitler's tending toward megalomania and giganticism, Speer's toward a modest and discreet neoclassicism, Speer was able to satisfy Hitler's wishes and to treat him as a mentor, while developing a relatively consistent style of his own. In part, the association with Hitler awakened latent talents and interests. While a student at Berlin, for example, Speer had come in contact with leading German archeologists and had developed some enthusiasm for the monumental architecture of classical and Near Eastern antiquity. This enthusiasm revived in long conversations with Hitler about architecture in ruins: about what materials to use in order to ensure that, in decay, Nazi public buildings would look as dignified and powerful as the remains of Babylon and Rome. Speer also came to share Hitler's interest in building great cities and particularly in remodeling Berlin along huge cross axes so that it could accommodate "infinite numbers of people" (Lane, 1968, p. 189, n. 21). Through his designs for the Nazi party congresses at Nuremberg (temporary structures, 1933; permanent, 1934ff.), Speer discovered a gift for creating effective stage settings, and this too was encouraged by Hitler, who himself regarded architecture as a stage—for the party and its leader.

Speer's architecture reflected the ideals of his various mentors. Like the prewar work of Billing, Bestelmeyer, and Tessenow, Speer's buildings for the Nazi regime were relatively modest in scale, visually accessible, simple in outline, and bare and streamlined in their surfaces. They were, however, urban in character, and although they lacked obvious historical references, their heavy masonry and vertical proportions implied a link to ancient empires. They were also austere and melancholy, vivid only when, as in Nuremberg, the inclination to stage design could be given full rein in rows of flags and searchlights, and in the choreography of the mass meeting itself.

In 1942, Speer succeeded FRITZ TODT as minister of armaments and war production, becoming one of the most powerful men in the Nazi government. Indicted and convicted of war crimes by the International Military Tribunal in Nuremberg in 1945, Speer served a twenty-year sentence in Spandau prison in Berlin. The memoirs and apologias which he has published after his release are profoundly interesting, but should be used with appropriate caution by the historian.

BARBARA MILLER LANE

WORKS

1928–1932, Ackerweg House, Heidelberg, Germany. 1928–1932, Deutsche Akademische Austauschdienst Offices; 1928–1932, Adolf Hitler House (remodeling); 1928–1932, Nazi Party Business Office (remodeling); 1933, Chancellery (remodeling of interior); 1933, Paul Joseph Goebbels Offices (remodeling); Berlin. *1933, Temporary Buildings for the Nazi Party Congress; 1934, Party Congress Grounds (partially destroyed in 1945), Zeppelinfeld; Nuremberg, Germany. *1937, German Pavilion, World's Fair, Paris. *1938, New Chancellery, Berlin.

BIBLIOGRAPHY

ARNST, KARL; KOCH, GEORG F.; and LARSSON, LARS OLOF 1978 *Albert Speer: Arbeiten, 1933–1942.* Frankfurt, Berlin, and Vienna: Ullstein.

LANE, BARBARA MILLER 1968 *Architecture and Politics in Germany: 1918–1945.* Cambridge, Mass.: Harvard University Press.

LANE, BARBARA MILLER 1973 "Inside the Third Reich." *Journal of the Society of Architectural Historians* 32:341–346.

LARSSON, LARS OLOF 1978 *Die Neugestaltung der Reichshauptstadt: Albert Speers Generalbebauungsplan für Berlin.* Stockholm: Almqvist & Wiksell.

PETSCH, JOACHIM 1976 *Baukunst und Stadtplanung im Dritten Reich.* Munich: Hanser.

RITTICH, WERNER 1938 *Architektur und Bauplastik der Gegenwart.* Berlin: Rembrandt.

SPEER, ALBERT (1969)1970 *Inside the Third Reich: Memoirs.* Translated by Richard and Clara Winston. New York: Macmillan.

SPEER, ALBERT (1975)1976 *Spandau: The Secret Diaries.* Translated by Richard and Clara Winston. New York: Macmillan.

SPEER, ALBERT 1981 *Infiltration.* New York: Macmillan.

STEPHAN, HANS 1939 *Die Baukunst im Dritten Reich.* Berlin: Junker & Dünnhaupt.

TEUT, ANNA (editor) 1967 *Architektur im Dritten Reich.* Berlin: Ullstein.

SPEETH, PETER

Peter Speeth (1772–1831) trained first as a mason and then, from 1784, as an architect under Georg Weber and NICOLAS DE PIGAGE in Frankfurt. From 1804 he worked for Fürst von Leningen at Amorbach before entering the service of the short-lived Habsburg court of the Grand Duke Ferdinand of Tuscany at Würzburg. His Würzburg prison (1812–1827) is the most developed German example of CLAUDE NICOLAS LEDOUX and JEAN JACQUES LEQUEU's search to express a building's character and function through associational use of classical forms and emphatic manipulation of mass and volume. With its exaggerated contrasts of scale, apparent monumentality, expanses of unbroken wall surfaces played off against small apertures and emphatic rustication, the prison has a ponderous and forbidding aspect. The Guard House (1813–c.1824) at the Zeller Gate exploits the associations of the baseless Doric and rustication to evoke strength and authority. After Würzburg fell in 1815, Speeth turned to teaching. Called in 1826 to Russia by the Czar, he died there after designing the Metropolitan Church at Kishinev (begun 1826).

BARRY BERGDOLL

WORKS

1805–1806, Thibault d'Allerit House, Amorbach, Germany. 1811, 6 Ebrachergasse (reconstruction; façade only survives); 1812, 9 Turmgasse; *1812–1813, Director's House, Music School; Würzburg, Germany. 1812–1817, Catholic Parish Church, Saint John the Baptist, Unterhohenried, near Hassfurt, Germany. 1812–1827, Prison Annex Building (façade only survives); 1813–c.1824, Guard House, Zeller Gate; 1821, 31 Sanderstrasse; Würzburg, Germany. Begun 1826, Metropolitan Church, Kishinev, Russia.

BIBLIOGRAPHY

HAUG, INGRID 1969 "Peter Speeth, Architekt, 1772–1831." Unpublished Ph.D. dissertation, Rheinische-Friedrich-Wilhelms Universität, Bonn, Germany.

NERDINGER, WIFRID (editor) 1980 *Klassizismus in Bayern, Schwaben, und Franken: Architektur-Zeichnungen 1775–1825.* Munich: Münchner Stadtmuseum. Catalogue of an exhibition.

PRIMAVESI, JOHANN GEORG 1806 *XII. Ansichten des Heidelberger Schlosses.* Mannheim, Germany: Primavesi.

SPENCE, BASIL

Basil Spence (1907–1976) was born in India but educated in Scotland, becoming a prize pupil at the Edinburgh School of Architecture before transferring to the Bartlett School, London University, and working in the office of EDWIN LUTYENS. His early work in Scotland was done in partnership with William Kinninmonth. After 1945, he gained a reputation as a designer of decorative exhibition displays. His career was made by his success in the competition for the rebuilding of Coventry Cathedral (1950) which captured the popular imagination as a symbol of religious and artistic regeneration and made Spence's name a household word. The works of art commissioned for the Cathedral compete for attention with the building itself, which aspires to a Gothic spirit through modern forms. In the University of Sussex and many other works of the 1960s, Spence attempted to create monumental groups whose arrangement emulates Lutyens. However, the poverty of architectural vocabulary of the modern idiom (in this case derived from LE CORBUSIER's *Maison Jaoul*) deprives them of their proper force, although Spence had a surer handling of form than some of his contemporaries. His preference for traditional materials however, will assist the appreciation of his work in years to come. Contrary to the general trend of his time, Spence did not regard architecture primarily as a social service. Rather, he sought to give personal artistic expression to his buildings and succeeded in being, if nothing else, highly controversial with designs such as the Knightsbridge Barracks. The British Embassy in Rome was an extreme example of this tendency to create sculptural forms.

Spence was in many ways a modernist *malgré lui* whose affinities lay with Scandinavian eclecticism. In succession to his former master, he became a kind of architect laureate who helped to make a particular version of modern architecture more popular than it might otherwise have been.

ALAN POWERS

WORKS

1938, Spence House (rebuilding), Edinburgh. 1950, Coventry Cathedral (restoration), England. 1951, Heavy Industries Exhibition, Sea and Ships Pavilion, Festival of Britain, London. 1955, Church, Clermiston, Scotland. 1958, Wray House, Wimbledon, London. 1960, Undergraduate Housing, Queen's College, Cambridge. 1962, Falmer House, University of Sussex, Brighton, England. 1964, Library and Swimming Center, Hampstead Civic Center, London. 1965, Chemistry Building, University of Exeter, England. 1966, Crematorium, Mortonhall, Edinburgh. 1969, Biology and Recreation Buildings, University of Sussex, Brighton, England. 1970, Household Cavalry Barracks, Knightsbridge, London. 1971, Chancery, British Embassy, Rome. 1975, Bank of Piraeus, Athens. 1976, Queen Anne's Mansions Office Development, London.

BIBLIOGRAPHY

LEWIS, PETER 1962 "The Very Model of a Monumental O. M." *Queen* 221:66–68.
SHEPPARD, RICHARD 1977 "Obituary." *Journal of the Royal Institute of British Architects* 84, no. 1:40.
SPENCE, BASIL 1956 "The Modern Church." *Journal of the Royal Institute of British Architects* 63:369–376.
SPENCE, BASIL (1962)1964 *Phoenix at Coventry: The Building of a Cathedral.* London: Bles.
SPENCE, BASIL 1973 *New Buildings in Old Cities.* England: University of Southampton.
SPENCE, BASIL ET AL. 1964 *The Idea of a New University: An Experiment in Sussex.* Edited by David Daiches. London: Deutsch.
SPENCE, BASIL, and SNOEK, HENRY 1963 *Out of the Ashes: A Progress Through Coventry Cathedral.* London: Bles.

SPIERS, RICHARD PHENÉ

Richard Phené Spiers (1838–1916) was born in Oxford and educated at King's College, London, and at the Ecole des Beaux-Arts, Paris (1859–1861). He was master of the Architectural School at the Royal Academy, London, from 1870 to 1906. A classicist at a time when English architecture was experiencing a Gothic Revival, Spiers failed to be influential. He built little but drew much; many of his travel sketches of old buildings are in contemporary English architectural periodicals.

RICHARD CHAFEE

WORKS

1879, Robert Collier House, Stables, and Studio, Chelsea, London.

BIBLIOGRAPHY

ANDERSON, WILLIAM J., and SPIERS, RICHARD PHENÉ 1902 *The Architecture of Greece and Rome.* London. Revised and rewritten as two books: William Bell Dinsmoor, *The Architecture of Ancient Greece.* New York: Scribners, 1927 (reprinted New York: Norton, 1975), and Thomas Ashby, *The Architecture of Ancient Rome.* London: Batsford.
BOLTON, ARTHUR T. 1916 "Richard Phené Spiers: Architect and Archaeologist." *Architectural Review* 40, Oct.:96–100.
CHAFEE, RICHARD n.d. *Architectural History.* Forthcoming article.
FERGUSON, JAMES 1891–1899 *A History of Architecture.* Edited by Richard Phené Spiers. 5 vols. 3d ed. London.
"The Late R. Phené Spiers." 1916 *The Builder* 111, Oct.:224–225.
LETHABY, W. R. 1916 "Richard Phené Spiers." *Journal of the Royal Institute of British Architects* Series 3 23:334–335.
PHYSICK, JOHN, and DARBY, MICHAEL 1973 *Marble Halls.* London: Victoria and Albert Museum.
PUGIN, AUGUSTUS, and BRITTON, J. 1874 *Specimens of the Architecture of Normandy.* Edited by Richard Phené Spiers. London.
SPIERS, RICHARD PHENÉ (1887)1905 *Architectural Drawing.* Rev. ed. London: Cassell.
SPIERS, RICHARD PHENÉ (1890)1897 *The Orders of Architecture: Greek, Roman, and Italian.* 3d ed. London: Batsford.
SPIERS, RICHARD PHENÉ 1905 *Architecture East and West.* London: Batsford.

SPILLER, JAMES

Son of a London builder, James Spiller (?–1829) was in JAMES WYATT's office by 1780. His known works are few and none are from his later years, the portico at Drury Lane Theatre, London (1820), now being a doubtful attribution. Spiller was temperamental, suffered ill health and deafness, and had difficulties with clients. But he was a competent designer and, at Saint John's Church (1792–1797), London, strikingly original in a neoclassical idiom. JOHN SOANE, a long-time friend, provided him with some employment. Spiller was also surveyor to the Royal Exchange Assurance Company; in 1807 he tangled with S. P. COCKERELL over the development of the Foundling Hospital Estate, London.

FRANK KELSALL

WORKS

1781–1783, London Hospital (additions); *1788–1790, The Great Synagogue; 1792–1797, Saint John's Church (steeple and porches added 1812); *c.1797, Elm Grove; 1800–1801, The Royal Institution; London. 1805, Tolmers Park, Hertfordshire, England. *c.1810, Mells Park (completed by John Soane), Somerset, England.

BIBLIOGRAPHY

BOLTON, ARTHUR T. 1927 *The Portrait of Sir John Soane, R.A.* London: Sir John Soane's Museum.
OLSEN, DONALD J. 1964 *Town Planning in London.* New Haven and London: Yale University Press.

SPRATS, WILLIAM

William Sprats (1758/1759–1810) was a British soldier imprisoned during the Revolutionary War. Sprats later became a master joiner in Litchfield, Connecticut, where his transitional late Georgian style was the forerunner of an architectural flowering in the Federal period. Legend assigns several notable buildings to him, but only those listed below are documented. The Litchfield Courthouse (1795–1798), a prototype of the porticoed churches of federal Connecticut, is also attributed to Sprats, but all that is recorded is that he "assisted" his patron, Julius Deming, in making a plan and that Deming specified that Sprats should do the joinery "if he can be procured." About this time, Sprats left Connecticut for Vermont.

ELIZABETH MILLS BROWN

WORKS

c.1790, Henry Champion House, Colchester, Conn. 1792, Zenas Cowles House, Farmington, Conn. 1793, Julius Deming House, Litchfield, Conn. *1801–1802. Meetinghouse, Georgia, Vt.

BIBLIOGRAPHY

WARREN, WILLIAM LAMSON 1954 "William Sprats and His Civil and Ecclesiastical Architecture in New England." *Old-Time New England* 44:65–78 and 103–114.
WARREN, WILLIAM LAMSON 1955 "The Domestic Architecture of William Sprats and Other Litchfield Joiners." *Old-Time New England* 46:36–51.
WARREN, WILLIAM LAMSON 1957 "William Sprats, Master Joiner, Connecticut's Federalist Architect." *Connecticut Antiquarian* 9:11–21.

SPROATT and ROLPH

Sproatt and Rolph, a Toronto architectural office, were the masters of the collegiate Gothic style in Canada. Henry Sproatt (1866–1934) was born and educated in Toronto, and was apprenticed to Arthur R. Denison of that city, and to Harding and Gooch and the Parfitt Brothers of New York City. Ernest Ross Rolph (1871–1958) was born in Toronto and trained there under David Roberts, Junior. Their significant work in Toronto includes the Library, residences, and Great Hall at Victoria College (1901–1912), Hart House and Soldiers Tower, University of Toronto (1912–1925), for which they received the American Institute of Architect's Gold Medal for educational buildings in 1925, and the Canada Life Assurance Company Headquarters (1929–1931).

ROBERT HILL

BIBLIOGRAPHY

MIDDLETON, JESSE E. 1923 Volume 3, page 54 in *The Municipality of Toronto.* Toronto: Dominion Publishing Company.
"Obituary for E. R. Rolph." 1958 *Journal of the Royal Architectural Institute of Canada* 35, June:239.
"Obituary for H. Sproatt." 1934 *Journal of the Royal Institute of British Architects* Series 3, 42, no. 1:93.

STAAL, J. F.

In the first period of his architectural practice, during his collaboration with A. J. KROPHOLLER (1902–1910), the works of Jan Frederik Staal (1879–1940), born in Amsterdam, were related to the severe rationalism of H. P. BERLAGE. This changed after 1915 when he admitted ever more decoration in his designs and became one of the most important architects of the Amsterdam school. At the end of the 1920s, some of Staal's buildings showed a relationship with W. M. DUDOK's work. Staal finally acquired the form characteristics of Dutch functionalism.

Staal also wrote many architectural articles.

WIM DE WIT

WORKS

1902–1905, Insurance Company De Utrecht Office Building (with A. J. Kropholler), Amsterdam. 1906–1909, Insurance Company De Utrecht Archive Building (with Kropholler), Utrecht. 1917–1918, Five Villas,

Bergen, Netherlands. *1925, Dutch Pavilion, Exposition Internationale des Arts Décoratifs, Paris. 1929–1931, High-rise Apartment Building De Wolkenkrabber, Victorieplein, Amsterdam. 1929–1940, Exchange, Coolsingel, Rotterdam, Netherlands.

BIBLIOGRAPHY

Americana. 1975 Otterlo, Netherlands: Rijksmuseum Kröller-Müller.
Amsterdamse School: 1910–1930. 1975 Amsterdam: Stedelijk Museum. Exhibition catalogue.
Bouwen '20–'40: De Nederlandse Bijdrage aan het Nieuwe Bouwen. 1971 Eindhoven, Netherlands: Stedelijk Van Abbemuseum. Exhibition catalogue.
FANELLI, GIOVANNI (1968)1978 *Moderne architectuur in Nederland: 1900–1940.* Translated from Italian by Wim de Wit. The Hague: Staatsuitgeverij.
Nederland bouwt in baksteen: 1800–1940. 1941 Rotterdam, Netherlands: Museum Boymans-van Beuningen.
ROY VAN ZUYDEWIJN, H. J. F. DE 1969 *Amsterdamse Bouwkunst: 1815–1940.* Amsterdam: de Bussy.
STEUR, A. J. VAN DER 1929 "Bij het werk van J. F. Staal." *Wendingen* 10, nos. 5-6.
VRIEND, J. J. 1959 *Architectuur van deze eeuw.* Amsterdam: Contact.

STACY-JUDD, ROBERT

Born in London, Robert Stacy-Judd (1884–1975) studied at Acton College, Regent's Street Polytechnic Institute, Southend Technical Institute, and South Kensington Science and Art Institute in England. He practiced architecture in California and throughout his career sought a unique and indigenous American architectural form. He looked to Mayan culture for form and inspiration. Most of his built and proposed works used Mayan motifs.

PATRICIA C. PHILLIPS

WORKS

n.d., Aztec Hotel, Monrovia, Calif. n.d., First Baptist Church, Ventura, Calif. n.d., La Jolla Yacht and Beach Club, Calif. n.d., Village of Krotona Institute of Theosophy, Ojai, Calif.

BIBLIOGRAPHY

SKY, ALISON, and STONE, MICHELLE 1976 *Unbuilt America.* New York: McGraw-Hill.
STACY-JUDD, ROBERT B. 1934 "Some Local Examples of Mayan Adaptations." *Architect and Engineer* 116, no. 2:21–30.

STAM, MART

Following secondary school, Martinus Adrianus Stam (1899–) studied drawing in Amsterdam. He began his architectural career by working as a draftsman and designer in the offices of outstanding architects: J. W. VAN DER MEY in Amsterdam, VAN DER VLUGT AND BRINKMAN in Rotterdam, those of HANS POELZIG and BRUNO TAUT in Berlin, and KARL MOSER in Zurich. Stam was one of several European architects invited by LUDWIG MIES VAN DER ROHE to design housing for the Werkbund's exhibition in Stuttgart. Engaged by HANNES MEYER, Stam taught the aesthetics of planning at the Dessau Bauhaus during 1928–1929. Thereafter, he accompanied ERNST MAY to Russia, spending almost five years planning new towns. Subsequently, he practiced architecture in Amsterdam with his wife, Lotte Beese, and with W. VAN TIJEN.

Stam was director of the Institute for Industrial Arts Education in Amsterdam for eleven years from 1937 to 1948, of the Dresden Academy of Arts from 1948 to 1950, and of the Kunsthochschule in East Berlin from 1950 to 1952. Thereafter, he continued in private practice in Amsterdam until 1966, when he retired to Switzerland. In those years, he designed apartment houses, office buildings, city plans, exhibition pavilions, a sports center, and residences.

Stam was a founder and active member of the Congrès Internationaux d'Architecture Moderne (CIAM) in 1928. He was well-prepared to pursue his social ideals in CIAM, having worked in the preceding four years with HANS SCHMIDT, ELEAZAR LISSITZKY, and Hannes Meyer. He also edited the left-wing publication *ABC* and headed *de 8 en Opbouw*, a radical architectural organization, from 1926 to 1928. There were two parallel philosophies in the CIAM which sought to prevail to achieve their goals: the intuitive aesthetic and the scientific analysis, the latter a viewpoint promulgated by Stam. The controversy, internal to CIAM, faded with the decline of that organization, but the dichotomy of these approaches continued to be a source of debate in the profession and in education. Unfortunately, Stam and his contributions to the development of a social architecture have been given little recognition.

REGINALD R. ISAACS

WORKS

1920, Budge Foundation Old People's Home (with WERNER MOSER), Frankfurt. 1922, German Bookprinters' Association Building (with MAX TAUT), Berlin. 1926–1930, van Nelle Factory (with van der Vlugt and Brinkman), Rotterdam, Netherlands. 1927, Terraced Housing, Weissenhof Estate, Stuttgart, Germany. 1929–1931, Hellerhof Housing Development, Frankfurt. 1936, Apartment Building (with Lotte Beese, W. van Tijen, and others), Anthonie van Dijckstraat, Amsterdam. *1939, Dutch Pavilion,

World's Fair, New York. 1956, Housing Complex (with Merkelbach and Elling); 1959, Princesse Apartment Building, Beethovenstraat; 1963, Mahuko Office High-rise Building, De Tijd-Maasbode; 1964, Sports Center, De Boelelaan; Amsterdam. 1965, Country House, Hierden, Netherlands.

BIBLIOGRAPHY

BLIJSTRA, REINDER (compiler) 1970 *Mart Stam: Documentation of His Work, 1920-1965.* Translated and edited by C. V. Amerungen and others. London: Royal Institute of British Architects Publications.
JOEDICKE, JÜRGEN, and PLATH, CHRISTIAN 1968 *Die Weissenhofsiedlung.* Stuttgart: Krämer.
OORTHUYS, GERRIT 1970 *Mart Stam.* London.
RASCH, BABO 1977 "Wie die Weissenhofsiedlung entstand." *Deutsche Bauzeitung* Nov.: 28-35.
SEGAL, WALTER 1970 "Mart Stam." *Architects' Journal* 151:1352-1354.
STAM, MART 1924-1925 "Kollektive Gestaltung." *ABC* 1, no. 1:1.
STAM, MART 1935 "De stoel gedurende de laatste 40 jaar." *De 8 en Opbouw* 1:1.
STAM, MART 1938 "Zierikzee." *De 8 en Opbouw* 1:7.
STAM, MART 1946 "Behoudzucht." *Open Oog* 2:2-12.

STANTON, WILLIAM

The nephew and successor of Thomas Stanton, a well-established London mason, William Stanton (1639-1705) in turn became Warden of the Mason's Company in 1681 and 1684 and Master in 1688-1689. Like other masons of the period, he was capable of producing designs for houses as well as executing those of other, more professional, architects. Stanton was the chief contractor for Belton House in Lincolnshire in 1685, probably to the designs of WILLIAM WINDE, but he himself is thought to have built Denham Place, Buckinghamshire (1688-1701): a "double-pile" house of the type made popular by Sir ROGER PRATT. Stanton was also a prolific sculptor of monuments, though he was overshadowed in this sphere by his son, Edward.

GERVASE JACKSON-STOPS

WORKS

(A)1688-1701, Denham Place, Buckinghamshire, England. (A)1704-1705, Culverthorpe (north front), Lincolnshire, England.

BIBLIOGRAPHY

ESDAILE, K. A. 1929 "The Stantons of Holborn." *Archaeological Journal* 135.
HARRIS, JOHN 1957-1958 "The Building of Denham Place." *Records of Buckinghamshire* 16.
KNOOP, D., and JONES, G. P. 1935 *The London Mason in the Seventeenth Century.* London: Manchester University Press.

STAPLETON, MICHAEL

The leading Dublin master builder and stuccoist of the late eighteenth century, Michael Stapleton (?-1801) was actively involved in house building. Stapleton was a notable Irish follower of JAMES WYATT's decorative style, but he was less original as a designer than is sometimes suggested. His finest interior decorations are seen in the chapel of Trinity College, Dublin (1794).

NICHOLAS SHEAFF

WORKS

1777-1780, Powerscourt House (principal rooms); 1784, Theater (interior), Trinity College; 1785, Belvedere House; 1789, Houses, 44-45 Mountjoy Square; 1791, Michael Stapleton House, 1 Mountjoy Place; 1794, Trinity College Chapel (interior); Dublin.

BIBLIOGRAPHY

CURRAN, C. P. (1939)1967 "Michael Stapleton: Dublin Stuccodore." In *Dublin Decorative Plasterwork of the Seventeenth and Eighteenth Centuries.* London: Tiranti.
IRISH ARCHITECTURAL RECORDS ASSOCIATION 1965 *Irish Architectural Drawings.* Dublin: Municipal Gallery of Art. Exhibition catalogue.
McPARLAND, EDWARD 1976 "Trinity College, Dublin." *Country Life* 159, part 3:1310-1313.

STARK, WILLIAM

The early life of William Stark (1770-1813) is obscure. Born at Dunfermline, Scotland, he visited St. Petersburg in 1798 before practicing in Glasgow and, from 1813, Edinburgh. He became renowned as a Greek Revivalist and an enlightened institutional and town planner, his report on Edinburgh, printed 1814, forming the basis of its expansion undertaken by his pupil WILLIAM HENRY PLAYFAIR.

R. WINDSOR LISCOMBE

WORKS

*1804-1805, Hunterian Museum; 1807-1808, Saint George's Church, Buchanan Street; Glasgow, Scotland. 1809-1810, Saline Church, Fife, Scotland. *1810-1811, Courthouse, Gaol, and Public Offices; *1810-1811, Lunatic Asylum; Glasgow, Scotland. 1812-1820, Lunatic Asylum, Dundee, Scotland. 1812-1813, Old Church, Muirkirk, Ayrshire, Scotland.

BIBLIOGRAPHY

CROOK, J. MORDAUNT 1970 "Broomhall, Fife." *Country Life* 147:244-245.
GOMME, ANDOR, and WALKER, DAVID 1968 Pages 69-71, 279-280 in *The Architecture of Glasgow.* London: Lund Humphries.

STARK, WILLIAM 1807 *Remarks on the Construction of Public Hospitals for the Cure of Mental Derangement.* Glasgow, Scotland: Ballantyne.

STARK, WILLIAM 1814 *Report to the Lord Provost, Magistrates and Council of Edinburgh for Laying out the Grounds for Buildings between Edinburgh and Leith.* Edinburgh: Privately printed.

YOUNGSON, ALEXANDER J. 1966 Pages 149–152 in *The Making of Classical Edinburgh.* Edinburgh University Press.

STARÝ, OLDŘICH

Oldřich Starý (1884–1971) was one of the most important organizers and militants of Czech avant-garde architecture between the two world wars and in the postwar socialist era. He developed his style both from *neue Sachlichkeit* principles, which he applied particularly to family houses included in the Czechoslovak Werkbund Exhibition in Brno (1928) and in Prague's Baba District (1932), and from the elegant architecture of the International style as displayed in the Czechoslovak Werkbund Palace in Prague (1934–1935).

VLADIMÍR ŠLAPETA

WORKS

1916–1917, Buildings, Iron Ore Pits, Ejpovice, Czechoslovakia. 1917, Buildings, Limestone Pits, Srbsko, near Beroun, Czechoslovakia. 1923, Professor's House, Prague. 1925, Municipal Residences, Kladno, Czechoslovakia. 1928, Exhibition of Modern Culture (family house), Brno, Czechoslovakia. 1932, Czechoslovak Werkbund Exhibition (two houses with studio), Baba District; 1934–1935, Czechoslovak Werkbund Palace; Prague.

BIBLIOGRAPHY

KOULA, JAN EMIL 1944 *Oldřich Starý.* Prague. Exhibition catalogue.

STASOV, VASILI PETROVICH

Vasili Petrovich Stasov (1769–1848) was born in Moscow, where he studied under and worked for VASILI I. BAZHENOV and MATTEL F. KAZAKOV. Stasov's arrangements for Alexander's Coronation of 1802 resulted in his being sent on a study tour to France, England, and Italy for six years. He returned to Russia in 1808 where he designed a great number of neoclassical buildings, such as the church bell tower at Gruzino (1822) and the cast-iron Moscow Gate in St. Petersburg (1834–1838).

THOMAS J. McCORMICK

WORKS

1811, High School; Tsarskoye Selo, Russia. 1816–1819, Pavlovsky Barracks, St. Petersburg, Russia. 1817–1822, Chinese Village (completion); 1819–1821, Riding School; 1820–1823, Orangery; Tsarskoye Selo, Russia. 1822, Bell Tower, Church, Gruzino, Russia. 1823, Stables, Tsarskoye Selo, Russia. 1827–1835, Trinity Cathedral, St. Petersburg, Russia. 1832–1835, Food Storehouses, Moscow. 1834–1838, Moscow Gate, St. Petersburg, Russia.

BIBLIOGRAPHY

AKADEMIĨA ARKHITEKTURY SSSR 1950 *Arkhitektor V. P. Stasov.* Moscow.

GRABAR, I., LAZAREV, V. N.; and KEMENOV, V. S. (editors) 1958 Volume 8, part 1 in *Istoriĩa russkogo iskusstva.* Moscow.

HAMILTON, GEORGE H. (1954)1975 *The Art and Architecture of Russia.* 2d ed. Baltimore: Penguin.

PILYAVSKI, V. I. 1970 *Zodchii Vasilii Petrovich Stasov.* Leningrad: Soyuz sovetskikh arkhitektosor SSR.

STAUB, JOHN F.

John Fanz Staub (1892–1981) was born in Knoxville, Tennessee, and graduated from the University of Tennessee and the Massachusetts Institute of Technology. As an employee of Harrie T. Lindeberg, Staub moved to Houston, Texas, in 1921, where he established practice. He was particularly well known as a designer of elegant, expensive homes in a broad range of historical styles.

ROXANNE WILLIAMSON

WORKS

1923, River Oaks Country Club; 1926, Ima Hogg House (Bayou Bend), Houston, Tex.

BIBLIOGRAPHY

BARNSTONE, HOWARD 1979 *The Architecture of John F. Staub: Houston and the South.* Austin: University of Texas Press.

STEARNS, JOHN G.

See PEABODY and STEARNS.

STEGMANN, POVL

Povl Stegmann (1888–1944) was graduated from the Technical School in Århus, Denmark, in 1908, entered the Royal Academy in Copenhagen in 1909, and graduated in 1919. He was a poet and one of the pioneers of the Danish Functional Tradition, "a repressed romantic" as he called himself. To overcome historicism, he tried to grasp "the idea hidden in the stone axe," and his aim was to combine the practical wisdom of the old craftsmen with the human experience of his ancestors. The prismatic shape of the Århus University buildings was most likely his contribution to the project. He has left his marks on Danish architectural education as a conscientious teacher at the technical schools in Århus (1924–1937) and in Ålborg, of which he was the headmaster from 1937 until his death. Stegmann never compromised with his democratic principles and was shot by the Nazis.

LISBET BALSLEV JØRGENSEN

WORK

1931–1937, Århus University (with KAY FISKER and C. F. MØLLER), Denmark.

BIBLIOGRAPHY

JØRGENSEN, AXEL 1952 "Stegmann, Povl Christian." Volume 3, pages 277–278 in *Weilbach Kunstnerleksikon.* Copenhagen.
Povl Stegmann 1888–1944. 1953 Ringkobling, Denmark: Rasmussens Bogtrykkeri.

STEIGER, RUDOLF

Rudolf Steiger (1900–) studied architecture in Zurich with KARL MOSER. After working in Berlin in 1924, he settled in Zurich where he belonged to a group of architects who defended the ideas of modern architecture and who collectively built the Neubühl housing project (1929–1932). His talent was to translate technical problems into forms. In 1937, he formed an office with MAX ERNST HAEFELI and WERNER MOSER. They integrated new values into modern architecture, such as an expressive use of materials, revealed at best in the Cantonal Hospital in Zurich (1942–1951).

Steiger played an important role in formulating the programs of the Congrès Internationaux d'Architecture Moderne for the "Functional City" in the 1930s.

MARTIN STEINMANN

WORKS

1924, House Sandreuter (with Flora Steiger), Riehen, Switzerland. 1928–1930, Sanatorium (with Arnold Itten), Montana, Switzerland. 1929–1932, Neubühl Estate (with CARL HUBACHER, PAUL ARTARIA, HANS SCHMIDT, Max Ernst Haefeli, Werner Moser, and Emil Roth); 1930–1932, Commercial Building Z (with Hubacher); Zurich. 1936, General Motors Plant (with Hubacher), Biel, Switzerland. 1938, Widmer House (with Flora Steiger), Rüschlikon, Switzerland. 1939, Congress Building (with Haefeli and Moser); 1942–1951, Cantonal Hospital (with Architektengemeinschaft für das Kantonsspital), Zurich; 1959, House Steiger (with Flora Steiger); 1960–1964, Palme Commercial Building (with Haefeli and Moser); Zurich.

BIBLIOGRAPHY

STEIGER, RUDOLF 1970 *46 Jahre Bauen und Planen.* Zurich: printed privately.
VON MOOS, STANISLAUS, and STEINMANN, MARTIN (editors) 1980 "Haefeli, Moser, Steiger." *Architese* 10, no. 2:3–74.

STEIN, CLARENCE S.

Clarence S. Stein (1883–1975) was born in Rochester, New York, and studied architecture at Columbia University and the Ecole des Beaux-Arts in Paris. Although trained as a traditional architect, Stein soon turned to the newly emerging science of regional planning, seeking to use it to resolve contemporary urban crowding problems. Uniting a circle of interested New York based architects and writers including Lewis Mumford, HENRY WRIGHT, EDITH ELMER WOOD, Robert D. Kohn, and Benton McKaye, he formed the Regional Planning Association of America to promote the cause. Soon interesting investors, including real estate developer Alexander Bing, the group adapted British garden city principles to two American experiments: Sunnyside Gardens, Queens, New York (1924), a residential complex featuring housing clustered around large community gardens; and Radburn, New Jersey (1926), planned as a complete town whose construction was halted during the Depression. The design for the latter settlement included a unique circulation plan separating pedestrian and vehicular traffic, superblocks of mixed housing densities, and extensive interior parks surrounded by residences.

These ideas, labeled "the Radburn idea," were widely emulated abroad. In addition, Stein promoted this basic formula in his advice for the Greenbelt Towns planned during the New Deal by the Resettlement Administration at Chatham Village (Pittsburgh [1930]) and Baldwin Hills (Los Angeles [1941]). Stein publicized this work in his widely read book, *Towards New Towns for America* (1951).

Other pioneering aspects of his Radburn work were his early shopping center studies undertaken with CATHERINE KROUSE BAUER. The village's commercial complex served as a model for modern, postwar versions. In conjunction with his private work, Stein promoted the cause of regional planning in the public sector during his three-year tenure as chairman of the New York State Commission of Housing and Regional Planning. The Commission's *Report* (1926) has become a landmark in regional planning. It featured the first comprehensive statewide study and plan that was partially executed. In addition to his concern with urban planning, Stein engaged in some standard architectural work, including the design for Temple Emanu-el, (New York [1929]) undertaken with Robert D. Kohn.

EUGENIE L. BIRCH

WORKS

1915, San Diego World Fair Site Plan (with BERTRAM GROSVENOR GOODHUE), Calif. 1924, Sunnyside Gardens (with Henry Wright), Queens, N.Y. 1926, Radburn (with Wright), N.J. 1929, Temple Emanu-el (with Robert D. Kohn), New York. 1930, Chatham Village (with Wright), Pittsburgh. 1931, Phipps Garden Apartments I, Sunnyside Gardens, Queens, N.Y. 1932, Hillside Homes, New York. 1935, Phipps Garden Apartments II, Sunnyside Gardens, Queens, N.Y. 1941, Baldwin Hills Village, Los Angeles. 1951, Site plan (with ALBERT MAYER and Julian Whittlesey), Kitimat, British Columbia.

BIBLIOGRAPHY

BIRCH, EUGENIE L. 1980 "Radburn and the American Planning Movement: The Persistence of an Idea." *Journal of the American Planning Association* 46:424–439.
GOLDBERGER, PAUL 1975 "Clarence Stein, Planner of Garden Cities, 92, Dies." *New York Times,* Feb. 8.
MUMFORD, LEWIS 1976 "A Modest Man's Enduring Contributions to Urban and Regional Planning." *Journal of the American Institute of Architects* 65:19–29.

STEIN, RICHARD G.

Richard G. Stein (1916–) trained under WALTER GROPIUS at Harvard and subsequently worked for Gropius and MARCEL BREUER. He has taught architecture at Cooper Union for over thirty years while maintaining an active practice in Manhattan.

In the 1970s, Stein became widely recognized here and abroad as one of the profession's most articulate spokesmen for energy conservation through building design. He has lectured extensively and published numerous articles on energy related issues. He is the author of *Architecture and Energy* (1977) and of several pioneering studies documenting the total amount of energy required by the construction industry, including the extraction and manufacture of raw materials, the construction process, and operational energy use.

Stein's architectural works consistently reflect a carefully articulated structural clarity, acknowledging a debt to his Bauhaus teachers while bringing a special thoughtfulness and sensitivity to the user's needs. A catalogue published in conjunction with an exhibit of the architect's work (Cooper Union, 1980) best illustrates these qualities.

C. STUART WHITE, JR.

WORKS

1961, Wiltwyck School for Boys, Yorktown, N.Y. 1962, Public School 55, Staten Island, N.Y. 1967, Manhattan Children's Treatment Center, Ward's Island, N.Y. 1968, Intermediate School 183, Bronx, N.Y.

BIBLIOGRAPHY

HARAK, RUDOLPH DE, and PLASKOFF, ROBIN 1980 *Richard G. Stein: Forty Years of Architectural Work* New York: Cooper Union Press. Exhibition catalogue.
STEIN, RICHARD G. 1977 *Architecture and Energy.* Garden City, N.Y.: Doubleday.

STEINBACH, ERWIN VON

See ERWIN VON STEINBACH.

STEINER, RUDOLF

Rudolf Steiner (1861–1925), a Goethe scholar, educator, and founder in Germany of the spiritual science of Anthroposophy, developed in the early years of our century an architecture that was programmed to demonstrate his occult philosophy. Not a trained architect himself, Steiner relied upon professionals to carry out his conceptions. The significance of his works rests largely in the ways they reflect certain ideals of emotive and symbolic expression in the arts that were evident in Germany between 1900 and 1918 and that nurtured the growth of an Expressionist architecture.

Steiner's ideas on the expressive potentials of art and architecture were most thoroughly demonstrated in a complex of buildings constructed from 1913 onward in Dornach, Switzerland, outside Basel, for his Anthroposophical Society. The dominant building at the Dornach site was the Goetheanum, a central meeting hall and theater that was originally to have been built in Munich. As its name suggests, the Goetheanum had been erected in homage to Goethe, aspects of whose thought were embodied both in the building's formal conception and in the teachings of Anthroposophy. The building was mysteriously destroyed by fire in 1922; a second, less complex but larger Goetheanum begun two years later and completed by Steiner's followers, stands today amidst the earlier buildings.

Student years in Vienna at the Technische Hochschule (1879–1889) mark the beginning of Steiner's involvement with Goethe. The opportunity to prepare an edition of Goethe's natural scientific writings for *Kürschners Nationalliteratur* was extended to Steiner in 1882 upon the recommendation of Karl Julius Schröer, a professor of German literature and former teacher of Steiner's at the Hochschule. Two subsequent publications on Goethe, *Grundlinien einer Erkenntnistheorie der Goetheschen Weltanschauung* (1886) and *Goethe als Vater einer neuen Ästhetik* (1888), contain those aspects of Goethean thought that were to become the basis for Steiner's Anthroposophy: the thesis that all knowledge depends upon what can be visually perceived in the material world and that by penetrating beyond material characteristics insight may be gained into the greater spiritual laws permeating all things. Proceeding from a Goethean tradition of natural philosophy (*Naturforschung*) Steiner based his Anthroposophy, and in turn his architectural works, on three central monistic precepts: (1) that reality consists of the singular unity of spirit and matter; (2) that within the natural realm is a wealth of creative ideas the spiritual secrets of which are penetrable by means of reason; (3) that within the whole of reality are polar forces the interaction of which is the basis of all life. Steiner was not alone in developing a mode of inquiry based on these principles for they are contained as well in contemporary writings of the theologians Martin Buber and Rudolf Otto. In Anthroposophy (composed of the Greek words *anthropos* and *sophia* which together mean wisdom of man), one is encouraged to extend a knowledge of the sensible or material realm to a knowledge of the supersensible or spiritual realm by means of a sensitive perception of physical phenomena. Incorporated into Anthroposophical teachings are the monistic attitudes of world religions as well as those found in occult literature.

Goethe studies were furthered between 1890 and 1896 when, as a fellow at the newly founded Goethe-Schiller Archive in Weimar, Steiner was engaged in editing Goethe's scientific writings. Among Steiner's numerous publications over these years is his chief philosophical work, *Die Philosophie der Freiheit* (1894), which was based on the Goethean natural scientific method of investigation. Writings by Steiner from the Weimar period and those from his early years in Berlin (1897–1910) are evidence of his deepening involvement with philosophical investigations into natural phenomena and with the precepts of monistic thought which are an integral part of both natural philosophy and systems of occult science.

The means of fathoming the spiritual essence of all things was for Steiner a vitalistic identification with physical objects, of which the most revealing were held to be works of art. This relationship he explained as a natural affinity between a soul-bearing subject and a soul-shaping object, a clear reference to the aesthetics of empathy of The-odor Lipps and its postulate of a psychological give-and-take between object and viewer. Of more immediate influence upon Steiner were the elaborations of empathy theory contained in the writings of Wilhelm Worringer, *Abstraktion und Einfühlung* (1907) and *Formprobleme der Gotik* (1912). The Lippsian view that an object's expressive features, its expression (*Ausdruck*), stimulates an impression (*Eindruck*) that affects the viewer physically and psychically, was amplified by Steiner to the extent that an object or an appropriate art work was said to be capable of eliciting an inner spirit desiring to be released into consciousness. Steiner often indicated that the union of ourselves with an object, to which we are drawn because of an inner spiritual urge, acts to shape that spiritual force within us.

Steiner's designs, both those at Dornach and his less well-known works of the period 1907–1913, were guided by notions of empathetic expression and by associated precepts of natural philosophy. Similar creative objectives exist in the work of contemporary Symbolist, *Jugendstil,* and Expressionist artists whose ideas on matters physical and metaphysical were drawn from a monistic philsophical tradition. Steiner's endeavors to fashion an architectural equivalent to the spiritual revelations of Anthroposophy may be equated with one of the central aims of Symbolist and Expressionist arts: to create works of cosmic meaning for mankind.

Three projects chart Steiner's architectural interests which climaxed in his first Goetheanum: (1) seven planetary columns and circular signets designed for the Theosophical Congress in Munich (1907); (2) a subterranean chamber for the Theosophical Society in Stuttgart (1901–1912); (3) the *Johannesbau* project for Munich (1912–1913). These works belong to a period when Steiner was involved with Theosophy, lecturing extensively, writing numerous articles, and editing the Theosophical periodical *Gnosis* (*Luzifer-Gnosis*). Over this period, he distanced himself more and more from official Theosophical circles, having been oriented more toward western philosophy and Christian theology than toward Theosophy's exclusive amalgam of Eastern religions and philosophies. Following his break with Theosophy, Steiner founded the Anthroposophical Society in February 1913, and in September of that year he set in motion the construction of the Dornach buildings.

The seven columns of 1907 are the earliest evidence of Steiner's belief that spiritual laws could significantly be embodied in the formative arts. Set up in a prescribed sequence within an assembly hall of the Theosophical Congress in Munich, the columns represented the seven ancient planetary spheres (Saturn, Sun, Moon, Mars, Mercury, Jupiter, and Venus) which according to occult doctrine regulate all development in seven successive stages, a theme recurrent in ancient Indian, central Asian, and Near Eastern religions. To convey a sense of evolutionary progression, Steiner designed different forms in relief for each of the capitals which were composed to represent varied interactions of polar forces. The monistic concept of universal forces which determine the shapes and metamorphoses of natural forms was thereby demonstrated by compositional changes presented serially on the column capitals.

The changing motifs of the capitals and the two-dimensional circular signets of linear design which Steiner devised in conjunction with them, have an inherent order which can be related to two monistic systems of special relevance to Steiner, the primal plant (*Urpflanze*) and its metamorphosis described by Goethe, and the "qualities" or vital forces of God described by the seventeenth-century mystic philosopher Jacob Boehme. Just as Steiner acknowledged the connections of his architectural forms with Goethe's ideas on metamorphosis but was never explicit about them, so too his commentaries on Boehme's philosophy were of a more general nature and made no mention of architecture. However, in Steiner's columns and signets, as in Goethe's primal plant and Boehme's discourse on the qualities of God, three essential principles are evident: (1) seven is the guiding number; (2) growth and change is in accord with an alternating system of expanding and contracting movements; and (3) all forms are generated around a fixed center. Through his columns and signets Steiner attempted to translate into artistic form principles which for Goethe and Boehme were intrinsic to physical and metaphysical realms.

Steiner further explained that the capitals corresponded to sounds of "spiritual music," a reference to the ancient Pythagorean and Platonic notion of the numerical ratios and musical harmonies of the heavenly spheres whereby each planet signifies a different note. The capital series was therefore said to represent "frozen music," a metaphoric description of architecture which was repeated by nineteenth-century German philosophers, most notably Schelling, Goethe, and Schopenhauer. The planetary columns marked the beginning of architectural interests which developed over the next years and culminated in the first Goetheanum.

After designing the columns for the Munich congress, Steiner sought to devise a total setting in which the significance of the columns would be appropriately amplified. He first realized his ideal

in 1912 with the construction of a chamber located in the cellar of a new building for the Theosophical Society in Stuttgart. Built entirely of stone, the chamber was based on a design for a lodge hall which Steiner had projected in 1909 for the Theosophical Society at Malsch (outside Breslau). Like the original design, the subterranean hall was a windowless elliptical space. Two rows of seven sandstone columns carried arches from which arose a domical vault bearing signs of the zodiac and various astral bodies. Marking the crown of the vault was a polyhedric glass light fixture. The cavernous enclosure, the elliptical plan, the numerical progression of seven, the cosmological symbolism on the vault, and the crystalline globe represent a fascinating conjunction of elements. They allude to a spectrum of architectural and literary traditions included among which are Mythraic ritual and notions of cosmic symbolism contained in Hindu, Near Eastern, and occult writings as well as in Goethe's *Wilhelm Meisters Wanderjahre* and his *Märchen*.

Steiner's efforts at Munich and Stuttgart to give explicit form to occult principles were not unlike the efforts of the Neoplatonic philosopher and mystic Giordano Bruno, whose writings often included mnemonic signs and symbols intended to illuminate occult truths. A more immediate parallel to Steiner is Mani, a Persian painter and founder of the occult sect of Manichaeism. Both Mani and Steiner interpreted a wide range of spiritual beliefs primarily through art. The Anthroposophy which Steiner was shaping in these years also resembles Manichaeism in its syncretic character, incorporating aspects of Near Eastern, Indian, and Western religions. Steiner's aim was to formulate a spiritual science of the most comprehensive kind and to enrich its teachings with appropriate architectural and artistic forms.

While the Stuttgart hall was nearing completion, Steiner moved closer to his ideal of a grand space for the revelation of spiritual mysteries. He began to devise plans in 1912 for a domical auditorium and theater that would have been the center of a housing development in Munich. The building, which never materialized apparently because of zoning restrictions, was to have served primarily for the presentation of Steiner's cycle of four "mystery plays" which were inspired by Goethe's mystery drama, the *Märchen,* and which were introduced to members of Steiner's circle between 1910 and 1913. The projected theater, called the *Johannesbau* (after the name of the main protagonist in Steiner's cycle, Johannes Thomasius) was a further effort to create an architecture expressive of an occult program. From this time onward, dramatic arts were one of Steiner's major vehicles for the presentation of occult truths. To the repertory of mystery plays was added in later years the complete production of Goethe's *Faust,* another source of spiritual revelations.

Sketches of 1912/1913 for the interior of the *Johannesbau* indicate that Steiner was evolving a setting in which all forms, and in particular his columns, would exist in harmony with one another. Clearly, the static disposition of the forms and symbols at Stuttgart did not convey adequately the idea of active forces in the universe. Visual activity which had been contained in the column capitals were now spread to the arches and to the wall surfaces above them. Notations on the sketches indicate that the linear movements of relief forms were meant to elicit an empathetic awareness of metamorphosis and its inherent principles. An expressive architecture was being worked out that would reflect universal laws. The successor of the *Johannesbau* project was the Goetheanum at Dornach.

The first Goetheanum (1913–1920) embodied more completely than the other buildings erected at Dornach the aims of emotive and symbolic expression which Steiner had been elaborating since 1907. These dual ideals were being explored in works, both projected and realized, by a number of artists and architects active in Germany between 1900 and 1918 and whose roots were the *Jugendstil* and Symbolist arts. Among the outstanding examples of these ideals were the fountains, funerary monuments, and architectural projects of the *Jugendstil* designer and sculptor HERMANN OBRIST; the fantasies published by the architect OTTO KOHTZ; the various schemes for an "art-of-the-temple" postulated by the *Jugendstil* artist and illustrator Hugo Höppener known as Fidus; the festival theater imagined by PETER BEHRENS; the crystalline visions of the artist WENZEL HABLIK; and the Glass Pavilion of BRUNO TAUT at the 1914 Deutscher Werkbund Exposition in Cologne. With these and other artists of the time, Steiner shared two of the central aims of architectural Expressionism, that of exploiting the empathetic as associative aspects of formal expression and the related Romantic ideal of the *Gesamtkunstwerk,* whereby diverse artistic media and sensory effects are synthesized for the purpose of a heightened spiritual awareness.

Steiner regarded his Goetheanum as a temple of spiritual wisdom in the tradition of Solomon's Temple and the Temple of the Holy Grail and so conceived his cult hall that its various formal and structural features would demonstrate universal laws through empathetic and symbolic means. To this end, the building's reinforced concrete base and its timber upper portions were designed both on the interior and exterior to achieve a sculptural mobility and a fluctuation between forms fluid and crystalline. The building protectively encircled its internal spaces, extended winglike projections to the outside, and was brought to a resolution in the double domes which crowned the large main auditorium and the smaller apsidal stage. For Steiner, the Goetheanum was in the lineage of an "organic" living architecture. Features such as the double rows of planetary columns in the auditorium and stage spaces and the continuous entablature which they supported were said in their changing forms to capture Goethean ideas of the metamorphosis of plants. Accompanying the dynamics of structure were the chromatic interior effects of the various woods, stained glass windows, and paintings in the domes, the whole of which was conceived to be in resonance with the music from the organ and the spoken words of recitations and lectures. Forms were also conceived to be attuned to the dialogue and movement of Steiner's mystery plays and to eurythmic dances, an art form of movement and speech which Steiner had developed for the Goetheanum. Unfortunately, neither the plays nor the dance programs were performed there because of the tragic fire of 1922. To create an interior that would harmoniously unite the formative, musical, and dramatic arts and thereby constitute a *Gesamtkunstwerk* was Steiner's ultimate aesthetic mission at the Goetheanum. Influenced by the writings of various Romantics and most notably by Richard Wagner, he believed that architecture, sculpture, and painting drawn into synthesis with music could effectively convey a sense of the divine force in the world. Synaesthetic blendings of forms, colors, and sounds were the means of expanding one's spiritual perception and of creating an architecture that would be at one with and hence demonstrative of cosmic laws.

Today among the focal buildings at Dornach are the Glass Studio, where the stained glass windows of Goetheanum I were made (1914), the Power Plant (1914–1915), the Grossheintz-Duldeck House (1915–1916), the De Jaager House (1921–1922), and the second Goetheanum, begun in 1924 and finished in intermittent stages by Steiner's followers. Of the early structures, the Power Plant and the Grossheintz-Duldeck House convey Steiner's evolution toward an architecture more integrally sculptural than the first Goetheanum. Built entirely of reinforced concrete, these buildings unite prismatic and fluid forms in order to symbolize the interaction of opposing cosmic impulses which Steiner had begun to elaborate in the first Goetheanum and on which he occasionally lectured. Goetheanum II, a compact sculptural mass, is a further development of the formal themes present in the earlier buildings. Only the general massing of Goetheanum II was indicated in Steiner's plasticine model of 1924. Little was specified by Steiner about detailed sculptural accents, the mode of entry, or the disposition of internal spaces. In accord with Steiner's beliefs and with aspects of the first Goetheanum, these were worked out by the architects Hermann Ranzenberger and Ernst Aisenpreis, the mathematician Albert von Baravalle, and the sculptor Carl Kemper.

Collectively, the extant buildings at Dornach only partially reflect Steiner's emotive and symbolic aims which paralleled those of Expressionism and which had found their most complete realization in Goetheanum I. Steiner's contribution to the growth and dispersal of Expressionist ideals was primarily through his writings and lectures. His architecture, on the contrary, exerted minimal influence upon the practice of Expressionism. Nevertheless, his little-known early designs, the Dornach buildings, and, most significantly, the first Goetheanum, are not mere curiosities of occult history but are symptomatic of Symbolist and Expressionist currents in German architecture in the years before 1918, which after World War I were to emerge in Expressionist circles.

EUGENE A. SANTOMASSO

WORKS

1907, Seven Planetary Columns, Theosophical Congress, Munich. 1910–1912, Subterranean Chamber, Theosophical Society Building, Stuttgart, Germany. 1913–1920, Goetheanum I; 1914, Glass Studio; 1914–1915, Power Plant; 1915–1916, Grossheintz-Duldeck House; 1919–1920, Van Blommestein Studio House; Dornach, Switzerland. 1919–1921, Vreede House, Arlesheim, Switzerland. 1920–1921, Three Eurythmy Houses; 1921, Transformer House; 1921–1922, De Jaager Studio House; 1923–1924, Brodbeck House (extensions); 1923–1924, Publishing House; 1924–1925, Goetheanum II (not completed until 1964); Dornach, Switzerland.

BIBLIOGRAPHY

BIESANTZ, HAGEN; KLINGBORN, ARNE; and FANT, ÅKE 1980 *The Goetheanum: Rudolf Steiner's Architectural Impulse.* Translated by Jean Schmid. London: Steiner.

FANT, ÅKE; KLINGBORN, ARNE; and WILKES, A. JOHN 1969 *Die Holzplastik Rudolf Steiners in Dornach.* Dornach, Switzerland: Philosophisch-Anthroposophischer Verlag am Goetheanum.

KEMPER, CARL 1966 *Der Bau: Studien der Architektur und Plastik des ersten Goetheanums.* Stuttgart, Germany: Verlag Freies Geistesleben.

SANTOMASSO, EUGENE A. 1973 "Origins and Aims of German Expressionist Architecture: An Essay into the Expressionist Frame of Mind in Germany, Especially as Typified in the Work of Rudolf Steiner." Unpublished Ph.D. dissertation, Columbia University, New York.

SHARP, DENNIS 1963 "Rudolf Steiner and the Way to a New Style in Architecture." *Architectural Association Journal* 79:372–383.

STOCKMEYER, E. A. KARL 1957 "Von Vorläufern des Goetheanums." Pages 85–91 in *Rudolf Steiner: Bilder okkulter Siegel und Säulen. Der Münchner Kongress Pfingsten 1907.* Dornach, Switzerland: Steiner.

ZIMMER, ERICH 1971 *Rudolf Steiner als Architekt von Wohn- und Zweckbauten.* Stuttgart, Germany: Verlag Freies Geistesleben.

STENHAMMAR, ERNST

Ernst Stenhammar (1859–1927) was a Swedish architect whose practice consisted mainly of office and hospital buildings. As a member of an artistically gifted family (his father was an architect; his brother Wilhelm, a famous composer) he early decided to become an architect, and in 1884 he finished his education at the Royal Academy of Arts in Stockholm.

After several years of designing apartments, he specialized in office buildings. His first prominent project was the Central Palace (1895–1898), one of the first office buildings for rent in Stockholm, following the American pattern of frame structure, open floors, secondary walls, and large windows. This type was further developed in the Myrstedt and Stern Building at Kungsgatan in Stockholm (1908–1910), the first pure frame construction of reinforced concrete in Stockholm with a stone front, slightly Gothicizing. He developed his office architecture in a number of big bank buildings, for which he used different kinds of glazed domes. A fine example is the head office of the Wermland Bank at Karlstad (1906–1908), where series of open, glazed rooms are placed in a sequence behind a closed and sparsely decorated front of brick and granite. His interest in technical solutions is also evident in his many hospital buildings, also heavily influenced by the American way of organizing hospitals.

FREDRIC BEDOIRE

BIBLIOGRAPHY

ÅMAN, ANDERS 1976 *Om den offentliga vården.* Stockholm: Liber Förlag.

ANDERSSON, HENRIKO, and BEDOIRE, FREDRIC 1981 *Bankbyggande i Sverige.* Stockholm: Liber Förlag.

STENMAN, ELIS

Elis Stenman (?–1942) and his wife built their home (1922–1942), in Pigeon Cove, Massachusetts, out of more than 100,000 newspapers. The walls and roof were made of sheets of newspaper pasted and folded into designs. Furniture and a fireplace were created from tightly rolled cylinders of newspaper used like logs. Curtains were woven of colored newspaper folded into strips.

JANET KAPLAN

BIBLIOGRAPHY

WAMPLER, JAN 1977 Pages 118–121 in *All Their Own: People and the Places They Build.* Cambridge, Mass.: Schenkman.

STEPHENSON, DAVID

David Stephenson (1757–1819) entered the Royal Academy Schools in London in 1782. In the following year, he returned to his birthplace, Newcastle-on-Tyne, to establish his practice. As an accomplished neoclassical architect, Stephenson executed mostly civic and religious buildings.

BRIAN LUKACHER

WORKS

1786–1789, All Saints Church; 1787–1788, Theatre Royal; Newcastle, England. 1806–1809, Farmhouses, Estate of the Duke of Northumberland, Alnwick, England.

STEPHENSON, GEORGE, and STEPHENSON, ROBERT

George Stephenson (1781–1848) and Robert Stephenson (1803–1859)—father and son—were the leading figures in England in the revolution in transport brought about by the steam locomotive and the railroad in the early nineteenth century. Their main contribution to architecture was thus an indirect one, though it did include several major bridges.

George was born in the Northumberland mining village of Wylam and began work at about the age of eight without having had any formal schooling. Indeed, he probably had little aptitude for book learning or theory. His chief qualities were keen powers of observation and imaginative reasoning in relation to anything mechanical, coupled with the confidence and ambition to develop the potential that he saw in the use of the steam engine for locomotion. Later, he recognized the handicap of his lack of learning and was already sufficiently prosperous by 1815 to send Robert to a private school in Newcastle and, for a short period,

to Edinburgh University. Thus, with the exception of three years when Robert worked as a mining engineer in South America, father and son were able to form a powerful complementary partnership.

Already in 1814, George had built a locomotive to haul colliery wagons in which he had, for the first time, used the flanged wheels that subsequently became universal. In 1825, he completed the first railroad to carry passengers between Stockton and Darlington, with assistance from Robert in the initial survey. The Liverpool to Manchester line followed. Robert was then primarily responsible for lines from London to Birmingham and Newcastle to Berwick, among others. These involved major bridges as well as other civil engineering works, notably over the Tyne at Newcastle and over the Tweed at Berwick. His most important bridge was the Britannia Bridge over the Menai Straits (1845–1850) carrying the Chester to Holyhead line. For this he adopted a novel tubular form, with the trains running through twin tubes set side-by-side high above the water. Their design was the result of an epoch-making collaboration with WILLIAM FAIRBAIRN and Eaton Hodgkinson, though the solid-walled tubular form soon gave way to lighter truss forms and became widely adopted only in the 1860s.

ROWLAND MAINSTONE

WORKS

1845–1850, Conway and Britannia Tubular Bridges, North Wales. 1846–1849, High Level Bridge, Newcastle, England.

BIBLIOGRAPHY

CLARK, EDWIN, and STEPHENSON, ROBERT 1850 *The Britannia and Conway Tubular Bridges.* London: Weale.
ROLT, L. T. C. 1960 *George and Robert Stephenson.* London: Longmans.
SMILES, SAMUEL (1862)1905 Volume 3 in *Lives of the Engineers.* New York: Scribners.

STEPHENSON, ROBERT STORER

Following several years in the office of McKIM, MEAD, AND WHITE, Robert Storer Stephenson (1858–1929) founded his own firm in New York about 1890. He was best known for his work in domestic architecture and built many fine residences in the prevailing eclectic styles in Connecticut, New Jersey, New York, and Massachusetts.

C. STUART WHITE, JR.

WORKS

c.1891, Trinity Church, East Orange, N.J. *1907, Frederick F. Brewster Estate (Edgerton), New Haven. c.1914, John A. Garver House, Oyster Bay, N.Y. c.1914, Thomas H. Gillespie House, South Orange, N.J.

BIBLIOGRAPHY

DANA, RICHARD H., JR. 1913 "Edgerton—A Study in the Tudor Style." *Architectural Record* 34, no. 4:273–291.
PARKE, RICHARD H. 1964 "Doomed Mansion Calls Up the Past." *New York Times* Sept. 5, p. 21.
PRICE, C. MATLACK 1914 "A Recent Country House on Long Island—The Garver Residence at Oyster Bay." *Architectural Record* 35, no. 3:181–201.

STERN, RAFFAELLO

Born in Rome, Raffaello Stern (1774–1820) continued the classical directions of his father Giovanni Stern. He integrated the principles of Johann Joachim Winckelmann into a more formal and moderate architecture in a Roman environment. After beginning his practice in engineering and restoration, he was put in charge of the construction of the Baraccio Nuovo by the Museum of Chiaramonti in 1817. Through his commanding knowledge of archeology, he converted an original sense of classical Roman into an elegant style with linear decorations in reliefs and stucco. The roof was made of small hollow shell vault cases containing sculptures.

FARHAD NIROUMAND-RAD

BIBLIOGRAPHY

LAVAGNINO, E. 1956 Volume 1, pages 51–52 in *L'arte moderna.* Turin, Italy.
MEEKS, CARROLL L. V. 1966 *Italian Architecture: 1750–1914.* New Haven: Yale University Press.

STEUART, GEORGE

George Steuart (c.1730–1806) worked mainly for the third and fourth dukes of Atholl. Interior decorative painting was his primary art. He acted as agent for the third duke in London and soon contrived to build a mansion for him (1769–1770). Steuart designed several important country houses, the grandest being Attingham Hall, Shropshire, for Lord Berwick. Characteristic of Steuart's work is its attenuated classical decoration, yet Castle Mona, Isle of Man, for the fourth duke, is a Gothic palace. Observant, clever, self-taught, the architect became sufficiently adept to annoy ROBERT ADAM who resented his competition. Steuart had no pupils and exerted little architectural influence, though New Saint Chad's Church (1790–1792), circular in shape, is of unusual interest. He was born in Perthshire and died on the Isle of Man.

PAUL F. NORTON

WORKS

1779–1781, Barons Court, County Tyrone, Ireland. 1783–1785, Attingham Hall, Shropshire, England. 1786–1791, Stoke Park, Erlestoke, Wiltshire, England. 1788–1790, All Saints Church, Wellington, Shropshire, England. 1790–1792, New St. Chad's Church, Shrewsbury, England. 1801–1806, Castle Mona, Douglas, Isle of Man, England.

BIBLIOGRAPHY

NORTON, PAUL F., and HILL, MARY 1967 *New Saint Chad's and Its Architect.* Shrewsbury, England: K. W. Thomas.
RIX, M. M., and SERGEANT, W. R. 1962–1963 "George Steuart, Architect, in the Isle of Man." *Journal of the Manx Museum* 6:177–179.

STEVENS, FREDERICK WILLIAM

Frederick William Stevens (1848–1900), the leading Victorian architect of Bombay, designed High Victorian Gothic buildings long after the style had ceased to be fashionable in Britain. Increasingly, his Gothic acquired an oriental character. His most celebrated work, the Victoria Terminus Station in Bombay (1876–1888), is one of the largest and most impressive Gothic Revival secular buildings in the world. Born in Bath, England, he was articled to Charles E. Davis. In 1867, he became assistant engineer in the Public Works Department in Bombay. In 1884, he retired from government service but remained in Bombay until his death.

GAVIN STAMP

WORKS

1871–1875, Royal Alfred Sailors' Home, Bombay. 1874–1876, Government House, Naini Tal, India. 1876–1888, Victoria Terminus Station; 1888–1893, Municipal Buildings; 1894–1896, Church Gate Station; Bombay. 1894–1896, Standard Insurance Building, Calcutta.

BIBLIOGRAPHY

"The Late F. W. Stevens, C.I.E." 1900 *Journal of the Royal Institute of British Architects* Series 3 7:374–375.
STAMP, GAVIN 1977 "Victorian Bombay: Urbs Prima in Indis." *Art and Archaeology Research Papers* 11, June:22–27.

STEVENS, JOHN CALVIN

Born in Boston, John Calvin Stevens (1855–1940) entered the architectural offices of Francis H. Fassett there; in 1885, Stevens (junior partner in the firm of Fassett & Stevens from 1880 to 1884) and Albert W. Cobb established the firm of Stevens and Cobb, which was dissolved in 1891. In addition to designing public and private buildings, the partners published *Examples of American Domestic Architecture* (1889), which emphasized the architect's responsibility for infusing the democratic spirit into architecture.

Stevens is especially noted for his contributions to the picturesque cottage architecture of the 1880s; Vincent Scully has accorded him a place of critical importance with respect to a move toward "geometric and spatial discipline in [residential] design" (1955, p. 113). Representative of this move are the project for a House by the Sea (1885) and most notably the James Hopkins Smith House (1885) near Portland, Maine, whose mass is unified by a broad gambrel roof, a continuous envelope of shingles on the second story, and a solid base of rubble masonry.

In 1906, Stevens's son, John H., joined him in practice. Examples of the firm's work include the Sweat Memorial Art Museum (1909) in Portland, Maine, and the Portland City Hall (1911) designed in collaboration with the New York firm of CARRÈRE AND HASTINGS.

SUSAN STRAUSS

WORKS

1883, Stevens House, Portland, Maine. 1885, James Hopkins Smith House, Falmouth Foreside (near Portland), Maine. 1888, Eastern Maine Insane Hospital, Bangor. 1909, Sweat Memorial Art Museum; 1911, City Hall (with Carrère and Hastings); 1934, United States Post Office; Portland, Maine.

BIBLIOGRAPHY

SCULLY, VINCENT, JR. (1955)1971 *The Shingle Style and the Stick Style.* Rev. ed. New Haven and London: Yale University Press.

STEVENS, JOHN CALVIN, and COBB, ALBERT W. 1889 *Examples of American Domestic Architecture.* New York: Comstock.

STEVENSON, JOHN JAMES

John James Stevenson (1831–1908) was one of the leading architects working in the vernacular revival style of the 1870s and 1880s in England that became known as the Queen Anne style. Stevenson was born in Glasgow and studied under DAVID BRYCE and GEORGE GILBERT SCOTT. He settled in London in 1869, and from 1871 to 1876 was in partnership with the school architect EDWARD ROBERT ROBSON. Stevenson's own house, the Red House (1871), was one of the first buildings erected in the Queen Anne style, and it was influential in changing the character of London domestic architecture from stucco to brick. Of his country houses, Ken Hill, Norfolk (1880), is the best known; it embodies ideas set forth in his illustrated work *House Architecture* (1880).

BETTY ELZEA

WORKS

*1871, Red House, Bayswater; 1878, Houses, Lowther Gardens, South Kensington; 1878, House and Studio (for Colin Hunter), Melbury Road; London. 1878, Munstead, Godalming, Surrey, England. 1880, Ken Hill, Norfolk, England.

BIBLIOGRAPHY

ASLIN, ELIZABETH 1969 *The Aesthetic Movement: Prelude to Art Nouveau.* New York: Praeger.

GIROUARD, MARK 1979 *The Victorian Country House.* Rev. & Enl. ed. New Haven: Yale University Press.

GOODHART-RENDEL, H. S. 1953 *English Architecture Since the Regency: An Interpretation.* London: Constable.

PHYSICK, JOHN, and DARBY, MICHAEL 1973 *Marble Halls: Drawings and Models for Victorian Secular Buildings.* London: Victoria and Albert Museum.

STEVENSON, JOHN JAMES 1880 *House Architecture.* 2 vols. London: Macmillan.

TROUT, F. W. and REDFERS, HARRY 1907–1908 "The Late J. J. Stevenson, F.S.A." *Journal of the Royal Institute of British Architects,* Series 3 15:482–483.

STEWARDSON, EMLYN

See COPE and STEWARDSON.

STIRLING, DAVID

David Stirling (19th century) was born in Galashiels, Scotland. Trained there, he went to British North America about 1847 and designed buildings in diverse architectural styles. During the next forty years, he lived and worked in the Atlantic provinces and Ontario, his most productive period being in Halifax during the 1860s.

GARRY D. SHUTLAK

WORKS

1855, County Courthouse, Pictou, Nova Scotia. 1857–1860, Osgoode Hall, Toronto. 1862–1863, Halifax Club; 1863–1868, Provincial Building; Halifax, Nova Scotia. 1867–1868, Bank of Prince Edward Island,

Charlottetown. 1867–1869, The Poor's Asylum; 1868, School for the Blind; 1870, Fort Massey Presbyterian Church; Halifax, Nova Scotia. 1875–1878, Lunatic Asylum, Charlottetown, Prince Edward Island.

BIBLIOGRAPHY

Additional material is available in the David Stirling Notebook, Queen's University Archives, and David Stirling's Architectural Plans (1.3.3), both in the Public Archives of Nova Scotia, Halifax.

BLAKELEY, PHYLLIS R.   1949   *Glimpses of Halifax: 1867–1900*. Halifax: Public Archives of Nova Scotia.

HOUSE OF ASSEMBLY JOURNALS   1850–1878   Halifax, Nova Scotia: Queen's Printer.

TUCK, ROBERT C.   1978   *Gothic Dreams: The Life & Times of a Canadian Architect, William Critchlow Harris 1854–1913*. Toronto: Dundern.

STIRLING and GOWAN

James Stirling (1926–) and James Gowan (1923–) were both born in Glasgow, Scotland, where Gowan received his architectural training, Stirling's being at Liverpool University, where the curriculum was based on that of the Ecole des Beaux-Arts in Paris. The partnership of Stirling and Gowan lasted from 1956 to 1963 and produced a small number of influential buildings which helped to change the course of British architecture from a prevailing blandness of surface and design to the rigorous use of materials and stylish pseudo-functionalism known as Brutalism.

The low-rise flats of Ham Common (1957) in London started a trend for brick used with exposed concrete beams. Their next major building, the Engineering Department at Leicester University (1959–1963), introduced a much imitated use of hard red brick and industrial glazing, designed with many chamfered faces on the basis of axonometric drawings. The Leicester Building provided the basis for Stirling's History Faculty, Cambridge, and his Florey Building, Queen's College, Oxford.

Since the dissolution of the partnership, Stirling's extrovert architecture has undergone many transformations of style and has been as provocative for its appearance as for its frequent structural failures. In recent years, he has aligned himself with the European rediscovery of neoclassicism and has found much work in Germany.

Gowan has worked on smaller projects with less publicity but has received much admiration from critics and fellow architects for his careful detailing and originality of approach. He has also been an active teacher of architecture. It is generally agreed, however, that neither architect has individually recaptured the remarkable qualities that distinguished their partnership, although Stirling won the Pritzker Prize in 1980.

ALAN POWERS

WORKS

STIRLING AND GOWAN

1956, House, Isle of Wight, England. 1957, Low-rise Flats, Ham Common; London. 1958–1961, Dining Hall, Brunswick Park Primary School; London. 1959–1963, Engineering Department, Leicester University, England. 1960–1964, Home for the Elderly, Blackheath, London.

JAMES GOWAN

1967, Low-rise Housing, Creed Road, Greenwich; 1968, Low-rise Housing, Trafalgar Road, Greenwich; 1969, Luxury Flat, Fountain House, Mayfair; 1970, Unit Warehouses, Pages Walk; 1971, Unit Warehouses, Crimscott Street; London. 1972, Rural Housing, Bembridge, Isle of Wight, England. 1973, Warehouse and Offices, Evelyn Street, London. 1978, Housing, East Hanningfield, Essex, England. 1981, Charles Schriber Villa, Chester, England.

JAMES STIRLING

1964, History Building, Cambridge University. 1964, Andrew Melville Hall, University of St. Andrews, Scotland. 1965, Dorman Long Headquarters, Middlesborough, England. 1966, Florey Building, Queen's College, Oxford. 1967–1976, Housing Runcom New Town, Cheshire, England. 1969–1972, Olivetti Training School, Haslemere, Surrey, England. 1976, Regional Centre for Tuscany (with others), Florence, Italy. 1977, Art Gallery (addition), National Museum, Stuttgart, Germany. 1977, Dresdner Bank, Marburg, Germany. 1980, Dusseldorf Kunstsammlung, Germany. 1980, Science Center, Berlin. 1980, Wallrat-Richardtz Museum, Cologne, Germany. 1981, Tate Gallery (extension), London.

BIBLIOGRAPHY

BANHAM, REYNER   1966   *The New Brutalism*. New York: Reinhold.

FRAMPTON, KENNETH   1975   "Transformations in Style." *Architecture + Urbanism* 5, no. 2:128–138.

GOWAN, JAMES   1978   "Sketches for a Wall of a Room." *Architectural Association Quarterly* 10, no. 2:41–53.

"Inside James Stirling." 1976 *Design Quarterly* 100:special issue.

"James Stirling." 1980 *Architectural Design* 50, nos. 7–8:2–58.

James Stirling: Buildings and Projects, 1950–1974. 1975 London: Oxford Unversity Press.

"James Stirling: Royal Gold Medal for Architecture." 1980 *Journal of the Royal Institute of British Architects* 87, no. 3:35–42.

LYALL, SUTHERLAND   1981   "Architectural Purist." *New Society* 56, no. 966:320–321.

STAMP, GAVIN   1976   "Stirling's Worth." *Cambridge Review* 98, no. 2230:77–82.

STIRLING, JAMES   (1956)1979   "Ronchamp: Corbusier's Chapel and the Crisis of Rationalism." *Architecture and Urbanism* 105, no. 6:3–10.

"Three German Projects by James Stirling." 1979 *Techniques et Architecture* 326:23, 66–67.

STOKES, I. N. PHELPS

Isaac Newton Phelps Stokes (1867–1944) studied architecture at Columbia University in New York and the Ecole des Beaux-Arts in Paris, then established a New York firm within JOHN MEAD HOWELLS (1897). Improved low-income housing was his priority, and New York State reform housing legislation in 1901 was made possible in part through his efforts. Presaging present-day renewal, Stokes advocated government-subsidized slum clearance and a park–tenement scheme. He opposed restrictive legislation in favor of working within the present real-estate speculation system and encouraging sound economic planning through architectural competition. His published collection of prints, *The Iconography of Manhattan Island, 1498–1909* (1915) is an invaluable resource.

GWEN W. STEEGE

WORKS

1897, University Settlement House; 1901, Tuskegee House; 1914, Saint Paul's Chapel, Columbia University; New York.

BIBLIOGRAPHY

LUBOVE, ROY 1964 "I. N. Phelps Stokes: Tenement Architect, Economist, Planner." *Journal of the Society of Architectural Historians* 23:75–87.

STOKES, I. N. PHELPS (1915)1928 *The Iconography of Manhattan Island: 1498–1909.* 6 vols. New York: Dodd.

STOKES, I. N. PHELPS (n.d.)1941 *Random Reflections of a Happy Life.* Rev. ed. New York: Privately printed.

STOKES, LEONARD

Leonard Aloysius Scott Stokes (1858–1925) was an inventive Roman Catholic architect of the English Free Style school. He designed many churches and convents in an Arts and Crafts Gothic manner; a series of adventurously rationalist telephone exchanges; and schools, houses, and other work in both late medieval and eighteenth-century styles, sometimes strangely combined within the same building.

Articled to S. J. Nichol in 1874, he was then successively assistant to GEORGE E. STREET, J. P. St. Aubyn, T. E. Collcutt, GEORGE F. BODLEY, and

THOMAS GARNER, setting up his own practice in 1882. Stokes was president of the Architectural Association (1889–1892) and president of the Royal Institute of British Architects (1910–1912), and was awarded the Royal Gold Medal for Architecture in 1919. From 1916, due to severe paralysis, he virtually retired from practice.

T. RORY SPENCE

WORKS

1887–1889, Nazareth House Convent, Southsea, Hampshire, England. 1888–1889, Church of Our Lady, Folkestone, Kent, England. 1888–1889, Wilfred Meynell House, Bayswater, London. 1889–1890, Church of Saint Clare, Liverpool, England. *1890–1891, House (Broxwood Court), near Dilwyn, Hertfordshire, England. 1893–1894, Church of Saint Augustine, Sudberry, Suffolk, England. 1893–1894, Nazareth House Convent, Bexhill-on-Sea, Sussex, England. 1895–1896, Church of All Souls, Peterborough, Cambridgeshire, England. 1896–1897, Church of the Holy Ghost, Balham; 1898–1899, Philip Stokes House, Streatham; London. 1899–1901, Convent of All Saints, London Colney, Hertfordshire, England. 1900–1901, Telephone Exchange, Southampton, England. 1901–1902, Ascot Priory Convent, Berkshire, England. Leonard Stokes House (Littleshaw), Woldingham, Surrey, England. *1904–1906, Telephone Exchange, Soho, London. 1904–1907, Lord Digby House (Minterne), near Cerne Abbas, Dorset, England. 1905–1906, Lincoln Grammar School, England. 1906–1907, Western Telephone Exchange, Glasgow, Scotland. 1906–1908, Chelsea Town Hall, London. 1910–1911, Church of Saint Joseph, Pickering, Yorkshire, England. 1910–1912, Downside School, near Bath, Somerset, England. 1913–1915, Emmanuel College North Court, Cambridge. 1914–1925, Georgetown Cathedral, Guyana.

BIBLIOGRAPHY

DRYSDALE, GEORGE 1927 "The Work of Leonard Stokes." *Journal of the Royal Institute of British Architects* 34, no. 5:163–177.

ROBERTS, H. V. MOLESWORTH 1946 "Leonard Aloysius Stokes." *Architectural Review* 100:173–177.

SERVICE, ALASTAIR (editor) 1975 *Edwardian Architecture and Its Origins.* London: Architectural Press. Including a reprint of Roberts (1946), with different illustrations.

SPENCE, T. RORY 1976 "Stokes, Leonard Aloysius Scott (1858–1925)." Volume 7, pages 115–117 in Margaret Richardson (editor), *Catalogue of the Drawings Collection of the Royal Institute of British Architects.* Farnborough, England: Gregg.

STONE, EDWARD DURELL

The prolific architectural career of Edward Durell Stone (1902–1978) divides conveniently into two distinct and antithetical periods. The earlier is marked by a deep commitment to the principles and objectives of the Modern movement. Stone's stylistic reversal occurred in the early 1950s when he rejected his early avant-garde predilections and began to evolve an extremely personal idiom characterized by the proliferation of ornament and the use of lavish materials.

Born in Fayetteville, Arkansas, Stone studied art at the University of Arkansas. In 1926, following two years of combined study at the Boston Architectural Club and employment in the office of Henry R. Shepley, a Beaux-Arts architect, Stone entered the architecture school of Harvard University; in 1927, he transferred to the Massachusetts Institute of Technology to study with JACQUES CARLU, professor of modern design.

Upon his return from Europe in 1929 (he had won the Rotch Scholarship, which provided two years of travel in Europe), Stone assisted in the design of Rockefeller Center in New York City, undertaking his first major work: the interior of Radio City Music Hall. The International style tendencies in Stone's early period are epitomized in the Mandel House (1933) in Mount Kisco, New York, a strictly modern, concrete, steel, and glass block structure combining elementary geometric volumes, continuous strip windows, flat roof, and open plan. Shortly after Stone had established his office in New York City in 1936, he and PHILIP GOODWIN collaborated on the design for the Museum of Modern Art there—a design emphasizing the International style requirement of open and flexible planning.

A transition period in the late 1940s was marked by a rejection of the Platonic purity of form toward which the early structures had strived and by an interest in indigenous materials and siting. The Robert L. Popper House (1949) in White Plains, New York, is representative.

The highly embellished personal style of the later period is represented by the United States Embassy in New Delhi (1954), the motifs of which are repeated with slight variation in the United States Pavilion for the Brussels World's Fair (1958), the State University campus at Albany, New York (1962), and the John F. Kennedy Center in Washington (1969). The embassy is a formal composition consisting of a white columned box, the façades of which are articulated by concrete grilles—non-load-bearing partitions that take the form of pierced screens in front of or behind structural members—a feature that became ubiquitous in Stone's work. In the realm of tall buildings, the General Motors Building (1968) in New York City represents Stone's departure from the glass and steel idiom of his early years; it is sheathed in marble and has bay windows.

Stone served as professor of architecture at New York University (1927–1942) and Yale University (1946–1952), as visiting critic at Princeton University, the University of Arkansas, and Cornell University, and on the advisory committees of the Massachusetts Institute of Technology and Columbia University.

SUSAN STRAUSS

WORKS

1933, Richard H. Mandel House, Mount Kisco, N.Y. 1936, Henry R. Luce Mepkin Plantation, Moncks Corner, S.C. 1939, Museum of Modern Art (with Philip Goodwin), New York. 1946, El Panama Hotel, Panama City. 1949, Robert L. Popper House, White Plains, N.Y. 1954, United States Embassy, New Delhi. 1958, United States Pavilion, World's Fair, Brussels. 1962, State University of New York Campus, Albany. 1968, General Motors Building, New York. 1969, John F. Kennedy Center for the Performing Arts, Washington.

BIBLIOGRAPHY

GOLDBERGER, PAUL 1978 "Edward Durell Stone Services Will be Held Tomorrow." *New York Times* August 8 (section C):10.
"Obituary." 1978 *American Institute of Architects Journal* 67:104–105.
STONE, EDWARD DURELL 1962 *The Evolution of an Architect.* New York: Horizon.
STONE, EDWARD DURELL 1967 *Recent and Future Architecture.* New York: Horizon.

STONE, NICHOLAS

Nicholas Stone (1587–1647), a sculptor, mason, and architect, was one of the outstanding English artists of his period. The son of a Devonshire quarryman, he trained in London, then in 1606 went to Amsterdam to work with HENDRICK DE KEYSER, whose daughter he married. On his return to England in 1613, Stone soon established himself as the leading monumental sculptor in the country. His career as a mason also flourished: in 1619–1622, he was master mason for INIGO JONES's Banqueting House; in 1626, he was appointed master mason and architect to Windsor Castle; and in 1632, he became king's master mason. His interests extended also to fortification, on which he published a treatise, *Enchiridion of Fortification* in 1645.

Stone's work as a sculptor is exceptionally well documented, as an office notebook for the period 1614–1641 and an account book for the years 1631–1642 survive in the Sir John Soane's Museum, London. Much of his large and varied output survives, showing him to have surpassed all his English contemporaries in vigor, originality, and technical skill. However, comparatively little of his documented work as an architect is extant, and as there is often some uncertainty as to his role as designer in the surviving buildings associated with him (the York Water Gate, for example, has also been attributed to Jones and to BALTHAZAR GERBIER), his stature as an architect is less easy to assess. Stone's style showed some influence from Inigo Jones, but he was richly and robustly eclectic, looking more to SEBASTIANO SERLIO than to ANDREA PALLADIO, and creating what H. M. Colvin describes as a "vernacular classical architecture of considerable charm and accomplishment."

IAN CHILVERS

WORKS

1626, York Water Gate (originally part of York House), Embankment Gardens, London. *c.1631, Chapel on south side of chancel, Chilham Church, Kent, England. 1632–1633, Botanic Garden (Danby Gate and two subsidiary gateways), Oxford. 1632–1633, Cornbury Park (wing; subsequently remodeled), Oxfordshire, England. *1635–1638, Goldsmiths' Hall, Foster Lane, London. *1636, Gateway to park at east end of terrace, Windsor Castle, Berkshire, England. 1637, Saint Mary the Virgin (porch), Oxford. *1638, Tart Hall, Buckingham Gate, London. *1638–1639, Copthall (extensions), Essex, England. 1638–1639, Kirby Hall (remodeling of north front), Northamptonshire, England.

BIBLIOGRAPHY

BULLOCK, ALBERT EDWARD 1908 Some Sculptural Works of Nicholas Stone. London: Batsford.
HARRIS, JOHN; ORGEL, STEPHEN; and STRONG, ROY 1973 The King's Arcadia: Inigo Jones and the Stuart Court. London: Arts Council of Great Britain.
KNOOP, DOUGLAS; and JONES, G. P. 1935 The London Mason in the Seventeenth Century. Manchester (England) University Press.
LEES-MILNE, JAMES 1953 The Age of Inigo Jones. London: Batsford.
NEWMAN, JOHN 1970 "Copthall, Essex." In Howard Colvin and John Harris (editors), The Country Seat: Studies in the History of the British Country House Presented to Sir John Summerson. London: Allen Lane.
NEWMAN, JOHN 1971 "Nicholas Stone's Goldsmiths' Hall: Design and Practice in the 1630s." Architectural History 14:30–39
SPIERS, WALTER LEWIS 1919 "The Note-Book and Account-Book of Nicholas Stone." Walpole Society 7.
SUMMERSON, JOHN (1953)1977 Architecture in Britain: 1530–1830. 6th ed. Harmondsworth, England: Penguin.
WHINNEY, MARGARET D. 1964 Sculpture in Britain: 1530–1830. Harmondsworth, England: Penguin.
WHINNEY, MARGARET D., and MILLAR, OLIVER 1957 English Art: 1626–1714. Oxford: Clarendon.

STONOROV, OSKAR

The work of Oskar Stonorov (1905–1970) exemplifies his commitment to a socially responsive and responsible architecture. As the need for public housing grew, Stonorov sought more and more innovative means for creating positive communities within established economic guidelines. His efforts in this domain represent the practical application of an optimistic spirit expressed symbolically in an early, prize-winning design for the Moscow Palace of the Soviets (1931).

Stonorov was born in Frankfurt, West Germany. His diverse education included a study of anatomy and mathematics at the University of Florence and sculpture in the studio of Aristide Maillol. He emigrated to the United States in 1929 after study at the Eidgenössische Technische Hochschule (ETH) in Zurich (1925–1928). Alternating private practice and partnerships with Alfred Kastner (1932–1936), GEORGE HOWE, (1942–1943), and LOUIS I. KAHN (1942–1948), Stonorov remained in Philadelphia throughout his career, serving in such capacities as its Housing Association Director. In 1951, he organized the exhibition Sixty Years of Living Architecture: The Work of Frank Lloyd Wright, which opened at the Palazzo Strozzi in Florence and traveled throughout Europe and North America (1951–1954).

During the Depression, Stonorov worked diligently to ensure that economic provisions for low-cost housing were included in the National Recovery Act. His first major work in Philadelphia, the Charles Mackley Houses (1932), tapped these hard-won resources as well as the minds of the hosiery workers who would occupy the multifamily dwellings. Weighing their expressed needs and desires against his own sensibilities, Stonorov designed a community-oriented complex of apartments which defied the "bare bones" dictate of the day. The cast concrete structures incorporated bright, airy living spaces and recreational facilities as well as a cooperatively run nursery school and grocery store which reflected the philosophical stance of the workers' union.

After World War II, Stonorov expanded this concept of community planning in the Better Philadelphia Exhibition (1947; with EDMUND BACON). As an educational tool, the exhibition convinced the public that their personal efforts coupled with intelligent and sensitive overall planning could revitalize the city. Philadelphia's continued adherence to this plan, which streamlined traffic systems, rehabilitated neighborhoods, and incorporated community shopping malls, has made it a pioneer in urban planning.

Stonorov's dedication to a socially committed

architecture persisted throughout his varied career. In his last major work, the United Auto Workers Family Education Center (1970) in Onoway, Michigan, sculptural, structural, and functional concerns for community metaphorically affirm the concept of union. Stonorov died in a plane crash with union president Walter Reuther on May 9, 1970, en route to the center.

JAN SCHALL

WORKS

1931, Weyman Biological Laboratory, Southern Highlands, N.C. 1932, Carl Mackley Houses (Housing Development for the Federation of Full-Fashioned Hosiery Workers; with W. P. Barney), Philadelphia. 1936, Frank B. Foster House (remodeling and additions); Oskar Stonorov House, Avon Lea; Phoenixville, Pa. 1941, Sidney Biddle House, Philadelphia. 1941–1943, Carver Court Housing (with George Howe and Louis I. Kahn), Coatesville, Pa. 1945, Prefabricated steel house for the Harman Corporation. 1949, Cherokee Village (housing development), Philadelphia. 1949, Solidarity House (United Auto Workers Office Building), Detroit, Mich. 1952, Alexander Frey House, Pocono Hills, Pa. 1962, Hopkinson House (apartments); 1962, Schuylkill Falls (public housing development); 1963, Schenk Memorial Building (Lutheran Church); Philadelphia. 1964, Charlestown Elementary School, Pa. 1965, Plaza Apartments; 1966, Casa Fermi Housing for the Elderly; 1969, Community Health Care Center and Teaching Hospital, Temple University; Philadelphia. 1970, United Auto Workers Family Education Center (now the Walter and Mary Reuther Memorial Family Education Center), Onoway, Mich. 1970, Casa Vivarelli, Pistoia, Italy.

BIBLIOGRAPHY

"City Rebuilding at People's Level." 1956 *Architectural Forum* 105:148–150.

CLIFF, URSULA 1971 "Oskar Stonorov: Public Housing Pioneer." *Design and Environment* 2:50–57.

"Good Land Use + Good Architecture = Long Earning Life." 1956 *House and Home* 19:162–167.

GUTHEIM, FREDERICK A. (editor) 1937 "Architecture, Art, and Life." *Magazine of Art* 30:306–309.

GUTHEIM, FREDERICK A. 1972 "Special Issue Dedicated to the Work of Oskar Stonorov." *L'Architettura: Cronache e Storia* 18:special issue.

"Philadelphia Plans Again: The Better Philadelphia Exhibition." 1947 *Architectural Forum* 87:66–88.

STONOROV, OSKAR, and BOESIGER, WILLY (editors) 1937 *Le Corbusier, et Pierre Jeanneret, Oeuvre Complète, vol. I: 1910–1929.* Zurich: Girsberger.

STONOROV, OSKAR, and KAHN, LOUIS I. 1942 *Why City Planning Is Your Responsibility.* New York: Revere Copper & Brass.

STONOROV, OSKAR, and KAHN, LOUIS I. 1944 *You and Your Neighborhood: A Primer for Neighborhood Planning.* New York: Revere Copper & Brass.

ZIEGLER, ARTHUR JR. 1967 "Housing: Still Man's Primary Need." *Charette* 47:7–20.

STOREY, ELLSWORTH P.

Ellsworth Prime Storey (1879–1960) was born in Chicago. He spent two summers as an apprentice in the office of Frost and Granger in that city and graduated from the University of Illinois with a degree in architecture in 1903. He moved immediately to Seattle, Washington, where he practiced independently, concentrating on residential work, including small-scale, affordable houses. His individualistic designs, which typically made use of naturally treated native materials, were based on the Arts and Crafts ideal. His expressive use of wood and skillful site planning, admired by younger architects, contributed to the emergence of a Pacific Northwest regional style.

ELISABETH WALTON POTTER

WORKS

1903, Ellsworth Storey House; 1905, Ellsworth Storey House; *1909, Hoo Hoo House, Alaska-Yukon-Pacific Exposition; 1911, Episcopal Church of the Epiphany (chapel and rectory); 1911–1912, Cottage Group, Lake Washington Boulevard South; 1915–1916, Cottage Group, 36th Avenue South; 1916, University Presbyterian Church; 1926, Sigma Nu Fraternity House; Seattle, Wash. 1934–1940, Mount Constitution Observation Tower; 1934–1940, Park Buildings, Cascade Lake; Moran State Park, Orcas Island, Wash.

BIBLIOGRAPHY

DE CHAZEAU, EUNICE STOREY 1959 "Ellsworth Storey Story." Unpublished manuscript, College of Architecture and Urban Planning, University of Washington, Seattle.

O'GORMAN, JAMES F. 1960 "The Hoo Hoo House, Alaska-Yukon-Pacific Exposition, Seattle, 1909," *Journal of the Society of Architectural Historians* 19, no. 3:123–125.

STEINBRUECK, VICTOR 1960 "Seattle's Storey Cottages." *Pacific Architect and Builder* 66, no. 6:21–24.

WOODBRIDGE, SALLY BRYNE, and MONTGOMERY, ROGER 1980 *A Guide to Architecture in Washington State.* Seattle: University of Washington Press.

STORM, WILLIAM GEORGE

William George Storm (1826–1892), a Toronto architect, was born in England and arrived in Canada in 1830. He was apprenticed to WILLIAM THOMAS from 1844, and worked with FREDERIC W. CUMBERLAND as partner from 1852. Their Toronto work includes University College (1856–1858) and Osgoode Hall (1857–1860). Storm's later work includes Saint Andrew's Presbyterian Church, Toronto (1875), and Victoria College, Toronto (1890–1892).

ROBERT HILL

BIBLIOGRAPHY

"Obituary." 1892 *Canadian Architect and Builder* 5, Aug.:81.

ROBINSON, C. BLACKETT 1885 "The City of Toronto: William George Storm." Volume 1, pages 355–357 in *History of Toronto and County of York*. Toronto: The author.

STRACK, JOHANN HEINRICH

A pupil of KARL FRIEDRICH SCHINKEL and friend and collaborator of FRIEDRICH AUGUST STÜLER, Johann Heinrich Strack (1805–1880) continued the tradition of Schinkel's refined classicism of the 1820s into the self-confident years after German unification. His fine decorative sense, betraying the influence of Karl Boetticher's ornamental theories, is especially evident in his many Berlin villas and private houses. For the Borsig family, he designed a *Rundbogenstil* factory as well as his finest Italianate villa.

BARRY BERGDOLL

WORKS

*c.1837, Villa Wegener (interior decoration); *1843, Raczynski Palais, Königsplatz; Berlin. 1845–1849, Schloss Babelsberg (extension; with M. Gottgetreu), near Potsdam, Germany. *1846–1850, Petrikirche; *1849, Borsig Villa, Moabit; Berlin. 1853–1855, Donnerschloss, Altona, Germany. *1853–1856, Andreas-Kirche, Stralauer Platz; 1856–1858, Kronprinzenpalais (remodeling); *1858–1860, Borsig Cast-Iron Factory (fragments in Garden of Technische Universität); c.1860, Fintelmann's House; 1866–1876, National Gallery (exterior design by Friedrich August Stüler); 1868, Brandenburg Gate (side wings); *1868–1870, Borsig Villa (Garden Hall); 1869–1873, Victory Column (moved in 1938 to Grossen Stern), Königsplatz; 1876–1880, Joachimsthaler *Gymnasium* (executed by Jacobsthal & Giersberg; now the Conservatory); *1879, Hallesches Gate; Berlin.

BIBLIOGRAPHY

BÖRSCH-SUPAN, EVA 1977 *Berliner Baukunst nach Schinkel, 1840–1870*. Munich: Prestel.

DUVIGNEAU, VOLKER 1966 "Die Potsdam-Berliner Architektur zwischen 1840 und 1875, an ausgewählten Beispielen." Ph.D. dissertation, Ludwigs-Maximilians-Universität, Munich.

KOHTE, JULIUS 1907 "Zum Gedächtnis Heinrich Stracks und Karl Boettichers." *Wochenschrift des Architektenveriens Berlins* 2:1–4, 9–14.

STRACK, JOHANN HEINRICH 1843 *Das altgriechische Theatergebäude*. Potsdam, Germany: Riegel.

STRACK, JOHANN HEINRICH 1858 *Architektonische Details*. Berlin: Ernst & Korn.

STRACK, JOHANN HEINRICH, and GOTTGETREU, M. 1857 *Schloss Babelsberg*. Berlin: Ernst.

STRACK, JOHANN HEINRICH, and KUGLER, FRANZ 1833 *Architektonische Denkmäler der Altmark Brandenburg*. Berlin: Sachse.

STRAUMER, HEINRICH

Heinrich Straumer (1876–1937), a German architect and engineer, was born in Chemnitz. A student of PAUL WALLOT in Dresden, he established his own practice in Berlin in 1906, building churches, office buildings, housing, the Entomological Museum, and the Agricultural College. The Funkturm on the exhibition grounds (1926) is his best-known monument.

RON WIEDENHOEFT

BIBLIOGRAPHY

"Heinrich Straumer." 1927 *Die Baugilde* 9:13–28.

"Heinrich Straumer." 1932 *Wasmuths Lexikon der Baukunst* 4:479.

STRAUVEN, GUSTAVE

A Belgian, Gustave Strauven (1878–1919) worked as a draftsman in the office of VICTOR HORTA from 1896 to 1898. Later, in independent practice in Brussels, he achieved success as a designer of Art Nouveau houses of pronounced neo-rococo character. His celebrated Saint-Cyr House in Brussels (1903?), a vertiginous assemblage of stone, brick, glass, wood, and tortuous ironwork, astounds by virtue of a calculated exuberance which is not, however, unparalleled in Strauven's other works.

ALFRED WILLIS

WORKS

1899, Spaak Houses; 1900–1901, Van Dyck House; 1903, Saint-Cyr House; 1903–1904, Beyers House; 1906, Apartment House (with shops), avenue Bertrand; Brussels.

BIBLIOGRAPHY

BORSI, FRANCO 1970 *Bruxelles 1900*. New York: Rizzoli.

BORSI, FRANCO, and WIESER, HANS *Bruxelles: Capitale de l'Art Nouveau*. Rome: Colombo.

Bruxelles: Construire et reconstruire: Architecture et aménagement urbain: 1780–1914. 1979 Brussels: Crédit Communal de Belgique.

DELEVOY, ROBERT ET AL. 1972 *Bruxelles 1900*. Brussels: Ecole Nationale Supérieure d'Architecture et des Arts Visuels.

PUTTEMANS, PIERRE 1978 *Modern Architecture in Belgium*. Brussels: Vokaer.

RUSSELL, FRANK (editor) 1979 *Art Nouveau Architecture*. New York: Rizzoli.

STREET, GEORGE EDMUND

George Edmund Street (1824–1881) was a leader of the High Victorian generation of British architects. A prolific and innovative artist, he was also one of the most thoughtful architectural theorists of his day.

Street was born in Woodford, Essex (now Greater London), the son of a London solicitor. He attended several schools in the London suburbs until the age of fifteen, when his father retired and moved the family to Devon. There, he took painting lessons and explored the local architectural antiquities with his brother Thomas, but despite this background he found his first employment in the family law office in London. It was not until 1841 that Street began to prepare seriously for a career in architecture, when he was articled to Owen Carter of Winchester, a competent but unremarkable architect who produced both classical and Gothic designs. Street was Carter's pupil for two years and his assistant for a third before moving to London in 1844.

In London, Street found a place in the office of GEORGE GILBERT SCOTT. This was an exciting place in the late 1840s, buzzing with work on the design for the Nicholaikirche in Hamburg. Street's fellow assistants were GEORGE FREDERICK BODLEY and WILLIAM WHITE, and there were new ideas in the air. The purist Gothic Revival of AUGUSTUS WELBY NORTHMORE PUGIN and the Ecclesiological Society had rapidly fallen into disfavor, and in this milieu the more confident eclecticism of High Victorian architecture was born.

Street played an important role in the swift reshaping of architectural taste that occurred at mid-century. Some of his first independent work, executed while he was still employed by Scott, was conservatively Puginian. For example, the little Church of Saint Peter at Treverbyn, Cornwall, of 1848–1850 is gentle and picturesque in composition and faithful to the precedents of English Decorated Gothic that were strongly preferred by the purists of the 1840s. But an even earlier work in Cornwall, Saint Mary at Biscovey (1847–1848), is early English in detail and forthright—almost primitive—in spirit. It heralds the High Victorian vitality of the 1850s and 1860s.

In 1849, Street established his own office. His early Cornish connections were quickly supplanted by more important ties to Oxfordshire, where he served as diocesan architect from 1850 until his death. Between 1850 and 1852, he lived in Wantage in nearby Berkshire (now Oxfordshire), before moving to Oxford itself. Having begun to establish a national reputation, he moved to London in 1856.

Street's designs and writing of the first dozen years of his practice comprise one of the most complete anthologies of the programmatic, theoretical, and visual character of High Victorian architecture. In terms of program, his work reflects an increasing interest in secular and urban architecture and a concomitant decline in concern for the religious associations of Gothic. Street's architectural theory ignored the narrow historical and geographic confines with which Pugin and the Ecclesiological Society had bound the Gothic Revival, and it embraced a more favorable attitude toward eclecticism. Street viewed architectural history as a dynamic system of varied forces, driven by a still active modernizing process that he and his contemporaries called "development." The visual results of these ideas were an increase in vigor and monumentality, intended to fulfill the requirements of secular and urban programs, and an increase in the variety of means with which to accomplish this.

Street first outlined his position in three seminal articles in the *Ecclesiologist* in 1850–1853. His later publications reiterated the same themes while supplying a wealth of information about Gothic architecture on the Continent, thus expanding the horizons of High Victorian design. Street followed in the footsteps of JOHN RUSKIN to Venice, and he published an influential book on northern Italian Gothic in 1855. He also reported on his extensive travels in France and Germany in many articles, and his second book, on Spanish Gothic, appeared in 1865.

Street's buildings of this period are quintessentially High Victorian: they use a wide variety of foreign medieval precedent in responding with vigor to the visual challenges of the nineteenth-century urban environment. His best-known early

Street.
Crimean Memorial Church.
Istanbul.
1863–1868

Street.
Royal Courts of Justice.
London.
1870–1881 (not completed until 1882)

work, Saint James the Less, Westminster (1859–1861), is a powerful urban church which combines a French apsidial plan and plate tracery, a campanile and polychromy of Italian origin, and a north German sensitivity to the monumental potential of brickwork. Like WILLIAM BUTTERFIELD, Street at first employed constructional polychromy to bring his designs to life, but this usage soon declined, and the power of most of his mature works comes from his fondness for the simple and muscular forms of early French Gothic, a taste which he shared with WILLIAM BURGES. The "early French" appears in Street's design for the Lille Cathedral competition of 1855–1856, in which he placed second. He fared similarly in the competition for the Crimean Memorial Church (Istanbul, 1856) with another early French design, and the executed version of 1863–1868, for which Street ultimately received the commission, is an exceedingly powerful variation on the same theme.

By the late 1860s, High Victorian vigor was losing its popularity, and Street's work also changed, reflecting some of the ideas of the new Queen Anne taste. His understanding of this movement came from firsthand experience, for between 1852 and 1862 he had trained or employed three of its leading designers of the new generation: PHILIP S. WEBB, WILLIAM MORRIS, and R. NORMAN SHAW. Street's greatest commission, the Royal Courts of Justice in London, was designed during this transitional period, and it demonstrates obliquely the influence of the younger men. The competition design of 1866–1867 is a last, brilliant effort at High Victorian stylistic synthesis, specifically intended to unite the irregular vigor of Gothic with the quasi-classical symmetry and monumentality appropriate for a public building. But Street's long series of revised designs increasingly display the unabashed picturesque that Shaw and his contemporaries had made fashionable. The final design (1870–1881), approved with the support of William Ewart Gladstone, the prime minister, is a curious mixture of heavy, High Victorian detail and irregular, almost relaxed composition.

Other later works reflect more explicitly the desiderata of late Victorian architecture. The High Victorian conviction that art was served by national interbreeding had waned, and Street's own home, Holmdale, at Holmbury Saint Mary, Surrey (1873–1876), is a relatively pure old English half-timbered manor, with obvious debts to Shaw. Foreign precedents are usually restricted to special circumstances, as seen notably in the very Italian design for Saint Paul's American Church, Rome (1872–1876).

Street received all the honors of his profession.

He was elected an associate of the Royal Academy in 1866 and a full member in 1871. He was awarded the Gold Medal of the Royal Institute of British Architects in 1874, and in 1881, the year of his death, he served both as president of that institution and as professor of architecture at the Royal Academy.

Street died in London, after suffering two strokes. His death at the age of fifty-seven was surely hastened by the physical and emotional strain of the Law Courts commission. The great building was opened a year after his death.

DAVID B. BROWNLEE

WORKS

1847–1848, Saint Mary's, Biscovey; 1848–1850, Saint Peter's, Treverbyn; Cornwall, England. 1849–1850, Vicarage, Wantage; 1852–1875, Theological College, Cuddeson; Oxfordshire, England. 1853–1854, Vicarage, Colnbrook, Buckinghamshire, England. 1854–1861, Saint Mary's Convent, Wantage, Oxfordshire, England. 1854–1865, All Saint's, Boyne Hill, Maidenhead, Berkshire, England. 1854–1879, Saint Peter's, Bournemouth, Hampshire, England. 1858–1865, Saints Philip and James, Oxford. 1859–1860, Saint John the Evangelist, Howsham, Humberside, England. 1859–1861, Saint James-in-the-Less, Westminster, London. 1859–1866, Saint Michael's (reconstruction), Saint Michael Penkevil, Cornwall, England. 1860–1862, All Saints Church, School, and Vicarage, Denstone, Staffordshire, England. 1861–1863, Uppingham School Hall; 1861–1881, Uppingham School Chapel (not completed until 1882); Leicestershire, England. 1862–1881, Saint John's (not completed until 1885), Torquay, Devon, England. *1863–1872, All Saints', Clifton, Bristol, Avon, England. 1864–1881, Convent of Saint Margaret (not completed until 1890), East Grinstead, West Sussex, England. 1865–1872, Saint Saviour's, Eastbourne, East Sussex, England. 1867–1869, Saint Margaret's Church and Vicarage, Liverpool, England. 1867–1873, Saint Mary Magdalene's, Paddington, London. 1867–1881, Holy Trinity (nave and west façade; not completed until 1888), Bristol, Avon, England. 1868–1878, Christ Church Cathedral (reconstruction and Synod Hall), Dublin. 1870–1881, Royal Courts of Justice (original design, 1866–1867; revised design, 1868; reduced design and design for embankment site, 1869; not completed until 1882); 1871–1881, Saint John the Divine (not completed until 1888), Kensington; London. 1872–1876, Saint Paul's American Church, Rome. 1873–1876, The Hall (Wigan Rectory), Greater Manchester, England. 1873–1876, Holmdale (G. E. Street House), Holmbury Saint Mary, Surrey, England. 1873–1877, Saint Andrew's Church, East Heslerton, North Yorkshire, England. 1877–1879, Saint Mary's, Holmbury, Saint Mary, Surrey, England. 1879–1881, Misses Monk House, Chelsea, London. 1880–1881, Saint Paul's American Church (rectory), Rome. 1880–1881, Holy Trinity American Church (not completed until 1884), Paris.

BIBLIOGRAPHY

BROWNLEE, DAVID B. 1980 "George Edmund Street and the Royal Courts of Justice." Unpublished Ph.D. dissertation, Harvard University, Cambridge, Mass.

CLARKE, BASIL F. L. 1968 "Street's Yorkshire Churches and Contemporary Criticism." Pages 209–225 in *Concerning Architecture: Essays on Architectural Writers and Writing Presented to Nikolaus Pevsner.* London: Allen Lane.

GERMANN, GEORG 1972 "George Edmund Street et la Suisse." *Zeitschrift für schweizerische Archäologie und Kunstgeschichte* 29, nos. 2–3:118–130.

HITCHCOCK, H. R. 1960 "G. E. Street in the 1850's." *Journal of the Society of Architectural Historians* 19, no. 4:145–171.

JACKSON, NEIL 1980 "The Un-Englishness of G. E. Street's Church of St. James-the-Less." *Architectural History* 23:86–94.

KING, GEORGIANA G. (editor) 1916 *George Edmund Street: Unpublished Notes and Reprinted Papers.* New York: Hispanic Society.

KINNARD, JOSEPH 1963 "G. E. Street, the Law Courts and the 'Seventies." Pages 221–234 in *Victorian Architecture.* Edited by Peter Ferriday. London: Cape.

LONG, E. T. 1968 "Churches of a Victorian Squire." *Country Life* 144, no. 3734:770–772.

MEEKS, CARROLL L. V. 1953 "Churches by Street on the Via Nazionale and the Via del Babuino." *Art Quarterly* 16, no. 3:215–227.

PORT, MICHAEL H. 1968 "The New Law Courts Competition, 1866–1867." *Architectural History* 11:75–93.

STREET, ARTHUR EDMUND (1888)1972 *Memoir of George Edmund Street, R.A., 1824–1881.* Reprint. New York: Blom.

STREET, GEORGE EDMUND 1850 "On the Proper Characteristics of a Town Church." *Ecclesiologist* 11:227, 233.

STREET, GEORGE EDMUND 1852 "The True Principles of Architecture, and the Possibility of Development." *Ecclesiologist* 13:247–262.

STREET, GEORGE EDMUND 1853a *An Urgent Plea for the Revival of True Principles of Architecture in the Public Buildings of the University of Oxford.* Oxford and London: John Henry Parker.

STREET, GEORGE EDMUND 1853b "On the Revival of the Ancient Style of Domestic Architecture." *Ecclesiologist* 14:70–80.

STREET, GEORGE EDMUND (1855)1874 *Brick and Marble Architecture in the Middle Ages: Notes on Tours in the North of Italy.* 2d ed. London: Murray.

STREET, GEORGE EDMUND (1865)1969 *Some Account of Gothic Architecture in Spain.* Edited by Georgiana G. King. Reprint. New York: Blom.

STREET, GEORGE EDMUND 1866–1868 "The Study of Gothic Foreign Architecture and Its Influence on English Art." Volume 1, pages 397–411 in Orby Shipman (editor), *The Church and the World.* London: Longmans Green.

STREET, GEORGE EDMUND 1867a "Architecture in the Thirteenth Century." Volume 4, pages 1–45 in *Afternoon Lectures on Literature and Art.* Edited by Robert H. Martley and R. Denny Urbin. London: Bell & Daldy; Dublin: Hodges, Smith, & McGee.

STREET, GEORGE EDMUND 1867b *Explanation and Illustrations of His Designs for the Proposed New Courts of Justice.* London: J. E. Taylor.

STREET, GEORGE EDMUND 1871 "A Lecture Delivered at the Royal Academy Last Session." *Architect* 6:299–301, 310–312, 323, 325.

STREET, GEORGE EDMUND 1872 "A Second Lecture Delivered at the Royal Academy Last Session." *Architect* 7:78–80, 88–90, 103–104.

SUMMERSON, JOHN 1970a "A Victorian Competition: The Royal Courts of Justice." Pages 77–117 in *Victorian Architecture: Four Studies in Evaluation.* New York: Columbia University Press.

SUMMERSON, JOHN 1970b "The Law Courts Competition of 1866–1867." *Journal of the Royal Institute of British Architects* 77, no. 1:11–18.

SUMMERSON, JOHN 1970c "Two London Churches." Pages 47–76 in *Victorian Architecture: Four Studies in Evaluation.* New York: Columbia University Press.

STRICKLAND, WILLIAM

William Strickland (1788–1854) was one of the most talented of the first generation of native Americans who sought to make a living as a professional architect. Throughout the colonial period, almost anyone competent beyond the ordinary in the arts of building might be called "architect," and from time to time Europeans who claimed that title appeared briefly on the American scene. But it was well into the nineteenth century before architecture became a recognized profession, distinct from the building trades and with generally accepted duties, fees, and standards of conduct.

Strickland was born in Navesink, New Jersey, where his father was a successful carpenter. He showed an early aptitude for drawing, and at the age of fourteen he was apprenticed to the English architect BENJAMIN HENRY LATROBE, who had immigrated to America in 1796. The commission that had initially brought Latrobe to Philadelphia was also the means of introducing him to the Strickland family. This was the Bank of Pennsylvania on which John Strickland worked as carpenter and where on the scaffoldings and unfinished walls his son liked to play.

Latrobe found young William an able, if sometimes undependable, pupil. Their association lasted only about three years, but that was long enough for Strickland to learn the fundamentals of design and engineering from the best trained and most accomplished architect then active in America. By 1807, William was living in New York

City, where his father was employed on the construction of the Park Theater. While John Strickland worked as carpenter, William painted scenery as assistant to Hugh Reinagle, a contemporary who had learned his art at Philadelphia's New Theater. Little, if anything, certainly by Strickland's hand survives from his New York years, but evidence of the drafting skills with which he supported himself during this period may be seen in the oil painting of Philadelphia's Christ Church that was exhibited in 1811 at the Pennsylvania Academy of the Fine Arts and is now owned by the Historical Society of Pennsylvania.

Although Strickland is most closely identified with the renewed interest in classical forms that goes under the sometimes misleading name of Greek Revival, like his teacher and most of his contemporaries, he occasionally used a number of other styles for their associative value. Thus, for his first major architectural commission, the Masonic Hall of Philadelphia (1808–1811), he produced an early example of American Gothic, a style doubtless selected as a reminder that the medieval guilds were believed to have contributed importantly to the rise of Freemasonry. After having been used for

a time by the Franklin Institute, Strickland's Masonic Hall—now without its tower, which had not been restored after the fire of 1819—was demolished about 1852 to make way for a more elaborate Gothic structure designed by the firm of Sloan and Stewart. While it stood, the first Masonic Hall was a major Chestnut Street landmark, however, and its favorable acceptance must have given its designer sufficient confidence to take a wife. On November 3, 1812, he married Rachel M. Trenchard from Bridgetown, New Jersey.

The successful completion of the Masonic Hall might have been expected to bring other commissions in its wake. That it did not immediately do so was at least in part attributable to the unsettled conditions associated with the approaching conflict with England. As surveyor and engineer, Strickland worked diligently on the defenses of Philadelphia during the War of 1812. But once hostilities were over, he returned to the practice of architecture with a design for the Temple of the New Jerusalem (1816–1817), commissioned by the Swedenborgian community of Philadelphia. Demolished long ago, this little square structure was basically Federal or late Georgian in concept, but the combination of pointed openings with a low dome has understandably led to the use of such descriptive adjectives as Moorish or Saracenic.

Scarcely had he finished his work for the Swedenborgians when Strickland won the competition to design the Second Bank of United States (1818–1824). The Parthenon at Athens provided the model for the octastyle Doric porticoes on the north and south façades of the Second Bank, but on the sides the peripteral colonnade of the original was omitted in the interest of light and space. With its impressive barrel-vaulted central room, the interior was also dictated by the modern requirements of a bank, and references to antique models were largely limited to decorative details. Except for its author's favorite low, Roman dome, the scheme Latrobe submitted in the competition for the Second Bank was similar to that of Strickland, but no firm evidence has been found to substantiate the former's claim that his sometime pupil had plagiarized the winning design. In its use of the Ionic order of the Erechtheum, Latrobe's Bank of Pennsylvania may have marked the advent of the Greek Revival in America, but its adoption of the entire façade of the Parthenon made the Second Bank the first mature statement of the new style. America had seen nothing like it before.

Even had the Second Bank not been linked so closely to the political fortunes of Andrew Jackson, the size and quality of the building that housed it must have brought its architect favorable public attention, especially in his own city. Well before the bank was finished Strickland was elected a member of the American Philosophical Society and of the State in Schuylkill fishing club. He was one of the early members, as well as the first recording secretary, of the Franklin Institute, and as long as he lived in Philadelphia he served on the Board of the Musical Fund Society, for which in 1824 he designed the hall that still stands, much altered, on Locust Street.

As in the case of Belmont (1850; later the Ward-Belmont School), several of the houses in Nashville that have been attributed to Strickland are impressive in size and detail, but for the most part the few domestic designs that can be associated with his name are not representative of his most distinguished work. From first to last, he remained pre-eminently an architect of public buildings. For these he regularly achieved exteriors of considerable dignity and monumentality through the imaginative use of Greek details found in the pages of the *Antiquities of Athens* (5 vols., 1762, 1789, 1794, 1816, 1830), the collection of engravings originally conceived by JAMES STUART and NICHOLAS REVETT but later supplemented by others. In fact, Strickland is said to have

been fond of assuring assistants that for his models a successful architect need look no further than the *Antiquities of Athens.*

Among Strickland's most notable neoclassic designs was that for the United States Naval Asylum (after 1879 the United States Naval Home), for which he was appointed designer and supervising architect late in 1826. As the model for the Ionic order for the handsome central portico he chose the much admired Temple on the Ilissus, destroyed by the Turks about 1778, but known from the pages of the *Antiquities of Athens.* Iron was used for the open balconies on both front and rear of the wings, and elsewhere masonry construction made the Naval Asylum as nearly fireproof as the state of the art permitted.

While work on the Naval Asylum was progressing, Strickland was commissioned to design the new Arch Street Theater (1828), another in the long series of playhouses that occupy so prominent a place in the architectural history of Philadelphia. Early in his career he must have learned some of the requirements of good theatrical design while painting scenery in New York City, but his qualifications to design "The Arch" had been most clearly demonstrated by his success in rebuilding the New Theater ("Old Drury") on Chestnut Street after the disastrous fire of 1820. The Chestnut Street Theater was demolished in 1856, but some of the elements of Strickland's original façade could still be distinguished after The Arch had been remodeled in 1863.

Construction at the Naval Asylum dragged on until 1833, but at the end of 1829 Strickland resigned as supervising architect. Earlier that same year he had been appointed architect of the new United States Mint that was to be built at the corner of Chestnut and Juniper streets, and his professional services were also in demand elsewhere in the city. Except for the columns from the twin Ionic porticoes that were given to the Jewish Hos-

Strickland.
United States Naval
  Asylum.
Philadelphia.
1826–1833

Strickland.
Chestnut Street Theater.
Philadelphia.
1820–1822

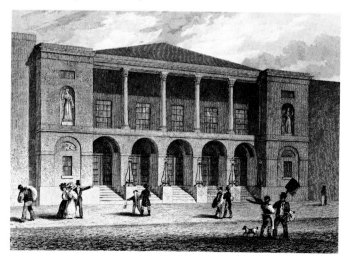

Strickland.
United States Mint.
Philadelphia.
1829–1833

pital (later the Albert Einstein Medical Center), the Mint was demolished in 1904 and the site used for an arcade. When first built, however, its impressive marble exterior, central court for light, and iron and masonry construction to resist fire, made the Philadelphia Mint an advanced building for its time. That opinion appears to have been shared by officials of the Treasury Department, who later commissioned Strickland to design a branch mint in Charlotte, North Carolina, and a mint in New Orleans, Louisiana, both begun in 1835.

Like most architects, Strickland was frequently called upon to make additions or alterations to existing structures. About 1817, he remodeled the Medical Department that Latrobe had designed in 1807 as an addition to the great Federal mansion that the University of Pennsylvania had purchased from the state in 1800, after it had been declined

Strickland.
Independence Hall (steeple).
Philadelphia.
1828

for an official residence by President John Adams. Apparently the University was satisfied with the alterations made to its medical school because it selected Strickland as architect for the two new buildings with which it proposed to replace the President's House in 1829–1830. Federal, rather than neoclassic in style, the *retardataire* character of College and Medical halls can be explained as a conscious effort to recall the earlier landmark they replaced.

Strickland's awareness of the historical aspects of architectural style was perhaps demonstrated most clearly by the steeple he designed for Independence Hall in 1828. This was so successful that even historians have all but forgotten that the steeple of Edmund Woolley's tower (added 1750–1753) had to be removed in 1781 because of rotting timbers. Though it differs markedly from the original, which had no clock, the present steeple deserves mention as one of the first efforts at historic restoration in America.

Much of Strickland's professional career was involved with projects a later day would consider the province of the engineer. In 1827, after only a year, he resigned his position as engineer in charge of the Eastern Division of the Pennsylvania Mixed System (so called because it involved an inconvenient combination of railroad and canal), but he later served as consultant for a number of similar projects, among them the Fair Mount Dam (1828), the Columbia and Philadelphia Railway (1830), and the Wilmington and Susquehanna Railroad (1835). From 1828 to 1840 he was supervising engineer for the Delaware Breakwater, a major project that still protects the Philadelphia harbor.

In such commissions as the Athenaeum (1836–1838) in Providence, Rhode Island, or the First Congregational Unitarian Church (1828) and the Mechanics' Bank (1837) in Philadelphia, Strickland demonstrated how effectively he could adapt his favorite neoclassical style to structures of widely differing functions and comparatively modest size. After his initial efforts at the Masonic Hall and the Temple of the New Jerusalem, he appears to have attempted Gothic designs only when custom or the client required it, and then never with perhaps complete success. To be sure, the rector was so pleased with the design for Saint John's Episcopal Church (1836) in Salem, New Jersey, that a few years later he asked that it be repeated for Christ Church (1840) at Easton, Maryland, when he was called to that parish. Although few historians would place such designs among Strickland's most noteworthy commissions, his naive and tentative handling of Gothic forms gives the Salem and Easton churches a distinctive appeal

of their own. Much the same might be said of better known Saint Stephen's (1822–1823) in Philadelphia; and if the Western Penitentiary in Pittsburgh (1820–1827) was judged a failure, it had to do more with the impracticality of its round plan than with any faults of its castellated style.

On at least three occasions, Strickland tried his hand at using elements of the Egyptian style made popular through the publications that were among the more beneficial results of Napoleon's Egyptian campaign of 1798–1799. But though the Mississippi might be called the American Nile and cities along its banks given such names as Cairo and Memphis, lotus and papyrus columns had little chance of supplanting the classical orders as a kind of national style. Because most of the surviving Egyptian monuments had to do with the cult of the dead, designs based on them were thought most appropriate for cemetery gateways or funerary monuments; by the same token, Hebrew and Christian congregations were apt to avoid Egyptian motifs as too obviously pagan for their places of worship. For a gateway to Laurel Hill Cemetery (c.1836), then on the outskirts of Philadelphia, the developers may have preferred a classical design to his Egyptian one, but Strickland appears to have been the only American to have served as architect for both a synagogue and a church in the Egyptian style. Not only do these two commissions bracket his career—the synagogue coming comparatively early and the church near the end—they also illustrate how the style progressed from applied ornament to forms that function as a more integral part of the design. Mikveh-Israel (1822–1825) stood on Cherry Street in Philadelphia only until 1860, but the First Presbyterian Church (1848–1851) is still a prominent feature of downtown Nashville. In both instances the choice of a style probably had to do more with differentiating synagogue and church from other nearby places of worship than it had to conforming to the view, held in some quarters, that the Temple of Solomon resembled Egyptian structures.

One of the last of Strickland's Philadelphia commissions, and possibly his most original design, was for the Merchants' Exchange (1832–1834). At the apex of the triangle formed by Walnut, Dock, and Third streets, he placed a semicircular portico made up of Corinthian columns based on the order of the Choragic Monument of Lysicrates, the small Athenian structure that also served as model for the cupola of the Exchange. Much earlier, the Choragic Monument had been admired by Stuart who included it in the first volume of the *Antiquities of Athens,* and who had relied on it for several of his own designs, but Strickland was the first to employ this "pretty Athenian toy"—to use Jefferson's phrase—as part of the design of an American building.

Since the financial panic of 1837 all but ended new construction, Strickland was probably glad to be asked to design a stone sarcophagus for George Washington in that year. As it turned out, this was only the most visible of a considerable number of similar commissions with which he was associated in the course of his career; monuments like those to Benjamin Carr (1831) in Saint Peter's churchyard, Philadelphia, or to James Polk (1850) in Nashville remain among the most appealing examples of the neoclassical style. And if times were hard and architectural commissions scarce, at least the enforced leisure provided Strickland with opportunities for study and travel. In 1838, he took his wife and two young daughters on an extended

Strickland.
First Presbyterian Church.
Nashville, Tennessee.
1848–1851

Strickland.
Philadelphia
*   (Merchants') Exchange.*
1832–1834

European trip that included Liverpool, Paris, Rome, and London.

On his return to America, Strickland soon found himself involved in a number of projects, many of them abortive and none financially rewarding: an unsuccessful scheme for the development of the city of Cairo, Illinois, was followed first by the publication of a book on public engineering projects in the United States and then by unavailing political activity on behalf of John Tyler. Meanwhile, continuing efforts to secure substantial architectural commissions from private groups, and especially from the federal government, proved futile.

Under these circumstances, Strickland must have welcomed the appointment as designer and supervising architect of a new capitol (1845–1859) for Tennessee, and in the spring of 1845 he moved his family to Nashville. The plan of the capitol had perforce to be based on the requirements of the Tennessee legislature, but as so often before, Strickland sought his decorative details in the pages of Stuart and Revett: the Choragic Monument again provided a model for the tower, and the Ionic order of the portico that adds dignity and interest to each of the four sides is taken from the Erechtheum.

While supervising the building of the capitol, Strickland found time to accept a number of other commissions. The Polk Monument and the First Presbyterian Church have already been noted, and earlier he had given Roman Catholics in Tennessee their first cathedral (erected 1845–1847; now called Saint Mary's) and one of his most effective neoclassical designs. A number of houses in the

area have also been attributed to Strickland, though in their use of the newer Italianate forms, some, at least, may show the hand of Francis, Strickland's eldest son, who is known to have continued supervising construction of the capitol after his father's death.

Probably as a result of a fall the previous day, Strickland died April 7, 1854. Nearly twenty years before, he had been elected first president of the transient American Institution of Architects (founded 1836), and had he lived until 1857, he might well have played a part in organizing the American Institute of Architects, with all that implied for the profession he had done so much to establish. As it was, in the course of a long professional career he had achieved widespread recognition but scant financial success. In death he was honored by being buried in a niche in the Tennessee capitol, but the administrators of his estate could not find assets with a value of more than twenty-six dollars.

GEORGE B. TATUM

WORKS

*1808–1811, Masonic Hall; *1816–1817, Temple of the New Jerusalem (later the Academy of Natural Sciences); *1817, Medical Department (improvements), University of Pennsylvania; 1818–1824, Second Bank of the United States; *1820–1822, Chestnut Street Theater; Philadelphia. *1820–1827, Western State Penitentiary, Pittsburgh. *1822–1825, Mikveh-Israel Synagogue; 1822–1823, Saint Stephen's Episcopal Church; 1824, Musical Fund Society Hall; *1824, Triumphal arches for Lafayette's visit to Philadelphia; 1826–1833, United States Naval Asylum (after 1879 the United States Naval Home); *1828, Arch Street Theater; *1828, First Congregational Unitarian Church; 1828, Independence Hall (steeple); *1829–1830, Medical and College Halls, University of Pennsylvania; *1829–1833, United States Mint; Philadelphia. *1830–1834, New Almshouse, Blockley Township, Pennsylvania. 1832–1834, Philadelphia (Merchants') Exchange. 1835, Branch Mint, Charlotte, N.C. 1835–1836, Mint, New Orleans, La. 1836–1838, Athenaeum, Providence, R.I. 1828–1840, Delaware Breakwater, off Lewes. 1836, Saint John's Episcopal Church, Salem, N.J. 1837, Mechanics' Bank (now the Norwegian Seamen's Church); 1842, Saint Peter's Episcopal Church (tower and steeple); Philadelphia. 1845–1847, Cathedral of the Blessed Virgin of the Seven Dolors (now Saint Mary's Church); 1845–1859, State Capitol; 1848–1851, First Presbyterian Church; (A)1850, Belmont (now Ward-Belmont School); (A)1853, Belle Meade; Nashville, Tenn.

BIBLIOGRAPHY

BENDINER, ALFRED 1959 "The Architecture of William Strickland, in His Building for the Congregation Mikveh Israel, Philadelphia, 1824." *Year Book of the American Philosophical Society* 1959:529–533.
CARROTT, RICHARD G. 1978 *The Egyptian Revival: Its*

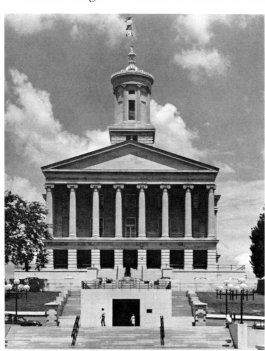

Strickland.
State Capitol.
Nashville, Tennessee.
1845–1859

Sources, Monuments, and Meaning, 1808–1858. Berkeley: University of California Press.

DEKLE, CLAYTON B. 1969 "The Tennessee State Capitol." *Tennessee Historical Quarterly* Fall:213–238.

DOLL, EUGENE E. 1957 "Trial and Error at Allegheny: The Western State Penitentiary, 1818–1838." *Pennsylvania Magazine of History and Biography* 81:3–27.

GILCHRIST, AGNES ADDISON (1950)1969 *William Strickland, Architect and Engineer: 1788–1854.* Enl. ed. Reprint. New York: Da Capo.

HAMLIN, TALBOT 1944 *Greek Revival Architecture in America.* New York: Oxford University Press.

"Historic Philadelphia: From the Founding Until the Early Nineteenth Century." 1953 *Transactions of the American Philosophical Society* 43: part 1.

PIERSON, WILLIAM H., JR. 1970 *American Buildings and Their Architects: The Colonial and Neoclassical Styles.* Garden City, N.Y.: Doubleday.

STANTON, PHOEBE B. 1968 *The Gothic Revival and American Church Architecture: An Episode in Taste, 1840–1856.* Baltimore: Johns Hopkins University Press.

STRONG, EDWARD

A member of a long dynasty of master masons and quarry owners originating from the Gloucestershire-Oxfordshire borders, Edward Strong the Younger (1676–1741) is known to have designed the north gateway to Saint Bartholomew's Hospital (1702) and probably also Addiscombe House in Surrey (1702–1703), much praised by John Evelyn. Both show the influence of NICHOLAS HAWKSMOOR's buildings at Greenwich Hospital, where the Strongs had taken the chief mason's contract in 1696.

GERVASE JACKSON-STOPS

WORKS

1702, Saint Bartholomew's Hospital (north gate), Smithfield, England. (A)1702–1703, Addiscombe House, Surrey, England.

BIBLIOGRAPHY

DOWNES, KERRY 1966 *English Baroque Architecture.* London: Zwemmer.

WHITTERIDGE, GWENETH 1949 "The Henry VII Gateway into Smithfield." *Saint Bartholomew's Hospital Journal.*

STRONG, THOMAS THE YOUNGER

A brother of EDWARD STRONG, Thomas Strong the Younger (1685–1736) was another master mason employed on CHRISTOPHER WREN's City churches, who could on occasion act as architect in his own right. Designs by him for Ardington House, Oxfordshire (1719–1720), have recently emerged, and close stylistic analogy makes it almost certain that he was responsible for two neighboring houses—Lockinge Manor (c.1725–1730) and Maiden Earley (c.1730). The markedly vertical emphasis of Thomas and Edward Strong's buildings could have been influenced by Dutch houses of the period, both brothers having accompanied the painter Thornhill on a tour of the Netherlands in 1711.

GERVASE JACKSON-STOPS

WORKS

1719–1720, Ardington House; *(A)c.1725–1730, Lockinge Manor; Oxfordshire, England. *(A)c.1730, Maiden Earley, Berkshire, England.

BIBLIOGRAPHY

JACKSON-STOPS, GERVASE 1981 "Ardington House, Oxfordshire." *Country Life* 170:1282–1285.

STUART, JAMES

James Stuart (1713–1788) was born in London. In 1742 he went to Italy where he met NICHOLAS REVETT, Gavin Hamilton, and MATTHEW BRETTINGHAM II, with whom a visit to Greece was discussed. In 1748, he and Revett issued proposals for "a new and accurate description of the Antiquities &c. in the Province of Attica." Funds were raised from English travelers in Rome and assistance was given by Sir James Gray, British resident in Venice, and Sir James Porter, ambassador at Constantinople. Both were members of the Society of Dilettanti, to which Stuart and Revett were elected in 1751. From that year until 1753, they surveyed buildings in Greece, notwithstanding the dangers and difficulties inflicted on them by the Turks then in occupation. The first volume of *The Antiquities of Athens* (1762) by Stuart and Revett contained only minor buildings; volumes 2–4 were published after Stuart's death. Nevertheless, Stuart's personality and influence, reinforced probably by the exhibition of his watercolor drawings of Athens, spread the *gusto greco,* and the book when it appeared was seen to be of great importance. In 1758, Stuart built for Lord Lyttelton at Hagley Park, Worcestershire, a small Doric temple thought to be the first example of the Greek Revival. In the same year, he was appointed surveyor to Greenwich Hospital, a post he held till he died, but he left to his assistant, WILLIAM NEWTON, a great part of the very important work of rehabilitation of the chapel there after a fire (1780–1788).

Stuart.
Hadrian's Arch from The
Antiquities of Athens.

He received commissions to build two large houses—Belvedere, Erith, Kent, for Sir Sampson Gideon in about 1775, and Montagu (later Portman) House, 22 Portman Square, London, for Elizabeth Montagu a leading "Bluestocking" between 1775 and 1782. As at Greenwich, his patrons found him an unreliable architect, and, perhaps because he was already middle-aged when his Grecian fame came to him, he allowed others to exploit his ideas rather than carry them further himself. However, a patronage stemming largely from his connection with the Society of Dilettanti kept him in considerable prosperity; he designed garden temples, furniture, interior decoration, and some church monuments. Surviving drawings by his accomplished hand link his name tantalizingly with schemes, often unexecuted, for Kedleston Hall, Derbyshire (c.1757), Wimbledon House, Surrey (mid-1750s), Wimpole Hall, Cambridgeshire (c.1775), and other unidentified places which may not have been completed or have perished. The main body of his papers appears to have been lost and information about so influential a figure is regrettably scanty.

LESLEY LEWIS

WORKS

c.1755, Wentworth Woodhouse (interior decoration), Yorkshire, England. 1758, Doric Temple, Hagley Park, Worcestershire, England. 1759-1765, Spencer House (interiors), Green Park; *1760-1765, Holderness (later Londonderry) House (decoration and possibly the original design), Hertford Street; 1764-1766, Lichfield House (altered by Samuel Wyatt in 1791-1794), Saint James's Square; London. 1764, Nuneham Park (interior decorations), Oxfordshire, England. 1764-1770, Shugborough (interior decoration and park buildings), Staffordshire, England. *c.1775, Belvedere, Erith, Kent, England. *1775-1782, Montagu (later Portman)

House, Portman Square, London. c.1780, Temple of the Winds, Mount Stewart, County Down, Ireland. 1780-1788, Greenwich Hospital Chapel (restoration with William Newton), London.

BIBLIOGRAPHY

HARDY, JOHN, and HAYWARD, HELENA   1978 "Kedleston Hall, Derbyshire." *Country Life* 163, no. 2:262-266.
HARRIS, JOHN   1979 "Newly Acquired Designs by James Stuart in the British Architectural Library, Drawings Collection." *Architectural History* 22:72-77, plates 16a-28c.
LANDY, JACOB   1956 "Stuart and Revett: Pioneer Archaeologists." *Archaeology* 9:252-259.
LAWRENCE (LEWIS), LESLEY   1938 "Stuart and Revett: Their Literary and Architectural Careers." *Journal of the Warburg Institute* 2, no. 2:128-146.
LEWIS, LESLEY   1947 "The Architects of the Chapel at Greenwich Hospital." *Art Bulletin* 29:260-267.
STUART, JAMES, and REVETT, NICHOLAS   (1762)1968 Volume 1 in *The Antiquities of Athens*. Reprint. New York: Arno.
THORNTON, PETER, and HARDY, JOHN   1968 "The Spencer Furniture at Althorp." *Apollo* 87:440-451.
WATKIN, DAVID   1982 *'Athenian' Stuart, 1713-1788.* London: Allen & Unwin. Forthcoming publication.
WIEBENSON, DORA   1969 *Sources of Greek Revival Architecture.* London: Zwemmer.

STUBBINS, HUGH ASHER JR.

Hugh Asher Stubbins Junior (1912-) was born in Powderly, Alabama. Following receipt of a Bachelor of Science degree in architecture from the Georgia Institute of Technology (1933) and a Master of Architecture degree from Harvard University (1935), Stubbins worked in the office of Royal Barry Wills, an architect of small houses, designing primarily in a New England Colonial style. His partnership with Marc Peter (1938-1939) brought national recognition in the form of awards in design competitions.

In 1940, Stubbins established an office in Cambridge, Massachusetts, and became assistant to WALTER GROPIUS at the Graduate School of Design, Harvard. In 1946, he was appointed associate professor of design, and in 1953, upon Gropius's resignation, Stubbins was designated chairman of the architecture school. Stubbins acknowledged Gropius's influence as a philosophical one. He credits MARCEL BREUER with having influenced his conceptions of siting, scale, and expression of technology. The University of California at Santa Cruz College #5 (1967) and the Countway Library of Medicine at Harvard (1965) suggest the influence of Breuer and that of ALVAR AALTO, whom Stubbins credits with having exposed him to the subtleties of silhouette, color, scale, and texture of materials. Stubbins's commissions have been diverse, including the expressionistic Kongresshalle (Berlin, 1957) with its catenary roof construction, schools, and large office buildings.

Commissions for the Federal Reserve Bank in Boston (1978) and the Citicorp Center in New York (1978) allowed the firm to move into large-scale urban planning. The forty-six-story Citicorp breaks with convention in its being lifted 127 feet off the ground on four stilts and in its being terminated with a crown, cut at a sharp angle facing south. The space at the base is reserved for public use; in one corner is the sculptural Saint Peter's Church.

In attempting to develop an architecture and a design methodology that respond to the modern world, Stubbins has steadfastly conceived of architecture in terms of problem solving; he does not subscribe to a conception of architecture either as the articulation of tradition or as the search for a new style, but instead has emphasized the historicity of architecture. The present is viewed as a link between past and future; although the architecture of a given moment necessarily represents an interpretation of the priorities and purposes of a given society, in light of its unique past, it must be flexible enough to accommodate future users.

SUSAN STRAUSS

WORKS

1957, Kongresshalle, Berlin. 1960, Loeb Drama Center, Harvard University; 1962, Graduate Student Housing, Massachusetts Institute of Technology; Cambridge, Mass. 1962–1969, Dormitories and Dining Halls, University of Massachusetts, Amherst. 1962–1975, Dormitories and Theater, Mount Holyoke College, South Hadley, Mass. 1965, Countway Library of Medicine, Harvard University, Boston. 1965, Physics Building and Dormitory, Princeton University, N.J. 1967, College #5, University of California, Santa Cruz. 1968, Museum of Fine Arts (Decorative Arts Wing), Boston. 1972, Hampshire College Master Plan, Amherst, Mass. 1976, Pusey Library, Harvard University, Cambridge, Mass. 1978, Citicorp Center (with EMERY ROTH and Sons), New York. 1978, Federal Reserve Bank, Boston. 1978, Saint Peter's Church, New York.

BIBLIOGRAPHY

"An Architect's House in Massachusetts." 1948 *Architectural Record* 103, Mar.:88–96.
"Art Building, Mount Holyoke College." 1972 *L'Architecture d'Aujourd'hui* 44, no.160:19.
"Berlin Congress Hall." 1957 *Architectural Record* 122, Dec.:143–150.
"The Countway Library: Fresh Approach to Old Problems." 1965 *Progressive Architecture* 44, Nov.:166–177.
"The Current Work of Hugh Stubbins." 1959 *Architectural Record* 126, Oct.:167–182.
"Designing with Deference." 1963 *Architectural Record* 133, Mar.:133–144.
HEYER, PAUL 1978 *Architects on Architecture: New Directions in America.* New York: Walker.
"Kongresshalle in Berlin." 1958 *Baumeister* 55, Jan.:16–21.
MCCALLUM, IAN 1957 "Machine Made America." *Architectural Review* 121, May:365–366.
Schmertz, Mildred F. "Citicorp Center: If You Don't Like Its Crown Look at Its Base." *Architectural Record* 163, no. 7:107–116.
"School Houses." 1977 *Baumeister* 74, no.2:115–157.
"Skyscraper for People: New York Citicorp Complex." 1978 *Contract Interiors* 137, no. 10:126–139.
STUBBINS, HUGH A., JR. 1976 *Architecture: The Design Experience.* New York: Wiley.

STÜLER, FRIEDRICH AUGUST

Friedrich August Stüler (1800–1865) came to Berlin at eighteen, enrolling silmultaneously in the University and the Bauakademie. Beginning with the supervision of the remodeling of Prince Karl's Palace (1827), Stüler was engaged on KARL FRIEDRICH SCHINKEL's Berlin projects. In 1841, he prepared a plan to develop the Spreeinsel behind Schinkel's Altes Museum into a museum complex. Only the Neues Museum (1843–1855)—deferent externally to Schinkel's building but lavishly decorated inside to reflect the diverse collections—was completed to Stüler's plans. Following an 1842 tour of English churches with HEINRICH STRACK, Stüler drew plans for a basilican cathedral on the Lustgarten as a response to the king Friedrich Wilhelm IV's desire to create a Protestant architecture to rival the neo-Gothic style of the Catholic Cologne school. In over one hundred churches and model designs done with August Soller, Stüler realized a synthesis of early Christian, Lombard, and Romanesque forms in brick and terra cotta, developing the model of Schinkel's suburban churches. After LUDWIG PERSIUS's death in 1845, Stüler was charged with giving form to the king's ideas at Sanssouci, where a series of villas rely on the Renaissance models of PERCIER AND FONTAINE. In city houses and apartment buildings, he defined a characteristic Quattrocento façade style, which was given monumental expression in the National Museum in Stockholm (1850–1866).

BARRY BERGDOLL

WORKS

1834–1837, Saint Peter and Saint Paul (with A. D. Shadow), Nikolskoe, Berlin. *1840, Börse, Frankfurt am Main, Germany. 1843–1855, Neues Museum; 1844–1845, Jacobskirche; 1844–1846, Matthäuskirche;

1844–1856, Saint Johannes Kirche (alterations), School, and Parish House; 1845–1853, Royal Schloss Chapel (dome with Shadow); 1845–1856, War Ministry; Berlin. 1846–1863, Hohenzollern Castle, near Bisingen, Württemberg, Germany. 1848–1855, Markuskirche, Berlin. 1850–1866, National Museum, Stockholm. 1851–1857, Schloss (interiors), Schwerin, Germany. 1851–1859, Officer's Barracks (now the Egyptian Museum), Schloss Charlottenburg; 1854–1858, Bartholomäuskirche (completed by Friedrich Adler); Berlin. 1856, Protestant Church, Hechingen, Germany. 1857–1860, Holy Trinity Church, Cologne, Germany. 1857–1861, University of Königsberg, Germany (now Russia). 1859–1861, Lukaskirche (executed by Georg Moller); 1859–1866, Synagogue (interiors with Eduard Knoblauch); Berlin. 1862–1864, Academy of Sciences, Budapest. 1866–1876, National Gallery (altered in execution by Johann Heinrich Strack), Berlin.

BIBLIOGRAPHY

Börsch-Supan, Eva 1977 *Berliner Baukunst nach Schinkel, 1849–1870.* Munich: Prestel.

Dehio, Ludwig 1961 *Friedrich Wilhelm IV. von Preussen: Ein Baukünstler der Romantik.* Berlin: Deutscher Kunstverlag.

Fritsch, K. E. O. 1900 "Zum hundertsten Geburtstage August Stülers." *Deutsche Bauzeitung* 34:58–63, 66–72, 73–80.

Hannman, Eckart 1974 "Die Burg Hohenzollern als Denkmal des Historismus." *Burgen und Schlösser* 15:32–40.

Heck, Oscar 1968 "Die evangelische Kirche zu Hechingen und die Baukunst des Berliner Nachklassizismus." *Nachrichtenblatt der Denkmalpflege in Baden-Württemberg* 11:104–106.

Hitchcock, H. R. 1931 "The Romantic Architecture of Potsdam." *International Studio* 99:46–49.

Königlich-Preussischen Ober-Baudeputation (editor) 1852 *Entwürfe zu Kirchen, Pfarr und Schulhäusern.* Potsdam, Germany: Riegel.

Müller-Stüler, Dietrich 1943 "August Stüler: Presusische Baukunst um die Mitte des 19. Jahrhunderts." *Kunst im Deutschen Reich* 7:74–89.

Muthesius, Stefan 1974 *Das englische Vorbild.* Munich: Prestel.

Persson, Eva 1964 "Nationalmuseum och dess Fasadskulpturer." *Konsthistorisk Tidskrift* 23:105–116.

Plagemann, Volker 1967 *Das deutsche Kunstmuseum, 1790–1870.* Munich: Prestel.

Stüler, Friedrich August 1853–1866 *Bauwerke.* 3 vols. Berlin: Ernst & Korn.

Stüler, Friedrich August 1861 *Vortrag über die Wirksamkeit Friedrich Wilhelm IV. in dem Gebiete der bildenen Künste.* Berlin: Ernst & Korn.

Stüler, Friedrich August; Prosche, E.; and Willebrand, H. 1869 *Das Schloss zu Schwerin.* Berlin: Ernst & Korn.

Waesemann, H. 1865 "A. Stüler's Entwürfe und Bauausführung." *Zeitschrift für Bauwesen* 15:507–512.

Wallé, Peter 1900 "Zur Erinnerung an August Stüler." *Centralblatt der Bauverwaltung* 20:38–41.

STURGIS, JOHN HUBBARD

John Hubbard Sturgis (1834–1888), artist, architect, anglophile and world traveller, brought to Boston architecture a new international perspective creatively based in the English Arts and Industry tradition. The Sturgis family was pre-eminent in the China trade by 1834 when the architect was born in Macao, the second son of Russell Sturgis, Director of the far eastern office of Russell and Company. With the death of his mother, Mary Greene Hubbard in 1837, in Manila, John, already fluent in Portuguese, was sent to be educated at Boston Latin School. When the Opium Wars closed China in the 1840s, the maritime focus of Boston shifted to Europe. Russell Sturgis thus returned from China, married Julia Overing Boit of Newport in 1846 and in 1848 accepted partnership in Baring's Bank, moving permanently to London. In 1850, John joined his family and it was here that his ties with England began.

Although a Bostonian, John Sturgis was educationally and ideologically British. Between 1850 and 1860 he was educated on the continent, attending school in Munich and Belgium in 1853. He completed the Grand Tour in Africa, Egypt and on the Nile (in part with Richard Morris Hunt), arriving in Palestine in 1855. Sturgis studied in London 1855–1857 and with the architect James K. Colling. By 1858, after deciding upon an architectural career and following his marriage to Frances Anne Codman of Boston, he assisted Colling in Liverpool and Wales.

After returning to America as a partner in the largest architectural office in Boston 1861–1866 he worked alone and together with Gridley J. F. Bryant and Arthur D. Gilman on early Back Bay houses on Arlington Street, Beacon Street, and Commonwealth Avenue. Having formed a partnership in 1866 with Charles Brigham, a young draftsman in the Bryant and Gilman office, Sturgis returned to England from 1866 to 1870. With Brigham in charge of their Boston office during this period Sturgis designed on a transatlantic basis, returning to Boston in 1870 to win the commission for his best known work, the Museum of Fine Arts on Copley Square. This first public art museum in America was both structurally and programmatically based on the South Kensington Museums in London.

His success with this building, on which he used English terra cotta for the Gothic ornament, established his role as the purveyor of English taste amongst the Boston aristocracy. Although most of his executed work was domestic in nature, the plan and foliate ornament of his tiled and banded Church of the Advent in Boston (1874–1878), creatively synthesized from contemporaneous English designs by JAMES BROOKS, JOHN L. PEARSON, and GEORGE E. STREET, were unique in American high Anglican ecclesiastical architecture. From the 1860s onward Sturgis completed a series of innovative seaside and country cottages. Distinguished by cascading, broken roof planes which descend over wide verandas from irregular chimneys, they incorporated exterior terra cotta, encaustic tile, and molded bricks imported from England.

After 1870 the domestic designs of Sturgis are closely allied to those of the English architects Bruce Talbert,, RICHARD NORMAN SHAW and WILLIAM E. NESFIELD (who also studied with J. K. Colling). His literate understanding of the Queen Anne Revival is emphatically English in comparison with that of his Boston colleagues, but his work is also marked by deft allusions to American Colonial and Federal design which he viewed as a British phenomenon. Frequently using details from measured drawings of the Hancock House (1737) which he completed before its demolition in 1863, he redesigned a series of eighteenth-century houses with consummate skill to serve the needs of late nineteenth-century living. At this time his Edward Hooper House (1872) and Arthur Astor Carey House (1882) in Cambridge were prototypical versions of nineteenth-century Colonial Revival design for new construction, both reflecting the influence of the Hancock House drawings.

In the 1880s skillfully planned domestic designs by John Sturgis with rich paneling and carved ornament set the artistic standard for Boston. The Frederick L. Ames House at 306 Dartmouth Street (1882), legendary in its day, palatial in scale and fully comparable to English work by Norman Shaw, is generally considered to be his masterpiece. His conceptual influence on the development of American museums is perhaps best characterized by the interiors he designed for Mrs. Jack Gardner at 152–154 Beacon Street (1882). Art objects from this house became in 1900 the core of Boston's next great museum of the decorative arts, Fenway Court.

MARGARET HENDERSON FLOYD

WORKS

1862, Ogden Codman, Jr., House (The Grange), Lincoln, Mass. 1863, Russell Sturgis House (Sunnywaters), Manchester-by-the-Sea, Mass. 1864, Greenvale, Portsmouth, R.I. 1864, Samuel A. Ward House (Land's End); *1866, Edward D. Boit, Jr., House (The Rocks); Newport, R.I. *1867, Henry Cabot Lodge Cottage; *1867, George Abbott James House (Lowlands); Nahant, Mass. 1868, Edward N. Perkins House (Pinebank), Jamaica Plain, Mass. 1869, Hollis Honnewell House (The Cottage), Wellesey, Mass. 1870, Martin

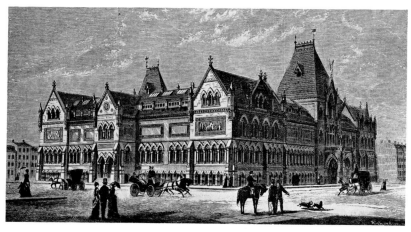

Brimmer House, Beverley, Mass. 1870–1876, Museum of Fine Arts, Copley Square; 1872, Franklin Gordon Dexter House, 55 Beacon Street; Boston. 1872, Edward Hooper House, Reservoir Street, Cambridge, Mass. 1872, Charles Joy House, 86 Marlboro Street, Boston. 1873, Codman Building, 55 Kilby Street; 1874–1878, Church of the Advent, Brimmer Street; Boston. 1874–1886, The Homestead, Geneseo, N.Y. 1876, Boylston House, Brookline, Mass. 1876, Warren Delano House, Barrytown, N.Y. 1876, John Carey House (Gardener's Cottage), Newport, R.I. 1876, James Lawrence House (Homestead), Groton, Mass. 1876, James Lawrence House, 84 Marlboro Street, Boston. *1876, Charles Sprague Sargent House, Brookline, Mass. 1880, E. Rollins Morse House, 167 Commonwealth Avenue; 1881, Massachusetts Hospital Life Insurance, 50 State Street; 1882, Frederick L. Ames House; Boston. 1882, Arthur Astor Carey House, Cambridge, Mass. 1882, Theodore A. Davis House, Newport, R.I. 1882, Mrs. Jack Gardner House, 152–154 Beacon Street; 1882, Nathaniel Thayer House, 239 Commonwealth Avenue; Boston. 1882, Trinity Church, Independence, Mo. 1882, Young Men's Christian Association, Berkeley Street, Boston. 1885, Railway Station, Dedham, Mass. 1886, Netherfield, Prides Crossing, Mass. 1886, John E. Thayer House, Lancaster, Mass. 1886, E. V. R. Thayer House, 17 Gloucester Street; 1887, Boston Athletic Club, Exeter Street; Boston. 1887, Railway Station, Stoughton, Mass.

Sturgis.
Drawing of the Museum of
  Fine Arts.
Boston.
1870–1876

BIBLIOGRAPHY

The "Scrapbook" of John Hubbard Sturgis, containing mounted drawings and photographs of his work, can be found in the Avery Architectural Library, Columbia University, New York. Letters and personal papers of John Hubbard Sturgis are in the Boston Athenæum.

"The Museum of Fine Arts, Boston." 1980 *American Architect and Building News* 8:205–215.

BUNTING, BAINBRIDGE 1967 *Houses of Boston's Back Bay.* Cambridge, Mass.: Belknap.

FLOYD, MARGARET HENDERSON 1973 "A Terra Cotta Cornerstone for Copley Square: Museum of Fine Arts, Boston, 1870–1876, by Sturgis and Brigham." *Journal of the Society of Architectural Historians.* 32:83–103.

FLOYD, MARGARET HENDERSON 1979 "Measured

Drawings of the Hancock House by John Hubbard Sturgis: A Legacy to the Colonial Revival." Pages 87–111 in *Architecture in Colonial Massachusetts.* Boston: Colonial Society of Massachusetts.

FLOYD, MARGARET HENDERSON 1981 "John Hubbard Sturgis and the Redesign of The Grange for Ogden Codman." *Old Time New England* 71:41–65.

FLOYD, MARGARET HENDERSON n.d. "John Hubbard Sturgis of Boston and the English Architectural Image." Manuscript in preparation.

KING, MOSES (editor) (1878) 1889 *King's Handbook of Boston.* Rev. ed. Cambridge, Mass.: King.

LAMB, MARTHA J., MRS. (editor) 1879 *The Homes of America.* New York: Appleton.

STURGIS, JOHN HUBBARD 1871 "Terra Cotta and its Uses." *Proceedings of the American Institute of Architects* 5:39–43.

STURGIS, JULIAN 1893 *From the Books and Papers of Russell Sturgis.* Oxford University Press.

WHITEHALL, WALTER MUIR 1970 *Museum of Fine Arts, Boston: A Centennial History.* 2 vols. Cambridge, Mass.: Belknap.

STURGIS, RUSSELL

Russell Sturgis (1836–1909), born in Baltimore, grew up in New York and his interest in JACOB WREY MOULD's buildings and in the theories of JOHN RUSKIN led him to choose architecture as a profession. After a year in LEOPOLD EIDLITZ's office, he went to Munich in 1859 to study at the Academy of Fine Arts and Sciences, where medieval styles and the practical aspects of construction were stressed. Beginning practice in New York in 1863, Sturgis shared office space with PETER B. WIGHT; in 1868, he established separate quarters. Among his assistants were George Fletcher Babb (see BABB, COOK, AND WILLARD), Charles F. McKim and William R. Mead (see MCKIM, MEAD, AND WHITE).

Sturgis designed in the popular styles of the post-Civil War period. His best known work is Farnam Hall (1869–1870), executed for Yale University in New Haven, a restrained version of the High Victorian Gothic, its plain masses carefully balanced by picturesque detail. Later, he produced an example of unornamented functionalism in iron, the destroyed Austin Building (1876) in New York, and a Queen Anne mansion (1884) for Charles Farnam in New Haven. By 1885, Sturgis had retired from building, devoting himself, until his death, to developing Columbia University's Avery Library and to architectural criticism. He was an early champion of the Chicago school.

CHARLOTTE A. KELLY

WORKS

1869–1870, Farnam Hall, Yale University; 1870, Durfee Hall, Yale University; 1871, Henry Farnam House; New Haven. 1874–1875, Farmers' and Mechanics' Bank (now Manufacturers' Hanover Bank), Albany, N.Y. 1874–1876, Battell Chapel, New Haven. *1875, Plymouth Congregational Church, Minneapolis, Minn. 1875–1881, First Baptist Church, Tarrytown, N.Y. *1876, Austin Building, New York. 1884, Charles Farnam House; 1885–1886, Lawrance Hall, Yale University; New Haven. c.1898, Dean Sage House (now St. Louis Senior Citizens' Center), Brooklyn, N.Y.

BIBLIOGRAPHY

DICKASON, DAVID HOWARD 1953 *Daring Young Men: The Story of the American Pre-Raphaelites.* Bloomington: Indiana University Press.

SCHUYLER, MONTGOMERY 1909a "Russell Sturgis." *Architectural Record* 25:146, 220.

SCHUYLER, MONTGOMERY 1909b "Russell Sturgis's Architecture." *Architectural Record* 25:404–410.

SCHUYLER, MONTGOMERY 1909c "Architecture of American Colleges, II: Yale." *Architectural Record* 26:393–416.

SCHUYLER, MONTGOMERY 1909d "Russell Sturgis." *Scribner's Magazine* 45:635–636.

WIGHT, PETER B. 1909 "Reminiscences of Russell Sturgis." *Architectural Record* 26:123–131.

STURM, L. C.

Leonhard Christoph Sturm (1669–1719) was born in Altdorf near Nuremberg as son of the mathematician, theologian, and philosopher Johann Christian Sturm. Educated at the Universities of Altdorf (1683–1688) and Jena (1689) as mathematician, he became involved with architecture only after his move to the University of Leipzig in 1690. Patronized by Georg Bose, who also provided funds for study trips to Berlin and Dresden, he had an opportunity to study Nicolaus Goldmann's manuscript of an architectural treatise which was in Bose's possession. Sturm published it in 1696 and again, in modified form, in 1699 and 1721. Earlier, in 1694, Sturm had published a treatise on the Temple in Jerusalem, maintaining that its dimensions and proportions had been revealed by God and that this knowledge eventually was taken over by the Greeks. Sturm's training as mathematician is clearly evident in this text. In subsequent publications as well, this aspect of architectural theory—correct proportions—is stressed.

Appointed professor of mathematics and architecture at the Ritterakademie in Wolfenbüttel (a school for the education of princes) in 1694, he continued his interests in architecture through travels to Holland (1697 and 1699) and France (1699) and published, in 1719, his observations in the form of letters addressed to nobles as *Reise-Anmerckungen.* In 1702, Sturm accepted a position as professor of mathematics at the University of Frankfurt/Oder. During his tenure there, he designed triumphal arches, medals, and other decorations in connection with university celebrations in 1706. He also was asked to evaluate the structural soundness of ANDREAS SCHLÜTER's tower for the Mint in Berlin. Alternate designs by Sturm were published in his *Prodromus* (1714). In 1710, he was involved in the construction of the Schelfkirche (Sankt Nikolai auf dem Schelfe) in Schwerin, which had been begun in 1708 by Jakob Reutz. His involvement in this project resulted in basic observations on the nature and requirements for Protestant church architecture, which he published in 1712 and 1718. The interior by Sturm is characterized by a two-story colonnade separating the choir from the nave. Sturm also designed the high altar for this church. The baroque decoration was removed in 1858. Moving to Schwerin in 1710, Sturm was involved with the completion of the *Neue Schloss* in Neustadt on the Elbe (begun as early as 1618) and presented plans for a new residence (1712), which was not built. His plans for this building are contained in the Prodromus. In 1712, he went again to Holland, this time to study waterworks. Moving from Schwerin to Rostock in 1716 and later (1718?) to Hamburg, he sought employment in Blankenburg, the residence of Duke Ludwig Rudolf of Braunschweig. He died in Blankenburg a few days after his arrival.

Sturm's importance rests not so much on his very few architectural works as on his theoretical writings, especially the edition of Goldmann's treatise. Through his writings on Protestant church architecture he established a sober architectural antidote to the exuberance of south German and Austrian baroque architecture. Drawings by Sturm are preserved in Wolfenbüttel and Nuremberg (Germanisches Nationalmuseum).

EGON VERHEYEN

WORKS

*1690, Caspar Bose Garden and Orangerie, Dresden, Germany. 1694–1702, Corner Pavilions (enlargement from three to five axes), Salzdahlum, Germany. *1706, Temporary Buildings, University of Frankfurt. 1710–1713, Schelfkirche, Schwerin, Germany.

BIBLIOGRAPHY

BERCKENHAGEN, EKHART 1966 *Barock in Deutschland: Residenzen.* Berlin: Hessling.

KUSTER, ISOLDE 1942 "L. C. Sturm." Unpublished Ph.D. dissertation, University of Berlin.

MITTENBÜHLER, ROBERT L. 1969 *Aesthetic Currents in German Baroque Architecture.* Unpublished Ph.D. dissertation, Syracuse University, New York.

STURM, L. C. 1694 *Sciagraphia Templi Hierosolymitani.* Leipzig: Krügeri.

STURM, L. C. (1695)1708 *Erste Ausübung der vortrefflichen und vollständigen Anweisung zu der Civil-Bau-Kunst Nicolai Goldmanns.* Leipzig: Richter.

STURM, L. C. 1712 *Architektonisches Bedenken von der protestantischen Klein Kirchen Figur und Einrichtung.* Hamburg, Germany.

STURM, L. C. 1714 *Prodromus Architecturae Goldmannianae.* Augsburg, Germany: Wolff.

STURM, L. C. (1718)1752 *Vollständige Anweisung grosser Herren Paläste starck, bequem anzugeben.* Augsburg, Germany: Wolff.

STURM, L. C. 1719 *Architectonische Reise-Anmerckungen.* Augsburg, Germany.

WACKERNAGEL, MARTIN 1915 *Die Baukunst des 17. und 18. Jahrhunderts in den germanischen Ländern.* Berlin: Akademische Verlagsgesellschaft; Athenaion.

STÜRZENACKER, AUGUST

August Stürzenacker (1871–1943) was trained in Karlsruhe where his career in state and municipal service began under Josef Durm. Durm's German Renaissance and neo-Romanesque preferences are strongly reflected in Stürzenacker's early works for the Harbor Direction and his Rhenish Romanesque-style crematorium. In his Karlsruhe Railroad Station (1913–1914), the lively surface ornament of the early work is subordinated to a more functionally expressive composition with strong classical overtones, similar in spirit to the late work of JOSEPH MARIA OLBRICH. Restrained classicism and elegant decoration unite harmoniously with FRIEDRICH WEINBRENNER's earlier work in Stürzenacker's additions to the *Kurhaus* at Baden-Baden (1912–1917).

BARRY BERGDOLL

WORKS

1899–1901, Director's Building, Harbor Direction; 1899–1901, Electricity Works, Municipal Rhine Port; 1903, Crematorium, Main Cemetery; *1903–1905, Schiller School; Karlsruhe, Germany. 1908–1935, New Bath Buildings, Badenweiler, Germany. 1912–1917, *Kurhaus* (rebuilding and additions), Baden-Baden, Germany. 1913–1914, Railroad Station, Karlsruhe, Germany.

BIBLIOGRAPHY

GÖRICKE, JOACHIM (1971)1980 *Bauten in Karlsruhe.* 2d ed. Karlsruhe, Germany: G. Braun.

STÜRZENACKER, AUGUST 1918 *Das Kurhaus in Baden-Baden und dessen Neubau 1912–1917.* Karlsruhe, Germany: Müllersche Hofbuchandlung.

SUARDI, BARTOLOMMEO

See BRAMANTINO.

SULLIVAN, LOUIS H.

Louis Henry Sullivan (1856–1924) wanted to produce a new style of architecture. His quest for a mode of design independent of the historic styles became the consuming passion of his life. In transcending every other aspect of his being, it explained and justified his theory, his work, and his life. In his writings, Sullivan tried to lead other architects to the same goal. His architecture served as a visual demonstration of his theory. Sullivan's life was tragic because in advocating the new architecture he refused all compromise.

Sullivan's theoretical writings span the forty years between 1885 and 1924 and run into the hundreds of thousands of words. Because he chose not to write in a straightforward expository style, it is not always easy to grasp his message. Nonetheless, whenever the reader gives Sullivan's writings the care and attention required to discover his essential ideas, the basic themes can be discerned in spite of Sullivan's lyrical, poetic, and metaphorical manner of expression. Even so, Sullivan's thought is hardly simplistic. In seeking to erect a complete philosophical system to support and explain his notion of a new style and to provide the rationale and methodology for effecting it, Sullivan reached far and wide into nineteenth-century philosophy, history, literature, poetry, religion, and educational theory. As the search for the intellectual sources of Sullivan's thought has been given considerable attention (Paul, 1962; Weingarden, 1980; Menocal, 1981), we will confine our remarks to elucidating the major themes embraced by Sullivan's conception of "the new architecture":

Our art is an organism. To see it emerge from the matrix of humanity, to see it born of its conditions, to rock its cradle, to guard and ward it, to forecast its hope and promise,—such shall be our friendly task. For the NEW ARCHITECTURE is that child,—moaning a little in its first days of old, old looking prophetic infancy, and gurgling a little now and then, but growing, growing, a wholesale happy little one, pawing here and there but chuckling, and sleeping a little and waking a little,—but come to stay, and grow, and bring sunshine to our hearts (1901–1902, xiv).

Sullivan's reasons for wanting to alter architectural design so radically were essentially the same ones expressed by other nineteenth-century writers who had been affected by evolutionary theory. In announcing that artistic expression should be derived from and conditioned by the physical and cultural milieu of its time, Sullivan was echoing an evolutionary theory of art that was already well established by the time he began to think of a career in architecture.

Scientific Darwinism imagined the healthy organism adapting to and expressing in its shape and form its physical environment. This concept had been extended to the cultural sphere by writers like the French art historian and philosopher Hippolyte Taine, from whom Sullivan claimed to have acquired his theory of cultural Darwinism. The idea that the work of art should adapt to and, at the same time, proclaim the essence of its cultural environment was formalized in such expressions as "the spirit of the time" and "the spirit of the people." The latter was a particular favorite of Sullivan who, following Taine and the American poet Walt Whitman, often substituted for it the term "the genius of the people."

Even though Sullivan firmly believed that a new architectural style expressing the cultural environment existing at the time of its creation would appear sooner or later, he did not choose to explore the idea in all of its ramifications. Thus, even though Sullivan clearly implied that the style he envisioned would not be universal in range because the genius of the people would naturally vary from place to place, he never bothered to distinguish precisely between new styles of national, regional, and personal scope. Certainly, he believed that his new style was his own property and thus personal, for he frequently spoke of it in that way and, on one occasion, even railed against an architect who plagiarized his ornament (Paul, 1962, p. 157, n. 12). As Sullivan often spoke of an American style, one must presume he believed that his unique personal manner was naturally to become a subdivision of a national style when it arose, though in fact he never specifically says so. He is also silent about the appearance of regional styles, though again one may reasonably assume that he supposed such styles would also arise.

Whether or not Sullivan thought the Europeans would develop national, regional, and personal styles of their own, we do not know, for he is mute on that question. One must suppose, however, that he believed such a possibility unlikely for several reasons. Apparently he was convinced, perhaps as the result of his study in France, that the historic styles were so firmly entrenched in Europe and the weight of tradition so heavy, as to all but preclude the rise of a new style there in the foreseeable future. Even more important was Sullivan's conviction, often expressed, that the democratic atmosphere of the United States provided the most hospitable environment for the evolution of a new architecture. In Europe by contrast, democracy was not only in short supply but its antagonist, which he called feudalism—the enemy of free expression in the arts as in life—remained firmly in control.

For Sullivan democracy was not merely a form of government but an attitude of mind that emphasized individual freedom and carried with it the related concept of individual responsibility. Sullivan constantly used the term democracy to underline his conviction that a free society must sooner or later give rise to a responsible freedom in design from which a new style of architecture would be born. From this it followed that the first stirrings of the new architecture were predestined to occur in the world's foremost democracy, the United States.

Sullivan's predictions about the necessary evolution of a new architectural style were not always correct, to be sure. This is especially evident as regards his belief in the manifest destiny of democracy to stimulate and nurture a creative architecture. Nonetheless, he remained highly optimistic in his hopes for the imminent appearance of an American architecture, at least well into the 1880s.

By the turn of the century, however, his writings began to exhibit a new pessimism that appeared in the form of undisguised attacks on the architectural establishment. In "Kindergarten Chats" (1901) and later writings, Sullivan became quite open in his denunciation of architects working in the historic styles, who by 1900 had come to be nearly all American architects except for Sullivan and FRANK LLOYD WRIGHT, their students, a few sympathetic midwestern colleagues, and a number of California architects.

But if taking on nearly all the professional architects in the country was not enough, Sullivan also attacked the architectural schools, for in them he found much to condemn. His primary educational targets, however, were the twin evils, as he saw them, of increasing emphasis on formula in the guise of the historic styles, and the suppression in the architectural student of any natural instinct toward originality in design. Whether Sullivan was right or wrong to have been so persistent and uncompromising in his attacks on the architectural and educational establishment is now a moot question. To him the battle was necessary, and for his belligerency he was soon to suffer bitterly.

Much of Sullivan's writing in a positive vein was directed at trying to make clear his method for translating "the genius of the people" into the art of architecture. It was a task that proved to be exceedingly difficult because of the way evolutionary theory had evolved in the scientific and cultural worlds. The problem went back to the Darwinian concept of the organism adapting to and expressing the conditions of its environment. In a scientific age, it was naturally easier for men to understand the environment in purely physical terms. Thus, the perfectly adapted work of architecture came to be thought of in evolutionary terms as a building whose plan, volume, masses, and details reflected and expressed such physical factors as site, use, circulation, structure, and materials. Although the roots of this scientific interpretation of architecture go back to the eighteenth century and beyond, it was in the writings of such nineteenth-century architects as A. W. N. PUGIN and EUGÈNE EMMANUEL VIOLLET-LE-DUC that these concepts were given wide appeal. Because this special brand of evolutionary theory depended upon a reasoned analysis of environmental conditions when it was applied to architecture, it was often called rationalism, and its proponents rationalists.

Like most architects of his day, Sullivan was thoroughly familiar with rational theory. But Sullivan had also come to know the more subjective evolutionary theories of Taine and others as they were applied to culture in general and to the fine arts in particular. Facing two evolutionary theories, one scientific and the other cultural, and sensing that neither standing alone would be adequate to support a fully developed theory of evolutionary architecture, Sullivan set out to combine them into a synthesis of the objective and the subjective, of the intellectual and the emotional, of the head and the heart.

In doing so, Sullivan faced a dilemma. Were he to give both aspects of evolutionary theory equal weight, the subjective side of the equation might well be lost on architects for whom the objective side of their art had been overemphasized for so long. Thus, in presenting his theory, Sullivan chose to stress the subjective. Indeed, he did so not only in the ideas expressed but also in the style of his writing which, in its poetic effects, resembled the verse of Walt Whitman, whom Sullivan especially admired. Unfortunately, the result was quite the contrary of what Sullivan planned, for the effect of his lyrical style was to obscure his message from all but the most dedicated.

One wonders, however, whether Sullivan's message really would have been any better understood considering the dominant position occupied by scientific rationalism in the architectural theory of his day, even had he chosen to approach his subject in a more direct way. Yet how could he? At a time when architects everywhere were immersed in rational thought, would Sullivan have been any better understood had he described in objective language how the architect might move from subjective experience to architectural design? Sullivan apparently did not think so for he rarely left the realm of the poetic.

In fact, in those few places where Sullivan did write in a more expository fashion, as, for example, in his much read "The Tall Office Building Artistically Considered" (1896), the objective part of his message was taken—more often than not—to be the entire message. Sullivan's theory thus mistakenly came to be identified with scientific rationalism and his architecture to be interpreted and evaluated in terms of that theory of design.

This unfortunate association of Sullivan's ideas with rational theory led as well to confusion about the true meaning of the famous dictum "form follows function," first announced in "The Tall Office Building Artistically Considered" (1896). It is true, of course, that Sullivan did mean by his dictum that the forms of a building should *in part* arise out of and express such physical functions as use, plan, structure, and materials. Yet, it is also obvious from the small amount of space he devoted to a discussion of physical functions that the objective in art was not his priority. Clearly, it was the subjective or spiritual in art on which Sullivan placed the higher value. Perhaps his attitude is best expressed in the essay of 1894, "Emotional Architecture as Compared with Intellectual: A Study in Objective and Subjective," in which he suggests that it is the task of scientific functionalism to provide the vehicle of art and of subjective functionalism to clothe that vehicle with a form of beauty:

Thought . . . eventually arrives at a science of logical statement that shall shape and define the scheme and structure that is to underlie, penetrate and support the form of an art work. . . . Expression . . . is to clothe the structure of art with a form of beauty; for she is the perfection of the physical . . . and the uttermost attainment of emotionality. . . . It is the presence of this unreality that makes the art work real; it is by virtue of this silent subjectivity that the objective voice of an art song becomes sonorous and thrilling. Unless . . . subjectivity permeate an art work that work cannot aspire to greatness.

By function Sullivan most often meant an irrational force in nature that he sometimes called the "Infinite Creative Spirit," the "Function of all functions" (1901–1902, xxx). Every object existing in the world of the senses was in part an expression of this ultimate function. But each object was also the product of a specialized spiritual function that actually gave rise to it. "That which exists in the spirit ever seeks and finds its physical counterpart in form, its visible language" (*ibid., xii*). Objective forms in the visible world thus followed their subjective functions according to an immutable natural law. And it was this natural law that was to become for Sullivan the rule "so broad as to admit of NO EXCEPTION" (1924*a*, p. 221), by which form ever followed function: "All these words [organ, organize, organization, organism] imply the initiating pressure of a living force and a resultant structure or mechanism whereby such an invisible force is made manifest and operative. The pressure, we call function: the resultant, Form" ("Kinder-

garten Chats," ([1934]1980, p. 48).

The job of the architect, therefore, was to align himself with the forces of nature and thereby to discern those subjective and objective functions that demanded expression in the art of architecture:

He must impart to passive materials a subjective or spiritual quality which shall make them live. . . . Therefore to vitalize building materials, to animate them with a thought, a state of feeling, to charge them with a social significance and value, to make them a visible part of the social fabric, to infuse into them the true life of the people, to impart to them the best that is in the people, as the eye of the poet, looking beneath the surface of life, sees the best that is in the people—such is the real function of the architect;—for understood in these terms, the architect is one kind of poet, and his work one form of poetry,—using the word in its broad, inclusive actual sense (1901–1902, xlii).

In the words of Hugh Morrison, who wrote about Sullivan's architecture nearly a half century ago, "Once it is understood that the conception of functionalism as set forth by Sullivan . . . calls for emotional and spiritual realities as well as physical realities, much confused thinking will be avoided" (1935, p. 279).

As we know from *The Autobiography of an Idea* (Sullivan, 1924) and other sources (Connely, 1960), Sullivan was an insular person with relatively few friends who devoted himself largely to his intellectual and spiritual quest for a new architecture. If we may believe the *Autobiography,* this search began as an unconscious awakening in Sullivan the child, as he experienced the depth and power of nature. Later, as a youth, Sullivan found it necessary to liberate himself from the trammels of a conventional education. During his middle years, he concentrated on developing, then perfecting, a personal style of American architecture. His later life was devoted to presenting his art and philosophy of architecture to laymen, architects, and especially to the future architects of America.

Born in Boston, Louis Sullivan was educated in the elementary schools of that city. He spent the summers near Boston on the farm of his maternal grandparents, Henri and Anna List. Sullivan's mother was a skilled pianist and amateur artist, and his father, Patrick, a dancing master. Sullivan's deep love of nature thus may be traced to his summers in the country, and his musical and artistic gifts to the example of his parents.

At the English High School in Boston that Sullivan attended from 1870–1872 he was moved boldly into the world of ideas by the inspired instruction of his much revered first-year teacher, Moses Woolson. An occasional lecture by Harvard botanist Asa Gray added a scientific dimension to

Sullivan's hitherto untutored love of nature, thus helping to lay the foundations for his theories of architecture and ornament. Dissatisfied with the architectural curriculum as presented by WILLIAM R. WARE in 1872–1873, when Sullivan studied at the Massachusetts Institute of Technology, the aspiring architect decided to seek professional employment. The place selected to look for work was not Boston, however, but Philadelphia. The firm chosen was Furness & Hewitt (see FRANK FURNESS), who had been recommended to Sullivan by none other than RICHARD MORRIS HUNT of New York City whose office Sullivan visited on his way to Philadelphia. That job lasted through the summer and into the autumn of 1873 when Sullivan was laid off.

From there the young man traveled to Chicago to join his parents and brother Albert, now living in that city. Arriving on the day before Thanksgiving 1873, Sullivan soon found employment with the architect WILLIAM LE BARON JENNEY. It was in Jenney's office that he met the somewhat older office foreman, JOHN EDELMANN, who was to become his close friend and mentor. In the spring of 1874, Edelmann left Jenney to found his own architectural firm of Johnston & Edelmann, and Sullivan, now ready to continue his education, set sail for Europe in June 1874 where, in Paris, he would enroll in the atelier of JOSEPH AUGUSTE EMILE VAUDREMER at the Ecole des Beaux-Arts. It was during Sullivan's preparations for the entrance examinations that he was tutored in mathematics by Monsieur Clopet whose teaching inspired him to search for an architectural principle so broad as to admit of no exception. "If this can be done in mathematics, why not in architecture?" (*Autobiography*, 1924, p. 221).

After his return to Chicago in July 1875, Sullivan dropped out of sight. No doubt he worked occasionally for Johnston and Edelmann, at least until the summer of 1876 when the firm was dissolved and Edelmann left the city for a period of years. There is evidence to indicate that when Edelmann returned to Chicago in 1879 and was hired as chief draftsman by DANKMAR ADLER, the young Sullivan was already working for Adler as a draftsman. Thus, when Edelmann again decided to leave Chicago early in 1881, he was in the position to promote the interests of his younger friend with the boss. No doubt, it was then that Adler made Sullivan his chief draftsman. Later on in the spring of 1882, Adler invited Sullivan into a one-third partnership, and one year later, on April 1, 1883, they became full partners in the famous firm of ADLER AND SULLIVAN.

During the ensuing twelve years, Sullivan and Adler worked together as a smoothly functioning team with Sullivan responsible for design and Adler for business and engineering. It was during these years that Sullivan managed to arrive at, then perfect, a personal mode of artistic expression. Sullivan's two best-known apprentices were also trained in the Adler and Sullivan office during this time. Frank Lloyd Wright was hired in 1888 and left in 1893, but GEORGE G. ELMSLIE, who came in 1890, remained with Sullivan for nearly twenty years.

At the depth of the depression of the 1890s, Adler decided to leave the practice of architecture for a secure, well-paying position elsewhere, and the partnership was dissolved. After that, Sullivan practiced alone. Toward the end of the century, he received a number of substantial commissions of which the Schlesinger and Mayer Department Store in Chicago (1898–1903) was the most distinguished. After that, however, his work slowed dramatically so that during the last twenty years of his life, he designed fewer than fifteen structures. These included three houses, a church, and a department store. Most, however, were modest banks in small towns scattered across the Midwest. None were tall buildings.

When Alder left the partnership in July 1895, Sullivan was only thirty-nine years old. At that time, the designing partner, who until then had known only success, was in a state of optimistic euphoria about the future course of American architecture and the place in it of his personal style. That much is certain from Sullivan's writings during the first six years of the 1890s. Thus blinded by success and flushed with optimism, Sullivan refused to resume the partnership when early in 1896 Adler decided to return to architecture. This rejection of Adler was not in itself the cause of the disastrous turn in Sullivan's fortunes after 1903, for Adler was to die prematurely in 1900. But Sullivan's refusal to reunite with Adler was symptomatic of his growing propensity to overvalue his own capabilities as both architect and businessman and to isolate himself from the realities of architectural practice in the years following the Columbian Exposition. Whether this isolation resulted from Sullivan's singleminded advocacy of a new architecture or from a cancerous defect of personality, we shall probably never know for certain despite much morbid speculation about it (Connely, 1960; Menocal, 1981). Perhaps it was something of both. One wonders, though, if a definitive answer is really necessary, for by 1900 Sullivan had already etched for himself a solid and unimpeachable place in the history of architecture. He had become the first American to devise and perfect a personal style of architecture whose forms and details were distinct from those of the historic styles.

Moreover, the style that Sullivan created was not only a personal style but was modern as well, using the term "modern" to denote an original style in which there is no conscious or intentional reference to the historic styles for inspiration. In this sense, all of the new architectural styles that appeared in America and Europe after about 1890 are modern and thus are integral parts of the Modern movement. Accordingly, it is Sullivan and the small group of like-minded European innovators born before 1860 who must be regarded as the first generation of modern architects.

Like his European counterparts, Sullivan never seriously considered eschewing ornament as a part of his modern style. "For the NEW ARCHITECTURE," Sullivan wrote in 1901, "a new decoration must evolve to be the worthy corollary of its harmonies, a decoration limitless in organic fluency and plasticity, and in inherent capacity for the expression of thought, feeling and sentiment" (1901–1902, xlix).

Considering the course of modern architecture in the twentieth century, one well may wonder how it is possible to regard Sullivan's ornamented architecture as modern. Yet, if that question is inverted, one might inquire equally as to how the unornamented buildings of twentieth-century architects could ever have been considered architecture in the full sense of the term. Is it not the more curious that after thousands of years of ornamented architecture during all periods and in all styles, architects in the twentieth century should ever have conceived of an architecture without ornament? When in 1892 Sullivan wrote "Ornament in Architecture," he had already answered that question for himself:

I take it as self-evident that a building, quite devoid of ornament, may convey a noble and dignified sentiment by virtue of mass and proportion. It is not evident to me that ornament can intrinsically heighten these elemental qualities. Why then should we use ornament? . . . I should say it would be greatly for our aesthetic good if we should refrain from the use of ornament for a period of years, in order that our thought might concentrate acutely upon the production of buildings well-formed and comely in the nude. . . . If we shall have become well grounded in pure and simple forms . . . we shall have discerned the limitations as well as the great value of unadorned masses.

Now if this spiritual and emotional quality is a noble attribute when it resides in the mass of a building, it must, when applied to a virile and synthetic scheme of ornamentation, raise this at once from the level of triviality to the heights of dramatic expression (1892, reprinted in [1901–1902] 1918).

In developing his modern style, Sullivan also clung to other attributes of the architectural art that, in being timeless, transcended the limited stylistic notions of "historic" and "modern." One of these was monumentality which, as a concept specific neither to time nor place, remained outside the realm of evolutionary theory. That Sullivan chose to design in terms of monumentality was simply because that is the way he had been taught to design in Boston, Philadelphia, Chicago, and Paris. Thus, Sullivan cast his modern style in terms of balance, symmetry, and stately rhythms; of clearly defined axes and carefully ordered plans; of regular fenestration; and of logical and straightforward compositions and refined materials. He conceived of mass, volume, and space in terms of dignity and grandeur. To Sullivan these and other elements of monumentality in architecture were neither old nor new, neither historic nor modern, but timeless and eternal. As such, they had nothing in particular to do with his search for a personal style or with his conception of a modern or American architecture.

Sullivan's architectural development divides itself into four distinct periods. His work up to 1887 was experimental. The period from 1887 to 1890 was a time of transition during which he moved vigorously toward an original style. In 1890, Sullivan finally arrived at his goal, and in the 1890s, he refined and perfected the new style. His late work after 1900 was a colorful autumnal flowering in tapestry brick, glazed terra cotta, and stained glass.

During the first three years of the 1880s, Sullivan produced designs of a fairly unified visual character. Whatever their use, the buildings of those years exhibited many common stylistic features. Most prominent was a combination of light stone and red brick. Wall surfaces consisted of a number of planes and thus were sculptural. Shapes were controlled by a fairly rigid geometry both in line and plane. Few buildings contained obvious historical references though in general there was the suggestion of classicism in composition and in such details as a pilasterlike treatment of piers. Arches were always round, never pointed, but minor elements such as columns and cresting seem medieval in inspiration. Sullivan's architectural ornament was also stylistically cohesive during this period and, like the architecture, began to change only in 1883 at about the time of full partnership.

Why this early period of cohesive design should be identified so closely with the years before the founding of Adler and Sullivan on April 1, 1883, is not known. Perhaps Adler had not yet completely passed the crayon to Sullivan. A more likely explanation, however, is that during these years Sullivan's designs were still much affected by the work and ideas of his friend John Edelmann. Certainly, Edelmann's architectural sketches in a notebook kept by Sullivan during the mid–1870s (Avery Library) resemble Sullivan's buildings of 1880–1883 in many respects. Furthermore, Edelmann's Blackstone-Power Block, erected in Cleveland in 1882, echoes many of the visual attributes of Sullivan's Chicago buildings of the early 1880s. Several other commercial structures erected in Cleveland between 1882 and 1884 by Edelmann were of a more advanced design than most of Sullivan's buildings. In the opening up of their façades through the use of large windows separated by cast-iron mullions set into walls of narrow piers and metal-backed spandrels, they were progressive. In this respect, the Cleveland buildings resemble quite closely the only building in Chicago by Sullivan to diverge markedly in its visual expression from his other early designs. That was the Rothschild Store of 1881. It should also be pointed out that between 1873 and 1883, Edelmann developed a style of decoration that is difficult to distinguish from Sullivan's early ornament.

These visual correspondences between the documented work of Sullivan and Edelmann strongly support the idea that during the early years Sullivan was inspired, if not assisted in his designs and ornament, by his mentor John Edelmann. Yet, if true, there still remains the question of what inspired the unusual and adventurous early architectural and ornamental styles of Edelmann and Sullivan. Although Sullivan had studied in Paris, the similarities between his early style and that of Edelmann, who had not been abroad, suggests that the immediate sources lay closer to home. Supporting this view are two drawings by Sullivan showing his characteristic ornament of the mid-1870s that predate his year in Paris. A number of similar drawings survive that were made by Sullivan while a student at the Ecole des Beaux-Arts which he sent to Edelmann as patterns for stencil decorations in buildings then being erected in Chicago by Johnston and Edelmann.

The most likely source of the early designs, both architectural and ornamental, by Edelmann and Sullivan was the avant-garde style—if such it may be called—that characterized the work of a number of leading American architects during the decade from about 1868 to 1878. It was an experimental style that aimed at originality by mixing together elements of the English High Victorian Gothic, and the French néo-grec and Second Empire. Sometimes the results were more English, at other times more French, but more often than not they were a curious and exciting mixture of the two.

This short-lived American style apparently was an attempt to break out of the straitjacket of the historic styles, at least in their more scholarly and archeological aspects, and to produce a more inventive and creative mode of architectural design, though one that did not entirely discard the authority of the historic styles. Certainly the best-known architect to work in the style was the New Yorker Richard Morris Hunt. Less well known was his pupil, the Philadelphia architect Frank Furness. In Hunt's work, the mixed avant-garde style may be traced back at least to his Presbyterian Hospital (New York), begun in 1868. After that, he developed the style in such works as the Stuyvesant Apartments (New York, 1869–1870); the Osborne and Sturgis Houses (New York, 1869–1870); the Martin Brimmer Houses (Boston, 1869–1870); Chateau-sur-Mer (Newport, Rhode Island, 1869–1873); Stevens House (New York, 1870–1872); Lenox Library (New York, 1870–1877), Marshall Field House (Chicago, 1871–1873); Delaware and Hudson Canal Company (New York, 1873–1876), Tribune Building (New York, 1873–1876) and the Lenox Library (Princeton, New Jersey, 1876–1879). As for Furness, his best-known buildings in the style were all erected in Philadelphia: The Pennsylvania Academy of Fine Arts (1871–1876); Guarantee Trust Building (1873–1875); Thomas Hockley House (1875–1876); Centennial National Bank (1876), and Provident Life Building (1876–1879).

Because this avant-garde style had a limited appeal beyond New York and Philadelphia in the 1870s, Edelmann and Sullivan could have known and studied it in publications and midwestern examples. Indeed, an important specimen of the style, the Marshall Field House by Richard Morris Hunt, was already standing on Prairie Avenue when Sullivan and Edelmann first met in 1873. But their contact with the style need not have been limited to the Midwest, for New York and Philadelphia were only an overnight train ride away. In fact, we know absolutely that Sullivan visited Hunt's office in New York in 1873 when traveling to Philadelphia, and again in 1874 on his way to France. And of course, Sullivan was actually working for Furness during the summer and autumn of 1873 when the Pennsylvania Academy of Fine Arts was under construction and the Guarantee Trust Building projected.

Between 1883 and 1887, Sullivan's architecture became more varied than it had been in the early 1880s by virtue of stylistic quotations from the popular styles of the day. In two important commercial buildings in Chicago, the Troescher and Ryerson of 1884, Sullivan seemed to be trying to carry forward into a style more his own the positive attributes of his early commercial structures,

Sullivan.
Jewelers' Building.
Chicago.
1881–1882

Sullivan.
Rothschild Store.
Chicago.
1881

Sullivan.
Guaranty Building (with
Adler).
Buffalo, New York.
1894–1896

especially the Rothschild Store of 1881. Both buildings, however, were also characterized by a decorative richness that may be traced to Richardsonian (see H. H. RICHARDSON) Romanesque and Queen Anne sources. These references appeared in the quarry-faced stone arches of the Troescher and the balusterlike top floor columns of the Ryerson, and in the elaborate skylines with top floors accentuated horizontally by a rhythm of colonnettes and narrow windows in both of them. Otherwise, Sullivan's buildings were usually presented as an inventive combination of elements borrowed from the up-to-date styles of the time, especially the Romanesque, Queen Anne, and Châteauesque.

Perhaps the best illustration of Sullivan's in-

ability to find a point on which to focus in pursuing his ambition of a personal style is seen in the design he prepared during the late summer of 1886 for the Auditorium Building. To accompany its basic rectangular configuration, already established at that early date, Sullivan proposed a mixture of Romanesque arcades, Queen Anne oriels and turrets, and Châteauesque roofs, spires, and dormers. Sullivan's failure to gain approval of his eclectic design precipitated a crisis that finally forced him to focus on the essentials of his art and thus to work his way out of the creative impass that had resulted from his eclectic and indecisive approach to design. The catalyst was certainly H. H. Richardson and more specifically his Marshall Field Wholesale Store then under construction in Chicago. What Sullivan learned from Richardson was not only how to organize a façade into a logical and integrated composition but, even more important, how to simplify the architectural problem into its constituent artistic parts and then to blend the parts into a unified and cohesive whole. The immediate result was the final design for the Auditorium Building of January 1887.

The long-range effect of this crucial experience was to enable Sullivan at last to glimpse the ray of light that between 1887 and 1890 was gradually to lead him to a mature personal style of architecture. Now began a three-year period of experimentation based on the principles of design implicit in Richardson's warehouse. What Sullivan did was to carry the logic and simplicity of Richardson's idea one step further. By turning to ashlar walls and thus eliminating Richardson's heavily textured surfaces, and by nearly doing away with architectural ornament, Sullivan was able to "concentrate acutely upon the production of buildings well formed and comely in the nude." And comely in the nude they were. In the severely simple Ryerson Tomb (designed in November 1887), Sullivan began to explore the "limitations as well as great value of unadorned masses." His exploration of this theme continued with the Walker Warehouse (1888–1889), the Falkenau Flats (1888), the Chicago Cold Storage Exchange (1890–1891), Kehilath Anshe Ma'ariv (1890–1891), the Seattle Opera House project (1890), and the Dooly Block in Salt Lake City (1890–1891). Of course Sullivan's progress was not so unitary as this list would suggest and there were false starts and dead ends: the Standard Club (Chicago, 1887–1889), Pueblo Opera House (Colorado, 1888–1890), the Jewish Training School (Chicago, 1889–1890), and Hotel Ontario (projected for Salt Lake City, Utah, 1890). Nonetheless, there was in the more simplified of Sullivan's buildings of this period the clear working out of a theme.

The decisive change marking the maturity of Sullivan's architecture occurred in 1890 when he designed the Getty Tomb. It was then that Sullivan, having finally discerned "the limitations . . . of unadorned masses," returned to an ornamented architecture by applying to the stone cube of this tomb "a virile and synthetic scheme of ornamentation." That ornament, now the eloquent expression of a sophisticated, mature, and personal mode of decoration, when added to the restrained masses of the Getty Tomb, resulted in the integrated original style that Sullivan had sought for so long.

The next building of significance in which Sullivan again overlaid his geometry of mass with the smile of ornament was the Wainwright Building in St. Louis (1890–1891) which, like the Getty Tomb, was essentially a cube. But there the comparison stops, for the Wainwright was many times larger than the tomb and belonged to a new building type that constituted the design challenge of the age, the skyscraper. Yet, in spite of the considerable differences between tomb and tall office building, Sullivan designed each in terms of his mature style of architecture and ornament, a style that, in being largely independent of the historic styles for inspiration, was not only original but modern.

During the 1890s, Sullivan modulated and expanded but never essentially altered the style he announced in the Getty Tomb and Wainwright Building. For reasons known only to himself, Sullivan occasionally referred to the historic styles in his modern work of the 1890s in such places as the Renaissance-inspired cupola of the Schiller Building (Chicago, 1891–1892) and the side entrance of the Chicago Stock Exchange Building (1893–1894), to mention but two examples. Yet for Sullivan to have recalled historic prototypes here and there in a body of work that after 1890 was largely independent of the historic styles is hardly sufficient reason to impugn in the slightest the overall achievement of a man who singlehandedly created the first sustained modern style of architecture in America. Even Sullivan's famous pupil, Frank Lloyd Wright, was not able all at once to free his own work completely of historic references even though he had Sullivan's foundations on which to build.

Sullivan's modern buildings of the 1890s are best examined in two groups: low structures and tall buildings. In one way, the low buildings are the more interesting as they argue effectively against the idea that Sullivan's modern style was invented for and is meaningful only in connection with tall commercial buildings. That Sullivan's new style with its geometrically controlled ornamented masses had universal applicability to all

Sullivan.
Auditorium Building (with
Adler).
Chicago.
1887–1890

Sullivan.
Stock Exchange (with
Adler).
Chicago.
1893–1894

Sullivan.
Saint Nicholas Hotel (with
Adler).
St. Louis, Missouri.
1892–1894

Sullivan.
Tall Building Project (with
  Adler; never built).
St. Louis, Missouri.
1893?

Sullivan during the 1890s furnish sufficient evidence by which to distinguish four successive phases of stylistic evolution. To identify these stages of artistic development is not merely to perform an academic exercise; to do so is to contradict the claim that Sullivan's contribution to the aesthetics of tall building design was simply one of making such buildings look tall or, as he put it in "The Tall Office Building Artistically Considered," to make each of them "a proud and soaring thing, rising in sheer exultation . . . from bottom to top . . . without a single dissenting line" (1896, reprinted in [1901–1902] 1918, p. 206).

Writers on architecture most often concentrate on Sullivan's tall buildings of the first phase (1890–1892) which includes the Wainwright Building, Schiller Building, Fraternity Temple project (Chicago, 1891), and Union Trust (St. Louis, 1892–1893), and the third phase (1895–1897) in which we find the Guaranty Building (Buffalo, New York, 1894–1896), two tall building projects for St. Louis (1895, 1896), and the Bayard Building (New York, 1897–1898). All seem to fit the paradigm of accentuated height.

But in the tall buildings of the second (1893–1894) and fourth phases (1898–1903), Sullivan chose instead to emphasize the horizontal character of the structural opening in the metal frame. The best-known building of this type is the Schlesinger & Mayer Department Store (Chicago, 1898–1903) which belongs to the fourth phase. But the Chicago Stock Exchange (1893–1894), a product of phase two, was fenestrated in a similar manner, not often noticed because of its vertically oriented bay windows (but see Morrison, 1935, pp. 170–171).

There are two projects which can be firmly dated to 1893–1894 by their ornamental details that have the same fenestration as the Stock Exchange without its misleading bay windows. The most interesting of them, which was proposed to stand next to Adler and Sullivan's Union Trust

building types of an ornamental character is obvious from such splendid low-rise designs of the 1890s as the Charnley House (not solely the product of Frank Lloyd Wright despite assertions to the contrary, 1890–1891), the Albert Sullivan House (1891–1892), and the Transportation Building (1891–1893), all in Chicago, and the Wainwright Tomb (1891–1892) and Coliseum project (1897) in St. Louis, Missouri.

The large number of tall buildings designed by

Sullivan.
Union Trust Building
  (with Adler).
St. Louis, Missouri.
1892–1893

Sullivan.
Union Trust Building
  (with Adler).
St. Louis, Missouri.
1892–1893

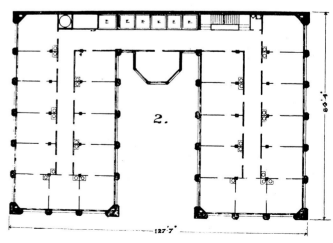

Building of 1892–1893 in St. Louis, is particularly revealing. Its general shape, a severe rectangular solid with walls treated as flat planes, serves to emphasize the abstract geometry of massing that underlay Sullivan's modern style of the 1890s. Its fenestration, consisting of thirteen floors of paired sash windows set in unmolded openings that accentuate the horizontal character of the metal frame, is full of dissenting lines. Its contrast with the more plastically conceived, vertically oriented surfaces of the Union Trust Building which appears in the same rendering is striking indeed.

If Sullivan, therefore, did not provide a consistent formula for organizing the multistoried tall building into a proud and soaring thing, what was it exactly that he did to warrant the judgment of Morrison and others that he "gave definitive artistic form, for the first time, to the high building" (Morrison, 1935, p. 140)? What Sullivan really did was to demonstrate how, by abandoning the historic styles and their attendant proportional systems, the architect could give to the skyscraper an aesthetic unity or oneness that up to that time tall buildings largely had lacked.

When confronted with the problem of the tall building in the 1870s and 1880s, most architects subdivided their designs vertically into horizontal units. They did so in order to approximate in each stage the proportions associated with the classic styles of architecture, proportions originally worked out for buildings that were wider than they were high, buildings that employed the orders of architecture. Now, in 1890, at the very beginning of Adler and Sullivan's skyscraper period, the designing partner succeeded in giving visual unity to the Wainwright Building, erected in St. Louis, Missouri, in 1891. There, Sullivan carried broad corner piers straight up from street to entablature in order to provide strong vertical accents at the edges. He pulled the building together forcefully at the top by way of a deeply textured entablature and projecting cornice. At the base he further integrated the design by means of two floors of ashlar stone which were accentuated hori-

Sullivan.
Wainwright Building
*   (with Adler).*
Chicago.
1890–1891

zontally, first by the slow and steady rhythms of the shop windows and entrances, and then by the more rapid rhythms of the smaller windows of the second story. Finally, at the center of each façade Sullivan wove together narrow, smooth-surfaced, vertically oriented piers and broader, heavily textured spandrels into a tight rectilinear pattern that framed the windows. The total effect was visual integration and aesthetic unity. What Sullivan thus proposed in the Wainwright and elaborated in subsequent tall buildings was a general principle for reuniting the separate parts of the tall building, thereby making the skyscraper appear to be what in fact it was, a single structure. What he did not propose was a formula in any sense of the word. That much is clear from the tall buildings by Sullivan that followed the Wainwright, no two of which are exactly alike, but all of which are integrated designs, unified and whole.

Because of events that Sullivan was unable to control, his work of the twentieth century seems more like an afterglow than an unerring progression toward a well-defined goal. His American colleagues were then mostly marching to the beat of a different drummer, while the European moderns, especially the Austrians and Germans, were taking the new architecture in a direction of which Sullivan surely would have disapproved had he known about it.

This does not mean, however, that Sullivan's late work is without interest or value. Quite the opposite. Even though his gemlike banks and other buildings of these years no longer belonged to the mainstream of design either in America or the rest of the Western world in the way that his work had belonged before 1900, these works are important for a number of reasons. For one thing, they demonstrate that Sullivan's ornamented mod-

ern style was susceptible to internal evolution. Thus, had there been a demand for Sullivan's kind of architecture and had he produced more students, it is likely that modern styles derived from Sullivan's initial inspiration of the 1890s would still be alive in America today. Indeed, a variation of Sullivan's ornamented modern style was created by his best-known student, Frank Lloyd Wright, who carried it forward with modulation and vigor into the 1950s.

The late buildings are also precious as elegant and colorful works of art produced by a man who was significant not only as an innovator and teacher but also as an artist of impressive depth and imagination. When all of Sullivan's more famous earlier buildings have been removed from the large metropolitan centers of American cities, it will be especially to the rich and inspiring prairie banks that future generations will have to turn in order to experience first-hand the visual and spiritual realities of the art of America's first modern architect.

PAUL E. SPRAGUE

Sullivan.
National Farmers' Bank.
Owatonna, Minnesota.
1906–1908

WORKS

*1880–1881, Borden Block; *1880–1881, John Borden House; *1881, Rothschild Store; Chicago. *1881–1882, Academy of Music, Kalamazoo, Mich. 1881–1882, Jewelers' Building; *1881–1883, Revell Building; *1882, Charles Kimball House; *1882, Rosenfeld Building II; *1882, Marx Wineman House; *1882–1883, Rothschild Flats; 1883, Ann Halsted House; 1883, Kaufman Store and Flats; *1883–1884, Blumenfeld Flats; *1883–1885, McVicker's Theater (remodeling I); *1884, Martin Barbe House; 1884, Ann Halsted Flats; *1884, Knisely Building; *1884, Rubin Rubel House; *1884, Charles Schwab House; *1884, Morris Selz House; *1884, Abraham Strauss House; *1884–1885, Ryerson Building; *1884–1885, Scoville Building; *1884–1885, Troescher Building, *1885, Chicago Opera Festival Auditorium; *1885, Benjamin Lindauer House; *1885–1886, Zion Temple; 1886, Joseph Diemel House; *1886, Hugo Goodman House; *1886, West Chicago Club; Chicago. 1886–1887, Deussenberg Block, Kalamazoo, Mich. 1887, Dexter Building; 1887–1889, Ryerson Tomb; *1887–1889, Standard Club; 1887–1890, Auditorium Building; *1888, Falkenau Flats; *1888–1889, Walker Warehouse; Chicago. *1888–1890, Opera House Block, Pueblo, Colo. *1889–1890, Jewish Training School; 1890, Auditorium Banquet Hall; 1890, Getty Tomb; 1890–1891, James Charnley House (with Frank Lloyd Wright); Chicago. *1890–1891, Chicago Cold Storage Exchange Warehouse. *1890–1891, Dooly Block, Salt Lake City, Utah. 1890–1891, Kehilath Anshe Ma'ariv Synagogue; *1890–1891, McVicker's Theater (remodeling II); Chicago. 1890–1891, Wainwright Building, St. Louis, Mo. *1891–1892, Schiller Building; *1891–1892, Albert Sullivan House; *1891–1893, Transportation Building; Chicago. 1891–1892, Wainwright Tomb, St. Louis, Mo. *1892–1893, Meyer Building, Chicago.

1892–1893, Union Trust Building; *1892–1894, St. Nicholas Hotel; St. Louis, Mo. *1893–1894, Stock Exchange, Chicago. 1894–1896, Guaranty Building, Buffalo, N.Y. 1897–1898, Bayard Building, New York. 1898–1899, Gage Building (façade); 1898–1903, Schlesinger & Mayer Department Store; Chicago. 1906–1908, National Farmers' Bank, Owatonna, Minn. *1908–1909, Henry Babson House, Riverside, Ill. 1909–1910, Harold Bradley House, Madison, Wis. 1910–1911, People's Savings Bank; 1910–1914, Saint Paul's Methodist Episcopal Church; Cedar Rapids, Iowa. 1911–1914, Van Allen Department Store, Clinton, Iowa. 1913–1914, Merchants' National Bank, Grinnell, Iowa. 1916–1918, People's Savings & Loan Association Bank, Sidney, Ohio. 1919, Farmers' and Merchants' Union Bank, Columbus, Wis. 1922, Krause Music Store (façade), Chicago.

BIBLIOGRAPHY

ADAMS, RICHARD 1957 "Architecture and the Romantic Tradition: Coleridge to Wright." *American Quarterly* 9:46–52.

ADLER, DANKMAR 1892 "Light in Tall Office Buildings." *Engineering Magazine* 4:171–186.

BUSH-BROWN, ALBERT 1960 *Louis Sullivan.* New York: Braziller.

COLLINS, PETER 1965 *Changing Ideals in Modern Architecture: 1750–1950.* Montreal: McGill University Press; London: Faber.

CONDIT, CARL 1952 *The Rise of the Skyscraper.* University of Chicago Press.

CONDIT, CARL 1964 *The Chicago School of Architecture.* University of Chicago Press.

CONNELY, WILLARD 1960 *Louis Sullivan as He Lived.* New York: Horizon.

CROOK, DAVID 1967 "Louis Sullivan and the Golden Doorway." *Journal of the Society of Architectural Historians* 26, no. 4:250–258.

DUNCAN, HUGH 1965 *Culture and Democracy.* Totawa, N.J.: Bedminster.

EGBERT, DONALD DREW (1950)1956 "The Idea of Organic Expression and American Architecture." Pages 336–396 in Stow Persons (editor), *Evolutionary Thought in America.* New Haven: Yale University Press.

EGBERT, DONALD, and SPRAGUE, PAUL 1966 "In Search of John Edelmann." *Journal of the American Institute of Architects* 45, Feb.:35–41.

GEBHARD, DAVID 1957 "William Gray Purcell and George Grant Elmslie and the Early Progressive Movement in American Architecture from 1900 to 1920." Unpublished Ph.D. dissertation, University of Minnesota, Minneapolis.

HITCHCOCK, H. R. (1942)1973 *In the Nature of Materials: The Buildings of Frank Lloyd Wright, 1887–1941.* Reprint. New York: Da Capo.

HOFFMANN, DONALD 1967 "The Brief Career of a Sullivan Apprentice: Parker N. Berry." *Prairie School Review* 4, no. 1:7–15.

JORDY, WILLIAM 1972 *Progressive and Academic Ideals at the Turn of the Twentieth Century.* Volume 3 in *American Buildings and Their Architects.* Garden City,
N.Y.: Doubleday.

KAUFMANN, EDGAR JR. (editor) 1956 *Louis Sullivan and the Architecture of Free Enterprise.* Art Institute of Chicago.

KIMBALL, FISKE 1925 "Louis Sullivan: An Old Master." *Architectural Record* 57:289–304.

MANSON, GRANT 1955 "Sullivan and Wright: An Uneasy Union of Celts." *Architectural Review* 118:297–300.

MANSON, GRANT 1958 *Frank Lloyd Wright to 1910.* New York: Reinhold.

MENOCAL, NARCISO 1981 *Architecture as Nature: The Transcendentalist Idea of Louis Sullivan.* Madison: University of Wisconsin Press.

MORRISON, HUGH (1935)1962 *Louis Sullivan: Prophet of Modern Architecture.* Reprint. New York: Norton.

MUMFORD, LEWIS (1931)1955 *The Brown Decades.* 2d ed., rev. New York: Dover.

NICKEL, RICHARD 1957 "A Photographic Documentation of the Architecture of Adler and Sullivan." Unpublished M.A. thesis, Illinois Institute of Technology, Chicago.

PAUL, SHERMAN 1962 *Louis Sullivan: An Architect in American Thought.* Englewood Cliffs, N.J.: Prentice-Hall.

SCHUYLER, MONTGOMERY 1961 *American Architecture and Other Writings.* Edited by William Jordy and Ralph Coe. Cambridge, Mass.: Harvard University Press.

SEVERENS, KENNETH 1975 "The Reunion of Louis Sullivan and Frank Lloyd Wright." *Prairie School Review* 12, no. 3:5–21.

SPRAGUE, PAUL 1968 "The Architectural Ornament of Louis Sullivan and His Chief Draftsmen." Unpublished Ph.D. dissertation, Princeton University, N.J.

SPRAGUE, PAUL 1979 *The Drawings of Louis Henry Sullivan.* N.J.: Princeton University Press.

SULLIVAN, LOUIS 1892 "Ornament in Architecture." *Engineering Magazine* 3:633–644.

SULLIVAN, LOUIS 1894 "Emotional Architecture as Compared with Intellectual: A Study in Objective and Subjective." *Inland Architect* 24, no. 4:32–34.

SULLIVAN, LOUIS 1896 "The Tall Office Building Artistically Considered." *Lippincott's Magazine* 57:403–409.

SULLIVAN, LOUIS 1901–1902 "Kindergarten Chats." *Interstate Architect* nos. 2–3.

SULLIVAN, LOUIS (1924a)1956 *The Autobiography of an Idea.* Reprint. New York: Dover.

SULLIVAN, LOUIS (1924b)1967 *A System of Architectural Ornament According to a Philosophy of Man's Powers.* Reprint. New York: Eakins.

SULLIVAN, LOUIS (1934)1980 *Kindergarten Chats (revised 1918) and Other Writings.* Edited by Isabella Athey. Reprint. New York: Dover.

TSELOS, DIMITRI 1967 "The Chicago Fair and the Myth of the 'Lost Cause'." *Journal of the Society of Architectural Historians* 26:259–268.

TURAK, THEODORE 1974 "French and English Sources of Sullivan's Ornament and Doctrine." *Prairie School Review* 11, no. 4:5–30.

WEISMAN, WINSTON 1961 "Philadelphia Function-

alism and Sullivan." *Journal of the Society of Architectural Historians* 20, no. 4:3–19.
WEINGARDEN, LAUREN 1980 "Louis H. Sullivan: Investigation of a Second French Connection." *Journal of the Society of Architectural Historians* 39:297–303.
WRIGHT, FRANK LLOYD (1942)1977 *An Autobiography*. Rev. ed. New York: Duell.
WRIGHT, FRANK LLOYD (1949)1971 *Genius and the Mobocracy*. New York: Horizon.

SUNDAHL, ESKIL

Eskil Sundahl (1890–1974), a Swedish architect, was educated at the Royal Institute of Technology and at Royal Academy of Arts in Stockholm. He was soon employed by his teacher ERIK LALLERSTEDT. Around 1920 he started his own practice, and among his first independent works there are some fine examples of Swedish classicism of the 1920s. In 1924, his office was assimilated with the Swedish Cooperative Union, which now began to expand rapidly with building projects such as shops, different kinds of food factories and warehouses, dwellings for workers on Kvarnholmen and at Gustavsberg outside Stockholm, and so on. Famous is the Katarina Elevator with two bridges and a roof terrace on the office building of the Cooperative Union at Slussen, Stockholm (1936), a symbol of Swedish Functionalism. The Architects' Office of the Cooperative Union (c.1926) early adapted the ideas of the Bauhaus and LE CORBUSIER. Sundahl and several of his collaborators were involved in the Stockholm Exhibition of 1930, and in 1931 Sundahl was one of the authors of the functionalist polemical pamphlet "acceptera." The Architects' Office of the Cooperative Union, of which Sundahl was the leader until 1958, was a kind of architects' collective which soon became the biggest architects' office in Sweden, with seventy collaborators in 1935.

FREDRIC BEDOIRE

BIBLIOGRAPHY
RÅBERG, PER G. 1972 *Funktionalistiskt genombrott*. Stockholm: Norstedt.
RUDBERG, EVA 1981 *Uno Åhrén: En föregångsman i 1900-talets arkitektur och samhällsplanering*. Stockholm: Statens nåd för byggnadsforskning.
Swedish Cooperative Union and Wholesale Society's Architect's Office: 1935–1949. 1949 Stockholm: Kooperativa förbundets bokförlag.

SUOMALAINEN, TIMO

Timo Suomalainen (1928–) and his brother Tuomo (1931–), who have been practicing together since 1956, immediately became internationally known for their Temppeliaukio Church in Helsinki (1960–1969). In order to preserve the open rock outcrop surrounded by apartment buildings, the church was cut into the bedrock. The walls are left unfinished, and the space is capped with a huge copper-and-glass dome. A sensitivity to the site is central in their works, nature being the inspiration for the richness of form, color, and sense of materials, they want to avoid conscious symbolism and rigid systems. In their architectural development the works of OSCAR NIEMEYER have been influential, and they have high regard for the works of FRANK LLOYD WRIGHT, LE CORBUSIER (his early works), EERO SAARINEN, and REIMA PIETILÄ.

PIRKKO-LIISA LOUHENJOKI

WORKS
1960–1969, Temppeliaukio Church; 1962–1967, Haaga Vocational School; Helsinki. 1964–1965, Ristiniemi Cemetery Chapel, Hamina, Finland. 1969–1971, Majakumpare Apartment House, Laurinlahti, Espoo, Finland. 1973–1976, Hotel Mesikämmen, Ähtäri, Finland. 1978–1979, Multipurpose Building for Wildlife Park, Ähtäri, Finland. 1976–1981, Espoonlahti Church, Kivenlahti, Espoo, Finland. 1979–1981, Gate Building, Wildlife Park, Ähtäri, Finland.

BIBLIOGRAPHY
"Haagan ammattikoulu Haaga vocational School." 1967 *Arkkitehti* 64, no. 12:34–37.
"Taivallahden Kirkko, Helsinki, Edesvikens Kyrka, Helsingfors' Taivallahden Church, Helsinki." 1970 *Arkkitehti* 67, no. 4:49–59.

SÜSSENGUTH, GEORG

Georg Süssenguth (1862–?) studied at the Technische Hochschule in Berlin-Charlottenburg and later became a professor there. In 1894, he established a partnership with Heinrich Reinhardt; together, they specialized in town halls and other government and municipal buildings. Their early works, executed in a rosy stone and highly decorated, were romantically medieval in appearance. In the Hamburg Railroad Station of 1906, however, their style changed, and their later buildings were marked by an absence of decoration and by a functional arrangement of spaces. Under the influence of PAUL MEBES and others, Reinhardt and Süssenguth's last works before World War I adopted a reduced and abstracted neoclassicism.

BARBARA MILLER LANE

WORKS
1896–1897, Town Hall, Steglitz, Berlin. 1898–1901,

Municipal Museum, Altona, Hamburg, Germany. 1899–1901, City Hall, Dessau, Germany. 1899–1905, Town Hall, Charlottenburg, Berlin. 1906, Railroad Station, Hamburg, Germany. 1910–1913, Town Hall, Spandau; 1911–1914, Reichsmarineamt; n.d., Church, Treptow; Berlin. n.d., High Schools, Mariendorf, Germany. n.d., Housing Developments; n.d., School; Berlin. n.d., Town Hall, Köthen, Germany. n.d., Town Hall, Treptow, Berlin.

BIBLIOGRAPHY

Architekten und Ingenieur-Verein (editors) 1964–1980 *Berlin und seine Bauten.* 11 vols. Berlin: Ernst.

"Der Entwurf für das neue Rathaus in Dessau." 1898 *Zentralblatt der Bauverwaltung* 18:54–55.

"Hauptbahnhof Hamburg." 1910 *Berliner Architekturwelt* 12:130–140.

LANE, BARBARA MILLER 1981 "Government Buildings in European Capitals, 1870–1914." In Hans J. Teuteberg (editor), *Urbanisierung im 19. und 20. Jahrhundert: Historische und geographische Aspektae.* Cologne, Germany, and Vienna: Böhlau.

"Das Rathaus in Spandau." 1913 *Zentralblatt der Bauverwaltung* 33:701–705, 710–711, 713, 717–720.

THIERBACH, HANS 1914 "Neue Bauten von Reinhardt & Süssenguth." *Berliner Architekturwelt* 16:479–518.

Wasmuths Monatshefte für Baukunst und Städtebau 1914–1915 1:93.

"Der Wettbewerb um den Entwurf für das Empfangsgebäude auf dem neuen Hauptbahnhofe in Hamburg." 1901 *Zentralblatt der Bauverwaltung* 21:53–55, 65–68.

SWAN, ABRAHAM

Abraham Swan (18th century) was a carpenter and joiner, but he became influential as an architectural compiler whose architecture, reflected in his books, is Palladian laced with rococo decoration. His principal books were *The British Architect* (1745) and *A Collection of Designs in Architecture* (1757), the former exerting a considerable influence in the United States due to editions published there.

JOHN HARRIS

BIBLIOGRAPHY

SWAN, ABRAHAM (1745)1967 *The British Architect.* Reprint of 1758 ed. New York: Da Capo.

SWAN, ABRAHAM 1757 *A Collection of Designs in Architecture Containing New 1757 Plans and Elevations of Houses, for General Use.* London: The author.

SWART, PIETER DE

Pieter de Swart (1709?–1772) received his architectural training from JACQUES FRANÇOIS BLONDEL in Paris in the rococo style of Louis XV. From 1747 to 1751, he worked for Stadtholder William IV on the interior of the Royal Palace *Huis ten Bosch,* The Hague, Netherlands.

After William's death in 1751, de Swart designed several delicate mansions with sandstone façades in The Hague. Examples are the house at 14–16 Vijverberg (1755–1756), with rococo interior decorations, and the Palace Van Nassau Weilburg (1767–1774), now the Royal Theater, with a curving front, a transition to the Louis XVI style.

MARIET J. H. WILLINGE

WORKS

1747–1751, Ten Bosch House (interiors); 1755–1756, 14–16 Lange Vijverberg; 1759–1761, Lutheran Church (façade); The Hague. 1760, Town Hall (interior), Leeuwarden, Netherlands. 1760–1764, Anthony Patras House (now the Palace Lange Voorhout); 1761, Huguetan House (wings), Lange Voorhout; 1767–1774, Karl van Nassau Weilburg Palace (now the Royal Theater); The Hague. 1768–1769, Government House, 's-Hertogenbosch, Netherlands. *1768–1772, Delftse Poort, Rotterdam, Netherlands.

BIBLIOGRAPHY

OZINGA, M. D. 1936 "Pieter de Swart: Hofarchitect van Prins Willem IV." *Bulletin Nederlandse Oucheidkundige Bond* 1939:124–143.

OZINGA, M. D. 1939 "Pieter de Swart: Architect der Stadhouderlijke Familie en zijn school." *Bulletin Nederlandse Oudheidkundige Bond* 1939:99–123.

ROSENBERG, JAKOB; SLIVE, SEYMOUR; and KUILE, E. H. TER (1966)1972 *Dutch Art and Architecture: 1600–1800.* Rev. ed. Harmondsworth, England: Penguin.

SWARTWOUT, EGERTON

Born in New York, Egerton Swartwout (1872–1944) was graduated from Yale University in 1891. He subsequently entered the firm of McKIM, MEAD, AND WHITE, where he remained until 1901 when he formed a partnership with Evarts Tracy. In conjunction with Tracy, Swartwout designed the Missouri Capitol (1913), Jefferson City, the Mary Baker Eddy Memorial (1917), Boston, Massachusetts, and the Elks' Memorial Building (1922), Chicago.

STEVEN McLEOD BEDFORD

WORKS

1913, Missouri Capitol (with Evarts Tracy), Jefferson City. 1917, Mary Baker Eddy Memorial (with Tracy), Boston. 1922, Elk's Memorial Building (with Tracy), Chicago. 1923, United States Post Office, Denver, Colo. 1929, Bailey Memorial Fountain, Brooklyn, N.Y.

BIBLIOGRAPHY

SWARTWOUT, EGERTON 1924 "Plans in Competition and in Reality." *American Architect* 126:413–421.

SWIERCZYŃSKI, RUDOLF

Rudolf Swierczyński (1887–1943) studied architecture in Warsaw; Darmstadt, Germany; and Dresden, Germany. In his early career, his forms were inspired by local historic architecture. He designed most of his works between 1915 and 1925 in this so-called Polish Cottage style. Features of old country houses were applied indiscriminately to less appropriate structures. After 1925, Swierczyński began to accept more modern forms of architectural expression, yet he never fully adopted the International style.

Through his teaching at the Technical University of Warsaw, he strongly influenced the next generation of Polish architects who practiced between 1950 and 1970.

LECH KŁOSIEWICZ

WORKS

1921–1925, Housing Estate, Zoliborz; 1928, Ministry of Transportation Building; 1929, Ministry of Foreign Affairs Building; 1936, General Patent Office; Warsaw.

BIBLIOGRAPHY

Warsaw School of Architecture: 1915–1965. 1967 Warsaw: P.W.N.

SWITZER, STEPHEN

Although trained in French formal garden design under GEORGE LONDON and HENRY WISE, Stephen Switzer (1682–1745) became a major theorist and popularizer of the new English landscape garden ideas. Influenced by the writings of Alexander Pope and Joseph Addison, he criticized the expense and excessive formality of the French style. As a transitional figure, he still advocated geometrical designs near the house and a straight main axis throughout the garden. But beyond that, he required winding paths through informal wildernesses, with caves, cascades, and grottoes. As he wrote in his important *Ichnographia Rustica,* the "natural gardener" must "submit to Nature, and not Nature to his Design"; "all the adjacent Country [should] be laid open to View" so that "a whole Estate will appear as one great Garden" (vol. 2, p. 201; vol. 1, p. xviii; vol. 3, p. vi).

RICHARD O. SWAIN

BIBLIOGRAPHY

BROGDEN, WILLIAM A. 1974 "Stephen Switzer: 'La Grand Manier.'" In Peter Willis (editor), *Furor Hortensis: Essays on the History of the English Landscape Garden in Memory of H. F. Clark.* Edinburgh: Elysium.

HUNT, JOHN DIXON, and WILLIS, PETER (editors) (1975)1976 *The Genius of the Place: The English Landscape Garden, 1620–1820.* New York: Harper.

HUSSEY, CHRISTOPHER 1967 *English Gardens and Landscapes, 1700–1750.* London: Country Life; New York: Funk & Wagnalls.

PEVSNER, NIKOLAUS 1968 Volume 1 in *Studies in Art, Architecture, and Design.* New York: Walker.

SWITZER, STEPHEN (1718)1980 *Ichnographia Rustica: Or, the Nobleman, Gentleman and Gardener's Recreation.* Reprint. New York: Garland. The quotations in the text are from the second edition, published in 1742.

SYRKUS, HELENA, and SYRKUS, SZYMON

Szymon Syrkus (1893–1964), born in Warsaw, studied art and architecture at the Technische Hochschule in Vienna (1911–1912), the Academy of Fine Art in Cracow, Poland (1918–1920), the Ecole des Beaux-Arts and the Academie Colarossi (1923–1924) in Paris, and elsewhere (1915–1922). He served in the Polish army for two years as a technical engineer (1915–1917) and was interned at Auschwitz during World War II.

In 1926, Syrkus married Helena Niemirowska (1900–), born in Warsaw. She studied architecture at the Institute of Technology at Warsaw (1918–1923) and philosophy and humanities at the University of Warsaw (1923–1925). Their mutual dedication to avant-garde notions of social housing resulted in a long partnership that ended only with the death of Szymon in 1964.

Associating themselves with a group of radical Modernists, they collaborated on the publication of *Praesons,* a journal that explored the theories of functionalist architecture. They represented the Polish branch of the Congrès Internationaux d'Architecture Moderne (CIAM) from 1928 to 1956 and worked steadily to develop and realize the assertions of the Athens Charter. They believed that architecture must be combined with its environment and with all the benefits of modern industry, if it is to meet social demands and adapt to change. Szymon and Helena Syrkus sought to develop a rational framework for urban planning, one that would maximize the efficiency of production and standardize design according to the nature of the city's functions.

The Syrkuses, as members of the Praesons Design Team, were commissioned to design the Rakowiec Housing Development for the Warsaw Housing Cooperative in 1936. Their work, resulting in the development of a modular system that facilitated large-scale construction, served as the seminal project for the Pre-fabricated Slab Systems for Housing Units project of 1960.

In 1945, the Syrkuses produced plans for a "Socialist Warsaw," the result of their involvement in PAU (Underground Architecture and Town Planning Studio), of which they both held the position of chairperson during the Nazi occupation of Poland.

The Kolo Housing Development, built in Warsaw between 1947 and 1949, marked another important achievement; it was classified as a historic monument in 1978. The Syrkuses' housing theory was perhaps most clearly expressed in the Tatary Housing Development at Lublin in 1960.

LYNDA GREENBERG

WORKS

1929, Old People's Home, Kutno, Poland. 1934, Experimental Theater, for Irena Solska, Zoliborz, Warsaw. 1935, Association of Workers Housing Cooperative, Grudziadz, Poland. 1947–1949, Kolo Housing Development, Warsaw.

BIBLIOGRAPHY

MUMFORD, LEWIS 1938 *The Culture of Cities.* New York and London.

SARTORIS, ALBERTO 1932 *Gli elementi dell'architettura funzionale.* Milan.

SYRKUS, SZYMON 1927 "Debate on the Modern Theater." In *International Theatre Exhibition.* New York.

SYRKUS, SZYMON 1931 *Osiedie w Celle i w Kassel.* Katowice, Poland.

SYRKUS, SZYMON, and SYRKUS, HELENA 1932 "Production des Logements en Masse." *L'Architecture d'Aujourd'hui* 1.

SYRKUS, SZYMON, and SYRKUS, HELENA 1934 "Nuovo teorie di teatro." *Quadrante* 11.

SYRKUS, SZYMON, and SYRKUS, HELENA 1949 "Planning and Housing in Warsaw." *Architect's Yearbook.*

SYRKUS, SZYMON, and SYRKUS, HELENA 1959 "Sozialer Wohnungsbau und Baurationalisierung in Warshau: Wohnquartier Kolo." *Das Werk.*

TAIT, T. S.

T. S. Tait (1882–1954) studied at the Glascow School of Art (under CHARLES R. MACKINTOSH in 1897–1899 and 1907–1909). He was apprenticed to James Donald, ex-chief draftsman to ALEXANDER THOMSON, whose drawings he copied. In 1904, he became JOHN J. BURNET's personal draftsman, and his partner in 1918.

He worked on the Kodak House, London (1910) and the north wing of the British Museum, London (1914). Tait's Silver End (1926–1928), an estate village for Crittal Metal Windows, shows the influence of PETER BEHRENS's New Ways and W. M. DUDOK's Hilversum Town Hall.

ROSEMARY IND

WORKS

1910, Kodak House, Kingsway; 1914, British Museum (northwing); 1920–1925, Adelaide House, London Bridge; 1926, Church of Christ Scientist, Kensington Palace Gardens; London. 1926–1928, Silver End, near Braintree, Essex, England. 1930, House, Newbury, Berkshire, England. 1931, House, Aldbourne, Wiltshire, England. 1932–1938, Hospital for Infectious Diseases, Paisley, Renfrewshire, Scotland. 1933, Royal Masonic Hospital, Ravenscourt Park; 1933–1934, Curzon Cinema, Mayfair; 1935, German Hospital, Dalston; London. 1938, Glasgow Exhibition, Scotland. 1938, Saint Dunstan's Hospital for the Blind, Brighton, England. 1939, Saint Andrew's House, Edinburgh.

BIBLIOGRAPHY

REILLY, C. H. 1931 "Some Younger Architects of Today: Thomas Smith Tait." *Building* Oct.:444–450.
YOUNG, ANDREW MCLAREN, and DOAK, A. M. (editors) (1965)1977 *Glasgow at a Glance*. Rev. ed. London: Hale.

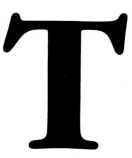

TAKEDA, GOICHI

Born in Fukuyama, Hiroshima Prefecture, Japan, and graduated from Tokyo University, Goichi Takeda (1872–1938) was appointed an assistant professor of architecture at Tokyo University at a young age. He went to Europe to study European architecture (1901–1903). After his return to Japan, he became the head of the Nagoya School of Technology. He was a member of the organizing committee of the department of architecture for Kyoto University and was appointed a professor of architecture when it was established in 1920. He was not interested in neoclassicism, but the late Art Nouveau and Secession movements in Europe influenced his design of the Fukushima House in 1905. He was, in addition, a pioneer of morphology as well as color theories. He had a wide range of interests in design, ranging from buildings, bridges, towns, furniture, craft work, to industrial production.

SAKA-E OHMI
*Translated from Japanese by
Bunji Kobayashi*

WORKS

1909, Memorial Library of Kyoto-fu; 1910, Kyoto Exhibition Hall of Merchandise; 1930, Research Institute of Eastern Culture (branch); Kyoto.

BIBLIOGRAPHY

TAKEDA, GOICHI 1900 "On the Appearance of a Building." *Journal of the Architectural Institute of Japan* June.
TAKEDA, GOICHI 1909 "Styles of Commercial Buildings Being Built in Tokyo." *Journal of the Architectural Institute of Japan* Aug.
TAKEDA, GOICHI 1911 "Architecture and Color." *Journal of the Architectural Institute of Japan* Apr.

TALENTI FAMILY

From obscure stylistic origins outside his native Florence, Francesco Talenti (1300?–1369?) rose to dominate mid-fourteenth century architecture by completing GIOTTO DI BONDONE's Campanile and building the nave of Florence Cathedral. Active as both an architect and a sculptor, he was documented as *capomaestro* of the enormous Duomo workshop from 1351 to 1364 and from 1366 to 1368. Francesco's personal style is seen in the upper stories of the Campanile, the piers, and gallery of the cathedral, while other construction during his tenure as *capomaestro* was subcontracted or the result of collaborative designs. His son, Simone di Francesco (1341?–1381?), assisted him in the cathedral workshop and developed a highly ornate style which spread into Florentine late Gothic civic architecture.

Francesco was first recorded in 1325 working as a low-paid master mason under the Sienese architect Nicola di Nuto at Orvieto Cathedral. The lack of any other documentation until 1351 means that his training can only be surmised from stylistic relationships in his later work. Francesco seems to have been deeply impressed by the Orvietan decorative taste. He transformed the complex, geometric motifs from the medium of Orvieto's Cosmati-type mosaic inlay into Tuscan marble incrustation and tracery. LORENZO MAITANI's façade portals at Orvieto, framed with multiple-threaded twisted columns with massive, rolling base moldings influenced Talenti's conception of the jambs of the Porta dei Cornacchini, the north side portal of Florence Cathedral built around 1355–1359. His vocabulary of moldings and cornices—decorated with double-leaf friezes, dentilation, beading, and egg-and-dart motifs—derives from Maitani's and Nuto's work. Talenti's window tracery, crocket, and finial motifs indicate an acquaintance with the Siena Baptistery façade (begun 1316) and the Siena Duomo Nuovo (begun 1339). On the basis of such comparisons, it seems that for almost twenty years Talenti worked in the ambient of lower Tuscany and Umbria.

Although not documented as chief architect of the Florentine *Opera del Duomo* until 1351, Francesco must have returned to Florence in the early 1340s because the bifora zone of the Campanile, certainly Francesco's design, was begun around 1343 after Andrea Pisano's (see PISANO FAMILY) dismissal as chief architect. The third level of the Campanile consists of two cubes pierced by elaborately decorated bifora windows, with the surrounding marble revetment echoing the proportions of the windows' balustrade, lancet, and gable. Talenti thus abandoned the modular grid system of the lower stories' revetment and loosened the marble decoration from its architectonic function. In toto, the bifora ornament produces a planar, silhouette effect, parallel to contemporary stylistic development in Sienese architecture. In 1351, Talenti advanced to the trifora section of which detailed documentation is preserved in the *Opera del Duomo* records. His trifora lunette, with star-patterned tracery enclosed by interlaced round and pointed arches, and the trefoil balustrade show increased tension in the overlapping planes and marked ambiguity in figure/field relationships. In 1353, Talenti also completed a wooden model of the bell tower which showed a tall spire capping the shaft, but this was never executed. The crowning balustrade, projecting forcefully on three tiers of consoles, was finished in 1358.

Talenti's achievements in the Duomo, which was begun in 1296 by ARNOLFO DI CAMBIO, are more controversial. In 1355, Francesco's church model which planned the form of the "chapels in the rear" and corrected the "defect of the windows" was accepted. In 1357, his pier model was chosen in a competition among several well-known masters including ORCAGNA. Recent excavation evidence suggests that Talenti changed the Arnolfian plan of the nave by designing three larger vaulted nave bays which interlocked with Arnolfo's already laid out east end. As these began to take shape directed by Talenti and a second co-chief architect, Giovanni di Lapo Ghini, the side aisles were heightened for the vaulting and the incrustation of the exterior side walls proceeded. (Scholars disagree concerning the height of the side wall incrustation before this time.) The side portals, neither one designed in a single campaign, owe their general shape to Talenti's work from 1355 to 1364. Whatever modifications he intended for Arnolfo's façade are uncertain since a drawing (Museo dell'Opera del Duomo, Florence) representing Talenti's façade in 1587 shows a jumble of incomplete structure and decoration. In the late 1350s, Talenti directed the numerous facets of both the Duomo and Campanile construction with consummate administrative skill but finally he lost his position as *capomaestro* to Ghini. Talenti returned to the *Opera* in 1366–1368 to design the cornice or narrow gallery beneath the vaults, thus putting the finishing touch on his nave design.

Simone di Francesco Talenti first appears in the Duomo documents in 1357 when he vowed to help finish the prototype capital for the nave piers without any payment. In the avid competition for a new design for the east end in 1366, Simone submitted a model which was not discussed seriously and not supported by his father. Simone continued working under his father's aegis until matriculating in the stonemason's guild in 1368, and he was probably responsible for some tracery and revetment designs on the cathedral's flanks as well as two apostle figures in a cycle of sculpture destined to replace the early fourteenth-century sculpture on the central portal of the façade. Simone's major work in the late 1360s was the ground floor arcade which closed in the church of Or San Michele. The lunette designs are based on Francesco's trifora, but here they are even more profusely decorated with dense textural effects. During his brief tenure as *capomaestro* of Florence Cathedral in 1377, his activity centered on sculptural decoration. Simultaneously, Simone was occupied with the most important civic architectural commission of the time, the Loggia dei Lanzi in Piazza della Signoria, Florence. Simone designed and erected the northeast corner pier which provided the prototype for the construction of the rest of the loggia by Benci di Cione and others. Simone's massive square pier with attached colonnettes, developed from pier types in Or San Michele and his father's Duomo pier, is less compact than earlier pier forms. The loosely bound moldings break up the verticality of the shaft at several stages, and miniature lions (a frequent motif in his work) decorate the base. This design shows an attempt to synthesize Sienese and Florentine ideas from mid-fourteenth-century architecture and create a new, distinctly late Trecento style.

KATHLEEN GILES ARTHUR

WORKS
FRANCESCO TALENTI

1343–1358, Campanile (bifora and trifora levels); 1355–1368, Florence Cathedral (nave), Florence.

SIMONE TALENTI

1366?, Church of Or San Michele (ground floor arcade); 1376–1379, Loggia dei Lanzi (with Benci di Cione and others); Florence.

BIBLIOGRAPHY

KIESOW, GOTTFRIED 1961 "Zur Baugeschichte des Florentiner Domes." *Mitteilungen des Kunsthistorischen Institutes in Florenz* 10:1–22.
KREYTENBERG, GERT 1974 *Der Dom zu Florenz.* Berlin: Mann.
KREYTENBERG, GERT 1977 "Tre cicli di Apostoli dell'antica facciata del Duomo fiorentino." *Antichita Viva* 16:13–39.
SAALMAN, HOWARD 1964 "Santa Maria del Fiore: 1294–1418." *Art Bulletin* 46:471–500.
TOKER, FRANKLIN K. D. 1978 "Florence Cathedral: The Design Stage." *Art Bulletin* 60:214–231.
TRACHTENBERG, MARVIN L. 1971 *The Campanile of Florence Cathedral: Giotto's Tower.* New York University Press.
VALENTINER, W. R. 1957 "Simone Talenti scultore." *Commentari* 8:235–243.
WEINBERGER, M. 1940–1941 "The First Façade of the Cathedral of Florence." *Journal of the Warburg and Courtauld Institutes* 4:67–79.
WHITE, JOHN 1966 *Art and Architecture in Italy: 1250–1400.* Baltimore: Penguin.

TALLMADGE, THOMAS EDDY

Thomas Eddy Tallmadge (1876–1940) designed domestic and ecclesiastic buildings, taught architectural history, and was active in the burgeoning preservation movement. He had a scholarly interest in American architectural history with special emphasis on developments in Chicago.

Tallmadge, born in Washington, in 1876, moved to Evanston, Illinois, with his family in 1881. In 1894, he enrolled in the architectural program at the Massachusetts Institute of Technology, taking his degree in 1898. He worked as a draftsman in the Chicago office of DANIEL H. BURNHAM and Company, then in 1905, persuaded another employee, Vernon Spencer Watson, to join him in independent practice.

The firm of Tallmadge and Watson designed suburban homes in the Prairie mode. Characteristic of their work was the presence of a historical reference, as in the Italianate Linthicum House (1907–1908) or the Tudor gables of the Condict House (1909), both in Evanston. By the mid-teens their work exhibited an incipient and increasing medievalism. The firm also built churches, beginning with the streamlined Gothic style of the First Methodist Episcopal Church of Evanston (1910) and culminating with the Federalist design of the First Congregational Church of Evanston (1927).

In 1936, with Watson's early retirement, the firm was dissolved. The following year, Tallmadge formed an association with William Alderman.

In a parallel career, Tallmadge taught at the Armour Institute in Chicago (now the Illinois Institute of Technology) from 1906 to 1926. His related publications included the landmark article "The 'Chicago School,'" (1908) and *The Story of Architecture in America* (1927), the first comprehensive work on the subject.

Tallmadge was accepted as a fellow of the American Institute of Architects in 1923 and received an honorary Master of Arts degree from Northwestern University in 1926. On January 1, 1940, Tallmadge was killed in a train wreck. His writings in progress remained unfinished. Friends in the architectural community published the fragmentary manuscript as *Architecture in Old Chicago* (1941), a final tribute to an architect of local significance and an historian of national repute.

DEBRA N. MANCOFF

WORKS

1906, Vernon S. Watson House, Oak Park, Ill. 1907-1908, John C. Linthicum House; 1908, Kretsinger House; Evanston, Ill. 1909, Gustavus Babson House, Oak Park, Ill. 1909, Wallace Condict House; 1910, First Methodist Episcopal Church; Evanston, Ill. 1910-1913, H. H. Rockwell House; 1912, Second Gustavus Babson House; 1915, J. W. Bingham House; Oak Park, Ill. 1922-1923, First Baptist Church Parish House, Evanston, Ill. 1926, North Congregational Church (now Dole Branch, Public Library), Oak Park, Ill. 1927, First Congregational Church, Evanston, Ill. 1928-1929, Louis Sullivan Tombstone, Graceland Cemetery, Chicago. 1931, First Methodist Episcopal Chapel, Evanston, Ill. *1933, Colonial Village, Century of Progress, Chicago. 1934-1940, Saint Mark's Parish House (not completed until 1945); 1938, Harry Paskind House; Evanston, Ill.

BIBLIOGRAPHY

BROOKS, HAROLD ALLEN 1976 *The Prairie School: Frank Lloyd Wright and His Midwest Contemporaries.* New York: Norton.

CONDIT, CARL W. 1964 *The Chicago School of Architecture: A History of Commercial and Public Building in the Chicago Area, 1875-1925.* University of Chicago Press.

MANCOFF, DEBRA N. 1978 "Thomas Eddy Tallmadge: Historian for the 'Chicago School.'" Unpublished M.A. thesis, Northwestern University, Evanston, Ill.

"Recent Work of Tallmadge and Watson." 1911 *House Beautiful* 29, no. 5:158-159.

TALLMADGE, THOMAS EDDY 1908 "The 'Chicago School.'" *Architectural Review* 15, no. 4:69-76.

TALLMADGE, THOMAS EDDY (1927)1936 *The Story of Architecture in America.* Rev. ed. New York: Norton.

TALLMADGE, THOMAS EDDY (1941)1975 *Architecture in Old Chicago.* University of Chicago Press.

"The Work of Tallmadge and Watson, Architects." 1915 *Western Architect* 22, July-Sept.:47-50.

TALMAN, JOHN

John Talman (1677-1726) was an architect *manqué* who never built anything, but whose designs are the most extraordinary Italian baroque inventions outside Italy. He added to the collection of drawings of his father, WILLIAM TALMAN, and achieved a reputation as an antiquarian early interested in Gothic architecture. He was the first director of the Society of Antiquaries in London.

JOHN HARRIS

TALMAN, WILLIAM

William Talman (1650-1719) was an example, not uncommon in the annals of English architecture, of a gentleman and man of means taking up the professional practice of designing. His father bequeathed London property to him in 1663, and in 1678 he obtained the sinecure of King's Waiter in the Port of London. His patron may have been the second Earl of Clarendon. How Talman received his training is unknown, but a study of his work would indicate some links with HUGH MAY, in particular his remodeling of the Upper Ward of Windsor Castle (1675-1684) and the building of Cassiobury Park, Hertfordshire (c.1677). The baroque planning and decoration of both buildings are reflected in Talman's own work more than in any other architect of the William III era. Talman was not, however, officially employed under May at Windsor. It is impossible to believe that he was announced to the architectural fraternity with the rebuilding of the south and east fronts of Chatsworth, Derbyshire (1687), for he must surely have performed before this, but only Stanstead Park, Sussex (1686), has any basis of secure attribution, and this is a very different sort of house, of his Uppark, Sussex, type (c.1690), derived from the red-brick, hipped-roof, WILLIAM SAMWELL-ROGER PRATT type of Restoration house. There is, however, Hackwood Park, Hampshire (1683), to consider, built for the first duke of Bolton. It was prophetic in both plan and decoration, with pairs of pavilions extending the ends of the main body of the house, each linked by colonnades, and with quadrant colonnades breaking forward from the front to offices flanking a courtyard. Elements of this plan appear in projects by Talman for a Trianon at Hampton Court (c.1700).

From Chatsworth on extends a majestic series

of country houses, additions, and installations. Chatsworth's south front heralded the advent of the baroque house clasped by a giant order. Inside, there appear suites of rooms in which the arts of painter as decorator of ceilings, carver, and sculptor are brought together in ensembles that owe much to May's work at Windsor Castle. From Chatsworth, Talman moved to the redecoration of the rooms at Burghley House, Northamptonshire (c.1688–1690), again with spectacular arrangements of painting and carving. In 1689, he built Swallowfield, Berkshire, for Lord Clarendon, and the surviving gateway there, once the porch of the house, reveals Talman's eclectic taste, for it is in a Milanese baroque style and may have been derived from engravings. There is no doubt at all that Talman possessed a huge library and collections of engravings and drawings, indeed, the nucleus of what became under his son John's (see JOHN TALMAN) aegis the celebrated Talman Collection that included all ANDREA PALLADIO's drawings. As far as can be discovered, William never traveled abroad, so his eclecticism and the astonishing variety of his building owes everything to his omnivorous reading.

He was not always able to execute what he proposed. For Kiveton Park, Yorkshire, for example, his first designs (c.1698) proposed a baroque plan that was certainly not carried out, and William III's Trianon would have been unique, not only as an example of Franco-Italianate baroque, but also for its unity of architecture and garden. He made many designs for Welbeck Abbey, Nottinghamshire, and for Houghton, Nottinghamshire, about 1703, and even if these were unexecuted, they are, in parts, prophetic of future planning, such as a main block linked at the corners to pavilions by quadrants. This eclectic baroque vein ran through the greenhouse at Castle Ashby, Northamptonshire (1695), probably the garden front of Dorchester House, Weybridge (c.1700), and Drayton Park, Northamptonshire, where Talman rebuilt the south courtyard front in 1702. This is most exquisite, and it reflects the style of one of the Trianon designs made by John Talman as an exercise. It is extraordinary how much of Talman's work has disappeared, but Dyrham Park, Gloucestershire (1698), survives. The east front here was built at the same time that a baroque, but whimsical garden was laid out by GEORGE LONDON.

Throughout the years of the Williamite court, London and Talman went together. It was London who first planned the great gardens of Castle Howard, Yorkshire, where Talman lost the commission to the emerging genius of JOHN VANBRUGH. It was London who laid out the spectacular gardens at Wanstead, Essex, and it is difficult not to attri-

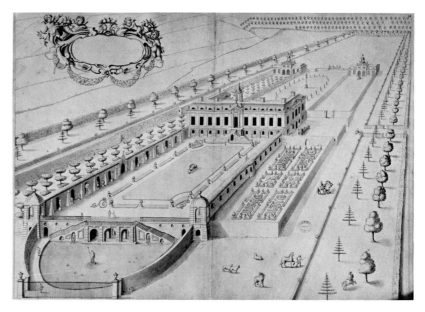

Talman.
Design for a Trianon At
Hampton Court.
Middlesex, England.
c.1700

bute the splendid architectural episodes in these to Talman.

In May 1689, Talman was appointed Comptroller of the works to King William III, an appointment that must have been supported by the evidence of considerable architectural expertise, for Talman was now second in command to CHRISTOPHER WREN. It is possible that Talman got the job through the earl of Portland, for he was Portland's Deputy as Superintendent of the Royal Gardens, a special post created for the earl, and Talman must have worked upon the earl's great country seat at Bulstrode Park, Buckinghamshire. Talman as Comptroller virtually had command of Hampton Court Palace, but the extent of his responsibility for designs is unclear. Most must obviously go to Wren, but Talman certainly completed the state apartments (1699–1702) and had charge of laying out the gardens from 1689. There was much rivalry between Talman and Wren, and however much an aficionado of Talman one is, he must be discredited for maligning his supervisor. Talman was an unpleasant character, haughty and imperious, aware of his station and probable wealth, and he had little truck with dukes and noblemen who might have wished him to kow-tow to them. For this reason, many buildings may have been designed by Talman that were built by others after his dismissal. This was certainly the case with Buckingham House, London, a most influential building carried out by William Winde from 1702. There are many buildings of extraordinary interest that can be attributed to Talman, notably Blyth Hall, Nottinghamshire (1684), with its proto-Palladian tower or pavilion plan, and Waldershare Park, Kent (c.1705), a magnificent rendition of parts of Hampton Court grafted onto the Trianon style of Drayton.

The death of William III in 1702 led to Talman's dismissal from the works and the rise of a new junta under Vanbrugh and NICHOLAS HAWKSMOOR. Talman was a committed Williamite and undoubtedly had a special relationship with the king. He was the country house architect of the Williamite court par excellence, building and altering more than perhaps everyone else in the top hierarchy combined. He can be described as a maverick architect, for his works, from the first to the last, display stylistic gymnastics to such an extent that one building can be totally dissimilar from another. For this very reason a study of his works is a testing exercise.

JOHN HARRIS

WORKS

1683, Hackwood Park, Hampshire, England. (A)1684, Blyth Hall, Nottinghamshire, England. 1686, Stanstead Park, Sussex, England. 1687, Chatsworth House (rebuilding south and east fronts), Derbyshire, England. c.1688–1690, Burghley House (apartments), Northamptonshire, England. 1689, Hampton Court Palace (gardens), Middlesex, England. 1689, Swallowfield, Berkshire, England. c.1690, Uppark, Sussex, England. 1695, Castle Ashby (greenhouse), Northamptonshire, England. 1698, Dyrham Park, Gloucestershire, England. c.1698, Kiveton Park, Yorkshire, England. 1699–1702, Hampton Court Palace (state apartments), Middlesex, England. 1700, Fetcham Park, Surrey, England. c.1700, Dorchester House (garden front), Weybridge, England. c.1700, Kimberley Hall, Norfolk, England. 1702, Drayton Park (south courtyard front), Northamptonshire, England. c.1705, Waldershare Park, Kent, England. c.1706, Wanstead House (garden), Essex, England.

BIBLIOGRAPHY

WHINNEY, M. D. 1955 "William Talman." *Journal of the Warburg and Courtauld Institutes.* 18:123–139.

TALUCCHI, GIUSEPPE

Giuseppe Talucchi (1782–1863), a neoclassic architect from the Piedmont region in Italy, studied with FERDINANDO BONSIGNORE. He completed the seventeenth-century Collegio dei Nobili of GUARINO GUARINI and furthered San Filippo Neri in Turin. Talucchi designed the Ospedale of San Luigi (1818–1833), now the Archivo di Stato, and the Psychiatric Hospital (1835, with Lorenzo Panizza), and he remodeled the Accademia Albertina in Turin, the Cathedral of Sant'Agata, Santhià (1836), and the parish church of Vigone.

HENRY A. MILLON

WORKS

1818–1833, Ospedale of San Luigi (now the Archivo di Stato); 1823–1824, San Filippo (chapels flanking main altar); 1835, Psychiatric Hospital (with Lorenzo Panizza); 1838, Odeon, Accademia Filarmonica; Turin, Italy. n.d., Moncalieri, Villa Cambiano, Italy.

BIBLIOGRAPHY

MALLÈ, LUIGI 1961 *Le Arti Figurativi in Piemonte.* Turin, Italy: Casanova.
TALUCCHI, V. 1917 *Brevi cenni sulla vita e sulle opere dell'arch. G. Talucchi.* Turin, Italy: G.M.T.

TAMBURINI, FRANCISCO

Little is known of the origins of Francisco Tamburini (?–1892). Born in Iesi in the Italian Marches—no one is certain—he was professor of design at the Royal Academy of Fine Arts in Naples when, on July 1, 1883, he signed a contract with the Argentinian government in Rome.

At the beginning of 1884, he arrived in Buenos Aires and, assigned the function of inspector of architectural works of the nation, oversaw the civil constructions of the federal state. His first work was the government seat or the Casa Rosada (1884–1900) in Buenos Aires, for which he readapted two Louis Treize-style pavilions, recently built on the main façade, and united them by a monumental arch marked by loggie in the neo-Renaissance Italian style that he made predominant in those parts of the palace whose construction he managed personally to complete: the majestic northern façade, of graceful proportions, and its cortile or "patio of the palm trees."

This language of loggie, cortiles, and harmoniously shaped volumes reappears in other works, such as the Police Department (1885–1889) and the residence of President Juárez Celman in Buenos Aires (1886).

Despite the brevity of his sojourn, Argentina owes to Tamburini its monumental public edifices, still in use, and several unbuilt projects as well. His principal work is the Colón Theater (1887–1908) of Buenos Aires, whose original design displays the same architectural idiom. After Tamburini's death in 1892, supervision of this work was continued by his disciple Víctor Meano and concluded by the Belgian architect Jules Dormal who, with a sense of eclecticism, modified the ornamental cover but not the general concept of the theater nor its monumental hall, considered among the best in the world.

ALBERTO S. J. DE PAULA
Translated from Spanish by
Florette Rechnitz Koffler

WORKS

1884–1889, Central Military Hospital (now the National Hospital for Tuberculosis); 1884–1900, Casa Rosada (Government House; completed by Joaquín Belgrano); 1884–1892, Normal School for Teachers (Mariano Acosta); 1885–1895, School of Medicine and Maternity Shelter, University of Buenos Aires; 1885–1889, Police Department and Firemen's Headquarters; *1886, Miguel Juárez Celman House; Buenos Aires. 1887–?, Penitentiary Jail; 1887–1889, Bank of the Province of Cordoba (Central House); 1887–1891, Rivera Indarte Theater; Córdoba, Argentina. 1887–1908, Colón Theater; *1888–?, Basail House; Buenos Aires. 1888–?, Marcos Juaréz Family Villa; 1888–?, Molina Family Villa; Córdoba, Argentina.

BIBLIOGRAPHY

BUSCHIAZZO, MARIO J. 1967 *Architecture in Argentina.* Buenos Aires: Valero.

PAULA, ALBERTO S. J. DE 1982 *The Official Architecture in Argentina during Roca's First Presidency.* Buenos Aires: National Academy of History. Forthcoming publication.

WAISMAN, MARIANA 1973/1974 "The Building of the Provincial Bank." *Review of Economy* 24:13–71.

TANGE, KENZO

Born in Imabari, Japan, Kenzo Tange (1913–) was graduated with honors from the department of architecture of Tokyo University in 1938. After gaining professional experience with KUNIO MAEKAWA, Tange returned to the university for graduate study (1942–1945). In 1949, upon winning the open competition for the Hiroshima Peace Center (his first executed building), he established a private practice and accepted a professorship at Tokyo University.

In 1961, Tange founded URTEC, a team of architects and urbanists. It is no accident that the team was developed on the model of The Architects Collaborative (TAC) headed by WALTER GROPIUS, for Tange, like most of the architects of his generation, was influenced by the principles of the Congrès Internationaux d'Architecture Moderne and by the central figures in that organization including LE CORBUSIER, Gropius, and SIEGFRIED GIEDION.

Committed as he is to realism in architecture, Tange has at all times sought to express the social, political, and technological realities of a specific situation. With respect to his work in Japan, this has meant confronting accelerated political and economic change following World War II. Although Tange's development parallels the reconstruction and coming of age of Japan as a leading industrial nation, the impact of his design and theory has been international in scope; his work aims at truths beyond the unique Japanese experience.

Tange's design methodology has evolved from a functionalist to a structuralist approach. Having rejected an orthodox functionalist position defined by a static correspondence between function and space, Tange began to work with the idea of typification of functions. Premised upon the notion that buildings have numerous arbitrary demands imposed upon them, typification indicates selection of the most human, essential, and future-oriented uses as determining factors in design. Recognition of the complex nature of function led to his introducing the concept of structure, which identifies relations between functional units as positive entities and seeks to define the nature of those relations. It seems likely that Tange's application owes something to the principles of literary structuralism as well as to traditional Japanese planning theory, which values the "spaces between" and plans them with as much care as the architecture itself.

A greater emphasis upon the urban environment appears to have been the result of this evolution and reflects Tange's belief that an order higher than the individual exists and must be given realization. The structural approach, which Tange considers to be justified ultimately by its humanity or its apparent ability to resolve problems of scale, takes as its point of departure the idea that space must be determined by communication systems or human activity patterns. Taking into account the human element, Tange distinguishes hard (inflexible or static) from soft environments (ones in which there is a dialogue between the environment and its users and that include possibilities for growth and change). In sum, the structural approach represents the result of a search for a design methodology and image that emerge from and reflect the union of contemporary technology and human existence.

Initially, Tange focused on defining the role of tradition in the creative act. He has studied and written about the Japanese architectural tradition; his publications include *Katsura: Tradition and Creation in Japanese Architecture* (1960b) and *Ise:*

Tange.
Hiroshima Peace Center.
Japan.
1949–1955

Prototype of Japanese Architecture (Tange and Kawazoe, 1962). Although he acknowledges the value of tradition as a catalytic force in creative work, Tange adamantly rejects the idea that tradition can be converted into a creative impulse, and he cautions against the formularization of historical prototypes; the lessons to be learned from the past are ones of principle rather than form. References to the past extend beyond the Japanese: for example, Tange has used concrete in an essentially Corbusian manner, and his belief that architecture or the built environment can be instrumental in building human character harks back to the idealism of the early modernists. Recognition by the architect that although architecture does not create living patterns, it must translate existing ones into livable and readable spaces is what Tange means by the creative continuity of tradition.

Formal design changes have paralleled the evolution of the design theory. Buildings of Tange's early career—the Hiroshima Museum, the Tokyo Metropolitan Government Offices (1952–1957), Tange's own home (1953), the Tsuda College Library (1953–1954) in Tokyo, and the Toshoinsatsu Printing Plant in Numazu—are rather conventional rectangular forms with light structural frames. During the same period, Tange explored the possibilities of more plastic form, experimenting with shell concrete structures and advanced geometries as in the Children's Library (1951–1952) in Hiroshima and the Shizuoka (1955–1957) and Ehime (1952–1953) Convention Halls. The next phase was marked by an increased confidence with the use of concrete. A development can be identified from the Kurayoshi City Hall (1955–1956) and the Sumi Memorial Hall (1955–1957), in which superstrength concrete beams appear for the first time, to the Kurashiki (1958–1960) and Imbari (1957–1958) City Halls and the

Rikkyo Library (1959–1961), in which the form of the building and its structure are one: all elements have been subordinated to a massive concrete sculptural whole.

The development of megestructures, including the prototypical Boston Bay project, which was conceived by Tange and his students at the Massachusetts Institute of Technology during his visiting professorship there in 1959–1960, the World Health Organization project, and the series of projects for Tokyo Bay, made a decisive break with previous urban design projects. Kenzo Tange and his team were propelled to a position as leaders of the Japanese metabolists. Published in *A Plan for Tokyo, 1960: Toward a Structural Reorganization,* the Tokyo Bay project represented a generalized attempt to demonstrate the importance of a structural approach to architecture and urbanism rather than a specific plan for Tokyo. The plan proposed a linear extension of linked hubs forming a civic axis over Tokyo Bay along which growth and change would be possible. Architecture would include residences of the type introduced in the M.I.T. project—massive, tentlike forms with dwelling units lining the sloping side walls and communal facilities between—and suspended office blocks spanning service towers set approximately 200 feet apart. Tange's philosophies of urban design have evolved from the Master Plan for Hiroshima to his ideas of Japan in the twenty-first century. The urban design lineage includes the Tokyo project and elaborations of and variations on that theme: the reconstruction project for Skopje City Center (1965–1966), the master plan and trunk facilities for Expo '70, the plan for the Fiera District Center, Bologna, Italy (1971–1974), and the Yerba Buena Center plan for San Francisco (1967–1968).

Tange began to develop suspended structures in Saint Mary's Cathedral, Tokyo (1961–1964), and the National Gymnasia for the Tokyo Olympics (1961–1964). It was in these two buildings that Tange began to clarify his notion that typification of function in connection with spiritual content results in the expression of symbol. Other changes occurred in Tange's design methodology based on the premises of the Tokyo plan. The Yamanashi Communications Center (1961–1967) marks the beginning of a period during which both Corbusian and traditional references disappeared, and creation of an integrated unity in which the parts would be subordinated to the whole was abandoned as a goal in favor of an architecture that would suggest incompleteness, flexibility, and the possibilities of growth and change. Representative are the main office building of the Dentsu Company(1965–1967), the Shizuoka Press and Broadcasting Center (1966–1967; here the structural core provides support for the whole building, which becomes a bridgelike structure), the Kuwait Embassy in Tokyo (1966–1970), the International School of the Sacred Heart (1966–1968) in Tokyo, and the University of the Sacred Heart (1965–1967) in Taipei. Whereas in the earlier phases structure and space were integrated, in this later phase, Tange's intention has been to disassemble the building, to analyze individually the parts, and then to reassemble the parts into a functioning system.

SUSAN STRAUSS

WORKS

1949–1955, Hiroshima Peace Center, Japan. 1951–1952, Children's Library, Hiroshima, Japan. 1952–1953, Ehime Convention Hall, Japan. 1952–1957, Metropolitan Government Offices; 1953, Kenzo Tange House; Tokyo. 1953–1954, Toshoinsatsu Printing Plant, Numazu, Japan. 1953–1954, Tsuda College Library, Tokyo. 1955–1956, Kurayoshi City Hall, Japan. 1955–1957, Shizuoka Convention Hall, Japan. 1955–1957, Sumi Memorial Hall, Japan. 1955–1958, Prefectural Office, Kagawa, Japan. 1957–1958, Imbari City Hall, Ehime, Japan. 1958–1960, Kurashiki City Hall, Okayama, Japan. 1959–1961, Rikkyo Library, Japan. 1959–1964, Ichinomiya Housing Project, Kagawa, Japan. 1960–1962, Nichinan Cultural Center, Miyazaki, Japan. 1960–1964, Tsukiji Redevelopment Plan; 1961–1964, National Gymnasium, Tokyo Olympics; 1961–1964, Saint Mary's Cathedral; Tokyo. 1961–1967, Yamanashi Communications Center, Japan. 1965–1966, City Center (reconstruction), Skopje, Yugoslavia. 1965–1967, Densu Offices, Tokyo. 1965–1967, University of the Sacred Heart, Taipei. 1966–1967, Shizuoka Press and Broadcasting Center; 1966–1968, International School of the Sacred Heart; 1966–1970, Kuwait Embassy; Tokyo. 1966–1970, Expo 1970 (master plan, trunk facilities, and Festival Plazza), Osaka, Japan. 1967–1970, Olivetti Technical Center, Kanagawa, Japan. 1967–1970, Shizuoka and Shimizu Regional Plans, Shizuoka, Japan. 1969, Central Station, Skopje, Yugoslavia. 1970–

Tange.
Hanae Mori.
Tokyo.
1976–1978

1974, Minneapolis Arts Complex (with Parker Klein), Minn. 1971, University (hospital and dormitory), Oran, Algeria. 1972–1974, Bulgarian Embassy and Chancery; 1973–1977, University of Tokyo Headquarters; Tokyo. 1974, Abbasabad City Center (with LOUIS KAHN), Tehran. 1974, Sacred Garden, Buddha's Birthplace, Lumbini, Nepal. 1974–1977, Sogetsu Hall and Offices; 1975, Iranian Embassy; Tokyo. 1976, Institute of Architecture and Urbanism, Oran, Algeria. 1976–1978, Hanae Mori, Tokyo. 1977, Crown Prince's Palace; 1977, King's Palace; Jeddah, Saudi Arabia.

BIBLIOGRAPHY

ALTHERR, ALFRED 1968 *Three Japanese Architects: Mayegawa, Tange, Sakakura.* Teufen, Switzerland: Niggli.

BANHAM, REYNER 1976 *Megastructure: Urban Futures of the Recent Past.* London: Thames & Hudson.

BORRÀS, MARIA LUISA 1970 *Arquitectura contemporánea japonesa.* Barcelona, Spain: Poligrafia.

BOYD, ROBIN 1962 *Kenzo Tange.* New York: Braziller.

BURCHARD, JOHN ELY 1961 "New Currents in Japanese Architecture." *Architectural Record* 129:129–144.

HOZUMI, NOBUO, and DODD, JEREMY 1965 "Junzo Sakakura, Kunio Mayekawa and Kenzo Tange." *Architectural Design* 35, no. 5:entire issue.

KULTERMANN, UDO 1960 "Kenzo Tange." *Das Kunstwerk* 1960:39–50.

"Special Feature: Kenzo Tange and URTEC." 1979 *Japan Architect* 51, nos. 8–9:entire issue.

TANGE, KENZO 1956 "Creation in Present Day Architecture and the Japanese Architectural Tradition." *Japan Architect* 31:25–33.

TANGE, KENZO 1960a "Architecture and Urbanism." *Japan Architect* 35:29–39.

TANGE, KENZO 1960b *Katsura, Tradition and Creation in Japanese Architecture.* New Haven: Yale University Press.

TANGE, KENZO 1970 *Kenzo Tange 1946–1969.* Edited by Udo Kultermann. New York: Praeger.

TANGE, KENZO 1976 "Development of Design Concept and Methodology." *Japan Architect* 51:11–19.

TANGE, KENZO 1978 "Five Errors of Architects Today." *Japan Architect* 53:4.

TANGE, KENZO, and KAWAZOE, NOBORU (1962)1965 *"Ise"—Prototype of Japanese Architecture.* Cambridge, Mass.: M.I.T. Press.

TANIGUCHI, YOSHIRŌ

Born in Kanazawa, Ishikawa Prefecture, Japan, from one of the families of the *Kutani* kiln of ceramic makers, Yoshirō Taniguchi (1904–1979) was graduated from Tokyo University in 1928. He was a professor of architecture at the Tokyo Institute of Technology until 1965. He was an architect as well as an essayist. His works, using modern structures and building materials, still have some Japanese expression in their external appearance and details. His design, ranging from a small memorial for a novelist to a large edifice such as the Palace of the Crown Prince, always requires, to appreciate it, a certain understanding of its cultural heritage. Taniguchi became a member of the Japan Academy of Arts in 1962 and was awarded the Order of Cultural Merits in 1973.

HIROSHI YAMAGUCHI

WORKS

1938, Dormitories, Hiyoshi, Keiō University, Yokohama, Japan. 1948, Memorial Hall for Shimazaki Tōson, Magome, Gifu Prefecture, Japan. 1949, Student's Hall, Keiō University, Tokyo. 1956, Factory Number 2, Chichibu Cement Company, Saitama Prefecture, Japan. 1969, Tokyo National Museum of Modern Art; 1974, Reception Hall, Akasaka Palace; Tokyo.

BIBLIOGRAPHY

SHINKENCHIKU-SHA (editor) 1981 *Taniguchi Yoshirō Sakuhin-shū.* Kyoto: Dankō-sha.

TANNEVOT, MICHEL

Michel Tannevot (c.1685–1762) was one of the most prominent builders of *hôtels* and smaller, middle-class houses in eighteenth-century Paris. His residences were known particularly for their commodious plans and elegant rococo interiors, the decorations of which were frequently designed by others, such as NICOLAS PINEAU. Elected to the Académie d'Architecture in 1718, Tannevot often addressed that body on theoretical issues. His studies on the proportions of the orders survive in the Bibliothèque de l'Institut de France. His major essay at monumental public architecture was his project for the competition of 1753 for the Place Louis XV in Paris.

RICHARD CLEARY

WORKS

1726, Hôtels des Vieux; 1742, Hôtel Tannevot; Paris. 1742, Pavilion, Bagnolet Gardens, near Paris. 1751, Hôtel de Montbazon (remodeling), Paris.

BIBLIOGRAPHY

FERAY, JEAN 1963 "L'Hôtel Tannevot et sa décoration attribuée à Nicolas Pineau." *Bulletin de la Société de l'Histoire de l'Art Français* 1963:69–84.

GALLET, MICHEL 1972 *Paris Domestic Architecture of the Eighteenth Century.* Translated by James Palmes. London: Barrie & Jenkins.

HAUTECOEUR, LOUIS 1950 *Première moitié du XVIIIᵉ siècle, le style Louis XV.* Volume 3 in *Histoire de l'architecture classique en France.* Paris: Picard.

KALNEIN, WEND GRAF, and LEVEY, MICHAEL 1972 *Art and Architecture of the Eighteenth Century in France.* Translation of Kalnein by J. R. Foster. Baltimore: Penguin.

LEMONNIER, HENRY (editor) 1911–1929 *Procès-verbaux de l'Académie Royale d'Architecture: 1671–1793.* 10 vols. Paris: Champion.

TARAVAL, LOUIS GUSTAVE

Known primarily as a draftsman and engineer, Louis Gustave Taraval (1738–1794) studied with ETIENNE LOUIS BOULLÉE. In addition to serving as inspector for the Bâtiments du Roi, he was influential in the publication of the works of many architects, including PIERRE CONTANT D'IVRY and JEAN FRANÇOIS CHALGRIN.

GÉRARD ROUSSET-CHARNY
*Translated from French by
Richard Cleary*

TATHAM, CHARLES H.

Charles Heathcote Tatham (1772–1842), born in London, was less important as an architect than as a propagator of knowledge about antique decorative detail. Trained briefly in the office of SAMUEL PEPYS COCKERELL, he was employed by HENRY HOLLAND to study architectural ornament in Rome in 1794–1796 and published a series of outline engravings (1799) which exercised considerable influence on Regency cabinetmakers and silversmiths. He also formed for Holland a large collection of antique Roman fragments subsequently purchased by JOHN SOANE. He designed several art galleries and mausolea in an uncompromisingly astringent classical style and died at Greenwich, near London, in 1842.

DAVID WATKIN

WORKS

1800–1801, Sculpture Gallery and Museum, Castle Howard, England. *1803–1805, Wilton Park (alterations), Buckinghamshire, England. 1803–1806, Cleveland House (picture gallery and alterations), London. 1807, Brocklesby Park (picture gallery; since remodeled), Lincolnshire, England. 1807–1808, Trentham Park (bridges, lodge, and mausoleum), Staffordshire, England. 1809, Mausoleum, Ochtertyre, Perthshire, Scotland. c.1820, Mausoleum, Rooksbury, Hampshire, England.

BIBLIOGRAPHY

PROUDFOOT, CHRISTOPHER, and WATKIN, DAVID 1972a "The Furniture of C. H. Tatham." *Country Life* 151:1481–1486.

PROUDFOOT, CHRISTOPHER, and WATKIN, DAVID 1972b "A Pioneer of English Neo-Classicism, C. H. Tatham." *Country Life* 151:918–921.

TATHAM, CHARLES H. 1799 *Etchings, Representing the Best Examples of Ancient Ornamental Architecture; Drawn from the Originals in Rome, and Other Parts of Italy; During the Years 1794, 1795, and 1796.* London: Printed for the author.

TATHAM, CHARLES H. 1806 *Etchings Representing Fragments of Antique Grecian and Roman Architectural Ornaments; Chiefly Collected in Italy, Before the Late Revolutions in that Century, and Drawn from the Originals.* London: Barfield.

TATLIN, VLADIMIR EVGRAFOVICH

Vladimir Evgrafovich Tatlin (1885–1953) was trained as a painter and employed as a stage designer, but he is best known for an architectural project, the Model for a Monument to the Third International (1919–1920), which represented the postrevolutionary aesthetic in Russia: industrial, kinetic, innovative, symbolic.

Born in Moscow but raised in Kharkov, Tatlin studied at the local schools, including the Penza Art School, and served in the Imperial Navy from 1902 to 1906. In 1910, Tatlin entered the Moscow College of Painting, Sculpture, and Architecture, where he met Alexander Vesnin (see VESNIN FAMILY). In 1911, he followed the painter Mikhail Larionov to St. Petersburg, where he exhibited brightly colored Cubist compositions with the Union of Youth Group (1912–1913) and made successful Cubist stage designs for a production of Ostrovsky's *A Life for the Tsar* (1913).

In the spring of 1913, Tatlin visited Berlin and Paris, where he was inspired by Picasso's synthesis of found materials into several musical reliefs. On his return to Russia, Tatlin created "counterreliefs" that were experimental assemblages of metals, glass, and wood. By 1915, he suspended them across a corner, allowing the surrounding and penetrating space to participate actively in these "corner reliefs." The exploration of facture, tectonics, and construction in the reliefs came to be known as Tatlin's "culture of materials" and lay the foundations for the Constructivist style of the 1920s. Tatlin exhibited the reliefs in Moscow and St. Petersburg during 1915–1916 and used them in designs for the Café Pittoresque in Moscow and for lighting displays at the 1918 anniversary celebration of the Revolution.

In 1919, Tatlin was commissioned by the Commissariat of Enlightenment to design a monument to the Third International Communist Congress (Komintern) to be held in Moscow in 1921. Ignorant of construction methods, Tatlin worked with an architect and two artists on a model, which stood five meters high on exhibition at the Eighth Pan-Russian Moscow Congress of Soviets (December 1920–January 1921). The model was made of wood and netting, but the final version was to rise in iron and glass 400 meters above Petrograd's Neva River; it was also to surround four rotating thermal chambers that were to serve as legislative, administrative, and propaganda centers for the Komintern. Although never erected because of economic problems and stylistic confusion, the "Tower" symbolized the emergence of Russia as a technological society and a focus of power in the international communist movement. The Tower also inspired many architects and artists to make a rapid and dramatic transition from traditional styles to technological and sociopolitical formula-

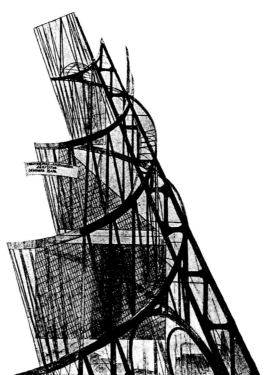

Tatlin.
Model for a Monument to the Third International.
Moscow.
1919–1920

tions in their work, numbering among them ELEAZAR LISSITZKY, IVAN LEONIDOV, and Vesnin.

In the early 1920s, Tatlin's fortunes varied with the volatile political climate from invited professorships to summary firings. In 1923, Tatlin's production of Velemir Khlebnikov's "Zangezi" was plagued by mechanical failures, and the enlarged reliefs that served as stage designs were criticized for their nonobjective and "misguided" forms. In 1924, demonstrating his pronouncements on utilitarian art, Tatlin designed an oven and modular workers' clothes, but these never fulfilled his goal of mass-production. Embittered by these experiences, Tatlin withdrew from active participation in Soviet artistic life, teaching only at the Kiev School of Theater and Cinema and the Moscow Art Studios in the late 1920s.

From 1929 to 1932, Tatlin developed his flying machine, *Letatlin—letat'* (to fly) and Tat*lin*—which was based on the principles of an air glider. As with the Tower, Tatlin had not formulated the technical apparatus in rational detail, and the 1933 exhibition of Letatlin met with derisive criticism, an attitude that pervaded much of Soviet criticism of Tatlin during the 1930s.

During the 1940s, Tatlin worked as a stage designer for various theaters in Moscow and returned to the figurative painting (nudes and still lifes) that had dominated his work before 1911. In his final years, Tatlin was dependent for survival on the generosity of his friends. Tatlin had intended his major designs (the Tower, Letatlin, and the utilitarian objects) to be contributions to Soviet life, but even his proper historical place has been denied by the Soviets, whose dogmatic insistence on social realism excludes Tatlin's vision.

GAIL HARRISON ROMAN

WORK

*1919–1920, Model for a Monument to the Third International, Moscow.

BIBLIOGRAPHY

ANDERSEA, TROELS (editor) 1968 *Vladimir Tatlin.* Stockholm: Moderna Museet.

BOWLT, JOHN E. 1979 "L'oeuvre de Vladimir Tatline." *Cahiers du musée national d'art moderne* 2:216–227.

ELDERFIELD, JOHN 1969 "The Line of Free Men: Tatlin's 'Towers' and the Age of Invention." *Studio International* 178, no. 916:162–167.

ERENBURG, IL'IA (1921–1922)1963 "Ein Entwurf Tatlins." *Bruno Taut, Frühlicht 1920–1922.* Berlin: Ullsteinn.

HARRISON, GAIL S. 1981 "Vladimir Tatlin's Project for a Monument to the Third International: A Paradigm of Russian Revolutionary Thought." Unpublished Ph.D. dissertation, Columbia University, New York.

LOZOWICK, LOUIS 1922 "Tatlin's Monument to the Third International." *Broom* 3, Oct.:232–234.

PUNIN, NIKOLAI 1919 "O pamiatnikh novogo tipa." *Iskusstvo kommuny* 14, Mar. 9:2–3.

PUNIN, NIKOLAI 1920 *Pamiatnikh III internationala: Proekt V. E. Tatlina.* Leningrad (St. Petersburg): Privately printed.

PUNIN, NIKOLAI 1921 *Tatlin: Protiv kubizma.* Leningrad (St. Petersburg): Gosizdat.

PUNIN, NIKOLAI 1922 "Tatlinova bashnia: Tour de Tatline." *Veshch/Gegenstand/Objet* 1–2:22.

RODCHENKO, ALEXANDER 1967 "Vladimir Tatlin." *Opus International* 4:15–18.

SKHLOVSKY, VICTOR 1921 "Pamiatnikh III internatsionala." *Zhizn' iskusstva* 1921:650–652.

STRIGALEV, ANATOLII 1973 "O proekte 'pamiatnika III internatsionala' khudozhnika V. Tatlina." In I. Kriukuv (editor), *Voprosy sovetskikh izobrazitel'nykh iskusstva i arkhitektury.* Moscow: Gosizdat.

UMANSKIJ, KONSTANTIN 1920 "Russland: Der Tatlinismus oder die Maschinenkunst." *Der Ararat: Glossen, Skizzen und Notizen zur neuen Kunst* 5–6:29–34.

ZYGAS, K. PAUL 1977 "Review of N. Punin's Pamiatnik III Internationala." *Oppositions* 10:75.

ZYGAS, K. PAUL 1977 "Punin's and Sidorov's Views of Tatlin's Tower." *Oppositions* 10:68–71.

ZYGAS, K. PAUL 1976 "Tatlin's Tower Reconsidered." *Architectural Association Quarterly* 2:15–27.

TATSUNO, KINGO

Born in Karatsu, Saga Prefecture, Japan, Kingo Tatsuno (1854–1919) was graduated from the Kōbu Daigakkō (later Tokyo University) as one of the first four graduates in architecture in 1879. In the same year, he went to London where he worked in the office of WILLIAM BURGES. He returned to Tokyo in 1883 and was appointed professor of architecture at the same college.

As the first native professor of architecture in modern Japan, he worked hard in many fields of architecture such as education, design and design practice, and administration. His works featured the color contrast of brick and stone as well as the use of many domes which came to be called the Tatsuno style. He was one of the founders of the Architectural Institute of Japan.

HIROSHI YAMAGUCHI
Translated from Japanese by Bunji Kobayashi

WORKS

1896, Bank of Japan Main Office, Tokyo. 1903, Bank of Japan (only exterior walls remain), Osaka, Japan. 1914, National Railway Central Station (later damaged and repaired), Tokyo.

BIBLIOGRAPHY

FUJIMORI, TERUNOBU (editor) 1980 Volume 3 in

Nihon-no Kenchiku: Meiji, Taishō, Shōwa. Tokyo.
SHIRATORI, SHŌGO (editor) 1926 Kōgakuhakase Tatsuno Kingo-den. Tokyo.

TAUT, BRUNO

Born in Königsberg, Prussia, Bruno Taut (1880–1938) experienced difficult years as son of an unsuccessful merchant. Already as a student at the *Gymnasium* he had to contribute to the family's income. He graduated from the *Baugewerkschule,* the traditional college for master builders, architectural designers, and engineers. He went to Berlin in 1903, working for BRUNO MÖHRING and attending his architectural lectures.

Between 1904 and 1908, he went to work for and studied with THEODOR FISCHER, the renowned leader of southern German architecture in Stuttgart. Taut returned to Berlin in 1908 and became a student of the city planner Theodor Goecke at the Technical University.

In 1909, he opened his first office together with Franz Hoffmann. The meeting in 1913 with the poet PAUL SCHEERBART and art critic Adolf Behne led to lifelong friendships and influenced Taut in many ways. Particularly, Scheerbart's ideas on glass architecture are reflected in Taut's Expressionist designs.

In 1914, MAX TAUT joined the office to form the firm of Brothers Taut and Hoffmann. However, the brothers practiced independently as far as design was concerned. Taut also became consulting architect for the German Garden City Association.

Twentieth-century architecture in Central Europe took a new direction in the short span of twenty years between 1913 and the early thirties. The pioneering architectural movement in Germany was called by their leaders *Das Neue Bauen* or modern architecture.

Bruno Taut's position within this movement was pivotal. His leadership was of particular importance within what became known as the Berlin School. Historical eclecticism began to disintegrate. However, the *Jugendstil,* the German form of Art Nouveau, represented in Berlin primarily by HENRI VAN DE VELDE and AUGUST ENDELL, proved to be just a transitory movement in the renewal process. It was the many-sided movement of Expressionism that ushered in the new age.

Whereas the term Expressionism is germane rather to painting and sculpture, architectural expressionism is a much more varied phenomenon. The clearest form can be found in *Die Gläserne Kette* (Akademie der Künste, 1963), which consists of letters from Taut's friends including

sketches that conjured up all kinds of futuristic fantasies. Taut also published and edited several issues of a journal, *Frühlicht* (1920–1921), which made the public familiar with the fledgling modern movement. His own major publications began with the book *Die Stadtkrone* (1919). The *Volkshaus,* or peoples' community center, took a dominant position in the envisioned thrilling urban environment.

At the same time, his large book of lithographs, *Alpine Architektur* (1919a), caused a great sensation. It showed the envisioned rebuilding of the Alps in a fantastic manner; one sees arched valleys, cathedral domes, including space frames, all in colored glass and defying the structural possibilities of the time. The book centers on a manifesto calling for an end to all war and posing the overwhelming challenge of preventing war by large and "impossible" tasks. Taut's passionate devotion to idealistic concepts made him appear more utopian than was borne out by later events. He was also very devoted to land reform and envisioned self-contained rural settlements linked by a net of freeways and advocated preservation of agricultural land between the clustered settlements.

During the short period as practicing architect before World War I, Taut was astonishingly busy with industrial as well as residential buildings which show a sparing use of Secessionist elements, but other work manifests his Expressionist ideas. Among some exhibition pavilions for industry was the famous glass house at the *Werkbund* Exposition in Cologne (1914). It showed the sure hand of an independent artist of great magnitude. Glass in all forms and colors with cascading water inside were used.

During the revolution, Taut also organized a group called *Arbeitsrat der Kunst* that tried to find a relationship with the events during the establishment of the first German Republic after World War I. Among its members were WALTER GROPIUS, LUDWIG HILBERSEIMER, the LUCKHARDT BROTHERS, ERIC MENDELSOHN, ADOLF MEYER,

*Bruno Taut.
Glass House, Werkbund
Exhibition.
Cologne, Germany.
1914*

HANS POELZIG, HANS SCHAROUN, and the Taut brothers. He also belonged to the *Novembergruppe,* an association of progressive architects. In 1924, he organized another group, *Der Ring,* consisting of twenty-five architects including HUGO HÄRING and LUDWIG MIES VAN DER ROHE. This group brought about new housing policies in Berlin. Taut further became active in the famous *German Werkbund* which brought him in close contact with efforts to apply high standards to industrial production and standardization of construction.

Taut's professional life can be divided into six discernible phases. The first two, which were just described, were his training and early practice before World War I and the Expressionistic work until the years directly after the war. The third and most productive phase was the period of large-scale housing work approximately from 1924 to 1931. The fourth period was his brief stay in Russia. The fifth and sixth periods were the years in exile, first in Japan, then in Turkey.

Taut spent the years of 1921–1924 as director of the building and planning department of Magdeburg. Building activities had not yet picked up, but Taut nevertheless caused a sensation by gaining support for the creation of polychrome façades over the dreary old residential blocks. Besides various projects for the city, the only executed large building was the exhibition hall (1921) in reinforced concrete with J. Goderitz. As important as this brief stay in Magdeburg was from a developmental point of view, it was nevertheless only an interlude between the revolution and the recovery of the country.

Taut returned to Berlin in 1924 to begin his spectacular success in design and planning of large-scale housing, mostly for nonprofit housing associations. Two developments stand out as examples of housing that provides for a happier life within the boundaries of an often dreary city of early industrialism. Anyone visiting the large development in Britz (1927) with the horseshoe around a pond or the *Uncle Tom* development embedded in pine forests in Zehlendorf (1926–1931)

will, even today, be impressed by the buildings' livability and close relationship to nature. MARTIN WAGNER worked with him in the planning for Britz and designed part of the development, as did OTTO RUDOLF SALVISBERG and Hugo Häring in Zehlendorf. More than ten thousand units were erected within the time span of not much more than five years (1925–1930).

An essential part of Taut's work must be seen in his use of color which he had reintroduced to architecture during his Expressionist period. This provided for a great amount of articulation in the visual environment of standardized living units.

Another interlude occurred when Taut accepted a professorship at the Technical University in Berlin (1930–1932). Taut advocated investigation of planning and methodological design based on the analysis of housing types. The seminar also pursued the study of related community facilities such as central heating plants, laundries, day-care centers, and assembly rooms. Although Taut discouraged his students from thinking that design can be derived from formula, he was farsighted enough to see the value of systematization of all valid ponderabilia.

After three semesters of teaching activity, he went as consulting architect of the city government to Moscow. His stay in Russia lasted only one year, until February 1933, and ended without the results he had hoped for. Although he had visited Russia several times before and had worked on a hotel project in Moscow before his moving there, he kept hoping that his dreams of building for peace, justice, and happiness could find fulfillment by joining the architectural avant-garde in Russia. Although the promise of the revolution was still there, 1932 was a year when Russia had to react to new threats from the fascistic developments in Central Europe. Taut, who was critical of the doctrinaire application of the International style and advocated to base modern design on the characteristics of indigenous design, was unable to change policies.

His work in Moscow included preliminary de-

Bruno Taut.
Housing Development (with
Martin Wagner).
Britz, Berlin.
1927

Bruno Taut.
Housing Development (with
Hugo Häring and Otto
Rudolf Salvisberg).
Zehlendorf, Berlin.
1926–1931

signs of a theater and a well-developed design for a hotel. He engaged in consulting activities and hoped to bridge the gap between design office and construction site.

When Taut returned to Berlin, he was thinking of a leave rather than a departure. In the meantime, he thought of resuming his teaching in Berlin, only to discover that the Nazis were about to arrest him as a cultural Bolshevist.

Via Switzerland and the Mediterranean countries and back through Siberia, he went to Japan at the invitation of the Japanese Society of Architects and with the help of several young Japanese architects. Taut lived in Japan for three years.

The Japanese lifestyle caused Taut to make new adjustments, facing in addition the difficulties of the life of a refugee. Contrary to his hopes, he could not attain an academic appointment. He gave, however, a number of lectures and did very small design work in cooperation with architects and two institutions for arts and crafts. Thus, he considered his stay in Japan as a "vacation from architecture." As his main activity, he wrote and published several books in Japan, foremost the opulently illustrated *Houses and People of Japan* (1937). Taut, who had been impressed by Japanese woodcuts in his younger years, became truly enamored with Japan's culture. He also began a profound summary of his architectural thinking with an important architectural theory which he finished in Turkey.

Taut's writings, besides being a survey of Japan's architectural history and customs, concentrated on his understanding of the contrast between *Tenno* and *Shogun* architecture, particularly between *Katsura* and *Ise* on the one side and *Nikko* on the other.

To escape the humid climate that proved to be particularly disagreeable to his asthma during the hot summers, he looked for a way out and accepted a call to Turkey where he spent the last two years of his life. This final period found him extremely busy and probably overworked. He received the professorship at the Academy of Fine Arts which Hans Poelzig was to have filled had he not died before reaching Istanbul. He also became head of the architectural office of the Ministry of Education.

Taut designed several schools in Ankara (1938) and Trabzon (1938), as well as a project for the Institute of Chemistry at the University of Istanbul (finished by his collaborator Franz Hillinger). He also participated in the international competition for the parliament building in Ankara. Perhaps his most important public building was for the Faculty of Languages on the campus of the University of Ankara (1936–1938). Taut intro-

Bruno Taut.
Bruno Taut House.
Ortaköy, Istanbul, Turkey.
1937–1938 (completed after
Taut's death)

duced a modernism that was consistent with his ideas on historic continuity. He successfully integrated elements of indigenous design with the modern idiom. For example, he reintroduced traditional horizontal rows of brick between the courses of stone masonry. Practical considerations such as day-lighting, conservation of energy, sun protection where needed, and careful detailing contributed greatly to giving modern design in Turkey a good name without losing all touch with architectural traditions.

His swan song was the jewel of a house on the Bosporus where he planned to live, but it was not finished before his death. This home in Ortaköy rises on a post-supported platform that projects from a steep hillside. Above the main floor rises a studio as a free-standing octagon affording a panoramic view.

Taut worked feverishly until the last. His architectural theory was finished and served as a text for his classes. The catafalque for Kemal Atatürk (1938) was done while he was already deathly ill. He succumbed in an asthma attack on December 24, 1938.

Taut's literary production varied in form and purpose. The extent, from popular political magazines and trade journals to books of various kinds, was prodigious and always influential. The repeated theme is an entirely new definition of architecture. He recast the term "proportion" to mean much more than the traditional theories on formal relationships. A piece of furniture, a building, or a whole city needs to have a balanced relationship between all imponderabilia that make a whole work of art out of all its parts. Taut's constant striving for this all-comprising unity irrespective of circumstances and trends of the day gives his work a strong continuity without which many designs or utterances would have to appear contradictory. His extreme sensitivity and complexity needed all these aspects of a holistic philosophy and practice. This universality lends new importance to the concept that one cannot be a true realist without also being an idealist.

H. H. WAECHTER

WORKS

1913, Monument to Steel (with Franz Hoffmann), International Building Trades Exhibition, Leipzig. 1913–1914, Garden City *Am Falkenberg,* Berlin. 1914, Glass House, *Werkbund* Exhibition, Cologne, Germany. 1921, Architectural Exhibition Hall (with J. Goederitz); 1921, Garden City Reform; Magdeburg, Germany. 1924–1931, Housing Development *Freie Scholle,* Tegel; 1926–1927, Bruno Taut House, Dahlewitz; 1926–1930, Housing Development, Weissensee; 1926–1931, Housing Development (with Hugo Häring and Otto Rudolf Salvisberg), Zehlendorf; 1927, Housing Development (with Martin Wagner), Britz; 1927–1928, Housing Development *Carl Legien* (with Franz Hillinger), Prenzlauer Berg; 1927–1930, Office Building for the German Transportation Workers (with Max Taut); 1928, Apartment Block, Neukölln; 1928, Housing Development, Grell Strasse; Berlin. 1936–1938, University Building, Ankara. 1937–1938, Bruno Taut House (completed after Taut's death), Ortaköy, Istanbul, Turkey. 1938, Catafalque for Kemal Atatürk; 1938, High School; Ankara. 1938, High School (with Franz Hillinger), Trabzon, Turkey. 1938, Middle School, Ankara.

BIBLIOGRAPHY

AKADEMIE DER KÜNSTE 1963 *Die Gläserne Kette.* Berlin: The academy. Exhibition catalogue.

AKADEMIE DER KÜNSTE 1980 *Bruno Taut: 1880–1938.* Berlin: The academy. Exhibition catalogue.

BLETTER, ROSEMARIE HAAG 1973 "Bruno Taut and Paul Scheerbart's Vision." Unpublished Ph.D. dissertation, Columbia University, New York.

CONRADS, ULRICH (editor) (1964)1970 *Programs and Manifestos on 20th Century Architecture.* Translated by Michael Bullock. Cambridge, Mass.: M.I.T. Press.

CONRADS, ULRICH, and SPERLICH, HANS G. 1962 *The Architecture of Fancy.* Translated and expanded by Christiane C. Collins and George Collins. New York: Praeger.

JUNGHANNS, KURT 1970 *Bruno Taut: 1880–1938.* Berlin: Henschelverlag.

LANE, BARBARA MILLER 1968 *Architecture and Politics in Germany: 1918–1945.* Cambridge, Mass.: Harvard University Press.

PEHNT, WOLFGANG 1973 *Expressionist Architecture.* New York: Praeger. Originally published in German in 1973.

PITZ, HELGE, and BRENNE, WINFRIED 1980 *Siedlung Onkel Tom, Zehlendorf, Einfamilienhäuser 1929, Architekt: Bruno Taut.* Berlin: Mann; Rome: Il Punto Editrice.

SEGAL, WALTER 1972 "About Taut." *Architectural Review* 151:25–27.

SHARP, DENNIS 1966 *Modern Architecture and Expressionism.* New York: Braziller.

Space Design 1970 12:3–82. Entire issue devoted to Taut.

TAUT, BRUNO (1919a)1972 *Alpine Architecture.* Edited by Dennis Sharp. Translated by Shirley Palmer. New York: Praeger.

TAUT, BRUNO ET AL. 1919b *Die Stadtkrone.* Jena, Germany: Diederichs.

TAUT, BRUNO 1920 *Die Auflösung der Städte.* Hagen, Germany: Volkwang-Verlag.

TAUT, BRUNO (editor) (1920–1921)1963 *Frühlicht.* Berlin: Ullstein. Republication of Taut's magazine.

TAUT, BRUNO 1924 *Die Neue Wohnung.* Leipzig: Klinkhardt & Biermann.

TAUT, BRUNO 1927a *Bauen: Der neue Wohnbau.* Leipzig: Klinkhardt.

TAUT, BRUNO (1927b)1930 *Ein Wohnhaus.* Stuttgart, Germany: Keller.

TAUT, BRUNO 1929a *Modern Architecture.* London: Studio; New York: Boni.

TAUT, BRUNO 1929b "The Nature and Aims of Architecture." *Creative Art* 4:169–174.

TAUT, BRUNO 1929c *Die Neue Baukunst in Europa und Amerika.* Stuttgart, Germany: Hoffmann.

TAUT, BRUNO 1934 *Nippon Seen with European Eyes.* Tokyo: Meiji-Shobo.

TAUT, BRUNO (1936a)1977 *Architekturlehre.* Edited by Tilmann Heinisch and Goerd Peschken. Hamburg, Germany: VSA Verlag. Originally published in Tokyo.

TAUT, BRUNO (1936b)1939 *Fundamentals of Japanese Architecture.* 3d ed. Tokyo: Kokusai Bunka Shinkokai.

TAUT, BRUNO (1937)1958 *Houses and People of Japan.* 2d ed., rev. Tokyo: Sansaido.

WAECHTER, H. H. (Victor Semper) 1940 "Bruno Taut och arbetararkitekturen." *Hyresgästen* 13, July 1.

WAECHTER, H. H. 1973 "Prophets of Future Environments." *Journal of the American Institute of Architects* 60:32–37.

WAECHTER, H. H., and WAECHTER, ELISABETH 1951 *Schools for the Very Young.* New York: Dodge.

TAUT, MAX

Max Taut (1884–1967) was born in Königsberg, Prussia, attended the local high school, and graduated from the *Baugewerkschule.* After work with HERMANN BILLING in Karlsruhe, he began an independent practice in Berlin in 1911. After World War I, he went into practice with his brother, BRUNO TAUT, and with Franz Hoffmann, a partnership that lasted until Hoffmann's death in 1950.

Max Taut was one of the founders of the Expressionist architectural movement in Germany. He took part in the *Novembergruppe,* the *Arbeitsrat für Kunst,* the avant-garde association *Der Ring,* and was a member of the German *Werkbund.* He

*Max Taut.
Wissinger Family Vault.
Stahnsdorf, Berlin.
1920*

*Max Taut.
Co-Operative Department
    Store.
Berlin.
1932*

contributed to his brother's *Die Gläserne Kette* (glass chain) and to the *Frühlicht* magazine with his brilliant drawings. However, he showed no inclination for theoretical or polemic writing. He was one of a few who were able to realize some expressionistic designs such as the Wissinger Family Vault in 1920 (the only sketch of the *Glass Chain* that was built) and the office building for the Federation of German Labor Unions in Berlin (1923). His enormous reputation as an architect rested on a consistent performance in the creation of well-planned, well-functioning, and well-built structures. His peers and his later students saw in Taut the prototype of a master builder.

Taut's aesthetic vocabulary consisted primarily of an honest expression of all structural elements with beautiful proportions. The care with which he handled construction detail and material showed his mastership. He did all designs with his own hands into old age. He never followed trends or fashions, and he cultivated with great clarity the character of the structure and the nature of materials. He was daring in his concepts but refrained from exaggerations. Throughout his career, he was striving to find generally perceptible solutions to often complex tasks.

During the Weimar Republic, Taut was known as the architect for the labor unions. He designed the headquarters of the printers' union in Berlin (1925) and emphasized its concrete frame. Then followed some school buildings and the much publicized office building of the Prussian Mines Administration (1930), a building that shows great sensitivity and exudes an airy and comfortable atmosphere. Another office building for the German Federation of Labor Unions, in Frankfurt am Main (1931), is an imposing structure with a ten-story center part. The last important structure during this period was a nine-story co-operative department store in Berlin, a clear and intelligent expression of encased steel frame con-

struction. Some work in housing and two houses at the Stuttgart Werkbund Exhibition (1927) should also be mentioned.

Then came the years under Hitler that enforced on him inactivity as an architect. But after World War II he was ready for another stretch of pioneering work that also proved to be very profitable for the education of young architects. This influence was also felt when he became professor at the Art Academy and established there with Wilhelm Büning a new school of architecture. His new architectural work gravitated toward large housing developments and apartment buildings, many multi-storied, in Berlin and West Germany.

H. H. WAECHTER

WORKS

1911, School; 1913, Koswig Textile Factory; Finsterwalde, Germany. 1913, Werdandi-Bund Pavilion (with F. Sesselberg), Building Exhibition, Leipzig. 1920, Wissinger Family Vault, Stahnsdorf, Berlin. 1923, Federation of German Labor Unions Office Building; 1925, Headquarters of the Printers Union; Berlin. 1926, Federation of German Labor Unions Hall, Gesolei Exhibition, Düsseldorf, Germany. 1927, Housing Development, Reinickendorf, Berlin. 1927, Werkbund Exhibition (two houses), Stuttgart, Germany. 1928, Housing Development; 1929, Dorotheen High School; Kopenick; 1929, School Complex, Lichtenberg; 1930, Prussian Mines' Administration Building, Dahlem; Berlin. 1931, Federation of German Labor Unions Office Building, Frankfurt am Main, Germany. 1932, Co-Operative Department Store; 1932, Co-Operative Wholesale Bakery, Spandau; Berlin. 1949–1952, Reuter Housing Development, Bonn. 1953, Ludwig-Georg-Gymnasium, Darmstadt, Germany. 1955, Apartment Building (Methfesselstrasse), Berlin. 1955–1964, August Thyssen Housing Development, Duisburg, Germany. 1957, Low-Rent Apartment Development, Steglitz; 1964, Central Children's Home; Berlin.

BIBLIOGRAPHY

AKADEMIE DER KÜNSTE 1964 *Max Taut*. Berlin: The

academy. Catalogue of an exhibition held from July 18–August 9, 1964, celebrating Max Taut's eightieth birthday.

BEHNE, ADOLF 1931 "Max Taut's Gewerkschaftshaus in Frankfurt am Main." *Wasmuths Monatshefte für Baukunst* 15:481–496.

"Die Lichtenberger Schulen." 1932 *Wasmuths Monatshefte für Baukunst* 16:257–269.

HELLWAG, GRITZ 1930 "Aufgaben für den Siedlungs-architekten zur Eichkamp-siedlung von Max Taut." *Das Schöne Heim* April:261–264.

POSENER, JULIUS 1967 "Max Taut in Memoriam." *Bauwelt* 11:274.

SAGE, KONRAD, and WEDEPOHL, E. 1967 "Max Taut in Memoriam." *Der Architekt* 16:145–146.

TAUT, MAX 1927 *Bauten und Pläne.* With an introduction by Adolf Behne. Berlin: Hübsch.

ZERVOS, CHRISTIAN 1928 "Un grand édifice de Max Taut." *Cahiers d'Art* 3:135–139.

TAYLOR, ANDREW

Andrew Thomas Taylor (1850–1937), a Scottish-born and -trained architect and educator, worked in Montreal during the last decades of the nineteenth century. The output of his office was prodigious and he was influential in shaping the direction of Montreal's architecture.

Perhaps best known for his designs for the McGill University campus, Taylor was also one of the first to bring Romanesque and Classical Revival styles to the city. As chief architect for the Bank of Montreal, he was responsibile for bank branches across Canada.

He returned to London in 1904 and was subsequently knighted for his political work there.

JULIA GERSOVITZ

WORKS

1884–1885, Henry Taylor Bovey Residence (Sunnandene), 3467 Avenue du Musée; *1885, H. C. Scott and H. G. Strathy Residences, Drummond Street; 1888, C. J. Fleet Residence, Avenue du Musée; 1889–1893, George Drummond Residence, Sherbrooke Street West; 1892, Bank of Montreal, West End Branch; 1893–1900, Redpath Library, McGill University; 1894, MacDonald Chemistry and Mining Building, McGill University; 1896, MacDonald Physics Building, McGill University; 1896, Montreal Diocesan College; 1898, MacDonald Engineering Building, McGill University; 1900–1901, Marborough Apartments, 370 Milton Street; Montreal.

BIBLIOGRAPHY

Canadian Architect and Builder. 1904 9, no. 11:174; 17, no. 12:xi.

"Taylor, Andrew Thomas." (1898)1912 Page 1088 in H. J. Morgan (editor) *The Canadian Men and Women of the Time.* Toronto.

TAYLOR, ROBERT

Robert Taylor (1714–1788) ranks with JAMES PAINE and WILLIAM CHAMBERS as one of the outstanding figures in the second generation of English Palladian (see ANDREA PALLADIO) architects. Though once dismissed as conservative and unadventurous, he now deserves recognition for his imaginative and ingenious planning and his handsome astylar villas, which in simplicity of treatment are prototypes of neoclassicism.

The son of Robert Taylor, a successful master mason, Taylor was apprenticed at age eighteen to the sculptor Henry Cheere. Following this, he made a journey to Rome, cut short by his father's death. Soon after 1750, Taylor turned from sculpture to architecture and won extensive patronage from city merchants and bankers for whom he designed London offices and houses as well as suburban and country villas. In 1764, he became surveyor to the Bank of England but his extensive work there was largely lost in subsequent alterations by JOHN SOANE and HERBERT BAKER.

Taylor made brilliant play with ovals, octagons, and canted bays in his plans, of which the best example is the huge domed oval staircase at Sharpham House, in Devon. According to his obituary in the *London Chronicle,* his own house in Spring Gardens was "a great curiosity for the economy of space, fanciful shapes and multiplied accommodations." Taylor's early interiors contain exuberant rococo decoration and he had a penchant for octagonal glazing bars and door panels. His later decoration is more neoclassical and Adamesque (see ROBERT ADAM). At Purbrook House in Hampshire, he introduced the first known recreation of a Roman atrium in England.

As a result of his extensive practice and financial acumen, Taylor became a very rich man, bequeathing the bulk of his fortune of £180,000 to Oxford University for the establishment of an institute of modern languages—the Taylorian Institute.

MARCUS BINNEY

WORKS

*1754–1755, 35–36 Lincoln's Inn Fields, London. 1755, Harleyford Manor, near Marlow, Buckinghamshire, England. (A)1756–1758, Barlaston Hall, Staffordshire, England. *c.1760, Grafton House, Piccadilly, London. c.1760–1765, Asgill House, Richmond, Surrey, England. c.1760–1765, Danson Hill, Bexleyheath, Kent, England. 1766–1788, Bank of England (extensive additions); *before 1767, 34 Spring Gardens; *1768–1775, 1–14 Grafton Street (3–6 survive); London. *1770, Purbrook House, Hampshire, England. c.1770, Sharpham House, Devon, England. 1772–1776, Ely House, 37 Dover Street; London. 1772–1777, Maidenhead

Bridge, Berkshire, England. 1774–1780, Lincoln's Inn, Stone Buildings; 1775–1777, Six Clerks' and Enrollment Offices, Chancery Lane; London. 1776, Assembly Room, Belfast, Ireland. 1777–1790, Gorhambury, Hertfordshire, England. *1778, Long Ditton Church, Surrey, England. 1778–c.1780, Heveningham Hall (interiors by James Wyatt), Suffolk, England. 1788–1795, Guildhall (executed by William Pilkington with some alterations), Salisbury, Wiltshire, England.

BIBLIOGRAPHY

BINNEY, MARCUS 1967 "The Villas of Sir Robert Taylor." *Country Life* 142, July 6:17–21, July 13:78–82.

BINNEY, MARCUS 1969 "Sir Robert Taylor's Bank of England." *Country Life* 146, Nov. 13:1244–1248, Nov. 20:1326–1330.

BINNEY, MARCUS 1981 "Sir Robert Taylor's Grafton Street." *Country Life* 170, Nov. 12:1634–1637, Nov. 19:1766–1769.

TECTON

The architectural firm of Tecton was formed in London in 1932. It consisted of a Russian immigrant, BERTHOLD LUBETKIN, and six Architectural Association graduates: Anthony Chitty, Lindsey Drake, Michael Dugdale, Val Harding, Godfrey Samuel, and Francis Skinner. Lubetkin had worked in Paris from 1925 to 1930, spending two years with AUGUSTE PERRET and the remainder in private practice, before moving to England. His experience thus gained of the latest Continental developments was to form the inspiration of Tecton's reforming practice. Their earliest impact on an English architectural scene where Modernists were still very much in the background and patronage tended to exclude them, was through zoo buildings, particularly those in Regent's Park. Their chief victory was the erection of two modern apartment blocks in the midst of conservative Highgate, the first of which was greatly admired by LE CORBUSIER. The progressive London Borough of Finsbury gave the firm its most important commissions, notably for a Health Centre (1935–1938) and for apartments. Tecton split up in the late 1940s, politically divided over the need for direct political involvement. Lubetkin and Skinner shared committed views, and they practiced together for a time. Lubetkin, however, retired from architecture soon afterward, and the Tecton legacy descended chiefly through Denys Lasdun, an assistant in the office who, at the split, went into partnership with Drake.

BRIAN HANSON

WORKS

1932, Gorilla House, London Zoo, Regent's Park; 1933–1934, Penguin Pool, London Zoo, Regent's Park; 1933–1935, Highpoint I Flats, Highgate; London. 1934, House, Bognor, West Sussex, England. 1934, House, Haywards Heath, Sussex, England. 1934, House (with Pilichowski), Plumstead, Kent, England. 1934–1935, Giraffe and Elephant Houses, Whipsnade Zoo; 1934–1936, Berthold Lubetkin House, Whipsnade; Bedfordshire, England. 1935, House, Farnham Common, Surrey, England. 1935, House, Sydenham Hill; 1935–1938, Finsbury Health Center; 1936–1938, Highpoint II Flats, Highgate; London. 1937–1939, Penguin Pool and Giraffe House, Dudley Zoo, Worcestershire, England. 1947–1951, Flats, Priory Green; 1947–1951, Flats, Spa Green, Rosebery Avenue; London.

BIBLIOGRAPHY

COE, PETER, and READING, MALCOLM 1981 *Lubetkin and Tecton: Architecture and Social Comment.* London: Arts Council of Great Britain. Exhibition catalogue.

"Finsbury Makes a Programme." 1939 *Architectural Review* 85:5–6.

GOULD, JEREMY H. 1977 *Modern Houses in Great Britain: 1919–1939.* London: Society of Architectural Historians of Great Britain.

HANCOCKS, DAVID 1971 *Animals and Architecture.* London: Evelyn; New York: Praeger.

"Health Center for the Borough of Finsbury." 1939 *Architectural Review* 85:7–22.

JACKSON, JEANETTE (exhibition organizer) 1975 *Hampstead in the Thirties: A Committed Decade.* London: Hampstead Artists Council. Exhibition catalogue.

JORDAN, ROBERT FURNEAUX 1955 "Lubetkin." *Architectural Review* 118:36–44.

LUBETKIN, BERTHOLD 1937 "Modern Architecture in England." *American Architect* 150:29–42.

LUBETKIN, BERTHOLD, and BRETT, LIONEL 1951 "Canons of Criticism, II." *Architectural Review* 109:135–137.

TECTON 1939 *Air Raid Precautions.* London: Finsbury Borough Council.

TECTON (1939)1941 *Planned A.R.P.* Brooklyn, N.Y.: Chemical Publishing.

THOMAS, JOHN 1976 "Tecton: A Bibliography." *Architectural Association Quarterly* 8, no. 3:40–50.

YORKE, FRANCIS REGINALD STEVENS (1938)1947 *The Modern House in England.* London: Architectural Press.

TEDESCHI, ENRICO

Enrico Tedeschi (1901–1978) performed a decisive role in architectural education and research in Argentina and other Latin American countries. Born in Rome, he studied in Milan and Rome and was one of the founders of *Metron,* the influential magazine of the organic movement in Rome, where he worked successfully after World War II as an architect, planner, and professor at the university.

In 1948, invited by the University of Tucumán

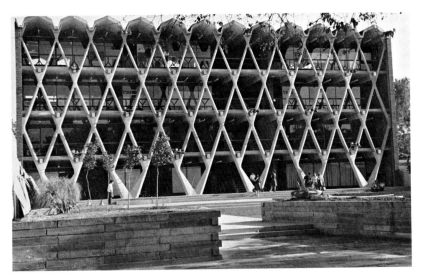

Tedeschi.
School of Architecture,
   University of Mendoza.
Argentina.
1961–1963

together with other well-known architects, he went to Argentina where he remained for the rest of his life. This team created a revolutionary teaching program for the school of architecture and a grandiose project for the university campus. A very active professor, Tedeschi stayed until 1975 in several Argentine universities, teaching history and theory of architecture, design, and planning. In the meantime, he lectured in several countries and published many books and articles. His *Introducción a la historia de la arquitectura* (1951) advocated a re-establishment of the connection between history and design, thus providing the theoretical support that had been lacking in Argentina for this discipline. For the theory of architecture, Tedeschi established a historical approach, rejecting normative theories as inadequate both for education and for designing. His book *Teoría de la Arquitectura* (eight editions since 1963) is currently used in many Latin American universities. In 1958, he founded with others an Institute for Architectural History, over which he presided until 1965, inviting Nicolaus Pevsner, Giulio Carlo Argan, and Vincent Scully, among others, to provide young scholars with a high-level education.

In 1960, he created the school of architecture at Mendoza University; as dean (1960–1975), he applied his ideas on architectural education, a creative and critical activity closely connected with research. Advanced students developed issues in several fields of regional architecture, and a team for research on solar architecture was created with an architectural approach: design as a basis for an energy-saving type of building and for efficiency in the use of solar energy. In 1975, he left teaching and incorporated this team with IADIZA, an institute for research on arid zones. A solar house prototype (1978) and a small housing project were built. IADIZA has the first library on the subject in Latin America.

Tedeschi was appointed chief planner in two important cities: Mendoza (1960–1962) where he prepared the basis for a master plan and a paradigmatic urban record, and Córdoba (1966–1968) where he put in practice part of the plans for the historical center. During 1972–1976 he presided over a national board for research on housing. He built sparsely, but every one of his buildings stated a thesis. The most interesting one, the School of Architecture at Mendoza (1961–1963), is a light construction with a structure of electricity poles of prestressed concrete diagonally assembled to resist the heavy earthquakes of the region.

His standing in Argentine architectural culture is due both to the architectural ideology (historic, critical, organic) he transmitted to his many disciples and to his effectiveness in opening ways of putting new ideas into practice.

MARINA WAISMAN

WORKS

*1938, Exhibition, Basilica Palladiana, Vicenza, Italy. 1944–1945, Rome Master Plan (revision). 1945–1946, Master Plan for Caserta, Italy. 1946–1947, Plan for Capua (reconstruction), Italy. 1948, Master Plan for the University City (with others), Tucumán, Argentina. 1950–1952, Seven Houses, Tafí del Valle y Tucumán, Argentina. 1961–1963, School of Architecture, University of Mendoza, Argentina. 1965–1967, Houses and Hotel at San Luis, Argentina. 1970–1971, School of Electronic Engineering; 1970–1973, School of Law; University of Mendoza, Argentina.

BIBLIOGRAPHY

TEDESCHI, ENRICO 1947 *I servizi colletivi nella comunita organica.* Rome: Metron.
TEDESCHI, ENRICO 1948 *L'Architettura in Inghilterra.* Florence: Edizioni "U."
TEDESCHI, ENRICO 1950 *Estadística para el urbanismo.* Argentina: University of Tucumán.
TEDESCHI, ENRICO 1951 *Una introducción a la Historia de la Arquitectura.* Argentina: University of Tucumán.
TEDESCHI, ENRICO 1955a *Asoleamiento en la Arquitectura.* Argentina: University of Tucumán.
TEDESCHI, ENRICO 1955b *Frank Lloyd Wright.* Buenos Aires: Nueva Visión.
TEDESCHI, ENRICO 1961 *La Plaza de Armas del Cuzco.* Argentina: University of Tucumán.
TEDESCHI, ENRICO 1962 *La arquitectura en la sociedad de masas.* 3d ed. Buenos Aires.
TEDESCHI, ENRICO (1963)1980 *Teoría de la Arquitectura.* 8th ed. Buenos Aires: Nueva Visión.

TEDESCO, JACOPO

Jacopo (or Lapo) Tedesco (13th century), a Lombard architect active in Assisi, in 1228, may have have designed the Church of San Francesco; other possibilities are Frate Elia, Fra Giovani della Penna, and Filippo Campello. The designer seems, in any case, to have been an Italian familiar with late twelfth-century French structures such as the Cathedral of Angers.

CHRISTINE SMITH

TEFFT, THOMAS ALEXANDER

Thomas Alexander Tefft (1826–1859) was born in Richmond, Rhode Island, where at seventeen he taught school. Henry Barnard, the educational reformer, persuaded Tefft to enter Brown University, and found him a job with JAMES BUCKLIN, a Providence architect. At Brown, Tefft was influenced by professors Charles Coffin Jewett, Francis Wayland, and George W. Greene.

After graduation in 1851, Tefft began his independent architectural career, receiving commissions throughout the eastern United States. At the same time, he lectured and was active in promoting a professional architectural association and architectural education. Inspired by the Great Exhibition of 1851, Tefft advocated the establishment of a school of design and an art museum in Providence.

From 1851–1856, Tefft designed approximately 150 buildings, including residences, libraries, churches, schools, factories, and railroad stations. He used several styles; Romanesque, or as he said "German round arch" for city churches, board and batten Gothic for village churches, Italian palacial for town houses, and Italian villa or Tudor for the country. In a lecture on rural art, Tefft advised architects to show humility. A house should command a good view of sunrise and sunset, and a pleasant view from the front door. The landscaping should be such that "the whole will be convenient and natural." Cottages should be board and batten or ornamental shingles in one pattern for the side and another for the roof. He was particular about color and liked to use it inside and out.

In Providence, the Tully Bowen House (1852–1853) is an example of his palace style, though the iron railings he designed have disappeared. Guzman Hall at Providence College (1850s) was an Italian villa constructed of stone.

Several of Tefft's churches exist, though altered, notably the Central Congregational Church (1850s) and "Mr. Tucker's Church" (1854), a Baptist church in Alexandria, Virginia. Both churches are Romanesque.

The railroad station in Providence (1848) was his best-known work and showed his love of decorated brickwork and the Lombard Romanesque adapted to a new use.

Thanks to many editions of Henry Barnard's book (1848) on schools, Tefft's school designs are widely known. On a larger scale, he designed the Richmond Female Institute (1853) and he prepared a design (1856) for a building at Vassar College, which was unexecuted at his death.

Tefft's best-known factory stands in Cannelton, Indiana (1850s), where he worked with the engineer Alexander McGregor. Here the towers were put to use supplying water and toilets on each floor. Later he based the American Antiquarian Society in Worcester, Massachusetts (1853) on an Italian palace.

In 1856, Tefft traveled to Europe, where he was warmly received by CHARLES BARRY, whom he had long admired. He visited England, France, Italy, Switzerland, Germany, and perhaps Russia. He died in Florence in 1859.

Thomas Alexander Tefft developed ideas in advance of anyone in New England, even though his ideas reflected concepts used at the Great Exhibition in the work of A. J. DOWNING and JOHN RUSKIN, and in books in general. His early death—followed closely by the Civil War—made his influence slight and his name obscure until the twentieth century.

BARBARA WRISTON

WORKS

1846–1847, Lawrence Hall; 1846–1848, Library; Williams College, Williamstown, Mass. *1848, Railroad Station; 1850s, Bradley House (now Guzman Hall); 1850s, Central Congregational Church; Providence, R.I. 1850s, Factory, Cannelton, Ind. 1852–1853, Tully Bowen House, Providence, R.I. 1853, American Antiquarian Society, Worcester, Mass. *1853, Richmond Female Institute, Va. 1854, Baptist Church, Alexandria, Va.

BIBLIOGRAPHY

BARNARD, HENRY 1848 *School Architecture, or Contributions to the improvement of school-houses in the United States.* 2nd ed. New York: A. S. Barnes.
GLASS, ANITA 1960 "Early Victorian Domestic Ar-

Tefft.
Railroad Station.
Providence, Rhode Island.
1848

chitecture on College Hill." Unpublished M.A. thesis, Brown University, Providence, R.I.

LITTLE, MARGARET RUTH 1971 "The Architecture of a Lamented Genius." Unpublished M.A. thesis, Brown University, Providence, R.I.

MALMSTROM, R. E. n.d. *Lawrence Hall at Williams College.* Williamstown, Mass.: Williams College Museum of Art.

OVERBY, OSMOND 1964 "The Architecture of College Hill, 1770–1900." Unpublished Ph.D. thesis, Yale University, New Haven.

STONE, E. M. 1869 *The Architect and Monetarian: A brief memoir of Thomas Alexander Tefft, including his labors in Europe to establish a universal currency.* Providence: Rider & Brother.

TEFFT, THOMAS ALEXANDER 1856 "New York Crayon." *Architecture* May-July.

"Thomas A. Tefft and Brick Architecture in America." 1886 *American Architect and Building News* 19, no.546:282–283.

WRISTON, BARBARA 1940 "The Architecture of Thomas Tefft." *Bulletin of the Museum of Art, Rhode Island School of Design,* 28, no. 2:37–45.

WRISTON, BARBARA 1942 "Thomas Alexander Tefft: Architect and Economist." Unpublished M.A. thesis, Brown University, Providence, R.I.

WRISTON, BARBARA 1963 "The Use of Architectural Handbooks in the Design of Schoolhouses from 1840–1860." *Journal of the Society of Architectural Historians* 22, no. 3:155–160.

WRISTON, BARBARA 1965 "Who was the Architect of the Indiana Cotton Mill, 1849–50?" *Journal of the Society of Architectural Historians* 24, no. 2:171–173.

TELFORD, THOMAS

Thomas Telford (1757–1834) was internationally recognized in his later years as one of the leading civil engineers of his time. He was a natural choice, in 1820, to become first president of the newly founded Institution of Civil Engineers. In his youth, no clear demarcation between civil engineering and architecture existed. Thus he first gained the confidence of influential patrons as an architect.

A Lowland Scot, born at Westerkirk in Dumfriesshire, he lost his father, a shepherd, before he was a year old. He attended the parish school and, after an apprenticeship as a mason, he moved first to Edinburgh and then to London to gain wider experience. His real architectural career began with the adaptation of Shrewsbury Castle as a residence for William Pulteney. Pulteney's patronage led to further architectural commissions in and near Shrewsbury, including houses, churches, and a new county jail, mostly in a restrained classical style well exemplified by Saint Mary Magdalene, Bridgnorth (1792–1794).

Probably through Pulteney, Telford had acted as county surveyor of bridges for Shropshire and, in 1793, he was appointed also as general agent for the new Ellesmere Canal. He then largely abandoned architecture for civil engineering.

As a civil engineer, Telford was responsible also for numerous other canal schemes, for fen drainage, for major harbor works, for many miles of new roads through difficult country in Scotland and North Wales, and for a very large number of bridges and aqueducts called for by the road and canal works. Most relevant here are some of the bridges and aqueducts in which he made notable innovations, especially in the use of iron. In an early aqueduct at Longdon on Tern (1793–1794), he first used a cast-iron trough to carry the water, and the same was done on a much greater scale in the Pont Cyssylte Aqueduct carrying the Ellesmere Canal over the River Dee (1794–1805). His first iron bridge at Buildwas, England (1795–1796), already marked a considerable advance on the pioneering Coalbrookdale Bridge. It led, in 1800, to a daring but unexecuted project for a 600-foot span over the Thames. A few years later, in the 150-foot span Bonar Bridge (1811–1812), he achieved the definitive form for the cast-iron arched bridge—with ribs lightened by perforations to give a latticed appearance, adequate lateral bracing, and lozenge-framed spandrels. The best example of this form is Mythe Bridge (1823–1826), near Tewks-

*Telford.
Saint Mary Magdalene.
Bridgnorth, England.
1792–1794*

*Telford.
Menai Bridge.
North Wales.
1819–1826*

bury. For his greatest bridge (1819–1826), carrying his Holyhead Road over the Menai Straits, he originally proposed a 500-foot span iron arch of the same form but later turned to the suspension form as offering considerable savings in cost. He finally built the bridge with a main span of 580-feet carried by eyebar chains. This finally established the suspension form as the appropriate one for long-span road bridges. Most of his bridges were, nevertheless, of stone. For the longer spans he usually reduced weight by substituting longitudinal bearer walls for a solid spandrel fill to carry the roadway. He also followed JEAN RODOLPHE PERRONNET's lead in reducing the rise of his arches both actually and visually, by adopting shallower profiles for the outer faces. Over Bridge (1825–1828) near Gloucester, and Dean Bridge (1829–1831) in Edinburgh, best exemplify this trend.

Telford's influence as an engineer was immense—both through the example of his works and what was written about them and through what he passed on directly to pupils and assistants.

ROWLAND MAINSTONE

WORKS

1792–1794, Saint Mary Magdalene, Bridgnorth, England. 1793–1794, Longdon on Tern Aqueduct, near Shrewsbury, England. 1794–1805, Pont Cyssylte Aqueduct, north Wales. 1795–1796, Buildwas Bridge, England. 1811–1812, Bonar Bridge, Scotland. 1819–1826, Menai Bridge, north Wales. 1823–1826, Mythe Bridge, near Tewkesbury, England. 1825–1828, Over Bridge, near Gloucester, England. 1827–1828, Saint Katherine's Docks (warehouses), London. 1829–1831, Dean Bridge, Edinburgh.

BIBLIOGRAPHY

GIBB, ALEXANDER 1935 *The Story of Telford.* London: Maclehose.

PENFOLD, ALASTAIR (editor) 1980 *Thomas Telford: Engineer.* London: Telford.

PROVIS, WILLIAM A. 1828 *An Historical and Descriptive Account of the Suspension Bridge Constructed over the Menai Strait.* London: The author.

ROLT, L. T. C. 1958 *Thomas Telford.* London: Longmans.

SMILES, SAMUEL (1861)1968 Volume 2 in *Lives of the Engineers.* Reprint. New York: Kelley.

TELFORD, THOMAS 1838 *Life of Thomas Telford, Civil Engineer.* Edited by John Rickman. Includes text and atlas. London: Payne & Foss.

TEMANZA, TOMMASO

Although he was trained as an architect and earned his living in that profession, Tommaso Temanza (1705–1789) acquired his fame largely through his lives and histories of Venetian architects and sculptors published during the second half of the eighteenth century. In these works, he attempted to re-establish the rules and classical principles of architecture. Although he traveled to Rome only late in his life and never saw Greece, his insistence on the classical rules of architecture gives him an important place next to other neoclassical theorists such as FRANCESCO MILIZIA and FRANCESCO ALGAROTTI.

Temanza was born in Venice and was trained by his uncle Giovanni Antonio Scalfarotto and by Giovanni Poleni, two of the leading exponents of the neo-Palladian (see ANDREA PALLADIO) style in early eighteenth-century Italy. His first buildings date from mid-century. A new façade for the Church of Santa Margherita, Padua, is based on the sepulchral monuments of VINCENZO SCAMOZZI. In addition, he was responsible for the Church of Santa Maria Maddalena in Venice (1748), a variation on the forms of the Pantheon in Rome. Temanza was also employed by the Venetian Republic as a military engineer and "prefect of the public waters," overseeing the canals.

Temanza's literary career began with the publication of a book on the Roman antiquities of Rimini (1741). He followed that with book-length lives of the Renaissance architect-sculptor JACOPO SANSOVINO (1752), Palladio (1762), and Scamozzi (1770). These, and other briefer lives, were collected in a single volume, *Vite dei Piu Celebri Architetti e Scultori Veneziani* (1778). This was the first work of Venetian scholarship to deal exclusively with architecture and sculpture. The word "scholarship" is used advisedly. Unlike earlier artistic biographers such as GIORGIO VASARI, Temanza was extremely careful to acknowledge his documentary and archival sources.

Temanza's relation to Venetian architecture of the past marks off his neoclassical position. SEBASTIANO SERLIO is condemned for the excessive variety of his forms, and those who followed it more assiduously, such as Palladio and Sansovino, were generally praised. Also praised were the architects of the Venetian fifteenth century. Scalfarotto, Temanza's teacher, was singled out for his architecture, which resembled that of BARTOLOMEO BON. Among Temanza's other favorites were MAURO CODUCCI and ANTONIO RIZZO; although not familiar with their names, he knew and praised their buildings.

Among those who followed Temanza's opinions were his friend Francesco Malizia and the architect Matteo Lucchesi as well as ANTOINE QUATREMÈRE DE QUINCY and Leopoldo Cicognara. Temanza's works are still used by scholars. Although most of the architects and sculptors he wrote about were not known to him, his archival research and his knowledge of Venice and its people provide a guide for many of our opinions today.

NICHOLAS ADAMS

WORKS

1748, Santa Maria Maddalena, Venice. n.d., Santa Margherita (façade), Padua, Italy.

BIBLIOGRAPHY

IVANOFF, NICOLA 1963 "Tommaso Temanza." *Bolletino del Centro Internazionale degli Studi di Architettura Andrea Palladio* 5:202–211.

TEMANZA, TOMMASO 1741 *Delle antichità di Rimini, libri due.* Venice, Italy: Pasquali.

TEMANZA, TOMMASO 1778 *Vite dei più celebri architetti e scultori veneziani che fiorirono nel secolo decimo sesto.* Venice, Italy: Palese.

TEMANZA, TOMMASO 1781 *Antica pianta dell'indita città di Venezia.* Venice, Italy: Palese.

TENGBOM, IVAR

Ivar Justus Tengbom (1878–1968) was one of the most important and influential of twentieth-century Swedish architects, and one of the best known abroad. In Sweden, he exercised a decisive influence on the generation between the world wars, encouraging through his teachings and example the establishment of a modernized neoclassicism. Tengbom's reputation abroad is illustrated by his foreign honors: he was an honorary member of the Prussian Academy of Art, the Royal Institute of British Architects, the Architectural League of New York, the American Institute of Architects, the Soviet Academy of Art, and the Academy of San Luca in Rome; he held honorary degrees from the Technische Hochschulen of Stuttgart, Darmstadt, and Vienna. In 1938, he received the Royal Gold Medal from the Royal Institute of British Architects.

Tengbom was born in Vireda, Småland, and married the prominent Swedish graphic artist and sculptor Hjördis Nordin. Their son Anders, born in 1911, became a successful architect in collaboration with his father; a grandson, Svante, also carries on the family profession. Ivar Tengbom began his studies at the Chalmers Technical Institute in Göteborg, and continued them at the Academy of Art in Stockholm, where he received the Royal Gold Medal. From 1900 to 1906, Tengbom traveled extensively throughout continental Europe; most important to him, however, were his trips to Denmark, where he got to know well the work of MARTIN NYROP and HACK KAMPMANN.

In Sweden, after a brief association with ERIK LALLERSTEDT, Tengbom set up independent practice, first in partnership with Ernst Torulf, then alone. From 1907, he was also active in the Royal Building Administration, and he became its director in 1924. In 1916, he was named professor at the Academy of Art, and later became its president.

Tengbom's work was varied. He moved from the National Romantic style of the Högalid Church (designed 1911, executed 1917–1923), which was deeply influenced by the work of LARS WAHLMAN and Nyrop, to the slick functionalism of the Citypalatset Block (1930–1932). But most of his buildings were characterized by an austere, workmanlike, well-planned, very refined and elegant neoclassicism. The milestone in the development of this style was his Stockholm Concert House (1923–1926), which reduced its neoclassical models to a simple cubic mass, fronted by a single giant order. The Concert House used rich and highly polished materials on the interior, and displayed Tengbom's mastery of functional planning and modern acoustics. The Concert House, the Tändstickpalatset (1926–1928), and other works of the 1920s foreshadowed the stripped classicism which came into general use in Europe and the United States in the 1930s. Tengbom often collaborated with the sculptor Carl Milles, whose lithe and graceful, but representational, figures were particularly well-suited to a modernized neoclassical setting. Tengbom's combination of historicism, functionalism, careful craftsmanship, and restrained elegance has brought him enduring respect and admiration in Sweden, but his importance has been overlooked by recent historians of modern European architecture.

BARBARA MILLER LANE

WORKS

1909, Enskilda Bank; 1909–1910, Town Hall; Borås, Sweden. 1911, Church, Arvika, Sweden. 1911, Sachsska Children's Hospital (later altered), Årstalunden; 1912–1915, Enskilda Bank Headquarters; 1913–1914, E. Trygger House; 1917–1923, Högalid Church; 1919, Reederei Company Offices; 1919, K. Tillberg House; Stockholm. 1921, Enskilda Bank, Vänersborg, Sweden. 1921, Sporrong and Company; 1923–1926, Concert House (interior later altered); 1925–1926, Grand Hotel (remodeled; later altered); 1925–1926, Handelshögskolan (additions in 1976 by others); 1926–1928, Swedish Match Company Offices (Tändstickpalatset); 1928, Skandia Insurance Company (addition); 1928–1934, Esselte Building (offices and press); 1930–1932, Citypalatset Block; 1930–1932, Sydbank (office and apartments); Stockholm. 1933, Church, Höganas, Sweden. 1934, Savings Bank, Örebro, Sweden. 1940, Swedish Institute of Classical Studies, Rome. 1943–1944, Åtvidaberg Offices; 1946–1949, Bonnierhuset (general offices and printing office; later altered); 1948–1952, Arvfurstens Palace (restoration, rebuilding, and additions); 1949, Bondeska Palace (restoration); 1956–1958,

Royal Palace (restoration of Museum of Antiquities); 1958, Stockholm Savings Bank (remodeling); Stockholm.

BIBLIOGRAPHY

AHLBERG, HAKON 1925 *Moderne Schwedische Architektur.* Berlin: Wasmuth.

ANDERSSON, HENRIK O., and BEDOIRE, FREDRIC (1973)1977 *Stockholms Byggnader.* Rev. ed. Stockholm: Bokförlaget Prisma.

"Bank in Stockholm Designed by Ivar Tengbom." 1948 *Architect and Building News* 193:124–125.

BOKLUND, HARALD (editor) 1923 *Hundra Blad Svensk Byggnadskonst.* Malmö, Sweden: Byggnadstidningens.

"The Concert House, Stockholm." 1929 *Architectural Review* 65:184–193.

LINN, BJÖRN 1981 "Ivar Tengbom." In Thomas Hall (editor), *Stenstadens Arkitekter.* Stockholm: Akademilitteratur.

ÖSTBERG, RAGNAR 1908 *Auswahl von schwedischer Architektur der Gegenwart.* Stockholm: Aktiebolaget Ljus.

RASMUSSEN, STEEN EILER 1940 *Nordische Baukunst.* Berlin: Wasmuth.

TENGBOM, IVAR 1931 "How Yesterday Made Possible Today's Swedish Architecture." *American Architect* 140, no. 2598:32–37, 98–100.

TENGBOM, IVAR 1941 "Svenska Instistitutet I Rom." *Byggmästaren* 6:69–75.

TENGBOM, IVAR 1944 "Atvidabergs-Huset." *Byggmästaren* 14:239–260.

TEODOLI, GIROLAMO

The eighteenth-century dilettante Girolamo Teodoli (1677–1766) occupied a position of prominence as an architect in Rome throughout his life. Teodoli's noble birth—he was a relation of Pope Innocent XIII—brought him early acceptance in artistic circles, for in 1695, at the age of eighteen, he was granted honorary membership in the Roman Academy of Saint Luke. In 1726, he became a regular member of the Academy, of which he was subsequently elected *principe* on three separate occasions. Teodoli's excellent connections with the Roman aristocracy, his outgoing personality, and his distinction as a teacher ensured him a brilliant academic career and the recognition of his professional colleagues. He is reputed to have been an especially learned theoretician, an accomplishment which is underscored by the presence of the treatises of VITRUVIUS and ANDREA PALLADIO which appear in the background of his portrait in the Academy of Saint Luke. In certain respects, Teodoli's noble birth and dual interests in teaching and architectural theory tended to set him apart from most contemporary Roman architects, who were more concerned with obtaining commissions

Teodoli.
Santi Marcellino e Pietro.
Rome.
1751–1752

and the practical realities of the profession. His position resembles more that of contemporary English dilettantes such as LORD BURLINGTON.

Teodoli designed relatively few buildings that were actually built. His first major work was the Teatro Argentina (1731), one of the most important theaters of eighteenth-century Rome. Like CARLO FONTANA's Teatro Tor di Nona, on which it was modeled, the Teatro Argentina had a horseshoe-shaped groundplan, and six levels of boxes. The theater still stands, but extensive renovations in the nineteenth century replaced Teodoli's late baroque forms with neoclassical ones.

Teodoli's best-known work is the Church of Santi Marcellino e Pietro, which was erected between 1751 and 1752. Its Greek-cross plan recalls a long series of Renaissance and baroque centralized churches, especially PIETRO BERRETTINI DA CORTONA's Santi Luca e Martina. Santi Marcellino e Pietro detaches itself from this tradition, however, in its emphasis on spare planar surfaces and basic geometric shapes. Teodoli exploited the corner site to accentuate the cubic mass of the exterior and reveal the stepped profile of the dome. The exterior betrays the limitations of Teodoli's inventive powers; his treatment of the orders is correct but uninspiring, and in place of a consistent and distinctively personal approach to design one sees the most eclectic and conflicting references to sources as disparate as the Pantheon and FRANCESCO BORROMINI's Sant'Ivo. Similarly, because of its studied proportions and lack of ornament, the interior appears cool, overly restrained, and unimaginative.

The lack of vigor which is evident in Teodoli's executed designs was remarked upon by contemporary critics such as FRANCESCO MILIZIA. Teodoli's significance in the history of architecture rests more on his reputation as a teacher and his role as representative and spokesman for his professional colleagues than on his distinction as a practicing architect.

JOHN PINTO

WORKS

1731, Teatro Argentina; *1738, San Nicola in Arcione (renovation); 1751, San Salvatore in Lauro (sepulchral monuments of Cardinals Simonetti and Marefosco); 1751–1752, Santi Marcellino e Pietro; Rome. 1755, San Pietro, Vicovaro, Italy. 1759–1761, Santa Maria di Montesanto (bell tower and monastery), Rome.

BIBLIOGRAPHY

ELLING, CHRISTIAN 1975 *Rome: A Biography of Her Architecture from Bernini to Thorvaldsen.* Tübingen, Germany: Wasmuth.
MILIZIA, FRANCESCO 1785 *Memorie degli architetti antichi e moderni.* 4th ed. Bassano, Italy: Remondini di Venezia.
MISSIRINI, MELCHIORE 1823 *Memorie per servire alla storia della romana Accademia di S. Luca fino alla morte di Antonio Canova.* Rome: Stamperia De Romanis.
TIRINCANTI, GIULIO 1971 *Il Teatro Argentina.* Rome: Palombi.

TERRAGNI, GIUSEPPE

Although Giuseppe Terragni (1904–1943) died young and with few completed works to his credit, his buildings exerted an enormous influence on his own and subsequent generations of architects.

The son of a mason, Terragni was born in Meda, near Milan and apparently became interested in architecture as a youth. He attended the technical high school and then enrolled in the Milan Politecnico, where his 1926 thesis consisted of research on MICHELANGELO. Even within the confines of a stuffily academic institute, the young students were infected by new currents in architecture drifting down across the Alps. In Italy, Terragni had especially close connections with a number of Italian Futurists, and he also drew inspiration from the visionary designs of fellow Comasque ANTONIO SANT'ELIA. Terragni and classmates Ubaldo Castagnoli, Luigi FIGINI AND Gino POLLINI), Guido Frette, Sebastiano Larco, and Carlo Rava formed the *Gruppo* 7 in 1926, bursting on the scene with a series of manifestos proclaiming a new era of architecture. As early twentieth-century manifestos go, theirs was not especially radical, but it was electric in staid Italian architectural circles. Within a short time, the *Gruppo* 7 had joined forces with other young architects from Rome to found the *Movimento italiano per l'architettura razionale.* By 1927, the architects were exhibiting designs conceived within the formal vocabulary of the Modern movement, or, as it was called in Italy, Rationalism.

Terragni's first building, the Novocomum Apartments in Como (1927–1928), proved to be one of the earliest Italian examples of the modern idiom. He combined the novel material of reinforced concrete (a highly polemical matter at the time) with traditional masonry as infill. External protruding balconies emphasized the building's horizontal quality, and on the two corners facing the street glass cylinders penetrated the rectilinear structure in a manner reminiscent of experiments he had conducted in designs for a gas works some months earlier, as well as of ILIA GOLOSOV's project for a Workers' Club in Moscow. More important, however, Terragni responded to the rounded corners of the adjacent structure, managing both to insert the Novocomum comfortably into the setting and to experiment with Constructivist and Purist themes.

With this building, Terragni also established another pattern: the façade he submitted to the conservative Building Commission bore decorous pedimented windows, molded stringcourses, portals flanked by columns, and little resemblance to the final structure. Despite the local furor when the straw matting and scaffolding came down and the building was unveiled, Terragni stubbornly resisted outside pressures on this and subsequent designs and, if nothing else, wore his opponents down in wars of attrition. He later battled the Fascist Party (PNF) for years on the issue of a façade decoration for his Casa del Fascio in Como. Intransigent and convinced of his own aesthetic judgment, Terragni was also an avid fascist who entered competitions to design buildings for various PNF agencies, who designed fascist exhibition installations, and who wrote endless polemical letters on a range of issues. His political associations have proved more of a problem for historians than they were for him, for it is clear from his writings that he was a sincere and dedicated fascist. He was also active in promoting the modernistic vision of architecture, attending the 1933 Congrès Internationaux d'Architecture Moderne (CIAM) and participating in the discussions which led to the Charter of Athens.

After several years of small commissions, Terragni received his first major project in 1932 for the Casa del Fascio of Como (1932–1936). His brother Attilio, architect, mayor of Como, and staunch member of the PNF, offered to donate his own services as chief designer and those of Giuseppe as his assistant. Attilio secured the commission, but there is no question that it was Giuseppe's building from the outset. Drawings in the Terragni archives suggest that Giuseppe worked on the project as early as 1929, although he submitted the first designs only in late 1932. The Casa, with its austere but highly differentiated façades, marble revetments, and extensive fenestration, turned out to be the flagship of the Modern movement in Italy. In plan it is a perfect square and in elevation a spare orthogonal grid; Terragni opened up the center with an internal courtyard under a glass ceiling, lined it with four floors of galleries and offices, and opened the atrium to the adjacent piazza with a row of sixteen glass doors. Terragni devised the doors to open simultaneously, allowing an uninterrupted flow of people from the atrium to the piazza, an ideal set-up for PNF mass meetings. He managed to design it as he wanted despite constraints imposed by the PNF.

In the next few years, Terragni acquired a number of commissions for apartment buildings in Milan in collaboration with PIETRO LINGERI. In 1934, he joined with A. Carminati, P. Lingeri, MARCELLO NIZZOLI, E. Saliva, M. Sironi, and L. Vietti to enter competitions for the Palazzo del Littorio in Rome. The team submitted two entries, one (Solution B) a sleek and daringly modern glass, steel, and reinforced concrete structure, while in the other (Solution A), the offices and functional spaces were shielded behind an eighty meter porphyry wall which was cobwebbed with isostatic lines and from which Mussolini's platform jutted. In a later design, the team developed the themes of Solution B and introduced even more glass and leaner lines.

Two other works rank with the Casa del Fascio: the Sant'Elia Nursery School (1936–1937) and the Giuliani–Frigerio Apartments (1939–1940), both in Como. For the nursery school, Terragni abandoned the closed block typical of his earlier designs and shifted to a low, horizontal structure resting lightly on the ground, with slender pilasters and extensive glass surfaces to render the structural system transparent. Terragni's last major project was for a Dante Museum and Study Center in Rome which Mussolini approved; it was never built because the war intervened. He sought an architectural interpretation containing a richness of imagery comparable to the three *canticas* of *The Divine Comedy,* a work which had gained special importance in the nationalist fever of Fascist Italy.

With Italy's entry into World War II, Terragni entered the Italian armed forces, serving in Greece and on the Russian front. He returned home in January 1943, suffering from total exhaustion, and

died of a stroke a few days after the fall of the fascist government in July 1943.

DIANE GHIRARDO

Terragni.
Casa del Fascio.
Como, Italy.
1932–1936

WORKS

1927–1928, Novocomum Apartments; 1930, Vitrum Store; 1931–1933, Monument to the Fallen of World War I; 1932–1936, Casa del Fascio; Como, Italy. *1933, Triennale, Monza, Italy. 1933, Toninello Apartments (with Pietro Lingeri), Milan. *1933, Vacation House, Monza, Italy. 1933–1935, Ghiringelli Apartments (with Lingeri); 1933–1935, Rustici Apartments (with Lingeri); 1934–1935, Lavezzari Apartments (with Lingeri); Milan. 1935. Pedraglio House; 1936–1937, Sant'Elia Nursery School; Como, Italy. 1936–1937, Villa Bianco, Seveso, Italy. 1938–1939, Casa del Fascio di Lissone (with A. Carminati), Lissone, Italy. 1939–1940, Giuliani–Frigerio Apartments, Como, Italy.

BIBLIOGRAPHY

EISENMANN, PETER 1970 "From Object to Relationship: Giuseppe Terragni." *Casabella* 34:38–41.
EISENMANN, PETER 1971 "From Object to Relationship II: Giuseppe Terragni." *Perspecta: The Yale Architectural Journal* 13–14:36–65.
GHIRARDO, DIANE 1980 "Politics of a Masterpiece: The *Vicenda* of the Decoration of the Façade of the Casa del Fascio, Como, 1936–39." *Art Bulletin* 62:466–478.
LABÒ, MARIO 1936 "La Casa del Fascio di Como." *Quadrante* 35:entire issue on the Casa del Fascio.
LABÒ, MARIO 1947 *Giuseppe Terragni.* Milan: Il Balcone.
MANTERO, ENRICO (editor) 1969 *Giuseppe Terragni e la città del razionalismo italiano.* Bari, Italy: Dedalo Libri.
SCHUMACHER, THOMAS 1977 "From Gruppo 7 to the Danteum: A Critical Introduction to Terragni's *Relazione sul Danteum.*" *Oppositions* 9:89–107.
VERONESI, GIULIA 1953 *Difficoltà politiche dell'architettura in Italia 1920–40.* Milan: Facoltà d'architettura del Politecnico di Milano.
ZEVI, BRUNO 1968 "Omaggio a Terragni." *Architettura, cronache e storia* 14:entire issue on Giuseppe Terragni.

TERZI, FILIPPO

Born in Bologna, Italy, Filippo Terzi (1529–1597) spent his youth in Pesaro, where he studied mathematics and engineering at the Della Rovere court. His first documented activity (1563) regarded the demolition of some buildings in Pesaro, though he probably had already been active for some time as both a church decorator and a civil engineer. In Pesaro, documents show he worked on some hydraulic projects and city fortifications. He also worked on the fortresses at Senigalia and Urbino, establishing his reputation as a military engineer.

In 1576, Terzi contracted to serve Portugal's King Don Sebastiano for four years. During that time, he prepared the ill-fated Portuguese expedition to Morocco, where he himself was captured by the Moroccans at Alcácer Quebir in 1578. Liberated by the Portuguese king Cardinal Don Enrico and awarded a royal pension, Terzi nonetheless joined the forces of the Spanish King Philip II in 1580 and returned to Portugal as Philip's master of royal works. In this period, Terzi added a pavilion to the Royal Palace in Lisbon after having prepared two triumphal arches for Philip II's entry into Lisbon on June 29, 1581. In the following year, Terzi began work on his most important commission, the Church of São Vicente de Fora (1582–1605) in Lisbon. The massive interior recalls Terzi's Italian heritage, whereas the organization of the interior, with its choir placed behind the sanctuary and a vestibule behind the façade, shows the direct influence of projects by JUAN DE HERRERA. The façade, on the other hand, is quite original. Numerous horizontal and vertical divisions, two towers, and twenty-four openings are bound together by a series of flat pilasters. On the middle and upper stories, the severely reduced capitals are joined together by an undecorated frieze. The façade was to become a model for numerous later façades in both Portugal and Brazil.

Engineering duties continued to occupy Terzi in this period. He built the fortress at Setubal (1580s), assisted in the preparation of the Spanish Armada, examined a bridge on the Mondego River in 1583, reconstructed the aqueduct of Saint Sebastian at Coimbra, and built the aqueduct in Vila do Conde. At Thomar, Terzi erected a new five-kilometer long aqueduct (1584–1613) and completed Diego di Torralva's masterpiece, the Cristo Cloister. Earlier scholarship had given the design of the cloister to Terzi, but, as Guiseppe Fiocco (1938) has shown, Terzi was directed to complete the cloister according to Torralva's design. Terzi's designs were never as vibrantly active as Torralva's, but Terzi's straightforward, even severe style appealed to Philip II's preference for aus-

tere monumentality. Two works in this style are attributed to Terzi: the monastery of Serra do Pilar with its circularly planned Ionic cloister (begun in 1598, after Terzi's death) and the Paco do Bispo at Coimbra with its two-story open loggia (renovated 1592).

GARY M. RADKE

WORKS

Before 1576, Fortress, Pesaro, Italy. Before 1576, Fortress, Senigalia, Italy. Before 1576, Fortress, Urbino, Italy. 1580s, Aqueduct, Vila do Conde, Portugal. 1580s, Aqueduct of Saint Sebastian (reconstruction), Coimbra, Portugal. 1580s, Castle, Setubal, Portugal. 1580s, Cristo Cloister (completion), Thomar, Portugal. *1580s, Pavilion, Royal Palace; *1581, Triumphal Arches (for the entry of Philip II); 1582–1605, São Vicente de Fora; Lisbon. 1584–1613, Aqueduct, Thomas, Portugal. 1592, Paco de Bispo, Coimbra, Portugal. (A)1598, Monastery, Serra do Pilar, Portugal.

BIBLIOGRAPHY

BATTELLI, GUIDO 1929 "Filippo Terzi: Architetto e ingegnere italiano in Portogallo." *Biblos* 5, no. 78:412–417. Coimbra, Portugal.

DOS SANTOS, REYNALDO 1953 Volume 3 in *História da arte em Portugal.* Porto, Portugal: Portucalense Editora.

FIOCCO, GIUSEPPE 1938 "Il Chiostro Grande nel Convento di Cristo a Tomar e l'opera di Filippo Terzi." *Rivista d'arte* 20:355–363.

KUBLER, GEORGE, and SORIA, MARTIN 1959 *Art and Architecture in Spain and Portugal and Their American Dominions: 1500 to 1800.* Harmondsworth, England, and Baltimore: Penguin.

TRINDADE COELHO, HENRIQUE, and BATTELLI, GUIDO 1935 *Filippo Terzi, architetto e ingegnere militare in Portogallo (1577–97): Documenti inediti dell'Archivio di Stato di Firenze e della Biblioteca Oliveriana di Pesaro.* Florence.

TESSENOW, HEINRICH

Heinrich Tessenow (1876–1950) was raised in Rostock, Germany. He trained in Munich with KARL HOCHEDER and FRIEDRICH VON THIERSCH, and worked with MARTIN DÜLFER at the Technische Hochschule in Dresden (1909–1910). He taught at the School of Arts and Crafts in Vienna (1913–1919) and the Academy of Arts in Dresden (1920–1926), before becoming professor at the Technische Hochschule in Charlottenburg in 1926. Thereafter he worked in Berlin.

Tessenow was a leading member of the German Arts and Crafts movement, which differed from the earlier English movement in the lingering influence of KARL FRIEDRICH SCHINKEL. He was also influential in the German *Werkbund,* founded in 1907 to improve the design and quality of architecture and standardized goods. Although functionalism was initially the guild's priority, it later became secondary to the symbolism of the "classic national style," which was represented in the revival of medieval German architecture and applied arts.

As pictured in his *Der Wohnhausbau* (1909), Tessenow's ideal house is always on a small scale, with a hip roof with eaves close to the ground. The over-all volumes are squat and awkward, but the construction is fastidiously exact. The unique beauty of these houses derives from this juxtaposition of the uncouth and the sublime.

The Dalcroze Institute for Physical Education in Hellerau (1910) is his most famous work. His style continued to be a refined, stripped classicism, but he abandoned his earlier symmetry. His neoconservative garden city ideas did not keep him from joining *Der Ring,* Germany's most formally radical architectural group in the 1920s. During the 1930s, *Der Ring,* the Bauhaus, and the *Werkbund* were suppressed as parts in a Marxist plot. Tessenow's activity resumed during the German housing boom after World War II.

His ultimate impact came through no single architectural monument, but through a lifetime of influential teaching and a series of influential publications.

JAMES WARD

WORKS

1906–1907, Workers' Housing, State Electricity Company, Trier, Germany. 1910, Dalcroze Institute for Physical Education, Hellerau, Germany. 1910, Schmidt House, Hopfengarten, near Magdeburg, Germany. 1910–1911, Single-family Terraced Houses, Am Schänkenberg, Hellerau, Germany. 1919–1920, Graf Doret Mansion, Czomahaya, Hungary. 1924, Bridge, River Elbe, Meissen, Germany. 1927, City Swimming Hall, Gartenstrasse; 1930–1931, Memorial to the War Dead (renovation and remodeling of Karl Friedrich Schinkel's Neue Wache); Berlin. 1936, Barracks, Magdeburg, Germany. 1936, Hall Layouts, Olympic Art Exhibitions, Berlin. 1936, Hindenburg Memorial, Magdeburg, Germany. 1937, Single-family houses, Iserhorstweg, Neustrelitz-Kiefernheide, Germany.

BIBLIOGRAPHY

CAMPBELL, JOAN 1978 *The German Werkbund: The Politics of Reform in the Applied Arts.* N.J.: Princeton University Press.
HEGEMANN, WERNER 1925 "Arbeiten von Heinrich Tessenow und Seinen Schülern." *Wasmuths Monatshefte für Baukunst* 9:365–381.
POSENER, JULIUS 1977 "Two Masters: Hans Poelzig und Heinrich Tessenow." *Lotus International* 16:20–25.
SCHEFFLER, KARL 1925 "Neue Arbeiten von Heinrich Tessenow." *Kunst und Künstler* 24:55–60.
TESSENOW, HEINRICH (1909)1927 *Der Wohnhausbau.* 3d ed. Munich: Callwey.
TESSENOW, HEINRICH 1917 "Das Ornament." *Kunst und Künstler* 15:32–36.
TESSENOW, HEINRICH 1919 *Handwerk und Kleinstadt.* Berlin: Cassirer.
TESSENOW, HEINRICH 1921 *Das Land in der Mitte: Ein Vortrag.* Hellerau, Germany: Hegner.
TIETZE, HANS 1913 "Heinrich Tessenow." *Kunst und Kunsthandwerk* 16:585–591.

TESSIN FAMILY

The history of Swedish architecture in the period from 1640 to 1740 was to a great extent determined by three members of the Tessin family, father, son, and grandson. After having successfully taken part in the Thirty Years War, Sweden became an attractive alternative to many artists in Germany, Holland, and France, who followed the Swedish generals when they turned back home from the Continent. Among those who came was Nicodemus Tessin the Elder (1615–1681) who arrived in Sweden in 1636. Like many others of his kind, he started as a fortification engineer, but as the need for fortresses was considerably less than that for modern, dignified public buildings and private residences, Tessin the Elder was employed by the high nobility and the royal family to furnish them in these respects.

In 1646, Tessin the Elder was appointed royal architect. Supported by Queen Christina, he was able to go to Italy, France, and Holland in 1651 for purposes of studies of art and architecture. He realized that his experiences of the north European art of building would not be enough if he was to respond to the demands of his future masters. Tessin the Elder certainly knew to take full advantage of his trip. When back in Sweden again in 1653, he was not only a mature baroque architect but he had also started to collect prints, drawings, and books on architecture and had established close contacts with colleagues abroad. This was evident ten years later when he made a design for a new garden for the Royal Palace at Drottningholm, which comes so close to the recently inaugurated garden for Vaux-le-Vicomte, ANDRÉ LE NOSTRE's breakthrough as a garden-architect, that Tessin must have been advised by le Nostre himself or must have obtained copies of his drawings. Tessin the Elder was the architect of the Palace of Drottningholm commissioned by Queen Hedvig Eleonora. Here, for the first time in Sweden, he developed the typical French baroque manner with its pavilion system, galleries, and monumental staircase and with a magnificent state bedroom, still marvelously well preserved. The Italian, espe-

Nicodemus the Younger and Carl Gustav Tessin.
Royal Palace (completed with others).
Stockholm.
1697–1753

cially the Roman, classicism is well adopted in his designs for the Bank of Sweden in Stockholm and the Cathedral of Kalmar begun in 1660, which to some extent echoes the church architecture of GIACOMO BAROZZI DA VIGNOLA. In 1601, he was appointed town architect of Stockholm, a position he held to his death in 1681.

After the death of Nicodemus Tessin the Elder, his son, Nicodemus Tessin the Younger (1654–1728), immediately took over as town architect of Stockholm. He had received a thorough education from his father completed by a five-year stay in Rome (1673–1678) and a two-year visit to Paris (1678–1680). During 1687–1688, he made a second visit to Paris and Rome. Taking great interest in the Swedish architect, the abdicated converted Swedish Queen Christina, who had settled in Rome, introduced him to GIOVANNI LORENZO BERNINI and CARLO FONTANA. The main and lasting experience of his travels was that the Italian classicism should be a model for the architect as far as the great outlines of the architecture and façades were concerned and that the French baroque as exemplified by Lebrun should guide the distribution of rooms, their decoration and furniture, and, last but not least, the gardens.

Tessin the Younger had the opportunity to bring his ideas into practice when finishing his father's work at Drottningholm where he became a capable leader of painters, sculptors, stucco workers, and gardeners. He did so even more when in the 1690s he erected his own house in the city of Stockholm, just opposite the southern wing of the old Royal Castle. Here, he presented himself as the brilliantly gifted eclectic, masterly controlling all the elements of contemporary Italian and French baroque to arrive at an astoundingly coherent and harmonious piece of architecture.

In 1697, the old Royal Castle of Stockholm was destroyed by fire. Almost too quickly, Tessin the Younger had his designs ready for the new Royal Palace, his biggest and most important task. Unfortunately, at the same time as the walls began to rise, Sweden sank into poverty and misery as a result of the wars during the reign of Charles XII,

which ruined the country. The lack of money and workmen brought the whole enterprise to a standstill and forced Tessin to employ himself with minor jobs and with immense projects of nearly utopian character (city plan for the surroundings of the Royal Palace of Stockholm, design for an adaptation of the Louvre square court into a round one, Apollo temple at Versailles), of which none was executed.

At the end of his life, however, he experienced the pleasure of seeing the bricklayers return to work at the Royal Palace in the middle of the 1720s. He also had the satisfaction of knowing that after his death his son Carl Gustav Tessin (1695–1770) would carry on his work as high commissioner of public buildings. But Carl Gustav had primarily an administrative capacity and made his main career as a politician and diplomat. In the field of art and architecture, he left the practical parts to Carl Hårleman (see HÅRLEMAN FAMILY) and dedicated his life to connoisseurship and enlarging his father's and grandfather's collections of prints, drawings, and books. He left the architectural drawings to Hårleman as working material and for purposes of study. Together, they form the important Tessin-Hårleman Collection of around 10,000 items of Italian, French, and Swedish architectural drawings from the sixteenth to the eighteenth centuries, now in the National Museum in Stockholm.

As an architect Carl Gustav Tessin never reached above the level of an amateur; together with Hårleman, he made some designs for his own country estate (Åkerö Manor). Yet, his name belongs to the history of Swedish architecture as a supervisor and supporter of Hårleman's work at the Royal Palace in Stockholm and as an intermediary link between international, especially French, art of all kinds and Swedish culture.

ULF G. JOHNSSON

WORKS

NICODEMUS TESSIN THE ELDER

c.1660, Royal Palace, Drottningholm, Sweden. c.1660s, Kalmar Cathedral, Sweden. 1671, Caroline Mausoleum, Riddarholms Church (not completed until 1740); 1676, Bank of Sweden; Stockholm.

NICODEMUS TESSIN THE YOUNGER

1690s, Nicodemus Tessin the Younger House, Stockholm. 1694, Steninge Castle, Sweden. 1697–1728, Royal Palace (not completed until 1753 by Carl Gustav Tessin and others), Stockholm. n.d., Gardens (with Johan Hårleman), Royal Palaces, Stockholm, Drottningholm, Ulriksdal, and Karlberg, Sweden.

CARL GUSTAV TESSIN

1720s?–1753, Royal Palace (completion, with others) Stockholm.

BIBLIOGRAPHY

JOSEPHSON, RAGNAR 1930 *L'architecte de Charles XII, Nicodème Tessin.* Paris and Brussels: Van Oest.
JOSEPHSON, RAGNAR 1930–1931 *Tessin; Nicodemus Tessin D. Y., tiden, mannen, verket.* Stockholm: Norstedt.
KOMMER, BJÖRN R. 1974 *Nicodemus Tessin der Jungere und das Stockholmer Schloss.* Heidelberg, Germany: Winter.
WRANGEL, FREDRIK ULRIK 1912 *Tessinska palatset: ett bidrag till öfverståthållarehusets i Stockholm historia.* Stockholm: Palmqvist.

TESTA, CLORINDO

Argentine architect-artist Clorindo Testa (1923–) initiated an empirical approach to architecture in Argentina that has redefined the concept of urban interior space and exterior continuity. Born in Naples, Testa graduated from the National University of Buenos Aires in 1948 when the Beaux-Arts tradition of copying from VITRUVIUS persisted. In 1949, he returned to Italy and devoted three years solely to painting. Rejecting the anachronism of the Beaux-Arts approach, he won his first major architectural competition for the Civic Center at Santa Rosa (1955–1963), with a tactile application of rough concrete—the first brutalist structure in Argentina.

Testa works as an independent agent, joining forces with different groups of architects each time he enters an architectural competition, but his genius for form and spacial manipulation always dominates. The contrasting environment of an exterior of rough reinforced concrete and a high-tech interior distinguishes his best designs, including the Bank of London and South America (1960–1966). Here, the closed façade gives way to an expansive interior of six open floors where cantilevered platforms cut into space like a three-dimensional collage. For Testa, engineering is an essential aspect of design conception; it has enabled him to win numerous competitions with designs that leave spectators in awe.

ELIZABETH D. HARRIS

WORKS

1955–1963, Civic Center and Bus Station (with Francisco Rossi, Augusto Gaido, and Boris Dabinovic), Santa Rosa, La Pampa, Argentina. 1960–1966, Bank of London and South America (with SEPRA); 1962–1980, National Library (with FRANCISCO BULLRICH and Alicia Cazzaniga de Bullrich); Buenos Aires. 1965, National Museum of Fine Arts, Montevideo. 1970–1975, Bank of Holland, Buenos Aires.

BIBLIOGRAPHY

BAYÓN, DAMIÁN, and GASPARINI, PAOLO 1977 *Panorámica de la Arquitectura Latino-Americana.* Barcelona: Editorial Blume.
BULLRICH, FRANCISCO 1969 *New Directions in Latin American Architecture.* New York: Braziller.

TEULON, SAMUEL SANDERS

Samuel Sanders Teulon (1812–1873) was one of the most original High Victorian Gothic architects. He was born in Greenwich, England, the son of a cabinetmaker of Huguenot descent. He attended the Royal Academy Schools, was articled to George Legg, and was later an assistant in the office of George Porter of Bermondsey. He started practice in 1838 and produced a large number of buildings in a vigorous and highly original Gothic style. His clients included the Queen, the Archbishop of Canterbury, and the dukes of Bedford, Marlborough, and Saint Albans. His brother, William Milford Teulon (1823–1900), was also an architect.

ROGER DIXON

WORKS

1849–1852, Tortworth Court, Gloucestershire, England. 1851–1852, Christ Church, Croydon, London. 1852–1853, Saint Margaret's Church (school and vestry hall), Angmering, Sussex, England. 1854, Cottages for Crown Labourers, Layton's Gate, Windsor Great Park, England. *1854, Saint Andrew, Lambeth, London. 1856, Saint John the Baptist, Burrington, Lincolnshire, England. 1856, Saint Thomas, Wells, England. 1856–1860, Shadwell Park (additions), Norfolk, England. 1857–1860, Christ Church, Wimbledon, London. 1858–1860, Saint James, Leckhampstead, Berkshire, England. 1859–1862, Elvetham Hall, Hampshire, England. 1861–1863, Saint John the Baptist, Huntley, Gloucestershire, England. 1862–1865, Bestwood Lodge, Nottinghamshire, England. 1866, Buxton Memorial Fountain, Victoria Tower Gardens, Westminster; 1866–1873, Saint Mary, Ealing; 1869–1871, Saint Stephen, Hampstead; London.

BIBLIOGRAPHY

BURTON, NEIL 1980 "The Church of St. Stephen, Rosslyn Hill, Hampstead." In *Historic Buildings Papers.* Greater London Council.
EASTLAKE, CHARLES L. (1872)1970 *A History of the Gothic Revival.* Edited by J. Mordaunt Crook. Leicester (England) University Press.
GIROUARD, MARK (1971)1979 *The Victorian Country House.* Rev. ed. New Haven: Yale University Press.
GRAVES, ALGERNON (1905)1970 *The Royal Academy of Arts.* Reprint. East Ardsley, England: S.R. Publishers.
"The Late Mr. S. S. Teulon, Architect." 1873 *The Builder* 31:384.
MUTHESIUS, STEFAN 1972 *The High Victorian Movement in Architecture: 1850–1870.* London: Routledge.

"Samuel Sanders Teulon." 1892 Volume 8, page 32 in Wyatt Papworth (editor), *Dictionary of Architecture*. London: Architectural Publication Society.

THATCHER, FREDERICK

Frederick Thatcher (1814–1890) was born in Hastings, England, became an associate of the British Institute of Architects in 1836, and proceeded to New Zealand in 1843. Much influenced by the Ecclesiological Society, he was closely associated with Bishop G. A. Selwyn and Governor Sir George Grey. He showed special skill in adapting timber construction to the early English idiom.

JOHN STACPOOLE

WORKS

1841, Halton Parsonage, Hastings, England. 1846, Saint Mary's Church, New Plymouth, New Zealand. 1846–1847, Saint John's College Chapel, Auckland, New Zealand. 1847, All Saints' Church, Howick, New Zealand. 1847, Colonial Hospital, Auckland, New Zealand. 1848, Colonial Hospital, New Plymouth, New Zealand. 1848, Church of Saint Barnabas, Parnell, New Zealand. 1849, Saint John's College Dining Hall, Auckland, New Zealand. *1851, Christ Church, Nelson, New Zealand. 1857, Chapel of Saint Stephen, Old Deanery; 1858, Kinder House; *1860, Church of Saint Mary; 1863–1865, Selwyn Court; Parnell, New Zealand. 1865–1866, Mansion House, Kawau Island, New Zealand. 1866, Old Saint Paul's Church, Wellington.

BIBLIOGRAPHY

ALINGTON, MARGARET 1965 *Frederick Thatcher and St. Paul's*. Wellington: Government Printer.
KNIGHT, C. R. 1972 *The Selwyn Churches of Auckland*. Wellington: Reed.

THAYS, CARLOS

The landscape architect Carlos Thays (1849–1934), who achieved his most notable works in Argentina, was born in Paris and was a disciple of Edouard André, in whose studio he designed works for various European countries. In 1888, he was introduced to the Argentinian pioneer Miguel Crisol, with who Thays signed a year's contract for planning and directing the construction of the Sarmiento Park of Córdoba. In June 1889, he arrived in Argentina.

Between 1891 and 1914, as the result of a competition, he occupied the position of director of parks and public avenues of the City of Buenos Aires; he planted trees on streets, enlarged and remodeled the February 3rd Park (1892–1913) by 565 hectares, and originated numerous squares and avenues. In the Botanical Garden (1892–1898), he brought together the flora of the Argentine provinces and of other parts of the world, and delineated the three types of landscape design: symmetrical, mixed, and picturesque. He designed the urban parks of the main Argentinian cities and of neighboring countries and, through his teachings, spread interest in them all throughout the Southern Cone.

His private works include parks, gardens, hothouses, and ornamentation for over forty palaces and residences in Buenos Aires and other cities and for about fifty rural establishments, especially haciendas, in the province of Buenos Aires.

His projects of the greatest magnitude are the national park of Iguazú (Argentina, 1911) with its virgin forests, waterfalls, and natural landscapes, and an urban center drawn according to a radial plan. As an urbanist, he sketched picturesque drawings for the residential area of Palermo Chico (Buenos Aires, 1912), the spa community of Carrasco (Montevideo, 1912), and others, as well as for the Maritime Boulevard of Mar del Plata (Argentina, 1903–1909) and its ancient ornamental works. He planned tourist centers such as the Winter Mansion (1909) and the Club Hotel Sierra de la Ventana (1911), both in Argentina, and introduced concepts pointing toward urbanism and architecture as functions of restraint and in relation to the values of the landscape and the forest. He died in Buenos Aires.

ALBERTO S. J. DE PAULA
Translated from Spanish by Florette Rechnitz Koffler

WORKS

1882, Bridge, Park of Marquis de Bourg, Prye, France. 1885?, Aquarium, Budapest. 1889–1891, Crisol Park (now Sarmiento), Córdoba, Argentina. 1892–1898, Botanical Garden; 1892–1913, February 3rd Park (enlargement and remodeling); 1893, Plaza de Mayo (remodeling); Buenos Aires. 1895, General Mansilla Square and Urquiza Park, Paraná, Entre Ríos, Argentina. 1896, San Martin Park, Mendoza, Argentina. 1899–1905, Colón Park, Buenos Aires. 1900, Belgrano Park, Salta, Argentina. 1901, Palace Square, San Luís del Maranhao, Brazil. 1901–1913, Independence Park, Rosario, Santa Fe, Argentina. *1903–1909, Boardwalk; 1903–1909, Colón Square; *1903–1909. General Paz Avenue; 1903–1909, Maritime Boulevard; Mar del Plata, Argentina. 1904–1907, La Ventana Farm (bridges, hothouses, kiosk, park, and pool), Tornquist District, Buenos Aires, Argentina. 1908–1914, Winter Mansion Tourist Center (ornamental park), Corrientes, Argentina. 1911, Central Park and Artigas Boulevard, Montevideo. 1911, Club Hotel Sierra de la Ventana (hothouses, park, and ornamentation of tourist center), Tornquist District, Buenos Aires, Argentina. 1911, National Park of Iguazu, Misiones Province, Argentina. 1912, Bosch Palace Gardens (now the Embassy of the United States of America); 1913–1915, Palaces of Fernández de Anchorena (gardens, hothouses, terraces, and ornamentation; now the Apostolic Nunciature); Buenos Aires. 1914–1917, Sans Souci Palace of C. M. de Alvear (parks and hothouses), San Fernando, Argentina. 1918, Ferreyra Palace (park and hothouse), Córdoba, Argentina.

BIBLIOGRAPHY

GOMEZ, RAUL ARNALDO 1979 "Architect Thays and the Mar del Plata Gardens." *Bulletin of the Institute of American and Argentinian History of Art* no. 3, Sept.

(T)HE (A)RCHITECTS (C)OLLABORATIVE

Founding of The Architects Collaborative (TAC) in 1945 represented the translation into professional practice of WALTER GROPIUS's ideal of collaboration. Out of his concept of team design and collective effort, the firm evolved into one of the largest architectural businesses in the United States and symbolized corporate structure in architecture. Hundreds of apprentice architects have received their first exposure to practice at TAC.

This group of young architects—Jean Bodman Fletcher, Norman Fletcher, Sarah Harkness, John Harkness, Louis McMillan, and BENJAMIN THOMPSON—formed their experiment in cooperative design around Gropius in Cambridge, Massachusetts. Among their first projects was a group of houses for themselves at Six Moon Hill, Lexington, Massachusetts (1948), that physically linked the young partners in their collaborative effort. A successful institutional project followed with the Harvard University Graduate Center, Cambridge, Massachusetts (1948–1949); it was a personal triumph for Gropius, who sought this scale and recognition since his arrival in the United States in 1936. The plan of the complex is a loose pinwheel of buildings disposed around a central courtyard. It attempted to respond to the existing grids and quadrangles of the Harvard campus. Educational facilities became a basic building type for TAC, and the firm also received numerous commissions for hospitals. Large-scale planning was involved in the 15,000 units of Gehag Housing in West Berlin (1959, 1970, 1974). The design of the Pan Am Building (1958–1963) in New York, for which Gropius and PIETRO BELLUSCHI were consultants, mobilized opposition to such large-scale intrusions into an existing character of a dense urban fabric. By the mid-1970s, TAC had developed extensive projects in the Middle East, Greece, and Yugoslavia; by 1979, 45 percent of its billings were from foreign operations.

The design approach of the firm has been relatively consistent with emphasis on tectonic expression, seen often as exposed floor slabs with masonry infill walls. Plan disposition generally has strongly reflected diagrams of circulation. The Johns Manville World Headquarters, Jefferson County, Colorado (1973–1976), designed by Joel Hoskins, however, was an outstanding project of the early 1970s, and it contrasted with what had become standard treatment for stereotypical schools, hospitals, office buildings, and resort complexes.

ANTHONY ALOFSIN

WORKS

1948, Six Moon Hill, Lexington, Mass. 1948–1949, Harvard University Graduate Center, Cambridge, Mass. 1955–1956, Hansa Apartment Block, Berlin. 1956, United States Embassy, Athens. 1958–1963, Pan American Building, New York. 1959, 1970, 1974, Gehag Housing, Berlin. 1961–1967, John Fitzgerald Kennedy Office Building, Boston. 1962–1981, University of Baghdad, Iraq. 1965–1970, Rosenthal Glass Factory, Amberg, Germany. 1967–1970, The Architects Collaborative Headquarters, Cambridge, Mass. 1968, Kuwait Fund Headquarters, Kuwait City. 1968–1973, New England Medical Center, Boston. 1969–1973, American Institute of Architects Headquarters, Washington. 1970–1976, Shawmut National Bank, Boston. 1971–1979, Bauhaus Archive, Berlin. 1973–1976, Johns Manville World Headquarters, Jefferson County, Colo. 1976–1981, Benardin Hotel Resort Complex, Piran, Yugoslavia. 1977, Joan Payson Whitney Gallery of Art, Portland, Maine. 1978–1981, Government Service Insurance System Headquarters, Manila, Philippines.

(T)he (A)rchitects (C)ollaborative. Pan American Building. New York. 1958–1963

(T)he (A)rchitects (C)ollaborative. Johns Manville World Headquarters. Jefferson County, Colorado. 1973–1976

BIBLIOGRAPHY

Building Design and Construction. 1980 Reprint. Cambridge, Mass: The Architects Collaborative.

The Architects Collaborative 1972 *The Architects Collaborative: 1945–1972.* Barcelona, Spain: Gili.

"TAC: The Heritage of Walter Gropius." 1980 *Process: Architecture* no. 19:special issue.

THEODOROS OF SAMOS

Together with RHOIKOS, Theodoros of Samos (?–540 B.C.) was architect of the fourth Heraion at Samos, the first colossal dipteral Ionic temple, begun around 575 B.C. Famous for his mechanical skill, Theodoros invented a lathe upon which the columns of the temple were turned. He wrote a book on the building, now lost, apparently the first architectural treatise of the Western world. Theodoros was associated also with construction of the foundations of the fourth temple of Artemis at Ephesos (c.565 B.C.; with CHERSIPHRON). He was responsible as well for the assembly hall (*skias*) at Sparta (c.550 B.C.), of which nothing is known today.

B. M. BOYLE

WORKS

*c.575–550 B.C., Fourth Temple of Hera (with Rhoikos), Samos, Greece. *Begun c.565 B.C., Fourth Temple of Artemis (with Chersiphron), Ephesos, Greece. *Begun c.550 B.C., Assembly Hall, Sparta, Greece.

BIBLIOGRAPHY

English translations of the ancient texts can be found in the volumes of the Loeb Classical Library series, published by Harvard University Press and Heinemann.

DINSMOOR, WILLIAM B. (1902)1975 *The Architecture of Ancient Greece.* Reprint of 1950 ed. New York: Norton. Originally published with the title *The Architecture of Ancient Greece and Rome.*

LAWRENCE, ARNOLD W. (1957)1975 *Greek Architecture.* Harmondsworth, England: Penguin.

PAUSANIAS, *Graeciae descriptio,* Book 3.12.10.

PLINY, *Historia naturalis,* Book 36.86, 90, 95.

VITRUVIUS, *De architectura,* Book 7.Praef.12.

THEODOTOS

Theodotos (?–360 B.C.) was architect of the temple of Asklepios at Epidauros, begun around 375 B.C. This was one of the first Doric temples to have six columns on the ends but only eleven, rather than twelve, on the flanks. The temple was distinguished by its famous pedimental sculptures by Timotheos, and by a chryselephantine statue on the interior by Thrasymedes. More interesting

than the building itself, today only a ruin, are its surviving expense accounts, which contain much information on building practices of the time.

B. M. BOYLE

WORK

*375–370 B.C., Temple of Asklepios, Epidauros, Greece.

BIBLIOGRAPHY

BURFORD, ALISON 1969 Pages 54–59, 138–145 in *The Greek Temple Builders at Epidauros.* University of Toronto Press.

DINSMOOR, WILLIAM B. (1950)1975 *The Architecture of Ancient Greece.* Reprint. New York: Norton.

LAWRENCE, ARNOLD W. (1957)1973 *Greek Architecture.* 2d ed. Harmondsworth, England: Penguin.

THEVENIN, JACQUES JEAN

Jacques Jean Thévenin (18th century), a French architect-builder in the Bâtiments du Roi active during the 1770s and 1780s, built a number of private houses in Paris. His pre-eminent work is the neoclassical Queen's Dairy with grotto at Rambouillet designed in collaboration with HUBERT ROBERT (1785–1788).

RICHARD CLEARY

WORKS

*1770, Barracks for the Gardes françaises; *1773–1778, Pavilion for the Perrier Brothers; *1782, Two Hôtels, Rue d'Artois (Lafitte); Paris. 1785–1788, Buildings (including the experimental farm and the Queen's Dairy), Château Rambouillet, France.

BIBLIOGRAPHY

GALLET, MICHEL 1972 *Stately Mansions: Eighteenth Century Paris Architecture.* Translated by James Palmes. New York: Praeger.

GUTH, PAUL 1958 "La Laiterie de Rambouillet." *Connaissance des Arts* 75:74–81.

LANGNER, JOHANNES 1963 "Architecture pastorale sous Louis XVI." *Art de France* 3:170–186.

LONGNON, HENRI 1909 *Le Château de Rambouillet.* Paris: Laurens.

THIBAULT, LOUIS MICHEL

Louis Michel Thibault (1750–1815) was born in Picquigny, France, and died in Cape Town, South Africa. He studied at the Royal Academy of Architecture in Paris under ANGE-JACQUES GABRIEL. Around 1781–1782, he studied military engineering in Paris at the expense of Colonel C. D. de Meuron, commanding officer of the newly raised Swiss regiment into which Thibault had enrolled. He was eventually promoted to lieutenant of engineers. Thibault arrived at the Cape with his regiment in 1783, but transferred to the service of the Dutch East India Company at the Cape in 1785. He was appointed inspector of the company's buildings, that is, official architect to the colony, in 1786). He was an eclectic neoclassical architect reflecting in his work the tastes of his clients, first Dutch, later English, yet overriding both with original, bold, plastic compositions using classical forms in a predominantly French manner, redolent of, variously, J-J Gabriel, Le Canu, FRANÇOIS DE NEUFFORGE, and CLAUDE NICOLAS LEDOUX.

RONALD LEWCOCK

WORKS

1786, Cape Town Castle (Kat balcony and alterations; with ANTON ANREITH). (A)1787–1788, Papenboom, Newlands, South Africa. (A)1791, Groot Constantia Wine Cellar (with Anreith), Cape Peninsula, South Africa. (A)c.1792, Koopmans de Wet House, Cape Town. (A)c.1792, Stellenburg (façade and gates), Wynberg, South Africa. (A)c.1792–1793, Groot Constantia, Cape Peninsula, South Africa. (A)c.1795, Tokai, Constantia, South Africa. 1801–1803, Freemasons Lodge de Goede Hoop, South Africa. 1804, Government Avenue Guard House, Cape Town, 1804–1805, The Drostdy, Graaf-Reinet, South Africa. 1804–1807, The Drostdy, Tulbach, South Africa. 1805–1807, Parade Fountain, Cape Town. (A)c.1806, Rustenburg (façade, pavilions, and gateway), South Africa. 1811–1815, Supreme Court and Government Offices; 1814, Customs House; Cape Town. (A)1815, Ballotina, Tulbach, South Africa.

BIBLIOGRAPHY

FRANSEN, HANS, and COOK, MARY ALEXANDER (1965)1978 *The Old Houses of the Cape: A Survey of the Existing Buildings in the Traditional Style of Architecture of the Dutch-Settled Regions of the Cape of Good Hope.* Rev. ed. Cape Town: Balkema.
LEWCOCK, RONALD 1963 *Early Nineteenth Century Architecture in South Africa.* Cape Town: Balkema.
PUYFONTAINE, HUGNETTE ROY DE 1972 *Louis Michel Thibault, 1750–1815: His Official Life at the Cape of Good Hope.* Cape Town: Tafelberg.

THIERSCH, FRIEDRICH VON

Beginning in 1879, Friedrich von Thiersch (1852–1921) taught at the Technische Hochschule in Munich for forty years, becoming one of the leading figures in south German architecture. His monumental buildings, often executed in neo-Romanesque styles, deeply affected the work of THEODOR FISCHER and PAUL BONATZ, who were among his many students.

BARBARA MILLER LANE

WORKS

1881, Rhine Bridge, Mainz, Germany. 1887–1897, Law Courts (extended 1902–?); 1887–1889, Parcushaus; 1889–1890, Stores and Residence for L. Bernheimer (with MARTIN DÜLFER); 1894–1895, Neresheimer House; Munich. 1900–1903, Garnison Church, Ludwigsburg, Germany. 1901, Bourse, Munich. 1904–1907, Kurhaus, Wiesbaden, Germany. 1905, Isar Bridges, Munich. 1909, Festhalle, Frankfurt am Main.

BIBLIOGRAPHY

EITEL, H. 1952 *Friedrich von Thiersch.* Munich: Der Baumeister.
Friedrich von Thiersch: Ein Münchner Architekt des Späthistorismus, 1852–1921. 1977 Munich: Lipp. Exhibition catalogue.
MARSCHALL, HORST K. 1981 *Friedrich von Thiersch (1852–1921): Ein Münchner Architekt des Späthistorismus.* Munich: Prestel.
THIERSCH, FRIEDRICH VON (1883)1977 *Die Königsburg von Pergamon.* Munich: Lipp.
THIERSCH, HERMANN 1925 *Friedrich von Thiersch: Der Architekt.* Munich: Bruckmann.

THIRY, PAUL

Paul Thiry (1904–) was born in Nome, Alaska. He attended the University of Washington, Seattle, and the Ecole des Beaux-Arts in Paris. He has practiced in Seattle since 1929, alone or with partners. He was made Officier d'Académie, France (1950), and Fellow, American Institute of Architects (1951). He was a Member of the Executive Board, Puget Sound Regional Planning Council (1945–57). He received an Honorary Diploma from the Colegio de Arquitectos, Santiago, Chile (1965) and a Citation for Community Design from the American Institute of Architects (1965). He was Architect-in-Residence, American Academy in Rome (1969) and he was made a Member, American Institute of Planners (1975).

MARY D. EDWARDS

WORKS

1940–1944, Federal Public Housing Authority Projects (with others), Port Orchard, Wash. 1940–1948, Our Lady of the Lake Catholic Church and School (with others), Seattle, Wash. 1943–1944, United States Navy Advance Base Depot (with others), Tacoma, Wash. 1947–1948, Electrical Engineering Building, University of Washington, Seattle. 1948–1950, Christ the King Catholic Church and School, Seattle, Wash. 1950–1958, Regents Hill Women's Residence, Washington State University, Pullman. 1955, Northgate Public Elementary School; 1957–1962, Century 21 Exposition; Seattle, Wash. 1961, United States Embassy, Santiago. 1962, Libby Dam, Powerhouse, Visitors Center and Facilities, Mont. 1964, United States Capitol (extension of west front), Washington. 1966, Saint Demetrios Greek Orthodox Church and Center, Seattle, Wash. 1966–1968, National Capital Transit Agency, Washington. 1967–1972, Riverfront Development, Spokane, Wash. 1968–1974, Lewis and Clark College Campus, Portland, Ore. 1969, Fourth Infantry Division Monument, Sainte Marie du Mont, France. 1969, Jewish Community Center, Mercer Island, Wash. 1970, Christ Episcopal Church, Tacoma, Wash. 1971, Washington Mutual Savings Bank Headquarters, Seattle. 1975, Enlisted Men's Club, Naval Air Station, Whidbey Island, Wash.

BIBLIOGRAPHY

DEAN, ANDREA O. 1977 "A Dam Designed as a Powerful, Respectful Work of Architecture." *Journal of the American Institute of Architects* 66, no. 4:36–41.

HEINZE, ANTON 1956 *Contemporary Church Art.* New York.

KOEHLER, R. E. 1961 "Profile III: Paul Thiry." *Pacific Architect and Builder.*

McCOY, ESTHER 1965 "West Coast Architects IV: Paul Thiry." *Art and Architecture* 82, no.1:12–17.

SMITH, GEORGE E. KIDDER 1976 *A Pictorial History of Architecture in America.* 2 vols. New York: American Heritage.

THIRY, PAUL 1955 "Contemporary Church Architecture." *Journal of the American Institute of Architects* 24:158–162.

THIRY, PAUL 1959 "Total Designs." *Journal of the American Institute of Architects* 32:19–28.

THIRY, PAUL 1966 "Our Cities Today: Chaos or Challenge?" *Journal of the American Institute of Architects.*

THIRY, PAUL 1968 "Libby Dam: An Engineer Talks Esthetics." *Journal of the American Institute of Architects* 50, no. 5:59–66.

THIRY, PAUL 1974 "Planning of Washington as a Capitol." *Journal of the American Institute of Architects* 61, no. 4:44–50.

THIRY, PAUL; BENNETT, RICHARD, M.; and KAMPHOEFNER, HENRY L. 1953 *Churches and Temples.* New York: Reinhold.

THIRY, PAUL, and THIRY, MARY 1977 *Eskimo Artifacts.* Seattle, Wash.: Superior.

THOMAS, THOMAS, and THOMAS, GRIFFITH

Thomas Thomas (1787/1788–1871) was born in Wales but traveled to London where he may have studied with PETER NICHOLSON. Thomas went to New York in 1833 where he began a successful career as an architect. In 1837, he met with other prominent American architects to form the National Institute of Architects, a precursor to the American Institute of Architects.

Griffith Thomas (1820–1879) was one of Thomas Thomas's three sons, all of whom worked in the building trades. Griffith came to New York in 1838 to join his father in a firm known from 1839 to 1872 as Thomas and Son. It is difficult to distinguish the work of the two men, but it is thought that the elder was more the classicist and the younger more a master of the palazzo mode made popular by CHARLES BARRY in his London clubs.

In the 1850s, Thomas and Son did a large number of shop buildings on Broadway. By the 1860s, the firm broadened out to do the odd opera house and hospital, but still primarily built for commercial interests concentrating on banks, stores, and insurance company offices. By the 1860s, Griffith Thomas was the head of the firm and was regarded in the contemporary press as an early advocate of the Second Empire style. Griffith Thomas was a master of cast-iron buildings and regarded as an innovator in the use of iron framing techniques in his New York Life Insurance Company Building (1868–1870). In the last decade of Griffith Thomas's career, he built many brownstone rowhouses in New York.

DENNIS D. FRANCIS
JOY M. KESTENBAUM
and MOSETTE GLASER BRODERICK

WORKS

*1850–1851, Chemical Bank, 270 Broadway; *1852–1853, Broadway Bank, 237 Broadway; *1854, Greenwich Savings Bank, Sixth Avenue; *1854–1856, Bank for Savings, 67 Bleecker Street; *1854–1856, New York Society Library, 67 University Place; *1856–1858, Fifth Avenue Hotel (with William Washburn); *1858, G. Spring's Brick Presbyterian Church (with LEOPOLD EIDLITZ?); *1858–1859, Lord & Taylor, 462–464 Broadway; 1859, Astor Library (extension), Lafayette Street; *1862–1863, Continental Life Insurance Company Building, 100–102 Broadway; *1866, Grand (Pike's) Opera House, Eighth Avenue at 23rd Street; *1867–1868, National Park Bank, 214–216 Broadway; 1868–1870, New York Life Insurance Company Building, 346–348 Broadway; 1876–1877, American News Company Building, 39–41 Chambers Street; New York.

BIBLIOGRAPHY

CLAIBORNE, DEBORAH ANN 1972 . "The Commercial Architecture of Griffith Thomas in New York." Unpublished M.A. thesis, Pennsylvania State University, University Park.

"Griffith, T." 1879 *American Architect and Building News* 5, Jan.:29–30.

NEW YORK LANDMARKS PRESERVATION COMMISSION 1973 *Soho Cast-Iron District, Designation Report.* New York: The commission.

WEISMAN, WINSTON 1954 "Commercial Palaces of New York: 1845–1875." *Art Bulletin* 36, no. 4:285–302.

THOMAS, WILLIAM

The elder brother of the sculptor John Thomas, William Thomas (1799–1860) was raised and apprenticed as a carpenter and joiner in Chalford, Gloucestershire, England, before his 1829 emergence as an architect in partnership with Richard Tutin in Birmingham, England. In 1832, he moved to Leamington Spa, England, where his practice was largely devoted to speculative housing for the middle class. A local bank failure forced Thomas into bankruptcy in 1840. Three years later, after sending his *Designs for Monuments and Chimney Pieces* to the press, Thomas and his family moved to Toronto. Opening offices in Hamilton, Ontario (1848), and Halifax, Nova Scotia (1858), Thomas established the largest architectural firm in British North America (now Canada). His work, primarily in Ontario, included a remarkable number of substantial churches (reputedly over thirty), public buildings, commercial blocks, and residences. Notable students from his office included WILLIAM G. STORM and two of Thomas's sons, WILLIAM TUTIN THOMAS and Cyrus Pole Thomas. Elected about 1847 as the first president of the Toronto Society of Arts and in 1859 as the first president of the Association of Architects, Civil Engineers, and Provincial Land Surveyors of the Province of Canada, Thomas is credited with being one of the founders of the architectural profession in Canada.

NEIL EINARSON

WORKS

1834, Baptist Chapel; 1834, Wesleyan Chapel; 1835, Lansdowne Circus; Leamington Spa, Worcestershire, England. c.1836–1839, Victoria House (now the Masonic Rooms); 1837–1840, Victoria Terrace, Pump Room and Baths; 1839, A.S. Field Office and Residence; Leamington Spa, England. 1839–1840, Saint Matthew's, Duddeston; *1839–1840, Warwick House; Birmingham, England. 1844–1845, Commercial Bank of the Midland District, Toronto. 1844–1846, Saint Paul's, London, Ontario. 1845, Bishop's Palace; 1845–1848, Saint Michael's; *1846, New Connexion Methodist Church; Toronto. 1846–1848, Niagara District Courthouse, Town Hall, and Market, Niagara-on-the-Lake, Ontario. *1848–1849, Bank of British North America, Hamilton, Ontario. 1848–1849, Kent County Courthouse, Chatham, Ontario. *1849, Union School, London, Ontario. 1850–1851, Saint Lawrence Hall, *Arcade and *Market, Toronto. *1851, Saint George's, Guelph, Ontario. *1851, Town Hall and Market House, Peterborough, Ontario. *1855–1856, Zion Congregational Church, Toronto. 1856–1857, Town Hall and Market, Guelph, Ontario. *1857, Town Hall and Market, Stratford, Ontario. 1858–1859, Saint Matthew's; 1858–1860, County Courthouse (not completed until 1862); Halifax, Nova Scotia. 1859–1860, Don Jail (not completed until 1864), Toronto.

BIBLIOGRAPHY

ARTHUR, ERIC (1965)1974 *Toronto: No Mean City.* 2d ed., rev. University of Toronto Press.
BARNETT, W. E. ET AL. 1969 *St. Lawrence Hall.* Toronto: Nelson & Sons.
EINARSON, NEIL 1980 "William Thomas (1799–1860), of Birmingham, Leamington Spa and Toronto." Unpublished M. Phil. thesis, University of Essex, England.
HERITAGE TRUST OF NOVA SCOTIA 1970 *A Sense of Place: Granville Street, Halifax, Nova Scotia.* Halifax, Nova Scotia: The trust.
MACRAE, MARION, and ADAMSON, ANTHONY 1963 *The Ancestral Roof: Domestic Architecture of Upper Canada.* Toronto: Clarke, Irwin.
MACRAE, MARION, and ADAMSON, ANTHONY 1975 *Hallowed Walls: Church Architecture of Upper Canada.* Toronto: Clarke, Irwin.
RITCHIE, T. 1967 "The Architecture of William Thomas." *Architecture Canada* 44:41–45.
THOMAS, WILLIAM 1843 *Designs for Monuments and Chimney Pieces.* London: Weale.

THOMAS, WILLIAM TUTIN

William Tutin Thomas (1828–1892) was born in Toronto. He trained under his architect father, WILLIAM THOMAS, and practiced in Montreal from 1864 until his death. His early designs were influenced by CHARLES BARRY; his later work was more personal and inventive, ranging from the austere Gothic of Saint George's Church (1870) to the exuberant eclecticism of the Mount Stephen Residence (1881–1884).

JULIA GERSOVITZ

WORKS

1866, Tiffin Stores, Saint James Street West and Dollard Street; (A)*c.1867, Harrison Stephens Residence, Dorchester Street; 1869, Recollet House, Notre Dame Street West and Saint Helen Street; *1870, Bishop's See; 1870, Caverhill Block, Saint Pierre Street; 1870, Saint George's Church, Dominion Square; 1872, Mrs. Philip Holland Residence, 1196 Sherbrooke Street West; 1894, Exchange Bank of Canada (British Empire Building), Notre Dame Street West and Saint François-Xavier Street; 1874, Lord Shaughnessy Residence, Dorchester Boulevard; 1881–1884, Lord Mount Stephen Residence, Drummond Street; *1889–1893, Duncan McIntyre Residence (Craiguie), Peel Street; Montreal.

BIBLIOGRAPHY

"Obituary." 1892 *Canadian Architect and Builder* 5, no. 7:70.

THOMAS DE CORMONT

See ROBERT DE LUZARCHES.

THOMON, THOMAS DE

Thomas de Thomon (1754–1813) was born in Nancy, France. He may have studied under CLAUDE NICOLAS LEDOUX in Paris. On tour in Italy, he was particularly impressed by the Temples at Paestum, and the influence of both Ledoux and Paestum are evident in his masterpiece, the Bourse in St. Petersburg, Russia. He had settled in Russia in the 1790s and became court architect to Alexander I in 1802. The Bourse (1805–1816) is one of the most original and impressive neoclassical works, dramatically situated on a river site which also includes ramps and quais by the architect. Thomon also produced striking watercolors in the style of GIOVANNI BATTISTA PIRANESI and wrote a treatise on painting and a book on his works in Leningrad and elsewhere in Russia.

THOMAS J. MCCORMICK

WORKS

*1802–1805, Great Theater, St. Petersburg. *1803, Theater, Odessa, Russia. 1804–1805, Warehouses, Salni Embankment, St. Petersburg. 1805–1808, Memorial Chapel to Paul I, Pavlovsk, Russia. 1805–1811, Column of Glory, Poltava, Russia. 1805–1816, Bourse, St. Petersburg.

BIBLIOGRAPHY

ACADEMIE DE FRANCE À ROME 1978 *Piranèse et les Français.* Edited by Georges Brunel. Rome: Edizioni dell'Elefante.

BERCKENHAGEN, EKHART (editor) 1970 *Die Französischen Zeichnungen der Kunstbibliothek Berlin.* Berlin: Hessling.

BERCKENHAGEN, EKHART 1975 *St. Petersburg um 1800: Architekturzeichnungen Thomas de Thomon.* Berlin: Kunstbibliothek. Exhibition catalogue.

GRABAR, IGOR 1912 "Les débuts du classisme sous Alexandre et ses sources françaises." *Starye Gody* 13:68–96.

GRABAR, IGOR; LAZAREV, V. N.; and KEMENOV, V. S. (editors) 1963 Volume 8, part 1 in *Istoriya russkago iskusstva.* Moscow: Knebel.

HAMILTON, GEORGE (1954)1975 *The Art and Architecture of Russia.* 2d ed. Harmondsworth, England: Penguin.

LOUKOMSKI, GEORGES 1945 "Thomas de Thomon (1754–1813)." *Apollo* 42:297–304.

OSHCHEPKOV, C. D. 1950 *Arkhitektor Tomon.* Moscow: Akademii arkhitektury SSR.

THOMON, THOMAS DE 1809a *Recueil de plans et façades des principaux monuments construits à Saint-Pétersbourg et dans les différentes provinces de l'Empire de Russie.* St. Petersburg (Leningrad): Pluchard.

THOMON, THOMAS DE 1809b *Traité de peinture précédé de l'origine des arts.* St. Petersburg (Leningrad).

THOUBNIKOFF, ALEXANDRE 1908 "Thomas de Thomon." *Starye Gody* 9:494–512.

VOGT, ADOLF MAX 1974 *Russische und französische Revolutions-Architektur.* Cologne, Germany: DuMont Schauberg.

THOMPSON, BENJAMIN

Benjamin Thompson (1918–), who was born in St. Paul, Minnesota, is president of Benjamin Thompson and Associates of Cambridge, Massachusetts. A graduate of the Yale School of Architecture, Thompson was one of the founders of The Architects' Collaborative (TAC) with WALTER GROPIUS in 1945. Between 1963 and 1967, he was chairman of the architecture department at Harvard.

His practice is broad and diversified, ranging from complex renovations and rehabilitations of old structures to large-scale commercial area developments and comprehensive urban plans. His buildings for educational institutions include residential and science buildings for Williams College (1966–1968), dormitories for Colby College (1967), music center for Amherst College (1970), new campus for Kirkland (Hamilton-Kirkland 1966–1972), addition to the Harvard Law School, and the library of the Harvard School of Education. Among his commercial designs are Design Research (1969) in Cambridge, Massachusetts, which he founded in 1953, the Faneuil Hall Marketplace (1978) in Boston, and Harborplace (1980) in Baltimore, Maryland. His firm's buildings have received numerous national and professional awards.

Among projects to be opened in 1982–1984 are the U.S. Embassy in Ottawa, Canada; the South Street Seaport development in New York City; Fulton's Landing, Brooklyn; and the St. Paul Music Theater, St. Paul, Minnesota.

WHITNEY S. STODDARD

THOMPSON, FRANCIS

Almost nothing is known of the life of Francis Thompson (19th century), an early railway architect; O. F. Carter (1968) considers he was also a London tailor. Thompson worked around Derby (1839–1841); Derby Trijunct (since rebuilt) was one of the first great railway stations; the adjoining contemporary hotel and railway workers' houses survive. From 1846 to 1850, he worked on the Chester-Holyhead line, where he collaborated with Robert Stephenson (see STEPHENSON AND STEPHENSON) on the tubular Britannia Bridge over the Menai Strait, Wales; Thompson designed the pylons at either end and also Chester Station with Robert Stephenson (see STEPHENSON AND STEPH-

ENSON) on the tubular Britannia Bridge over the Menai Strait, Wales; Thompson designed the pylons at either end and also Chester Station with its magnificent Italianate façade. Three surviving smaller stations are outstanding: Wingfield (closed), Holywell Junction (closed), and Great Chesterford, all simple but subtle Italianate classical.

DAVID W. LLOYD

WORKS

*1839–1841, Derby Trijunct Station; 1840, Midland Hotel, Derby; 1840, Wingfield Station, South Wingfield; 1841–1842, Railway Workers' Housing and Brunswick Inn, Railway Terrace, Derby; Derbyshire, England. 1845, Audley End and Great Chesterford Stations, Essex, England. 1845, Cambridge Station. 1846–1850, Britannia Bridge (pylons), North Wales. 1847–1848, Chester Station, Cheshire, England. 1847–1848, Holywell Junction, North Wales.

BIBLIOGRAPHY

BIDDLE, GORDON 1973 *Victorian Stations.* Newton Abbot, England: David & Charles.
BINNEY, MARCUS, and PEARCE, DAVID (editors) 1979 *Railway Architecture.* London: Orbis.
GARTER, OLIVER F. 1968 "Railway Thompson." *Architectural Review* 143, Apr.:314–315.
Hitchcock, H. R. (1954)1972 *Early Victorian Architecture in Britain.* Reprint. New York: Da Capo.

THOMPSON, MARTIN E.

Martin Euclid Thompson (1787–1877) rose from carpenter to New York architect in the early nineteenth century, when architects were first accepted on a level with other artists. Born in Elizabeth, New Jersey, he was apparently self-taught.

In his first known design, the Phenix Bank (c.1818)—a small Doric columned structure—he introduced the Greek Revival to Wall Street. His first important commission was the United States Branch Bank (1822–1824), which he designed in the traditional English style. It was the second building in New York to be built of marble (City Hall being the first).

In 1826, Thompson and ITHIEL TOWN were chosen to represent architects among the founding members of the National Academy of Design, the first institution in the United States established by professional artists. The partnership of Town and Thompson, formed the same year, was the first important architectural firm in New York. The firm's "architectural room" in the Merchants' Exchange (1825–1827) contained the first public library of its kind.

The first use of the Greek Doric temple style in church architecture in New York was in the Church of the Ascension on Canal Street (1828). The firm also received contracts for the steeples of Saint Mark's-in-the-Bowery, New York (1827) and the First Reformed Dutch Church in New Brunswick, New Jersey (1828).

After dissolving the partnership in 1828, Thompson built several residences, including a villa in the Greek temple style in Pelham, New York (1828–1829), for the banker Elisha W. King; a charming Corinthian country house for James Colles in Morristown, New Jersey (1836–1837); and an Italianate villa-style residence for James Lenox in New Hamburg, New York (1837–1838). The Robert Ray House on lower Broadway, New York (1830), his first elegant town house, was designed in the traditional English style.

Thompson's last use of the Greek temple style was the remodeling of the old jail in City Hall Park, New York in 1831 for use as the Hall of Records. With front and rear porticoes in the Ionic style, it was judged a fitting complement to City Hall.

In 1833, Thompson was hired as architect and builder of the Naval Hospital in Brooklyn, New York (1833–1841). Its recessed portico, with eight square stone columns form a colonnade. The square granite-pier concept is a feature which had been employed by Ithiel Town in the small Tappan store in Pearl Street in 1826 and had been developed to a monumental scale by Thompson.

Responding to the taste of the period, Thompson turned to the modern Gothic style of architecture in his design for the New York Institution for the Blind (1837–1842). Erected on a site in mid-Manhattan, it was in a more mature Gothic than the New York State Arsenal in Central Park, which has been attributed to Thompson.

Thompson's career demonstrated his remarkable ability to adapt to the demands of current taste and technology. At first employing conservative English styles, his planned buildings related to the commercial development of the City. Demand for his experienced skills came as a rapidly growing population required residences and enlarged facilities for educational and commercial structures. He became interested in the Greek Revival at the outset, making his most important contribution to the architecture of the city in this style.

After the death of his wife in 1864, he retired to Glen Cove, Long Island, where he died in 1877.

BETTY J. EZEQUELLE

WORKS

*c.1818, Phenix Bank; *1822–1824, United States Branch Bank; *1825–1827, Merchants' Exchange; *1827, New York Institution for the Instruction of the Deaf and Dumb; 1827, Saint Mark's-in-the-Bowery (steeple); *1828, Church of the Ascension; New York. 1828, First Reformed Dutch Church, New Brunswick, N.J. *1828–1829, King Mansion, Pelham, N.Y. *1829, Columbia College (grammar school and houses on Chapel Street); *1830, Robert Ray House; *1831, Hall of Records; New York. 1833–1841, Naval Hospital, Brooklyn, N.Y. 1836–1837, James Colles House, Morristown, N.J. *1837–1838, James Lenox House, New Hamburg, N.Y. *1837–1842, New York Institution for the Blind; 1841, Stores, Murray Street and Park Place; New York.

BIBLIOGRAPHY

Martin E. Thompson's manuscript account book, 1825–1852, is in the Avery Architectural Library, Columbia University, New York.

CLARK, ELIOT 1954 *History of the National Academy of Design: 1825–1953.* New York: Columbia University Press.
COLES, ROBERT R., and VAN SAATVOORD, PETER LUYSTER 1967 *History of Glen Cove.* n.p.: Privately printed.
COWDREY, MARY BARTLETT (editor) 1943 *The National Academy of Design Exhibition Record: 1826–1860.* New-York Historical Society.
HAMLIN, TALBOT F. 1939 "Martin E. Thompson." Volume 18, pages 467–468 in *Dictionary of American Biography.* New York: Scribners.
HAMLIN, TALBOT F. (1944)1964 *Greek Revival Architecture in America.* Reprint. New York: Dover.
LAFEVER, MINARD 1829 *The Young Builder's General Instructor.* Newark, N.J.: Tuttle.
"Public Buildings." 1829 *New-York Mirror: A Weekly Journal Devoted to Literature and the Fine Arts* 7, Sept. 26:89–90.
STOKES, I. N. 1915–1928 *The Iconography of Manhattan Island: 1498–1909.* 6 vols. New York: Dodd.
WODEHOUSE, LAWRENCE 1972 "Martin Euclid Thompson: Architect of the United States Branch Bank." *Antiques* 102:410–413.

THOMSEN, EDVARD

Edvard Thomsen (1884–1980), a Danish architect, started his career about 1910 and took part in most of the important architectural currents of his time. Influenced by strong classicistic tendencies, he built Oregaard Grammar School (1922–1924), considered one of the most lucid contributions to that era. It is controlled by a rational lightness, which he continued to apply as he assumed functionalist ideas.

VILLADS VILLADSEN

THOMSON, ALEXANDER

Alexander Thomson (1817–1875), or "Greek" Thomson as he became known, was one of the finest Scottish architects of the nineteenth century. Although he was highly regarded during his own lifetime, it was not until after his death that his work received the attention it fully deserves. Only then was his original handling of materials and forms and his expressive use of a wide vocabulary of motifs and detail recognized as setting him apart from his neoclassical contemporaries, establishing him as an innovative figure and forerunner of the Modern movement.

Thomson, the seventeenth child of twenty children of John Thomson, was born near Glasgow, the city in which he was to spend his entire professional life. Alexander's first job was with a publisher, but in 1836 he became an apprentice to the architect John Baird I, and eventually his chief draftsman from 1845 to 1849. In 1849, he formed a partnership with John Baird II (no relation to John Baird I), which lasted until 1857. From that year until 1871, he was in partnership with his brother in the firm of Alexander and George Thomson. During the last two years of his life, he worked with Robert Turnbull in the firm of Thomson and Turnbull.

"Greek" Thomson had a prolific output as an architect, producing his best work in the latter period of his career between 1856 and 1870. By this time, he had freed himself from the rigors of orthodox classicism and had begun to experiment with new techniques and materials. He designed all manner of buildings needed in the expanding city of Glasgow at the time: mansion houses, city terraces and tenement blocks, churches, and warehouses and offices. Whereas Thomson's early mansions on the outskirts of Glasgow show a picturesque Gothic flavor, his mature designs are bold and personal interpretations of Grecian and Romanesque themes. His finest villas are 25 Mansionhouse Road, Langside (1856–1858), Holmwood in Cathcart (1856–1858), and 202 Nithsdale Road, Pollokshields (1870). With the horizontal emphasis created by low roofs, flat gables, and long walls, these houses seem to herald the early domestic works of FRANK LLOYD WRIGHT built half a century later.

Thomson's many terraces and tenement blocks within Glasgow are at least as varied as his mansion houses, each representing an independent solution to a particular urban problem. His finest works of this kind are Moray Place (1857–1859) and Great Western Terrace built ten years later. With exquisitely incised horizontal bands of detailing on the stonework façades, Moray Place is quite tiny in scale and proportion compared to the vastness of Great Western Terrace. Indeed, the latter achieved a breadth of treatment and sense of scale previously unattained in Glasgow terraces.

In 1856, Thomson designed the Caledonia Road Church, the first of his three major United Presbyterian churches in Glasgow. In that building, he asserted a dignity of proportion within a personal treatment of the Greek and Egyptian manner which was to become the major feature of his successive ecclesiastical designs. Thomson's next church, and in fact his masterpiece, was the Saint Vincent Street Church (1857–1859). The impression of monumentality which this building exudes is due not only to the bold yet subtle massing of geometric forms on a steeply sloping site or the horizontal strength of a portico in juxtaposition to a tower and spire as strikingly original as that at Caledonia Road, but also to the meticulous refinement of the stonework construction and detail. Thomson's third major religious work, the Queen's Park Church (1867–1869), was tragically destroyed by fire in 1942—the only serious wartime casualty that Glasgow suffered and one of Britain's saddest architectural losses. With its horizontally linked bands of square-headed windows separated by square piers with simple capitals and restrained classical detailing, the church was a fine example of his mature style. As was often the case in Thomson's later work, the building owed much to the influence of the German neoclassicist KARL FRIEDRICH SCHINKEL.

The majority of Thomson's work can be found in the south side of Glasgow, but his warehouse and office buildings, not surprisingly, are located in the center of the city. Indeed, only JOHN J. BURNET made a greater contribution to the Victorian and Edwardian architecture of central Glasgow. Thomson's commercial structures represent a re-

freshing change in his work: a lightness of treatment within complex yet unified elevational compositions. His finest works of this kind, the Buck's Head (1863) and Egyptian Halls (1871–1873) are both iron-framed (like many nineteenth-century commercial buildings in that industrial city) and have richly articulated façades of cast iron and glass.

Although Thomson's genius is best seen in his architecture, his various published statements as president of the Glasgow Institute of Architects (1871) or his Haldane Lectures of 1874 demonstrate a strong theoretical basis to his work. When Thomson opened his presidential address with the question, "Why is there no modern architecture?," he continued with a most profound statement: "Some will answer that the field is exhausted, but genius and enterprise have converted many an exhausted field into a stage from which deeper and richer fields have been reached and wrought." Thomson appears to intimate that his own architecture had reached its climax. He also seemed to be anticipating the emergence of innovators to a profession stifled for much of the nineteenth century by stylistic preoccupations. Indeed, Glasgow was about to witness the work of three architects of great genius: Burnet, James Salmon (see SALMON AND GILLESPIE), and CHARLES RENNIE MACKINTOSH.

Thomson, who rarely left Scotland and never Britain (his widow was to establish the famous Thomson Traveling Scholarship), died in 1875, and with him so did the Glasgow classical tradition. Although his successor, JAMES SELLARS, produced a number of interesting schemes, they re-

Thomson.
1–10 Moray Place.
Glasgow, Scotland.
1857–1859

Thomson.
Saint Vincent Street
Church.
Glasgow, Scotland.
1857–1859

mained uninspired and totally lacking the vitality of Thomson's work.

It is wrong to consider Thomson as a mere nineteenth-century revivalist architect. He believed implicitly that the ideals expressed in classicism should form the basis of a modern Scottish style. Although this was not to be, through his work classical architecture once more flourished in Scotland and became absorbed into a fresh tradition.

                                            JOHN MCASLAN

WORKS

1849, 3–11 Dunlop Street; 1852–1853, The Knowe, Pollokshields; *1853, 36–38 Howard Street; *1856, Pollok School, Pollokshaws; *1856–1857, Caledonia Road Church; 1856–1858, Holmwood, Cathcart; 1856–1858, 25–25a Mansionhouse Road, Langside; 1857, 37–39 Cathcart Road; *1857, 190–192 Hospital Street; 1857, Queen's Park Terrace; 1857, Walmer Crescent; 1857–1859, 1–10 Moray Place; 1857–1859, Saint Vincent Street Church; *1859, Chalmers Free Church; *1859, 126–132 Sauchiehall Street; *1860, Cairney Building; *1860, 249–259 Saint Vincent Street; 1863, Buck's Head Building; 1864, Grosvenor Building; 1865, Grecial Building; 1865, 27–53 Oakfield Avenue; 1866, Northpark Avenue; 1867–1869, Great Western Terrace; *1867–1869, Queen's Park Church; 1870, 202 Nithsdale Road, Pollokshields; 1871, Blackies Printing Works; 1871, 200 Nithsdale Road, Pollokshields; 1871, Westbourne Terrace; 1871–1873, Egyptian Halls; 1872, Cowcaddens Cross Building; 1873, 84–112 Nithsdale Road (completed by R. Turnbull), Pollokshields; 1875, 265–289 Allison Street; 1875, 87–97 Bath Street; 1875, 148 Bath Street; 1875, 12–24 Norfolk Street; Glasgow, Scotland.

BIBLIOGRAPHY

BARCLAY, D. 1904 "'Greek' Thomson: His Life and Opinions." *Architectural Review* 15:183–194.

BILLING, J. M. M. 1939 "Alexander 'Greek' Thomson: A Study of the Re-creation of a Style." *Quarterly Journal of the Royal Incorporation of Architects in Scotland* 62:20–29.

BLOMFIELD, REGINALD 1904 "Greek Thomson: A Critical Note." *Architectural Review* 15:194–195.

BUDDEN, L. B. 1910 "The Work of Alexander Thomson." *The Builder* Dec. 31:815–819.

EDWARDS, A. T. 1914 "Alexander (Greek) Thomson." *Architects and Builders Journal* May 13:350–352.

GILDARD, T. 1888–1894 "'Greek' Thomson." *Proceedings of the Royal Philosophical Society of Glasgow* 19:191–210; 26:99–107.

GOMME, ANDOR, and WALKER, DAVID 1968 *Architecture of Glasgow.* London: Lund Humphries.

GOODHART-RENDEL, H. S. 1949 "Rogue Architects of the Victorian Era." *Journal of the Royal Institute of British Architects* 56:251–259.

JOHNSON, N. R. J. 1933 "Alexander Thomson: A Study of the Basic Principles of His Design." *Quarterly Journal of the Royal Incorporation of Architects in Scotland.* 43:29–38.

LAW, G. 1954 "'Greek' Thomson." *Architectural Review* 65:307–316.

MCFADZEAN, RONALD 1979 *The Life and Work of Alexander Thomson.* London: Routledge.

SMITH, W. J. 1951 "Glasgow: 'Greek' Thomson, Burnet and Mackintosh." *Quarterly Journal of the Royal Incorporation of Architects in Scotland* Aug.:56–60.

SUMMERSON, JOHN (1953)1970 *Architecture in Britain: 1530–1830.* Harmondsworth, England: Penguin.

THOMSON, ALEXANDER 1866 "An Inquiry as to the Appropriateness of the Gothic Style for the Proposed Buildings for the University." *The Builder* May 19:368–371.

THOMSON, ALEXANDER 1874 "The Haldane Academy Lectures, Art and Architecture: A Course of Four Lectures." *British Architect* 1:274–278, 354–357; 2:50–52, 82–84, 272–274, 288–289, 317–318.

THOMSON, JAMES

James Thomson (1835–1905) developed an immense commercial and domestic practice in Glasgow, on suceeding to John Baird's practice in 1859. He briefly continued Baird's experiments in cast-iron façades. Stylistically, he progressed from pure Italianate to a rich free Italianate and finally to early German Renaissance elevator buildings. His country houses were castellated or Scots Jacobean, sometimes with French rococo interiors.

                                            DAVID M. WALKER

WORKS

1858–1873, Crown Circus, Crown Terrace, and Princess Terrace, Glasgow. 1861, Greenock Provident Bank, 11 William Street, Greenock, Scotland. 1863, Cast-Iron Building (with R. McConnel), 217–222 Argyle Street; *1875–1877, Grand Hotel, Charing Cross; 1878, Scottish Union and National Insurance Building; *1879, Royalty (later Lyric) Theatre Buildings (with Frank Matcham); Glasgow. 1886, Belmont Castle and Stables, Perthshire, Scotland. 1887, J and D MacDougall's Building, Glasgow. 1892, Clydesdale Bank, 25 Bank Street, Dumfries, Scotland. 1892, Clydesdale Bank, 340–344 Argyle Street, Glasgow. 1894, Kinnaird House, Stirlingshire, Scotland. 1895, Schaw Hospital, Bearsden, Dunbartonshire, Scotland. 1899, Clydesdale Bank, Cathcart Square; 1899, Connal's Building; Glasgow. 1899–1900, Clydesdale Bank, Stirling, Scotland.

BIBLIOGRAPHY

GOMME, ANDOR, and WALKER, DAVID 1968 *The Architecture of Glasgow.* London: Lund Humphries.

THORNHILL, JAMES

Dorsetshire-born, James Thornhill (1675–1734) succeeded his master, Thomas Highmore, as the king's sergeant painter in 1720. Working in the style established by Antonio Verrio and Louis Laguerre, he was England's leading decorative artist. In addition, he was said by a contemporary to have designed several houses. His pretensions in this direction are indicated by his reported attempt to gain the vacant surveyorship of the king's works (1719). Many of his designs survive, surprisingly showing a strong Palladian (see ANDREA PALLADIO) influence, but Moor Park (1720–1728), the only house which can be attributed to him, is firmly in the English baroque style. Thornhill sat as member of parliament for Melcombe Regis from 1722 to 1734.

JOHN BOLD

WORK

1720–1728 Moor Park, Hertfordshire, England.

BIBLIOGRAPHY

CROFT-MURRAY, EDWARD 1962 *Early Tudor to Sir James Thornhill*. Volume 1 in *Decorative Painting in England: 1537–1837*. London: Country Life.
DOWNES, KERRY 1966 *English Baroque Architecture*. London: Zwemmer.

THORNTON, WILLIAM

Best known as the first architect of the United States Capitol, William Thornton (1759–1828) was also a physician, writer and pamphleteer, artist, inventor, scientist, social reformer, horse breeder, and government official. Born at his father's plantation on Tortola, British West Indies, Thornton was sent to Lancashire, England, at the age of five after his father's death. He entered medical school at Edinburgh and after receiving his degree in 1784 returned to Tortola in 1786.

Late that year he arrived in Philadelphia; he became an American citizen in 1788. His first architectural design was for the Library Company Building of Philadelphia (competition 1789); the façade was based largely on Plate 9, in ABRAHAM SWAN's *A Collection of Designs in Architecture* (1757), Book II.

After marrying in 1790, Thornton returned to Tortola, where he learned by July 1792 of the Capitol building competition. Drawing especially on the three designs for Wanstead House in COLEN CAMPBELL's *Vitruvius Britannicus* I (1715) and III (1725), he produced his first design for the Capitol and returned to Philadelphia by November 1792. Given permission to submit drawings after the July 15 deadline, his second design, prepared after having seen some of the rejected submissions, was warmly approved by George Washington and THOMAS JEFFERSON; in April 1793 it was accepted.

Due to structural difficulties in his design, the plan was thoroughly revised by ETIENNE SULPICE HALLET and the final plan was largely based on Hallet's own fifth design for the Capitol. The cornerstone was laid on September 18, 1793, with Hallet as supervising architect.

Appointed a district commissioner on September 12, 1794, Thornton moved to Washington, where he tried to fend off any alterations in the Capitol. In late 1795, with Hallet dismissed and GEORGE HADFIELD as supervising architect, Thornton began a revised (third) design for the Capitol, which followed the foundations as built. This final version has the well-known façade consisting of a monumental octastyle pedimented portico surmounted by a Pantheon dome, with more delicately detailed wings on each side, all on a rusticated base.

Thornton remained in Washington the rest of his life, as a district commissioner until 1802 and thereafter in a number of government positions, including head of the Patent Office (1802–1828). His most mature architectural designs date from these years. The two preliminary floor plans (c.1797) for Colonel John Tayloe III's Town House (The Octagon [1798–1800]) reveal his interest in oval and circular rooms. The brick exterior detailing is, however, not too different from the vernacular builders' style of the day.

For Thomas Peter, however, he provided both plans and elevation designs for his house Tudor Place in Georgetown (c.1805–1816), which was to incorporate existing wings erected around 1797. At least five different study plans survive, in which Thornton experimented with oval and circular spaces. Though for the final exterior design Thornton may have been influenced by a house by John Soane shown in George Richardson's *The New Vitruvius Britannicus* (1802–1803), I, pl. LVI. The stucco surface of the exterior of Tudor Place, which helped to give it elegant monumentality, was an uncommon treatment. Beautifully detailed, carefully thought out, and geometrically impressive, Tudor Place was one of Thornton's finest achievements.

Thornton's mature interest in simple, monumental architectural forms, and clearly defined yet spatially interesting interior volumes, represented the most advanced thinking of his day; however, his influence was negligible due largely to the strong local builders' vernacular. Probably because of his many other interests, he actually designed relatively few buildings for a man of his talent.

DANIEL D. REIFF

WORKS

*1789–1790, Library Company Building, Philadelphia.

1793–1827, United States Capitol (altered; completed by others); 1798–1800, John Tayloe III Town House (The Octagon); Washington. c.1800–1805, Woodlawn Plantation, Mount Vernon, Va. c.1805–1816, Tudor Place, Georgetown, Washington. 1817–1821, Pavilion 7, University of Virginia, Charlottesville.

BIBLIOGRAPHY

BENNETT, WELLS 1916 "Stephen Hallet and his Designs for the National Capitol, 1791–94." *Journal of the American Institute of Architects* 4:290–295, 324–330, 376–383, 411–418.

BROWN, GLENN 1896 "Dr. William Thornton, Architect." *Architectural Record* 6:53–70.

BROWN, GLENN (1900)1970 *History of the United States Capitol.* Reprint. New York: Da Capo.

BROWN, GLENN 1913 "Letters from Thomas Jefferson and William Thornton, Architect, Relating to the University of Virginia." *Journal of the American Institute of Architects* 1:21–27.

BUTLER, JEANNE FOLLEY 1976 "Competition 1792: Designing a Nation's Capitol." *Capitol Studies* 4:63–70.

CAMPBELL, COLEN (1715–1725)1967 *Vitruvius Britannicus or the British Architect.* Reprint. New York: Blom.

CAMPIOLI, MARIO E. 1976 "Building the Capitol." Pages 202–231 in Charles E. Peterson (editor), *Building Early America.* Radnor, Pa.: Chilton.

Documentary History of the Construction and Development of the United States Capitol Building and Grounds. 1904 Washington: U.S. Government Printing Office.

KIMBALL, FISKE 1936 "William Thornton." Volume 18, pages 504–507 in *Dictionary of American Biography.* New York: Scribner.

KIMBALL, FISKE, and BENNETT, WELLS 1923 "William Thornton and the Design of the United States Capitol." *Art Studies* 1:76–92.

MADDEX, DIANE 1973 *Historic Buildings of Washington, D.C.* Pittsburgh: Ober Park Associates.

MCCUE, GEORGE 1974 "The Octagon: Town House that Preceded the Town." *Historic Preservation* 26, April–June:27–31.

MCCUE, GEORGE 1976 *The Octagon: Being an Account of a Famous House—Its Great Days, Decline, and Restoration.* Washington: AIA Foundation.

PETER, ARMISTEAD, III 1970 *Tudor Place, Designed by Dr. William Thornton and Built Between 1805 and 1816 for Thomas and Martha Peter.* Washington: Privately printed.

PETERSON, CHARLES E. 1953 "Library Hall: Home of the Library Company of Philadelphia, 1790–1880." *Transactions of the American Philosophical Society* New Series 43, part 1:129–147.

REIFF, DANIEL D. (1971)1977 *Washington Architecture, 1791–1861: Problems in Development.* 2d ed. Washington: U.S. Commission of Fine Arts.

RICHARDSON, GEORGE (1802–1803)1970 *The New Vitruvius Britannicus.* Reprint. New York: Blom.

STEARNS, ELINOR, and YERKES, DAVID N. 1976 *William Thornton: A Renaissance Man in the Federal City.* Washington: AIA Foundation

SWAN, ABRAHAM 1757 *A Collection of Designs in Architecture Containing New 1757 Plans and Elevations of Houses, for General Use.* London: The author.

THORPE, JOHN

John Thorpe (c.1563–1655?) was a land and building surveyor who has become one of the few famous architectural personalities of his time in England because of the survival of a book of his drawings (Sir John Soane's Museum, London). The drawings, consisting of more than 200 sheets, include plans, elevations, perspective views, and details of various kinds, and constitute an invaluable source for the history of English architecture. Some drawings represent well-known houses, others are imaginary (including a fanciful design for a house in the shape of Thorpe's initials), and still others are copies of illustrations in foreign architectural books, with which Thorpe obviously had a good acquaintance. The majority are plans of country houses, some being surveys of existing buildings, others evidently projects for new ones, several unidentified. Most of the drawings appear to have been done for record purposes, but HORACE WALPOLE, who in 1782 first brought them to public attention in the third edition of his *Anecdotes of Painting in England,* presumed that Thorpe was the architect of the buildings represented and pronounced him "a very capital artist, who designed or improved most of the principal and palatial edifices erected in the reigns of Elizabeth and James I." This view of Thorpe as the super-architect of the age was largely maintained throughout the nineteenth century, and vestiges of the legend remained until John Summerson's article of 1949, which for the first time brought solid documentation to the subject.

Thorpe came from a family of masons in Kingscliffe, Northamptonshire. A plan of Kirby Hall, Northamptonshire, in Thorpe's book of drawings is inscribed "Kerby whereof I layd the first stone 1570," and as he was then a small child, it is presumed that he was performing a ceremonial function for his father, who in all likelihood was the master mason. One of John's brothers, another Thomas Thorpe (?–1625/1626), continued the family tradition (he worked with ROBERT LYMINGE at Blickling and built a gateway at Hunstanton Hall, Norfolk, in 1623–1624), but there is no evidence that John ever trained as a mason. By 1583, he had entered the Office of Works, and he served as a clerk at various royal palaces, the earliest authenticated drawing by him being a survey of the Outer and Green Courts of Eltham Palace, dated 1590 (Public Record Office, London). In

1601, he left the Office of Works and practiced as a surveyor, probably retiring in the 1630s. For most of his professional life he lived in London.

Only one architectural work is documented as having been designed by Thorpe (a gallery at Belvoir Castle, Leicestershire, for which a drawing is preserved in the castle muniment-room), but his name has been plausibly connected with other, fairly minor buildings, and it is probable that he supplied plans for houses, even if he was not involved in the actual building operations. It is also very likely that Thorpe was the "I.T." (mentioned on the title-page) who translated Hans Blum's Latin treatise on the orders (1550) into English as *The Booke of Five Collumnes of Architecture* (1601).

IAN CHILVERS

WORK

*1625–1627, Gallery (between Rosse and Stanton Towers), Belvoir Castle, Leicestershire, England.

BIBLIOGRAPHY

COLVIN, HOWARD (editor) 1975 *1485–1660*. Part 1, volume 3 in *The History of the King's Works*. London: H. M. Stationery Office. Part 2, volume 4 is forthcoming.
GOTCH, J. ALFRED (1901)1914 "Sixteenth Century House-Planning as Illustrated by John Thorpe's Drawings." Chapter 11 in *Early Renaissance Architecture in England*. 2d ed. London: Batsford.
LEES-MILNE, JAMES 1951 *Tudor Renaissance*. London: Batsford.
ROBERTS, DAVID L. 1973 "John Thorpe's Designs for Dowsby Hall and the Red Hall, Bourne." *Lincolnshire History and Archaeology* 8:13–34.
SUMMERSON, JOHN 1949 "John Thorpe and the Thorpes of Kingscliffe." *Architectural Review* 106:291–301.
SUMMERSON, JOHN (1953)1977 *Architecture in Britain: 1530–1830*. 6th ed. Harmondsworth, England: Penguin.
SUMMERSON, JOHN 1966 "The Book of Architecture of John Thorpe in Sir John Soane's Museum." *Walpole Society* 40:entire issue.
WALPOLE, HORACE (1782)1969 Volume 1 in *Anecdotes of Painting in England*. Edited by Ralph N. Wornum. Reprint of 1876 ed. New York: Arno.

THUMB FAMILY

An Austrian family of masons, the Thumbs (17th-18th centuries), together with the Beer (see MICHAEL BEER) and Moosbrugger (see CASPAR MOOSBRUGGER) families, became internationally known through the development of the Voralberger school of design. The Thumbs exhibited in their work the transition from the high baroque to rococo.

Michael Thumb (c.1640–1690), an architect and contractor, worked in Swabia, producing a number of outstanding baroque designs. His first commissions were for Jesuit colleges in Landshut and Mindelheim, Germany. His design for the Schonenberg Pilgrimage Church (1682–1686) near Ellwangen, Germany, introduced a new architectural concept in the style: a galleried wall-pillar nave which was derived from his three-dimensional research on space. His earliest church design, for the Austin Priory of Wettenhausen (1670–1686) led him to a more personal conception of the ecclesiastical baroque style. Obermarchtal Church, which as commissioned in 1686, demonstrated a pure application of his spatial baroque concepts and was enhanced by the participation of renowned artists and craftsmen such as the stuccoist Wessobruner.

Christian Thumb (?–1726), brother of Michael, practiced architecture mainly in the Austrian region of the Bregenzer Wald (Forest of Bregenz), exerting a potent influence on Swiss baroque architecture. In 1684–1686, he completed the Schönenberg Pilgrimage Church, which had been modified in 1683 by P. Heinrich Mayer. Between 1695 and 1700, he executed the Chapel for Friedrichshafen Castle on Lake Constance in southern Germany. He designed and oversaw the construction of two major baroque churches: Schussenried (1700) in Bavaria and Giessen (1701) in central Germany.

Peter Thumb (1681–1766), son of Michael Thumb, practiced primarily around Lake Constance in Germany, working until the 1720s with his father-in-law, Franz Beer. His first designs were somewhat conventional, using expressions of the well-established Voralberger school. His first conception of baroque is exemplified in his projects for Ebersmunster Church (1708–1712) and Saint Peter's Church (1724–1727) in the Black Forest. Around 1730, his work began to depart from the traditional vocabulary of the seventeenth-century baroque style, exhibiting a true inventiveness as seen in the Neu Birnau Pilgrimage Church (1745–1751). Here, the church nave was no longer combined with an aisle, and the vaulting emphasized a strong centrality, contrasting with the cursive effect of the side galleries. The frescoes of G. B. Göz and the stucco work of J. A. Feuchtmayr acted as complements to the design concepts. Peter Thumb started to work on the Benedictine Library at Saint Peter's in 1739 but he did not complete it until 1753, a masterpiece of rococo decoration composed of colorful stuccos. In 1758, he was commissioned to build the library of Saint Gall Abbey, Switzerland, where he had already worked as supervisor and designer of the new abbey church. The Library at Saint Gall, like that of Saint

Peter's, had in its galleries a sense of flow, a quality of alternating concave and convex lines. Saint Gall, however, appeared as a more mature work, displaying a light framework of rocaille ornamentation, colored and brilliant. Collaborating with the Gigl brothers for stucco ornamentation, with Joseph Wannenmacher for the historical and symbolic fresco painting, and with additional master craftsmen for the cabinetmaking and furnishing, Peter Thumb borrowed from the earlier high baroque to create his own style of rococo, referred to as "jubilant baroque" characterized by decorative gaiety and dramatic agility. The design for Saint Gall Library was a singular achievement and a pivotal moment for the baroque.

Michael Thumb (1725–1769), son of Peter Thumb and principal architect for the bishop of Constance, worked with his father and later supervised the completion of Saint Gall Library.

MARC DILET

WORKS
MICHAEL THUMB

1660s, Landshut College, Germany. 1660s, Mindelheim College, Germany. 1670–1686, Austin Priory, Wettenhausen, Germany. 1682–1686, Pilgrimage Church (completed in the 1690s by Christian Thumb), Schönenberg, near Ellwangen, Germany. 1686, Church, Obermarchtal, Germany.

CHRISTIAN THUMB

1695–1700, Chapel, Friedrichshafen Castle, Lake Constance, Germany. 1700, Church, Schussenried, Germany. 1701, Church, Giessen, Bavaria, Germany.

PETER THUMB

1708–1712, Ebersmünster Church, Germany. 1724–1727, Saint Peter's Church, Black Forest, Germany. 1739–1753, Benedictine Library, Saint Peter's, Black Forest, Germany. 1745–1751, Neu Birnau Pilgrimage Church, Germany. 1758–1766, Saint Gall Library and Abbey Church (completed by Michael Thumb, Peter's son), Switzerland.

BIBLIOGRAPHY

HITCHCOCK, H. R. 1968 *Rococo Architecture in Southern Germany.* London: Phaidon.
LIEB, NORBERT, and DIETH, FRANZ 1941 *Die Vorarlberger Barockbaumeister.* Munich.

TIBALDI, PELLEGRINO

Pellegrino Tibaldi (1527–1596), also called Pellegrino Pellegrini, was among the most radically inventive and influential mannerist architects practicing in northern Italy. He was born in Puria di Valsolda, near Lugano, the son of Tebaldo Tibaldi, a minor architect active for many years in Bologna.

Tibaldi spent his youth in Bologna where he began his career as a painter. In the late 1540s, he traveled to Rome and joined the atelier of Perino del Vaga, decorating the papal apartments of the Castel Sant'Angelo. He developed a powerful figure style inspired by the Roman works of MICHELANGELO. Emerging as an independent artist around 1550, he soon secured a series of commissions for fresco decorations in Rome and in Loreto. Among his patrons was Cardinal Giovanni Poggi, for whom he designed his earliest known architectural work, the small Doric Cappella Poggi in San Giacomo Maggiore in Bologna (1555?).

In the late 1550s, Tibaldi accepted commissions as a painter and decorator in Ancona in the Marches, and he was subsequently employed there on fortifications. It was probably at this time, in 1562 or 1563, that he came to the attention of CARLO BORROMEO, archbishop of Milan and legate of the Marches, who made him his personal architect. In 1564, Borromeo charged Tibaldi with two major commissions: the Collegio Borromeo in Pavia (1564–1568) and the Cortile della Canonica (executed between 1570 and 1604). For the Collegio, Tibaldi designed a triple-storied façade of seventeen bays in which windows and overscaled niches are disposed in willfully discordant rhythms. The restlessness of the façade is effectively resolved in the courtyard, where two stories of arcades on coupled columns convey an orderly, light, and airy purity. For the Canonica, by contrast, Tibaldi devised a courtyard where huge-scale, thorough-going rustication and the use of grotesque ornamental masks evoke an aura of somber majesty. With these innovative works, Tibaldi declared his independence from Vitruvian (see VITRUVIUS) orthodoxy and his adherence to an autonomous, graphic mode of generating form that had its source in Michelangelo.

In 1567, Tibaldi replaced VINCENZO SEREGNI as chief architect of the Cathedral of Milan, initiating seventeen years of intense productivity as well as conflict in the Fabbrica. With Borromeo's full support, the architect made major contributions to the church, including the main altar and side altars, the presbytery and the crypt (called the Scurolo), the baptistery, pulpits, marble flooring, and stained glass windows. In these works and in his unexecuted project for a gigantic classical façade, Tibaldi made no concessions to the Gothic style of basilica. Opposition to Tibaldi by native Milanese architects was spearheaded by MARTINO BASSI, who published a critique of his work in 1572.

Tibaldi received two important commissions for churches in Milan that were only partly realized according to his designs. San Fedele, begun in

1569, offered an exemplary aisleless church for the Milanese chapter of the Jesuits. The nave is comprised of two square bays in which six giant freestanding Corinthian columns assist in supporting the corners of high sail vaults. Tibaldi's drawings show that he intended that the east end of the church, enlarged after his death, should possess a narrow transept, a hemispherical dome on a low drum, and a relatively shallow semicircular apse. San Sebastiano, erected as a votive church following the plague of 1576, rises from a circular plan with five recessed chapels and three portals, and was to have been covered by a coffered dome resembling the Pantheon's.

Tibaldi was also responsible for a number of buildings in Piedmont and Lombardy. In 1577, he provided plans for the Jesuit Church of the Santi Martiri in Turin, which closely follows the San Fedele scheme, and for San Gaudenzio in Novara, a barrel-vaulted Latin-cross church without aisles. At Carravaggio near Milan, he designed the sanctuary church of the Madonna (1575–1579), whose groin-vaulted nave of five bays, short transepts, and deep monastic choir recall pre-Renaissance and northern European planning concepts. For the sanctuary at Saronno, he conceived a broad, double-order façade with a pair of colossal terminal figures flanking the entrance (1583).

With the death of Borromeo in 1584, Tibaldi's artistic sovereignty in Milan collapsed, and within a year he resigned his post as cathedral architect. His services were at once solicited by Philip II of Spain, whose invitation he accepted in the fall of 1587. During the following nine years, he worked primarily as a painter at the Escorial. Tibaldi died only weeks after returning to Milan in 1596.

As the chief artistic agent of Carlo Borromeo's post-Tridentine church reforms in the archdiocese of Milan, Tibaldi enjoyed nearly unlimited building opportunities. His challenging works along with those of GALEAZZO ALESSI, successfully conveyed the architectural vocabulary and principles of late Renaissance Rome to Milan, thereby setting a new and modern course for the architecture of Lombardy.

RICHARD J. TUTTLE

WORKS

1555?, Cappella Poggi, San Giacoma Maggiore, Bologna, Italy. 1564–1568, Collegio Borromeo, Pavia, Italy. 1564/1570–1596, Cortile della Canonica (not completed until 1604), Palazzo Arcivescoville; 1569–1583, San Fedele; Milan. 1575–1579, Sanctuary of the Madonna, Caravaggio, Italy. 1577, Santi Martiri, Turin, Italy. 1577, San Gaudenzio, Novara, Italy. 1577–1595, San Sebastiano, Milan. 1583?, Madonna dei Miracole (façade), Saronno, Italy. 1583?, Villa Gallio, Gravedonia, Italy.

BIBLIOGRAPHY

BASSI, MARTINO 1572 *Dispareri in materia di architettura et perspettiva. Con pareri di eccellenti et famosi architetti, che li risolvono.* Brescia, Italy: Marchetti.
BRIGANTI, GIULIANO 1945 *Il Manierismo e Pellegrino Tibaldi.* Rome: Cosmopolita.
HIERSCHE, WALDEMAR 1913 *Pellegrino dei Pellegrini als Architekt.* Parchim, Germany: Freise.
PERONI, ADRIANO 1958 "Contributo al Pellegrini Architetto." *Arte Lombarda* 3, no. 2:84–97.
ROCCO, GIOVANNI 1939 *Pellegrino Pellegrini, "l'Architetto di S. Carlo" e le sue opere nel duomo di Milano.* Milan: Hoepli.
SCOTTI, AURORA 1972 "Architettura e riforma cattolica nella Milano di Carlo Borromeo." *L'Arte* 18-19/20:54–90.
WITTKOWER, RUDOLF 1974 *Gothic vs. Classic.* New York: Braziller.

TIFFANY, LOUIS C.

Louis Comfort Tiffany (1848–1933) was a prolific artist best known for his work in glass, who, without formal training, expressed himself as an architect. As the foremost exponent of Art Nouveau in America he was a pioneer of the modern movement. Born in New York, he remained there until his death. He was the son of the founder of Tiffany and Company. As a designer of interiors he met and worked with STANFORD WHITE and other prominent architects including Thomas Hastings (see CARRÈRE AND HASTINGS) and J. C. CADY.

Few of his architectural works survive. The Tiffany Mansion (1884–1885) in New York was demolished in 1936. The Chapel for the Columbian Exposition in Chicago (1893) was taken apart but enough has been preserved that it may someday be restored. It has been compared to LOUIS SULLIVAN's *Golden Gate* as one of the most original works of that fair. His masterpiece, Laurelton Hall (1903–1905), was demolished after a fire in 1957, but the great loggia of the main entrance was preserved and has been installed in the courtyard of the American Wing of the Metropolitan Museum of Art.

The surviving elements of these structures demonstrate Tiffany's use of decorative materials to create colors and forms inspired by nature. Like the vases and lamps he designed, they represent his expression of individualism and antihistoricism.

ROBERT KOCH

WORKS

*1884–1885, Tiffany Mansion (with Stanford White), New York. *1893, Tiffany Chapel, Columbian Exposition, Chicago. *1903–1905, Laurelton Hall; 1921, Sarah Hanley House; Oyster Bay, N.Y.

BIBLIOGRAPHY

DeKay, Charles 1914 *The Art Work of Louis C. Tiffany*. Garden City, N.Y.: Doubleday.

Doros, Paul E. 1977 *The Tiffany Collection from the Chrysler Museum at Norfolk*. Norfolk, Va.: The museum.

Johnson, Diane Chalmers 1979 *American Art Nouveau*. New York: Abrams.

Koch, Robert (1964)1966 *Louis C. Tiffany: Rebel in Glass*. 2d ed. New York: Crown.

McKean, Hugh F. 1980 *The "Lost" Treasures of Louis Comfort Tiffany*. New York: Doubleday.

Purtell, Joseph 1971 *The Tiffany Touch*. New York: Random House.

Speenburgh, Gertrude 1956 *The Arts of the Tiffanys*. Chicago: Lightner.

TIGERMAN, STANLEY

Using a vocabulary of popular cultural symbols, sensual and theatrical imagery, and bright colors, Chicago architect Stanley Tigerman (1930–) has created private luxury homes, public housing complexes, libraries, art galleries, and commercial malls in the midwestern United States, Canada, and Bangladesh. Humorous and pornographic references enliven works such as Animal Crackers (1976–1978), a house based on the shape of the cookie box; Daisy House (1975–1977), designed in the shape of male genitalia for the owner of strip joints; and the projected Kosher Kitchen for a suburban "Jewish-American princess." Influential in Chicago's architectural community, Tigerman has been a member of the Chicago Seven group and has exhibited widely.

Janet Kaplan

WORKS

1962–1964, Pickwick Village Townhouses; 1963–1969, Woodlawn Gardens Low-rise Housing; Chicago. 1966–1969, Nun's Island Low-rise Housing, Montreal. 1966–1976, Polytechnics, Bangladesh. 1970–1973, Vollen Barn, Burlington, Wisc. 1972–1973, Frog Hollow, Berrien Springs, Mich. 1972–1973, Hot Dog House, Harvard, Ill. 1974, Richard Gray Gallery; 1974–1978, Illinois Regional Library for the Blind and Physically Handicapped; 1974–1978, Piper's Alley Commercial Mall, Old Town; Chicago. 1975–1977, Daisy House, Porter, Ind. 1976–1978, Animal Crackers (Blender House), Highland Park, Ill. 1976–1978, Ukrainian Institute of Modern Art, Chicago. 1976–1980, National Archives Center of the Baha'i's of the United States, Wilmette, Ill.

BIBLIOGRAPHY

Benham, Reyner 1976 *Megastructure*. London: Thames & Hudson.

Dahinden, Justus 1972 *Urban Structures for the Future*. New York: Praeger.

Schmertz, M. F. 1974 "Upgrading Barns to Be Inhabited by People." *Architectural Record* 155, no. 7:120–122.

Schmertz, M. F. 1975 "Weese versus Mies." *Architectural Record* 157, no. 4:83–90.

Sky, Alison, and Stone, Michelle 1976 *Unbuilt America*. New York: McGraw-Hill.

Sky, Alison 1976 "Stanley Tigerman on Being Just a Little Less Serious." *Architectural Record* 160, no. 9:111–118.

Stern, Robert A. M. (1969)1977 *New Directions in American Architecture*. Rev. ed. New York: Braziller.

Tigerman, Stanley 1976 "Eleven Works by Stanley Tigerman." *Architecture and Urbanism* 67:71–120. In Japanese and English.

Tigerman, Stanley 1978 "Beyond Scale: Two Projects for the Physically Handicapped." *Design Quarterly* 105:15–29.

Tigerman, Stanley 1979 "Chicago's Architectural Heritage: A Romantic Classical Image . . . and Work of the Current Generation of Chicago Architects." *Arquitectura* Mar.–Apr.:14–47. In Spanish.

TIJEN, WILLEM VAN

Willem van Tijen (1894–1974) was one of the most important trendsetters in the field of social housing in the Netherlands. During his long professional life, he acted upon the idealistic principles of the Modern movement in architecture for the construction of a New World.

At the age of six, van Tijen lost his father, a factory owner with utopian socialist ideals. From his native Wormerveer, an old industrial town north of Amsterdam, he moved to Hilversum, a villa town south-east of the capital. His career as architect of social housing started only after long and distant wanderings. In 1914, van Tijen was drafted into the army. In 1917, he escaped military service by accepting a job in the Dutch East Indies where he worked on the construction of a dam in Sumatra. After a visit to California to qualify as an irrigation technician, he was matriculated as one of the first students of the new Technological University at Bandoeng, Dutch Indies. After receiving the diploma of civil engineer, he became responsible for the construction of a flood-control dam in the Tjipoenegara-river on north Java (1924–1926). A severe attack of poliomyelitis, however, forced him to return to Holland, where he decided to become a housing engineer, in spite of the economic crisis. Van Tijen made contact with progressive architects of the association *Opbouw* in Rotterdam, and in 1930 he visited, with J. H. van den Broek (see Van den Broek en Bakema), the social housing of Ernst May in Frankfurt. He also traveled to the Bau-Ausstellung in Berlin and came to know WALTER GROPIUS and LUDWIG MIES VAN DER ROHE.

His first executed social housing is a project of fifty houses in Zutphen, De Pol (1932), the first consistent *strokenbouw* (rowhouse) in the Netherlands. In the 1930s, his principles could be put into practice only in an experimental way. Van Tijen realized the first high-rise galleried flats with a steel structure (1934), workers' apartment houses, and a block of apartment houses (1938) in Rotterdam.

During the compulsory building stop of World War II, van Tijen completed a number of studies that were of the utmost importance for postwar housing. In 1941, he edited, together with van den Broek, J. A. Brinkman (see BRINKMAN AND VAN DER VLUGT), and H. A. Maaskant, a book about the possibilities for living in the destroyed area of Rotterdam. They did research on the development of the open building block and new living forms based on social-psychological criteria.

Van Tijen played an important role in the reconstruction of Rotterdam as one of the advisers of the reconstruction plan and also directly through his designs for industrial buildings and housing, for instance, the apartment building at the Zuidplein. In 1957, in collaboration with the Bouwcentrum, he executed the experimental Iedershuis (Everybody's home) and participated in a study on functional principles of the dwelling, which later were incorporated into the state regulations for social housing.

From 1937 to 1954, van Tijen was in partnership with H. A. Maaskant; from 1954 to 1959, his partners were Maarten Boom and Jacobus Posno. Until the end of his life he proclaimed his faith in a rational approach to building and planning problems and in the establishment of a human building standard through design.

CEES L. BOEKRAAD

WORKS

1932, Worker's Housing (De Pol), Zutphen, Netherlands. 1933, Apartment Building, Parklaan, Rotterdam, Netherlands. 1934, Apartments (with galleries; with Brinkman and Van der Vlugt), Berglaan; 1934, Worker's Apartments, Frans Bekkerstraat; 1938, Apartments (with H. A. Maaskant), Kralingseplaslaan; Rotterdam, Netherlands. 1939, National Aircraft Laboratory (with Maaskant), Amsterdam. 1947-1948, Oostzeedyk and Goudsesingel Industrial Buildings (with Maaskant); 1949-1950, Zuidplein Apartments; Rotterdam, Netherlands. 1958, Housing, Geuzeveld, Amsterdam. 1960-1968, Technological University Campus Plan, Twente, Netherlands.

BIBLIOGRAPHY

BOS, A. (editor) 1946 *De stad der toekomst, De toekomst der stad. Een stedebouwkundige en sociaal-culturele studie over de groeiende stadgemeenschap.* Rotterdam, Netherlands: Voorhoeve.

De 8 en Opbouw; De organische woonwijk in open bebouwing. 1932 Amsterdam: Nederlands Instituut voor Volkhuisvesting en Stedebouw.

STUDIEGROEP WONINGARCHITEKTUUR VAN DE B.N.A. 1955 *Gronden en achtergronden van woning en wijk.* Amsterdam: van Saane.

TIJEN, W. VAN (chairman) 1957 *Functionele grondslagen van de woning.* Rotterdam, Netherlands: Bouwcentrum.

TIJEN, W. VAN 1970 *Een boekenkast opgeruimd. Veertig jaar persoonlijke architectuurbelevenis tot en voor(?) nu.* Amsterdam.

TIJEN, W. VAN; MAASKANT, H. A.; BROEK, J. H. VAN DEN; and BRINKMAN, J. A. 1941 *Woonmogelijkheden in het nieuwe Rotterdam.* Rotterdam, Netherlands: Brusse.

TITE, WILLIAM

Best known for the Royal Exchange, London (1841-1844), William Tite (1798-1873) was one of the earliest and most prolific railway architects. Early stations, such as Gosport with its fine colonnade, are boldly classical; some later ones, such as Windsor Riverside, under the castle, are romantic Tudor; many smaller ones are simple Italianate. Brookwood Cemetery, started 1854, is an outstanding early landscaped cemetery.

DAVID W. LLOYD

WORKS

*1838, Nine Elms Station, London. 1839-1840, Southampton Terminus Station, England. 1841, Gosport Station, Hampshire, England. 1841-1844, Royal Exchange, London. *1846-1851, Lime Street Station, Liverpool, England. 1847-1848, Carlisle Station (altered), Cumbria, England. 1851, Windsor Riverside Station, Berkshire, England. 1854 and later, Brookwood Cemetery Landscaping and Auxiliary Buildings (with SYDNEY SMIRKE), Surrey, England. 1859, Saint James, Gerrards Cross, Buckinghamshire, England.

BIBLIOGRAPHY

BIDDLE, GORDON 1973 *Victorian Stations.* Newton Abbot, England: David & Charles.

BINNEY, MARCUS, and PEARCE, DAVID (editors) 1979 *Railway Architecture.* London: Orbis.

HITCHCOCK, H. R. (1954)1972 *Early Victorian Architecture in Britain.* Reprint. New York: Da Capo.

'T KINDT, DAVID

David 't Kindt (1699-1770) who was born in Ghent, Belgium, became a master carpenter in 1726 and later served as Ghent's director of works (1755-1770). With BERNARD DE WILDE, he introduced French rococo detailing to Ghent. His oeuvre includes public buildings, *hôtels,* and many smaller houses. His son, Louis, was also a prominent architect–builder.

RICHARD CLEARY

WORKS

1738–1739, Guardhouse; 1741, Prison; 1745, Hôtel de Hertaing; 1745–1746, Hôtel d'Oombergen (now the Koninklijke Vlaamse Akademie); *1747, Church of Saint Nicolas (sacristy); 1749, David 't Kindt House; 1753, Hôtel Faligan; *1754, Barracks; 1768, Hôtel d'Hane-Steenhuyse (façade), Ghent.

BIBLIOGRAPHY

ACKERE, JULES VAN 1972 *Baroque and Classic Art in Belgium (1600–1789): Architecture, Monumental Art.* Brussels: Vokaer.

BERGMANS 1930–1932 "David 'T Kindt." Volume 25, pages 362–363 in *Biographie nationale publiée par l'Académie Royale des Sciences, des Lettres, et des Beaux-Arts de Belgique.* Brussels: Bruylant.

TODT, FRITZ

Fritz Todt (1891–1942) studied engineering at the Technische Hochschulen in Munich and Karlsruhe. After serving in World War I, he worked in bridge and highway construction in south Germany and was an early recruit to the Nazi party. In 1933, Hitler put him in charge of the German Autobahn network. Todt soon gained additional supervisory powers over building construction, navigable waterways, power, plants and fortifications, so that in 1940, when he became minister of armaments, he was in a position to affect and control nearly all aspects of the war effort. When Todt died in 1942, his offices were taken over by ALBERT SPEER.

BARBARA MILLER LANE

WORKS

1926–1933, Dams and Bridges, Isar River, Germany.

BIBLIOGRAPHY

HELLWIG, L. W. 1940 *Persönlichkeiten der Gegenwart: Luftfahrt, Wissenschaft, Kunst.* Berlin: Pape.

SPEER, ALBERT (1969)1970 *Inside the Third Reich: Memoirs.* Translation by Richard and Clara Winston. New York: Macmillan.

STOCKHORST, ERICH 1967 *Fünftausend Köpfe: Wer war was im Dritten Reich.* Bruchsal-Baden, Germany: Blick & Bild.

TOLEDO, JUAN BATISTA DE

Juan Batista de Toledo (?–1567), a Spanish architect, determined the Plateresque character of Spanish architecture which had been neglected in favor of the Italian Renaissance. He started his practice in Rome, where he was possibly MICHELANGELO's apprentice at Saint Peter's. Later, Toledo was the architect of Don Pedro de Toledo in charge of construction of Toledo Street and the Church of San Giacomo degli Spanoli in Naples. In 1559, he was called to the court of Philip II of Spain because of his education in principles of Italian architecture. Toledo was a faithful interpreter of anti-Reformation programs and received absolute authority from the court and the church of Spain in 1561.

Toledo was appointed for the construction of El Escorial, Philip II's tribute to Santo Lorenzo. He planned the entire ground floor, modeled on the Alcazar.

From 1562, Toledo worked on the general composition of the south elevation and court of Evangelisti which recalls the courtyard of Antonio da Sangallo the Younger (see SANGALLO FAMILY) of the Farnese Palace in Rome. The same characteristics can be found in his work on the castle of Aranjuez in Madrid (1561).

FARHAD NIROUMAND-RAD

BIBLIOGRAPHY

CLARK, A. F. 1958 *All the Best in Spain and Portugal.* New York: Dodd, Mead.

KUBLER, GEORGE, and SORIA, M. 1959 *Art and Architecture in Spain, Portugal, and Their Dominions.* Harmondsworth, England: Penguin.

TORO and FERRER

Osvaldo Toro (1914–) and Miguel Ferrer (1915–) changed the direction of Puerto Rican architecture by winning the Caribe Hilton Hotel (1946–1949) competition for the first luxury tourist hotel in Puerto Rico. They met in 1938 while working for the Puerto Rican Reconstruction Administration shortly after Toro had graduated from Columbia University and Ferrer from Cornell University. Opposed to the government's eclectic attitude toward architecture, they established a private firm in 1945.

Noted for their Supreme Court Building (1955) and numerous hotels, Toro and Ferrer have exploited the indoor–outdoor potential of the island's climate with balconies and open courtyards while emphasizing humanly scaled interiors.

ELIZABETH D. HARRIS

WORKS

1946–1949, Caribe Hilton; 1955, Puerto Rican Supreme Court Building; San Juan. 1955–1980, Puerto Rico International Airport, Carolina. 1959, La Concha Hotel,

San Juan. 1965, Banco Popular Center, Hato Rey, Puerto Rico. 1975, Americana Aruba Hotel, Netherlands Antilles.

BIBLIOGRAPHY

"Bright New Home for Justice." 1957 *Architectural Forum* 107, Aug.:128–131.

"The Caribe Hilton, An Object Lesson with What You Can Do with $7,000,000." 1950 *Interiors* 109, Apr.:74–87.

FERNANDEZ, JOSÉ ANTONIO 1965 *Architecture in Puerto Rico.* New York: Architectural Book Publishing.

TORRES CLAVÉ, JOSEP

Josep Torres Clavé (1906–1939) was born in Barcelona, Spain, and graduated from the School of Architecture there in 1929. Joint founder with other architects of the Catalan Architectural and Technical Group for the Progress of Contemporary Architecture (GATCPAC), he was the editor of the group's extraordinary magazine *A.C.* (Documents of Contemporary Activity 1931–1937). The Bloc House (1934–1936) and the Central Antituberculosis Dispensary (1934–1936), both in Barcelona, Spain (with JOSEP LLUIS SERT and J. B. Subirana), are among his principal works. He was co-author with GATCPAC and LE CORBUSIER of the (Macia) Plan for Barcelona.

At the beginning of 1936, he became committed to the radical transformation of Catalan architecture and urbanism. He served as secretary of the new Syndicate of Architects of Catalonia, was director of the School of Architecture of Barcelona (1936–1938), and became the technical secretary of the Group Collective of the Construction Industry of Barcelona.

SALVADOR TARRAGÓ CID
Translated from Spanish by
Judith E. Meighan

WORKS

1934–1936, Casa Bloc; 1934–1936, Central Antituberculosis Dispensary (with Josep Lluis Sert and J. B. Subirana); Barcelona, Spain.

BIBLIOGRAPHY

"Josep Torres Clavé: Arquitecto y revolucionario." 1980 *2C Construcción de la Ciudad* 15–16.

TORROJA MINET, EDUARDO

Eduardo Torroja Minet (1899–1961) was a prominent Spanish figure in the field of structural engineering and design. He was a member of the Madrid "Generation of 1925," advocates of the Modern movement. A prolific builder, he developed and made extensive use of the shell-structure form which contributed new abstract properties to architecture. His best known works are the Fronton Recoletos and the Zarzuela Hippodrome, both of 1935 in Madrid. In the 1940s and 1950s, Torroja designed numerous bridges, viaducts, and hangars. He founded and directed the Technical Institute of Construction and Cement in Costillares, Spain, in 1951 and wrote *Philosophy of Structure* in the same year.

ELIZABETH A. T. SMITH

WORKS

1925, Tempul Aqueduct, Jerez de la Frontera, Spain. 1933, Cantarramas Retaining Wall, Madrid. 1933, Market of Algeciras, Spain. 1933, Quince Ojos Viaduct, University City; 1933–1935, Stadium Streetcar Station, University City; 1935, Church of Villaverde; 1935, Fronton Recoletos; 1935, Zarzuela Hippodrome; Madrid. 1939, Martín Gil Viaduct over Esla River, Zamora, Spain. 1939, Tordera Bridge, Barcelona, Spain. 1943, Las Corts Soccer Stadium, Barcelona, Spain. 1949, Hangar at Cuatro Vientos, Madrid. 1951, Technical Institute of Construction and Cement, Costillares, Spain. 1952, Chapel of the Ascension, Xerralló, Spain. 1952, Church, Pont de Suert, Spain. 1956, Cañelles Dam, Lérida, Spain. n.d., Instituto Escuela (now known as Instituto Nacional de Enseñanza Media "Ramíro de Maeztu"), Madrid.

BIBLIOGRAPHY

ARNICHES, C.; DOMINGUEZ, M.; and TORROJA, E. 1948 "El Hipodromo de la Zarzuela en Madrid." *Revista Nacional de Arquitectura* 8:337–347.

BOHIGAS, ORIOL 1970 *Arquitectura española de la segunda república.* Barcelona, Spain: Tusquets.

BOZAL, VALERIANO 1978 *Historia del arte en España.* 2 vols. Madrid: ISTMO.

TORROJA, EDUARDO 1958a *Philosophy of Structure.* Translated by J. J. Polivka and Milos Polivka. Reprint. Berkeley: University of California Press.

TORROJA, EDUARDO 1958b *The Structures of Eduardo Torroja: An Autobiography of Engineering Accomplishment.* New York: Dodge.

TOURTELLOTTE, JOHN E.

John Everett Tourtellotte (1869–1939), born in Thompson, Connecticut, was apprenticed to the Worcester, Massachusetts, architectural firm of Cutting and Bishop for four years before moving west. In 1890, he arrived in Boise, Idaho, where he commenced practice as an architect and builder. In 1896, he became associated with Charles F. Hummel, with whom he formed a partnership in 1901. In 1913, Tourtellotte opened an office in Portland, Oregon, and was later joined by Frank K. Hummel, son of his partner, who remained in charge of the Boise office. The firm's most important project was the Idaho State Capitol in Boise, completed in the tradition of the American Renaissance in 1912, but it also produced a sizable body of work throughout Idaho, eastern Washington, and Oregon. The output included, in addition to a long list of residences and notable commercial buildings and churches in Boise, innumerable public school buildings and many of the region's large hotels of the pre-Depression era.

ELISABETH WALTON POTTER

WORKS

1902, Warden's House, Idaho State Penitentiary; 1903-1904, First Methodist Church; 1905, Overland Block (Eastman Building); 1905, Timothy Regan House; 1905-1919, Idaho State Capitol; 1906, Saint John's Roman Catholic Cathedral; Boise, Idaho. 1906, Liberal Arts and Administration Building, University of Idaho, Moscow. 1909, Administration Building (Eaton Hall), Willamette University, Salem, Ore. 1910, Frank Dietrich House; *1910-1911, Idaho Trust and Savings Building (Yates Block); 1911, Will Regan House; Boise, Idaho. *1917, Pilot Butte Inn, Bend, Ore. 1922-1926, John Jacob Astor Hotel, Astoria, Ore. 1924-1925, Lithia Springs Hotel (Mark Anthony Hotel), Ashland, Ore. 1926, Redwoods Hotel, Grants Pass, Ore. 1928-1929, Douglas County Courthouse, Roseburg, Ore. 1930, Hotel Boise, Idaho.

BIBLIOGRAPHY

FRENCH, HIRAM TAYLOR 1914 Volume 2, pages 658–660 in *History of Idaho*. Chicago and New York: Lewis.

HIBBARD, DON J. 1978 "Domestic Architecture in Boise, 1904-1912: A Study in Styles." *Idaho Yesterdays* 22, no. 3:2–9.

HITCHCOCK, H. R., and SEALE, WILLIAM 1976 *Temples of Democracy: The State Capitols of the USA.* New York and London: Harcourt.

LOCKLEY, FRED 1928 Volume 2, pages 485–486 in *History of the Columbia River Valley from the Dalles to the Sea.* Chicago: Clarke.

"Obituary." 1939 *Oregonian* May 10, p. 11.

VAUGHAN, THOMAS, and FERRIDAY, VIRGINIA GUEST (editors) 1974 *Space, Style and Structure.* 2 vols. Portland: Oregon Historical Society.

TOWN, ITHIEL

Eminent in both architecture and bridge engineering, Ithiel Town (1784-1844) was one of the most important early leaders of the Greek and Gothic Revivals in America. Independently and with his associates, he was responsible for a large number of prominent and influential buildings; several initiated patterns that were extensively copied. He was keenly interested in many aspects of structure, including the strength of materials, fireproof construction, the application of his lattice truss to roof framing, and the economical use of lighter timbers and stucco. Energetic, intense, and high-strung, he had an exceptional memory, a persuasive manner, and wide-ranging, progressive ideas in architecture and art, mathematics and engineering. He assembled by far the largest American library of art, architecture, and engineering books and prints, which he opened liberally to others. Able, innovative, and practical, he was widely respected.

Town was born in Thompson, Connecticut. His father, a farmer, died when Town was eight, and for several years he lived with an uncle. At seventeen, he taught a country school, but he soon became a carpenter. By 1805 or 1806, he was in Boston, where he studied with ASHER BENJAMIN. In 1810, he built Harvard's Botanic Garden House, a fine Federal-style house with an unusual method of roof framing.

Around 1813, or possibly earlier, Town's center of activity shifted to New Haven, Connecticut. Here, he built two important churches on the Green. The impressive Center Church (1812-1815) was modified from a design that Benjamin supplied; subtleties in the tower, unusually light framing timbers, and ingenuity in raising the spire attested to Town's skill. His remarkable Trinity Church (1813-1816) was an influential advance in American use of Gothic. Other work includes designs for Federal-style meetinghouses at Plainfield and Thompson, Connecticut (both 1815), and the Steamboat Hotel in New Haven (1816).

After 1816, for several years Town's chief activity shifted to bridges—perhaps previously a concurrent interest—and he moved about continually. With Isaac Damon he constructed several bridges over the Connecticut River, and from 1818 to mid-1825 he spent much time in the South, especially North Carolina, where he built a number of important bridges and developed his lattice truss. A major American invention, patented in 1820, it became widely used for covered bridges. By mid-decade, Town ceased to build bridges himself, but as an engineer he advised on plans and licensed and promoted his patent. He traveled constantly along the eastern seaboard and, from the early 1830s, to the Midwest. It was the wealth acquired from his patent and bridges that made possible his great library.

From Boston to Savannah Town saw America's architecture, and the new work in Philadelphia and Boston inspired him. He was particularly moved by the "simplicity, elegance, and grandeur" of the Greek styles, and at the age of forty he returned to architecture. This time, however, it was not as a builder-architect, but as a designing, directing professional. Back in New Haven briefly, he planned an exquisite Ionic temple for the Eagle Bank (designed 1824, commenced 1825); he also designed the Tontine Hotel (1825?–1827?) and a house for Mrs. Eli Whitney (1825–1826), both with Greek-columned porches. Yale College awarded him an honorary master's degree. In September 1825, failure of the Eagle Bank doomed his temple and plunged New Haven into a depression.

The next month, Town opened an office in New York, which was booming with optimism over the new Erie Canal. A friend of the painter Samuel F. B. Morse, he entered immediately into the city's artistic life, becoming an original member of the New-York Drawing Association (1825), then of the National Academy of Design (1826); in the 1830s, he was an officer of the older American Academy of Fine Arts, and in 1835, he published a proposal for a single academy, which would have the advantages of both.

The ten years in New York were the high point of Town's architectural career. His work gave major impetus to the Greek and Gothic Revivals both there and in western New England and through its quality and influence became of national importance. Most of his buildings were austere, forceful expressions of the Grecian style; some introduced practical modifications of Greek forms and effectively used massive anta-type square piers to suggest columns, freestanding or attached. Town continued to pursue his very active bridge business with amazing energy and endurance.

He immediately began introducing important new ideas in the city: a Doric distyle-in-antis temple for the large New York Theatre (1826); for Arthur Tappan a storefront (1826) with monolithic, anta-type piers, influenced by Boston post-and-lintel construction and soon widely copied; and a novel open-court plan for Jones Court (1826–1827). In Northampton, Massachusetts, he created the prototype of the American temple-form house with wings in Henry G. Bower's country house (1826-1827); for the rear portico and wings he employed practical square pillars.

In 1827–1828, Town was associated with MARTIN E. THOMPSON. The precise nature of the Town and Thompson association is not known, though it may have been limited to local joint efforts, usually executed by Thompson; Thompson's name has not been identified with Town's Connecticut buildings. Works credited jointly include the Doric Church of the Ascension (1828–1829), New York, and the Flushing Institute (1827–1828) on Long Island.

In Connecticut, Town designed several important early Greek Revival temples: the austerely

Town.
Drawing of Center Church,
Trinity Church, and
Connecticut State House.
New Haven.

monumental New Haven State House (1827–1831); Hartford's ingeniously practical City Hall and Market House (1828–1829), where he modified the Greek temple form for the double function and limited site and introduced shallow peripteral pilasters; and Samuel Russell's impressive house in Middletown (1828–1830), with a Corinthian main portico and massive square pillars in the rear. To Town is attributed New Haven's Third Congregational Church (1828–1829), apparently the prototype for a much copied façade pattern; distyle in antis with flanking paired antae suggesting a hexastyle portico. For most of these buildings Town used stucco over stone chips or brick, an economical technique he introduced from the South.

During the next six years (1829–1835), Town worked in partnership with ALEXANDER J. DAVIS as the firm of TOWN AND DAVIS, adding JAMES H. DAKIN for eighteen months in 1832–1833, when he optimistically opened branch offices in Washington and Baltimore. As directing head of the firm, Town was in general control of major works, although he was frequently away for long periods, delegating details to the younger partners and sharing the design process with them. He strongly influenced both brilliant young men, as well as JAMES GALLIER, SR., a draftsman for several months. In 1829–1830, he spent ten months in England (mostly London), France, and Italy, experiencing European architecture firsthand and sending back many books.

The firm produced many significant, influential designs of various types, public and institutional, ecclesiastical, commercial, and domestic. Most were intensely rational interpretations of the Greek Revival, often developing ideas already broached by Town. Many were characterized by powerful square antae used to suggest columns; as engaged piers like exaggerated pilasters, as huge square pillars, or as structural members.

Outstanding were the state capitols for Indiana in Indianapolis (1831–1835) and North Carolina in Raleigh (1833–1840; begun by WILLIAM NICHOLS, finished by David Paton) and New York's Custom House (1833–1842; modified by others in execution). Severe and monumental, with domes to symbolize their governmental functions, the designs were distinguished by excellent proportions and carefully studied detailing; all had bold antae in deep pilastrades—peripteral in Indianapolis and New York, on the flanks in Raleigh. Town gave overall supervision to construction in Indianapolis and initially in Raleigh, but he lost the supervision of the Custom House.

In the Rockaway Marine Pavilion (1833–1834), undertaken with Dakin, tall square pillars formed spectacular long colonnades. Many stores were designed on the Tappan pattern, from Hartford to New Orleans; in storefronts of the Lyceum of Natural History, New York (1835–1836), Town introduced metal for secondary members.

Handsomest of the Town and Davis churches was the French Church du Saint Esprit, New York (1831–1834), but most of their churches were variations of the distyle-in-antis pattern, including the South Congregational, Middletown, Connecticut (1829–1830), and the West Presbyterian in New York (1831–1832).

Town and Davis were among the earliest in New York to employ Greek columns and antae for townhouse doorways. Outstanding among their numerous houses were Samuel Ward's House (1831–1833) in New York and Ralph Ingersoll's (1829–1830) in New Haven.

Town made significant contributions to the advance of the American Gothic Revival. Working with the Reverend Nathaniel S. Wheaton, he designed the fine Christ Church Cathedral in Hartford (1827–1828); its latticed scissors trusses are the earliest surviving example of Town's application of his bridge truss to roof construction. With Robert Gilmor he planned America's first major asymmetrical Gothic country house, Glen Ellen (1832–1834), Towson, Maryland, with detailing by Davis. Likewise of much importance was the New York University Building (1833–1837). Its overall design was suggested by Professors David Douglass and Cyrus Mason; plans and detailing were chiefly by Town and Dakin, superintendence by Dakin, and the chapel by Davis.

With the award of his second bridge patent in April 1835, Town's primary attention turned again to bridge engineering. Several important bridges were planned, including one a mile long over the Ohio River at Louisville, Kentucky. The firm was discontinued in May 1835. For seven years, the two men mostly went their separate ways, although Davis did some drafting for Town, and they collaborated at times; they entered the Illinois Capitol competition (1837) jointly and worked nominally together on Ohio Capitol designs (1839). Town kept a New York address for two years, where William H. Bayless (nephew of Thomas Cole) was briefly his apprentice. He accomplished a few known architectural works, chiefly the design (with William Parker Elliot) for the Patent Office in Washington (1836–1840, 1849–1867, executed with modifications by ROBERT MILLS and others), and the Gothic New York Orphan Asylum (1836–1839; chapel by Davis).

New Haven became Town's headquarters again in early summer 1836 when he moved his great library to his unfinished house (1835?–1837), built according to his ideas of fireproof construction: floors deafened, brick walls and partitions constructed hollow without wooden furring (a technique he introduced from England); posthumously he was awarded a patent for molding hollow bricks. He was made an Honorary and Corresponding Member of the Royal Institute of British Architects (1836) and encouraged the founding of the American Institution of Architects.

The Panic of 1837 and its ensuing depression dimmed bridge-building prospects, and though several important bridges were completed, Town's favorite Ohio Bridge project failed. In January 1842, Town returned to New York with several Gothic projects in mind and in March reassociated with Davis. During their brief second partnership, the chief accomplishment was the façade, principally by Davis, for the Wadsworth Atheneum, Hartford, Connecticut (1842–1844; plan by HENRY AUSTIN).

Town began selling his library, some 11,000 books and 25,000 prints, privately and in a series of auctions.

After a trip to England and France during the second half of 1843, he reopened a New York office the next spring, but he died in New Haven in June 1844.

JANE B. DAVIES

WORKS

1810, Botanic Garden House, Harvard University, Cambridge, Mass. 1812–1815, Center Church (after design by Asher Benjamin); 1813–1816, Trinity Church; New Haven. 1815, Congregational Meetinghouse, Plainfield, Conn. *1815, Congregational Meetinghouse, Thompson, Conn. *1816, Steamboat Hotel; *1825–1826, Mrs. Eli Whitney House; *1825?–1827?, Tontine Hotel; New Haven. *1826, Arthur Tappan Store; *1826, New York Theatre; New York. *1826–1827,

Henry G. Bowers House, Northampton, Mass. *1826–1827, Jones Court, New York. 1826–1830, Fort Griswold Monument, Groton, Conn. 1827–1828, Christ Church Cathedral (with Nathaniel S. Wheaton), Hartford, Conn. *1827–1828, Flushing Institute (with Martin E. Thompson), Long Island, N.Y. *1827–1831, Connecticut State House, New Haven. *1828–1829, Church of the Ascension (with Thompson), New York. *1828–1829, City Hall and Market House, Hartford, Conn. *(A)1828–1829, Third Congregational Church, New Haven. 1828–1830, Samuel Russell House, Middletown, Conn. 1829–1830, Ralph Ingersoll House (with Alexander B. Davis), New Haven. *1829–1830, South Congregational Church (with Davis), Middletown, Conn. *1830–1833, General Hospital (with Davis), New Haven. *1831–1832, County Courthouse and Town Hall (with Davis), Middletown, Conn. *1831–1832, West Presbyterian Church (with Davis); *1831–1833, Samuel Ward House (with Davis); *1831–1834, French Church du Saint Esprit (with Davis); New York. *1831–1835, Indiana State Capitol (with Davis), Indianapolis. *1832–1834?, Glen Ellen (with Davis and Robert Gilmor), Towson, Md. *1833–1834, Marine Pavilion (with James H. Dakin), Rockaway, N.Y. *1833–1837, New York University Building (with Dakin, Davis, and others), New York. 1833–1840, North Carolina State Capitol (with Davis and others), Raleigh. 1833–1842, United States Customhouse (with Davis and others); *1835–1836, Lyceum of Natural History (with Davis); New York. *1835?–1837, Ithiel Town House, New Haven. *1836–1839, New York Orphan Asylum (chapel by Davis), New York. 1836–1840, 1849–1867, United States Patent Office (with William Parker Elliot and others), Washington. 1842–1844, Wadsworth Atheneum (façade; with Davis), Hartford, Conn.

BIBLIOGRAPHY

The chief manuscript sources for Ithiel Town are in the Town papers at the New Haven Colony Historical Society and at Yale University, New Haven; the Alexander J. Davis papers at the Avery Architectural Library, Columbia University, at the Metropolitan Museum of Art, New York, at the New York Public Library; and in the George Dudley Seymour Papers at Yale University, New Haven.

BROOKS, H. ALLEN, JR. 1954 "The Home of Ithiel Town: Its Date of Construction and Original Appearance." *Journal of the Society of Architectural Historians* 13, no. 3:27–28.
DAVIES, JANE B. 1965 "A. J. Davis' Projects for a Patent Office Building, 1832–1834." *Journal of the Society of Architectural Historians* 24:229–251.
HAMLIN, TALBOT F. (1944)1964 *Greek Revival Architecture in America.* Reprint. New York: Dover.
HITCHCOCK, H. R., and SEALE, WILLIAM 1976 *Temples of Democracy: The State Capitols of the U.S.A.* New York: Harcourt.
KELLY, JOHN FREDERICK 1948 *Early Connecticut Meetinghouses.* 2 vols. New York: Columbia University Press.
NEWTON, ROGER HALE 1942 *Town & Davis, Architects: Pioneers in American Revivalist Architecture, 1812–1870.* New York: Columbia University Press.
PIERSON, WILLIAM H., JR. 1970 *The Colonial and Neoclassical Styles.* Volume 1 in *American Buildings and Their Architects.* Garden City, N.Y.: Doubleday.
PIERSON, WILLIAM H., JR. 1978 *Technology and the Picturesque: The Corporate and Early Gothic Styles.* Volume 2A in *American Buildings and Their Architects.* Garden City, N.Y.: Doubleday.
SIGOURNEY, LYDIA H. 1839 "The Library of Ithiel Town, Esq." *Ladies Companion* 10:123–126.
TOWN, ITHIEL 1835 *The Outlines of a Plan for Establishing in New-York an Academy and Institution of the Fine Arts.* New York: Hopkins.
TOWN, ITHIEL 1842 *Important Notice to All Colleges, State, and Other Public Libraries, Athenaeums, & Other Institutions . . . Private Sale. . . .* New York: Vinten.

TOWN and DAVIS

One of the earliest American architectural firms, the partnership of ITHIEL TOWN and ALEXANDER J. DAVIS was formed in New York in February 1829 and continued to May 1835. For eighteen months in 1832–1833, it became Town, Davis, and Dakin, when JAMES H. DAKIN was added and Davis spent several months at temporary branch offices in Washington and Baltimore. After seven years apart, Town and Davis revived their association for a final year, March 1842 to July 1843.

The firm was a leading force in the new Revival styles, chiefly Greek, but also Gothic, Tuscan, and Egyptian. It produced many outstanding and influential designs for buildings of wide variety: two state capitols, a customhouse, patent office, county courthouse, hospital, insane asylum, and prison; churches, monuments, hotels, banks, and stores; a university, academy, and other institutional buildings; and city, suburban, and country houses.

Unique in New York in its day, the office had the finest architectural library in America, and it united the diverse talents of men intent on professional careers: the experienced, practical Town; the imaginative, innovative Davis; and the able, enterprising young Dakin. Town was unquestionably the head of the firm. His prestige, ability, and contacts brought many of the commissions. Although frequently away from the office for several weeks or months, he was usually there for the designing of important works. He shared the design process with his partners; some designs were worked out jointly, while others were done independently during his absences. Credit for design authorship is often difficult to determine, but Davis's records and drawings contain numerous indications, and responsibility can also be deduced from the partners' whereabouts.

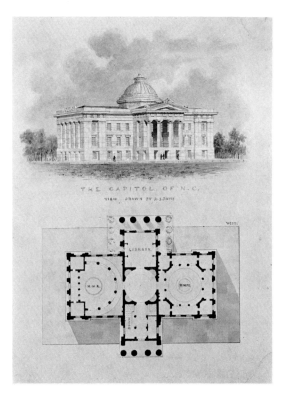

Town and Davis.
North Carolina State
    Capitol (with others).
Raleigh.
1833–1840

THE CAPITOL OF N.C.
VIEW DRAWN BY A.J.DAVIS

Davis and Dakin, both creative designers and skilled draftsmen, handled the details. For much of 1832–1833, the office also employed a draftsman, successively JAMES GALLIER SR., John Sole, and Charles B. Dakin. In addition, Davis taught a sequence of five students in the office in 1829–1832.

Town and Dakin undertook superintendence of several of the firm's large works, although most of the designs were executed by builders, with working drawings provided when requested. Town contracted for the Indiana Capitol (1831–1835), made long trips to Indianapolis to supervise construction, and sent men from the East as superintendents. He likewise supervised much of the construction of the North Carolina Capitol (1833–1840) at Raleigh. Dakin superintended the Marine Pavilion (1833–1834) at Rockaway, New York, and the New York University Building (1833–1837), except the chapel.

Fees were based on drawings provided and work performed, not on a percentage of building costs. Town and Davis, when practicing together, divided equally the office expenses and most architectural fees, while each continued private work of bridge engineering and drawing, respectively. When Dakin was in the firm, he received 40 percent for his full-time work, Town and Davis each 30.

These fruitful years of collaborative effort were a strong influence on the careers of the men in the office and on the development of American nineteenth-century architecture.

JANE B. DAVIES

WORKS

1829–1830, Ralph Ingersoll House, New Haven. *1829–1830, South Congregational Church, Middletown, Conn. *1830–1833, General Hospital, New Haven. *1831–1832, County Courthouse and Town Hall, Middletown, Conn. *1831–1832, West Presbyterian Church, New York. 1831–1833?, Aaron N. Skinner House, New Haven. *1831–1833, Samuel Ward House; *1831–1834, French Church du Saint Esprit; New York. *1831–1835, Indiana State Capitol, Indianapolis. *1832–1833, Second Avenue Presbyterian Church, New York. *1832–1834?, Glen Ellen, Towson, Md. 1832–1835, Cannon Block, Troy, N.Y. 1833, La Grange Terrace (interiors), New York. *1833–1834, Albany Female Academy, Albany, N.Y. *1833–1834, Marine Pavilion, Rockaway, N.Y. *1833–1837, New York University Building (with others), New York. 1833–1840, North Carolina State Capitol (with others), Raleigh. 1833–1842, United States Customhouse (with others), New York. 1834, Vesper Cliff (remodeling), Owego, N.Y. *1834–1848, Pauper Lunatic Asylum (one octagon still extant; with others); *1835–1836, Lyceum of Natural History; New York. 1842–1844, Wadsworth Atheneum (façade), Hartford, Conn. *1843–1844, Henry H. Elliott and Robert C. Townsend Houses, New York.

BIBLIOGRAPHY

The chief manuscript sources for the firm of Town and Davis are in the Alexander J. Davis collections of the Avery Architectural Library, Columbia University, New York; the Metropolitan Museum of Art, New York; and the New York Public Library.

DAVIES, JANE B. 1965 "A. J. Davis' Projects for a Patent Office Building, 1832–1834." *Journal of the Society of Architectural Historians* 24:229–251.
DAVIES, JANE B. 1967 "Six Letters by William P. Elliot to Alexander J. Davis, 1834–1838." *Journal of the Society of Architectural Historians* 26:71–73.
GALLIER, JAMES (1864)1973 *Autobiography of James Gallier, Architect.* With an introduction by Samuel Wilson, Jr. Reprint. New York: Da Capo.
HAMLIN, TALBOT F. (1944)1964 *Greek Revival Architecture in America.* Reprint. New York: Dover.
NEWTON, ROGER HALE 1942 *Town & Davis, Architects: Pioneers in American Revivalist Architecture, 1812–1870.* New York: Columbia University Press.
SCULLY, ARTHUR, JR. 1973 *James Dakin, Architect: His Career in New York and the South.* Baton Rouge: Louisiana State University Press.

TOWNSEND, CHARLES HARRISON

Born in Birkenhead, Cheshire, the son of a solicitor and a Polish violinist, Charles Harrison Townsend (1851–1928) was articled in 1870 to Walter Scott of Liverpool. He went into partnership with Thomas Lewis Banks in London from 1884 to 1888, after which he set up his own practice.

Each of Townsend's three major public buildings in London projects a memorable image of a monumental quality unique in free arts and crafts architecture and deriving from the combined influences of his beloved Art Workers Guild, his knowledge of the past and of the work of H. H. RICHARDSON, and his personal exploration of organic and evocative form and decoration.

His approach, though modified to an undistinguished vernacular in many country buildings, was carried further in the union of architect, artist, and craftsman; through the jewellike interiors of his village churches; and his designs for wall papers, fabrics, and fittings.

ANTHONY BALLANTINE

WORKS

1890, Tourelle, Salcombe, Devon, England. 1892, All Saints (west front and alterations), Ennismore Gardens, Knightsbridge; 1892–1895, Bishopsgate Institute; London. c.1893, Congregational Chapel; c.1894, Blatchfield; Blackheath, Guildford, Surrey, England. 1896, Linden House, Düsseldorf, Germany. 1896–1901, Horniman Free Museum, Forest Hill, London. 1897, Cliff Towers, Salcombe, Devon, England. 1899–1901, Whitechapel Art Gallery, London. 1900, Dickhurst, near Haslemere, Surrey, England. 1902–1904, Saint Mary the Virgin, Great Warley, Essex, England. 1902, Village Cross, West Meon, Hampshire, England. 1904, Union Free Church, Woodford Green, Essex, England. 1906, Arbuthnot Institute Hall, Shanley Green, Surrey. 1910, Village Hall, Panshanger, Hertfordshire, England.

BIBLIOGRAPHY

Many articles on Charles Harrison Townsend's work appeared in the architectural press and in the Studio *during the 1890s and 1900s.*

BELL, ROBERT ANNING 1929 "Charles Harrison Townsend." *The (London) Times,* Jan. 4.

MALTON, JOHN 1973 "Art Nouveau in Essex." Pages 159–169 in Nikolaus Pevsner and J. M. Richards (editors), *The Anti-rationalists.* London: Architectural Press.

MUSGRAVE, NOEL 1966 "Survival of the Richest: The Whitechapel Art Gallery." *Journal of the Royal Institute of British Architects* 73:315.

SERVICE, ALASTER 1974 "Arts and Crafts, Extremist: Charles Harrison Townsend (1851–1928)." *Architectural Association Quarterly* 6, no. 2:4–12.

SERVICE, ALASTER 1975 "Charles Harrison Townsend." Pages 162–182 in Alastar Service (editor), *Edwardian Architecture and Its Origins.* London: Architectural Press.

TOWNSEND, CHARLES HARRISON 1896 "An Artistic Treatment of Cottages." *Studio* 6:24–34.

TOWNSEND, CHARLES HARRISON 1901 "The Art of Pictorial Mosaic." *Journal of the Royal Institute of British Architects* Series 3 8:221–241.

TOWNSEND, CHARLES HARRISON 1912 "The Royal Institute Library and Some of Its Contents." *Journal of the Royal Institute of British Architects* Series 3 19:429–456.

TOWNSEND, CHARLES HARRISON 1916 "The Civic Survey." *Journal of the Royal Institute of British Architects* Series 3 23:177–180.

TRAMELLO, ALESSIO

Although not well known—his work is to be found exclusively in the northern Italian town of Piacenza—Alessio Tramello (1460–1550?) is one of the best provincial architects of the Renaissance in Italy. He was responsible for some strikingly original works that belong generally to the Lombard school of monumental Bramantesque (see DONATO BRAMANTE) architecture that are richly embroidered with elements from the architecture of the Piacenza region.

Tramello's birth date is not known precisely. It is possible that he learned architecture from GIOVANNI BATTAGGIO or from one of his school. He is recorded in the documents as an architect between 1488 and 1521. Two churches in Piacenza, San Sisto (1499–1514) and San Sepolcro (1510) demonstrate Tramello's architectural character.

In San Sisto, the barrel vault over the nave is coffered and, classical in inspiration (possibly derived from LEON BATTISTA ALBERTI's Sant Andrea, Mantua, or Bramante's Santa Maria presso San Satiro, Milan), but the round windows in the clearstory of the nave and the dwarf gallery in the drum over the crossing recall Lombard works in general (in Milan or Pavia, for example). Overall, the effect is of a highly eclectic classical-Lombard building of peculiar originality.

San Sepolcro with its neighboring monastery (begun 1502) is similarly unusual. The bays of the nave are alternately square and oblong and create a richly articulated volume in which the individual sections are clear and logical but their combination seems curiously varied and erratic. Whereas Tuscan architects of the late fifteenth century tended toward regular plans and rich decorative sculpture, Tramello and other architects of this period in northern Italy, such as BIAGIO ROSSETTI, evaded regularity in their plans.

In his last major work, the Church of the Madonna di Campagna in Piacenza (begun 1522), Tramello adapted his own longitudinal plan at San Sepolcro to the Greek cross. The massy forms, however, recall Bramante's choir at Santa Maria delle Grazie, Milan, or, perhaps, Bramante's Saint Peter's, as seen through Zaccagni's (see ZACCAGNI FAMILY) Steccata in nearby Parma.

Tramello's influence beyond Piacenza was negligible yet his work is so consistent by its own standards of internal logic that he may be compared in the quality of his designs with the better known Tuscans Giuliano da Sangallo (see SAN-GALLO FAMILY) or IL CRONACA.

Little is known about Tramello's life. He is thought to have died in Piacenza around 1550.

NICHOLAS ADAMS

WORKS

1499–1514, San Sisto; 1510, San Sepolcro; 1522, Madonna di Campagna; Piacenza, Italy.

BIBLIOGRAPHY

ANCONA, P. D' 1953 *Umanesimo e Rinasqmento.* Turin, Italy.
GAUZ, JÜRG 1968 *Drei Sakralbauten in Piacenza und die oberitalienische Architektur um 1500.* Frauenfeld, Switzerland: Huber.
GAZZOLA, P. 1935 *Opere di A. Tramello architetto piacentino.* Rome.
HEYDENREICH, LUDWIG H., and LOTZ, WOLFGANG 1974 *Architecture in Italy: 1400–1600.* Harmondsworth, England: Penguin.

TREHEARNE and NORMAN

A. F. A. Trehearne (1874–1962) and C. F. Norman (1883–1925) became partners in 1906, forming a highly successful commercial practice. The majority of their work was in the new London street, Kingsway, and the surrounding area where they built twenty-four large buildings between 1912 and 1930. The façades are competent but unexciting, although certain details confirm the tradition that THOMAS S. TAIT ghosted for the firm. Both partners were active members of the Society of Architects, a rival body to the Royal Institute of British Architects. Trehearne remained active until 1960; the practice is still in existence.

ALAN POWERS

WORKS

1912–1930, Africa House; 1912–1930, Adastral House; 1912–1930, Alexandra House; 1912–1930, Central House; 1912–1930, Connaught House; 1912–1930, Imperial House; 1912–1930, Ingersoll House; 1912–1930, Prince's House; 1912–1930, Regent House; 1912–1930, Shell Corner; 1912–1930, West Africa House; 1912–1930, Windsor House; 1912–1930, York House; Kingsway, London. 1920–1922, London School of Economics. 1939, Melton Court Flats, South Kensington, London.

TRESGUERRAS, FRANCISCO EDUARDO DE

Francisco Eduardo de Tresguerras (1759–1833), one of Mexico's greatest architects, was born in Celaya, southwest of Guanajuato. His work was so influential that most buildings in the area even vaguely reminiscent of his style are attributed to him.

Tresguerras was given a religious education before studying in Mexico City under the painter Miguel Cabrera at the Academia de San Carlos. After returning to Celaya, he married and devoted himself to painting. His architectural career began almost incidentally. A supposed letter by Tresguerras in which he described, half-facetiously, how simple it was to become an architect, implying that that was the reason why he became one, is often quoted. By this time, however, he was a true Renaissance man; he was proficient in woodcarving, engraving, surveying, music, and poetry, not to mention that he was a competent painter and sculptor.

Throughout his life, Tresguerras studied both historical and contemporary treatises on art and architecture, and indeed, his works are based on the theories of such architects as VITRUVIUS, SEBASTIANO SERLIO, GIACOMO BAROZZI DA VIGNOLA, and undoubtedly ANDREA PALLADIO. Tresguerras never traveled to Europe to see the monuments he was studying, relying completely on second-hand knowledge. However, his work displays a strong understanding of classical and Renaissance architecture in addition to a sound sense of proportion and a tendency toward plasticity and massing of elements which can best be seen in his mature work.

Tresguerras's earliest major architectural work is the reconstruction of the Convent Church of Santa Rosa de Viterbo in Querétaro (1780s) where his interest in surface texture can be seen on the dome. Surrounding the drum, alternating with niches, are rusticated double columns, a motif that is repeated on the lantern.

The Palace of the Conde de Casa Rul in Guanajuato (?–1803) is Tresguerras's most European work. It was finished by 1803 and is reminiscent of CLAUDE PERRAULT's east front of the Louvre with its giant order above a ground story; likewise, its center bay projects slightly and is topped by a pediment. It is Tresguerras's most elegant work and perhaps more than any other of his works reflects his debt to and knowledge of European styles.

Tresguerras's best known work is the Church of El Carmen in Celaya (1802–1807). His interest in plasticity and massing of elements is evident here, particularly in the tower and the portico. On one level, the tower is accented by projecting entablatures over single columns that flank arches; it is crowned by a conical peak. The portico is a mass of Tuscan columns, entablature, and pediment—an impressive base for the tower. The dome recalls MICHELANGELO's dome at Saint Peter's in Rome with its paired columns and projecting entablatures around the drum. The side portal has been described as French in influence, with a concave and convex arrangement of columns on two levels.

That Tresguerras has been called "el Miguel Angel mexicano" is indicative of his reputation as one of Mexico's greatest architects. His work inspired a number of architects to work in his style; even today their work complicates the efforts of those attempting to get a complete picture of Tresguerras's oeuvre.

JOHN H. WILSON

Tresguerras.
Convent Church of Santa
Rosa de Viterbo
(reconstruction).
Querétaro, Mexico.
c.1780s

WORKS

c.1780s, Convent Church of Santa Rosa de Viterbo (reconstruction); c.1790s, Santa Clara (interior); 1797, Neptune Fountain; Querétaro, Mexico. 1802–1807, El Carmen, Celaya, Mexico. Completed 1803, Palace of the Conde de Casa Rul, Guanajuato, Mexico. 1809, Rio de la Laja Bridge, Celaya, Mexico. 1810, Convent of La Enseñanza, Irapuato, Mexico. 1827, Column of Independence, San Luis Potosí, Mexico. n.d., Convent Church of La Conception (dome), San Miguel de Allende, Mexico. n.d., Teatro Ruiz de Alarcón, San Luis Potosí, Mexico.

BIBLIOGRAPHY

BAXTER, SYLVESTER 1897 "A Great Mexican Architect." *American Architect* 55:51–52, 67–68, 75–76, 83.
GALLO, EDUARDO L. (editor) 1873–1874 *Hombres ilustres mexicanos.* 4 vols. Mexico, Cumplido.
MAZA, FRANCISCO DE LA 1950 "Dibujos y proyectos de Tresguerras." *Anales del Instituto de Investigaciones Estéticas* 18:27–33.
MAZA, FRANCISCO DE LA 1960 "En el segundo centenario de Tresguerras." *Anales del Instituto de Investigaciones Estéticas* 29:9–14.
SANFORD, TRENT ELWOOD 1947 Chapter 28 in *The Story of Architecture in Mexico.* New York: Norton.
TERREROS, MANUEL DE 1927 "El arquitecto Tresguerras." *Anales del Museo Nacional* 5:55–63.
TOUSSAINT, MANUEL (1948)1967 *Colonial Art in Mexico.* Translated and edited by Elizabeth Wilder Weismann. Austin: University of Texas Press.

TROOST, PAUL LUDWIG

Paul Ludwig Troost (1878–1934) studied with Ludwig Hoffmann and at the Technische Hochschule in Darmstadt, Germany, and then worked in the offices of MARTIN DÜLFER in Munich. Troost combined Hoffman's neoclassicism and Dülfer's decorative skill in a series of houses, in the interior decoration of luxury liners for the north German Lloyd shipping firm, and in his work for Adolf Hitler. Troost designed the first official buildings of the Third Reich: the House of German Art (1933–?) and two administration buildings (1933–?) on the Königsplatz in Munich. After Troost's death, his buildings were completed by his widow, and ALBERT SPEER replaced him as Hitler's chief architect.

BARBARA MILLER LANE

WORKS

1905?, Benno Becker House, Bogenhausen; 1905?, Terminus Hotel (interior decoration; with Martin Dülfer); Munich. 1907–1908, House, Nuremberg, Germany. 1917, Haus Heinecken (interior decoration); 1925, Jacobihalle (interior decoration); Bremen, Germany. 1931–?, Brown House (remodeling; temporary Nazi headquarters); 1933–?, Ehrentempeln der Ewigen Wache für den Helden von 9. November (two Nazi party monuments); 1933–?, Füherbau (Adolf Hitler's headquarters); 1933–?, Verwaltungsbau der Reichsleitung der NSDAP (Nazi party administrative building); 1933–?, Haus der deutschen Kunst (Nazi party art museum); Munich.

BIBLIOGRAPHY

LANE, BARBARA MILLER 1968 *Architecture and Politics in Germany: 1918–1945.* Cambridge, Mass.: Harvard University Press.
Moderne Bauformen. 1910 9:363–368.
"Paul Ludwig Troosts Bauten für die NSDAP." 1934 *Monatshefte für Baukunst und Städtebau* 18:205–212.
SPEER, ALBERT (1969)1970 *Inside the Third Reich: Memoirs.* Translated by Richard and Clara Winston. New York: Macmillan.
TROOST, GERDY 1941–1943 *Das Bauen im neuen Reich.* 2 vols. Bayreuth, Germany.

TROST, HENRY CHARLES

Henry Charles Trost (1860–1933) graduated from art school at seventeen and then served three years as a draftsman in his native city, Toledo, Ohio. He practiced in Colorado, Kansas, Texas, Arizona,

New Mexico, and Mexico. He was in Chicago in the 1880s, and some of his designs show the influence of LOUIS H. SULLIVAN and FRANK LLOYD WRIGHT, but he also worked in traditional styles. Trost was the chief designer in the firm of Trost and Trost, which included his brother, Gustavus Adolphus Trost, and his nephew, George Ernest Trost.

ROXANNE WILLIAMSON

WORKS

1899–1900, First Owls Club, Tucson, Ariz. 1906, W. W. Turney House (El Paso Museum of Art); 1909, Trost House; 1910, Mills Building; El Paso, Tex. 1923, Franciscan Hotel, Albuquerque, N. Mex.

BIBLIOGRAPHY

ENGELBRECHT, L. C. 1969 "Henry Trost: The Prairie School in the Southwest." *Prairie School Review* 6, no. 4:5–29.

TROUARD, LOUIS FRANÇOIS

Louis François Trouard (1729–1794) obtained the Grand Prix of the French Académie d'Architecture in 1753. After a trip to Italy which permitted him to study antique and baroque architecture, his father, a wealthy monumental mason for the Bâtiments du Roi, entrusted him with the construction of a large house, surviving at the entrance of the Faubourg Poissonnière, in which he combined French elegance with the simplicity of Roman taste.

He worked successively for the Ponts et Chaussées, the Economats, and the Bâtiments du Roi. Between 1765 and 1770, he built the Church of Saint Symphorien de Montreuil and the Chapelle de la Providence or Catéchismes in the chevet of the Church of Saint-Louis in Versailles. He realized an elegant Gothic pastiche in the Cathedral of Sainte-Croix in Orléans between 1766 and 1773. While serving as architect for the Economats, he fell victim to an intrigue and was replaced by Antoine François Legrand who built the beautiful Church of Port-Marly in 1778.

He outfitted a *hôtel* on the Rue Boissy-d'Anglais behind ANGE JACQUES GABRIEL's western façade fronting the Place de la Concorde in Paris. In 1769, he became a member of the Académie d'Architecture.

GÉRARD ROUSSET-CHARNY

BIBLIOGRAPHY

GALLET, MICHEL 1976 "Louis-François Trouard et l'architecture religieuse dans la région de Versailles au temps de Louis XVI." *Gazette des Beaux-Arts* 88:201–218.

TROWBRIDGE and LIVINGSTON

The New York architectural firm of Trowbridge and Livingston, active in the first decades of the twentieth century, is best known for such buildings as the Saint Regis Hotel (1901–1904), the B. Altman and Company Department Store (1905–1914), the J. P. Morgan and Company Bank (1913–1914), and the Hayden Planetarium (1934–1935), all in New York City. Founded in 1894 as Trowbridge, Colt, and Livingston, the partners were Samuel Breck Parkman Trowbridge (1862–1925), Stockton B. Colt (1863–1937), and Goodhue Livingston (1865–1951). All graduated from Columbia College's School of Mines in New York and had started their careers in the offices of GEORGE B. POST.

Breck Trowbridge, who supervised the erection of the American School of Classical Studies in Athens, also studied at the Ecole des Beaux-Arts in Paris.

After Colt left the firm in 1899, the business continued as Trowbridge and Livingston until the early 1940s. Although the firm worked primarily in the then popular eclectic classical styles—the Beaux-Arts, the neo-Renaissance, the neo-Federal—some of their 1930s buildings show influence of the Art Deco style. For their clients, men of substance and wealth, they designed banks, hotels, and public buildings, as well as city and country residences.

The firm won several design competitions, most notably those for the Saint Regis Hotel (1901–1904), originally planned by John Jacob Astor as an apartment house, the Chemical National Bank Building (1905–1907), and the Bankers Trust Company Building (1910–1912), all in New York. In 1909, they were awarded the Medal of Honor by the American Institute of Architects for the French Renaissance-inspired New York mansion designed for Henry Phipps (1902–1906).

Both men were active in the professional societies of their time; Trowbridge served as president of the Architectural League of New York in 1913. He was also a founder and trustee of the American Academy in Rome, a founder and president for two terms of the Society of Beaux-Arts Architects (New York); in 1913, he was appointed by President Theodore Roosevelt as Commissioner of the first National Council of Fine Arts.

The buildings designed by Trowbridge and Livingston are handsome and dignified. Remaining within the limits of the neoclassical vocabulary, the architects' often imaginative use of forms and detail produced work characterized by fine craftsmanship and restrained elegance. From the imposing solidity and decorative understatement of J. P. Morgan's Wall Street building (1913–1914) to the small, charming Beaux-Arts townhouse on New York's East 63rd Street (designed originally as an artist's studio and stable in 1899–1900), the best of their buildings are distinctive and admirable additions to the cityscape.

KATHERINE C. MOORE

WORKS

TROWBRIDGE, COLT, AND LIVINGSTON

*1894–1895, Mrs. Richard Gambrill House, 30 Park Avenue, New York *c.1895, Ardsley Casino, Ardsley-on-Hudson, N.Y. 1895–1896, N. L. McCready House (now Harkness Ballet Foundation), 4 East 75 Street; *1898–1899, American Cotton Seed Oil Company Building 27–29 Beaver Street; 1898–1899, Saint Luke's Home for the Aged (now Hogan Hall, Columbia University), 2910–2914 Broadway; New York.

TROWBRIDGE AND LIVINGSTON

1899–1900, C. Ledyard Blair Stable and Artist's Studio, 123 East 63 Street, New York. *c.1900, Amory S. Carhart House, Tuxedo Park, N.Y. *c.1900, James Scrymser House, Seabright, N.J. 1901–1904, Saint Regis Hotel; 1902–1903, S. B. P. Trowbridge House, 123 East 70 Street; *1902–1906, Henry Phipps House, 1063 Fifth Avenue; 1904–1905, Firehouse (now the New York Fire Department Museum) 100 Duane Street; *1905–1907, Chemical National Bank, 270 Broadway; 1905–1914, B. Altman and Company Department Store; 1906–1908, B. Altman and Company Stables (now United States Postal Service Office), 207–213 East 36 Street; *1906–1908, C. D. Jackson House, 4 Riverside Drive; New York. *c.1907, Frederick W. Sharon House, Menlo Park, Calif. *c.1907, Harry Tevis House, Los Gatos, Calif. 1907–1908, Massachusetts Mutual Life Insurance Company Building, State and Main Streets, Springfield. 1907–1909, Palace Hotel, San Francisco. 1909–1910, Benson Bennett Sloan House (now the American Federation of the Arts), 41 East 65 Street; *1909–1910, George S. Brewster House, 746–748 Park Avenue; 1909–1911, John B. Trevor House (now the Consulate General of the Union of Soviet Socialist Republics), 11 East 91 Street; 1910–1912, Bankers Trust Company Building, 14 Wall Street; *1911–1914, George Blumenthal House, 50 East 70 Street; New York. 1912, Goodhue Livingston House, Southampton, N.Y. 1912–1913, New York Free Dispensary Building (now the Judson Health Center of Gouverneur Hospital), 34 Spring Street; 1913–1914, J. William Clark House (now the Automation House), 49 East 68 Street; 1913–1914, J. P. Morgan and Company Building, 23 Wall Street; 1913–1915, Orme Wilson House, 11 East 64 Street; New York. 1914–1915, George S. Brewster House (now the Fox Run Country Club), Muttontown, N.Y. *1914–1915, Walter Belknap James House, 7 East 70 Street, New York. 1915–1917, 1928–1930, 1930–1932, American Red Cross National Headquarters, Washington. 1916, Dennistoun M. Bell House, Amagansett, N.Y. 1916–1917, John S. Rogers

House (now the New York Society Library), 53 East 79 Street; 1920–1922, New York Stock Exchange (addition), 9–13 Wall Street; New York. 1922, Bonnie Briar Country Club, Larchmont, N.Y. 1922–1935, American Museum of Natural History and the Hayden Planetarium, New York. 1923–1924, Mellon National Bank, Pittsburgh. 1925–1926, Bank of America Building (now the National Bank of North America), 44 Wall Street; 1925–1928, Equitable Trust Company Building (now the Morgan Guaranty Trust Company of New York), Broad and Wall streets; New York. 1926–1929, Mitsui Bank Headquarters (now the Tokyo Branch of the Mitsui Bank), Japan. 1929, Pool and Squash Court Building, Trinity College, Hartford, Conn. 1930–1931, Four Mitsui Bank Branch Buildings, Osaka (two), Nagoya, and Yokohama, Japan. 1930–1932, Gulf Building; 1931–1934, Federal Building; Pittsburgh. 1936–1938, Oregon State Captiol (with Francis Keally), Salem.

BIBLIOGRAPHY

Additional material on Trowbridge and Livingston is in the Alumni Association Archives, Trinity College, Hartford, Conn.; Art Room, New York Public Library; Building Permit Docket Books, New York City Department of Buildings, Municipal Building; Wurts Collection, Museum of the City of New York; The Athenaeum, Philadelphia; The Columbiana Library, Columbia University, New York; files of the Society for the Preservation of Long Island Antiquities.

"Altman Store Now Covers Whole Block. . . ." 1914 *New York Times* Jan. 4, section 8, page 7, column l.

The Architects and Their Works. 1908 New York: Darnet.

"The Bankers Trust Building." 1912 *Architecture* 25:69–71, 76, 78.

"The Banking House of J. P. Morgan." 1915 *Architecture and Building* 47:5–14.

BOYD, JOHN TAYLOR, JR. 1916 "Two Country Houses at Southampton, L.I." *Architectural Record* 39:197–211.

BOYD, JOHN TAYLOR, JR. 1920 "The New York Zoning Resolution and Its Influence upon Design." *Architectural Record* 48:192–217.

CRAWFORD, WILLIAM 1925 *Thirty Years of Building.* New York: The author.

DAVID, ARTHUR C. 1904 "The St. Regis—The Best Type of Metropolitan Hotel." *Architectural Record* 15:552–623.

DAVID, ARTHUR C. 1907 "The New Fifth Avenue." *Architectural Record* 22:1–14.

"Hayden Planetarium, New York City." 1936 *Architecture* 73:133–138.

"Hitch in Altman's Plan. . ." 1905 *New York Times* May 18, page 1, column 2.

HITCHCOCK, H. R., and SEALE, WILLIAM 1976 *Temples of Democracy.* New York: Harcourt.

KLABER, JOHN J. 1915 "Some Recent Bank Plans: The Work of Thomas Bruce Boyd." *Architectural Record* 37:97–115.

LIVINGSTON, GOODHUE 1930 "Notes on the History of the Firm of Trowbridge and Livingston." Unpublished manuscript.

NEW YORK LANDMARKS PRESERVATION COMMISSION 1965, 1967, 1970, 1974 *Findings and Designations.* New York: The commission.

"The Residence of George S. Brewster, Esq., Brookville, L.I." 1919 *Architectural Review* 8:6–7.

TROWBRIDGE AND LIVINGSTON ARCHITECTURAL FIRM 1938 *Photographs of Buildings Under Construction.* 27 vols. New York. Mounted and bound by the New York Public Library.

VAN TRUMP, J. D. 1977 "The Skyscraper Style in Pittsburgh: Deco Form and Ornament (1920–40)." *Carnegie Magazine* 51:198–219.

TRUMBAUER, HORACE

Horace Trumbauer (1868–1938) was born in Philadelphia. At sixteen, he went to work for George W. and William D. Hewitt, leading Philadelphia architects. After six years, he left to found his own firm in 1890. His first important commission came in 1893 for a large residence in a Philadelphia suburb, followed rapidly by others, notably for members of the Widener and Elkins families. To these were added large townhouses in Philadelphia, New York, and Washington: summer houses in Newport, Rhode Island; churches, office buildings, and a hotel in Philadelphia and New York; the Harry Widener Library (1914) at Harvard University; the Philadelphia Free Library (1917–1927); the Philadelphia Museum of Art (1931–1938); and his greatest commission, the two main campuses of Duke University in Durham (1927–1938), North Carolina.

In this extraordinary practice which served some of the nation's wealthiest clients, he was assisted first by Frank Seeberg and later by Julian Abele, a Philadelphian whom Trumbauer first met at the University of Pennsylvania and whom he sent to the Ecole des Beaux-Arts. Abele, the first black to graduate from the Ecole was to head the office from 1908 to its final closing in 1938, the year Trumbauer died.

Trumbauer might be termed the supreme eclectic of the American Renaissance. No matter the style he turned to, he handled it with consummate ease, even the Gothic as seen in the Men's Campus of Duke University. His preference was the classicism of the French eighteenth century, and in this style he produced several of the most beautiful buildings of the era. He was very faithful to some of his models, for which he has been derided, but on close examination it is obvious that such was his mastery of scale, proportion, and detail that he improved on them. His eschewing the myth of originality did not endear him to his colleagues any more than did his success with wealthy clients,

and he was not admitted to the American Institute of Architects until 1931, at the end of his career.

HENRY HOPE REED

WORKS

1892–1893, William Welsh Harrison House, Glenside, Penn. 1898–1901, Chestnut Hill Casino, Chestnut Hill, Penn. 1896, George W. Elkins House; 1898, William Lukens Elkins House; 1898, Peter Arrell Brown Widener House; Elkins Park, Penn. 1900–1901, Mrs. E. G. H. Slater House, Washington. 1904, E. C. Knight, Jr., House, Newport, R.I. 1904–1906, I. Townshend Burden House, New York. 1906, Racquet Club, Philadelphia. 1907, George J. Gould House, New York. 1908, Theodore W. Cramp House, Philadelphia. 1909, George W. Elkins House, Elkins Park, Penn. 1911–1912, Duveen Brothers Building (with René Sergent), New York. 1912, Ritz-Carlton Hotel, Philadelphia. 1913, Mrs. Emory S. Carhart House, New York. 1914, Harry Widener Library, Harvard University, Cambridge, Mass. 1915, Cornelius Vanderbilt House (alterations), New York. 1915–1921, Edward Townsend Stotesbury House, Chestnut Hill, Penn. 1917–1927, Philadelphia Free Library; 1923–1926, Public Ledger Building; 1924, First Baptist Church; Philadelphia. 1925, New York Evening Post Building, New York. 1926, William B. Irvine Auditorium, University of Pennsylvania, Philadelphia. 1927, First Church of Christ Scientist, West Palm Beach, Fla. 1927–1938, Duke University, Durham, N.C. 1931, Wildenstein and Company, New York. 1931–1934, Mrs. Horace Dodge Residence, Grosse Pointe, Mich. 1931–1938, Philadelphia Museum of Art (with C. Clark Zantzinger and Charles Borie); 1932, Curtis Clinic, Jefferson Medical College; Philadelphia.

BIBLIOGRAPHY

BRANAM, ALFRED, JR. 1976 *Newport's Favorite Architects.* Long Island City, N.Y.: Classical America.

MAHER, JAMES T. 1975 *The Twilight of Splendor* Boston: Little, Brown.

TSUMAKI, YORINAKA

Yorinaka Tsumaki (1859–1916) was born in Edo (presently Tokyo), the son of a *hatamoto,* a hereditary retainer of *shōgun.* After the Meiji Restoration, he entered Kōbu Daigakkō (later Tokyo University) in 1878. He went to the United States in 1882 and was graduated from Cornell University in 1884 with a degree in architecture. Sent by the Japanese government to Berlin, he stayed there from 1886 to 1888, working in the offices of HERMANN ENDE and W. Böckmann. After his return to Japan, he worked as an architect for the Ministry of Home Affairs and the Ministry of Finance until his retirement in 1913. He was the leader of a large team of architects engaged in designing the governmental office buildings. His profound knowledge of Western architecture and his spirit as the son of a *hatamoto* could be seen in his works, which were an eclectic mixture of Western and Japanese styles.

TAKASHI HASEGAWA

WORKS

*1894, Prefectural Office; *1899, Chamber of Commerce; Tokyo. 1904, Yokohama Specie Bank, Japan. *1912, Japanese Red Cross Society, Tokyo.

BIBLIOGRAPHY

FUJIMORI, TERUNOBU (editor) 1981 Volume 4 in *Nihon-no Kenchiku: Meiji, Taishō, Shōwa*. Tokyo.

TURNER, C. A. P.

By 1900, reinforced concrete was widely used in America. It was, however, being employed in imitation of earlier arcuated and trabeated traditions which were based upon masonry, timber, and, in the nineteenth century, iron.

In the hands of Claude Allen Porter Turner (1869–1955), a new structural form emerged that used the unique properties of reinforced concrete. This new form was the flat slab floor, in which loads are sustained by the slab in bending in two directions whence they are carried directly to supporting columns without benefit of beams. The heavy shearing forces resulting from the transfer of the floor loads to the columns are resisted by enlarging the column heads, hence, Turner's designation of his patented system as the "mushroom slab." Apparently, he considered such a system as early as 1898, but its first application was not until 1906 in the Johnson-Bovey Building in Minneapolis. The mushroom slab was an immediate success, and by 1913, more than a thousand flat slab buildings had been built. Load tests in both Europe and America validated the efficiency of the system especially for heavy loadings.

Turner was not the only engineer experimenting with the possibilities of monolithic concrete slab construction in the early 1900s. In 1902, a patent covering concrete floors was issued for the Norcross System. It was primitive compared to Turner's system, patented in 1908, but nevertheless, in a series of court cases it was declared the basic patent. Further use of Turner's flat slab was prevented by court order in 1916. Thus, Turner never received the recognition his pioneering work deserves.

Turner was born in Lincoln, Rhode Island, and received a bachelor's degree from Lehigh University in 1890. After graduation, he sought professional experience in bridge work with the New York and Northeastern Railroad and several bridge companies before moving to Minneapolis in 1897 where he spent the remainder of his career. In addition to his building designs, he was responsible for a series of notable bridges and other engineering works.

Turner wrote many engineering papers and two books. In his first book, he presented information on the mushroom slab and the legal conflict with the Norcross patent.

EMORY KEMP

BIBLIOGRAPHY

CONDIT, CARL W. 1961 *American Building Art: The Twentieth Century*. New York: Oxford University Press.
HOOL, GEORGE A., and JOHNSON, NATHAN C. 1918 *Concrete Engineer's Handbook*. New York: McGraw.
TAYLOR, A. and THOMPSON, S. E. 1911 *Concrete: Plain and Reinforced*. New York: Wiley.
TURNEAURE, FREDERICK E., and MAURER, E. R. (1907)1909 *Principles of Reinforced Concrete Construction*. 2d ed., rev. & enl. New York: Wiley.
TURNER, C. A. P. 1909 *Concrete Steel Construction*. Minneapolis, Minn.: Farnham.
TURNER, C. A. P. (1922)1934 *Elasticity: Structure and Strength of Materials*. Minneapolis, Minn.

TURNER, PHILIP JOHN

A native of Stowmarket, England, Philip John Turner (1876–1943) went to Montreal in 1907. Turner was associated with the school of architecture at McGill University from 1907 until 1941, during which time he lectured frequently throughout Canada and the United States on numerous subjects including library planning and ecclesiastical architecture. In private practice, he specialized in residential, financial, and religious buildings. The H. S. Thomas House (1910) with steep slate roof and half-timbered gable end, reflects his interest in the Arts and Crafts movement. He designed many branch buildings in Quebec and Ontario for the Molsons Bank. The Sorel Branch (1912) is a clever adaptation of a villa design to the requirements of a small bank, with manager's residence above, fronting the town square. Saint Philip's Anglican Church (1929), considered his finest work, closely resembles in design the medieval parish churches of rural England.

ROBERT LEMIRE

WORKS

1910, H. S. Thomas House, Outremont, Quebec. 1912, Molsons Bank, Drummondville, Quebec. 1912, Molsons Bank; Sorel, Quebec. 1914, Elliot House; 1914, W. E. Mowat House; 1914, I. P. Rexford House; Westmount; Quebec. 1914, F. C. Skelton House, Montreal. 1915, Molsons Bank, Norwich, Ontario. 1915,

Molsons Bank, Port Arthur, Ontario. 1919, Molsons Bank, Bedford, Quebec. 1919, Molsons Bank, Hamilton, Ontario. 1919, Molsons Bank, Saint Thomas, East, Ontario. 1920, C. B. Howard Garage, Sherbrooke, Quebec. 1923, W. I. Gear House, Westmount, Quebec. 1923, S. S. Stevenson House, Point Cavagnol, Como, Quebec. 1924, Crown Trust Building; 1929, Saint Philip's Anglican Church; Montreal.

BIBLIOGRAPHY

TURNER, PHILIP J. 1915 "Houses at Montreal, Quebec." *Construction* 8, no. 6:265–273.

TURNER, PHILIP J. 1916 "The Smaller Branch Bank Building." *Construction* 9, no. 11:367–379.

TURNER, PHILIP J. 1927a *Christ Church Cathedral Montreal.* Montreal: McGill University.

TURNER, PHILIP J. 1927b *The Development of Architecture in the Province of Quebec Since Confederation.* Montreal: McGill University.

TURNER, PHILIP J. 1927c *Liverpool Cathedral.* Montreal: McGill University.

TURNER, PHILIP J. 1928 *The Old English Inn.* Montreal: McGill University.

TURNER, PHILIP J. 1929 *Library Buildings: Their Planning and Equipment.* Montreal: McGill University.

TURNER, PHILIP J. 1931a *The Chapel of St. Nicholas, Gipping Suffolk.* Montreal: McGill University.

TURNER, PHILIP J. 1931b *Parish Churches of Rural England.* Montreal: McGill University.

TURNER, PHILIP J. 1931c *University and College Libraries of Canada.* Montreal: McGill University.

TURNER, PHILIP J. 1936a "Modern Church Architecture in England." *Journal of the Royal Architectural Institute of Canada* 13, no. 2:20–27.

TURNER, PHILIP J. 1936b "The Library of the Royal Institute of British Architects, London, England." *Journal of the Royal Architectural Institute of Canada* 13, no. 9:172–175.

TUSCHER, MARCUS

Marcus Tuscher (1705–1751) was born in Nuremberg, Germany, and was trained as a painter and engraver. He lived in Italy (1728–1741), in London (1741–1743), and in Copenhagen, where he was appointed court painter. Since the years in Italy, he was preoccupied with architectonic and ornamental designs as well, and in the Copenhagen years there is some evidence, however vague, that he had some influence on the forming of Amalienborg Plads, Copenhagen.

VILLADS VILLADSEN

TVEDE, GOTFRED

Gotfred Tvede (1863–1947), a Danish architect, was trained at the Academy in Copenhagen in the 1880s. As the son of an architect, he inherited both talent and a prosperous office. Among his numerous buildings, of which most bear witness to a merely average skill, are the Kongelig Brand Insurance Company, the main office of the East Asiatic Company, and the Domus Medica in Copenhagen.

VILLADS VILLADSEN

TYL, OLDŘICH

Oldřich Tyl (1884–1939) was one of the pioneers of constructivism in Prague. His buildings exhibit a wealth of ideas, perfect layout, and equilibrium of proportions. His most outstanding artchitectural work is the Prague Fair Building, designed together with Josef Fuchs, one of the very first large constructivist buildings in Europe.

VLADIMÍR ŠLAPETA

WORKS

1923, First Women's Lodging House; 1924–1928, Prague Fair Building (with Joseph Fuchs); 1928, Young Women's Christian Association Hostel; 1928–1932, Bondy Department Store; Prague.

BIBLIOGRAPHY

STARÝ, OLDŘICH 1939 "Oldřich Tyl." *Architektura* 1:85–88.

TYNG, ANNE GRISWOLD

Born in China, Anne Griswold Tyng (1920–) studied architecture at Harvard Graduate School of Design and the Graduate School of Arts and Sciences at the University of Pennsylvania. From 1947 to 1973, she worked in association with LOUIS I. KAHN. Since 1973, she has had an independent practice in Philadelphia. Tyng has done extensive research on forming principles defining links between geometry, atomic and psychic structures, biology, and symmetry and asymmetry.

PATRICIA C. PHILLIPS

WORKS

1952–1953, Philadelphia City Planning Commission and Redevelopment Authority (associate consultant architect). 1954. Mill Creek Redevelopment Plan (associate consultant architect), Pa.

BIBLIOGRAPHY

SKY, ALISON, and STONE, MICHELLE 1976 *Unbuilt America.* New York: McGraw-Hill.

TYNG, ANNE GRISWOLD 1975 "Simultaneous Randomness and Order: The Fibonacci-Divine Proportion as a Universal Forming Principle." Unpublished Ph.D. dissertation, University of Pennsylvania, Philadelphia.

UNGERS, O. M.

Influential German architect and educator of the post World War Two period, Oswald Mathias Ungers (1926–) was born in Kaisersesch/Eifel, Germany. After his secondary schooling in Mayen was interrupted by military service, Ungers attended the Technical College in Karlsruhe (1947–1950) where he studied under EGON EIERMANN. Mathias Ungers has practiced architecture in Cologne, Berlin, and Frankfurt, West Germany, and Ithaca, New York. Ungers has taught and been dean of architecture at the Technical University of Berlin (1963–1968).

Mathias Ungers believes that architecture must reflect the quality of the place, its history and evolution. He finds in the palace garden of Schloss Glienicke near Potsdam, in the Park Wörlitz in Weimar, and in the cathedral in Trier, the essence of architecture, its morphology and transformation, characteristics that Ungers seeks in his own work. Ungers has built over thirty projects, from single-family houses to educational complexes, most in and around Cologne, though it is in his competition proposals that he has best explored the idea of a morphological approach to architecture.

GERARDO BROWN-MANRIQUE

WORKS

1951–1953, Apartment and Factory Buildings 'Z', Aachener Strasse, Cologne, Germany. 1953–1962, Science Institute, Oberhausen, Germany. 1956–1959, Studentenheim 'Ni,' Lindenthal; 1957, House 'M' (two family), Dürener Strasse; 1959, Ungers House, Belvedere Strasse, Müngersdorf; Cologne, Germany. 1959–1960, Apartment Block, Mozart Strasse, Wuppertal, Germany. 1959–1962, Apartment Complex, Jakob-Kneip-Strasse, Poll; 1962, Printshop and Publishing House, Braunsfeld; Cologne, Germany. 1962–1966, Apartment Complex, Märkisches Viertel, Berlin. 1963–1966, Apartment Complex, New City, Seeberg, Cologne, Germany. 1974, Master Plan. Fourth Ring Area, Lichterfilde, Berlin. 1975–1980, Masterplan, Mertenhof; 1975–1980, Mertenhof (renovation); Widdersdorf, Cologne, Germany. 1978–1981, Apartment Building, Schillerstrasse, Charlottenburg, Berlin. 1979–?, Badische Landesbibliothek, Karlsruhe, Germany. 1980–1981, Frankfurt Messehalle, Germany.

BIBLIOGRAPHY

ARCHER, B. J. (editor) 1980 *Houses for Sale.* New York: Rizzoli.
AYMONINO, CARLO 1975 "Il contributo di Oswald Mathias Ungers all Architettura." *Controspazio* 7, no. 3:2–43.
BISCOGLI, L. 1966 "Germania di Oggi: O. M. Ungers." *Casabella* 305:36–59.
CONRADS, ULRICH 1962 "Focus IV: O. M. Ungers." *Zodiac* 9:172–181.

CONRAD, ULRICH, and MARSCHALL, WERNER 1962
Modern Architecture in Germany. London: Architectural Press.

GIESELMANN, REINHARDT, and UNGERS, O. M. 1970
"Towards a New Architecture." Pages 165–166 in
Ulrich Conrads (editor), *Programmes and Manifestoes
on 20th Century Architecture.* London: Lund Humphries.

GREGOTTI, VITTORIO 1976 "Oswald Mathias Ungers." *Lotus* 11:12, 14–41.

KLOTZ, HEINRICH 1977 *Architektur in der Bundesrepublik—Gespräche mit Günter Behnisch, Wolfgang
Döring, Helmut Hentrich, Hans Kammerer, Frei Otto,
Oswald Mathias Ungers.* Frankfurt: Ullstein.

"O. M. Ungers—Sozialer Wohnungsbau: 1953–1966."
1967 *Baumeister* 64:557–572.

PEHNT, WOLFGANG 1970 *German Architecture:
1960–1970.* New York: Praeger.

Rational Architecture. 1978 Brussels: Archives d' Architecture Moderne.

ROSSI, ALDO 1960 "Un giovane architetto tedesco:
Oswald Mathias Ungers." *Casabella* 244:22–35.

UNGEWITTER, G. G.

An influential promoter of the Gothic Revival in
Germany, Georg Gottlob Ungewitter (1820–
1864) was trained in the Applied Art School in
Kassel and under FRIEDRICH VON GÄRTNER and
FRIEDRICH BÜRKLEIN in Munich. In 1842, he
formed a partnership with Gustav L. Martens in
Hamburg, where he built a series of houses in a
brick style derived from the work of ALEXIS DE
CHÂTEAUNEUF and BÜLAU. Converted in 1845 to
the cause of the Gothic Revival by the influential
writings of Auguste Reichensperger, Ungewitter
denounced the quest for a synthetic new style in
favor of the universal applicability of Gothic design principles. The influence of A. W. N. PUGIN
and EUGÈNE EMMANUEL VIOLLET-LE-DUC is apparent in the emphasis on structural rationality
and truth to materials in his many publications; he
also provided models of German vernacular
wood-and-brick construction. Ungewitter's own
work was limited to restorations and several small
churches much influenced by English Gothic Revival models in their vigorous massing. His influence was exerted primarily through pattern books
and as professor in Kassel's Applied Art School
from 1851.

BARRY BERGDOLL

WORKS

1847, House (with Gustav L. Martens), Hermanstrasse
3; 1847, Gut Bergried House (with Martens), Steinkirchen; Hamburg, Germany. 1848, House (with Martens), Lübeck, Germany. 1859–1861, Protestant
Church, Neustadt near Marburg, Germany. 1860–?,
Protestant Church, Malsfeld, Germany. 1862, Protestant Church (west tower), Eschwege, Germany. 1862,
Roman Catholic Church, Bockenheim, Frankfurt.
1862, Roman Catholic Church, Momberg, Germany.
*1862–1863, Scholl House, Bahnhofstrasse, Kassel,
Germany. 1863–1867, Protestant Church (nave), Schleirebach, Germany.

BIBLIOGRAPHY

MUTHESIUS, STEFAN 1974 *Das englische Vorbild.* Munich: Prestel.

REICHENSPERGER, AUGUSTE 1866 *Georg Gottlob Ungewitter und sein Wirken als Baumeister.* Leipzig: Wiegel.

SCHUCHARD, JUTTA 1979 *Carl Schäfer 1844–1908:
Leben und Werk des Architekten der Neugotik.* Munich:
Prestel.

STATS, VINCENZ, and UNGEWITTER, G. G.
(1856)1858 *The Gothic Model Book.* London: Evans.
Originally published in German.

UNGEWITTER, G. G. (1846)1899 *Vorlegeblätter für
Ziegel- und Steinarbeit.* Glogau, Germany: Flemming.

UNGEWITTER, G. G. (1849)1864 *Vorlegeblätter für
Holzarbeiten.* 2d ed. Glogau, Germany: Flemming.

UNGEWITTER, G. G. (1851)1869 *Entwürfe zu
gotischen Möbeln.* 2d ed. Glogau, Germany: Flemming.

UNGEWITTER, G. G. 1858–1864 *Entwürfe zu Stadt-
und Landhäusern.* 2 vols. 2d ed. Glogau, Germany:
Flemming.

UNGEWITTER, G. G. (1859–1864)1901–1903 *Lehrbuch der gotischen Konstruktion.* 2 vols. 4th ed. Leipzig:
Tauchnitz.

UNGEWITTER, G. G. 1866 *Sammlung mittelalterlicher
Ornamentik in geschichtlicher und systematischer Anordnung.* Leipzig: Wiegel.

UNWIN, RAYMOND

In the early part of his career Sir Raymond Unwin
(1863–1940), with his partner Barry Parker, made
significant contributions to the design of small
dwellings, and to their layout. Until his death
Unwin continued to promote, and to direct others,
in the art of town planning. He was born near
Rotherham, Yorkshire, and educated at Magdalen
College School, Oxford, before being trained first
in engineering and then in architecture. In his
youth he knew WILLIAM MORRIS, and was involved in the Socialist League—working for a time
alongside Edward Carpenter in Sheffield, Yorkshire. Later he became a member of the Fabian Society, writing one of its *Tracts,* and he used to lecture to the "Labour Church" on, amongst other
things, the life and work of William Morris.

Unwin's earliest architectural work was for
mining communities for the Staveley Coal and
Iron Company. With BARRY PARKER—his second
cousin and brother-in-law, who he entered into an
informal partnership with in 1896—he designed a

series of individual dwellings in the Arts and Crafts tradition, as well as schemes for cooperative dwellings, and larger town plans. They designed New Earswick village for the Rowntrees in 1901, the first Garden City at Letchworth in 1903, and Hampstead Garden Suburb for Henrietta Barnett in 1905–1907. At this time Unwin moved to Hampstead, leaving Parker to continue development at Letchworth. Although the two continued to undertake domestic commissions together until 1914—when Unwin became chief town planning inspector at the Local Government Board (later Ministry of Health)—Unwin's main attentions were before this being directed toward town planning. He published his influential *Town Planning in Practice* in 1909, the year that the first Housing and Town Planning Act was passed, and he organized the International Town Planning Exhibition and Conference for the Royal Institute of British Architects the following year. From 1911 to 1914 he lectured in town planning at Birmingham University, and was one of the founders of the Town Planning Institute in 1913. As Director of Housing for the Ministry of Munitions during World War I he designed settlements at Gretna, Mancol Village, Queensferry, and elsewhere. After the war he served on the influential Tudor Walters Committee, which reported on housing, and continued at the Ministry of Health until 1928.

In 1922 Unwin began a fruitful contact with the United States, as a consultant on the New York Regional Plan. In 1934 he was invited to report on low-cost housing in the United States, helping to prepare a report which was timely for the New Deal legislation of 1935. He died in Connecticut in 1940, after nearly four years as Visiting Professor in the planning and housing division of Columbia University. His funeral took place in New York.

Unwin succeeded Ebenezer Howard as President of the International Federation for Housing and Town Planning, 1928–1931. He was Chief Technical Adviser to the GLC Regional Planning Committee from 1929 to 1933, laying the groundwork for the Greater London Plans of the next decade. He was president of the Royal Institute of British Architects (1931–1933) during the difficult Depression years and was knighted in 1932. Unwin's vision was never parochial, he worked always as a kind of diplomat, attempting to foster international solutions to world-wide planning problems.

BRIAN HANSON

WORKS

RAYMOND UNWIN

1893, Saint Andrew's Church (glass mosaic reredos by

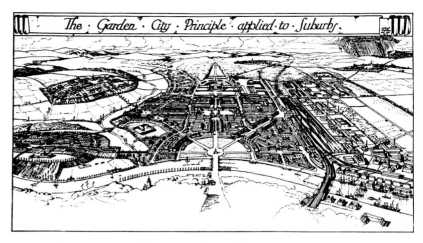

Barry Parker), Barrow Hill, near Steveley, Derbyshire, England. 1905–1907, Folk Hall (The Institute); 1911, Primary School; New Earswick, Yorkshire, England.

Unwin.
Diagram from Nothing Gained by Overcrowding.

RAYMOND UNWIN AND BARRY PARKER

1896, Macnar House, Hill Crest, Marple, Cheshire, England. 1899–1902, C. F. Goodfellow House, Northwood, Staffordshire, England. 1903–1906, Cooperative Housing, Saint Botolph's Avenue, Sevenoaks, Kent, England. 1904, H. Vause House, Rugby, Warwickshire, England. 1905, The Cottage, Newton, near Cambridge. 1906, R. Linke Cottage, Letchworth, Hertfordshire, England. 1907, Oakdene, Rotherfield, Sussex, England. 1907–1909, Whirriestone, Rockdale, Lancashire, England. 1908, Stanley Parker House, 102 Wilbury Road; 1910, Aitken Cottage; Letchworth, Hertfordshire, England.

BIBLIOGRAPHY

ASHWORTH, WILLIAM 1954 *The Genesis of Modern British Town Planning*. London: Routledge & Paul.
ATKINSON, GEORGE 1971 "Raymond Unwin: Founding Father of the BRS." *Journal of the Royal Institute of British Architects* 78:446–448.
BATCHELOR, PETER 1969 "The Origin of the Garden City Concept of Urban Form." *Journal of the Society of Architectural Historians* 28, no. 3:184–200.
CREESE, WALTER 1963 "Parker and Unwin: Architects of Totality." *Journal of the Society of Architectural Historians* 23, no. 3:161–170.
CREESE, WALTER 1966 *The Search for Environment: The Garden City Before and After*. New Haven: Yale University Press.
CREESE, WALTER 1967 *The Legacy of Raymond Unwin: A Human Pattern for Planning*. Cambridge, Mass.: M.I.T. Press.
EVANS, PAUL 1976 "Raymond Unwin and the Municipalisation of the Garden City." *Transactions of the Martin Centre* 1:251–254.
HAWKES, DEAN 1976 "Garden Cities and New Methods of Construction: Raymond Unwin's Influence on English Housing Practice, 1919–1939." *Transactions of the Martin Centre* 1:275–296.
HAWKES, DEAN 1978 "The Architectural Partnership of Barry Parker and Raymond Unwin: 1896–1914." *Architectural Review* 163:327–332.

PARKER, BARRY 1901 *The Art of Building a Home: A Collection of Lectures and Illustrations* London: Longmans, Green.

PARKER, BARRY 1940 "Sir Raymond Unwin." *Journal of the Royal Institute of British Architects* 47:208–210.

PEPPER, SIMON, and SWENARTON, MARK 1978 "Home Front: Garden Suburbs for Munitions Workers." *Architectural Review* 163:366–375.

SWENARTON, MARK 1981 *Homes for Heroes.* London: Heinemann.

UNWIN, RAYMOND (1902)1908 *Cottage Plans and Common Sense.* London: Fabian Society.

UNWIN, RAYMOND 1909a In *Town Planning and Modern Architecture at the Hampstead Garden Suburb.* London: Unwin.

UNWIN, RAYMOND (1909b)1971 *Town Planning in Practice: An Introduction to the Art of Designing Cities and Suburbs.* 2d ed. New York: Blom.

UNWIN, RAYMOND (1912a)1918 *Nothing Gained by Overcrowding: How the Garden City Type of Development May Benefit Both Owner and Occupier.* London: Garden Cities and Town Planning Association.

UNWIN, RAYMOND 1912b "The Town Extension Plan." In *Warburton Lectures.* Manchester (England) University Press.

UNWIN, RAYMOND 1924 "Higher Building in Relation to Town Planning." *Journal of the Royal Institute of British Architects* 31:125–150.

UNWIN, RAYMOND 1934 "The American Housing Corporation." *The Listener* 12, July 11:56–59.

UPJOHN, RICHARD

Richard Upjohn (1802–1878), eminent American architect, was born in England where he trained as a cabinetmaker and established his own business in furniture construction and architectural carpentry in Dorset, the county of his birth. In 1829, after financial reverses, he emigrated to the United States. On their arrival, Upjohn, his wife, and their small son were forced to depend on assistance from relatives. Because his brother was settled in New Bedford, Massachusetts, Upjohn at first lived and worked there. The decision to stay in New England rather than attempt life in New York meant that Upjohn was spared the disappointment of many Englishmen of similar training who, in the 1830s, came in numbers to New York seeking employment in the building crafts and architectural offices, but were forced to return to England because of widespread unemployment occasioned by the depression of those years.

Upjohn settled in Boston in 1834 where, as he developed a modest independent practice, he worked in the office of ALEXANDER PARRIS. He was assisted in his attempt to establish himself by the practicality and taste manifest in his earliest projects. Two Greek Revival houses in Bangor, Maine (1833–1836), and a Gothic Revival house in Gardiner, Maine (1835), remarkable in their careful and restrained use of eclectic patterns and precedents, were his earliest independent works. The Gardiner house, his first essay in the style with which Upjohn would be identified, is reticent, emphasizing general forms rather than ornament. Upjohn did not copy stylish features. He adapted the principles of design characteristic of the style he was using to the needs and means of his clients, accommodated himself to the materials and workmanship available, and followed his own preference for simplicity. Comparison of these early houses with those in J. C. Loudon's *Encyclopaedia of Cottage, Farm and Villa Architecture* (1833), an English book that was internationally known, reveals that Upjohn employed few of the decorative details commonly applied to make houses classical or Gothic.

The commission for Saint John's, Bangor (1835–1836, later destroyed and replaced by another church from the Upjohn office), was the beginning of his work as a church architect, in which he was to excel and on which his fame would largely depend. Gothic had been used in American churches before Saint John's, but these earlier buildings had been Gothic only in detail. Most were rectangular rooms without aisles. Many had galleries, some of which bisected the windows in the side walls. A tower, often with a steeple, was set in the middle of the front and forward of the entrance wall. In 1830, a commentator described these towers as "uniformly thrust forward and made the first and main object of our attention . . . [the tower] stands out either wholly or in part from the façade which is thus broken up and is incapable of receiving either majesty or beauty of expression." Saint John's was a church of this kind, save that its decorative details were richer and more accurately Gothic than was usual. Upjohn had taken reference to English books that contained measured drawings of Gothic details, and he also, undoubtedly, remembered Gothic buildings he had seen in England. As he was financially able to do so, he had begun to acquire a library, a resource that would, along with his own tastes, qualify his early Gothic Revival manner.

George Washington Doane left Trinity parish in Boston to become bishop of New Jersey, and Doctor J. M. Wainwright, who had known and sponsored Upjohn in Boston, became rector of Trinity parish in New York, described as "the oldest and wealthiest foundation in the city." Both of these Protestant Episcopal clergymen were to commission Upjohn churches; Trinity Church was begun in 1841, and the cornerstone of Saint

Richard Upjohn.
Trinity Church.
New York.
1841–1846

Richard Upjohn.
Trinity Church.
New York.
1841–1846

Mary's, Burlington, New Jersey, was laid in 1846. Between these years, the patronage of these men and the fame of their churches assisted Upjohn to establish his reputation, develop his characteristic preferences and knowledge, and expand his role in the Gothic Revival. By 1846, he had become a leading figure in the architecture of the Protestant Episcopal Church in the United States and in the architectural profession.

Trinity was in need of repair when Doctor Wainwright became rector. Upjohn was called in 1839 to advise the vestry, and because the old church was found to be irreparable, he submitted, before the year was out, the first of what were to be several designs for a new church. Two years elapsed before the present church was begun, and during this time, Upjohn read and increased his knowledge of the literature on Gothic and on the revival that was appearing in England. His design for Trinity underwent radical changes. A notable building was the result; it brought the American Gothic Revival in church architecture out of its earliest phase.

The responsibility for Trinity Church elicited growth in Upjohn's talent, for he had never before undertaken so large a task. It appears that when Upjohn read *The True Principles of Pointed or Christian Architecture* (1841) by A. W. N. PUGIN, a book widely influential in the nineteenth century, he found in it not only ideas to strengthen his own convictions about the nature of Gothic, its reli-

gious significance, and its proper revival but also an illustration of an ideal church (Plate H in Pugin). The tower, spire, and nave elevations of Trinity so closely resemble Pugin's model that it was noted in 1844 in an article by ARTHUR D. GILMAN, who also asserted that Trinity would surpass any church "erected in England since the revival of the pointed style," an inaccurate estimate but one indicative of the prominence of Trinity among American buildings. Several of Pugin's finest churches had been completed by 1844, and he had included in *True Principles* an illustration of a church in his own more developed taste (Plate K in Pugin), in which the tower was located to one side of the longitudinal axis of the nave, a suggestion Upjohn did not at once accept.

In size and in the accuracy and abundance of decorative detail, Trinity established a new standard for the American Gothic Revival. Upjohn had, in fact, designed a church not unlike Saint Luke's, Chelsea, London (1819–1825). His studies for the task had confirmed his conviction, as a devout churchman, that Gothic best represented the Church. Less often emphasized but of singular importance is the fact that Upjohn had had virtually no experience to prepare him for so monumental a design and for the management of the construction of so large a building. His success in both demonstrated his talent and knowledge of building, immediately identifying him as an important architect. Trinity Church was a landmark in American architecture; as late as 1872 a writer in an English journal, *The Architect,* discussed it as a building that had never been surpassed, despite the many subsequent churches in New York and elsewhere; he wrote that "with the erection of Trinity Church a new era might be looked for to open in the prospects of American church architecture."

Upjohn's performance at so prominent a place brought him to the attention of the Protestant Episcopal clergy, many of whom were associated with the General Theological Seminary in New York. Visitors to the Seminary reviewed the progress at Trinity and talked to its architect, for Upjohn had an office in its grounds. Leading churchmen recommended its architect when questions of propriety in church design arose; the correspondence in the Upjohn papers reveals that Bishops Onderdonk, Doane, and Whittingham, all of whom had visited England and appreciated the Gothic Revival as it was manifest there, suggested that reference be taken to Upjohn when a church, a rectory, or a question of proper liturgical appointments for an older church arose. Acting on the advice of Whittingham, the rector in Newark, Delaware, applied to Upjohn "upon the principles that it need cost no more to put our four brick walls into the proper proportion than to convert them into the ordinary deformation and barbarisms." Upjohn, in turn, sought the support of these sponsors of correct design; in 1843, for example, he asked Doane to intercede with the rector in Rahway, New Jersey, who was "totally unaware" of "what a parish church should be" in order that "another will not be added to the tasteless abortions already abounding."

E. M. Upjohn, in his biography, examined an incident in 1846 when Upjohn decided to reject a commission for a Unitarian church in Boston because, as an Episcopalian, he could not in good conscience design for another sect. Temperate though he was, Upjohn felt deeply the significance of Gothic. He had been reading certain English authorities. In their declarative introduction to the translation, in 1842, of the *Durandus Rationale Divinorum Officiorum,* John Mason Neale and Benjamin Webb, who were in control of the Ecclesiological Society, asserted that a "separatist" should not design a church and that "no churchman should allow himself to build a conventicle, and even sometimes to prostitute the speaking architecture of the Church to the service of her bitterest enemies." It was this advice that may have moved Upjohn to take his controversial decision about the Boston church. Upjohn's vocabulary, when writing to a knowledgeable churchman such as Bishop Doane, indicates that both he and Doane accepted not only the ideas but the language of the

English writers among whom were Pugin and the leaders of the Ecclesiological Society.

Upjohn, through his practice and study, was developing and solidifying his theory of the correct response to Gothic inspiration. He combined his personal preference for simple masses of good proportion with a decision to employ carefully studied and well-executed ornament used, not as superficial embellishment, but as decoration of construction. In 1850, a gentleman approached him about a house only to find the design Upjohn provided too plain for his taste. The client then turned to ALEXANDER JACKSON DAVIS, a decision which occasioned a sharp response from Upjohn, in which he displayed his approach to Gothic and an assertiveness and willingness to express his views. This begins to explain how a man of such mild disposition could assume the position of leadership he was to hold for so long among American architects. Upjohn said of the decision to have a castellated house that, although the owner's preference to have more diversity of form was attractive,

the house is too small for such a profusion of outlines and it is questionable whether the principal parts of a house so built can on looking at it be separated from the merest office and what should be subordinate parts of the structure are too often made the principal. Real fitness of purpose in design being found to give way to mere fancy. This is why we have such a variety of what are commonly termed "pretty houses" and other pretty buildings growing up over the country . . . whatever building erected should be truly characteristic of its purpose . . . I do not wish to be understood to be opposed to Pointed architecture when it is properly treated. It is capable of more variety of form and construction than any other style, but I am decidedly opposed to the mimic castles, abbeys, and other buildings of the present age in this country and in Europe. Such things are detestable and unworthy of the attention of anyone capable of appreciating *truth* in architecture. My decision may be against me in a pecuniary point of view, but as there is much good yet to be done by a right development of the arts I for me will make it my study, so far as I am capable, to design in the most truthful manner.

Upjohn refused to charge for the services he had rendered.

None of the ideas that Upjohn expressed in this letter were original to him. J. C. Loudon and other English writers had set forth similar arguments, citing as they did so the earlier writers from whom they had derived them. Pugin, in *True Principles,* condemned houses "designed to be picturesque." But the cohesiveness of Upjohn's argument and the intransigence with which he defended it are remarkable.

Upjohn was also willing to consider and use

styles other than Gothic when circumstances and "truth" suggested them, to welcome those who admired them and use them "truthfully," and to participate in criticism of architects who failed in the expression of "truth." In 1845, Arthur D. Gilman felt sufficiently at ease with Upjohn to write asking for a job and to comment that "Lafever, of whom you probably know something, perhaps a good deal, has been filling our devoted town with 'illuminated Gothic' bandboxes which will probably last until he gets home . . . certainly not much longer," and he went on to say that if Upjohn did not get the commission in question in Boston he hoped Lafever would not get it for "I think this is an event which you would deplore as heartily as any other." Gilman, who apparently felt Upjohn would not be disturbed by his comment on Trinity, sent him a copy of the article. It also contains an admiring passage on CHARLES BARRY's use of the Renaissance style in his London clubhouses, early American praise for the Italianate which Upjohn was on occasion to employ.

Surrounded by a coterie of informed and powerful clients, with the evidence of his competence, knowledge, taste, and probity manifest in his work at Trinity Church, Upjohn moved rapidly into a position of prominence. Many of his major churches were built between 1844 and 1850, a time when the Protestant Episcopal community prospered and expanded in wealth and membership. Between the beginning of Trinity Church and the design of Saint Paul's, Buffalo, New York (1850–1851), Upjohn designed and built seventeen major and twenty smaller churches and a number of domestic, commercial, and collegiate commissions. At the beginning of this period, his works resemble Trinity Church; the Church of the Ascension, New York (1840–1841), and Christ Church, Brooklyn, New York (1841–1842), are dominated by large towers set in front of the body of the building and both, but especially the Church of the Ascension, are distinguished by sparse ornament and the clarity with which the masses of the internal space are expressed externally.

Preoccupation with the building of Trinity Church resulted in an hiatus during which Upjohn accepted no other work. When in 1884 he began the Church of the Holy Communion, New York, completed in 1846, Upjohn and his client, the Reverend W. A. Muhlenberg, who had traveled in England, departed from Trinity as a model and accepted instead the parish church form recommended by the Cambridge Camden Society. They built a smaller, asymmetrical building with a steeply pitched roof. A new phase of the ecclesiastical Gothic in America had begun.

In July 1845, Bishop Doane, who had settled

Richard Upjohn. Church of the Holy Communion. New York. 1844–1846

in Burlington, New Jersey, wrote to Upjohn, "Have you seen the late papers of the Gothic Architecture Society of Oxford? Mine have just come and I find in Shottesbrooke Church as near as possible what I want for Saint Mary's." An approximation of the recommended English type was not enough for Doane who had visited England, heard the arguments of the churchmen there, and seen and admired English medieval and revived Gothic buildings. He planned for Burlington a compound of buildings with a church at its center. For the first time, an actual English building, in this case one measured and drawn by WILLIAM BUTTERFIELD at the order of the Oxford Architectural Society, would serve as the model for an American church. Upjohn was to struggle with the commission for years as Doane worried over every aspect of its execution, details, and costs.

Saint Mary's and the Church of the Holy Communion thus enlarged and developed Upjohn's style through direct contact with English sources but, though he worked with precise drawings of the model in the case of Burlington, he did not copy it. Saint Mary's (1846) is more an Upjohn church than a replica. In its design there appear for the first time characteristic features that were his own, among them the broach spire Shottesbrooke did not have, a feature he would use in some of his subsequent works.

Richard Upjohn. Saint Mary's Church. Burlington, New Jersey. 1846

Richard Upjohn. Saint Mary's Church (interior). Burlington, New Jersey. 1846

In the course of his career, Upjohn was to employ a variety of medieval styles and the Renaissance and Italianate modes. In all of them, a personal quality based upon his response to composition and practical problems emerges. Upjohn himself revealed the character of his preferences when on February 15, 1859, at a meeting of the American Institute of Architects, he commented upon a paper by J. Coleman Hart on "Unity in Architecture." Upjohn was fifty-seven at the time and he could look back on twenty years of vigorous practice, years in which he had seen tastes change as architecture moved from the Trinity Church manner into late nineteenth-century Gothic and the introduction of other stylistic sources. He said that

although most of his life has been spent in the study of Gothic architecture and although he intended to continue to devote his time and exertions toward its revival yet he could not but acknowledge that many of the most impressive Christian monuments were not Gothic. The Lombard and other Romanesque styles . . . furnished some of the most ennobling and impressive religious edifices . . . he had been affected by the majesty and simplicity of the Pantheon at Rome in a degree almost equal to that of the religious impressions produced by the best cathedrals.

His devotion to Gothic appears to have been at least in part religious and historical while at the same time he responded to expression of forms through simply stated volumes which Gothic could not provide.

Between 1844 and 1846, three projects prompted Upjohn to produce Romanesque buildings: the Harvard College Chapel (designed 1846 but never built); the Church of the Pilgrims,

Richard Upjohn. Saint Paul's Church. Baltimore. 1854–1856

Brooklyn, New York (1844–1846, a Congregational Church, now our Lady of Lebanon and much altered); and the Bowdoin College Chapel and Library (1845–1855), Brunswick, Maine, which remains a notable example of his work. Upjohn collected books that would be instructive in the preparation of his designs. In 1835 and 1836, when he could barely afford to do so, he had bought costly works on English Gothic. Georg Moller's *Denkmäler der deutschen Baukunst* had been published in German in 1821, translated into English in 1824, and translated and republished in 1836 by W. H. Leeds who added notes from L. Stieglitz's *Von altdeutscher Baukunst*. Upjohn owned this Leeds edition; he probably acquired it when he had in hand commissions that would broaden his practice to include Romanesque with which Moller dealt and to which Upjohn was instinctively sympathetic. It was a style suitable for buildings for others than members of the Protestant Episcopal community.

Upjohn and his client, the president of Bowdoin College, mention in their correspondence Thomas Hope's *An Historical Essay on Architecture* (1835). Both Moller and Hope provided careful and precise drawings of elevations and details, plans and views, with which Upjohn could work in composing his infinitely more simple but personal and effective version of the Romanesque. The least successful and earliest of his Romanesque essays was the Church of the Pilgrims. The Bowdoin College building, where Upjohn managed to adapt Romanesque and at the same time meet the complex requirement of a building to contain several uses, was a success. The Harvard College Chapel scheme foreshadows Saint Paul's Church, Baltimore, Maryland (1854–1856); the latter was designed after Upjohn's trip to Europe in 1850 and so is more accurately Lombard than the earlier chapel design. Upjohn was impressed by Lombard building; in 1853, when contributing to a volume of suggested church designs published by the General Convention of Congregational Churches, he offered a building in the Italian style which he proposed have exterior walls "faced in red and white bricks laid in alternate courses . . . or of stone of two colors." Within a year after this rather primitive and timid church proposal, Upjohn had moved on to employ the style with ease and command. Saint Paul's is accomplished. The site on which it stands slopes abruptly to the east, with the result that the north wall of the church forms a sober sequence of brick walls, round headed windows, arches, and corbels. The west front is severe but rich, an assured and commanding façade, perfectly adjusted to the small but urbanistically important situation.

The interiors of Upjohn's buildings, particularly his preference for heavy and complex carpentry in the roofs of Gothic churches, of which that of the First Parish Church in Brunswick, Maine (1845–1846), is an example often cited, reveal the element in Upjohn's taste which made him perhaps less than comfortable with Gothic, despite his loyalty to it. He was surely more at ease with the heavier expression of Romanesque and the forceful, often personal decoration characteristic of High Victorian design. It should be remembered that from 1850 on Upjohn was a contemporary, not of A. W. N. Pugin but of Butterfield, GEORGE GILBERT SCOTT, GEORGE E. STREET, and WILLIAM BURGES.

Another stylistic stimulus completed the process that brought Upjohn out of his early phase and into his mature middle years. The Church was growing, and small parishes required buildings for which versions of the Trinity formula were not suitable; many of the parishes were poor, most were small, and the churches were to be set in rural or suburban situations. In 1846, a Philadelphia parish undertook to build a church from designs sent by the English Ecclesiological Society. Confusion within the Society, which was being reorganized, led to a fortunate mistake; instead of plans for a Gothic Revival church by one of the Society's accredited architects, measured drawings of a thirteenth-century parish church in Cambridgeshire, Saint Michael's, Longstanton, were sent to Philadelphia. It was a beautiful little building, which could be reproduced in American materials and with American workmanship. Certain of its salient features could be adapted to less expensive materials without loss of character.

The plans from which Saint James the Less was being built and the church under construction must have been known to Upjohn, who was working in nearby Burlington. As the best known church architect in the United States, he was constantly being asked to provide or give plans for small parish churches. The influence of Saint James the Less is first seen in Upjohn's work at Calvary Church, Stonington, Connecticut (1847–1849), and thereafter in many of his smaller churches for Protestant Episcopal parishes. The steeply sloping roof, the bellcot and buttresses on the west wall, but most of all the simplicity, dignity, and sensitive way in which the small church was handled without overburdening ornament would have appealed to Upjohn's expressed preference for "truth" and assisted him in his search for the kind of pattern designs so frequently requested from him. Unlike his task in Burlington, where the client wished a specific English church reproduced, improvisation on the theme of Longstanton per-

Richard Upjohn.
First Parish Church.
Brunswick, Maine.
1845–1846

mitted Upjohn to pursue his own tastes and at the same time satisfy the higher needs of the Church for Gothic expression.

In 1847, a prospectus for a book by Upjohn on "country churches and rural houses" appeared, but his *Rural Architecture* was not published until 1852. Upjohn stated that his purpose was "to supply the want which is often felt, especially in the newly settled parts of our country, of designs for cheap but still substantial buildings for the use of parishes, schools, etc. In the examples given I have kept in view the uses of each building, and endeavored to give it the appropriate character." He included complete drawings for a wooden church, replete with drawings for simple, but correct church furniture, a wooden chapel, a wooden or brick school house, and a wooden parsonage. For each, estimates of cost and material quantities were given, and step by step directions for construction and management of building procedures were included down to the final instruction that "all rubbish made and accumulated during the erection of the building . . . be removed at the completion of the same."

It is not possible to assess the influence of this book on American provincial architecture; many of the buildings it inspired have now perished and such as survive are scattered through the country. But even in these simplest of buildings the qualities of good proportion, functional plan, careful and expressive use of materials, reasonable adaptations of the patterns in ecclesiastical ornament as recommended by English authorities, and sensible economy must have been felt. Upjohn had brought architectural competence within the reach of everyone. At the same time, he was designing small churches in response to requests for help; in 1852 and 1853, *The New York Ecclesiologist* mentioned sixteen examples in what it acknowledged was a partial listing. Other architects and *The New York Ecclesiologist* also published books on pattern buildings and practical advice to church builders.

The designs in his book and the modest

Richard Upjohn.
Chapel of Saint Mary the
Virgin.
Nashotah, Wisconsin.
1859–1860

churches of Upjohn's mature years illustrate again his ability never to copy and to adapt a pattern, especially that of Saint James the Less, to the materials, workmanship, and money available to small American parishes. Saint Thomas, Amenia, New York (1849–1850), Zion Church, Rome, New York (1850–1851), Christ Church, Elizabeth, New Jersey (1854), and The Chapel of Saint Mary the Virgin, Nashotah, Wisconsin (1859–1860), are examples in stone and brick. Saint John Chrysostom, Delafield, Wisconsin (1851–1853), is a remarkable translation of it to wooden construction. Unlike Saint James the Less, many of these churches have their door in the west, perhaps because few have aisles, a luxury which the wealthy parish in Philadelphia was able to afford. When he could, Upjohn recommended the expression on the exterior of the chancel as space different in function from the nave, a solution justified by history and the liturgy. He proposed it even for the modest wooden church in his pattern book. He returned to his own broach spire when he could; in the simplest of his designs, he used as the only elegance of design the double-pitch roof he had early developed.

Upjohn continued to enjoy a demanding practice. In 1850, he traveled abroad visiting Italy, Germany, France, and England, where he called upon the leaders of the Ecclesiological Society and showed them his plans for Saint Paul's Church, Buffalo (1850–1851), which they grudgingly approved while doubting that "wooden pillars within the stone shell" was suitable for any but "forest lands." His son, RICHARD MITCHELL UPJOHN (1828–1903), after training with his father, made an extended study tour in Europe before he joined the office in 1853.

The buildings of the next nineteen years differ from his earlier work: congregations had become larger and richer; urban churches required corner sites if they were to have light and ornamental treatment to be prominent. The Gothic Revival had changed, and the work of the firm moved with it into a High Victorian manner more varied in outline and ornament. The hand and taste of R. M. Upjohn becomes evident, but initially the influence of the senior Upjohn is still visible. The double-pitch roof, an asymmetrical plan with the tower and spire set at one side of the main axis, a minimum of external ornament, and carefully laid and severe masses of masonry characterize the exteriors of the churches of the early 1850s, and within, the intricate carpentry of the roof appears. The later, more elaborate city churches such as Saint Peter's, Albany, New York (1859–1860), Central Congregational Church, Boston (1865–1867), Saint Thomas's Church, New York (1868–1870), and Saint Philip-in-the-Highlands, Garrison, New York (1861–1862), display a later taste. An English critic, who visited in New York, was aware of this change; in *The Architect* (1872), he described Trinity Church as "thoroughly dignified and monumental" and lamented that American architects had taken a retrograde step in response to the writing of JOHN RUSKIN and the architecture of Street with the result that their buildings could be called American Gothic because they were "incongruous mixtures" of old features. He attributed Saint Thomas's in New York to R. M. Upjohn and called it "acrobatic Gothic."

Upjohn was also an architect of houses. Designs for at least seventy-five are known to have come from his office, a figure that does not include the modest parsonages built from the plan he provided in *Rural Architecture*. His first and for various reasons best-known house is Kingscote, Newport, Rhode Island (1839), which is both early and stylistically unusual for its architect. Kingscote has been related to the work of Alexander Jackson Davis who in the 1830s was creating a fashion in domestic architecture in the Gothic style. But English writing and illustration on the subject of houses forms so large a part of the literature that architects as informed as Davis and Upjohn were acquainted with Louden's *Encyclopaedia* which abounded with suggestions for the design of houses, plans, discussions of convenience, and relationships between the landscape and the dwelling. Building materials and workmanship as well as the means and tastes of clients differed between England and the United States, but the principles Louden put forward and the designs by the many architects who contributed to his book could be transplanted and made to accommodate to Ameri-

Richard Upjohn.
Saint John Chrysostom.
Delafield, Wisconsin.
1851–1853

can requirements. The extent of Upjohn's use of Loudon becomes obvious as soon as the parsonage proposed in *Rural Architecture* is compared with the design for "A Cottage in the Old English Style" by John Robertson in the Supplement to Loudon's *Encyclopaedia* published in 1842. Upjohn deleted a number of extravagant features; he eliminated the oval entry porch, the domestic wing, the anteroom and he divided the veranda into two each with access from the house. He added a bay window and thus balanced the composition of one front, and he put the kitchen and larders in an extension with a bedroom above. The parsonage is practical, adapted for the modest means of its users, a rational translation of the English cottage.

As Upjohn showed in his churches and stated in his letter, quoted above, to the client who chose A. J. Davis, his tastes which began with the asymmetrical and delicate, decorative charm of Kingscote assumed, in the 1840s, a more rigorous and intrinsically architectural bias. It is also possible that, as he pondered the question of the uses of the styles, Upjohn concluded that Gothic belonged only to churches and that domestic and certainly all fanciful use of it was frivolous and so impermissible. Finally his letter shows that he had outgrown the "mimic castle" and decorative cottage in which the exterior belied the purpose of the interior and the whole was but a miniature of something that had never been.

The Italianate and Romanesque styles offered an opportunity to develop spatial volumes for use in living, ways to express them externally with dignity and with asymmetricality to avoid the confusion that could develop when Gothic, a style which bespoke the function of church, was used for other than churches. Charles Barry's country houses and city clubs suggested designs for the countryside and façades for the city house.

Upjohn's domestic architecture forms a body of work that, though it has been overshadowed by the number and quality of his churches, represents his talent and illustrates his search for authenticity in the fitting of style to purpose which Pugin had advocated and practiced in his own domestic architecture.

Upjohn was the founder in 1857 of the American Institute of Architects; his policies and aims controlled its development. He sought continued education for the architect, and accordingly, the accumulation of a library was begun. He asked that the members prepare papers to be read in an atmosphere of polite criticism and tolerance for divergent views. He proposed the Institute establish rules to govern the relationship of architect and client and members of the profession to each other. He said he "had labored in the profession for the last twenty-five years . . . in an isolated position" and that he was cheered by the possibilities of unity. When in his founding address he spoke of architecture and its aims, he described his philosophy and, hence, his buildings. "The finest and fairest design may be spoiled by the destruction of its breadth," he said. "It is possible to make that which is in itself ample—large and dignified by size—small by puerile treatment." "Reality" and "truth" should dominate design. He spoke of the United States, calling it "a broad land, all is barren space, a wild, a wilderness" without precedents of its own upon which the architect might draw, and so the American architect should think "intently" on his work that "the purpose of every structure we build should be marked so as to need no other inscription than what it truly presents. Its exterior and interior expression ought to make plain the uses for which it was erected."

PHOEBE B. STANTON

WORKS

1833–1836, Houses, Bangor, Maine. 1835, Oaklands, Gardiner, Maine. *1835–1836, Church of Saint John's, Bangor, Maine. 1839, Kingscote, Newport, R.I. 1840–1841, Church of the Ascension, New York. 1841–1842, Christ Church, Brooklyn, N.Y. 1841–1846, Trinity Church; 1844–1846, Church of the Holy Communion; New York. 1844–1846, Church of the Pilgrims, Brooklyn, N.Y. 1845, Grace Church, Providence, R.I. 1845–1846, First Parish Church; 1845–1855, Chapel and Library, Bowdoin College; Brunswick, Maine. 1846, Christ Church, Norwich, Conn. 1846, Saint Mary's Church, Burlington, N.J. 1846, Trinity Chapel, New York. 1847, Grace Church, Brooklyn, N.Y. 1847, Saint James's Church, New London, Conn. 1847, Saint Mary's Church, South Portsmouth, R.I. 1847–1849, Calvary Church, Stonington, Conn. 1848, Chapel of the Cross, Chapel Hill, N.C. 1848, Christ Church, Raleigh, N.C. 1849–1850, Saint Thomas's Church, Amenia, N.Y. 1850–1851, Saint Paul's Church, Buffalo, N.Y. 1850–1851, Zion Church, Rome, N.Y. 1851, Church of Saint John-in-the-Wilderness, Copake Falls, N.Y. 1851, Saint Paul's Church, Brookline, Mass. 1851–1853, Church of Saint John Chrysostom, Delafield, Wisc. 1852, Rectory, Christ Church, Easton, Md. 1852, Saint Andrew's, Four Mile Point, Tenn. 1852, Taunton Academy, Taunton, Mass. 1853, Christ Church, Binghampton, N.Y. 1853, Saint Andrew's, Prarieville, Ala. 1853, Saint Luke's Church, Martin's Station, Ala. 1854, Christ Church, Elizabeth, N.J. 1854–1856, Saint Paul's Church, Baltimore. 1855–1856, The Low and White Houses, Pierrepont Place, Brooklyn, N.Y. 1855, All Saints Church, Frederick, Md. 1857, Saint Luke's Church, Clermont, N.Y. 1857, Saint Luke's Church, Jacksonville, Ala. 1857, Saint Thomas's Church, Taunton, Mass. 1859–1860, Chapel of Saint Mary the Virgin, Nashotah, Wisc. 1859–1860, Saint Peter's Church, Albany, N.Y. 1861, Greenwood Cemetery (entrance lodge), Brooklyn, N.Y. 1861–1862, Saint Philip-in-the-Highlands, Garrison, N.Y. 1865–1867, Central Congregational Church, Boston. *1868–1870, Saint Thomas's Church, New York.

BIBLIOGRAPHY

"American Conference of Architects." 1871 *The Architect* 5:179–180.

"American Institute of Architects." 1857–1859 *The Crayon* 4:182–183; 5:109–111, 199–201; 6:84–89, 97–100.

CHEROL, JOHN A. 1980 "Kingscote in Newport, Rhode Island." *Antiques* 118:476–485.

"Church Architecture in New York." 1872 *The Architect* 8:87–88.

"The Death of Mr. Richard Upjohn." 1878 *American Architect and Building News* 4:61.

LANCASTER, CLAY 1961 *Old Brooklyn Heights*. Rutland, Vt.: Tuttle.

"New York Church Architecture." 1858 *Putnam's Monthly* 2:233–248.

PATRICK, J. 1980 "Ecclesiological Gothic in the Antebellum South." *Winterthur Portfolio* 15, no. 2:117–138.

PIERSON, WILLIAM H., JR. 1978 *Technology and the Picturesque: The Corporate and Early Gothic Styles*. Volume 2A in *American Buildings and Their Architects*. Garden City, N.Y. Doubleday.

STANTON, PHOEBE B. 1968 *The Gothic Revival and American Church*. Baltimore: Johns Hopkins University Press.

UPJOHN, E. M. (1939)1968 *Richard Upjohn: Architect and Churchmen*. Reprint. New York: DaCapo.

UPJOHN, H. 1933 "Architect and Client a Century Ago." *Architectural Record* 74:374–382.

UPJOHN, RICHARD (1852)1975 *Upjohn's Rural Architecture*. Reprint. New York: DaCapo.

WARE, WILLIAM R. 1867 "Architecture and Architectural Education in the United States." *Civil Engineer and Architect Journal* 30:107–109.

UPJOHN, RICHARD MICHELL

Richard Michell Upjohn (1828–1903) was born in Shaftsbury, England, and came to the United States a year later with his parents Elizabeth and

Richard Michell Upjohn. Connecticut State Capitol. Hartford. 1872–1878

RICHARD UPJOHN. The fame of the father, who became the outstanding ecclesiastical architect of mid-nineteenth century America, has overshadowed the son's career. Their work has frequently been confused, and uncertainty may, in some instances, always persist.

From an early age, Upjohn assisted his father and by 1846 he had assumed many practical duties in the office, which he ran during his father's trip to Europe in 1850 to 1851. When the elder Upjohn returned, Richard Michell himself went abroad for almost a year to study European architecture. In 1853 he became a junior partner, along with his brother in law CHARLES BABCOCK, in the firm of R. Upjohn and Co. Henceforth, he took an increasing role in the design process, but he did not become a full partner until 1864. Only after his father's retirement in 1872 can Richard Michell's own work be certainly identified.

Having been trained so closely by his father, the young Upjohn maintained the firm's specialty in building churches. The earliest building which he claimed as his design was the Madison Square Presbyterian Church, New York (1853–1854), which shows how much the style formulated by the father affected the son.

But Richard Michell Upjohn achieved his own distinction. His ability to draw was superior to his father's, due to the more extensive training which he had received. Examples from his hand such as the drawing for the tower of Saint Peter's Church, Albany (1876) are masterpieces of detail and subtlety. Around 1860, he introduced the Victorian Gothic to the office repertoire for domestic, ecclesiastical, and public architecture. Notable early examples are Grace Church, Manchester, New Hampshire (1860) and the north gates of Greenwood Cemetery, Brooklyn, New York (1861–1865).

His most important and conspicuous work, the Connecticut State Capitol, Hartford (1872–1878) is an outstanding monument of the Victorian Gothic in America. Following his usual practice here, Upjohn also designed interior fittings and furniture. Over-all, the capitol shows the influence of historical French architecture and, like many of his later works, was very decorative and complex in design.

Upjohn was a founding member of the American Institute of Architects in 1857 and later served as president of the New York chapter of the A.I.A. He was also a founding member of the Long Island Historical Society. This interest in American history was manifested as well in the paper which he read before the American Institute of Architects in 1869, "Colonial Architecture of New York and the New England States," one of the earliest studies of the subject. Hobart Upjohn, his youngest son, was the third generation to become an architect and received most of his training in the Upjohn office.

JUDITH S. HULL

WORKS

1853–1854, Madison Square Presbyterian Church, New York. 1860, Grace Church, Manchester, N.H. 1860–1862, Surgeon N. Pinckney House, Easton, Md. 1861–1865, Greenwood Cemetery (north gates), Brooklyn, N.Y. 1865–1868, Central Congregational Church, Boston. 1870, William Mathews House, Rye, N.Y. 1872–1878, Connecticut State Capitol, Hartford. 1875–1878, Greenwood Cemetery (lodge and east gate), Brooklyn, N.Y. 1878–1879, Saint Luke's Church, Saranac, N.Y. 1885, Saint Paul's Church, Fond-du-Lac, Wis. 1887–1888, Saint George's Church, Brooklyn, N.Y.

BIBLIOGRAPHY

CURRY, DAVID PARK, and PIERCE, PATRICIA DAWES (editors) 1979 *Monument: The Connecticut State Capitol.* Hartford: Old State House Association.
HAMLIN, TALBOT 1948 "Richard Michell Upjohn." Volume 19, pages 126–127 in *Dictionary of American Biography.* New York: Scribner.
UPJOHN, EVERARD (1939)1968 *Richard Upjohn: Architect and Churchman.* Reprint. New York: Da Capo.
UPJOHN, RICHARD MICHELL 1869 "Colonial Architecture of New York and the New England States." *Proceedings of the Third Annual Convention of the American Institute of Architects* November 17:47–51.

URABE, SHIZUTARŌ

Born in Kurashiki, Okayama Prefecture, Shizutarō Urabe (1909–) graduated from Kyoto University in 1934. He did not start his own practice until 1962. His prize-winning work is the Kurashiki Ivy Square which was completed in 1974. Urabe revived a group of old brick factory buildings by converting them into a sort of cultural center for youth, preserving one corner as an art gallery and putting in a restaurant, coffee shop, and lecture rooms, thus contributing to the historic preservation of the city.

HIROSHI YAMAGUCHI
*Translated from Japanese by
Bunji Kobayashi*

WORKS

1963, Kurashiki Kokusai Kankō Hotel, Japan. 1969, Nishitetsu Grand Hotel, Fukuoka, Japan. 1972, Civic Hall; 1974, Kurashiki Ivy Square; Kurashiki, Japan.

BIBLIOGRAPHY

Gendainihon Kenchikuka Zenshū. 1973 Volume 12. Tokyo.

URBAN, JOSEPH

Joseph Urban (1872–1933) was an architect, set and interior designer, and illustrator. Trained under CARL HASENAUER at the Vienna Academy, he emigrated to the United States in 1911, where he designed sets for the Boston and Metropolitan Operas, designed hotel decorations, theaters, and houses, and was color coordinator at the Chicago Century of Progress Exposition (1933–1934). The The New School for Social Research (1929–1930), probably his most significant building, is closer to International Modernism. He prepared unexecuted designs for the Metropolitan Opera House (1926–1928) and the Palace of the Soviets (1932). Urban used smooth surfaces, compact masses, and geometric forms of traditional ornament. He was close to the *Sezession* movement and directed the New York branch of the Wiener Werkstätte. Urban advanced theater design and introduced dramatic buildings into prosaic surroundings.

CAROL HERSELLE KRINSKY

WORKS

1927, Paramount Theater and Shops, Palm Beach, Fla. *1927, Ziegfeld Theater; 1927–1928, International Magazine Building; 1929–1930, New School for Social Research; New York. 1930, M. M. Post House, Palm Beach, Fla.

BIBLIOGRAPHY

TAYLOR, DEEMS 1934 "Scenic Art of Joseph Urban: His Protean Work in the Theatre." *Architecture* 69:275–290.
TEEGEN, OTTO 1934 "Joseph Urban." *Architecture* 69:250–256.
URBAN, JOSEPH 1929 *Theaters.* New York: Theatre Arts.

*Urabe.
Kurashiki Ivy Square.
Japan.
1974*

UTZON, JØRN

Utzon.
Sydney Opera House.
Australia.
1956–1968 (not completed
until 1973)

Born in Copenhagen, Jørn Utzon (1918–) began his studies in 1937 at the Royal Academy of Art in Copenhagen under Steen Eiler Rasmussen and KAY FISKER. Following receipt of a degree in architecture in 1942, Utzon worked in the Stockholm office of ERIK GUNNAR ASPLUND (1942–1945) and in the Helsinki office of ALVAR AALTO (1946). In 1949, Utzon worked for a short time at Taliesin under FRANK LLOYD WRIGHT. He has undertaken study tours of Europe and North Africa (1947–1948) and the United States and Mexico (1949).

For Utzon, architectural form is not determined a priori by the architect; it has its own existence, and as an organic entity that must accommodate human life, it must be structured according to the same physical laws that govern its inhabitants. In reflecting the forms and materials of nature, organic architecture endeavors to unite the inhabitants with their natural environment. The villages in Morocco made a lasting impression upon Utzon; later, he translated the apparent unity of architecture and landscape into a modern aesthetic in the Kingohusene Housing Estate near Elsinore, Denmark, (1957–1960), and the housing development at Fredensborg, Denmark (1962–1963). His fascination with the platform—a fundamental element of Mayan and Aztec architecture—which Utzon describes as the "backbone of architectural compositions," led to the designs for the Utzon House at Helleback, Denmark (1952–1953) and for the Sydney Opera House. Utzon has won a number of Swedish design competitions including the 1959 contest for the Elineberg Housing Estate.

In 1957, Utzon won the competition for the design of the Sydney Opera House, by far his best known, albeit most controversial, work. The conception, which is highly sculptural and spiritedly responds to its open site on Bennelong Point, is comprised of a series of terraces from which two sequences of reinforced concrete shells structured as elliptical paraboloids rise to cover the concert halls. From 1957 and the design of the Opera House until the design of the Bagsvaerd Church (1976), Copenhagen, Utzon was preoccupied with a number of competitions and projects including a National Museum for Copenhagen (1960), a town development plan for Elviria, Denmark (1960), and an art museum for Silkeborg (1963). In 1964, he won first prize in a competition for the design of a municipal theater for Zurich. Like Kingohusene, the Bagsvaerd Church reacts to its siting by turning away and inward to its courtyards. Organized by means of its circulation routes, the plan demonstrates its ordering principles from the outside. Bagsvaerd illustrates Utzon's concern with craftsmanship, the use of materials, in this case as in most of the work, bare wood and concrete, as well as his understanding of principles of architectural planning.

SUSAN STRAUSS

WORKS

1952–1953, House, Holte, Denmark. 1952–1953, House, near Lake Fureso, Denmark. 1952–1953, Jørn Utzon House, Helleback, Copenhagen. 1954–1960, Elineberg Housing Estate (with E. Andersson and H. Andersson), Denmark. 1956–1968, Sydney Opera House (completed by others in 1973), Australia. 1957–1960, Klingohusene Housing Estate, near Elsinore, Denmark. 1959, Melli Bank, Teheran. 1962–1963, Danish Cooperative Building Company Housing Development, Fredensborg. 1964, Municipal Theater, Zurich. 1976, Bagsvaerd Church, Copenhagen.

BIBLIOGRAPHY

"Atriumhäuser bei Helsingor, Danemark." 1961 Werk 48, Feb.:46–49.
BOYD, ROBIN 1966 "Utzon: The End." Architectural Forum 124, no. 6:90.
"Competition for a New Theatre for the City of Wolfsburg, Germany." 1966 L'Architettura Cronache e Storia 12, no. 130:249.
"Court Houses at Elsinore, Denmark." 1960 Architectural Design 30:347–348.
"Denmark: Three Houses." 1955 Architects' Yearbook 6:173–181.
GIEDION, SIGFRIED 1965 "Jörn Utzon and the Third Generation." Zodiac no. 14:36–47.
HELMER-PETERSON, KELD 1959 "Jörn Utzon: A New Personality." Zodiac no. 5:70–105.
"Jeunes Architectes dans le Pays Nordiques." 1957 L'Architecture d'Aujourd'hui 28, Sept.:34–46.
"Jörn Utzon." 1966 Bauen und Wohnen 20, Sept.:10–14.
"Platforms and Plateaus: Ideas of a Danish Architect." 1962 Zodiac 10:112–140.
"Schauspielhaus Zurich." 1965 Deutsche Bauzeitung 70:829–830.
"The Sydney Opera House: What Happened and Why." 1967 Architectural Record 141, no. 5:189–192.
"Three Buildings by Jörn Utzon." 1965 Zodiac no. 14:48–93.
WINTER, JOHN 1979 "Utzon at Bagsvaerd." Architectural Review 165, no. 985:146–149.

VACCARINI, GIOVANNI BATTISTA

Giovanni Battista Vaccarini (1702–1768) was a Sicilian architect whose work shaped the built environment of eighteenth-century Catania. Like many Sicilian architects, Vaccarini was associated with the church; he signed himself as Secondary Canon of the Cathedral of Catania and an abbot.

Born in Palermo, Vaccarini was sent to Rome in the 1720s for his architectural training. In Rome, he was exposed to the followers of CARLO FONTANA who, although accepting the tradition of the high baroque masters PIETRO BERRETTINI DA CORTONA, GIOVANNI LORENZO BERNINI and FRANCESCO BORROMINI, were influenced by the waves of French classicism being felt throughout the arts. Vaccarini must have been drawn to this group, but just as surely, he was attracted to the last masters who were continuing the curvilinear compositions and ornamental complexities derived from Borromini: architects like ALESSANDRO SPECCHI, FILIPPO RAGUZZINI, and FRANCESCO DE SANCTIS.

In 1730, Vaccarini was appointed architect of the city of Catania and exerted a strong influence on architecture in the city. Although thirty-seven years had elapsed since the earthquake of 1693, many buildings were still in ruins or just being constructed when Vaccarini assumed his post. His arrival in the city checked the exuberant ornamentation which flowered in Catania after the earthquake. Through Vaccarini's influence, Roman baroque formulae became more common, adding a note of restraint and sophistication to Catania's architecture. His buildings illustrate both his sources in Rome and his hope for the stylistic evolution of Catanese architecture. The model for the plan of San Giuliano (1739–1751) is the plan of Santa Maria di Montesanto on the Piazza del Popolo in Rome; the plan of Sant'Agata (1735–1767) is based on the plan of Sant'Agnese in Piazza Navona in Rome. The double S-curve façade of Sant'Agata is based on San Carlo alle Quattro Fontane, also in Rome. The tassels on Sant'Agata's façade are modeled on those of the Baldachin in St. Peter's. Yet these models are transformed and adapted to Sicilian requirements. The façade of Sao Giuliano, one of the first convex façades in Sicily, is the perfect solution to the problem of linking the body of the church with nuns' terrace above, a typically Sicilian feature. The nuns' private walk and choir also contribute to the unusual proportions of Sant'Agata. Vaccarini tried, as in the façade of Sant'Agata, to unite the dynamism of Sicilian architectural tradition with the ornamen-

Vaccarini.
Church of the Badia of
Sant'Agata.
Catania, Italy.
1735–1767

tal formulae and spatial experiments he learned in Rome.

In addition to Sant'Agata and San Giuliano, Vaccarini constructed secular and religious buildings throughout the city of Catania. Outside the city, he built bridges and roads. After twenty years of working in Catania and southeastern Sicily, he returned to Palermo in 1750, where he worked on the first project for restoring the Cathedral (1752) which had suffered earthquake damage. He died in Palermo and was buried in the Church of the Crociferi near PAOLO AMATO and GIACOMO AMATO.

STEPHEN TOBRINER

WORKS

1730, University (courtyard); 1733–1757, Cathedral (façade); 1735, Elephant Fountain; 1735, Municipio; 1735–1767, Church of the Badia of Sant'Agata; 1737, Benedictine Monastery (work); 1738, Vaccarini House; 1739–1751, San Giuliano; c.1740–1750, Palazzo del Principe di Reburdone; c.1740–1750, Palazzo Nava; c.1740–1750, Palazzo Serravalle; c.1740–1750, Palazzo Valle; Catania, Italy. 1742, Jesuit College (courtyard); 1748, Cutelli College (courtyard); 1748, Palazzo San Giuliano; Catania, Italy. c.1750, San Giovanni Evangelista (restoration), Palermo, Italy.

BIBLIOGRAPHY

ALAJMO, ALESSANDRO GIULIANA 1950 *L'architetto della Catania settecentesca: G. B. Vaccarini e le sconosciute vicende della sua vita.* Palermo, Italy: Industrie grafiche.
BLUNT, ANTHONY 1968 *Sicilian Baroque.* London: Weidenfeld & Nicolson.
BOSCARINO, SALVATORE 1961 *Studi e rilievi di architettura siciliana.* Messina, Italy: Raphael.
FICHERA, FRANCESCO 1934 *G. B. Vaccarini e l'architet-*

tura del Settecento in Sicilia. 2 vols. Rome: Reale Accademia d'Italia.
PISANO, NICOLÒ 1958 *Barocco in Sicilia.* Syracuse, Italy: Isola d'Oro.

VAGNETTI, LUIGI

Architect, town planner, and university professor, Luigi Vagnetti (1915–1980) was a committed Italian scholar. Formed in the Roman school of Arnaldo Foschini, he focused on researching environmental qualities, in relation with the expressive tradition of *genius loci,* reviving it in appropriate contemporary forms.

As professor in the universities of Rome, Palermo, Genoa, and Florence, he organized, in addition, cultural activities and appraised research methods. He was one of the first in Italy to undertake town planning surveys. Vagnetti also promoted a re-evaluation of architectural draftsmanship. He was known as an expert in the history of perspective and wrote important works on the history of architectural education.

GIANCARLO CATALDI

WORKS

1939–1954, Public Works Exhibition Center, Rome. 1948–1950, Cassa di Risparmi Headquarters; 1949–1952, Palazzo and Teatro Grande; Leghorn, Italy. 1951, Samaritani Chapel, via della Camilluccia; *1951–1953, De Marzio House, via Misurina; Rome. 1954–1959, Bank of Italy Headquarters, Cremona, Italy. 1955–1979, Santa Maria Incoronata Sanctuary, near Foggia, Italy. 1956–1960, Municipal Elementary School, Anghiari, Italy. 1959–1963, Maria Rimoldi Institute, via Teulada, Rome. 1960–1974, Nostra Signora della Fiducia Parish Church, Bologna, Italy. 1967–1971, Offices, Stores, and Apartments (with others), via della Libertà, Palermo, Italy.

BIBLIOGRAPHY

BACIGALUPI, VINCENZO; BOAGA, GIORGIO; and BONI, BENITO 1965 *Guida dell'architettura contemporanea in Roma. Guide to Contemporary Architecture in Rome.* Bilingual. Rome: Associazione Nazionale Ingegneri ed Architetti Italiani.
CATALDI, GIANCARLO 1977 "Nuova sede del Ministero PP.TT. all'EUR." *L'Industria delle Costruzioni* 69–70:3–22.
MARCONI, PLINIO 1942 "Due progetti per gruppi di case popolari." *Architettura* 7:1–4.
MORETTI, BRUNO 1940 "Alcune opere dell'architetto Gigi Vagnetti di Roma." *Rassegna di Architettura* 9:3–11.
MURATORI, SAVERIO 1952 "Architetto Luigi Vagnetti: Il Palazzo Grande di Livorno." *Architetti* 3, no. 14:11–18.
VAGNETTI, LUIGI 1955 *Il Disegno dal Vero e la sua*

funzione nella formazione dell'architetto. Genoa, Italy: Vitali & Ghianda.

VAGNETTI, LUIGI 1958 *Disegno e Architettura.* Genoa, Italy: Vitali & Ghianda.

VAGNETTI, LUIGI 1963 *Tre lezioni di Disegno dal Vero.* Rome: Officina poligrafica Laziale.

VAGNETTI, LUIGI 1965 *Il linguaggio grafico dell'architetto, oggi.* Genoa, Italy: Vitali & Ghianda.

VAGNETTI, LUIGI 1972 "Il rilevamento del centro antico di Genova; prolegomeni per lo studio di un tessuto urbano." *Quaderni dell'Istituto di Progettazione Architettonica dell'Università di Genova* 8–10:1–211.

VAGNETTI, LUIGI (1974)1980 *L'Architetto nella storia di Occidente.* Reprint. Padua, Italy: Cedam.

VAGNETTI, LUIGI 1979 "De naturali et artificali perspectiva; biografia ragionata delle fonti toeriche e delle ricerche di storia della prospettiva; contributo alla formazione della conoscenza di un'idea razionale, nei suoi sviluppi da Euclide a Gaspard Monge." *Studi e Documenti di Architettura* 9–10:1–520.

VALADIER, GIUSEPPE

The lifetime of Giuseppe Valadier (1762–1839) virtually spans the neoclassical period, and his career is among the most important in Italy during the epoch. He was born in Rome, where his grandfather had emigrated from France in the early eighteenth century. Son and grandson of silversmiths and heir to French and Italian traditions, Valadier continued his training at the Accademia di San Lucas where, at the age of thirteen, he won a prize in the Concorso Clementino (1775). His father had worked in a circle of papal artists under Pius VI (1755–1799), and before Giuseppe's twentieth birthday, he too had been brought into papal employment as *architetto dei sacri palazzi* (1781). After his appointment at the Vatican, we have no notice of him until 1784, when he built the Villa Pianciani at Terraja, between Spoleto and Todi.

In 1786, Valadier assumed the title of *architetto camerale* and with it the additional responsibilities due to the disastrous earthquake of that year, which damaged so much of the homeland of Pius VI Braschi in the Romagna. Of this work, Valadier's restoration of the cathedral at Urbino in 1789 is the most notable. The seventeenth-century dome of the Renaissance church had suffered serious damage, and Valadier had to rebuild it entirely and to remodel and repair other parts of the interior. The local architect Camillo Morigia also had a significant role: he designed the façade, which Valadier finished after 1800. Valadier articulated the dome with coffers divided from one another by ribs that correspond to pairs of engaged columns around the drum and to the diagonal and cardinal axes of the crossing space. This severe union of components and orientation is complemented by the division of the vault of the nave into five bays by ribs corresponding to the arcades below it. This motif came from GIACOMO QUARENGHI's recently built church of Santa Scolastica at Subiaco (1774–1777), but Valadier's more rigorous application of elements creates a dynamic ambiguity between the effect of an open cage of ribs and the closed coffer system of the dome.

The other significant activity in this period of Valadier's career concerns the Palazzo Braschi in Rome. The triangular site between Piazza Navona and Via Papale (the present-day Corso Vittorio Emanuele II) was acquired by Pius VI for his nephews in 1790. The definitive plan was created by COSIMO MORELLI and presented to the pope in 1790, but Valadier may have been consulted because the much-praised staircase in Morelli's plan corresponds in details and dimensions to Valadier's stair design for a theater, submitted to the Accademia di San Luca in 1788–1789. That stair design does not appear on Valadier's own proposal for the palace of 1790, which is built around a circular courtyard reminiscent of GIACOMO BAROZZI DA VIGNOLA's villa at Caprarola. Valadier's proposal acknowledges the triangular site with three major entrances and develops the scheme on the *piano nobile* by using radiating ovoid spaces above them. Construction of the palace was interrupted during the French occupation and taken up again upon the return of Duke Braschi to Rome in 1800. The great staircase was completed in 1802–1804.

In early February 1798, the French occupied Rome, the pope was forced to leave the city, and on the Campidoglio a republic was declared. Pius VI was made prisoner and died in exile in 1799. Because of his French background, Valadier continued to work albeit in less than ideal circumstances: he was, for example, involved in the exportation to Paris of Italian works of art, as provided in the accords of Tolentino. The works were never sent, and in the wake of this fiasco he was forced to leave Rome with his wife and children. In July 1800, the newly elected Pius VII (1800–1823) returned to Rome and recalled Valadier to papal service as architect in charge of the Tiber, its bridges, and it banks. At this time, he was also nominated as a member of the Accademia di San Luca.

From 1800, Valadier worked for Prince Poniatowski, rebuilding his villa on Via Flaminia; the garden which Valadier designed was finished in 1818. The villa was later remodeled for a new owner, Luigi Vagnuzzi, by the architect's pupil LUIGI CANINA between 1824 and 1844. For the Torlonia family, Valadier designed the façade of the Church of San Pantaleo, located opposite Palazzo Braschi and finished in 1806. The medieval church had been rebuilt in the seventeenth century, but the façade remained unfinished. For its tall narrow proportions Valadier employed a two-story division marked by a thick frieze. The most obvious source for the façade is ANDREA PALLADIO's Zitelle, but the reinterpretation has been informed by a concern for decorative ensembles with structural rationale. Thus, the rusticated network of the façade is organized to suggest pilasters supporting an arch around a thermal window, and these elements express the single stage of the interior elevation.

Shortly after the return of Pius VII to Rome, Valadier was appointed to restore the Milvian Bridge and to systematize Via Flaminia; but the damage caused by the Tiber flood of 1805 made more extensive repairs necessary. The disheveled medieval tower at its north end was remade into a rusticated bastion. The approach road was realigned, and the arched passage under it was widened to permit two carriages to pass. The approach roads—Via Flaminia, Via Cassia, and Via Trionfale—were to be brought together at an elliptical piazza surrounded by rows of elm trees. The latter part of the project was never begun but, like Valadier's plan of 1805 for developing the area between Piazza del Popolo and the Milvian Bridge, would be taken up again during the period of the Napoleonic occupation.

In 1801, the French government officially embraced the Roman Catholic religion, and the ties between Rome and Paris were strengthened by the coronation of Napoleon by Pius VII in 1804. But in 1809, the Papal States were annexed to the Napoleonic empire. The supervision of public works was entrusted to Camillo de Tournon, prefect of the Department of Rome; to Baron de Montalivet, minister of the interior; and to Luigi Onesti Braschi, nephew of Pius VI and leader of the newly elected Roman Senate. Braschi's visit to Paris and his homage to Napoleon in the name of Rome insured the loyalty of artists patronized by his family, such as Valadier who, with RAFFAELLO STERN, was commissioned to regularize the area from the Milvian Bridge to the Piazza del Popolo. The project was adapted from the aforementioned plans by Valadier of 1805 but, perhaps because it did not address the economic problems at which other public works programs were aimed, it was not approved.

At the end of 1810, Valadier was named one of the *direttori dei lavori pubblici di beneficenza* whose initial duties were to carry out a program of building restoration as well as to study the navigability of the Tiber. Other projects of 1810–1811 involved systematizing or restoring the Forum, the Colosseum, the Column of Trajan, the Pantheon, and the Piazza della Rotonda, Piazza di Trevi, Piazza Colonna, as well as the demolition of the Palazzetto Venezia and the spina at the Vatican. Valadier, together with Filippo Aurelio Visconti, published a report of the restoration of the temple of Antoninus and Faustina with engravings by V. Feoli as the first of the *Raccolta delle più insigni fabbriche di Roma antica e sue adiacenze,* 1813, which was issued serially until 1826. In addition to these reports on Roman monuments and institutions, Valadier published original designs. In 1796, he had co-authored a *Raccolta di diversi inventioni,* including projects for twenty-four buildings of which Valadier was responsible for eight. In 1807, Valadier published his *Progetti architettonici;* and this was followed by his *Opere di architettura* in 1833.

In 1814, after the restoration, Pius VII visited his native Cesena and ordered the construction of a new church, Santa Cristina, entrusting the project to Valadier. Consecrated in 1825, it is the only church by Valadier that was not subsequently rebuilt or remodeled. It is built on a small circular plan preceded by a façade whose advancing flanks are joined by a simple Doric portico. A recessed section above the portico makes the dome more evident from the façade. From the inside, the dome with its severe coffering appears to be supported by an undecorated attic and a very plain entablature resting on Ionic columns.

Valadier.
San Pantaleo (façade).
Rome.
1806

Valadier's work at Piazza del Popolo constitutes without question his most significant contribution to Italian architecture. The formal organization of the piazza in the late sixteenth century included a fountain and an obelisk together in the middle of the space. The fifteenth-century Church of Santa Maria del Popolo stood to the north. In the seventeenth century, Carlo Rainaldi, GIOVANNI LORENZO BERNINI, and CARLO FONTANA were involved in the planning and execution of the twin churches that defined the major north–south axis of the piazza as a trident radiating from the northern city gate. In 1733, Leone Pascoli suggested the construction of a church to match Santa Maria del Popolo, thus to create twin churches at the north end of the piazza; he also proposed buildings that would form a cross-axis in the middle of the space. Aspects of this composition were later incorporated in the theme of the Academy's Concorso Clementino in 1772, in which a conservatory or monastery was to be placed opposite Santa Maria del Popolo, and according to which along the east and west sides were to be placed barracks for cavalry and infantry. In 1793, in response to a papal order for barracks to be built on the west side of the piazza, Valadier proposed that they be located behind uniform façades preserving the original trapezoidal shape of the piazza. The main axis of the space would be strengthened by raising the obelisk on a rusticated arch that permitted an uninterrupted north–south view. Fountains would be located at the sides of the arch. Neither the Republican government nor the restoration papacy of 1800 showed traceable interest in this extensive project, which was revived only during the Napoleonic occupation.

A large part of the public works policy of the Napoleonic regime was designed to alleviate the unemployment problem in Rome, and the imperial decree of 1811 providing for a million francs for the embellishment of Rome was nothing less than an attempt to resolve this problem. Article Seven provided for Piazza del Popolo: the Augustinian Convent of Santa Maria del Popolo and its dependencies were to be demolished and a promenade was to be built in its place, the famous "jardin du Grand César." The land between the piazza and the river was also to be cleared.

A new project that Valadier had begun for the piazza in 1810 was approved by decree in July 1811. The emphasis of the design was now on expanding space: whereas the façades of the barracks in the project of 1793 had shut off any visual contact with the natural topography, the plan of 1811 included walks and gardens to the east and west of the piazza, extending vistas laterally over the fences that supplanted the tall façades of the early

design. These fences preserved the trapezoidal shape of the piazza, but behind them are semicircular areas that subtly recall the cross-axes of the eighteenth-century schemes.

In December 1811, work was begun at Piazza del Popolo although much of the design remained unresolved, including the manner in which the piazza would be related to the Pincian Hill. A proposal of Prince Gabrielli, a member of the Commission pour les Embellissements which oversaw the enterprise, was intended to address this issue; Valadier elaborated his scheme between September and October 1812, before the intervention in December of Louis Marie Berthault at the request of the Conseil des Bâtiments in Paris.

Valadier's final project included several elements that Berthault would incorporate, such as the continuous ramps decorated by fountains and balusters organized symmetrically on the Pincio and crowned by a monumental temple. Berthault's lasting contribution to the design consisted of opening the piazza laterally by removing the fences separating the piazza from the gardens in Valadier's 1811 design. These spaces were made part of the piazza, which was given a strong cross-axial emphasis. The rigid, diagrammatic character of Berthault's garden designs is evident in the project approved in March 1813 and in a variant of April 1813 that provided for carriage traffic as well as pedestrians.

When the pontifical government returned in May 1814, the Piazza del Popolo enterprise was among the few to be continued. Valadier was reinstated as director of the works, and he presented a new project at the end of 1815, which was approved in January 1816. Valadier's final efforts were applied to combining the lateral spaces developed by Berthault with ramps and to systematizing the four angles that delimited the entire piazza. The south corners of the piazza, next to Via del Babuino and Via di Ripetta, were monumentalized by corresponding apartment blocks built for speculation by Giovanni Torlonia and Giuseppe Valenti. A monastery replaced the Augustinian Cloister of Santa Maria del Popolo; and corresponding to it on the northwest corner of the piazza, Valadier built the barracks, the so-called *Caserna dei cherubbinieri*." The sixteenth-century fountain on the piazza was removed and replaced by four lions spouting water from the corners of the obelisk. Fountains, reliefs, and statues were also located on the semicircular borders of the piazza. Rostral columns, sphinxes, and other neoclassical motifs complemented the decorative ensemble that weakened the original directional aspect of the piazza and reinforced its newly static aspect. The work was finished in 1824. On the

Valadier.
Arch of Titus (restoration).
Rome.
1819–1821

Valadier.
Palazzo Lezzani (façade).
Rome.
1832

Pincio, the Casina Valadier, which was intended as a *caffé,* was finished in 1817.

In 1818, Valadier was named *ispettore del consiglio d'arte per le fabbriche camerali.* Probably in this connection, he restored a spur of the Colosseum (1820) and embarked on the more famous restoration of the Arch of Titus (1819–1821), which established a new standard of historical preservation by recording the monument carefully in published designs showing its state before and after restoration and by using travertine rather than the original white marble for the restored parts. Valadier published his work in the *Narrazione artistica dell'operato finora nel restauro dell'arco di Tito* (1822). In 1819, Valadier and Giuseppe Camporese (see CAMPORESE FAMILY) submitted a report on the Teatro Valle; a definitive project for rebuilding the theater appeared in 1820, and work began in 1821, with decorations by Felice Giani. The theater was inaugurated in December 1822. During the building, a serious collapse occurred, straining relations between the architects and inspiring Valadier to write *Sulla improvisa caduta di un arco sul palcoscenico del Teatro Valle* (n.d.).

Few of Valadier's activities in Rome were not controversial, and this is true of his involvement in the restoration of San Paolo fuori le mura. Under Pius VII, restorations had been undertaken since 1814. In July 1823, a devastating fire reduced the church to a ruin and the pope, who had been Valadier's patron, died less than a week later. The church architects quickly made provisory repairs and produced a report advocating the repristination of the old building. They were seconded by the Abbot Angelo Uggeri, who argued that the arcades of the nave ought to be replaced by flat architraves on the model of Old Saint Peter's.

Uggeri, an architect and archeologist, was appointed secretary of the commission to supervise the restoration as provided by Leo XII in 1825. Opposed to Uggeri and the church architects was Valadier, who found the basilica so ruined as to demand an entirely new but smaller replacement built within the existing remains. Preliminary study for his proposal is embodied in his book *Della basilica di S. Paolo sulla Via Ostierse* (1823).

Under the auspices of the Accademia di San Luca in 1824, a competition for the reconstruction was held, and designs were exhibited on the Capitol. In Valadier's proposals the former transept would have become the main axis of the church, the apse and truncated nave would be made into a transept, and what had been the north transept arm became a monumental entrance. The whole church retained its cruciform shape on a much reduced scale. To this scheme the famous archeologist Carlo Fea was firmly opposed, arguing that the replacement of an ancient building with a smaller one had no auspicious precedent. In the end, the commission went to one of the church architects, PASQUALE BELLI, who had to contend with the inconsistent and shifting ideals of various theoretical camps; upon his death, the work was assumed by LUIGI POLETTI. The interior was finished and consecrated in 1854 by Pius IX.

In his later years, Valadier's activity as *architetto del camerlengato* from 1824 included the restorations of San Martino ai Monti (1826–1829), Sant'Andrea in Via Flaminia (1828–1829), and the temple of Fortuna Virilis (1829–1835). The private commissions of his last years included the palace for Giuseppe Lezzani on the Via del Corso (1832), which required the unification of three separate houses behind a new façade. Because a bearing wall coincided with the geometric center of the façade, Valadier used an even number of window bays, accenting the outermost bays with drafted masonry, Palladian windows, and projecting balconies with extraordinarily fine railings. The separation of the flanking windows from the tighter grouping of windows in the center is perhaps Venetian in origin.

The façade for the Church of San Rocco (1834) is also Venetian, for it was clearly inspired by Palladio's San Giorgio Maggiore (1566); but this was as much the responsibility of the *visitatore apostolico,* Cardinal Pallotta, as of Valadier, who wrote the *Breve cenno intorno alla nuova facciata della chiesa di S. Rocco* (n.d.).

At the end of his life, Valadier published his lectures at the Accademia di San Luca and a report on the building in which it is located (*L'architettura pratica dettata nella scuola e cattedra dell'insigne Accademia di S. Luca,* Rome, 1828, 1831, 1833; and

Cenni sull'origine e sullo stato attuale della insigne Accademia di S. Luca, Rome, 1838). He died in Rome where he is buried in the Church of San Luigi dei Francesi.

TOD A. MARDER

WORKS

1784, Casino and Church of Villa Pianciani, Terraja, Italy. 1789, San Crescentino (restoration), Urbino, Italy. 1800–1818, Villa Poniatowski, Rome. 1805, Ponte Milvio (restoration and reconstruction), Rome. 1806, San Pantaleo (façade), Rome. 1811–1824, Piazza del Popolo; 1814–1822, Santa Cristina, Cesena, Italy. 1819–1821, Arch of Titus (restoration); 1819–1822, Teatro Valle (reconstruction); 1820, Colosseum (restoration); Rome. 1823–1839, Collegiate Church (not completed until 1869), Monsampietrangeli, Italy. 1826–1829, Santa Maria ai Monti (restoration); 1828–1829, Sant'Andrea in Via Flaminia (restoration); 1829–1835, Temple of Fortuna Virilis (restoration); 1832, Palazzo Lezzani (façade); 1834, San Rocco (façade); Rome.

BIBLIOGRAPHY

DEBENEDETTI, ELISABETTA 1978 "Tre taccuini inediti di Giuseppe Valadier." *Miscellanea: Quaderni sul neoclassico* 4:147–171.

DEBENEDETTI, ELISA 1979 *Valadier: Diario architettonico.* Rome: Bulzoni.

FISCHER, MANFRED F. 1972 "Classicism and Historicism in 19th-century Roman Architecture: The Rebuilding of S. Paolo fuori le Mura." *Actes du XXIIe congrès international d'histoire de l'art* (Budapest 1969) 2:603–608.

HOFFMANN, PAOLA 1967 *Il Monte Pincio e la Casina Valadier.* Rome: del Mondo.

LAPADULA, ATTILIO 1969 *Roma e la regione nell'epoca napoleonica.* Rome: Instituto Editoriale Pubblicazioni Internazionali.

MARANI, STEFANO 1975 "Intorno alla ricostruzione della basilica di San Paolo fuori le mura a Roma." *Storia architettura* 2, no. 3:23–36.

MARCONI, PAOLO 1964 *Giuseppe Valadier.* Rome: Officina Edizioni.

MOLAJOLI, BRUNO 1971 "L'architettura neoclassica a Roma e nell' Italia centrale." *Bollettino del Centro Internazionale di Studi di Architettura A. Palladio* 13:208–222.

SCHULZE-BATTMAN, ELFRIEDE 1939 *Giuseppe Valadier: Ein klassizistischer Architekt Roms, 1762–1839.* Dresden, Germany: Zetzche.

VALERIANO, GIUSEPPE

Born in L'Aquilia, Italy, Giuseppe Valeriano (1542–1595) was trained under the local painter Pompeo Cesura whom he accompanied to Spain as an assistant on a variety of artistic and architectural endeavors. Valeriano entered the Jesuit Order in 1572 and, thereafter, devoted his efforts to designing the religious buildings of that order. He returned to Italy in 1581 on the instructions of the Jesuits' Father General, going first to Rome to assist in the construction of several Jesuit projects. He directed work on the Chapel of the Beata Vergine della Strada in the Church of the Gesù and also was involved in the construction of the Collegio Romano. This building is usually given to BARTOLOMMEO AMMANNATI but is attributed to Valeriano by some authorities. The exact extent of his participation in the project is uncertain, but he almost certainly was responsible for its courtyard. The open arcades of the two stories of loggias are framed by classical pilasters, Ionic in the lower story and Corinthian in the upper. The effect is of simple severity, enlivened by the use of a balustrade in the second story.

In 1582, Valeriano was sent to Naples to superintend the building of the Jesuit College at the Gesù Vecchio. Although actual construction did not begin until 1605 and lingered on for more than forty years, the project, in its essentials, seems to correspond to Valeriano's intentions. The collegiate courtyard repeats the form of that of the Collegio Romano but substitutes superimposed Doric and Ionic pilasters for the Ionic and Corinthian combination used at the Roman institution. Originally, only two stories of loggias were intended for the three sides of the courtyard with a third story in the wing facing the entrance being used to house the clergy; today's rather oppressive effect would have been avoided.

At the same time that Valeriano was preparing his designs for the Neapolitan college, he was asked to submit plans for a new Jesuit church in Naples. In 1584, work began on the Gesù Nuovo with the purchase and partial demolition of the Palazzo di Salerno built for Roberto Sanseverino in 1470 by Novello da San Lucano. Valeriano used the lower part of the palace's façade for the front of his new church and reused much of the masonry. The internal arrangement is reminiscent of the Roman Gesù of GIACOMO BARROZI DA VIGNOLA, but Valeriano gave the structure a more centralizing focus inspired, perhaps by MICHELANGELO's designs for St. Peter's. Construction on the Gesù Nuovo did not begin until 1593; the project was completed in 1601 under the direction of Pietro Provedo.

While he was at work for the Jesuits in Rome and Naples, Valeriano dispatched plans for the Church of Saint Michael in Munich. The Michaelskirche was built in the late Italian Renaissance manner of the pattern of the great Gesù in Rome. As in the Roman prototype, the Munich church has a single barrel-vaulted nave, a form which served as the model for the Vorarlsberg architects of the later Bavarian baroque.

Valeriano's interests in architectural theory are evident in a number of designs for ecclesiastical buildings in southern Italy and Sicily. Among these are proposals for the Jesuit College in Cosenza which would have featured a pentagonal church and a hexagonal cloister.

CHARLES RANDALL MACK

WORKS

c.1582, Chapel of the Beata Vergine della Strada in the Gesù; 1582, Collegio Romano (courtyard?); Rome. 1582–1595, Collegio (not completed until c.1645), Gesù Vecchio; 1584–1595, Gesù Nuovo (not completed until 1601); Naples. 1583–1595, Saint Michael's (not completed until 1597), Munich. 1589–1595, Gesù (Church of Saints Andrea and Ambrogio; not completed until 1639), Genoa, Italy.

BIBLIOGRAPHY

BLUNT, ANTHONY 1975 *Neapolitan Baroque and Rococo Architecture.* London: Zwemmer.

ERRICHETTI, MICHELE 1959 "L'architetto Giuseppe Valeriano (1542–1596) progettista del Collegio Napoletano del Gesù Vecchio." *Archivio storico per le provincie Napoletane.* New Series 39:325–352.

GOLZIO, VINCENZO 1937 "Giuseppe Valeriani." Volume 34, page 914 in *Enciclopedia Italiana.* Rome: Istituto della Enciclopedia Italiana.

MONTINI, RENZO UBERTO 1956 *La Chiesa del Gesù.* Naples: Azienda autonomia di soggiorno cura e turismo.

PANE, ROBERTO 1975 *Il Rinascimento nell'Italia meridionale.* Milan: Edizioni di comunità.

PIRRI, PEITRO 1970 *Giuseppe Valeriano S. I.: Architetto e pittore 1542–1596.* Rome: Institutum Historicum.

VALLE, GINO

Trained at the University of Architecture in Venice, Italy, and at the Urban Design Program of Harvard University, Gino Valle (1923–) joined the family practice, Studio Valle (father and sister), in Udine, Italy, in 1952 which consisted of architecture, urban design, and industrial design. From the outset, there was a duality of influence in his work: the Friulani region vernacular (the Quaglia House, 1954) and modernism (Migotto House, 1954). An early resolution of these may be seen in the Savings Bank at Latisana, Italy (1956). It is not until the Zanussi Factory office building at Porcia, Italy (1961) that his own vocabulary becomes fully developed. The Monument to the Resistance in Udine, carried out in a difficult urban setting, is a powerfully expressive work ranking high among the best of such. His practice has occurred largely in the Friulani region of Italy, but his thought has over time taken him away from that regional vernacular toward modernism. Valle brings an un-

usual elemental power to his modernism, as in the offices at the Fantoni Factory at Osoppo (1973–1978).

JOHN R. MYER

WORKS

1954, Migotto House (with Nani Valle and Provino Valle), Sutrio, Italy. 1954, Quaglia House (now Pozzi House; with Nani Valle and Provino Valle), Pasian di Prato, Italy. 1956, Savings Bank, Latisana, Italy. 1961, Zanussi Factory, Porcia Italy. 1969, Monument to the Resistance (with Federcio Marconi and Dino Balsadella), Udine, Italy. 1978, Fantoni Factory, Osoppo, Italy.

VALLIN DE LA MOTHE, JEAN BAPTISTE MICHEL

Trained as architect in Paris and Italy, Jean Baptiste Michel Vallin de la Mothe (1729–1800) worked mainly in Russia (1759–1775), where his buildings for Catherine the Great introduced the ideas of ANGE JACQUES GABRIEL and JACQUES FRANÇOIS BLONDEL. He was the first teacher of architecture at the Academy in St. Petersburg and became an *associé correspondant* of the French Academy. He furthered such talents as Ivan Yegorovich Starov.

CHARLOTTE LACAZE

WORKS

1760–1783?, Roman Catholic Cathedral of Saint Catherine (completed by Antonio Rinaldi?); 1762–1765, Gostiny Dvor (Merchants' Court; partially reconstructed in 1885); 1764–1767, First Hermitage of Catherine the Great; St. Petersburg, Russia. *1765?, Foreign Affairs Building, Moscow. 1765, New Holland Port Gateway and Warehouses, St. Petersburg, Russia. 1765–1771, Château and Church for Count Cyril Razumovsky, Potchep, Chernigov District, Russia. 1765–1772, Palace of the Academies; 1766, Hôtel de Ribas (later the Palace of the Prince of Oldenburg); *1766, Palace of Count Chernychov; St. Petersburg, Russia.

BIBLIOGRAPHY

BRAHAM, ALLAN 1980 *The Architecture of the French Enlightenment.* Berkeley and Los Angeles: University of California Press.

GALLET, MICHEL 1980 *Soufflot et Son Temps.* Paris: C.N.M.H.S. Exhibition catalogue.

HAMILTON, GEORGE HEARD (1954)1975 *The Art and Architecture of Russia.* 2d ed. Harmondsworth, England: Penguin.

HAUTECOEUR, LOUIS 1912 *L'Architecture classique à St Pétersbourg a la fin du XVIIIe siècle.* Paris: Champion.

HAUTECOEUR, LOUIS 1952 Volumes 3 and 4 in *Histoire de l'architecture classique en France.* Paris: Picard.

KRASENNIKOV, A. F. 1972 "Lesnye sklady na ostrove Novaja Gollandija v Peterburge." *Arkhitekturnoe nasledstvo* 19:96–101.

LISOVSKIJ, V. G. 1972 *Akademija Khudozhestv.* Leningrad: Lenizadt.

RÉAU, LOUIS 1922 "Un grand architecte français en Russie: Vallin de la Mothe (1729–1800)" *L'Architecture* 35:173–180.

RÉAU, LOUIS 1954 "L'Architecture française en Russie de Leblond à Ricard de Monferrand." Pages 319–329 in *Urbanisme et Architecture.* Paris: Laurens.

Réunion des Sociétés des Beaux-Arts des Departments 1890 14:724–726, 744–746.

VALPERGA, MAURIZIO

A typical member of the Savoy court, Maurizio Valperga (17th century) was count, sergeant major, ducal councillor, military architect, and first ducal engineer (1667). Father of the engineers Andrea and Anton Maurizio, he worked with CARLO DI CASTELLAMONTE on the first enlargement of Turin. His architectural works have been largely transformed.

MARTHA POLLAK

WORKS

1619, San Carlo, Turin, Italy. 1633–1644, Certosa (partially executed), Collegno, Italy. 1637, Eremo dei Camaldolesi (embellishments); 1663, Palazzo Galleani di Canelli e Barbaresco, 6–8 via Alfieri; n.d., Palazzo Reale (works); Turin, Italy.

BIBLIOGRAPHY

BRAYDA, CARLO; COLI, LAURA; and SESIA, DARIO 1964 *Ingegneri e architetti del settecento in piemonte.* Turin, Italy: Società degli ingegneri e degli architti.

VALVASSORI, GABRIELE

Gabriele Valvassori (1683–1761), son of a Bergamesque carpenter, was born in Rome. As a boy of fifteen, he entered the Accademia di San Luca to follow its six-year course in architecture, finishing in 1704. He is first mentioned in a professional capacity in 1717, as a subordinate of CARLO BIZZACHERI, architect of the Pamphili family. At Bizzacheri's death in 1721, Valvassori assumed his post and, until 1739, directed various architectural tasks undertaken by Prince Camillo Pamphili. During this period and after, he was also architect to the Colonna family and of various convents.

Valvassori's earliest important project was the rebuilding of the church of San Salvatore della Corte, Rome, rededicated to the Madonna della Luce (1730–1768). The spatial organization of this church, a double transept plan with transepts of different heights and side aisles that are visually isolated from the central space, is unusually complex for this period. The structural cage of dominant verticals intersected by horizontals, rounded corners, and unorthodox entablatures, as well as the over-all whiteness of the interior, look back to FRANCESCO BORROMINI's skeletal designs, but they also reveal a very personal plastic and decorative sense.

The Corso wing of the Pamphili palace (1730–1735), Rome, is Valvassori's key work. The design of the façade is the only instance among rococo palaces of an exterior that is as imposing as befits its building type and at the same time reflects the charm and decorative brilliance of the interior apartments. The Corso front shows the emphasis on the openings rather than the wall, the grouping of windows in a complex rhythmic sequence, and the stacking of openings at the center and ends of the façade, which are characteristic of eighteenth-century palace fronts. The novel and ingenious designs of the window and door frames and their accompanying balconies (of Borrominesque inspiration) make use of lively rococo forms, successfully adapted to a large front by a massive plasticity. Valvassori's synthesis of the principles of composition and vocabulary of the local rococo style and the monumentality of the baroque approach makes the Pamphili palace an achievement unmatched in this period.

Very little is known about Valvassori's professional activity between 1736 and 1750 other than that he was elected *accademico di merito* by the Accademia di San Luca in 1737 and also became a member of the Congregazione de' Virtuosi al Pantheon. It is possible that he was absent from Rome during the 1740s. In 1750, he appears again, engaged in two relatively minor commissions, the

Valvassori. Doria-Pamphili Palace. Rome. 1730–1735

decoration of a chapel in Santa Maria dell' Orto (1750), and the rebuilding of the convent of Santi Quirico e Giulitta (1750–1753), his last known work.

NINA A. MALLORY

WORKS

1730–1735, Doria–Pamphili Palace; 1730–1768, Madonna della Luce; 1731, Collegio Cerasoli; 1732, Gate in Villa Pamphili, Porta San Pancrazio; 1750, Chapel of San Giovanni Battista, Santa Maria dell' Orto; 1750–1753, Convent of Santi Quirico e Giulitta; Rome.

BIBLIOGRAPHY

FASOLO, FURIO 1949 *Le chiese di Roma nel '700*. Rome: "L'Erma" di Bretschnedier.
FASOLO, FURIO 1951 "Disegni inediti di un architetto romano del settecento." *Palladio* 4:186–189.
LORET, M. L. 1933 "L'architetto di palazzo Doria Pamphili." *L'illustrazione vaticana* 4:303–304.
LORET, M. L. 1933 "La decorazione della galleria e l'architettura del palazzo Doria Pamphili." *L'illustrazione vaticana* 4:428–429.
MALLORY, NINA A. 1977 *Roman Rococo Architecture from Clement XI to Benedict XIV (1700–1758)*. New York and London: Garland.
PORTOGHESI, PAOLO (1966)1970 *Roma Barocca: The History of an Architectonic Culture*. Translated by Barbara Luigia La Penta. Cambridge, Mass.: M.I.T. Press.
RAVA, ARNOLDO 1934 "Gabrielle Valvassori, architetto romano (1683–1761)." *Capitolium* 10:385–398.

*Van Alen.
Chrysler Building.
New York.
1929*

VAN ALEN, WILLIAM

Born in Brooklyn, New York, William Van Alen (1883–1954) began work as an office boy in the firm of New York architect Clarence True. At the same time, he attended Pratt Institute in Brooklyn. He subsequently worked for the firms of Copeland and Dole and CLINTON AND RUSSELL before winning the 1908 Lloyd Warren Fellowship. In Paris, Van Alen studied in the atelier of VICTOR A. F. LALOUX at the Ecole des Beaux-Arts. In 1911, he returned to New York, where he formed a partnership with H. Craig Severance. The partnership became known for its distinctive designs for multistory commercial structures that abandoned the previously established formula of base, shaft, and capital. The partnership dissolved around 1925, and Van Alen continued to practice on his own, producing the Child's Restaurant Building (1926) as well as the Reynolds Building (1928) in New York. Van Alen is best known for his design of the Chrysler Building (1929), often praised as the greatest of all Art Deco-style skyscrapers and the perfect monument to American

capitalism. Clothed in exotic woods and metals, the final building was the result of a bizarre race in which Van Alen was pitted against his former partner in a competition for the world's tallest building. Van Alen won in the fall of 1929 when a spire, which had been fabricated within the skyscraper, was erected, making the building, at 1,045 feet, taller than 40 Wall Street (927 feet).

STEVEN MCLEOD BEDFORD

WORKS

Before 1924, Bainbridge Building; before 1924, Bar Building; before 1924, Gidding Building; before 1924, Prudence Building; 1926, Child Restaurant Building; 1928, Delman Building, 558 Madison Avenue; 1928, Reynolds Building; 1929, Chrysler Building; 1936, House of a Modern Age; New York. 1941, Defense Housing, Newport, R.I.

BIBLIOGRAPHY

NATIONAL INSTITUTE FOR ARCHITECTURAL EDUCATION 1964 *Winning Designs 1904–1963: Paris Prize in Architecture.* New York: The institute.
"Obituary." 1954 *New York Times* May 25, p. 27.
SOLON, LEON V. 1924 "The Passing of the Skyscraper Formula for Design." *Architectural Record* 55:135–144.
SWALES, F. S. 1929 "Draftsmanship and Architects V: As Exemplified by the Work of William Van Alen." *Pencil Points* 10:514–526.

VAN BAURSCHEIT, JAN PIETER

Of German descent, Jan Pieter van Baurscheit (1699–1768) was one of the most brilliant interpreters of rococo art in the southern Netherlands. In 1728, after having been trained as a sculptor by his father, he decided to devote himself to architecture. Strongly influenced by DANIEL MAROT, who brought the style of Louis XIV to The Hague, he made a name for himself at Antwerp through the originality of his art, which combined the ornamental luxury of the rococo of Austrian inspiration with the rules of classical composition. It is nevertheless from Flemish traditions that he drew his themes, such as the monumental treatment of the central bay. To the artistic temperament of the Netherlands—Italianized but not sensitive to the subtleties of the rococo—Van Baurscheit adapted a refined aesthetic with mastery.

PIERRE LENAIN
*Translated from French by
Shara Wasserman*

WORKS

1730, Anthony van Dishoeck House (later Town Hall),

Vlissingen, Netherlands. *1730–1736, Van den Brande House (later the Provincial Library), Middelburg, Netherlands. 1737, Hôtel de Fraula, Antwerp, Belgium. 1740–1744, Town Hall, Lier, Belgium. 1745, Hôtel van Susteren (later Royal Palace); 1749, Hôtel van Susteren-Dubois (later Hôtel Osterrieth); c.1749, Hôtel Den Grooten Robijn; Antwerp, Belgium.

VAN BOGHEM, LOUIS

Louis van Boghem (c.1470–1540) was born in Brussels to a family of stone merchants and sculptors. His career is documented from 1503 onward. From 1512 until his death, he was architect of the prince of Brabant and the Outre-Meuse. His major work was the construction of the Church of Brou near Bourg-en-Bresse, France (1513–1532). Commissioned by Margaret of Austria, it is an exuberant outcropping of Brabantine Gothic in central France.

ELIZABETH SCHWARTZBAUM

WORK

1513–1532, Church of Brou, near Bourg-en-Bresse, France.

BIBLIOGRAPHY

BRUCHET, MAX 1927 *Marguerite d'Autriche: Duchesse de Savoie.* Lille, France: Danel.
NODET, VICTOR 1911 *L'église de Brou.* Paris: Laurens.

VANBRUGH, JOHN

Sir John Vanbrugh (1664–1726) was a writer of brilliant Restoration comedies who became the most famous architect of the English baroque period. His ability and enthusiasm in designing massively picturesque and flamboyant country houses, the raciness of his comedies, the circumstances of his life, and the ebullient character evident both in his formal works and in his correspondence have combined to give him the popular image of a talented but scarcely disciplined amateur, disguising the seriousness of mind and purpose which underlay almost all of the actions of his adult life. In the world of literature and the stage his plays are still admired and some still performed, while among his architectural works Blenheim Palace has attracted interest and comment, though not consistently favorable, from its inception to the present day. Since the revival of interest in baroque art from the 1920s onward, Vanbrugh's originality has come to be understood and appreciated to an extent greater than in his own lifetime, although no more than is justly due to him.

Vanbrugh was born in January 1664 in the City of London, where his father was engaged in the wholesale cloth trade. His grandfather was of Flemish ancestry but had come in the interest of trade by way of Haarlem to London, where he married the daughter of a Protestant refugee from Antwerp, also a cloth merchant. The architect's mother, however, was the youngest daughter of Sir Dudley Carleton, whose uncle, of the same name, was a diplomat and a patron of the painter Rubens and became Viscount Dorchester. The family into which the architect was born thus combined in equal measures two distinct communities. One was a mercantile and commercial group which, although Dutch and Flemish in origin and family name, had made itself loyally British. The other was from the backbone of seventeenth-century England: the provincial landed gentry, the Church, and the army. His mother's family connections, moreover, made him a kinsman—remote but acknowledged—of several English noblemen. To one, the seventh earl of Huntingdon, he owed his first brief commission in the army in 1686. To Robert Bertie, later fourth earl of Lindsey and finally duke of Ancaster, he owed not only architectural commissions in mature life but in 1688 the mixed blessings of his journey to France and his subsequent imprisonment there. Most important was the third earl of Carlisle, who in 1699 would launch his final career by commissioning, as his first architectural work, the palatial house at Castle Howard. Carlisle also was instrumental in Vanbrugh's appointment as Comptroller of the Royal Works, which sealed his credibility as an architect, and as one of the senior Heralds in the College of Arms.

In 1667, the year after the Great Fire of London, Vanbrugh's family moved to Chester, where his father acquired a business in the refining of sugar. He was probably sent away to school or to a private tutor, but we know nothing of his education except its results, a command of the English and French languages, a taste for books, and good handwriting. He learned to keep accounts in his first employment, about 1681, as "servant" to a cousin in London who ran a wine and brandy business. But the cousin went bankrupt, and after his first brief spell as a soldier Vanbrugh was attached to the household of Robert Bertie.

In the summer of 1688, he and Bertie were in Holland, and both seem to have gone to France, where in September Vanbrugh was arrested, accused, in his own words, "of speaking something in favour of the enterprise the King was then upon the point of executing." The King was William III, then Prince of Orange, and the enterprise was the Glorious Revolution, in which his uncle James II fled to France and William and Mary took the throne of England. Thus were established the Protestant succession of the British monarchy and the responsibility of the monarch through Parliament to the British people, the aims of the Whig party of which Vanbrugh was to be a staunch and active supporter. But evidently in France, on the eve of the English *coup* and hostilities between the two countries, such loyalty was unwisely expressed, and Vanbrugh found himself a political prisoner. He proved to be of little value in the trading of captives between England and France, and it was over four years before he secured his release, not by the practice but by the exposure of double dealing.

So long an experience of confinement was a sobering one, and it added a seriousness of mind to the ambition for success he learned or inherited from his father's family. The direction of that ambition was not yet determined, and there is no evidence to support the legend that Vanbrugh studied architecture in France. Part of his imprisonment was spent at Vincennes, and the late medieval curtain wall and north gate tower there seem to have directly influenced the wall and gate to the east court at Blenheim; moreover, the precinct of Vincennes included a château designed by LOUIS LE VAU, the one seventeenth-century French building Vanbrugh therefore must have known. Early in 1692, he was moved to the relative comfort of the Bastille, and after his release he spent some time at liberty in Paris; evidence both of style and of touristic popularity suggest that he would have visited the Invalides and the palace of Versailles. It was also in the Bastille that Vanbrugh sketched out the comedy that later became *The Provok'd Wife*.

On his return to England in April 1693, Vanbrugh held a sinecure in the duchy of Lancaster, and from 1695 a captaincy in a marine regiment. He retained a lifelong military image of himself but probably never saw active service; from 1698 he was on the reserve, and much of his time was spent in London until 1702, when he resigned both his sinecure and his commission to become Comptroller of Works. Meanwhile, his first comedy, *The Relapse,* had been staged in London at the end of 1696, followed by *The Provok'd Wife* and some adaptations of French comedies which, for all their sparkling language, never attained the same success as the first two plays. Altogether, his career as a dramatist lasted only ten years, and during that time he found his true avocation in architecture.

It was acceptable and not unusual for a gentleman to take up architecture; what are remarkable in Vanbrugh's case are the suddenness ("without thought or lecture," in Jonathan Swift's phrase) with which he did so and the thoroughness with

which he consolidated his position. Swift satirized him as aiming to do better than mudpies and cardhouses, but in truth he must have aimed to build better houses than the leading domestic architect of the 1690s, WILLIAM TALMAN, whom he supplanted both as Lord Carlisle's architect and, with Carlisle's help, as Comptroller. Talman had already begun to make designs for Castle Howard when Vanbrugh proposed himself to his kinsman as an alternative—untrained, untried, but supremely confident. Both his correspondence and the testimony of contemporaries show Vanbrugh as likable and persuasive, but even more significant than ties of family friendship must have been his introduction to NICHOLAS HAWKSMOOR which perhaps took place through Vanbrugh's cousin William, treasurer to the newly started Greenwich Hospital on which Hawksmoor was assistant to Sir CHRISTOPHER WREN. Delegacy was as natural to Hawksmoor as was delegation to Vanbrugh, who with Lord Carlisle's agreement found in Hawksmoor a draftsman, a detail designer, an organizer, and a negotiator.

Talman had begun Chatsworth in 1687 for the earl of Devonshire, one of the group who invited William and Mary to the throne of England. In both style and imagery, in the monumentality of its façades and the richness of its decoration, Chatsworth marks the assumption in architecture of royal prerogatives by the Whig nobility; Castle Howard was to eclipse Chatsworth. Apart from short periods of office, Carlisle's political ambition lay not in London but in the development as a moral duty of his Yorkshire estates, and his palace there was to be related to York, then at its most fashionable, rather as Hampton Court was to London or Versailles to Paris. This was the message of Castle Howard's sprawling length, its two sets of wings, its excess of state rooms over sleeping accommodation, the martial emblems in the metopes of its entrance front, the *Fall of Phaeton* as an allegory of the fall of Absolutism painted in the dome above the hall, and that dome itself, inserted like the crossing of a Renaissance church into the middle of the house, as the first great Vanbrughian afterthought.

Castle Howard was begun in 1700 with the northeast wing; the main block was started in 1702. The house was finished in 1712 except for the northwest wing, which Carlisle had postponed in favor of expenditure on gardens and outbuildings. Eventually it was built to a deliberately different design by Sir THOMAS ROBINSON for the fourth earl (his brother-in-law) in 1753–1759; fortunately lack of money saved Vanbrugh's extant building from remodeling by Robinson.

Castle Howard depends first on its siting on a

*Vanbrugh.
Castle Howard (kitchen
wing).
Yorkshire, England.
1700–1712*

*Vanbrugh.
Castle Howard (south
front).
Yorkshire, England.
1700–1712*

*Vanbrugh.
Castle Howard (north
front).
Yorkshire, England.
1700–1712*

long ridge of land facing north and south, and on the dramatic skyline formed by the dome and the towers and turrets of the wings and service blocks; the northeast wing has a small cupola of the type common in later seventeenth-century domestic architecture and the northwest would have had a pair to it, while the kitchen block has (and the stables would have had) corner towers with pyramidal roofs which may be reminiscences of the old Henderskelfe Castle which the new house superseded. At closer range, Castle Howard impresses by the giant pilaster orders of the main block, Doric on the north, entrance, front, and Corinthian on the long south range facing the garden; it is shaped further by the crisp cutting of detail and the banded rustication. The detail itself was designed, and most of the drawings for the building were made, by Hawksmoor, but the French character of the varied surfaces must owe as much to Vanbrugh's firsthand knowledge, limited though it may have been, as to Hawksmoor's familiarity with engravings.

The interior decoration of Castle Howard was undertaken by a team that included, besides local craftsmen, Italian stuccoists and painters; with the exception of the hall and dome, which have been restored, much of the original decoration was destroyed by fire in 1940. It is possible to speculate but not to decide on whether Carlisle's visit to the Veneto in 1690 or Vanbrugh's to Saxony (to take the Order of the Garter to the future George II) in 1706 influenced the decoration; certainly it had none of the illusionist ceilings and paneled walls of houses like Chatsworth, and its relegation of enrichment to architecturally discrete fields anticipated English decoration of the 1730s. Castle Howard also had more domestic interior virtues. Vanbrugh reported that his patron, after he had begun to live in the house, had found it free from drafts and exceptionally warm even in freezing weather; although good joinery and thick walls undoubtedly contributed to these comforts, the architect took credit for features of his design which he believed could be repeated elsewhere: this must mean the placing rather than the capacity of hearths and the warming effect of the great series of south windows which already in the first

drawings had appeared to Lord Devonshire "like an orange house."

The wooden model made for Castle Howard was sent to London for inspection by King William, an extraordinary sign of the determination of Vanbrugh's onslaught on the architectural profession. This determination appears most clearly in the first house he designed for himself in London (1701); it earned the ridicule of Swift, who compared it rather mysteriously to a goose pie, and the nickname has stuck to it. Certainly, it was unusual for a small town house, having superimposed rusticated arcades in the middle three bays and a flat parapet over the second story, and it is not too difficult to imagine its roughly cubed shape as a raised meat pie. Moreover, Vanbrugh chose a remarkably public site, managing to obtain permission to build his house amid the ruins of old Whitehall Palace which had burned down in 1698; he thus set a precedent for several grander houses built there during the eighteenth century.

In May 1702, through Carlisle's agency, Talman was dismissed as Comptroller and succeeded by Vanbrugh. The post was potentially a sinecure, but Vanbrugh took its duties seriously; he also joined the board of Greenwich Hospital in 1703. He set out to learn the business of architecture, helped not only by Hawksmoor but by the purchase in 1703 of Roland Fréart's 1650 French translation of ANDREA PALLADIO's *Quattro Libri dell' Architettura*. How far he came to see himself as a professional architect can be gauged from his comment in 1719 when the painter Sir James Thornhill was in competition with him—neither being successful—for the Surveyorship of Works. Painters, Vanbrugh wrote, know of architecture only "the great expensive part, as columns, arches, bas reliefs etc. which they just learn enough of, to help fill up their pictures. But to think that such a volatile gentleman as Thornhill shou'd turn his thoughts and application to the duty of a surveyor's business, is a monstrous project."

Vanbrugh's appointment in 1703 as Clarenceux King of Arms, also through Lord Carlisle, was less honorable; when he sold the office in 1725, he told a friend he had obtained it "in jest." Nevertheless, although he did not reside in the College of Arms, he seems to have discharged or delegated his duties, admittedly lucrative and unexacting, with reasonable care. He was a more rounded character than most of the heralds, and Carlisle may have wished to enliven a rather crabbed institution as well as to further his kinsman's career.

In 1704–1705, Vanbrugh designed and built the Queen's Theatre, or Opera House, in the Haymarket, near Saint James's Square. The acoustics of the auditorium, which burned down in 1789, were at the start disastrous, and Vanbrugh's last two full-length plays were inaudibly performed there in 1705. Three years later, the insertion of a false ceiling improved the sound at the expense of appearance. Vanbrugh's financial involvement both in the building itself and in the staging there of opera lost him a considerable amount of money over several years. There is no evidence that he ever made designs for stage sets, but he must have supplied a drawing for the "prospect of Blenheim Castle" shown as an *intermezzo* in 1707.

In August 1704, the duke of Marlborough had led the British and Austrian armies to victory over the forces of France and Bavaria at Blindheim on the Danube. This event, not the end but the turning point of the War of the Spanish Succession, seemed in England to warrant a special reward for Marlborough. He was granted the manor of Woodstock and apparently the gift of a house there. Marlborough had initially been prepared to pay for the house himself when he approached Vanbrugh with the idea of something resembling but surpassing Castle Howard; the prospect of a bounty to which no limit had been set changed Blenheim from a private habitation to "a Monument of the Queen's Glory," as Vanbrugh put it, or a commemoration of the deed not the doer. The scale of the house (1705–1716) was to be vast and was to increase in execution. But by 1710 the project was in serious trouble. The flow of government money was stopped; both Marlborough and his duchess were losing favor with Queen Anne and the nation, and the conspicuous magnificence of their as yet unroofed mansion became the focus of their misfortune. By May 1712, when the Treasury stopped all payments, the main buildings were roofed but not habitable; at the end of that year the Marlboroughs, dismissed from their offices, went into voluntary exile. Work was resumed in 1716 after Marlborough's reinstatement, but in November, the duchess, who distrusted all architects and detested both Vanbrugh and his works, provoked his resignation. With the aid of James Moore, a cabinetmaker, and, in 1722–1725, of Hawksmoor, she made Blenheim a home. She engaged in futile litigation against everyone who had been connected with the work under Vanbrugh— four hundred defendants; ultimately, the Treasury paid for the greatest part of Blenheim, while the duchess grudgingly paid but easily could afford the remaining fraction. In spite of "that B.B.B.B. old B.," as Vanbrugh called her, the architect received the fees due to him.

Most of the construction of Blenheim is well-documented by accounts and letters, its design less so. When work began, Vanbrugh was an architect of six years' experience and application; nevertheless, Hawksmoor later wrote that at that stage "the

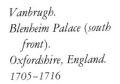

Vanbrugh. Blenheim Palace (south front). Oxfordshire, England. 1705–1716

builders could not stir an inch without me," and as official assistant Hawksmoor was responsible for drawings, detailing, and central management. Blenheim repeats several features of Castle Howard: the long range of state rooms on the south front facing the garden, the use of internal corridors both for convenience and for their scenic perspective value, the reinforcement of a heroic scale of massing by the application of a giant pilaster order, and the arrangement of quadrant passages linking the *corps de logis* to wings set at right angles to it so as to make a broad court on the north, entrance, side. But at Blenheim, Vanbrugh's brief included the provision of a gallery, which he placed on the west side of the house; it was balanced by the private apartments on the east in such a way that these features appear from the court as wings but on the outside form parts of the *corps de logis*.

Contemporaries referred to Blenheim "Castle" rather than "Palace," and although this is not unconnected with the French term *château,* meaning "great house," it accords well with Vanbrugh's growing interest in what he called the "castle air." The eruption of both plan and elevations at Blenheim into corner towers and the proliferation of the roofline into lanterns and pinnacles are without doubt deliberate reminiscences of the great romantic houses of the late Elizabethan age which, in their turn, were based on a revival of late Gothic ideas of chivalry and castles. In literature, some parallel is to be found in the admission by some critics in Vanbrugh's time that Shakespeare and Spenser must be judged by their own rules and standards rather than those of antiquity, at a time when those writers were remote enough from the medievalism of Spenser's poetry and Shakespeare's historical plays to be noteworthy.

But Blenheim is not medieval in its architectural vocabulary except for a row of battlements in the kitchen court nor is it as disjointed as its picturesque outlines might at first suggest. Originally, the giant order was to have been Doric, appropriate to military and heroic subjects, but after the building and the order were started, Vanbrugh,

having decided to increase the height, was obliged to use instead the proportionately slenderer Corintian Order. The detail is handled with the impeccable but idiomatic assurance Hawksmoor brought to it, and even the clamorous rooftop enrichment is built up from basically classical forms. Neither the corner towers nor several intermediate sections of the elevations show the giant order, but Vanbrugh adopted the device, used notably by Le Vau at Vaux-le-Vicomte and in the College of the Four Nations in Paris, of a single-story Doric order running through the articulation of the larger order. This second order appears fully in the quadrants and linking colonnades on the north side; its entablature continues through the middle of the north front and along the sides and the south front. Although it disappears in the corner towers, which are textured by banded rustication, it is still implied in the big labels placed, at the same level,

Vanbrugh.
Blenheim Palace (kitchen court).
Oxfordshire, England.
1705–1716

Vanbrugh.
Blenheim Palace (north front).
Oxfordshire, England.
1705–1716

Vanbrugh.
Blenheim Palace (hall).
Oxfordshire, England.
1705–1716

below the upper windows. Through such formal devices the varied textures and shapes of the whole building are coherently related: towers, colonnades, linking bays, and the central block from which the hall projects both outward into the portico and upward into a clearstory.

Appropriately for a martial and political monument, Blenheim is ornamented by trophies of arms and heraldic details such as the British lion clutching the French cockerel and ducal coronets surmounting overturned fleurs-de-lys; above the garden front stands a colossal bust of Louis XIV surrounded by trophies, all captured by Marlborough in Tournai in 1709 and sent back to Blenheim three years later. Much of the detailing, including the interior of the hall, was designed by Hawksmoor.

Vanbrugh coined his term "the castle air" for Kimbolton Castle, near Huntingdon, a courtyard house whose interior ranges had been rebuilt in the 1690s. He told the owner, the earl of Manchester, that to have used "pillasters, and what the orders require could never have been born with the rest of the Castle"; instead, his ashlar façades, astylar and crenellated but regular, would "make a very noble and masculine shew." As a precedent, he cited the neo-Norman refacing of the Upper Ward of Windsor Castle by HUGH MAY in the 1670s. Vanbrugh attempted to forearm his patron, who was then in Venice, against Italian criticism by appealing to native English tradition and to the still almost universal principle of symmetry. But in a further letter he wrote of Kimbolton as a demonstration that "tis certainly the figure and proportions that make the most pleasing fabrick, and not the delicacy of the ornaments."

Vanbrugh's work at Kimbolton (1707–1710) comprised the rebuilding of the south and west ranges and part of the east. The design of the overbearing Doric portico built in 1719 in the middle of the east front is not his but is due to ALESSANDRO GALILEI, whose signed drawing for it survives. Hawksmoor made some drawings for Kimbolton, but there is no evidence that he was involved in designing there. As Vanbrugh gained in knowledge and experience, his reliance on

Hawksmoor decreased. We should not imagine that Vanbrugh was motivated by the desire to dispense with his help; that he was able to do so in subsequent works, however, was certainly a consequence of his adoption of a style much less dependent on ornament than that of Castle Howard and Blenheim. So, too, is Hawksmoor's style in subsequent independent works, but ultimately the difference between his style and Vanbrugh's is definable without the help of higher criticism: Hawksmoor had invented the plainer style as early as the 1690s, and Vanbrugh learned how to use it.

The "castle air" was also to be found in the second house Vanbrugh designed for himself, Chargate, near Esher in Surrey (1709–1710). In 1714, he sold this house to the earl of Clare, who renamed it Claremont and subsequently, as Duke of Newcastle, commissioned Vanbrugh to remodel and greatly extend it (1715–1720). The original Chargate was modest in size; it was H-shaped in plan, and like Kimbolton it was astylar and crenellated. Towers and chimneys formed further projections in both plan and silhouette and gave the house the appearance of a toy castle or the stage setting for historical plays; in this respect, the neomedievalism of Chargate is more literal than that of Blenheim.

It is, however, impossible to separate the strands in Vanbrugh's imagination which run directly to the Middle Ages from those which represented that period through the romanticism of later Tudor and Jacobean architecture—the style which HORACE WALPOLE called "King James's Gothic." In 1708, Vanbrugh had made a literal incursion into that manner with the design of the main staircase at the south end of the hall at Audley End, Essex, a house built in 1603–1616. Archeological investigation has recently introduced doubt about both the date of the staircase and Vanbrugh's involvement with it. Nevertheless, his engagement there in 1708 is documented, and the screen, of two tiers of open arches, offers the same kind of transparency between major spaces as that between the hall and the staircases at Castle Howard and Blenheim; the formula would be recreated in one of Vanbrugh's late works, the hall at Grimsthorpe.

In about 1710 Vanbrugh began work on Kings Weston, near Bristol, which was structurally complete by 1714 although much of the interior was not executed until the 1760s. With Kings Weston, Vanbrugh's adoption of a plainer style was complete. In plan the house is roughly square, with a deep recess at the back which provides light for the central staircase. Each elevation is symmetrical, but each has a different pattern of articulation by projections or recesses. An order is used only on

Vanbrugh.
Kimbolton Castle (rebuilding of west, south, and part of the east ranges).
Huntingdon, England.
1707–1710

the entrance front, for an applied portico; most of the windows have no architraves but seem merely punched out of the walls like those illustrated in Palladio's *Architettura*. The house depends inevitably on its "figure and proportions," on the soft shading of its ashlar façades, and on the battlemented arcade in the center of its roof which contains all the chimneys.

Whig allegiance did not preclude Vanbrugh's membership from 1711 to 1715 in the commission for building new London churches, although no churches were built to his designs. In comparing his memorandum to his fellow commissioners' with one composed by Wren, most writers single out Vanbrugh's emphasis on grandeur and magnificence and neglect the characteristic common sense embodied in his "Proposals." Some of his observations read as if they had been phrased by Hawksmoor, who was a servant and not a member of the commission. Conceivably, the document resulted from collaboration, but the original is in Vanbrugh's hand and must be accepted at face value. To attribute to Vanbrugh, however—as has been done—a share in the design of Hawksmoor's churches is to misunderstand both the relationship between the two architects and the nature of the style which Hawksmoor invented and Vanbrugh adopted.

Vanbrugh's personal charm seems in general to have earned him friends, but his capacity for speaking his mind made him some enemies. The duchess of Marlborough's enmity has already been mentioned; others arose from his growing professionalism and his distaste for the incompetent. His loyalty to the duke of Marlborough, however, after the latter's dismissal, caused Vanbrugh the loss of the comptrollership on March 31, 1713 after the misdirection of a private letter in which he had written in the duke's favor. On the accession of George I in August 1714, Marlborough was reinstated and Vanbrugh received a knighthood; officially this was a reward for his services as a herald, but Marlborough was his sponsor and this was surely the "something lasting" for which in 1710 the duke had counseled him to wait. In January 1715, Vanbrugh was reinstated as Comptroller, in a newly constituted Board of Works which was intended to assist the Surveyor, Wren, who was now eighty-three. In June, Vanbrugh was additionally appointed Surveyor of Gardens and Waters; this office, in charge of royal gardens and ornamental waters and also the water supply of the palaces, was created for him by Lord Carlisle and was not entirely a sinecure. Vanbrugh and Carlisle alike were concerned both with the reform of the Office of Works and with the development of gardens. It was perhaps at the

Vanbrugh. Kings Weston. Avon, England. c.1710–1714

same time that Vanbrugh was offered the surveyorship but in his own words "refused it out of tenderness" for Wren. Until 1719, he attended most of the board's meetings, motivated at first by concern for Wren as much as his own ambition, and later, when Wren was superseded by WILLIAM BENSON, by mistrust of the latter. As Comptroller he was in charge of the completion of rooms in the northeast corner of Hampton Court; he also tried without success to interest George I in the colossal enlargement of Kensington and Saint James's Palaces as well as the extension of Hampton Court. But when in 1719, after little more than a year in office, Benson was dismissed as Surveyor, Vanbrugh, who had exposed his incompetence, did not succeed to the post. As the Royal Works entered a period of undistinguished achievement, he turned more to private architecture, his friends, and his family.

At the age of fifty-five he had married, in January 1719, Henrietta Maria Yarburgh, nearly thirty years his junior, whom he had known for several years. The marriage seems to have been a conventionally happy one, and in spite of an inclination toward delicate health Lady Vanbrugh outlived her husband by half a century. The only child of the marriage to survive infancy, Charles, was born in 1720.

Lady Vanbrugh's second cousin, Henrietta Godolphin, had married the duke of Newcastle in 1717. Vanbrugh had played some part in the arrangement of this match, but for him the architectural patronage of the duke was of greater significance. He refitted Newcastle House in Lincoln's

Vanbrugh.
Bridge, Blenheim Palace.
Oxfordshire, England.
1705–1716

Vanbrugh.
Vanbrugh Castle.
Greenwich, England.
1718–c.1721

Inn Fields, London (1714–1717) and Nottingham Castle (1719) for the duke and, as already mentioned, sold him not only his own house at Chargate but also the idea of its transformation into Claremont, a mansion of characteristically Vanbrughian extent. In 1716–1717, he removed the medieval trimmings from the house and added two long wings with round-headed window arcades, extending altogether three hundred feet along the contour of the land. In 1719–1720, he added, asymmetrically behind one wing, the two-story Great Room, approximately one hundred feet long and the largest single room he ever built. All this was demolished in 1769 to make way for a new house. Although Vanbrugh's influence can be traced in some buildings on the Claremont estate, nothing survives of his work there except some garden walls and the Belvedere, built in 1715 on a hill behind the house. This four-turreted and crenellated summerhouse has a roof terrace which for-

merly afforded wide views over the countryside and perhaps suggested to the architect the "castle" he later built for himself at Greenwich. The charming pedimented gallery pew he built for Newcastle in 1723–1725 survives in Old Esher church.

The sale of Chargate in 1714 left Vanbrugh with no country home. However, between 1713 and 1716 he made occasional use of rooms he had fitted up in the ruins of Woodstock Manor facing the building works at Blenheim. In 1709, he had offered the duchess of Marlborough a paper of "Reasons" for preserving the manor; first, the historical and sentimental associations of the home of Henry II's mistress, and second, its picturesque quality in an otherwise bare part of the view from Blenheim. Its convenience for surveillance of the Blenheim works or for the lodging of their architect was not stressed nor was the view it offered of one of the features of Blenheim about which Vanbrugh cared inordinately—the Great Bridge or viaduct over the valley north of the house, which had been begun in 1706 but stood until 1721 without the necessary earthworks to complete the road. By that time a different approach route to the house had been established, and the intended arcaded superstructure which would have clarified Vanbrugh's acknowledgment in his design to the covered bridge in Palladio's *Architettura* was never built. Utility must always have come well below visual effect in the attractions of the bridge, and Vanbrugh perhaps considered it also as a giant emblem of *Brug* (bridge), his own name. The duchess of Marlborough counted thirty-three rooms inside the bridge, and some have fireplaces; Vanbrugh, however, told her that "if at last there is a house found in that Bridge your Grace will go and live in it." The interior has been inaccessible since the level of the lake was raised in the 1760s.

However great the pleasure Vanbrugh acknowledged in building Blenheim as "a Palace for another," his taste for his own habitation was very different in scale. A considerable number of designs survive, from his hand or his office, for small and picturesque houses, the majority probably made toward 1720. Three or four such private houses by or attributed to him, mostly near London, survived into the late nineteenth century. There are also several similar designs in another hand, possibly copies of his originals, in a collection of drawings compiled in the eighteenth century by someone connected with Kings Weston.

In March 1717, Vanbrugh rented a house in Greenwich; the locality pleased him, and in 1718 he began to build Vanbrugh Castle on a site at the top of Greenwich Hill with an extensive view of both London and the lower reaches of the River

Thames. He moved into the castle with his wife at the beginning of 1720, but with the expectation of children to come he must already have decided to enlarge the house. Thus by the end of 1721, the original modest symmetrically planned house had been doubled in size by the addition of a second range, equally symmetrical in itself but so different in plan that the asymmetry of the whole anticipates the picturesque castles of the late eighteenth century. Both parts are of brick, three stories high; the turrets of the first and the chimneys of the second building combine with the corbel tables under the parapets to give the definitive formulation of the "castle air." The original single-story kitchens do not survive, but successive additions as well as demolitions were made until the early twentieth century; after many years as a school, the house with its small intimate rooms has recently been restored to domestic use.

Nothing now survives of the four other houses which Vanbrugh built (1719–1725) in the field south of the castle with a pseudo-medieval gatehouse intended for members of his family. Two of the houses were crenellated "towers" and one a bungalow, while Vanbrugh House (known as Mince-Pie House) had the richness of contour that is common to Vanbrugh Castle, to Blenheim, and to Seaton Delaval (1720–1728) but was devoid of specifically medieval detail. The buildings in Vanbrugh's field were placed with a seeming casualness and interspersed with planted trees, and this modest private estate was the precursor of both the picturesque village and the garden suburb of succeeding centuries.

Seaton Delaval, Northumberland, is both the most compact and linguistically the most complex of Vanbrugh's larger houses. The main block was gutted by fire in 1822 and remains uninhabited although it has been reroofed, glazed, and secured. Seaton Delaval was designed with a great room above the two-story hall; this room originally ran the whole length of the attic, like the great upper chamber at Wollaton, the late Elizabethan house closest in feeling to both Blenheim and Seaton. The latter has, as much as Blenheim, "the rise and fall, the advance and recess, with other diversity of form" which ROBERT ADAM and JAMES ADAM found in Vanbrugh's buildings, but whereas Blenheim sprawls on a vast scale, Seaton consists of a single nearly square block joined to the service wings by a single-story arcade forming a long rectangular forecourt. The corners of the main building are marked by octagonal turrets, features not uncommon in Elizabethan houses. These rise only as far as the main roofline; above this level are the attic room, two groups of chimneys, and the upper stages of the two staircase towers placed at the

Vanbrugh.
Seaton Delaval.
Northumberland, England.
1720–1728

sides of the house. These varied projections in plan and elevation, and the diverse rustication of the stair towers and the north (entrance) front, suggest a picturesque recreation of an Elizabethan "castle." Other aspects of Seaton, however, are unequivocally eighteenth-century: the neo-Palladian proportions and detail of windows, and the elegant tetrastyle portico on the south front. These features are in fact characteristic of Vanbrugh's later architecture and of his response to the extraordinary growth of interest in Palladio during the first quarter of the eighteenth century in England.

Of the interior of Seaton Delaval little remains beyond the walls, some small rooms, and the two-story blind arcading around the hall. The saloon on the garden front must originally have been a room as elegant as the portico outside it: it occupied the whole width of the garden front and was divided into three sections by screens of columns. The hall and the two oval staircases, being lined with ashlar, have survived better than the other interiors; nevertheless, in these places fire and weathering have added a degree of coarseness to detailing that was never as refined as that of Castle Howard and Blenheim. This coarseness is quite appropriate both to the safeguarded romantic ruin that Seaton Delaval has become and to the rugged landscape of northeastern England which Vanbrugh himself once contrasted with relish to the "tame sneaking south." Some of the house's character, however, results from the paucity of Vanbrugh's personal supervision: he visited Seaton three times at the most and depended otherwise on local craftsmen and a local clerk of works. Castle Howard could not have been built successfully in this way, and Vanbrugh should be credited not only for the setting, massing, and internal planning of Seaton but also for a design which could successfully be carried out by correspondence and by proxy. In 1721–1722, he prepared designs for refacing and regularizing Lumley Castle, Durham, and for remodeling internally the north range; again, the work was entrusted to local craftsmen, and much of the interior work was of a conventional kind. The structure of the castle, however, largely dates from the fourteenth century, and the "castle air" which had to be designed at Kimbolton was taken over ready-made at Lumley and transformed into a curious hybrid by the blocking of original lancet windows and the insertion of regular sash windows and small oval lights.

The extent of Vanbrugh's medievalism should not be exaggerated, in spite of his appreciation of old Woodstock Manor and his passionate appeal in 1719 for the preservation of the Tudor "Holbein" Gate of Whitehall Palace, which delayed its demolition for another forty years. Nor was medievalism his prerogative alone: he shared this interest with Hawksmoor, WILLIAM DICKINSON, and even Wren, and a fragile thread runs through English architecture from the sixteenth century to the eighteenth, in which the survival of the Gothic style is scarcely distinguishable from its revival. Vanbrugh's relation to Palladianism was more complex, more individual, and more central to his art.

When, in 1703, he had asked a friend abroad to buy for him Fréart's translation of Palladio, Vanbrugh specifically mentioned "the plans of most of the houses he built." Very probably he already knew the book and wished to use it as a practical manual; his debt to Palladio was considerable. His larger house plans bear a general resemblance to Palladio's, and his remark of 1707 about the priority of shape and proportion over delicate ornament may reflect his study of both the text and the illustrations of Palladio's treatise as well as his absorption of the plainer style developed by Hawksmoor. By 1715, both architects, and also THOMAS ARCHER, the most obviously baroque of English architects, had introduced into designs the three-light Venetian window or *serliana* which is accepted as one of the hallmarks of neo-Palladian-

ism. The first major neo-Palladian publication, however, volume one of COLEN CAMPBELL's *Vitruvius Britannicus* (1715), contains no designs with the motif. Vanbrugh's later architecture is not only plainer than his earlier, its detail is also predominantly derived from sixteenth-century Italian rather than French or baroque models. He could never be called a Palladian in the sense of a follower of a stylistic revival, and several members of the early Palladian group, including Campbell, became rivals rather than colleagues in the Office of Works. Palladio's effect on Vanbrugh was earlier, more personal, and, as the Temple at Castle Howard will show, more fundamental than on those who saw in the Italian master either a guarantee of good taste without sensibility or the source of a stock of instantly reproducible designs.

The third earl of Shaftesbury's *Letter Concerning Design* (1712) demanded a new British style, but did not characterize it except (by implication) as antibaroque, anti-French and anti-Wren; with felicitous timing, Campbell promoted the Palladian Revival as the answer to this demand. It must be accepted that, although Vanbrugh was as much a Whig as Shaftesbury or those to whom his *Letter* was directed, the architect of Blenheim had little prospect of success in promoting an alternative national style of his own in the face of both Campbell's publicity in books and his intrigues within the Office of Works. Nevertheless, although in fact he failed, between 1715 and about 1720 Vanbrugh himself seems not only to have entertained this aim but also to have believed that he could achieve it. The surveyorship might have given him a degree of influence comparable to that which Shaftesbury at least believed Wren to have exerted, and the plainer manner of Vanbrugh's later works had some of the reproducibility which helped to establish neo-Palladianism. Moreover,

Vanbrugh.
Temple, Castle Howard.
Yorkshire, England.
1725–1726 (not completed
until 1728)

Vanbrugh.
Eastbury.
Dorset, England.
1718–1726

for Vanbrugh, authoritarian control in architecture was evidently acceptable in the right hands—his own rather than those of Benson or JAMES THORNHILL: his opinion of Thornhill's claims to architecture has already been mentioned.

Reproducibility of style was put to the test in one class of buildings, to which the combination of visual economy and structural massiveness was singularly appropriate. These were the buildings constructed for the Board of Ordnance from about 1716 onward at Woolwich, Chatham, Devonport, Berwick-on-Tweed, and elsewhere. Their designer has not been identified, and there may have been more than one, since their indebtedness to Vanbrugh is not uniform. In the same years, and in the same style of arched windows, portholes, and unmolded string courses, he was probably responsible for the great kitchen at Saint James's Palace (1716–1717) and the new pumphouse by the Thames supplying Windsor Castle (1718). Contemporary references by the antiquary William Stukeley give certainty to his authorship of the Water Tower on Kensington Palace Green (1722), which was similar in style to Vanbrugh Castle, and the rough stone wellhouse on the Great North Road at Skelbrooke, Yorkshire (c.1720).

Vanbrugh was concerned from about 1715 with the design of a house at Eastbury, Dorset (1718–1738), an estate which George Doddington had bought in 1709. Of the several projects known, some predate the "New Design for a Person of Quality" of 1716 illustrated in the second (1717) volume of Campbell's *Vitruvius Britannicus*. Building had commenced by 1718, but the definitive design of the main block shown in Campbell's third (1725) volume may not have been reached until after 1720 when Doddington died and was succeeded by his nephew George Bubb. The house was finally completed in 1738 by ROGER MORRIS without the central attic designed by Vanbrugh but with the addition of a pediment to his giant hexastyle portico of ringed Doric columns. Eastbury was larger and more ostentatious, but no less plain, than Seaton Delaval; it was also expensive, costing with its gardens and outbuildings almost half as much as Blenheim. In 1775, George Bubb Doddington's heir, unable to maintain such a house, demolished it with gunpowder, leaving only part of the west wing and a section of the forecourt arcading. Campbell also records two of the garden buildings, of which the more remarkable was the Temple. This in reality was no more than a hexastyle Corinthian portico, but its order was on nearly the scale of that of the house: although "Palladian," indeed, almost neoclassical in severity, it was thus Vanbrughian in scale.

Vanbrugh was also considering Grimsthorpe

Castle, Lincolnshire, as early as 1715, the date he inscribed on a survey plan of it; the occasion may have been the elevation of its owner, his old friend Robert Bertie, earl of Lindsey, to the dukedom of Ancaster. Vanbrugh may already at that date have designed the façade and interior of a new hall on the north side of Grimsthorpe, a house which in spite of the defensive connotations of its name was merely a large residence in four ranges around a rectangular courtyard. In July 1723, the duke died, but Vanbrugh understood that his son would "go on upon the General Design I made for his Father last Winter and which was approved of by himself." In the absence of documentary evidence it is therefore usually assumed that all the executed work at Grimsthorpe dates from Vanbrugh's last years, that is to say the rebuilding of both the two-story hall and the rectangular three-story towers flanking it at the north corners. The "General Design," recorded in volume 3 of *Vitruvius Britannicus,* was for a complete and symmetrical rebuilding of the house, with south and west elevations closer than any other by Vanbrugh to Campbell's style of Palladianism; the south front indeed would have amounted to a revision of Campbell's design for Houghton which appears in the same volume. However, the fenestration rhythms are un-Palladian, and all the Grimsthorpe basement windows have bold rustication and gross keystones. The work seems to have stopped in 1726 soon after Vanbrugh's death, only the north range being completed. The hall replaced a room built in the 1680s; both inside and outside its single theme is a continuous arcade on both stories. On the outside wall the arches form windows and on the inside wall they are blind, while at the ends they are open to form Vanbrugh's characteristic screens between the hall and the symmetrically placed staircases leading to the towers. Vanbrugh's most Italianate

Vanbrugh.
Grimsthorpe Castle (gallery door).
Lincolnshire, England.
1722–1726

Vanbrugh.
Grimsthorpe Castle (north range).
Lincolnshire, England.
1722–1726

detail is to be found in the towers, both in the Venetian windows and pedimented frames of the exterior and, within, in the stair landing doorcases. These, with downward tapering imposts, derive from those designed by MICHELANGELO for the side palaces of the Capitol in Rome and since 1702 available in engravings.

From 1718–1719, Vanbrugh was occupied at both Castle Howard and, for Viscount Cobham, at Stowe, Buckinghamshire, with garden buildings and perhaps with garden design also. Lord Carlisle's daughter later, in a printed poem, credited her father with the whole invention of Castle Howard; although this cannot have been the case, the placing of buildings and other features there owed a good deal to the collaboration between the earl and his architects. The garden designer at Stowe, as at Claremont and Eastbury, was CHARLES BRIDGEMAN, but at Stowe especially the early phases of the landscape garden appear to be the result of discussion between Bridgeman, Cobham, and Vanbrugh. Of the latter's buildings at Stowe, the Rotonda (1719), an open peripteral temple, survives, although the dome has been rebuilt to a lower profile and its original appearance can best be judged from the replica, perhaps also from Vanbrugh's design, at Duncombe, Yorkshire. He probably designed also the portico on the north front of the mansion at Stowe (c.1720); it bears a generic resemblance as close to that at Blenheim as to the one designed a few years later at Lyme Park, Cheshire, by GIACOMO LEONI, and the fact that

Leoni also worked at Stowe does not therefore show that he designed the portico there.

At Stowe, Lord Cobham gradually developed a political and philosophical program of meaning in the gardens; at Castle Howard, the iconography seems to have been personal to Lord Carlisle. The big obelisk at the entrance of the avenue to the house, however, was a tribute to Marlborough, erected in 1714; its form was probably due to Vanbrugh, as were the Pyramid Gate (1719) and the curtain wall with pseudo-medieval bastions of about the same date. The Pyramid Gate was the first of several hilltop structures; some were to be designed by Hawksmoor, but as remarkable as any of them is the Temple (to use the simple name Vanbrugh gave it). This was built in 1725–1728 under the faithful eye of Hawksmoor, although its interior decoration, by the stuccoist Francesco Vassali (1737–1739) may be independent of either architect. Vanbrugh's last building is his most profound, most literal, but also most personal and unorthodox derivation from Palladio. Formally, its domed central cube and four projecting porticos are derived from Palladio's Villa Almerigo or Rotonda outside Vicenza, the conscious prototype of four English Palladian villas. Vanbrugh's version is much smaller and more erect, but its Virgilian feeling, entirely concordant with that of the landscape around it, is due partly to the simplicity of its "figure and proportions" and partly to Vanbrugh's understanding that Palladio's building, like his own, was designed not as a residence but primarily for the contemplation of diverse aspects of the owner's estates.

Late in August 1725, Vanbrugh was seized by an asthmatic complaint. He recovered, but after a normally active winter he succumbed to a short illness, probably of a similar nature, on March 26, 1726. He was buried in the family vault in Saint Stephen Walbrook, London. His widow retained the house in Whitehall but chose not to live in Vanbrugh Castle, instead building herself a cottage nearby.

Apart from the designs for Castle Howard and Blenheim which passed through Hawksmoor's hands, the chief surviving deposits of Vanbrugh's designs are in the Victoria and Albert Museum, London, and in an album at Elton Hall. The latter contains a mixture of designs by Vanbrugh and by the Anglo-Irish Palladian architect EDWARD LOVETT PEARCE, who was Vanbrugh's cousin and probably briefly, in the early 1720s, his pupil. Otherwise there were no pupils or, except for the Board of Ordnance designer, no followers.

Neither the more flamboyant nor the plainer aspects of Vanbrugh's architecture were to mid-eighteenth-century taste, but after about 1770 his dramatic massing and his anticipation of effects of the sublime and the picturesque came to be appreciated by figures as significant as Horace Walpole, the Adam brothers, and Sir Joshua Reynolds. In 1809, JOHN SOANE called him "the Shakespeare of architects," and late English neoclassicism hides a vein of his massive simplicity which came to the surface in the work of nineteenth-century engineer architects who carried on the style of the Ordnance buildings. Literary scholars, interested in his plays, were the first to investigate his biography, and it was not until the reappraisal of the 1920s that his architectural expression came to be seen as anything other than universal solecism. The greatest single step forward was the publication in 1928 of his correspondence. Since then not only has his architecture been revalued and at last understood, but more recently archives have yielded much information about his family connections on both sides. The rediscovery of his account book (Journal of all Receipts, Payments and other Transactions) for 1715–1726 has made possible, uniquely among English eighteenth-century architects, a detailed picture of daily life both familial and professional.

KERRY DOWNES

WORKS

1700–1712, Castle Howard (west wing designed by Thomas Robinson in 1753–1759), Yorkshire, England. *1701, Vanbrugh House, Whitehall; *1704–1705, The Queen's Theatre (Opera House), Haymarket; London. 1705–1716, Blenheim Palace (completed by the Duchess of Marlborough and Nicholas Hawksmoor in 1722–1725), Oxfordshire, England. 1707–1710, Kimbolton Castle (rebuilding of west, south, and part of the east ranges), Huntingdon, England. 1708, Audley End (staircase and screen), Essex, England. *1709–1710, Chargate, Surrey, England. c.1710–1714, Kings Weston, Avon, England. 1714, Obelisk, Castle Howard, Yorkshire, England. *1715–1720, Claremont (destroyed except for the Belvedere), Surrey, England. 1716–1717, Great Kitchen, Saint James's Palace, London. (A)1718, Pumphouse, Windsor, England. 1718–c.1721, Vanbrugh Castle, Greenwich, England. *1718–1726, Eastbury (completed by Roger Morris in 1738), Dorset, England. 1719, Pyramid Gate, Castle Howard, Yorkshire, England. *c.1719–1724, Stowe (rotonda, portico on north front, additions to the house, and garden buildings), Buckinghamshire, England. *1719–1725, Vanbrugh Fields Estate, Greenwich, England. (A)c.1720, Wellhouse, Skelbrooke, Yorkshire, England. 1720–1728, Seaton Delaval, Northumberland, England. 1721–1722, Lumley Castle (refacing and remodeling north range), Durham, England. 1722, Somersby Hall, Lincolnshire, England. *(A)1722, Water Tower, Kensington Palace, England. 1722–1726, Grimsthorpe Castle (north range), Lincolnshire, England. 1723–1725, Newcastle Pew, Esher Old Church, Surrey, England. 1725–1726, Temple (not completed until 1728), Castle Howard, Yorkshire, England.

BIBLIOGRAPHY

CAMPBELL, COLEN (1715–1725)1967 *Vitruvius Britannicus.* Reprint. New York: Blom.

COLVIN, H. M. (editor) 1976 *The History of the King's Works: V. 1660–1782.* London: H.M. Stationery Office.

COLVIN, H. M., and CRAIG, MAURICE J. (editors) 1964 *Architectural Drawings in the Library of Elton Hall by Sir John Vanbrugh and Sir Edward Levett Pearce.* Oxford University Press.

DOWNES, KERRY 1966 *English Baroque Architecture.* London: Zwemmer.

DOWNES, KERRY 1967 "The Kings Weston Book of Drawings." *Architectural History* 10:7–88.

DOWNES, KERRY 1977 *Vanbrugh.* London: Zwemmer. Includes the complete text of John Vanbrugh's "Account Book."

GREEN, DAVID 1951 *Blenheim Palace.* London: Country Life.

HUSEBOE, ARTHUR R. 1974 "Vanbrugh: Additions to the Correspondence." *Philological Quarterly* 53:135–140.

HUSSEY, CHRISTOPHER 1967 *English Gardens and Landscapes 1700–1750.* London: Country Life.

KIMBALL, FISKE 1944 "Romantic Classicism in Architecture." *Gazette des Beaux-Arts* Period 6 25:95–112.

ROSENBERG, ALBERT 1966 "New Light on Vanbrugh." *Philogosical Quarterly* 45:603–613.

VANBRUGH, JOHN 1927–1928 *Complete Works.* Edited by Bonany Dobrée and Geoffrey F. Webb. London: Nonesuch Press. Volume 4 contains the letters of John Vanbrugh.

WHISTLER, LAURENCE 1954 *The Imagination of Vanbrugh and his Fellow Artists.* London: Batsford.

VAN BRUNT, HENRY

One of the leading American architects of the post-Civil War period and the principal critic and theorist of the profession, Henry Van Brunt (1832–1903) was born in Boston. Van Brunt attended Boston Latin School and Harvard College, from which he was graduated in 1854. He early manifested a strong literary bent, but turned instead to architecture for a career. He first entered the office of George Snell, a Boston architect, where he stayed from 1855 to 1857. In the fall of 1857, he joined with Charles Dexter Gambrill and GEORGE B. POST to study in the new atelier formed by RICHARD MORRIS HUNT in New York. He remained there till 1860. From his study at the Ecole des Beaux-Arts in Paris, from his travels, and from his work with HECTOR MARTIN LEFUEL, Hunt had brought back the most serious, disciplined, and cosmopolitan notions of architectural

training, and his pupils entered a world of style and professional idealism hitherto unknown in this country. This episode marked a turning point in professional training and practice in America, which Van Brunt was later to expound upon in his writings on Hunt and on the state of the architectural profession in the last decades of the century.

Following naval service in the Civil War, Van Brunt formed a professional partnership in Boston with WILLIAM R. WARE(see also WARE AND VAN BRUNT), who had joined a second group of students in Hunt's atelier. Ware and Van Brunt became one of the leading firms in Boston, specializing in institutional, ecclesiastical, and library work. Van Brunt was the acknowledged design partner in the firm, and his work followed the major movements in style in the late nineteenth century, from Gothic Revival through Romanesque and Queen Anne to Classical Revival. His work was most successful in its earliest Gothic phase, with Harvard's Memorial Hall (1865–1878) in Cambridge, Massachusetts, one of the noblest and richest examples of the style in the country. Other noteworthy works of this period were the buildings of the Episcopal Theological School in Cambridge, Massachusetts (1868–1880); the First Church in Boston (1865–1867); and Saint Stephen's Church, Lynn, Massachusetts (1881–1882).

Both partners were strongly committed to professional and educational responsibilities and inaugurated an atelier in their office. Whereas Ware soon became fully involved in the teaching of architecture, Van Brunt combined design with active leadership in the profession. He was secretary of the newly founded American Institute of Architects in 1860 and became president in 1898. He was also a founding member and vice president of the Boston Society of Architects. More important still was his architectural criticism. Beginning in 1859 and continuing to the end of the century, Van Brunt published a number of essays and reviews in which he commented with analytical cogency and

historical awareness upon the conditions and problems of contemporary American architectural practice. The depth of his understanding was enhanced by his wide reading and varied experience, and culminated in the rich articles of the 1890s on the architecture of the 1893 World's Columbian Exposition in Chicago and its implications. Van Brunt was also the first translator into English of EUGÈNE EMMANUEL VIOLLET-LE-DUC's highly influential *Discourses on Architecture* (1875–1881).

In 1885, Van Brunt was asked by his friend Charles Francis Adams, who had recently become president of the Union Pacific Railroad, to design a number of stations in the West. In that year, Frank Howe, who had joined the firm of Ware and Van Brunt in 1868, was sent to Kansas City to set up an office, and two years later Van Brunt himself moved there permanently with his family. Van Brunt and Howe was then the leading firm west of the Mississippi, and the significance of the firm was acknowledged in Van Brunt's selection as one of the chief architects of the World's Columbian Exposition of 1893 in Chicago.

In 1900, Van Brunt set off with his family on a fifteen-month tour of Europe. After his return he was appointed one of the planners of the Louisiana Purchase Exhibition of 1904 in St. Louis, Missouri, but he took sick during a trip East and died in Boston in 1903.

WILLIAM A. COLES

WORKS

1865–1867, First Church (with William R. Ware), Boston. 1865–1878, Memorial Hall (with Ware), Harvard University; 1868–1880, Episcopal Theological School (with Ware); 1870–1871, Weld Hall (with Ware), Harvard University; Cambridge, Mass. *1873–1875, Union Railway Station (with Ware), Worcester, Mass. *1876–1877, Gore Hall Library (stack addition), Harvard University, Cambridge, Mass. 1880–1881, Music Hall, Wellesey, Mass. 1881–1882, Saint Stephen's Church, Lynn, Mass. 1881–1882, Simpson Infirmary, Wellesley, Mass. *1881–1883, University of Michigan Library, Ann Arbor. 1886–1887, Union Pacific Station, Ogden, Utah. 1886–1888, Union Pacific Station, Cheyenne, Wyo. 1887–1889, Rindge Public Library, Cambridge, Mass. *1888–1889, Kansas City Club; *1889–1890, Bullene, Moore, and Emery Store; *1889–1890, Coates House Hotel; Kansas City, Mo. *1892–1893, Electricity Building, World's Columbian Exposition, Chicago. 1893, Union Station, Portland, Ore. *1893–1894, Kansas City Star Building, Mo. 1893–1894, Spooner Library, Lawrence, Kans. 1895–1896, August Meyer House, Kansas City, Mo. *1899, Union Station, Omaha, Neb. 1901, S. B. Armour House, Kansas City, Mo.

BIBLIOGRAPHY

COLES, WILLIAM A. 1967 "Richard Morris Hunt and His Library as Revealed in the Studio Sketchbooks of

Henry Van Brunt." *Art Quarterly* 30:224–238.

COLES, WILLIAM A. (editor) 1969 *Architecture and Society: Selected Essays of Henry Van Brunt.* Cambridge, Mass.: Belknap.

HENNESSEY, WILLIAM JOHN 1979 "The Architectural Works of Henry Van Brunt." Unpublished Ph.D. dissertation, Columbia University, New York.

PILAND, SHERRY 1976 "Henry Van Brunt of the Architectural Firm of Van Brunt and Howe: The Kansas City Years." Unpublished M.A. thesis, University of Missouri, Kansas City.

VAN BRUNT, HENRY 1893 *Greek Lines.* Boston: Houghton Mifflin.

VIOLLET-LE-DUC, EUGÈNE EMMANUEL 1875–1881 *Discourses on Architecture.* Translated by Henry Van Brunt. 2 vols. Boston: Osgood.

WIGHT, PETER B. 1894 "Henry Van Brunt: Architect, Writer, Philosopher." *Inland Architect and News Record* 23:29–30, 41–42, 49–50, 60–61.

VAN CAMPEN, JACOB

Painter and architect, clever mathematician, savant, Seigneur of Randenbroek, Jacob Van Campen (1595–1657) was born in Haarlem, Netherlands. He died at the age of sixty-two, unmarried but wealthy. He was buried in the Saint Jorischurch in Amersfoort, and his tomb, handsomely sculptured probably by Rombout Verhulst, is still to be found there.

The young Jacob Van Campen was trained as a painter. Unfortunately, very little is known of these early years. Van Campen entered the Guild of Saint Luke in Haarlem in 1614. In this town he surely met famous men as LIEVEN DE KEY, Haarlem town architect, and Salomon de Bray. With another inhabitant of Haarlem, PIETER POST, he would work for several years. His first architectural design is the façade of a double house (1625), built for the wealthy merchants Balthasar

and Ioan Coymans in Amsterdam. The building was executed in an Italianate style: the elevation shows two tiers of pilasters: first the Ionic order, superposed by the Corinthian order topped by a low attic, the last feature being remarkable in a time when central gables were frequently used. In designing this façade—the groundplan is by someone else—Van Campen used the measurements of ANDREA PALLADIO and details by VINCENZO SCAMOZZI. Another early work, probably designed by Van Campen, is the lovely House Ten Bosch (1628) at Maarssen, near Utrecht. The groundplan is traditional, but the façade with a giant order and pediment is designed entirely according to the principles given in Scamozzi's *Dell' Idea dell' Architettura Universale* (Venice, 1615), a first in Dutch architecture.

The Girls' Court (1633) at the Municipal Orphanage (Burgerweeshuis) in Amsterdam was designed along the old, irregular buildings of the orphanage to form three wings with a giant Ionic order under a cornice. The measurements and details again follow Scamozzi's principles. Van Campen employed the "feminine" Ionic order as suitable for a girls' court.

Constantijn Huygens, the learned diplomat and secretary of Stadtholder Frederik Hendrik, played an important role in Van Campen's life and his way of thinking. As a result of this friendship, an exchange of ideas took place that resulted in the creation of a number of the most important buildings of the time. Through Huygens, Van Campen received the commission to design a house for Prince Johan Maurits van Nassau that resulted in the creation of the famous Mauritshuis (1633) in The Hague, next to Huygens's own house, built in a similar style. (Whether Jacob Van Campen assisted in designing Huygens's house is not known, but it seems quite probable.) The plans of Van Campen were carried out by Pieter Post during

Van Campen.
Ten Bosch House.
Maarssen, Netherlands.
1628

Van Campen.
Mauritshuis.
The Hague.
1633

Johan Maurits's stay in Brazil. The Mauritshuis was the first building in Holland in which the principles of the classical style could be found not only in the façade but also in the groundplan and in the decoration. Except for a few alterations in the windows and the removal of the chimneys, the small palace is, on the exterior, largely unchanged. The beautiful interiors were demolished during a fire in 1704. The house is built of brick with a giant Ionic order of sandstone. Over the three middle bays rises a pediment with sculptured reliefs.

Several important commissions followed in quick succession: the Amsterdam Theater (1637) after the example of Palladio's Teatro Olympico at Vicenza, the Accijnshuis (Excise House) in Amsterdam (1638), and the alteration and extension of Frederik Hendrik's old palace, Noordeinde, The Hague (1640). The latter was changed into a modern building with a pediment and side wings with arcaded galleries and orders of pilasters carried along all the façades. Van Campen also acted as adviser in the creation of the Marekerk in Leiden. From 1645 dates his design of the Nieuwe Kerk in Haarlem to abut the tower by Lieven de Key (1613). The groundplan consists of a Greek cross inscribed in a square. The ceiling above the cross is barrel-vaulted, whereas the four corners have flat ceilings. A harmonious, spatial atmosphere is created by the disposition of piers and pillars.

Van Campen's main work and certainly his masterpiece is the Amsterdam Town Hall (1647–1665), now Royal Palace. This new town hall replaced an old medieval building that had become too small for the growing and prosperous city of Amsterdam. Van Campen designed both the building and the decoration. The designs were executed in marble by the sculptor Artus Quellien, his principal assistant Rombout Verhulst, and other skilled artists. The size of the building—the street was enlarged to create this city center—and the rich decorations all express the city's glory; the building was simultaneously a monument of the Peace of Munster after eighty years of war with Spain. The building is erected around two inner courts. The exterior consists of a rather low arcade and two tiers of pilasters of the Roman and the Corinthian orders, following the principles of Scamozzi. A hugh pediment with sculptured reliefs shows the oceans of the world, paying homage to Amsterdam. Behind the low arcade, the Vierschaar (High Court of Justice) was situated. Narrow stairs led up to the Burgerzaal (Citizens' Hall) and the Galleries, all ornated with beautiful sculptured reliefs. Van Campen left his work after difficulties in 1654, after which construction was taken over by Daniel Stalpaert. Van Campen never saw his townhall finished: he died in 1657.

CATHARINA L. VAN GRONINGEN

WORKS

1625, Huis Coymans, 177 Keizersgracht, Amsterdam. (A)1628, Ten Bosch House, Maarssen, Netherlands. 1633, Girls' Court, Municipal Orphanage, Amsterdam. *(A)1635, Elswout House, Overveen, near Haarlem, Netherlands. *1637, Theater; 1638, Accijnshuis; Amsterdam *(A)1638, Saxenburg House, Bloemendaal, Netherlands. 1638–1646, Saint Laurens Church (organcase), Alkmaar, Netherlands. 1639–1640, Marekerk (windows and portico; with Arent van 's Gravesande), Leiden, Netherlands. 1640, Noordeinde Palace (rebuilding); The Hague. 1641–1643, Hofwijck (with Constantijn Huygens), Voorburg, Netherlands. 1645–1649, Nieuwe Kerk, Haarlem, Netherlands. 1647–1655, Town Hall (not completed until 1665), Amsterdam. 1655, Laurenskerk (chairs), Alkmaar, Netherlands.

BIBLIOGRAPHY

FREMANTLE, KATHARINE 1959 *The Baroque Townhall of Amsterdam.* Utrecht, Netherlands: Haentjens.
KLUIVER, J. H. 1974 "De orgelarchitectuur van Jacob van Campen." *Koninklijke Nederlandse Oudheidkundige Bond—Bulletin* 73, no. 1:1–18.
MEISCHKE, R. 1966 "De vroegste werken van Jacob van Campen." *Koninklijke Nederlandse Oudheidkundige Bond—Bulletin* 65, no. 5:131–145.
MEISCHKE, R. 1975 "Amsterdams Burgerweeshuis." *Nederlandse monumenten van geschiedenis en kunst* 1975:182–183.
ROSENBERG, JAKOB; SLIVE, SEYMOUR, and KUILE, E. H. TER (1966)1977 *Dutch Art and Architecture.* Harmondsworth, England: Penguin.
SWILLENS, P. T. A. 1961 *Jacob van Campen: Schilder en bouwmeester.* Assen, Netherlands: Van Gorcum.
TERWEN, J. J. 1979 "The Buildings of Johan Maurits van Nassau." In E. van den-Boogaart (editor), *Johan Maurits van Nassau-Siegen, 1604–1679: A Humanist Prince in Europe and Brazil.* The Hague.

VANDELVIRA, ANDRES DE

Of remote Flemish descent, Andres de Vandelvira asserted himself in the middle of the sixteenth cen-

*Van Campen.
Town Hall.
Amsterdam.
1647–1655 (not completed until 1665)*

tury among the masters of the Spanish Renaissance. He was engaged initially with work in Castille, but in 1536 he began a brilliant career in Andalusia, in the cities of Breza and Ubeda, where he founded a true school. In his very personal style, Vandelvira united Castillian severity, the delicacy of Andalusian motifs, and even the Arab taste of Cordoba with the themes developed by the Italian schools of the period, specifically those of DONATO BRAMANTE. One of his five sons, Alonso, an architect in Seville between 1589 and 1609, is the author of a valuable treatise on the cutting of rocks.

PIERRE LENAIN
Translated from French by
Shara Wasserman

WORKS

1536-1559, Church of the Savior; 1540-1575, Hospital of Santiago; c.1560, Palace of Molina; c.1560, Palace of Vazquez; Ubeda, Spain. n.d., Cathedral; n.d., Convent of Saint Francis (apse); n.d., Town Hall (sections); Breza, Spain.

VAN DEN BROEK and BAKEMA

It has recently been said that Jacob B. Bakema (1914-1981) built half of the Dutch buildings since World War II. This may not be true, but surely suggests an active man whose designs are scattered all over the Netherlands and sometimes into Germany and beyond. These buildings reveal the poetic verbiage of Bakema, especially those words coming from Team 10 (a postwar offshoot of the Congrès Internationaux d'Architecture Moderne), which picture him as a messianic deliverer from the rationalized messages of the CIAM.

Although Bakema actually collaborated with CIAM in the Dutch group Opbouw (meaning edification, erection) he soon became a frequent contributor to *Forum,* the vehicle that before and after *Team 10 Primer* stood as the peak of human values and of architectural standards in Holland. Although the structural rationalism of EUGÈNE EMMANUEL VIOLLET-LE-DUC was still a lively issue, functionalism, at least that which cancelled out human imagination, was rendered obsolete in the pages of *Forum* and *Team 10 Primer.* Some of Bakema's buildings, however, adhere to the functional characteristics of oversimplification, sameness, and repetition.

Bakema has always been known as a "social architect," which means that he concentrates on the places of architecture in society and vice versa. This tradition was brought to life in Holland in the older generation by H. P. BERLAGE. Berlage was a socialist; Bakema knew the dire needs of the impoverished and spoke out against social inequities.

In any discussion of Bakema, it is necessary to include J. H. van den Broek (1898-1978), although he never wrote as extensively as Bakema on architecture and his thoughts are thus more inaccessible. Van den Broek was born in Rotterdam and educated at the Rijkswerkschool, Nijmegen, (1913-1917) and at the Technical University, Delft (1919-1924). Before his involvement with other *zakelijkheid* architects van den Broek went into private practice (1927-1937); then into partnership with Johannes Brinkman (1937-1948), and finally Architecten gemeenschap van den Broek en Bakema (1948-until his death in 1978). Van den Broek taught, traveled, received many awards, and was a member of Team 10 in 1963, but did not write under its auspices.

Bakema, on the other hand, a prolific writer, was born in Groningen, and was educated there at the Technical School (1932-1937); at the Academy of Architecture, Amsterdam (1937-1941); and the Technical University, Delft (1939-1940). During World War II he was a prisoner, but escaped and became involved in the underground movement in Groningen. Before joining with van den Broek, Bakema worked with Cor van Eesteren, WILLEM VAN TIJEN and Huig A. Maaskant, and Brinkman and in the Rotterdam Municipal Housing Department (1945).

In the late 1940s van den Broek and Bakema opened what was to become a very large office, with up to two hundred employees. Control of design was always with the principals because of the fifty-one percent advantage they had in the holding company they formed. The large production of buildings recalls the interpretation of Manfredo Tafuri that urban building can be almost entirely explained as capitalist enterprise with speculative aims.

Because of the large output of the partnership it is difficult to describe precisely the product, although one might list bridges within building complexes; the use of concrete and rounded corners; and the mixture of small and large scale are often prevailing tendencies.

The main objective of the functionalism of Bakema and van den Broek was to provide simple shapes, thereby subsuming the artist's ego and concentrating on building types, such as the strokenbouw (row building). The Siedlung Klein Driene (1950-1958) in Hengelo, with F. J. van Gool and J. M. Stocla, carries out the repetitive membering of the Strokenbouw, but is slightly creative in its manipulation of space. Long and short rows of housing units are largely identical and with a facing row of partially enclosed landscape, surround a central space.

More recent housing occurs at Leeuwarden and Kampen (1959–1968) where a heavier, more crafted look appears. Inner galleries are generous enough to allow contact among residents and guests. Although the idea of a strokenbouw is still present, the block is set in the midst of thick greenery.

The reformed church at Nagela (1958–1960) is both awesome, modest, and far from bare simplicity or repetition, although certain purist tones connect it to the modernist tradition. The bell tower dominates the rising lines of concrete and is framed with a low concrete wall. The body of the church is a blank wall toward the front suggesting the strict obedience practiced by the congregation, although a fair amount of light penetrates in the rear wall.

The latest building (only partially constructed) is the office building complex for the computer complex Siemens in Munich. Although designed for commerce, it is a city within a city. Formal interest lies mainly in the lesenes (stripped pilasters) and the color, which makes a clear and lively reading: yellow for "traffic" (hand rails, stairways and doors), red for technical installations, and blue for ventilations. But the main part of the building is of white aluminum. Social interest resides in its nonauthoritarian atmosphere. Bakema is responsible for its pretentionless functional architecture.

The urban project on which the reputation of van den Broek and Bakema almost exclusively depends is the Lijnbaan, a shopping center in the heart of Rotterdam (1949–1953). An open arcade reserved for pedestrians, it was intimately linked with the city's life style. This, together with its link to the Beaux-Arts Rotterdam Town Hall that survived the war, makes it a significant urban plan of the twentieth century. Bakema definitely designed the series of intermittent wood roofs, which give some protection from the weather and are visually attractive. The buildings are noteworthy for their fine detailing of the "new" materials—steel, large glass panes, and concrete.

The only other specifically urban project given as much publicity is the unbuilt Pampus (designed 1965). Drawings show that it was designed to the last detail with buildings arranged around outside *pleinen* (plazas), resembling *de Stijl* and pinwheels. One attractive feature is that all housing units had views of the surrounding waters.

Bakema was a loquacious man with an expansive output of writing. His international renown stems from ideas expressed in the *Team 10 Primer* and two monographs on the two architects by Jürgen Joedicke (1963; 1976). But the book that guarantees Bakema a large readership among Dutch students at the Technisch Hogeschool of Delft is *Woning en Woonomgeving* (1977), a compendium of Bakema's writing up to the early 1970s. They are not systematized, but as loosely as they represent his interests and beliefs, they still have value in terms of social and visual meaning. Bakema wrote that good housing required shops, industries, schools, and churches, and medical and social centers—a development even more comprehensive than the neighborhood unit.

SUZANNE FRANK

WORKS

1948–1951, Department Store ter Meulen-Wassen-van Vorst; 1949–1953, Shopping Center Lijnbaan; Rotterdam, Netherlands. 1950–1958, Siedlung Klein Driene (with F. J. van Gool and J. M. Stocla), Hengelo, Netherlands. 1955–1960, Montessori School, Rotterdam, Netherlands. 1957–1960, Dwelling Tower, Hansaviertel, Berlin. 1958–1960, Reformed Church, Nagele, Netherlands. 1959–1961, Shopping Center and Maisonette Dwellings, Bergen, Netherlands. 1959–1962, Housing Leeuwarden North, Netherlands. 1959–1968, Housing, Leeuwarden and Kampen, Netherlands. 1961–1962, Auditorium Center, Technische Hochschule Delft, Netherlands. 1961–1973, Office for Postal Services, Arnhem, Netherlands. 1962–1972, Housing 'tHool, Eindhoven, Netherlands. 1963–1969, Het Dorp Housing for Handicapped People, Arnhem, Netherlands. 1963–1972, Town Hall, Terneuzen, Netherlands. 1964–1969, Hermes (Students' Club), Rotterdam, Netherlands. 1969–1974, Heineken Brewery, Zoeterwoude, Netherlands.

BIBLIOGRAPHY

BAKEMA, J. B. 1977 *Woning en Woonomgeving.*
Bouwen voor een open Samenleving. 1962 Rotterdam, Netherlands: Museum Boymans-van Beuningen.
GUBITOSI, CAMILLO, and IZZO, ALBERTO (editors) 1976 *Van den Broek/Bakema.* Officina Edizioni Roma.
JOEDICKE, JÜRGEN (editor) 1963 *Das Werk van den Broek und Bakema.* Stuttgart, Germany: Karl Krämer.
JOEDICKE, JÜRGEN 1976 *Architectengemeenschap van den Broek en Bakema: Architecture-Urbanism.* Stuttgart, Germany: Karl Krämer.
NEWMAN, OSCAR 1961 *CIAM '59 in Otterlo: Dokumente der modernen architektur herausgegeben von Joedicke (Jürgen).* Stuttgart, Germany: Karl Krämer.
SALOMONS, IZAK 1980 "De Siemensgebouwen in Munich." *Forum* 1:15–23.
SMITHSON, ALISON (editor) (1962)1968 *Team 10 Primer.* Reprint. Cambridge, Mass.: M.I.T. Press.
VAN DE VEN, CORNELIS 1980 "De laatste werken van de architecten-gemeenschap van den Broek en Bakema, 1970–1980." *Plan* 8:14–41.

VANDENHOVE, CHARLES

A student of VICTOR BOURGEOIS at the Ecole de La Cambre in Brussels, Charles Vandenhove (1927–) devoted himself to the creation of an architectural language appropriate to prefabricated building techniques. Under the influence of LOUIS I. KAHN and ALDO VAN EYCK, he abandoned this avenue of research in the late 1960s. His interpretations of Palladian (see ANDREA PALLADIO) private residences led to interests in the complexities of old cities and in vernacular construction. His most recent works have paved the way for a new urban language based on traditional vernacular culture.

MAURICE CULOT
Translated from French by
Shara Wasserman

WORKS

1961–1977, Charles Vandenhove House, 60 Rue Chauve-souris, Liège. 1962–1981, Liège University Hospitality Center; 1963–1980, Liège University Institute of Physical Education; Sart Tilman, Angleur Tiliff, Belgium. 1967, Schoffeniels House, Riessonart; 1969, Dufays House, Saint André; 1974, Wuidar House, Esneux; Liège Province, Belgium. 1979–1981, Hors-Château Quarter (renovation), Liege, Belgium.

VAN DER MEY, J. M.

Johan Melchior van der Mey (1878–1949) was born in Rotterdam, the Netherlands. Working in the office of EDUARD CUYPERS in Amsterdam, he became acquainted with MICHEL DE KLERK and PIET KRAMER. From 1909 to 1919, he worked as aesthetic adviser to the Board of Works and Public Buildings in Amsterdam. In addition to this job, he received in 1912 the commission for the Scheepvaarthuis. From 1919 on, van der Mey worked mostly in the field of housing, but he did not receive many commissions.

WIM DE WIT

WORKS

1912–1916, Scheepvaarthuis; 1914, Bridge over Waalseilandsgracht; 1925, Housing, 26–50 Titiaanstraat; 1928–1930, Housing and Shops, Hoofdorpplein; Amsterdam.

BIBLIOGRAPHY

EVERS, HENRI (1905–1911)1916–1918 *De architectuur in hare hoofdtijdperken.* 2 vols. 2d ed. Amsterdam: Wolters.
FANELLI, GIOVANNI (1968)1978 *Moderne architectuur in Nederland: 1900–1940.* Translated from Italian by Wim de Wit. 's-Gravenhage, Netherlands: Staatsuitgeverij.
GUGEL, EUGEN (1886)1916–1918 *Geschiedenis van de bouwstijlen in de hoofdtijdperken der architectuur.* 2d ed. Rotterdam, Netherlands: Bolle.
Nederland Bouwt in Baksteen: 1800–1940. 1941 Rotterdam, Netherlands: Museum Boymans van Beuningen.
Nederlandse Architectuur, 1910–1930: Amsterdamse School. 1975 Amsterdam: Stedelijk Museum.
OUD, J. J. P. (1926)1976 *Holländische Architektur.* Reprint. Mainz, Germany: Kupferberg.
ROY VAN ZUYDEWIJN, H. J. F. DE 1969 *Amsterdamse Bouwkunst: 1815–1940.* Amsterdam: De Bussy.

VAN DER NÜLL and SICCARDSBURG

The Viennese architects Eduard van der Nüll (1812–1868) and August Siccard von Siccardsburg (1813–1868) first met during studies at Vienna's Polytechnical Institute. Van der Nüll left for work in Lemberg (now Lvov, Ukraine) as a governmental builder in 1832, while Von Siccardsburg was appointed as an assistant at the Institute in 1833. In 1835, Van der Nüll returned to study at the Akademie der bildenden Künste, where he and Von Siccardsburg were awarded a joint scholarship in 1839 to travel to Italy, France, England, and Germany. They were appointed professors at the Akademie in 1844 and had a significant influence upon Vienna's next generation of architects.

Von Siccardsburg was a master of technical and constructional matters, while Van der Nüll specialized in ornamentation. Both architects took part in the Vienna Industrial Exhibition of 1845, overseen by Jacob Reuter. Their first commissions were private ones—the Sophien-Bad of 1846, and the Carl-Theater of 1847, both in Vienna. After the declaration of public competitions in Austria in 1848, Van der Nüll and Von Siccardsburg received commissions in the Vienna Arsenal for the colossal outbuildings, workshops, and the headquarters. The success of these buildings resulted in further military commissions in 1851 and 1852 and in the designs for the alteration of the Military Academy. Their most famous work, however, is the sumptuous Opera House in Vienna (1861–1869), built in a decorative and freely adapted neo-Renaissance style.

Van der Nüll and Von Siccardsburg won an award in the 1857 Ringstrasse competition, but they did not take part in its execution. Van der Nüll committed suicide in April 1868 during the final stages of its construction, and Von Siccardsburg died a few months later. The Opera House was completed by two of their students, Joseph Storck and G. Gugitz.

IVAN S. FRANKO

Van der Nüll and Siccardsburg. Imperial Opera House. Vienna. 1861–1868 (not completed until 1869)

WORKS

1846, Sophien-Bad; 1847, Carl-Theater; 1847–1855?, Vienna Arsenal (outbuildings, workshops, and headquarters); 1851–1860?, Artillery Barracks; 1855?, Lagerhaus von Haas; 1855?, Palace of Count Larisch; 1861–1868, Imperial Opera House (not completed until 1869); Vienna.

BIBLIOGRAPHY

AUER, HANS 1885 *Das k.k. Hof-Opernhaus in Wien von van der Nüll und von Siccardsburg.* Vienna: Lehmann.
COLLINS, GEORGE R., and COLLINS, CHRISTIANE C. 1965 *Camillo Sitte and the Birth of Modern City Planning.* New York: Random House.
EITELBERGER VON EDELBERG, RUDOLF VON 1879 *Kunst und Künstler Wiens der neueren Zeit.* Volume 1 in *Gesammelte Kunsthistorische Schriften.* Vienna: Braumüller.

VAN DER ROHE, LUDWIG MIES

See MIES VAN DER ROHE, LUDWIG.

VAN DER SWAELMEN, LOUIS

A propagator of Modernism in the 1920s, Louis Martin Van der Swaelmen (1883–1929), a landscape architect, played a decisive role in the planning of the first garden-cities in Belgium.

Initially a student of law, philosophy, botany, and painting (1901–1904), he was later a refugee in Holland (1914–1918), where he became close to H. P. BERLAGE. In 1916, he published the *Préliminaires d'art civique,* which constituted the first coherent functionalist theory of city planning in Belgium.

He was among the theoreticians who influenced the Congrès Internationaux d'Architecture Moderne (CIAM).

MAURICE CULOT
Translated from French by
Shara Wasserman

WORKS

1921–1930, Floral Dwelling (plan), Watermael-Boitsfort; 1922–1925, La Cité Moderne (plan), Berchem-Sainte Agathe; 1923–1926, Kapelleveld (plan), Woluwe-Saint-Lambert; Brussels.

VAN DER VLUGT and BRINKMAN

Michiel Brinkman (1873–1925) was a particularly gifted practitioner of the Dutch version of *Sachlichkeit,* promulgated by H. P. BERLAGE. Active in his office after he established it in Rotterdam in 1910 were his son, Johannes Andreas Brinkman (1902–1949) and Leendert Cornelis Van der Vlugt (1894–1936), who joined the firm in 1915. When his father died, Johannes made Van der Vlugt a principal in the firm; together they would be responsible for some of the most luminous examples of the International style in the Netherlands. On the death of Van der Vlugt, the younger Brinkman associated himself with J. H. van den Broek (see VAN DEN BROEK AND BAKEMA). The production of the successive firms was enormous and comprised every building type, incorporating the most advanced architectural thinking of the time, and reflecting the idea that the architect must be socially accountable. The work is of consistently high quality, attaining on occasion almost unsurpassable heights, as in the case of the housing complex in Spangen, Rotterdam (1919–1921), by the elder Brinkman, and the Van Nelle Factory (1926–1930) in the same city, by the son in partnership with Van der Vlugt.

Michiel Brinkman received his architectural education at the Academy of Fine Arts in Rotterdam. Designer of industrial buildings such as the *De Maas* flour plant (1913) and the Corn Elevator Company (1916) as well as institutional projects such as the Koningin Wilhelmina- and Koningin Emma School (1919–1920) and the Church on the 's Gravendijkwal (1919–1920), all in Rotterdam. His most enduring monument is the municipal housing project in the Spangen quarter (1919–1921). The complex covers more than 12,600 square meters and accommodates 264 families. The housing blocks line the perimeter of the plot to enclose a generous courtyard with private and public gardens and interior streets. Access to the courtyard, from which entry to all the dwellings is gained, occurs at four points via polygonal openings in the street walls. Shorter rows of dwellings, which also contain a public bath, a central heating plant, and communal laundry facilities, give a rich texture to the inner enclosure. A masterful sequence of spaces has been attained with an economy of means through the novel site plan.

The organizations of the floor-through dwellings is equally ingenious, with three-bedroom flats on the first and second stories, and duplexes above. The duplexes are entered via a gallery which runs around the inner face of the complex at the third story. Constructed of concrete, the gallery is broad enough to provide a supplemental play area for children and a thoroughfare for delivery carts; it is clearly a harbinger of those "streets in the sky" that British architects such as PETER SMITHSON and ALISON SMITHSON hailed in the 1950s as the ideal solution to the social problems engendered by large-scale housing projects. Window boxes have been cast into the low walls of the gallery; filled with plants, they provide, with the gray concrete, a colorful contrast to the prevailing yellow of the brick. The detailing of the brick walls is straightforward but inventive, with the rhythmic alternation of the fenestration resulting in a lively surface pattern. At Spangen, Michiel Brinkman created a stately community for the working class which is rationally conceived and aesthetically satisfying.

With its bearing walls modulated by low-relief planes, Spangen has a massive character and belongs to the first phase of *Sachlichkeit*. The work of the successor firm, on the other hand, constructed of point supports and light, mass-produced curtain walls, represents the *neue Sachlichkeit*. It is unlikely that Van der Vlugt and the younger Brinkman came to this vision of architecture through their conventional education: Van der Vlugt, like Michiel, attended the Academy in Rotterdam while Johannes was trained at the Technical University in Delft. Their impulse toward international modernism more likely arose through participation in *Opbouw,* a group founded in 1920 that became the stronghold of the new functionalism in the Netherlands. Besides Van der Vlugt, J. J. P. OUD, MARTINUS STAM, and CORNELIS VAN EESTEREN were members. Believing that modern industrialized society forced architecture into directions totally divorced from the experiences of the past, the group's goals resembled those of avant-garde movements elsewhere in Europe. Not surprisingly, *Opbouw* would form the core of the Dutch delegation to the Congrès Internationaux d'Architecture Moderne (CIAM).

In his MTS (Technical School) at Groningen (1922), done in collaboration with J. W. Wiebenga, Van der Vlugt heralded the transformation that would occur when he became a principal in the firm. The school is very precocious; except for the symmetrical layout, it may be the most progressive executed work for its date in all of Europe. The structure, clearly separated from the enclosure, lies behind a thin membrane of transparent and opaque planes. In its uncompromisingly severe horizontal layering, the school is similar to LUDWIG MIES VAN DER ROHE's project of the same year for a concrete office block; it set a promising precedent for the work Van der Vlugt would do with the younger Brinkman.

Almost immediately, the partnership had a stunning series of successes, thanks in part to the support of Cornelis Hendrick Van der Leeuw, an enlightened architectural patron in the tradition of Karl Ernst Osthaus and the Kröller-Müller family. A man of wide knowledge and artistic daring, Van

Brinkman.
Spangen Housing
Development.
Rotterdam, Netherlands.
1919–1921

der Leeuw had studied with Sigmund Freud and, like a great many Dutch intellectuals and artists, was an active member of the Theosophical Society, at that time an important spiritual and cultural force in the Netherlands. When he employed the firm, Van der Leeuw was a director of the Van Nelle company, manufacturers of coffee, tea, and tobacco products; in the 1940s, he would serve as president of the Technical University at Delft. The partners designed his house on the Kralingse Plaslaan, Rotterdam (1927–1928), and his summerhouse, *Sterkamp* (1929–1931), at Ommen, as well as the buildings for Van Nelle described below. Through his good offices, they also completed several commissions for the Theosophical Society: the auditorium (1925–1926) and administration building (1926) in Amsterdam, and the Administrative Complex at Ommen (1927). All are sensitive interpretations of the *neue Sachlichkeit* or, as it was sometimes called, the *Nieuwe Bouwen* (New Building).

The first commission for Van Nelle was an office with storerooms in Leiden (1925–1927). With its flat roof, strip windows, tile- and stucco-covered planar surfaces, factory sash, uncompromising geometric shapes, its neon signage the only "decoration," it was an exquisite example of the International style and prepares us for what is undoubtedly Van der Vlugt's and Brinkman's most splendid work and surely the most lyrical and

Brinkman and Van der
Vlugt.
Van Nelle Tobacco Factory
Office Building.
Leiden, Netherlands.
1925–1927

elegant industrial complex in the world: the Van Nelle Factory (1926–1930), Rotterdam. This is in fact a group of buildings serving administrative, recreational, packaging, and shipping as well as manufacturing functions. The challenge of articulating the various components of the program while simultaneously integrating them to form a harmonious whole was confidently met in a design that has the sophistication and sleek beauty of the very machines it houses.

Upon arrival at the site, bounded by a railroad track and a canal, one first encounters the interlocking concave and convex spaces of the administration wing, the complicated composition of which proclaims its public nature. In this section, there are not only offices and a company dining room, but also the area where customers redeem the coupons that are packed with the company's products—a double-height space that corresponds with the curving balcony linking the upper offices to form a flowing yet intricate spatial configuration. Specially made fixtures and tubular steel furniture are found throughout this wing, which is connected to the factory by a second-story bridge. This glazed "street-in-the-sky" is experienced as a Cubist composition of transparent planes; it leads to a stair-and-elevator tower which is crowned by the circular, nautically detailed executive suite where the directors may oversee the complex.

The factory itself, 220 meters long, is a simple rectangular volume set parallel to the canal. Its taut glass and metal curtain wall, behind which can be glimpsed the large mushroom columns which support the structure, is interrupted only by the projections of service wings containing stairs and bathrooms and by the glassed-in conveyor belts which send goods to the shipping plant. The factory is tripartite in silhouette, stepping down from eight to five to three stories to serve the different needs of the tobacco, coffee, and tea sections.

The scale and complexity of Van Nelle is unusual for the time, as is the visual richness achieved within the modernist canon of industrialized materials and simple geometric shapes. Compared with its almost exact contemporary, the Bauhaus by WALTER GROPIUS, its singular poetry is revealed. Both buildings accommodate a variety of functions, but Van Nelle is more diverse in massing. The carefully calibrated curves of the administration wing bear testimony to the lingering presence of Expressionism in the Netherlands. Also deriving from Expressionist experiments is the way the buildings are by night a cage of light, while by day their reflective surfaces mirror the swiftly moving clouds and constantly changing light of the Dutch skies. Still other avant-garde directions which tended to lose their integrity

when they were assimilated into the International style are distinctly recognizable here. Throughout the plant are accents of the primary colors favored by De Stijl. The deliberate and dramatic display of human and mechanical movement behind large transparent surfaces reveals both Futurist and Russian Constructivist influences. Because of the latter, some historians have claimed that Martinus Stam, who had first-hand knowledge of progressive Russian architecture and who was with the firm from 1925 to 1928, was the chief designer. But the client, Van der Leeuw, who closely followed the progress of the work, has always adamantly insisted that the main credit belongs to the two principals.

Equally powerful but completely opposite in its opaque solidity is the Grain Silo (1927–1931), Rotterdam, whose stark concrete walls were executed by means of sliding formwork. At the base, however, the building opens up and the unbroken upper wall, cantilevered out over the large expanse of factory sash, demonstrates with great flair the possibilities of modern construction techniques.

Yet a third exterior treatment appears in the Bergpolder Flats (1932–1934), Rotterdam, designed in cooperation with fellow Opbouw member WILLEM VAN TIJEN. Here, the tradition of gallery access established by Brinkman senior has been modernized, with metal balconies and walkways spinning a delicate linear armature over the long sides of the slab. This incredibly elegant building looks as though it contains luxury flats but in fact shelters workers' dwellings, financed by one of the publicly funded housing societies that made such important contributions to Dutch architecture in the 1910s and 1920s. Previously, workers' housing had been at most four stories high, but Bergpolder, its nine stories served by a skip-stop elevator, offered a radically new solution. At the ground level are shops, storage spaces, and a laundry; above are floor-through apartments, each with its own balcony and front door. At one end of the slab project cantilevered stairways sheathed in translucent glass; at the other, open stairs leading from gallery to gallery create a De Stijl-like play of plastic form. Meant to be a prototype for production on a large scale, Bergpolder unhappily remained a rare example, though a very appealing one, a graceful precursor of LE CORBUSIER's Unités d'Habitation.

A similar integument of steel perches over the aggressive curves of the vast Feyenoord Stadium in Rotterdam, designed in 1934 and completed just before Van der Vlugt's death. Once again, the partners displayed their uncanny skill at giving striking form to huge complexes. Yet, while they understood better than most of their contemporaries the demands of the large, comprehensive commission, they were equally at home with the minute in scale. Because there were no appropriate interior fittings available commercially at the time, they designed furniture and fixtures for such commissions as the houses for Van der Leeuw and the Van Nelle complex. The impeccably detailed glass-and-steel outdoor telephone booth they fashioned in 1931–1932 is still in production today and graces every Dutch city, an example of clean and logical modern design at its best.

One year after Van der Vlugt died, the firm became Brinkman and van den Broek; since 1948, it has been called Van den Broek and Bakema. The ability to orchestrate a series of large-scale forms into a unified whole, and the insistence on efficient and handsome design and social responsibility, established at the beginning of the twentieth century by Michiel Brinkman and carried on by his son and by Van der Vlugt, thus continues.

HELEN SEARING

WORKS

MICHIEL BRINKMAN

1913, De Maas Flour Factory (extended in 1930 by Brinkman and van der Vlugt); 1916, Corn Elevator Company (grain elevator); 1919–1920, Koningin Wilhelmina- and Koningin Emma School; 1919–1920, 's Gravendijkwal Church; 1919–1921, Spangen Housing Development; Rotterdam, Netherlands.

LEENDERT CORNELIS VAN DER VLUGT

1922, M.T.S. School (with J. W. Wiebenga), Groningen, Netherlands.

BRINKMAN AND VAN DER VLUGT

1925–1926, Theosophical Society Meeting Hall, Amsterdam. *1925–1927, Van Nelle Tobacco Factory Office Building, Leiden, Netherlands. 1926, Theosophical Society Administration Building, Amsterdam. 1926–1927, Municipal Housing; 1926–1930, Van Nelle Factory; 1927, Heldring and Pierson Bank; Rotterdam, Netherlands. 1927, Theosophical Society Administrative Complex, Ommen, Netherlands. 1927–1928, C. H. Van der Leeuw House; 1927–1931, Graansilo Company (grain silo), Rotterdam, Netherlands. 1928, Rotterdam Company Workers' Housing, Schiedam, Netherlands. 1928–1929, Sonneveld House, Rotterdam, Netherlands. 1929, Private Chapel and Columbarium, Staverden, Netherlands. 1929–1931, De Bruin House, Schiedam, Netherlands. 1929–1931, R. Mees and Sons Bank, Rotterdam, Netherlands. 1929–1931, C. H. Van der Leeuw Summerhouse, Ommen, Netherlands. 1930–1932, Dutch Postal Service Telephone Booth; 1930–1932, Van Stolk and Son Office Building; Rotterdam, Netherlands. 1931, Van Ommeren Travel Bureau, Paris. 1931–1938, Van Dam Hospital (extended by van den Broek and Bakema in 1957–1960); 1932–1934, Bergpolder Flats (with Willem van Tijen); Rotterdam, Netherlands. 1933, Henry Wassenaar, Netherlands. 1933, De Maas Grain and Coal Silos, Rotterdam, Neth-erlands. 1933, Rotterdam Golf Club, Netherlands. 1934, Holland–America Line Travel Office, Paris. 1934–1936, Feyenoord Stadium; 1934–1936, Nuova Tennis Club; 1934–1936, Volker Bouwindustria (middle-class housing); Rotterdam, Netherlands.

BIBLIOGRAPHY

BAKEMA, J. B. 1968 *L. C. van der Vlugt.* Amsterdam: Meulenhoff.

BENEVOLO, LEONARDO (1960)1977 *The Modern Movement.* Volume 2 in *History of Modern Architecture.* Translated by H. J. Landry from the third revised edition. Cambridge, Mass.: M.I.T. Press.

EIBINK, A., GERRETSEN, W. J., and HENDRIKS, J. P. L. 1937 *Hedendaagsche Architectuur in Nederland.* Amsterdam: Kosmos.

De 8 en Opbouw 1936 7, no. 10: entire issue.

FANELLI, GIOVANNI (1968)1978 *Moderne architectuur in Nederland 1900–1940.* Translated from the Italian by Wim de Wit. The Hague: Staatsuitgeverij.

GRINBERG, DONALD I. 1977 *Housing in the Netherlands.* Rotterdam: Delft University Press.

LEERING, J. 1971 *Bauen '20–40: Der Niederlandische Beitrag zum Neuen Bauen.* Amsterdam: Spruyt.

MUSEUM BOYMANS-VAN BEUNINGEN [1962] *Bouwen voor een Open Samenleving.* Rotterdam: Gemeentedrukkerij.

OUD, J. J. P. (1926)1976 *Holländische Architektur.* Reprint. Mainz, Germany: Kupferberg.

VAN LOGHEM, J. B. 1932 *Bouwen Holland.* Amsterdam: Kosmos.

VAN DE VELDE, HENRY

Henry Van de Velde (1863–1957) was destined for a law career, but he chose instead to study at the Beaux-Arts Academy in Antwerp, the city of his birth, from 1882 to 1884. He continued his painting studies with Carolus Duran in Paris for another year. With no more than this academic preparation but with almost ten years' experience as an interior decorator in Antwerp and Brussels, he began to practice as an architect and designer in Brussels in 1895. That year he built his own home. *Villa Bloemenwerf;* its interior and all its furnishings including furniture, carpets, and table service were designed by him. This was followed in 1896 by a house in the Art Nouveau style for the famed art dealer S. Bing in Paris. His growing reputation as an innovative designer led to commissions for shops, offices, and museum interiors. Notable among his commissions was one for the museum in Hagen, Germany, directed by, and later named for, Karl Ernst Osthaus; another was for Count Harry Kessler to redesign the interiors of his Weimar home. Such an array of distinguished and satisfied clients quickly promoted his practice.

Van de Velde's first exhibit was in Dresden in

1897; its success stimulated him to move to Germany in 1900, and in 1902, he exhibited at the Weimar Court of Ernst-Ludwig, grand duke of Saxe-Weimar, whom he served as an adviser. In 1906, he designed the granducal Saxon School of Arts and Crafts building in Weimar, of which he became director in 1908.

There, Van de Velde organized a curriculum that emphasized the individuality and innovative abilities of the students. He was able to establish a lively collaboration with the crafts unions and businesses, solving many artistic problems in doing so. His critics, however, believed that the school should have developed step by step beyond the little things that were made—batik, bookbinding, and pottery—to develop out of the pettiness into a genuine artistic architectonic line.

Van de Velde continued his private practice, designing museums, houses, monuments, and interiors. He clashed with AUGUSTE PERRET over the replanning of the Théâtre des Champs-Elysées, Paris; first designed by Van de Velde in 1910, it represented the artistic school, but Perret's redesign emphasized the structural. This was not the only clash: by 1914 and especially at the annual meeting of the Werkbund in July, a schism developed between HERMANN MUTHESIUS and Van de Velde. Muthesius's approach to art and design was evidenced in his Cologne Werkbund Exhibition work and in his strong plea for a new unity of style by imposing standardization, a more uniform approach. He appeared unwilling to see the artists' side, his own mind being too rigid and lacking in spiritual understanding. It was Van de Velde's conviction that no style could be imposed by organizational means. WALTER GROPIUS, recently elected to the Werkbund Board, supported Van de Velde in defense of the artistic style more as a rebuke to the person of Muthesius, whom he described as disagreeable and offensive, than as an attack on the content of Muthesius's thesis.

Despite the concerted rejection of Muthesius's ideas, Van de Velde's subjective approach to design, which derived from the turn-of-century *Jugendstil* movement, was defeated by the greater recognition of the *Neue Sachlichkeit*. Furthermore, Gropius's forceful support of Van de Velde in the meeting did not mean approval of his teaching method and school organization. A half century later Gropius explained:

Van de Velde was a great artist, but I did not believe in his way of teaching. The students who went through his curriculum in Weimar show also the specific van de Velde stamp. They are, so to speak, smaller editions of van de Velde himself. Van de Velde, conscious of his strength, believed that one man could change the style of a whole country. My own notion, on the contrary, was that in education we have to provide the students with objective physiological and psychological facts, with the knowledge of which he has to build up himself in order to become an independent artist. This difference is, for me, the most important problem in art education.

Van de Velde's personal approach in art and architecture was strong and had its influence. I like particularly the comprehensiveness of his approach to buildings and all their contents [Gropius, letter to Günther Stamm, December 18, 1967].

Van de Velde himself would not disagree with the identification of an approach unique to himself; he wrote in his autobiography (1962): "The idea of a 'new style' has been so closely connected with my life for forty years that I must consider it my personal adventure."

Van de Velde's comprehensiveness as noted by Gropius was evident in the manner in which he sought and achieved a sensitive aesthetic compatibility of his building designs with their interiors, and of the interiors with the furniture, wall and floor covering, ceiling trim and motifs, glazing, hardware, fabrics, and lighting fixtures, and beyond these to the binding of books on the shelves, place settings, dishes, picture frames, and mirrors.

Van de Velde subsequently designed the Theater for the 1914 Werkbund Exposition in Cologne, which was his last major work of the pre–World War I period. As an alien he was forced to leave his post as director of the Weimar Arts and Crafts School. Concerned with the future of the school, he recommended that Gropius be engaged to continue it. This thoughtful, generous gesture by Van de Velde in a most disheartening moment of his own life would prove to be a first action toward the postwar establishment of the Bauhaus by Gropius.

Van de Velde remained in Germany until 1917, when he moved to Holland. Establishing his practice there, he designed houses, apartments, a museum, and the Belgian Pavilions for the 1937 Paris World's Fair and the 1939 New York Fair. His last notable work was a library for the University of Ghent, Belgium.

REGINALD R. ISAACS

WORKS

1896, L'Art Nouveau Shop (interiors), Paris. 1896, Van de Velde House, Avenue Vanderaey, Brussels. 1898, Keller und Reiner Art Gallery (interiors), Berlin. 1901, Folkwang Museum (interiors; now the Karl Ernst Osthaus Museum), Hagen, Germany. 1903, Kessler House (remodeling); 1904, Kunstgewerbeschule; Weimar, Germany. 1906, Osthaus House, Hagen, Germany. 1906, Saxon School of Arts and Crafts; 1912, Durkheim House; Weimar, Germany. *1914, Werkbund Exhibition Theater, Cologne, Germany. 1921, Van de Velde House, Wassenaar, Netherlands. 1927, Van de Velde House, Tervueren, Belgium. 1930, Wolfers House, Brussels. 1937, Belgian Pavilion (with I. Eggeriey), World's Fair, Paris. 1939, Belgian Pavilion (with VICTOR BOURGEOIS), World's Fair, New York. 1939, Library, University of Ghent, Belgium.

BIBLIOGRAPHY

CURJEL, HANS (editor) 1955 *Henry van de Velde.* Munich: Piper.

DELEVOY, ROBERT ET AL. 1963 *Henry Van de Velde.* Brussels: Paleis Voor Schone.

HAMMACHER, A. M. 1967 *Le Monde de Henry van de Velde.* Antwerp, Netherlands: Mercator.

HÜTER, KARL-HEINZ 1967 *Henry van de Velde.* Berlin: Akademie-Verlag.

LENNING, HENRY 1951 *The Art Nouveau.* The Hague: Nijhoff.

MESNIL, JACQUES 1914 *Henry van de Velde et le Théâtre des Champs-Elysées.* Brussels: Oest.

OSTHAUS, KARL ERNST 1920 *Van de Velde.* Hagen, Germany: Folkwang.

PEVSNER, NIKOLAUS 1963 "Gropius and Van de Velde." *Architectural Review* 133:165–168.

VAN DE VELDE, HENRY 1894 *Déblaiemant d'Art.* Brussels: Mannom.

VAN DE VELDE, HENRY 1895 *L'Art Futur.* Brussels.

VAN DE VELDE, HENRY (1901)1903 *Die Renaissance im modernen Kunstgewerbe.* 2d ed. Berlin: Cassirer.

VAN DE VELDE, HENRY 1962 *Geschichte meines Lebens.* Edited by Hans Curjel. Munich: Piper.

VAN DOESBURG, THEO

Although he was not an architect, the life and work of Theo Van Doesburg (1883–1931) have some significance for the history of modern architecture. A jack-of-all-trades, he was a painter, designer, typographer, critic, writer, and teacher in the manner of the Russian ELEAZAR LISSITSKY and the Hungarian LÁSZLÓ MOHOLY-NAGY.

Born in Utrecht, he was given the name Christiaan Emil Marie Küppers, after his biological father, a German photographer. Throughout his life, however, he called himself Theo van Doesburg, after his Dutch stepfather, Theodorus Doesburg, a minor Amsterdam industrialist. Confusion about his name compounded, as Van Doesburg at times called himself both I. K. Bonset and Aldo Camini.

A zealous promotor of the "new," Van Doesburg collected avant-garde ideas from around the world and proselytized with the zeal of a Savonarola. He saw himself as a crusader struggling to cleanse mankind of the cultural impurities of conventional social and artistic norms and practices, these to be replaced by universally valid forms of Modernism, as he defined it. As early as 1914, he

wrote that he imagined himself "making a daring, spiritual crusade throughout artistic and intellectual Europe" (Baljeu, 1974 p. 10). A purged and properly transformed visual environment, he assumed, would inevitably result in an improved, indeed perfected, moral climate.

A strident polemicist, he engaged in endless disputes with his peers: personal charges and countercharges, professional gossip and slander. A few details about his life, his beliefs, and about his work can be sifted out of the confusion of gritty fact and windy hyperbole associated with Van Doesburg's career. Against the wishes of his parents, he began painting at about the age of sixteen, and for several years he worked in a muddy, Rembrandtesque manner. The period culminated in his first exhibition, which took place in The Hague in 1908. Thereafter, his work became a cross between Vasily Kandinsky and Italian Futurism. Around 1912, while still painting, he began publishing art criticism in newspapers and periodicals, especially in the weekly *Eenheid* (unity). Although Holland remained neutral during World War I, the country mobilized for the contingency of war, and Van Doesburg served in the army border guard near Belgium from 1914 to 1916. After returning to civilian life, he began an association with some Dutch artists, most importantly with the architect J. J. P. OUD and the painters Piet Mondriaan and Bart van der Leck. Along with others, the four established the periodical *De Stijl,* under Van Doesburg's severe editorship, which lasted from October 1917 until his death in March 1931. The avant-garde periodical was surely his most significant contribution to the history of modern art; on page one of the first number he outlined his editorial line when he wrote that "This periodical hopes to make a contribution to the development of a new awareness of beauty. It wishes to make modern man receptive to what is new in the visual arts."

During 1921 and 1922, he lectured in Weimar, Germany, where he also taught informal classes and engaged in private debates with WALTER GROPIUS, director of the Bauhaus. Van Doesburg volunteered to guide the development of the institution, an offer that Gropius declined.

Van Doesburg wrote a great deal about the new architecture and its social implications, but he actually did little architectural design. His earliest known work, some interior decorations, was done in collaboration with Oud for his design for the De Vonk summer house at Noordwijkerhout (1917). In collaboration with CORNELIS VAN EESTEREN, Van Doesburg designed three projects for houses (1923) for a De Stijl exhibition sponsored by the Leonce Rosenberg Art Gallery in

Paris. And with Hans Arp and his wife Sophie Tauber-Arp, Van Doesburg remodeled Aubette (1926–1928), an eighteenth-century building built in Strasbourg by FRANÇOIS BLONDEL; the three installed a variety of recreational spaces, including a cinema and dancehall. During the last years of his life, Van Doesburg designed a home and studio (1929–1931) for himself and his wife, Nelly, at Meudon, near Paris. The boxlike composition, partially elevated on stilts, resembles LE CORBUSIER's Citrohan houses of the early twenties.

The Rosenberg projects and Aubette were, undoubtedly, his most important architectural works. Rosenberg invited members of the De Stijl group to design projects for two houses and one studio-house. They were exhibited in October and November of 1923, immediately after the first Bauhaus exhibition in Berlin during the summer of 1923, and shortly before GERRIT T. RIETVELD began work on his famous Schroeder House (1924) in Utrecht. Breaking with traditional notions of architecture as the symmetrical organization of hollowed masses, the Paris projects consist of spaces loosely defined by interlocking vertical and horizontal planar systems, seemingly weightless volumes projecting 360 degrees outward from a central volumetric core. Discontinuous planes and boxes channel space through and beyond usable interior space, while dynamic colors—reds, yellows, and blues—help establish spatial relations.

Aubette was conceived as a huge walk-in painting defined by planes of primary colors, along with white, gray, and black. The cinema consisted of a long, rectangular space divided into a central aisle and side booths, with suspended lighting and screen located at one end. Floor, walls, and ceiling were coloristically and spatially integrated into a highly controlled environment, which anticipated the total design of post-World War II big-business corporate headquarters. Van Doesburg and his collaborators produced hundreds of schemes for Aubette, from ashtrays and furniture to the overall layout.

Some historians and critics have visualized and described Van Doesburg as a scorned prophet, shouting the truth in a wilderness of conventional deceit, while others now view him as just one of the many self-proclaimed messiahs who shouted their way through the 1920s.

THEODORE M. BROWN

WORKS

1917, De Vonk Summer House (interior decorations; with J. J. P. Oud), Noorwijkerhout, Netherlands. *1926–1928, Aubette (remodeled; with Hans Arp and Sophie Tauber-Arp), Strasbourg, France. 1929–1931, Van Doesburg House and Studio, Meudon, France.

BIBLIOGRAPHY

BALJEU, JOOST 1974 *Theodore Van Doesburg.* New York: Macmillan.
BANHAM, REYNER (1960)1967 *Theory and Design in the First Machine Age.* 2d ed. New York: Praeger.
BROWN, THEODORE N. 1958 *The Work of G. Rietveld, Architect.* Utrecht: Bruna & Zoon.
FANELLI, GIOVANNI 1968 *Architettura Moderna in Olanda 1900–1940.* Florence, Italy: Marchi & Bertolli.
JAFFE, HANS LUDWIG C. 1956 *De Stijl/1917–1931.* Amsterdam: Meulenhoff.
OVERY, PAUL 1969 *De Stijl.* London: Studio Vista.
PETERSEN, AD (editor) 1968 *De Stijl.* 2 volumes. Amsterdam: Athenaeum. Facsimile reprint of the periodical, complete from 1917–1932.

VAN EESTEREN, CORNELIS

Cornelis (Cor) van Eesteren (1897–) was born in Kinderdijk, Netherlands, on the bank of the river Noord. His family of building contractors still work there and throughout the country. Kinderdijk, between Rotterdam and Dordrecht, enjoys international fame in construction, especially of machines and ships. After high school, lessons in drawing, and a short practice as a carpenter's apprentice, Van Eesteren decided to become an architect. In 1915, he entered the service of WILLEM KROMHOUT, once a Dutch Modern movement architect and at that time a modest Expressionist. Apparently, he did not influence his trainee very much from a stylistic point of view. Two years later, Van Eesteren graduated with honors from the Rotterdam Academy of Fine Arts and Technical Sciences. In 1918, he was occupied with town planning in Alblasserdam, the municipality to which Kinderdijk belongs. He also briefly worked for architects in The Hague and Amsterdam. In this period, he designed a building for the Royal Netherlands Academy of Sciences in a style that was influenced by FRANK LLOYD WRIGHT and H. T. WIJDEVELD. The interior of the building was well organized. Van Eesteren was awarded the *Prix de Rome,* which enabled him to visit Germany in 1922 to study brick architecture. But Van Eesteren preferred the problems of his own time and went to Weimar, where he came in contact with the Bauhaus people. He also met THEO VAN DOESBURG, the leading figure of *De Stijl,* who was in Weimar at that time. The German and Dutch avant-garde influenced him very much, but the final aim of Van Eesteren was to obtain more knowledge about town planning.

In 1923, he worked in Paris with Van Doesburg and met Piet Mondrian. Van Doesburg designed the color schemes for two houses by Van Eesteren. Both men drew up the manifesto *Vers une construction collective,* which was also signed in its first version by G. T. RIETVELD. Van Eesteren and Van Doesburg participated in the famous *De Stijl* exhibition in Léonce Rosenberg's *Galerie de l'Effort moderne* in 1923. For this occasion, they made three functionalist designs and models: the Rosenberg House, the Private House, and the Studio House. In this period, Van Eesteren also designed the House on the River and a house in Park Zorgvliet, The Hague. His models and drawings show a distinct feeling for space and the interrelation of interior and exterior space.

In 1924, he became office manager for JAN WILS, for the period in which Wils had to design and build the Amsterdam Olympic Stadium for the games of 1928. But Van Eesteren's studies of town planning went on. In 1925, he received first prize in the international competition for a plan to remodel *Unter den Linden* in Berlin. At the same time, he was engaged in a plan for the *Rokin,* a street in Amsterdam, and for the center of Paris. In all these plans, Van Eesteren chose high buildings and uninterrupted traffic flows in the centers of the cities. In 1929, Van Eesteren, already well known for his knowledge and international relations, became chief architect of the town planning department of the City of Amsterdam, but he also held many part-time functions. From 1930 to 1947, he was president of the Congrès Internationaux d'Architecture Moderne (CIAM), and from 1947 to 1967 he was professor of town planning at Delft's Technical University.

Van Eesteren supervised for nearly half a century the town planning of Amsterdam, a tremendous task of which the General Extension Plan is the most important part. The first version was completed in 1934. He was one of the first town planners to research how a town had developed and what it needed for its inhabitants. He analyzed which categories of people had to be accommodated, each according to its own lifestyle. Densities of people not streets or houses were his starting point. According to Van Eesteren, a planner has to know in advance where people will live and work, where they will recreate and which routes for traffic have to be designed to control the movement of people. The underlying principle was to restore the unity in human life after a period of technical predominance. Many of his principles were known in the CIAM milieu; they became self-evident and were widely applied elsewhere.

PIETER SINGELENBERG

WORKS

1923, House, Alblasserdam, Netherlands. 1926, House, Nunspeet, Netherlands. 1928–1940, School Buildings and Residential Blocks (with Charles Karsten and Benjamin Merkelbach), The Hague. 1929–1934, General Extension Plan (with additions until c.1964), Amsterdam. 1949, Nagele Village (with Merkelbach and other architects from *De 8*), Netherlands.

BIBLIOGRAPHY

BALJEU, JOOST 1974 *Theo van Doesburg.* London: Studio Vista.
BLIJSTRA, REINDER 1971 *C. van Eesteren.* Translated by Ray Edwards. Amsterdam: Meulenhoff.
FANELLI, GIOVANNI 1978 *Architetturi, Edilizia, Urbanistica: Olanda, 1917–1940.* Impruneta, Italy: Francesco Papafava.
GIEDION, SIGFRIED (1941)1971 *Space, Time, and Architecture; the Growth of a New Tradition.* 5th ed., rev. and enl. Cambridge, Mass.: Harvard University Press.
JAFFÉ, HANS LUDWIG C. 1956 *De Stijl, 1917–1931; The Dutch Contribution to Modern Art.* Amsterdam: Meulenhoff.
STEINMANN, MARTIN (editor) 1979 *CIAM. Internationale Kongresse für Neues Bauen, Congrès Internationaux d'Architecture Moderne. Dokumente 1928–1939.* Stuttgart, Germany, and Basel: Birkhäuser.

VAN EYCK, ALDO

Aldo van Eyck (1918–) was born in Driebergen, Holland. He attended a number of Dutch and English schools between 1924 and 1938 and then studied at the Eidgenössische Technische Hochschule in Zurich between 1939 and 1943. He worked with the Public Works Department of Amsterdam from 1946 to 1950. Since 1952, Van Eyck has been in private practice in The Hague and Amsterdam, and since 1971 he has been in partnership with Theo Bosch.

Van Eyck's reputation has been formed mainly on the basis of his designs and his writing as an editor of the Dutch *Forum* between 1959 and 1967. He also served as a lecturer in Holland and in the United States. Since 1967, Van Eyck has been teaching at the Technical University, Delft. He has participated in many exhibitions, for example, the Biennale in Venice in 1976, and has received many prizes.

If any single characteristic may be accredited to Van Eyck it is his stress on the imaginative and the insistent drive to unshackle the mind from the bounds of rationalism. Thus, he has turned away from the functionalism of the Congrès Internationaux d'Architecture Moderne (CIAM) toward groups that have had no or little influence: the children's world and the primitive tribesman.

The spontaneity and joyful world of children has been a constant source of inspiration, and explains the 650 playgrounds Van Eyck designed.

Van Eyck has had close affiliations with primitive peoples and he has assumed some of their native practices into his own ideology. One such tribe is the Dogon of West Africa, and Van Eyck has shared his interest in several articles. One of the most striking features of the Dogon is their nonpossessiveness of their homes. Although each has a place to sleep and eat and share company, the Dogon tribesman can experience the home as a special place in each and all of his fellow tribesmen's homes.

Van Eyck's message is basically an existential one, one that he shares with Gaston Bachelard. Van Eyck believes with Bachelard in the home as a mimetic symbol, the carrier of the personalized idea. Van Eyck sees the home as the spiritual core of existence allowing for inner experiences. In *Team 10 Primer,* he has noted a diagram where the home harbors the mind's processes, such as ideas, dialogue, awareness, the interior of vision, and imagination, as well as places for past and future.

The Orphanage in Amsterdam (1957–1960) is probably the best example of Van Eyck's architectural works, while his playgrounds have been publicized in *Forum* and other buildings have received ample treatment in *Lotus International.* Van Eyck's main purpose for the orphanage was to "untwist these little children" by providing a splendid world for the imagination. The pools of flowing space are anchored down by geometric domical centers. Thus, the unchanneled space provides freedom and the domical centers form the counterpoint; this is the "twin phenomenon" Van Eyck speaks about. Although Van Eyck probably does not want visitors to dote on the material of the place because of its rationalistic cast, the concrete has a special significance. It is an antidote to the very personalized, warmhearted clustering effect of the interior spaces for the children he loves: rough and tough like the immediate concrete world that surrounds the orphanage.

Van Eyck's place in architectural history is frequently defined by his contributions to Team 10 although he still moves powerfully beyond that. Along with the other prime movers of Team 10— ALISON SMITHSON AND PETER SMITHSON, J. B. Bakema (see VAN DEN BROEK AND BAKEMA), and Shadrach Woods (see CANDILIS JOSIC WOODS), Van Eyck started in the late 1940s to break the bounds of functional logic. Although his ambling spaces in the orphanage and in the schools of Nagele (1955–1956) run parallel to the plans of the Free University in Berlin designed by Candilis Josic Woods, Van Eyck is in spirit closer to LOUIS I. KAHN. Both Kahn and Van Eyck were interested in exploring how concrete could be used in personalized and formal ways. But one should

remember that Van Eyck wished to distinguish himself from Kahn.

SUZANNE FRANK

WORKS

1946, Tower Space, Zurich. 1947–1979, 650 Playgrounds, Amsterdam. 1948, Heldring and Pierson Bank, The Hague. 1950, Ahoy Entrance Sign, National Maritime Exhibition, Rotterdam, Netherlands. 1953, Blue-Violet Room, Stedelijk Museum; 1954, Sixty-four Houses for the Aged (with Jan Rietveld); 1955, House (with GERRIT THOMAS RIETVELD), Herman Gorterstraat; Amsterdam. 1955–1956, Three Schools (with H. P. D. van Ginkel), Nagele, Netherlands. 1957–1960, Children's Home, Amsterdam. 1958, House, Water's Edge, Baambrugge, Netherlands. 1966, Sculpture Pavilion, Arnhem, Netherlands. 1968–1970, Pastoor van Arskerk, The Hague. 1969–1970, Housing (with Sean Wellesley Miller), Lima. 1970–1975, Housing (with Theo Bosch), Zwelle, Netherlands. 1974–1980, Hubertus Home (with Hanna van Eyck), Amsterdam.

BIBLIOGRAPHY

BARBIERI, UMBERTO 1980 "Labyrinth en Vierkant." *Plan* 11.

BLIJSTRA, REINDER 1966 *Dutch Architecture after 1900.* Amsterdam: van Kampen.

BOHIGAS, ORIOL 1976 *Once Arquitectos.* Barcelona, Spain: La Gaya Ciencia.

FRAMPTON, KENNETH 1975 "Des Vicissitudes de l'idéologie." *L'Architecture d'Aujourd'hui* 177:62–65.

HEER, J. DE 1980 "Amsterdamse speelplaatsen." *Plan* 11.

JENCKS, CHARLES 1973 *Modern Movements in Architecture.* Garden City, N.Y.: Doubleday.

NICOLIN, PIERLUIGI 1976 "Aldo Van Eyck: The Web and the Labyrinth." *Lotus International* 11:107–108.

SMITHSON, PETER 1975 "Church at the Hague." *Architectural Design* 45:345–350.

VAN EYCK, ALDO 1949 "Wij Ontdekken Stijl." *Forum* 4:115–116.

VAN EYCK, ALDO (1951)1954 "CIAM 6. Bridgewater: Statement Against Rationalism. 1947." In Sigfried Giedion (editor), *A Decade of Architecture.* New York: Wittenborn.

VAN EYCK, ALDO 1958 "De Bal Kaatst Terug." *Forum* 13:104–112.

VAN EYCK, ALDO 1960–1961 "There is a Garden in Her Face." *Forum* 15:107–117.

VAN EYCK, ALDO 1961 "CIAM '59." In Oscar Newman (editor), *Contemporary Otterlo.* Stuttgart, Germany: Kramer.

VAN EYCK, ALDO 1966 "University College in Urbino by Giancarlo De Carlo." *Zodiac* 16:170–187.

VAN EYCK, ALDO 1968 *Team 10 Primer.* Edited by Alison Smithson. Cambridge, Mass.: M.I.T. Press.

VAN EYCK, ALDO 1969 "The Enigma of Multiplicity." *Harvard Educational Review* 39, no. 4:126–143.

VOELCKER, JOHN 1955 "Polder and Playground." *Architects Yearbook* 6:89–94.

VAN HENEGOUWEN, JAN

Jan van Henegouwen (14th century), who is also known as Jan I van den Dom and who is listed in a Utrecht chronicle as Magister Johannes de Hannonia, seems to have been called from Hainault to Utrecht by his compatriot Bishop Guy d'Avesnes. He is credited with the design of the lower, square stories of the western tower of the Cathedral of Saint Martin, Utrecht, on which he began construction in 1321. The tower, influential by its great height, was completed in 1382 by Jan II van den Dom.

ELIZABETH SCHWARTZBAUM

WORK

1321, Saint Martin's Cathedral (tower), Utrecht, Netherlands.

BIBLIOGRAPHY

KUILE, ENGELBERT HENDRICK TER 1942 *De Dom van Utrecht*. Maastricht, Netherlands: Leiter-Nypels.
MULLER, SAMUEL 1906 *De Dom van Utrecht*. Utrecht, Netherlands: Breijer.

VAN HERENGRAVE, HERMAN

Herman van Herengrave (16th century) was town mason of Nijmegen, Netherlands. As such designed the Latin or Apostolic School (1544–1546) in that town. It is built mainly in the Gothic style, with a remarkable mixture of early Renaissance details. In a later work, the older part of the Town Hall of Nijmegen (1554–1555), the Renaissance elements are more obvious, although that style is not yet fully developed. The decorations, antique medallions, and frontons are by the sculptor Cornelis Sass of Utrecht.

MARIET J. H. WILLINGE

WORKS

1544–1546, Latin or Apostolic School; 1554–1555 Townhall; Nijmegen, Netherlands.

BIBLIOGRAPHY

FOCKEMA ANDREAE, S. J.; KUILE, E. H. TER; and HEKKER, R. C. 1957 Volume 2 in *Duizend jarr bouwen in Nederland*. Amsterdam: Albert de Lange.
GORISSEN, F. 1956 *Stede-atlas van Nijmegen*. Arnhem, Netherlands: S. Gouda Quint.

VAN OBBERGEN, ANTON

The Flemish architect Anton Van Obbergen (active c.1577–c.1611) had CORNELIS FLORIS as his teacher. He moved to Danzig (now Gdańsk, Po-land) in 1568, where he directed the fortification of the Castle of Weichselmunde. He later distinguished himself as an able builder of fortresses, a distinction which put him in demand in Denmark, Germany, and in Poland. In 1592, he replaced HANS VREDEMAN DE VRIES as military engineer of the city of Danzig, where he worked until his death. The arsenal in Danzig (1602–1605) is the most lavish of his buildings.

Van Obbergen's art had a decisive influence on the style of the area. Engaged as a technician as well as an artist, he was the most brilliant importer of the Renaissance in Denmark and above all in Danzig.

PIERRE LENAIN
Translated from French by
Shara Wasserman

WORKS

1577–1585, Château Kronborg (begun by J. Steenwinkel), Helsinger, Denmark. 1597–1598, Patrician Houses (with J. Strakowski); 1602–1605, Arsenal (with J. Strakowski); 1608–1611, City Hall (remodeling); Danzig, Poland.

VAN OSDEL, JOHN MILLS

John Mills Van Osdel (1811–1891), born in Baltimore, learned building skills from his carpenter father. He also studied architectural books and later became associate editor of *American Mechanic.* He went to Chicago in 1837 to build Mayor Ogden's mansion and became that city's first architect, opening an office in 1844. He designed its first City Hall (1848) and Court House (1853). Of the hundreds of structures—public, commerical, and residential—that he built before and after the Great Fire of 1871 few survive. He pioneered fireproofing, was a leader and counselor in his profession, and served on many civic and government bodies.

MARGOT GAYLE

WORKS

*1837, William B. Ogden Mansion; *1848, City Hall and Market; *1851, Second Presbyterian Church; *1853, Court House; *1856, Ironfront Warehouses; 1872, McCarthy Building, Washington and Dearborn Streets; 1872, Peter Page Leather Goods Store, Lake and State Streets; *1873, Kendall Fireproof Building; *1873, Tremont House Hotel; *1875, Palmer House Hotel; Chicago.

BIBLIOGRAPHY

CONDIT, CARL W. 1968 *American Building: Materials and Techniques from the First Colonial Settlements to the Present.* University of Chicago Press.

ERICSSON, HENRY 1942 *Sixty Years a Builder*. Chicago: Kroch.

John Van Osdel: A Quarter Century of Chicago Architecture. 1898 Chicago: Swift.

LOWE, DAVID 1975 *Lost Chicago*. Boston: Houghton Mifflin.

RANDALL, FRANK A. 1949 *A History of the Development of Building Construction in Chicago*. Urbana: University of Illinois Press.

TALLMADGE, THOMAS EDDY 1941 *Architecture in Old Chicago*. University of Chicago Press.

VAN PEDE, HENRI

The work of Henri van Pede (16th century), a Flemish architect and sculptor, was little known during his lifetime. Director of works in Brussels from 1516 and later city architect, he was called to work on the replacement of the Broodhuis (Bread House) on the Great Square of Brussels, working from projects designed by A. Keldermans (see KELDERMANS FAMILY). His personal career is illustrated by the Town Hall of Audenarde (1525–1530), a work much inspired by the Town Hall in Brussels, which places this artist among the last representatives of the late Gothic school of Brabant. The last years of his life seem to have been devoted to the remodeling and restoration of the Château of Louvain, commissioned by Charles V.

Van Pede belonged to that generation of architects who were marked by strong local Gothic traditions at a time when Italian tastes little by little entered the art of Flanders, beginning with painting.

PIERRE LENAIN
*Translated from French by
Shara Wasserman*

WORKS

1512–1536, Replacement of Broodhuis by the King's House, Brussels. 1525–1530, Town Hall of Audenarde, Belgium. 1531–1532, Ducal Chapel (reconstruction), Château of Louvain, Belgium.

VAN RIJSSELBERGHE, OCTAVE

Brother of the neo-impressionist painter Theo Van Rijsselberghe, Octave Van Rijsselberghe (1855–1929) studied at the Academy of Fine Arts in Ghent, Belgium, and trained in the Brussels office of JOSEPH POELAERT. Although his career began with a series of designs executed in an Italianate classical manner, he later built in a personal Art Nouveau style. In all of his designs, Van Rijsselberghe evidenced a predilection for robust massing. His appointment as chief architect to the *Compagnie des Grands Hôtels Européens* in 1900 assured the European scope of his professional reputation.

ALFRED WILLIS

WORKS

1892, Goblet d'Alviella House; *1893, Theo Van Rijsselberghe House; 1894, Paul Otlet House (interiors by H. Van de Velde); Brussels. 1896, Paul Signac Studio, Saint Tropez, France. 1903, Villas; 1905, Hôtel Bellevue (damaged and restored); Westende, Belgium. 1912, Octave Van Rijsselberghe House, Brussels.

BIBLIOGRAPHY

BORSI, FRANCO 1977 *Bruxelles 1900*. New York: Rizzoli.

DUMONT, ALEXIS 1952 "Notice sur Octave Van Rysselberghe." *Annuaire de l'Académie Royale de Belgique* 118:147–164.

PUTTEMANS, PIERRE 1976 *Modern Architecture in Belgium*. Brussels: Vokaer.

STEVENS, JACQUES, and HENVAUX, EMILE 1975 "Octave Van Rysselberghe (1855–1929)." *Aplus* Mar.:16–55.

STYNEN, HERMAN 1979 *Urbanisme et société: Louis Van der Swaelmen (1883–1929), animateur du mouvement moderne en Belgique*. Brussels: Mardaga.

VAN DER SWAELMEN, LOUIS 1929 "Octave Van Rijsselberghe, architecte." *La Cité* 7:145–148.

VAN RUYSBROECK, JAN

Jan van Ruysbroeck (?–1485), who is also known as Jan van den Berghe, was a sculptor as well as an architect. His earliest known work is a fountain for the Hospital of Our Lady in Oudenaarde, Belgium (1443–1445). He designed the tower of Saint Michael on the Brussels Town Hall (1449–1455) and the tower of the Church of Sainte-Gertrude, Louvain, Belgium (completed 1453). In 1459, he was named architect of the duchy of Brabant.

ELIZABETH SCHWARTZBAUM

WORKS

1443–1445, Hospital of Our Lady Fountain, Oudenaarde, Belgium. 1449–1455, Town Hall (tower of Saint-Michel), Brussels. Before 1453, Sainte-Gertrude (spire), Louvain, Belgium. 1479–1485, Notre-Dame, Anderlecht, Belgium. 1470–1485, Sainte-Gudule, Brussels.

BIBLIOGRAPHY

BATTARD, MARIUS 1948 *Beffrois, halles, hôtels de ville dans le nord de la France et la Belgique*. Arras, France: Brunet.

BOCK, VON HENNING 1972 "Architektur: Niederlande, Deutschland, Frankreich, England, Skandinavien." Pages 339–379 in Jan Bialostocki (editor), *Spätmittelalter und beginnende Neuzeit*. Berlin: Propyläen.

DES MAREZ, G. 1907 "L'ancien beffroi de la Ville de

Bruxelles." *Annales de la Société d'Archéologie de Bruxelles* 21:463–475.

DUVERGER, JOSEF 1933 *De Brusselsche steenbickeleren.* Ghent, Belgium: Vyncke.

EVEN, EDWARD VAN 1875 *Les auteurs de la tour de Sainte-Gertrude.* Louvain.

VAN 'S GRAVESANDE, ARENT

Arent van 's Gravesande (1600?–1662) was municipal architect to various towns in Holland: The Hague (1636–1639), Leyden (1639–1651), and Middelburg (from 1656). He had previously worked on the palaces of Stadtholder Frederick Henry. Characteristic of his style is the use of giant pilasters. Well-known examples are the Sant Sebastiaansdoelen (1636) in The Hague and the Lakenhal in Leyden. His Marekerk (1639–1649) in Leyden, an octagonal central church, is inspired by Italian examples. He completed the Oostkerk in Middelburg, a work started in 1646 by PIETER POST and Bartolomeus Drijfhout.

MARIET J. H. WILLINGE

WORKS

1636, Sant Sebastiaansdoelen, The Hague. 1639, Town Hall, Middelharnis, Netherlands. 1639–1640, Lakenhal; 1639–1649, Marekerk; 1640, Hofje van Brouchoven; 1655, Bibliotheca Thysiana; Leyden, Netherlands. 1657, Oostkerk, Middelburg, Netherlands.

BIBLIOGRAPHY

FOCKEMA, ANDREAE, S. J.; KUILE, E. H. TER; and HEKKER, R. C. 1957 Volume 2 in *Duizend jaar bouwen in Nederland.* Amsterdam: Lange.

OERLE, H. VAN 1943 "De bouwgeschiedenis van de Thisiusbibliotheek aan het Rapenburg." Pages 170–179 in *Leids Jaarboekje.* Leiden, Netherlands.

OZINGA, M. D. 1929 *De Protestantsche Kerkenbouw in Nederland van Hervorming tot Franschen tijd.* Amsterdam: Paris.

SLOTHOUWER, D. F. 1946 *De paleizen van Frederik Hendrik.* Leiden, Netherlands: Sijthoff.

TERWEN, J. J. 1964 *De ontwerpgeschiedenis van de Marekerk te Leiden.* Pages 231–256 in *Opus Musivum.* Assen, Netherlands: Van Gorcum.

VAN THIENEN, JAKOB

Known from a brief mention as Master of Sainte-Gudule in late fourteenth-century accounts of the city of Brussels, Jakob van Thienen (14th–15th centuries) was probably responsible for completing the south aisle of the Collegiate Church of Sainte-Gudule, Brussels (c.1400). In 1405, he worked with Jean Bornoy on the Town Hall of Brussels, of which he is credited with the design of the left wing (begun 1402), the first section to be completed.

ELIZABETH SCHWARTZBAUM

WORKS

1383–c.1410, Notre-Dame au Lac (aisles of the nave), Tienen, Belgium. c.1400, Sainte-Gudule (south aisle); 1402–c.1405, Town Hall (left wing); Brussels.

BIBLIOGRAPHY

DUVERGER, JOSEF 1933 *De Brusselsche steenbickeleren.* Ghent, Belgium: Vyncke.

LEFÈVRE, PLACIDE 1956–1957 "La collégiale des Saints Michel et Gudule a Bruxelles." *Annales de la Société Royale Archéologie de Bruxelles* 99:16–72.

VAN 'T HOFF, ROBERT

After the completion of his architectural education in England, Robert van 't Hoff (1887–1979), who was born in Rotterdam, Netherlands, visited the United States in 1914 where he studied FRANK LLOYD WRIGHT's work. In the Netherlands in 1915–1916, he built two villas in Huis ter Heide, near Utrecht. Their concrete structure and flat, cantilevered roofs clearly evidence the influence of Frank Lloyd Wright. During construction of these villas, Van 't Hoff became acquainted with THEO VAN DOESBURG and J. J. P. OUD, and when Van Doesburg established the magazine *De Stijl* in 1917, Van 't Hoff was listed as contributor. In 1920, he left *De Stijl* and around the same time ended his architectural practice. Three years later he moved to England.

WIM DE WIT

WORKS

1911, Bosch en Duin Villa, Amersfoortse Weg, Huis ter Heide, Netherlands. 1911, De Zaaier Farm, Lunteren, Netherlands. 1913, Augusts John Studio-House, Mallord Street, London. 1914–1916, A. B. Henny Villa, Amersfoortse Weg; 1915–1916, J. M. Verloop Villa, Ruysdaellaan; Huis ter Heide, Netherlands.

BIBLIOGRAPHY

Bouwen '20–'40. 1971 Eindhoven, Netherlands: Van Abbemuseum.

FANELLI, GIOVANNI (1968)1978 *Moderne architectuur in Nederland: 1900–1940.* Translated from Italian by Wim de Wit. 's-Gravenhage, Netherlands: Staatsuitgeverij.

GIEDION, SIEGFRIED (1941)1967 *Space, Time and Architecture.* 5th ed., rev. & enl. Cambridge, Mass.: Harvard University Press.

JAFFÉ, HANS L. C. 1956 *De Stijl: 1917–1931.* Amsterdam: Meulenhoff.

JONKER, GERT 1979a "Robert van 't Hoff maker van

het kleinst denkbare oeuvre." *Bouw* 12:6–8.

JONKER, GERT 1979*b* "En poging tot reconstructie van de werken van Robert van 't Hoff." *Bouw* 13:17–23.

Nederlandse Architectuur, 1880–1930, Americana. 1975 Otterlo, Netherlands: Rijkmuseum.

ZEVI, BRUNO (1953)1974 *Poetica dell'architettura neoplastica.* 2d ed. Milan: Einaudi.

VANTONGERLOO, GEORGES

Georges Vantongerloo (1886–1965) was born in Antwerp, Belgium. As a sculptor he became a prominent member of *de Stijl* in 1917. His abstract sculptures were based on mathematical ratios expressed in architectonic forms. His architectural projects include a bridge for Antwerp designed as a habitable structure (1928), a "Skyscraper City" (1930) similar to his sculptures in its cubiform structure, and a "Subterranean Aerodrome" (1931).

REGINALD MALCOLMSON

VANVITELLI, LUIGI

Luigi Vanvitelli (1700–1773), widely recognized as one of the great figures of eighteenth-century Italian architecture, is famous primarily for one building—the royal palace at Caserta, just north of Naples. Begun in 1751, Caserta combines the Italian Renaissance tradition of rectilinear geometric planning with the French practice, seen in the Louvre and at Versailles, of housing the chief administrative, military, and cultural organs of the state in a large building that served as the royal residence.

Born in Naples on May 12, 1700, Vanvitelli's father was the Dutch landscape painter Gaspar van Wittel. Within a year of Vanvitelli's birth the family moved to Rome, where he studied literature, philosophy, geometry, and physics as well as design and the monuments of ancient Rome. He learned landscape and figure drawing from his father. His architectural mentor was FILIPPO JUVARRA, whose buildings in Turin and Lisbon provided models for the campanile that Vanvitelli built at Loreto for the Santa Casa (1750–1754), although FRANCESCO BORROMINI's campanile for Sant'Andrea delle Fratte (1665) in Rome, was equally influential. An expert in the sumptuously curvilinear architecture of the late Baroque, Vanvitelli also became a practical builder–engineer and the creator of simple rectilinear structures in the Roman tradition of DOMENICO FONTANA.

In 1732 Vanvitelli entered the competition in Rome for the design of a new façade for the church of San Giovanni in Laterano. Though he failed to win, his excellent showing against ALESSANDRO GALILEI who won, and against a second prominent Roman architect, NICOLA SALVI, who received the Trevi Fountain commission as a consolation prize, guaranteed Vanvitelli's reputation. Awarded the commission to build a lazaretto in the harbor at Ancona, Vanvitelli created a fine, impressive polygon based on the classic shape of the Renaissance bastion (1733–1738). In the same city, he also built the church of the Gesù (1743) and the Arch of Clement (1738).

Yet Vanvitelli's fame—and also a certain accompanying notoriety—remained anchored to Rome. There he created an enviable reputation despite severe attacks by many critics, particularly concerning design to stabilize MICHELANGELO's dome of Saint Peter's, which had developed cracks. Vanvitelli's plan was successfully adopted and he emerged with a strengthened reputation. Other work in Rome included the wings for the Odescalchi Palace, completed with Salvi in 1750, and the curious, controversial enlargement of Santa Maria degli Angeli (1749), the church Michelangelo had erected out of the ruinous Baths of Diocletian. More serene in effect, and more like Caserta in style, is the cloister of Sant'Agostino (1746–1750). Yet the critics attacked even this large, pleasant building, whose rectangular court is accented with offset openings in the manner of Borromini.

Thus, Vanvitelli's Roman career had been problematic. By the age of fifty he had completed no major building on his own. At this point, as an obvious opportunity to prove himself, he accepted the summons to Naples to erect a huge royal palace for Carlo di Borbone, king of the Two Sicilies. Vanvitelli worked expeditiously, and by December 1751, the drawings were ready. Carlo, who had architectural talents, may have assisted with the design and may have dictated the general layout. The scheme is in fact very close to ROBERT DE COTTE's second project for Buen Retiro (1714–1715), a royal palace near Madrid that King Carlo had known as a child.

The construction of Caserta began in 1752, and by 1774 the outer shell of the palace was finished. The huge palace, 800 feet wide and 600 deep, was to contain not only the royal family but, as at Versailles, the court, leading administrative and military bodies, a theater, a large chapel, and rooms for important state functions. A plan for a new town, Caserta Nuova, was partially implemented with the building of a pair of quadrants around a grand avenue that was to lead straight to Naples. Here too, Vanvitelli was clearly inspired by Versailles, with its Place d'Armes and its Avenue de Paris.

The gardens, which stretched behind the palace for two or more miles, are dominated by a descending spine of waters and a combination canal and roadway that featured cascades decorated with marble sculptured groups of mythological figures. Although he planned to continue the canal to Naples as a water supply for the city neither this nor the avenue to Naples was ever completed.

Caserta's great feature is its plan. A rectangle with the standard Renaissance proportions of 3:4, it consists of straight ranges of rooms laid out according to an over-all uniform grid. On the two ground floors are storerooms and offices, on the main floor reception rooms and royal apartments, and on the upper floors lodging for courtiers and servants. The outer ranges of these rooms make up the perimeter of the rectangle. Its central axes are composed of further ranges forming a central cross within the rectangle. The points where these ranges interlock are marked by major interior spaces—theater, vestibules, reception rooms, apartments, and the like.

The entrance system is stunning. The façades surround tall, terra-cotta colored, rusticated basement, above which rises the red brick bulk of the main floors. These are subdivided by a giant composite order of pilasters and engaged columns in limestone. In the center of the main façade a triumphal arch is set into a temple front and around the window and balcony from which the king could greet crowds below. Beneath, the basement level has its own great archway, followed by a 600-foot vaulted triumphal corridor, wide and tall enough to accommodate the largest royal coaches. The corridor passes directly through the building to the garden on axis with the canal. The eye is drawn to the flank of Monte Tifata where the garden begins with a rocky cascade. Meanwhile the triumphal corridor is inflected with niches, grouped engaged columns, and sculpture. At each of its three main crossing spaces, diagonally offset arches lead into the courtyards, as at the convent of

Sant'Agostino in Rome. In its central octagon a stair hall leads off to the right, rising past statues of royal virtues into a frescoed vault of Apollo and his muses.

The innumerable state rooms of the palace are somewhat less impressive. Work on their decoration continued after Vanvitelli's death in 1773 as well as past that of his son and pupil, Carlo, in 1821. The process was finally halted with the fall of the Bourbon dynasty in 1860. Even then the interior was incomplete, as it still is today.

Vanvitelli also found time for other buildings during his Neapolitan period. He built an aqueduct system (1752–1764) to supply the palace gardens at Caserta, and in 1756, a façade and stairs for the Palazzo Calabritto, Naples. In 1761–1762 he began construction of his major Neapolitan church, the Annunziata, completed by Carlo Vanvitelli in 1782. With its single colossal Corinthian colonnade forming the interior, the Annunziata, like Caserta, represents a step from late Baroque toward neoclassicism. In 1757–1763,

Vanvitelli.
Royal Palace.
Caserta, Italy.
Begun 1752

Vanvitelli.
Royal Palace (campania).
Caserta, Italy.
Begun 1752

he designed the Foro Carolino (now Piazza Dante), a broad half-oval in the city's main Renaissance street, the via Toledo. Vanvitelli was active in other Neapolitan projects, and built, as well, in nearby towns and at Brescia, Milan, and Genoa.

Vanvitelli's achievements reflected not only the advent of neoclassicism but that of neoclassicism's architectural programs. The first era of absolute monarchy, symbolized by Louis XIV, was past, and a new, not less absolute, but enlightened type of rule was symbolized by Louis XIV's more liberal descendants, including Vanvitelli's patron Carlo di Borbone. As the palace of an enlightened absolute king, Caserta was designed to draw power from the landed aristocracy and to concentrate it on the crown. At Caserta, the monarch dealt directly with his people through a large administrative machine. The functional aim was control of large numbers of workers and visitors. In these respects Caserta foreshadows the palatial congress halls, ministries, barracks, office buildings, and other institutions of the period of neoclassicism, for example the projects of ETIENNE-LOUIS BOULLÉE.

G. L. HERSEY

WORKS

1733–1738, Lazaretto and Pier; 1738, Arch of Clement; Ancona, Italy. 1739, Church and Cloister of the Olivetani, Perugia, Italy. 1743, Church of the Gesù, Ancona, Italy. 1746–1750, Cloister of Sant'Agostino; 1749, Church of Santa Maria degli Angeli (enlargement); 1750, Odescalchi Palace (wings; with NICOLA SALVI); 1750, St. Peter's (decorations for the tribune); Rome. 1750–1754, Santa Casa (campanile); Loreto, Italy. Begun 1752, Royal Palace; 1752–1764, Aqueduct to Naples; Caserta, Italy. *1753–1754, Cavalry Barracks; *1755, Palazzo Calabritto (façade and stairs); 1757–1763, Foro Carolino (now Piazza Dante); 1759, Church of San Marcellino; Begun 1761, Church of the Annunziata (completed by Carlo Vanvitelli in 1782); 1766, Casacalenda Palace; 1772, Perelli Palace; Naples.

BIBLIOGRAPHY

DEFILIPPIS, FELICE 1968 Il palazzo reale di Caserta e i Borboni di Napoli. Naples: Mauro.
DE FUSCO, RENATO (editor) 1973 Luigi Vanvitelli. Naples: Edizioni scientifiche italiane.
FAGIOLO DELL'ARCO, MARCELLO 1863 Funzioni simboli valori della reggia di Caserta. Rome: Dell'Arco.
HERSEY, GEORGE L. "Caserta: Myth and Order in an Absolute Palace." Manuscript in preparation.
VANVITELLI, LUIGI 1756 Dichiarazione dei disegni del reale palazzo di Caserta. Naples: Regia Stamperia.
VANVITELLI, LUIGI 1976 Le Lettere di Luigi Vanvitelli della Biblioteca palatina di Caserta. Edited by Franco Strazzullo with an introduction by Roberto Pane. Galatina, Italy: Congedo.
VANVITELLI, LUIGI (the Younger) (1823)1975 Vita di Luigi Vanvitelli. Edited by Mario Rotili. Naples: Edizioni scientifiche italiane.

VARDY, JOHN

John Vardy (?–1765), a follower of WILLIAM KENT, was a skilled draftsman and designer in the Palladian (see ANDREA PALLADIO) manner. His origins are unknown, but his long career in the Office of Works is documented. He was successively clerk of works at Greenwich (1736–1744); Hampton Court (1745–1746); Whitehall, Westminster, and Saint James's (1746–1754); and Kensington (1754–1761). He was also clerk of works at Chelsea Hospital (1756–1765) and surveyor to the Royal Mint (1749–1763). The most important of his many privately commissioned designs was for the Palladian Spencer House (1756–1765), but he also showed himself to be an accomplished designer of interiors in the rococo style. In 1744, he published Some Designs of Mr Inigo Jones and Mr William Kent, an Anglo-Palladian pattern book.

JOHN BOLD

WORKS

1756–1765, Spencer House, London. 1761–1763, Hackwood Park (alterations), Hampshire, England. *1763–1765, Stanmore House, Middlesex, England.

BIBLIOGRAPHY

COLVIN, H. M. (editor) 1976 The History of the King's Works: 1660–1782. London: H.M. Stationery Office.

VASANZIO, GIOVANNI

Giovanni Vasanzio (c.1550–1621), or Jan van Santen, was born in Utrecht and went to Rome around 1595, where he remained until his death. He began his career as a maker of inlaid furniture, but once in Rome, he seems to have entered the circle of FLAMINIO PONZIO and devoted himself to the practice of architecture. Upon Ponzio's death, Vasanzio succeeded his master as papal architect to Paul V Borghese, but because CARLO MADERNO remained architect of St. Peter's and GIOVANNI BATTISTA SORIA received most of Cardinal Scipione Borghese's ecclesiastical commissions, the position carried but little authority.

Vasanzio's works, which all date from the last decade of his life, are almost exclusively comprised of villas, fountains, and gardens. His only notable sacred commission called for the completion of the façade of San Sebastiano fuori le mura (1612), begun by Ponzio in 1609. In his design of the upper story, Vasanzio created a crisp, classical elevation without the dense ornamental surface treatment that characterizes most of his buildings.

More typical and more ambitious is the Villa

Borghese on the Pincian Hill (1613–1615). In plan, this building follows the design of the traditional Renaissance *villa suburbana* as introduced a century earlier in BALDASSARE PERUZZI's Villa Farnesina, but the façade elevation with its profusion of niches and statuary juxtaposed to areas of flat walling recalls more recent mannerist prototypes like PIRRO LIGORIO's Casino of Pius IV and ANNIBALE LIPPI's Villa Medici. Even more mannerist in its ornamental vocabulary is the large Aviary that Vasanzio built a short distance away. That this retardatory structure actually postdates the main villa by two years suggests the extent to which Vasanzio rejected the progressive reforms of his age.

Vasanzio's second most important commission called for the enlargement of the Villa Mondragone in Frascati (1614), begun by Martino Longhi the Younger (see LONGHI FAMILY) in 1573. Here, the architect contributed an entrance portal, a wing with loggias, and a water theater. All three of these structures make extensive use of rustication, an ornamental device that again looks back to mannerist prototypes of the mid-sixteenth century. The new wing or porticus may be considered Vasanzio's most novel design despite his probable reliance on ANDREA PALLADIO's Basilica in Vicenza (1550) for the basic structural concept.

Notwithstanding the involvement of Maderno, the Casino dell' Aurora at the Borghese Garden Palace on the Quirinal Hill should probably be attributed to Vasanzio.

Among his many commissions for fountains, two works stand out: the architectural Fontana dell' Acqua Paola at the Ponte Sisto (1613, formerly in Via Giulia), and the Fontana del Galera (1620) in the Vatican Gardens, constructed in the form of a three-masted warship.

Although he completely sublimated his northern European heritage in developing a wholly Roman manner, Vasanzio was always content to practice picturesque variations on well-established architectural themes. Unlike his more distinguished contemporary Maderno, he not only failed to challenge prevailing tastes, but his work was consciously anachronistic in flavor.

JOHN VARRIANO

WORKS

1612, San Sebastiano fuori le mura (rebuilding completed); 1612–1613, Casino dell'Aurora, Borghese Garden Palace on the Quirinal; 1613–1615, Villa Borghese on the Pincio; 1613, Fountain, Acqua Paola at Ponte Sisto; (A)1614, Fountain of the Eagle, Vatican Gardens; 1614, Villa Mondragone (expansion), Frascati; 1615–1616, Fountains of Velo and Pioggia, Quirinal Gardens; 1617, Aviary, Villa Borghese on the Pincio; 1618, Fuomo at Monteporzio (restoration); 1618–1619,

Vasanzio.
Villa Borghese on the
  Pincio.
Rome.
1613–1615

Park and Fishpond, Casale of Cecchignola; 1620, Fountain of the Galera, Vatican Gardens; Rome.

BIBLIOGRAPHY

BAGLIONE, GIOVANNI (1641)1635 Pages 175–176 in *Le vite de' pittori, scultori, et architetti.* Reprint. Rome: Calzone.

HIBBARD, HOWARD 1971 *Carlo Maderno and Roman Architecture: 1580–1630.* University Park: Pennsylvania State University Press.

HOOGEWERFF, GODEFRIDUS 1928 "Giovanni van Santen, architetto della Villa Borghese." *Roma* 6:1–12, 49–64.

HOOGEWERFF, GODEFRIDUS 1942 "Giovanni Vansanzio fra gli architetti romani del tempo di Paolo V." *Palladio* 6:49–56.

HOOGEWERFF, GODEFRIDUS 1943 "Architetti in Roma durante il pontificato di Paolo V Borghese." *Archivio della R. Deputazione Romana di Storia Patria* 66:135–147.

ONOFRIO, CESARE D' 1957 *Le fontane di Roma.* Rome: Staderini.

VASARI, GIORGIO

Giorgio Vasari (1511–1574) was one of the most versatile artists in sixteenth-century Italy. Best known for his *Lives of the Most Excellent Painters, Sculptors, and Architects* (1550), Vasari was a talented painter and architect whose organizational skills and tireless energy facilitated the swift completion of several large-scale projects which combined painting and architecture. A consummate court artist, Vasari served Duke Cosimo I de'Medici (1519–1574), who sought to make Tuscany as important (and splendid) as the major European royal houses. Consequently, Vasari's Florentine buildings were linked to his patron's search for status and legitimacy through architectural magnificence, thus making his designs primary instruments of ducal politics.

Born in Arezzo, Vasari was taken to Florence in 1524 by the Medici where he enjoyed a privileged artistic education. His teachers included Andrea del Sarto, Rosso Fiorentino, and, for a short time, MICHELANGELO. A decade later, Vasari's first architectural project, the organ loft for Arezzo's Cathedral (1535–1537) shows a somewhat slavish admiration for Michelangelo by employing massive volutes inspired by his teacher's designs for the tomb of Pope Julius II. The source did not guarantee success; its details contrast in size and scale with its own ornament and statuary. Despite this inauspicious start, Michelangelo remained a fertile source for Vasari's architectural ideas and later encouraged him to continue his study of architecture.

In the 1540s, Vasari's activity as a painter took him to Bologna, Rome, Venice, and Naples. There was scarcely any time to develop an architectural career, and the only major building from this decade is the house in Arezzo which Vasari remodeled and decorated (1540–1548) as his own residence. The exterior is simple and unornamented, but Vasari originally planned to cover the main façade with graffito decorations which were never executed. The interior, however is more elaborate, using in the main *salone* an architectural framework derived from Michelangelo's New Sacristy at San Lorenzo in Florence.

Vasari's architectural career began to flourish in Rome under the patronage of Pope Julius III. In his autobiography in the *Lives,* Vasari claimed to have laid out a rural residence for Julius (then Cardinal del Monte) near his native Monte Sansovino. Upon Julius's ascension to the papacy, Vasari moved to Rome where he collaborated with other architects on two important projects. Vasari's preliminary design for the first, the del Monte Chapel in San Pietro in Montorio (1550), employed an elaborate system of architectural and sculptural decoration, but it was executed in a more sober vein by BARTOLOMEO AMMANNATI. For the Villa Giulia (1551–1553), a papal retreat not far beyond the walls of Rome, Vasari, as coordinating architect, prepared the first designs which were then reviewed by Michelangelo and later completed by GIACOMO BAROZZI DA VIGNOLA and Ammannati. In both cases, however, it is difficult to judge Vasari's share in their design since their execution was left to his collaborators.

In 1555, Vasari returned to Florence where he served Duke Cosimo as artistic superintendent at the Medici court, thereby involving him in projects that ranged in size and permanence from temporary architectural decorations to large urban buildings. Almost immediately, Vasari began a series of projects within the Palazzo Vecchio which tested his skills as an architect, painter, and administrator. The most elaborate was the transformation of the main hall, the Sala di Cinquecento, which was redesigned to compete in magnificence with the Ducal Palace in Venice. In 1563, its roof was raised seven meters, a gallery was inserted at the southern end of the hall, and an architectural setting was created for a series of decorations executed from Vasari's designs which celebrated Florence's dominion over Tuscany. In addition, a modern coordinated system of staircases was constructed to separate the private quarters from the state rooms while linking both with the main entry. During the 1560s, the ducal residence was transferred across the Arno river to the Pitti Palace which Vasari linked to the Palazzo Vecchio by building the Corridoio, a raised, private passage more than a half mile long. Although this structure has always been considered a novelty, prototypes for it can be found in Rome and in ducal palaces in Mantua and Ferrara. Vasari also provided designs for the Studiolo (1570), a small room which housed precious objects. The decorations for this treasure chamber as well as for the adjacent main hall were executed with the assistance of Vasari's large staff.

Vasari's masterpiece, the Uffizi, was begun in 1560 to provide offices for thirteen Florentine magistracies which were scattered throughout the city. Its most striking feature, a direct visual connection between the Palazzo Vecchio and the Arno River, was accomplished by creating a pair of repetitive façades linked by an open loggia. The design was based, in large part, on a street which had been created to rid the city of an undesirable neighborhood, and each magistracy was given an individual house facing the street. This was directly reflected in the façades which are made up of three-bay units flanked by piers. Vasari's sources here are Roman—a three-story façade similar to DONATO BRAMANTE's Belvedere; a loggia inspired by BALDASSARE PERUZZI's Palazzo Massimo—but the effect is emphatically Florentine in its use of *pietra serena* details projecting in relief from the façade's surface. There are scarcely any direct prototypes for an administrative building like this, though Bramante's project for a tribunal palace in Rome shows separate apartments for the judicial courts, and repetitive houses linked by arcades are found in the Procuratie Vecchie in Venice. The Uffizi was the structure most representative of Duke Cosimo's Florence: an administrative structure in a state that prized organization and efficiency.

Vasari's religious architecture was often constrained by existing construction. The tetrastyle plan of Santa Maria Nuova, a pilgrimage church outside Cortona, had been fixed by an earlier architect, but its three-dimensional appearance is entirely due to Vasari, who completed it (1554).

Here several different traditions were married. For example, its two-story exterior recalls LEON BATTISTA ALBERTI's façade of Santa Maria Novella in Florence, but the shape of its interior enclosure—a series of domes and vaults within a Greek cross—shows close parallels with Venetian churches like San Giovanni Crisostomo. Vasari's elegant details were inspired by a more immediate source, FRANCESCO DI GIORGIO MARTINI's Santa Maria del Calcinaio, also in Cortona.

Construction problems tested Vasari's ingenuity in completing the Madonna dell' Umilità in Pistoia (1561–1569). In 1495, VENTURA VITONI began the church with its octagonal central hall, but a lack of funds prevented its completion. Only the dome remained unbuilt, and, after shoring up Vitoni's arches and adding an additional story to his base, Vasari added a cupola whose two shells were separated and supported by discontinuous internal ribs. The result was a curious hybrid which crossed the exterior of FILIPPO BRUNELLESCHI's dome of Florence Cathedral with the substructure of the Florentine Baptistery. The dome's excessive height was due to its political message—the imposition of Florentine control over subject cities—but its technical problems (cracking, movement) solved by Ammannati's later repairs were due to imperfections in both Vitoni's original construction and Vasari's addition.

Vasari's design for Saints Flora and Lucilla in Arezzo (1565–1586), also known as the Badia, resulted from a different set of circumstances. Its most important feature, a Venetian-inspired plan similar to San Marco, may be understood in two ways: as a reflection of the taste of the Badia's monastic order, the Cassinese, who originated in the Veneto, or as Vasari's conscious emulation of the *maniera greca,* his term for both Romanesque and Byzantine architecture, and the style of the original Badia in Arezzo. Its graft of foreign elements onto local traditions is not convincing, and Vasari's failure to mention the Badia in the *Lives* may be due to his collaboration on its design with Don Vicenzo Borghini, a member of the Cassinese order.

Vasari also executed a significant number of church renovations in Tuscany. Religious practice during the Counter Reformation required unimpeded access to the main altar to facilitate frequent communion and the layman's direct involvement with the Mass. In 1554, a scheme was proposed for the renovation of Arezzo's Cathedral, but a conservative clergy blocked its execution. A decade later, Vasari began the renovation of another church in Arezzo, the Pieve, where the high altar was designed as a sepulchral monument for the Vasari family. This project, removed to the Badia in 1865, became the model for the more extensive changes to Santa Croce (1565) and Santa Maria Novella (1565, greatly altered in 1861) in Florence. In both churches, Vasari removed medieval rood screens which blocked views of the high altars, and the interiors were completely whitewashed, thus covering any earlier fresco decoration. The side aisles were also united with the nave by creating a series of repetitive tabernacles whose altarpieces were specifically commissioned for the renovations. Though these projects generally conformed to the beliefs of Duke Cosimo, who closely monitored their development, Vasari's aim was primarily architectural—to give a medieval church interior the same unified effect found in Renaissance examples like San Lorenzo.

Siting was a crucial factor in Vasari's last building, the Loggia in Arezzo. Begun in 1570 as an investment by the Confraternity of the Misericordia, the Loggia gave a new focus to the Piazza Grande by replacing a group of structures which had fallen into disrepair during the construction of the town's fortress. Despite its private patronage, the Loggia was the most important civic building in sixteenth-century Arezzo. Its lower floor contained shops with mezzanines above them, while the upper level accommodated a wide range of functions—the Monte di Piete (a state-run loan bank), state chancellery, and five row houses sometimes occupied by government administrators. An ingenious section was designed to fit the sharply sloping site; the offices and row houses were entered from the rear at a higher level than the shops facing the square below. Vasari's sympathy for older structures—a characteristic not often stressed by his critics—can be seen in the

Vasari.
Uffizi.
Florence.
1560–1580s

derivation of the lower level of the Loggia's façade from the adjacent medieval Misericordia palace.

Vasari was recognized as a major architect in his own time, but the impact of his buildings on later generations was minimal. Another legacy, the commentary on architecture in the 1550 and 1568 editions of the *Lives,* has always been a basic source for the study of Renaissance architecture. Vasari's theoretical statements were unsystematic and unoriginal, drawing mainly on VITRUVIUS, Alberti, and SEBASTIANO SERLIO, but his criticism of individual architects was professional and informed. In comparison to the first edition, judgments in the second are sounder and the discussion of architecture has been greatly expanded. Old prejudices against medieval buildings were modified, and assessments of some architects were changed. Vasari's growth as a critic was due to his own practice (which largely fell between the two editions) and his personal knowledge of numerous structures and their designers. Despite factual errors, the *Lives* has been called a remarkable achievement for an age lacking modern standards of historical accuracy.

LEON SATKOWSKI

WORKS

1535–1537, Cathedral (organ loft), Arezzo, Italy. *1537, Triumphal Arch (for the entry of Emperor Charles V), Piazza San Felice, Florence. 1540–1548, Giorgio Vasari House, Arezzo, Italy. *1548?, Layout of Farm or Garden for Cardinal del Monte, Monte Sansovino, Italy. 1551–1553, Villa Giulia (with Giacomo Barozzi da Vignola and Bartolomeo Ammannati), Rome. 1554, Santa Maria Nuova (completion), Cortona, Italy. 1556, Grotta Grande (façade; completed by Bernardo Buontalenti), Boboli Gardens; 1556–1574, Palazzo Vecchio (renovations); 1560–1580s, Uffizi; Florence. 1561–1569, Madonna dell' Umilità (cupola), Pistoia, Italy. 1562–?, Piazzo dei Cavaliere, Pisa, Italy. 1564, Pieve (renovation); 1564, Saints Flora and Lucilla; Arezzo, Italy. 1564, Tomb of Michelangelo, Santa Croce, Florence. 1565, Santa Croce (renovation); 1565, Santa Maria Novella (renovation); Corridoio, Italy. 1568–?, Santa Maria della Quercia, Lucignanao, Italy. 1569–1572, Madonna della Vittoria, Foiano della Chiana, Italy. 1570–1574, Loggia (not completed until 1596), Arezzo, Italy.

BIBLIOGRAPHY

BOASE, T. S. R. 1979 *Vasari: The Man and the Book.* N.J.: Princeton University Press.
HALL, MARCIA B. 1979 *Renovation and Counter Reformation; Vasari and Duke Cosimo in Sta Maria Novella and Sta Croce.* Oxford: Clarendon.
SATKOWSKI, LEON 1979 *Studies on Vasari's Architecture.* New York: Garland.
VASARI, GIORGIO (1550)1973 *Le opere de Giòrgio Vasari, con nuove annotazioni e commenti.* 9 vols. Edited by G. Milanesi. Reprint. Florence: Sansoni. Origi- nally published in 1550 with the title *Le vite de piv eccelenti architetti.* There are many English transla- tions and selections from Vasari's *Lives,* the standard one by G. du C. de Vere was published in London by the Medici Society in 1912–1915.
VASARI, GIORGIO 1960 *Vasari on Technique, Being the Introduction to the Three Arts of Design.* Translated by Louia S. Maclehose. Reprint. New York: Dover. A translation of Vasari's introduction to the *Lives,* with notes and commentary by G. Baldwin Brown.
VENTURI, ADOLFO 1939 "Giorgio Vasari." Volume 11, part 2, pages 385–454 in *Storia del arte italiana.* Milan: Hoepli.

VASCONI, FILIPPO

Filippo Vasconi (1687–c.1730) was a Roman archi- tect and printmaker; he was a nephew of CARLO FONTANA and an associate of FILIPPO JUVARRA. Although Vasconi won first prize in architecture in each of three years (1705–1707) of the Concorso Clementino at the Accademia di San Luca, noth- ing is known of his architecture. Drawings by Vasconi are in the Kunstbibliothek in Berlin as well as at the Accademia di San Luca. He engraved plates, primarily architectural views, for Juvarra and many others in Rome.

HENRY A. MILLON

BIBLIOGRAPHY

JACOB, SABINE 1975 Numbers 763–773 in *Italienische Zeichnungen der Kunstbibliothek Berlin.* Berlin: Staat- liche Museen Preussischer Kulturbesitz.
MARCONI, PAOLO; CIPRIANI, ANGELA; and VALERIANI, ENRICO 1974 Volume 1, pages 7–8, plates 153–156, 174–177 in *I disegni di architettura dell'archivio storico dell'Accademia di San Luca.* Rome: de Luca.
MYERS, M. 1975 *Architectural and Ornament Draw- ings.* New York: Metropolitan Museum.

VASIL'OV and TSOLOV

Born in Oriakhovo, Bulgaria, Ivan Tsokov Vasil'ov (1893–1979) grew up in Sofia. He studied art (1910–1912) at the Munich Academy of Art and architecture (1913–1919) at the Polytechnic Insti- tute in Karlsruhe, Germany. After practicing briefly in Germany (1917–1919) and with Stancho Belkovski (see BELKOVSKI AND DANCHOV) from 1922 to 1924, Vasil'ov joined with Dimitur Tsolov (1896–1970) in a long, successful career.

Born also in Oriakhovo, Bulgaria, Tsolov fought in World War I before departing for Vi- enna in 1920 to study architecture. Graduating in 1925 from the Polytechnic Institute in Munich, he returned to Sofia, co-edited the first professional periodical, *Arkhitektura,* and organized and chaired (1949–1965) the Housing Program at Sofia Polytechnic Institute.

Until absorbed by the State Central Architectural Design Organization of Bulgaria in 1948, Vasil'ov and Tsolov completed over 350 buildings, mostly with their interiors and furniture expressly designed to create a total environment. Dedicated to developing a specifically Bulgarian architecture, the partners often interpreted nineteenth-century vernacular features into contemporary residential forms. Inspired by Romantic classicism, they ascertained monumentality for civic edifices by employing symmetrical compositions and delineating spaces and volumes sparingly with classicial details, as in the Bulgarian National Bank (1934–1939), or profusely with classical colonnades, as in the Public Library *Kiril i Methodii* (1937–1949), both in Sofia. Their methods, adapted to Socialist Realism—the Communist Party's official style— still guide Bulgarian architects today.

MILKA T. BLIZNAKOV

WORKS

IVAN VASIL'OV

1922–1923, Georgiev's House (now the Austrian Embassy), 16 Vladimir Poptomov Street, Sofia. 1926–1929, Summer Palace, Bania, near Karlovo, Bulgaria. 1935, Pobornikov's House, Kniazhevo, near Sofia. 1939, Ivan Vasil'ov's House, Gornobanski Road, near Sofia. 1939–1941, Office Building (now the Sofia Town Hall), 30 Moskovska Street. 1950–1953, Apartment Building (with V. Brunekov), 10 Sofiăska Komuna Street; 1952–1954, Apartment House (with Milka Bliznakov and others); 1956–1957, Urban Design for Deveti Septevri Plaza (with others); Sofia. 1957, Shipka Memorial (interior reconstruction; with others), Bulgaria. 1960–1961, Zavodproekt Office Building (with others), Stamboliiski Street, Sofia.

DIMITUR TSOLOV

1937–1944, Ministry of Defense (addition and redesign), Sofia. 1950–1954, Council of Ministries Vacation Complex, Zlatni piasutsi, near Verna, Bulgaria. 1955–1956, Hotel Balkan (with others), Sofia. 1960–1964, Sports Palace Diana (with others), Iambol, Bulgaria.

VASIL'OV AND TSOLOV

1927, Pupeshkov House, Klementina Street; *1927–1928, Dorst House, Nevski Plaza; 1927–1929, Saint Nedella's (rebuilding); 1928, Draganov House; Sofia. 1929–1930, Library and Theater Complex, Vratsa, Bulgaria. 1930, Chaprashikov House (now a residence for Party officials), 19 Oborishche Street; 1930–1932, Sofia University Library; 1931–1932, Peev House (now the residence of the Niederland Embassy), 31 Oborishche Street; 1932, Kantardzhiev House (now the Swedish Embassy), 29 Oborishche Street; 1934–1939, Bulgarian National Bank and Archeological Museum; 1935–1938, Housing Cooperative, Tolbukhin Street and Slavianska Street; 1936–1937, Theater-Cinema Royal (now the Theater Narodna Stsena); 1937–1949, Public Library Kiril i Metodil; Sofia. 1938–1941, Business Academy, Svishchov, Bulgaria.

BIBLIOGRAPHY

ANASTASOV, KHRISTO 1965 "Profesor Dimitur Tsolov: Arkhitekt, pedagog, nauchen rabotnik." *Arkhitektura* no. 6:21–27.

BRUNEKOV, VLADIMIR 1981 "Ivan Vasil'ov. *Narodna Kultura* 17, Apr.:3.

BŬLGARSKA AKADEMIIA NA NAUKITE 1965 *Kratka istoriia na Bŭlgarskata arkhitektura.* Sofia: The academy.

GREKOV, P. ET AL. 1967 *Zhilishchni sgradi.* Sofia.

GREKOV, P. ET AL. 1970 *Arkhitektura Sotsialisticheskoĭ Bolgarii.* Moscow: Stroiizdat.

KALINOV K., and KONDOV, V. 1968 "20 godini 'Sofproekt' 1948–1960." *Arkhitektura* 6–7:6–8.

KAPITANOV, B. 1961 "Arkhitekt Ivan Vasil'ov." *Arkhitektura* no. 3:1–3.

"Laureati na Dimitrovska nagrada: Arkhitekt Ivan Tsokov Vasil'ov, prof. arkh. Dimitur Tsolov Marinov, inzh. Stoian Kolev Shoshev i inzh. Ilia A. Doganov." *Arkhitektura i Stroitelstvo* nos. 7–8:40.

MAMBRIANI, ALBERTO 1969 *L'architettura moderna nei paesi Balcanici.* Bologna, Italy: Cappelli.

NENKOV, BORIS 1952 "Bulgarskata arkhitektura sled purvata svetovna voina." *Arkhitektura i stroitelstvo* no. 4:9–14.

NIKOLOV, KOSTA 1953 "Narodnata bibiloteka 'Vasil Kolarov' Sofia." *Izvestiia na Instituta po gradoustroistvo i arkhitektura* 5–6:287–292.

PASKALEV, NEDELCHO 1978 *Ivan Vasil'ov.* Sofia: Takhnika.

TANGUROV, YORDAN S. ET AL. 1972 *The Architecture of Modern Bulgaria.* Sofia: Technika.

TONEY, LIUBEN 1962 *Arkhitektura v bulgariia: 1944–1960.* Sofia: Bŭlgarska Akademiia na Naukite.

TSOLOV, DIMITUR 1929 "Konkursa na B. Z. Banka-Sofia." *Arkhitekt* 8–9:7–21.

TSOLOV, DIMITUR 1952 "Novoto zhilishchno stroitelstvo na bul. Stamboliiski v Sofia." *Izvestiia na instituta po gradoustroistvo i arkhitektura* 3–4:387–390.

TSOLOV, DIMITUR 1957a "Arbanashkata Kŭshcad." *Izvestiia na instituta po gradoustroistvo i arkhitektura* 10–11:75–80.

TSOLOV, DIMITUR 1957b "Predstavitelniiat hotel v Sofia." *Arkhitektura* no. 4:103–109.

TSOLOV, DIMITUR 1958 "Zhilishchnata arkhitektura i obuchenieto." *Arkhitektura* no. 6:23.

TSOLOV, DIMITUR and KRUSTANOVA, R. 1957 *Mebeli, eksperimentaeni obraztski.* Sofia: Bŭlgarska Akademiia na Naukite.

TSOLOV, DIMITUR; KRUSTANOVA, R.; and POPOV, N. 1953 "Vŭprosa za masovoto proizvodstvo na tipovi mebeli za zhilishcheto v Bŭlgaria." *Izvestiia na instituta po gradoustroistvo i arkhitektura* 3–4:387–390.

VASIL'OV, IVAN 1953a "Dom na Suvetite." *Nauka i tekhnika za mladezhta* 9:14–15.

VASIL'OV, IVAN 1953b "Narodna bibioteka 'Vasil Kolarov'." *Tekhnika* 6:6–9.

VASIL'OV, IVAN 1958a "Khotel-Restorant 'Shipka'"

na vrukh Stoletov." *Arkhitektura* no. 3:15–19.

VASIL'OV, IVAN 1958*b* "Prinos kŭm arkhitekturno-gradoustroiskvenoto preshenie na sgradata za gom na Sofiĭskiĭa gradski naroden Sŭvet." *Arkhitektura* no. 1:20–22.

VASIL'OV, IVAN 1974 "Kak be suzdadena sgradata na narodnata biblioteka." *Arkhitektura* no. 6:36–37.

VASIL'OV, IVAN, and TSOLOV, DIMITUR 1928 "Kŭm proektite na arkhitektite Iv. Vasil'ov i D. Tsolov." *Arkhitekt* 3–4:1–17.

VASQUEZ DE CASTRO, ANTONIO

Antonio Vasquez de Castro (1929–) was born in Madrid and received his architectural degree in 1955.

An architect pledged to progressive social and cultural movements, he has divided his activity between building, teaching, and involvement in professional organizations, gaining prominence in all three fields.

The designs of Vasquez de Castro are characterized by the extreme precision and realism of his proposals, in which he pays special attention to construction problems. For example, his interest in light, prefabricated structures is evident in his Tabibloc system. His low-cost housing in Cano Roto, Madrid (1957–1972) has served as a model for other such projects in Spain.

In almost all his works, Vasquez is assisted by Iñiguez de Onzono. The poetry of Vasquez's buildings lies in the occasional abandonment of rationality and efficiency in favor of a human touch.

MIGUEL ANGEL BALDELLOU
Translated from Spanish by
Judith E. Meighan

WORKS

1957–1972, Low-cost housing (*pueblo dirigado*), Cano Roto; 1966, Office Building, Cañamo; 1971, Housing, Entrevias; 1972, Linear housing, Aravaca; 1980, Housing *La Fosforera;* Madrid.

BIBLIOGRAPHY

FLORES LOPEZ, CARLOS 1961 *Arquitectura española contemporánea*. Madrid: Aguilar.

BENEVOLO, LEONARDO (1963)1971 *History of Modern Architecture*. Cambridge, Mass.: M.I.T. Press.

Encyclopedia of Modern Architecture. (1963)1970 London: Thames & Hudson.

VASSE, FRANÇOIS ANTOINE

François Antoine Vassé (1681–1736) was trained in the sculpture atelier of the Marine Arsenal in Toulon. After 1698, he worked in Paris and became a collaborator and, after PIERRE LE PAUTRE's death in 1716, chief decorator of ROBERT DE COTTE. With GILLES MARIE OPPENORD, he was the leading decorator and creator of the *style Régence.* Vassé's work on de Cotte's foreign commissions helped spread the style abroad. In 1715, Vassé was named *dessinateur général de la Marine* responsible for all decorations of the fleet. His most important pupil was his son, the sculptor Louis Claude Vassé, who executed some of his designs.

CHARLOTTE LACAZE

WORKS

1701–1711, Notre Dame (episcopal chairs, choir screen, and altar; bas relief executed by Louis Claude Vassé after 1736), Paris. 1708–1712, Chapel (relief, chair, and lectern), Versailles, France. *1710?, Cabinet chinois, Lacour des Chiens Hôtel, Paris. 1713–1714, Buen Retiro (decoration); 1713–1714, Royal Palace (decoration); Madrid. 1715, Palace of Elector of Cologne (bronzes and fireplaces), Bonn. 1718–1719, Galerie Dorée, Hôtel de Toulouse (formerly the Hôtel de la Vrilliere; now the Banque de France), Paris. *1718–1719, Salon (decoration), Château of Petit-Bourg, Seine-et-Oise, France. 1719–1722, Lady Chapel (decoration and sculpture), Notre Dame; *1721–1722, Capuchine Monastery (sculptural decoration for portal); Paris. *1725, Queen's Chamber (fireplace), Versailles, France. 1729, Cathedral of Sainte-Croix (high altar), Orléans, France. 1729–1734, Salon d'Hercule (decorations and doors); 1730, Chapel (marble statue, La Gloire de Louis XV); Versailles, France.

BIBLIOGRAPHY

BAUER, HERMANN 1962 *Rocaille; Zur Herkunft und zum Wesen eines Ornament-Motifs*. Berlin: de Gruyter.

ERIKSEN, SVEND 1974 *Early Neo-Classicism in France*. London: Faber.

HAUTECOEUR, LOUIS 1950 *Première moitié du XVIIIe siècle: Le style Louis XV*. Volume 3 in *Histoire de l'architecture classique en France*. Paris: Picard.

KALNEIN, WEND GRAF, and LEVEY, MICHAEL 1972 *Art and Architecture of the Eighteenth Century in France*. Harmondsworth, England: Penguin.

KIMBALL, FISKE 1949 *Le Style Louis XV: Origine et évolution du Rococo*. Paris: Picard.

LAUDET, FERNAND 1932 *L'Hôtel de Toulouse: Siège de la Banque de France*. Paris: Firmin-Didot.

LE MOËL, MICHEL 1970 "Catalogue de plans et dessins d'architecture concernant Notre-Dame de Paris aux 17e et 18e siècles, conservés aux Archives Nationales et à la Bibliothèque Nationale." *Paris et Ile-de-France: Mémoires* 21:155–172.

MARIE, JEANNE and ALFRED 1976 Pages 472–489 in *Versailles aux Temps de Louis XIV*. Paris: Imprimerie Nationale.

NEUMANN, ROBERT M. 1978 *Robert de Cotte: Architect of the Late Baroque*. Unpublished Ph.D. dissertation, University of Michigan, Ann Arbor.

RÉAU, LOUIS 1930 "Un sculpteur oublié du XVIIIe

siècle: Louis-Claude Vassé 1716–1772." *Gazette des Beaux Arts* 4:31–56.

VLOBERG, MAURICE 1926 *Notre-Dame de Paris et le Voeu de Louis XIII.* Paris: The author.

VAUBAN, SEBASTIEN LE PRESTRE DE

Sébastien Le Prestre, marquis de Vauban (1633–1707), dominated the field of military engineering in France during the second half of the seventeenth century. As Louis XIV's favorite military architect (until he dared to criticize the king's tax system), he is said to have built or rebuilt more than 120 fortresses and to have surrounded France with a cordon of powerful strongholds.

The Le Prestres, an old family of mostly notaries and small merchants, had purchased the fief of Vauban in the middle of the sixteenth century and thereafter called themselves Le Prestre de Vauban. Vauban's birthdate is unknown, but he was baptized on March 4, 1633. He received his early formal training in a Carmelite college. At the age of seventeen, through family connections, he was accepted as cadet in the regiment of the Prince of Condé. After serving Condé for two years during the civil war called the Fronde, he was captured by royal forces. Apparently, he had already earned a reputation of sorts, for Cardinal Mazarin himself converted the young captive to the royal cause.

During the next few years, good fortune coupled with personal courage and ability repeatedly brought Vauban to the king's attention. In 1655, he was granted an engineer's commission and two years later, at the age of twenty-four, he was put in charge of the siege operations against the Spanish-held town of Montmédy. His success there marked the end of his military apprenticeship.

A period of peace during the 1660s permitted Vauban to develop those skills which were to make him the most admired military architect of the seventeenth century, as Louis XIV sent him back and forth across France to repair and improve the kingdom's defenses. When the War of Devolution broke out, he quickly won renewed recognition as siege engineer. At first, he served under Louis-Nicolas de Clerville, the inspector-general of fortifications; but during the siege of Lille (1667), which, in the king's presence, was captured in seven days, it was recognized that most of the success was due to the young subordinate's work. And when the king decided to refortify Lille, he passed over Clerville and entrusted the planning of the new defenses to Vauban.

From the 1670s onward, France was almost constantly at war and Vauban, now the king's fa-vorite, knew little rest. He doubled as siege engineer and as planner and builder of fortifications. In 1678, after Clerville's death, he was elevated to the rank of inspector-general of fortifications and in 1703, he received the marshal's baton.

Vauban's contemporary fame rested primarily upon his legendary achievements as siege engineer and the repute that no fortress could withstand a Vauban-led assault. His successes in this field were due largely to his famed "system of parallels," a logical and systematic refinement of past siege methods. It enabled him to advance his forces in a series of carefully calculated and methodically executed movements, under the protection of trenches dug parallel to the defensive lines, until his sappers, breaching batteries, and assault troops were securely established at the counterscarp. His treatise on the subject went through several editions and became the standard handbook for eighteenth-century siege engineers.

As builder of fortifications, Vauban was the spiritual heir of Blaise François de Pagan (1604–1665), a military architect who turned theoretician after he had lost his sight in 1643. Pagan's *Traité de fortification* (1645) described the design of defenses in depth and became the determinant in the development of Vauban's fortificatory style. Vauban was not an inventor and he introduced no revolutionary innovations into the design of fortresses. His strength lay in the refinement of known principles of fortification and their skillful adaptation to the demands of specific sites. He was a practical builder and brilliant technician rather than abstract designer. As quoted by Thomassin, one of his assistants, Vauban was fond of saying: "The art of fortification does not consist of rules or systems, but of common sense and experience." Nevertheless, his work was classified according to "three systems," not by him but by his successors. Such a classification, however, is valid only when applied to fortifications built in flat and open terrain.

The "first system" is characterized by very large bastions with flanks that vary in length from about 90 meters at the citadel of Lille (1668) to 160 meters at that of Strasbourg (1681). Vauban's curtain lengths were equally variable, ranging from 70 to 340 meters. Such lack of standardization is in keeping with the architect's pragmatic approach to fortification and his penchant to experiment and to modify his designs in accordance with the demands of the site, the expected size of the garrison and the caliber of the defensive weapons to be used. The bastions' ample dimensions were intended to accommodate large bodies of infantry, not massed artillery as in the past. Vauban felt that the defenders rarely, if ever, could match the firepower of the besieger and that their artillery was employed most efficiently in the defense of the curtains. The best and most effective defense, he said, was vigorous sorties by footsoldiers to disrupt the enemy's siege preparations.

Curtains were protected by tenailles fitted between bastions and, beyond them, by powerful ravelins. Most striking was Vauban's fortification of the covered way which, up to his time, had been little more than a footpath behind a shoulder-high parapet. By providing it with traverses against enfilading fire from the field and with spacious assembly areas, he converted it into a powerful first line of defense from which large bodies of men could mount their disruptive sorties.

The "second system" may be seen at Besançon (1687) and Belfort (1689); it was used for the first time in 1686 and illustrates Vauban's growing concern with a defense in depth. The system is characterized by bastions which have been detached from their curtains and moved outward into a widened ditch. Along the straight curtains, behind the bastions, casemated artillery towers resemble six-

Vauban.
New City Foundation.
Neuf-Brisach, France.
1689–1699

Vauban.
Plan of New City
Foundation.
Neuf-Brisach, France.
1689–1699

teenth-century cavaliers in their function of defending their respective bastions, or offending them should they fall to the enemy.

The "third system" is shown at Neuf-Brisach (1698–1699), Vauban's most mature work; essentially it is a refinement of the second. The ditch has been widened even more, the central section of the curtains has been recessed for improved flanking and the powerful ravelins are now backed up by redoubts whose function duplicates that of the gun towers behind the bastions. The system thus combines a series of effectively flanked passive restraints with staging areas for aggressive counterattacks (sorties). The elements of the fortified belt have been arranged and spaced so as to enable the defenders to contest each part step by step and to continue their resistance even after the loss of a bastion, which, in the past, usually had meant final defeat.

All terraces up to the massive earthen parapets are faced with masonry shirts, revetments that are buttressed on the inside and have exterior faces with a 20 percent batter, their thickness decreasing from about three meters at the base to 1.5 meters at the top. Vauban felt that this combination of masonry mass and angle offered the best resistance to artillery fire.

Neuf-Brisach was more than just a fortress; it was also a garrison town that had to house a civilian as well as a military population. The problem of combining the two disparate elements was solved admirably in Vauban's urban plan. The huge, central *place d'armes* doubled as market place and as parade grounds or mustering area for the town's military forces; around it the civilian inhabitants were accommodated in spacious, square building blocks, while the garrison was housed in barracks placed parallel to the eight sides of the town's circumference and near its defenses. Here, as for his other new foundations, Vauban preferred the checkerboard plan to the radial schemes which were in vogue with baroque planners. On a smaller scale, Vauban's designs for well-proportioned and functional military barracks, for an occasional church of rather sober appearance, and for the severely rusticated portals leading into his towns and citadels (reminiscent of those of MICHELE SANMICHELI's a century and a half earlier), all show him to be a more than adequate civil architect.

Although competent in several fields, including that of hydraulic engineering (Aqueduct of Maintenon, [1684–1685] which provided Versailles with much of its water), Vauban was first and foremost a siege engineer. He participated in or led a total of forty-eight sieges in his career and occasionally, as before Ath in 1697, he was confronted with the ironical task of having to conquer

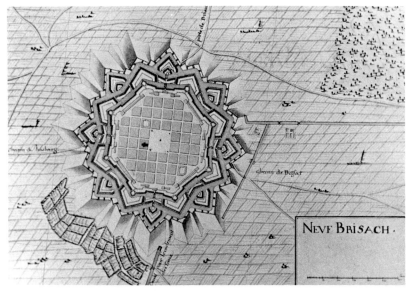

NEUF BRISACH.

a stronghold which he himself had fortified. He knew that no fortress, no matter how strongly built or well-defended, could hold out indefinitely against a protracted siege that is pressed home with force and conviction. The purpose of a fortress was only to delay an enemy long enough to allow the king to muster sufficient forces to meet the aggressor.

His attack-oriented bias is reflected in Vauban's published writings. His *Mémoire pour servir d'instruction dans la conduite des sièges et dans la défense des places* (written between 1667 and 1672) is a treatise of instructional nature that stresses attack methods; a short appendage on defense deals primarily with problems of logistics and command. His later treatise, *De l'attaque et de la défense des places,* written c.1706 and first published in 1737, is more comprehensive and gives about equal weight to attack and defense. But here also the reader will look in vain for a general exposition of the author's theory of fortification.

Vauban was not a theoretician and his fortresses must speak for themselves. The bulk of his work consisted in the strengthening and modernization of extant older fortifications, usually providing them with extensive outworks in the form of ravelins, lunettes, and horn- and crownworks, the latter two being his favored types. Here as in his new constructions he took full account of the increased range of the artillery of his day; he tried to offset its growing power by rearranging and amplifying traditional fortificatory elements in such a way as to convert what had been a linear defense into a defense in depth. By vastly strengthening the outworks of his fortresses, he de-emphasized the importance of the magistral line and took a long first step in the direction of the eventual dissolution of continuous urban enceintes.

HORST DE LA CROIX

WORKS

More than 120 works are attributed to Vauban. Of these, approximately thirty were new constructions of enceintes, citadels, forts, and new city foundations. The remaining works consisted of the renewal, strengthening, and enlargement of extant older fortifications. In many cases, the dating is uncertain, as work continued for decades at some sites. Interruptions were frequent, strongholds were lost and reconquered, earlier work was improved or strengthened at a later date, and major structural damage suffered during a siege often required massive reconstruction. Thus the dates given to the monuments must be regarded as approximate; they refer to those years in which major work was done at a given site, although construction may have begun earlier and the actual completion date may have been later.

1668, Citadel, Arras, France. *1668, Ath, Belgium. 1668, Bergues, France. *1668, *Enceinte,* Knocke, France. 1668, Citadel, Lille, France. 1668, Montmédy, France.

*1668–1671 and later, *Enceinte,* Dunkirque, France. 1669, Rocroi, France. 1669, Sedan, France. *1673, *Enceinte,* Philipsbourg, France. *1673–1675, *Enceinte,* Breisach, Germany. 1675–1676, Metz, France. 1676, Le Quesnoy, France. *1678, Menin, Belgium. 1678–1681, *Enceinte,* Maubeuge, France. 1679, Fort de Bellegarde, France. 1679, New City Foundation, Longwy, France. 1679, New City Foundation, Montlouis, France. *1679, *Enceinte,* Phalsbourg, France. *1679 and later, Toulon, France. 1681, Antibes, France. 1681, Blaye, France. 1681, *Enceinte,* Port-Vendre, France. *1681, Citadel, Strasbourg, France. 1681–1683, Citadel, Bayonne, France. 1681–1683, New City Foundation, Sarrelouis, France. 1681–1685, Fort, Saint Martin-de-Ré, France. 1682, *Enceinte,* Socoa, France. *1683, Brest, France. 1683, Verdun, France. 1684–1685, Aqueduct of Maintenon, France. 1685, Cherbourg, France. 1685, Fort Hoedic, France. 1685, Fort Houat, France. *1686–1689, New City Foundation, Fort Louis, France. *1686–1689, New City Foundation, Huningue, France. 1687, Besançon, France. *1687, New City Foundation, Montroyal, France. *1687–1689, *Enceinte,* Landau, Germany. 1689, *Enceinte,* Belfort, France. 1692, *Enceinte,* Briançon, France. 1692, New City Foundation, Mont Dauphin, France. 1693, Fort Saint Vincent, France. 1694, Fort, Camaret, France. 1689–1699, New City Foundation, Neuf-Brisach, France.

BIBLIOGRAPHY

BLOMFIELD, REGINALD LOUIS 1938 *Sébastien Le Prestre de Vauban: 1633–1707.* London: Methuen.

CASSI RAMELLI, ANTONIO 1966 *Sebastiano Le Prestre, Marchese di Vauban.* Rome: Istituto Italiano dei Castelli.

HALÉVY, DANIEL (1923)1925 *Vauban.* Translated by C. J. C. Street. New York: Macveagh.

KIMBER, THOMAS 1852 *Construction of Vauban's First System of Fortification.* 2d ed., rev. London: Parker, Furnivall.

LAZARD, PIERRE E. 1934 *Vauban: 1633–1707.* Paris: Alcan.

LECOMTE, CHARLES 1903 "Du service des ingénieurs militaires en France pendant le règne de Louis XIV." *Revue militaire du génie* 1903:1–163.

LLOYD, E. M. 1887 *Vauban, Montalembert, Carnot: Engineer Studies.* London: Chapman & Hall.

MICHEL, GEORGES 1879 *Histoire de Vauban.* Paris: Plon.

PARENT, MICHEL, and VERROUST, JACQUES 1971 *Vauban.* Paris: Fréal.

RÉBELLIAU, ALFRED 1962 *Vauban (Les temps et let destins).* Paris: Fayard.

ROCHAS D'AIGLUN, ALBERT DE (editor) 1910 *Vauban, sa famille et ses écrits, ses oisivetés et sa correspondance.* 2 vols. Paris: Berger-Levrault.

SAULIOL, RENÉ (1924)1931 *Le Maréchal de Vauban: Sa vie, son oeuvre.* 2d ed. Paris: Lavauzelle.

TOUDOUZE, GEORGES 1954 *Monsieur de Vauban.* Paris: Berger-Levrault.

VAUBAN, SÉBASTIAN LE PRESTRE DE (1737)1828–1829 *De l'attaque et de la défense des places.* 2 vols. Paris: Anselin.

VAUDOYER, ANTOINE LAURENT THOMAS, and VAUDOYER, LEON

Antoine Laurent Thomas Vaudoyer (1756–1846) and his son Léon Vaudoyer (1803–1872) were both born in Paris. The first was destined for a military career but instead enrolled at the Ecole Royale d'Architecture, a pupil of Antoine François Peyre (see PEYRE FAMILY); in 1783, he won the Grand Prix. A spherical *Maison d'un cosmopolite* he designed in 1785 suggests that he was strongly influenced by ETIENNE LOUIS BOULLÉE. His career was to be that of an administrator and teacher rather than practician. He opened an *atelier libre* in 1789, the first of its kind. After the suppression of the Académies in 1793, he joined with JULIEN DAVID LEROY and LOUIS PIERRE BALTARD to continue teaching; in 1795, their school became the Ecole Spéciale d'Architecture, the forerunner of the Ecole des Beaux-Arts, of which he was *secrétaire/archiviste* from 1806 to 1846. He was a rigid and doctrinaire teacher but, as his annotations and critiques in 1804 and 1806 of Charles François Viel's pamphlets make clear, more astute than is sometimes thought. He was joined in his atelier by his cousin LOUIS HIPPOLYTE LEBAS in 1819, the year in which Léon entered it and enrolled at the Ecole des Beaux-Arts.

Léon Vaudoyer won a competition for the tomb of General Foy in 1825, a baseless Doric affair of which he was not afterward proud and, in 1826, the Grand Prix. In Rome, together with FÉLIX DUBAN, PIERRE FRANÇOIS HENRI LABROUSTE, and LOUIS JOSEPH DUC, he became identified with the radical opposition to much that his father had represented. Returning to France in 1832, he began work under Lebas and opened an atelier, but he traveled widely in the following years, to Italy again (1836), England (1837), Spain and Algeria (1839), and Germany (1840). After his father's death, he took over his atelier and his most important commission, the conversion of the Priory of Saint Martin des Champs into the Conservatoire des Arts et Métiers.

There are indications that he was seeking here to interpret Saint-Simonist ideas, as is even more evident in his determinedly populist writings on architecture, the earliest being the article "Cirque" in Pierre Leroux and Jean Reynaud's *Encyclopédie nouvelle*. He was intent to show that the Greek ideal had been sustained but also successively transformed and given a particular, local expression throughout the history of architecture in southern Europe, so that contemporary architecture in France could be conceived as a renewed synthesis of Graeco-Roman (pagan), Byzantine (Christian), Gothic (spiritual) and Renaissance (rational) art forms. This amalgam was given form in his greatest work, the Cathedral of Marseilles. He failed, perhaps, in his bright promise, but his writings provide one of the few guides to the thinking of a most enterprising group of academic rebels and are inevitably of high interest.

Léon Vaudoyer was the first to refer in print to the work of CLAUDE NICOLAS LEDOUX as *architecture parlante* (1852). His son, Alfred Lambert Vaudoyer, was also an architect, as was his grandson, Léon Jean Georges Vaudoyer.

R. D. MIDDLETON

WORKS

ANTOINE LAURENT THOMAS VAUDOYER
*1806–1807, Salle des Séances, Palais de l'Institut, Quai Conti; *1812–1813, Marché des Carmes; Paris.

LÉON VAUDOYER

c.1830, Poussin Monument, San Lorenzo in Lucina, Rome. 1831–1832, General Foy's Tomb (with David d'Angers), Père Lachaise Cemetery; 1845–1872, Conservatoire des Arts et Métiers; 1846, Vaudoyer Family Tomb, Montparnasse Cemetery; Paris. 1855–1872, Sainte Marie Majeure (not completed until 1893), Marseilles, France.

BIBLIOGRAPHY

ALLAIS, HONORÉ PIERRE DÉSIRÉ; DETOURNELLE, ATHANASE; and VAUDOYER, A. L. T. (1806)1834 *Projets d'architecture et autres productions de cet art, qui ont mérités les Grands Prix*. Paris: Morel.

BALLU, THEODORE 1873 *Institut de France. Academie des Beaux-Arts. Notice sur M. Léon Vaudoyer*. Paris: Firmin-Didot.

BAUDOT, ANATOLE DE, and PERRAULT-DABOT, ALFRED n.d. Volume 3 in *Archives de la Commission des Monuments Historiques*. Paris: Laurens & Schmid.

BEULE, CHARLES ERNEST; BALTARD, VICTOR; DUC, JOSEPH LOUIS; and DAVIOUD, GABRIEL JEAN ANTOINE 1872 "Funérailles de M. Léon Vaudoyer." *Bulletin mensuel de la Société Centrale des Architectes*. Paris: La Société.

BLANC, CHARLES 1876 "Léon Vaudoyer 1803–1872." Pages 225–248 in *Les artistes de mon temps*. Paris: Firmin-Didot.

COCKERELL, FREDERICK P. 1875–1876 "Biographical Notices of Deceased Foreign Members: Léon Vaudoyer." Pages 215–218 in *Royal Institute of British Architects. Sessional Papers*. London: The institute.

DAVIOUD, GABRIEL JEAN ANTOINE 1873 "Notice biographique sur Léon Vaudoyer." *Revue générale de l'architecture* 30:67–72.

LUCAS, CHARLES 1894–1895 "Lettre inédite de Léon Vaudoyer." *Construction Moderne* 10:109–111.

Notice des oeuvres de Léon Vaudoyer 1873 Paris: Chamerot. Exhibition catalogue.

SEDILLE, PAUL 1873 "Exposition des oeuvres de Léon Vaudoyer." *Chronique des Arts* March: 77–79.

SOUBIES, ALBERT 1906 "Vaudoyer, 1756–1846." Pages 90–92 in *Les membres de l'Academie des Beaux-Arts. Deuxième série 1816–1852.* Paris: Flammarion.

VAN ZANTEN, DAVID T. 1977 "Architectural Composition at the Ecole des Beaux-Arts from Charles Percier to Charles Garnier." In Arthur Drexler (editor), *The Architecture of the Ecole des Beaux-Arts.* New York: Museum of Modern Art; London: Secker & Warburg.

VAUDOYER, A. L. T. 1811 *Plan, coupe et élévation du Palais de l'Institut Impérial de France.* Paris: Dusillon.

VAUDOYER, A. L. T. 1823 "Dissertation sur l'architecture." Unpublished manuscript, Library of the Royal Institute of British Architects, London, no. 728.84.

VAUDOYER, A. L. T., and BALTARD, LOUIS PIERRE 1834 *Grands Prix d'Architecture. Projets couronnés par l'Académie Royale des Beaux-Arts de France.* Paris.

VAUDOYER, LÉON 1840 "Cirque." Volume 3, pages 626–630 in Pierre Leroux and Jean Reynaud (editors), *Encyclopédie nouvelle: Dictionnaire philosophique, scientifique, littéraire et industriel.* Paris: Gosselin & Furne.

VAUDOYER, LÉON 1844 *Instruction sur les moyens de prévenir ou de faire cesser les effets de l'humidité dans les bâtiments.* Paris: Carilian-Coeury.

VAUDOYER, LÉON 1847 *Patria. La France ancienne et moderne morale et matérielle,* vol. 2. Paris: J. J. Dubochet, Le Chevalier.

VAUDOYER, LÉON 1848 "Colonnes monumentales de la barrière du Trône." *Magasin Pittoresque* 16:195–197.

VAUDOYER, LÉON 1859 "Les bizarreries de Ledoux, architecte." *Magasin Pittoresque* 27:27–29.

VIOLLET-LE-DUC, EUGÈNE LOUIS 1872 "Mort de M. Vaudoyer." *Gazette des architectes et du bâtiment.* Series 2 1, no.3:23.

VAUDREMER, EMILE

The most talented of the pupils of the prolific Blouet-Gilbert (see ABEL BLOUET) atelier, Joseph-Auguste-Emile Vaudremer (1829–1914), a native Parisian, won the second Grand Prix in 1854 with a design for a "Building intended for the sepulchre of the rulers of a great Empire." His project was based on Hadrian's Mausoleum, also the subject of his unorthodox reconstruction for the fourth-year *envoi,* an assigned archeological study. He toured Italy and Sicily, studying especially early medieval monuments which had earlier captured Blouet's imagination, and also traveled to Greece. After working under FÉLIX DUBAN and VICTOR BALTARD, he was appointed city architect in the thirteenth and fourteenth *arrondissements* of Paris. His first independent design, the Santé Prison (1862–1885), is in the utilitarian tradition of his teacher's radially planned and austerely articulated prison design. His best known work, the Church of Saint Pierre, established Vaudremer's individuality among those Ecole-trained architects who were also influenced by EUGÈNE EMMANUEL VIOLLET-LE-DUC's rationalism. Adroitly but simply composed on a confined triangular site between intersecting boulevards, the church served the village of Montrouge, newly incorporated into the city limits, and was clearly a critique of Baltard's Saint-Augustin, on which Vaudremer had worked. Dominated by a single campanilelike tower at the apex of its site, the church has a monumental public presence, yet in Vaudremer's characteristic fashion it is soberly dignified in articulation and ornamentation. Within the framework of a Tuscan-style basilican plan are amalgamated Sicilian, Italian Romanesque, and even Syrian sources.

His influential school designs developed the clear distinction of materials already evident at Saint Pierre and were considered by JULIEN GUADET a model for utilitarian structures in their functional planning. From 1860 to 1880, Vaudremer ran an influential atelier frequented by, among others, the Americans LOUIS SULLIVAN, WALTER COOK, and WILLIAM ROTCH WARE.

BARRY BERGDOLL

WORKS

1862–1885, Santé Prison; 1864–1872, Saint-Pierre de Montrouge; 1876, Groupe scolaire, rue d'Alésia; 1876–1892, Notre-Dame d'Auteuil; Paris. 1877, Saint-Ferdinand des Ternes (façade; with Debray), Neuilly, France. 1877–1880, Temple de Belleville (Protestant), 97 rue Julien Lacroix, Paris. c.1879, Bishops Palace, Beauvais, France. c.1884, Lycée, Passy, Paris. 1884–1887, Girl's Lycée, Montauban, France. 1885–1886, Lycée, Grenoble, France. 1885–1888, Lycée, Molière, 71 rue de Ranelagh; 1885–1890, 1895–1899, Lycée Buffon; 1890–1895, Greek Orthodox Church, rue Bizet; 1895–1896, Hôtel, rue Chardin; 1901–1903, Saint Antoine des Quinze-Vingts (with Lucien Roy), Paris. 1914, Vaudremer Gravestone, Avignon, France. n.d., Apartment House, boulevard Henri-Martin, Paris. n.d., Convent, Vaugirard, France. n.d., Hôtel, avenue d'Antin; n.d., Hôtel, rue Magellan; Paris.

BIBLIOGRAPHY

ALAUX, JEAN-PAUL; BRACHET, LOUIS; and COOK, WALTER 1915 "Emile Vaudremer." *Journal of the American Institute of Architects* 3:292–299.

CHABAT, PIERRE 1872 "Eglise Saint-Pierre de Montrouge." *Encyclopédie d'Architecture* Series 2 1:168, plates 41, 47, 55, 66, 72, 77, 84, 89.

DREXLER, ARTHUR (editor) 1977 *The Architecture of the Ecole des Beaux-Arts.* Cambridge, Mass: Massachusetts Institute of Technology.

EGBERT, DONALD DREW 1980 *The Beaux-Arts Tradition in French Architecture.* N.J.: Princeton University Press.

"M. Emile Vaudremer." 1895 *Construction Moderne* 10:337–339.

GROMORT, GEORGES 1922 *L'Architecture*. Volume 2 in *Histoire Générale de l'Art Français de la Révolution à nos jours*. Paris: Librarie de France.

HAUTECOEUR, LOUIS 1957 *La Fin de l'Architecture Classique: 1848–1900*. Volume 7 in *Histoire de l'Architecture Classique en France*. Paris: Picard.

HERMANT, JACQUES 1914 "Emile Vaudremer." *L'Architecture* 27:65–68.

MAGNE, LUCIEN 1889 *L'Architecture Française du Siècle*. Paris: Imprimerie Nationale.

MIDDLETON, ROBIN, and WATKIN, DAVID (1977)1980 *Neoclassical and 19th Century Architecture*. New York: Abrams.

NARJOUX, FÉLIX 1882 Volume 2 in *Paris Monuments Elevés par la Ville: 1850–1880*. Paris: Morel.

VAUDREMER, EMILE 1871 *Monographie de la Maison d'arrêt et de correction pour hommes, construite à Paris par Emile Vaudremer*. Paris.

VAUGHAN, HENRY

Henry Vaughan (1845–1917), a leader of the "Boston Gothicists" in the late nineteenth and early twentieth centuries, laid the foundations of the last and perhaps greatest phase of the American Gothic Revival, over which he continued to exert a strong influence until his death. Primarily an ecclesiastical architect, Vaughan's recreations of English parish churches, such as the half-timbered Saint Andrew's in Newcastle, Maine (1883), set new standards for American church design and inspired many younger architects, particularly RALPH ADAMS CRAM.

Vaughan was a solitary and self-effacing man and little is known about his private life. He was born in Cheshire, attended secondary school in Scotland, and was apprenticed to GEORGE FREDERICK BODLEY, a key figure of the late phase of the Gothic Revival in England. As Bodley's head draftsman, Vaughan came to Boston in 1881 to design a chapel for the Sisters of Saint Margaret and remained here, setting up his own practice.

The chapel for Saint Paul's School in Concord, New Hampshire (1886–1894), with its spireless Perpendicular Tower, is a major monument of the late Gothic Revival in America. Academic works for Saint Paul's, Groton School, and Bowdoin College established Vaughan as one of the foremost revivalists of the English collegiate style. He also designed in the Elizabethan, Jacobean, and English Georgian styles. In collaboration with Bodley, Vaughan designed the Cathedral of Saint Peter and Saint Paul (1907–1917), Washington; cathedral architect until his death, Vaughan completed the Bethlehem Chapel (1910–1912) and the Sanctuary (1915–1918).

Vaughan's chief patron was the eccentric millionaire Edward F. Searles of Methuen, Massachusetts, for whom he designed, among other things, two castles, a railroad station, a music hall, a factory, and several churches and schools.

WILLIAM MORGAN

WORKS

1881–1882, Saint Margaret's Convent (chapel), Boston. 1883, Saint Andrew's Church, Newcastle, Maine. 1886–1894, Chapel of Saint Peter and Saint Paul, Concord, N.H. 1888, Saint Mary's Church, Dorchester, Mass. 1890, Saint Barnabas Church, Falmouth, Mass. 1893, Church of the Holy Name, Swampscott, Mass. 1894, Searles Science Building, Brunswick, Maine. 1895–1898, Christ Church, New Haven. 1899–1900, Saint John's Chapel, Groton, Mass. 1902, Church of the Good Shepherd, New York. 1902, Holy Cross Monastery, West Park, N.Y. 1902, Hubbard Library, Brunswick, Maine. 1902, New Upper School, Concord, N.H. 1902, Saint Mary's-by-the-Sea, Northeast Harbor, Maine. 1907–1917, Cathedral of Saint Peter and Saint Paul (with George Frederick Bodley) 1910–1912, Cathedral of Saint Peter and Saint Paul (Bethlehem Chapel); Washington. 1909–1910, Amasa Stone Memorial Chapel, Cleveland, Ohio. 1913–1920, Church of the Redeemer, Chestnut Hill, Mass. 1915–1918, Cathedral of Saint Peter and Saint Paul (Sanctuary), Washington. 1916, Jonathan Bourne Whaling Museum, New Bedford, Mass. 1916–1918, Cathedral of Saint John the Divine (Chapels of Saint Boniface, Saint James, and Saint Ansgar), New York.

BIBLIOGRAPHY

MORGAN, WILLIAM 1971 "The Architecture of Henry Vaughan." Unpublished Ph.D. dissertation, University of Delaware, Newark.

MORGAN, WILLIAM 1973 "Henry Vaughan: An English Architect in New Hampshire." *Historical New Hampshire* 28:120–140.

VAUTHIER, LOUIS LEGER

The French engineer Louis Léger Vauthier (1815–1901) was educated at the Ecole Polytechnique and arrived in Recife, Brazil, in 1840. Architect of the Santa Isabel Theater and urban expansion of Recife, he advanced building and city planning techniques. Returning to Paris in 1846, he remained in contact with Brazil until his death.

ELIZABETH D. HARRIS

WORKS

1840–1846, Carmo Convent (adaptation of a hospital); 1840–1846, Santa Isabel Theater; 1840–1846, Santo Amaro Bridge; 1840–1846, Secondary School; Recife, Brazil.

BIBLIOGRAPHY

FREYRE, GILBERTO 1940 *Um Engeuheiro francês no Brasil*. Rio de Janeiro: Olympio.

VAUX, CALVERT

Calvert Vaux (1824-1895), a leading American architect and landscape designer, was born in London. After receiving his general education at the Merchant Taylors' School in London, Vaux was articled to Lewis Nockalls Cottingham. He then accompanied his fellow pupil and friend, George Truefitt, on a sketching tour of France and Germany. At an exhibition of the Architectural Association of London in 1850, Vaux was introduced to ANDREW JACKSON DOWNING, who invited Vaux to return with him to the United States and to become his architectural associate. From their office in Newburgh, New York, they maintained an active practice specializing in the designing and landscaping of country residences in the English picturesque tradition. In addition, Vaux assisted Downing with the plans for the grounds surrounding the Capitol, the Smithsonian Institution, and the White House in Washington, D.C. The project was left unfinished upon Downing's untimely death in 1852.

As Downing's successor, Vaux remained in Newburgh and soon formed a three-year partnership with FRANK CLARKE WITHERS. At this time, he established important and enduring ties with artists of the Hudson River school. Vaux's work of this period is summarized in his publication of 1857, *Villas and Cottages*. Based on the popular genre of Downing's pattern books, it includes domestic designs in the Italian villa and cottage styles prepared by Vaux alone or in collaboration with Downing or Withers. It was published in a revised edition of 1864 and later reprinted.

In 1856, Vaux moved his office and residence to New York, where he had obtained several significant commissions, including the townhouse of John A. C. Gray (1855-1858) and the Bank of New York (1856-1858). A naturalized citizen, Vaux became a member of the newly formed American Institute of Architects (1857) and began an active participation in the artistic, social, and urban concerns of the city. In 1857, a public competition was announced for Central Park and Vaux invited FREDERICK LAW OLMSTED to collaborate with him. In April 1858, their joint plan, *Greensward*, was selected over thirty-three entries. Inspired by the picturesque tradition of English landscape gardening and the work of Downing, *Greensward*, a masterpiece of urban planning, was a major force in the development of the public parks movement in the United States. Vaux was appointed consulting architect and later landscape architect, and for many years, both alone and with Olmsted, he supervised the execution of their designs. In addition, Vaux was in charge of the bridges, cottages, rustic shelters, and other architectural features, among the most notable of which is the Terrace (1858-1871), the architectural termination of the Mall. He was assisted by a staff which included JACOB WREY MOULD and Alfred Janson Bloor.

Following the recognition of his work in Central Park, Vaux received numerous landscaping commissions. In 1865, he prepared a preliminary report for Prospect Park in Brooklyn, New York, and the following year, Olmsted and Vaux were appointed landscape architects. Simultaneously, they established a private landscape partnership known as Olmsted, Vaux, and Company (1865-1872), operating from the same office as the architectural firm of Vaux, Withers, and Company (1863-1872). In conjunction with Olmsted and Withers, his former partner, Vaux pursued a varied career combining public work in the landscaping and designing of structures for several city park systems, including New York, Brooklyn (1866-1873), Buffalo (1868-1876), and Chicago (1871-1873), with private work for institutions, campuses, private estates, and residential communities, among the most successful of which was Riverside, Illinois (1868-1870). Vaux collaborated with Olmsted on the plans for several important parks after the termination of their formal partnership in 1872.

In the 1870s, Vaux prepared designs for major public buildings in the High Victorian Gothic style. In 1872, he collaborated with Mould on the master plans for the Metropolitan Museum of Art (1874-1880) and the Museum of Natural History (1874-1877). Only one wing of each museum was erected. In collaboration with the English-born engineer George K. Radford, Vaux won a major competition in 1873 for the Main Building of the Philadelphia Centennial Exposition, but their ambitious design was not selected for construction due to its high cost.

During the last phase of his career, Vaux continued his working method of combining an architectural with a landscaping partnership. He formed Vaux and Radford (1876-1892) and, with Samuel Parsons, Jr., a horticulturist from Flushing, New York, he formed Vaux and Company (1880-1895). Among the notable designs of this period were the numerous lodging homes and school buildings for the Children's Aid Society of Greater New York (1879-1892), the High Victorian Gothic New York townhouse of Samuel J. Tilden (1881-1884), and the landscaping of Greystone (1879-1880), Tilden's country estate in Yonkers, New York. While maintaining his private practice, Vaux resumed his public employment with the New York Department of Public Parks. He was reappointed landscape architect, a position he held from 1881–1882 and again from 1887 until his death in 1895. Assisted by Parsons, he executed his and Olmsted's plans for Morningside Park (from 1887) and Riverside Park (preliminary plan 1873, continued through 1880s), designed many small parks and squares, and fought to preserve the integrity of park lands he had worked so hard to create.

Vaux's career spanned a period of great growth in America and reflected a shift from rural to primarily urban concerns. An accomplished domestic architect who worked in a variety of Victorian styles, Vaux also experimented with alternative housing and designed a Model Tenement (1880–1882) in New York. However, Vaux's greatest achievement lay in the field of landscape architecture. Though he never achieved the stature or renown of Olmsted, he is considered, along with Downing and Olmsted, among the founders of this profession in America.

DENNIS STEADMAN FRANCIS and
JOY M. KESTENBAUM

WORKS

*1851–1852, William L. Findlay Residence (with A. J. Downing), Newburgh, N.Y. 1851–1852, Daniel Parish House (with Downing), Newport, R.I. c.1852–1853, Dr. William A. M. Culbert House (with Downing), Newburgh, N.Y. 1852–1853, Francis Dodge House (with Downing); 1852–1853, Robert Dodge House (with Downing); Washington. 1852–1853, Fowler-Moore House (with Downing); c.1852–1855, William E. Warren House, Newburgh, N.Y. 1853, Nathaniel P. Willis Residence, Cornwall-on-Hudson, N.Y. c.1853–1855, Lydig M. Hoyt House, Staatsburg, N.Y. *c.1854–1855, Henry H. Chamberlain House (with F. C. Withers), Worcester, Mass. *c.1855–1858, John A. C. Gray Townhouse (with Withers); *1856–1858, Bank of New York (with Withers); New York. 1856–1858, Federico Barreda Residence, Newport, R.I. 1858–1876, Central Park (with Frederick Law Olmsted), New York. 1862, Grounds of Institute of Living (formerly Retreat for the Insane; with Olmsted), Hartford, Conn. 1865, Eugene A. Brewster House (with Withers), Newburgh, N.Y. *1865–1866, Charles Kimball Townhouse (with Withers), Brooklyn, N.Y. *c.1865–1867, Edwin L. Godkin Townhouse, New York; 1866, Grounds of Polytechnic Institute (formerly Free Institute of Industrial Science), Worcester, Mass. 1866, Grounds of Gallaudet College (formerly Columbia Institution for Deaf and Dumb; with Olmsted), Washington. 1866–1873, Prospect Park and Brooklyn Park System, Brooklyn, N.Y. 1867, John James Monell Residence (with Withers), Beacon, N.Y. 1867–1872, Hudson River State Hospital and Grounds (with Withers and Olmsted), Poughkeepsie, N.Y. 1868–1870, Plan of Riverside (with Olmsted), Ill. 1868–1876, Park System (with Olmsted), Buffalo, N.Y. 1871–1873, South Park (with Olmsted), Chicago. 1873–1879, Grounds of Par-

liament Buildings, Ottawa. 1873–1888, Riverside Park (with Olmsted and Samuel Parsons), New York. 1874–1876, Henry Baldwin Hyde Residence, Babylon, N.Y. 1874–1877, Jefferson Market Courthouse (with Withers); 1874–1877, Museum of Natural History (with Jacob Wrey Mould); 1874–1880, Metropolitan Museum of Art (with Mould); New York. 1876, George J. Bull Residence, Worcester, Mass. 1879–1880, Grounds of *Greystone*, Samuel J. Tilden Estate, Yonkers, N.Y. *1879–1880, Thomas Worthington Whittredge House, Summit, N.J. 1879–1892, Lodging houses and buildings for Children's Aid Society (some demolished; with George K. Radford); *1880–1882, Improved Dwellings Model Tenement (with Radford); 1881–1884, Samuel J. Tilden Townhouse (now National Arts Club; with Radford); 1881–1889, Trinity Cemetery Grounds and Gatehouse (with Parsons and Radford); New York. 1882–1883, Edwin Booth House and Grounds, Middletown, R.I. 1884–1885, Shearith Israel Cemetery Grounds and Chapel, Brooklyn, N.Y. 1887–?, Morningside Park (with Olmsted), New York. 1887–1894, Downing Park (with Olmsted), Newburgh, N.Y. 1887–1895, State Reservation (with Olmsted), Niagara Falls, N.Y. 1890–1891, Grounds of *Wilderstein*, Rhinecliff, N.Y. *1890–1892, Samuel D. Coykendall Residence (with Radford), Rondout, N.Y. *1891, Isaac Gale Johnson Grounds; 1894, New York University Grounds; 1895, New York Botanical Garden (with Parsons); Bronx, N.Y.

BIBLIOGRAPHY

The correspondence and miscellaneous papers of Calvert Vaux can be found in the Manuscript Division of the New York Public Library and in the collection of the Historical Society of Pennsylvania, Philadelphia.

"Calvert Vaux." 1895 *Harper's Weekly* 39:1130.

FRANCIS, DENNIS STEADMAN 1976 "Further Notes on Calvert Vaux, Landscape Architect." *APT Bulletin* 8:81–82.

FRANCIS, DENNIS STEADMAN 1980 *Architects in Practice, New York City, 1840–1900*. New York: Committee for the Preservation of Architectural Records.

MAGONIGLE, H. VAN BUREN 1933 "A Half-Century of Architecture: A Biographical Review." *Pencil Points* 14:477–479.

PARSONS, MABEL (editor) 1926 *Memories of Samuel Parsons*. New York: Putnam's.

SIGLE, JOHN DAVID 1967 "Calvert Vaux, An American Architect." Unpublished M.A. thesis, University of Virginia, Charlottesville.

SIGLE, JOHN DAVID 1968 "Bibliography of the Life and Works of Calvert Vaux." *American Association of Architectural Bibliographers: Papers*. 5:69–106.

VAUX, CALVERT (1864)1970 *Villas and Cottages*. Reprint. New York: Dover.

VEGAS and GALIA

The work of Martin Vegas (1926–) reveals the impact of North American architecture on Venezuela. With no formal training in architecture available in Venezuela, he studied with LUDWIG MIES VAN DER ROHE at the Illinois Institute of Technology, and upon his return joined forces with the Uruguayan-born Jose Miguel Galia (1924–), who had studied with JULIO VILAMAJÓ. Vegas and Galia combined Vilamajó's sensitivity toward climate and regional materials with Mies's classic preciseness, bringing Internationalism to Venezuela. They designed Edificio Polar (1954) with curtain walls hung from four ferroconcrete piers, and the Commerce and Agricultural Bank (1955), which combined reinforced concrete and brick in an office tower with alternating glass façades, balconies, and hanging gardens. The Eastern Professional Center of Sabara Grande (1956), a twelve-story parallelepied, effectively used exterior sun breakers, and later their honest handling of materials and instinctive sense of structural integrity dominated in the brick faced Twin Morochos Apartments (1958).

ELIZABETH D. HARRIS

WORKS

1954, Edificio Polar; 1955, Commerce and Agriculture Bank; 1955, San Bernardino Apartments; 1956, Club for the State of Monagas; Caracas. 1956, Colinas de Bello Monte Apartments and Auto Showroom, Bello Monte, Venezuela. 1956, Eastern Professional Center of Sabara Grande; 1957, Metropolitan Bank Headquarters; 1958, Twin Morochos Apartments; 1960, Los Chaguaramos Apartments; Caracas. 1962, Department Store; 1965, Private Home; Choao, Venezuela. 1977, Orinoco, Office Building, Caracas.

BIBLIOGRAPHY

MOHOLY-NAGY, SIBYL 1964 *Carlos Raúl Villanueva and the Architecture of Venezuela.* London: Tiranti.
SMITH, C. RAY 1966 "In South America: After Corbu What's Happening." *Progressive Architecture* 47:140–161.

VENNECOOL, STEVEN

Only a few works can be attributed to Steven Vennecool (1657–1719), who was born in Amsterdam. The Town Hall of Enkhuizen is one of the best preserved examples of late seventeenth-century architecture in the Netherlands. The original exterior as well as the interior have hardly been changed since. In 1695, together with Jacob Roman, Vennecool rebuilt the originally medieval House Middachten, De Steeg, Netherlands, of which particularly the oval staircase is noteworthy.

MARIET J. H. WILLINGE

WORKS

1686–1688, Town Hall, Enkhuizen, Netherlands. 1691, Triumphal Arch, The Hague. 1695, House Middachten, De Steeg, Netherlands. 1697, Town Hall (renovation), Amsterdam.

BIBLIOGRAPHY

FOCKEMA ANDREAE, S. J.; KUILE, E. H. TER; and HEKKER, R. C. 1957 *Duizend jaar bouwen in Nederland, deel 2.* Amsterdam: Allert de Lange.
GELDER, HENDRIK ENNO VAN (editor) 1955 *Kunstgeschiedenis der Nederlanden, deel 2.* Utrecht: De Haan.
JANSE, H. 1979 "Het geslacht Vennecool, bouwmeesters en handelaren in bouwmaterialen." *Bulletin KNOB* 1:39–40.
ROSENBERG, JAKOB; SLIVE, SEYMOUR; and KUILE, E. H. TER 1966 *Dutch Art and Architecture: 1600–1800.* Harmondsworth, England: Penguin.

VENTURI, ROBERT

Robert Venturi (1925–), partner of the Philadelphia firm of Venturi, Rauch, and Scott Brown, is probably best known for his two books, *Complexity and Contradiction in Architecture* (1966) and *Learning from Las Vegas* (1972, written together with Denise Scott Brown and Steven Izenour). At a time of growing discontent with some of the assets of orthodox modern architecture, these books— despite or with the help of their often provocative puns (e.g. "Less is a Bore," varying LUDWIG MIES VAN DER ROHE's "Less is More")—helped to redefine the territory of architecture by emphasizing issues such as history, language, form, symbolism, and the dialectics of high and popular art. Both books combine a sophisticated artistic and cultural outlook on the art of building with a difficult commitment to what appears to be at once an ironic and a sympathetic vision of the American Dream. While often referred to as marking the "watershed" that separates the modernist past from the "absolutely delightful" postmodernist future (PHILIP C. JOHNSON in *Time,* January 8, 1979), these books can with equal justification be placed into the specifically modern tradition of architectural polemics documented by authors such as ADOLF LOOS or LE CORBUSIER, with whose *Vers une architecture* (1923) Venturi's *Complexity and Contradiction in Architecture* has been compared. On closer analysis, Venturi's preoccupations (for example, his critique of the simplifications of late modern urban renewal strategies, or his interest in Pop Art as a means of artistic appropriation of mass culture) become part of the broader spectrum of critical evaluations of the Modern movement's legacy, as it is offered, for example, in certain writings of the Team 10 group, especially in England and Italy, from the mid–1950s onward.

Venturi.
Vanna Venturi House,
Chestnut Hill.
Philadelphia.
1962

Complexity and Contradiction in Architecture concentrates, as its title suggests, on problems of formal language and style. *Learning from Las Vegas* in turn starts off from Venturi's famous "Is not Main Street almost all right?" (*Complexity and Contradiction,* p. 102) and studies the reality of the American Strip in what is probably its most exuberant version. As a result of this "Form Analysis as Design Research," the authors propose a number of programmatic (if often paradoxical) definitions applicable to architectural design and architectural criticism at large. Among these, "The Duck and the Decorated Shed" and "Ugly and Ordinary as Symbol and Style" have since entered the vocabulary of many architects and critics.

Venturi's practice has had a clear focus in the design of individual houses. The scale and intricate nature of this architectural genre has profoundly influenced his thinking about the relationships of functional requirements, historical reference, and representation in architecture. With the unexecuted project of a Beach House (1959) began a long and multifaceted series of house designs which had its first climax in Venturi's mother's residence in Chestnut Hill, Pennsylvania (1962). Shingle style houses such as the Low House in Bristol, Rhode Island, by MCKIM, MEAD, AND WHITE (1887; published, among many others, by Vincent Scully in his book *The Shingle Style and the Stick Style* [1955]), may well have provided an inspiration for the overall form. Yet, while many among Venturi's contemporaries—CHARLES WILLARD MOORE, Robert Stern, and others— developed their own elaborations on late nineteenth-century Shingle style houses into narrative, picturesque architectural landscapes, Venturi likes to keep his compositions under the control of axial symmetry and to establish a clear, almost archetypal identity of the overall form against which the details, following the intrincacies of the program, can then play. So a sense of gravity reigns.

The Shingle Style or, more generally, the tradition of the American Salt Box—is but one area of inspiration. Later houses combine very different architectural images, oscillating from Italian mannerist sources (Venturi spent more than a year at the American Academy in Rome) to EDWIN LUTYENS's Country House in Nashdon, England, or to Le Corbusier's Villa Savoye in Poissy, France, and at times incorporating references to commercial Art Deco architecture, as in the Brant House in Greenwich, Connecticut (1971–1973).

In his projects for public buildings, Venturi and his partners have preferred ordinary and conventional building techniques to extraordinary and original solutions. Applied ornament and decoration, not a dramatic and (so they argue) culturally irrelevant and economically irresponsible display of "structure," "form," and "space," are proposed to indicate the buildings' public function. The classical example is the Guild House, a home for elderly people in Philadelphia (1960–1963). Structurally, the symmetrical, six-story street façade is ordinary and conventional, as is the rest of the building—in tune with what may be assumed to be the needs and expectations of the building's inhabitants. Yet, the shape and size of the windows evoke LOUIS I. KAHN and Palladianism (see ANDREA PALLADIO), while the glazed brick of the entrance story and the huge letters above the entrance refer rather aggressively to industrial and supermarket aesthetics.

Paradoxically, it is the use of emphatically conventional, "ordinary" imagery of a 1950s institutional building that makes the Humanities Building at the State University of New York at Purchase (1968) look extraordinary in the context of the more explicitly heroic and original modern architecture that surrounds it. Not only does this building document the Venturian ideas about the "Ordinary" and the "Boring" as a means of architecture's sociocultural and aesthetic invigoration, but the handling of its interior spaces (especially the lobby) also betrays the architect's admiration for ALVAR AALTO and Le Corbusier, while a look at the plan reveals an echo of Kahnian geometries.

The firm's concern for context and its almost instinctive propensity toward monumentality achieved by the simple means of establishing clear hierarchies and tensions among the elements of their otherwise unspectacular façades is particularly evident in the unexecuted project for the North Canton Town Center (1965) and the famous competition entry for the Mathematics Building at Yale University, New Haven (1970). In later works, such as the addition of a gallery and workshop wing to the Allen Art Museum, Oberlin, Ohio (1973–1976), a more explicit use has been

made of decorative ornament as a means of distinguishing representative from secondary façades. At times, the solutions are more artistic and conceptual than purely architectural; yet, paradoxically, the reconstruction of Benjamin Franklin's house in Philadelphia as a "ghost structure" recalling Alberto Giacometti's "Palais à 4 heures du matin" (1932–1933, Museum of Modern Art, New York) was perhaps the only authentic architectural monument realized in the context of the Bicentennial celebrations (1972–1976).

It may come as no surprise that given the firm's interest in sociological documentation and analysis of the American environment, urban design has become a central issue in its activity. In some of its planning work, for example, the South Street Rehabilitation Plan for Philadelphia (1970), the "City Edges Study" for Philadelphia (1973), the Galveston Development Project (1975), or the Pennsylvania Avenue Project for Washington, (1978–1979; partly realized), the office manages to combine the skills of architects, visual artists, and architectural historians with those of cultural geographers. In this way, the firm in its capacity as planner, tries to abolish the split between high art and mass culture. At the same time, it continues to practice design as a medium of elaborate visual metaphors of the contradictory symbiosis of aesthetic standards and taste cultures that constitute the imagery of a pluralist society.

Robert Venturi, born in Philadelphia, studied architecture at Princeton University (1943–1950; under JEAN LABATUT, among others) and followed Donald Drew Egbert's history classes on Beaux Arts Architecture there. From 1950 to 1958, he worked successively for OSCAR STONOROV, EERO SAARINEN, and Louis I. Kahn. From 1954 to 1956, he was a member of the American Academy in Rome. After his return, he taught a course on architectural theories at the University of Pennsylvania School of Architecture (the basis of *Complexity and Contradiction in Architecture*). Later, a graduate seminar taught at Yale together with Denise Scott Brown and Steven Izenour (1968) was to provide the material for *Learning from Las Vegas* and further studies of the everyday environment.

Since the early 1970s, Venturi has written only a few articles and has devoted most of his time to designing and building. The sixteenth office with John Rauch in South Street, Philadelphia was founded in 1964. John Rauch, born in Phildelphia (1930), has been the managing partner of the firm. Denise Scott Brown joined them in 1967. Born in South Africa and graduated from the Architectural Association in London (1955), she has been involved with Venturi in the development of architectural theory since the early 1960s and has directed the office's planning projects since 1968.

STANISLAUS VON MOOS

Venturi.
Guild House (with Cope
and Lippincott).
Philadelphia.
1960–1963

Venturi.
Humanities Classroom
Building, State
University of New York
at Purchase.
1968

WORKS

1960–1963, Guild House (with Cope and Lippincott); 1962, Vanna Venturi House, Chestnut Hill; Philadelphia. 1965, Fire Station Number 4, Columbus, Indiana. 1968, Humanities Classroom Building, State University of New York at Purchase. 1970, Dixwell Fire Station, New Haven. 1970, Trubek and Wislocki Houses, Nantucket Island, Mass. 1971–1973 Brant House, Greenwich, Conn. 1972–1976, Franklin Court, Independence National Historical Park, Philadelphia. 1973–1976, Allen Art Museum (renovation and addition), Oberlin, Ohio. 1974–1977, Pennsylvania State University Faculty Club, State College, Pa. 1975, Tucker House, Mount Kisco, N.Y. 1975–1978, Brant House, Bermuda. 1978, Institute of Scientific Information Office Building, Philadelphia. 1979, BASCO Showroom, Bristol Township, Pa.

BIBLIOGRAPHY
COHEN, STUART 1974 "Physical Context/Cultural

Context: Including It All. *Oppositions* 2:1–40.

COLQUHOUN, ALAN 1978 "Sign and Substance: Reflections on Complexity, Las Vegas, and Oberlin." *Oppositions* 14:26–37.

COOK, JOHN W., and KLOTZ, HEINRICH 1973 *Conservations with Architects.* New York: Praeger.

GOLDBERGER, PAUL, and FUTAGAWA, YUKIO 1976 *Global Architecture 39: Venturi and Rauch.* Tokyo: A.D.A.

MOORE, CHARLES W., and PYLE, NICHOLAS (editors) 1974 *The Yale Mathematics Building Competition.* New Haven: Yale University Press.

MOOS, STANISLAUS VON, and WEINBERG-STABER, MARGIT 1979 *Venturi and Rauch: Architektur im Alltag Amerikas.* Zurich: Kunstgewerbemuseum der Stadt Zurich. Exhibition catalogue.

SCULLY, VINCENT 1974 *The Shingle Style Today.* New York: Braziller.

SCOTT BROWN, DENISE 1967 "Team 10, Perspecta 10, and the Present State of Architectural Theory." *Journal of the American Institute of Planners* 33, no. 1:42–50.

SCOTT BROWN, DENISE 1969 "On Pop Art, Permissiveness and Planning." *Journal of the American Institute of Planners* 35, no. 5:184–186.

SCOTT BROWN, DENISE 1976a "On Architectural Formalism and Social Concern: A Discourse for Social Planners and Radical Ohio Architects." *Oppositions* 5:99–112.

SCOTT BROWN, DENISE, and IZENOUR, STEVEN 1976 *Signs of Life: Symbols in the American City.* New York: Aperture. Exhibition catalogue.

VENTURI, ROBERT 1953 "The Campidoglio: A Case Study." *Architectural Review* 113, no. 5:333–334.

VENTURI, ROBERT 1966 *Complexity and Contradiction in Architecture.* New York: Museum of Modern Art.

VENTURI, ROBERT 1976 "Plain and Fancy Architecture by Cass Gilbert at Oberlin." *Apollo* 2:86–89.

VENTURI, ROBERT 1978 "Architecture as Shelter with Decoration on It, and Another Plea for a Symbolism of the Ordinary in Architecture." *Architecture + Urbanism* 1:3–80.

VENTURI, ROBERT; SCOTT BROWN, DENISE, and IZENOUR, STEVEN (1972)1977 *Learning from Las Vegas.* 2d ed. Cambridge, Mass.: M.I.T. Press.

"Venturi and Rauch: 25. "Öffentliche Bauten."" 1977 *Werk/Architese* 64, nos. 7–8:special issue.

"Venturi, Rauch and Scott Brown." 1981 *Architecture + Urbanism* 12:special issue.

VERMEXIO FAMILY

The Vermexios were a seventeenth-century family of builders and architects, originally of Spanish origin, who lived and worked in Syracuse in Sicily. Although members of the family appear in many documents, only one existing building can be positively attributed to a Vermexio.

Andrea Vermexio (?–1643) first appears as a *muratore* in a document of 1594. His only surviving work is the Church of Monte Virgini in Syracuse, which is attributed to him on the basis of a 1622 document. In the document and others relating to the building, he is referred to as "magistro . . . muratore" and is nowhere credited with its actual design. The building, severely damaged in the earthquake of 1693, retains only a single portal and pilaster from the early seventeenth century, and these are without any particular character.

Giovanni Vermexio (?–1648), Andrea's son, designed several buildings in Syracuse, the most important of which is the Municipio or Palazzo del Senato. The building, begun in 1629, has had a checkered history. It was more or less a family enterprise, with Giovanni as the architect and his brother, Francesco Vermexio (?–?), working as a master mason. In the 1640s, the building threatened to collapse, and Giovanni was replaced as supervisor of the construction by Giuseppe Guido. Although scholars have yet to examine its later history, there is little doubt that the Municipio was damaged by the earthquake of 1693. What we see today may be eighteenth-century restoration work rather than Vermexio's original building. The Municipio is an imposing blocklike building articulated with Michelangelesque (see MICHELANGELO) orders and aperture surrounds. The model for the main portal was GIACOMO BAROZZI DA VIGNOLA's doorway for Caprarola. The architectural character of the upper and lower stories and the western and southern façades of the building all differ, challenging the integrity of the design of the whole construction.

At the same time that Giovanni was working on the Municipio, he began the Church of Santa Lucia, which is still incomplete today. Giovanni worked on the church from 1629 to 1631, when construction was halted because it was thought that the church's position outside the walls could be used to bombard the city. The present church was built after Giovanni's death on the foundation stones that he laid and dates stylistically from the late seventeenth century. Giovanni may have also designed the Cappella Torres in the Cathedral of Syracuse, but construction on the chapel began after his death. Therefore, the extent to which his designs were followed by his successor, Giuseppe Guido, is still unknown.

STEPHEN TOBRINER

WORKS

ANDREA VERMEXIO

1622, Church of Monte Vergini, Syracuse, Italy.

GIOVANNI VERMEXIO

1629, Municipio; 1629, Santa Lucia Outside the Walls; Syracuse, Italy.

BIBLIOGRAPHY

AGNELLO, GIUSEPPE 1959 *I Vermexio, architetti ispano-siculi del Secolo XVII.* Florence: "La Nuova Italia" Editrice.

BLUNT, ANTHONY 1960 Review of *I Vermexio, architetti ispano-siculi del Secolo XVII. Burlington Magazine* 102:124–125.

VERRIER, ETIENNE

Etienne Verrier (1683–1747) was a military engineer and the principal designer of Fortress Louisbourg, Louisbourg, Nova Scotia. Born in Aix-en-Provence, France, the son of a master sculptor, Verrier learned military engineering in France from the disciples of SEBASTIAN LE PRESTRE DE VAUBAN and was commissioned an engineer in 1707. Between 1725 and 1745, as chief engineer at Louisbourg, he planned and revised the layout of the town; he completed the bastioned enceinte with its ornate town gates, the barracks with clocktower and governor's wing, the hospital, the lighthouse, two major harbor batteries, and harbor installations; and he designed an unbuilt parish church. More than a hundred plans and his many reports and accounts, together with data from archeological investigations, have provided the basis for much of the vast reconstruction at Louisbourg National Historic Park.

F. J. THORPE

VESNIN FAMILY

Of the three Vesnin brothers, Russian architects who worked together in various combinations during the first twenty years of their joint practice, Viktor Vesnin (1882–1950) seems to have been by far the most radical in both an architectural and a political sense. Not only did he project a remarkable series of industrial buildings before the October Revolution, but he also participated in the 1918 May Day Red Square celebrations and designed a timber monument to Karl Marx for the Red Square May Day setting of the following year. His progressive spirit may well have derived from the fact that he was educated at the Institute of Civil Engineering in St. Petersburg rather than at the Academy there.

Leonid Vesnin (1880–1937), on the other hand, studied at the Academy of Fine Arts in St. Petersburg (1901–1909) and was thus possibly the more academic of the three. Given Leonid Vesnin's background, we may assume that he played a major part in the design of the neo-Romanesque Myasnitskaya Post Office (1911) in Moscow. He probably also played a prominent role in formulating the neoclassical manner of the early practice which led, in 1914, to the realization of a large neoclassical villa for D. V. Sirotkin in Nizhny-Novgorod, a building which is now the Gorky Museum.

Although trained as an architect at the Institute of Civil Engineering in St. Petersburg, Aleksandr Vesnin (1883–1959) appears to have been the most artistic of the Vesnins, since he divided his early professional activities between painting, architecture, and stage design. His debut as a painter was the decorated ceiling of the large hall of the Sirotkin villa, while his career as a scenographer began with sets for the Maly theater. In 1920, he collaborated with the Constructivist artist Ljubov Popova and the director Vselvold Meyerhold on the design of an unrealized suspended aerial construction for the Third International. He followed this experiment with two remarkable sets for Tairov's Kamerny Theater, a 1922 setting for Racine's *Phèdre,* and a permutable Constructivist environment built for G. K. Chesterton's *The Man Who Was Thursday* which was staged in 1923.

Aside from his activities in the theater, Aleksandr Vesnin was instrumental in 1920 in establishing the architectural faculty at the reorganized State Higher Art and Technical Workshops, known as the Vkhutemas. In 1924, Aleksandr and Viktor Vesnin designed the canonical project of Russian Constructivist architecture, namely, their Pravda Newspaper Building which emphasized the extra-tectonic elements of its form such as the elevators, the loud speaker, the searchlight, the digital clock, and so on. In the following year, in association with MOISEI YAKOVLEVICH GINSBURG, Aleksandr Vesnin founded the Constructivist OSA group (Association of Contemporary Architects) and in the following year joined Ginsburg as co-editor of the OSA journal, *Sovremenia Architektura* (Contemporary Architecture).

By 1917, the year of the Revolution, Viktor Vesnin had already arrived, in the five-story Dynamo Stock Company Building, erected in Lubyansky Square, Moscow, at the stripped trabeated manner which was to be the touchstone of the earliest Vesnin Constructivist works; above all, it was to inform their epoch-making design for the 1923 Palace of Labor competition, comprising in one structure an 8,000-seat amphitheater, a 2,500-seat theater, numerous smaller auditoria, a library, reading rooms, offices, dining facilities, and a radio station. There followed a long series of extraordinary projects and three major realizations before the untimely death of Leonid Vesnin in 1933. The first of these achievements is the 1925 Institute of

Mineralogy in Moscow designed by V. Vesnin alone. In the following year, construction began on their large-span, curtain-walled Mostorg Department Store, which opened in Moscow at the end of 1927. The heroic culmination of this early joint practice was their Dnieper Dam and Hydro-Electric Station (1929–1930), won in competition and worked out in collaboration with N. Kolli, G. Orlov, and S. Andreevsky. Victor Vesnin and the same team were to realize a remarkable wooden Constructivist canteen for the construction workers on the Dnieper site.

Their most brilliant Constructivist competition designs were their 1929 entry for the Lenin Library and their 1931 Kharkov State Theater. That year also saw the construction of their Film Actors Club in Moscow. These achievements were followed in the first half of the 1930s by two other major constructions. The first of these was the Palace of Culture, Vostochnaya Ulitsa, Moscow (1933; now known as ZIL); the second was the Social Realist interior design for the Paveletskaia Subway Station built in Moscow in 1935. This eventual shift toward Social Realism was already presaged in the details of the Palace of Culture; the deployment of conventional architectural features within a modern skeleton became more and more evident in their major projects of the 1930s: their entry in the Palace of the Soviets competition of 1931 and their designs for the Narkomtiazhprom competition submitted between 1934 and 1936.

KENNETH FRAMPTON

WORKS

1911, Post Office, Myasnitskaya Street, Moscow. 1914–1915, Sirotkin House, Nizhny-Novgorod, Russia. 1917, Dynamo Stock Company; *1919, Karl Marx Monument, Red Square; 1925, Institute of Mineralogy; 1926–1927, Mostorg Department Store; Moscow. 1929–1930, Dnieper Dam and Hydro-Electric Station, Russia. 1931–1934, Film Actors Club; 1933–1937, Palace of Culture; Moscow.

BIBLIOGRAPHY

BARKHIN, MIKHAIL GRIGOR'EVICH 1975 Volume 2 in *Mastera Sovetskoĭ arkhitektury ob arkhitecture.* Moscow.

CHINYAKOV, A. 1967 "Brat'va Vesniny." *Arkhitektura SSSR* no. 3:41–54.

IL'IN, MIKHAIL ANDREEVICH 1960 *Vesniny.* Moscow.

KOPP, ANATOLE 1970 *Town and Revolution.* New York: Braziller.

KROHA, J., and HRŮZA, J. 1973 *Sovetska architektonika avant garda.* Prague: Odeon.

LISSITZKY, ELEAZAR 1970 *Russia: An Architecture for World Revolution.* Translated by Eric Dluhasch. Cambridge, Mass.: M.I.T. Press.

SHVIDOVSKY, O.A. 1970 *Building in the USSR: 1917–1932.* London: Studio Vista; New York: Praeger.

VESPIGNANI, VERGILIO

Roman-born Vergilio Vespignani (1808–1882) was a leading practitioner of both neoclassical and eclectic architectural styles in nineteenth-century Rome. He was trained under LUIGI POLETTI with whom he also collaborated on several projects. Vespignani's neoclassical manner is well represented by his Porta Pia façade (1852–1868) and by the Porta San Pancrazio (1857); his later medievalizing eclecticism is seen in a number of church restorations executed during the reign of Pope Pius IX. Vespignani was a member of the Accademia di San Luca and served as its president in 1874. He furnished the illustrations to Edward Dodwell's *I Setti Colli* (1829) and also worked with Luigi Rossini on *Le antichità* (1831). A number of his architectural projects were completed by his son Francisco Vespignani.

CHARLES RANDALL MACK

WORKS

1852–1868, Porta Pia (exterior façade); 1854, San Paolo fuori le Mura (façade, narthex, and atrium portico; with others); Rome. 1855, Theater, Orvieto, Italy. 1855, Theater, Viterbo, Italy. 1857, Porta San Pancrazio; 1861, San Carlo ai Catinari (restoration of chancel); 1864, Santa Maria Maggiore (confessional); 1864–1870, San Lorenzo fuori le Mura (restoration); 1864–1870, Verano Cemetery (chapel and porticoes); 1869–1888, San Pietro in Vincoli (high altar and baldacchino); 1869–1888, Santa Maria in Trastevere (presbytery tabernacle); 1869–1888, San Tommaso di Canterbury (rebuilding; with others); 1874, San Marcello (restoration); 1874–1882, San Giovanni in Laterno (restoration of apse; completed by Francesco Vespignani in 1886); Rome.

BIBLIOGRAPHY

MEEKS, CARROLL 1966 Pages 121, 251, in *Italian Architecture: 1750–1914.* New Haven: Yale University Press.

VESTIER, NICOLAS

Nicolas Jacques Antoine Vestier (1765–1816), the son of the painter Antoine Vestier, studied at the Ecole des Beaux-Arts in Paris. Primarily a residential architect, Vestier built in 1798, probably collaborating with BERNARD POYET, the rowhouses of the Rue des Colonnes in Paris. Two of his sons, Archimède and Phidias, also became architects.

RICHARD CLEARY

WORKS

1790s, Théâtre de Ribier; 1798, Houses, rue des Colonnes; 1812–1914, Orphanage of Mont Valérien; Paris.

BIBLIOGRAPHY
MAYEUX, HENRI 1908 "L'exposition théâtrale au Pavillon de Marsan." *L'Architecture* 21, no. 32:275.
POISSON, GEORGES 1969 "Napoléon et le Mont-Valérien." *Archives de l'Art Français* 24:309–321.

VIECO SANCHEZ, HERNAN

Hernan Vieco Sanchez (1925–) graduated in architecture from the National University of Colombia in 1948, studied urbanism in France, and collaborated on the Paris UNESCO Complex before returning to Colombia.

Prominent architect of public housing, professor, and urbanist, Vieco incorporates traditional materials into his angular designs expressing Colombia's heritage in modern architecture.

ELIZABETH D. HARRIS

WORKS

1948–1950, City Hall, Venadillo, Colombia. 1948–1950, Private Homes (two), Bogotá. 1960, Timinez Housing Project, Colombia. 1966, Marulandia Housing Development, Bogotá.

BIBLIOGRAPHY
ARANGO, JORGE, and MARTINEZ, CARLOS 1951 *Arquitectura en Colombia*. Bogotá: Ediciones Proa.
BERTY, ANNE 1981 *Architectures Colombiennes*. Paris: Moniteur.

VIGANÓ, VITTORIANO

Vittoriano Viganó (1919–) graduated from the Milan Politecnico in 1945 and came to international prominence with his Istituto Marchiondi in Milan (1953–1957). A proponent of the Italian strain of New Brutalism, Viganó has also been a teacher at the Milan Politecnico, involving himself in various areas of design, from interiors to urban planning.

THOMAS L. SCHUMACHER

WORKS

1947–1948, Condominium, Viale Piave; 1953, Galleria Schettini, Via Brera, Milan. 1953–1957, Istituto Marchiondi Spagliardi, Milano Baggio, Italy. 1955, Galleria Apollinaire, Via Brera; 1958, Galleria Grattacielo, Via Brera; 1958–1959, Condominium, Via Gran Can Bernardo; Milan. 1964–1965, Calvi House, Redavalle-Broni, Italy.

BIBLIOGRAPHY
BANHAM, REYNER 1966 *The New Brutalism*. New York: Reinhold.
GALARDI, ALBERTO 1967 *New Italian Architecture*. New York: Praeger.

GREGOTTI, VITTORIO 1968 *New Directions in Italian Architecture*. New York: Braziller.
VIGANO, VITTORIANO 1961 *Il Mobile e L'Architettura degli Interni in Italia dal 1945 al '60*. Milan.

VIGARANI, GASPARE

Gaspare Vigarani (1588–1663) was an Italian architect, stage designer, and military engineer, author also of a treatise on fortifications. Trained in Reggio Emilia, he was appointed supervisor of works in 1635 by Francesco d'Este, duke of Modena, for whom he produced a series of court festival and theatrical decorations and under whose patronage he worked on a number of important buildings in Modena itself and in Reggio. He also built fortifications at Carpi and Gualtieri. In 1659, he was called by Louis XIV to Paris where, with his sons Carlo and Lodovico, he organized theatrical decorations for the court and built the Theater of the Tuileries. Gaspare returned to Modena, but his son Carlo remained in Paris and in 1665 did some work on the Theater at Versailles.

DAVID CAST

WORKS

1646, San Girolamo, Reggio Emilia, Italy. 1647–1655, San Giorgio, Modena, Italy. 1651–1666, San Agostino, Reggio Emilia, Italy. 1654, Teatro della Spelta, Modena, Italy. 1659, Theatre des Tuileries, Paris.

BIBLIOGRAPHY
MICHEL, A. 1921–1922 *L'art en Europe au XVIIIe siècle*. 2 vols. Volume 6 in *L'histoire de l'art depuis les premiers temps chrétiens jusqu'à nos jours*. Paris: Colin.
ROUCHES, G. 1913 *Inventaire des lettres et papiers manuscripts de Gaspare, Carlo et Lodovico Vigarani (1634–1681)*. Paris: Champion.

VIGNOLA, GIACOMO BAROZZI DA

Born Giacomo Barozzi, but called after his birthplace west of Bologna, Vignola (1507–1573) was trained first as a painter, chiefly in Bologna, and then as an architect. In the 1530s, he went to Rome to study the antiquities and work as a painter at the Vatican, and in 1541–1543 he was in France, where he was associated with FRANCESCO PRIMATICCIO and where he met SEBASTIANO SERLIO. Thereafter, he worked in Rome, Caprarola, Piacenza, and Bologna. He was honored with burial in the Pantheon, as RAPHAEL, BALDASSARE PERUZZI, and others had before him. These bare facts suggest a solid, satisfying career, but that was not the case. His impractical nature and somewhat thorny personality, the shifting nature of sixteenth-century ecclesiastical patronage, and the repeated necessity of working with other architects, or with structures begun by others, all gave him much difficulty, and his course was erratic.

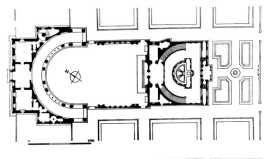

Vignola.
Floor plan of Villa di Papa Giulia (with Ammannati and Vasari).
Rome.
1550–1555

Vignola.
Façade of Villa di Papa Giulia (with Ammannati and Vasari).
Rome.
1550–1555

Vignola.
Villa di Papa Giulia (with Ammannati and Vasari).
Rome.
1550–1555

Still, Vignola was a major architect, perhaps the chief broker between the architecture of the first and last decades of his century. His work was derived in part from that of DONATO BRAMANTE and Antonio Sangallo (see SANGALLO FAMILY) and in part from a synthesis of mannerist forms, but at his best, as in the plan and spatial cohesion of the Gesù or in the masterful conquest at Caprarola of the parti he inherited, he touched greatness. Although his buildings tend to lack the kind of stylistic coherence of his celebrated contemporary ANDREA PALLADIO and although his creative talents were far outdistanced by MICHELANGELO's profoundly original genius, he is in a sense also immortal because of the far-reaching effects of both his best designs and his potent book, *La regola delli cinque ordini dell'architettura,* first published in 1562 and one of the three or four most influential treatises on architecture ever written.

His career opened with his appointment, by Pope Paul III in 1541, as the architect of San Petronio in Bologna. He took up this post after returning from France, but although his 1545 design for the façade exists, it was not executed and the building remained essentially untouched by him. At the same time, he was connected with work on minor and utilitarian structures in Bologna and its environs, and began to become involved in the problem of regularizing the façades of the shops more or less lined up along the east side of the Piazza Maggiore in the city. This, the Portico (Palazzi) dei Banchi, not finished until the early 1560s, is a major structure of Italian urbanism. A uniform arcade of shops, together with two passageways, is divided from an upper story by a grand entablature passing uninterruptedly along the entire length of the building. Michelangelesque pilasters divide the bays below; above, the bays are empaneled rather in the manner of those at Caprarola and contain windows with typically Vignolan teapot-top crowns. The result is in harmony with the rest of the piazza, well-proportioned and functional, though not excessively monumental. Also in Bologna, he worked on the idiosyncratic Palazzo Bocchi (1545–1555); an engraving of his design for the façade exists, and the standing fabric, aggressively mannerist in its configurations, conforms to this design, in the ground story at least, to a considerable degree.

Vignola's first commissions in Rome were given him by Pope Julius III and included the Villa (of 1550–1555) that stands north of the Porta del Popolo and now houses the national museum of the pre-Roman and Etruscan antiquities of central Italy; he may also have been connected with the construction of the modern Acqua

Vergine whose waters were displayed in the Villa's dramatic sunken nymphaeum. BARTOLOMEO AMMANNATI and GIORGIO VASARI were also involved in the design of the Villa (the latter calls attention to himself in this connection); collaboration such as this was often visited on Vignola, who surely did not welcome it. But the main block of the building—the façade, the apartments behind it, and the first or northwesternmost semicircular court—are Vignola's; the balance—the freestanding walls past the semicircular court and the multistoried nymphaeum court beyond—were executed by Ammannati but, with the exception of the curved staircases leading down to the nymphaeum, probably to Vignola's plan. Vasari's precise contributions, as well as other details of attribution, are not clear.

The façade is dominated by a rusticated entranceway flanked by niches, the whole vaguely reminiscent of an ancient triumphal arch; this arrangement is repeated, without the rustication, in the upper story. The balance of the composition is symmetrical and relatively plain, though the ground story windows recall those of the Palazzo Bocchi, the upper those of the Portico dei Banchi. Abbreviated wings project from this block from a point well behind the plane of the façade, but the whole gives no hint of the transition to curving forms that begins a mere room's width behind the entrance portal. The façade block is hardly more than a screen for a large courtyard whose wide, semicircular portico is the dominant architectural feature of the whole building. Seen from the inside, it resembles somewhat the first two stories of the southern half of the interior of the Pantheon, though its more direct inspiration was probably Bramante's Cortile del Belvedere at the Vatican. The quasi-triumphal arch motif is repeated, in a flattened version, at the center of the arc, from which spacious annular-vaulted porticoes curve to pavilions originally giving onto gardens outside the freestanding walls.

The axis of symmetry established by the centers of the entranceway and the semicircle continues southeast through the whole composition. The U-shaped courtyard ends in a wall which screens the final feature, a second, shorter, theater-shaped court focused on the sunken nymphaeum. Thus there is far more courtyard than enclosed space, there are changes of level, and above all there are surprises in that the courtyards and their dominating curved elements are both masked by planar walls. Yet, the controlling longitudinal axis is of the traditional Roman kind, and the whole building is as enclosed and private as an atrium house and its garden. It is more than a caprice and quite different from handsome adjustments of pavilions

to courtyards such as at PIRRO LIGORIO's Casino Pio. The Villa Giulia is a true retreat (albeit a generously scaled one, some 100 meters in length), a distant descendant of Pliny's villa (*Letters,* 2.17). No doubt the pope, Ammannati, and Vasari also contributed to it, but the overall plan, and the design of the main block and its spreading semicircular portico, are Vignola's.

Not far to the northwest of the villa, beside the Via Flaminia, Vignola built the small Church of Sant' Andrea, in 1550–1553, also for Julius III. Of deceptively simple shape, it is important as a study of the problems of modernizing traditional forms. It consists of a plain, oblong block with a projecting rectangular apse and an oval drum and dome, all with robust cornices of a late antique type seen for example on the Curia, or Senate House. Because it stands free, unlike most Roman churches, its sturdy blockiness is emphasized; from the front, it looks like a small-scale Pantheon. Its few windows are undecorated, and the impost line of the pendentives is marked on the exterior only by a stringcourse and two plain running bands. That, together with the cornices, is all the exterior surface treatment Vignola allowed himself except for the façade. There, the forms are very flat, the substantiality of the wall emphasized only by the simple entranceway and its flanking niches. The rhythm of the insubstantial pilasters, on the other hand, is rather striking: they are tightly paired at the corners, much further apart where they define the bays with the niches and still further apart for the entrance bay. Vignola was not the first to arrange the orders in such a nontraditional fashion, but his Sant' Andrea dispositions, which successfully establish the primacy of the unifying vertical center line by means of nonstructural spacing, is a landmark in the translation of the functional temple front into a freer, more complex, and supple element of design.

The single-volume interior is set on the long axis of the oval, entrance to apse. Its forms are almost as simple as those of the exterior. The

Vignola.
Sant' Andrea, Via
   Flaminia.
Rome.
1550–1553

warped pendentives rise from an impost line lacking an entablature; between them are bath windows whose triple divisions continue those defined by pilasters and panels aligned below. The cornice from which the dome springs is similar to those of the exterior. The building has been said to be the first church with an oval plan, but that is incorrect. That it influenced the baroque masters who subsequently worked with the oval can hardly be doubted. But in a curious way, in spite of its noncircular vault, it is rather Renaissance in quality: baldly geometric, its interior walls rationally subdivided, subdued in detail and in color, it is a kind of sixteenth-century Pazzi Chapel, a building more abstract and theoretical in inspiration than most of its contemporaries.

Vignola soon went north to Piacenza and shortly thereafter to Caprarola, though Rome remained his base. There, from 1568 until his death, he labored on his chief work, the Gesù. The project had a muddled history going back to 1550; in 1554, Michelangelo had been consulted. But when adequate financing became available in 1568, thanks to Cardinal Alessandro Farnese, Vignola took charge, backed by the cardinal although his plan was not popular with the Jesuits. The cardinal stipulated that the church was to have a single nave, with chapels where aisles normally would be, and that the whole structure was to be vaulted. From this directive and from the contemporary tendency to define the interior spaces of churches more simply and clearly than in the past, Vignola took his cue. The result, the home church of the Jesuit Order, is a monumental structure some 75 meters long, embracing a space made physically and visually coherent by reducing the entrances to the side chapels to small-scale features, by the provision of transepts which though broad are proportionately very shallow, and by a consistent vault span (18 meters) running from entrance to chancel. Only slight projections—the dome piers—intrude into a unified volume which, except for the main entrances in the west façade, is

apparently independent of its surroundings; there are no openings, for example, in the transept walls. Comparisons with LEON BATTISTA ALBERTI's Church of Sant' Andrea in Mantua are inevitable, but there, the design of the nave chapels and their function in the fabric of the building are quite different. And where Alberti's majestic nave piers and arcades mediate between the central volume and the imposing chapels that flank it, Vignola places what is by contrast a wall, in which the modest openings to the low chapels are only minor elements in the overall effect. Above, the entablature runs uninterrupted around the entire interior, helping to unify the space; the building had reached this level when, in 1573, Vignola died.

In such a design the focus is inevitably, and properly, upon the apse and its central altar. But at the Gesù this effect is lessened somewhat by the broad, rather short nave; a comparison with Renaissance basilican church plans will show how much longer, proportionately, their naves were. What the Jesuits wanted was a preaching church, one for large congregations as much as for the ceremonies of the sacraments. Thus the almost undivided volume of the Gesù appeared largely in response to a functional requirement. The Jesuits carried these architectural principles with them wherever they went, and because of this the Gesù is the clear source of a hundred churches large and small.

But this is not to imply that the building is without subtleties. The beltlike entablature carries another elevated horizontal zone (in which the grilles of the openings of the narrow gallery can be seen) that furthers the unification of the space. Each corner of the shallow transepts is rounded, diminishing even further any sense of their depth and suggesting that their volumes are fundamentally one with the main space. And before the interior was given its lining of baroque splendor (a process still going on in the nineteenth century as it goes on in St. Peter's to this day), the nave vault was apparently finished with white stucco, while the paired pilasters of the nave wall were of travertine, not encased in marble as they are now. With some exceptions, the colorful and dramatic décor of the building one sees today was added toward the end of the seventeenth century; one must look under it, so to speak, for Vignola's building, which was a far less heady concoction than it now appears to be, restrained, subtle, and very effective.

The façade is not Vignola's but GIACOMO DELLA PORTA's, whose design was chosen by Cardinal Farnese in 1571 and who supervised the construction of the building after Vignola's death. It is somewhat hard to see, at this distance, why della Porta's less subtle design was preferred, ex-

Vignola.
Il Gesù (vaulting and
façade by Porta).
Rome.
1568–1573

cept for the fact that taste was changing. One of Vignola's designs makes it clear that he thought of the façade as a more highly modulated entity, in plan at least, than did della Porta. But the latter's proposal elevated all the orders on pedestals, giving the building a greater sense of verticality, while its generously scaled scroll buttresses (Vignola, in the design just mentioned, had proposed simple triangles with concave silhouettes) suggested that expansive reach of the interior volume. In addition, della Porta repeatedly paired his orders, in harmony with Vignola's nave wall design. Although Vignola's proposal is the more balanced and coherent one, neither solution is particularly successful. However, both represent attempts to shake off the uneasy, unresolved aspect of so many mannerist façade compositions and supply answers to the problem of designing complex yet coherent church façades.

Nor is the façade of Sant' Anna dei Palafrenieri entirely Vignola's. He began this Vatican church toward the end of his life, in 1565, but it was not consecrated until 1583, still unvaulted; it was not finished until much later. The end bays of the façade have the broad, flat pilasters and enframed, recessed panels Vignola favored, but the upper portion of the center bay is of a later time. The plan of the church is unusual in that a single oval space is fitted into a surrounding rectangular enclosure. The wall of the interior oval is not tangential to the enveloping box, for it expands on the major axes into two altar recesses and two entrance bays (one on the flank); there are chapels in the left-over corner spaces. The building is about 20 meters long overall, half again as long as Sant' Andrea in Via Flaminia, where the proportions of the plan are much the same as at Sant' Anna. The unity of the oval interior is emphasized by keeping the entrances to the corner chapels small—one is reminded of the handling of the nave chapels at the Gesù—and by the powerful reinforcement of the unitary spatial nature of the place by the four interior recesses, which anchor absolutely the reciprocating tensions of the lateral and longitudinal axes whose point of intersection is the generative source for the design. All commentators connect this interior with the ovals of GIOVANNI LORENZO BERNINI, FRANCESCO BORROMINI, and later architects; a comparison of the interiors of Sant' Anna and San Carlo alle Quattro Fontane is revealing, especially because of the similar way Vignola and Borromini relate columns to walls and to the cornices that in both buildings travel around the wall at the impost level of the arches of the entrance and altar recesses.

Of the numerous other buildings and projects Vignola designed or had a hand in, two huge palaces, one at Piacenza and the other at Caprarola, record his style and thought as fully as do the Villa Giulia and the Gesù. Begun in 1558, the Palazzo Farnese at Piacenza was commissioned by the Habsburg Margaret of Parma, wife of the Farnese duke. Had it ever been finished, it would have been one of the most imposing monuments of Italian architecture, some 88 by 112 meters (the Farnese palace in Rome measures about 58 by 77 meters); not enough money was available, and only about a third of it was built. The huge but quite plain city-side façade, largely of brick, was to have been articulated only at the entrance, over which a tower was to have been built; the effect would have been rather like Bernini's scheme for the Louvre or a moated, towered Caserta. On the opposite side, from which gardens led to the Po in the fashion of the Rome palace, there were loggias. In the vast courtyard, Vignola proposed a theater of semi-elliptical plan, a feature recalling both Bramante's Belvedere and Raphael's Villa Madama. This was not the only unusual feature of the courtyard, for the corner angles were masked by vertical tiers of large niches set on the diagonal, and the bay piers were in part articulated with flattish, straplike forms that outlined the piers and arches, and were set around tiers of niches, panels, and blind windows. Again Borromini's work comes to mind, for example, the exterior walls of the San Carlo Monastery or the handling of the piers at San Giovanni in Laterano.

At Caprarola, however, Vignola's Palazzo Farnese stands complete. Of all the buildings of that family, the Caprarola palace is the most insistent iconographically and symbolically, an unequivocal statement of the authoritarian Farnese ideology. Before becoming pope, Paul III had begun a moated castle of pentagonal plan (51 meters on a side) on a hill overlooking the village of Caprarola, facing Rome some 55 kilometers to the southeast. In 1559, Vignola took over the castle, then perhaps one story high, and continued the work according to his own designs and to Alessandro Farnese's requirements; when the architect died, the palace was substantially finished.

In transforming the pentagonal fortress into a grand villa-palace, Vignola did some of his best work. Documents show that he laid out the main street of the village, the Via Nicolai, which lies on the extension of the main northwest–southeast axis of the pentagon. From the end of the street access to the villa can be gained only by an extensive sequence of ramps, plazas, and stairs, all fitted into a wide trapezoidal area also axially aligned with the center line of the pentagon. At the end of this sequence, double flights of stairs rise to converge before a bridge that crosses the moat and

Vignola.
Palazzo Farnese.
Caprarola, Italy.
1559–1573

Vignola.
Courtyard of Palazzo
*   Farnese.*
Caprarola, Italy.
1559–1573

leads to the main entrance to the *pianterreno*. The result is one of the most effective architectural approaches in Europe, one emphasized by the narrowness of the long axial street, the compactness of the village with its small-scale structures, and, above all, the dominating position, high up on the hill, of the villa proper. The entire design speaks of authority and control, of the distance the Farnese put between themselves and the rest of the world.

Both BALDASSARE PERUZZI and Antonio Sangallo had considered the problem of transforming the five-sided fortress into a building for aristocratic family life; they both thought of inserting a pentagonal courtyard inside it, and Sangallo seems to have considered centering a circular courtyard in it, but only in a very general way and without thinking out the complex spatial and structural adjustments such a scheme required. Vignola, on the other hand, apparently took up the circular scheme from the beginning and, perhaps with a nod to the classical villa—the Island Casino of Hadrian's comes to mind—proceeded brilliantly to solve the problems inherent in a circle-pentagon relationship; it is such problems that show how far apart geometry and architectural reality are, being separated by many practical and aesthetic considerations. So while the exterior is a regular polygon—by the law of tangents, it looks rectangular from fairly close up—the visitor soon discovers that a third of the interior volume is a centered, circular courtyard, and that the apartments of the primo and secondo piani are ingeniously set out along the five sides of the pentagon in files nearly tangent to the circular courtyard corridors at five points (where there are doorways). The rest of the small amount of left-over space is variously filled in, en-niched, or used for tight, circular service stairs. The enfilades and corner dispositions of the *piano nobile* are such that the building can be circumnavigated not only via the circular courtyard

corridor but also by way of the grand *saloni* and their dependencies. At the southern and eastern corners—that is, at the ends of the main façade—Vignola placed respectively a circular staircase, which rivals Bramante's, and a chapel. All five sides of the terzo piano have central corridors flanked by numerous small rooms; this level rises above the uppermost zone of the circular court.

The detailing is restrained throughout. In both the circular courtyard and in the grand staircase the orders are used in pairs, and in the courtyard at *piano nobile* level the spandrels are recessed in the usual Vignola way and the piers have oval, recessed panels set vertically. Here and there, the curving Vignolan window tops appear, but there is little else that can be called exuberant. Rustication is used sparingly—at the entrances, the exterior corners, and the basement level of the courtyard. Pilasters and recessed panels govern the exterior articulation of the walls and that of most of the interior ones as well. The architectural drama of the building, in the interior, comes from the experience of the circular corridors, open to the courtyard and lit from above, the frequent views into and across the court from various points in the building, and the traverse of the splendid spiral staircase, with its tightly paired columns, helical vault, and dizzying void. In the formal rooms and corridors, the figural decoration, largely planned by Vignola, emphasizes and re-emphasizes the fame and pretensions of the Farnese.

Vignola's many other works and projects are listed and documented in Walcher Casotti's book (1960), together with those wherein his degree of participation is uncertain. Chief among the certain works, both in Rome and dating from the 1560s, are the façade of Santa Maria del Orto and the Orti Farnesiani on the Palatine. His monumental entrance gate to the latter was taken down in 1882 but has been re-erected beside the Via di San

Gregorio; part of the villa proper still stands on the north slopes of the hill, opposite the Basilica of Maxentius and Constantine: two elegant garden pavilions, a grotto *all'antica,* stairs, and terraces. The lower story of the gate bears some resemblance, in its tripartite character and rustication, to the entranceway of the Villa Giulia and that at Caprarola; above, there is an open arch flanked by female herms and buttressed by forms very similar to those seen in his Gesù façade proposal, the whole topped by a segmental pediment carrying the Farnese arms. The façade of Santa Maria del Orto is unusually wide for its height. The rhythms of the lower story expand upon those of Sant' Andrea in Via Flaminia through the addition of extra bays and pilasters, and only the columns and segmental pediment that enframe the entrance arch come forward. The second story, a relatively thin and narrow three-bay wall, is connected to the spreading first story below by means of sweeping, overscaled buttresses. The whole is sprinkled with large obelisks, and the overall effect is not a particularly happy one.

Vignola's written work consists of a treatise on perspective, published posthumously in 1583, and the famous book of *regole* or rules, which first appeared in 1562. At that time, an architect could consult VITRUVIUS, Alberti, or Serlio; their works were for all practical purposes the only texts available. Vitruvius was perhaps appealed to more in argument than in architectural practice. He is quite obscure in places though useful on the orders; a difficulty was that the Roman buildings that could be studied and measured rarely conformed to his prescriptions, most of them having been built well after Vitruvius's time in a quite non-Vitruvian style. Alberti's book was intellectual and theoretical but, however penetrating, somewhat out of tune with the Cinquecento and in any event not the kind of thing to appeal particularly to a man like Vignola. Serlio's work, which had appeared in installments between 1537 and 1551, and which became very influential, was based in part upon the work of Peruzzi, whose pupil Serlio had been. His is a practical book, as is Vignola's, but Vignola's has clearer—in some cases much clearer—illustrations, and the quite brief text has a firmer though not discouraging scholarly tone.

The reader, after an introduction, is given thirty-two engraved plates, each with a short, explanatory caption. The proportions are selected from what Vignola considered the best he had found in the ancient monuments. Details are set out unambiguously, as are workable modular schemata for the orders. Some of Vignola's own work appears. The result is a straight-forward guide to design, one that became immensely popular, especially in France but hardly less so elsewhere. This popularity persisted through the eighteenth century and well into the nineteenth; an American *Vignola* appeared as late as 1902–1906 (W. R. Ware's; it was reprinted in 1977). With one's Vignola in hand, propriety and correct proportions were assured, and one was connected directly with a meticulous interpreter of antiquity and, through him, with Sangallo and Bramante. Palladio's great *Quattro libri* appeared eight years later. A different kind of book, one that influenced domestic architecture in particular, it did not replace Vignola's treatise, largely because it is less concise, more personal, and more theoretical.

Vignola, it has been said, was by temperament a master craftsman. He was a better draftsman than most; good examples of his work can be seen in his Caprarola paintings of architecture viewed in perspective as well as in the plates of his treatises. He seems to have concerned himself with every detail of his buildings, a practical trait that gives authority to his writings. He knew how to build well and he was a master of architectural planning; his responses to difficult commissions can be studied with considerable profit. As a designer he excelled: "his buildings are never mere façades, or clever but partial solutions; rather they are the completely thought-out answer to the problem given" (Coolidge, 1950, p. 12). As a thorough-going professional he commanded respect; as a person he was less effective. He was nobody's man, and in a difficult time, tried as he was by uneasy collaboration and by major buildings unfinished or abandoned, he made a lasting mark.

He did this in part by absorbing the lessons he read in the ancient monuments and the works of the High Renaissance masters, using them not for specific plans and forms so much as for guides to what was permissible, to what was proper. In that sense he was very much of a classicist; like Palladio, he sought for an architecture of propriety, though along a much different path. Vignola in his own way was as experimental as GIULIO ROMANO, though once again with very different results. This gift for experiment appears in his plans and all that they lead to, and it is his plans above all that show that his designs are not just assemblies of Serlio-like entranceways and Bramantesque walls and orders. Not since imperial antiquity had an architect investigated relationships between curved and straight-sided figures so meaningfully. He was much attracted to the focal and axial properties of concavities, especially on a large scale and in conjunction with rectangles and polygons. If he could rationally insert a semicircular, circular, or oval space into a building, he did, and he was as good or better at this than any architect before the seventeenth century. That these shapes were fitted into enclosing, straight-sided ones marks him as a mannerist architect as much as do his rusticated entranceways and his somewhat jarring window tops. These, together with his all but ubiquitous flat, shallow pilasters and his recessed, Bramantesque wall and spandrel panels, are not, however, the essentials of his style. Those are found rather in his formal rhythms, his plans, the spaces he projected from them, and the architectural interaction of those spaces. The coherence of his work has to be sought, but it is there. The key to it lies more in the ways in which he solved his problems and gave them architectonic forms than in the manner in which those forms are embellished.

WILLIAM L. MacDONALD

WORKS

1545–1555, Palazzo Bocchi (unfinished), Bologna, Italy. 1550–1553, Sant' Andrea, Via Flaminia; 1550–1555, Villa di Papa Giulia (with Bartolomeo Ammannati and Giorgio Vasari); Rome. 1558ff., Palazzo Farnese (unfinished), Piacenza, Italy. 1559–1573, Palazzo Farnese (on and within a fortress begun, but not finished, by others), Caprarola, Italy. 1560s, Orti Farnesiani, Rome. Completed 1561, Portico dei Banchi, Bologna, Italy. 1565ff., Sant' Anna dei Palafrenieri (completed by others); 1566–1569, San Maria del Orto (façade); 1567–1573, St. Peter's (architect); 1568–1573, Il Gesù (vaulting and façade by Giacomo della Porta); Rome.

BIBLIOGRAPHY

The effect of Vignola's tenure upon St. Peter's is under discussion; the documents and discussions of this and other problems connected with his career are cited in Walcher Casotti's book and other works listed below.

ACKERMAN, JAMES S., and LOTZ, WOLFGANG 1964 "Vignoliana." Pages 1–24 in Lucy F. Sandler (editor), *Essays in Memory of Karl Lehmann.* New York: Institute of Fine Arts.

COOLIDGE, JOHN 1950 "Vignola's Character and Achievement." *Journal of the Society of Architectural Historians* 9, no. 4:10–14.

HEYDENREICH, LUDWIG H., and LOTZ, WOLFGANG 1974 Pages 267–277 and 382–383 in *Architecture in Italy: 1400 to 1600.* Harmondsworth, England: Penguin.

KITAO, TIMOTHY K. 1962 "Prejudice in Perspective: A Study of Vignola's Perspective Treatise." *Art Bulletin* 44, no. 3:173–199.

LEWINE, MILTON 1965 "Vignola's Church of Sant'Anna de' Palafrenieri in Rome." *Art Bulletin* 47, no. 2:199–229.

LOTZ, WOLFGANG 1939 *Vignola-Studien.* Würzburg, Germany: Kitriltsch.

PARTRIDGE, LOREN 1970 "Vignola and the Villa Farnese at Caprarola." *Art Bulletin* 52, no. 1:81–87.

VASARI, GIORGIO (1568)1973 *Le opere di Giorgio Vasari, con nuove annotazioni e commenti.* 9 vols. Edited by G. Milanesi. Reprint. Florence: Sansoni. Originally published in 1550 with the title *Le vite de piv eccelenti architetti.* There are many English translations and selections from Vasari's *Lives,* the standard one by G. du Vere was published in ten volumes in London by the Medici Society in 1912–1915.

VIGNOLA, GIACOMO BAROZZI DA 1562 *La regola delli cinque ordini d'architettura.* There are many translations, versions, and variations on the title. Sometimes the work is simply entitled *Vignola,* which was taken to mean "Handbook of Architecture," and it is not uncommon to find that the text has been altered or rewritten, and the plates redrawn and their number expanded or reduced.

WALCHER CASOTTI, M. 1960 *Il Vignola.* 2 vols. Trieste, Italy: Istituto di storia dell'arte.

VIGNON, ALEXANDRE PIERRE

Alexandre Pierre Vignon (1763–1828) was trained by JULIEN DAVID LEROY; he was also a close friend of CLAUDE NICOLAS LEDOUX. Minor commissions during the French Revolution earned Vignon the title of *Inspecteur général des bâtiments de la République* (1794). In 1807, Napoleon I chose Vignon's uncompromising neoclassical design for his *Temple de la Gloire* (Madeleine) in Paris.

CHARLOTTE LACAZE

WORKS

*1792, Salle des Machines (executed by Jacques Pierre Gisors), Tuileries Palace; *1793–1794, Arsenal (remodeled the manege), Tuileries Palace; 1807–1828, Temple de la Gloire (now Madeleine Church; not completed until 1842 by JEAN JACQUES HUVÉ); Paris.

BIBLIOGRAPHY

BOYER, FERDINAND 1933 "Notes sur les architectes Jacques-Pierre Gisors, Charles Percier, Pierre Vignon." *Bulletin de la Société de l'Histoire de l'Art Français* 1933:258–269.

BOYER, FERDINAND 1934 "Les Tuileries sous la Convention." *Bulletin de la Société de l'Histoire de l'Art Français.* 1934:197–241.

GRUEL, LEON 1910 *La Madeleine depuis son établissement à la Ville Evêque.* Paris: Champion.

HAUTECOEUR, LOUIS 1953 *Revolution et empire: 1792–1815.* Volume 5 in *Historie de l'architecture classique en France.* Paris: Picard.

KRIÉGER, ANTOINE 1937 *La Madeleine.* Paris: Desclée de Brouwer.

LAPAUZE, HENRY 1903 *Procés-Verbaux de la Commune générale des arts de peinture, sculpture, architecture, et gravure (18 juillet 1793) et de la Société Populaire et Républicaine des Arts (3 nivose II-28 floréal III).* Paris: Imprimerie nationale.

VAUTHIER, GABRIEL 1910 "Pierre Vignon et l'église

de la Madeleine." *Bulletin de la Société de l'Histoire de l'Art Français* 1910:380–422.

VIGNON, ALEXANDRE PIERRE 1793 *A la Convention nationale, sur la nouvelle salle dans le Palais des Tuileries.* Paris: Cagnion.

VIGNON, ALEXANDRE PIERRE 1806 *Mémoire à l'appui d'un projet pour placer conformément aux intentions de S.M., la Bourse, le Tribunal de commerce et la Banque de France dans les constructions de la nouvelle église de la Madeleine.* Paris: the author.

VIGNON, ALEXANDRE PIERRE 1814 *Sur le rétablissement des académies des beaux-arts.* Paris: Veuve Perroneau.

VIGNON, ALEXANDRE PIERRE 1816 *Monuments commémoratifs projetés en l'honneur de Louis XVI et de sa famille.* Paris: Veuve Perroneau.

VIGNON, ALEXANDRE PIERRE n.d. *A la Société républicaine des Arts.* Paris: de Guffroy.

VIGNON, ALEXANDRE PIERRE n.d. *Observations sur le Palais que doit occuper le Tribunat.* Paris: Porthmann.

VIGNON, ALEXANDRE PIERRE n.d. *Pétition présentée à la Convention nationale, par P. Vignon, architecte de sa nouvelle salle.* Paris: Imprimerie Nationale.

VIGNY, PIERRE DE

Pierre de Vigny (1690–1777) began his career as a draftsman in the offices of the Bâtiments du Roi under the direction of ROBERT DE COTTE. During a trip he made to the Levant in 1722, he prepared a project for a new palace for Monsieur de Bonnac, the French ambassador to Constantinople. After having crossed Italy, where he admired baroque art, on his return to Paris, he executed around 1726 a strange work, the Hôtel de Chenizot on the Ile Saint-Louis. The general disposition of this building and the two chimeras supporting the balcony above the entrance portal express his denial of classical restraint.

From 1728 to 1732, he constructed in Paris for Pierre Crozat, brother of the celebrated collector, the buildings of the Cour du Dragon in the district of Saint-Germain-des-Prés. Paul Ambroise Slodtz carved the dragon, now preserved in the Louvre. The balcony nested under the arch of the monumental portal giving on to the rue de l'Egout.

The 1740s were the most active of Vigny's career: he decorated the apartment of the duc de Chevreuse in the Hôtel de Luynes and built the stables of the Gardes du Corps at Coulommiers, the Church of Saint Martin du Tertre in Valois, and numerous Parisian apartment houses of which that at 42 rue François Miron is one of the best preserved. Called to Reims, he made repairs to the cathedral from top to bottom.

The general hospital of Lille was his principal work. This ambitious project, conceived in 1738, was three-quarters realized in the course of a cen-

tury. It is an imposing work possessing a cold elegance.

In his *Dissertation sur l'architecture* published in 1752, he praised the liberating genius of FRANCESCO BORROMINI, but his own eclectic taste made him a precursor of the architects of the nineteenth century.

GÉRARD ROUSSET-CHARNY
Translated from French by Richard Cleary

BIBLIOGRAPHY

GALLET, MICHEL 1973 "L'architecte Pierre de Vigny (1690–1772): Ses constructions, son esthétique." *Gazette des Beaux-Arts* Series 6 82:263–286.

VILAMAJÓ, JULIO

Julio Vilamajó (1894–1948) was the first Latin American architect to open the door to objective regionalism by using local materials and traditional building practices in the urbanization of Uruguay's Villa Serrana (1943–1947) in Minas. Influential in both Uruguay and Argentina, he began his career by designing neo-Tuscan villas after winning Uruguay's *Gran Premio* in architecture at the University of the Republic and traveling to Europe.

In 1929, once he had absorbed LE CORBUSIER's purism theories, he moved toward planar designs with an emphasis on structure and exterior texture. By the late 1930s, he had become a leading innovator and three months before his death was chosen to become one of the United Nations' ten architects.

ELIZABETH D. HARRIS

WORKS

1930, Casa Vilamajó; 1932, Banco Republica; 1935–1938, Engineering School, University of the Republic; Montevideo. 1943–1947, Villa Serrana, Minas, Uruguay.

BIBLIOGRAPHY

BULLRICH, FRANCISCO 1969 *New Directions in Latin American Architecture.* New York: Braziller.

"Dibujos de Julio Vilamajó." 1965 *Montevideo Universidad de Arquitectura Revista* 6, Aug.:7–10.

LUCCHINI, AURELIO 1970 *Julio Vilamajó: su Arquitectura.* Montevideo Universidad de la República, Instituto de Historia de la Arquitectura.

VILAR, ANTONIO UBALDO

Antonio Ubaldo Vilar (1888–1966) became Argentina's foremost representative of European functionalism after his 1926 design for the Banco

Popular Argentino in Buenos Aires in the then fashionable neo-Hispanic style.

The clear-cut volumes, plain white wall surfaces, chromed railings and banisters of his buildings of the thirties are examples of Argentina's best modern architecture. His work is the result more of cold functional logic, technical excellence, and skillful construction methods than of aesthetic impulse. His designs for low-cost industrialized housing, which he described as "minimum and decent," are particularly noteworthy.

FEDERICO F. ORTIZ

WORKS

1934–1938, Various Standardized Apartment Buildings; 1935–1936, Apartment Building, Avenida del Libertador and calle Oro; Buenos Aires. 1936–1942, Ninety-two Service Stations for the Automóvil Club Argentino. 1938, House, calle Rivera Indarte, San Isidro, Buenos Aires. 1938–1942, Eight Radio Stations with Studios, LR4 Splendid Radio Network. 1938–1942, Police Hospital, Buenos Aires.

BIBLIOGRAPHY

Documentos para una historia de la arquitectura argentina. 1980 2d ed. Buenos Aires: SUMMA.

ORTIZ, FEDERICO, and GUTIERREZ, RAMÓN 1972 *La Arquitectura en la Argentina: 1930–1970.* Madrid: Ediciones y Publicaciones Populares.

SCARONE, MABEL 1970 *Antonio U. Vilar.* Instituto de Arte Americano, University of Buenos Aires.

VILLAGRAN GARCIA, JOSÉ

Architect and educator José Villagran Garcia (1901–) has been recognized as the father of functional architecture in Mexico. A year after graduating from the Universidad Nacional de Mexico in 1923, Villagran Garcia began his teaching career, reforming the university's Beaux-Arts curriculum. He introduced the instruction of composition combining practice with doctrine by insisting on a meticulous analysis of function and historical knowledge of how architecture has accommodated need. Above all, he imbued students such as JUAN O'GORMAN with the ideal that architecture must be a product of artistic imagination and technical knowledge.

In 1923, he became chief architect for the Mexican Department of Public Health and two years later he designed the Hygiene Institute in Poptla, Mexico's first modern structure based on his functionalist principles. A tactile application of materials has also been paramount in his work exhibited by his use of unfinished reinforced concrete in the cubicle sun breakers of the Surgery Annex in Tlalpam (1941).

He traveled throughout Central and South America to give seminars in structural theory, restoration, and his speciality, hospital construction. In 1968, he received the country's most prestigious award, the *Premio Nacional de Artes,* bestowed by the president of Mexico for a lifetime of dedication to the creation of dynamic architecture reflective of Mexico's culture.

ELIZABETH D. HARRIS

WORKS

1925, Hygiene Institute, Poptla, Mexico. 1934, Hogar Number 5 School, Mexico City. 1941, Surgery Annex, Huipulco Tuberculosis Sanitarium, Tlalpam, Mexico. 1951–1953, School of Architecture and Art Museum, Ciudad Universitária, Mexico. 1952–1956, Las Americas Office Building, Cinema and Garage Complex; 1962, Hotel Maria Isabel; Mexico City. 1976, National Institute of Cardiology, Tlalpam, Mexico.

BIBLIOGRAPHY

Arquitectura Mexico 1956 12, no. 55. Entire issue dedicated to José Villagran Garcia.

BORN, ESTHER 1937 *The New Architecture of Mexico.* New York: Architectural Record and William Morrow.

CETTO, MAX C. 1961 *Modern Architecture in Mexico.* Translated by D. Q. Stephenson. New York: Praeger.

VILLANUEVA, CARLOS RAÚL

Meshing the indigenous and colonial architectural traditions of South America with a European tradition of design theory, Carlos Raúl Villanueva (1900–1975) introduced a brand of modernism uniquely suited to the climate, people, and terrain of Venezuela. Both his architectural innovations and their philosophical underpinnings remain as touchstones for younger architects.

Villanueva was born in London, where his father was a member of the Venezuelan diplomatic service. He was educated at the Lycée Condorcet in Paris and returned to Caracas, in 1928 following the receipt of his architecture degree from the Ecole Nationale des Beaux-Arts in Paris. From 1929, the year he began private practice in Caracas, until his death, Villanueva was instrumental in guiding the development of the burgeoning city. Consistently, his carefully considered architecture mediated between the chaotic swell of urban structures and the vast spaces of an awesome landscape. He served as architect to the Ministry of Public Works, Caracas, between 1929 and 1939, as president of the Venezuelan National Board for Historic and Artistic Protection and Conservation, and as founder director of the National Planning

Commission. His contributions to the architectural profession were equally generous. In addition to founding the school of architecture at the University of Venezuela in Caracas in 1944 and serving as a professor there for much of his life, he was also the founding president of the Venezuelan Association of Architects. Villanueva's contributions earned him numerous honors and awards.

Several of Villanueva's architectural aims were first realized in the bullring at Maracay (1931). Its massive form and ornamental Moorish arcade affirm the enduring bullfight tradition, while the use of cast concrete and externally articulated load-bearing piers acknowledge modern concerns.

Villanueva began to express his concept of the architect as a responsive catalyst in the process of shaping a fluid world in his redevelopment of Caracas's rambling slum area, El Silencio (1941). Here, six-story apartment dwelling and service structures, graced and linked by a continuous, street-level arcade, are arranged around a central plaza from which vehicular traffic has been virtually eliminated. At Maracaibo, his General Rafael Urdaneta Housing Development (1934–1944) filled a need for low-cost, low-rent housing with a sensitivity to indigenous, aboriginal housing patterns and a dedication to upgrading living standards. Several three-story multiple dwellings and 1,000 single-family houses concentrically encircle community facilities. Interspersed yard space, the orientation of structures primarily toward prevailing winds, and the use of axial, mobile shutters in place of glass windows facilitate natural cooling. Villanueva's contributions to public housing culminated in the 23 de Enero (1955–1957) and El Paraiso Development (1954), which echo the dramatic landscape surrounding Caracas.

In University City, Caracas, a project which occupied much of his career, Villanueva masterfully wove poetic content into the fabric of form and function. A cantilevered, covered walkway meanders throughout the campus, alternately defining intimate spaces, circling sunlit gardens, and spilling into expansive plazas. Villanueva conceived this richly varied environment as a series of musical "movements" and orchestrated the whole in precast, prestressed concrete units. The incorporation of latticed concrete panels diffuses the brilliant sunlight into lyrical patterns which play upon interacting surfaces yet permit the flow of cool breezes. Although Villanueva's commitment to the holistic integration of the plastic arts is apparent throughout the university complex it is, perhaps, nowhere more strikingly evinced than in his Aula Magna (1952). There, Alexander Calder's polychromed "clouds," suspended at varying levels from the ceiling, simultaneously distribute sound evenly throughout the acoustically meticulous auditorium and visually harmonize the space.

The humanized spaces of Villanueva's housing developments and university complex give way to grandeur in his Olympic Stadium at University City (1950–1952). With breathtaking bravura, the cast concrete form, braced from below by concrete columns, sweeps upward to establish the seating area for 30,000 people and then doubles back dramatically upon itself to soar anew in a daring cantilevered span.

JAN SCHALL

WORKS

1931, Bullring, Maracay, Venezuela. 1935, Museo de los Caobos, Caracas. *1937, Venezuelan Pavilion, World's Fair, Paris. 1939, Gran Colombia School; 1941, Redevelopment of the El Silencio Quarter; Caracas. 1943–1944, General Rafael Urdaneta Housing Development, Maracaibo, Venezuela. 1944–1947, Master plan, University City; 1945, Medical Center, University City; 1950–1952, Olympic Stadium, University City; 1951, Villanueva House; Caracas. 1952, Aula Magna (main auditorium), Library, Plaza Cubierto and Walks, and the Botanical Institute, University City; 1953, Small Concert Hall, University City; 1954, El Paraiso Housing Development (with Carlos Celis and José Manuel Mijares); 1954, Humanities, Science, and Physics buildings, University City; 1955, School of Dentistry, University City; 1955–1957, 23 de Enero High-Rise Housing Development (with C. C. Cepero and José Manuel Mijares); 1957, School of Architecture and Urbanism, School of Pharmacy, and Olympic Swimming Stadium, University City; Caracas. 1958, Villanueva House, Caraballeda, Venezuela. *1967, Venezuelan Pavilion (with E. Trujillo), Expo '67, Montreal.

BIBLIOGRAPHY

BAYÓN, DAMIÁN, and GASPARINI, PAOLO 1979 *The Changing Shape of Latin American Architecture: Conversations with Ten Leading Architects.* New York: Wiley.

"Caracas University City." 1954 *Arts and Architecture* 71:14–19.

"Carlos Raúl Villanueva, Hon. FAIA." 1975 *Journal of the American Institute of Architects* 64:60.

DAMAZ, PAUL F. 1963 *Art in Latin American Architecture.* New York: Reinhold.

HITCHCOCK, H. R. 1955 *Latin American Architecture Since 1945.* New York: Museum of Modern Art.

MOHOLY-NAGY, SIBYL 1964 *Carlos Raúl Villanueva.* New York: Praeger.

PETER, JOHN 1958 *Masters of Modern Architecture.* New York: Braziller.

VILLANUEVA, CARLOS RAÚL 1950 *La Caracas de ayer y de hoy, su arquitectura colonial y la reurbanizacion de "El Silencio."* Paris.

VILLANUEVA, CARLOS RAÚL 1964 "La Ciudad y su Historia." *Bolletin de Universidad Central, Caracas* 1964:91–96.

VILLANUEVA, CARLOS RAÚL 1969 "Formation-Fonction-Position." *Arquitectura, Formes y Fonctions* 15:9–78.

VILLANUEVA, JUAN DE

Juan de Villanueva (1739–1811) was a Spanish neoclassical architect who carried on the ideas of VENTURA RODRÍGUEZ TIZÓN in Spain. He spent the years 1759–1765 at the Accademia di San Luca in Rome and in 1768 became architect for the Jeronymites of the Escorial in Spain. His architecture is compact, regular, and rational, in keeping with the enlightened spirit of the age. Villanueva's masterpiece is the Prado Museum in Madrid (1787–1789). Making imaginative use of a classical vocabulary, Villanueva created the greatest example of picturesque classical architecture in Spain. Villanueva was active in the Spanish Academy and served as royal architect from 1797 until his career was truncated by the change of regime in 1808.

ELIZABETH A. T. SMITH

WORKS

1768, Residence of Marqués de Campovillar, El Escorial, Spain. 1770, Sacristy; 1770–1783, Palafox Chapel; Burgo de Osma Cathedral, Spain. 1771, Casa de Infantes; 1773, Casita de Abajo; 1773, Casita de Arriba; El Escorial, Spain. 1775, Residence of Marqués de Llano; 1780, House for the Agustinos, calle de Reloj; 1781, Entrance to the Botanical Gardens, Madrid. 1784, Casita del Príncipe, El Pardo, Spain. 1787–1788, Prado Museum; 1787–1789, Ayuntamiento (north façade); 1788–1811, Academy of History (not completed until 1847); 1789, Oratory, Church of Caballero de Gracia; 1789, Royal Observatory; 1791, Convent of San Fernando (reconstruction); 1791, Plaza Mayor (restorations); 1809, Cemetery and Chapel, Puerta de Fuencarral; n.d., Patio de las Escribanías, Court Prison (now Ministry of Foreign Affairs); Madrid.

BIBLIOGRAPHY

CABELLO LAPIEDRA, LUIS 1918 "D. Juan de Villanueva." *Arquitectura* 1, Nov.:185–195.
CHUECA GOITIA, FERNANDO, and MIGUEL, CARLOS DE 1949 *La vida y las obras del arquitecto Juan de Villanueva.* Madrid: Carlos-Jaime.
GAYA NUÑO, J. A. 1966 *Arte del siglo XIX.* Madrid: Plus-Ultra.
KUBLER, GEORGE, and SORIA, MARTIN 1959 *Art and Architecture in Spain and Portugal and Their American Dominions: 1500–1800.* Baltimore: Penguin.
SCHUBERT, OTTO 1924 *Historia del barroco en España.* Translated from German by Miguel Hernández Alcalde. Madrid: Editorial Saturnino Calleja.

VILLARD DE HONNECOURT

Of all the preserved medieval architectural treatises the most important by far is that of Villard de Honnecourt. His lodge-book, which is now in the Bibliothèque Nationale in Paris, not only covers important monuments of the most seminal period of Gothic architecture and sculpture but also ranges over more categories within medieval architecture than any other sketchbook except that of Wolfgang Rixner. Wilars de Honecort, as the author called himself, was born in the last quarter of the twelfth century in the small town of Honnecourt-sur-l'Escaut in northern France. The Benedictine monks of the local abbey taught him to write a faultless French and awakened his interest in history, geometry, and Archimedean physics. Around 1190 he probably became a journeyman in the lodge of the enormous Cistercian church construction at Vaucelles which was consecrated in 1235 and which he illustrated in his lodge-book. His interest in Cistercian architecture persisted and he gave us the only graphic analysis of the Bernardine plan "made up of squares." His theoretical interest encompassed an early Gothic chevet solution which he "discussed with Pierre de Corbie." The ambulatory fuses rectangular and semicircular chapels and thus is a prime visual example of the Scholastic demand for unity gained through variety. Villard visited and perhaps worked in Meaux, whose plan he illustrated accurately. On his way there he probably visited Laon where the cathedral was undergoing its third building campaign. He was deeply affected by the elegance of the West towers which were "the finest I have seen." There followed trips to Reims and to Chartres, where he sketched reliefs and the just completed western rose window for which he drew up an alternate design.

The pattern of his travels shows that he was anxious to keep up with *modernitas* while simultaneously looking for short-term contracts. Omnivorous, he freely skipped over many arts. He drew from manuscripts and ivories and made many sketches of sculpture, metalwork, and gadgets which he must have seen in the nearby foundry centers of Liège and Dinant. His enormous catapult with a counterpoise weighing approximately twenty tons and wooden springs is the major thirteenth-century drawing of military machinery. Villard also was fascinated with animals and copied some of his most beautiful drawings from bestiaries.

The variety of his drawings reflects the intense cultural ferment of the early thirteenth century and the importance of the innovative Gothic style which involved French architects in projects as distant as Bosnia, Serbia, and Norway. Shortly after 1220 Villard himself left for Hungary, most likely to aid in the construction of the Cistercian abbey at Pilis near the capital of Esztergom. On his way there he may have passed through Bamberg, where his drawings of Laon may have occasioned an abrupt change in the design of the western tower of the cathedral. He also passed through Lausanne where he not only met several of his compatriots but also crudely sketched an alternate design for the south transept rose which was completed around 1227. Returning from his voyage of around 3700 kilometers, he almost certainly subcontracted work for parts of Reims Cathedral. Under the supervision of Jean-de-Loup, he seems to have worked on the triforium of the choir, the tracery of the side-aisle windows, sundry cornices and mullions, and segments of the nave ribs which were never used. After the work stoppage of 1233 he most likely served as a consultant in the planning of the choir of Saint Quentin, the largest collegiate church of France. He may also have participated in the construction of the choir of Cambrai, of which he gives a precise plan in his lodge-book. Both projects were located less than half a day's ride from Honnecourt. Since Villard did not include any sketches of the stupendous new sites at Amiens, Beauvais, and Rouen which were only a few days away from his center of activity, it is likely that he died in the mid 1230s. Before his death he presumably organized his sketches working with a colleague who added several drawings and explanatory texts in Latin. After Villard's death the sketchbook came into the hands of clerics and in the fifteenth century it still had 82 pages. Around 1560 it passed into the Félibien family and may have had some influence on the Gothic revival of the 1600s through ANDRÉ FÉLIBIEN DES AVAUX's important *Entretiens* published in 1669. In 1795, now only 66 pages long, it entered the *Fonds latin* of the Bibliothèque Nationale.

The manuscript is the main graphic witness of the personality pattern of the thirteenth-century humanist–architect. Like all great builders from the Renaissance to the present, the medieval architect had to be a master of several trades. Being in charge of major sculptural programs on façades, of sophisticated machinery, scaffolding, form work, and tremendous roofs, and being interested even in medicine, he followed the classical tradition. Above all, he also had to be a theoretician. Villard himself defines his manuscript as a treatise on masonry, machinery, carpentry, and the principles of geometry, and wants to give "sound advice" and intriguing *exempla*. The practical tips range from the beveling of an oblique springer without a template, the construction of a double arch lacking a central support, the making of a floor with short timbers, the straightening of sagging structures, the strengthening of hoisting wheels and screw jacks, and, amazingly, an automatic sawmill with a reciprocal drive. Playful gadgets include a hand warmer with gimbals, a singing bird powered by

Villard De Honnecourt. Drawing of west tower of Laon Cathedral.

syphoned liquid, an important clockwork in the form of an angel precisely pointing at the sun, and, alas, a perpetual motion machine. For surveying Villard suggests a crossbow with a wired arrow; for halving the volume of a vessel he inscribes a smaller square at a 45-degree angle within a larger square, and draws the second, cylindrical vessel into the perimeter of the smaller square.

Echoing VITRUVIUS whose *De Architectura* was well known from the Carolingian period onward, Villard unsuccessfully tried to predetermine the proportions of human figures through geometric overlays so that "work will be facilitated." Above all, he began to understand the quadrature principle which became the most basic Gothic design device around 1220. The rotation of successive squares inscribed in an original square at 45-

Villard De Honnecourt. Drawing of "Ideal" Chevet, Saint Stephen. Meaux, France.

Villard De Honnecourt. Drawing of checker players, animals, Tantalus cup, and warming apple.

Villard De Honnecourt. Drawing of choir at Reims Cathedral with masons' marks.

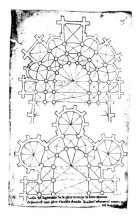

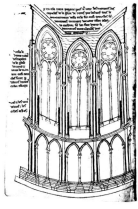

degree angles is used in several figural sketches, in the plan of the Laon tower, and in theoretical drawings done in collaboration with the second master.

The sketchbook of Villard de Honnecourt thus stands at the beginning of the codification of Gothic theory and deals with many of its practical and decorative challenges. In spite of his obvious lack of leadership, Villard looked at new designs with critical assurance saying: "This is good masonry" or "I drew it because I liked it best." He modified existing structures, usually heightening the proportions or changing the design altogether. His sketchbook therefore becomes a mirror of the formidable stature of the cathedral builders who were completely secure in their aesthetic and professional environment. P. Frankl not unjustly called Villard a "Gothic Vitruvius."

FRANÇOIS BUCHER

BIBLIOGRAPHY

The lodge-book (c.1175–1240) of Villard de Honnecourt in the Bibliothèque Nationale in Paris contains approximately 1215–1233 entries. The 66-page parchment (240 x 160 mm.), whose purpose was the organization of didactic materials, has suffered losses in the section on carpentry, but includes architecture, machinery, figures, sculpture, architectural theory, and animal sketches. The text is in French; theoretical material and Latin titles were added by a second master.

BOWIE, THEODORE (editor) (1959)1962 *The Sketchbook of Villard de Honnecourt.* 2d rev. ed. Bloomington: Indiana University Press.

BUCHER, FRANÇOIS 1979 Volume 1, pages 15–193 in *Architector: The Lodge Books and Sketchbooks of Medieval Architects.* New York: Abaris. Includes a critical text with corrected translations, additional facts, and an updated bibliography.

HAHNLOSER, HANS R. (1934)1972 *Kritische Gesammtausgabe des Bauhuttenbuches ms. fr. 19093 der Pariser Nationalbibliothek.* 2d rev. ed. Graz, Austria: Akademische Druck- und Verlagsantalt. Still the *editio princeps.*

VINCI, LEONARDO DA

See LEONARDO DA VINCI.

VINGBOONS, PHILIPS

Philips Vingboons (1607/1608–1678) was the son of the painter David and brother of the architect Justus and engraver Johannes. He is widely known through two folios with engravings of his works, published in 1648 and 1674. His name is bound to a special type of small house, which can be recognized by its gables with frontons between richly decorated wings and pilasters. This kind of façade can be seen in Amsterdam as well as in the northeastern part of Holland. He also designed many country houses.

MARIET J. H. WILLINGE

WORKS

1638, 168 Herengracht; 1639, 319 Keisersgracht; 1639, 548 Singel; 1642, 95 Kloveniersburgwal; Amsterdam. *1642, Vredenburg, Beemster, North Holland, Netherlands. 1661, New Tower, Kampen, Netherlands. 1662, Deventer Townhall (new wing), Overijssel, Netherlands. 1662, 364–370 Herengracht; 1664, 412 Herengracht; Amsterdam. 1664, Vanenburg House, Putten, Gelderland, Netherlands. 1669, 466 Herengracht; 1670, 450 Herengracht; Amsterdam.

BIBLIOGRAPHY

BALEN, C. L. VAN 1939 "Het probleem Vinckboons-Vingboons opgelost." *Oud Holland* 56:97–112.

EEGHEN, I. H. VAN 1952 "De familie Vingboons-Vingboons." *Oud Holland* 67:217–232.

FOCKEMA ANDREAE, S. J.; KUILE, S. H. TER, and HEKKER, R. C. 1957 Volume 2 in *Duizend jaar bouwen in Nederland.* Amsterdam: Albert de Lange.

GELDER, HENDRIK E. VAN (editor) (1936)1955 Volume 2 in *Kunstgeschiedenis der Nederlanden.* Rev. ed. Utrecht: de Haan.

KOLLEMAN, G. 1970 "Philip Vingboons en zijn ontwerp voor het Raadhuis op de Dam." *Ons Amsterdam* 1970:312–315.

KUYPER, W. 1976 "Vingboons' Capitool." *Spiegel Historiael* 11:614–622.

VINGBOONS, PHILIPS 1648 *Afbeeldsels der voornaemste gebouwen uyt die Philips Vingboons geordineert heeft.* Amsterdam.

VINGBOONS, PHILIPS 1674 *De granden . . . afbeeldingen en beschrijvingen des aldervoornaamste en aldernieuwste gebouwen uyt alle die door Philippus Vingboons geordineert zijn.* Amsterdam: Danckerts.

VIOLLET-LE-DUC, EUGENE EMMANUEL

Eugène Emmanuel Viollet-le-Duc (1814–1879) may be viewed as scholar, archeologist, architect, or theorist. He was a determined and enterprising man. To his contemporaries in France he appeared as the principal exponent of medieval architecture, the restorer of many of the most famous Gothic monuments, notably Notre Dame de Paris, the author of two compendious dictionaries on medieval art. The Gothic Revival in France was based on these works, the illustrations especially, though it was in Germany and England that they were to be exploited most actively for architectural details. But Viollet-le-Duc aimed to be more than a revivalist or even a medievalist. He despised archeology. He wanted the theory of architecture which he abstracted in his study of Gothic—and in particular Gothic construction—to serve as the basis for a renewal of contemporary architecture. He saw himself as a prophet of the future. Leaders of the Modern movement; men as diverse as FRANK LLOYD WRIGHT, AUGUSTE PERRET, and LE CORBUSIER, leaned heavily on the verities propounded by him.

Viollet-le-Duc was born to a comfortably placed family in Paris, of some pretension. The "-le-Duc" was added to the family name in 1740 to commemorate a liaison with the Montmorency-Luxembourgs. His father was on the civil list, in charge of the royal residences, later to be granted an official house within the precincts of the Tuileries. When Viollet-le-Duc was born, the family lived at 1 rue Chabanais, a house built by his mother's father, a building contractor. The Viollet-le-Ducs lived on the second floor. On the third floor lived his mother's sister, married to the painter Antoine Théodoze Clérambourg. In the attic lived his mother's brother, Etienne Jean Delécluze, who had studied painting under Jean Louis David. Delécluze became art critic to the *Journal des Débats* in 1822 and retained that position through life. The household was surprisingly stimulating. Viollet-le-Duc's father, who himself wrote poetry, had an admirable collection of early French literary works, and on Friday evenings he entertained in his library a host of notable young writers, critics, and publishers, all of whom, and more, gathered on Sunday afternoons in Delécluze's attic; P. L. Courier, C. A. Sainte-Beuve, and Henri Stendhal were among them, though more important for the young Viollet-le-Duc's future career were Ludovic Vitet and Prosper Mérimée. Most of the guests were contributors to *Le Globe,* a radical journal, which, at the end of 1830, passed firmly into the hands of the Saint-Simonists.

Viollet-le-Duc's introduction to architecture was less stirring, though scarcely less elevated. Hardly more than sixteen years old, he began working for Marie Huvé, architect of the interior of the Madeleine and a close friend of his father, who lived at 2 rue Chabanais. Soon after, having determined to pursue the career of an architect, he moved to the office of ACHILLE LECLÈRE, another of his father's friends. Other architects with whom his father was in close contact all suggested that Viollet-le-Duc enroll at the Ecole des Beaux-Arts, but he rejected their advice. Already he mistrusted established procedures. Already he hated that institution.

He explored France in the years that followed—Provence in July and August 1831, in the company of his uncle Delécluze; Normandy in September and October 1832, all by himself, grieving for the sudden and shattering death of his mother; the Pyrénées from May to September 1833, with Emile Millet, a young musician who remained one of his closest friends until he emigrated to America thirty years later; Normandy again in September 1834 with his younger brother Adolphe, and Elizabeth Tempier, whom he had married on May 3; and yet again to Normandy in May and June 1835 with Léon Gaucherel, a student at the Ecole de Dessin (later the Ecole des Arts Décoratifs) where Viollet-le-Duc began teaching in August 1834 and where he was to continue until 1850. During these tours, he sketched more landscapes and picturesque views than buildings. But early in 1836, he decided to travel to Italy, to see for himself those monuments that had sustained the classical tradition. He was by then the father of an eight-month-old son, Eugène-Louis (his daughter Sophie was to be born in 1838), but leaving his family behind with his father in the Tuileries, he set off with Gaucherel.

They left on March 12, following the route south through Lyons, taking a boat from Genoa to Livorno and thence to Naples, which they explored, and thence to Sicily, where they spent three months before traveling north again to Rome. By then Mme. Viollet-le-Duc had grown restive and insisted on joining them. She arrived in Livorno in August, with Adolphe as companion. They went then to Pisa and Florence and south to Rome where they stayed for no less than nine months before returning home via Venice, Verona, Milan, and Geneva. Viollet-le-Duc had been away, in all, seventeen and a half months. The Italian journey is clearly of interest in Viollet-le-Duc's career, but it was not decisive. He left France a typical young romantic, delighting, if we are to judge by the drawings done in Normandy, in the rich intricacy of the late Gothic architecture; he returned respectful of a wide range of classical styles.

Viollet-le-Duc's mind was to be focused soon enough by Prosper Mérimée, newly appointed *inspecteur général des monuments historiques,* in succession to Ludovic Vitet. Viollet-le-Duc worked first, on his return from Italy, under Achille Leclère at the Conseil des Bâtiments Civils and as assistant on the Hôtel des Archives in Paris, and on a project for the completion of Saint-Just in Narbonne. But on February 13, 1840, at the instigation of Mérimée, he was asked by the Commission des Monuments Historiques to prepare plans for the restoration of the Madeleine at Vézelay. This marks the beginning of his career proper.

Mérimée is remembered today as the author of *Carmen* and a handful of other novellas, a man of

Viollet-le-Duc.
City of Carcassonne
(fortification).
France.
n.d.

fashion and wit, but he was also a man of mind. He was perceptive in a way that Viollet-le-Duc was not. He had a sensibility Viollet-le-Duc lacked. Equally, he was lazy and disdainful of technicalities in a way that Viollet-le-Duc was not. They complemented one another perfectly. Mérimée remained through life Viollet-le-Duc's intellectual mentor and closest friend. Their relationship was at first formal, but when Mérimée found that work was proceeding well at Vézelay, he invited Viollet-le-Duc to accompany him on his tours of inspection through France. Their first journey together was made in 1843. There were to be many more, followed by an expedition to England in 1850, and in 1854, with Emile Boeswillwald, to Germany and Czechoslovakia. Mérimée's *Notes d'un voyage* served as the model for Viollet-le-Duc's early writings, though more important for his future was the introduction Mérimée provided into that circle of enthusiastic and already active medievalists on the Commission des Monuments Historiques, among them Charles Forbes, the comte de Montalembert, and Victor Hugo, whose *Notre Dame de Paris* had been published in 1831. It is worth noting that Viollet-le-Duc's father had introduced him already to Isidore Justin Séverin, Baron Taylor, for whose *Voyages pittoresques dans l'ancienne France* (1820–1878) he was to do no less than 249 drawings between 1838 and 1845. Between 1842 and 1845, Viollet-le-Duc was awarded twelve commissions for the restoration of medieval monuments. He was thus drawn irrevocably into the orbit of the medievalists. But his career was not determined by Mérimée alone. In 1840, he had been appointed second inspector to the restoration of the Sainte Chapelle in Paris, then proceeding under the direction of FÉLIX DUBAN. The first inspector was JEAN BAPTISTE ANTOINE LAS-

SUS, a pupil of HENRI LABROUSTE, who, like many other of Labrouste's disciples, had turned from classical architecture to the study of French Renaissance architecture and thence to the national style par excellence, thirteenth-century Gothic. Labrouste himself was no great admirer of Gothic, but his rational doctrines were clearly susceptible of reinterpretation in medieval terms. Lassus taught Viollet-le-Duc to consider Gothic as the outcome of an intellectual endeavor. Together, they worked also on the restoration of Saint-Germain l'Auxerrois, where most of the leading enthusiasts of Gothic art, led by Alphonse Napoléon Didron, were involved. There, Viollet-le-Duc designed the stained glass for one of the side chapels. But infinitely more significant was his collaboration with Lassus in a limited competition for the restoration of Notre Dame de Paris. The judges were Mérimée, Duban, and Hubert Rohault de Fleury (see ROHAULT DE FLEURY FAMILY). On April 30, 1844, Viollet-le-Duc and Lassus were appointed to restore the cathedral and build a new sacristy. Work began in the following year and continued through until 1864. There, he trained the architects and the craftsmen who were to sustain the vast nineteenth-century program of Gothic restoration in France and also the whole of the Gothic Revival in architecture. There, he tested the ideas that had been transmitted by Lassus. He himself was to emerge conspicuously as the theorist of the Gothic movement in the next few years.

During the 1840s, he wrote a number of articles for that wholly partisan journal edited by Didron, the *Annales Archéologiques,* on the fortifications of Carcassonne and the church of the Jacobins at Toulouse, on medieval treasures and tiles, but especially a series of nine articles, "De la construction des édifices religieux en France depuis le commencement du christianisme jusqu'au XVIe siècle," published between 1844 and 1847, in which he first outlined the theory he was to develop in his *Dictionnaires.* The whole emphasis, as the title makes plain, is on structure, and thus on the more material and practical aspects of architecture. He was concerned to explain medieval building in the most simple, rational terms. "If the architects of the twelfth and thirteenth centuries made naves high," he wrote, "it was not with any puerile symbolic intent, rather to provide air and light for those great elevated vessels in a gloomy and damp climate; in this, as in all things, they simply followed their reason" (III, 1845, p. 325). The history of medieval architecture appeared to him thus as little more than the development of an efficient and economical structural system. The Gothic cathedrals of the thirteenth century were the climax of this process. The pointed arch evolved, Viollet-le-Duc argued, to control the forces set up in masonry vaults with precision. The ribs of the Gothic vault carried entirely and independently the weight of the webs above, so that the vertical component of the thrust could be directed downward, to point supports or columns, while the horizontal component could be taken up by flying buttresses and in turn ingeniously counterpointed by the weight of pinnacles set on the outer buttresses and thus redirected downward. The whole was a balance of forces in equilibrium. The resulting structural scaffold allowed bay sizes to be varied and planning to become much more flexible. Viollet-le-Duc was led, ultimately, to entertain the idea that Gothic architecture was simply the clear expression of function, that every form and molding was designed to strictly determined, practical ends. Thus, moldings were designed to throw off rain water or express a division between floors, nothing more. Ornament itself was used only to heighten some adroit manipulation in stone. Even sculpture was subservient to structural expression, if indeed it was not a part of it. He went on to suggest that just as the Gothic cathedrals of France were a fitting expression of the needs of Frenchmen of the thirteenth century, so Greek architecture could be seen to be the proper and satisfying expression of the needs of the ancients. Good architecture was the result of a careful consideration of the materials at hand and the appropriate methods of building in relation to the climate and the social aspirations of a particular race.

Viollet-le-Duc's ideas were not original. Around 1830, the Saint-Simonists had formulated a theory which held that the architectures of ancient Greece and thirteenth-century France were fitting expressions of what they recognized as the only two organic societies in history. The rational analysis of Gothic architecture had an even longer history in France. From the early Renaissance at least, and possibly back to the Middle Ages themselves, Gothic architecture had been analyzed in terms of structural finesse. That this knowledge was not readily available to Viollet-le-Duc need not be in doubt; that most respected and widely used treatise, JACQUES FRANÇOIS BLONDEL's *Cours d'architecture* (1771–1779) contains an analysis of Gothic vaulting, indeed of all Gothic construction, as detailed and as single-minded as Viollet-le-Duc's own. JEAN BAPTISTE RONDELET, who was to teach building construction at the Ecole des Beaux-Arts for over twenty years, outlined the principles of Gothic construction with even greater finesse in that standard work of reference, the *Traité théorique et pratique de l'art de bâtir* pub-

lished first between 1802 and 1803.

Despite the objectivity of Viollet-le-Duc's analysis of Gothic construction, he aimed, when he wrote his articles for the *Annales Archéologiques,* to further the Gothic Revival in architecture that Didron and his associates were so actively fostering. One of the consequences of their campaign was the building of Sainte-Clotilde in Paris. This was designed in a late Gothic style to the taste of none of them. The members of the Académie, who had opposed it from the start, liked it even less. Auguste Nicolas Caristie initiated a debate on the subject of the revived Gothic style, summarized in a pamphlet by Désirée Raoul Rochette, permanent secretary to the Académie, that stirred the most violent polemic and brought forth a sheaf of further pamphlets and articles. Viollet-le-Duc responded with vigor. But he, along with many other supporters, found that they had no proper argument. After 1846, any faith he might have had in a Gothic Revival had gone. Within a few years he had ceased to contribute to the *Annales Archéologiques,* turning instead to the less partisan *Revue Générale de l'Architecture,* though after 1853 he was to be associated rather with the *Encyclopédie d'Architecture* and the related *Gazette des architectes et du bâtiment,* started in 1863 by his son. He sought with some desperation an architecture Gothic in inspiration, but recognizably of the nineteenth century. He himself was not up to the challenge. His first important building, a four-story apartment block at 28 rue de Liège, Paris, built between 1846 and 1849 for Henri de Courmont, administrator of the Monuments Historiques and friend of Mérimée, has a conven-

Viollet-le-Duc.
H. Courmont House.
Paris.
1846–1849

tional enough plan, with a street façade robustly detailed for the most part, though with an admixture of rather too brittle and pretty elements, Gothic in inspiration. He was responsible for at least thirty completed buildings, some in a French Renaissance style, not to mention a handful of miscellaneous tombs and monuments. He did develop a style of his own that derived, but was in no sense an imitation of Gothic, but he never succeeded in fashioning a forceful, convincing image in architecture. There is an uncertainty in all these works, even in the ambitious projects for Saint Pierre de Chaillot, Paris (1866 and 1868), that made them unsuitable as models for imitation.

Viollet-le-Duc's energies as an architect were directed rather toward restoration. Work on Notre Dame began in 1845. The following year, he was made *chef du bureau* to the Monuments Historiques and appointed as architect to the restoration of the Abbaye de Saint-Denis. The year after that, he was already supervising work on twenty-two sites, and he took Eugène Millet into his office as an assistant. By 1853, Viollet-le-Duc had been appointed one of the three *inspecteurs généraux des Edifices Diocésains,* which vastly increased his responsibilities in connection with the restoration, maintenance, and extension of medieval buildings. This institution soon became, to all intents, Viollet-le-Duc's own. His disciples and supporters, to a man, worked for it. The zeal and the effort required of Viollet-le-Duc in all this is to be grasped only with the greatest difficulty. From 1842 onward, for the next twenty-five years, he traveled on tours of inspection through France, for four or five months each year, certainly never less than three, inspecting buildings, meeting local architects and contractors, resolving difficulties with local authorities and landowners, making endless reports, writing innumerable letters. The task was grueling. He traveled at night in order not to waste time. Yet, he was able to direct the restoration and completion of many major medieval monuments.

Viollet-le-Duc's wisdom and high rectitude were soon recognized. By 1849, he had been made Chevalier de la Légion d'Honneur, and even César Daly, editor of the *Revue Générale de l'Architecture,* who had constantly warned that the ambitions of Viollet-le-Duc and Lassus at Notre Dame were of the intemperate kind, hailed him as the most brilliant champion of the Middle Ages. Thereafter, he was venerated simply as *le maître.* By 1855, he had been made a corresponding member of the Royal Institute of British Architects, and nine years later he was awarded its Gold Medal. Professional institutions and academies throughout Europe and even in America vied thereafter to make him an honorary member. Though he would accept such honors from abroad, he twice refused—in 1868 and 1873—to stand as a candidate for the Académie des Inscriptions et Belles Lettres. He was an architect, he insisted, and should sit on the appropriate institution in France. Not that he was without the strongest official support in all his doings. Throughout the Second Empire, prompted by Mérimée, who had known the Empress Eugénie even before her marriage, Viollet-le-Duc acted the courtier, helping out with amateur theatricals at Compiègne, designing the decorations for official ceremonies at Notre Dame. He was also responsible for the design of the imperial train in 1856, and was almost awarded the commission for building the Opéra in Paris in 1860. In 1864, he designed a palace for General MacMahon in Algiers and, in 1867, a tomb for Eugénie's sister, the Duchess of Alba, outside Madrid. Neither of these was built. There were other imperial commissions, though the most significant by far was the restoration of Pierrefonds (1858–1870) as a summer retreat for the court.

The *Dictionnaire raisonné de l'architecture française du XIᵉ au XVIᵉ siècle,* in which he embodied all his knowledge, all his observation and experience of medieval architecture, began to appear in 1854, continuing through 1868. The ten volumes seem, at first, designed as an archeological handbook. The buildings and architectural features are described and illustrated with indefatigable care. Yet, the work was not intended as such but rather as a work of propaganda for the development of a nineteenth-century architecture based on a scientific exposition of Gothic. The theme and the method had been explored in the *Annales Archéologiques;* what he offered on this occasion was no more than amplification—often extremely repetitive, owing to the nature of his chosen format, and obsessive. As before, he saw the vault as the prime generator of the architecture, and over and over again he returned to an explanation of it. But the determination to explain everything in

Viollet-le-Duc.
Château de Pierrefonds
(restoration).
Oise, France.
1858–1870

architecture as a solution to a structural problem was now extended. Even the *claires-voies* outside the apse of Saint Urbain at Troyes were analyzed in this manner. The windows there occupied the whole space between the adjacent buttresses and lay in the same plane as the edge of the roof. The relieving arches of the windows, he therefore assumed, were designed to support the roof trusses. But the broad stone gutter, which ran along the edge of the roof, serving also as an access gallery for repairs, required additional support. The *claires-voies* were thus, he suggested, erected as additional props. Viollet-le-Duc described the arrangement at length, never for a moment considering that it might be more elaborate than necessary, that it might perhaps have an aesthetic raison d'être of its own. Even in dealing, in the article on "Proportion," with the theory of triangulation with which the very sections of the cathedrals were ordered, he sought to prove that the basis of visual pleasure was not independent but was the same as that required for stability. In the article on "Style" in the eighth volume, he went even further, seeking to show that the earth, indeed all matter, was built up on a system of equilateral triangulation, to form crystals and rhomboids, which ultimately were to be regarded as the essence of style. The partiality of his interpretations is often infuriating, though one never ceases to admire his determination; his partiality, moreover, is only the reverse side of his imagination and perception. He had the power to illuminate in all his explanations. And he sought always to make them very simple. Unrestrained by any false reverence for Gothic, he illustrated a section through the choir of Beauvais Cathedral in the article on "Construction" as it would have been with flying buttresses of timber. He aimed there to make the role of the structure more apparent. But in the same article he showed a section through the nave of Notre Dame at Dijon not only with flying buttresses of timber, but also with columns of iron. Here, he was at once indicating how the Gothic principle might be taken up, using different materials, to produce a new effect. This was his message for the nineteenth century.

There was more to this than structure and materials. Viollet-le-Duc required a comparable reinterpretation of social aspirations. Anticlerical by now, he was unwilling to recognize Gothic architecture as the product of any purely religious organization. Reacting against the power of the monasteries, he suggested, the bishops of the twelfth and thirteenth centuries had allied themselves with the communities in the towns, growing daily more strong; the great cathedrals of France were thus to be seen as the products of burgeoning civic aspiration and effort. But Viollet-le-Duc's aim was not simply to interpret the Middle Ages in the terms of historians such as Augustin Thierry; rather, he wanted to show that the principles of architecture developed at that time were applicable to a nineteenth-century secular society.

The *Entretiens* were even more openly didactic in aim and were, from the first, bound up with Viollet-le-Duc's teaching ventures. They did not offer a coherent theory of architecture but rather an array of essays and commentaries outlining his preoccupations and prejudices. When, in 1856, Labrouste decided to close his atelier, his students split up; approximately fifteen, led by ANATOLE DE BAUDOT, approached Viollet-le-Duc and asked him to open an atelier. On January 15, 1857, he started to teach at 1 rue Bonaparte. This was considered an event of some importance. His aims were outlined in both the *Revue Générale de l'Architecture* and the *Encyclopédie d'Architecture*. This program served as the outline for the *Entretiens*. Within a few months, he had written the first four, dealing with the relationship of art to society and its development by the Greeks and Romans, and sent them to Mérimée for approval. Mérimée found much to disapprove, though not Viollet-le-Duc's conclusions. Some of Mérimée's comments Viollet-le-Duc incorporated, unaltered, into his revised versions of the *Entretiens*. The first four were published in 1858, but the remaining six that make up the first volume, taking his historical survey right through to the nineteenth century, came out only sporadically. The first volume was completed in 1863; by then, it represented a program for a far more ambitious teaching venture.

Viollet-le-Duc, having spent far too little time in his atelier, had soon closed it, taking his best pupils, such as de Baudot and EDMOND DUTHOIT into his office; now, spurred and strongly abetted by Mérimée and Courmont, he planned to restructure the Ecole des Beaux-Arts itself. With the support of the Emperor and his ministers, they saw a decree promulgated on November 13, 1863, for the radical reform of the school. The Ecole was to be separated from the Académie; the professors were no longer to sit on the juries. More important, Viollet-le-Duc was appointed *professeur d'histoire de l'art et esthétique*. He gave his first lecture on January 29, 1864. Opposition, as might be imagined, was strong and well organized, for the new Grand Prix regulations had tactlessly reduced the age limit of candidates from thirty to twenty-five, thus stirring a clutch of angry ring-leaders, the most active of whom was JULIEN GUADET. The din during Viollet-le-Duc's lecture was intolerable, but in a moment of calm he touched his audience vitally when he drew a parallel between the Greek ability to give form to their myths in the

Viollet-le-Duc.
Château de la Flachère.
Saint Verand, Rhone,
France.
1863–1869

Viollet-le-Duc.
Church, Place Thiery-Ruby,
Aillant sur Tholon.
Yonne, France.
1864–1867

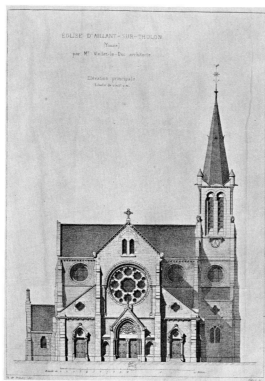

Viollet-le-Duc.
Tomb for the Duc de
Morny, Père Lachaise
Cemetery.
Paris.
1865–1866

temples of Olympia and the possibility of the architects of the nineteenth century to give form to such inventions as steam power and electricity, in particular in their exhibition buildings. Viollet-le-Duc's audience was to hear nothing more of this kind.

The catcalls and interruptions continued unabated in the lectures that followed. After the seventh, on March 18, he resigned. He felt humiliated and disheartened. He traveled at once to Italy, staying a few weeks, then to Corsica and Algiers. On his return, he took up the attack once again, writing his famous pamphlet, "Intervention de l'Etat dans l'enseignement des Beaux-Arts." He also wrote the eleventh and twelfth *Entretiens* in which he audaciously suggested how a new architecture relating to materials such as iron might be arrived at. In the eleventh *Entretien,* he illustrated a hall with brackets and columns of iron; in the twelfth, a whole array of such structures, including his well-known *hôtel de ville* with V-columns of iron, and, the most famous of all his designs, the polygonal concert hall for 3000, made up of an exposed system of iron struts, columns, and ribs to support galleries and a vault of brick webs. The whole might have been based on the geometries of the equilateral triangle, but it was, absolutely, lacking in style. It acted nonetheless as a catalyst for radical architects in the future. The publication of these designs coincided, more or less, with the opening of yet another teaching venture, the opening, on November 10, 1865, of the Ecole Centrale d'Architecture (later the Ecole Spéciale d'Architecture), under the direction of Emile Trelat. Viollet-le-Duc soon rejected what he regarded as Trelat's airy attempts to evolve a new symbolism in architecture. In 1868, he issued the fourteenth *Entretien,* "Ce qui reclame au XIXᵉ siècle l'enseignement de l'architecture," published again in 1869 as a separate pamphlet. In the next year came the fifteenth and sixteenth *Entretiens,* on decoration and monumental sculpture.

At this time, there occurred a crisis in his life. The disappointment of his various attempts to teach the young and his own growing fatigue in the face of work led him to think of retreat or retirement. After 1868, he refused to take on any new commissions in the provinces. At the same time, he initiated the habit of spending a few weeks, then months, of each year in the Alps, at first based at Chamonix, where he was later to build a chalet for himself, then at Lausanne, where he was to put up a house (1874–1878). Restless when not fully occupied, he began a study of Mont Blanc, surveying and measuring the mountain mass, publishing the results in 1876 in the form of a detailed map and a book, *Le massif du Mont*

Blanc, that offered nothing less than a gigantic restoration study of the mountain. On one of his alpine expeditions in 1870, Viollet-le-Duc fell down a crevasse near Mattmark. He was shocked and shaken but emerged eventually feeling more determined than ever to concentrate his energies to useful ends.

A few days later, war was declared between Prussia and France, and his experiences as an artillery officer in the field outside Paris and afterward in the face of the Commune, from which he fled to Venice and then on to Florence, strengthened his resolve more than ever. He reproached himself for his mindless support of the Empire which had, he felt, brought such humiliation upon France, and broke off forthwith from the sophisticated society with which he had so assiduously associated. He embarked on an ambitious program of publication. He quickly finished off the last four *Entretiens,* bringing the second and final volume to an end in 1872. He also rushed through the remaining five volumes of the *Dictionnaire raisonné du mobilier français,* covering the decorative arts, clothes, and armor. These were published between 1871 and 1875. Together with his disciple Felix Narjoux and the editors of the *Encyclopédie d'architecture,* he offered a selection of eighty-five dwellings, illustrated on two hundred plates, the *Habitations modernes* (1875–1877). In the introduction and conclusion, Viollet-le-Duc hints at some of his criteria, but the selection is of the arbitrary kind, not what a careful reading of the second volume of the *Entretiens* would lead one to expect. This found a more fitting sequel in an altogether surprising work of these years, *L'Art russe, ses origines, ses éléments constitutifs, son apogée, son avenir,* issued in 1877. Viollet-le-Duc analyzed what he recognized as the "constituent elements" of Russian architecture and sought to demonstrate how these might be combined with the material requirements and materials of the nineteenth century to produce an architecture traditional in spirit yet contemporary in appearance. Viollet-le-Duc had been persuaded to undertake the work by Viktor Butovskii, director of the Stroganov School in Moscow, who visited Paris in 1872. He furnished Viollet-le-Duc with all the information and prints required for his research, though in March 1877, a few months before publication, Viollet-le-Duc sent Maurice Ouradou to Moscow to check some of the observations he had made. The book was translated into Russian in 1879, and it is just possible that Viollet-le-Duc kindled a spark that was to fire the Constructivists of the twentieth century.

During these years, Viollet-le-Duc thought also to enter politics, but though he was assured of success as a deputy he was all too soon disillusioned by the manner of operation required for such success. He nonetheless developed very strong opinions as to the way things should be done. Goaded beyond endurance, he wrote a private letter to Pierre Baragnon, editor of the *Tâche Noire,* in 1874, in which he poured scorn on the moral turpitude of the government in its dealings with the clergy. As a consequence, he felt bound to resign from the Service des Edifices Diocésains and give up most of his restorations in France. This was a courageous step to take, though it might be argued that Viollet-le-Duc should have taken it earlier. In November of the same year, he stood as Republican candidate for Montmartre in the municipal elections and became and remained a councillor to the end of his life. He also wrote for several political papers, though his articles are not, on the whole, of the political kind. But despite all this activity, he spent more and more time in Lausanne, where he died in 1879.

R. D. MIDDLETON

WORKS

1840–1859, Church of the Madeleine (restoration), Vézelay, Yonne, France. 1843–1849, Notre Dame (sacristy with J. B. A. Lassus); 1845–1864, Notre Dame (restoration with Lassus); 1846–1849, H. Courmont House, 28 rue de Liège; Paris. 1850–1875, Cathedral (restoration), Amiens, Somme, France. 1852–1858, Saint Gimer, Carcassonne, Aude, France. 1854–1856, Dollfus House (now Maison de Repos Geisbuhl), Dornach, Mulhouse, France. 1855–1866, Salle Synodale (restoration), Sens, Yonne, France. *1856, Durand House, 43 M. de Pré, Neuilly, France. 1856–1866, Château de Coucy (restoration), Aisne, France. 1857, Maignan House, Saint Brieuc, Côtes du Nord, France. *1857–1858, Constant Troyon House and Studio, 11 Boulevard Rochechouart; 1857–1861, A. Milon House, 15 rue de Douai; Paris. 1857–1865, Griois House (now the Château du Tertre), Ambrières les Vallées, Mayenne, France. 1858, Woronzow Tomb, Odessa, Russia. 1858–1860, Ecole polonaise, 80 Boulevard du Montparnasse; Paris. 1858–1870, Château de Pierrefonds (restoration), Oise, France. 1859–1861, Chapelle du Petit Séminaire, rue de Vaugirard, Paris (moved in 1898 to Fontenay aux Roses, Seine, France). 1859–1863, Sellières Chapel, Cires le Mello; 1860–1863, Sabatier House (now Ecole Secondaire d'Agriculture du Prieuré), Pierrefonds; Oise, France. 1860–1866, Saint Denis de l'Estrée, Saint Denis, Seine, France. 1860–1868, Château de Montdardier (supervised by Edmond Duthoit), Le Vigan, Gard, France. 1860–1869, Château de Chamousset (with Duthoit), Saint Laurent du Chamousset, Rhone, France. 1860–1873, Cathedral (restoration), Reims, Marne, France. 1860–1871, Saint Raymond (restoration), Toulousse, Haute Garonne, France. 1860–1879, Walls (restoration), Avignon, Vaucluse, France. 1861–1869, Château de Pupetières (supervised by D. Darcy), Chabons, Isère, France. 1862–1863, Viollet-le-Duc House, 68 rue Condorcet, Paris. 1862–1865, Monument to Napoléon and His Brothers (with Barye, Thomas, Maillet, and V. Dubray), Place du Diamant, Ajaccio, Corsica. 1862–1879, Cathedral (restoration), Clermont Ferrand, Puy de Dôme, Avignon, Vaucluse, France. 1863–1865, Sauvage House, 23 rue Chauchat, Paris. 1863–1869, Château de la Flachère (supervised by A. de Baudot), Saint Verand, Rhone, France. 1864, Monument to Louis Napoléon and Eugènie, Place Napoléon, Algiers, 1864–1866, Château d'Abbadia (supervised and continued by Duthoit), Hendaye, Pyrénées Orientales, France. 1864–1867, Church (supervised by A. A. Lefort), Place Thiery-Ruby, Aillant sur Tholon, Yonne, France. 1864–1879, Château de Roquetaillade (supervised and continued by Duthoit), Mazeres, Gironde, France. 1865–1866, Tomb for the Duc de Morny, Père Lachaise Cemetery, Paris. 1865–1867, Château Jacquesson (now part of the Slavia Brewery), 128 Avenue de Paris, Chalons sur Marne, France. 1866–1867, Notre Dame (presbytery), Place du Parvis, Paris. 1868–1871, Saint Raymond (restoration); 1871–1875, Donjon (restoration); Toulouse, Haute Garonne, France. *1872–1873, Châlet de la Côte, Le Brévent, Chamonix, Haute Savoie, France. 1873–1876, Cathedral (restoration); *1874–1878, Viollet-le-Duc House (La Vedette), 29 Avenue de Leman; Lausanne, Vaud, Switzerland. 1874–1879, Château d'Eu (interior decoration, furniture, and outbuildings), Seine Maritime, France. 1876–1877, Scots Kirk (supervised by J. L. Verrey), Avenue de Rumine, Lausanne, Vaud, Switzerland. 1879, Millet Tomb, Saint Germain en Laye Cemetery, Seine et Oise, France.

BIBLIOGRAPHY

AUZAS, P. M. (editor) 1965 *Eugène Viollet-le-Duc—1814–1819.* Paris: Caisse Nationale des Monuments Historiques. Exhibition catalogue.

Catalogue des livres composant la bibliothèque de feu M. E. Viollet-le-Duc. 1880 Paris: Labitte.

FOUCART, BRUNO (editor) 1980 *Viollet-le-Duc.* Paris: Editions de la Réunion des musées nationaux. Exhibition catalogue.

GOUT, PAUL 1914 *Viollet-le-Duc: sa vie, son oeuvre, sa doctrine.* Paris: Champion.

GUBLER, JACQUES (editor) 1979 *Viollet-le-Duc: Centenaire de la mort à Lausanne.* Lausanne, Switzerland. Musée historique de l'Ancien-Evêché. Exhibition catalogue.

MIDDLETON, ROBIN DAVID 1976 "Viollet-le-Duc's Academic Ventures and the Entretiens sur l'architecture." In Adolf M. Vogt, Christina Reble, and Martin Frohlich (editors), *Gottfried Semper und die Mitte des 19. Jahrhunderts.* Basel: Birkhauser.

SUMMERSON, JOHN 1949 "Viollet-le-Duc and the Rational Point of View." Pages 135–158 in *Heavenly Mansions.* London: Cresset.

VIOLLET-LE-DUC, EUGÈNE EMMANUEL (1854–1868) 1979 *Dictionnaire raisonné de l'architecture française du XIe au XVIe siècle.* 10 vols. Reprint. Paris: Saint-Julien-du-Sancey.

VIOLLET-LE-DUC, EUGÈNE EMMANUEL (1858–1872) 1959 *Discourses on Architecture.* 2 vols. London: Allen & Unwin. Originally published in French with the title *Entretiens sur l'architecture.*

VIOLLET-LE-DUC, EUGÈNE EMMANUEL 1858–1875 *Dictionnaire raisonné du mobilier français de l'epoque carolingienne à la renaissance.* 6 vols. Paris: Morel.

VIOLLET-LE-DUC, EUGÈNE EMMANUEL (1875)1876 *Habitations of Man in All Ages.* Translated into English by B. Bucknall. London: Low, Marston, Searle, and Rivington. Originally published in French with the title *Histoire de l'habitation humaine depuis les temps préhistoriques jusqu'à nos jours.*

VIOLLET-LE-DUC, EUGÈNE EMMANUEL (1876)1877 *Le Massif du Mont-Blanc: Etude sur sa construction géodésique et géologique, sur ses transformations et sur l'état ancien et moderne de ses glaciers.* Translated into English by B. Bucknall. London: Low, Marston, Searle, and Rivington.

VIOLLET-LE-DUC, EUGÈNE EMMANUEL 1877 *L'art russe, ses origines, ses éléments constitutifs, son apogée, son avenir.* Paris: Morel.

VIOLLET-LE-DUC, EUGÈNE EMMANUEL, and NARJOUX, FELIX (1875–1877)1979 *Habitations modernes.* 2 vols. Reprint. Brussels: Mardaga.

VIOLLET-LE-DUC, EUGENE L. 1902 *Lettres inédites de Viollet-le-Duc recueillies et annotées par son fils.* Paris: Imprimeries réunies.

VIOLLET-LE-DUC, GENEVIÈVE (editor) 1971 *E. Viollet-le-Duc: Lettres d'Italie, 1836–1837, adressées à sa famille.* Paris: Laget.

VIOLLET-LE-DUC, GENEVIÈVE (editor) 1972 *Viollet-le-Duc: Voyage aux Pyrénées 1833. Lettres à son père et journal de route: Dessins, lavis et aquarelles de l'auteur.* Lourdes, France: Amis du musée pyrénéen.

VIOLLET-LE-DUC, GENEVIÈVE, and AILLAGON, JEAN JACQUES (editors) 1980 *Le voyage d'Italie d'Eugène Viollet-le-Duc 1836–1837.* Paris: Levrault. Exhibition catalogue.

VIRASORO, ALEJANDRO

Alejandro Virasoro (1892–1978) in the mid-1920s broke away radically from the then prevailing academic and eclectic canons of design. Recognized today as Argentina's premier pioneer of modern design, his work raised considerable objections from the professionsl establishment. His confrontation in 1926 with Alberto Coni Molina, sometime president of the Sociedad Central de Arquitectos, in the *Revista de Arquitectura,* was memorable and enlightening.

Virasoro admitted being impressed by the work of scenographer Leon Bakst, but he stubbornly denied any affiliation with Art Deco. He organized his own construction company as a workers cooperative, suffered financial collapse in the early 1930s, and built little thereafter.

FEDERICO F. ORTIZ

WORKS

1925, Architects Home, calle Agüero; 1926. Banco El

Hogar Argentino, calle Bartolomé Mitre; 1929, La Equitativa del Plata Office Building, Avenida Roque Sáenz Peña & calle Florida; 1929, Apartment Building, Avenida Las Heras; Buenos Aires. 1929, Housing, Banfield, Province of Buenos Aires. 1931, De Cusatis Hospital, avenida Pueyrredón, Buenos Aires.

BIBLIOGRAPHY

Documentos para una historia de la arquitectura argentina. 1980 2d ed. Buenos Aires: Ediciones SUMMA.

MARTINI, JOSÉ XAVIER, and PEÑA, JOSÉ MARIA 1969 *Alejandro Virasoro.* Instituto de Arte Americano e Investigaciones Estéticas, University of Buenos Aires.

ORTIZ, FEDERICO, and GUTÍERREZ, RAMON 1972 *La Arquitectura en la Argentina: 1930-1970.* Madrid: Ediciones y Publicaciones Populares.

VISCONTI, LUDOVICO

Ludovico Tullio Joachim Visconti (1791–1853), son of the Italian scholar Ennio Quirinio Visconti, was trained in Paris in the atelier of CHARLES PERCIER. During the Restoration and the Monarchy of July, he designed several large houses (notably the Hôtel Pontalba [1828]) and fountains in Paris (Fontaines Gaillon [1828]; Louvois [1839]; Molière [1844]; and des Quatres Evèques [1844]) with increasingly florid Renaissance details. He is best remembered for his tomb of Napoleon in the Invalides (commenced in 1841 but incomplete upon his death) and his design for the New Louvre, begun in 1852 but redesigned after his death by HECTOR M. LEFUEL, who completed the building in 1857.

DAVID T. VAN ZANTEN

WORKS

1828, Gaillon Fountain; 1828, Hôtel Pontalba; 1839, Louvois Fountain; 1841–1853, Tomb of Napoleon, Hôtel des Invalides; 1844, Molière Fountain; 1844, Quatres Evèques Fountain; 1852–1853, New Louvre (not completed until 1857 by Hector Lefuel); Paris.

BIBLIOGRAPHY

AULANIER, CHRISTIANE 1953 *Le nouveau Louvre de Napoléon.* Volume 3 in *Histoire du Palais et du Musée du Louvre.* Paris: Editions des Musees nationaux.

VITONI, VENTURA

In his *Lives of the Artists,* GIORGIO VASARI singles out Ventura Vitoni (1442–1522) for special praise as a student of the High Renaissance architect DONATO BRAMANTE. Born in Pistoia, Italy, and trained there as a carpenter, he worked for Bramante, in Vasari's opinion in Rome around 1500. The true story of the life of this little known architect is yet to be ascertained, but Vasari had, as we shall see, particular reasons for inflating Vitoni's reputation.

All Vitoni's works are found in Pistoia. His major work there is a church dedicated to the Madonna dell'Umiltà, begun in 1495. The main vestibule of the church is built in a manner reminiscent of FILIPPO BRUNELLESCHI or Giuliano da Sangallo (see SANGALLO FAMILY), but the imposing octagon, added by Vitoni beginning in 1509, recalls newer Roman developments. In fact, this massive work, with its porphyry Doric pilasters at the first floor level and Corinthian pilasters above that, was completed by Vasari himself much later in the sixteenth century. Vitoni's octagon may well have reminded Vasari of Saint Peter's and other monumental works of the Roman High Renaissance. This apparent Bramante connection provided the excuse for Vasari to place Vitoni within Bramante's circle—something that is not documented.

We know, in fact, relatively little about Vitoni. His other works, such as the Church of San Giovanni Battista, Pistoia (1487–1516), recall more the work of Brunelleschi and the Florentine Renaissance of the fifteenth century rather than work of Bramante in the sixteenth. Nonetheless, a period in Rome, as suggested by Vasari, cannot be ruled out for Vitoni. He died in Pistoia in 1522.

NICHOLAS ADAMS

WORKS

1487–1516, San Giovanni Battista; begun 1495, Madonna dell'Umiltà; Pistoia, Italy.

VITOZZI, ASCANIO

A descendant of the Braschi lords from Orvieto, Italy, Ascanio Vitozzi (1539–1615) was an architect, engineer, and military officer. He participated in the battle of Lepanto as captain, and in the conquest of Portugal with Philip II. He probably studied architecture under GIACOMO BAROZZI DA VIGNOLA, and between 1569–1570 he conducted the work of damming the Tiber in Rome. He fought in Piedmont as captain of artillery, and in 1584 was nominated architect and engineer to the duke of Savoy.

During his long Piedmontese career, Vitozzi designed and supervised the construction of numerous buildings. The most important extant ones are Santa Maria del Monte, Santa Trinità, and Corpus Domini in Turin, and the Sanctuary of Vicoforte di Mondovi. Santa Maria del Monte (1585–1596) recalls the plan of the sanctuary in

Todi. It is highly visible because of its hillside location above the Po which emphasizes the already exaggerated verticality of the building. The plan of the Santa Trinità (1598) is a star hexagon, foreshadowing the better known Sant' Ivo in Rome; the interior decoration of the church has been repeatedly altered. The Corpus Domini Church (1607) shelters the site of an important local miracle, commissioned and maintained by the city. It is single-aisled with side chapels, and its rich and extensive decorations date from the eighteenth century. Programmatically, the Sanctuary at Vicoforte (1596) is Vitozzi's most important building since it was to serve as the Savoy mausoleum. Although Vitozzi completed only a section of the building, his ideas are made clear in a contemporary engraving. Its oval plan shows singular spatial intuition and anticipates seventeenth-century developments in design.

Vitozzi made a crucially important contribution to the urbanism of Turin. His 1606 design for the Piazza Castello façades recalls the Piedmontese tradition of porticoed streets but also takes a large step ahead by establishing a large-scale urban environment and palatial residences. The façades for the Contrada Nova (1615) formed a uniform and straight street, axial to his earlier Piazza Castello. These urban designs influenced later important city planning enterprises in Turin. The gallery connecting Palazzo Reale to the Castello (1606), a wall building which looked out on the countryside as well as on the major square, helped in further establishing the urban character of Piazza Castello, originally a plain *piazza d'armi*.

Vitozzi contributed also to military architecture, fortifying Cherasco, a castrum-plan town, for the Savoy duke, and undertaking various trips to fortresses in the Provence. His *Relatione et Parere del capitan Ascanio Vitozzi delle fortificationi et ripari da farsi in Antibo et a S. Paolo di Provenza*, written from Nice in 1589 to the duke of Savoy, is among his preserved papers.

MARTHA POLLAK

WORKS

*1584, Palazzo San Giovanni; 1584, Piazza Castello (façades, constructed after 1606); 1585–1596, Santa Maria dei Capuccini (church and convent); Turin. 1596, Sanctuary and Convent, Vicoforte di Mondovì, Italy. 1598, Santa Trinità; 1606, Galleria, between the Piazza Castello and Palazzo Reale; 1607, Corpus Domini, Turin, Italy. 1610, Fortifications, Cherasco, Italy. 1615, Contrada Nova (façades), Turin, Italy.

BIBLIOGRAPHY

BAUDI DI VESME, A. 1932 "L'Arte negli stati sabaudi." *Atti SPABA* 14:742.

BERTAGNA, U. 1974–1976 "Vicende costruttive delle chiese del Corpus Domini e dello Spirito Santo in Torino." *Palladio* 1974–1976:23–35, 75–113.

CARBONERI, NINO 1966 *Ascanio Vitozzi: Un architetto tra manierismo e barocco.* Rome: Officina.

LOTZ, WOLFGANG 1955 "Die ovalen Kirchenräume des Cinquecento." *Römisches Jahrbuch für Kunstgeschichte* 7:9–99.

PROMIS, C. 1871 "Gli ingegneri militari." *Miscellanea di Storia Italiana* 12:584–591.

SCOTTI, A. 1969 *Ascanio Vitozzi: Ingegnere ducale a Torino.* Florence: La nuova Italia.

VITRUVIUS

   I.   Biography
   II. Writings

I. Biography

Vitruvius's treatise, *De Architectura,* sheds light on a crucial era, the first century B.C. It is the only corpus of Greco-Roman architecture and engineering that exists, and there is no evidence to show that there was ever another. Vitruvius (c.90–c.20 B.C.) partly reveals himself as an architect who, for his time, was outmoded. All that is known of him, with one minor exception, is to be found in his book. Vitruvius is most exposed in the dedication and prefaces to the chapters (book-rolls) of his work. They were written toward the end of his life, when he was old, defeated, and no doubt estranged. For the rest one must glean, bit by bit, the unintended disclosures that adumbrate his career.

The Man. The compiler of *On Architecture* was builder, engineer, and scholar, but the scribes of the oldest manuscripts of his treatise could supply only his family name. The Vitruvii, nevertheless, though not numerous, were of long standing in Latium and Campania and later on in Africa. The first of the line known to history was a certain Vitruvius Vaccus, who was already a man of distinction in the Auruncan city of Fundi in the late fourth century B.C. and was able to maintain a second mansion on the Palatine at Rome. Our Vitruvius of the first century B.C. in all likelihood was of a branch that had become practiced in the arts of building and mechanics. He writes proudly of his education, of his apprenticeship and training by his parents and kinsmen, and of the honor of his profession (VI.3.4). He says nothing of a wife and children, but in the following century members of the family were still active. A certain Vitruvius seems to have served as naval architect for the fleet at Misenum, while one Lucius Vitruvius Cerdo, a freedman of the clan, designed and built the arch of the Gavii in Verona.

During the second century B.C. and on into the first, Greek architects from the Hellenistic east, notably Hermodorus in Cyprus, were being invited to immigrate to Rome to embellish the growing cosmopolis, and Italian architects were similarly being commissioned by Hellenistic monarchs. The Seleucid king, Antiochus IV (175–163 B.C.), for example, employed one DECIMUS COSSUTIUS to rebuild the Olympieion of Athens and to construct an aqueduct at Antioch. The brothers Gaius and Marcus Stallius were called to restore the Athenian Odeum by King Ariobarzanes of Cappadocia (63–52 B.C.). The reciprocal coming and going of architects was no doubt frequent and fruitful, and there are indications that the young Vitruvius may have taken advantage of similar opportunities.

Although his treatise does not signal any voyages, Vitruvius appears to have examined, in the Roman province of Asia, a number of buildings, otherwise unnoticed, that had been built of sun-dried brick (II.8.9–10). His interest was in the remarkable longevity of the material. In each case he was careful to let the reader know its present state of use: the palace of King Croesus at Sardis (560–547 B.C.) "which the citizens have turned over to the guild of the elders"; the palace of King Mausolus at Halicarnassus (377–353 B.C.), "of extraordinary strength to this day"; the palace of the Attalid kings at Tralles (190–133 B.C.), "now always granted to the man who holds the priesthood of the city." These were surely observations of Vitruvius on the spot, probably made around 60 B.C. Yet for him they must have been a very minor aspect of the architecture that he found all around him. He would, first of all, have sought the great Hellenistic sanctuaries of Asia that were to permeate his conception of temples as they should be built at home.

There at Rome he had no doubt studied Hermodorus's temple of Jupiter Stator, built in the 140s B.C., and now, at last, he could inspect its prototype, the Ionic temple of Athena at Priene, PYTHEOS's masterpiece of nearly two hundred years before. Yet it was not Pytheos but a follower of his, whose architecture caught Vitruvius's full attention. This was HERMOGENES, who, in the early second century had built at least two temples, one at Teos, the other at Magnesia, that were revolutionary in their openness. The widening between columns, the broadening of peristyles, and the opening of pediments and delicately scrolled acroteria all produced an effect of airiness that suited Vitruvius's inclination.

From the sixth century B.C. onward Greek architects in Ionia and Attica had occasionally drawn up programmatic accounts of exceptional buildings, which they published as booklets. The practice in the east was continued by the Hellenistic builders more regularly, it appears, and was more self-assertive. None of these have survived, but it may be presumed that Vitruvius sought them out at this time, perhaps with help of the famous library of Pergamon (VII.Pr.4). Surely the commentaries of Pytheos, Hermogenes, and his contemporaries Menesthes and Arcesius were to be found there. One may suppose, moreover, that his esteem for the example of these older architects moved Vitruvius to begin to compile his treatise.

It appears also that on this voyage or perhaps another he had visited Athens. Vitruvius always paid special attention to obsolete materials and techniques. He noted, for example, that part of the city wall, "which faces toward Hymettus and Pentelicon," was still built of sun-dried brick and that on the Areopagus there was "to this day" an example of a roof of clay (II.8.9; II.1.5). He also found it "particularly noticeable in Athens" that the springs were so unpalatable "that the inhabitants were obliged to drink from wells" (VIII.3.6). Vitruvius again turned to some of the more modern architecture of the city: the unfinished Olympieion of Cossutius, the Porticus of Eumenes of Pergamon, the Odeum of Ariobarzanes (unmentioned before or after) "as you leave the theater on the left side," and the octagonal tower of ANDRONIKUS OF KYRRHOS, a Syrian expert on sundials (VII.Pr.15; V.9.1; I.6.4). Of the older buildings, he labored to describe the odd forms of the Erechtheion and the temple of Athena at Sunium in terms of the contemporary Roman temples, like that of Veiovis, having the pronaoi centered on one long side of the cellae (IV.9.4.).

Vitruvius implies his early architectural practice without naming it. Judging from chapters II and IV one can readily infer that up to the 50s B.C. he was chiefly engaged in designing private dwellings. The materials and methods of building that occupy chapter II are concerned mainly with domestic architecture, even so far as to praise the many-storied tenements of Rome. Architects in Vitruvius's time, however, were not expected to design houses except for the tolerably well-to-do. Vitruvius assumed that the normal house is the old-fashioned atrium-house, be it large or small. Chapter VI, on houses, treats its subject more orderly and comprehensively than any other; it ends with the architect's mutual relations with his client and his foreman. This is the only instance of his own attitude toward the process of building, and it is pertinent:

The approval of any work is to be considered under three heads: fine workmanship, liberality and planning. When the work shows its richness, the owner will be praised for the outlay he has authorized. When it displays craftsmanship, the foreman will be approved for his skill. But when pleasing proportions and symmetries have mastery, the architect will be in his glory. It is proper for him to be ready to consult with both workmen and laymen, because not only architects but every man can recognize good work. The difference is that the others need to see it finished, while the architect, once he has conceived his design, but not built it, knows precisely what its beauty, its utility and its fitness will be. [VI.8.9–10]

There was another side to Vitruvius's technical expertise. He had been taught engineering as part of architecture, the designing and constructing of the engines of his time, among which were engines of war. This was a time of unceasing conflict, and he was drawn, it seems, to its rewards. In any case, he had become expert in the construction of the artillery of the day, which was indispensable to every army. This consisted chiefly of catapults and ballistae, intricate machines for launching heavy arrows and stone balls, which were powered by the torsion of twisted ropes of sinew or hair. An innovation of the Hellenistic wars, they were constantly being improved and refined, and Vitruvius presented two of his latest models (X.10–12). His proficiency in this field somehow reached the ears of Julius Caesar as he was enlisting his legions for the conquest of Gaul and was looking for technicians. Vitruvius was enrolled in his staff. It was a decisive turn in his career. Between the years of 58 and 44 B.C., at least for a decade, he followed Caesar's fortunes as one of his military architects.

He probably established a base or bases for the production and repair of artillery and would have been ready for other occasional duties at the front. At first, his base would have been somewhere in Cisalpine Gaul, south of the Alps, where Caesar usually wintered, administering his provincial tasks, enlisting recruits and requisitioning supplies. On one occasion there, Vitruvius, in the presence of Caesar, watched an attempt to burn down the timber tower of a fortress, which proved incombustible (II.9.14–17). Vitruvius found the wood to be larch, learned that it was shipped down the Po to Ravenna and along the coast as far as Ancona. He noted for his treatise that it could be used against the danger of fire in Rome. It is likely also that in one of these years he took time to observe the marshland ports of Ravenna, Altino, and Aquileia and the alder piles that supported their buildings (I.4.11). On Caesar's campaigns north of the Alps only the Gallic fortifications of stone, strengthened by horizontal and vertical timber framework, were thought worthy of recommendation for his ideal city (I.5.3).

After the Gallic wars Vitruvius remained in service with Caesar until the latter's death in 44 B.C. In 49 B.C., at the siege of Marseilles, he had been detached to assist the legate in charge of the blockade and assault works, but as a fellow technician he took pains to commend the ingenuity of the military architects on the defense (X.16.11–12). Again, three years later, he was with Caesar in Africa at the campaign of Thapsus. He shared his billet with a Numidian prince, with whom he discussed the wonders of his country; he also discovered, at Utica, a law that required sun-dried bricks to be seasoned for five years before use (VIII.3.5; II.3.2).

The ides of March, 44 B.C., must have left Vitruvius adrift for a while. He was probably in his late forties, a *senior* for a Roman. For the last ten or more years he had been in the provinces, a military engineer not an urban architect. Meanwhile a new generation of young architects, with other ideas and ethics, as Vitruvius thought, were vying for commissions in the renovation of old Rome that Caesar had projected. Some, at this time, were at work on the Julian Basilica and the Julian Forum with its temple of Venus, while others were in the planning stage for a new theater and the conversion of the old parade ground. Vitruvius had been left behind, even by Caesar. Nine months before his assassination Caesar had chosen as master architect and city planner one Caecilius (or Pomponius), a newcomer. Little of what Vitruvius saw and heard could have been to his taste or expectation. The architecture rising all about him would have seemed to him heavy, compressed, and garish. The vision of his youthful studies was to be a tacit condemnation.

In the meantime, Vitruvius turned to Caesar's heir, Octavian, who had need for a seasoned military architect in his wars for supremacy. Vitruvius was appointed to his former command with three other artificers to construct and repair artillery. His salary, on recommendation of Octavian's older sister, Octavia, was converted to a pension for life, which allowed him both to augment and to edit his treatise (I.Ded.2–3) and to accept occasional other commissions.

The connection with Octavia is something of a mystery, but it might have been the interest in artillery of her son, Marcellus, who had aided another artillery man, Athenaeus Mechanicus, well acquainted with Vitruvius. Later, Marcellus's gallant mother, now wedded to Marc Antony, shuttled back and forth from Rome to Athens in the early 30s B.C., conveying money, men, and artillery to husband and brother. It is pleasant to think that she was accompanied by the aging architect who supervised his ordnance and found time to inspect the old city.

Still later in the 30s B.C., when Agrippa, Octavian's trusted confidant, undertook to restore, enlarge, and reorganize the water system of Rome, it is reported that Vitruvius was enlisted. Among other things, he devised a standard gauge for the lead pipes that distributed the flow from the aqueducts. Although the gauge could not measure the velocity of the flow, it was in use from then on. This crumb of information from Frontinus's *De Aquis Urbis Romae* (about A.D. 100) is the only authentication of the existence of Vitruvius outside his treatise.

He was near sixty when the civil strife was ended at Actium in 30 B.C. Three years later, Octavian changed his name to Augustus. Vitruvius grumbled about his old age and tried to defend what he considered his lack of celebrity. "As for me," he wrote, "nature has denied me stature, age has marred my face and ill health has sapped my strength" (II.Pr.4). "Other architects solicit and beg to practice architecture, but I have been taught that it is respectable to undertake a charge after being asked and not to ask it" (VI.Pr.5). Still, antiquated as he may have felt, Vitruvius did not fail, shortly after 27 B.C., to accept the commission for the only building of his own that he chose to insert into his treatise.

This was a basilica on one side of the forum of a new colony for veterans of Augustus's armies, *Colonia Iulia Fanestris,* modern Fano, where the Via Flaminia reached the Adriatic. The specifications included a temple for Augustus and a tribunal for the magistrates of the colony. Neither the forum nor the basilica has come to light at Fano, but Vitruvius's dimensioned description, concise but complete, includes structure, form, and space. It offers the only technical commentary on a single building by an ancient architect that has come down to us. The nearest to it in Latin would be Julius Caesar's descriptions of Gallic fortifications and of his bridge across the Rhine, though Vitruvius would have had in mind the commentaries of Pytheos and Hermogenes, which he so prized. It was preceded by a general statement of the elements of a typical basilica.

Yet basilicas of the greatest dignity and beauty can also be constructed in the style of the one that I designed and supervised at *Colonia Iulia Fanestris.* Its proportions and symmetrical relations were established as follows. The main roof over the nave is 120 feet long and sixty feet wide between its columns. The aisles around the nave, between the outer walls and the columns are twenty feet wide. The columns, of unbroken height, including their capitals are fifty feet high and five feet thick (at the bottom), having behind them pilasters, twenty feet high, two and a half feet wide and one and one half thick. These support the beams which carry the upper flooring of the aisles. Above these come other pilasters, eighteen feet high, two feet wide and one foot thick, which carry the beams that support the rafters and roofs of the aisles. These are dropped below the main roof, and the intervals between the two roofs and the intercolumniations are left open as windows.

The columns at the ends of the main roof are four, including the corner columns. On the long side, adjacent to the forum, there are eight, including the corner columns, and on the other side, six, including the corner columns. This is because the two middle columns on that side have been omitted, so as not to obstruct the view of the pronaos of the temple of Augustus, which opens from the center of the wall of the basilica, facing the middle of the forum and the temple of Jupiter. The tribunal, which is made part of the pronaos, is shaped as a hemicycle, whose curvature is less than a semicircle. In front, the chord of the hemicycle is 46 feet, while the rise of its arc inward is fifteen feet, so that those who stand before the magistrates do not hinder the businessmen in the basilica.

The architraves above the columns round about are of three, two-foot timbers, joined together. These are returned from each third column on the inner row to the piers, which project from the pronaos and limit the ends of the hemicycle right and left. Above the architraves, plumb above each column, supports are set in the form of dadoes, three feet high and four feet wide on sides. Above these run beams of oak, composed of two two-foot timbers, upon which rest the tie beams and struts (of the trusses), directly over the columns, the piers and walls of the pronaos, supporting a single roof the length of the basilica and another from the middle over the pronaos and temple.

Thus the combination of the doubly sloping roofs on the outside and the lofty, open-timbered spaces within provide views of beauty, while the disregard of any ornamental entablatures and of an upper story of walls and columns (as in the typical basilica) does away with a waste of labor and reduces a good part of the cost. Moreover, extending the columns without interruption up to the beams that carry the roof seems to add an air of magnificence and authority. [V.1.6–10]

Although Fano was a new and modest colony and Vitruvius's budget apparently was stringent, he was able to create one nobly spatial ambience, enveloping and unifying the functions of a basilical hall, a tribunal, and a temple. Concern for variations of light, air, and sound are evident, and the axial relation across the forum, temple to temple, would have stressed its center so as to shape the whole square. The stark forms of the major elements of the interior were an innovation, to which Vitruvius draws attention, particularly the towering columns.

Columns of this sort had been used for the same purpose in a basilica built about a century before at Pompeii. Whether or not Vitruvius may have seen or heard of it, both basilicas must have been designed in mind of older, utilitarian Greek structures, such as PHILON's arsenal at Piraeus, three centuries past. The basilica at Fano was a far cry from the contemporary basilicas at Rome, staggered on either side of the forum, with storied façades lavishly adorned and the thickets of marble columns and piers within. Their architects, one might think, were being challenged by Vitruvius with grander forms and volumes from another day.

In any case, the basilica at Fano was, in all probability, his last architectural endeavor and his description of it the final addendum to his treatise. The dedication of his treatise to Octavian had been added before 27 B.C., whereas the temple in the basilica was dedicated to Augustus. The publication of his treatise and his death could not have come much later. His treatise was his monument and it portrays, better perhaps for its uniqueness, the experience of a studious architect-engineer with strong convictions, somewhat out of step with the breadth of his profession and the limits of his time.

The Treatise. The monument that Vitruvius left for posterity was based on the author's own experience and on whatever writings of earlier or contemporary architectural specialists he had been able to discover. His bibliography cites at least sixty-three. His scholarship has a curiously modern ring:

I express unlimited thanks to all the authors who in the past compiled the notable instances of their skill, providing me with abundant material of every sort. Drawing from it, like water from a spring, and adding it to my objective, these resources help me to write more efficiently and more fluently and give me confidence to venture to match their authority with my new treatise. [VII.Pr.10]

His treatise had apparently occupied him off and on for the last thirty-five or forty years of his life. As finally published, it comprised ten chapters (or book-rolls), the first bearing a dedication to Octavian and each of the other nine having prefaces of varying length. The treatise, as we have it, shows signs of its growth during its long gestation: additions, divisions, and shifts, which the author was not always able to conceal. The initial six chapters, without their prefaces and other additions, appear to have formed a unity that covered architecture alone and was conceived as the visualization of the construction of an entire contemporary town or colony with the indispensable buildings it was to contain.

Thus, chapter I at this stage started with the divisions of architecture (I.3) and proceeded with the siting of the town (I.4), the defenses of the town (I.5), the layout of the grid of streets (I.6), and the sites for public buildings. Chapter II, on building materials, seems at one time to have been chapter I, and as it stands breaks the continuity between chapters I and III. Vitruvius defended the position of chapter II, declaring that chapter I was entirely devoted to the education of the architect and the principles of architecture (II.1.8), but this is not so in its final state. However this may have been, chapter II begins with the origins of buildings (II.1) and introduces the scientist's conception of raw matter, composed of atoms gathered together into the four elements (II.2). It then treats of bricks (II.3), sands (II.4), lime (II.5), pozzolana (II.6), stone (II.7) and the methods of using it compared with bricks (II.8), and finally timber (II.9–10).

Chapters III and IV, having to do with temples, were probably at some time together as one but were separated to fit the general lengths of the other chapters. Chapter III opens with a discourse on proportions derived from members of the human body (III.1) and follows with succinct classifications of types of temple forms (III.2) and of proportions of columns and intercolumniations (III.3). The temple starts from the foundations, below and above grade (II.4), and the Ionic order is chosen for its specific proportions (III.5). Chapter IV, in continuation, proceeds with the proportions of the Corinthian capital (IV.1.1–2 and 11–12). Vitruvius then relates the origins of the three orders (IV.2) and treats the Doric order and his version of it. His proportions for the combined pronaos and cella (IV.4) come next, followed by their orientation (IV.5) and the proportions of Doric, Ionic, and Attic doorways (IV.6). After these "legitimate" temples, Vitruvius deals with the proportions of Tuscanic (IV.7), circular, and other uncommon temples (IV.8), and closes with altars (IV.9).

Chapters V and VI pass from sacred to functional structures, from Hellenistic temples to Italian public and private forms and spaces. Vitruvius's attention is now directed not from the outside as before but from the inside. The envelope that defined the gods is no longer important to citizens. Chapter V includes the essential public buildings of the town, first of all the forum (V.1.1–3) with its basilica (V.1.4–5) and its treasury, jail, and senate house (V.2). The theater is next in importance with its siting, foundations, access to and fro, and acoustics (V.3), whether one prefers the plans of either Roman (V.6) or Greek (V.7) models. Rules are provided for porticoes and walks (V.9), public baths (V.10), and an outdoor gymnasium (V.11). Harbors and harbor works are described for towns that border on the sea.

Chapter VI, on dwellings, completes the town. The varieties and sites of houses require that their symmetries and modules be particular to each (VI.2). The principal rooms have their own proportions and relations (VI.3) and their determined exposures (VI.4). The rooms of a house are either private or public, and the status of a proprietor decides their number, size, and embellishments (VI.5). The dimensions of farmhouses depend on the size of the farm, and the storage rooms and workrooms and the stables and lodgings must be situated with regard to the quarters of the sky (VI.6). Greek houses follow Greek customs and naturally have their own plans (VI.7). Houses on sloping sites require buttressed foundations and underground spaces; arched and vaulted (VI.8.1–8). Finally, any house that has been well designed, well built, and well decorated must be a union of architect, workmen, and owner (VI.8.9–10).

These six chapters may well have been the first draft of Vitruvius's treatise that he seems to have submitted to Julius Caesar before or during their long association. If so, the other four chapters will have been added to the six and rearranged afterward, over the years. Chapter VII was both connected to the foregoing chapters by its subject and linked with them by its bibliographical preface on architects, the longest of the ten. The chapter was probably the first of the later series. It treats of the surfacing of buildings: of kinds of concrete floors (VII.1), of stucco and its uses on vaults and walls (VII.2–3), with special care for damp rooms and dining rooms (VII.4). The author then justifies his preference for realism in mural decorations and for restraint in the application of costly pigments (VII.5). This brings him to marble dust (VII.6), natural (VII.7) and manufactured pigments (VII.8–13) and their substitutes (VII.14).

The remaining three chapters are not in chronological sequence but in the order of Vitruvius's divisions of architecture: building, fabricating timepieces, and constructing machinery (I.3.1). Chapter VIII is concerned with the building of aqueducts, wells, and cisterns. Yet about three-fourths of the whole is devoted to the water: first, the underground water, which has to be tapped (VIII.1); then, the visible water of streams and springs (VIII.2)—at this point Vitruvius interpolates a lengthy disgression on the marvelous properties of certain waters, fruit of his own observations and of his learning (VIII.3); last, the testing for acceptable water (VIII.4). Having reached aqueducts, he describes the instruments for leveling (VIII.5); the materials and methods of conducting water and lifting it over depressions, not omitting his pipe gauge (VIII.6.1–11); and last, the sinking of watertight wells and cisterns (VIII.6.12–15).

Chapter IX leaves buildings to deal with instruments for measuring time. Knowledge of the sun and its motions alone was necessary for the designing of ancient sundials and clocks, marked for days, hours, and minutes. Yet, Vitruvius could not resist pre-empting about two-thirds of his subject with the irrelevant lore acquired from his teachers and predecessors: the zodiac and the planets (IX.1), the phases of the moon (IX.2), the constellations of the northern and southern heavens (IX.4–5), and astrology with portents of the weather (IX.6). Once arrived at the principles of sundials, he began to draw the necessarily elaborate diagram of the analemma for Rome, but, as he says, "I am omitting details . . . lest I should offend by writing too much" (IX.7); he went on to mention various forms of sundials, none of which the reader could contrive (IX.8.1). He was more interested and more critical of three kinds of waterclocks, which he had improved (IX.8.2–14). These two chapters may have been the last that Vitruvius penned. Whether he was hurried, weary, or bored, he was obviously padding.

Chapter X, on mechanics, the longest of the chapters, is crowded with Vitruvius's experience of the engineering which led him in his later years to serve Julius Caesar, Octavian, and Agrippa. Mingled with earlier sources, it constitutes a selected textbook of the technology of his day, divided equally between peace and war. An introduction touches on the principles and vocabulary, Greek and Latin, of mechanics and some of its everyday uses (X.1). First, pulleys for hoisting (X.2.1–10) and the many applications of the fulcrum are explained (X.3). The raising of water follows, with waterwheels and bucket-chains, operated manually (X.4) or by the impulsion of sluices and millstreams (X.5). Archimedes's endless water screw is brought in (X.6) and Ctesibius is mentioned for his force-pump (X.7), to which Vitruvius added a water-organ (X.8) and two rather unwieldy odometers for land and sea (X.9). As to war, Vitruvius's catapults and ballistae are minutely described, even to the tuning of their torsion cylinders (X.10–12). The siege machines of the attackers cover battering rams, slung or on rollers, in towers or armored sheds, under which ditches and moats were filled up (X.13–15). Meanwhile, the devices of the defenders, responding with makeshift expedients, could be narrated only by onlookers, such as Vitruvius at Marseilles (X.16).

To clarify for the reader some of his difficult descriptions Vitruvius attached ten or perhaps twelve diagrams at the end of six of the chapters (or rolls) of his treatise. They illustrated in chapter I, a wind rose and a layout of streets; in chapter III, the convex curve of a column, the horizontal curves of a temple, and the volute of his Ionic capital; in chapter IV, the musical scale of Aristoxenus and possibly the geometrical schemes of the Roman and Greek theaters; in chapter VIII, the surveyor's trestle-level; in chapter IX, Plato's doubling of the square and the Pythagorean proposition; and in chapter X, the Archimedean screw. None of these drawings survived copying and the passage from rolls to folios in the dark ages left only one manuscript of the treatise extant. Certain medieval scribes, able to comprehend some of Vitruvius's references, attempted to replace one or another of the diagrams, but with little success. The drawings awaited the nineteenth century to be finally deciphered.

In the introductory paragraphs of chapter I of Vitruvius's published treatise he outlines the education of the well-qualified architect, implying that it was something like his own. What he proposed was a version of the Hellenistic and Roman *enkyklios paideia* or liberal arts. The budding architect was to study literature, drawing, geometry and arithmetic, philosophy, music, medicine, law, and astronomy. "I think," he declared, "that men cannot rightly profess themselves architects offhand, but only unless they have climbed from boyhood the steps of these studies and thus, nourished by many arts and sciences, have reached the highest domain of architecture."

The impact of Greek logic on Roman minds in Vitruvius's day had stirred them to justify rationally their attitudes and occupations. Cicero was one of these and Vitruvius another, but the first contemporary Roman who conceived a standard curriculum for all, based on Greek models and suited to Romans, was the polymath Terentius Varro. His *Nine Books* (or chapters) of the liberal arts, written in the mid-30s B.C., fixed the scheme of the trivium (grammar, logic, and oratory) and quadrivium (geometry, arithmetic, astronomy, and music) with medicine and architecture added. The headings were practically identical to those of Vitruvius, except, of course, architecture, which is replaced by drawing. Vitruvius mentions Varro's *Nine Books* (VII.Pr.14) and acclaims him along with Lucretius and Cicero (IX.Pr.17). There can be little doubt that Vitruvius was inspired by Varro to establish his own system of liberal arts for architects and to place it as the frontispiece of his book. It was to knit together his insistence on study as well as practice. To his mind the chapters were his fundamental textbook of architecture, whereas the prefaces and digressions would continually remind the student of his liberal education.

In the progressive study of the practical curriculum, Vitruvius was fond of introducing examples appropriate to his theme. These digressions—historical, anthropological, physical or biological—

are in effect items from his learning that provide refreshment for his readers. For instance, in the introduction to chapter I the legendary history of the columnar figures called Caryatids and Persians animates the curriculum (I.1.5–6) and man's sensitivity to temperature and wind helps explain the siting of a town and its streets (I.4.1–10, I.6.1–3). The opening of chapter II relates the rise of early man (II.1.1–3) and, midway, bricks are enhanced by the history of Mausolus and Artemisia of Halicarnassus (II.8.11–15). Consider the charmingly sophisticated myths of the origins of the three orders early in chapter IV (IV.1.3–10) or Vitruvius's fascination with resonators in theaters in chapter V (V.5.1–8), or how in chapter VI, after compassing the climates of the earth that affect dwellings, he praises Italy chauvinistically as the best (VI.1.1–12). In short, each chapter divulges a canny, professional touch.

The prefaces, on the other hand, concern mostly himself and his principles and practices. He joins with or pits himself against the times and his colleagues by setting himself beside the bygone architects, philosophers, scientists, and literati. The prefaces were obviously attached to the chapters after they had been arranged in their final order. All but two of them emphasize, in one way or another, the importance to Vitruvius, not only of the treatise itself but of the immortality it would bring him. He believed that his buildings had not brought him fame, and he was apprehensive of his shortcomings as a writer and the hybrid vocabulary of his calling. I beg "those who may read these chapters to pardon what may seem to affront the rules of grammar, for it was not as a great philosopher that I have striven to write this work, nor as a skilled orator, nor as a writer, trained to the highest degree of his art, but as an architect barely initiated to literature" (I.1.17). Moreover, "the terms necessarily devised for the special needs of architecture, strike readers as obscure and outlandish. They are not obvious in themselves nor of common usage. Therefore, as I introduce expressions from this jargon in enumerating the members of a building, I shall give brief explanations, so as to fix them in memory" (V.Pr.2).

It is evident that his contemporaries would have found the more pretentious passages of his treatise clumsy and that the lingo of architects might have been trying, but the latter at least proved to be one of Vitruvius's exemptions from oblivion. When, from the Renaissance onward, architects and antiquaries sought to study and depend upon their ruins and their designs, they found in the treatise of Vitruvius the specific architectural vocabulary they needed. The terms—Greek, Latin, and hybrid—served their purposes, and they have continued to serve architects in a wider context up to the present.

The outcome of Vitruvius's endeavor to generate well-educated architects for the future cannot be estimated. The architects of the Julio-Claudian era are virtually unknown. From Nero to Hadrian the known imperial builders, SEVERUS AND CELER, RABIRIUS and APOLLODORUS, were, like Vitruvius, ready to construct temples, basilicas, baths, theaters, urban villas, palaces, lay out vast squares and landscaped gardens, dig canals, and engineer roads, bridges, and artillery, but their intellectual propensities are not recorded. The first person known to have read *De Architectura*, or to have it read for him, was Pliny the Elder (A.D. 23/24–79) who, in his encyclopedic *Natural History*, cited it in his bibliographies on botany and mineralogy. In later times, the treatise was taken apart. Some 150 years after Pliny, a certain M. Cetius Favorinus, in northeast Italy, excerpted from it all he could find about private dwellings of all sorts and anything else that was pertinent. At about the same time in the third century, a Q. Gargilius Martialis did the same for a book on gardens, and a century later a practical farmer, Rutilius Palladius followed Vitruvius and Gargilius in his work on agriculture. In the fifth century, Sidonius Apollinaris referred to the treatise, and in the seventh, Bishop Isidore of Seville did the same. He was the last of the encyclopedic scholars who clung to the diminishing culture of the ancient world.

Still the work of Vitruvius was not lost. The archetype of all our manuscripts survived and from about A.D. 850 it began to spread over Europe. In the Middle Ages, north of the Alps, the treatise was copied not so much for the author's liberal arts or the ancient, Mediterranean architecture of temples, open basilicas, outdoor theaters, and houses with atria and peristyles but for advice on such things as building materials, recipes for pigments, stucco and wall-painting, the methods of finding and supplying water, lessons on astronomy and mechanics, even for resonators in churches. It was not until the Renaissance that *De Architectura* became a handbook of antiquity and its revival. That however is another story, the story of the architects who made use of it.

FRANK E. BROWN

II. Writings

The text of Vitruvius's treatise was preserved during the middle ages by copyists who produced manuscripts that became increasingly removed from the original text. Over time, the original illustrations, which were probably appended at the end of the work, disappeared. Finally, the work itself was all but forgotten until in 1414 or 1416 Poggio Bracciolini discovered a copy at the monastery of Saint Gall.

Following this find, the first group of men to become interested in the treatise were humanists such as Petrarch and Decembrio. As the work became better known, artists and writers such as ANTONIO AVERLINO FILARETE and FRANCESCO COLONNA produced literary works influenced by Vitruvius's treatise in which they attempted to recreate the lost world of classical antiquity, and architects such as LEON BATTISTA ALBERTI, LORENZO GHIBERTI, and Colonna used the treatise to develop principles and techniques from which it would become possible to produce architectural forms based on those of the classical past.

The first publication of the treatises in Latin in 1486 by Fra Giovanni Sulpitius, appears to have been produced for the humanist scholars who were originally interested in the work. However, this period was quickly followed by that of popular editions of the treatise, the two major publications being the first illustrated edition of 1511 by FRA GIOCONDO and the first vernacular edition of 1521 by CESARE DI LORENZO CESARIANO. Editions influenced by these two were produced in Italian, French, and German through the 1540s.

At the same time, architects such as RAPHAEL, Antonio da Sangallo (see SANGALLO FAMILY), and BALDASSARE PERUZZI were translating and illustrating sections of Vitruvius's work in unpublished treatises in which they attempted to solve some of the textual inaccuracies that had developed in the medieval manuscripts and to interpret text descriptions with accurate illustrations.

By 1540, the work of correcting and interpreting the original text and of rendering it meaningful to the contemporary period began in earnest with such published editions as GUILLAUME PHILANDER's 1544 *Annotations to Vitruvius,* the 1559 Vitruvius abstract and commentary of Gardet and Bertin, and the interesting interpretations of GIOVANNI ANTONIO RUSCONI and Daniele Barbaro. At the same time, the major sixteenth-century architectural treatises based on Vitruvius's theory were being written. All these mid-century works appeared in many re-editions until 1660.

During the seventeenth century, a shift toward practical works on architectual problems began to replace architectural interest in Vitruvius's treatise. New editions of the work were undertaken by classical scholars, who were concerned with encyclopedic compendia and interpretations of obscure textual passages.

Not until the end of the seventeenth century did Vitruvius's treatise achieve innovations in two works, both by the same man, CLAUDE PERRAULT.

His encyclopedic translation and commentary of 1673 is the first of the learned Vitruvius editions that would be produced by men who were both architects and classical scholars, while his *Epitome,* published the following year is a reconstruction of Vitruvius's treatise that forms a compact statement on taste and heralds the many architectural treatises written for the amateur in the eighteenth century.

The vast majority of Vitruvius editions were published in the nineteenth century. Most of these continued to be produced as encyclopedic works for and by the learned architect or as philological works for the classical scholar. One final original edition, a "functionalist" interpretation was published in 1909 by the architect AUGUSTE CHOISY.

The audience for Vitruvius's treatise has again shifted, and recent translations of the treatise recall the first popular printed editions of Giocondo.

DORA WIEBENSON

BIBLIOGRAPHY

English translations of the ancient texts can be found in the volumes of the Loeb Classical Library series, published by Harvard University Press and Heinemann.

BECCATTI, G.   1951   *Arte e gusto negli scrittori latini.* Florence: Sansoni.

BEYEN, HENDRIK GERARS   (1930)1960   *Die pompejanische Wanddekoration vom zweiten bis zum vierten Stil.* 2 vols. The Hague: Nijhoff.

CALLEBAT, LOUIS (translator)   1973   *De l'architecture, livre VIII.* Paris: Les Belles Lettres.

CARRINGTON, ROGER CLIFFORD   1936   *Pompeii.* Oxford: Clarendon.

DRACHMANN, AAGE GERHARDT   1963   *The Mechanical Technology of Greek and Roman Antiquity.* Copenhagen: Munkegaard.

EBHARDT, BODO   1918   *Die zehn Bücher der Architektur des Vitruv.* Berlin: Burg.

FENSTERBUSCH, CURT (translator)   1964   *Zehn Bücher über Architektur.* Darmstadt, Germany: Wissenschaftliche Buchgesellschaft.

FRONTINUS, *De Aquis Urbis Romae.*

GRANGER, FRANK (translator)   1955–1956   *Vitruvius, On Architecture.* Cambridge, Mass.: Harvard University Press.

GROS, PIERRE   1976   *Aurea Templa: recherches sur l'architecture religieuse de Rome à l'époque d'Auguste.* Rome: Bibliothèque des écoles françaises d'Athènes et de Rome.

MARSDEN, E. W.   1971   *Greek and Roman Artillery: Technical Treatises.* New York: Oxford University Press.

MAU, AUGUST   (1899)1904   *Pompeii, Its Life and Art.* New York: Macmillan.

MORGAN, MORRIS HICKEY (translator)   (1914)1960   *Vitruvius, The Ten Books of Architecture.* Cambridge, Mass.: Harvard University Press.

PLINY THE ELDER, *Natural History.*

RUSSELL, JAMES   1968   "The Origin and Development of Republican Forums." *Phoenix* 22:304–336.

SCHEFOLD, KARL   1957   *Die Wände Pompejis.* Berlin: W. de Gruyter.

SOUBIRAN, JEAN (translator)   1969   *De l'architecture, livre IX.* Paris: Les Belles Lettres.

SWINDLER, MARY H.   (1929)1976   *Ancient Painting.* New York: AMS.

VAGNETTI, LUIGI (editor)   1978   "2000 anni di Vitruvio." *Studi e documenti di architettura* no. 8. Special issue.

VARRO, MARCUS, *Nine Books.*

VITTONE, BERNARDO ANTONIO

Bernardo Antonio Vittone (1702–1770), citizen of Turin, Italy, designer of over a score of churches in Piedmont, was the most gifted architect of his generation in Italy and perhaps in all of Europe. A nephew of GIAN GIACOMO PLANTERY, he may have begun in architecture with his uncle, but before 1731 he certainly studied under FILIPPO JUVARRA, cited by Vittone as his teacher (*Istruzioni Elementari,* p. 285).

After working independently as an architect in Turin for a number of years, Vittone went to Rome in the fall of 1731 to study at the Accademia di San Luca, where he remained until April 1733. In May 1732, his design for *A City in the Sea* won first prize in the Concorso Clementino, and on 16 November 1732 he was elected to membership in the Academy. The consignment of his offering to the Academy, a design of a *Temple to Moses,* on April 6, 1733 confirmed his election less than two weeks before his return to Turin.

Before going to Rome, Vittone had been well prepared by Juvarra, the most significant architect alive in Italy, and by the city of Turin, where the most interesting new architecture in Italy could be found, which insured that his stay in Rome would be profitable. Werner Oechslin (1967, 1971, 1972*a*, 1972*b*) has demonstrated how thoroughly Vittone studied fashionable topics in Rome, absorbing and digesting architectural thought that was beginning to show a re-evaluation of the seventeenth century. His designs done in Rome demonstrate appreciation of and a familiarity with monumental architectural elements of combinatorial potential, such as rostral columns, obelisks, architectural fragments in ruins, triumphal arches, equestrian statues, reconstructions of the tomb of Hadrian, items of archeological notoriety, the published work of JOHANN BERNARD FISCHER VON ERLACH, and drawings kept in the archives of the Accademia di San Luca. Vittone's works are academic Roman, and, except in details, undistinguished. After his return to Turin, and for the remainder of his life, his works, except for his treatises, subordinate his academic experience to what he had learned from GUARINO GUARINI and Juvarra. In the months before his return to Turin, Vittone spent much time studying and copying from the many volumes of drawings by CARLO FONTANA in the collection of Cardinal Alessandro Alabani. (Two volumes of Vittone's drawings from this period are in the Musée des Arts Décoratifs in Paris.) Albani sent a letter of recommendation to Marchese Ferrero D'Ormea, secretary of internal affairs in Turin, but no major commissions or appointments resulted.

Vittone's name does not appear in documents again until 1735 (Pommer, 1967, p. 108, suggests he worked once again for Juvarra) when he had completed the preparation of one of the treatises left by Guarini at his death in 1683 (only some plates without text had been published in 1686). The preparation of the *Architettura Civile,* which appeared in 1737, may have extended Vittone's interest in Guarini (a number of his early works show an appreciation of the earlier architect's work), though there is evidence that he did not understand some of the sections on stereotomy (Muller, 1968).

The next five years, from 1737 to 1742, was the period of a number of Vittone's master works and the initial exploration of themes that would occupy him throughout his career: the Cappella della Visitazione, at Valinotto (1738), clearly related to Guarini's work; San Bernardino in Chieri (1740); Santi Marco e Leonardo in Turin (1741); Santa Maria Maddalena in Foglizzo (1741); Santa Chiara in Bra (1741); and Santa Chiara in Turin (1742).

It is also at this early stage of Vittone's career that his principal civil commissions from the crown were received: Ospedale di Carità, Casale (c.1737); Collegio delle Provincie, Turin (1737); Ricovero dei Catecumeni, Pinerolo (1740); Monastero degli Infermi, Turin (1740, project); and, four years later, the Albergo di Carità, Carignano (1744).

For the remainder of his life, he worked primarily on religious structures, largely outside Turin. He built only five buildings in Turin: four churches (Santi Marco e Leonardo, Santa Chiara, Santa Maria di Piazza, and Sant' Antonio Abate) and the Collegio delle Provincie. His other work, principally small churches and monastic buildings, is dispersed in smaller towns, villages, and rural sites throughout Piedmont.

Two of his treatises were published—*Istruzione elementari per indirizzo de'giovani allo studio dell'Architettura Civile,* 2 volumes, Lugano, 1760,

and *Istruzione diverse concernanti l'officio dell'Architetto Civile,* 2 volumes, Lugano, 1766—while others remained in manuscript (Rodolfo, 1933). In 1760, he gathered a number of his drawings in a manuscript album entitled *L'Architetto Civile,* now in the Biblioteca Reale in Turin (Carboneri, 1964).

The captions to the illustrations of his own work in the published volumes offer valuable insight into Vittone's intentions. His comments on examples by others reveal something of his theoretical base.

The small wayside chapel of 1738, on a rustic site at Valinotto, built for the Turinese banker Antonio Faccio, was a modest early opportunity which Vittone converted into a major achievement. Its three-tiered form, hexagonal plan, plunging light, double dome, and interlaced arches (shared also by his contemporary design for San Luigi Gonzaga at Corteranzo and his project for Santa Chiara in Alessandria) show an affinity with Guarini's San Lorenzo, Turin, and his other tiered churches, but also an appreciation of FRANCESCO BORROMINI (Sant' Ivo, plan), pierced vaults (San Lorenzo, Turin, perhaps Sant' Antonio Abate, Parma, by Ferdinando Galli Bibiena [see GALLI DA BIBIENA FAMILY], and similar open vaults), and, most likely, frescoed vaults depicting views through openings in the surface (Consolata, Turin).

A number of the themes Vittone studied throughout his life made their first appearance in this church: geometric form with symbolic references, the placement of a structure within a structure, screening elements through which other portions of the building or structure may be seen, light that falls vertically into chapels or on upper levels, light from hidden sources that illuminates surfaces or specific elements, multiple levels (some of which are actual passageways, other real or imaginary viewing levels), lightened or skeletal structure, pierced vaults, vertical continuities, and subsidiary spaces aggregated to a principal central space.

From the chapel entrance the whole is visible. Aggregated alternating large and small bays extend the hexagonal central space that focuses on the altar. A pair of piers screen the lighted semicircular annular vaulted space behind, while above the altar light falls through a pierced hemicircular vault, as it also falls in each of the other five bays.

Above the central space, interlaced masonry flying arches with painted soffits spring and cross well below the painted surface of the inner dome which itself is open in the center; above it is revealed the painted surface of the outer dome lighted by windows hidden behind the vault of the inner dome. Yet further above, the image of the

Vittone.
Section of Assunta.
Grignasco, Italy.
1750

Holy Trinity rests on the brilliantly lighted vault of the lantern.

Vittone, well aware of this tour de force, described the three vaults in his *Istruzione diverse* (p. 186): "one above the other, all pierced and open such that the viewer in the church may see the spaces that exist between them and enjoy, with the aid of light that is introduced by unseen windows, the variety of the [heavenly] hierarchies represented in these vaults increasing gradually to the top of the lantern where the Holy Trinity is seen." The viewer remains surprised and pleased, experiencing what at large scale would be awesome, but what at Valinotto is personal and intimate yet reverent.

At San Bernardino in Chieri (1740–1744), Vittone was asked to add drum and cupola to a church (in plan a Greek cross with elongated choir) that had already been completed through the main entablature. Vittone capped a pedestrian plan with one of the most astonishing cupolas of the eighteenth century. He increased from eight to twenty the number of supports that would normally support a ribbed dome of eight panels inscribed within the square of the Greek cross. He

added four piers above the corners of the square and a pair of piers above each of the arms. They were all linked on the exterior as a continuous drum with a weaving surface. On the interior he treated the octagonal dome as a structure nestled within the larger square. The additional spaces or lanterns outside the octagonal drum and dome enabled Vittone to open the vaults above each of the arms to the lanterns or light boxes above them. Most significant, the pendentives were pierced with openings leading up to the triangular light boxes. The astonishing view contrasts a traditional solid ribbed dome with an open supporting structure, all pierced with light flooding through the vaults and pendentives.

In Santa Chiara at Bra (1742), Vittone reached the culmination of the first phase of his career. An increasing absorption of Juvarra's ideas is evident in Santa Chiara which, while reinterpreting Juvarra's Sant' Andrea in Chieri (Pommer, 1967), also includes Vittone's notions of multiple levels, skeletal structure, structure within structure, pierced vaults, aggregated spaces, and hidden light. In plan, the church is circular, with four less-than-semicircular lobe-shaped chapels aggregated to the central space: an inner dome is supported on four equally spaced piers with pairs of superimposed orders. Arches leading to the chapels spring from the entablature of the lower order and at their crest support an upper, brightly lighted open gallery that encircles the central space. Above the gallery (and the chapels beneath), four ribbed domes with lanterns are supported by arches that spring from the rear of the central piers and the exterior walls.

At the upper level, the church seems more expansive, more open, lighter, and airier than seen from below. The panels of the inner dome are pierced, and through the openings frescoes of the apotheoses of Santa Chiara and San Francesco may be seen on the inner surface of the outer dome, illuminated by hidden windows from lanterns above the gallery domes. The ponderous masses of

Vittone.
San Bernardino (interior).
Chieri, Italy.
1740–1744

Vittone.
Santa Chiara (interior).
Bra, Italy.
1742

the enclosed lower level have been transformed to light and weightlessness, an analogue of the world beyond.

Of less interest, perhaps, are Vittone's civil buildings which, even though carefully planned (Passanti, 1951), follow traditional patterns of distribution. Both the Ospedale at Casale (1737) and the Ricovero at Pinerolo (1740) were designed with rusticated porticoes—the one at Pinerolo (not executed) composed of arches springing from pairs of rusticated piers, while at Casale arches spring from a single pier. At Pinerolo, the upper levels were unarticulated; at Casale, there was a sophisticated layering of pilasters and pilaster strips with a stringcourse to separate the levels (a similar treatment was accorded the upper levels of the Collegio delle Provincie in Turin). In the Albergo at Carignano (1744), giant pilasters were placed on a raised basement while a stringcourse again separated two levels of nearly equal height. All speak modestly, but Casale has the most characteristic Piedmontese accent.

The axially placed chapel in the Albergo at Carignano, however, contains Vittone's first use of a fully gouged-out pendentive (or inverted squinch; Wittkower, 1958), drawn no doubt from his experiment with pierced pendentives at San Bernardino at Chieri four years earlier. The removal of the center of the pendentive, rupture of the cornice ring, and consequent rupture of the drum, opened the "corners" to light, emphasized the vertical, and lightened the apparent weight of the dome, vault, and ribs—recurrent themes for Vittone. Hollowed-out pendentives recur in three churches in the 1750s: at Santa Maria di Piazza, Turin (1751); Santi Pietro e Paolo, Mondovì (1755); and Santa Croce (now Santa Caterina), Villanova di Mondovì (1755), where the pendentive has all but disappeared. The curved drum seems to be a second exterior structure rising from the shoulders of the main arches, while the star-shaped inner cupola appears to be supported on short piers containing circular windows resting atop the main crossing arches.

Vittone designed and built churches on plans that were circular (Santi Marco e Leonardo, Turin [1741–1742]); oval (San Gaetano, Nice, France [1740]); elongated octagons (Santa Maria Maddalena, Foglizzo, [1741]); longitudinal (Parish Church, Pecetto [1730]); Santi Giovanni e Vincenzo, Sant' Ambrogio di Torino [1757]; Greek crosses (*City in the Sea,* all four churches in the piazza centrale; church in new piazza, Pinerolo [1750?]), as well as the more numerous that were based on hexagons (frequent in the early years— Gonzaga, Corteranzo, 1738; Visitazione, Valinotto [1738]; Assunta, Grignasco [1750]; San Michele,

Vittone.
Capella della Visitazione
   (interior).
Valinotto, Italy.
1738

Borgo d'Ale [1770]), and octagons (Santa Chiara, Turin [1742]; San Michele, Rivarolo Canavese [1758]—another masterpiece).

The hexagonal churches at Grignasco from 1750 and Borgo d'Ale from 1770, the last year of Vittone's life, will serve as examples of his middle and late periods for comparison with the chapel at Valinotto and Santa Chiara at Bra.

At Grignasco, Vittone eschewed both the alternating bays of Valinotto, San Luigi Gonzaga, and the project for Santa Chiara at Alessandria, and multiple levels. The similar side walls of entrance bay and chapels converge toward a convex rear wall with a trapezoidal window above the entablature. The main piers are hollow behind, containing light boxes that divert side light through superimposed openings in the piers and chapel vault. Strong vertical accent is achieved through the fully round columns that mark the apices of the hexagon and lead through a sharply defined entablature with ressant, and a salient attic pedestal above to the salient ribs of the dome. A single order of pilasters with stilted arches defines the tall aggregated chapels while, with the drum eliminated, vault and chapel arches interact as the dome ribs spring from below the crown of the arches leading to the chapels. The curves of the great gores of the dome provide space in the lunette above the chapel arches for large fan-shaped windows that extend from the soffit of the gore to the extrados of the chapel arch. The emphasis on breadth and height (extent of the volume enclosed), on movement through converging and curving walls and vault

surfaces, and on relationships through repetition establishes forceful directness and simplicity.

From the exterior, the church recalls designs by Guarini with its stolid, two-tiered, centralized mass, both broad and high, with repetitive, reinforcing, but discontinuous curved surfaces, generated from points outside the structure. Vittone thought worth noting (*Istruzione diverse,* p. 178) the convergence of the walls of the chapels toward a point outside the chapels which he said also emphasized a perspective diminution. At Grignasco, geometry is at the heart of the plan and massing; the exterior form reveals much of the interior volume—light boxes behind piers, chapels, dome, each element rising to shape the whole.

At Borgo d'Ale, the great bulk of both levels of San Michele rises without setbacks from the sidewalk, the form emphasized by the projecting entablatures of the two levels. The exterior form is defined completely by intersecting concave bays of alternating width—broad bays with arched windows mark the chapels; narrow bays with smaller rectangular windows indicate the piers between chapels. A lone convex bay with salient pediment marking the entrance projects forward at the lower level from within a broad concave bay. The discontinuous curves, baying outward and inward on the exterior, reminiscent this time of a tamed Guarini, do not reappear on the interior where, instead, six shallow, aggregated apsidal spaces reverse the curvature of the exterior walls. The chapel arches do not rise as high as those at Grignasco, and there is a gallery above. The entablature of chapel and main order are separated. At each corner of the hexagon, above the main columns and pilaster bunch, are ressants emphasizing continuity with the ribs of the dome. The lunettes above the chapels are pierced by ovals that open to the gallery which is itself lighted by the large arched windows of the exterior. Once again, by modest means, Vittone has suggested that the ribbed and paneled dome and its supports may be read as an independent structure within an exterior envelope.

Toward the end of his life, Vittone seemed to recognize neoclassicism in an altered decorative detail and perhaps in more simplified plans and elevations, though his assistant MARIO LUDOVICO QUARINI had already built in the new manner with Vittone's approval. However, among Vittone's last works, the chapel of San Secondo in the Church of San Secondo at Asti (1769) demonstrates a continuing interest in themes he explored at Valinotto more than thirty years earlier. Working in constricted circumstances (the long, narrow space of the chapel existed before his intervention) for the impecunious Compagnia di San Secondo, Vittone created a central-plan, domed space with aggregated narthex and choir, pierced vaults (dome and barrel vaults) lighted from hidden windows (one of which is now closed), the appearance of a screen of columns behind the altar separating a side-lighted space between the altar and exterior wall (originally enhanced by windows, now blocked up at the upper level behind the second level of the altar), painting that suggests further piercing of the structure (pendentives, arches, and dome), and large windows in the lunettes below the dome that lighten the structure. The modest chapel testifies both to undiminished ability over a lifetime and to a continuity of attitude.

Vittone had little influence after his death and, as interest in the classical world expanded, was soon forgotten. At the time of his death, hundreds of unsold copies of his publications were still either in his possession or at the printer's shop in Lugano. His rehabilitation began in 1920 (Olivero); today, he is recognized as one of the three great masters of Piedmontese baroque.

HENRY A. MILLON

WORKS

1730, Parish Church, Pecetto, Italy. 1737, Ospedale di Carità, Casale Monferrato, Italy. 1738, Capella della Visitazione, Valinotto, Italy. 1738?, Collegio delle Provincie, Turin, Italy. 1738, Gonzaga, Corteranzo, Italy. 1740, San Gaetano, Nice, France. *1740, Santi Vincenzo e Anastasio, Cambiano, Italy. 1740–1744, San Bernardino, Chieri, Italy. 1741, Santa Maria Maddalena,

Foglizzo, Italy. *1741–1742, Santi Marco e Leonardo, Turin, Italy. 1742, Santa Chiara, Bra, Italy. 1742, Santa Chiara, Turin, Italy. 1744–1749, Albergo di Carità, Carignano, Italy. 1750, Assunta, Grignasco, Italy. 1750, Santa Maria di Piazza, Turin, Italy. 1754, Church, Casotto, Certosa, Italy. 1754–1756, Santa Chiara, Vercelli, Italy. 1755, San Croce (now Santa Caterina), Villanova Mondovì, Italy. 1755, San Salvatore, Borgomasino, Italy. 1757–1764, Santi Giovanni e Vincenzo, Sant'Ambrogio di Torino, Italy. 1758, San Michele, Rivarolo Canavese, Italy. 1761, Assunta, Riva di Chieri, Italy. 1769, Chapel of San Secondo, Asti, San Secondo, Italy. 1770, San Michele, Borgo d'Ale, Italy.

BIBLIOGRAPHY

ARGAN, GIULIO C. 1970 "Bernardo Vittone." Pages 347–356 in *Studi e Note del Bramante al Canova*. Rome: Bulzoni.

BARACCO, C. 1938 "Bernardo Vittone e l'architettura guariniana." *Torino* 16:22–27.

BELLINI, AMEDEO 1974 "Un'opera sconosciuta di Bernardo Vittone: La Cappella di San Secondo nella omonima chiesa di Asti." Volume 2, pages 355–379 in Vittorio Viale (editor), *Bernardo Vittone e la disputà*. Turin, Italy: Accademia delle Scienze.

BRAYDA, CARLO 1947 "Opera inedite di Bernardo Vittone." *Bollettino della Società Piemontese di Archeologia e Belle Arti* 1:86–88.

BRINCKMANN, ALBERT E. 1931 *Theatrum Novum Pedemontii: Ideen, Entwürfe und Bauten von Guarini, Juvarra, Vittone wie anderen bedeutenden Architekten des piemontesischen Hochbarocks*. Düsseldorf, Germany: Schwann.

CARBONERI, NINO 1948 'Gallo e Vittone nella Chiesa dei Santi Pietro e Paolo in Mondovì Breo." *Bollettino della Società Piemontese di Archeologia e Belle Arti* 2:99–111.

CARBONERI, NINO 1963a "Appunti sul Vittone." *Quaderni dell'Istituto di Storia dell'Architettura* 1963, nos. 55–60:59–74.

CARBONERI, NINO 1963b "Architettura." Pages 1–8 in Vittorio Viale (editor), *Mostra del Barocco piemontese*. Turin, Italy.

CARBONERI, NINO, and VIALE, VITTORIO 1967 *Bernardo Vittone Architetto*. Turin, Italy: Pozzo-Salvati-Gros Monti. Exhibition catalogue with full bibliography.

CAVALLARI MURAT, AUGUSTO 1942 "Alcune architettura piemontese del settecento in una raccolta di disegni del Plantery, del Vittone, e del Guarini." *Torino* 21:7–11.

CAVALLARI MURAT, AUGUSTO 1956 "L'architettura sacra del Vittone." *Atti e Rassegna Technica* 10:35–52.

GAMARINO, FRANCESCO 1947 "Architettura barocca nel Monferrato." *Bollettino della Società Piemontese di Archeologia e Belle Arti* 1:116–127.

GOLZIO, VINCENZO 1959 "L'architetto Bernardo Antonio Vittone Urbanista." *Atti del X Congresso di Storia dell'Architettura Torino* 1959:101–112.

GRISERI, ANDREINA 1967 *Le Metamorfosi del Barocco*. Turin, Italy: Einaudi.

MILLON, HENRY 1958–1959 "Alcune osservazioni sulle opere giovanili di Bernardo Antonio Vittone." *Bollettino della Società Piemontese di Archeologia e Belle Arti* 12–13:144–153.

MILLON, HENRY 1972 "La formazione piemontese di B. Vittone fino al 1742." Volume 1, pages 443–456 in Vittorio Viale (editor), *Bernardo Vittone e la disputà*. Turin, Italy: Accademia delle Scienze.

OECHSLIN, WERNER 1967 "Un tempio di Mosè—I Disegni offerti da Bernardo Vittone all'Accademia di San Luca nel 1733." *Bollettino d'Arte* 52:167–173.

OECHSLIN, WERNER 1972a *Bildungsgut und Antikenrezeption im frühen Settecento in Rom, Studien zum römischen Aufenthalt Bernardo Antonio Vittones*. Zurich: Atlantis-Verlag.

OECHSLIN, WERNER 1972b "Il soggiorno romano di Bernardo Antonio Vittone." Volume 1, pages 393–441 in Vittorio Viale (editor), *Bernardo Vittone e la disputà*. Turin, Italy: Accademia delle Scienze.

OECHSLIN, WERNER 1974 'Vittone e l'architettura europea del suo tempo." Volume 2, pages 29–80 in Vittorio Viale (editor), *Bernardo Vittone e la disputà*. Turin, Italy: Accademia delle Scienze.

OLIVERO, EUGENIO 1920 *Le opere di Bernardo Antonio Vittone*. Turin, Italy: Tipografia del Collegio degli Artigianelli.

OLIVERO, EUGENIO 1936 *Brevi cenni sui rapporti fra la Reale Accademia di San Luca in Roma e l'Arte in Piemonte*. Turin, Italy.

POMMER, RICHARD 1967 *Eighteenth Century Architecture in Piedmont*. New York University Press.

PORTOGHESI, PAOLO 1960–1961 "Metodo e poesia nell' architettura di Bernardo Antonio Vittone." *Bollettino della Società Piemontese di Archeologia e Belle Arti* 14–15:99–114.

PORTOGHESI, PAOLO 1962 "La Chiesa di Santa Chiara a Bra nell'opera di B. A. Vittone." *Quaderni dell'Istituto di Storia dell'Architettura* no. 54:1–22.

PORTOGHESI, PAOLO 1966 *Bernardo Vittone, un Architetto tra illuminismo e Rococò*. Rome: Edizioni dell'Elefante.

RODOLFO, GIACOMO 1937 "L'Architettura barocca in Carignano." *Atti della Società Piemontese di Archeologia e Belle Arti* 16:130–186.

TAMBURINI, LUCIANO 1968 *Le chiese di Torino dal Rinascimento al Barocco*. Turin, Italy: Le Bouquiniste.

VIALE, VITTORIO (editor) 1972–1974 *Bernardo Vittone e la disputà fra classicismo e barocco nel settecento*, 2 vols. Turin, Italy: Accademia delle Scienze.

VITTONE, BERNARDO ANTONIO 1760a "L'Architetto Civile." Unpublished manuscript, Biblioteca Reale, Turin, Italy.

VITTONE, BERNARDO ANTONIO 1760b *Istruzione Elementari*. . . . Lugano, Switzerland.

VITTONE, BERNARDO ANTONIO 1766 *Istruzione diverse*. . . . Lugano, Switzerland.

WITTKOWER, RUDOLF 1967 "Vittone's Drawings in the Musée des Arts Décoratifs." Pages 165–172 in *Studies in Renaissance and Baroque Art Presented to Anthony Blunt*. London: Phaidon.

WITTKOWER, RUDOLF (1958)1972 *Art and Architecture in Italy: 1600–1750*. Harmondsworth, England, and Baltimore: Penguin.

VITTORIA, ALESSANDRO

Active in the Veneto, Italy, during the late Renaissance, Alessandro Vittoria (1525–1608) was one of the best pupils of JACOPO TATTI SANSOVINO. Although primarily a sculptor, Vittoria imbued his works, notably his altars, with a rich architectural quality. Vittoria's "architecture," however, seems almost fantastic in form at times; possibly without direct experience of Rome and Florence, unlike his contemporary ANDREA PALLADIO and his teacher Sansovino, he turned toward elaborate varied forms.

Born in the northern Italian town of Trent, Vittoria moved to Venice at the age of eighteen and was employed by Sansovino. From 1547, he was active on his own account.

A work such as his altar for the Church of San Francesco della Vigna, Venice (1561–1562), demonstrates Vittoria's architectural character. Not only are the forms of the figures taken from MICHELANGELO but bizarre architectural elements such as the triple corbel volutes that support the statues also recall Michelangelo. The unsteady, unstable character of these elements, often defined as mannerist, is quite different from the noble simplicity of Palladio's forms.

Vittoria was active in a number of architectural projects. Under the inspiration of Michelangelo's Julius Tomb, he provided caryatids for the entrance to the Libreria di San Marco, Venice (1555), and in Padua he was active in the construction of the monument to Alessandro Contarini as assistant to MICHELE SANMICHELI between 1555 and 1558. As decorator, he provided stucco ornament for the stairway of the Libreria of San Marco (1560) and the Scala d'Oro of the Palazzo Ducale in Venice (1561).

NICHOLAS ADAMS

WORKS

1555, Libreria di San Marco (caryatids), Venice, Italy. 1555–1558, Monument to Alessandro Contarini, Padua, Italy. 1560, Libreria di San Marco (stucco decoration); 1561, Scala d'Oro, Palazzo Ducale; 1561–1562, San Francesco della Vigna (altar); 1600, Scuola dei Luganegheri (altar), San Salvatore; Venice, Italy.

BIBLIOGRAPHY

POPE-HENNESSEY, JOHN W. 1963 *Italian High Renaissance and Baroque Sculpture.* 3 vols. London: Phaison; Greenwich, Conn.: New York Graphic Society.

FRIEDRICH VON GÄRTNER, who provided the first designs for Voit's major work, the Neue Pinakothek (1846–1853). This museum of contemporary painting featured external frescoes by Wilhelm von Kaulbach commemorating King Ludwig I's patronage of the arts. Voit designed many neo-Romanesque churches in the Bavarian Pfalz, but he is chiefly known for the Glaspalast (1853–1854)—inspired by the Crystal Palace in London—for the Allgemeine Deutsche Industrieausstellung.

BARRY BERGDOLL

WORKS

1825–1826, Protestant Cemetery Chapel (with J. M. Boit and Balthasar von Hössler), Augsburg, Germany. 1831–1834, Protestant Church, Binnthal, Germany. 1836–1841, Saint Michael, Homburg, Germany. 1840–1843, Protestant Church, Wilgartswiesen, Germany. 1842–1843, Saint Martin, Waldsee, Germany. 1842–1844, Town Hall, Annweiler, Germany. c.1842–1844, Town Hall, Landau, Germany. *1844–1845, Arts and Crafts School, Luisenstrasse; *1846–1853, Neue Pinakothek (original plan in 1842 by FRIEDRICH VON GÄRTNER); *1853–1854, Glaspalast; *1860–1862, Palm House, Botanical Garden; 1874–1876, Wittelsbacher Bridge; Munich.

BIBLIOGRAPHY

HEDERER, OSWALD 1976 *Friedrich von Gärtner, 1792–1847; Leben, Werk, Schüler.* Munich: Prestel.
HÜTSCH, VOLKER 1981 *Der Münchener Glaspalast, 1854–1931: Geschichte und Bedeutung.* Munich: Münchener Stadtmuseum.
KOHLMAIER, GEORG, and SARTORY, BARNA VON 1981 *Das Glashaus: Ein Bautypus des Neunzehnten Jahrhunderts.* Munich: Prestel.
KOTZUR, HANS J. 1977 "Forschungen zum Leben und Werk des Architekten August von Voit." Unpublished Ph.D. dissertation, Heidelberg University, Germany.
LÜBKE, WILHELM; GUHL, E.; and CASPAR, E. 1860 *Denkmäler der Architektur.* Stuttgart, Germany: Ebner & Seubert.
MITTLEMEIER, WERNER 1977 *Die Neue Pinakothek in München, 1843–1854: Planung, Baugeschichte und Fresken.* Munich: Prestel.
PLAGEMANN, VOLKER 1967 *Das deutsche Kunstmuseum: 1790–1870.* Munich: Prestel.
PLAGEMANN, VOLKER 1970 "Die Bildprogramme der Münchner Museen Ludwigs I." *Alte und Moderne Kunst* 15:16–27.
ROTH, ENGEN 1971 *Der Glaspalast in München: Glanz und Ende, 1854–1931.* Munich: Süddeutscher Verlag.

VOIT, AUGUST VON

The son of an architect, Richard Jacob August von Voit (1801–1870) was trained in Munich under

VOLK, JOHN

Born in Gratz, Austria, John Volk (1901–) came to the United States in 1909. He attended Columbia's School of Architecture. He worked in New York for H. P. Knowles, for whom he completed Mecca Temple (New York City Center).

In 1925, Volk established an office in Palm Beach, Florida. He designed in ADDISON MIZNER's Spanish style until the early 1930s when the less costly Colonial and Regency became popular. He has built over one thousand buildings, including luxury homes, airports, hospitals, and large resort complexes in the Bahamas, Florida, and Wyoming.

VICTORIA NEWHOUSE

WORKS

1948, Good Samaritan Hospital (with later additions), Palm Beach, Fla. 1957, Royal Poinciana Playhouse and Shopping Plaza, Palm Beach, Fla. 1966, Parker Playhouse, Fort Lauderdale, Fla.

BIBLIOGRAPHY

HOFFSTOT, BARBARA D.   (1974)1980   *Landmark Architecture of Palm Beach.* Rev. ed. Pittsburgh: Ober Park Associates.

PRICE, PAUL   1972   "John L. Volk: The Man Behind Those Mansions." *Palm Beach Post-Times, Home Section* Jan. 2, pp. 1, 4.

VORONIKHIN, A. N.

Andrei Nikiforovich Voronikhin (1759–1814), a serf on the Stroganov estate near Perm, Russia, enjoyed his master's patronage and was sent to Moscow to study painting and to St. Petersburg and Europe to study architecture. After several years in Rome and Paris, where he was a pupil of CHARLES DE WAILLY, he returned to Russia in the 1790s, producing two major classically inspired works: the Cathedral of the Virgin of Kazan, St. Petersburg (1801–1811), derived from St. Peter's in Rome and the Pantheon in Paris, and the Academy of Mines, St. Petersburg (1806–1811), derivative of Paestum.

THOMAS J. MCCORMICK

WORKS

1790s, Stroganov Dacha, near St. Petersburg, Russia. 1790s, Stroganov Palace (remodeled State Rooms); 1801–1811, Cathedral of the Virgin of Kazan; 1806–1811, Academy of Mines; St. Petersburg, Russia.

BIBLIOGRAPHY

ARKIN, DAVID E.   1953   *Zakharov i Voronikhin* Moscow.

BERCKENHAGEN, EKHART   1975   *St. Petersburg um 1800: Architekturzeichnungen Thomas de Thomon.* Berlin: Kunstbibliothek. Exhibition catalogue.

GRABAR, I.; LAZAREV, V. N.; and KEMENOV, V. S. (editors)   (1958)1963   Volume 8, part 1 in *Istoriía russkogo iskusstva.* Moscow.

GRIMM, GERMAN G.   1963   *Arkhitektor Voronikhin.* Leningrad.

HAMILTON, GEORGE H.   (1954)1975   *The Art and Architecture of Russia.* 2d ed. Baltimore: Penguin.

PANOV, V. A.   1937   *Arkhitektor A. N. Voronikhin.* Moscow.

TARASSOFF, N.   1909   "L'Ecole des Mines à St-Petersbourg." *Starye Gody* Mar.:139–145.

VOYSEY, CHARLES F. A.

There seem to be certain moments in the history of architecture that have brought forth remarkable constellations of personages, and one of those moments was the closing years of the nineteenth and the opening years of the twentieth centuries. In Great Britain, Glasgow and London emerged as major architectural centers, and in London itself one of the most publicized of the architectural practitioners was Charles F. A. Voysey (1857–1941). Here was an architect who, though widely known and respected, had not made his mark by designing any major public or private buildings in London nor had he ever received any of the really sumptuous commissions for regal country houses. His practice, with the fewest of exceptions, was devoted to moderate-sized country houses, designed not for the rich, but for the upper middle class and the intelligentsia.

Voysey was an enigma in his time, and in many ways he still is. His contemporaries saw him as a major exponent of the late English Arts and Crafts movement, yet he proudly pointed out that much of his work, especially in the decorative arts, was the result of the machine. His simple-volumed white stucco houses were, in the 1930s and later, taken up by the apologists of the Modern movement as precursors of the new architecture. These and other aspects of Voysey's career illustrate that he does not easily fit into any preconceived mold. As a person he was a dour puritan who never smiled. At the same time, there is infectious charm and even at times a naïvete about his architecture and decorative art that takes us into the world of our childhood experiences. Voysey loomed large on the architectural scene because he was able to create buildings and designs that mingled so many essential middle class ideals: the fondness for the rural countryside or suburbia, the suggestion of puritanism in his play on vernacular forms, and finally the deep seated reality of childhood as opposed to the "embarrassment" of adult life.

The architect's adherence to puritanism and his fondness for the rural scene may well be a reflec-

Voysey.
Wallpaper Factory,
*   Sanderson and Sons.*
Chiswick, England.
1902

Voysey.
Wallpaper Factory,
*   Sanderson and Sons.*
Chiswick, England.
1902

tion of his own childhood. Until he was fourteen, he and his seven brothers and sisters lived in the remote village of Healaugh in Yorkshire, where his father was the local vicar. In 1871, his father left the Anglican Church and founded his own Theistic Church. Charles attended the Dulwich School for two years and then worked with a private tutor for eighteen months. At the age of seventeen, in 1874, Charles was apprenticed to the architect J. P. SEDDON. In 1880, he joined the office of GEORGE DEVEY, and here he was exposed to the newly emerging Queen Anne Revival and the open use of vernacular domestic architecture as a source for contemporary design.

In 1881, he established his own practice in Westminster, and the following year he married Mary Maria Evans. Through his friendship with ARTHUR H. MACKMURDO he was able to obtain commissions to design wallpaper, fabrics, and rugs for several of England's leading manufacturers. His decorative designs of these first years of architectural practice were his principal source of income until he began to receive architectural commissions at the end of the decade. Several of Voysey's unbuilt designs were published in the late 1880s, and their publication slowly began to bring in commissions. In 1888, he designed a house for M. H. Lakin in Bishop's Itchington which was built the following year. By the early 1890s, his practice was firmly established. For his country houses he looked to the common vernacular cottages as a source, and he then rearranged their volumes, spaces, and surfaces so that they became highly abstract compositions. In contrast, his designs for London and its suburbs tended to embrace both vernacular and "New Art" elements. His small Britten Studio (West Kensington,

1891) and his frequently illustrated Forster House (Bedford Park, 1891) are more avant-garde "New Art" than they are vernacular. His larger compositions of the 1890s and early 1900s illustrate the range of his designs. The Grove Townhouses (Kensington, 1891–1892) illustrate how Voysey in the fashion of R. NORMAN SHAW and EDWIN LUTYENS was able to compose interior spaces as a series of ascending platforms. His later Wallpaper Factory Building for Sanderson and Sons (Chiswick, 1902) illustrates how the dull repetition of windows and walls of a factory could be made geometrically abstract and miniaturized to the world of a dollhouse.

The architect's many country houses of the 1890s represent variations on a single theme. His favorite form was a single rectangular two-story volume covered by a high pitched roof. The walls were white, of rough cast stucco, the roofs were slate; horizontal groupings of windows were surrounded by stone frames. Though vernacular in feeling, these houses strongly reveal the controlling hand of the architect; everything, including the characteristic green barrels to receive rain water from the roof has been carefully conceived. What is not conveyed through photographs or drawings is Voysey's manipulation of scale. Many of his low towers such as that of the Sturgis Stable (near Guildford, 1896) appear as enlarged mantel clocks. The houses, too, often seem to be dollhouses which have been taken from the children's nursery, magically enlarged, and then placed in the pastoral countryside.

Smallness of scale was a device which Voysey continually employed, whether in more modest dwellings such as his own house, The Orchard (Chorley Wood, 1899) or larger country dwellings like the Briggs House (near Lake Windermere, 1898), or the Walters House (near Woking, 1903). Though several of these dwellings contain two-story halls, the space encountered within is always small in scale.

Although Voysey's imagery remained consistent throughout the years of his productive career, he did not remain repetitive or stagnant. Voysey has been credited (or derided) for setting the stage for much of England's town council and speculative housing of the 1920s and 1930s, but his own few instances of multiple housing are as inventive in their design as were his free-standing country houses. His most extensive housing project, that for Briggs and Son (Normanton, 1904) is village-like and picturesque, but its picturesqueness is kept tightly in place by the puritanism of volumes and surfaces.

In his work after 1900, he never lost his touch of miniaturizing. The Tytus House (Tyringham,

Massachusetts, 1904) is a half-timber and stone rural manner house, reduced to the scale of an American suburban Arts and Crafts bungalow; the Cotterell House (Combe Down, 1909) is a stone dollhouse castle, enlarged just sufficiently to accommodate real human beings. In the early 1900s, Voysey produced several of his most fascinating designs for small dwellings. In his Simpson House, Littleholme, (Kendal, 1909) and in his proposed house for C. F. A. Voysey (Slindon, 1909) he provided a single open living floor on the ground floor.

From the inception of his career, Voysey had been occupied with a wide range of decorative arts, from wall paper, fabric, and rug designs to furniture and even prefabricated fireplaces. He approached the design of all of these objects in the same fashion as his architecture. Like WILLIAM MORRIS and OWEN JONES before him he delighted in taking recognizable animal and plant forms and transforming them into a scheme which formed a convincing two-dimensional pattern. In contrast to Morris and others, his designs do not generally hint at the English Medieval Gothic tradition. At times there is an occasional nod to the Pre-Raphaelite or the proto Art Nouveau, and in a few instances to the flat stylized mode of depiction associated with illustrations in children's books at the turn of the century.

As a group, the English Arts and Crafts designers excluded the heavy crudeness in furniture design associated with the American phase of the movement. In fact, Voysey's furniture is perhaps the most refined and delicate of all of the English exponents. Like theirs, his source was the vernacular and commonplace, but when he had finished the design of a chair or table, it ended up being both traditional and "New Art." A good share of Voysey's furniture was designed for commercial manufacture. He welcomed the machine as a tool to produce this furniture, and he took it into account in his designs. The element of exposed and exaggerated joinery, of how the individual pieces were put together, was not something which interested him. Generally, he specified traditional hidden joinery, realized through traditional means such as dowels and mortise and tenon joints. Thus, the keynote of uncluttered simplicity marks all of his furniture designs. As in his architecture, he avoided ornamentation. If it was introduced as with his cutout heart motif, or his occasional use of tall spindly columns topped by a flat shelf, the sense was playful and childlike. As with his buildings, the only change in his designs for furniture was one of continual refinement.

Voysey's ability and enthusiasm for design embraced a wide range of objects. He produced the first cover for the magazine *Studio* (1893) and the advertisements and sales brochures for several companies. He produced a full set of silver tableware, weather vanes, hinges, locks and keys, clocks and boxes. Without exception, all of these designs, like those for his wallpapers and fabrics, were based upon recognizable subject matter which conveys the sense of the child's world as *the* golden moment of life.

World War I brought a close to Voysey's activities as an architect and designer. In the early years immediately after the war, he produced several designs including a cottage for G. B. Simonds (Bradfield, 1919), but none of these were built. At the time when the suburban fringes of English cities were being filled with Voyseyesque cottages, the architect himself was without commissions. His work was exhibited in London in 1931, and he emerged as an important figure in Nikolaus Pevsner's *Pioneers of the Modern Movement* (London, 1937). In 1940, he received the Gold Medal of the

Voysey.
Burke House.
Beaconsfield, England.
1905–1906

Voysey.
Horniman House
*   (Lowicks).*
Near Frensham, England.
1894

Royal Institute of British Architects, and the following year he died.

DAVID GEBHARD

WORKS

1888–1889, M. H. Larkin House, Bishop's Itchington, England. 1890, Cazalet House (Walnut Tree Farm), Castlemorton, England. 1891, Studio Britten, West Kensington; 1891, Forster House, Bedford Park; 1891–1892, Grove Town Houses, Kensington; London. 1893, Wilson House, Colwell, England. 1896, Sturgis Stable, near Guildford, England. 1897, Grane House, Shackleford, England. 1897, Methuen House, near Haslemere, England. 1898, Briggs House, near Lake Windermere, England. 1899, C. F. A. Voysey House, Chorley Wood, England. 1899, H. G. Wells House, Sandgate, England. 1902, Wallpaper Factory, Sanderson and Sons, Chiswick, England. 1903, Walters House, near Woking, England. 1904, Houses and Institute for H. Briggs and Son, Normanton, England. 1904, Titus House, Tyringham, Mass. 1905–1906, Burke House, Beaconsfield, England. 1905–1906, Turner House, Frinton-on-Sea, England. 1906, Essex and Suffolk Equitable Insurance Co. (interior), London. 1906–1907, Muntzer House, Guildford, England. 1909, Cotterell House, Combe Down, England. 1909, Knight House, Henley-in-Arden, England. 1909, Simpson House, Kendal, England. 1911, Store for Atkinson & Co., London.

BIBLIOGRAPHY

BAER, C. H. 1911 "C. F. A. Voysey Raum Kunst." *Moderne Bauformen* 10:247–256.

BETJEMAN, JOHN 1927 "Charles Francis Annesley Voysey, the Architect of Individualism." *Architectural Review* 70:93–96.

BRANDON-JONES, MARTIN S. 1949 "Voysey and Blomfield, A Study in Contrast." *The Builder* 176:39–42.

BRANDON-JONES, MARTIN S. 1957 "C. F. A. Voysey." *Architectural Association Quarterly* 72:239–262.

BRANDON-JONES, MARTIN S. 1978 *C. F. A. Voysey, Architect and Designer: 1857–1941.* London: Lund Humphries.

DARYLL, A. B. 1906 "The Architecture of Charles Francis Annesley Voysey." *Magazine of Fine Arts* 2:191–195.

GEBHARD, DAVID 1971 "C. F. A. Voysey—To and From America." *Journal of the Society of Architectural Historians* 30:304–312.

GEBHARD, DAVID 1975 *Charles F. A. Voysey, Architect.* Los Angeles: Hennesey & Ingalls.

KLOPFER, PAUL 1910 "Voysey's Architektur—Idyllen." *Moderne Bauformen* 9:141–148.

PEVSNER, NIKOLAUS 1968 "C. F. A. Voysey." Volume 2, pages 140–151 in *Studies in Arts, Architecture and Design.* New York: Walker.

SIMPSON, DUNCAN 1979 *C. F. A. Voysey and the Architecture of Individuality.* London: Lund Humphries.

TOWNSEND, HORACE 1899 "Notes on Country and Suburban Houses Designed by C. F. A. Voysey." *Studio* 16:157–164.

VREDEMAN DE VRIES, HANS

Painter, decorator, architect, and theoretician, Hans Vredeman de Vries (1526/1527–1606) was known above all for his remarkable collection of engravings which circulated throughout Europe. He was a student of the painter R. Griesten in Amsterdam for five years and became well known in Antwerp and Mechelen both as a painter and as a designer of royal festivities. He was later forced to flee from the Spanish repression of Protestants. His career took him in turn to Frankfurt, Braunschweig, Danzig, Hamburg, Wolfenbüttel, and Prague, and ended with his return to the Netherlands.

His architectural principles, which reveal a profound knowledge of perspective and of the theories of SEBASTIANO SERLIO, were responsible for popularizing throughout Europe many motifs inherited from the school of Fontainebleau. His original art style, complicated and rich, was the principal contribution to Northern Mannerism and inspired the English Jacobin style and baroque decoration.

PIERRE LENAIN
Translated from French by
Shara Wasserman

WORKS

*1549, Temporary Triumphal Arches to the Glory of Charles V (with others), Antwerp, Belgium. c.1550, Various Works for Royal Festivities, Mechelen, Belgium. 1570, Great Triumphal Arch, Antwerp, Belgium. 1596, Prague Castle (art gallery). n.d., Fortifications (supervised construction), Antwerp, Belgium.

VULLIAMY, LEWIS

Born in London, Lewis Vulliamy (1791–1871) was the son of the clockmaker Benjamin Vulliamy. First articled to ROBERT SMIRKE, he became a student at the Royal Academy in 1809, winning the Silver Medal in 1810, the Gold Medal in 1813, and the traveling scholarship in 1818. He spent four years in Europe. On his return he began to exhibit at the Royal Academy and built up a substantial practice, chiefly new churches for the Church Commissioners and other patrons in an archeologically incorrect Gothic style. In 1822, he published *The Bridge of Sta. Trinita at Florence* and later *Examples of Ornamental Sculpture in Architecture, drawn from originals in Greece, Asia Minor, and Italy in the years 1818, 1819, 1820, 1821.* His most important secular works in London were the Greek Revival Law Society (1828–1836), the Corinthian façade of the Royal Institution (1838), and the

Italian Renaissance Dorchester House (1850–1863) for R. S. Holford. For Holford, he also built Westonbirt House (1863–1870), in the Jacobean style with Renaissance interiors and an elaborate formal garden. He remained in practice until his death and was employed on additions to many country houses. OWEN JONES was one of his pupils.

JILL ALLIBONE

WORKS

1825, Boothby Pagnell Hall, Lincolnshire, England. 1826–1831, Saint Bartholemew, Sydenham; 1828–1829, Saint Barnabas, Addison Road; *1828–1829, Saint James, Clapham Common; 1828–1836, The Law Society, Chancery Lane; London. 1829–1831, Saint John the Divine, Richmond-upon-Thames, Surrey, England. *1830, Edith Weston Hall, Rutland, England. 1830–1832, Saint Michael, Highgate; 1831–1833, Christchurch, Woburn Square; London. *1833–1836, Carlton Lodge, Great Carlton, Lincolnshire, England. 1834, Hickey's Almshouses, Richmond-upon-Thames, Surrey, England. 1838, The Royal Institution (façade), Albemarle Street; *1838–1839, Saint James, Shoreditch; 1838–1839, Christchurch, Rotherhithe; London. 1839–1840, Friday Hill House, Chingford, Essex, England. 1840–1842, Saint James the Less, Bethnal Green; 1842–1849, Lock Hospital, Chapel, and Asylum, Paddington; London. 1848, Chestal House, Dursley, Gloucestershire, England. 1848–1849, All Saints, Ennismore Gardens; *1850–1863, Dorchester House, Park Lane; 1852–1853, Saint Margaret's (now Kilmorey) House, Isleworth; London. 1853, Shernfield House, Frant, Sussex, England. 1863–1870, Westonbirt House, Gloucestershire, England.

BIBLIOGRAPHY

"The Works of the Late Mr. Lewis Vulliamy, Architect." 1871 *The Builder* 29:142.
REDGRAVE, SAMUEL 1878 Pages 452–453 in *A Dictionary of Artists of the English School*. London.

WACHSMANN, KONRAD

Konrad Wachsmann (1901–1980), architect, inventor, educator, and pioneer of industrialized building systems in the United States and Europe, was born in Frankfurt an der Oder, Germany. Apprenticed as a cabinetmaker, he later became a pupil of HEINRICH TESSENOW and HANS POELZIG in Dresden and Berlin (1922–1925). In 1932, he won a Prix de Rome in architecture.

Later, Wachsmann worked on advanced laminated arch structures in timber and practiced as an architect in Berlin, building a summer house (1928) for Albert Einstein with whom he developed a lifelong friendship. In the 1930s, he was a designer for engineering companies in Spain and Italy, and before World War II he had a brief association with LE CORBUSIER, who admired Wachsmann's structural ideas. In 1940, he came to the United States and was associated with WALTER GROPIUS in Cambridge, Massachusetts, with whom he developed the General Panel Corporation in California in 1942; for this enterprise, Wachsmann not only designed the building system but also planned and supervised the assembly line and production process, as well as the site assembly of several thousand housing units with prefabricated plumbing and service units.

Appointed professor and director of the Department of Advanced Building Research in the Institute of Design at Illinois Institute of Technology in 1950, he set up a program based on his ideas of industrialized building, combining research, team work, and design of experimental structures and systems analysis. At this time, he undertook a special research project for the United States Air Force: the design of a building system for the erection of service hangars for B-52 aircraft on a global scale. In 1955, he made a world tour sponsored by the Department of State, lecturing in schools of architecture.

Wachsmann was invited to the University of California in 1962 where he continued to teach as a professor of building research until his death in 1980. Among the many spectacular projects of this period, the most outstanding was a City Hall for California City (1966), a tension structure whose roof supported on cables was to have a 500-foot clear span. In later years he was a much sought after lecturer in schools of architecture in the United States and Europe.

REGINALD MALCOLMSON

WORKS

1926, Prefabricated Hotel, Curacao, West Indies. 1927, Prefabricated Tennis Court Pavilion, Berlin. 1928, Albert Einstein Country House, Caputh, near Potsdam,

Germany. 1936, Office Building and Recreational Complex, Rome. 1942, General Panel Corporation Building System (with Walter Gropius), California. 1945–1947, Factory, Burbank, Calif. 1948, Marshall House, 6643 Lindenhurst, Los Angeles. 1966, City Hall, California City.

BIBLIOGRAPHY

WACHSMANN, KONRAD (1959)1961 *The Turning Point in Building.* Translated by Thomas E. Burton. New York: Reinhold.

WAGHEMAKERE FAMILY

Herman (c.1430–1503) and his son Domien (c.1460–1542) de Waghemakere dominated architectural production in Antwerp, Belgium, from 1473, when Herman was appointed Master of Works of Antwerp Cathedral, until Domien's death in 1542. Herman's most important work was the Church of Saint Jakob, Antwerp (begun 1491). Domien, trained by his father, followed him as Master of Works of Antwerp Cathedral and of Saint Jakob, and also served as town architect of Antwerp. From about 1514 to 1531, he worked in collaboration with Rombout II Keldermans (see KELDERMANS FAMILY).

ELIZABETH SCHWARTZBAUM

WORKS

HERMAN DE WAGHEMAKERE

1473–1485, Saint Gommarius (ambulatory, choir, and Chapel of Our Lady), Lier, Belgium. 1473–1503, Cathedral of Our Lady (Chapel of Holy Circumcision, north tower to second gallery, and completed the nave and north aisle), Antwerp, Belgium. 1482–1487, Saint Willibrord, Hulst, Netherlands. 1491–1502, Saint Jakob (completed by Domien de Waghemakere); 1501, Fleischhaus (completed by Domien de Waghemakere); Antwerp, Belgium.

DOMIEN DE WAGHEMAKERE

1494, Saint Gommarius, Lier, Belgium. 1502–1542, Cathedral of Our Lady (completed north tower with spire and restored the building after the fire of 1533); 1502–1542, Saint Jakob (completed); Antwerp, Belgium. 1514–1523, Maison du Roi (with Rombout Keldermans II), Brussels. 1517–1533, Town Hall (unfinished: with Rombout Keldermans II), Ghent, Belgium. 1521, The Steen (with Rombout Keldermans II); 1531, New Stock Exchange (with Rombout Keldermans II); Antwerp, Belgium.

BIBLIOGRAPHY

BOCK, HENNING 1972 "Architektur: Niederlande, Deutschland, Frankreich, England, Skandinavien." Pages 339–370 in Jan Bialostocki (editor), *Spätmittelalter und beginnende Neuzeit.* Berlin: Propyläen.

DONNET, E., and VAN CAUWENBERGH, E. 1931 *Sint Gommariuskerk te Lier.* Lier, Belgium.

LEEMANS, HERTHE 1972 *De Sint-Gummariuskerk te Lier.* Antwerpen-Utrecht: De Nederlandsche Boekhandlung.

MANIKOWSKY, F. VON 1909 "Die Architektenfamilie De Waghemakere in Antwerpen." *Deutsche Kunst und Denkmalpflege* 2, no. 11:81–84.

VAN BRABANT, J. (1972)1977 *De Onze-Lieve-Vrouwkathedraal van Antwerpen.* 2d ed. Antwerp, Belgium: Vlaamse Toeristen-bond.

WAGNER, MARTIN

Martin Wagner (1885–1957) was a city planner with a special interest in low-cost housing. His already strong social orientation was encouraged by a series of lectures given (c.1906) by philosopher-sociologist Georg Simmel at the Berlin University. WALTER GROPIUS accompanied Wagner to these lectures, later noting that Simmel's philosophy influenced their lives and careers thereafter. Wagner received degrees in City Planning from the Institute of Technology in Dresden (1912) and from the Technische Hochschule in Berlin (1915). During the period 1910–1916, he was associated as Stadtbaurat with the planning and building departments of several German cities. After serving as a private in World War I, during which he was awarded the Iron Cross for bravery, he returned to city planning, working primarily in Berlin.

According to ERNST MAY, Wagner was a confirmed socialist; he wanted to create building organizations which would make housing available to all, and from 1920 to 1926 he was active in organizing the German Building Guild (*Baugewerkschaft*) and building cooperatives (*Bauhüttenbewegung*). Seeking to reduce construction costs through rational methods, a necessity for low-income housing in depressed postwar Germany, he introduced such modern building techniques as prefabricated slab construction. During this period, Wagner founded the periodical *Wohnungswirtschaft* to promulgate such ideas as would contribute to low-cost housing.

In 1926, Wagner became head of Berlin's building department; he cooperated with prominent architects in the designs of housing developments, office buildings, baths, exhibition pavilions, and other works integrated with his plans for Berlin. Though vilified by the press as a red architect, Wagner was recognized in 1931 by election to the Prussian Academy of Arts.

He was an organizer of *Der Ring,* whose purpose was the improvement of the architectural profession. It was this association, together with his activities as a member of the *Werkbund* Board, his responsible city office, and his outspoken views, that led to Wagner being particularly vulnerable to attack. When Hitler ordered the reorganization of the *Werkbund* in March 1933, Wagner and Gropius immediately resigned from its board, and a few months later Wagner was expelled from membership, losing his city position as well.

Wagner departed Germany for Turkey, where from 1935 to 1938 he was counselor and professor of city planning at the Academy of Arts in Istanbul. In 1938, on the recommendation of Gropius, he was invited to Harvard University, where he taught regional planning for twelve years, retiring as emeritus professor in 1950.

Wagner's rich and varied experience was appreciated by his students; his contributions to professional journals were widely read. These were among the first articles from United States planners to be published in postwar Germany. In his later years, he attacked everything which seemed to him not progressive enough both in Germany and in the United States, even if it imperiled personal friendships with alumni, colleagues, and others; nevertheless, none would deny his lifelong integrity. In the end, he was very bitter, feeling that he was prevented from greater involvement. His writing became his only outlet.

REGINALD R. ISAACS

WORKS

1918–1919, Lindenhof Siedlung, Schönberg, Germany. 1925–1931, Gross-Siedlung Britz (with BRUNO TAUT); 1926, Forest Development (with Taut), Zehlendorf; 1927, Siemensstadt (with HUGO HÄRING, OTTO BARTNING, HANS SCHAROUN, and Walter Gropius); Berlin. 1927, Exhibition Buildings (with Haring), Witzleben, Ministergarten, Germany. 1927, Police Administration Building (with others); 1929, Casino am Funkturm; Charlottenburg, Germany. 1929, Columbus House (with ERICH MENDELSOHN); 1930, Strandbad Wannsee; Wandseebadweg, Berlin. 1931, Alexanderplatz (with Mendelsohn); 1932, Wachsende Haus Exhibition; Berlin.

BIBLIOGRAPHY

WAGNER, MARTIN 1915 *Städtische Freiflächenpolitik.* Berlin: Heymann.

WAGNER, MARTIN 1918 *Neu Bauwirtschaft.* Berlin: Heymann.

WAGNER, MARTIN 1923 *Alte oder Neue Bauwirtschaft.* Berlin: Vörwarts-Buchdruckerei.

WAGNER, MARTIN 1925 *Amerikanische Bauwirtschaft.* Berlin: Vörwarts-Buchdruckerei.

WAGNER, MARTIN 1929 *Städtebaulichen Probleme in Amerikanischen Städten.* Berlin: Deutsche Bauzeitung.

WAGNER, MARTIN 1932 *Das Wachsende Haus.* Berlin: Bong.

WAGNER, MARTIN 1932 "Zur Ökonomie von Städtebau und Bauwirtschaft." In Siegfried von Kardorff (editor), *Der internationale Kapitalismus und die Krise.* Stuttgart, Germany: Enke.

WAGNER, MARTIN 1946 "American Versus German City Planning." *Journal of Land and Public Utility Economics* 22, no. 4:321–338.

WAGNER, MARTIN 1956 "Karl Friedrich Schinkel." *Bauwelt* 56, May 3:476–477, May 10:514–515.

WAGNER, MARTIN, and ALTMANN, HANS 1931 "Das Bauwesen im Neuen Gesetz Gross-Berlin." *Die Baugilde* 13, no. 5:377–383.

WAGNER, MARTIN, and HÄRING, HUGO 1929 "Der Platz der Republik." In Martin Wagner (editor), *Das neue Berlin,* Berlin: Deutsche Bauzeitung.

WAGNER, MARTIN, and HILBERSEIMER, LUDWIG 1929 "Das Form-problem eines Weltstadtplatzes." In Martin Wagner (editor), *Das neue Berlin.* Berlin: Deutsche Bauzeitung.

WAGNER, OTTO

Otto Wagner (1841–1918) accomplished in his life's work the passage from nineteenth-century historical "style architecture" to a new building art conceived for the modern metropolis. His work falls into three periods: (1) building largely speculative apartment houses for Vienna's great Ringstrasse development (1870–1895); (2) developing, under the combined impact of urban engineering and Art Nouveau aesthetics, an architecture to meet the practical and psychological requirements of the modern megalopolis (1895–1905); and (3) constructing and projecting, in a radically rationalistic urban style, buildings—commercial, residential, and monumental—deliberately conceived for businesslike, "de-historicized," modern man (1905–1915).

Wagner complemented his architectural activity with theoretical and practical works on city planning, with the teaching of architecture in a reformed spirit to meet modern conditions, and with vigorous political and entrepreneurial activity to promote the cause of modern art as a vital constituent of contemporary urban civilization. Wagner's interlocking activities mark him as one of the most effective and comprehensive formulators of the role of the building arts for the twentieth century, reflecting the economic interests and psychological needs of the political and economic elite.

Wagner was born into that elite. He came of a family of wealthy bourgeois bureaucrats. His vigorous, early widowed "idolized and revered mama," Wagner recalled, imbued him with the values of her class: "to strive for independence, money, and then again money, as the means thereto. . . . A remarkable philosophy, but the only right one," which, as she predicted, enabled

her son "to live by his own ideas" (Oswald, 1943, p. 24).

After a solid preparatory education in Vienna's Akademisches Gymnasium and the prestigious Kremsmünster boarding school, Wagner received architectural training at both the Vienna Polytechnic School (1857–1859) and the Academy of Fine Arts (1861–1863). An intervening year of study at the Royal Building Academy in Berlin with the successors of KARL FRIEDRICH SCHINKEL permanently stamped his style with an astringent classicism foreign to the weighty historicism favored by his Viennese teachers and contemporaries. At the Academy in Vienna, Wagner fell under the spell of two teachers, both major architects, who together designed Vienna's Opera House: August von SICCARDSBURG AND Eduard VAN DER NÜLL. Wagner attributed to the first of these his appreciation of utility; to the second, his refined skill in drawing.

When Wagner embarked upon his architectural career in the late 1860s, the boom that accompanied the development of the Ringstrasse, Vienna's great complex of public and private buildings for the newly ascendant liberal bourgeoisie, was at its height. For a quarter-century, Wagner worked energetically as a speculative architectural entrepreneur, building a whole series of relatively luxurious apartment houses. His "free Renaissance" style in their execution gave little reason to suspect in Wagner a modernist in the making. Although he received few commissions for public buildings in this period, Wagner showed in his many projects how fully he shared the spirit of massive monumentality that reigned on the Ringstrasse. Thus, Wagner's *Artibus* project of 1880, a utopian city of cultural institutions, outdid in its fantasy of gargantuan glory even the ambitious neobaroque of the Ringstrasse's imposing complex of theaters and museums.

Not until the 1890s, when he was already in his fifties, did Wagner emerge as a functional theorist and pioneer of modern urban architecture. The first step in his transformation came through involvement in city planning and in the building of Vienna's municipal railway system, which sensitized him to transportation and engineering as fundamental factors in modern urban construction. The second step was Wagner's identification with Vienna's Secession movement in the plastic arts. Its Art Nouveau aesthetic idiom, with its stress on dynamic line and two-dimensionality, gave Wagner a language admirably suited to his radical simplification of architectural forms.

As chief architect of the municipal railway, Wagner came to espouse a polycentric solution to the problem of the modern megalopolis. He designed more than thirty stations, conceiving each as a focal point of public life and movement for its neighborhood, somewhat as a parish church and market square might have been in an earlier age. Usually of a simple, subdued elegance, his stations were attuned to the prevailing character of the

built environment. Although the stations remained basically historical in style, Wagner allowed the new materials he employed in them—iron and glass—to show forth their aesthetic properties. Yet, even in his bridges, tunnels, and dams, Wagner in the 1890s tempered his radical structural, iron-and-concrete aesthetic by embellishing it with ornamental swags, wreaths, and stonework. To modern eyes, these pioneering works are marked by a persistent dissonance between a functional ethic and an aesthetic of embellishment.

Wagner's involvement in such public utility projects affected his outer career no less than his inner conception of architecture. In 1894, the Austrian Academy of Fine Arts had to fill one of its two most prestigious chairs—the one previously reserved for "a convinced representative of classical Renaissance." Its appointments committee chose Wagner—not for his three decades of masterful building in the Renaissance style, but for his ability "to bring the needs of modern life and the employment of modern building materials and construction into consonance with artistic demands" (Wagner, 1967, pp. 251–252).

With characteristic energy, Wagner took up his new role in architectural education in a new way. In a challenging textbook, *Modern Architecture* (1895), he assaulted the prevailing historical "style architecture." In the nineteenth century, he argued, the pace of social change had proceeded too swiftly for the development of style to match it; hence, the recourse to pre-existing styles that were unsuitable because they were devised to answer the needs of civilizations different from our own. Wagner called for the recognition of the primacy of function—his term for it was purpose (*Zweck*)—as the determinant of form. Modern man, as Wagner saw him, was energetic, rational, efficient, and urbane: a businesslike metropolitan bourgeois with little time, lots of money, and a taste for the monumental. Despite his strength, modern man's fast-moving world of time and motion bred in him a psychological weakness: a "painful uncertainty" about direction and a need for orientation in space. The architect must meet this problem, Wagner urged, by providing clearly defined lines of movement in everything he built.

The imperative to provide guidance to the city dweller affected Wagner's work at every level, from urban design, through building form, to domestic interior. It led him to consider the street as a primary determinant of building façades. Especially in an age where perspective on the street had become vehicular rather than pedestrian, Wagner maintained, the building façades should reinforce the trajectory of the street. Away, then, with the heavily ornamented and articulated fronts of Ring-strasse apartment houses, in favor of flat walls with flush window frames that would reflect in verticality the simplicity of the street as a contained horizontal plane. The building should add power to the street's unidirectional thrust rather than disturbing it by the assertion of its individual identity. The two-dimensional and linear forms favored by the painter Gustav Klimt, leader of the Secession—whom Wagner idolized as "the greatest artist who ever walked the earth"—offered Wagner an ornamental vocabulary consistent with his aspiration to create a flat, unindented façade. The motto inscribed by the Secession on its exhibition building expressed admirably the antihistorical side of Wagner's aesthetic outlook: "To the Age its Art; to Art its Freedom." But to it Wagner added, in affirmation of the principle of utility so central to his modern urbanism, a slogan earlier employed by GOTTFRIED SEMPER: *artis sola domina necessitas* (necessity is art's only mistress).

In 1898–1899, Wagner embodied, in a pair of adjacent buildings on the Linke Wienzeile, a threefold commitment that informed his new architectural ethos: to modern economic man; to the potentialities of new materials; and to the antihistorical aesthetic of Vienna's Secession. Like most apartment buildings of Vienna, Wagner's Wienzeile group consigned the ground floors to commercial uses. But whereas this business space had traditionally been governed by the residential style of the Renaissance palazzo model, Wagner treated his commercial ground story autonomously, with a front of iron and glass. Consonant with Wagner's sense of the primacy of the street, the lines of the ground stories are vigorously horizontal, while the upper stories present a flat surface of astonishing regularity compared to the then usual heavily articulated façades. Whereas utility proclaims its dominion below, beauty continues to assert, in the form of floral ornament, its claims to the residential portion above. The ornament is, to be sure, reduced from the usual three-dimensional stone and stucco embellishment to flat Art Nouveau wall painting or, at most, low-relief ceramic

Wagner.
Apartment House, Linke
Wienzeile.
Vienna.
1898–1899

appliqué. In the Wienzeile buildings, a tension between new utility below and new beauty above is evident, but the basis for their synthesis on the premise of a rational, street-reinforcing urban building that proclaims its functions in its façade had been achieved.

In one of his buildings most admired by posterity, the Postal Savings Bank Office (1904–1906, 1910–1912), Otto Wagner achieved the modern style, rich in material, lean in line, to which he had been aspiring for a decade. The architect made extensive use of a metal new to building, aluminum, in ways that exploited both its structural properties and its aesthetic values. The floors of this large office block—a new building type for Austria—were of reinforced concrete. Interior communication—stairways and corridors—were visually reinforced by painted or inlaid lines to orient the user. Exterior marble plaques with aluminum-studded bolts sheathed the building's exterior and much of its interior, enhancing the light, tectonic effect that Wagner achieved through a free interplay between rational structure and geometric ornament. Finally, Wagner designed the furniture in the spirit of the whole to make of the Postal Savings Office a commercial-bureaucratic *Gesamtkunstwerk*.

After this important work, Wagner turned again to residential building, appropriating to it the stripped, rational style he had perfected for the office block. In the Wienzeile apartments, he had scored a partial breakthrough of utilitarian forms into the conventionally dominant residential style of Vienna's multistoried buildings. In 1909–1910, in Neustiftgasse 40, Wagner resolved the resultant stylistic tension by imposing the office style on the home. The modular windows, sill-less and equal, suggest the uniform cellular space of a commercial building. Gone is all adventitious ornament, whether of Victorian sculpting or Art Nouveau painting. Geometry reigns supreme, on the surface as in the structure, in the residential stories above as in the commercial space below. Business sets the tone; the Renaissance residential palace on whose model Wagner and his erstwhile peers had built on the Ringstrasse has nearly reached its end.

In Wagner's thought, as well as in his practice, architecture and the city were always interrelated. When his ideas changed in one area, new viewpoints surfaced in the other. Thus it was that in 1910, after achieving his mature modern building style, Wagner turned once more to the problems of urban form. His ideas found expression in *Die Grosstadt (The Metropolis)*, a theoretical work, half-practical, half-utopian in character.

As in architecture, so in urban planning, Wagner believed that art "must . . . adapt the city's image to contemporary man." Wagner had no doubt that the modern economy made infinite urban growth inevitable; moreover, to him the values of modern men made it positively desirable. "Making a living, social position, comfort, luxury, the presence of intellectual and physical facilities; entertainment in the good and bad sense, and finally art motivate this phenomenon" (Wagner, 1911, pp. 3, 7).

The only solution for accommodating the urban millions was the great housing block. "Our democratic essence, which is forced upon us by the demand for cheap and healthy housing and the imposed economy of our life-style, has the uniformity of our dwelling houses as its consequence." The way to meet the problem thus created was "to raise uniformity into mon-

Wagner.
Postal Savings Bank Office.
Vienna.
1904–1906, 1910–1912

Wagner.
View of the Air Center of the Future Twenty-second District of Vienna, from Die Grosstadt.
1910

umentality" (Wagner, 1911, p. 3). By regulating the height of the houses, leaving them free of disturbing surface ornament, and placing them in massive but dynamic array, the houses would raise the street itself to monumentality.

To make the infinitely expansible city viable and livable, however, Wagner proposed a polycentric solution in urban form. Using Vienna as his model, he proposed that all new city districts be developed in relative autonomy, as modular subcities of 100,000 to 150,000 people. Each would make it possible for the inhabitants to work and to reside within a reasonable radius. Each apartment housing block would abut upon a green square, and each subcity as a whole would have a highly formal "air center" where its public buildings would be located. As in his first city plan of 1893, Wagner projected radial arteries and circular belts of rail and road to determine the direction of growth, yet to contain it in a single communications net. In *The Metropolis,* Wagner evoked once more the monumental spirit of the *Artibus* project of 1880. Now, however, he vested monumentality not in museums, as he had done as a child of the Ringstrasse era and its worship of historical high culture, but in the efficient, modern, urban fabric itself, its uniform streets and its housing blocks. Through these, Wagner celebrated the cause he served so devotedly as architectural pioneer: the rational organization of the city for commerce and consumption, for the getting and the spending that he viewed as fundamental to the life of modern man.

CARL E. SCHORSKE

WORKS

1869, Apartment House, 4 Bellariastrasse; 1877, Apartment House, 23 Schottenring; 1880–1881, Apartment House, 3 Rathausstrasse; 1882–1883, Apartment House, 6–8 Stadiongasse; 1883–1884, Länderbank; 1886–1888, First Villa Wagner, 26 Hüttelbergstrasse; 1888, Apartment House, 12 Universitätsstrasse; 1890, Palais Wagner, 3 Renweg; 1894–1901, Stations and other works, Vienna Municipal Railway; 1894–1898, Nussdorf Dam; 1895, Anker Building am Graben; 1895, Neumann Department Store, Kärntnerstrasse; 1898–1899, Apartment Houses, 38–40 Linke Wienzeile; 1898–1904, Quayside Installations, Danube Canal; 1902, Die Zeit Telegraph Office; 1904–1906, 1910–1912, Postal Savings Bank Office (first and second stages); 1905–1907, Church am Steinhof; 1909–1910, Apartment House, 40 Neustiftgasse; 1910–1913, Lupus Sanatorium; 1912, Apartment House, 4 Döblergasse; 1912–1913, Second Villa Wagner, 28 Hüttelbergstrasse; Vienna.

BIBLIOGRAPHY

GERESTSEGGER, HEINZ, and PEINTNER, MAX (1964)1979 *Otto Wagner, 1841–1918: The Expanding City and the Beginning of Modern Architecture.* New York: Rizzoli.

GIUSTI BÀCULO, ADRIANA 1970 *Otto Wagner: Dall'architettura di stile allo stile utile.* Naples: Edizioni scientifiche italiane.

LUX, J. A. 1914 *Otto Wagner: Eine Monographie.* Munich: Delphin.

OSTWALD, HANS 1948 *Otto Wagner: Ein Beitrag zum Verständnis seines baukünstlerischen Schaffens.* Germany: Verlag Buchdr. Baden.

WAGNER, OTTO 1892–1922 *Einige Skizzen: Projekte und ausgeführte Bauwerke.* 4 vols. Vienna: Schroll.

WAGNER, OTTO (1895)1914 *Die Baukunst unserer Zeit.* 4th ed. Vienna: Schroll. Originally published with the title *Moderne Architektur.*

WAGNER, OTTO 1911 *Die Groszstadt: Eine Studie über diese.* Vienna: Schroll.

Wagnerschule: Projekte, Studien und Skizzen aus der Spezialschule für Architektur des Oberbaurats Otto Wagner, 1902–1907. 1910 Leipzig: Baumgärtners.

WAGNER, WALTER 1967 *Die Geschichte der Akademie der Bildenden Künste in Wien.* Vienna: Rosenbaum.

WAHLMAN, LARS

Lars Israel Wahlman (1870–1952) is little known outside Sweden, yet his work embodied some of the most innovative ideas of his time, and he acted as a mentor to the architects of his own country for more than half a century. Wahlman was born in Hedemora, in the Dalecarlia district of Sweden, studied at the Royal Institute of Technology, principally with I. G. CLASON, joined the teaching staff there in 1895, and was professor of building science at the Institute from 1912 until his retirement in 1935. He traveled extensively (France and England, 1900; Netherlands and England, 1905; United States, 1924; Denmark, frequently throughout his career) and brought together in his buildings elements of the work of WILLIAM MORRIS, RICHARD NORMAN SHAW, MARTIN NYROP, H. P. BERLAGE, and H. H. RICHARDSON. Like some contemporary continental architects, Wahlman sought to find in primitive and rural architecture the models for a new style which would embrace all the arts, and which would give a new expression to national culture. But although Wahlman was greatly admired by Swedish National Romantics such as RAGNAR ÖSTBERG and CARL WESTMAN, he stood apart from any single movement, and his work remained strikingly original.

Wahlman specialized in villas and in churches, and he came to be regarded as the foremost church architect in Sweden. The villas, for which he preferred exceptionally dramatic sites, often employed rough timber construction, with the unfinished log face showing on the exterior. On the interior, plans were open and functional, and the decorative features (friezes, wood carving, elaborate leaded glass) were closely related to continental Art Nouveau work. Wahlman took part in all aspects of the building process, himself designing the furniture, hardware, tableware, and other kinds of implements.

Of Wahlman's churches, the best known is the Engelbrekt's Parish Church in Stockholm (designed 1906, constructed 1909–1914). The church is faced with rich dark red brick, decorated with touches of pink granite and red sandstone. On the windows and porches there are heavy carved stone columns reminiscent of Viking or Anglo-Saxon art. Crowned by a steep red tile roof which is edged in green copper, its building masses organized around a commanding tower, and set upon a hill whose slopes are terraced into steps and walls with detailing similar to the main building, the Engelbrekt's Church is one of Stockholm's most impressive monuments. The cavernous interior, spanned by paraboloid arches of roughly grooved granite, contains furnishings and fittings which evoke a distant medieval past; these too were designed by Wahlman.

The Engelbrekt's Church also reflects Wahlman's consistent desire to integrate the building into its environment. At his urging, a surrounding district of houses was designed to repeat materials and motifs from the church, so that the central area of the parish came to have the appearance of an integrated architectural whole. Wahlman always took an extensive interest in site planning, and he was one of the first modern Swedish architects to become a major landscape designer in his own right. In his later years, Wahlman was in almost as much demand as a garden designer as he was as an architect.

BARBARA MILLER LANE

WORKS

1894–1897, Hjularöd Castle, Scania, Sweden. 1900–1901, Wahlman House, Hedemora, Sweden. 1900–1902, Community Center, Tjolöholm Village; 1900–1904, Tjolöholm Castle; Halland, Sweden. 1901, Town Hall (restoration), Hedemora, Sweden. 1901–1907, Villa Cedergren, Stocksund, near Stockholm. 1902–1904, Villa Widmark, Lysekil, Sweden. 1903–1904, Villa Arvid Johansson, Sandviken, Sweden. 1903–1907, Yngstrom Residence (Norhaga), near Falun, Sweden. 1904–1905, Grand Hotel (club room), Stockholm. 1904–1906, Tallom (Lars Wahlman residence), Stocksund, near Stockholm. 1906, Memorial Chapel, Lützen, Germany. 1906–1907, Villa Lindström; 1907–1909, Villa von Greyerz; Stocksund, near Stockholm. 1908–1909, Villa Björkeberga, Djursholm, Sweden. 1908–1911, Villa Lyth, Lindingö, Sweden. 1909–1914, Engelbrekt's Parish Church, Stockholm. 1910–1911, Rott-

neby Manor Garden, Korsnäs, Sweden. 1913–1915, Djursholm Cemetery, Sweden. 1914–1917, Slottsskogen Arena, Göteborg, Sweden. 1915–1920, Cemetery and Chapel, Stora Skedvi, Dalecartia, Sweden. 1918–1921, Steneberg Park, Gavlë, Sweden. 1918–1923, Torpa Manor (restoration) and Garden, Västergotland, Sweden. 1921–1922, Göteborg Botanical Garden, Sweden. 1921–1923, Rättvik Cemetery, Sweden. 1921–1931, Church, Sandviken, Sweden. 1923–1924, Villa Aspnäs, Upland, Sweden. 1923–1926, Margaret's Church, Oslo. 1925–1929, Church, Nynäshamn, Sweden. 1927–1930, Saint Ansgar's Chapel, Björkö Island, Lake Mälaren, Sweden. 1928–1930, Church, Tranås, Sweden. 1931–1932, Synagogue (restoration); 1932, Oscar's Parish House; Stockholm. 1933–1934, Crematorium Chapel, Sandviken, Sweden. 1935–1940, Church, Östersund, Sweden. 1942–?, Mörby Chapel, Stocksund, Sweden. 1943–?, Crematorium Chapel, Jönköping, Sweden.

BIBLIOGRAPHY

AHLBERG, HAKON 1925 Moderne Schwedische Architektur. Berlin: Wasmuth.
ANDERSSON, HENRIK O., and BEDOIRE, FREDRIC (1973)1977 Stockholms Byggnader. Rev. ed. Stockholm: Bokförlaget Prisma.
The International Studio. 1908 34:330–334.
LIND, SVEN IVAR; ROMANS, BENGT; and STERNER, NILS 1950 Verk av L. I. Wahlman. Stockholm: Byggmästaren.
SEELING, HEINRICH 1923 "Reiseeindrücke aus Stockholm vom Schluss des Jahres 1922." Deutsche Bauzeitung 57, no. 28:133–136.

WALKER, C. HOWARD

Born and educated in Boston, C. Howard Walker (1857–1936) trained in the office of Sturgis and Brigham. In 1884, Walker set up on his own in Boston as Walker and Kimball. However, Walker was primarily known as a professor of the fine arts at the Massachusetts Institute of Technology, Harvard College, and the Child-Walker School of Fine Arts, of which he was a founder, rather than as a practicing architect. He was also an editor of the Boston Architectural Review.

MOSETTE GLASER BRODERICK

WORKS

1889, Tenement, 78–86 East Canton Street; 1897, Charles Rollins House, 497 Commonwealth Avenue; Boston. 1914, Carnegie Public Library, Sharon, Mass. 1916, High School of Commerce (with Kilham and Hopkins); 1918, Ditson Building (with Townsend, Steinle, and Haskell), 178 Tremont Street; n.d., British Consulate, State Street; n.d., Washington Irving High School; Boston.

BIBLIOGRAPHY

The sketchbooks (1870–1924) of C. Howard Walker can be

found in the Archives of American Art, Washington.

EMERSON, WILLIAM 1936 "C. Howard Walker, 1857–1936: An appreciation." *American Architect* 148:109.

SHELDON, GEORGE 1886–1887 *Artistic Country-Seats.* New York: Appleton.

WALKER, C. HOWARD 1898 "The Great Exposition at Omaha." *Century* 55:518–521.

WALKER, C. HOWARD 1904 "Louisiana Purchase Exposition at St. Louis, Missouri." *Architectural Review* 11:197–220.

WALKER, C. HOWARD 1915 *Parish Churches of England.* Boston: Rogers.

WALKER, C. HOWARD 1918 *An Architectural Monograph on Some Old Houses on the Southern Coast of Maine.* Saint Paul, Minn.: White Pine Bureau.

WALKER, C. HOWARD (1899–1900)1926 *The Theory of Mouldings.* Cleveland, Ohio: Jansen.

WALKER, RALPH THOMAS

From the 1920s through the 1950s, Ralph Thomas Walker (1889–1973) was one of America's most prominent, prosperous, and prolific architects. A leader in professional circles, he served on many national and international committees, published regularly, and received numerous honors. In 1957, the American Institute of Architects saluted their former president (1949–1951) as "the architect of the century." Yet, Walker's reputation has since faded, due in part to the moderatism of his modernism.

Walker's architectural education consisted of almost three years' apprenticeship, two years at Massachusetts Institute of Technology (1909–1911), and two in the Montreal atelier of Francis Swales. He worked for James Ritchie in Boston from 1913 to 1916 when he won the coveted Rotch Traveling Scholarship. Precluded from Europe by the war, he moved to New York, working briefly for several large firms. In 1919, he joined the office of MCKENZIE, VOORHEES, AND GMELIN, which in 1926 became Voorhees, Gmelin, and Walker, and after 1939, Voorhees, Walker, Foley, and Smith.

In the 1920s, Walker won recognition as a leading proponent and designer of Art Deco skyscrapers; among his most acclaimed projects were the Barclay-Vesey Telephone Building (1923–1926) and the Irving Trust Building (1929–1932), both in New York. He also pioneered in the design of modern laboratory and research centers, and after World War II his firm produced hundreds of such facilities for large corporate clients across the United States and abroad.

CAROL WILLIS

WORKS

1923–1926, Barclay-Vesey Telephone Building; 1928–1929, Western Union Building; 1929–1932, Irving Trust Building, 1 Wall Street; New York. 1937–1949, Bell Telephone Laboratories, Murray Hill, N.J. *1939, Eight Exhibition Buildings (including those for General Electric, Borden, and the Petroleum Industries), New York World's Fair. 1946–1949, Hayden Memorial Library, Massachusetts Institute of Technology, Cambridge, Mass. 1952, Argonne National Laboratories, Chicago. 1956, AFL-CIO Building, Washington.

BIBLIOGRAPHY

BOSSERMAN, JOSEPH NORWOOD (compiler) 1968 *Ralph Walker Bibliography.* Charlottesville, Va.: American Association of Architectural Bibliographers.

Ralph Walker: Architect. 1957 New York: Henahan House.

SWALES, FRANCIS 1930 "Draftsmanship and Architecture as Exemplified in the Work of Ralph T. Walker." *Pencil Points* 11, no. 8:609–622.

WALKER, RALPH 1957 *A Fly in the Amber.* New York: Aldus.

WALLACE, WILLIAM

William Wallace (?–1631) was a leading Edinburgh carver and master mason and an important figure in the dissemination of the Anglo-Flemish style of architectural decoration in Scotland following the Union of the Crowns. He held the post of King's master mason from 1617 until his death and in this capacity was employed in the erection of the King's Lodging, Edinburgh Castle (1615–1617), and the north quarter of Linlithgow Palace (1618–1621). He also undertook private commissions, including at least two major houses in and around Edinburgh, a number of churchyard monuments and Heriot's Hospital, Edinburgh (1628–1659), his best known work.

JOHN G. DUNBAR

WORKS

1615–1617, Edinburgh Castle (King's Lodging). 1618–1621, Linlithgow Palace (north quarter), West Lothian, Scotland. c.1620–1630, Moray House, Edinburgh. c.1620–1630, Winton House, East Lothian, Scotland. 1628–1659, Heriot's Hospital, Edinburgh.

BIBLIOGRAPHY

DUNBAR, JOHN G. 1966 *The Historic Architecture of Scotland.* London: Batsford.

MACGIBBON, D., and ROSS, T. 1887–1892 *The Castellated and Domestic Architecture of Scotland.* Edinburgh: David Douglas.

MYLNE, ROBERT S. 1893 *The Master Masons to the Crown of Scotland.* Edinburgh: Scott & Ferguson, Burness.

WALLANDER, SVEN

Sven Wallander (1890–1968) attended the Royal Academy of Arts in Stockholm, Sweden. In 1915, he made a proposal for a new main street in Stockholm, the Kungsgatan. This town plan, ratified in 1919, showed a curved street with uniform buildings in a kind of classicist-expressionistic manner, with two 17-story towers as a central theme. As the architect of several of the buildings on Kungsgatan in the 1920s, he used a mannerist classical architecture. Wallander became widely known as a manager and architect of the National Association of Tenants' Savings and Buildings Societies, founded in 1923. He worked in order to create more comfortable dwellings for workers and to develop more rational building principles such as standardization; an invention he used very early was the garbage chute. In the 1920s, his classical style gave way to plans of big open blocks, such as Kvarteret Metern on Södermalm in Stockholm. Among Wallander's later well-known works are the apartment buildings on Reimersholme in Stockholm (1942–1946) with the Hungarian architect Fred Forbat as collaborator.

FREDRIC BEDOIRE

BIBLIOGRAPHY

ANDERSSON, HENRIK O., and BEDOIRE, FREDRIC (1973)1977 *Stockholms byggnader.* 3d ed. Stockholm: Prisma.
HOLM, LENNART (editor) 1954 *Hyresgästernas Sparkasse—och Byggnadsföreningars Riksförbund.* Stockholm: HSB.
LINN, BJÖRN 1974 *Storgårdskvarteret.* Stockholm: Byggtjänst.
WALLANDER, SVEN 1968 *Mitt liv med HSB.* Stockholm: Wahlström & Widstrand.

WALLOT, PAUL

A student of RICHARD LUCAE and MARTIN GROPIUS, Paul Wallot (1841–1912) was initially a builder of houses in Frankfurt am Main. The German Reichstag, which he built in Berlin from 1884–1894, brought him fame, a teaching position at the Art Academy in Dresden, and many students, including Adolf Abel and HEINRICH STRÄUMER.

BARBARA MILLER LANE

WORKS

1877, House; 1881?, Exhibition Buildings; 1882?, Store, Offices, and Residence; Frankfurt am Main. 1884–1894, Reichstag (destroyed in 1933 and reconstructed in the 1970s); 1897–1904, Reichspräsidialgebäude; Berlin. 1901?, House, Darmstadt Artists' Colony, Germany. 1903, President of the Reichstag's Residence, Berlin. 1901–1907, Ständehaus (later Landtag), Dresden, Germany.

BIBLIOGRAPHY

MACKOWSKY, W. 1912 *Paul Wallot und seine Schüler.* Berlin: Wasmuth.
"Das neue Reichstagsgebäude." 1883 *Zentralblatt der Bauverwaltung* 3:63–66, 208–211, 383–386.
SCHLIEPMANN, H. 1913 *Paul Wallot.* Berlin: Wasmuth.
SCHMÄDECKE, JÜRGEN 1970 *Der Deutsche Reichstag.* Berlin: Hande & Spener.
SCHMITZ, HERMANN 1926 "Hauptströmungen der deutschen Architektur während der letzten sechzig Jahre." *Deutsche Bauzeitung* 60:3–16.

Walpole.
Strawberry Hill.
Twickenham, Middlesex,
England.
1747–1763

WALPOLE, HORACE

Horace Walpole (1717–1797) had had lessons in drawing from Bernard Lens and some slight architectural sketches survive from his hand, but he is principally remembered as the patron who employed JOHN CHUTE, Richard Bentley, JOHANN HEINRICH MÜNTZ, Thomas Pitt, ROBERT ADAM, and JAMES WYATT at various times in the building of his house, *Strawberry Hill,* Twickenham, Middlesex, England, the first major monument of the Gothic Revival in architecture. He popularized this manner of building by the publication in 1774 and 1778 of *A Description of the Villa of Horace Walpole at Strawberry Hill,* and it gained further currency through its close association with his widely read romance in the Gothic vein, *The Castle of Otranto,* first published in 1765.

Walpole was among the most prolific correspondents of the century and encouraged his friends and acquaintances in the study and practice of the Gothic style. But his influence went beyond that of establishing a fashionable trend in style in architecture. He made an effective contribution to the history of architecture in England by including accounts of the works of architects in his *Anecdotes of Painting in England,* published from 1762 to 1771, and he encouraged the study of genuine Gothic architecture in the researches of his friends Thomas Gray and JAMES ESSEX, the Cambridge architect who proposed to write a history of the style. He also applied antiquarian precedents to his own buildings, most successfully to the Chapel in the Woods at Strawberry Hill, built from 1768 to 1772. In its plan, Strawberry Hill also set a most important precedent for later domestic buildings in the Gothic Revival style. Walpole departed from the axial symmetry of the original house in his extensions of 1758 to 1761 when he added a battlemented wing of two stories which ended in a battlemented round tower of three stories. The resulting play of varied profiles and volumes in elevation and plan was central to the concept of the Picturesque in architecture in the subsequent century.

MICHAEL MCCARTHY

BIBLIOGRAPHY

CALLOWAY, S.; SNODIN, M.; and WAINWRIGHT, C. 1980 *Horace Walpole and Strawberry Hill.* London.
CROOK, J. MORDAUNT 1973 "Strawberry Hill Revisited." *Country Life* 153, no. 3963:1598–1602; no. 3964:1726–1730; no. 3965:1794–1797.
LEWIS, WILMARTH SHELDON 1934–1936 "The Genesis of Strawberry Hill." *Metropolitan Museum Studies* 5:57–92.
LEWIS, WILMARTH SHELDON 1960 *Horace Walpole.* New York: Pantheon.
LEWIS, WILMARTH SHELDON 1973 *A Guide to the Life of Horace Walpole.* New Haven: Yale University Press.

WALTER, THOMAS U.

Thomas Ustick Walter (1804–1887) was the grandson of Frederick Jacob Walter who arrived in Philadelphia in 1749 as a six-year-old orphan and was auctioned as a "German redemptioner." Having been apprenticed to a bricklayer, Frederick later became a partner of Jacob Graff (in whose house the Declaration of Independence was drafted) and, as a Revolutionary volunteer, participated in the legendary events at Valley Forge and Trenton. Three of his four sons also followed the building trade, including Joseph Saunders Walter (1782–1855) who married Deborah Wood of Philadelphia in 1803. Both Joseph and Deborah Walter had been baptized in the Schuylkill River by the Baptist pastor Thomas Ustick, after whom

they named the first-born of their seven children.

In the genealogical history of his family compiled in 1871, Walter stated that his early education was "liberal but not collegiate." His inclination toward the family trade led his father to take him as apprentice in bricklaying and stonemasonry from 1819 to 1824, the years in which the elder Walter and Daniel Groves were in charge of the construction of WILLIAM STRICKLAND's Second Bank of the United States, the nation's seminal project in the Greek Revival style. When the building was complete, young Walter married Mary Ann Elizabeth Hancocks of Philadelphia and joined his father in the construction business as a master bricklayer. His first known independently executed structure was a house for his own family built in 1827 on Race Street in Philadelphia. In the same year, Walter was also elected to membership in the Bricklayers' Company of the City and County of Philadelphia, founded in 1792. Between 1809 and 1842 the elder Walter was successively secretary of this organization, vice president, and president and frequently served as a member of the all-important measuring committee in which his son joined him in 1830 and 1833.

Meanwhile, young Walter had set his sights on the profession of architecture. While apprenticed to his father, he had attended a small private school operated by a retired sea-captain named David McClure to learn Euclidian geometry (1818–1819). He had also spent an unspecified amount of time in Strickland's office "as a student of Architecture" to acquire "the art of linear drawing" and "a general knowledge of the professional practice of Architects." When his apprenticeship was over in 1824, he began attending the School of Mechanic Arts (known as the Drawing School) opened that autumn by the newly founded Franklin Institute. The school was under the direction of JOHN HAVILAND, whose style Walter's later works recall more often than they do Strickland's. At the Institute, Walter studied mathematics, physics, architectural theory, and "the several branches of mechanical construction connected with building." In addition, he learned from William Mason the less scientific art of landscape painting in watercolor, a skill which made his later presentation perspectives singular works of art in themselves. By 1829, Walter was a member of the Franklin Institute, and he was named its professor of architecture in 1841. In that capacity, he prepared six lectures on the history and philosophy of architecture (of which the manuscript text survives) and published a number of short articles from time to time in the *Journal of the Franklin Institute*. In 1828, he had again associated himself with Strickland's office. He said that he was the architect's "pupil" for two years, but a surviving letter to him from Strickland reveals that he was still in the office as late as June, 1831, by which time he had begun to practice architecture in his own right. His first professional design, dated January 1, 1831, was for a Presbyterian Church in Louisville, Kentucky. Walter continued in the bricklayer's business with his father, however, probably as a hedge against the possibility of his failure in the architectural profession which was as yet neither generally understood nor fully accepted in America. His early designs, numbering some three dozen (though not all were executed), were of the simplest sort for the most part, and all bore the stamp of the master craftsman. They included a large number of houses, most notably the row called Portico Square (1831) still standing on Spruce Street between Ninth and Tenth Streets in Philadelphia, and a rope walk for the Philadelphia Navy Yard, his first United States Government commission. By far the most important achievement of his early career was the Philadelphia County Prison, called Moyamensing (1831–1835). Considerable attention was devoted to the heating, ventilation, and plumbing in the building, and Walter designed the water system in consultation with Frederick Graff, Jacob Graff's grandson, then in charge of the Philadelphia Water Works. The two cell blocks were designed according to the Auburn plan, the alternative in those days of penal reform to the cruel but much admired Pennsylvania plan elected for Haviland's Eastern State Penitentiary (1821–1836). Like that building, however, Moyamensing was conceived in the Gothic style. Highly romantic battlements, turrets, and pointed arches decorated an otherwise plain façade organized in the symmetrical, quasi-Palladian (see ANDREA PALLADIO) manner so common among craftsman-builders of the time. Simultaneously sophisticated and naïve, the prison brought Walter considerable local attention and gained him the respect and support of the civic and cultural leaders of Philadelphia.

It was doubtless this, in part, that won Walter

Walter.
Girard College for Orphans.
Philadelphia.
1833–1848

the first premium in the competition for the Girard College for Orphans (1833–1848), a professional triumph which brought him a national reputation and insured his final success as an architect. He turned over his place in his father's business to his brother Joseph (1807–1846), who was later to be one of Strickland's assistants in the planning of the new city of Cairo, Illinois. The College was a tour de force, whether viewed from the standpoint of practical structural engineering or from that of contemporary architectural aesthetics. When complete, it was also the last word in American Greek Revivalism and unquestionably its grandest monument. The main building, called Founder's Hall, was actually planned by Stephen Girard in his last will and testament: four fifty-foot-square vaulted classrooms and two vestibules on each of three floors. Built of brick (by Walter's father) reinforced with iron and clothed in marble, Walter's conception of the building was inspired by the Madeleine, not yet complete in Paris, although the Corinthian peristyle was taken from JAMES STUART and NICHOLAS REVETT's measured engravings of the Choragic Monument of Lysicrates in Athens. The evolution of the design brought Walter into close association with Nicholas Biddle, financial genius and arbiter of architectural taste. Shortly after the cornerstone of the College was laid on July 4, 1833, Walter also designed the extension of Biddle's country seat called Andalusia, which extension he surrounded on three sides by a copy in wood of the Doric peristyle of the Theseum (Hephaisteion) in Athens. Although the portico of Andalusia took the form of Biddle's favorite Greek temple and although Biddle was instrumental in bringing about the alteration of the original design for the College and seeing it through the debates of City Councils, it cannot be said that either building was more a reflection of Biddle's taste than of Walter's. In both projects, the old patron–builder relationship and the new client–architect one seems to have obtained simultaneously between the two men. Yet, it seems certain that Walter's association with Biddle constituted the last stage in his professional education, in which he added to his other accomplishments a mastery of contemporary values in aesthetic discrimination and that new sense of self-confidence which shines from the portrait of him made by John Neagle in 1835.

During the 1830s, Walter was keeping abreast of architectural developments in other American cities and in Europe. His growing library included works on Egyptian, Greek, Roman, and Gothic architecture, publications on mechanical theory (heating, ventilating, and so on), and all the issues of John C. Loudon's *Architectural Magazine*

(1834–1838) from London. In 1838, the building committee of Girard College sent him to Italy, France, England, and Ireland to observe the structural and stylistic character of some of those countries' major buildings. In particular, he was to study arrangements for stone roofs and for utilities in schools. The report of his findings on this journey, delivered to the authorities at the College in 1839, is a significant document in the history of American architectural theory and taste. At the same time, Walter's circle of professional acquaintances grew at home. In addition to Strickland and Haviland in Philadelphia, these included ITHIEL TOWN, ALEXANDER JACKSON DAVIS, JAMES DAKIN, and MINARD LAFEVER in New York, and ROBERT CARY LONG in Baltimore. To the last of these he first aired his idea for the creation of an "American Institute of Architects" on October 20, 1836, two years after the founding of the Royal Institute of British Architects in England. On November 2, he proposed the idea to his colleagues in New York who received it enthusiastically and joined in calling a convention of twenty-three architects to meet in New York on December 6. Only eleven responded, and, with Davis named as chairman and Walter as secretary, it was agreed to change the name of the new organization to the "American Institution of Architects." Walter was also prominent in composing the constitution and by-laws adopted in May, 1837. The Institution did not long survive, but it seems that Walter was the originator of the first professional organization for architects in the United States and invented the name of the present one. His efforts to advance the cause of professionalism in architecture also led him to lecture in communities in and around Philadelphia with the intent to educate the public in architectural history and taste. This practice he continued throughout his life and advocated to his colleagues on many occasions.

Walter rapidly gained the respect of the local scientific community as well, including such persons as Alexander Dallas Bache for whom he designed a magnetic observatory (1839) built in wood and entirely without hardware on the grounds of Girard College. From 1835, he was a member of the Academy of Natural Sciences of Philadelphia, and, from 1839, he numbered among the distinguished members of the American Philosophical Society. In 1840 and 1841, he also was among the diners of the elite Wistar Party, an association of brilliant minds who met weekly for simple suppers and illuminating conversation.

Walter's talents, training, and professional dedication; the prestige of his connection with Girard College; and his social, intellectual, scientific, and professional associations guaranteed suc-

cess. By 1843, he had designed more than two hundred projects, although not all were executed and many were constructed under supervision other than his. The projects included banks, a bridge, cemeteries and tombs, churches of most major Protestant denominations, factories, local government buildings, hospitals, houses, offices, railway depots, and stores. Many were in the prevailing Grecian style; several were Gothic and a few Egyptian, most notably the Debtors' Apartment at Moyamensing (1836) inspired by Haviland's New Jersey Penitentiary at Trenton (1833–1836); and a considerable number belonged to what can safely be called a vernacular style with little, if any, allusion to the historical styles at all. With only a few exceptions, such as the Matthew Newkirk House (1835) in Philadelphia, the budgets were always stringent. Whatever the style, therefore, Walter's designs were rarely academic, though he depended as much as any other architect of his time upon such guides as Stuart and Revett's *Antiquities of Athens*.

By 1841, Walter was among Philadelphia's new and well-to-do professional class. He lived in a mansion of his own design across from Matthew Newkirk's house on Arch Street, its basement sheathed in marble and its interior as lavish in Greek detail as that of Andalusia. However, in 1841, a series of personal disasters began. The short, local depression which followed upon the closing of the United States Bank in that year brought the architect to bankruptcy. He sold his house and many of his possessions, including the bulk of his architectural library. Although his fortunes were saved by the challenging commission obtained through the Dallett family of Philadelphia and its shipping interests to build a breakwater at La Guaira, Venezuela (1843–1845), the experience away from home was not to his liking. On this venture he took his eldest son, Joseph, who died (probably of typhoid fever) in Venezuela in June, 1844. The breakwater was never entirely a success, and, because of the insolvency of the Venezuelan government, Walter was never paid for the work even though no less a figure than the secretary of state, Daniel Webster, made earnest efforts in his behalf. Other losses of members of the family were climaxed by the death of Walter's wife in January, 1847, as the result of the birth of her last child. In mourning, Walter refrained from work for three days, a hardship in view of his energetic nature and his voluntary habit of working from early morning until at least midnight six days a week without holidays. Even Sundays were fully occupied in the activities of his religious life. Walter's religion was a major force in both his personal and his professional activities; it gave him equilibrium in the face of good fortune and ill and governed the ethics of his architectural practice. As a teacher at the Spruce Street Baptist Church, which he had built in 1829, he met Amanda Gardiner, whom he courted and married in 1848. His brother-in-law, Daniel Rice Gardiner, became one of his sons-in-law the following year.

Walter rapidly revived his architectural practice after his return to Philadelphia from Venezuela late in November 1845. His style having matured with his person, he easily assimilated new developments in American fashion. By this time, ANDREW JACKSON DOWNING had published his *Cottage Residences,* and Walter added the Italian villa to his repertory of styles. Two such buildings by him survive, both dating from 1851 and both considerably altered: *Glenelg* in Ellicott City, Maryland, and *Ingleside* in Washington. Walter continued in the other historical styles, however, the number of designs in the Gothic increasing and the number in Greek decreasing, as would be expected. His Gothic became more Puginesque (see A. W. N. PUGIN), although his innate Protestantism prevented his participation in the fullness of the revival represented by RICHARD UPJOHN and JAMES RENWICK. In his classical buildings, ornament became less dominant and more eclectic. Walter's attention concentrated more and more on the clarity of building masses. Two unexecuted projects—one for Saint George's Episcopal Church in New York (1846), the other for the façade of the Roman Catholic Cathedral of Saints Peter and Paul in Philadelphia (1850)—and the new front of the Spruce Street Baptist Church (constructed in 1851, after Walter's departure for Washington, by R. Morris Smith) verge on baroque monumentality. Walter also began to exploit further the architectural possibilities of cast iron during the 1840s, as, for example, in the sheathing of the Corinthian columns and capitals of the Chester County Court House in West Chester, Pennsylvania (1847), cast by Morris, Tasker, and Morris in Philadelphia. To further the production of tasteful architectural ornament by the iron and other industries, Walter collaborated with John Jay Smith, librarian of the Library Company of Philadelphia and the Loganian Library, in the production of two collections of patterns in 1846. These were the *Guide to Workers in Metal and Stone* and *Two Hundred Designs for Cottages and Villas,* both published in four volumes and neither containing more than a few designs by Walter himself. The chief significance of the two publications may lie in their having been among the first examples of anastatic printing (the forerunner of blueprinting) which Edgar Allen Poe pronounced the most momentous novelty of the age. In 1850, Walter was again the leading

architect in Philadelphia in spite of increasing professional competition in the city. During that year alone, he was responsible for no fewer than seventeen houses, four stores, twelve churches, five schools, two hotels, two county government projects, and other assorted commissions. He was also retained by Dr. David Jayne to complete the construction of the late WILLIAM L. JOHNSTON's design for the famous Jayne Building, 1849, which he enlarged both vertically and horizontally.

Walter presented his design for the extension of the United States Capitol on December 12, 1850, and was one of four winners of the competition announced on September 30 by the Senate Committee on Public Buildings chaired by Jefferson Davis. President Millard Fillmore disregarded the compromise design made at the Committee's request by ROBERT MILLS, and, acting in accordance with a bill passed by Congress on the day of the competition announcement, appointed Walter as designer and architect of the new wings of the Capitol. This displaced Mills, whose relation with Walter may be assumed to have been less than cordial since the latter's negative report of 1838 on the style and stability of the Treasury Building.

Walter moved to Washington in June 1851, and the cornerstone of the Capitol Extension was ceremoniously laid on July 4 of that year with an oration by Daniel Webster. The following Christmas Eve, the Library of Congress (then behind CHARLES BULFINCH's western colonnade) burned, and Walter reconstructed the central room entirely in cast iron during the following year, the flanking rooms being left unexecuted until required by the Library's expansion. In this and later work at the Capitol, especially the dome (1855–1865), he relied heavily on the able assistance of a German immigrant named August Gottlieb Schoenborn, who had been partially trained in architecture in his native country and hired as a draftsman by Walter shortly after his own arrival in Washington. Subject only to the authority of the secretary of the interior, Walter was in charge of the entire operation until early in 1853. As a result of imputed fraud among his superintendents, responsibility was transferred to the secretary of war. This was Jefferson Davis who appointed Capt. Montgomery C. Meigs as engineer in charge in March. Construction moved forward rapidly, and the old wooden dome was dismantled in 1855. Work began at once on the new cast-iron dome whose design was principally based upon that of A. A. Monferrand's Saint Isaac's Cathedral in Leningrad (completed 1857). In 1858, Meigs openly challenged Walter's authority as architect, and Secretary Floyd replaced Meigs with Capt. William B. Franklin. The onset of the Civil War put a stop to work for some nine months, during which responsibility for the Capitol Extension was returned to the Interior Department. By 1865, the Capitol was virtually complete, and work had begun again on the unfinished rooms of the Library of Congress. In May, James Harlan became the new secretary of the interior. Dedicated to economy, Harlan unilaterally canceled the cast iron contract for the Library and set the commissioner of public buildings, B. B. French, in authority over the architect. Walter resigned his post on May 31, retiring to Germantown, a suburb of Philadelphia where he had built a house in 1861. He fully expected to be recalled to Washington, but his hopes were dispelled in August when the post of architect of the Capitol was given to Edward Clark whom Walter had brought with him from Philadelphia in 1851. The government never paid Walter or his heirs any of his claims for services rendered in the design and construction of the extensions to the Treasury, Patent Office, and Post Office, the Hospital for the Insane (St. Elizabeth's), or the Marine Barracks in Brooklyn, New York (1858–1859), and Pensacola, Florida (1857), all executed during the enlargement of the Capitol.

Walter's work at the Capitol set the image and iconography of the American government building for a century to come and provided much needed impetus to the development of American architectural technology. In addition, it brought into focus the problem of architectural professionalism in the United States which Walter had already addressed in 1836. All of his major difficulties in Washington stemmed from the still ambivalent contemporary view of the architect. The problem was addressed again in 1857 by the founding of The American Institute of Architects in New York with Walter, its first vice president, in attendance. Unable to contribute much more than advice at first, Walter devoted much time to the organization in the years of his retirement. He was instrumental in the establishment of the Philadelphia Chapter (chartered 1872) after the decision of 1867 that the Institute should be a national organization rather than the local one it had become. In 1876, Walter followed Richard Upjohn as president of the A.I.A. and remained in that office until his death.

The investments which sustained Walter during his retirement began to decay with the general economy in 1869, and it became necessary for him to work again. Only one major work dates from the architect's later years: the Eutaw Place Baptist Church (1868–1870) in Baltimore for which he donated the design. He lost the competitions for the Baptist Home in Philadelphia (1872) and the new Library of Congress in Washington (1873),

Walter.
Capitol Dome.
Washington.
1855–1865

Walter.
United States Treasury
*   Building Extension.*
Washington.
1852

though both designs were accomplished in the popular style of the Second Empire in France. In 1873, he was forced to sell his splendid house in Germantown and move to more modest quarters in the city. He took a position that year in the office of the Wilson Brothers where he seems to have been little more than a draftsman in projects for suburban railroad stations. His prestige remained great, however, and he figured among the judges in the competitions for the Philadelphia City Hall and the Centennial Exposition. Finally, he was appointed second in command under JOHN MCARTHUR, the designer, in the supervision of the construction of the Philadelphia City Hall, so that much of the detail of that building may be ascribed to him. Though his authority in the building of the City Hall was considerable, he was referred to as a draftsman for the project in the Philadelphia newspapers when they reported his death in October, 1887.

It was said that Walter died very nearly a pauper. But he was genuinely mourned by his profession across the nation. No one had worked longer or harder for its confirmation as one of the most respected of professions in the United States. Such dedication combined with his authorship of the final design for the most symbolically significant building in the nation, the Capitol, made him the dean of American architects in the nineteenth century.

ROBERT B. ENNIS

WORKS

*1831, Bricklayer's Hall; 1831, Portico Square; 1831, Wills Hospital for the Blind and Lame; Philadelphia. 1831, Presbyterian Church, West Chester, Penn. *1831–1835, Philadelphia County Prison (Moyamensing). *1833, Amity Street Baptist Church, New York. 1833–1848, Girard College for Orphans, Philadelphia. *1834, Cohen's Bank, Baltimore. *1835, Matthew Newkirk House; *1835, Third Dutch Reformed Church; Philadelphia. *1836, Chester County Prison, West Chester Prison, Penn. *1836, Debtors' Apartment, Philadelphia County Prison (Moyamensing). *1837, Central High School, Reading, Penn. *1837, Merchant's and Mechanic's Bank, Wheeling, W. Va. *1838, James Dundas House, Philadelphia. 1838, Saint James Episcopal Church, Wilmington, N.C. 1839, Eleventh Baptist Church, Philadelphia. 1839, First Baptist Church, Richmond, Va. 1839, Norfolk Academy, Va. *1839, Observatory, Girard College, Philadelphia. 1841, Presbyterian Church, Petersburg, Va. 1843–1845, Breakwater, Laguaria, Venezuela. 1846, Chester County Courthouse, West Chester, Penn. 1847, City Hall, Norfolk, Va. *1848, Beth Israel Synagogue, Philadelphia. 1848, University of Lewisburg (Bucknell), Penn. *1849, Jayne Building (completed and enlarged William L. Johnston's design); *1849, Pennsylvania Medical College; Philadelphia. 1850, Patent Office Extension; 1850, United States Capitol Extension; 1851, Hewlings House (*Ingleside*); Washington. 1851, Tysen House (*Glenelg*), Ellicott City, Md. *1852, Library of Congress (in the Capitol); 1852, United States Government Hospital for the Insane (Saint Elizabeth's); 1852, United States Treasury Building Extension; 1855–1865, Capitol Dome; 1856, General Post Office Extension; Washington. 1857, Marine Barracks, Pensacola, Fla. 1858–1859, Marine Barracks, Brooklyn, N.Y. *1861, Thomas Ustick Walter House, Germantown, Penn. 1868–1870, Eutaw Place Baptist Church, Baltimore.

BIBLIOGRAPHY

Copies of the personal and professional papers of Thomas Ustick Walter are in the collection of The Athenaeum of Philadelphia.

BANISTER, TURPIN C. 1948 "The Genealogy of the Dome of the United States Capitol." *Journal of the Society of Architectural Historians* 7, nos. 1–2:1–31.
BROWN, GLENN (1902)1970 *History of the United States Capitol.* 2 vols. Reprint. New York: DeCapo.
DUNLAP, WILLIAM (1834)1965 *A History of the Rise and Progress of the Arts of Design in the United States.* New York: Blom.
ENNIS, ROBERT B. 1979 "Thomas U. Walter." *Nineteenth Century* 5, no. 3:59–60.
ENNIS, ROBERT B. 1982 *Thomas U. Walter, Architect, 1804–1887.* 2 vols. Philadelphia: The Athenaeum. Forthcoming publication.
GILCHRIST, AGNES ADDISON 1957 "Girard College: An Example of the Layman's Influence on Architecture." *Journal of the Society of Architectural Historians* 16, no. 2:22–25.
GOWANS, ALAN (1964)1976 *Images of American Living: Four Centuries of Architecture and Furniture as Cultural Expression.* New York: Harper.
HAMLIN, TALBOT (1944)1964 *Greek Revival Architecture in America.* New York: Dover.
JACKSON, JOSEPH 1923 *Early Philadelphia Architects and Engineers.* Philadelphia: Privately printed.
LISCOMBE, R. WINDSOR 1980 "T. U. Walter's Gifts of Drawings to the Institute of British Architects." *Journal of the Society of Architectural Historians* 39, no. 4:307–311.
RUSK, WILLIAM SENER 1939 "Thomas U. Walter and His Works." *Americana* 33, no. 2:151–179.
TATUM, GEORGE B. 1961 *Penn's Great Town: 250 Years of Philadelphia Architecture Illustrated in Prints and Drawings.* Philadelphia: University of Pennsylvania Press.

WALTERS, EDWARD

Edward Walters (1808–1874), the son of architect John Walters, was a pupil of LEWIS VULLIAMY. In 1832, JOHN RENNIE sent him to Constantinople to supervise the erection of works for the Turkish government. In 1839 he was established in his own practice in Manchester, where he remained until 1865. The leading Manchester architect from 1848 to 1860, he designed a number of distinguished warehouses and other buildings, including the railway stations between Ambergate and Manchester on a line he designed with W. H. BARLOW. He died at Oriental Terrace, Brighton.

JAMES STEVENS CURL

WORKS

1839–1840, Mosley Street Warehouse; 1840, Saint Andrew's Free Church; 1845, Schwabe Warehouse; 1847, Cavendish Street Independent Chapel; 1851, Aytoun Street Warehouse; 1853, Free Trade Hall; 1857–1860, 10, 12, and 34, Charlotte Street; 1860, Manchester and Salford Bank; Manchester, England.

BIBLIOGRAPHY

BOASE, FREDERIC 1965 Volume 3, column 1181 in *Modern English Biography, Containing Many Thousand Concise Memoirs of Persons Who have Died Between the Years 1851–1900.* London: Frank Cass.
HITCHCOCK, H. R. (1954)1972 *Early Victorian Architecture in Britain.* 2 vols. Reprint. New York: Da Capo.
PEVSNER, NIKOLAUS 1969 Volume 1 in *The Buildings of England: South Lancashire.* Harmondsworth, England: Penguin.
SHARP, DENNIS 1969 *Manchester.* London: Studio Vista.

WALTON, GEORGE

George Walton (1867–1933) was born in Glasgow, Scotland, the son of a painter. He trained as a bank clerk, taking evening classes, probably at the

Glasgow School of Art. In 1888, he gave up his banking career and opened a firm of interior decoration in Glasgow. His first commissions were for two tearooms for Miss Cranston in which he assisted CHARLES RENNIE MACKINTOSH (1896–1897).

In 1897, Walton moved to London, where he joined the Arts and Crafts Society; CHARLES F. A. VOYSEY became a close friend. His first architectural work was *The Leys* at Elstree, Hertfordshire (1901), for which he also designed the furnishings and which was considered by his contemporaries to be his best work. His other major commission was the *White House,* Shiplake (1908).

After World War I, Walton carried out fewer and smaller jobs. His last work was a memorial chapel at Cap d'Antibes (1931).

HANNAH WALTON

WORKS

1896, J. C. Annan House (interiors), Lenzie, Dunbarton, Scotland. 1896–1897, Two restaurants for William Rowntree, Scarborough, Yorkshire, England. *1896–1897, Two tearooms for Miss Cranston (with Charles Rennie Mackintosh), Glasgow, Scotland. 1898, S. Leetham House, Elm Bank (interiors), York, England. *1898, Kodak Offices, Clerkenwell Street, London. 1898–1902, Kodak Shops in London, Glasgow, Brussels, Milan, and Vienna. 1901, J. B. B. Wellington House, The Leys, Elstree, Hertfordshire, England. 1902, The Philippines (interiors), Brasted Chart, Kent, England. 1905, Alma House (interiors), Cheltenham, Gloucestershire, England. 1905, Finnart House (additions), Weybridge, Surrey, England. 1907–1910, George Davison House, Wern Fawr, Harlech, Wales. 1908, White House, Shiplake, England. *1910–1911, Saint David's Hotel, Harlech, Wales. 1920, War Memorial, Saint Peter's Church, Glasgow, Scotland. 1923, Houses, Sterne Street, London. *1931, Davidson Memorial Chapel, Cap d'Antibes, France.

BIBLIOGRAPHY

DAN, HORACE, and WILLMOTT, MORGAN 1970 *English Shopfronts Old and New.* London: Batsford.
FINE ART SOCIETY 1979 *Glasgow 1900.* London: The society. Exhibition catalogue.
HOWARTH, THOMAS 1952 *Charles Rennie Mackintosh and the Modern Movement.* London: Routledge & Kegan Paul.
LARNER, GERALD, and LARNER, CELIA 1979 *The Glasgow Style.* Edinburgh: Harris.
MCGRATH, RAYMOND 1934 *Twentieth Century Houses.* London: Faber.
MUTHESIUS, HERMANN (1904)1979 *The English House.* London: Staples. Originally published in German.
PEVSNER, NIKOLAUS 1968 Volume 2 in *Studies in Art, Architecture and Design.* London: Thames & Hudson.
SPARROW, WALTER SHAW (editor) 1904 *The British Home of To-day.* London: Hodder & Stoughton.
Studio Yearbook of Decorative Art 1906–1913.

WARCHAVCHIK, GREGORI

Gregori Warchavchik (1896–1975) pioneered functionalist architecture in Brazil and gained international recognition with the First Modern Exhibition House in São Paulo in 1930 and a year later with a similar home in Rio de Janeiro. Born in Odessa, Russia, he studied in his home town and later at the Fine Arts Institute in Rome, but moved permanently to Brazil in 1923. In 1925, a manifesto on his functionalist principles entitled "Apropos of Modern Architecture" appeared in newspapers in São Paulo and Rio de Janeiro. In order to substantiate his ideas, he built Vila Mariana (1927–1928), his family home in São Paulo. At first criticized and later praised for its stark simplicity and open planning, this house initiated Brazil's modern architectural movement.

In 1930, Warchavchik helped modernize the architectural curriculum at the National School of Fine Arts in Rio de Janeiro and commuted from São Paulo to teach on weekends. An article on Warchavchik's work appeared in *Cahiers d'Art* (1931) by Christian Zervos, and ALBERTO SARTORIS included his houses in the first edition of *Elementi dell'Architettura Funzionale.* Although Warchavchik was never given a government commission, his buildings revolutionized the development of twentieth-century architecture in Brazil.

ELIZABETH D. HARRIS

WORKS

1927–1928, Vila Mariana; 1930, First Modern Exhibition House; São Paulo, Brazil. 1931, Modernistic House, Rio de Janeiro. 1938, Apartment Building for *CIA de Melhoramentos Gropouva;* 1939, Apartment Building, Alameda Barão de Limeira; São Paulo, Brazil. 1943, Raul Crespi Beach House; 1943–1944, Apartment House, Avenida do Estado; Guaruja, Brazil.

BIBLIOGRAPHY

FERRAZ, GERALDO 1965 *Warchavchik e a introdução da nova arquitectura no Brasil: 1925 a 1940.* Preface by P. M. Bardi. São Paulo, Brazil: Museu de Arte.

WARD, JASPER D.

Jasper D. Ward (20th century) received a bachelor of architecture degree from the Massachusetts Institute of Technology in 1948. He worked for SKIDMORE, OWINGS, AND MERRILL and for Kelly and Gruzen in New York, and in 1958 opened his own practice in Louisville, Kentucky. He has taught at Pratt Institute, Columbia University, and the University of Kentucky. Two of Ward's unrealized projects, Ballard Mills (1970) and Big Four Bridge (1968), proposed the megastructural adaptation of old structures into multi-unit housing.

PATRICIA C. PHILLIPS

WORKS

1956, Walter P. Swain House, Watchung, N.J. 1961, Universal CIT; 1963, Neighborhood House; 1968, Portland Elementary School; Louisville, Ky.

BIBLIOGRAPHY

SKY, ALISON, and STONE, MICHELLE 1976 *Unbuilt America.* New York: McGraw-Hill.

WARDELL, WILLIAM WILKINSON

Because of ill health, William Wilkinson Wardell (1823–1899) emigrated to Melbourne, Australia, in 1857. He left a fairly good London architectural practice, composed mainly of churches influenced by A. W. N. PUGIN, although he was trained and articled as a civil engineer. In Melbourne, he was appointed chief architect (1859), then inspector general of public works (1861) to the State of Victoria. His many works were both Gothic (for example, Saint Patrick's Cathedral [1858–1899]) and classical (for example, Government House [1872–1876]) and of a great variety of building types. When dismissed in 1878, he was encouraged to practice in Sydney. He continued to employ Gothic as well as Italianate, Palladian (see ANDREA PALLADIO), and Venetian styles in a variety of free interpretations. It all came together in the English, Scottish, and Australian Bank, Melbourne, of 1885. He was a true eclectic.

DONALD LESLIE JOHNSON

WORKS

1849–1852, Church of Our Immaculate Lady, Clapham; 1851, Saint Joseph's Alms House, Hammersmith; London. 1858, 1865–1899, Saint Mary's Cathedral (not completed until 1940), Sydney. 1858–1899, Saint Patrick's Cathedral (not completed until 1927), Melbourne. 1860–1862, Church of Saint John, Toorak, Victoria, Australia. 1869, Royal Mint, Melbourne. 1872, Customs House, Williamstown, Victoria, Australia. 1872–1876, Government House, Melbourne. 1888, Clivedon, William Clarke House, East Melbourne. 1885, English, Scottish, and Australian Bank, Melbourne.

BIBLIOGRAPHY

HERMAN, MORTON 1956 *The Architecture of Victorian Sydney.* Sydney: Angus & Robertson.
HITCHCOCK, H. R. (1954)1972 *Early Victorian Architecture in Britain.* 2 vols. Reprint. New York: Da Capo.
McDONALD, D. I. 1970 "William Wilkinson Wardell: Architect and Engineer." *Victorian Historical Magazine* (Melbourne) 41:327–350.
McDONALD, D. I. 1976 "William Wilkinson Wardell." Volume 6, pages 354–355 in Geoffrey Serle and Russel Ward (editors), *Australian Dictionary of Biography.* Melbourne University Press.
WARDELL, V. A. 1940 "A Review of the Architectural and Engineering Works of W. W. Wardell, F.R.I.B.A., M.I.C.E." Unpublished manuscript in Mitchell Library, Sydney.

WARE, ISAAC

Isaac Ware (?–1766) is first recorded as apprenticed to THOMAS RIPLEY for seven years from August 1721. In April 1728, he obtained his first appointment to the Office of Works as clerk itinerant and draftsman, to be followed in 1729 with the Clerkship of the Works at Windsor Castle. It must have been about this time that Ware became acquainted with LORD BURLINGTON, for he was a subscriber to WILLIAM KENT's *Designs of Inigo Jones* (1727) and made drawings for Burlington's *Fabbriche Antiohe* (1730). By 1733, Ware's *Designs of Inigo Jones and Others* had appeared, and in this he published many drawings in Lord Burlington's collections. It was probably due to Burlington that Ware got the task of converting Lanesborough House into Saint George's Hospital, Hyde Park Corner, in 1733.

Between 1733 and the building of Clifton Hill House, Bristol, in 1746, there is a lack of documentation, but Ware was probably engaged in London speculative development. He was also busy as an author. His master Ripley had superintended the building of Houghton, Norfolk, from 1722, where Ware must have found his training. In 1735, Ware published *The Plans . . . of Houghton,* and three years later there appeared his immaculate edition of ANDREA PALLADIO's *Four Books of Architecture* dedicated to Lord Burlington. In 1741 he was drawing plans of Rokeby House, Yorkshire, for Sir THOMAS ROBINSON, the talented amateur architect, for whom Ware may well have acted in a similar capacity as did ROGER MORRIS for LORD PEMBROKE or, indeed, HENRY FLITCROFT for Lord Burlington. Finally in 1756, he translated Lorenzo Sirigatti's *La Practica di Prospettiva* and began to issue his monumental *Complete Body of Architecture* in parts. The latter was encyclopedic and attempted to cover the whole theory and practice of Georgian architecture in no less than 748 pages amply illustrated with Ware's designs. It was one of the most influential books upon taste in architecture for nearly forty years.

Ware's admiration for Lord Burlington is confirmed by a number of his buildings, not the least Oxford Town Hall (1751), and by the designs submitted for the London Mansion House competition in 1735. These were of Burlingtonian purity and incorporated episodes of antiquity-inspired neo-Palladian planning. The main body of Ware's practice does not, however, commence until after the mid-1740s, and a glance at his buildings will show that he was not always dedicated to Burlington's doctrinaire style and was able to evolve his own. Wrothan Park, Middlesex (1754), was an example of COLEN CAMPBELL's Great House reduced, that is, of Wanstead III reduced to a villa body with domed wings; Amisfield House, East Lothian (1756), was a huge, high, porticoed house of massive dignity and spectacular quality. Ware's best townhouse was undoubtedly Chesterfield House in South Audley Street, built for the fourth earl of Chesterfield from 1748. It was here, possibly for the first time, that Ware showed his willingness to depart from the Palladian canon in interior decoration, for many rooms were in a full-blooded French rococo taste. The same style was to be found at Belvedere House, Kent, in the Great Room there after 1751, as well as at Woodcote Park, Surrey, for the sixth Lord Baltimore (c.1755). This divergence from normal Palladian decoration was a manifestation of the rococo, and it is significant that Ware belonged to a coterie of artists, including Hayman, William Hogarth, and Louis François Roubiliac, who congregated at Slaughter's Coffee House in Saint Martin's Lane, all of whom were influenced by rococo art. This deviation from principle is manifest in Ware's *Complete Body*.

Not enough is known about Ware to be dogmatic on the facts of his career. He may well have traveled abroad, and to this end was possibly helped by Lord Burlington, but there is no evidence that Ware belonged, as did Henry Flitcroft or William Kent, to what is known as the Burlington House Group or the Chiswick Coterie. By 1742, Ware was able to purchase an estate, Westbourne House, Paddington, London (c.1750), where he built himself a substantial house, subsequently lived in by S. P. COCKERELL. He adopted the apprenticeship system, according to the records of the Carpenter's Company, whose master he became in 1763. His most notable pupil was CHARLES CAMERON, and thus Ware's influence is discernible in Russia.

JOHN HARRIS

WORKS

1733, Saint George's Hospital (conversion from Lanesborough House), Hyde Park Corner, London. 1746, Clifton Hill House, Bristol, England. Begun

Ware.
Design for a ceiling,
  Chesterfield House.
London.
Begun 1748

1748, Chesterfield House; c.1750, Westbourne House; London. 1751, Belvedere House, Kent, England. *1751, Oxford Town Hall, England. 1754, Wrotham Park, Middlesex, England. c.1755, Woodcote Park, Surrey, England. 1756, Amisfield House, East Lothian, Scotland.

BIBLIOGRAPHY

BURLINGTON, LORD   1730   *Fabbriche Antiohe disegnate da Andrea Palladio Vicentino.* London.
KENT, WILLIAM   (1727)1967   *Designs of Inigo Jones.* Reprint. Farnborough, England: Gregg.
SIRIGATTI, LORENZO   1756   *The Practice of Perspective.* Translated by Isaac Ware. London: The author. Originally published with the title *La Practica di Prospettiva.*
WARE, ISAAC   (1733)1971   *Designs of Inigo Jones and Others.* Reprint. Farnborough, England: Gregg.
WARE, ISAAC   1735   *The Plans . . . of Houghton in Norfolk.* London: The author.
WARE, ISAAC (translator)   1738   *The Four Books of Architecture: by Andrea Palladio.* London: The author.
WARE, ISAAC   1756   *A Complete Body of Architecture.* London: Osborne and Shipton.

WARE, WILLIAM R.

William Robert Ware (1832–1915), the founder of modern architectural education in America, was born in Cambridge, Massachusetts. Ware attended Harvard College, from which he was graduated in 1852. After two years as a private tutor in New York City, Ware studied civil engineering for two years at Harvard's Lawrence Scientific School and then entered the architectural office of EDWARD

CLARKE CABOT. In 1859, he and FRANK FURNESS joined the students' atelier of RICHARD MORRIS HUNT in New York, where HENRY VAN BRUNT, his future partner, was already studying. There, he experienced Beaux-Arts training under America's first graduate of the Paris Ecole. Ware began practice in Boston in 1860 together with Edward S. Philbrick, a civil engineer, but in 1863 he joined Henry Van Brunt to form the architectural partnership of WARE AND VAN BRUNT, which lasted until 1881.

Both Ware and Van Brunt were scholarly in temperament, and from the beginning they adopted Hunt's sympathetic and generous atelier training in their own office. Among their pupils were John G. Stearns and Robert S. Peabody (see PEABODY AND STEARNS), CHARLES B. ATWOOD, and Frank Howe (who succeeded in partnership with Van Brunt upon Ware's retirement). The Ware and Van Brunt atelier soon attracted the notice of officials of the Massachusetts Institute of Technology (M.I.T.), who were interested in founding the first university program in architecture in the United States. As the architectural profession in the country was becoming officially organized and concerned about professional standards in ever more complex conditions of practice, the lack of institutional training in architecture had become very evident. Ware's views on education were solicited, and in 1865 he was appointed professor of architecture and head of the new program. The opening of the school was delayed until the fall of 1868 so that Ware might travel extensively in Europe, studying architecture and systems of architectural instruction and assembling the necessary books, photographs, drawings, and casts to use in teaching. Instruction at M.I.T. was influenced by the teaching practices at the Ecole des Beaux-Arts, especially after Eugène Létang, a graduate of the Paris school, arrived in 1872 to become the principal design instructor. Ware, however, felt the need to modify French methods of instruction to suit far less monumental conditions of practice in the United States and to provide a liberal education for students, especially emphasizing a historical understanding of the growth and development of architecture which would complement training in pure design and structural engineering.

In 1881, Ware was called to Columbia College in New York to found a department of architecture in the School of Mines. Though the school prospered and Ware's pupils from there and from M.I.T. went on to teach in most of the other university schools of architecture which were then being founded, it never fully kept pace with the escalating ambitions of such men as Charles F. McKim (see McKIM, MEAD, AND WHITE) who wanted more thorough Beaux-Arts design training to prepare men for the new opportunities in monumental work which followed the 1893 Chicago Fair. After Ware's retirement in 1903, the Columbia curriculum was revised in this direction.

In addition to his teaching, which influenced the entire direction of American professional instruction, Ware was generally active in professional affairs. A member of the American Institute of Architects, he formulated the official rules for architectural competitions which were adopted by the Institute, and he himself served as judge or adviser for many competitions. Though teaching supplanted design early in his career, he did design the building of the American School of Classical Studies in Athens.

Ware was an active lecturer and writer, much concerned to diffuse appreciation of architecture to a wide audience of both professionals and laymen. Among his many publications are *Greek Ornament* (1878); *Modern Perspective* (1882); *The American Vignola* (1901), still the standard American treatment of the classical orders; and *Shades and Shadows* (1912–1913).

WILLIAM A. COLES

WORKS

1865–1867, First Church (with Henry Van Brunt), Boston. 1865–1878, Memorial Hall (with Van Brunt); 1868–1880, Episcopal Theological School (with Van Brunt); 1870–1871, Weld Hall (with Van Brunt); Cambridge, Mass. *1873–1875, Union Railway Station (with Van Brunt), Worcester, Mass. 1886–1888, American School of Classical Studies, Athens.

BIBLIOGRAPHY

CHEWNING, J. A.   1979   "William Robert Ware at MIT and Columbia." *Journal of Architectural Education* 33, Nov.:25–29.

EVANS, CLARE T.   n.d.   "Professor William Robert Ware, 1832–1915." Unpublished manuscript, Avery Architectural Library, Columbia University, New York.

WARE, WILLIAM R.   1866   *An Outline of a Course of Architectural Instruction.* Boston: Wilson.

WARE, WILLIAM R.   1866–1867   "On the Condition of Architecture and of Architectural Education in the United States." *Papers of the Royal Institute of British Architects* 1866–1867:81–90.

WARE, WILLIAM R.   1878   *Greek Ornament.* Boston: Tilton.

WARE, WILLIAM R.   1881   "Architecture at Columbia University." *Architect and Building News* 10, Aug.:61–62.

WARE, WILLIAM R.   (1882)1900   *Modern Perspective.* Rev. ed. New York: Macmillan.

WARE, WILLIAM R.   1888   "Instruction in Architecture at the School of Mines." *School of Mines Quarterly* 10, Nov.:28–43.

WARE, WILLIAM R. (1901)1977 *The American Vignola.* Reprint. New York: Norton.

WARE, WILLIAM R. 1912–1913 *Shades and Shadows.* Scranton, Pa.: International Textbook.

WARE, WILLIAM ROTCH

William Rotch Ware (1848–1917) was the nephew of WILLIAM ROBERT WARE. Born in Cambridge, Massachusetts, he was educated at Phillips Academy and Harvard College. He later studied architecture at the Massachusetts Institute of Technology and worked for a while in the architectural practice his uncle shared with HENRY VAN BRUNT. From 1874 until 1876, he was at the Ecole des Beaux-Arts in Paris, working in Joseph-Auguste Vaudremer's atelier.

Returning to Boston in 1876, Ware assumed, at his uncle's insistence, the assistant editorship of the newly established *American Architect and Building News.* In 1880, Ware became editor and served in that capacity until his retirement in 1907. He also became publisher of the *American Architect* in 1893. Ware never practiced architecture, much to his regret, but he was responsible for introducing the public to the works of H. H. RICHARDSON, PEABODY AND STEARNS, WILLIAM R. EMERSON, and McKIM, MEAD, AND WHITE. He was particularly interested in architectural drawing, and he established an in-house drafting office at the *American Architect* in 1886 to serve both the magazine and the profession. Ware's greatest influence came through the editorial columns of the *American Architect,* where he championed such causes as the professionalization of architecture, architectural education, reform of the competition system, and the preservation of historic structures. In addition to his duties at the *American Architect,* Ware edited and published the *Monographs of American Architecture* (1885–1888), *Architectural Odds and Ends* (1892), and *The Georgian Period* (1899–1902).

MARY N. WOODS

BIBLIOGRAPHY

"Obituary" 1917 *American Architect* 111:273–276.

WALKER, C. HOWARD 1917 "Obituary." *Journal of the American Institute of Architects* 5:242.

WARE and VAN BRUNT

One of the leading Eastern architectural firms in the post-Civil War decades, Ware and Van Brunt was founded in 1863 when HENRY VAN BRUNT returned from Civil War duty and joined WIL-LIAM ROBERT WARE in architectural practice. Both men had studied at Harvard and completed their architectural training in the atelier of RICHARD MORRIS HUNT in New York. Van Brunt was the acknowledged design partner in the firm; indeed, from 1865, Ware was fully occupied with founding, directing, and teaching in the new school of architecture at the Massachusetts Institute of Technology. The firm's work centered on ecclesiastical and institutional work, and their most noteworthy commissions were among their earliest: the First Church in Boston (1865–1867); Harvard's splendid Memorial Hall (1865–1878), perhaps the best Victorian Gothic edifice in the country (though today somewhat mutilated by fire and neglect); the buildings of the Episcopal Theological School in Cambridge, Massachusetts (1869–1880); Weld Hall, Harvard University (1871–1872); the stack addition to Gore Hall, the Harvard University Library (1876–1877), where the stack principle of book storage was first introduced to the United States; and several buildings at Wellesley College in Massachusetts. The work of the firm reflected the eclectic mixture of styles of the period: English Gothic Revival, Queen Anne, and Flemish Renaissance, all handled with rational sobriety and conscientiousness and, it must be said, showing generally more discipline and scholarly reserve than imaginative flair in design. In addition, the firm designed a number of

Ware and Van Brunt. First Church. Boston. 1865–1867

houses in the Back Bay and suburbs of Boston.

In 1881, when Ware was called to New York to found the architecture program at Columbia College, Ware and Van Brunt was dissolved, and Frank Howe, who had entered the firm in 1868, was elevated to a full partnership in the successor firm of Van Brunt and Howe. Later in that decade, an office was opened in Kansas City, Missouri, and eventually all the work of the firm shifted to the West, where Van Brunt and Howe were one of the most prestigious firms and where the nature of their practice broadened considerably.

WILLIAM A. COLES

WORKS

1865–1867, First Church, Boston. 1865–1878, Memorial Hall; 1869–1880, Episcopal Theological School Buildings; 1871–1872, Weld Hall; Cambridge, Mass. *1873–1875, Union Railway Station, Worcester, Mass. *1876–1877, Gore Hall (stack addition), Harvard University Library, Cambridge, Mass. 1880–1881, Music Hall; *1880–1881, Stone Hall; Wellesley, Mass. 1881–1882, Saint Stephen's Church, Lynn, Mass. 1881–1882, Simpson Infirmary, Wellesley, Mass.

BIBLIOGRAPHY

COLES, WILLIAM A. (editor) 1969 *Architecture and Society: Selected Essays of Henry Van Brunt.* Cambridge, Mass.: Belknap.
HENNESSEY, WILLIAM JOHN 1979 "The Architectural Works of Henry Van Brunt." Unpublished Ph.D. dissertation, Columbia University, New York.

WARREN, MILES

Born in Christchurch, New Zealand, Frederick Miles Warren (1929–) studied architecture at the University of Auckland after a period in the office of CECIL WOOD. Since 1958, he has practiced with M. E. Mahoney in Christchurch. The firm has won three gold and three silver medals of the New Zealand Institute of Architects.

JOHN STACPOOLE

WORKS

1958, Dorset Street Flats; 1960, Hall of Residence, Christchurch College; 1961, Memorial Garden Crematorium; 1961, Wool Exchange; 1962, Student Union and Ngaio Marsh Theatre, Canterbury University; Christchurch, New Zealand. 1963, Student Union, Auckland University, New Zealand. 1964, Student Union, Massey University, Palmerston North, New Zealand. 1964, Miles Warren Offices and House, Christchurch, New Zealand. 1964, Wool Exchange, Dunedin, New Zealand. 1965, Government House, Honiara, Solomon Islands. 1965, Government Office Condominium, Port Vila, New Hebrides; 1965, Mendana Hotel, Honiara, Solomon Islands. 1965, Town Hall, Christ-church, New Zealand. 1967, Canterbury Frozen Meat Company Offices, Christchurch, New Zealand. 1969, Maidment Theatre, Auckland, New Zealand. 1970, Travelodge Hotel, Queenstown, New Zealand. 1972, Williams City Centre, Wellington. 1973, City Library, Timaru, New Zealand. 1973, I.C.I. Offices; 1974, Sports Hall, Christ's College; Christchurch, New Zealand. 1974–1979, Chancery, New Zealand Embassy, Washington. 1976, Latimer View House, Christchurch, New Zealand. 1978, Army Memorial Museum, Waiouru, New Zealand. 1979, Canterbury Library, Christchurch, New Zealand.

BIBLIOGRAPHY

BROWN, ROSS 1979 "An Appraisal: New Zealand Army Museum, Waiouru." *New Zealand Architect* 3:28–36.
"Christchurch Town Hall." 1972 *Architects' Journal* Oct.: 292–303.
ECKARDT, WOLF VON 1979 "The Well-mannered Embassy." *New Zealand Architect* 5:22–27.
"Ownership Flats for Williams Development Holdings Ltd." 1975 *Architects' Journal* Apr.:47–51.
"Three Christchurch Office Buildings by Warren and Mahoney." 1972 *Architects' Journal* Sept.:267–279.
WARREN, MILES 1978 "Style in New Zealand Architecture." *New Zealand Architect* 3:2–15.

WARREN, RUSSELL

Russell Warren (1783–1860), an accomplished architect and engineer best known for his work in the late Federal and Greek Revival styles, was associated first with the firm of William Tallman and JAMES C. BUCKLIN in Providence and, in 1835–1836, with ALEXANDER JACKSON DAVIS in New York, where he met Ithiel Town (see TOWN AND DAVIS).

Born in Tiverton, Rhode Island, he went to Bristol, Rhode Island, in about 1800, where by 1806–1810 he was designing imposing Federal mansions for the wealthy DeWolf family and other Bristol merchants. In 1828, he designed with Bucklin the handsome granite Greek Revival Providence Arcade. In the following years, he built Greek Revival houses, churches, banks, public buildings, schools, and libraries in Rhode Island, Massachusetts, and also Charleston, Savannah, and New York State. For these, he used variants of the full temple form as well as a square symmetrical scheme, often with an attic story and embellished with balustrades or parapets and pedimented or unpedimented porticos. As early as 1810, he was also using Gothic Revival elements, and later he experimented with Italianate and romantic mid-century eclectic forms. As an engineer he designed a number of bridges; his name is associated with the Warren truss.

ANTOINETTE F. DOWNING

WORKS

1805, Russell Warren House; *1808, James DeWolf House (The Mount); 1810, George DeWolf House (Linden Place); Bristol, R.I. 1828–1829, Providence Arcade, R.I. *1833, North Christian Church, New Bedford, Mass. 1833, Wheaton House, Warren, R.I. 1834, Levi Gale House, Newport, R.I. 1834, John Avery Parker House, Fall River, Mass. *1834, Warren Ladies Seminary, R.I. 1835, Elmhurst (altered), Newport, R.I. 1835–1837, Dutch Reformed Church, Newburgh, N.Y. 1836, Athenaeum Row, Providence, R.I. 1837, Gerbst House; 1837, Captain Joseph Talbot House; Bristol, R.I. 1839–1840, Lapham Institute (altered), Scituate, R.I. *1840, Foster House, Providence, R.I. 1840–?, Bosworth House; 1844, Second Baptist Church; Warren, R.I. 1853, New Bedford Institute for Savings, Mass. 1858, House of Representatives Room, Colony House, Newport, R.I.

BIBLIOGRAPHY

ALEXANDER, ROBERT 1952 "The Architecture of Russell Warren." Unpublished M.A. thesis, New York University.

WARREN and WETMORE

Warren and Wetmore was a successful New York City architectural firm in the first three decades of the twentieth century. Whitney Warren (1864–1943) had studied architecture briefly at the School of Mines of Columbia College before going to the Ecole des Beaux-Arts in Paris where he entered the ateliers of Pierre-Gérôme-Honoré Daumet, CHARLES LOUIS GIRAULT, and Pierre-Joseph Esquié. Charles D. Wetmore (1867–1941) was a graduate of the Harvard Law School. Warren and Wetmore did the majority of their work for commercial clients. The office was best known for its hotel designs and work for railroad companies. Warren's training was evident in the firm's early work. The New York Yacht Club (1898), the first published design attributed to Warren and Wetmore jointly, is an exuberant, highly personal essay in the Beaux-Arts style. In its middle years, the office developed the successful formula it employed for many of the hotels and apartment houses it designed. These buildings were tall masonry blocks with three or four stories at the top and bottom rendered in a restrained classical vocabulary. In some cases, such as the Biltmore Hotel in New York City (1914), the building was sheathed in brick with the decorative trim in contrasting stone. The Stewart and Company Store in New York City (1929, altered 1930), a design from Warren and Wetmore's last years, illustrates the firm's interest at this time in the composition of architectural mass and its attempts at modern

Warren and Wetmore.
Grand Central Terminal
(with Reed and Stem).
New York.
1913

decorative detail. The most famous project Warren and Wetmore were associated with was the Grand Central Terminal in New York City. Credit for this building, completed in 1913, should be shared between Warren and Wetmore and Charles A. REED AND Alan H. STEM. Reed and Stem won the original competition for the project and Warren and Wetmore were associated with them throughout the design and construction. The terminal was the centerpiece of a larger project called Terminal City which was to be developed around Grand Central. Warren and Wetmore designed many of the major elements of this innovative urban scheme which included hotels, apartments, and commercial buildings grouped around the terminal.

DENNIS McFADDEN

WORKS

1898, New York Yacht Club. 1904, J. A. Burden Residence; 1913, Grand Central Terminal (with Reed and Stem); 1914, Biltmore Hotel; New York. 1920, Louvain Library (restoration), Belgium. 1927, Aeolian Building; 1929, Stewart and Company Store; New York.

BIBLIOGRAPHY

"Charles D. Wetmore." 1941 *New York Times,* May 9, p. 21.
FITCH, JAMES MARSTON, and WAITE, DIANA S. 1974 *Grand Central Terminal and Rockefeller Center: A Historic-critical Estimate of Their Significance.* Albany: New York State Parks and Recreation.
"Whitney Warren, Architect, 78, Dies." 1943 *New York Times,* Jan. 25, p. 13.

WATELET, CLAUDE-HENRI

An amateur and patron of the arts, Claude-Henri Watelet (1718–1786) developed the garden of Moulin-Joli (1754–1786), the outstanding example of mid-eighteenth century French rococo–picturesque garden. Here existing views were framed in a seminaturalistic setting, and existing buildings were restored. His book on the French picturesque garden was influenced by Rousseauesque concepts.

DORA WIEBENSON

WORK

1754–1786, Moulin-Joli Garden, near Paris.

BIBLIOGRAPHY

HENRIOT, MAURICE 1922 "Un Amateur d'art au XVIIIe siècle, l'académicien Watelet." *Gazette des Beaux-Arts* Series 5 6:173–194.
HOFER, PHILIP 1956 *A Visit to Rome in 1764*. Boston Museum of Fine Arts.
QUÉNÉHEN, L. 1937 Pages 378–392 in *Histoire de Colombes à travers les âges*. Paris: Jouve.
WATELET, CLAUDE-HENRI 1764 *Essai sur les jardins*. Paris: Prault.
WIEBENSON, DORA 1978 Pages 15–19, 64–70 in *The Picturesque Garden in France*. N.J.: Princeton University Press.

WATERHOUSE, ALFRED

Alfred Waterhouse (1830–1905), a Quaker from Liverpool, rose to the top of the London-centered and predominantly Anglican High Victorian architectural profession. His reputation rested almost solely on secular designs whose hallmark was simple but clever planning.

Waterhouse attended the Grove House Friends' School in Liverpool before being articled to Richard Lane of Manchester in 1848. After serving his five years, he made an extended trip through Europe and returned to set up practice in Manchester in 1854.

Success in the Manchester Assize Courts competition of 1858–1859 earned him national recognition, and it was followed by other great public and institutional commissions. He very nearly won the competition of 1866–1867 for the Royal Courts of Justice in London, and he did win the two-stage contest for the Manchester Town Hall of 1867–1868. In 1866, he was appointed architect of the Natural History Museum in London. Waterhouse built new universities in Liverpool, Manchester, and Leeds, and he made numerous additions to the colleges of Oxford and Cambridge. He designed several major hospitals and prisons and many offices for the Prudential Assurance Company. He built a few important country houses, but only a handful of churches.

Waterhouse was a pragmatic artist who readily adopted iron and terra cotta as building materials. He exploited the stylistic liberty of High Victorian architecture and ultimately looked beyond Gothic to Romanesque and classical sources.

He wrote very little, but his material achievements earned him the highest honors of the Royal Institute of British Architects and the Royal Academy. Waterhouse established a London office in 1864, and in 1891 his son Paul became his partner. In 1901, a paralytic stroke forced him to retire.

DAVID B. BROWNLEE

WORKS

1854, Hothay Holme (now the Lakes District Council Offices, Ambleside, Cumberland, England. *1855–1856, Binyon and Fryer Warehouse, Manchester, England. 1856, Hinderton House, Hooton, Cheshire, England. 1857, Bradford Banking Company (now the Midland Bank), West Yorkshire, England. *1858–1861, Barcombe Cottage, Fallowfield; *1858–1864, Manchester Assize Courts; *1861, Royal Insurance Building; Manchester, England. 1862, Pilmore Hall; 1862–1864, Market and Public Offices; Darlington, Durham, England. 1863–1868, Strangeways Prison, Manchester, England. 1864, Barclays Bank, Darlington, Durham, England. *1864–1866, Clydesdale and North Scotland Bank, London. 1864–1866, Hutton Hall, Guisborough, Yorkshire, England. *1865–1866, New University Club, London. 1865–1873, Reading Grammar School, England. 1866, University Union, Cambridge. 1866–1868, Foxhill and Whiteknights Houses, Reading, England. 1866–1869, Balliol College Master's Lodge and South Front, Oxford. 1867–1870, Allerton Priory; 1867–1871, London and North-western Hotel, Lime Street Station; Liverpool, England. 1867–1877, Manchester Town Hall, England. 1868–1869, Saint Matthew's Church, Vicarage, School, and Cottages, Hampshire, England. 1868–1870, Gonville and Caius College Tree Court; 1868–1870, Jesus College Detached Range; Cambridge. 1869–1872, Blackmoor House, Hampshire, England. 1869–1888, Owen's College (now the University), Manchester, England. *1869–1897, Easton Hall; Cheshire, England. 1871–1872, Pembroke College South Range, Cambridge. 1871–1872, Town Hall (former), Knutsford, Cheshire, England. 1871–1873, Master's Lodge, Cambridge. 1871–1874, Seamen's Orphan Institution (now the Park Hospital), Anfield, Liverpool, England. 1872–1875, Municipal Buildings, Reading, England. 1872–1887, Girton College, Cambridge. 1874–1877, New Hall Oxford. 1874, Saint Elisabeth's Parsonage, Reddish, Manchester, England. 1875, Library and New Hall, Cambridge. *1875, New Court Chambers, London. 1876–1877, Saint Mary's, Twyford, Hampshire, England. 1876–1879, Prudential Assurance Buildings, London. 1877–1878, Iwerne Minster House (now the Clayesmore School), Dorset, England. *1877–1878, Yattendon Court, Berkshire, England. 1877–1905, Yorkshire College of Science (now the University; not completed until 1908), West Yorkshire, England. 1878–1881, Bedford Assize Courts and Shire Hall, England. 1879–1882, Hove Town Hall, East Sussex, England. 1880, 1 Old Bond Street, London. 1880–

1883, Saint Elisabeth's, Reddish; 1881, Prudential Assurance Building; Manchester, England. 1881–1883, Turner Memorial Home, Toxteth, Liverpool, England. *1881–1884, City and Guilds of London Central Technical Institution. *1881–1885, Saint Paul's School, London. 1882–1884, Blackmoor House (new wing), Hampshire, England. 1883–1884, Lyndhurst Road Congregational Church, Hampstead; 1884–1887, National Liberal Club; London. 1885, Prudential Assurance Building, Nottingham, England. 1885–1886, Prudential Assurance Building; 1887–1889, University Engineering Building and Victoria Building; Liverpool, England. 1888–1889, Metropole Hotel, Brighton, England. 1888–1891, King's Weigh House chapel (now the Ukrainian Catholic Cathedral), London. 1893, Saint Mary's Hospital; 1893–1905, Refuge Assurance Building (not completed until 1913); Manchester, England. 1894–1897, Saint Margaret's Clergy Orphan School, Bushey, Hertfordshire, England. 1896–1898, Royal Institution of Chartered Surveyors; 1896–1905, University College Hospital (not completed until 1906); 1899–1905, Prudential Assurance Buildings (extensions; not completed until 1906); 1901–1903, Staple Inn Buildings North; London.

BIBLIOGRAPHY

AXON, WILLIAM E. A.   1878   *An Architectural and General Description of the Town Hall, Manchester.* London and Manchester: Haywood.

COOPER, THOMAS   1905   "Alfred Waterhouse, R.A., LL.D." *Journal of the Royal Institute of British Architects* Series 3 12 no. 19:609–618.

GIROUARD, MARK   1981   *Alfred Waterhouse and the Natural History Museum.* New Haven: Yale University Press.

GIROUARD, MARK   1974   "Blackmoor House, Hampshire: The Property of the Earl of Selborne." *Country Life* 156, no. 4026:554–557; no. 4027:614–617.

JENKINS, FRANK   1967   "The Making of a Municipal Palace: Manchester Town Hall." *Country Life* 141, no. 3650:336–339.

SHEPPARD, F. H. W. (editor)   1975   Volume 38, chapter 13 in *Survey of London.* London: Athlone Press.

SMITH, STUART ALLEN   1976   "Alfred Waterhouse: Civic Grandeur." Pages 102–121 in *Seven Victorian Architects.* Edited by Jane Fawcett. London: Thames & Hudson.

SMITH, STUART ALLEN   "Alfred Waterhouse: The Great Years, 1860–1875." Unpublished Ph. D. dissertation, University of London.

WATERHOUSE, ALFRED   1890–1891   "The President's Address to Students: Colour in Architecture." *Journal of Proceedings of the Royal Institute of British Architects.* Series 2 7:121–126.

WATERHOUSE, ALFRED   1876–1877   "Description of the Town Hall at Manchester." *Sessional Papers of the Royal Institute of British Architects* 1876–1877: 117–131.

WATERHOUSE, ALFRED   1899   "Architects." Pages 342–358 in *Unwritten Laws and Ideals of Active Careers.* Edited by E. H. Pitcairn. London: Smith, Elder.

WATERHOUSE, ALFRED   1864–1865   "A Short Description of the Manchester Assize Courts." *Papers of the Royal Institute of British Architects* 1864–1865:165–174.

WATERHOUSE, ALFRED   1867   *Courts of Justice Competition: General Description of Design.* London: Eyre & Spottiswoode.

WEBB, ASTON

Aston Webb (1849–1930), one of the most prolific of English Edwardian architects, was the son of an engraver and watercolor painter. After serving an apprenticeship with the firm of Banks and Barry and winning the PUGIN Studentship for the study of English medieval architecture in 1873, Webb set up his own practice. After 1882, his major works were done in partnership with E. Ingress Bell.

Webb was adept at architectural competitions by reason of his clarity of planning and his structural knowledge, linked with an understanding of the stylistic requirements of each time and place. His early work is often built of florid terra cotta in a French-derived style. At Birmingham University (1901), he was Byzantine, while at Christ's Hospital (1893), Horsham, Sussex, and the Royal Naval College (1897) in Dartmouth, Devon, the style is CHRISTOPHER WREN. Much of Webb's work is coarse in detail compensated by boldness of general effect and picturesque grouping. After 1900, he led the trend toward purer classicism, his best work in this manner being the Royal College of Science (1906), Dublin, rather than the familiar re-fronting of Buckingham Palace (1912), London, and its ceremonial counterpart, Admiralty Arch (1903–1910).

Webb was a leading figure in professional affairs and improved links with American architects whose large practices resembled his own. His son Maurice W. Webb continued the practice after 1920 under the name Sir Aston Webb and Sons.

ALAN POWERS

WORKS

1875, Saint John's, Kingston Blount, Oxfordshire, England. 1879, House, 60 Bartholomew Close, London. 1886–1891, Victoria Law Courts (with E. Ingress Bell), Birmingham, England. 1888, House, 23 Austin Friars (with Bell); 1890, Metropolitan Life Assurance Company Building, Moorgate; London. 1893, Christ's Hospital (with Bell), Horsham, Sussex, England. 1893, French Protestant Church, Soho Square; 1893, Royal United Service Institution (with Bell), Whitehall; London. 1897, Yacht Club, Yarmouth, Isle of Wight, England. 1897, Royal Naval College, Dartmouth, Devon, England. 1899–1903, Victoria and Albert Museum, South Kensington, London. 1901, Birmingham University (with Bell), England. 1901, Queen Victoria

Memorial; 1903–1910, Admiralty Arch; London. 1903–1910, Saint Michael's Court, Caius College, Cambridge, England. 1906, Royal College of Science (with THOMAS N. DEANE), Dublin. 1907, Offices of Grand Trunk Railway of Canada, Cockspur Street, London. 1908, Webb Court, King's College; 1908, Bright's Building, Magdalene College; Cambridge, England. 1909, Royal School of Mines, South Kensington; 1912, Buckingham Palace (east front); London. 1913, George V Gateway, Leys School, Cambridge, England.

BIBLIOGRAPHY

CRESSWELL, H. B. 1955 "A Backward View." *Architect and Building News* 208, Aug. 11: 172–173.
CRESSWELL, H. B. 1958 "Seventy Years Back." *Architectural Review* 124, Dec.:403–405.
LUCAS, WILLIAM 1920 "The Architecture of Sir Aston Webb P.R.A." *Building News* 118:63–64.
"Obituary." 1930 *Journal of the Royal Institute of British Architects* 37:710–711, 744.
"Sir Aston Webb's Record: Public Buildings and Churches." 1905 *Architects' Magazine* 5, no. 57.

WEBB, JOHN

John Webb (1611–1672) was born in London of a Somersetshire family, and according to his own statement was "brought up by his Uncle Mr. INIGO JONES upon his late Maiestyes command in the study of Architecture." In fact, Webb's wife was Anne Jones, a close relation of the great Inigo. Webb entered into the employ of Jones about 1628, and for the rest of his master's life was his personal assistant. During that time, he never held an official post in the Office of Works. For this reason, he never emerged as a fully identifiable architect in his own right. From the early 1630s, however, he was in charge of two of Jones's great works: the restoration of old Saint Paul's Cathedral and the building of the Barber Surgeon's Theatre.

In 1638, he can be considered to have come

John Webb.
Amesbury House.
Wiltshire, England.
1659

into his own with a design for a lodge at Hale Park, Hampshire, and with grandiose designs for rebuilding the Strand façade of Old Somerset House. Both were unexecuted, but the latter, always attributed to Jones, is almost certainly by Webb. Their sources are identifiable and are used in an academic manner. The same must be said about the various designs for a palace at Whitehall or in Saint James's Park. Even the celebrated "P" scheme does not deserve to be attributed to Jones for the very same reasons, but naturally Jones looms as the powerful influence behind them, and there is no reason to doubt that their Salomonic connotations derive as much from Jones's readings as Webb's. A clue to the direction that Webb's career was to take is his design for Colonel Edmund Ludlow's House at Maiden Bradley before 1650 and probably not built. Ludlow was a Parliamentarian, and Webb was willing to treat with him, despite the loyalty and love that Inigo had for Charles I. This willingness on Webb's part to be a trimmer may have brought him work during the Interregnum, but it possibly denied him the coveted Surveyorship of the Works at the Restoration in 1660.

His major commission in the "dread" years was the reconstruction of the state rooms in the south front of Wilton House, Wiltshire, after the fire of around 1648. Designs for this are dated 1649, and with the Double and Single Cube Rooms, Webb has left us the only memorial of a full-blooded royal interior of the sort that Jones had designed for the king and queen in the 1630s. For this reason alone, the Wilton state rooms are precious and unique. It had been Webb's hope to carry the torch of Palladianism (see ANDREA PALLADIO) through the Restoration, but it was not to be, for exiles returning from France and Italy brought new ideas and influences to England, and the up-and-coming architect was the mathematician CHRISTOPHER WREN. Nevertheless, Webb was able to build several important Palladian monuments, all of which were to exercise tremendous influence in the early eighteenth century upon the neo-Palladianism. They were all engraved in the volumes of *Vitruvius Britannicus* edited by COLEN CAMPBELL in 1715, 1717, and 1725, but alas for poor Webb, all were thought to be works by Jones.

His first magisterial commission (Gunnersbury House, Middlesex, c.1658) was just before the Restoration. In this are echoes of Jones's works: the portico from the Queen's House, details from designs for the Prince's Lodging at Newmarket, and many other episodes make Gunnersbury the nearest equivalent to a country house by Jones. Amesbury House, Wiltshire, followed in 1660, and few would dispute that this was one of the finest

Palladian houses in the century, "of uncommon grandeur," to quote CHARLES R. COCKERELL's observations in the nineteenth century. There are hints in Amesbury of the emergent baroque: heavily rusticated and voussoired windows and rusticated wall facing. Webb was coming to terms with the new style, and his opportunity occurred in 1664 when he began a royal palace for Charles II at Greenwich. Unfortunately, only the western or Charles II wing was built, later to be incorporated into Wren's great design for the Royal Hospital for Seamen. Here occurred for the first time in English architecture the proper use of the giant order. In 1662 for the Queen Mother, Henrietta Maria, Webb built, the exquisite Gallery at Somerset House, a five-bay pilastered front above an arcade, and with it provided one of the most admired models for the urban façade in the age of neo-Palladianism.

All in all, his influence in his time was insignificant, but due to the fact that his and Jones's designs passed into the collection of LORD BURLINGTON, many were engraved, and thus Webb's influence upon the eighteenth century was profound and out of all proportion to his actual merit as a competent academic exponent of Jones's Palladianism.

JOHN HARRIS

WORKS

1649, Wilton House (reconstruction of south front state rooms), Wiltshire, England. 1651, Library and Repository, Royal College of Physicians, London. 1653, Drayton House (interiors), Northamptonshire, England. 1654, The Vyne (front and portico), Hampshire, England. 1655, Belvoir Castle (reconstruction after fire), Rutland, England. 1655, Chevening House (interiors), Kent, England. 1655, Lamport Hall, Northamptonshire, England. 1657, Northumberland House (interiors), London. 1658, Gunnersbury House, Middlesex, England. 1659, Amesbury House, Wiltshire, England. 1660s, Butleigh Court, Somerset, England. 1661, Queen's House (alterations), Greenwick; 1662, Somerset House (gallery); 1664, Palace for Charles II (incomplete), Greenwick; 1665, Cockpit Theatre (alterations), Whitehall; London.

WEBB, PHILIP S.

Anonymity and ordinariness in architecture and design were the ideals set down by Philip Speakman Webb (1831–1915). The sense of anonymity was cultivated not only in his designs but also in his life and professional activities. During his active career as an architect he allowed only a few of his buildings to be published. His historic fame has generally rested on his long and close association with WILLIAM MORRIS: his design of the famous Red House for Morris (Bexley Heath, Kent, 1859–1860); the numerous designs he made over the years for furniture and other decorative art objects for the Morris firm; and finally his later association with Morris in the establishment of the Society for the Preservation of Ancient Buildings (1877) and in the Socialist League.

Webb was born in Oxford where his father practiced medicine. In 1849, he was apprenticed to the Reading architect John Billing. After completing his training with Billing, he obtained a drafting position with the larger local firm of Bidlake and Lovatt, who maintained offices in Wolverhampton. He returned to Oxford in 1852 to work for an architect he had long admired, GEORGE E. STREET. Within a year, he was advanced to the position of chief draftsman in the office. In 1855, William Morris joined the Street office, and a lifetime friendship and close collaboration was established between the two. Morris and Webb accompanied Street when he moved his office to London in 1856, and later that year Morris was persuaded by Dante Gabriel Rossetti to abandon architecture and devote his efforts to becoming a painter. Before Webb left the Street office in 1859, he was joined by R. NORMAN SHAW, who succeeded him as chief draftsman in the firm.

The two buildings which firmly established his early reputation both date from the initial years of his practice. These were the much publicized Red House (1859–1860) for Morris, and Benfleet Hall (1860) near Cobham, designed for the painter Spencer Stanhope. Both of these small brick country houses were based upon late seventeenth- and eighteenth-century examples in which late vernacular Gothic forms had been affected by the classicizing influence of Renaissance forms and details. Webb's view of his architecture as expressing an "absence of style" meant that he, like A. W. N. PUGIN and such contemporaries as GEORGE F. BODLEY, GEORGE DEVEY, and WILLIAM E. NESFIELD, turned his attention to the modest vernacular architecture of the English countryside and small villages. Webb had first developed his own interest in the vernacular while working on one or another of the vicarages produced by the Street firm.

Along with his older colleague WILLIAM BUTTERFIELD, Webb felt that an essential ingredient of the vernacular was a cultivated commonplace, which often led to apparent ugliness. He would seem to have devoted as much of his design abilities to realize awkward and ungainly proportions, scale, and detailing as to any other facet of his architecture. The selection of the Queen Anne style of the late seventeeth and early eighteenth centuries was advantageous, for the architecture of this

Philip S. Webb.
Red House for William
Morris.
Bexley Heath, Kent,
England.
1859–1860

Philip S. Webb.
Standen.
Near East Grinstead,
Sussex, England.
1891–1894

and iron furniture, table glass, and metal candlesticks in the Morris, Marshall, and Faulkner exhibit. In the decades that followed, Webb continued to design with and for Morris. He frequently provided the drawings of animals and birds for the firm's glass windows, wallpapers, fabrics, and tile work. This close collaboration was in striking contrast to his architectural practice in which he not only preferred to work alone in his office and in supervising the construction of his buildings, but he also refused to become a member of any professional architectural organization.

Most of Webb's buildings were small suburban and country houses, but he did design several commercial buildings and one church. The first of the commercial buildings was a row of retail shops on Worship Street in London for Col. Gillum (1861–1862); this was followed by an office building for lawyers, Lincoln Inn Field, London (1868–1869); and in 1890, he designed a three-story raised basement office building for Bell Brothers in Middlesbrough. The shops on Worship Street and the office building on Lincoln Inn Field tend toward the Gothic, while the Bell Brothers Building with its dramatic silhouette of curved parapets is classical via Dutch and Belgian examples. The small Parish Church at Brampton (1874–1875), with decorative details by Morris and Edward Burne-Jones, perfectly sums up Webb's interest in producing studied anonymous buildings.

In many of his designs for suburban houses, he continued his close collaboration with Morris and Burne-Jones. The Howard House at No. 1 Palace Green, Kensington (1867–1870), exhibited a strikingly plain vertically awkward red brick Gothic exterior, while internally it was richly decorated by the three collaborators. Most of his suburban houses, though, were far less luxurious. The Studio-house for Prinsep in Kensington (c.1864–1865), the addition to the Bell House (Washington Hall) in Durham (1867–1870), and the Boyce House, Chelsea (1868–1869) indicate Webb's interpretation of the increasingly popular Queen Anne Revival. All exhibit picturesque, many-gabled, and chimneyed roofs; walls of brick with minimal stone trim; and windows and doors which sometimes hint at the Gothic, at other times are square-headed with classical double-hung windows.

The Queen Anne style was especially advantageous for country houses, and Webb made the most of its assets. Although he let his houses ramble somewhat loosely over their sites, he always provided a central rectangular block which dominated and held the elements together. In his interiors, he, like other Queen Anne Revival architects, had a fondness for a two-story living hall,

period was an unsettled mixture, with the late vernacular Gothic often in open or hidden conflict with the design principles of the imported classical tradition. In the Red House and at Benfleet Hall, Webb could be ordered and classical at one moment, and picturesque and Gothic at the next. Webb's own interest in the visual play between the Gothic and the classical was different from that of Butterfield or later of Shaw, for he consciously employed it not to establish a fashionable high art style but to further his goal of creating a normative nonstyle of his own. Although early in his career he traveled to the Low Countries and France with Street and Morris, and later in the 1880s to Italy, his architectural vocabulary remained relatively pure in its English sources.

As early as 1858, Webb had started designing furniture and other decorative art objects for and with William Morris. Much of the furniture for the Red House was designed by him, and when the firm of Morris, Marshall, and Faulkner was formed in April 1861 (with Webb as a partner), the first articles sold were table glass, furniture, and jewelry, all designed by Webb. At the London Exposition of 1882, Webb was represented by wooden which internally served the same purpose of unification as his central rectilinear volume did externally. In his first large country house, Arisaig, near Fort William, Inverness-shire, Scotland (1863), the two-story living hall and the exterior of the central block lean toward the Gothic. Beginning in the 1870s, Webb's country houses became more and more classical. Joldwynds, near Dorking, Surrey (1872–1873), and Rounton Grange, Yorkshire (1872), provided a classical vocabulary as expressed within the late seventeenth-century Queen Anne style. Later in the decade, Smeaton Manor, Yorkshire (1876–1879), seems more Georgian than Queen Anne. Clouds, near East Knoyle, Wiltshire (1881–1887), his largest country house, was insistently classical, though in plan and elevation it was still picturesque and complex. His final work of the 1890s, Standen near East Grinstead, Sussex (1891–1894), and Great Tangley Manor, Yorkshire (1892), perfectly sum up the qualities which EDWIN LUTYENS admired in Webb: "freshness and orginality" combined with "thoroughness."

DAVID GEBHARD

WORKS

1859–1860, Red House for William Morris, Bexley Heath, Kent, England. 1860, Ben Fleet Hall, Fairmile, near Cobham, England. 1861–1862, Stores for Col. Gillum, Worship Street, London. 1863, Arisaig near Fort William, Inverness-shire, Scotland. 1864–1865, Prinsep House, Kensington, London. 1865–1867, Washington Hall, Durham, England. 1867–1870, Howard House, Kensington, London. 1868, Trevor Hall (Church Hill House), East Barnet; 1868–1869, Boyce House, Chelsea; 1868–1869, Lawyer's Offices, Lincoln Inn Field; London. 1872, Rounton Grange, Yorkshire, England. 1872–1873, Joldwynds, near Dorking, Surrey, England. 1874–1875, Parish Church, Brampton, England. 1876–1879, Smeaton Manor, Yorkshire, England. 1876–1886, Clouds House, East Knoyle, Wiltshire, England. 1878, New Place, Welwyn, England. 1890, Bell Brothers Offices, Middlesbrough England 1891–1894, Standen, near East Grinstead, Sussex, England. 1892, Great Tangley Manor, Yorkshire, England.

BIBLIOGRAPHY

BRANDON-JONES, JOHN 1955 "The Work of Philip Webb and Norman Shaw." *Architectural Association Journal* 71:9–21, 40–47.
BRANDON-JONES, JOHN 1964 "Philip Webb." Pages 247–265 in Peter Ferriday (editor), *Victorian Architecture.* Philadelphia: Lippincott.
JACK, GEORGE 1915 "An Appreciation of Philip Webb." *Architectural Review* 38:1–6.
JACKSON, NEIL 1977 "A Church for SPAB." *Architectural Review* 162:69–71.
LETHABY, WILLIAM R. 1935 *Philip Webb and His Work.* London: O.U.P.
MACLEOD, ROBERT 1971 "William Morris and Philip Webb." Pages 40–44 in *Style and Society: Architectural Ideology in Britain: 1835–1914.* London: R.I.B.A.
MORRIS, G. H. 1897 "On Mr. Philip Webb's Town Work." *Architectural Review* 2:199–208.
ROOKS, NOEL 1950 "The Work of Lethaby, Webb and Morris." *Journal of the Royal Institute of British Architects* 57:167–175.
YOKOYAMA, TADAMI 1976 "Trip to 'Epoch Making' Red House." *Global Architecture Houses* 1:4–17.

WEBSTER, GEORGE

George Webster (1797–1864) was the son of the Westmoreland, England, builder and architect Francis Webster (1766–1827) and a partner in his mechanized marble cutting business (1820–1827). George appears to have trained with a northern English architect, from 1827 establishing his own large regional practice. More remarkable than his conventional neoclassical public buildings and neo-Gothic churches was his early revival of the Jacobean style in a series of houses. In 1845, he made his draftsman, Miles Thompson, a partner. Webster visited Italy on various occasions, assembling a collection of coins and antiquities.

R. WINDSOR LISCOMBE

WORKS

1824–1825, Rydal Church; *1825, Rigmaden; 1825–1827, Assembly Rooms (now Town Hall), Kendal; Westmoreland, England. 1825–1827, Eshton Hall, Yorkshire, England. 1825–1828, Underley Hall, Westmoreland, England; 1828–1829, Lindale Church; *1829, Moreton Hall, Whalley; *1832, Penwortham Priory (major remodeling), near Preston; Lancashire, England. *1832, Public Rooms (now Town Hall), Settle, Yorkshire, England. *1833, Dowker's Hospital; 1835–1837, Holy Trinity (Roman Catholic) Church; 1835–1837, Saint Thomas's Church; Kendal, Westmoreland, England. 1838–1841, Broughton Hall (major alterations), near Skipton, Yorkshire, England. 1839–1841, Saint George's Church, Kendal, Westmoreland, England. 1840?, Holker Hall (remodeling), near Cartmel, Lancashire, England. 1841–1842, Cleator Church, Cumberland, England. 1843–1853, Bardsea Church, Lancashire, England. 1855, Market Hall (now Public Library), Kendal, Westmoreland, England.

BIBLIOGRAPHY

ASLET, CLIVE 1980 "Holker Hall, Cumbria 2." *Country Life* 168:18–21.
COOPER, NICHOLAS 1973 "Growth of a Lakeland Town. Kendal, Westmoreland I." *Country Life* 154:762–764.
CORNFORTH, JOHN 1965 "Hutton-in-the-Forest, Cumberland—III." *Country Life* 137:352–356.
HAWORTH, JEFFREY P., and TAYLOR, ANGUS C. 1973 *The Websters of Kendal.* Exhibition Catalogue. Abbot Hall, Kendal, Westmoreland, England.

Hussey, Christopher 1950 "Broughton Hall, Yorkshire I." and "Broughton Hall, Yorkshire III." *Country Life* 107:876–879, 1034–1037.

WEEKS, JOHN

Born in London and educated at the Architectural Association School there, John Weeks (1921–) began his partnership with Richard Llewelyn-Davies in 1960 and is currently senior director of the firm Llewelyn-Davies Weeks Forestier-Walker, and Bor, in charge of the firm's hospital and health services planning practice.

As well as practicing architecture in a professional capacity, Weeks has been involved in the educational and theoretical field. He was studio master at the Architectural Association School in 1960 and part-time senior lecturer at the Bartlett School of Architecture, University of London, from 1961 to 1972. He is best known for his advocacy of "Indeterminacy in Architecture," involving as it does provision for irregular and unforeseeable growth and change. This "multi-strategy" architecture challenges standard ideas on finitude and is best exemplified in Week's Northwick Park Hospital (1961), Harrow, Middlesex.

CHRISTOPHER FAWCETT

WORKS

JOHN WEEKS AND RICHARD LLEWELYN-DAVIES

1952, Nuffield House, Musgrave Park Hospital, Belfast, Ireland. 1954, Diagnostic Center, Corby, Northhamptonshire, England. 1955, House, Mayford, Surrey, England. 1957, Mignot Memorial Hospital, Alderney, Channel Island, England. 1957, Rushbrooke Village Housing, Burg Saint Edmunds, Suffolk, England. 1958, Times Newspaper Office Building (with Ellis, Clarke and Galleraugh), London. 1960, Imperial College of Tropical Agriculture (students residence and dining room with Colin Laird Associates), Trinidad. 1960, Nuffield Institute of Comparative Medicine; 1960, Zoological Society (meeting halls and laboratories); London. 1961, Clinical Research Center; 1961, Northwick Park Hospital; Harrow, Middlesex, England. 1961, Stock Exchange (redevelopment with Fitzroy Robinson); 1961, Sun Alliance Insurance Building (with Robinson); 1963, Tate Gallery (extension); London. 1963, Town Center Development (phase I and Sports Center with Ian Fraser Associates), Basingstoke, Hampshire, England. 1966, Barmston Village Housing Project, Washington New Town, County Durham, England. 1968, Experimental Pathology Research Building, Saint Mary's Hospital, Paddington, London. 1968, Stantonbury Housing Scheme, Milton Keynes, Buckinghamshire, England. 1970, Medical Center, Flinders University (with South Australia Dept. of Public Works), Adelaide, South Australia. 1970, University Children's Hospital (with Felix Tanghe and Delarue), Leuven, Belgium. 1970, Youth Treatment Center, Birmingham, England. 1971, National Hospital for Nervous Diseases (sciences laboratories), London. 1971, Salmaniya Medical Center, Bahrain. 1971, York District Hospital, England. 1972, General Hospital, Doha, State of Qatar. 1972, Metal Box Company Headquarters, Reading, Berkshire, England. 1972, Singapore General Hospital (with INDECO), Outram Road. 1973, Normanby College Education Center, King's College Hospital, London. 1974, Health Sciences Center, University of Khon Kaen (with Kingston Reynolds, Thom and Allardice), Thailand. 1975, Cancer Research Foundation, Sutton, Surrey, England. 1975, Rayne Institute Research Laboratories, University College Hospital; 1976, Voluntary Research Trust Research Laboratory, King's College Hospital; London.

BIBLIOGRAPHY

Brett, Lionel 1970 *Parameters and Images.* London: Weidenfeld & Nicolson.
Jencks, Charles, and Baird, George (editors) 1969 *Meaning in Architecture.* London: Barrie & Jenkins.
Weeks, John 1963–1964 "Indeterminate Architecture." *Transactions of the Bartlett Society* 2:83–106.
Weeks, John, and Llewelyn-Davies, Richard (editors) 1965 "Health and Hospitals." *Architectural Review* 137, no. 820:special issue.
Weeks, John, 1969 "Multi-strategy Buildings." *Architectural Design* 39:536–540.
Weeks, John, 1970 "Hôpital Northwick Park-Londres." *L'Architecture d'aujourd'hui.* 41, no. 150:62–63.
Weeks, John, 1976 "Alvar Aalto." *The Listener.*

WEESE, HARRY MOHR

Harry Mohr Weese (1915–), born in Evanston, Illinois, was educated at the Massachusetts Institute of Technology and at the Cranbrook Academy of Art. A partner with Benjamin Baldwin from 1941 to 1942, he established his own firm, Harry Weese and Associates, in 1947 after serving as a naval engineering officer during World War II. Influenced by Eliel Saarinen and Eero Saarinen at Cranbrook, and by works of Alvar Aalto and Le Corbusier, Weese also draws inspiration from Chicago's historic architecture and has an interest in historic preservation.

ELSA GILBERTSON

WORKS

1956, 227 East Walton Apartments, Chicago. 1956–1959, United States Embassy and Staff Housing, Accra. 1959, Pierce Towers, University of Chicago. 1960, Eugenie Lane Apartments, Chicago. 1961, Arena Stage (part 1), Washington. 1961, Northside Junior High School; 1965, First Baptist Church; Columbus, Ind. 1965, International Business Machines Office Building, Milwaukee, Wis. 1967, Adler–Sullivan Auditorium Theater (restoration); 1967, John Fewkes Tower; 1967, Field Museum of Natural History (restoration); 1967, Orchestra Hall (renovation); Chicago. 1968, Library and College of General Studies, Rochester Institute of Technology, N.Y. 1969, Latin School, Chicago. 1969, Milwaukee Center for the Performing Arts, Wis. 1970, Academic Complex and Art Center, University of Wisconsin, Madison. 1970, Time Life Building, Chicago. 1972, Arena Stage (part 2), Washington. 1972, Given Institute of Pathobiology, Aspen, Colo. 1973, Crown Center Hotel, Kansas City, Mo. 1974, Hyde Park Townhouses, Chicago. 1974, Mercantile Bank Building, Kansas City, Mo. 1974, Village Hall, Oak Park, Ill. 1975, Campbell United States Courthouse Annex, Chicago. 1975, Sawyer Library, Williams College, Williamstown, Mass. 1976, First National Bank of Albuquerque, N.M. 1977, Metro System, Washington. 1977, Terman Engineering Center, Stanford University, Palo Alto, Calif. 1978, 200 South Wacker Drive Building, Chicago.

BIBLIOGRAPHY

"Current Work of Harry Weese." 1963 *Architectural Record* 133:127–142.

DANZIG, PHILIP I. 1966 "Names." *Architectural and Engineering News* 8, no. 10:100.

DEAN, ANDREA O. 1978 "Harry Weese of Chicago." *American Institute of Architects*. 67, no. 5:56–65.

"Harry Weese and Associates of Chicago." 1976 *Space Design* no. 138:5–36.

"Harry Weese: Humanism and Tradition." 1979 *Process: Architecture* no. 11:entire issue.

HEYER, PAUL (1966)1978 *Architects on Architecture: New Directions in America.* New ed., enl. New York: Walker.

"In the Spirit of the 'Chicago School'—An Apartment Building Designed for Light, Air and Views." 1968 *Architectural Record* 144, no. 1:109–112.

McQUADE, WALTER 1962 "A Continuing Tradition in Great Architecture." *Architectural Forum* 116:89–106.

MILLER, NORY 1972 "Exploring the Fundamentals in Fundamentalist Columbus, Indiana." *Inland Architect* 16, no. 10:9–13.

MILLER, NORY 1975 "The Loop Gets a Stunning Skyscraper Jail." *Inland Architect* 19, no. 1:7–13.

"United States Embassy—Accra, Ghana." 1957 *Architectural Record* 121:197–202.

WEIDLINGER ASSOCIATES

Weidlinger Associates is a group of consulting engineers who have worked on many architectural projects. Founded by Paul Weidlinger in 1949, the firm now has nine general partners. The main office is in New York with branches in Cambridge, Massachusetts; Menlo Park, California; and Chesapeake, Virginia. In addition to a civil-structural engineering practice, Weidlinger Associates conducts innovative research.

PATRICIA C. PHILLIPS

WORKS

1972, 1 Liberty Plaza, New York. 1975, Grand Coulee Dam Power Plant, Denver, Colo. 1976, American Telephone and Telegraph Longlines, Bedminster, N.J. 1976, Roosevelt Island, New York. 1976, University of Riyadh Recreational Facility, Saudi Arabia. 1980–1983, New York Exposition and Convention Center.

BIBLIOGRAPHY

Some of the information in this article was provided by Weidlinger Associates.

RUSH, RICHARD 1980 "Technics: Structuring Tall Buildings, Structure and Circumstance." *Progressive Architecture* 61, no. 12:50–57.

SKY, ALISON, and STONE, MICHELLE 1976 *Unbuilt America.* New York: McGraw-Hill.

WEINBRENNER, FRIEDRICH

Friedrich Weinbrenner (1766–1826) is considered the outstanding architect of classicism in the southwest of Germany. His work is largely defined by the planning and building for which he was responsible as *Bauinspektor* of Karlsruhe, the capital city of Baden and seat of the ducal court, an office he held from 1797 until his death. As with other great architects—KARL FRIEDRICH SCHINKEL in Berlin, GEORG LUDWIG FRIEDRICH LAVES in Hanover, LEO VON KLENZE in Munich—his architectural activity also included urban planning, as required by the transformation of medieval and baroque court seats into the modern middle-sized administrative centers of the post-Napoleonic restoration.

Until he was twenty, Weinbrenner received the traditional artisan's training as a carpenter in his father's shop. Only thereafter, on travels to Switzerland, Vienna and Dresden, and finally to Berlin, did he come in contact with the new architectural ideas from Paris and Rome. Through association with CARL GOTTHARD LANGHANS and with contemporaries such as FRIEDRICH GILLY and H. C. GENELLI, he decided to undertake a long trip to Italy. This extended into five years of study in Rome, from 1792 to 1797. The sketches and designs from those years bear witness, both in their literary inspiration and in their formal artistic attitude, to GIOVANNI BATTISTA PIRANESI's lasting influence and the Doric-Grecisizing adaptation it underwent at the hands of the international circle around the Roman academies. Designs for overscaled memorial monuments document the megalomaniac pomposity of the Napoleonic era, which later was to find its parallel in the national cult of monuments memorializing the German wars of liberation (Monument to Frederick the Great, 1794; Monument to the Battle of the Nations near Leipzig, 1814).

In 1797, immediately upon his return to Karlsruhe, Weinbrenner was engaged as a state official for building activities. From then on, his architectural work was devoted to reshaping the city, which had been founded in 1725 as the seat of the court of the absolutist princes of Baden. To counterbalance the concentric radial pattern of streets dominated by the castle, it was necessary to establish a sequence of plazas within an axially arranged reorientation which would make room for the representational demands of the new middle class community. Already in his *General-Bauplan* (general building plan) as well as in his first design for the Marktplatz (market place) Weinbrenner laid down the binding framework that would govern all subsequent architectural and planning decisions for the expansion of the town. With the widening of the street axis running south from the castle, a monumental urban space was projected, beginning with a gate (*Ettlinger Tor*) at the outer end and followed by a series of varied street and plaza spaces. Furthermore, the plazalike areas were to be accented by monuments.

The Marktplatz became the artistic and political center of the town. The porticoes of the Town Hall (1806–1820) and the Evangelical Church (1806ff), built in the antique mode, protruded from its unified building line. For another church project, the Roman Catholic Church of Saint Stephen (1807ff), Weinbrenner created an effective mass accent with a central-building variant of the Pantheon heightening the annex rooms with pediments. With a synagogue, begun in 1798 in a Doric-Orientalizing mixed style, Weinbrenner gave impressive representation to the religious faiths recognized by the liberal-constitutional state. As early as 1804, Weinbrenner had designed model façades for the middle class buildings on the outskirts of the projected urban entity. Planned in the tradition of absolutism, they were intended to define the new town organism as a unity; however, they were not always adhered to. In the vicinity of the Schlossplatz, the play on the canon of aesthetic examples was to be particularly effective through the erection of palatial townhouses. In spite of complicated, often wedge-shaped building lots, Weinbrenner here achieved sometimes quite convincing ground-plan types which represent ornamentally reduced variants of Palladian (see AN-DREA PALLADIO) forms. A project such as the remodeling of the diagonal Lange Strasse (1808) which recommended even rows of steep, round arcades in front of the straight lines of the house façades could be appreciated anew only within the aesthetics of surrealism. With other public buildings of bourgeois culture, such as museums and theaters, Weinbrenner was less successful. They were rebuilt soon after their erection by his numerous pupils in the less rigid forms of Romantic classicism.

EBERHARD DRÜEKE
Translated from German by
Beverley R. Placzek

WORKS

1798, Synagogue; 1805–1813, Palace of the Margrave; 1806–1816, Evangelical Church; 1806–1820, Town Hall; 1807–1814, Saint Stephen; Karlsruhe, Germany. 1817, Museum, Leipzig. 1822, Conversationshaus, Baden-Baden, Germany. 1826, Museum, Karlsruhe, Germany.

BIBLIOGRAPHY

VALDENAIRE, ARTHUR 1919 *Friedrich Weinbrenner: Sein Leben und seine Bauten.* Karlsruhe, Germany: Müller.
"Friedrich Weinbrenner 1766–1826." 1977 Karlsruhe, Germany: Staatliche Kunsthalle. Exhibition catalogue.
WEINBRENNER, FRIEDRICH 1810–1819 Volumes 1–3 in *Architektonisches Lehrbuch.* Tübingen, Germany: Cottaischen.

WEININGER, ANDREW

Andrew Weininger (1899–) was born in Karancs, Hungary. He was influenced by Impressionism and *de Stijl,* and studied with Johannes Itten at the Weimar Bauhaus in 1921, with THEO VAN DOESBURG in 1922, and with Oskar Schlemmer in the Bauhaus theater at Dessau. He is the author of a project for a spherical theater which places the spectators on the inner walls of a sphere around an arena stage to form "a new psychic, optical, acoustical relationship." Since 1958, he has been living and working as an artist in New York.

REGINALD MALCOLMSON

WELLS, MALCOLM

Malcolm Wells (1926–) studied civil engineering at Georgia Tech (1943–1945). In addition to five hundred architectural commissions, Wells has lectured and has written many publications. He provides consultation on underground and energy-efficient architecture and solar energy. Wells's guiding principle of "gentle architecture" has been a search to build without harming the natural environment.

PATRICIA C. PHILLIPS

WORKS

1953, Church of Christ, Collingswood, N.J. 1959, Radio Corporation of America Space Center, Princeton, N.J. 1966, Cherry Hill Free Public Library, N.J. 1973–1978, Plant Science Building, Cary Arboretum, New York Botanical Garden, Millbrook, N.Y.

BIBLIOGRAPHY

SKY, ALISON, and STONE, MICHELLE 1976 *Unbuilt America.* New York: McGraw-Hill.
WELLS, MALCOLM 1965 "Nowhere to Go But Down." *Progressive Architecture* 46, no. 2:174–179.

WELSCH, MAXIMILIAN VON

Johann Maximilian von Welsch (1671–1745), architect and engineer in Franconia and the Middle Rhine in the early eighteenth century, played a significant role in making this region one of the principal centers of the German baroque. Born in Kronach, von Welsch spent most of his childhood and adolescence in Bamberg. After attending the local Jesuit Academia Ottoniana (1690–1692), he entered the military service of the duke of Saxe-Gotha in 1693. This was the start of a brilliant, lifelong career as an infantry officer and military engineer; in 1714, von Welsch was ennobled by the emperor for his achievements in fortifications design. Although it is doubtful that he ever studied architecture extensively, service with the mercenary Saxe-Gotha regiments provided him with the opportunity to travel widely in central and western Europe. In 1704, von Welsch entered the employ of Lothar Franz von Schönborn, elector of Mainz and prince-bishop of Bamberg, and made Mainz his permanent home. Although primarily engaged as a fortifications engineer, his aptitude for architecture was recognized by his patron, who appointed him *Baudirektor* of Bamberg in 1706 and enlisted his services on the building enterprises of other family members. The Schönborn princes, all of them prolific builders, pursued a policy of collective design, soliciting plans and opinions from various architects and summoning them for frequent conferences. Along with JOHANN BALTHASAR NEUMANN, Johann Dientzenhofer (see DIENTZENHOFER BROTHERS), and JOHANN LUCAS VON HILDEBRANDT, von Welsch participated in the planning of Schloss Pommersfelden (1711–1718), Schloss Bruchsal (1720–1752), and the Würzburg *Residenz* (1719–1779). He was involved during the early stages at Bruchsal (1720) and Würzburg (1720–1723). Although his impact on the formulation of the overall plans was decisive, at both sites his influence was later eclipsed by Neumann. At Pommersfelden, he was responsible

for the stables (1714–1718) and the garden (1714). Von Welsch was much in demand among the central German nobility as a designer of small country palaces, gardens, and orangeries. Chief among these were Lustschloss Favorite (1707–1723) near Mainz, Lustschloss Biebrich (1708–1721), and the Orangerie and Schlossgarten at Fulda (1722–1730). Although his architecture exhibits an informed understanding of the major seventeenth-century developments of France, Italy, and Austria, von Welsch ultimately failed to integrate the conflicting tendencies of classicism and the baroque. Fundamentally classicistic, he experimented with baroque plasticity, but without the resolute mastery of Hildebrandt or JOHANN BERNHARD FISCHER VON ERLACH, both of whom influenced him profoundly. His work shows none of Neumann's interest in spatial dynamics and only occasional outbursts of Hildebrandt's energetic ornamentalism. A generation of minor architects working in central Germany in the mid-eighteenth century trained under von Welsch's aegis.

SAMUEL J. KLINGENSMITH

WORKS

*1707–1723, Lustschloss Favorite (garden and orangery); 1708–1721, Lustschloss Biebrich; near Mainz, Germany. 1709–1719, Wambolter Hof, Worms, Germany. *1710–1714, Belvedere in Tiergarten Schrattenhofen, near Oettingen, Germany. 1710–1715, Deutschordenskommende, Frankfurt-Sachsenhausen (portal, staircase), Germany. 1711–1718, Palais der Kurmainzer Regierung, Erfurt, Germany. *1712–?, Residenzschloss (garden), Usingen, Germany. 1714–1718, Schloss Pommersfelden (stables, garden), Germany. 1720–1721, Schönbornkapelle, Cathedral (exterior executed), Würzburg, Germany. 1720–1723, Court Chapel, Residenz, Würzburg, Germany. 1722–1730, Orangerie and Schlossgarten, Fulda, Germany. 1742–1747, Abteikirche, Amorbach, Germany.

BIBLIOGRAPHY

EINSINGBACH, WOLFGANG 1962 "Die künstlerischen Anfänge Maximilian von Welschs." *Forschungen und Fortschritte* 36:110–115.
EINSINGBACH, WOLFGANG 1963 "Johann Maximilian von Welsch: Neue Beiträge zu seinem Leben und zu seiner Tätigkeit für den Fürsten Georg August von Nassau-Idstein." *Nassauische Annalen* 74:79–170.
EINSINGBACH, WOLFGANG 1972–1973 "Zum Leben des Mainzer Barockarchitekten Maximilian von Welsch zwischen 1693 und 1704 und der Bericht über seine Reise in die Niederlande, nach Frankreich und England in den Jahren 1699–1700." *Mainzer Zeitschrift* 67–68:214–229.
HOTZ, JOACHIM 1976 "Barocke Planzeichnungen für das Schloss in Bruchsal: Gang und Stand der Forschung zur Architektenfrage." *Jahrbuch der Staatlichen Kunstsammlungen in Baden-Württemberg* 13:87–122.

KÖMSTEDT, RUDOLF 1963 *Von Bauten und Baumeister des fränkischen Barocks.* Berlin: Hessling.

KREISEL, HEINRICH 1953 *Das Schloss zu Pommersfelden.* Berlin and Munich: Hirmer.

LOHMEYER, KARL 1911 *Friedrich Joachim Stengel, fürstäbtlich fuldischer Ingenieur, Hofarchitekt und Baumeister . . . 1694–1787.* Düsseldorf, Germany: Schwann.

LOHMEYER, KARL 1925 "Barock und Klassizismus bei Welsch und Dinzenhofer." *Der Cicerone* 17:600–604.

LOHMEYER, KARL 1927 *Schönbornschlösser: Die Stichwerke Salomon Kleiners . . . mit einer Einleitung und der Lebensgeschichte Maximilian von Welschs.* Heidelberg, Germany: Winters.

LOHMEYER, KARL 1931 *Die Baumeister des rheinisch-fränkischen Barocks.* Vienna and Augsburg, Germany: Filser.

MEINTZSCHEL, JOACHIM 1963 *Studien zu Maximilian von Welsch.* Würzburg, Germany: Schöningh.

SEDLMAIER, RICHARD, and PFISTER, RUDOLF 1923 *Die fürstbischöfliche Residenz zu Würzburg.* Munich: Müller.

WENZEL, WERNER 1970 *Die Gärten des Lothar Franz von Schönborn, 1655–1729.* Berlin: Mann.

WERNERUS, MATTHIAS

Using concrete shaped over an armature of steel and fence wire, inlaid with glass, uncut gems, petrified wood, and whatever else people would bring him, Father Matthias Wernerus (1873–1931) built a grotto, cemetery shrines, and monument to Christopher Columbus (1926–1931) in Dickeyville, Wisconsin, to stand between the church and rectory of his rural parish.

JANET KAPLAN

BIBLIOGRAPHY

WAMPLER, JAN 1977 Pages 108–117 in *All Their Own: People and the Places They Build.* Cambridge, Mass.: Schenkman.

WESTMAN, CARL

Ernst Carl Westman (1866–1936) studied at the Royal Institute of Technology and the Academy of Art in Stockholm; in 1916, he became chief architect for the Department of Public Health in Stockholm. Westman is best known for his Stockholm Courthouse (1909–1915), an important monument of National Romanticism. Taking some of its motifs from late medieval castles and churches in Sweden, the building offered, at the same time, a new and very practical layout for the principal municipal courts. Westman was influenced by CHARLES F. A. VOYSEY and MARTIN NYROP, and his work was closely related to that of RAGNAR ÖSTBERG and LARS WAHLMAN.

BARBARA MILLER LANE

WORKS

1906, Swedish Medical Society Headquarters, Stockholm. 1907, Sanitorium, Romanäs, Sweden. 1909–1915, Courthouse, Stockholm. 1911, Courthouse, Nyköping, Sweden. 1914, Röhsska Museum of Applied Arts, Göteborg, Sweden. 1917–1919, Bünsow House, Djurgården, Stockholm. n.d., Fåhraeus House, Lidingö, Sweden. n.d., Hospital Buildings, Stockholm.

BIBLIOGRAPHY

AHLBERG, HAKON 1925 *Moderne Schwedische Architektur.* Berlin: Wasmuth.

AHLBERG, HAKON 1954 "Carl Westman och nationalromantiken." *Byggmästaren* 33, no. 11:254–257.

ANDERSSON, HENRIK O., and BEDOIRE, FREDRIC (1973)1977 *Stockholms Byggnader.* Rev. ed. Stockholm: Bokförlaget Prisma.

Deutsche Bauzeitung. 1923 57, nos. 17–18:80, no. 19:89, no. 28:133.

LANE, BARBARA MILLER 1981 "Government Buildings in European Capitals, 1870–1914." In Hans J. Teuteberg (editor), *Urbanisierung im 19. und 20. Jahrhundert: Historische und geographische Aspekte.* Cologne, Germany, and Vienna: Böhlau.

MÜHLKE, K. 1916 "Das neue Rathaus in Stockholm." *Zentralblatt der Bauverwaltung* 36, no. 64:430.

PALM, BERTIL 1954 *Arkitekten Carl Westman: 1866–1936.* Lund, Sweden: CWK Gleerup.

WHEELER, GERVASE

Gervase Wheeler (c.1815–1870) was the son of a London jeweler, who, having trained as an architect, emigrated to America in the 1840s and worked first in Hartford, Connecticut, and then in New York. The only known works by Wheeler are those built in America, and all but one seem to have been destroyed. He had returned to England by 1865, probably discouraged by the Civil War, and set up an office at 9 Conduit Street, London. His designs were favorably noticed and published by ANDREW JACKSON DOWNING in both *The Architecture of Country Houses* and in the periodical *The Horticulturalist.* Wheeler himself published his ideas in three books: *Rural Homes; or, Sketches of Houses suited to American Country Life, Homes for the People, in Suburb and Country,* and *The Choice of a Dwelling.* All went through a number of editions. In the absence of any identifiable works by Wheeler in England, his importance seems to lie in his translation of the English picturesque style of the early nineteenth century into the American timber-built vernacular, and in doing this he became one of the originators of the Stick style. He was also interested in the planning of American townhouses and lectured on this subject at the Royal Institute of British Architects in 1868.

JILL ALLIBONE

WORKS

1849, Henry Boody House, Brunswick, Maine. *1849, Olmstead House, Hartford, Conn. *1851, New York, University Buildings, Washington Square, New York. *1853, Italian Villa, Norwich, Conn. *1854, 111 Braodway, New York. *1854, Villa Mansion, Long Island, N.Y. 1855, Bowdoin College Chapel (alterations), Brunswick, Maine. *1856–1857, 430 Broome Street, New York. 1857, Stone Chapel (Goodrich Hall), Williams College, Williamstown, Mass. *1859–1860, 18 William Street, New York. *1860, Brooklyn Post Office Building, N.Y.

BIBLIOGRAPHY

DOWNING, ANDREW JACKSON (1850)1969 *The Architecture of Country Houses.* Reprint. New York: Dover.
SCULLY, VINCENT JOSEPH, JR. 1953 "Romantic Rationalism and the Expression of Structure in Wood: Downing, Wheeler, Gardner, and the 'Stick Style' 1840–76." *Art Bulletin* 35:121–142?
SCULLY, VINCENT JOSEPH, JR. (1955)1971 *The Shingle Style and the Stick Style.* Rev. ed. New Haven: Yale University Press.
WHEELER, GERVASE 1848–1849 "Design for a Villa in the Tudor Style." *The Horticulturalist* 3:560–561.
WHEELER, GERVASE 1849–1850 "Design and Description of an English Cottage." *The Horticulturalist* 4:77–79, 144.
WHEELER, GERVASE 1851 *Rural Homes; or, Sketches of Houses Suited to American Country Life.* New York: Scribner.
WHEELER, GERVASE 1853 "Design for an Italian Villa." *The Horticulturalist* New Series 3:373–375.
WHEELER, GERVASE 1855 *Homes for the People, in Suburb and Country.* New York: Scribner.
WHEELER, GERVASE 1868 "A New York Up-Town House." *The Builder* 11:262–263.
WHEELER, GERVASE 1871 *The Choice of a Dwelling.* London: Murray.

WHEELWRIGHT, EDMUND M.

Edmund March Wheelwright (1854–1912) was educated at the Massachusetts Institute of Technology and the Ecole des Beaux-Arts, Paris. He practiced in Boston, first alone, then in partnership with Parkman B. Haven. Stylistically eclectic and particularly active in civic building, Wheelwright was Boston city architect from 1891 to 1895. Several of his scholarly architectural writings were published, including *School Architecture* (1901).

GWEN W. STEEGE

WORKS

c.1900, Cambridge Bridge; 1900, Horticultural Hall; 1903, New England Conservatory of Music; 1908, Boston Opera House; Boston. c.1911, Bridge, Hartford, Conn.

BIBLIOGRAPHY

BROWN, FRANK CHOUTEAU 1907 "Boston Suburban Architecture." *Architectural Record* 21:245–280.
CHANDLER, FRANCIS WARD (editor) 1898 *Municipal Architecture in Boston, from Designs by Edmund M. Wheelwright.* Boston: Bates & Guild.
"Edmund W. Wheelwright Dead." 1912 *American Architect and Building News* 102, Aug. 28:3.
WHEELWRIGHT, EDMUND M. 1901 *School Architecture.* Boston: Rogers & Manson.
WODEHOUSE, LAWRENCE 1976 *American Architects from the Civil War to the First World War.* Detroit, Mich.: Gale.

WHIDDEN and LEWIS

The establishment of the firm of Whidden and Lewis marked the coming of age of architecture in Portland, Oregon. William Whidden (1857–1929), a native of Boston, studied at the Massachusetts Institute of Technology (M.I.T.) and spent four years at the Ecole des Beaux-Arts in Paris. Upon his return in 1882, he joined MCKIM, MEAD, AND WHITE in New York. Later that year, Whidden accompanied McKim to the Northwest where the firm had commissions from Henry Villard to design hotels and railroad stations in Tacoma, Washington, and Portland. Whidden stayed in Portland to supervise the hotel work. Due to the collapse of Villard's railroad empire near the end of 1883, construction on the Portland Hotel was halted with the stone walls projecting to the first story. Whidden returned to Boston and formed a partnership with William, E. Chamberlin, a schoolmate at M.I.T. and fellow draftsman at McKim, Mead, and White. In 1888, a syndicate of Portland's leading families acquired the unfinished Portland Hotel, and Whidden returned to oversee the project. A year later, another friend and M.I.T. alumnus, Ion Lewis (1858–1933), visited Portland and upon Whidden's invitation stayed and joined Whidden in partnership. Their practice grew quickly, and they soon became the prominent firm in Portland.

After graduation from M.I.T., Ion Lewis had joined the Boston architectural firm of PEABODY AND STEARNS. In 1882, he formed a partnership with Henry Paston Clark. Clark and Lewis became well known for their Shingle style work.

Whidden and Lewis introduced the latest Eastern styles to the Portland architectural scene: the Colonial Revival residence and the classical commercial business structure. The Milton W. Smith House (1890) is an early example of the former, and the Hamilton Building (1893) is an elegant work in the latter style.

Due to Whidden's association with the Portland Hotel, the firm had access to the city's leading developers and institutions. In 1891, they designed the Portland Public Library, a modest version of McKim, Mead, and White's Boston Library, and a year later, the firm completed designs for the Portland City Hall, a full block structure in the Renaissance Revival mode. Whidden and Lewis completed their major public work in 1909 with the design of the Multnomah County Courthouse. That year also marked the beginning of the firm's decline and the emergence of their protégé, ALBERT E. DOYLE. The firm continued until Whidden's death in 1929. Their only major works in the later years were the Wilcox Building (1911), the Courthouse Addition (1914), and the Stevens Building (1913-1914).

GEORGE A. MCMATH

WORKS

*1888-1890, Portland Hotel; 1890, Milton W. Smith Residence; *1890-1892, Portland Public Library; 1891, Arlington Club, Concord Building; 1893, Hamilton Building; 1892-1895, Portland City Hall; *1895, Portland Academy; *1897-1898, Meier and Frank Store; *1900, Good Samaritan Hospital (extended in 1908); *1903-1905, Lewis & Clark Exposition; 1907-1908, Corbett Building; 1909, Multnomah County Courthouse; 1910, Imperial Hotel; 1911, Wilcox Building; 1913-1914, Stevens Building; 1914, Multnomah County Courthouse (addition); Portland, Oregon.

BIBLIOGRAPHY

HOLDEN, WHEATON A. 1973 "The Peabody Touch: Peabody and Stearns of Boston, 1870-1917." *Journal of the Society of Architectural Historians* 32, no. 2:114-131.
MOORE, CHARLES (1929)1969 *The Life and Times of Charles Follen McKim.* Reprint. New York: Da Capo.
"Obituary (Lewis)." 1933 *Oregonian* Aug. 30.
"Obituary (Whidden)." 1929 *Oregonian* Jan. 28.
ROSS, MARION DEAN 1956 "Architecture in Oregon: 1845-1895." *Oregon Historical Quarterly* 57:33-64.
ROSS, MARION DEAN 1968 "125 Years of Building." *Journal of the American Institute of Architects* 49:120-126, 172, 178, 180, 182, 186.
SCULLY, VINCENT J., JR. 1955 *The Shingle Style.* New Haven: Yale University Press.
VAUGHAN, THOMAS, and FERRIDAY, VIRGINIA GUEST (editors) 1974 *Space, Style and Structure: Building in Northwest America.* 2 vols. Portland: Oregon Historical Society.
VAUGHAN, THOMAS, and MCMATH, GEORGE A. 1967 *A Century of Portland Architecture.* Portland: Oregon Historical Society.

WHITE, STANFORD

As the nineteenth century gave way to the twentieth, Stanford White (1853-1906) was said to be not only the best known man in New York City but also—a reputation far more difficult to achieve—the best loved. He was tall and handsome, with red hair going gray; he was companionable and tender-hearted; and he worked and played with what amounted to demonic energy. Nobody knew when he slept; he seemed to be everywhere at once, sometimes on his knees (in evening dress) to slip a few dollars under the doorsill of an artist who he had happened to hear was hard up, and sometimes on his knees (again in evening dress) to mix paints for the decoration of a ballroom in some big country house of his design. He was salmon-fishing in Canada, he was buying antiques in Paris, he was playing golf at Shinnecock, he was enjoying a late supper at Martin's, and he was also drawing, drawing, drawing—sketches and plans fell from his hand with an ease and grace that baffled his contemporaries.

Since 1879, White had been a partner in the firm of McKIM, MEAD, AND WHITE—the busiest architectural firm in New York, if not in the country and indeed the world. Its handiwork was to be observed block after block all the way up Fifth Avenue and Madison Avenue and in the sidestreets as well: residences, clubhouses, churches, banks, and office buildings, to say nothing of hospitals, stables, and even power stations. The firm executed its commissions as a single entity, but it was common knowledge that certain fine things were by White and others were by McKim; as for Mead, he was content to run the office, jovially boasting that it was his task to keep his two partners from making damned fools of themselves. Among White's fine things was the classic Washington Memorial Arch (1892) in Washington Square, through which one could glimpse, on the far side of the square, the Italianate Judson Memorial Church (1888-1893), also by White. In the bell tower of the church were artists' studios; perhaps only White at that time could have persuaded the trustees of a Baptist church to build in the Italian style and to grant artists habitation in a house of God. In Madison Square Park, one glanced up from the Farragut Memorial (1877-1881)—the bronze sculpture of Admiral Farragut was by Augustus Saint-Gaudens, the carved bluestone base by White—to admire the romantic buff-brick and terra-cotta confection of Madison Square Garden (1887-1891), which White had designed and in the tower of which he kept a studio for giving parties, not all of them of a fastidious nature. At the tip of the tower stood a superb copper Diana, designed by Saint-Gaudens; her nakedness, even at a height of over three hundred feet above the square, was an occasion for many letters of protest to the newspapers.

In those headlong, busy years at the turn of the century, McKim, Mead, and White gathered in commissions by the bushelful and employed an army of draftsmen in their overcrowded offices. Kindly put, the firm was an atelier, and few gifted young architects failed to pass through the premises on their way to setting up practices of their own; unkindly put, the firm was a factory, and much of the work they accomplished was of necessity repetitious and sometimes slipshod. Like most architects throughout history, they found it difficult to turn away a client, especially if the client was a fashionable, imperious one—a Morgan, say, or a Whitney, a Bennett, a Goelet, a Vanderbilt. Joseph Morrill Wells, whose hand is to be seen in the design of the exteriors of the Villard Houses and the Century Club, is said to have refused a partnership in the firm on the grounds that he did not want to sign his name to "so much damned bad work." (Wells died young, or the partnership would certainly have been his.) The remark was in part a sour joke—like many shy men, Wells took refuge in a sharp tongue—and in part the truth: White's coarse and ugly Stuyvesant Fish House, on the northwest corner of Madison Avenue and Seventy-eighth Street, stands directly across the way from the charming, correctly detailed Philip A. Rollins House, designed by McKim. They were houses planned in the same office at approximately the same time, but what a world of difference between them!

The word "fashionable" is nearly always used in a pejorative sense. That McKim, Mead, and White in its prime was the most fashionable firm in town is a fact that can be faced with equanimity. For architecture is an impure art, indissolubly linked to money and to the ways in which money chooses to express itself. Again and again, we observe young architects beginning their careers with commissions given to them by wealthy members of their families or by wealthy friends; in some cases, the commissions are among the most substantial that they will ever have. One thinks of that New York society figure, JAMES RENWICK, designing Grace Church at the age of twenty-six, and William Delano (see DELANO AND ALDRICH) being offered the commission for the Walters Art Gallery, in Baltimore, at a similar age, when he was but newly graduated from architectural school and had yet to design so much as a doghouse.

White was born into a world of exceptional privilege. His ancestors had settled in New England in the early seventeenth century and were among the founders of Hartford. His grandfather

White.
Farragut Memorial (base only).
New York.
1877–1881

White was a prosperous clipper-ship owner, with offices on South Street, in New York City; with the coming of steam, his firm went bankrupt and the family found itself, for the first time in several generations, in reduced circumstances. White's father, Richard Grant White, was one of the leading intellectuals of his day—a music and drama critic, a friend of Dickens and Browning, an authority on Shakespeare, and a tireless defender of the King's English against the vulgar inroads constantly being made upon it by his fellow Americans. Richard White was a tall, handsome, gentle man; his wife, Alexina Black Mease, was born in Charleston, South Carolina, and was of mixed English and Scottish ancestry. They had two sons—Richard, who grew up to be a mining engineer in the Far West, and Stanford. At an early age, Stannie—the affectionate diminutive was to follow him all his life—demonstrated unusual energy, unusual charm, and an unusually strong gift for drawing. He attended New York University and would have liked to embark on a career as an artist, but his father, knowing from personal experience how difficult it was to earn a living in the arts, argued against such a course; a family friend, the artist John LaFarge, himself often penniless, recommended the down-to-earth alternative of a career in architecture.

In 1872, at the age of nineteen, White secured a position as an apprentice draftsman in the architectural offices of H. H. RICHARDSON. His immediate superior was McKim, who in his spare time was already designing small houses for an assortment of friends and relatives. Richardson and McKim were among the tiny handful of Americans who had enjoyed the benefit of formal architectural training at the Ecole des Beaux-Arts in Paris; with no formal training whatever, White sat at the feet of Richardson and McKim and learned his art and craft from them. They were ideal teachers, and it soon became apparent that White was their ideal student. As McKim said, White could "draw like a house afire," and his eye for color, texture, and proportion was notably keen; his weakness lay in working up a plan with the clarity and practicality that was a hallmark of the Beaux-Arts school. When Richardson, busy with Trinity Church and other Boston commissions, moved his practice to Brookline, Massachusetts, McKim remained in New York and launched into practice on his own. White took McKim's place and accepted with characteristic high spirits the long hours and many journeys that were required of him.

On his return from a trip abroad in 1879—a trip that he shared in part with McKim and Saint-Gaudens—White was invited to become a partner in a new firm to be known as McKim, Mead, and White. Joyfully, he accepted the invitation. With an insouciance prophetic of their future, they chose as a motto for the firm a French slang phrase that must have struck their Victorian elders as somewhat alarming, not only because the French language itself was an object of suspicion but also because of the sentiment it embodied. "*Vogue la galère!*" they cried—words that can be

White.
Madison Square
Presbyterian Church.
New York.
1904–1906

freely translated as "Come what may!," "Here goes!," or even "What the hell!"

The three young partners were ambitious and gregarious (especially White, who was reputed to be able to be in at least two places at once and sometimes three), and they had not long to wait for clients. Their social connections were strong and readily exploitable; soon they were carrying out designs on a large scale for country and seaside houses that were either in a neo-Colonial style, conscientiously based upon eighteenth-century sources, or in the style known as Queen Anne, which, having nothing to do with Queen Anne, was characterized by a balanced but asymmetrical façade, often with a tower at one side and with big chimneys and porches (known at the time as "piazzas"). The floorplans of these houses were open, one room dissolving almost imperceptibly into the next and broad flights of stairs leading by easy stages into a commodious upper hall. Visiting a number of such houses in the course of a visit to America in 1905, Henry James deplored their lack of interior doors; there was, he complained, no longer any privacy in American life. The Low House (1886–1887), in Bristol, Rhode Island, crouched under a single gable of unprecedented length as if under the wing of some immense sea-bird; the Robert Goelet Cottage (1882–1883) in Newport, Rhode Island, lifted its shingled, dark-brown countenance to the sun with a self-confidence that RICHARD MORRIS HUNT's nearby European palazzi could not hope to equal.

Some architectural historians hold that the firm of McKim, Mead, and White was at its best in its beginnings, before their "come-what-may" essays in the American vernacular gave way to skillful plunderings of the Renaissance. The transition was inevitable, for architecture is always more nearly a mirror of the culture in which it exists than a means of altering it. The new rich emerging in the 1880s and 1890s and reaching, in the years before World War I, the apogee of their need for showing off were a more sophisticated group of rascals than their predecessors in an earlier gilded age; they were also in greater haste to conceal the untidy nature of their origins. More and more, they turned to Europe for instruction; as they purchased impoverished noblemen for their daughters to marry, so they purchased the furnishings and *objets d'art* of noblemen's houses to dwell among. When they put on airs, it was with the hope that the airs would smell of England, France, and Italy and not of Pittsburgh. McKim, Mead, and White were far from having to abandon one set of principles in order to embrace a second. They moved without regret from pioneering in one mode of expression in architecture to pioneering in another. They were every bit as eager as their patrons were to bring the Old World to the New and to cause it to flourish here; they raced pell-mell from the charming simplicities of the Newport Casino (1879–1880) to the august dignity of the University Club (1892).

The fantastic energy that had distinguished White in his youth seemed only to strengthen with the years. In 1906, he could be said to be in the fullness of his talent and at the very height of his professional career. He had just completed the Tiffany Building (1903–1906), a Venetian palace on a colossal scale, and the Colony Club, (1904–1906), delicately Georgian in detail; he was bringing to completion what is generally regarded as his masterpiece, the Madison Square Presbyterian Church (1904–1906), a Mediterranean basilica of a richness of carving and polychromy unprecedented in America. (Built to last a thousand years, it lasted but thirteen, being demolished to make way for an office building.) Busy as White was in his profession, he was no less busy in his private life—or rather in a multiplicity of private lives. There was White the party-giver and party-goer, omnipresent in the whirligig of New York society; there was White the serious patron of the arts, constantly to be seen at the opera, at concerts, and especially at the theater; and there was White the apparently happy family man, with a wife and son, a grand house on Gramercy Park, and an estate on Long Island that looked out over gardens and fields and woods to the blue distances of Long Island Sound.

And there was still another White, who carried out in secret what would have been for any ordinary man an exhausting succession of sexual encounters, most of them with extremely young women. Long before Nabokov had invented the word "nymphet," White was a worshipper of nymphets, and his worship embraced something far more complex than sexual satisfaction. A young woman, if her beauty appealed to him, must have that beauty perfected. An aspiring actress (for most of his women were, or pretended to be, actresses) must be made over to his heart's desire, not for his sake alone but for hers; he would pay for lessons in voice and in dance, he would pay to have her teeth straightened, and if she had the misfortune to fall "ill," not necessarily because of her relationship with him, he would see to the resolution of that problem as well. He met in her teens an actress and photographer's model named Evelyn Nesbit, whose astonishing beauty was matched by high intelligence and a passionate determination to make good. They were lovers and then more than lovers, for White came to fuss over her amorous and professional delinquencies like any father over any daughter's. In a hard-boiled attempt to further her career, Nesbit became the mistress of a cretinous young Pittsburgh millionaire named Harry K. Thaw. After a time, and to White's distress, Nesbit married Thaw. In his dour, distrustful fashion, Thaw had every reason to be envious of the most popular man in New York. On the evening of June 25, 1906, the Thaws attended the opening of a show called *Mamzelle Champagne* at Madison Square Garden. In the course of the performance (the male lead happened to be singing "I Could Love a Thousand Girls"), White entered the auditorium and took a seat at a table reserved for him at a short distance from the stage. Thaw made his way to White's table, took a revolver from under his overcoat, and shot White dead. After two trials, at both of which Nesbit testified in her husband's behalf, Thaw was declared insane and put away in an asylum. Eventually, he gained his freedom and lived on ignominiously until the 1940s. Nesbit survived until 1966, dying in poverty in Hollywood at the age of eighty-one. She and Thaw had long been divorced and she spoke often of her beloved "Stannie," whose name, exactly sixty years earlier, she had done everything she could to blacken. As for McKim, he never recovered from the tragedy of White's death. On hearing the news, he is recorded as having said only, "Oh, God!" He must have known more about White's secret life than anyone else; his exclamation hints not at surprise but at the confirmation of a fear long held in silence that he was never able to act upon.

BRENDAN GILL

WORKS

1877–1881, Farragut Memorial (base only; sculpture by Auguste Saint-Gaudens), New York. 1879–1880, Newport Casino, R.I. 1880–1887, Deacon Chapin Monument, Springfield, Mass. 1882–1883, Goelet Cottage, Newport, R.I. 1884?, Stanford White House, Gramercy Park, New York. 1885–1905, Schools, Library, Bank, Church, Fountain, and Three Houses, Naugatuck, Conn. *1886–1887, William G. Low House, Bristol, R.I. *1887–1891, Madison Square Garden; New York. 1887–1898, Boston Public Library. 1888–1893, Judson Memorial Church, Washington Square South, New York. 1889–1890, Johnson Gate, Harvard University, Cambridge, Mass. 1889–1892, Washington Memorial Arch, New York. 1890–1891, Brown and Meredith Apartment Block, Boston. 1890–1895, New York Herald Building. 1891–1892, King Model Houses; 1891–1894, Metropolitan Club; New York. 1891–1903, State Capitol, Providence, R.I. 1892?, Stanford White Estate, Saint James, N.Y. 1892–1901, New York University Buildings, Washington Heights. 1892–1901, Symphony Hall, Boston. 1893–1902, Seven Buildings, Columbia University, Morningside Heights, New York. 1894–1895, Factory and Housing, Roanoke Rapids, N.C. 1895–1899, Frederick W. Vanderbilt House, Hyde

Park, N.Y. 1896–1900, University Club, New York. 1896–1907, Rotunda (restoration) and Four Buildings, University of Virginia, Charlottesville. 1897–1899, Gymnasium, Radcliffe College, Cambridge, Mass. 1897–1900, Stuyvesant Fish House, New York. 1897–1902, Herman Oelrichs House, Newport, R.I. 1898–1900, State Savings Bank, Detroit, Mich. 1899–1901, Union, Harvard University, Cambridge, Mass. 1900–1903, Joseph Pulitzer House, New York. 1900–1905, Bank of Montreal (additions). 1901–1904, Interborough Rapid Transit Powerhouse, New York. 1902, White House (restoration), Washington. 1902–1906, J. Pierpont Morgan Library (not completed until 1907 by others); 1903–1906, Tiffany Building; 1904–1906, Colony Club (not completed until 1908 by others); *1904–1906, Madison Square Presbyterian Church; New York.

BIBLIOGRAPHY

For additional information on Stanford White, see the bibliography to McKim, Mead and White.

BALDWIN, CHARLES C. (1931)1971 *Stanford White.* Reprint. New York: Da Capo.

A Monograph of the Works of McKim, Mead and White. (1914)1973 With an essay by Leland Roth. New York: Blom.

ROTH, LELAND M. 1978 *The Architecture of McKim, Mead and White, 1870–1920: A Building List.* New York: Garland.

Sketches and Designs by Stanford White. 1920 With an outline of his career by his son Lawrence Grant White. New York: Architectural Book Publishing Company.

WHITE, THOMAS

Thomas White (c.1674–1748), who described himself in his will as a statuary, was born and died in Worcester, England. In 1718, he submitted designs for Worcester Guildhall (1721–1724). Other buildings have been attributed to him, but without documentary evidence. Seventeen works of sculpture by him are known.

MARCUS WHIFFEN

WORK

1718–1724, Guildhall, Worcester, England.

BIBLIOGRAPHY

GREEN, VALENTINE 1796 *The History and Antiquities of the City and Suburbs of Worcester.* 2 vols. London: Bulmer.

GUNNIS, RUPERT (1951)1968 "Thomas White." Pages 430–431 in *Dictionary of British Sculptors, 1660–1851.* Rev. ed. London: Abbey Library.

NASH, TREADWAY RUSSELL (1781–1782)1799 *Collections for the History of Worcestershire.* 2 vols. 2d ed., rev. London: White.

WHIFFEN, MARCUS 1945 "White of Worcester." *Country Life* 98:1002–1005.

WHITE, WILLIAM

William White (1825–1900), a British High Victorian Gothic Revival architect, worked in the office of GEORGE GILBERT SCOTT, where he met GEORGE E. STREET and GEORGE F. BODLEY, before setting up his own practice in Cornwall in 1847. His work included numerous churches, two cathedrals—in Madagascar and Pretoria—and a large country house, Humewood, County Wicklow, Ireland (1866–1870). His bold and original architecture makes extensive use of polychromy; Saint Saviour's, Aberdeen Park, London (1865), built almost entirely of brick, is one of his most interesting churches. White lectured and wrote extensively on architectural subjects, most notably in *The Ecclesiologist.* He was a Fellow of the Society of Antiquaries and a Fellow of the Royal Institute of British Architects.

ROGER DIXON

WORKS

1849–1850, Old Rectory, Saint Columb Major; 1852, Church, Saint Hilary; Cornwall, England. 1852ff., All Saints, Nottinghill, London. 1853, Saint Michael's Home, Wantage, Berkshire, England. 1855, Church; 1855, School; Hooe, Devon, England. c.1855, Penmellyn House, Saint Columb Major, Cornwall, England. 1856, Christ Church, Smannell, Hampshire, England. 1857, Bank, Saint Columb Major, Cornwall, England. 1858, Former Vicarage, Little Baddow, Essex, England. 1858–1859, Saint Michael, Lyndhurst, Hampshire, England. 1860–1864, Bishop's Court, Sowton, Devon, England. 1865, Saint Saviour, Aberdeen Park, London. 1866–1870, Humewood (completed 1873–1877 by James Brooks), County Wicklow, Ireland. 1873, Saint Mark, Battersea Rise, London.

BIBLIOGRAPHY

"Contemporary British Architects." 1890 *Building News* 58, no. 1830:186–187.

EASTLAKE, CHARLES LOCK (1872)1970 In J. Mordaunt Crook (editor), *A History of the Gothic Revival.* England: Leicester University Press.

GIROUARD, MARK (1971)1979 *The Victorian Country House.* Rev. ed. New Haven: Yale University Press.

"Obituary." 1900 *The Builder* 78, no. 2973:91.

"The Late William White, F.S.A." 1900 *Journal of the Royal Institute of British Architects* Series 3 7:145–146.

THOMPSON, PAUL 1968 "The Writing of William White." Pages 226–237 in John Summerson (editor), *Concerning Architecture.* London: Allen Lane.

WHITEHOUSE, MORRIS H.

Morris Homans Whitehouse (1878–1944), born in Portland, Oregon, was apprenticed to architectural firms in his native city for a number of years before completing work for a degree in architecture at the Massachusetts Institute of Technology. He was graduated from M.I.T. in 1906 and was the first recipient of the Guy Lowell traveling scholarship, which enabled him to spend a year at the American Academy in Rome. He returned to Portland to open his practice in 1908. His significant partnerships were formed with J. ANDRÉ FOUILHOUX, from 1909 to 1917, and with Glen Stanton and Walter E. Church, who joined Whitehouse as associates in the 1920s before becoming his partners in 1931. Whitehouse and Church added Earl Newberry and Frank Roehr as partners in 1942. The firm produced numerous important clubhouses and public buildings in both traditional and early modern styles, mostly in Portland and Salem, Oregon.

ELISABETH WALTON POTTER

WORKS

1910, Jefferson High School; 1911, Lincoln High School; 1911, Multnomah Amateur Athletic Club; 1913, Platt Building; 1913, University Club; 1913, Waverly Country Club; 1918, Eastmoreland Country Club; Portland, Ore. *1923, Gearhart Hotel, Ore. 1924, Oswego Country Club, Lake Oswego, Ore. 1927, Temple Beth Israel (with Herman Brookman, Bennes and Herzog), Portland, Ore. 1929, First Presbyterian Church, Salem, Ore. 1929–1930, Elizabeth Clark House, Oregon City. 1930–1933, United States Courthouse; 1931–1933, Sixth Church of Christ Scientist; Portland, Ore. 1936–1938, Oregon State Capitol (with Francis Keally, and Trowbridge and Livingston); 1939, Oregon State Library; Salem.

BIBLIOGRAPHY

DOWNS, WINFIELD SCOTT (editor) 1943 Volume 2, pages 121–123 in *Encyclopedia of Northwest Biography.* New York: American Historical Company.
MCMATH, GEORGE A. 1979 "National Register of Historic Places Inventory-/Nomination-Form, February 1, 1979." Unpublished manuscript, University Club, Portland, Ore.
"Whitehouse and Associates to Design Federal Building." 1930 *Morning Oregonian* June 5, p. 24.
"Whitehouse Honored by Architects." 1932 *Oregon Sunday Journal* January 17, section 4, p. 4.
VAUGHAN, THOMAS, and FERRIDAY, VIRGINIA GUEST (editors) 1974 *Space, Style and Structure.* 2 vols. Portland: Oregon Historical Society.

WICKMAN, GUSTAF

Beside FERDINAND BOBERG, Gustaf Wickman (1858–1916) was Sweden's most prominent representative of Art Nouveau architecture. After studies at the Chalmer's Arts and Crafts School in Göteborg, Wickman for some years worked in a very personal eclectic manner. He had his breakthrough in 1893 with the Swedish pavilion at the World's Columbian Exposition in Chicago, a building inspired partly by Swedish wooden bell towers, partly by the American Shingle style. In the United States, he was strongly influenced by H. H. RICHARDSON and LOUIS H. SULLIVAN, and his first important work in Sweden, a building for the Stockholm branch of the Skåne Bank (1897–1900), is a creation in Art Nouveau baroque, with influences from both Richardson and Sullivan.

Wickman became the architect for the new industrial and capitalistic establishment. He was, for example, the "town architect" of the mining society in Kiruna. In a series of bank buildings he developed the conceptions from the Skåne Bank further, inspired by the international Art Nouveau. He introduced the glazed banking hall in Sweden and developed an office architecture in accordance with American principles. His works are distinguished by a strong sense of three-dimensional form and plasticity. Plans and sections are often based on simple geometrical forms, with the shingled church in Kiruna (1902–1912) as the best example.

FREDRIC BEDOIRE

WORKS

*1893, Swedish Pavilion, World's Columbian Exposition, Chicago. 1897–1900, Skåne Bank; 1900–1902, Sundsvall Bank, 4 Fredsgatan; Stockholm. 1902–1912, Church, Kiruna, Sweden. 1903–1906, Skånska Banken, 10 Sødergaten, Malmö, Sweden. 1909–1911, Skandia Insurance Office, 2 Västra Hamngatan, Göteborg, Sweden.

BIBLIOGRAPHY

BEDOIRE, FREDRIC 1974 *En arkitekt och hans verksamhetsfält kring sekelskiftet: Gustaf Wickmans arbeten 1884–1916.* With a summary in English. Stockholm.
BEDOIRE, FREDRIC 1974 *Gustaf Wickman som Sjukhusarkitekt.* Stockholm: Fritzes Norbokh.

WIELEMANS, ALEXANDER

Alexander Wielemans von Monteforte (1843–1911) belongs to the less renowned and yet indispensable architects of the Ringstrasse era. Born in Vienna, the eldest son of an army engineer officer, he was acquainted with building and construction practice even before he began to study architecture under August von Siccardsburg and EDUARD VAN DER NÜLL. Wielemans collaborated with Friedrich von Schmidt from 1868 until 1874, when he won the competition for the Vienna Justizpalast (Law Courts) (1874–1881). This complex, especially famous because of its megalomaniac staircase hall, remained his chief work. During the riots of 1927 it was partly destroyed and afterward completed in another style. The impressive dimensions contain elements of movement and plasticity as well as pictorial use of decoration. Characterized by a clear turn toward light and shadow modeling of the façade, the Justizpalast was a milestone of late historicism. This success brought Wielemans commissions for several law buildings. He also erected parish churches, villas, townhouses, and palaces. The Town Hall of Graz (1887–1893) and the Breitenfelder Pfarrkirche in Vienna (1894–1898; designed 1886) give proof to Wielemans's ability to unify architectonic mass and rich surface modeling.

WALTER KRAUSE

WORKS

1874–1881, Justizpalast, Vienna. 1882–1883, Wodianer House, Budapest. 1882–1884?, Villa Gutmann, Baden, Austria. 1887–1893, Town Hall (with Theodor Reuter); 1889–1894, Zivil-Justizgebäude (now Landesgericht); Graz, Austria. 1894–1898, Breitenfelder Pfarrkirche; 1894–1898, Neu-Ottakringer Pfarrkirche; Vienna. 1903–1908, Zivilgerichtsgebäude, Brno, Czechoslovakia.

BIBLIOGRAPHY

AUER, HANS 1885 Der k.k. Justiz-Palast in Wien von A. von Wielemans. Vienna: Lehmann.

CZEIKE, FELIX 1974 Das grosse Groner-Wien-Lexikon. Vienna, Munich, and Zurich: Fritz Molden.

EGGER, GERHART, and WAGNER-RIEGER, RENATE 1973 Geschichte der Architektur in Wien. Vienna: Verein für Geschichte der Stadt Wien.

EGGERT, KLAUS 1971 Die Ringstrasse. Vienna, and Hamburg, Germany: Zsolnay.

MIKOLETZKY, LORENZ 1976 "Alexander von Wielemans (1843–1911)." Österreich in Geschichte und Literatur 20:155–167.

VINCENTI, C. V. 1876 Wiener Kunst-Renaissance. Vienna: C. Gerolds Son.

WAGNER-RIEGER, RENATE (editor) 1969 Die Wiener Ringstrasse—Das Kunstwerk im Bild. 2 vols. Vienna; Cologne, Germany; and Graz, Austria: Böhlau.

WAGNER-RIEGER, RENATE 1970 Wiens Architektur im 19. Jahrhundert. Vienna: Österreichischer Bundesverlag.

WIENER, PAUL LESTER

Born in Leipzig, East Germany, Paul Lester Wiener (1895–1967) studied in Vienna and Berlin, arriving in New York in 1913. Flowing, light-reflecting spaces accented with bright colors characterize his small buildings and interiors. Interest in housing and industrialized construction led him to form Town Planning Associates with JOSEP LLUIS SERT and Paul Schulz (1945). The Cidade dos Motores (1944–1946) and subsequent unbuilt urban plans in Peru, Colombia, Venezuela, and Cuba embodied the principles of regional development as espoused by the Congrès Internationaux d'Architecture Moderne, and included proposals for neighborhoods and public and residential buildings developed in great detail. Wiener's ideas on site planning and design were implemented in Washington Square Village, New York (1959–1962).

THOMAS G. BEDDALL

WORKS

1934–1935, Contempora House, Rockland County, N.Y. *1936–1937, American Pavilion (with Charles H. Higgins), 1937 Exposition, Paris. *1938–1939, Brazilian Pavilion (with LÚCIO COSTA and OSCAR NIEMEYER), New York World's Fair. 1943, Ratio Structures Housing (with Josep Lluis Sert and Paul Schulz), Sidney, N.Y. 1944–1946, Cidade dos Motores (with Town Planning Associates), near Rio de Janeiro. 1948, Chimbote and Lima City Plans (with T.P.A.), Peru. 1949, Medellín Urban Plan (with T.P.A.), Colombia. 1959–1962, Washington Square Village (with S. J. Kessler & Sons); 1960, Weitzmann Apartment (with Ala Damaz), New York. 1964, Scull House (with Richard Bender), East Hampton, N.Y. 1967, Colombian Center (with Damaz), New York.

BIBLIOGRAPHY

ANDERSON, JOHN 1960 "Game of Color Above the River." Interiors 120, no. 5:68–73.

"Brazil Builds a New City." 1946 Progressive Architecture 27, no. 9:52–74.

"Can Patios Make Cities?" 1953 Architectural Forum 99, no. 2:124–131.

GIEDION, SIEGFRIED 1960 "Washington Square Village, New York." L'Architecture d'aujourd'hui 31, no. 89:68–75.

NIELSON, BODIL W. 1967 "The Colombian Center." Interiors 126, no. 9:108–115.

"Portfolio: Contempora House." 1935 Architectural Record 78, no. 1:22–29.

"Rhythmic Functionalism." 1941 Interiors 101, no. 1:18–23.

WIENER, PAUL LESTER 1943 "Prefabrication: Ratio Structures." Architectural Forum 79, no. 6:83–88.

WIENER, PAUL LESTER, and SERT, JOSEP LLUIS 1951 "Urbanisme en Amerique Latine." L'Architecture d'aujourd'hui 21, no. 33:4–55.

WIENER, PAUL LESTER, and SERT, JOSEP LLUIS 1957 "Work of Town Planning Associates in Latin America: 1945–1956." Architectural Design 27, no. 6:190–213.

WIGHT, PETER B.

Peter Bonnett Wight (1838–1925) contributed to post-Civil War American architecture as an architect and as a designer of furniture and interior decoration, as a contractor of fireproofing, and as a critic and historian of contemporary architecture and fireproofing technology. His polychromatic and richly embellished National Academy of Design (1863–1865) in New York introduced Americans to the architectural and artistic ideals of JOHN RUSKIN and the Pre-Raphaelites in England and helped establish the High Victorian Gothic in America.

Born in New York, Wight graduated from the Free Academy (City College of New York) in 1855. After a postgraduate year there studying drawing, he apprenticed from 1856 to 1857 with Thomas R. Jackson and then worked briefly for Isaac G. Perry; both were New York architects. From 1858 to 1859, he worked in Chicago with the firm of Carter and Bauer. Wight returned to New York in 1859 and from 1863 to 1868 was associated with RUSSELL STURGIS.

Winning the competition for the National Academy of Design in 1861 established Wight's reputation. His comparatively conservative Yale School of Fine Arts (1864–1866) originally housed the first college art school in America. For the interior and furnishings of his Brooklyn Mercantile Library (1867–1869) and his T. P. Jacob House (1866–1868) in Louisville, Kentucky, Wight followed the lead of A. W. N. PUGIN, OWEN JONES, and other English design reformers. Wight's constructively designed furniture of medieval inspiration and his painted wall decoration anticipated the American Arts and Crafts movement by at least a decade.

Opportunities created by the great Chicago fire drew Wight to that city in 1871. As a partner in the firm of Carter, Drake, and Wight, he was instrumental in rebuilding the commercial city in the early 1870s. The Springer Block (1872) and the Lenox Building (1872), where his firm's former draftsmen DANIEL H. BURNHAM and JOHN W. ROOT had their first office, exemplified Wight's mature High Victorian Gothic. In 1873, in charge of the reconstruction of H. H. RICHARDSON's American Express Building, Wight reinforced the foundation piers with concrete and connecting I-beams; later, he took credit for the first grill foundation, designed for Burnham and Root's Montauk Block (1881–1882), for which he was consulting architect. His commercially produced wallpaper and furniture, and perhaps also the furniture and interior decoration of his E. W. Blatch-

ford House (1875–1876) in Chicago, helped further the American design reform movement in the mid-1870s.

Beginning in 1869, Wight read papers at professional meetings and published articles detailing effective and economical methods of fireproofing. In 1874, he and Drake patented a fireproof iron column, the first of several such inventions; and by 1881, he had formed the Wight Fireproofing Company in Chicago which specialized in hollow tile construction and the porous terra-cotta cladding of metal beams. Responsible for the fireproof construction of more than two hundred buildings, including WILLIAM LE BARON JENNEY's Home Insurance Building (1883–1885), Wight's company remained in business until 1891.

After 1891, Wight concentrated on writing for architectural journals. In the 1860s, he had contributed to *The New Path* (1863–1865) published by the reformist Association for the Advancement of Truth in Art of which he was a founder. Early to appreciate EUGÈNE EMMANUEL VIOLLET-LE-DUC's writings and such innovations as the apartment house, concrete as a building material, and unadorned, rationally designed commercial buildings, Wight wrote for all the major journals of his time. From 1904 to 1907, he was editor of *Fireproof,* published in Chicago from 1902 to 1907.

SARAH BRADFORD LANDAU

WORKS

c.1858, 1862, Middletown Bank (façade reconstructed in 1924, N.Y. *1861–1863, 1863–1865, National Academy of Design (façades re-erected, much modified, as the exterior of the Church of Our Lady of Lourdes, New York, in 1902–1904), New York. 1864–1866, Yale School of Fine Arts (now Street Hall), New Haven. *1865, 1867–1869, Brooklyn Mercantile Library, N.Y. *1866–1868, Thomas P. Jacob House, Louisville, Ky. 1872, Springer Block (altered by Adler and Sullivan in 1888); *1872, Lenox Building; *1872, Stewart-Bentley Building; *1873, American Express Building (reconstruction and interiors); Chicago. 1873, 1874, Williamsburgh Savings Bank (interior painted decoration of dome), Brooklyn, N.Y. *c.1874, 1875–1876, E. W. Blatchford House, Chicago.

BIBLIOGRAPHY

JONES, ELIZABETH F., and KINSMAN, MARY JEAN 1980 "Unknown Wight Designs in Louisville, Kentucky." *Nineteenth Century* 6, no. 4:57–60.

LANDAU, SARAH BRADFORD 1981 *P. B. Wight: Architect, Contractor, and Critic, 1838–1925.* The Art Institute of Chicago.

WIGHT, P. B. 1866 *National Academy of Design: Photographs of the New Building with an Introductory Essay and Description.* New York: Avery.

WIGHT, P. B. 1869 "Remarks on Fireproof Construction." *Architectural Review and American Builders' Journal* 2:99–108.

WIGHT, P. B. 1877 "Concrete as a Building Material—A Remarkable House at Port Chester." *American Architect and Building News* 2:266–267.

WIGHT, P. B. 1880 "The Condition of Architecture in the Western States." *American Architect and Building News* 7:107–109, 118–119.

WIGHT, P. B. 1884 "The Development of New Phases of the Fine Arts in America." *Inland Architect and News Record* 4:51–53, 63–65.

WIGHT, P. B. 1897 "The Origin and History of Hollow Tile Fire-proof Floor Construction." *Brickbuilder* 6:53–55, 73–75, 98–99, 149–150.

WIGHT, P. B. 1899 "Modern Architecture in Chicago." *Pall Mall Magazine* 18:292–308.

WIGHT, P. B. 1909 "Reminiscences of Russell Sturgis." *Architectural Record* 26:123–131.

WIJDEVELD, H. T.

Hendrik Theodor Wijdeveld (1886–) achieved his reputation mainly through his articles for the magazine *Wendingen* from 1918 to 1931 when he helped to give definition to the Amsterdam school. Wijdeveld helped to create a connection between this Dutch Expressionist movement and the one in Germany. His article for the first issue of *Wendingen* expressed the strength of the Amsterdam school. The Amsterdam school is characterized by the rhythm of the supple, molded masses of its buildings. A good example is the People's Theater of 1919, especially its central masses, which have an erotic suggestiveness in the direction of HERMANN FINSTERLIN, the German free-form artist par excellence. Another point of interest in this theater are its references to BRUNO TAUT and PAUL SCHEERBART in a crystalline, vaulted bay.

Wijdeveld's first building project was an entry in a competition; its masses were probably based on the skyscrapers of Manhattan. The most interesting part of this project was the provision of setback roofs as streets; thus, it was a multilevel city not unlike LOUIS I. KAHN's much later proposal for Philadelphia. The buildings were laid out in the form of a crucifix which gives the project a Christian flavor.

A much later design (1944) has strong references to LE CORBUSIER and FRANK LLOYD WRIGHT. This fifteen-mile wide city suggests Wright's mile-high tower or Le Corbusier's huge towers dotting the landscape of his *Ville radieuse*.

SUZANNE FRANK

WORK

1920, Housing, Indische buurt, Amsterdam.

BIBLIOGRAPHY

"Nic H. M. Tummers over het werk van H. Th. Wijdeveld." *Bouwkundig Weekblad* 1965 83, no. 19:19/333–19/364.

WILDE, BERNARD DE

A Flemish architect and decorator, Bernard De Wilde (18th century), along with DAVID 'T KINDT, was the most important figure of the rococo period in Ghent, Belgium. His brilliant and precocious career began in 1716 and centered in Ghent. His original artistic style, charged with the influence of the French Regency style but also stemming from native types, was characterized by strong horizontals and highly elaborate upper portions.

PIERRE LENAIN
*Translated from French by
Shara Wasserman*

WORKS

1735, Guild of Saint Sebastien House; 1738, City Guard House; 1743–1745, Chapel of Saint John; 1755–1760, Hôtel Faliggan; Ghent, Belgium.

WILKINS, WILLIAM

William Wilkins (1778–1839) initiated the archeological Greek Revival in Britain, promoted a studious Gothic style, and was an eminent classical scholar, art collector, and theater proprietor.

Born in Norwich, England, eldest son of architect William Wilkins, educated at Gonville and Caius College, Cambridge (1796–1880), his studies in classics and mathematics inspired his learned and finely proportioned designs. He exhibited at the Royal Academy from 1799. Elected to the Society of Antiquaries (1800), he toured Sicily, Greece, and Asia Minor (1801–1804) as University Scholar. While preparing *Magna Graecia* (1807), he added to Osberton House, Nottinghamshire (1805–1806), the earliest properly scaled Doric portico, and secured commissions for Downing College, Cambridge (1805–1822), and East India Company College, Haileybury (1805–1809), proportioning the new structures to accurately imitated sections of Athenian monuments, chiefly the Erechtheum, and pioneering the campus plan. Other successes included Nelson Pillar, Dublin (1807–1809), innovating Greek Doric columnar monuments, and transformation of The Grange, Hampshire (1808?–1809) into a quasi-Attic temple.

In 1809 he wrote on early English Renaissance

architecture, embodied in designs for Bylaugh Hall, Norfolk (1822), anticipating that fashion, and began translating Vitruvius Books 3–6: *Civil Architecture of Vitruvius* (1813). In 1812, he was appointed editor to the Society of Dilettanti.

In 1816 he testified before the Elgin Marbles Select Committee and published *Atheniensia*, a topography of ancient Athens. In 1817 he won the Army Monument, London, competition, unexecuted due to government retrenchment, evolving a more flexible Greek idiom as for United University Club, London (1822–1826), combining Greek motifs with Renaissance features.

Wilkins's career as a Gothicist began at Pentillie Castle, Cornwall (1810?–1811?), maturing through Dalmeny House, West Lothian (1814–1819), Tregothnan, Cornwall (1815–1818) and Dunmore Park, Stirlingshire (1820–1822) inspired by East Anglian Tudor houses, influential on WILLIAM BURN and CHARLES BARRY. More significant are his neo-Gothic additions to Trinity (1821–1827), Corpus Christi (1822–1826), and King's (1823–1828) colleges, Cambridge. The harmonious blend of new with old, epitomized by the King's College screen, reflected Wilkins's preservationist principles, expressed in a restoration scheme for Saint Mary's Abbey, Sherborne (1827).

While revering historical architecture, Wilkins was not a pedant. New Norfolk County Jail, Norwich (1820–1824) had radial cell blocks as did Huntington County Jail (1826–1828). Saint George's Hospital, London (1826–1828) incorporated progressive facilities and structural cast iron, like University College London (1826–1830). Funds lacking, only center erected, having an unprecedented decastyle Corinthian portico and neo-Renaissance dome; the College was equated with Saint Paul's Cathedral.

Thereafter, Wilkins's health and career declined. He published sundry pamphlets, advocating official patronage of the arts and educational reform. Compromised by government parsimony, his National Gallery and Royal Academy, London (1832–1838) was harshly criticized. Unplaced in the Houses of Parliament competition (1835), he retired to Cambridge 1837, consoled by his election as Royal Academy Professor of Architecture. Some of his lectures are probably in *Prolusiones Architectonicae* (1837). His pupils included BENJAMIN FERREY.

R. WINDSOR LISCOMBE

WORKS

1805–1806, Oberton House, Nottinghamshire, England. 1805–1809, East India Company College, Haileybury, Hertfordshire, England. 1805–1822, Downing College (incomplete), Cambridge. *1807–1809, Nelson Pillar, Dublin. *1808–1809, Lower Assembly Rooms,

Wilkins.
University College London.
1826–1830

Bath, England. 1808?–1809, The Grange, Hampshire, England. 1810?–1811?, Pentillie Castle (later additions with William Wilkins, Sr.), Cornwall, England. 1814–1817, Nelson Column, Great Yarmouth, Norfolk, England. 1814–1819, Dalmeny House, West Lothian, Scotland. 1815–1818, Tregothnan, Cornwall, England. 1817–1819, Freemasons' Hall, Bath, England. *1820–1822, Dunmore Park, Stirlingshire, England. 1820–1824, New Norfolk County Jail and Shire House, England. *1821–1822, Saint Paul's Church, Nottingham, England. 1821–1827, New Court Trinity College; 1822–1826, New Quadrangle, Corpus Christi College; Cambridge. *1822–1826, United University Club (with J. P. GANDY-DEERING), London. 1823–1828, New Buildings and Screen, King's College, Cambridge. *1825–1826, Theater Royal, Norwich, England. 1826–1828, Huntington County Jail, England. 1826–1828, Saint George's Hospital, London. 1826–1830, University College London. 1827–1830, Yorkshire Philosophical Society Museum (York Museum), England. 1832–1838, National Gallery and Royal Academy, London.

BIBLIOGRAPHY

CROOK, J. MORDAUNT 1964 *Haileybury and the Greek Revival: The Architecture of William Wilkins.* Hoddesdon, England: Haileybury.

CROOK, J. MORDAUNT 1970 "Grange Park Transformed." Pages 220–228 in Howard M. Colvin and John Harris (editors), *The Country Seat.* London: Allen Lane.

LISCOMBE, R. WINDSOR 1980 *William Wilkins 1778–1839.* London: Cambridge University Press.

LITTLE, BRYAN 1971 "Cambridge and the Campus." *Virginia Magazine of History and Biography* 74:190–201.

MARTIN, GREGORY 1971 "Wilkins and the National Gallery." *Burlington Magazine* 113:318–329.

WILKINS, WILLIAM 1807 *The Antiquities of Magna Graecia.* Cambridge University Press; London: Longman.

WILKINS, WILLIAM 1809 "Observations on the Porta Honoris of Caius College, Cambridge." *Vetusta Monumenta* 4: plates 21–23.

WILKINS, WILLIAM (1813)1817 *The Civil Architecture of Vitruvius: Comprising Those Books of the Author Which Relate to the Public and Private Edifices of the Ancients.* London: Longman. Introduction written anonymously by the fourth earl of Aberdeen.

WILKINS, WILLIAM 1816 *Atheniensia, or Remarks on the Topography and Buildings in Athens.* London: J. Murray.

WILKINS, WILLIAM 1817 "Remarks on the Architectural Inscription Brought from Athens, and Now Preserved in the British Museum." Pages 580–603 in Robert Walpole (editor), *Memoirs Relating to European and Asiatic Turkey.* London: Longman.

WILKINS, WILLIAM 1820 "On the Sculptures of the Parthenon." Pages 409–419 in Robert Walpole (editor), *Travels in Various Countries of the East.* London: Longmans.

WILKINS, WILLIAM 1828 *Report on the State of Repair of Sherborne Church.* Sherborne, England: Harker and Penny.

WILKINS, WILLIAM 1832 *A Letter to Lord Viscount Goderich on the Patronage of the Arts by the English Government.* London: Whittingham.

WILKINS, WILLIAM 1836 *An Apology for the Designs of the Houses of Parliament Marked Phil-Archimedes.* London: Clowes.

WILKINS, WILLIAM 1837 *Prolusiones Architectonicae; or, Essays on Subjects Connected with Greek and Roman Architecture.* London: Weale.

WILKINSON, LESLIE

London-born and London-trained, Leslie Wilkinson (1882–1973) was appointed to Australia's first chair of architecture at Sydney University in 1918. The climate encouraged him to adopt Spanish Revival modes in plain white plaster and red tiles for most of his work. He was profoundly influential through the 1930s. He received the first Royal Australian Institute of Architects Gold Medal in 1960.

DONALD LESLIE JOHNSON

WORKS

1923, Wilkinson House, Vaucluse; New South Wales, Australia. 1930, Inorganic Chemistry Building, Sydney University. 1933, Saint John's Church of England, Penshurst; 1934, House, Wiston Gardens, Double Bay; 1970–1971, Antony Coote House, Vaucluse; New South Wales, Australia.

BIBLIOGRAPHY

JOHNSON, DONALD LESLIE 1980 *Australian Architecture 1901–51: Sources of Modernism.* Sydney University Press.

JOHNSON, R. N. 1973 "Emeritus Professor Leslie Wilkinson." *Architecture in Australia* 62, Dec.:78–82.

WILL, PHILIP JR.

Philip Will, Jr. (1906–) was born in Rochester, New York, and attended Cornell University College of Architecture. He was a founding partner, with LAWRENCE B. PERKINS and E. T. Wheeler, of Perkins, Wheeler, and Will in Chicago (1935–1946), later Perkins and Will (1946–1964) and The Perkins and Will Partnership (1964–1970), with offices in New York (since 1951) and Washington (since 1962).

MARY D. EDWARDS

WORKS

1937, Philip Will, Jr. Residence, Evanston, Ill. 1939–1940, Crow Island School (with Eliel Saarinen and Eero Saarinen), Winnetka, Ill. 1952, Heathcote School, Scarsdale, N.Y. 1954, Rockford Memorial Hospital, Ill. 1958, Cornell University Engineering Campus, Ithaca, N.Y. 1960, Pure Oil Company Office Building, Palatine, Ill. 1960, Stamford Hospital, Conn. 1963, United States Gypsum Building, Chicago. 1964, National College of Agriculture, Chapingo, Mexico. 1965, Scott Foresman Building, Glenview, Ill. 1965, Lutheran School of Technology; 1966, First National Bank (with C. F. Murphy Associates); Chicago. 1966, Salsbury Laboratories, Charles City, Iowa. 1969, Abbott Laboratories, Lake County, Ill.

BIBLIOGRAPHY

PERKINS, LAWRENCE B., and WILL, PHILIP, JR. 1969 "The Perkins and Will Partnership." *Building Construction.*

STEPHENS, SUZANNE 1973 "Return of the Megastructure." *Architectural Forum* 139, no. 2:40–47.

WILL, PHILIP, JR. 1961 "The Future of the Architectural Profession." *Louisiana Architect.*

WILL, PHILIP, JR. 1962a "Ahead Lies a New Frontier." *Florida Architect.*

WILL, PHILIP, JR. 1962b "The Architect Serves His Community." *AIA Journal* 137, no. 5:65–69.

WILL, PHILIP, JR. 1973 "First National Bank de Chicago." *Informes de la Construcción* no. 255:19–28.

WILL, PHILIP, JR. 1975 "Medical Facilities." *Architectural Record* 158:109–124.

WILLARD, SOLOMON

Solomon Willard's (1783–1861) reputation has never equaled his numerous achievements as an architect, teacher, inventor, sculptor, and granite quarryman. During his relatively brief architectural practice (1822–c.1844) he devoted most of his time and energy to the construction of the Bunker Hill Monument (1824–1842). Willard was born in Petersham, Massachusetts, and trained there as a housewright. After settling in Boston in 1804 he distinguished himself as a wood carver, obtaining work under ASHER BENJAMIN, PETER BANNER, and ALEXANDER PARRIS. These commissions led to others in Providence, Baltimore, and Washington, where he constructed a model of the new United States Capitol for CHARLES BULFINCH. Inspired with an enthusiasm for the works of BEN-

JAMIN LATROBE, Willard and his friend, Parris, introduced the Greek Revival style to Boston around 1820. Although Willard's major works are few they reveal a variety of styles far beyond the range of his principal Boston colleagues, Parris and ISAIAH ROGERS. His United States Branch Bank (1822–1824), Norfolk County Courthouse (1824–1826), and Suffolk County Courthouse (1835) are Grecian Doric in style; the Bunker Hill Monument is Egyptian; and the Bowdoin Street Church (1830) is Gothic. Willard's work is characterized by a special reverence for the materiality of the native granite. He eventually abandoned his practice and moved to Quincy, Massachusetts, where he became a supplier of granite to other architects. He died there in 1861.

JACK QUINAN

WORKS

1819, Saint Paul's Cathedral (assistant to Alexander Parris); *1822–1824, United States Branch Bank; Boston. 1824–1826, Norfolk County Courthouse, Dedham, Mass. 1824–1842, Bunker Hill Monument, Charlestown, Mass. 1830, Bowdoin Street Church; *1835, Suffolk County Courthouse; Boston. 1844, City Hall, Quincy, Mass.

BIBLIOGRAPHY

EDWARDS, WILLIAM CHURCHILL (1946)1954 *Historic Quincy Massachusetts.* Rev. ed. Quincy, Mass.: Franklin Printing Service.
HAMLIN, TALBOT (1944)1964 *Greek Revival Architecture in America.* Reprint. New York: Dover.
WHEILDON, WILLIAM W. 1865 *Memoir of Solomon Willard.* Boston: Monument Association.
WILLARD, SOLOMON 1843 *Plans and Sections of the Obelisk on Bunker's Hill.* Boston: Dickinson.
WINSOR, JUSTIN 1880–1881 Volume 4 in *The Memorial History of Boston.* Boston: Osgood.

WILLCOX, WALTER ROSS BAUMES

Walter Ross Baumes Willcox (1869–1947) was born in Burlington, Vermont. After some study at the Massachusetts Institute of Technology and the University of Pennsylvania, he returned to practice in Vermont. In 1907, he moved to Seattle, Washington. His greatest influence was in education. Appointed head of architecture at the University of Oregon in 1922, he transformed the teaching of architecture, breaking with the Beaux-Arts system. In later years, he devoted much time to theories of taxation.

MARION DEAN ROSS

WORKS

c.1903, Horticultural Building, Amherst, Mass. c.1903, Library, Burlington, Vt. 1910–1911, North Trunk Sewer Viaduct and Footbridge; c.1913, Queen Anne Hill Retaining Walls; Seattle, Wash. *1923, Westgate Building; 1924–1925, First Congregational Church (now a cinema); Eugene, Ore.

BIBLIOGRAPHY

The W. R. B. Willcox Papers are in the Special Collections (1123) of the University of Oregon Library, Eugene.
ALDEN, CHARLES H. 1947 "Walter R. B. Willcox, F.A.I.A." *Journal of the American Institute of Architects* 8, no. 2:64–66.
GENASCI, DON, and SHELMAN, DAVID 1980 *W. R. B. Willcox (1869–1947): His Architectural and Educational Theory.* Eugene: University of Oregon, Department of Architecture.
POTTER, ELIZABETH WALTON 1978 "W. R. B. Willcox: A Note on the Seattle Years." In *Festschrift: A Collection of Essays on Architectural History.* Salem, Ore.: Northern Pacific Coast Chapter of the Society of Architectural Historians.
SMITH, NANCY K. 1968 "Annals of Oregon: W. R. B. Willcox." *Call Number* 29, no. 2:18–24.
WILLCOX, W. R. B. 1938 *The Curse of Modern Taxation.* New York: Fortune.

WILLIAM OF SENS and WILLIAM THE ENGLISHMAN

William of Sens and William the Englishman were the two architects of the Gothic choir of the Metropolitan Cathedral Church of Christchurch at Canterbury, England, from 1174 to 1189. Their year-by-year activities are recorded in the *Tractatus* of the monk Gervase of Canterbury (d. c.1210) whose eyewitness account is the most authentic and detailed record of all medieval building program.

The Norman choir at Canterbury burned in 1174, and after holding a competition to determine the most suitable architect to direct reconstruction, the monks selected William of Sens "on account of his lively genius and good reputation." William of Sens directed work on the new choir for four years until he was severely injured in September 1179 when the scaffolding collapsed while he was working on the high vaults and he fell 50 feet to the choir pavement. This William completed the choir from the western crossing through the eastern crossing, including the western transept.

After his accident, William of Sens tried to direct continuation of construction, entrusted to a monk, from his sickbed, but this proved unsuccessful so he "gave up the work, and crossing the sea, returned to his home in France."

William of Sens was replaced as architect by another William, "English by nation, small in body, but in workmanship of many kinds acute and honest." This second William had certainly worked under the first William and of necessity continued his basic concept but also his detailing, possibly because materials already prepared were on hand. The English William completed the choir vaults that were left unfinished when the French William fell, closed in the eastern transept, and built the circular axial chapel of the choir variously termed "Becket's Crown" (Corona) and the Chapel of the Trinity.

Nothing is known of the work of either William before or after Canterbury. Jean Bony (1949) has demonstrated that both were familiar with the most recent architectural innovations in northern France, especially in the dioceses under the jurisdiction of the Metropolitan of Reims. The traditional view that William of Sens's Canterbury is a "transplantation" of the cathedral of Sens is untenable. William of Sens's innovations at Canterbury, most notably paired main-arcade supports, Purbeck marble contrasted with light Caen limestone, and his particular variant of six-part vaults, point to such northern French buildings as the cathedrals at Arras and Cambrai and the abbey church of Notre-Dame at Valenciennes. William the Englishman introduced into England the true triforium passage, then a very new feature in French architecture (Saint-Vincent at Laon, Saint-Yved at Braine).

The work of the two Williams at Canterbury had an enormous impact on later Gothic architecture in England, especially in decorative detailing and in the use of Purbeck marble. However, it is an oversimplification to maintain that, for all their debt to France, either William simply built a French building in England or, for that matter, they introduced the Gothic architectural style into England.

CARL F. BARNES, JR.

BIBLIOGRAPHY

BONY, JEAN 1949 "French Influences on the Origins of English Gothic Architecture." *Journal of the Warburg and Courtauld Institutes* 12:1–15.
CHARTRAIRE, ETIENNE (1921)1926 "Sens and Canterbury." Pages 17, 109–120 in *The Cathedral of Sens.* Paris: Lauren. Originally published in French.
GERVASE OF CANTERBURY 1879 "Tractatus de combustione et reparatione Cantuariensis ecclesiae." Volume 1, pages 3–29 in William Stubbs (editor), *The Historical Works of Gervase of Canterbury.* London: Longmans.
WEBB, GEOFFREY (1956)1965 *Architecture in Britain: The Middle Ages.* 2d ed. Harmondsworth, England: Penguin.

WILLIAM OF WYKEHAM

Born to poor parents in the village of Wykeham, England, William of Wykeham (1324–1404) was able to receive an education with the help of Nicholas Uvedale, Lord of Wykeham. From 1338 to 1346, Wykeham was the secretary of Sir John Scures, Sheriff of Hampshire, and in 1346, at the age of twenty-three, he became secretary to his patron. It was there that he probably acquired his architectural training. Because of his conscientious work, he was recommended to King Edward III and transferred from Winchester to Windsor. He became chief warden and surveyor of the Royal Castles of Windsor, Leeds, Dover, and Hadleigh, and subsequently was named clerk of the works at Windsor (1356–1361). At this same time, William of Wykeham's ecclesiastical and political careers also began to develop. In 1349, he was appointed clerk in holy orders and in 1362 he was ordained priest. During the following year, he became archdeacon of Lincoln and provost and Prebenday of Wells. Wykeham became Keeper of the Privy Seal in 1364 and was named bishop of Winchester in 1366, a title he held for nearly forty years.

At this same time, William of Wykeham began work on his first architectural projects for the king—the rebuilding of a great part of Windsor Castle, Berkshire (1360–1369), which has undergone much remodeling since by CHRISTOPHER WREN and others, and the Castle of Queensborough on the Isle of Sheppy (1361–1367; now destroyed but known from ground plans and a drawing by Hollar). The latter was built as a defense against invasion not as a castle for royalty as was Windsor. Soon after, Wykeham found himself in the middle of a scandalous affair, and although nothing was substantiated, he left the service of the king.

This gave him a chance to work on a project of his own. At the end of the 1360s, William of Wykeham had begun to buy land in Oxford with a plan to build a college. Between 1380 and 1386, he built the main quadrangle of New College. He continued to buy land, and a few years later (1389), he added a cloister with an enclosed garden. The following year, after the completion of the main quadrangle at Oxford, William of Wykeham built a college at Winchester (1387–1393). This college was built on the same plan as the one at Oxford. After this had been completed, Wykeham worked on his final project—the Cathedral at Winchester (1394–1404; the tower had been built by Bishop Walkelyn in 1079).

William of Wykeham's lasting contribution—aside from his works, most of which have been remodeled or destroyed—was the architectural style in which he worked. Wykeham was among the first architects to use the Perpendicular style. This style was born out of the Decorated style and was used only in England. It is much stronger and more rigid than the Decorated style, and there is a great stress on straight horizontals and verticals. It is also characterized by thinner walls and vaults, larger windows, and more window tracery which formed frames for the stained-glass pictures that were then becoming popular. This style was, with little change, the architectural style of England for the next 250 years.

JUDITH COHEN

WORKS

1360–1369, Windsor Castle (reconstruction), Berkshire, England. *1361–1367, Castle of Queensborough, Isle of Sheppy, England. 1380–1386, New College (later altered), Oxford. 1387–1393, College; 1394–1404, Cathedral (remodeling); Winchester, England.

BIBLIOGRAPHY

CHAMPNEYS, BASIL 1888 "William of Wykeham." *Art Journal* 50:161–165, 259–262.
CLAPHAM, ALFRED W. 1912 "William of Wykeham as a Castle Builder." *Architectural Review* 31:128–130.
HAYTER, WILLIAM 1970 *William of Wykeham: Patron of the Arts.* London: Chatto & Windus.
WALCOTT, MACKENZIE E. C. 1852 *William of Wykeham and His Colleges.* Winchester, England: Nutt.
"William of Wykeham." 1843 *The Builder* 1, Dec.:2–3.

WILLIAMS, AMANCIO

Amancio Williams (1913–) has been successively engineer, aviator, and architect. He is the son of Argentina's most famous musical composer, Alberto Williams, and is perhaps best known for his House over the Brook built in the Mar del Plata area. This house, built with exceptional exactitude, is a veritable bridge structure in reinforced concrete (1943–1945) that spans a small stream. His architectural projects are of great purity and elegance, of which one of the most important is the Hall for Plastic Spectacle and Sound in Space (1943–1953), in which the profile of the interior space is a mathematical curve, the product of sound and light waves, that have been revolved through 360 degrees, giving a resultant ovoid form which is supported at its base and surrounded by a Saturnlike glass corridor containing foyers and an exhibition hall. The other major project is the Office Building for Buenos Aires (1948): the constructive elements are divided into a superstructure of concrete columns, girders, and trusses

and suspended elements in steel—cables, metal floor decks, and curtain walls—thereby permitting the expression of materials and static forces, concrete for compression, steel for tension. This project offers a poetic vision of architecture's plastic possibilities.

In 1968, Williams was selected to be the Argentine consultant to WALTER GROPIUS in designing the new German Embassy for Buenos Aires. Since 1975, he has been working on a major research project entitled "The City that Humanity Needs" in collaboration with architects in Uruguay and the United States.

REGINALD MALCOLMSON

WORKS

1943–1945, House over the Brook, Mar Del Plata, Argentina. 1960, Ignacio Pirovano Penthouse; *1966, Bunge & Born Exhibition Pavilion; Buenos Aires.

WILLIAMS, OWEN

(Evan) Owen Williams (1890–1969) was a heroic figure in interwar British architecture. Trained as an engineer, he was an inspiration in the 1930s to English architects seeking to realize an architecture of functionalism, particularly in his use of concrete. His experience of this material went back to 1912, and during World War I he made designs for concrete ships, which he returned to during World War II. The first well publicized, large-scale use of concrete in British building was at the Empire Exhibition in 1924, for which Williams was consulting engineer. He had a very matter-of-fact approach to design and, unlike a number of his contemporaries, believed in respecting the wishes—however reactionary—of his clients. He was fortunate, however, in often attracting clients who commissioned large-scale buildings, and offered little resistance to his ideas. His work was much publicized in the 1930s. After the war he worked on the early stages of the motorway network, the results of which rather spoiled his reputation in some quarters.

BRIAN HANSON

WORKS

1914–1918, Concrete Ships. 1919, Walls Factory, Acton, London. 1920, Tannery, Runcorn, Cheshire, England. 1921, Ice-making Plant, Hull, England. 1923, Palace of Industry, British Empire Exhibition, Wembley, London. 1925, Parc des Attractions, International Exposition, Paris. 1925–1930, Wansford Bridge, Huntingdon, England. 1930, Cumberland Garage, Marble Arch, London. 1932, Boots Factory, Beeston, Nottingham, England. 1933, Cement Factory, Thurrock, Essex, England. 1934, Empire Swimming Pool and Sports Arena,

Wembley; 1934, Pioneer Health Centre, Saint Mary's Road, Peckham; 1934, Sainsbury's Warehouse, Rennie Street, Southwark; 1935, Lilley and Skinner Warehouse, Pentonville Road; London. 1937, Odhams Printing Works, Watford, Hertfordshire; 1937, Synagogue, Dollis Hill, London. 1939–1945, Concrete Ships. 1948, Olympic Games Installations, Wembley Stadium; London. 1966, Viaduct, Port Talbot, Wales. 1968, Midland Link Motorways, England.

BIBLIOGRAPHY

GOLD, MICHAEL 1968 "Sir Owen Williams, K.B.E." *Zodiac* (Milan) 18:11–30.

"The Pioneer Health Centre, St. Mary's Road, Peckham, London." 1935 *Architectural Record* 77, no. 6:437–444.

ROSENBERG, STEPHEN; CHALK, WARREN; and MULLIN, STEPHEN 1969 "Sir Owen Williams." *Architectural Design* 39, July:348.

WILLIAMS, E. OWEN 1927 *The Philosophy of Masonry Arches*. London.

WILLIAMS, E. OWEN, and WILLIAMS, O. T. 1961 *The Design and Construction of the M1*. London.

WILLIAMS, WARREN HAYWOOD

No name more exemplifies the quality of architecture in Portland, Oregon, during the 1870s–1880s than the work of Warren Haywood Williams (1844–1888). His prolific output, designing independently or in partnership with others, produced the buildings that gave the city its distinctive architecture.

Born in New York, Williams was five when his father architect, Stephen Hedders Williams, moved to San Francisco. He apprenticed in that office later and was influenced by one of his father's noted associates, HENRY W. CLEAVELAND. In 1869, as partner in the firm Stephen H. Williams & Son, he came to Portland to supervise construction of the Odd Fellows' Temple (1869). Following the devastating fires of 1872 and 1873, he moved to the city where he joined E. M. Burton (1873–1875), designing commercial buildings, hospitals, churches, and residences. Later, he associated with Justus Krumbein (1875–1878). A notable building of this partnership was the large Cosmopolitan Block (1878). Among the significant buildings which Williams produced on his own were the Union Block (1879), Labbés Block (1880), Cooks' Building (1882), Portland Savings Bank (1885), Villard Hall (1885), and Temple Beth Israel (1888). Craigdarroch Castle (1885) in Victoria, British Columbia, was produced in association with Arthur Smith.

WILLIAM J. HAWKINS III

WORKS

*1869, Odd Fellows' Temple; *1873, Bank of British Columbia; *1874, Good Samaritan Hospital; *1874, Trinity Episcopal Church Parish; *1878, Cosmopolitan Block; *1879, Union Block; *1880, Labbés' Block, *1882, Cooks' Building; Portland Ore. 1885, Craigdarroch Castle, Victoria, B.C. *1885, Portland Savings Bank, Portland, Ore. 1885, Villard Hall, University of Oregon, Eugene. *1888, Temple Beth Israel, Portland, Ore.

BIBLIOGRAPHY

HAWKINS, WILLIAM JOHN, III 1980 "Warren H. Williams, Architect." *Portland Friends of Cast-Iron Architecture Newsletter* 17, Dec.

HUNTINGTON, WALLACE KAY 1974 "Victorian Architecture." *Space, Style and Structure* 1.

NELSON, LEE H. 1959 "Architects of Oregon: Piper and Williams." *Call Number* 20, no. 2:4–15.

NELSON, LEE, and SCHMITT, MARTIN 1955 "Sic Transit Observatorium." *Call Number* 16, no. 2:15–20.

ROSS, MARION D. 1956 "Architecture in Oregon, 1845–1895." *Oregon Historical Quarterly* 57, no. 1:33–64.

SEGGER, MARTIN 1979 *Victoria: A Primer for Regional History in Architecture, 1843–1929*. With photographs by Douglas Franklin. Victoria, British Columbia: Milestone.

WILLS, FRANK

Frank Wills (1822–1856), architect of Gothic Revival churches in Canada and the United States, was born in England and died in Montreal when at work on Christ Church Cathedral there.

Wills was from Exeter (he has in some accounts been wrongly associated with Salisbury) where he trained in the office of J. Hayward, an accomplished Devonshire architect. There, he met the Rev. John Medley who, on moving to Canada in 1845, was resolved to build a cathedral patterned after a Norfolk church, Saint Mary's, Snettisham. Wills followed to Canada and built Saint Anne's Chapel (consecrated March 1847) to serve Medley, by now bishop of New Brunswick, until the larger building could be completed. The quality of the architecture and the internal details of Saint Anne's and the accomplishment of the design of the cathedral demonstrate that Wills, though young, was informed in English Gothic Revival taste and possessed talent.

Wills moved to New York in 1847; he had completed the basic work on the cathedral, which would develop slowly as Medley could raise the money for it. In 1848, upon the creation of the New York Ecclesiological Society, whose seal he designed, Wills became its architectural expert and an editor of *The New York Ecclesiologist,* journal of the Society, which was destined to have a wide influence on Protestant Episcopal church building. For the journal he wrote articles on church architecture and on ecclesiological practice and opinion; he also published a design for a modest parish church to serve as a pattern for parishes in need of but unable to afford architectural counsel.

In 1850, as he ventured into independent practice, Wills published *Ancient Ecclesiastical Architecture,* a book which received considerable and favorable notice. In it he described the English medieval architectural styles and condemned much Gothic Revival architecture as vulgar, ornate, and not expressive of its purpose. He explained the traditional liturgical uses of the parts of the English church and cathedral, using Lincoln as his example of the latter. He championed the cause of chancel screens and discussed the history and characteristics of satellite buildings such as chapter houses, cloisters, and lych-gates.

This book reveals Wills's debt to A. W. N. PUGIN. Nowhere is this clearer than in the discussion of scale which repeats Pugin's argument (*True Principles,* p. 69) and acerbic tone. Though in some ways derivative, Wills's essay was in its clarity, applicability to the American church building problem, and its transplantation of the ideas of the English architectural and liturgical antiquary, an unusual event in the American Gothic Revival.

In 1851, Wills founded a partnership with HENRY C. DUDLEY, an older man who had also worked with Hayward in Exeter; in a letter, Wills described Dudley as "an English gentleman who for twenty years has been engaged in the erection of many of our best churches in England." Their association was short-lived but productive.

Wills's writing brought a spirited authority and controversialist into the North American Gothic Revival; his role as artistic advocate of *The New York Ecclesiologist* gave him authority and influence in Protestant Episcopal church circles at a time when many churches were being built; he played an important role in the establishment in North America of the English parish church model at the time of the High Church movement in the 1840s. Many churches are attributable to Wills and to the firm of Wills and Dudley, but many that are not were, in fact, directly taken from the model church Wills suggested in his publications. As his Fredericton buildings illustrate, Wills was an able designer; in 1908 he was remembered by Montgomery Schuyler who described him as "one of the most accomplished of the Anglican revivalists."

PHOEBE B. STANTON

WORKS

1845–1853, Christ Church Cathedral (with William

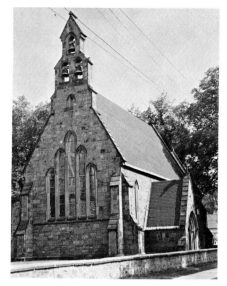

Butterfield); 1847, Saint Anne's Chapel; Fredericton, New Brunswick. 1849, Saint Peter's, Milford, Conn. 1853, Christ Church, Napoleonville, La. 1855, Chapel of the Cross, Annandale, Miss. 1855, Christ Episcopal, Oberlin, Ohio. 1855, Saint Mary's, Saint Francisville, La. 1855, Trinity Church, Scotland, N.C. 1856, Christ Church Cathedral (not completed until 1860 by others), Montreal.

BIBLIOGRAPHY

WILLS, FRANK 1850 *Ancient English Ecclesiastical Architecture.* New York: Stanford & Swords.
HUBBARD, R. H. 1954 "Canadian Gothic." *Architectural Review* 116:102–108.
PATRICK, JAMES 1980 "Ecclesiological Gothic in the Antebellum South." *Winterthur Portfolio* 15, no. 2:117–138.
STANTON, PHOEBE 1968 *The Gothic Revival and American Church Architecture.* Baltimore: Johns Hopkins University Press.

Wills.
Saint Anne's Chapel.
Fredericton, New
*   Brunswick.*
1847

Wills.
Saint Anne's Chapel.
Fredericton, New
*   Brunswick.*
1847

WILS, JAN

Jan Wils (1891–1972) was an important representative of the most progressive period in twentieth-century Dutch architecture.

He was born in Alkmaar, Netherlands. In 1909, he followed an evening course in drawing. In 1910, he designed his first house. In 1912, he was employed by the municipal works of Alkmaar and at the same time followed lectures at the Technical University of Delft. After working a year at an architects' office in The Hague, he was given the opportunity to work on the Holland-House (London, 1914–1916) with H. P. BERLAGE.

In the designs he made after leaving Berlage's office in 1916, Berlage's influence is initially quite apparent. This influence decreased rapidly, however, after his first contacts with THEO VAN

Wils.
Residential Area, Daal en
Berg.
The Hague.
1920

DOESBURG and J. J. P. OUD in 1916. He began to blend the vernacular of FRANK LLOYD WRIGHT, the Amsterdam school, and *De Stijl*. An interesting design of this period is the café-restaurant *De Dubbele Sleutel* (1918–1919) in Woerden, Netherlands, where Van Doesburg cooperated as color consultant. Another important work is the housing development, *Daal en Berg,* The Hague (1920). The back-to-back dwelling type used here was unconventional, and the plan resembles Lexington Terrace in Chicago by Wright. Wils used a smooth outer surface, and the project was realized with prefabricated elements of concrete with sintel, remarkable developments at that time.

In this period, Wils wrote articles for *De Stijl* as well as for *Wendingen,* the Amsterdam school publication. This indicates an interaction between the two movements despite their different premises. Wils could be seen as an intermediary: he combined the craftsmanship of the one movement with the principles and organization of building mass of the other. This is why he is sometimes compared with W. M. DUDOK. The next link in the functional-rationalist line, the *nieuwe zakelijkheid* (new functionalism), played an important role for Wils. The buildings designed between 1925 and 1935 are all of the same spirit and made his reputation.

The first is the Olympic Stadium of Amsterdam (1926–1928). This building was constructed of reinforced concrete with partitioning walls between the columns and an outer wall of masonry, which gives the building its fortresslike appearance.

Shortly afterward, the first Citroen Building was erected next door, initially to be constructed in concrete but erected in steel. The next noteworthy buildings are the OLVEH Company Building (1930–1931) and the Centrale Onderlinge Building (1934–1935), both in The Hague and both good examples of *nieuwe zakelijkheid* architecture.

The last building of this period is the City Theater in Amsterdam; Wils probably made use of a design for the same building made earlier by Jo-

HANNES J. DUIKER. In its day, the building stood as an example of efficient building, probably due to the use of a steel frame. People spoke of the "American way of doing business" that swept Europe.

In the years after World War II, it was no longer so easy to recognize architects in their buildings. This goes for Wils, too, although he still designed interesting structures after the war.

MARK À CAMPO

WORKS

1918–1919, Café-restaurant *De Dubbele Sleutel,* Woerden, Netherlands. 1920, Residential area, *Daal en Berg;* 1921, Dance Institute; 1925–1926, Block of flats, J. Israëlsplein; 1926–1928, Olympic Stadium; 1929–1931, Citroen Building, Amsterdam. 1930–1931, OLVEH Co. Building; 1934–1935, Office Centrale Onderlinge; The Hague. 1935–1936, Cinema City Theater, Amsterdam. 1952–1961, Hotel Bouwes, Zandvoort, Netherlands. 1955, County Labor Enforcement Office; 1956–1959, Chamber of Commerce; The Hague. 1959, Second Citroen Building, Amsterdam. 1963–1966, Crematorium, Okkenburg; Netherlands. 1968–1972, Home for the elderly *Prinsenhof,* Leidschendam, Netherlands.

WILSON, COLIN ST. JOHN

The architecture of Colin St. John Wilson (1922–), which is grounded in a theoretical rather than a stylistic organization of space, originates in a rigorous analysis of the activities to be accommodated. Born in Cheltenham, England, Wilson studied architecture at Cambridge and London Universities before working in the London County Council's housing division (1950–1955). He returned to Cambridge in 1956, becoming an influential teacher at the school of architecture there and practicing (until 1962) with JOHN LESLIE MARTIN. Wilson and Martin's Harvey Court, Cambridge (1960–1962), and Library Group, Oxford (1961–1964), are early examples of the recurrent organizational themes of the courtyard and the stepped terrace. Wilson's contemporary School of Architecture Extension, Cambridge (1958–1959), likewise employs Brutalist brick, wood, and concrete for interior and exterior surfaces while strictly following the geometry of the Golden Section.

Wilson's own house, Grantchester Road, Cambridge (1963–1964), accommodating his collection of contemporary art works, attains an almost classical calm in its modular use of concrete blockwork throughout. His lyrical use of top-lighting is especially strong in the diagonally fractured Cornford House (1966–1967) and in his public buildings. Although Wilson's largest urban projects remain unbuilt, the British Library

(1982–?), London, will incorporate many elements he has long studied in designs for civic, industrial, and office buildings to orient the individual within communal spaces.

THOMAS G. BEDDALL

WORKS

1958–1959, Architecture Department Extension (with Alex Hardy); 1960–1962, Harvey Court Residential Building (with Leslie Martin), Gonville and Caius College; Cambridge. 1961–1964, Three Libraries (with Martin), Manor Road, Oxford. 1962–1964, William Stone Residential Building (with Martin), Peterhouse College; 1963–1964, Two Houses, Grantchester Road; 1966–1967, Cornford House, Madingley Road; Cambridge. 1969–1971, Agricultural Research Council Biochemistry Laboratory (with Michael Brawne), Babraham, England. 1977–1979, British Museum West Wing Extension; 1982–?, British Library Building, Euston Road; London.

BIBLIOGRAPHY

CANTACUZINO, SHERBAN 1978 "A Necessary Giant: Proposed New Building for the British Library." *Architectural Review* 164, no. 982:336–344.
"Civic and Social Centre, Liverpool." 1967 *Architectural Design* 37, no. 6:265–269.
ECHENIQUE, MARCIAL 1969 "Colin St. John Wilson o la seriedad en el proceso arquitectónico." *Cuadernos de Arquitectura* 72:55–72.
"Extension to the School of Architecture, Cambridge." 1959 *Architectural Design* 29, no. 10:394–399.
"Library Group for Oxford University." 1960, 1965 *Architectural Design* 30, no. 10:399–403; 35, no. 9:440–448.
SILVER, NATHAN 1966 "Translating the Root Form for Today's Campus." *Progressive Architecture* 47, no. 4:156–175.
WILSON, COLIN ST. JOHN 1961 "Open and Closed." Pages 97–102 in *Perspecta* 7. New Haven: Yale University, School of Art and Architecture.
WILSON, COLIN ST. JOHN 1965 "Two Houses, Cambridge." *Architectural Design* 35, no. 11:546–549.
WILSON, COLIN ST. JOHN 1979 "Architecture: Public Good and Private Necessity." *Journal of the Royal Institute of British Architects* 86, no. 3:107–115.
WILSON, COLIN ST. JOHN, and MARTIN, LESLIE 1959 "The Collegiate Plan." *Architectural Review* 126, no. 750:42–48.

WILSON, HENRY

Henry Wilson (1864–1934) was born in Liverpool, England. He was a brilliant church interior designer, working in a variety of styles. At various times, he assisted JOHN OLDRID SCOTT, John Belcher, and JOHN D. SEDDING, whom he succeeded in 1891. From 1895 on, he devoted himself to visionary church decoration schemes, metalwork, jewelry, lecturing, and writing. He was associated with the circle of WILLIAM RICHARD LETHABY in the Liverpool Cathedral scheme (1902).

RODERICK O'DONNELL

WORKS

1888–1900?, Church of the Holy Trinity (furnishing), Chelsea; 1890–1891, Public Library, Ladbroke Grove; 1892, Church of Saint Peter, Ealing; London. 1893, Church of Saint Clement (tower), Bournemouth, England. 1895?, Church of Saint Augustine (furnishing), Hornsey, London. 1895–1924, Church of Saint Marin (additions and furnishings), Low Marple, Cheshire, England. 1897–1908, Church of Saint Bartholemew (furnishings), Brighton, England.

BIBLIOGRAPHY

SERVICE, ALASTAIR (editor) 1975 Pages 280–288 in *Edwardian Architecture and Its Origins*. London: Architectural Press.
SERVICE, ALASTAIR 1977 *Edwardian Architecture*. London: Oxford University Press.
TAYLOR, NICHOLAS 1966 "Byzantium in Brighton." *Architectural Review* 139:274–277.
VICTORIA AND ALBERT MUSEUM 1971 Pages 140, 143–144 in *Victorian Church Art*. London: The museum. Exhibition catalogue.
WILSON, HENRY 1899 "Art and Religion." *Architectural Review* 6:276–278.

WIMMEL and FORSMANN

Carl Ludwig Wimmel (1786–1845) studied architecture under Christian Friedrich Lange and FRIEDRICH WEINBRENNER before beginning a career in Hamburg's Buildings Department in 1814. In 1841 he became the first director of the department and exercised a decisive influence on the city's development. Abandoning his early neoclassical style, Wimmel joined the search for an astylar architecture pioneered by HEINRICH HÜBSCH and KARL FRIEDRICH SCHINKEL. While his utilitarian brick buildings reflect the more refined brick Rundbogenstil of his Hamburg rival ALEXIS DE CHÂTEAUNEUF, two major public buildings—the Johanneum and the Börse (both 1837–1840)—initiated a Renaissance Revival style which was widely imitated in Hamburg. Franz Gustav Joachim Forsmann (1795–1878), whose earlier Jenisch House (1831–1835) was indebted to Schinkel's classicism, collaborated with Wimmel in both designs.

BARRY BERGDOLL

WORKS

CARL LUDWIG WIMMEL

*1815–1823, General Hospital; 1816–1820, Saint Pauli

Church and Parsonage; *1817, Dammtor; *1818, Steintor; *1819, Millentor; 1821, Buildings, Botanical Garden; *1823–1827, English Reformed Church; 1823–1827, Housing, Zeughausmarkt; *1826–1827, Municipal Theater; 1827–1830, Esplanade; 1827–1830, House, Gross and Kleine Theaterstrassen; *1828–1830, Prison; *1833–1837, Holy Spirit Hospital; 1834–1837, Saint John Monastery; *1838–1839, Maria-Magdalena Convent; Hamburg, Germany. 1840–1842, House of the Boat Commander, Cuxhaven, Germany.

FRANZ GUSTAV JOACHIM FORSMANN

1831–1835, Jenisch House; 1846, Berenberg-Gossler House; 1846, Kellinghusen House, Jungfernstieg; Hamburg, Germany.

WIMMEL AND FORSMANN

1837–1840, Börse; *1837–1840, Johanneum; Hamburg, Germany.

BIBLIOGRAPHY

GERHARDT, JOACHIM 1950–1951 "Die Hamburger Börse." *Deutsche Kunst und Denkmalpflege* 1952:134–137.
GRUNDMANN, GÜNTHER 1957 *Jenisch Haus und Jenisch Park.* Hamburg: Hans Christians.
HANNMANN, ECKART 1975 *Carl Ludwig Wimmel: 1786–1845; Hamburgs erster Baudirektor.* Munich: Prestel.
GERHARDT, JOACHIM 1950–1951 "Die Hamburger Börse." *Deutsche Kunst und Denkmalpflege* 1952:134–137.
HANNMANN, ECKART 1975 *Carl Ludwig Wimmel: 1786–1845: Hamburgs erster Baudirektor.* Munich: Prestel.

WINDRIM, JAMES H.

James Hamilton Windrim (1840–1919), a Philadelphia architect, was a member of the first graduating class of Girard College (1856). His association with the college continued throughout his life, for he was appointed the architect of the Girard Estate in 1871 and subsequently designed and superintended the erection of many buildings on the campus.

Windrim received his early architectural training as a draftsman under Archibald Catanach, a stonemason who was the builder of JOHN NOTMAN's Holy Trinity Episcopal Church in Philadelphia (1856–1859).

In the early 1860's, Windrim was sent to Pittsburgh by the Pennsylvania Railroad to design and build the Union Depot and on his return to Philadelphia in 1867, he won the architectural competition for the Masonic Temple. By the age of twenty-eight, Windrim was a professional success, for he had been chosen to be the architect of the largest "public" building on Philadelphia's Penn Square. This competition is also of interest because it provided the recently formed New York-based American Institute of Architects with one of its earliest successes in its struggle to establish recognized professional standards.

Windrim later designed such prominent Philadelphia structures as the Academy of Natural Sciences (1872), the U.S. Centennial Agricultural Hall (1876), and the Richard Smith Memorial Gateway (1897). He was appointed Supervising Architect of the United States in 1889—a post he held until 1891, when he resigned to become the Director of Public Works for the city of Philadelphia.

JOHN POPPELIERS

WORKS

1867–1873, Philadelphia Masonic Temple; 1872, Academy of Natural Sciences; c.1872, Hood, Bonbright & Company Dry Goods Store; 1876, United States Centennial Agricultural Hall, Fairmont Park; c.1882, First Regiment Armory; 1882–1890, Girard College (Buildings 8, 9, and 10); *c.1892, Southern Home for Destitute Children; Philadelphia. 1893–1894, Pennsylvania State Library (with John T. Windrim), Harrisburgh, Penn. 1897, Richard Smith Memorial Gateway, Fairmount Park, Philadelphia.

BIBLIOGRAPHY

The Biographical Encyclopaedia of Pennsylvania of the Nineteenth Century. 1874 Philadelphia: Galaxy.
HENRY, FREDERICK P. (editor) 1909 *Founder's Week Memorial Volume.* Philadelphia: F. A. Davis.
"James H. Windrim." 1911 *Steel and Garnet* 1, Oct.:7–8.
KING, MOSES (1901)1902 *Philadelphia and Notable Philadelphians.* New York: Moses King.
POPPELIERS, JOHN 1962 "James Hamilton Windrim." Unpublished M.A. thesis, University of Pennsylvania, Philadelphia.
POPPELIERS, JOHN 1967 "The 1867 Philadelphia Masonic Temple Competition." *Journal of the Society of Architectural Historians* 26, no. 4:278–284.
TATUM, GEORGE B. 1961 *Penn's Great Town: 250 Years of Philadelphia Architecture Illustrated in Prints and Drawings.* Philadelphia: University of Pennsylvania Press.
YOUNG, JOHN RUSSELL (editor) 1895–1898 Volume 2 of *Memorial History of the City of Philadelphia.* New York Historical Company.

WISE, HENRY

Trained in the French formal garden style, Henry Wise (1653–1738) became one of its leading practitioners in late Stuart England. By 1687 he was GEORGE LONDON's partner in the famous Brompton Park Nurseries, which supplied the later gardens they designed, including those at Longleat (c.1685) and Chatsworth (1688). At the accession of Queen Anne in 1702, Wise became sole superintendant of the Royal Gardens, creating new designs at Hampton Court (1702), Kensington Palace (1702), and Windsor Castle (1702–1708). In 1705 he began his masterpiece, the great bastioned parterre behind JOHN VANBRUGH's Blenheim Palace. Wise retired from royal service in 1728 leaving the field to pupils CHARLES BRIDGEMAN and STEPHEN SWITZER, transitional designers to the new landscape garden style.

RICHARD O. SWAIN

WORKS

The dates listed below for each garden are the founding dates.
c.1685, Longleat Gardens (with George London), Wiltshire, England. 1688, Chatsworth Gardens (with London), Derbyshire, England. 1702, Hampton Court, Middlesex, England. 1702, Kensington Palace, London. 1702–1708, Windsor Castle (The Maestricht Garden), Berkshire, England. *1705–1716, Blenheim Palace (the parterre), Oxfordshire, England.

BIBLIOGRAPHY

GREEN, DAVID 1956 *Gardener to Queen Anne: Henry Wise (1653–1738) and the Formal Garden.* London: Oxford University Press.

HUNT, JOHN DIXON, and WILLIS, PETER (editors) (1975)1976 *The Genius of the Place: The English Landscape Garden, 1620–1820.* New York: Harper.

LONDON, GEORGE, and WISE, HENRY (editors) 1699 *The Compleat Gard'ner . . . by Monsieur De la Quintinye.* London: M. Gillyflower. Abridgment of John Evelyn's translation, published in 1693.

LONDON, GEORGE, and WISE, HENRY (translators and editors) (1796)1980 *The Retir'd Gard'ner.* Reprint. New York: Garland. A translation and adaptation "to our English Culture" of French works by François Gentil and Sieur Liger d'Auxerre.

SWITZER, STEPHEN (1718)1980 *Ichnographia Rustica: Or, the Nobleman, Gentleman and Gardener's Recreation.* Reprint. New York: Garland.

WILLIS, PETER 1977 *Charles Bridgeman and the English Landscape Garden.* London: Zwemmer.

WITHERS, FREDERICK CLARKE

Frederick Clarke Withers (1828–1901) was prominent among the group of English High Victorian Gothic architects who constituted a vital element of the New York architectural scene during the late nineteenth century. Born in Shepton Mallet, Somerset, Withers became an indentured pupil of Edward Mondey in Dorchester in 1844. Five years later, he entered the London office of Thomas Henry Wyatt (see WYATT AND WYATT) and DAVID BRANDON, as an assistant. In 1852, at the invitation of ANDREW JACKSON DOWNING, the American landscape architect, he immigrated to Newburgh, New York, to assist Downing, together with CALVERT VAUX, in the preparation of architectural designs.

When Downing died that summer, Withers formed a partnership with Vaux that lasted until 1856. Most of their work appeared in Vaux's *Villas and Cottages* (1857). From 1857, Withers maintained an independent practice in Newburgh where he attracted clients desiring large country houses. The Daniel B. St. John House (1857), Balmville, New York, and *Tioronda* (1860), Beacon, New York, brick dwellings in a sober Gothic style, are outstanding among these projects.

In Newburgh, Withers also innaugurated his career as a church architect, a role in which he distinguished himself. A devout Episcopalian, Withers became one of the most accomplished practitioners of Anglican ecclesiology in America. His book *Church Architecture* (1873) illustrated many of his ecclesiastical designs and epitomized the subject. His earliest church, the First Presbyterian Church (1857), Newburgh, adapted ecclesiological principles to non-Episcopal requirements. In the polychromatic brick Dutch Reformed Church (1859), Beacon, New York, High Victorian Gothic ideas appeared for one of the first times in America.

After a brief enlistment in the Union Army, Withers, in 1863, once again joined Vaux in New York, an arrangement that lasted until 1871. He was then also associated with FREDERICK LAW OLMSTED in the firm of Olmsted, Vaux and Company. The middle phase of Withers's career, which extended to the late 1870s, was his most productive and led to such works as Saint Luke's Episcopal Church (1869), Beacon, New York, the Church of Saint Thomas (1872), Hanover, New Hampshire, and the William Backhouse Astor Memorial Altar and Reredos (1876) in New York's Trinity Church, where Withers also remodeled the chancel.

As a secular architect Withers shunned the conservatism of his ecclesiastical designs and espoused High Victorian Gothic, which, rightly or wrongly, was identified with the theories of JOHN RUSKIN. The Newburgh Savings Bank (1866), Withers's first full-blown statement in this idiom, was followed by the Hudson River State Hospital (1867), Poughkeepsie, New York, and Chapel Hall (1868-1871) at Gallaudet College in Washington (where Withers designed several college buildings). The Third Judicial District Courthouse, Prison and Firetower (1874–1878) in New

Withers.
Third Judicial Courthouse,
Prison, and
Firetower (Jefferson Market
Courthouse).
New York.
1874–1878

York, commonly known as the Jefferson Market Courthouse, a work indebted to WILLIAM BURGES's 1866 competition design for the London Law Courts, was Withers's greatest building. Its polychrome Italianate forms and naturalistic sculpture, its clear expression of volumes and plan, and its architectonic control of picturesque massing make it a supreme example in the United States of Ruskinian ideals. Withers's domestic architecture of these years, such as the Eugene Brewster House (1865), Newburgh, and the President's House (1867), Gallaudet College, grafted elements from High Victorian Gothic design onto the antebellum Downing suburban villa.

During the last two decades of the century, Withers maintained an active practice (after 1888 in partnership with Walter Dickson), although his position as an artistic leader of his profession was reduced. Favored by conservative clergymen, he drew the plans for a number of churches in eastern cities, including Trinity Church (1891), Hartford, his largest church, and the Chapel of the Good Shepherd (1888), New York, reminiscent of the elemental brick churches of JAMES BROOKS in England. The Van Schaick Free Reading Room (1882), Bronx, New York, and the Hackensack Water Company Tower (1883), Weehawken, New Jersey, have a similar planometric severity. Withers's later houses were in the Queen Anne style, and the New York City Prison (1896), his last important commission, was a tall château-fortress design.

FRANCIS R. KOWSKY

WORKS

1857, First Presbyterian Church, Newburgh, N.Y. 1857, Daniel B. St. John House; 1859, Frederick Deming House; Balmville, N.Y. 1859, Dutch Reformed Church; 1860, Tioronda (Joseph Howland House); Beacon, N.Y. 1865, Eugene Brewster House; *1866, Newburgh Savings Bank; Newburgh, N.Y. 1867, Hudson River State Hospital, Poughkeepsie, N.Y. 1867, President's House, Gallaudet College; 1868–1871, Chapel Hall, Gallaudet College; Washington. 1869, Saint Luke's Episcopal Church, Beacon, N.Y. 1872, Church of Saint Thomas, Hanover, N.H. 1874–1878, Third Judicial District Courthouse, Prison, and Firetower, New York. 1875, College Hall, Gallaudet College, Washington. 1876, Trinity Church (William Backhouse Astor Memorial Alter and Reredos), New York. 1882, Van Schaick Free Reading Room (now Huntington Library), Bronx, N.Y. 1883, Hackensack Water Company Tower, Weehawken, N.J. 1888, Chapel of the Good Shepherd, New York. 1891, Trinity Church, Hartford, Conn. *1896, New York City Prison.

BIBLIOGRAPHY

Personal documents and drawings of Frederick Clarke Withers are in the collections of the New York Historical Society; The Avery Architectural Library, Columbia University, New York; the (Alan Burnham) American Architectural Archive, Greenwich, Connecticut; and the Fine Arts Library, University of Pennsylvania, Philadelphia.

KOWSKY, FRANCIS R. 1971–1972 "Gallaudet College: A High Victorian Campus." *Records of the Columbia Historical Society of Washington, D.C.* 49:71–72, 439–467.

KOWSKY, FRANCIS R. 1976 "The Architecture of Frederick Clarke Withers." *Journal of the Society of Architectural Historians* 35:83–107.

KOWSKY, FRANCIS R. 1980 *The Architecture of Frederick Clarke Withers and the Progress of the Gothic Revival in America after 1850.* Middletown, Conn.: Wesleyan University Press.

KOWSKY, FRANCIS R. 1980 "College Hall at Gallaudet College." *Records of the Columbia Historical Society of Washington, D.C.* 50:279–289.

VAUX, CALVERT (1857)1970 *Villas and Cottages.* Reprint. New York: Dover.

WITHERS, FREDERICK CLARKE 1873 *Church Architecture.* New York: Bicknell.

WITTET, GEORGE

George Wittet (1880–1926) was responsible for several early twentieth-century public buildings in Bombay, for which he usually employed his own version of Indian styles. Wittet was born in Scotland and worked for G. Washington Browne in Edinburgh and Walter Brierley in York before being invited to India in 1904 to assist JOHN BEGG in Bombay. In 1908, Wittet succeeded Begg as consulting architect to the government of Bombay. In 1919, he left government service but resumed his earlier appointment in 1925, shortly before his premature death.

GAVIN STAMP

WORKS

1905–1914, Prince of Wales Museum; 1914–1921, Gateway of India; ?–1916, College of Science; Bombay.

BIBLIOGRAPHY

BEGG, JOHN 1926 "George Wittet." *Journal of the Royal Institute of British Architects* Series 3 33:618–619.

WOLF, PAUL

Paul Wolf (1879–1957), German city planner, architect, and author, was born in Schrozberg, Württemberg, and studied under THEODOR FISCHER in Stuttgart. He began a career in public service in Kattowitz (1906–1907), became building director of Wilhelmshaven (1907–1910), and proceeded to ever greater responsibilities in Berlin-Schöneberg (1910–1914), Hanover (1914–1922), and Dresden (from 1922 on). His works include the Ceciliengärten Housing Area in Berlin, and in Hanover an urban development plan, the stadium, a power plant, and the Siedlung Laatzen. In Dresden, he was responsible for everything from schools and hospitals to swimming pools, the planetarium, and plans for urban expansion. He died in East Germany.

RON WIEDENHOEFT

BIBLIOGRAPHY

MITTMANN, REINHOLD 1957 "Dr. Ing. h. c. Paul Wolf." *Deutsche Architektur* 6:473.
"Paul Wolf." 1932 Volume 4, page 725 in *Wasmuths Lexikon der Baukunst*. Berlin: Wasmuth.
WOLF, PAUL 1919 *Städtebau: Das Formproblem der Stadt in Vergangenheit und Zukunft*. Leipzig: Klinkhardt & Biermann.
WOLF, PAUL 1926 *Wohnung und Siedlung*. Berlin: Wasmuth.

WOLFF, JACOB THE ELDER, and WOLFF, JACOB THE YOUNGER

Jacob Wolff the Elder (c.1546–1612) and his son, Jacob Wolff the Younger (1571–1620), were late Renaissance German architects whose most important works were done for the city of Nuremberg, where Jacob the Elder became master mason. Jacob the Elder was born in Bamberg and is first docu-

mented as a stonemason in the Bamberg Cathedral records of 1572. Between 1600 and 1607, he enlarged the Marienberg Castle for the bishop of Würzburg. Between 1602 and 1607, he and Peter Carl built the *überherrliche* (super-magnificent) house for Martin Peller, Nuremberg (partially rebuilt after its destruction in World War II). Although Peller, who had been a consul in Venice, preferred an Italian design, the final result incorporated Italian details into an essentially German-style gabled house.

Jacob Wolff the Younger, who traveled in Italy early in the seventeenth century, developed further the Italian elements of his father's style. His most notable work was the enlargement of the Nuremberg Town Hall (destroyed in World War II and rebuilt) on which he worked from 1616 until his death in 1620. Italian influence is detectable in the long horizontal façade which the three sculptural portals dominate. After Jacob's death, the work was supervised until 1622 by his brother Hans.

JOANNE E. SOWELL

WORKS

JACOB WOLFF THE ELDER

1600–1607, Marienberg Castle (enlargement), above Würzburg, Germany. 1602–1607, Martin Peller House, Nuremberg, Germany.

JACOB WOLFF THE YOUNGER

1616–1620, Nuremberg Town Hall (additions), Germany.

BIBLIOGRAPHY

HEMPEL, EBERHARD 1965 *Baroque Art and Architecture in Central Europe*. Baltimore: Penguin.

WOMERSLEY, PETER

The work of English architect Peter Womersley (1923–) consists mostly of small, one-off schemes in which he has experimented both aesthetically and structurally, moving from a predominant use of timber to that of concrete. Fascinated by the application of geometry to architecture, in which he divides simple, open volumes into smaller, interrelated spaces, Womersley has always acknowledged his debt to LUDWIG MIES VAN DER ROHE, but he has recently turned increasingly to FRANK LLOYD WRIGHT for inspiration in the imaginative expression of materials.

Womersley currently practices in Hong Kong.

PETER WILLIS

WORKS

Completed 1954, Farnley Hey, Yorkshire, England. 1957, House, Galashiels, Scotland. 1957, House,

Gattonside, Scotland. 1963, House, Port Murray, Scotland. 1967, Doctors' Group Practice Surgery, Kelso, Scotland. 1968, Transplantation Surgery Unit, Edinburgh. 1972, Bernat Klein Design Studio, Galashiels, Scotland.

BIBLIOGRAPHY

WILLIS, PETER 1977 *New Architecture in Scotland.* London: Lund Humphries.
WILLIS, PETER 1980 "Womersley, Peter." Pages 893–894 in Muriel Emanuel (editor), *Contemporary Architects.* New York: St. Martin's.

WOOD, CECIL

Cecil Walter Wood (1878–1947), was born in Christchurch, New Zealand, and articled to F. W. Strouts. In England from 1901 to 1907, he was employed by the London County Council and R. Weir Schultz. He returned to practice in Christchurch, working in the free English tradition, but was later much influenced by Scandinavian architecture.

JOHN STACPOOLE

WORKS

1915, Hare Memorial Library, Christ's College, Christchurch, New Zealand. 1920, Anderson House, Invercargill, New Zealand. 1920, Fleming House; 1922–1925, Public Trust Office; 1924, Weston House; 1925, Memorial Hall, Christ's College; 1926, Theosophical Society Hall; 1926–1928, Bishopscourt; Christchurch, New Zealand. 1927, Church of Saint Barnabas, Fendalton, New Zealand. 1928, Presbyterian Church, Cashmere, New Zealand. 1930, Church at Tai Tapu, New Zealand. 1930, Jacobs House, Christ's College, Christchurch, New Zealand. 1938–1942, Saint Paul's Cathedral, Wellington.

BIBLIOGRAPHY

MAINGAY, L. ST. J. 1964 "Cecil Walter Wood: Architect of the Free Tradition." Unpublished M. Arch. dissertation, University of Auckland, New Zealand.
STACPOOLE, JOHN, and BEAVEN, PETER 1972 *New Zealand Art: Architecture, 1820–1970.* Wellington: Reed.

WOOD, EDITH ELMER

Edith Elmer Wood (1871–1945), housing reformer, was born in Portsmouth, New Hampshire, and educated at Smith College. Following her graduation, she became a nonresident worker at the College Settlement in New York. As with many women of her era, however, her social work career was cut short by her marriage in 1894 to naval officer Albert Norton Wood. In the next few years, Wood performed the duties of a military wife at home and abroad and bore four children.

She also pursued a writing career, gaining an entry in *Who's Who* in 1903.

The beginning of her housing career occurred in 1906 in Puerto Rico, where she led an islandwide antituberculosis campaign. She soon concluded that the disease's eradication required the elimination of the dark, unventilated, native house. As part of this effort, she wrote a new housing code for San Juan.

In 1909, her husband retired and the family returned to the United States, ultimately settling in Washington, D.C., where she was drawn into the capital's housing reform movement. Increasingly dismayed by the results of contemporary solutions, she decided in 1914 to discontinue writing fiction and to become a professional housing expert. This decision sent her back to school to earn degrees at the New York School of Philanthropy and Columbia University. Her doctoral dissertation, *The Housing of the Unskilled Wage Earner* (1919), became a classic in modern housing reform literature, advocating a national policy to facilitate the construction of low-cost housing.

For the next twenty-five years, Wood worked as a writer, lobbiest, and government consultant in pursuit of this objective, which became a reality with the passage of the National Housing Act of 1937.

Wood was active in housing well into her seventies when ill health forced her total retirement. She died in April 1945 having lived long enough to see the construction of units of public housing designed according to her prescriptions.

EUGENIE L. BIRCH

BIBLIOGRAPHY

BIRCH, EUGENIE L. 1976 "Edith Elmer Wood and the Genesis of Liberal Housing Thought: 1910–1942." Unpublished Ph.D. dissertation, Columbia University, New York.
BIRCH, EUGENIE L. 1978 "Woman-Made America." *Journal of the American Institute of Planners* 44, no. 2:130–144.
WOOD, EDITH ELMER 1919 *Housing of the Unskilled Wage Earner.* New York: Macmillan.
WOOD, EDITH ELMER 1923 *Housing Progress in Western Europe.* New York: Dutton.
WOOD, EDITH ELMER 1931 *Recent Trends in American Housing.* New York: Macmillan.
WOOD, EDITH ELMER (1935)1969 *Slums and Blighted Areas in the United States.* Reprint. College Park, Md.: McGorath.

WOOD, SANCTON

Sancton Wood (1816–1886) was articled to ROBERT SMIRKE and worked in the classical style. He is chiefly known as the architect to railway companies in England and Ireland. His office was in London, where he acted in many arbitrations and as district surveyor to the parishes of Putney, Poehampton, and Saint Luke's Chelsea.

JILL ALLIBONE

WORKS

c.1840–1860, Railway Stations and Buildings, Eastern Counties Railway; Eastern Union Railway; Rugby and Stamford Railway; Syston and Peterborough Railway; England. c.1840–1860, Railway Stations and Buildings, Great Southern and Western Railway, Ireland. 1845, Cambridge Railway Station. 1846, Blackburn Railway Station, Lancashire, England. 1850, 42–44 Gresham Street; *1852, Queen's Assurance and Commercial Chambers; 1857, Terrace Houses, Lancaster Gate; 1864, Hackney Town Hall; London.

BIBLIOGRAPHY

BARNES, FREDERICK 1886 "The Late Mr. Sancton Wood." The Builder 50, May 29:795–796.
ROBINS, E. C. 1886 "Mr. Sancton Wood." The Builder 50, May 22:761.

WOOD, THOMAS

Thomas Wood (1643/1644–1695) was a master mason and sculptor, working mainly in and around Oxford. He seems to have done little work as an architect, but was almost certainly the designer of the Old Ashmolean Museum (1678–1683), Oxford (the first public museum in England), for which he was master mason. Although certain features of this handsome little building are somewhat clumsy and provincial-looking, it was one of the most advanced classical buildings of its time in Oxford, and has accordingly (but groundlessly) often been attributed to CHRISTOPHER WREN.

IAN CHILVERS

WORKS

1678–1683, Old Ashmolean Museum (now the Museum of History of Science), Oxford. 1683–1685, Deddington Church (rebuilding of tower), Oxfordshire, England.

BIBLIOGRAPHY

GUNNIS, RUPERT (1953)1968 Dictionary of British Sculptors: 1660–1851. Rev. ed. London: Abbey.
MALLET, CHARLES EDWARD (1924)1968 A History of the University of Oxford: Volume II. Reprint. New York: Barnes & Noble; London: Methuen.
VAISEY, D. G. 1971 "Thomas Wood and His Workshop." Oxoniensia 36:55–58.
VICTORIA COUNTY HISTORY 1954 The University of Oxford. Volume 3 in Oxfordshire. London: Institute of Historical Research.

WOOD FAMILY

John Wood the Elder. John Wood (1704–1754), also known as John Wood the Elder and John Wood I to distinguish him from his son of the same name, was born in Bath, England. John Wood was the son of George Wood, a mason and builder. He attended the Blue Coat School in Bath; little else is known of his early life. There is no evidence that Wood ever traveled abroad to study, which is in keeping with the sense of local history and tradition with which his architecture and his writings, in particular, are imbued. Records of Saint Marylebone, London, show that Wood resided on Oxford Street, London, during the years 1725–1727, while functioning as one of the principal builders on the Cavendish-Harley Estate for the earl of Oxford (to whom he later dedicated his book on Stonehenge). Concurrently, Wood was working in Yorkshire. From March 1723, until July 1730, Wood was granted leases in London to build five houses on Oxford Street, one on Margaret Street, and several more on Edward Street. Under commission of the duke of Chandos and Lord Bingley, he was building on Cavendish Square. Lord Bingley was at work on a large house on the west side of Cavendish Square, and it is probable that Wood acted as his surveyor. Lord Bingley had recently completed his country estate at Bramham Park in Yorkshire, and there is evidence that Wood was employed there in the design of the grounds.

In *An Essay Towards a Description of Bath, and of the British Works in its Neighborhood* published in 1742–1743, Wood states that while he was in Yorkshire in the summer of 1725 he began his designs for the improvement of Bath. A number of considerations fostered and facilitated his developing scheme for the improvement of his home town. Bath, a small town dependent on a moribund wool industry, was on the threshold of prosperity at this time with the qualities of its famous hot springs attracting royal visits. Wood had read a great deal concerning the origins of Bath, and from this he conceived of an expanded Bath with homage paid to its Roman foundations. He did not live to see the unearthing of the Roman baths, but he was determined to re-endow Bath with Roman monuments. Legislative acts had already been obtained to improve the roads leading to Bath, to "pave, clean and light" its streets, and to make the Avon River navigable from Bath to Bristol (1712). Thus, from his *Description of Bath,* "when I found the Work was likely to go on, I began to turn my Thoughts toward the Improvement of the City by Building, and for this Purpose I procured a Plan of the Town, which was sent me

John Wood the Elder.
Queen Square.
Bath, England.
1729–1736

into Yorkshire, in the summer of the year 1725, where I, in my leisure Hours, formed one design for the Ground, at the North West Corner of the City" (belonging to Robert Gay, an eminent London surgeon who had been Member of Parliament for Bath), and "another for the Land on the North East side of the Town and River" (that is, on the estate of the earl of Essex). These were alternative sites. Both included

a grand Place of Assembly, to be called the Royal Forum of Bath; another Place, no less magnificent, for the Exhibition of Sports, to be called the Grand Circus; and a third Place, of equal State with either of the former, for the Practice of medicinal Exercises, to be called the Imperial Gymnasium of the City, from a Work of that kind, taking its Rise at first in Bath, during the Time of the Roman Emperors.

Back in London, Wood proposed his improvements to the owners of the sites, and in November 1726, he became Robert Gay's agent. Wood acted as a speculative builder, leasing the land for building from the freeholder (in this case Gay) and subleasing to builders, giving them liberty in the interiors but maintaining control regarding the elevations. The builders would obtain agreements for long tenancies, borrowing money with these as security. Wood's initial venture into speculative building, a group of houses originally known as Barton Street, is now known as Gay Street. In 1727, the duke of Chandos commissioned Wood to erect a "court of houses" on the site of Saint John's Hospital. Later in the same year, Wood assisted in the canalization of the Avon River. Believing the local builders to be capable of substandard work at best, Wood contracted masons from Yorkshire and other craftspeople from London and its environs to do the work. The canal opened to traffic in 1727.

Wood established residence permanently in Bath in May 1727. Fluctuations in the political climate threatened the patronage of Wood's proposed improvements there, and when Gay rescinded his support, Wood responded by becoming the sole contractor for a large residential square. As such his was the last word in all considerations, both financial and aesthetic. Late in 1727, Wood leased land from Gay to the northwest of old Bath on which to build the east side of the square, which has come to be known as Queen Square. In 1728 and 1734, adjacent parcels of land were subsequently leased. Queen Square consists of a series of attached townhouses integrated into a unified and dignified palazzo design. It is the first example outside of London of this type of housing being handled in a Palladian (see ANDREA PALLADIO) manner. The square was conceived as a palatial forecourt; the houses on the north side form the dominant element. A rusticated ground floor serves as the foundation for the large order of engaged Corinthian columns which articulate the end wings and the pedimented center, with corresponding pilasters in the intervening wings. Originally, there were to have been auxiliary buildings of a less dominant character to balance the pedimented center to the east and to the west. Having subdivided his design into individual houses, Wood proceeded by subleasing these residential increments to the builders, who were bound by contract to follow Wood's elevation plans while allowed freedom in the plan and decoration of the interiors. Queen Square is related to the west London estates of the time, particularly the unresolved design in Grosvenor Square by EDWARD SHEPHERD of 1725–1735. With the completion of Queen Square in 1736, Wood had realized a portion of his plan for Bath.

Inspired by the success of Queen Square, Wood sought to execute his other improvements for Bath, namely the Forum and the Circus. With a man named Leake, a bookseller, Wood leased the site of the Abbey Orchard on the east side of Bath and began the construction of his "Royal Forum" in 1739. Had the Forum been executed according to his original design, it would have consisted of houses with classical palace façades (Corinthian order) facing sunken gardens complete with corresponding rusticated retaining walls. Unfortunately, Wood compromised with his subleases and did away with the Corinthian order and the rusticated substructure. The block of houses known as the South Parade remains today as the only portion of his "Royal Forum" to have been executed.

The Circus was not begun until February 1754, within months of Wood's death; hence, the majority of the actual construction was supervised by Wood's son, John Wood the Younger. Theoretically, Wood had intended the Circus to serve as an arena for spectator sports, but it was built as a residential enclosure. The Circus consists of thirty-three houses, grouped into three segments defined by the entering streets, and situated about a circular arc 318 feet in diameter. Wood took the form from the Roman Colosseum begun by Vespasian in the first century A.D. as he knew it via inexpensive and inaccurate engravings, and he inverted and miniaturized it. The elevations are likewise borrowed from the Colosseum: the three stories are articulated by superimposed orders of Doric, Ionic, and Corinthian columns, appearing in pairs complete with full architraves. Like those of Queen Square, the houses have identical fronts, while differing considerably within and behind. The Circus drew criticism on the basis of Wood's inaccurate archeology from a number of architects, including JOHN SOANE; yet, its brilliant architectural effect has left an enduring impression on the English town planning tradition, underscoring its considerable value.

For the most part, the architectural vocabulary of John Wood borrows from the design books in circulation during the second quarter of the eighteenth century. That is to say, the elevation and detail of his housing designs are essentially in keeping with the eclectic Palladianism then in vogue. His very real contribution lay in applying the more urban possibilities of Palladianism as it had been practiced in England to a more provincial setting. The style, which is so lucidly classic, is brilliantly sympathetic to a spa city whose desire was to revive its Roman past.

As Wood's reputation spread, he received commissions for civic buildings outside Bath as well as for private estates. Notable public buildings include the Exchange and Market in Bristol of 1741–1743, and the Exchange (now the Town Hall) in Liverpool of 1749–1754. The country estate of Ralph Allen, called Prior Park, exhibits Wood's consummate ability in the treatment of a single theme. Begun in 1735 on a site near Bath, it is said to have been intended to demonstrate the qualities of the local, that is oolithic limestone. The entrance is severe in appearance with an engaged Ionic portico. The rear façade is articulated by a hexastyle Corinthian portico. The lower subsidiary elevations were designed in a simple Tuscan manner. An altercation with Allen precipitated Wood's being replaced by Richard Jones (Allen's clerk) who made changes in the design of the east wing. Prior Park would have been one of the most resolved examples of British Palladianism had it been executed according to Wood's design.

John Wood the Elder. The Circus (completed by John Wood the Younger). Bath, England. Begun 1754

In addition to his architectural works, Wood wrote a number of books, including his aforementioned *An Essay Towards a Description of Bath* published in 1742–1743. In this work, the self-educated antiquarian fully expressed his romanticized notions. He identified the city of Bladud as the ancient seat of Apollo, and established a Druidic University at Stanton Drew. In 1741, Wood published a rather odd book entitled *The Origin of Building, or the Plagiarism of the Heathens Detected.* He posits that the development of classical architecture was anticipated in Biblical times and that the three classical orders had been revealed to the Jews and integrated in the Temple at Jerusalem. Wood does not cite his source for this thesis, but it takes its essentials from G. B. Villalpanda's com-

John Wood the Elder. Exchange and Market. Corn Street, Bristol, England. 1741–1743

John Wood the Elder.
Prior Park.
Near Bath, England.
1735–1748

mentaries on Ezekiel published in 1604, which sought to free classical architecture from the stigma of pagan origin, thus rendering its application more palatable on both religious and aesthetic grounds. *Choir Gaure, Vulgarly called Stonehenge, Described, Restored and Explained,* published in 1747, was based on a survey conducted by Wood for Lord Oxford in 1740. The essay attempts to prove that Stonehenge was "a temple of British Druids" ultimately based on the stone circles at Stanton Drew. His other works include *A Description of the Exchange of Bristol,* 1745, and *Dissertation Upon the Orders of Columns and Their Appendages,* 1750.

John Wood died at the age of 50. He was survived by his wife Jane, and his four children, John, Allen Thayer, Jane, and Elizabeth. His speculative building and architectural practice had been successful, and he left substantial property to his wife at his death.

John Wood the Younger. John Wood (1728–1781) also known as John Wood the Younger and John Wood II to distinguish him from his father was christened in Bath Abbey, on February 25, 1727/1728. It is reasonable to suppose that as a youth Wood received his training under the guidance of his father and that as a young man he served as his assistant. The first evidence for this dates to 1749, when his father was executing his Exchange in Liverpool. The elder Wood agreed "to leave his son Mr. John Wood at Liverpoole during the summer season to superintend and

carry on the said building." After his father's death in 1754, Wood was his natural successor as the most prominent architect in Bath. He supervised the completion of the Circus, which his father had begun in 1754, and further complemented his father's scheme, conceived in 1727, with his Royal Crescent.

Begun in 1767 and completed in 1775, the Royal Crescent was the first, largest, and most dignified of its kind of residential building, in addition to being Wood's first masterpiece. The Royal Crescent evolved from the Colosseum plan, as had the Royal Circus, but with some significant differences. It maintains the Colosseum's elliptical plan, halved and inverted. The Crescent consists of thirty attached townhouses, measuring 538 feet along its major axis. The elevation is majestic in scale: a plain ground story serves as a base for an order of 114 Ionic columns running through the two upper stories. The center house is emphasized by coupled columns and a semicircular window head. The individual houses are not identical, any possible visual tedium being relieved by the variety in the number of bays, and there are wide variations in their internal planning and detail. Wood's fine sense of design is especially evident in the interiors. The rooms are not wedge-shaped as might be presumed from the exterior, but rather rectilinear. The walls between the townhouses are increased in width in areas with the insertion of cupboards and alcoves. The grand sweep of columns, and the successful relationship of the building to the site made the Royal Crescent a design much emulated by architects who followed in the Bathonian town planning tradition.

Wood's second major accomplishment was the new Assembly Rooms in Bath. Begun in 1769 and costing twenty thousand pounds, the structure opened to the public in 1771. The Assembly Rooms served as a center of social functions: it was where Georgian Bathonians gathered to dance, drink tea, eat, and play cards, as described in the novels of Jane Austen. In keeping with his father's practice of speculative building, Wood in a sense

John Wood the Younger.
Royal Crescent.
Bath, England.
1767–1777

commissioned the structure himself, employing the tontine system, he issued seventy shares at the price of thirty pounds, bringing in over twenty thousand pounds to finance the building. The Assembly Rooms consist of a dignified stone block measuring approximately 150 feet square. There is a single range of windows along the north façade articulated by a Doric colonnade, which is now filled in, but which was originally used as a shelter for sedan chairs. The south façade is divided into three stories, with both sham and true windows. The roofline is punctuated by a deep entablature complete with a balustraded parapet and fine chimneys. The Ball Room in the Assembly Rooms measuring approximately 104 feet in length speaks of Wood's skill as an interior designer. His idea of placing the dominant decoration in the upper portion of the room ensured that it remained unobscured while the room was in use. Rich plasterwork articulating interior details is particularly evident in the five-paneled, coved ceiling, which crowns the range of engaged Corinthian columns running along the upper level of the north side of the room.

The Hot Bath (now the Old Royal Baths) in Bath, executed between 1773 and 1777, made clear that Wood was as accomplished in the design of a small, specialized structure as he was in his larger ones.

Like his father, Wood was also an author. In 1781, he published *A Series of Plans, for Cottages or Habitations of the Labourer* (second edition 1792; third edition 1806; reprinted 1837), a thoughtful assessment of the problems unique to working class housing, complete with suggestions and designs intended to ameliorate the situation.

The building of John Wood the Younger exemplifies the apogee of the Palladian impulse in Bath. After his death, succeeding architects, such as THOMAS BALDWIN, were more inspired by ROBERT ADAM than by Palladio.

Wood died in Batheaston, England, on June 16, 1781, and was buried in the family vault in Swainswick Church.

JANE ANNE WILEMAN

WORKS
JOHN WOOD THE ELDER

1722–1724, Bramham Park Gardens, Yorkshire, England. (A)1727–1728, Ralph Allen House, Lilliput Alley; 1727–1730, Chandos Buildings; 1727–1730, Chapel Courthouse; 1727–1730, Saint John's Hospital; Bath, England. *1728, Tiberton Court, Herefordshire, England. *1728–1730, Lindsey's (later Wiltshire's) Assembly Rooms; 1729–1736, Houses on Wood Street, John Street, and Old King Street; 1729–1736, Queen Square; *1732–1734, Saint Mary's Chapel; Bath, England. 1734, Belcombe Court, near Bradford-on-Avon, Wiltshire, England. *1734–1752, Llandeff Cathedral, Glamorganshire, Wales. 1735–1748, Prior Park; 1738, Lilliput Castle, Lansdown; near Bath, England. 1738–1742, General (now Royal Mineral Water) Hospital; 1740, North and South Parades; 1740, Pierrepont and Duke Streets; Bath, England. 1741–1743, Exchange and Market, Corn Street, Bristol, England. *1746, The Spa; 1748–1749, Titanbarrow Logia (now Whitehaven), Kindsdown Road; Bathford, near Bath, England. 1749–1754, The Exchange (now Town Hall), Liverpool, England. begun c.1750, Gay Street; begun 1754, The Circus (completed by John Wood the Younger); Bath, England.

JOHN WOOD THE YOUNGER

1755–1757, Buckland House, Berkshire, England. 1760–1761, Bitton Church, Gloucestershire, England. (A)1761, Woolley Church, Somerset, England. 1766, Stanlynch (now Trafalgar) House (wings only), Wiltshire, England. c.1767, Brock Street, Bath, England. 1767–1771, The Infirmary, Salisbury, Wiltshire, England. 1767–1775, Royal Crescent; 1769–1771, New Assembly Rooms; c.1770, Rivers Street; (A)1772–1776, Alfred Street, Bennett Street, and Russell Street; c.1773, Margaret Chapel, Brock Street; Bath, England. 1773–1774, Tregenna Castle, near Saint Ives, Cornwall, England. 1773–1777, Hot Bath (now the Old Royal Baths),

John Wood the Younger.
New Assembly Rooms.
Bath, England.
1769–1771

John Wood the Younger.
New Assembly Rooms (Ball Room).
Bath, England.
1769–1771

Bath, England. Consecrated 1779, Hardenhuish Church, Wiltshire, England. c.1780, Catherine Place, Bath, England. Before 1781, Almshouses, Saint Ives, Cornwall, England.

BIBLIOGRAPHY

BROWNELL, CHARLES E. 1976 "John Wood the Elder and John Wood the Younger: Architects of Bath." Unpublished Ph.D. thesis, Columbia University, New York.

COATES, A. BARBARA 1946 "The Two John Woods." Unpublished thesis, Royal Institute of British Architects, London.

GREEN, MOWBRAY A. 1904 *The Eighteenth Century Architecture of Bath.* Bath, England: Gregory.

HUSSEY, CHRISTOPHER 1947 "No. 9, The Circus, Bath." *Country Life* 102:978–981, 1026–1029.

ISON, WALTER (1948)1969 *The Georgian Buildings of Bath.* Reprint. Bath, England: Kinsmead.

ISON, WALTER 1954 "John Wood the Elder, of Bath." *Journal of the Royal Institute of British Architects* 61, July:367–369.

LITTLE, BRYAN 1954 "Wood of Bath." *Architect and Building News* 205:499–500.

STROUD, DOROTHY 1938 "The Assembly Rooms, Bath: Their History, Restoration, and Re-opening." *Country Life* 84:402–406.

SUMMERSON, JOHN (1949)1963 "John Wood and the English Town-planning Tradition." Pages 87–110 in *Heavenly Mansions.* New York: Norton.

SUMMERSON, JOHN (1953)1977 *Architecture in Britain: 1530–1830.* 6th ed., rev. Harmondsworth, England: Penguin.

WITHERS, MARGARET 1970 "No. 1 Royal Crescent." *Architect and Building News* 6, no. 7:74–77.

WITTKOWER, RUDOLF 1943 "Federigo Zuccari and John Wood of Bath." *Journal of the Warburg and Courtauld Institutes* 5:220–222.

WOOD, JOHN THE ELDER (1742–1743)1969 *An Essay Towards a Description of Bath, and of the British Works in Its Neighborhood.* 2 vols. Reprint. Bath, England: Kingsmead.

WOOD, JOHN THE ELDER 1747 *Choir Gaure, Vulgarly Called Stonehenge, on Salisbury Plain, Described, Restored and Explained.* Oxford: The Theatre.

WOOD, JOHN THE YOUNGER (1806)1972 *A Series of Plans for Cottages or Habitations of the Labourer, either in Husbandry, or the Mechanic Arts, Adapted as Well to Towns as to the Country.* Reprint. Farnborough, England: Gregg.

WOODHOUSE, CORBETT, and DEAN

The firm of Woodhouse, Corbett and Dean was active in Manchester, England from 1906 to 1912. John Henry Woodhouse (1847–1929) was nearing the end of a locally renowned career when the partnership was formed with rising architect Corbett, and Benjamin Sagar Dean (?–?)—about whom very little is known—and had designed some important buildings in the North and Midlands. Particularly prolific in the design of schools and private houses—some of them in partnership with Smith and Willoughby—he also designed a number of public buildings. His draftsmanship was greatly admired, and he was remembered as being very friendly towards the younger members of the profession. He was president of the Manchester Society of Architects from 1905 to 1907.

Albert Edward Corbett (1873–1916) was the son of the Salford Borough engineer, and he was educated as an engineer at Manchester School of Technology, before being apprenticed to a Manchester architect, John Brooke. He was familiar with the domestic work of most of his more famous contemporaries, and personally knew Edgar Wood, who practiced nearby. He felt that domestic architecture was before all else *building,* and that its strength lay in a practical root of sound and honest construction, and judicious use of materials. Corbett encouraged innovation within the traditions of good building, including the use of concrete with permanent brick shuttering for walls. He was responsive to suggestions from American domestic work, including the American Shingle style's use of large open central halls, such as were then influencing M. H. BAILLIE SCOTT's work. In 1912 Corbett retired from the firm to become an H.M. Inspector of Schools (expert in building construction). He was killed in action in World War I.

BRIAN HANSON

WORKS

JOHN HENRY WOODHOUSE
Before 1906, Bury Free Library and Art Gallery, Lancashire, England. Before 1906, Manchester Fire Station, England. Before 1906, Saint James's Church (rood screen and church hall), Brighouse, Yorkshire, England. Before 1906, School Board Offices, Salford, Lancashire, England.

WOODHOUSE, CORBETT, AND DEAN
After 1906, Young Men's Christian Association Building, Peter Street, Manchester, England.

BIBLIOGRAPHY

CORBETT, ALFRED E. 1904 "Modern Domestic Architecture." *Journal of the Royal Institute of British Architects* Series 3 11:117–125.

WOODS, SHADRACH

See CANDILIS JOSIC WOODS.

WOODWARD, BENJAMIN

Benjamin Woodward (1816–1861), a disciple of JOHN RUSKIN, was the leading personality and designer in the Irish firm of DEANE AND WOODWARD. Born in Tullamore, County Offaly (King's County), Woodward trained as a civil engineer, but a love of medieval art led him to adopt the architectural profession. In 1845, he entered the office of THOMAS DEANE in Cork to assist with the design of the firm's principal Gothic works of the 1840s.

In partnership with Thomas N. Deane, Woodward designed the firm's masterpieces of the 1850s, including the Oxford Museum (1854–1860), Trinity College Museum (1852–1857) and the Kildare Street Club (1858–1861) in Dublin, in which he shaped a Ruskinian Gothic style characterized by simple contained masses, rich sculptural decoration, and an emphasis on materials, surface texture, color, and window design.

EVE M. BLAU

WORKS

1846–1849, Queen's College, Cork, Ireland. 1847–1850, Killarney Lunatic Asylum, Ireland. 1852–1857, Trinity College Museum, Dublin. 1854–1860, Oxford Museum. *1855–1857, Crown Life Assurance Company Office, London. 1855–1857, Dundrum Police Court and Barracks, Dublin. *1856–1858, Llys Dulas, Anglesey, Wales. *1856–1858, Saint Anne's Parochial Schools, Dublin. 1857, Government Offices Competition Design, London. 1857, Oxford Union. 1857–1859, Dundrum Schools, Dublin. 1857–1859, Middleton Hall, Oxford. 1858–?, Brownsbarn, Thomastown, Ireland. 1858–?, Clontra; 1858–?, Glandore; County Dublin. 1858–1859, Saint Austin's Abbey, County Carlow, Ireland. 1858–1861, Kildare Street Club, Dublin. 1858–1863, Kilkenny Castle (extensive alterations), Ireland. *1859–1861, 15 Upper Philmore Gardens, London. 1860–1862, Trinity College Library, Dublin.

BIBLIOGRAPHY

ACLAND, HENRY, and RUSKIN, JOHN 1859 *The Oxford Museum.* London: Smith, Elder.
BLAU, EVE M. 1979 "The Earliest Work of Deane and Woodward." *Architectura* 9:170–192.
BLAU, EVE 1981 *Ruskinian Gothic: The Architecture of Deane and Woodward, 1845–1861.* N.J.: Princeton University Press.
COOK, E. T., and WEDDERBURN, ALEXANDER (editors) 1903–1912 *The Works of John Ruskin.* 39 vols. London: George Allen.
CURRAN, C. P. 1940 "Benjamin Woodward, Ruskin, and the O'Sheas." *Studies* 29:255–268.
EASTLAKE, CHARLES (1872)1970 *A History of the Gothic Revival.* Reprint. New York: Humanities Press.
FERRIDAY, PETER 1962 "The Oxford Museum." *Architectural Review* 132:409–416.
HERSEY, GEORGE L. 1972 *High Victorian Gothic: A Study in Associationism.* Baltimore: Johns Hopkins University Press.
HITCHCOCK, H. R. (1954)1972 "Ruskin or Butterfield: Victorian Gothic at Mid-century." Chapter 17 in *Early Victorian Architecture in Britain.* Reprint. New York: Da Capo.
MUTHESIUS, STEFAN 1972 *The High Victorian Movement in Architecture 1850–1870.* London: Routledge.
RICHARDSON, DOUGLAS 1978 *Gothic Revival Architecture in Ireland.* New York: Garland.

WREN, CHRISTOPHER

Christopher Wren (1632–1723) is the most famous of British architects; like ROBERT ADAM's, his name has become synonymous, however inaccurately, with the style of his period. He was also the most brilliant intellectually of his profession, and if he had died at the age of thirty rather than ninety he would have been remembered in history as an experimental scientist, mathematician, and astronomer. The fortunes of patronage and the accidents of history insured the advancement of his architectural career, but it was an exceptional talent that made that advancement possible. Wren has often been represented as a scientist who became an architect, and in the sense of a curriculum vitae this is accurate. But the two activities, and the contrasting intellectual and intuitive aptitudes which made them possible, co-existed in his temperament from boyhood to the end of his life. It was perhaps Wren's greatest good fortune to have received the commission to rebuild Saint Paul's Cathedral in London and to have carried his design through to completion within his own lifetime, an achievement contrasted by the construction of St. Peter's in Rome, which followed the designs of a succession of architects and lasted more than a century.

Wren's maturity and old age coincided with the period of the English baroque, of which he was one of the principal figures; NICHOLAS HAWKSMOOR was his pupil and JOHN VANBRUGH a colleague. On the other hand, it would be simplistic to categorize him as a baroque architect: the English baroque and the "Wren school" were not stylistically coherent groups but collections of individualists, and Wren's own architecture passed, in the course of four decades, through stages of development almost as diverse as those from the early Florentine Renaissance to the late Roman baroque of CARLO FONTANA, Wren's own contemporary.

In spite of confusion in parish records, the year of Wren's birth is beyond doubt. His father, also

Christopher, was a clergyman of the Church of England who held among other benefices the rectory of East Knoyle, Wiltshire; the provision there of "a very strong roof" was among a number of ingenious inventions credited to him. In 1635, Dr. Wren was appointed dean of Windsor and thereby acquired a house in the precinct of the royal castle. In 1642, the English Civil War erupted, and before the end of the year the deanery at Windsor was ransacked and the Wren family became refugees. Dr. Wren's brother Matthew, bishop of Ely, who had already been arrested the previous year for his outspoken criticism of the Puritan party, was committed to prison where he remained until early in 1660. The boy Christopher was from 1641 to 1646 a boarding pupil at Westminster School, receiving the traditional education in the Greek and Latin classics. He first learned mathematics from his brother-in-law William Holder, clergyman, scientist, and musician; after leaving Westminster, he continued to study privately and with Sir Charles Scarburgh, who was both a mathematician and an anatomist. Wren made for him paste-board working models of muscles, and by the time he entered Wadham College, Oxford, in 1649 or 1650, he had invented a weather-recording machine, a device for writing in the dark, a working model of the solar system, and a deaf-and-dumb alphabet.

Only a few drawings and Latin compositions survive from these early efforts, most of which had in common an interest in mechanisms and a concern with visible results. The next twelve years saw Wren rise to the peak of academic success. He received his B.A. and in 1653 his M.A. at Wadham College, and then spent four years in research as a Fellow of All Souls, until in 1657 he became professor of astronomy at Gresham College in the City of London. His colleagues and friends in the 1650s were a circle of scholars in the natural sciences, who were exceptional in two respects. They were committed to the new Baconian concept of scientific inquiry based on experiment, skepticism, and empirical procedure; and, in the disturbed political and religious atmosphere of the period, their society united in its common interest firm supporters of both the royalist and the republican causes, of both the episcopacy and the presbytery. They formed, in 1661, the nucleus of the Royal Society, of which Wren was a founder member.

In 1657, Wren had written of geometry and arithmetic as "the only Truths that can sink into the Mind of Man void of all Uncertainty." Later, when comparing the geometrical and associative "causes" of beauty, he stressed the superiority of geometry: his assertion that "geometrical figures are naturally more beautiful than other irregular [ones]" was reinforced by the claim that "in this all consent as to a law of Nature." Wren's conception of architecture was based on the distinction between natural laws, which are immutable and can be expressed mathematically, and the "rules" of artistic theory whether ancient or modern, which are mutable and arbitrary; this is true even when the "rules" involve geometry, since the application of mathematics to artistic design leaves room for interpretation. The concern that Wren developed for the visual effect, often arrived at by trial and error, was as characteristic of his century as of his own empirical methods; although he was suspicious of the unguarded imagination, there is too much of a protest in his assertion that "always the true test is . . . geometrical beauty."

Wren received no instruction in architecture. His habit and profession of inquiry qualified him to teach himself, from the study of VITRUVIUS and the Italian and French treatises and pattern books, and undoubtedly by asking questions of others. His acquired skepticism, however, disposed him to take nothing on trust or on the authority of writers ancient or modern. In the spiritual and moral spheres, Wren, who must have been profoundly affected by the execution of Charles I in 1649, accepted the values of his father and uncle: episcopacy and monarchy, piety and royalty. But in all other branches of knowledge, whether sciences or arts, his philosophy was one of a return to first principles, testing every notion for himself. The Royal Society's motto, "on the words of no man," was complemented by his own, "by number, weight and measure." If drawings and models provided the earliest evidence of his potential ability in architecture, the character of his scientific mind was of profound importance for his architectural achievement.

According to his son and first biographer, Wren had devised "New Designs tending to Strength, Convenience and Beauty in Building" before 1660. This implies that already his interest was not solely in the mechanical but also in the aesthetic aspects of the Vitruvian tripos. Thus, he brought to his first involvement in design the fruits of consideration, perhaps over several years, of its nature and principles, and although his first works may show inexperience, they are not the inventions of a dilettante: Wren indeed was professional in all that he did.

In 1661, Wren returned to Oxford as Savilian Professor of Astronomy, and the year was momentous for him in other respects as well. He had presented a relief model of the moon to Charles II, and apparently as a result the king asked him, as an outstanding geometrician, to advise on the fortification of Tangier, which had just come into British possession. As an inducement, the king offered him the reversion of the post of surveyor of the king's works whenever the holder, Sir John Denham, should die. Wren was not inclined to go to Africa and asked to be excused. King Charles was shrewd enough to have seen, perhaps more clearly than his brilliant subject, the latter's artistic potential, although by 1669 when Wren did succeed Denham, completed buildings provided more obvious evidence. Before the end of 1661 also, Wren had been consulted about the repair of Saint Paul's Cathedral, whose medieval fabric, imposingly but inadequately restored by INIGO JONES in the 1630s, had further deteriorated as a result of misuse and neglect during and after the Civil War.

In 1662, Wren lectured in Oxford, and in 1663 he drew illustrations for Thomas Willis's book on the anatomy of the brain, published in 1664. These years also saw his first architectural works. The chapel of Pembroke College, Cambridge (1663–1665) was a gift to the college from Wren's bishop uncle Matthew, who has been suggested as the designer because *Parentalia* mentions the work only in the uncle's *Life* and not in that of the nephew. But although Christopher's responsibility may not have extended to the interior plaster and woodwork, there can be no doubt of his authorship of the pilastered and pedimented street front; its scholarly eclecticism in antique references is tempered by an overall disregard of tradition in the application of a temple front to an elevation that contains no entrance.

The far more ambitious Sheldonian Theatre in Oxford (1664–1669) was designed not for drama but for university ceremonies; although it is thus an academic theater, it embodies references to the theaters of antiquity. Wren used his understanding of beam theory to devise a roof without internal supports, and the allegory of learning and virtue painted in illusionism on the ceiling by Robert Streater is enacted within a representation of the open *velaria* of a Roman theater, whose D-shaped plan is also the basis of the Oxford building. To this amalgam of archeological reconstruction, baroque illusion, and technological invention, Wren brought the pragmatism of a mind seeking new solutions to problems of design. Thus, although the south elevation, based on Roman temple fronts, provides an advertisement of the building's scholarly status and a frame for its ceremonial entrance, the design of the sides and the polygonal north end comprises a basement and an attic, with no principal story and therefore no order. This unprecedented arrangement was due to the internal requirements: two levels of tiered seating and a range of larger windows to illuminate, as if with

Wren.
Sheldonian Theatre.
Oxford.
1664–1669

the clear light of reason, both the real ceremonies below and the fictive ceiling figures above that comment on them.

The exterior is built of yellow sandstone; the interior is largely of wood, painted to resemble cedar or marble and extensively gilded. It is impressive more for its air of logic than for any sensuous characteristics, in accordance with Wren's claim of the superiority of geometrical beauty. In 1663, he had shown a model of the Sheldonian to the Royal Society, and some contemporaries seem to have understood it as an architectural demonstration of the society's aim of returning to first principles in all disciplines. The oval dormer windows which he provided around the north end to light the roof space were destroyed when the roof was rebuilt in 1801–1802; the central lantern was enlarged, to his own design, by EDWARD BLORE in 1838.

By the early summer of 1665, the character of the Sheldonian was already evident, and it was equally clear to its creator that his future lay in architecture. He left for Paris in June 1665, intending to meet FRANÇOIS MANSART and GIOVANNI LORENZO BERNINI. He certainly met the latter and "would have given my skin" for his design for the Louvre. Although many of his contacts were in the scientific world, he certainly met other architects and engineers in Paris, both French and Italian. Moreover, he collected engravings of French architecture, and in the course of a stay of about eight months saw most of the significant buildings in the Île de France. Upon the basis of his previous reading, his acute observation and quick intelligence gave him an architectural education for which a lesser mind would have needed much longer. Undoubtedly, he was also profoundly affected by the experience of Renaissance architecture of a scale and an extent impossible in England; above all, he was impressed by the vastness and the building organization of the still uncompleted Louvre Palace and by the domes of several

Paris churches, examples of a form of building previously unknown to him. He traveled no further, and his knowledge of Dutch and Italian buildings remained restricted to printed sources. From France he retained the sensation of architecture as a living art and a taste for the French conception of the wall as a variegated relief skin in which the masses of a building are clothed; it was this legacy more than anything else that tempered the geometrical severity which he claimed to be the essence of architecture.

Soon after Wren's return from Paris to London in March 1666, he was again asked to advise on the fabric of Saint Paul's Cathedral, the condition of which had not improved in the course of four years of piecemeal repairs. Early in May, he presented a long report, amplified three months later by a set of drawings. He proposed the total replacement of the most decrepit part, the crossing and tower, by a new domed space as wide as the old nave and aisles combined. Since the dome was to be a double shell, the outer structure, of timber covered with lead and topped by an open-work pineapple, would provide a considerable landmark. With its delicate relief detail, this project is essentially an architectural manifesto on paper with the domes of Paris fresh in Wren's mind, in particular JACQUES LEMERCIER's Church of the Sorbonne. It would have risen strangely above the already incongruous mixture of the old medieval forms and Inigo Jones's cosmetic Renaissance refacing of the nave. Yet, this pre-Fire project established for Wren the general lines to which, after many vagaries at the drawing board, his invention would finally return. Not only did he come back to the principle of an inner masonry dome with a taller leaded outer shell; a comparison of dimensions shows that all the main levels, both inside and outside, are very close between the first and the very last designs. The significant differences are in the visual and structural complexity of the completed building and the increase, by one-third, in its diameter.

Within a few weeks, in September 1666, the Great Fire of London burned to the ground three-quarters of the City. Most of the houses had timber frames, and in the fierce heat the masonry of the cathedral, churches, and public buildings was calcined. Wren produced within ten days an idealistic plan for a new city with broad straight streets and star-shaped public spaces, but although a Louis XIV or a Pope Urban VIII might have forced such a design on his people, neither enough money nor enough time was available to the middle-class metropolitan community or the fragile monarchy of Restoration England. London was inevitably rebuilt on the old street plan, but with the crucial difference that wooden houses were outlawed and many novel safety regulations in building were enforced, in whose constitution Wren certainly had a share.

Although he was immediately concerned as one of several advisers in the City, the real effect of the fire on Wren was not as a planner but as a church architect. He was at the time involved with the completion of the Sheldonian building and the design of a chapel and gallery for Emmanuel College, Cambridge (1668–1673). His appointment as the king's architect early in 1669 was to make him the most powerful figure in the nation, but the creative opportunities of this appointment were always to be circumscribed by the purse of a monarch dependent for money on the vote of Parliament, and many of his duties as surveyor were curatorial or administrative. Far greater possibilities were to be open to him as architect to the commissions for rebuilding churches and cathedral, and in this sense Wren's success was due to the accident of fire at one moment in his personal development. Since the Reformation, England and London in particular had had more than enough churches; now about fifty parish churches needed to be rebuilt in a short time, while at Saint Paul's the necessity of repair ceded to the question of total replacement. By 1670, when Parliament passed the act for rebuilding them, financed by a tax on coal coming into London, Wren had produced a provisional design for a new cathedral as well as the set of formulas which would serve for all the new churches, more than a dozen of which were begun in that year.

As a result of depopulation, real estate values, and bombing in World War II, only about half the churches still exist and only a quarter have not been more or less rebuilt. None retains its tall box pews, many have been falsified by Victorian or modern stained glass in place of clear windows, and by pastiche furniture or fanciful electric light fittings, and although every age must adapt buildings for its own usage, the historical imagination must be exercised in order to appreciate their original mixture of warmth and lucidity.

The parish churches were not only places of worship in an age of conformist church-going but also the centers, administrative and social, of local communities. In the old wooden London, they had been distinguished by the use of brick, flint, and stone in their construction, as much as by the towers and steeples that gave identity to both church and neighborhood. In the new brick city, the distinction of materials was less marked, but the towers and steeples were at first to have a comparable effect and ultimately a greater one. Many of the sites were irregular in shape or crowded between secular properties; thus, many of Wren's churches were to have only one appreciable elevation, a few none at all. In many cases, too, his favorite geometry did not extend to right-angled corners, especially where old unsquare foundations could be used again.

Wren encountered the problems of designing forty-five churches within an area of half a square mile; the traditional figure is fifty, but in a few cases of partial rebuilding work seems to have been undertaken independently. The project was phased, temporary wooden "tabernacles" being provided and the last permanent churches not being commenced until the mid-1680s and completed a decade later. Even so, the responsibility for design and administration was taxing; artistically, there was also the need for Wren not to repeat himself. Although his control was acknowledged, much of the work was undoubtedly delegated, most notably to Robert Hooke, who in the 1670s was in almost daily contact with Wren and certainly had designing responsibility for some, or parts, of the churches. Fittings and furniture were not Wren's responsibility; they were funded by the parishes who normally engaged craftsmen to design as well as make them. Wren solved the problem of architectural individuality by designing a number of basic types which could be adapted to the peculiarities of individual sites. All these types appeared in the first building campaign of 1670–1672. The simplest were single cells (Saint Edmund; Saint Nicholas, Cole Abbey) and cells with a single aisle on one side (Saint Margaret Lothbury; Saint Margaret Pattens; Saint Lawrence Jewry). Some of the smaller churches on irregular sites showed Wren at his most inventive. There were square and rectangular domed designs (Saint Mildred, Bread Street; Saint Mary Abchurch), elongated polygons with oval lanterns (Saint Antholin; Saint Benet Fink), and three in the form of a Greek cross within a square (Saint Mary-at-Hill; Saint Anne and Saint Agnes; Saint Martin Ludgate). This form had most recently been used in Holland but is also found in Tuscan and Venetian Renaissance churches; although conceivably Wren could have known of such examples, it is possible that a common but independent concern with geometry and lucidity underlies the English and the Continental examples.

Most of the larger churches were basilican and contained additional seating in wooden galleries over the side aisles (Saint Bride, rebuilt without galleries; Saint Andrew-by-the-Wardrobe). The largest of these, Christ Church, Newgate Street, was destroyed in 1940; the finest surviving examples were built outside the City and unconnected with the Great Fire. Saint Clement Danes (1680–1682) was a rebuilding of an old church; Saint James, Piccadilly (1676–1684) was built to serve a new suburb of Westminster. This was the church that Wren himself singled out later in life (1711) as an economical, convenient, and handsome building in which all could see, hear, and feel engaged in the service. His self-praise did not include the feeling of Imperial Roman grandeur reduced to a small scale, produced by the sequences of transverse barrel vaults covering the galleries and running into the main vault over the nave. All the vaults and domes in the parish churches are of wood and plaster, but in many cases the same wooden framework carries the vault on the inside and the roof on the outside, giving interior loftiness with a minimum of weight.

The smaller churches often had galleries, which were a feature of some Continental Protestant churches. Wren seems, however, to have reached the formula of Saint James, Piccadilly, less through foreign prototypes than by way of his own solution, in the Sheldonian Theatre, to a similar problem of accommodation. In the churches of the later 1670s, the solution was visually more elegant, and they have a sense of space as a three-dimensional continuum. This sense is lacking in Wren's earliest buildings: the Sheldonian gives rather the impression of a structure conceived as a set of flat frames hinged up together to make a box.

The sense of an interior as a spatial unity would probably first have been evident, had it been built, in the first model design for Saint Paul's. The new cathedral would be the first purpose-built Protes-

Wren.
Saint James.
Piccadilly, London.
1676–1684

Wren.
Saint Stephen Walbrook.
London.
1672–1717

tant one in England, and Wren's search for radical solutions led him to design two adjacent but independent spaces. A wooden model was completed in March 1670, of which only part of the eastern portion survives, a ten-bay barrel-vaulted hall, with side galleries and transverse vaults making an interior very much like the later Saint James, Piccadilly, but twice as long. There were no aisles; the spaces under the galleries were closed from the interior and formed instead open arcades to the churchyard. Less is known about the western portion, a vestibule with three entrance porticoes and a dome and peristyle. Both spaces would have been impressive, but Wren's conception of a cathedral amounted to an enlarged parish church for ceremonies and a domed ante-chamber for show, for a civic landmark, and for his own satisfaction as the fulfilment of his Parisian experiences.

Contemporary reaction to this design involved not only its unconventionality but also its lack of grandeur; Wren was led to envisage something more expensive and (in his son's words) "conformable to the best style of the Greek and Roman architecture." By March 1672, drawings had been made for a much bigger domed Greek-cross church with concave quadrants between the arms, comprising inside a linked sequence of spaces around the eight equal piers carrying the dome. This design showed a new understanding of the status of a cathedral church, unified in style and form and encompassing all the functions required of it. It showed Wren as a European architect; it invited comparison with St. Peter's in Rome and

the projects by Bernini and Mansart, under discussion during Wren's visit to Paris, for a gigantic Bourbon chapel at Saint-Denis.

At the same time, Wren designed Saint Stephen Walbrook, the most regular and complex of the City churches, in whose plan a grid of squares is combined with a central dome and a cruciform plan. This was the only church begun in 1672, and its lucid and faultless geometry is visually a small-scale rehearsal for the grander cathedral he now had in mind. A reworking of the Greek-cross design, with the addition of a large vestibule and a portico on the west, was embodied during 1673–1674 in the great model, built to a scale of 1/24, which survives at Saint Paul's. This design received royal approval, a rebuilding commission was appointed, and in 1674 the center of the dome was set out on site and some foundation work was started before the clergy's objections canceled the project. Some at least considered it too far from the traditional Latin-cross plan of medieval English cathedrals and too overtly emulous of Roman Catholic architecture in France and Italy.

Wren was asked to think yet again, and returning once more to first principles he produced a design subsequently named from the royal warrant (dated May 14, 1675) attached to the presentation drawings. This offered a Latin cross, a long aisled nave and shorter choir, a domed crossing with a wooden spire, and a western portico. Its plan alluded to medieval cathedrals, its portico and external elevations to Inigo Jones and the age of Charles I, its crossing to the Pantheon in Rome.

Wren, if nobody else, evidently considered the Warrant design no less provisional than its precursors; probably, he began to rework the design even before the royal approval, for by July 1675 he had done so twice over, not merely in details but in fundamental structure and principal dimensions, to produce the set of drawings on which construction started in that month. The dome and western towers did not reach their final form on the drawing board until about 1704, but the rest of the cathedral, inside and outside, was gradually built according to what may be called the Definitive design of 1675. In the course of Wren's architectural development, the designs of the mid-1670s, including both the Great Model and the Definitive designs, represent his High Renaissance period. The model could be completed in a year and thus has a unity of style unique for a building of its scale; in execution, the relief detail of the final building, on the other hand, became both more extensive and freer as work progressed. But the Definitive design, like the Great Model, differed from its immediate precursor not only in style but also in quality. The Warrant design was the prod-

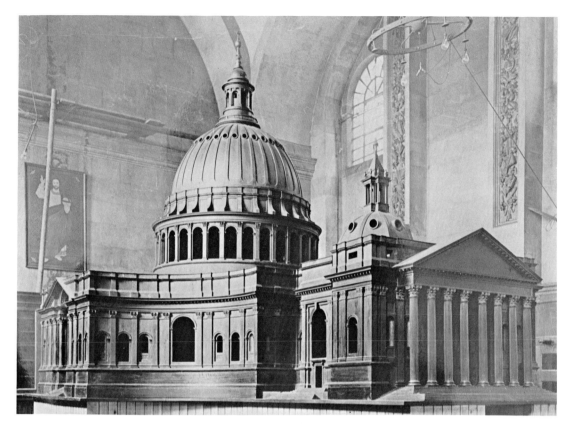

Wren.
Saint Paul's Cathedral
(Great Model).
London.
1675–1711

uct of intellect without the admixture of intuition that makes Saint Paul's the masterpiece of a great artist.

In place of the basilican cross section of the Warrant, a two-story elevation conceals from the outside both the clearstory walls and the flying buttresses that support the main vaults, which in the cathedral are of true masonry. The screen walls probably had a structural function during the building of the dome, but their principal contribution to the whole is to increase its apparent massiveness as a visual support for the enormous dome Wren intended to build. Coupled pilasters replaced the Warrant's buttress strips, and chapels were added on either side of the west end, where the last two bays inside were replaced by a single larger one as an introduction to the nave. Thus, both inside and outside the apparent, but not the usable, length of the nave was reduced from five bays to three, the same number as in the choir, giving the impression that the dome is over the center of the building; this was the nearest Wren could attain toward the theoretical ideal of the Greek cross with four equal arms.

Wren also departed from the spirit of the Warrant design in the phasing of construction. One of its specified advantages was that it was "so ordered that it might be built and finished by parts" whereas the Great Model was structurally indivisible. Wren undoubtedly feared that if the choir were built first the rest might never be started, and

Wren.
Saint Paul's Cathedral
(Great Model).
London.
1675–1711

he aimed to ensure that the whole would be too far advanced to be abandoned. By 1677, therefore, work had begun on the transept ends and west of the crossing, and foundations were laid for a west end in 1684.

The 1660s had seen Wren's establishment as a professional architect; the 1670s were no less momentous. The decade embraced nearly all of his married life; he married Faith Coghill, a childhood friend, in December 1669; she died in 1675 and two years later he married Lady Jane Fitzwilliam, who died in 1680. Three children grew to maturity. In 1673, he officially resigned his Oxford chair of astronomy and received a knighthood; this too was almost certainly the year of the sensitive marble bust of him carved by Edward Pierce now in the Ashmolean Museum, Oxford. As if to emphasize that he retained his scientific interests, he was vice-president of the Royal Society in 1677 and president in 1680. In addition to his concern with the cathedral and the churches, he designed the new library of Trinity College, Cambridge (1676–1684).

The site chosen for the library was at the back of the second court of the college. Wren's first idea was for a circular domed reading room with bookstacks arranged round it and staircases placed in the corners of the cubic block. As often happened with Wren, this design was not developed but replaced by a totally different one, in this case for a long, gallerylike upstairs library of the type traditional in monasteries and colleges. The architect's intentions are exceptionally well-documented by a set of drawings and a long letter. This includes such practical features as the choice of wood flooring for comfort in the reading bays and stone for quietness in the central aisle; it also explains Wren's conception of the ground floor space under the library as a recreation of the stoa of the ancient Greeks. Wren rejected a giant order, which would have related the building obviously to MICHELANGELO's side palaces of the Capitol in Rome; his stated reasons were expense and proportion. The resemblance between his two-order elevation and JACOPO SANSOVINO's Library of Saint Mark in Venice, although superficial, is nonetheless significant both of his High Renaissance taste in 1676 and of his awareness that a building in daily use by an academic community should not overawe in the manner of a St. Peter's or a Capitoline.

Although Wren scarcely visited the site, his drawings were so detailed and explicit that local craftsmen had no difficulty in faithful execution. He even provided patterns for moldings, capitals, and other details which were executed inside in wood or plaster and outside in fine yellow sandstone. One serious omission, however, was that the ceiling was finished flat, without visible crossbeams; this was made good in a restoration of 1851, so that it is possible to appreciate the three-dimensional character of his internal geometry. Not only the plan and elevations but also the cross-sections of the library embody a geometrical grid, and in this sense Trinity Library develops further the Cartesian unity and rationality of Saint Stephen Walbrook, in which every point in space is precisely identifiable. There is no reason to suppose that for Wren this was any less an expression of the order of the cosmos in the house of learning than in the house of God. Nevertheless, in the library not all is as it appears to be.

The ground floor stoa also forms a continuation of the existing arcades of the court, but in other aspects the library is very clearly differentiated from its neighbors. It is wider than the court it closes, its end bays being obliquely visible over the side ranges; it is also taller, both overall and in individual stories. This last difference led to Wren's brilliantly illusionistic solution for the library interior. The floor level is identical with that of the flanking ranges and immediately above the imposts of the lower library arcade, the arches of which have infilling tympana. The bookstacks and readers are therefore placed on a level inside the upper part of the first outside story, and only the upper part of the interior answers to the second, comprising the big arched windows, giving ample light above the bookcases.

As the king's architect, Wren was responsible for the new Custom House in London (1669–1671) and in the 1670s for some additions to royal palaces of a purely domestic character. It was also by royal command that he designed the Royal Observatory at Greenwich (1675–1676) for the use of the first Astronomer Royal. This picturesque turreted brick-and-stone building like an overgrown garden pavilion was built by the Board of Ordnance on the base of an old fort; Wren also

Wren.
Library, Trinity College.
Cambridge.
1676–1684

Wren.
Library, Trinity College.
Cambridge.
1676–1684

chose the location and was thus ultimately responsible for the naming of Greenwich Mean Time. The only major royal building of the decade, the refashioning of the Upper Ward at Windsor Castle, was entrusted by Charles II to Hugh May, Comptroller of Works at Windsor, where there was a separate establishment over which Wren had no authority. Large-scale secular building was not offered to him until 1682 with the foundation of the Royal Hospital at Chelsea, then a country village. The famous home for pensioned soldiers originated directly as a result of the establishment of a regular professional army, less directly in emulation of Louis XIV's foundation of the Hôtel des Invalides in Paris. For this project, philanthropic as well as politically ambitious, Wren gave his services free, as he did also for Trinity College Library and later for the naval hospital at Greenwich. He did, however, accept a gratuity as public acknowledgment of his authorship.

In the provision of light, spacious, and airy ward-blocks with large windows, Wren followed the recent example of Hooke's Bedlam Hospital built just north of the City in 1674–1676. But Chelsea is a home rather than an infirmary, and its economy combines those of the garrison and the college. Moreover, a royal foundation required an element of ostentation. The pensioned soldier found both community and privacy in the division of each ward into compartments opening at will into a gallery. Wren certainly knew JOHN WEBB's project for a palace at Greenwich, with a court open on one side and a domed vestibule and portico in the center of the opposite side. At Chelsea, he wedded to this formula the symmetrical placing of hall and chapel which had been introduced early in the seventeenth century to college architecture in his undergraduate home, Wadham College at Oxford. In Trinity Library he had eschewed the giant order; at Chelsea, not only the status but also the scale of the building required giant porticoes: full columns between the hall and chapel, and pilasters in the inner and outer centerpieces of the side ranges containing the wards. Apart from the superhuman Great Model he had designed nothing previously on this scale, and the court at Chelsea, about 230 feet square, shows an unresolved dichotomy between human and architectural scale, the former determining windows and small doors, the latter the frontispieces. The principal buildings were roofed by 1686; for James II, Wren added smaller lateral courts with two-story blocks on a more domestic scale. Except for the substitution in the 1780s of sash windows for the original casements, Chelsea has undergone very little visible alteration since it was opened in 1691.

Wren's other large project for Charles II, again inspired by Louis XIV, was for a new palace at Winchester (1685). Ostensibly, it was to be a hunting lodge close to the New Forest, but Winchester was also the ancient capital of England, and a politician as devious as Charles II saw advantages in a residence more easily accessible to France than to London. Versailles too had begun as a hunting lodge, but the palaces were similar in more important respects: formally, in the forecourt narrowed by a series of set-backs, and iconographically, in that both were to be large palaces outside the metropolis. Winchester, like Chelsea, showed an imperfect relation between size and scale; again like Chelsea, it was largely of brick with stone dressings and was to have a central portico and a dome. Work stopped at the king's death early in 1685, and the unfinished carcass, ultimately fitted up as a barracks, was demolished in 1894.

Wren's principal work for the short and troubled reign of James II (1685–1688) was at Whitehall Palace; since it was all either destroyed by, or demolished after, the fire that gutted the palace early in 1698, its significance is entirely historical. James began his reign by openly and blatantly showing his allegiance to Roman Catholicism, and the new range facing the Privy Garden at Whitehall included, besides a new council chamber, a "Popish" chapel of which the best record is the description in the diary of John Evelyn. Architecturally, the chapel was simple, with a shallow barrel-vaulted ceiling and a royal west end gallery. The decoration, however, was elaborate and excited Evelyn's admiration as much as the ceremonies offended his Protestant sensibility. The same combinations of carved and painted decoration, interior architecture, and illusionism, had amazed him at Windsor where the guiding hand was that of Hugh May; if May had not died early in 1684 he would have been the obvious person to take charge of the Whitehall chapel. Wren took upon himself most of May's duties, and although the illusionist vault and mural paintings and carved marble allegorical altar-piece were peripheral to his conception of architecture, he proved himself able to supervise them as well as the decoration of the adjoining state rooms and those in a further building by the waterside begun for Mary of Modena in 1688 and finished for William and Mary. The Privy Garden range also contained the only adequate approach there has ever been to Jones's Banqueting House, a large square, open-newel staircase lit from above by a wooden lantern, at the south end of Jones's building. After the accession of William and Mary, the Popish chapel lay unused; some fittings, including the organ case, now in Saint James, Piccadilly, were removed and thereby saved from the 1698 fire.

Within a few months of the change of sovereigns, Wren was in charge of work not only at Kensington but also at Hampton Court. At Kensington (1689–1696), he enlarged the house William and Mary had bought from the earl of Nottingham to make a suburban home in place of Whitehall, which William III found too damp for comfort. Wren's additions were, like the Privy Garden range at Whitehall, built of brick with stone dressings and high pitched roofs with dormer windows, very like the better London street architecture of the time. Success in palace building finally came to him with Hampton Court (1689–1700), which William and Mary quickly decided to make a principal residence. Again, Versailles comes to mind, at a similar distance from the capital, although Wren's first project was for a large closed court comparable with, but smaller than, the Square Court of the Louvre.

In designing Hampton Court, Wren showed the same capacity for speed as in preparing the London plan in 1666 and reworking Saint Paul's in 1675. Between February and June 1689, he worked through this grand project and several intermediate stages to a final design for a partial rebuilding; this retained half the Tudor palace, including the chapel and great hall, and provided new south and east ranges with an internal court. This smaller-scale solution reduced not only cost but also building time, an important consideration for William III, who lived in perpetual haste. The reliance on brick as the principal material, with stone dressings, also saved both money and time, although the facing brickwork is of very high quality. The combination was already well established in England, and although it may have reminded William of Dutch domestic architecture, it is a mistake to see Hampton Court as Dutch in style.

The façades of Hampton Court have often been criticized. In particular the center of the east front appears top-heavy, and the large number of

Wren.
Hampton Court Palace
(façade).
Middlesex, England.
1689–1700

bays makes inevitably monotonous elevations. Wren's own opinion is not known, but by the criteria of the Sheldonian building he succeeded in adapting to his brief the Palladian (see ANDREA PALLADIO) formula of basement, main story, and attic. But in dimensions and number of bays they are very close to the central block of Versailles, and from the river and the park (that is from the direction of London) they give the illusion, certainly not accidental, of a palace on a comparably vast scale. In his last years (1700–1702), William received embassies at Hampton Court, and he suffered there the riding fall that led to his death. Another significant element in Wren's brief was the king's dislike of stairs owing to a chronic asthmatic complaint; this led his architect to make the ground story below the state rooms as low as possible and consequently to produce elevations that look top-heavy. The façades are, as much as the sides of Saint Paul's, screens; here they conceal the convenient disposition of rooms including the separate "sides" or state suites for king and queen.

The Fountain Court within the angle of the two ranges is unrelated to the outside façades except in levels. It is on different axes, and its elevations comprise twelve bays in the width of nine on the outside. This faster rhythm, combined with greater surface enrichment, conforms with a dictum of Wren's that things seen closely may contain more detail. He also considered that "in things that are not seen at once, and have no respect one to another, great variety is commendable." At Trinity College, visual effect and geometrical consistency were finely balanced; as Wren's style became more baroque the empirical gained in ascendancy over the absolute, and at Hampton Court the outside and the inside, to be seen in different ways, are almost two separate buildings. As in Trinity Library, he again filled in the tympana of the court arcades so as to bring the upper floor down almost to the springing of the arches.

Figurative and emblematic sculpture and carving play an important part in the effect of the palace, with trophies, reliefs, frames, and originally many garden statues. Both king and architect were well aware of the impact of princely iconography in state building, and next to Saint Paul's the palace is Wren's most highly decorated building. The interiors too have decorative wood carving as well as illusionistic painting, though Wren was responsible for little of them. The king had spent much of the earlier years of his reign abroad in military campaigns, leaving the conduct of architectural as well as state affairs to Queen Mary. When she died at the end of 1694, the new palace was structurally almost complete; work stopped, and was only resumed three years later after the Peace of Ryswick had given the king at least temporary political security. In April 1699, Wren described the decoration of many rooms as "long since designed" and on heraldic evidence surviving drawings can be dated to the queen's lifetime; the estimate chosen for completing the interiors was, however, not Wren's but that of WILLIAM TALMAN, Comptroller of Works since 1689. Nevertheless, Hampton Court is essentially Wren's building, and again next to Saint Paul's it is his most complete large work.

The ambition of William III together with what Hawksmoor called the "fixed intention for magnificence" of his queen offered Wren the leadership in the creation of what is unquestionably the most beautiful English architectural ensemble of the late seventeenth and early eighteenth centuries, the Royal Hospital (1696–1716) (now the Royal Naval College) at Greenwich. It was intended to be to the developing navy what Chelsea was to the army, and the need for such an institution was brought home by the sea battles of the early 1690s. The grant of the site of Webb's abandoned palace at Greenwich was not difficult for the sovereigns; they did not pay for the buildings, which were funded by charitable subscriptions with the addition of special votes by Parliament. Wren became architect to the hospital (giving his services) by appointment, not as royal architect.

Greenwich was meant to eclipse Chelsea, and through Wren's genius it does so in splendor in spite of the limitations built into the site. Wren seems to have known before the grant of the site in October 1694 that it would exclude not only Inigo Jones's Queen's House to the south but also the strip of land of the same width (115 feet) between the house and the River Thames on the north. Several projects must have been made before the grant: one because it incorporates, as Webb's earlier palace project of the 1660s had done, a central domed building; others because they exceed the site in other directions. After the first enthusiastic consideration, Wren seems to have turned to other work until late in 1697; by then he was architect to the hospital, and work was well advanced on finishing as part of the whole the western side building, the only portion ever begun, of Webb's palace. Early in 1698, Wren produced plans for a hall, and the foundations were laid for the first entirely new block of the hospital. The commissioners had gained the use of all the land between the river and the Queen's House, except for the central strip; Wren was able to design two separate blocks on either side. That to the north, next to the river, consisted of the Webb building with a base block behind it on the west (King Charles Block) and a building round a court, with a copy of Webb's

Wren.
Hampton Court Palace
  (fountain court façade).
Middlesex, England.
1689–1700

façade, matching it on the east (Queen Anne Block). Further south, two courts have buildings on three sides; the fourth sides facing each other across the central strip of land consist of colonnades leading toward but not as far as the Queen's House. The north side of King William Court on the west contains the hall, the other (Queen Mary) contains the chapel; both have domed vestibules opening to the colonnades. Of necessity Greenwich Hospital has no middle, but the domes and colonnades, rather like the foreground trees in a Claude landscape, act as a frame for the Queen's House, too small and too far off, and for the space around it and the park behind it with, rather off the axis, Wren's own Greenwich Observatory.

Ideally, Greenwich should first be seen from the water, and this is the view over which Wren personally took most care. He had observed that colonnades were the only form of building which could be extended to any desired length without losing proportion. The twin domes were designed and redesigned, reaching their definitive form in 1701–1702. They thus anticipate by two or three years the west towers of Saint Paul's, which were constantly in his mind during this period. In both cases, the design grew in height, in complexity of plan, richness of shadow, and originality of inspiration; simple cylindrical forms were augmented by clusters of columns on the diagonals. The towers of the cathedral were to be seen in conjunction with the great central dome, whereas the cupolas of Greenwich appear only against the sky; although they are each suited to their situation, the Greenwich domes may be considered as a last rehearsal for Saint Paul's.

The axial view of the hospital from the river terrace is almost all for show and almost all of Portland stone, exceeding Chelsea in materials as well as in richness of design. Within and behind the courts, Greenwich presents other faces. Some parts were totally outside Wren's control: much of

Queen Mary Court was redesigned after his death by THOMAS RIPLEY in a dull Palladian style, and Ripley's chapel, later gutted by fire, received its present form from JAMES STUART. The hall was painted by James Thornhill in 1708–1727, and although Wren must have expected such decoration its exact nature was not determined by him. Much of the Queen Anne and King William buildings was constructed under Wren's authority but designed by Hawksmoor, whose relationship with his old master was particularly close at Greenwich. Hawksmoor was engaged first as personal, then as official, clerk to Wren, and drawings show that he helped in the design stages of what indubitably are Wren's creations: the hall, colonnades, and domes. Wren in his late sixties had lost nothing in imagination or commitment; nevertheless, he was at an age to be more selective between those things which mattered supremely to him and those which did not. The central view at Greenwich came into

the first category; in the courts, however, he must have been prepared to allow Hawksmoor a free hand in a way that he would not have done at Hampton Court or Saint Paul's. He would have retained total control, too, over his unexecuted designs for rebuilding Whitehall after the 1698 fire. The large surviving drawings for two different projects show that neither his liking for drawing nor his dexterity had diminished, and the sequences of courts he proposed show a greater sensitivity in scale and massing than he had previously attained.

The choir of Saint Paul's had been opened in 1697. By that date, the building was nearly complete to the main outside cornice, according to a design that had changed little in two decades except in decorative detail. Wren experimented in the early 1690s with a giant-order western portico in marked contrast to the superimposed orders of the rest of the exterior. According to his son, monoliths could not be obtained of sufficient size for the entablature, but the real problem was one of abutment at the sides of a projecting structure of such magnitude. Comparisons are usually made with the Corinthian portico added to the old cathedral by Inigo Jones, and it should therefore be noted that Wren's portico would have been nearly twice as high as Jones's, the order of which was only larger by a quarter than the lower of the two orders Wren finally adopted in unison with the other elevations. Even on this scale he solved the problem of spans by locking smaller stones together to form flat arches. The west front was completed by 1701 with the exception of the towers.

The period 1701–1704 saw very little progress on the dome and none on the towers: Wren was in fact deciding on the final form of both these features and in 1702–1703 went so far as to authorize the engraving of a design which he was already discarding. The problems were both statical and aesthetic: in the dome possible forms were limited by the already completed supporting structure, while at the same time both dome and towers needed to be considered in relation to each other and to the London skyline. The general increase in London building heights in the last hundred years, and even more the advent of high-rise blocks in the last thirty, have greatly impaired the impact of the church steeples, but these changes equally demonstrate what a large and impressive structure the dome of Saint Paul's remains. In 1675, Wren envisaged a complex profile, derived from Michelangelo's dome of St. Peter's, with large ribs and three tiers of lucarne windows in the dome itself and a ring of strongly projecting buttress piers round the drum; the towers on the other hand were to be simple shapes of concentric cylinders on the pattern of DONATO BRAMANTE's Tempietto. A quarter of a century later he decided on a dome of much simpler shape that could be comprehended at one glance, based on the Tempietto formula; the towers became much more complex, with clusters of columns which give them a Borrominian (see FRANCESCO BORROMINI) play of convex and concave and with a varied silhouette that is immediately seen in contrast with the dome. This combination shows him thinking in terms of the larger units and immediate impressions of late baroque architecture. The reversal of shapes between dome and towers, however, was not made in isolation. The dome was to be the bold simple form in the midst of a group, ranged across the City, of smaller complex ones; in this group the cathedral towers would be merely the grandest.

The steeple of Saint Mary-le-Bow, completed in 1680, stayed for some years as a solitary example of Wren's conception. Most of the other churches were given towers, some with small lanterns or spires, but none at all approaching Saint Mary's in height or richness. In 1697, the coal tax, due to lapse in 1700, was extended in order to pay for the completion of the cathedral and churches, and although the latter required mainly repairs or minor works it became possible, with the economic recovery of London, to think more grandly of embellishment. The leaded spire of Saint Augustine, Watling Street (1696), was followed by those of Saint Margaret Lothbury (1699) and Saint Margaret Pattens (1702) and a wonderful sequence of larger and more elaborate steeples and spires: Saint Dunstan-in-the-East (1695–1698); Saint Bride

(1702–1703); Christ Church, Newgate Street (1703–1704); Saint Magnus (1705–1706); Saint Vedast (1709–1712); Saint Michael, Crooked Lane (1709–1714); Saint Michael Royal and Saint Stephen Walbrook (both 1713–1718); and Saint James Garlickhythe (1714–1717). The hand of Hawksmoor has been seen in some of these late works, but this is unlikely for two reasons. First, he ceased to be employed in connection with the churches in 1701. Second, with the exception of the Borrominian Saint Vedast, whose play of con-

Wren.
Saint Paul's Cathedral
  (west front).
London.
1675–1684

Wren.
Saint Paul's Cathedral.
London.
1675–1711

vex and concave curves has always been accepted as Wren's work, the Wren steeples follow the prescription of LEON BATTISTA ALBERTI in that they are made up of little temples one above the other and derived principally from the orders. Hawksmoor's own steeples, on the other hand, derive less from the orders and more from abstractions of cubic masonry. Now that documentation has established the late date of this group of Wren's works, their complementary relationship to his cathedral is the more evident.

Saint Paul's was officially declared complete in 1711, though Wren was subsequently humiliated by the softening of the hard edge he gave the building by a balustrade, which he likened to the lace edgings preferred by ladies. As we see the interior of the cathedral today we need to remember that originally it was all painted nearly white, but that he would have liked a geometrical mosaic in the dome. Neither the later Victorian mosaics of the choir nor the modern altar canopy corresponds to his intentions, and the organ originally stood on a screen across the end of the choir; this marked off the space under the dome and emphasized the centrality which he had striven to retain ever since the Greek-cross design.

In 1715, Wren's authority in the King's Works was circumscribed and in 1718 he was dismissed from office. Undoubtedly, familiarity had allowed him to cut corners, but there is no evidence that even in his eighties he was incompetent. It was rather personal jealousy and political ambition that ended his reign of nearly forty years. A shift in taste away from France and baroque Italy coincided with a decline in both royal interest in building and the caliber of officers in the Works. Wren retired to a house at Hampton Court, although according to family tradition he died during a short stay in London. Little is known of his last five years; his son Christopher did not gather as much information from him as he wished, but he records that his father was still working on scientific problems.

Wren was not a traveler. His only trip abroad was that to France. Thereafter, his life was largely spent within the City and Westminster, and he seems to have lived mostly in his official house at Scotland Yard, a modest base court of Whitehall Palace not unlike the Oxford colleges of his youth. His architectural output consisted almost entirely of public buildings, secular or religious, although there are a number of private works on which he advised informally to a degree that is now difficult to assess. Decorative and domestic architecture did not greatly interest him; his ability is nevertheless indicated by his work for James II at Whitehall and by two documented country houses designed for crown servants like himself. Tring, Hertfordshire (c.1687–1690), exists inside a late Victorian house; it has a two-story hall divided from the staircase by a gallery across the middle of the house. Winslow, Buckinghamshire (1699–1702), is spatially simpler and more convenient. Neither was richly decorated. He may have designed, for a cousin of his wife, the wings of Easton Neston (c.1682), a commission subsequently delegated to Hawksmoor. The duchess of Marlborough believed that he was the architect of Marlborough House, London (1709–1711), but "the poor old man" as she called him seems to have outwitted her by giving to his son the conduct of this excessively plain house. Although he held a clerkship in the Works, the younger Christopher (1675–1747) lived in his father's shadow and was not really an architect. We owe to him, however, the first biography as well as a number of engravings and the preservation of many of the drawings from his father's hand or his office. Wren's chief pupils were Hawksmoor and WILLIAM DICKINSON, both of whom inherited with enthusiasm an interest in Gothic that in Wren was always rather grudging. He delegated to Dickinson the repair of Westminster Abbey (1700–1722), but his own Gothic designs include Tom Tower at Christ Church, Oxford (1681–1682), and some City church work (most notably the steeple of Saint Dunstan). His fragmentary writings on his art also show an interest in historical architecture which he shared both with Hawksmoor and with his European contemporary JOHANN BERNHARD FISCHER VON ERLACH.

Genius is harder to describe than to recognize, and for Wren many have failed in the attempt. His achievement was more than the range of his architectural and other work, than the ratiocination by which he made himself into an architect, than his pertinacity which saw Saint Paul's to completion, than the realization of a cathedral which, for all its stylistic eclecticism, is like no other building in the world. It owes a good deal to the ambiguity of his mind which, in architecture, constantly saw both the natural and the customary causes of beauty, the absolute of geometry and the empirical of association and visual effect, and recognized that the rules of the eye are not always those of the square of the compass. His style developed into that of a late baroque master. But, though Hawksmoor and less directly Vanbrugh learned "much if not everything from him, their curious 'heroic' baroque is a different thing, more declamatory, more coarsegrained than the architecture of their master, which kept to the end of his days something of the spirit of the lyric poets of his youth" (Webb, 1937, p. 140).

KERRY DOWNES

WORKS

1663–1665, Pembroke College Chapel, Cambridge. 1664–1669, Sheldonian Theatre, Oxford. 1668–1672, Emmanuel College Chapel and Gallery, Cambridge. *1669–1671, Custom House; (A)1670–1673, Temple Bar (moved to Theobalds, Hertfordshire, England); 1670–1674, Saint Mary Aldermanbury (rebuilt in Fulton, Mo.); *1670–1677, Saint Mildred, Poultry; *1670–1679, Saint Olave (tower extant), Old Jewry; *1670–1681, Saint Benet Fink; 1670–1681, Saint Lawrence Jewry; *1670–1685, Saint Dionis Backchurch; *1670–1687, Saint Michael, Wood Street; 1670–1695, Saint Mary-at-Hill; 1670–1703, Saint Bride, Fleet Street; 1670–1707, Saint Edmund, Lombard Street; London. 1671–1674, Williamson Building, The Queen's College, Oxford. 1671–1676, The Monument; 1671–1678, Saint Nicholas, Cole Abbey; *1671–1679, Saint George, Botolph Lane; 1671–1680, Saint Mary-le-Bow; London. 1671–1706, Saint Magnus; 1672–1717, Saint Stephen Walbrook; *1674–1677, Saint Stephen, Coleman Street; *1674–1681, Saint Bartholomew, Exchange; 1675–1676, Royal Observatory, Greenwich; 1675–1711, Saint Paul's Cathedral; 1676–1681, Saint Anne and Saint Agnes, Gresham Street; 1676–1684, Saint James, Piccadilly; London. 1676–1684, Library, Trinity College, Cambridge. *1676–1687, Saint Michael, Queenhythe; *1676–1712, Saint Michael Bassishaw; 1676–1717, Saint James Garickhythe; *1677–1682, All Hallows the Great, Thames Street; *1677–1684, All Hallows, Watling Street; 1677–1685, Saint Benet, Paul's Wharf; 1677–1685, Saint Peter, Cornhill; 1677–1686, Saint Martin Ludgate; *1677–1686, Saint Swithin, Cannon Street; *1677–1704, Christ Church (tower extant), Newgate Street; *1678–1687, Saint Antholin, Budge Row; 1679–1703, Saint Mary Aldermary; 1680–1682, Saint Clement Danes; *1680–1696, Saint Augustine (tower extant), Watling Street; 1681–1682, Tom Tower, Christ Church, Oxford. *1681–1686, Saint Matthew, Friday Street; *1681–1687, Saint Benet, Gracechurch Street; 1681–1687, Saint Mary Abchurch; *1681–1687, Saint Mildred, Bread Street; *1682–1689, Saint Alban (tower extant), Wood Street; 1682–1691, Royal Hospital, Chelsea; London. *1683–1685, Winchester Palace, Hampshire, England. 1683–1687, Saint Clement, Eastcheap; *1683–1687, Saint Mary Magdalen, Fish Street; 1684–1702, Saint Margaret Pattens; 1684–1704, Saint Andrew, Holborn; *1684–1714, Saint Michael, Crooked Lane; *1685–1688, Whitehall Palace (Privy Garden Range and Roman Catholic Chapel); 1685–1694, Saint Andrew, Wardrobe; 1686–1694, All Hallows (tower extant; rebuilt at Twickenham, Middlesex, England), Lombard Street; *1686–1694, Saint Mary Somerset (tower extant); 1686–1699, Saint Margaret Lothbury; 1686–1717, Saint Michael Royal; London. c.1687–1690, Tring Manor (recased), Hertfordshire, England. *1688–1693, Whitehall Palace (Queen's Apartments); 1689–1696, Kensington Palace; London. 1689–1700, Hampton Court Palace, Middlesex, England. 1695–1702, Saint-Dunstan-in-the-East (tower); 1695–1712, Saint Vedast, Foster Lane; 1696–1716, Royal Naval Hospital, Greenwich; London. 1699–1702, Winslow Hall, Buckinghamshire, England.

BIBLIOGRAPHY

BENNETT, J. A. 1972 "Christopher Wren: The Natural Causes of Beauty." *Architectural History* 15:5–22.
DEAN, C. G. T. 1950 *The Royal Hospital, Chelsea.* London: Hutchinson.
DOWNES, KERRY 1982 *The Architecture of Wren.* London: Granada.
ELMES, JAMES 1823 *Memoirs of the Life and Works of Sir Christopher Wren.* London: Priestley & Weale.
LITTLE, BRYAN 1975 *Sir Christopher Wren: A Historical Biography.* London: Hale.
POLEY, ARTHUR F. E. (1927)1932 *St. Paul's Cathedral, London: Measured, Drawn and Described.* 2d ed. London: The author.
SEKLER, EDUARD F. 1956 *Wren and His Place in European Architecture.* London: Faber.
SUMMERSON, JOHN 1953 *Sir Christopher Wren.* London: Collins.
SUMMERSON, JOHN 1961 "The Penultimate Design for St. Paul's." *Burlington Magazine* 103:83–89.
SUMMERSON, JOHN 1970 "Drawings of London Churches in the Bute Collection: A Catalogue." *Architectural History* 13:30–42.
WATKIN, DAVID 1972 *Architects.* Volume 4 in *Sale Catalogues of Libraries of Eminent Persons.* London: Sotheby Parke-Bernet.
WEAVER, LAWRENCE 1923 *Sir Christopher Wren.* London: Country Life.
WEBB, GEOFFREY F. 1937 *Wren.* London: Duckworth.
WHINNEY, MARGARET 1971 *Christopher Wren.* London: Thames & Hudson.
WREN, CHRISTOPHER (1750)1965 *Parentalia, or Memoirs of the Family of the Wrens.* Reprint. Farnborough, England: Gregg.
Wren Society 1924–1943 20 vols.

WRIGHT, EDMUND WILLIAM

Edmund William Wright (1824–1888) was born in Surrey, England, and was educated in England and France. After having trained with W. C. Stow, district surveyor of Bermondsey, London, he was employed by the British government before setting out for Adelaide, South Australia, in 1849. Wright was mayor of Adelaide in 1859 and was vice-president of the Institute of Architects which he helped to establish in 1886. In South Australia, he was the longest practicing architect of his period. Wright sought to improve building techniques and design by introducing new methods and materials. His own stated preference in style is reflected in his use of the architectural vocabulary of the Italian and French Renaissance, with careful attention to detailing and stonecarving in the finishing of his civic, religious, commercial, and domestic buildings.

ALAN FEENEY

WORKS

1860–1872, Brougham Place Congregational Church, North Adelaide, South Australia. 1865–1866, Adelaide Town Hall, South Australia. 1865–1866, *Athelney* (mansion), Hackney, South Australia. 1866–1872, Adelaide General Post Office; 1875–1878, Bank of South Australia; 1879, Bank of Adelaide; *1879–1880, Adelaide Stock Exchange; Adelaide, South Australia. 1880–1882, Paringa Hall (mansion), Somerton, South Australia. 1883–1889, Parliament House (west side), Adelaide, South Australia.

BIBLIOGRAPHY

BAGOT, W. H. 1958 *Some Nineteenth-Century Adelaide Architects.* Adelaide: Pioneers Association of South Australia.
CITY OF ADELAIDE 1921 *Municipal Yearbook.* Adelaide, South Australia.
The South Australian Register 1888 Aug. 6.

WRIGHT, FRANK LLOYD

Frank Lloyd Wright (1867–1959) is known as one of the great architects of all time; in seventy years of practice he designed about one thousand structures, some four hundred of them built. Already famous by his early forties, in later life his genius became widely recognized and honored. Wright, like many leading artists of his times, did not seek a canonical style; he innovated freely, guided by principles. They were rooted in early impressions which Wright later recorded.

Childhood impressions. As a small boy Wright was fascinated by his father, William, a New England clergyman, playing Bach or Beethoven. Under his father's guidance, Frank came to recognize musical structure and its influence on the flow of emotions which music aroused in him. When the boy was nine, his mother, Anna, who had been a schoolteacher, began to train him and his young sister according to Froebel's kindergarten method. Frank's artistry was awakened by the clear colors and regular shapes. Here, as in music, he related composition and expression. Remembering these childhood discoveries in *An Autobiography* (1943), Wright declared *"form* became *feeling."* At the same time, he learned that both tone and form were regulated by rhythm: the beat of music and the modular grid of Froebel patterns.

When Wright was eleven, his parents, after extensive wanderings in search of a living, settled in Madison, Wisconsin, near Anna Wright's family, the Lloyd Joneses. Strong Unitarians from Cardiganshire, Wales, they were self-reliant farmers, clannish, idealistic, and open to new thoughts. Anna sent her son to work long summers on his uncles' farms close to Spring Green. Sharing their world as he grew into his teens, Wright experienced the unity of mankind and nature as a reciprocating adjustment, an ongoing organic process. This process shaped farmstead and chapel; from early days Wright knew architecture not as a reflection or embellishment of life but as an active element of living, "organic architecture." He felt that human life was part of the whole natural order, and architecture was an organic part of human life, produced by it and reacting on it.

During these summers, young Wright gained the robust strength needed for a lifetime of unremitting work; Emerson's "what a man does, that he has" was often quoted by Wright. Unsettled, perhaps by moving from place to place, Wright never finished high school and attended the University of Wisconsin as a special student only. Yet, the boy had read widely and Emerson was his mentor; many of Wright's attitudes were forecast in the essay on "Self-Reliance," and he must have revered the close of that on "Art," the "division of beauty from use, the laws of nature do not permit"; this characterized Wright's entire architecture.

First architectural influences. When Frank Wright was eighteen, the course of life in Madison and on the farms was abruptly broken. His father divorced his mother and disappeared. The shock left lasting scars. Fortunately, soon thereafter a compelling experience came Wright's way. His uncle Jenkin Lloyd Jones, a well-known preacher in Chicago, summered with the family, and in 1885 he asked J. LYMAN SILSBEE, a successful Eastern architect venturing in the Midwest, to design a small chapel for the Jones's valley. Young Frank had heard much about architecture; his mother hoped it might be his profession and his aunts had given him JOHN RUSKIN's *Seven Lamps of Architecture* and *The Stones of Venice.* Now, befriended by Silsbee, he could witness architecture from design to actual construction. Soon Frank was making designs of his own in Silsbee's manner. His university courses seemed pointless compared to learning to be an architect; moreover, working full time, he could do more to help support his mother and sisters. Against his family's advice, Frank Lloyd Wright went to Chicago to try his hand as an apprentice architect.

Frank Lloyd Wright's first employer in Chicago was Silsbee. While Wright rapidly learned to be a skilled draftsman, he disliked the designs produced in the office. He found his niche as assistant to LOUIS H. SULLIVAN, then starting to detail his first masterpiece, the Auditorium Building. During nearly six years with the firm of ADLER AND SULLIVAN (1888–1893), Wright took part in creating works that became landmarks of modern

American architecture. Sullivan's partner, Dankmar Adler, was a resourceful engineer and manager; from him Wright learned to appreciate professional practice. Paul Mueller, a young man on the staff, later became Wright's builder for major constructions. Above all, Wright was devoted to Sullivan who confided to him a deeply felt philosophy of architecture as a manifestation of societal aims. Wright became enduringly inspired by Sullivan's ideals and fluent drawing yet he sensed that architecture required a strength and a directness that Sullivan did not always achieve.

Reading in the library of his uncle's Unitarian center, Wright was struck by a chapter of *Notre-Dame de Paris* in which Victor Hugo announced that technological progress would destroy traditional arts. On the same shelves, he found OWEN JONES's *Grammar of Ornament,* prefaced by a credo which began: "the Decorative Arts arise from, and should properly be attendant upon, Architecture." Wright especially admired EUGÈNE EMMANUEL VIOLLET-LE-DUC whose Positivist analyses of architecture were partially published in translation from the 1870s through the 1890s. The speculative theories of GOTTFRIED SEMPER were mentioned and discussed in the press. EDWARD L. GARBETT's *Rudimentary Treatise* on design in architecture (1850) recommended by Emerson and often reissued, predicted the dominance of tensile architecture, a vital theme in Wright's development. Whether directly or through hearsay these sources helped to clarify Wright's ideals of architecture, including "the nature of materials" which he always emphasized. To Wright this meant using structural materials understandingly, eliciting their inherent colors and textures; it did not imply the exposure of structural framework or utilities.

Marriage. As Sullivan relied more on his assistant, Wright's time for reading became scant. His mother and his sisters had joined him in Chicago and, in 1889, Wright married young Catherine Tobin. Sullivan helped him to buy a lot in semirural Oak Park and build a home; his mother and sisters settled next door. In the office, Wright worked on important commissions and on houses, less desired and less profitable. As his responsibilities increased, especially for houses, he often worked nights at home. With a fast-growing family and obligations, Wright designed other residences on his own in violation of his contract with the firm, and when this came to light Sullivan felt badly betrayed. In 1893, Wright was working from his own office; despite the general economic panic at that time he found clients.

Early independent buildings: 1889–1899. Wright's first independent buildings were marked by a broad eclecticism and anticipations of fresh design; his progress may be seen in two houses built ten years apart, 1889 and 1899. The first was Wright's own modest home in Oak Park, Illinois; its shingled exterior was not remarkable. The chimney that served furnace and stove opened also toward the living room in a small, conventional inglenook; around this core, at once functional and spatial, the main rooms were dynamically arranged, terminating in faceted bays. The central hearth and the extensions outward, a balanced pair, became a regular theme in Wright's architecture. As he mastered the use of the core, he found the accompanying extensions boxed in by walls, and to avoid this Wright began to establish his cores on clear-cut platforms set on the earth, sheltered under hip or gable roofs. With no dormers and few chimneys the roofs became quiet, gently angled, and wide, echoing the earth. Confident in this triad of platform, core, and roof, Wright conceived the enclosing walls as independent screens. Instead of doors and windows cut through walls, corners were left open, the walls were extended past one another and capped some distance below the roofs; these appeared floating above them. Ceiling and floor levels were stepped, so that all planes were inflected. In this unorthodox, articulated architecture the openings were closed by framed glass or blind panels, both often enriched by ornament. Wright called his systematic procedure "breaking the box." Its elements were displayed (some more clearly than others) in the villa of 1899 for the Husser's where, however, stylistic reminiscence remained prominent. Even earlier, it was said, DANIEL H. BURNHAM, the dominant architect in the Middle West, had invited Wright to polish his classicism at the Ecole des Beaux-Arts in Paris and return to lead design in the Burnham office; although it meant an assured future, Wright refused. By 1900, Frank Lloyd Wright demonstrated his own architecture and ideas without quoting from the past; though not every form and concept was novel, the whole was consistent and individual. Other enterprising architects in the Chicago area were aiming to simplify construction and detail and to use space ingeniously; together with Wright, they are called the Prairie school.

Achievements (1900–1909). Wright's achievements of 1900–1909 will be presented in three groupings: small homes, grand residences, and buildings for public use. All employed the same devices: central cores, solid or spatial; platforms; structural screens shaping the flow of space; and eloquent uses of materials and ornament. In his houses Wright began to employ perimeter heating and clearstory ventilation and lighting, derived from industrial and commercial building practices of the day. Many other features were inherited from English practice and European ideas of the preceding century yet the thrust of Wright's design was clearly American and progressive.

Wright relied on four main types of small house design. First came the house with living room, dining room, and study arranged in line and broadly open to each other. Along an inside wall stood the fireplace, the stairs nearby, and behind them service quarters were annexed. This was a known scheme; Wright merely made the openings between main rooms as wide and high as possible. Though furnishings indicated the use of each area and usually one was separated from the next by portieres, the whole space presented itself as one. A variant with double-height living area and balcony over the fireplace accentuated interpenetrations of space. A second, more original type needed ample views; it was centered on a core from which wings extended forming a +, a T, or an L in plan. Some of Wright's happiest successes were based on this scheme. A third type of small house design was planned for steep, inexpensive terrain, often with good views. Evolved from the double-height living area, the vertical house exploited split-level space to great advantage. The fourth scheme was boxy and symmetrical in contrast to the others. Corner walls bracketed horizontal bands of windows below flat roofs, and a central partition with fireplace divided the interior; Wright used these devices stiffly for economy's sake.

Many of Wright's early homes, both small and large, shared basic features. The platform on the ground rested on footings. Wright preferred not to dig cellar spaces, placing most services at grade, well lit and ventilated; kitchens were level with dining rooms on the main floor lifted above ground. Rising from the platform a wall pierced by few windows enclosed the low level up to a sill

course under the wide openings of the main floor and continued up to the full coping. Above or somewhat behind this main wall rested a lighter construction of window bands and blind panels. The broad-eaved roof was vented for cooling; there were no attics. Wright considered them, like cellars, costly and bootless. On the inside, varying ceiling heights were as a rule unconventionally low, tending to direct the eye toward the outside, establishing contact between inside and the unbounded environment.

In this decade, Wright designed five ample, luxurious homes, of which three were built. In 1903, the Dana House in Springfield, Illinois, arose around the shell of an older house (a legal requirement). Despite this limitation, Wright created spatial innovations on a grand scale complemented by elegantly ornamented glass panels. The Dana interiors were the richest and most handsome of the decade. Exterior massing and certain features, such as clustered piers enclosing heating devices, were further developed at the Darwin D. Martin House, Buffalo, a year later. The spectacular shaft of space which appeared vertically as one entered the Dana House was present in the Martin House as a very long horizontal vista, more conventional and evident. The Thaxter Shaw project for Montreal (1906) was the most subtle; its space axis would have run on a prolonged diagonal through a series of structural screens and incidents of plan and decoration. The beautiful Coonley House in Riverside, Illinois (1908), was at its best after Wright improved its garden façade to match the sweep and scale of the grounds. In the same year as the Coonley, Wright designed a project in fireproof concrete for Harold McCormick, for a bluff overlooking Lake Michigan at Lake Forest. Long, low pavilions, casually disposed, edged large garden courts; the principal rooms, rising from a terrace with a heroic retaining wall, opened toward the lake. In this project, there were echoes of Wright's first visit to Japan in 1905, which had broadened his horizons. Now Wright's Prairie school manner began to cede to fresh impulses.

Meanwhile, Wright had designed and built other houses, some famous such as the Willits and the Robie; clubhouses and country homes sheathed in horizontal board and batten; brick row houses and apartment blocks, none of which can be discussed here. However, his two great structures for public use will be cited, the Larkin Administration Building in Buffalo, New York, of 1904, and Unity Temple in Oak Park (1906). The Larkin Building was one of Wright's strong creations. Its numerous technological and commonsense practicalities, specified by the clients, were transformed by the architect into a harmoniously

Wright.
Prairie House Plan.

Wright.
Prairie House (double height living room).

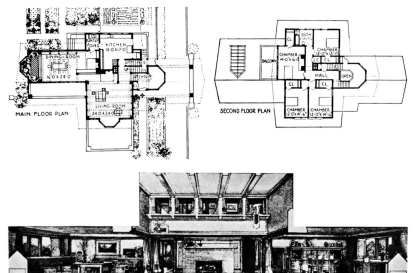

Wright.
Coonley House.
Riverside, Illinois.
1908–1912

functional whole. In the Larkin Building, Wright's cores of space and clearstory lighting assumed paramount importance; the central shaft of space was skylit and ringed by subsidiary levels cross-lit by clearstory strips, one light augmenting and softening the other. Throughout his life, Wright applied the basic lighting scheme worked out here, a late example being the circular Guggenheim Museum as designed. The Larkin utilities, including conditioned ventilation and fire stairs, were placed in blind corner shafts while balconies were devoted to clerical work with ample daylight. All furniture and fittings were especially designed in metal. The articulation of a small entry block with employees' lockers and washrooms above; the placement of areas for eating, recreation, and rest at the very top of the main block while executives' desks were in the open at ground level, accessible to the public, combined to form an image of efficiency and humane consideration unparalleled in commercial structures of that day.

Unity Temple, a gem of pure serenity, was small and far more economical than the Larkin Building. Instead of steel framing Wright had to use massive poured concrete walls with roofs and balconies of the same material more fully reinforced. Both buildings were sealed from the noise and soil of their surroundings and in both the closed corner towers were separate from the main blocks. Glass ceilings flooded both interiors with changing natural light, incorporating the vitality of outside nature, and both central volumes were surrounded by peripheral spaces with high side lighting. The Larkin was acoustically treated to inhibit the spread of sound, while at Unity even on the balconies one felt close to the speakers' platform. Furthermore, the two interiors differed in the expression of structural support. In Buffalo, the fireproofing of the steel columns was equally ornamented on all four faces, establishing the identity of each post. At Oak Park, the bulky piers, which were heating ducts as well as supports, bore ornamentation only on the two inner surfaces as if on folded screens. The four "screens" pointing toward the center spoke not of separate supports but of the central space. The change affirmed the

primacy of space over matter in Wright's architecture.

Wright's urge to develop the expression of space in architecture was a solitary impulse. His Prairie school colleagues for the most part were content with established devices. His devoted wife admired his genius at a distance; six children and community activities occupied her attention. In 1904, Wright had built a home for the Edwin Cheneys, and Mrs. Cheney (Mamah), a trained librarian and a liberal thinker, attracted Wright. In the following year, the Ward Willitses, friends and clients, invited the Wrights to accompany them to Japan; it has been surmised they meant to divert Wright's interest from Mrs. Cheney. After long hesitation, Wright asked for a divorce in 1908, but then, at his wife's request, agreed to wait one more year. Mr. Cheney accepted divorce but Mrs. Wright continued to refuse. Before any legal disentanglement was achieved, Wright left for Berlin in 1909 to negotiate a splendid publication of his architecture proposed by the well-known firm of E. Wasmuth. Mrs. Cheney joined him en route, and in Berlin they registered at the hotel as husband and wife. The news reached Oak Park quickly and became a public scandal. In distant Fiesole, Wright and two helpers prepared one hundred drawings while Mamah stayed in Germany. Drafting done, the pair toured Europe.

European publications: 1910–1911. Wright's work had been featured in the press, professional and popular, ever since 1900, and now he had a very handsome monograph of his work, issued as a pair of portfolios. In 1911, after Wright had left Europe, Wasmuth issued an excellent paperbound book of photographic illustrations and plans of Wright's works, less costly than the portfolios. At Wright's request, an introduction was written by the prominent English Arts and Crafts man, CHARLES R. ASHBEE, well regarded in Germany. Ashbee and Wright had become friendly when the former toured the United States in the winter of 1900–1901, and it was in the latter year that Wright wrote and delivered his talk, "The Art and Craft of the Machine," one of Wright's best statements. The Wasmuth publications were ac-

Wright.
Unity Temple.
Oak Park, Illinois.
1906

Wright.
Unity Temple.
Oak Park, Illinois.
1906

claimed, and in Europe Wright's fame grew.

From Wisconsin (1911) to Japan (1922). In the Chicago world, Wright's position was difficult; he had taken his provocative stance openly, yet his wife was still unwilling to break their marriage. Clients stayed away, though the Coonleys and a few others gave him work and his mother allowed him to build a handsome home, studio, and farm on property she owned near Spring Green. As soon as possible, he and Mamah Borthwick, formerly Mrs. Cheney, moved there despite his married status; his mother accompanied them. The other Lloyd Joneses were appalled. Wright's new house, Taliesin (1911), became famous; it lay casually around the crest of a hill, in plan somewhat like the McCormick project but built of local stone and plaster with wood trim. It was warm and noble as befitted the rich terrain where Wright had grown to manhood. In 1912, Wright designed his first skyscraper, for downtown San Francisco, a narrow slab, a form later widely adopted. Also unprecedented were its closed, rigid corners evolved from the Larkin as was its 24-story reinforced-concrete frame, half again as high as any then standing. The clients declined to take the risk.

Wright was known as a connoisseur of Japanese prints and this may have attracted the attention of Japanese clients. A group of investors, including the Imperial Household, administering the Emperor's private finances, were searching worldwide for an architect. On a site adjoining the

palace moat in central Tokyo they planned to build a luxurious hotel where foreign dignitaries and visitors would be housed and entertained in Western style. An emissary to Taliesin reported favorably on Wright's skills and ideas, and in 1913, accompanied by Mamah Borthwick, Wright went to Tokyo and the commission was secured. Wright was recognized as a world architect. Meanwhile, he agreed to design Midway Gardens, a complex of restaurants, clubrooms, and barrooms surrounding an open court with tables and bandshell for summer concerts, the whole set in South Side Chicago. Colorful, abstract murals, sculptures, and many fanciful details enlivened the building, which presented a novel side of Wright's talent.

As this work neared completion in 1914, Wright was hastily called to Taliesin where a bad fire had broken out. On the way, he met Edwin Cheney, also summoned since his children were visiting their mother. At the house both men faced a ghastly murder. An insane houseman had set a fire at lunchtime and, as those present tried to escape, axed them down. Mamah, the Cheney boy and girl, and four employees died at his hands, as he did himself soon after capture amid the ruins of the house. Two-thirds of Taliesin were gone and more than that of Wright's spirit. Slowly, he began to rebuild; any activity was some relief from his grief. An unknown woman came to condole; she stayed on, supportive, independent, somewhat commandeering. When Wright went to Japan in 1916 to construct the Imperial Hotel, she sailed with him. Strangely unbalanced, increasingly vindictive and unreasonable, she bedeviled Wright's existence for years. Yet, Wright felt responsible and indebted; when at last his first wife, Catherine, divorced him to marry another man, he made Miriam Noel his wife, though she left him soon thereafter only to reappear with threats and lawsuits. Thus enmeshed, Wright pursued his work.

The Imperial Hotel kept Wright in Japan for large portions of six years; many obstacles cropped up in constructing, equipping, decorating, and financing this unique work of architecture; the main difficulty was the site, more spongy than Chicago's soil and subject—like all Japan—to repeated earthquakes and the ensuing fires. With Paul Mueller's help, informed by earlier experiments in Tokyo, Wright determined on a reinforced-concrete frame that met the challenge. Clusters of concrete piles were sunk eight feet into the soil; free-floating below, they were firmly attached to the walls above, cross-braced by floor slabs. This structure was segmented in 60-foot sections; flexible joints allowed for movement; all utilities and services were similarly jointed. This limber structure supported two long exterior wings, three stories high, containing the bedrooms. Between them, surrounded by garden courts, a shorter, high, central mass housed the splendid public rooms. Two cross wings connected these three. The sophistication of detailing, from the Zen-inspired simplicity of the comfortable bedrooms to the festive opulence of the restaurants, theater, ballroom, and provisions for private functions, was unparalleled. Worn out by his exertions, Wright had to leave Japan before the last touches were added, but one year later when one of the major earthquakes of modern times devastated Tokyo, the hotel, like other reinforced-concrete structures, survived essentially intact amid surrounding rubble and ashes. What earthquakes could not do was accomplished more slowly by aerial bombing, neglect, and cupidity; the Imperial Hotel was torn down in 1967.

California: 1917–1924. Wright's trips to and from Japan included leisurely stops in California. There, he met a former acquaintance from Chicago, an enthusiast for the new little-theater movement and a patroness of musical talent, Aline Barnsdall. She had bought a hill in Hollywood where she wished to build an experimental theater, studios, apartments, and shops to serve her artistic benefactions. At the crest would rise a grand house for entertaining and occasional stays; she and her young daughter traveled widely. Designing was done mostly by mail; the private house and two studios, all that was built, were supervised by delegates. Surprisingly, a poetic masterpiece emerged; later, it was adapted as a community art center. When Wright returned to live in the United States, he began to perfect a building process using unskilled labor and low-cost materials. It consisted of small cast-concrete shells, assembled to form double walls with a central cavity, held together by a network of steel rods grouted into the shells on site. The shells could be ornate or plain, and the cavity could hold utilities, ducts, and flues; if the shells were pierced, air could pass through or central glass could transmit light alone. The system interested Edward L. Doheny, an oil magnate who hoped to develop mountainous terrain he owned just east of Pasadena. Wright projected a community of homes linked by contour-curving roadways and arched viaducts, all constructed as one. But Doheny was deeply involved in the Teapot Dome scandal, and the scheme came to naught.

Wright continued to propose his "textile block" (named for the steel network). A former client, now widowed and moving west, needed a small house suited to her dealing in antiques. The Millard House (1923) in Pasadena was based on the split-level designs of twenty years earlier, but in the concrete shells it gained a character all its own. Partly thanks to the double-height central space,

Wright.
Taliesin.
Near Spring Green,
Wisconsin.
1911

the house was an effective setting for the Renaissance furnishings Mrs. Millard collected and sold. The same system, further developed, was used for three hillside homes in Los Angeles. The most handsome, for Dr. John Storer (1923), employed an improved split-level plan; another, the Freeman House (1924), benefited from a new detail, subsequently often used by Wright. This was a corner window entirely without a corner post or muntin; glass panes met and were sealed with waterglass; later the detail was refined. It liberated space decisively. Wright's California houses used flat roofs and were more compactly massed than his homes of earlier days; this was occasioned by notable differences in sunlight, climate, terrain, and building materials; Mediterranean and Amerindian allusions were employed.

Changes: 1923–1924. In these years, Wright's personal life was changing fundamentally. His mother had stayed near him, even traveling to Japan when he fell ill; she died, age 81, at the beginning of 1923. Later that year, Wright married Miriam Noel. Early in 1924, Louis Sullivan died, feeble and impoverished; a dozen years earlier, the two men had become close to one another again. Later in 1924, Wright met Olga Lazovich (Olgivanna), a native of Montenegro, young, gifted, and divorced. They were at once attracted

Wright.
Drawing of Imperial Hotel.
Tokyo.
1915–1922

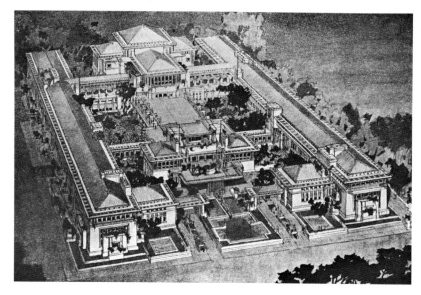

to each other and were married when Wright was again free four years later; they remained together throughout Wright's lifetime.

In Japan, Wright had been thinking about enclosing a cantilevered reinforced-concrete frame, like that used in the hotel, with curtain walls. Both elements lay to hand; in Germany, LUDWIG MIES VAN DER ROHE was on the same track though neither architect was able to execute the idea at that time. Less visionary than Mies's schemes, Wright's project (1923–1924) for the National Life Insurance Company was envisaged as four slab-shaped wings projecting from a taller spine of hallways and elevators. A veil of glass and insulated sheet copper covered all but the top where the concrete framework appeared; movable interior partitions were foreseen. Wright wanted to probe the nature of concrete more fully, despite the advance indicated in this project.

The Doheny project had been organized around curved automobile roadways of concrete. In 1925, Wright gave that concept more concise shape for another entrepreneur, Gordon Strong, wishing to attract visitors to his mountain resort outside Washington accessible by car. Wright suggested crowning the height by driving on a spiral, reinforced-concrete ramp to a lookout with wide vistas; the ramp was double, for up and down traffic. Further attractions, such as a radio transmission tower, a restaurant, and a planetarium (the first had recently opened at Jena) were also considered. The whole approach was up to date but nothing was built. Nevertheless, the spiral automobile ramp was Wright's initial essay in architecture shaped around the path of motion; later he transposed the idea to fit human movement, with remarkable results. Although there was another serious fire at Taliesin, two joys enriched 1925 for Frank Lloyd Wright; Olgivanna bore him a daughter, and the Dutch architectural magazine *Wendingen* published a beautifully produced book

on his life's work.

William Norman Guthrie, a Protestant minister, as early as 1908 had asked Wright to plan a small home for Sewanee, Tennessee, where he taught. The design did not suit, but it became a favorite of Wright's with four variants built and as many projected. In 1926, Guthrie had a different idea. Gigantic cathedrals and churches were being constructed by various sects in America. Guthrie wanted to outdo them with a super cathedral for all faiths, the largest church in the world. Some slight sketches by Wright survive of a pyramidal crystal rising to a height of 1450 feet from an irregular honeycomb of large chapels around a very large central space. Over a steel frame the glass skin was to be double like the skylights Wright had used successfully; at night, the thing would gleam like an immense jewel. Guthrie did not find patrons. In 1954, Wright used a much reduced and refined version of the concept for Beth Sholom Synagogue in Philadelphia.

Years of trouble: 1926–1927. In 1926, Miriam Noel's attacks became monstrous, and Wright's creditors nearly dispossessed him and did sell some of his valuable possessions. The newspapers gave highly colored reports. Wright, Olgivanna, and their baby had to go into hiding; the nightmare went on through much of 1927. At last, Miriam divorced Wright and, later, a group of his friends, including the Darwin Martins and the Coonleys, formed Frank Lloyd Wright Incorporated, paying his debts and a stipend to him; in return they owned his assets and earnings of his work. It gave him security, though not against Miriam's persecutions which lasted until she died in 1930.

In this drastic period, Wright began writing his autobiography at Olgivanna's urging. At the same time, he launched a series of articles in the *Architectural Record;* fourteen in all were published in 1927 and 1928. For the next several years, writing and lecturing took much of his time. Early in 1928, he went to Phoenix, Arizona, to help a former student, Albert C. McArthur, in detailing the Arizona Biltmore resort hotel and cottages, built partly in Wright's textile-block technique. Soon, he and his family were in California where he continued to write and where he pondered another large resort deeper in the Arizona desert proposed by Dr. Alexander Chandler.

The desert influence: 1928–1929. At last in August, Olgivanna and Wright were properly married; they, the baby, and Mrs. Wright's older daughter returned to the Arizona desert. The brilliant sunshine heightened all perception. In the geologically new, sharp mountains and rocks, and in the indigenous plants and animals Wright observed equilateral triangles and dotted lines. The

Wright.
Drawing of G. Strong
Project.
1925

Chandler designs incorporated these elements experimentally. Wright's inventiveness tinged other commissions at this time, a house in Tulsa for his cousin Richard Lloyd Jones, editor of the local newspaper; a hillside apartment block for Elizabeth Noble in Los Angeles; and in New York City another apartment building or group of buildings for William Norman Guthrie, now minister to old, conservative Dutch families and some others at Saint Mark's-in-the-Bouwerie. All these designs were stopped short when the stock market crashed. The Great Depression set in and only the Tulsa house was built.

The Lloyd Jones residence (1929) was an embodiment of the dotted line; its enclosure consisted of full-height glass panels and concrete-block piers, equally wide in continuous alternation. The boldly striped surface ended abruptly against the sky, and the flat roof remained invisible. Inside, the main floor was articulated by piers like the outer ones, but without glass. The exterior was stark, the screened and stepped interiors were pleasingly mysterious. The Noble apartment project looked like European modern architecture at first glance but its vigorously stepped glass walls, giving unusual fluidity to space, and its deft arrangement of half levels were original. The scheme called Saint Mark's Tower—at one point three separate units were considered—was especially noteworthy. Its structure consisted of four independent concrete walls anchored in the earth; in plan they thickened toward a common, open center and they were cross-braced at each level where the floor slabs cantilevered out. Each quarter plan was filled by one studio apartment with a square, two-story living room, kitchen adjacent, stairs leading to a triangular balcony with bedrooms and bath. The layout was based on equilateral triangles allowing easy movement through the fully used spaces. The tower was next proposed in linked groups rising from a big substructure for parking and shops. At Bartlesville, Oklahoma, a single unit for mixed office and apartment use was built in 1953. Three years later Wright made a final version of this scheme, the Golden Beacon, a forty-four story skyscraper, elegant in its height but unrealized.

The trough of the Depression: 1930–1934. In 1930, the Depression deepened. Wright was invited to give a series of lectures at Princeton University, published a year later as *Modern Architecture.* By then, he was working on a model for an international survey of the same name planned by the Museum of Modern Art in New York. There was much talk also of the forthcoming exposition in Chicago, A Century of Progress. Although Wright was not invited to participate, he presented several ideas for the entire show, without

avail. More profitably he was working on another use of reinforced concrete proposed for a small newspaper plant in Salem, Oregon. The simple, cubic volumes were encased in sheer glass, metal framed; inside, the structure consisted of point supports formed as tapered hollow tubes with wide flaring caps. The circular caps nearly touched at roof level, and the interstices were glazed as a series of skylights giving optimum natural light. Wright waited six years before a client used the concept.

The Museum of Modern Art exhibition opened in 1932. Wright's presentation, the House on the Mesa, was a doctrinaire essay in reinforced-concrete cantilevers. He was designing advanced proposals for theaters and at the same time investigating insulated sheet-steel panels for farm buildings. He also designed a modest home for the Malcolm C. Willeys; when in 1934 they built a second version Wright had not actually erected a structure for five years. In 1932, the Wrights announced the Taliesin Fellowship, a residential program for apprentices. A modest fee was charged to cover maintenance and the apprentices were given balanced work, partly in the drafting room, partly on the farm, and partly in the operation and housekeeping of the premises. In a short while, new buildings were started for and by the apprentices, and older structures were remodeled. Such learning-through-work programs with idealistic principles had been tried before in the United States and were not unlike the community near Paris headed by Georgi I. Gurdjieff in which Mrs. Wright had participated. Many early apprentices were drawn

Wright.
Price Tower.
Bartlesville, Oklahoma.
1953

by Wright's *An Autobiography* in which his philosophy of life and architecture was exemplified. It is a remarkable document, perhaps best in its first, brief edition (1932). In that same year, he brought out another book often reworked, *The Disappearing City,* in which Wright outlined his approach to the social and technological changes shaping the world. He was well aware that these tendencies could not be gainsaid but he believed that with forethought and planning they could be directed to yield a more natural, more satisfying life. In the gradual refinement of this text Wright learned that many of his thoughts might be conveyed better visually. When an opportunity arose to present his thesis in Rockefeller Center, New York City, he set the apprentices to work on a large model of "Broadacre City," four square miles containing a dispersed community with every kind of building. The abstract rendition of natural features with very small building models allowed the overall pattern to be seen readily. Larger models of individual buildings were grouped around this, and a great number of Wright's earlier designs were represented. The social, economic, and technological basis for the scheme was stated on the model, and was better explained in Wright's books. Not much of this theory was original, but the assemblage and visual presentation were, and Wright's undogmatic, open-ended approach lifted Broadacre City above the sociological fads and nostrums of the day. When Broadacre City was first shown in the midst of the Depression, it stimulated hopeful discussion, not only by the public and in the press, but among the apprentices at Taliesin who then saw architecture from an unfamiliar viewpoint.

Resurgence: 1935–1940. The exhibition of Broadacre City was the curtain raiser for an unpredictable resurgence of vitality in Wright's career. The fact that the Taliesin Fellowship was productive must have encouraged Wright, and as the economic situation became more tractable more commissions came his way. In 1934–1936, one could see in Wright's drafting room four entirely differ-

ent designs for buildings, since famous worldwide, spread on the boards: Fallingwater, a luxurious weekend house; the S. C. Johnson and Son Administration Building; the Hanna House, a family home based on an hexagonal grid; and the first Jacobs House, the start of a long series of inexpensive, ingenious do-it-yourself homes Wright called "Usonian." Together these four represented a burst of creativity exceptional in the annals of architecture.

Fallingwater, one of Wright's best-known works, was an effective implement for the enjoyment of nature as a way of life. In a beautiful and dramatic setting it was built as a weekend and vacation house for city dwellers; later, it was opened to the public. Wright chose to cantilever the living room over a waterfall in a small mountain stream called Bear Run. Three levels of reinforced-concrete trays were anchored in a tall stone core wrapped around the kitchen, above which two bedrooms were stacked vertically. The other accommodations were family bedrooms, each provided with a terrace reaching out in space. The house was backed into a cliff and on this, higher up, guest rooms, servants' quarters, and garages were built. Concrete, warmly tinted, rugged stonework, and bright earth-red paint on the metal frames of glass gave the house a distinct presence amid the green foliage or winter snows; Fallingwater was a clear statement of the harmony between mankind and nature. Moreover, it was one of the culminations of Wright's long exploration of concrete and cantilevering.

The S. C. Johnson and Son commissions began with a building for clerical work and executive offices plus some amenities, and ten years later a tower for research laboratories and other, lower adjuncts were built. Situated in a mediocre area of Racine, Wisconsin, the main Johnson Building, like its ancestor, the Larkin, closed its perimeter to the outside and received daylight through skylights and clearstory strips. Unlike the Larkin, the Johnson Building lay square and low on the land. The tapered mushroom columns first devised for Oregon were used after passing rigorous tests. Around them were wrapped solid brick enclosures resting on a platform. The light sources were sealed with horizontal glass tubing. Many corners of the simple masses were rounded, and the whole was a smooth object, shaped and colored to suggest warmth and easy flow of movement. Inside, the flood of daylight and the regular caps of the point supports unburdened by any roof created an air of open efficiency. The executive suites were disposed high around the entrance lobby. A feature of the design was the provision for entrance by automobile and convenient parking, built into

Wright.
Broadacre City Model.

Wright.
Kaufmann House
(Fallingwater).
Near Mill Run,
Pennsylvania.
1936–1939

the structure. Metal office furniture was made to accord with the fluency of the building.

Very different was the Hanna House (1937), built on the grounds of Stanford University. It provided for a busy professorial pair with three children and a steady stream of students, colleagues, and visitors. It was organized on a grid of hexagons, providing gentle paths of movement throughout but problematic for the building trades. Fortunately, the Hannas were able to supervise closely, resolving difficulties as they arose. The house fitted its site and operated efficiently. Certain changes foreseen from the start transformed it into a spacious home when the children left and into a useful university facility when the Hannas retired; thus, flexibility was its main trait, not only visually but also in the course of mutable duties.

Wright's Usonian homes, beginning with the first Jacobs House (1937), had been preceded by many approaches to low-cost construction: his blocky Prairie school minimal houses; precut lumber-framed houses called American System Built, erected around 1916 (though not supervised by Wright, away in Japan); concrete-block houses in California; and sheet-metal prefabrication proposed in 1937. These varied from factory-formed systems to on-site construction using generally available materials. The latter might involve client participation, lowering the cash requirement. In

this vein, Wright had been designing what he called Usonian houses, a name which suggested adaptability to a nationwide clientele. In essence, these houses depended on a series of related devices, all simple to grasp and execute. First, a concrete platform was laid down with heating pipes cast in, the whole resting on a layer of crushed stone. The concrete would be mixed with red coloring to give a warm, earthy cast to the interiors. On this were erected a brick core around the kitchen, incorporating flues, and one or two other brick supporting screens. A flat roof was constructed of three layers of two-by-fours, conventionally surfaced with asphalt felt; it was supported principally by the brick walls, the kitchen rising above it to provide a draft. The furnace

Wright.
S. C. Johnson and Son
Administration
Building.
Racine, Wisconsin.
1936–1946

room was usually slightly sunk. The roof was higher over the living-dining area, lower over bedrooms and bath. The difference in height allowed clearstory strips to let light into the innermost recesses, and similar strips brought light at the top of walls where privacy was welcome. Toward the garden, the windows were often floor-to-ceiling doors. The enclosing walls, largely free of loads, were three layers, firmly screwed together, of waterproof plywood and boards with roofing paper between. Electric conduit could be freely exposed or with more trouble set out of sight. Practically every skill required for such construction could be provided by many home owners eager to save expense. When noncorrodible pipes were used, the hot-water heating system was economical but ample, and the walls were good insulators. Not every client was a builder; over the years more sophisticated details were adopted and the line between the Usonian house and a small home designed by Wright became blurred.

The Usonian idea was realized when Herbert and Katherine Jacobs built their small home, with happy results. As other clients applied for similar plans, they were given individual consideration. Partly due to this success with inexpensive homes, Wright designed as many buildings in his last twenty years as in the preceding half century. He continued to develop new ways of meeting architectural demands and yet he rarely abandoned earlier solutions. Hence, his later work of every kind is hard to categorize.

As the Jacobs Usonian was rising in 1937, Wright was planning winter quarters for himself and the Fellowship, Taliesin West outside Scottsdale, Arizona. This soon became as famous as Taliesin itself; like the earlier structure it was consonant with its landscape and generously laid out, but different materials and a livelier tempo controlled the composition. Crisp bases of desert rock were cast with cement in wood forms; from these bases arose rough lumber strengthened by steel flitch plates, supporting overhead shelter of white canvas doubled around wood stretchers, reflecting heat and diffusing light. Many of the canvas panels were hinged for ventilation. All structures were built by apprentices. Over the years, Taliesin West became more used, and gradually the rough materials were replaced by glass, plastic fabrics, and metal beams and parapets. In the tradition established by Wright, from time to time new structures were added and parts were remodeled; forty years after its inception Taliesin West had assumed a new character.

In 1937, Wright started to design a campus for Florida Southern College, a growing, church-run institution lacking means. The buildings were to be student built, and were so in part; no regular supervision was supplied. The quality of Wright's design was apparent in the suavely dramatic disposition of the buildings. In 1940, Wright designed a smaller scheme for a working plantation in Yemassee, South Carolina, using cypress boards and screening in triangulated structures. The plans of these three groups of diversified buildings, Taliesin West, Florida Southern College, and Yemassee Plantation show many differences but a constant elegance.

Toward the end of 1937, Wright and the Fellowship were preparing a publication celebrating his resurgence; the *Architectural Forum,* a leading monthly magazine, had generously turned over its issue of January 1938 to Wright. Later in 1938, he presented an ambitious plan for a new civic center in Madison, Wisconsin, the state capital. Wright waived his fee but the plan was rejected and for years thereafter it was revived and thwarted in turn. In 1938, Wright also designed a novel house with a concrete platform and a cantilevered concrete slab roof partly pierced as a trellis. Between these parallel planes the main rooms were formed as freestanding cylinders of plywood, asymmetrically arranged; the intervening space became a sheltered patio in lieu of hallways.

The 1938 *Forum* served admirably as fanfare for Wright's 1939 appearance in London to deliver four lectures by invitation to a distinguished professional audience. Published that same year as *An Organic Architecture,* the texts included some of Wright's best statements. World War II broke out shortly thereafter and Wright could not be awarded the Gold Medal of the Royal Institute of British Architects until 1941; the British honors confirmed Wright's official international acceptance as an architectural genius. Also in 1939, Wright designed two important Usonian houses, the Rosenbaum House in Florence, Alabama, enlarged within ten years and long the family's satisfactory home; and a minimal masterpiece for two art teachers at a teachers college, the Misses Goetsch and Winckler. The elaborate house for Carlton D. Wall, not built until 1941, used Wright's hexagonal unit planning to perfection. In 1940 came the Lloyd Lewis and Gregor Affleck houses, both more luxurious than a Usonian type and both lifted up over their sites; the Lewis House was a classic of Wright's mature design. At the end of the year, Wright was given a one-man exhibition at the Museum of Modern Art in New York. A set of three books was published in tandem with the exhibition: in 1941, Frederick Gutheim's *Frank Lloyd Wright on Architecture: Selected Writings, 1894–1940;* in 1942, Henry-Russell Hitchcock's essential study, *In the Nature of Mate-*

rials: 1887–1941, the Buildings of Frank Lloyd Wright; and in 1943, an augmented edition of Frank Lloyd Wright's An Autobiography.

New directions: 1940s. Two projects of the winter of 1940–1941 introduced what became Wright's most debated innovation, a single elementary geometric form used as the main mass of a building. It seemed that Wright had jettisoned humanism and organicism in favor of form for form's sake. The Roy Peterson Project was a great equilateral triangle, later successfully adapted for Professor William Palmer and his wife at Ann Arbor, Michigan. For the Lloyd Burlinghams' wind-swept sand dune near El Paso, Texas, Wright proposed a double arc, almond shaped, enclosing a courtyard. The adobe walls curved as they rose to a ridged roof; plan and section were in resonance. The sheltered court was not needed when the arc plan was used elsewhere, as in houses for Kenneth Laurent in Rockford, Illinois (1949), or for Andrew B. Cooke House (1953) at Virginia Beach. Triangle and arc were joined by full circle, sphere (both infrequent), and spiral. How did Wright make use of such powerful, arbitrary shapes? Wright invaded or modulated the ideal mathematical figure, indicating that he wanted the strength and impact of a clear, regular shape, but he insisted on making it subservient to human uses and feelings. Evidently, Wright pursued this theme—among others—during the last decades of his career because it presented a major challenge. In the 1900s, he had decided to demonstrate the importance of space over matter; now it was the dominance of vitality over abstraction. These concepts seem abstruse but Wright found no shortage of appreciative clients for the buildings he derived from them.

At the end of 1941, the United States entered World War II; Wright could not countenance war, and with many apprentices away, the years 1942 to 1945 were not active at Taliesin. Nevertheless, several of Wright's most significant designs were evolved then, all built in due course. Another home for Herbert Jacobs and his family, now larger, was discussed at length; finally, in 1945, a design was agreed on, and was built two years later. It was an arc of stone shielding a sunken circular garden against the prevailing winds, with almost all glass on the garden side, to trap the sun. The earth excavated from the garden was banked against the back wall, insulating it but for a strip of clearstory windows which lit the bedroom balcony which hung free inside the tall windows; below was living room, dining area, and kitchen. A circular stone core contained utilities below and the bathroom, skylit, above. The Jacobs family were dedicated pioneers; both their Wright homes were originals, inevitably not fully resolved. The second Jacobs House could have used more shade in summer and more heat in winter on the balcony, but the clients were adaptable and the house was beautiful, the work of their own hands in large part.

The Douglas Grants lived outside Cedar Rapids, Iowa, amid rolling hills. They too did not build until 1947 and then did much of the work

Wright.
Taliesin West.
Near Scottsdale, Arizona.
1938

Wright.
Triangular House Plan.

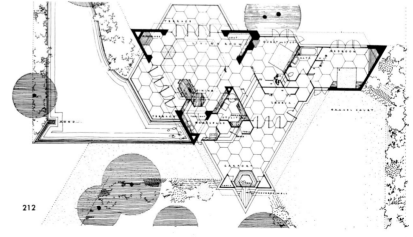

212

themselves, expertly. The house was a narrow rectangle leading to a two-story high living room with glass uninterrupted on three sides and a wide overhanging roof. Bedrooms, baths, and a number of adjacent services completed the accommodations. The living-room floor flowed out into the terrain and the terraces seemed part of the main room. From the entry, steep stairs led narrowly down, lit by clearstory; the open living room came as a surprise. This is one of Wright's simplest, best works.

Solomon R. Guggenheim commissioned his museum at this time. Guided by the Baroness Rebay, he had amassed an unusual collection of modern painting and sculpture programmatically limited to "nonobjective art," that is, art that did not represent an object either man-made or natural. Instinct or intellect provided the imagery which thus gained a quality not attainable in arts imitative of something else; this was, it was claimed, the art of the future. Wright related easily to these ideas, and much of the art related to his buildings, with strong centers and extensions reaching outward. Moreover much of nonobjective art avoided traditional frames and bases, each work standing by itself. Wright believed his architecture could supply the inobtrusive milieu called for and at the same time could liberate the act of viewing in unanticipated ways. He designed the expanding spiral ramp, since famous and debated. Guggenheim and Rebay were convinced they had a masterpiece, but like lesser clients they thought the time was wrong for building. Guggenheim set aside a generous building fund; he was an exact contemporary of Wright's and secured the money in his will, should he die before building started. He did, and his appointees soon changed the staff and the policy of the museum. Wright's building had to be erected yet the segregated fund had declined considerably in purchasing power over the years. At the end of his life, Wright saw his greatest, freest architectural concept rise in Manhattan, skimped, bound by inappropriate codes, and fated to be used contrary to the terms of the commission he had fulfilled. Wright did not live to see it open, but the frustration of his concept extended to such essentials as lighting and wall treatments. Despite this, Wright's Guggenheim Museum stands as one of the irrefutably grand achievements of modern architecture. Its qualities as a museum will remain in question until the intentions of donor and architect are fulfilled.

In the later 1940s, Wright made an intensive search for the possible uses of circles in architecture. His spiral proposals for a symbolic city center in Pittsburgh, Pennsylvania, stood beyond the scope of reality yet celebrated the tensile grace in-

herent in steel, the city's foremost product. A spiral self-service parking garage for the same city, not built, has been paralleled often in more recent structures. Two cooperative housing communities were planned by Wright on the basis of circular individual plots set in forested land held in common. The plans were skillfully irregular; patterns of cellular structure seemed put to new use. One of Wright's most elaborate mansions was designed in 1949 for Texas. The roofs were shallow inverted saucers, echoed in the main space by a floor stepped down toward the center, as if a large central zone were excised from a sphere and the caps brought nearer each other. Proposed for Mexico and Connecticut, suitably changed, the scheme never was built. A small spiral ramp was used for a store in San Francisco with a skylit roof and a provocatively closed façade, the famous Morris Store of 1948. Ten years after the British, the American Institute of Architects awarded its Gold Medal to Wright, and once again the *Architectural Forum* gave him an entire issue. A Unitarian group on the outskirts of Madison, Wisconsin, in 1947 asked Wright for a suitable meeting house and social center. Wright designed a soaring shed roof and a great window to the greenery outside; the interior could be used flexibly. The church became famous as a new symbol for reverence without ostentation.

Final accomplishments: 1950s.   No slackening of Wright's work occurred during the 1950s, although awkward liturgical ornament disturbed Beth Sholom Synagogue (1954) and Annunciation Greek Catholic Church at the edge of Milwaukee (1956). In both buildings, usable space was deftly lifted free of the ground. The great accomplishment of this decade was Marin County Civic Center outside San Francisco (1957), built after Wright's death in accord with his drawings officially approved following public hearings. Two elongated wings bridged the foothills, a domed unit intervening where they met. One wing housed county offices with clerical areas, the other contained courtrooms, chambers, and a jail. Meeting rooms and a civic library occupied the domical feature. Each wing centered on a long, skylit court with open corridors on either side; these courts exhausted used air from the mechanically ventilated rooms, and the chimney action pulled fresh air constantly from below; this was considerably more economical than total air conditioning. Outside the windows, a separate outer skin was pulled down like an awning to attachments at each level. The low structure harmonized with the hills and roads; it had a casual resemblance to Roman aqueducts which similarly bestrode the landscape.

An unexecuted scheme for California, dated 1955, would have housed an electronics assembly

Wright.
Marin County Civic Center.
San Raphael, California.
1957–1966

plant under mushroom columns amply developed from those at Racine. In Europe, a major exhibition of Wright's works, including many original drawings, opened in 1951 at the Palazzo Strozzi in Florence and then circulated widely. A year before he died, Wright appeared on television with Mike Wallace, and gave a lucid, engaging explanation of his work in popular terms. On April 9th, 1959, he died.

Wright's place in architecture. Out of common practice at the end of the nineteenth century Frank Lloyd Wright gradually forged an individual architecture of astonishing scope, power, and coherence. It diverged from the work of his contemporaries not only in appearance but in principle. Wright believed that forms, however appealing, have significance only as evidence of principle. Wright's principles derived from a faith in architecture as the natural link between mankind and environment. In his last London lecture, Wright said that "architecture . . . proceeds, persists, creates, according to the nature of man and his circumstances as they both *change.*" This was his vision of organic architecture.

EDGAR KAUFMANN, JR.

WORKS

1889–1911, Frank Lloyd Wright House and Studio, Oak Park, Ill. 1892, Blossom House, Chicago. 1893, Winslow House, River Forest, Ill. 1894, Roloson Row Houses; *1895, Francisco Terrace Apartments; Chicago. 1895, Moore House (remodeled by Wright in 1923), Oak Park, Ill. *1898–1901, River Forest Golf Club, Ill. *1899, Husser House, Chicago. 1900, Bradley House; 1900, Hickox House; Kankakee, Ill. 1902, Heurtley House, Oak Park, Ill. 1902, Hillside Home School Buildings, near Spring Green, Wis. 1902, Willits House, Highland Park, Ill. 1903, Barton House, Buffalo, N.Y. 1903, Dana House, Springfield, Ill. 1904, Cheney House; 1904, Mrs. Gale House; Oak Park, Ill. *1904, Larkin Company Administration Building, Buffalo, N.Y. 1904, Martin House, Buffalo, N.Y. 1905, Glasner House, Glencoe, Ill. 1905, Hardy House,

Racine, Wis. 1905, Smith Bank, Dwight, Ill. 1906, Unity Temple, Oak Park, Ill. 1907, Hunt House, La Grange, Ill. 1907, Tomek House, Riverside, Ill. 1908, Bitter Root Inn, Stevensville, Mont. *1908, Browne's Bookstore; 1908, Robie House; Chicago. 1908–1912, Coonley House and Annexes, Riverside, Ill. 1909, Baker House, Wilmette, Ill. 1909, Stewart House, Montecito, Calif. *1909, Thurber Art Gallery, Chicago. *1910, Universal Portland Cement Exhibition Stand, New York. 1911, Taliesin (major remodeling in 1914 and 1925), near Spring Green, Wis. *1914, Midway Gardens; 1915, Bach House; Chicago. *1915–1922, Imperial Hotel, Tokyo. 1916, Richards House, Milwaukee, Wis. 1917, Allen House, Wichita, Kan. 1917–1920, Barnsdall House and Annexes, Los Angeles. 1921, Jiyu Gakuen School, Tokyo. 1923, Millard House, Pasadena, Calif. 1923, Storer House; 1924, Ennis House; 1924, Freeman House; Los Angeles. *1928, Ocatillo Desert Camp, near Chandler, Ariz. 1929, Jones House, Tulsa, Okla. 1934, Willey House, Minneapolis, Minn. 1936–1939, Kaufmann House (Fallingwater), near Mill Run, Pa. 1936–1946, S. C. Johnson and Son Administration Building and Annexes, Racine, Wis. 1937, Hanna House, Stanford, Calif. 1937, Jacobs House (first), Madison, Wis. 1937, Kaufmann Office, Victoria and Albert Museum, London. 1938, Taliesin West, near Scottsdale, Ariz. 1938–1954, Florida Southern College Buildings, Lakeland. 1939, Goetsch-Winckler House, Okemos, Mich. 1939, Rosenbaum House, Florence, Ala. 1939, Suntop Homes, Ardmore, Pa. 1940, Baird House, Amherst, Mass. 1940, Lewis House, Libertyville, Ill. *1940, Pauson House, near Phoenix, Ariz. 1940, Pew House, Shorewood Hills, Wis. 1940, Pope House (moved in 1964), Mount Vernon, Va. 1940, Stevens Plantation, Yemassee, S.C. 1941, Affleck House, Bloomfield Hills, Mich. 1941, Wall House, Plymouth, Mich. 1947, Grant House, near Cedar Rapids, Iowa. 1947, Jacobs House (second), Middleton, Wis. 1947, Unitarian Church, Shorewood Hills, Wis. 1948, Lamberson House, Oskaloose, Iowa. 1948, Morris Gift Shop, San Francisco. 1948, Mossberg House, South Bend, Ind. 1948, Walker House, Carmel, Calif. 1948, Walters House, Quasqueton, Iowa. 1949, Anthony House, South Bend, Ind. 1949, Laurent House, Rockford, Ill. 1950, Berger House, San Anselmo, Calif. 1950, Carr House, Glenview, Ill. 1950, Gillin House, Dallas, Tex. 1950, Keys House,

Rochester, Minn. 1950, Muirhead House, Plato Center, Ill. 1950, Smith House, Bloomfield Hills, Mich. 1950, Wright House, Phoenix, Ariz. 1950, Zimmerman House, Manchester, N.H. 1952, Price Tower, Bartlesville, Okla. 1953, Cooke House, Virginia Beach. 1953, Price House, Bartlesville, Okla. 1953, Wright House, Bethesda, Md. 1954, Beth Sholom Synagogue, Elkins Park, Pa. 1954, Hoffman Automobile Showroom, New York. 1954, Price House, Paradise Valley, Ariz. 1955, Dallas Theater Center, Tex. 1955, Hoffman House, Rye, N.Y. 1955, Rayward House, New Canaan, Conn. 1956, Annunciation Greek Catholic Church, Milwaukee, Wis. 1956, Solomon R. Guggenheim Museum, New York. 1957–1966, Marin County Civic Center, San Raphael, Calif.

BIBLIOGRAPHY

Different methods have been used to date Wright's works. In this article Hitchcock's precedent has been followed wherever possible, using the start of construction for each building and for projects, the dates inscribed on the drawings. Storrer and others use the date when a design was first conceived, as near as can be estimated.

Frank Lloyd Wright's documents, drawings, photographs, and letters are preserved at Taliesin West, near Scottsdale, Arizona. Further material is available at the Avery Architectural Library, Columbia University, New York.

HEINZ, THOMAS A. 1982 *Frank Lloyd Wright.* New York: St. Martin's. Best color photographs of Wright buildings.

HITCHCOCK, H. R. (1942)1973 *In the Nature of Materials.* Reprint, New York: Da Capo. The standard study of Wright's work through 1941.

IZZO, ALBERTO, and CAMILLO GUBITOSI 1981 *Frank Lloyd Wright: Three-quarters of a Century of Drawings.* New York: Horizon. Lists works from 1942 to 1959.

STORRER, WILLIAM ALLIN (1974)1978 *The Architecture of Frank Lloyd Wright: A Complete Catalog.* Cambridge Mass.: M.I.T. Press. Only executed works are listed.

SWEENEY, ROBERT L. 1978 *Frank Lloyd Wright: An Annotated Bibliography.* Los Angeles: Hennessey & Ingalls. 2095 fully indexed items.

WRIGHT, FRANK LLOYD 1943 *An Autobiography.* New York: Duell, Sloan and Pearce. The standard edition of the chief biography. A shorter first edition, illustrated, was issued in 1932 in London, New York, and Toronto by Longmans, Green, and Company. An enlarged edition appeared in 1977 in New York by Horizon.

WRIGHT, HENRY

Henry Wright (1878–1936), landscape architect and town planner, was born in Lawrence, Kansas, and educated at the University of Pennsylvania. After his graduation, he moved to St. Louis, Missouri, where he practiced residential landscape design and was caught up in the nascent city planning movement. For many years, he was the chairman of the City Planning Association of St. Louis and a consultant to the City Planning Commission.

Employed by the United States Shipping Board during World War I, he moved to Washington, where he assisted in the site planning of several defense housing settlements, notably, Yorkship Village, Camden, New Jersey (1918). At this time, he worked with several like-minded architects including CLARENCE S. STEIN and Frederick L. Ackerman. All were convinced that British garden city principles and public housing schemes should be adopted in the United States. They were attracted by the cost efficiency, land conserving benefits, and beauty of the English models.

After the Armistice, they continued to propagate their ideas through the Regional Planning Association of America and its subsidiary, the City Housing Corporation, which they founded in 1923. They planned and built several model communities including Sunnyside Gardens (New York, 1924), Radburn (Fair Lawn, New Jersey, 1928), and Chatham Village (Pittsburgh, 1930).

In this period, Wright also collaborated in developing a classic but unexecuted State Regional Plan (1926) sponsored by the New York State Commission for Housing and Regional Planning established by Governor Alfred E. Smith. The plan was clearly influenced by the work of PATRICK GEDDES and his disciple Lewis Mumford.

The New Deal era offered Wright opportunities to extend his housing and planning interests into the national arena. Engaged as a consultant to both the Public Works Administration Housing Division and the Resettlement Administration, he promoted projects employing large-scale development and the superblock, key characteristics of his earlier work. The unexecuted design for Greenbrook, New Jersey (1935), is an example.

A prolific writer, Wright was a regular contributor to the *Architectural Record, American City, Survey,* and *National Real Estate Journal.* He published a thorough account of his philosophy in 1935 in *Rehousing Urban America* (1935).

An associate professor of architecture at Columbia University at the time of his death in 1936, he was perfecting his particular contribution to planning, the statistical analysis of subdivision and housing design, to document the cost efficiency of his concepts.

EUGENIE L. BIRCH

WORKS

1918–1919, Defense Housing, Newburgh, N.Y.; Bridgeport, Conn., and Camden, N.J. 1924, Sunnyside Gardens, New York. 1928, Radburn (with Clarence S. Stein), Fair Lawn, N.J. 1930, Chatham Village, Pittsburgh. n.d., St. Louis Country Club Subdivision, Mo.

BIBLIOGRAPHY

CHURCHILL, HENRY 1960 "Henry Wright: 1878–1936." *Journal of the American Institute of Planners* 26:293–301.

"Henry Wright, Town Planner, Dies Suddenly." 1936 *New York Times,* July 10.

WRIGHT, JOHN LLOYD

Like his older brother LLOYD WRIGHT, John Lloyd Wright (1893–1973) acquired his drafting and architectural skills in the Oak Park studio of his father, FRANK LLOYD WRIGHT. Like other members of the family, he attended the Hillside School at Spring Green and later attended the University of Wisconsin. In 1912, he joined his older brother in San Diego, California. There, he worked in the office of Harrison Albright, where he was responsible for the design of an early essay in reinforced concrete, the Golden West Hotel (San Diego, 1912). In nearby Escondido, he produced his first independent building, the Wood House (1912), a variation on his father's 1906 *Ladies Home Journal* scheme. Between 1913 and 1919, he worked for his father and accompanied him to Japan. He then returned to the Midwest, working as a designer in several firms, before setting up his own independent practice in 1926. In the late 1920s and early 1930s, he designed a number of buildings in northern Michigan and Indiana which partook of the Expressionist-Art Deco imagery found in the then contemporary work of BARRY BYRNE and BRUCE A. GOFF. At the end of World War II, he set up his practice in the San Diego area. His work from 1945 until his death was characterized by highly original versions of his father's Usonian houses and of the California Ranch House. His delight in the world of the child was expressed in his creation of "Lincoln Logs" in 1920 and his interlocking Wright Blocks (1949).

DAVID GEBHARD

WORKS

1912, Golden West Hotel, San Diego, Calif. 1912, Woods House, Escondido, Calif. 1927, Dunes Arcade Hotel, Ind. 1928, Cedar Street Apartments, Michigan City, Ind. 1934, Burnham House, Long Beach, Mich. 1938, Coolspring School, La Ponte County, Ind. 1938, Dunes State Park, Ind. 1941, Wright House; 1948, Cohn House; La Jolla, Calif. 1948, Eitel House, San Diego, Calif. 1952, Schmock House, La Jolla, Calif. 1958, Wishing Well Hotel, Rancho Santa Fe, Calif. 1967, Marston House, La Jolla, Calif. 1968, Fine House, Grossmont, Calif.

BIBLIOGRAPHY

"Earliest Work of John Lloyd Wright." 1970 *Prairie School Review* 7, no. 2:16–19.

WRIGHT, JOHN 1952*a* "Lichenaceous Ornament." *House and Home* 1, Jan.:136–137.

WRIGHT, JOHN 1952*b* "What's New?" *Journal of the American Institute of Architects* 18, Oct.:187–188.

WRIGHT, LLOYD

The eldest son of FRANK LLOYD WRIGHT, Lloyd Wright (1890–1978) was trained as a draftsman/delineator in his father's Oak Park Studio. For two years (1908–1909), he studied engineering and agronomy at the University of Wisconsin. During much of 1909, he worked with his father at Fiesole, Italy, in preparing the drawings for Frank Lloyd Wright's famous Wasmuth Portfolio. Upon his return, he joined the Boston planning/landscape architectural firm of Olmsted and Olmsted (see FREDERICK LAW OLMSTED). He was sent by the firm to San Diego in 1911 to help with the preparation of their design for the Panama California Exposition. When the Olmsted firm withdrew from this project, Lloyd Wright stayed on to work for IRVING J. GILL. With the conclusion of Gill's and Olmsted and Olmsted's work on the new industrial town of Torrence, California, he formed a landscape architectural practice with Paul Thiene. His professional activities as a landscape architect continued on through the 1920s. It was during these years that he was once again involved with his father in several Los Angeles projects, including the Barnsdall project and the series of precast concrete block houses designed between 1922 and 1924. By 1925, he had established himself as both an architect and landscape architect. He produced a remarkable project for a multilayered civic center for Los Angeles (1925), and through a number of projects and realized buildings he explored how one should build and live in the eastern California desert. A number of his best known structures were designed in the opening years of his practice. These include several precast concrete block houses: that for John Derby (1926) in Chevy Chase, California, and his own house and studio in Los Angeles (1927). Pre-Columbianism and Art Deco themes were strong in his Los Angeles Sowden House (1926) and in the Samuel–Navarro House (1926–1928) in Hollywood, California. With his intense interest in music, he provided the only two workable shells for the Hollywood Bowl, Hollywood, California (1924–1925; 1928).

The ability to complete large-scale projects continually eluded him. In 1930, he provided schemes for the new Los Angeles and Burbank Airports. Designs for skyscrapers were explored in such unrealized projects as a precast concrete-block Catholic Cathedral (1931) in Los Angeles, and much later for a tower addition to the Fairmont Hotel (1944) in San Francisco. Much of his work in the 1930s and on into the post-World War II years represented highly inventive variations on the theme of the California ranch house. Lloyd Wright's ability to couple landscape design and architecture is most perfectly summed up in his much publicized Swedenborg Memorial Chapel or Wayfarer's Chapel (1946–1971) at Palos Verdes, California.

DAVID GEBHARD

WORKS

1915–1916, Garden for Benjamin Meyer, Beverly Hills, Calif. 1915–1916, Garden for John L. Severence, Pasadena, Calif. 1922, Henry Bollman House, Hollywood, Calif. 1922, Martha Taggert House, Los Angeles. 1923, Oasis Hotel, Palm Springs, Calif. 1924–1925, Hollywood Bowl (first shell), Calif. 1926, Calori House; 1926, John Derby House; Chevy Chase, Calif. 1926, John Sowden House, Los Angeles. 1926–1928, Samuel–Navarro House, Hollywood, Calif. 1927, Lloyd Wright Studio–House, Los Angeles. 1928, Hollywood Bowl (second shell), Calif. 1935, Claudette Colbert House, Los Angeles. 1936, Raymond Griffith Ranch House, Canoga Park, Calif. 1946–1971, Swedenborg Memorial Chapel, Palos Verdes, Calif. 1950, Alfred Erickson House, Minneapolis, Minn. 1950, Arthur Erickson House, Edina, Minn. 1965, First Christian Church, Thousand Oaks, Calif.

BIBLIOGRAPHY

GEBHARD, DAVID, and VON BRETON, HARRIETTE 1971 *Lloyd Wright Architect.* Santa Barbara: University of California. Exhibition catalogue.
MCCOY, ESTHER 1966 "Lloyd Wright." *Arts and Architecture.* 83:22–26.
SCHINDLER, PAULINE (Gibling) 1932 "Modern California Architects." *Creative Arts* 10:111–115.

WRIGHT, STEPHEN

Stephen Wright (?–1780) was in LORD BURLINGTON's employ in 1731 and was an employee of the Office of Works from 1746. An underappreciated architect working in WILLIAM KENT's style, he was from at least 1752 under the patronage of the duke of Newcastle, for whom he rebuilt Clumber, Nottinghamshire (1766). He is best known for the exquisite University Library, Cambridge (1754), and for the organization of Oatlands, Surrey (1750s–1760s).

JOHN HARRIS

WORKS

1751, Sunbury Church, Middlesex, England. 1754, University Library, Cambridge. 1768, Clumber House, Nottinghamshire, England.

WRIGHT, THOMAS

Thomas Wright (1711–1786) was a remarkable person—the astronomer who first explained the Milky Way, a landscape gardener, an architect, a mathematician, and a notable antiquary whose *Louthiana, or an Introduction to the Antiquities of Ireland* appeared in 1748. As an architect he was a neo-Palladian whose work is reflective of WILLIAM KENT's staccato style; he was also close to Kent as a garden designer. His Nuthall Temple, Nottinghamshire (1754), is one of the most splendid of all the rotonda villas derived from ANDREA PALLADIO's Villa Capra. Wright was also the designer of many extraordinary and rustic garden buildings, represented in engravings in his rare "Designs of Arbours" (1755) and "Grottos" (1758). He was one of the pioneers of a style of gardening known as gardenesque.

JOHN HARRIS

WORKS

1743, Duchess of Kent's House, Old Windsor, Berkshire, England. 1748, Shugborough (wings), Staffordshire, England. c.1750, Stoke Gifford, Gloucestershire, England. 1754, Nuthall Temple, Nottinghamshire, England. c.1760, Horton House (front), Northamptonshire, England.

BIBLIOGRAPHY

HARRIS, EILEEN 1971 *Country Life* Aug. 26, Sept. 2, 9.
WRIGHT, THOMAS 1748 *Louthiana, or an Introduction to the Antiquities of Ireland.* London: Faden.
WRIGHT, THOMAS 1755–1758a "Designs of Arbours." In *Universal Architecture.* London: The author.
WRIGHT, THOMAS 1755–1758b "Grottos." In *Universal Architecture.* London: The author.

WURSTER, WILLIAM WILSON

William Wilson Wurster (1895–1972) was born in Stockton, California, and studied architecture at the University of California at Berkeley and regional planning at Harvard University. He spent the majority of his career in California, ultimately becoming a principal partner in Wurster, Bernardi, and Emmons, whose diversified practice included residences, housing projects, and institutional and commercial complexes. He also was a leader in architectural education, serving as dean of the school of architecture and planning, Massachusetts Institute of Technology (1944–1950), and chairman of the department of architecture, University of California, Berkeley (1950–1959). He later founded and became dean of the latter institution's College of Environmental Design (1959–1963).

EUGENIE L. BIRCH

WORKS

1942, Schuckl Canning Company Office Building, Sunnyvale, Calif. 1942, Stern Hall, University of California, Berkeley. 1954, Center for Advanced Studies in the Behavioral Sciences, Stanford University, Palo Alto, Calif. 1958–1965, Capitol Tower Apartments (with EDWARD LARRABEE BARNES and DeMars and Reay), Sacramento, Calif. 1959, Married Student Housing; 1959, Medical Plaza; Stanford University, Palo Alto, Calif. 1959, Strawberry Canyon Recreation Center, University of California, Berkeley. 1961, First Unitarian Church, El Cerrito, Calif. 1962–1967, Ghirardelli Square (renovation and remodeling), San Francisco. 1965, Woodlake Residential Community, San Mateo, Calif. 1970–1971, Bank of America World Headquarters (with SKIDMORE, OWINGS, AND MERRILL and PIETRO BELLUSCHI), San Francisco.

BIBLIOGRAPHY

PETERS, RICHARD C. 1980 "Wurster, William Wilson." Pages 908–909 in Muriel Emanuel (editor), *Contemporary Architects.* New York: St. Martin's.
"W. W. Wurster, Architect, Dies." 1973 *New York Times,* Sept. 30.

WYATT, BENJAMIN

Benjamin Dean Wyatt (1775–1850), eldest son of JAMES WYATT, took up an appointment in India in 1797–1803 with the East India Company. In 1807, he became private secretary to Sir Arthur Wellesley (later first duke of Wellington) in Ireland, returning to England and his father's office in 1809. His first success was Drury Lane Theatre, London (1811–1812), which contains carefully related, impressively formed internal spaces. Patronage by the Wellesley family brought him alterations to Stratfield Saye House, Hampshire (1822), and Apsley House, London (1828–1829). Together with his brother Philip he decorated several London houses and clubs in the Louis Quatorze style which he seems to have introduced in England in 1827 at Crockford's Club. In 1833, he became bankrupt and his last years are obscure.

DEREK LINSTRUM

WORKS

1811–1812, Drury Lane Theatre, London. 1816, Mansfield Park, Sussex, England. 1822, Stratfield Saye House (alterations), Hampshire, England. 1825–1827, York (Stafford, now Lancaster) House; 1825–1828, Londonderry House (with Philip Wyatt); London. c.1825–1830, Belvoir Castle (decoration; with M. C. Wyatt), Leicestershire, England. 1827, Crockford's Clubhouse (with P. Wyatt); 1827–1828, Oriental Club (with P. Wyatt); 1828–1829, Apsley House (with P. Wyatt); 1831–1834, Duke of York's Column; London.

BIBLIOGRAPHY

LINSTRUM, DEREK 1974 "The Waterloo Palace." *Architectural Review.* 155:217–223.
ROBINSON, JOHN MARTIN 1979 *The Wyatts: An Architectural Dynasty.* Oxford University Press.

WYATT, CHARLES

Charles Wyatt (1758/1759–1819), who belonged to the well-known architectural family, was a nephew of JAMES WYATT. He was born in Stafford, England, and became a cadet with the Bengal Infantry in 1780. He reached India in 1782, by which time he transferred to the Madras Engineers. He was asked to submit designs for a new Government House, Calcutta, during the governorship of Marquess Wellesley in 1798. Adapted from the designs for Kedleston Hall, Derbyshire, Wyatt's were chosen in preference to those of the East India Company architect, Edward Tiretta. Building began in 1799 and was largely complete by 1804. Wyatt returned to England that year, retired from the service in 1806, and later became a member of Parliament for Sudbury.

PAULINE ROHATGI

WORK

1799–1804, Government House, Calcutta.

BIBLIOGRAPHY

ARCHER, MILDRED 1959 "A Georgian Palace in India: Government House, Calcutta." *Country Life* 125, no. 3247:754–756.
CURZON, GEORGE NATHANIEL 1925 *British Government in India.* New York and London: Cassell.
ROBINSON, JOHN M. 1980 *The Wyatts: An Architectural Dynasty.* Oxford University Press.

WYATT, JAMES

James Wyatt (1746–1813) was England's most fashionable and prolific architect in the late eighteenth century. Adept at both classical and medieval styles, Wyatt built and remodeled country houses throughout England and Ireland. His talents touched virtually every Oxford College, and his cathedral restorations, although consistent with eighteenth-century architectural ideals, brought forth vehement antiquarian opposition. Wyatt's significance lies not only in the number of buildings he designed, but also in their diversity.

James Wyatt was born in Weeford, Staffordshire, the sixth son of the builder Benjamin Wyatt. The family firm, known by the 1760s as Benjamin Wyatt and Sons, received substantial commissions from the Midlands landed gentry and the new industrial society, including the design and construction of the Soho Manufactory, Birmingham (1762), for Matthew Boulton (see BOULTON AND WATT). The firm's buildings reflected the tall proportions and centralized compositions of contemporary English neo-Palladianism. However, through a concern for utility, Benjamin Wyatt and Sons eschewed unnecessary detail and favored undecorated surfaces.

This family background instilled several attitudes later crucial to James Wyatt's career. First, there was no suggestion of a separation between architect and builder; financial success was dependent on the ability to design, supply materials, provide craftsmen, and supervise construction. When James Wyatt's own practice was established, he frequently provided complete construction, even though it created difficult burdens, given the number of his commissions. Second, the Wyatts regarded architecture pragmatically, based partly on precedent and theory, but also on use. Third, good architecture and the new industrialism were seen as perfectly compatible. Throughout his career, James Wyatt experimented with new building techniques and materials, including the largely cast-iron internal construction of Kew Palace, Surrey (1800–1811), built for George III.

Family connections led to unusual opportunities for the young James Wyatt. As the promising son of Benjamin Wyatt, he evidently caught the attention of the Bagots of Blithfield, Staffordshire. Although there is no documentary evidence, it is assumed that James Wyatt traveled to Italy in 1762 in the company of Richard Bagot, secretary to Lord Northampton. He stayed in Italy for six years, measuring the buildings of antiquity in Rome and studying for two years in Venice with the aged Venetian architect Antonio Visentini. Visentini was a leading exponent of Venetian architectural conservatism, loyal to ANDREA PALLADIO, but tempering his style with graceful ornamentation. Wyatt's training with him thus reinforced his native English Palladianism; his experience of Rome familiarized Wyatt with the archeological motifs then coming into fashion.

Wyatt returned from Italy in 1768. During the next six years, he undertook independent commissions at the same time that he made designs for execution by the family firm, notably for Beaudesert (1771–1772) and the Burton Town Hall (1771–1773), both in Staffordshire. His family was also, in part, responsible for his most visible early commission, the Pantheon assembly rooms, London (1769–1772). His brother John was one of the shareholders, and his innovative architect brother SAMUEL WYATT made James's design for

the vast dome a technical possibility by devising its elaborate carpentry support. The Pantheon assembly rooms demonstrated the twenty-six-year-old Wyatt's determination to be an architect of technical daring in its dome and an architect of fashion in his extensive references to archeological sources and to the work of ROBERT ADAM. The dome was based on that of the Pantheon in Rome and the neoclassical abundance of columnar screens in the lower levels suggested the Hagia Sophia as a possible source. The plan reflected the work of Robert Adam in its sequence of intricately shaped rooms, and the interior was overlaid with delicate Adamesque decoration. The Pantheon made Wyatt's name, but its obvious dependence on Adam meant that Wyatt never repeated its style.

After the Pantheon, worldly success came rapidly to Wyatt. He became immediately an associate of the Royal Academy, a full member of the academy in 1785, and, briefly and somnolently, its president in 1805. His association with the family firm was over by 1774 when he took up residence in Newman Street, London. Wyatt undertook more than three hundred commissions during the next forty years, many more than he was able to handle efficiently. He gave his careful attention only to those whose nature or patron caught his interest. Despite the formidable chaos of his private practice, Wyatt received several official posts, beginning with his 1776 appointment as surveyor of Westminster Abbey. He became the favored architect of George III and Queen Charlotte and, in 1796, succeeded Sir WILLIAM CHAMBERS as surveyor-general and comptroller of the Office of Works. Although Wyatt continued to work assiduously on private commissions for the king and queen, the Office of Works and its many projects suffered. This was partly because no major commissions came to Wyatt through the office and its concerns rarely rose above the mundane. Investigations began in 1806; the full story of financial mismanagement and inattention to duty was told after Wyatt's death in 1813. The situation was so dire that the Office of Works was completely reformed the following year.

There is no clear line of development in Wyatt's work in either classical or medieval styles, although certain patterns can be noted. He introduced new styles throughout his career, but rarely with the intention of replacing the old. Rather, each style was added to his expanding repertory. Wyatt's earliest country house commission, Gaddesden Place, Hertfordshire (1768–1774), looks as if the architect had never left England. It incorporated the entire neo-Palladian vocabulary of a villa plan with central stair, a high base, and the main block connected by quadrant corridors to tripartite, pedimented wings. His next major country house, Heaton Hall, Lancashire (1772), was a major revision. The massive central focus and height of Palladianism were gone in favor of smaller units of strongly contrasted geometric shapes. Wyatt was seeking new neoclassical compositional principles of distinctly separated and more equalized parts.

Wyatt's classical works of the 1770s had increasingly rigid, sharply differentiated compositional units, complicated visually by the Adam heritage of niches, Palladian windows, relieving arches, inset reliefs, and sculpture. The Radcliffe Observatory, Oxford (1776–1794), has disparate geometric shapes, with part cut from part by shifts in scale and incisive string courses. In his country houses, Wyatt often avoided any graceful bridge between architecture and nature. At Bryanston, Dorset (1778–1780), C. R. COCKERELL found the result horrifying, writing in his diary (1824) that "it rises like a great box dropt upon the ground. I think Wyatt was the first who moulded these boxes." Indeed, even the façades were equally developed; no one part dominated, as in the Palladian formula.

Throughout this period, one of the busiest aspects of Wyatt's practice was the provision of designs for interior decorations and for furniture. He also designed objects in silver for production as a luxury line of Matthew Boulton's Soho Manufactory. Wyatt's interior designs remained based on those of Adam and were barely distinguishable from designs by several other architects who pared down the Adam style during the 1770s. Samuel Wyatt, THOMAS LEVERTON, JOHN JOHNSON, and GEORGE STEUART all did similar work, but with varying influences from Greek archeology or French neoclassicism. Wyatt was the architect of fashion, however, and his work was wildly popular.

After 1780, Wyatt's classical buildings had no consistent style. The starkly geometric Mausoleum at Cobham, Kent (1783–1784), directly preceded the richly decorated Brocklesby Mausoleum, Lincolnshire (1787–1794), and the highly Palladian Oriel College Library, Oxford (1787–1794). By the 1790s, Wyatt more frequently used sternly Greek forms, notably in the stout Paestum Doric colonnade of Stoke Park, Buckinghamshire (1795–1797). In other works of this time, he moved toward a simpler style, foregoing the earlier pictorialism of nonfunctional columns and sculptural detail in favor of flat surfaces and monumental cubic shapes, as at Castle Coole, Ireland (1790–1797), and Goodwood House, Sussex (1787–1806). The same ordering, reticence, and geometrical control are evident in his interior decorations of the

1790s. However, by the turn of the century, Wyatt was again seeking richness and variety. Dodington Park, Gloucestershire (1796–1813), was a summation of his compositional ideals, with its disparate façades and blocky shapes. But details were now richly decorated and Roman in their sympathies, suggesting a new robust classicism which became the norm for the next generation.

Although Wyatt designed most frequently in the classical mode, Gothic buildings constitute about one-fifth of his production. In fact, in his commissions between 1800 and 1813, Gothic country houses slightly outnumber classical houses. As early as 1771–1772, Wyatt created Gothic interior decorations for Beaudesert, Staffordshire. By 1775, he made substantial Gothic additions to Sheffield Park, Sussex, and in 1783, he began his first complete Gothic house, Lee Priory, Kent. The Gothic interiors of the 1770s and 1780s are small in scale and linear, linking them with the Gothic of Strawberry Hill and with Wyatt's contemporary neoclassical decoration. The connection is made explicit in the entrance hall of Heveningham Hall, Suffolk (c.1780–1784), where Wyatt merged Gothic fan vaults with neoclassical detail. Later Gothic commissions show a steady increase in size and in the muscularity of motifs both inside and out, culminating in Fonthill Abbey, Wiltshire (1796–1813), and Ashridge Park, Herfordshire (1808–1813). In both houses, medieval archeology, monumental scale, and picturesque massing are combined for maximum effect.

Wyatt and his patron, the flamboyant aesthete William Beckford, galvanized interest in the Gothic through the design and construction of Fonthill Abbey. Built in well-publicized secrecy, Fonthill emulated the scale and scenic impact of a real medieval abbey, with a tower 225-feet tall. Frequent shifts in the design meant that the construction was slipshod and the materials employed included ephemeral wood and composition cement. Fonthill's collapse in 1825 added to its romantic reputation and saved the abbey from the exacting eyes of the Victorians, who would have faulted its many inaccurate details and its sham structure.

Over his lifetime, James Wyatt designed in a variety of medieval styles. The earlier country houses were primarily adaptations of Early English Gothic, a style Wyatt continued to use for small churches and for situations where it was demanded by the patron. Such was the case at Fonthill, where Beckford wanted the association of a thirteenth-century abbey. Later country houses were more typically castellated, as at Norris Castle (1799), Belvoir Castle (1799–1813), Pennsylvania Castle (1800), and Kew Palace (1800–1811). Their rich massing and boldly austere forms left their impact

Wyatt.
Dodington Park.
Gloucestershire, England.
1796–1813

Wyatt.
Heveningham Hall
(interior, orangery, and
lodges).
Suffolk, England.
c.1780–1784

Wyatt.
Kew Palace.
Surrey, England.
1800–1811

on architects of the next two decades, particularly Sir ROBERT SMIRKE. Finally, Wyatt recognized the nationalist potential of the Tudor style, using it for the new House of Lords at Westminster Palace, London (1800–1808), and at Ashridge Park, where the elevation is based on the Elizabethan Wollaton House.

Wyatt's reputation as an expert in the Gothic style led to commissions in the 1780s and 1790s to restore four of England's most famous cathedrals: Hereford (1786–1796), Salisbury (1787–1792), Lichfield (1787–1793), and Durham (1795–1805). He approached the work with an attitude typical of his time and training. Wyatt wanted greater consistency and order than was present in the mix of styles of most medieval cathedrals. Like MARC ANTOINE LAUGIER in France, he sought to improve and augment the dominant style of each cathedral. Wyatt regarded the Early English style of the thirteenth century as an ideal and determined to remove many works of earlier and later periods, meeting with the frequent protests of antiquarians. In some instances, Wyatt was allowed to carry out his controversial plans. He succeeded, for example, in creating the grassy, leveled close of Salisbury Cathedral by removing all its gravestones. However, opposition to his proposal to demolish the

Galilee Chapel of Durham Cathedral was sufficient to prevent the action—and to delay Wyatt's election to the Society of Antiquaries in 1797. A generation later in 1841, A. W. N. PUGIN labeled him "James Wyatt the destructive" and the epithet "The Destroyer" has stuck until present time. Nevertheless, Wyatt gave timely aid to his country's cathedrals and saved them from potential structural ruin. Much of his work, in turn, has been obliterated by the pervasive restorations of the mid-nineteenth century.

James Wyatt died in a coach accident in 1813. He left the heritage of his buildings, but little else. Wyatt had many pupils, the most important being members of his own family, particularly his nephews LEWIS W. WYATT and JEFFRY WYATVILLE, and his son, BENJAMIN WYATT. Although he lived well, James Wyatt's fame was not matched by a fortune. After his death, his house was seized for debts and his wife was forced to make repeated pleas to government officials for a pension. Wyatt clearly lacked the business acumen that had made the provincial firm of Benjamin Wyatt and Sons a financial success. However, he more than achieved the fame and professional stature envisioned by his early Midlands patrons. The prodigious heterogeneity of James Wyatt's work met the needs of his own time and led directly to the eclectic attitudes of the early Victorian period.

FRANCES D. FERGUSSON

WORKS

1768–1774, Gaddesden Place, Hertfordshire, England. *1769–1772, The Pantheon, London. *1771–1772, Beaudesert (remodeling); *1771–1773, Town Hall, Burton; Staffordshire, England. 1772, Heaton Hall, Lancashire, England. c.1775–c.1787, Sheffield Park, Sussex, England. 1776–1794, Radcliffe Observatory, Ox-

ford. *1778–1780, Bryanston House, Dorset, England. c.1780–1784, Heveningham Hall (interior, orangery, and lodges), Suffolk, England. c.1783–1784, Mausoleum, Cobham; *c.1783–1790, Lee Priory; Kent, England. 1786–1796, Hereford Cathedral (restoration), England. 1787–1792, Salisbury Cathedral (restoration), Wiltshire, England. 1787–1793, Lichfield Cathedral (restoration), England. 1787–1794, Library, Oriel College, Oxford. 1787–1794, Mausoleum, Brocklesby Park, Lincolnshire, England. 1787–1806, Goodwood House, Sussex, England. 1790–1797, Castle Coole, County Fermanagh, Ireland. 1795–1797, Doric Colonnade, Stoke Park, Buckinghamshire, England. 1795–1805, Durham Cathedral (restoration), England. 1796–1813, Dodington Park, Gloucestershire, England. *1796–1813, Fonthill Abbey, Wiltshire, England. 1799, Norris Castle, Isle of Wight, England. 1799–1813, Belvoir Castle, Leicestershire, England. 1800, Pennsylvania Castle, Portland, England. 1800–1808, House of Lords, Westminster Palace, London. *1800–1811, Kew Palace, Surrey, England. 1800–1813, Royal Apartments (remodeling), Windsor Castle, Berkshire, England. 1808–1813, Ashridge Park, Hertfordshire, England. 1813, Chicksands Priory, Bedfordshire, England.

BIBLIOGRAPHY

CROOK, J. MORDAUNT, and PORT, MICHAEL 1972 Volume 6 in *The History of the King's Works.* London: H. M. Stationery Office.
DALE, ANTONY (1936)1956 *James Wyatt.* Rev. ed. Oxford: Blackwell.
DALE, ANTONY 1948 "James Wyatt and His Sons." *Architect and Building News* 193:294–296.
EASTLAKE, CHARLES (1872)1970 *A History of the Gothic Revival.* Edited by J. Mordaunt Crook. England: Leicester University Press.
ELMES, JAMES 1847 "History of Architecture in Great Britain." *Civil Engineer and Architect's Journal* 10:166–170, 209–210, 234–238, 268–271, 300–302, 337–341, 378–383.
FARRINGTON, JOSEPH (1923–1928)1978–1979 *The Diary of Joseph Farrington.* Edited by Kenneth Garlick and Angus Macintyre. 6 vols. New Haven: Yale University Press.
FERGUSSON, FRANCES 1973 "The Neo-classical Architecture of James Wyatt." Unpublished Ph.D. dissertation, Harvard University, Cambridge, Mass.
FERGUSSON, FRANCES 1977 "James Wyatt and John Penn, Architect and Patron at Stoke Park, Buckinghamshire." *Architectural History* 20:45–55.
FREW, JOHN M. 1979 "Richard Gough, James Wyatt, and Late 18th-century Preservation." *Journal of the Society of Architectural Historians* 38:366–374.
HARRIS, JOHN 1971 "C. R. Cockerell's 'Ichnographica Domestica.'" *Architectural History* 14:5–29.
HUNT, THOMAS FREDERICK 1827 "James Wyatt." Pages 13–17 in *Architettura Campestre.* London: Longmans.
"James Wyatt." 1813 *Universal Magazine* 20:342–343.
PUGIN A. W. N. (1841)1973 *True Principles of Pointed or Christian Architecture.* Reprint. New York: Saint Martins.
ROBINSON, JOHN MARTIN 1979 Pages 56–89 in *The Wyatts: An Architectural Dynasty.* London: Oxford University Press.
"Short Memoirs of the Life of James Wyatt, Esq." 1813 *Gentleman's Magazine* 83:296–297.
SUMMERSON, JOHN 1959 "The Classical Country House in 18th-century England." *Journal of the Royal Society of Arts* 107:539–587.
TURNOR, REGINALD 1950 *James Wyatt, 1746–1813.* London: Art and Technics.
WATKIN, DAVID 1968 *Thomas Hope, 1769–1831, and the Neo-Classical Idea.* London: Murray.

WYATT, LEWIS

Lewis William Wyatt (1777–1853) was the son of Benjamin Wyatt, agent to Lord Penryhn at Penryhn Castle in North Wales. He trained as an architect in the offices of his uncles, JAMES WYATT and SAMUEL WYATT. He branched out on his own in 1806 establishing an office in Albany, London.

Lewis Wyatt made his reputation as a designer of country houses. His finest work is Willey Park, Shropshire (1813–1815), with a central, atriumlike hall with scagliola Corinthian columns.

JOHN MARTIN ROBINSON

WORKS

1806–1824, Heaton Hall, Lancashire, England. 1807–1821, Hackwood Park, Hampshire, England. 1808–1810, Wonham Manor, Surrey, England. 1809, Mount Shannon, County Limerick, Ireland. 1810–1812, Rode Hall, Cheshire, England. 1812, Stoke Hall, Nottinghamshire, England. 1813–1815, Willey Park, Shropshire, England. 1813–1817, Stockport Parish Church; 1814–1817, Lyme Park; Cheshire, England. 1815, Cuerden Hall, Lancashire, England. 1816–1826, Oulton Park, Cheshire, England. 1818–1819, Radcliffe Chapel; 1818–1819, Winstanley Hall; Lancashire, England. 1822–1823, 12–17 Suffolk Street, London. 1823–1824, Bolton Hall, Yorkshire, England. 1828–1829, Cranage Hall, Cheshire, England. 1828–1829, Flintham Hall, Nottinghamshire, England. 1829, Eaton-by-Congleton Hall, Cheshire, England. 1829–1834, Sherborne House, Gloucestershire, England. 1832–1834, Hawkstone Hall, Shropshire, England.

BIBLIOGRAPHY

"Obituary of Lewis William Wyatt." 1853 *Gentleman's Magazine* 34:670.
ROBINSON, J. M. 1979 *The Wyatts: An Architectural Dynasty.* London: Oxford University Press.

WYATT, SAMUEL

Samuel Wyatt (1737–1807), the older brother of the more celebrated architect JAMES WYATT, in 1760 obtained a post as a carpenter at Kedleston,

Derbyshire, then being rebuilt by Nathaniel Curzon to the design of ROBERT ADAM, who soon promoted him to clerk of works. The experience he gained there was crucial to his artistic development and enabled him to become a fashionable neoclassicist in his own right. Wyatt specialized in small country houses in an elegant Adam-inspired manner, notable for their ingenious geometrical plans and idiosyncratic use of dome bows.

His most important achievement was the Albion Mill at Blackfriars, London (1783–1784), a project which grew out of his friendship with MATTHEW BOULTON AND JAMES WATT, the pioneer manufacturers of steam engines. The Albion Mill was the first building designed specifically to incorporate rotative steam engines and was an ingenious piece of construction supported on a floating foundation of shallow brick vaults.

JOHN MARTIN ROBINSON

WORKS

1776–1779, Baron Hill, Anglesey, Wales. 1777, Herstmonceux Place, Sussex, England. 1777–1798, Doddington Hall, Cheshire, England. 1777–1801, Thorndon Hall, Essex, England. 1778–1788, Hooton Hall, Cheshire, England. 1780–1782, Theatre Royal, Birmingham, England. 1780–1807, Holkham (farm buildings), Norfolk, England. 1782–1785, Penrhyn Castle, Caernarvonshire, Wales. 1783–1784, Albion Mill, Blackfriars, London. 1784, Delamere Lodge, Cheshire, England. 1785, Coton House, Warwickshire, England. 1785–1791, Tatton Park, Cheshire, England. 1787–1790, 6 Upper Brook Street, London. 1787–1792, Belmont Park, Kent, England. 1790–1796, Culford Hall, Suffolk, England. 1790–1806, Shugborough, Staffordshire, England. 1790–1810, Kinmel Park, Denbighshire, Wales. 1791–1794, 15 Saint James's Square, London. 1792, Dungeness Lighthouse, Kent, England. 1792–1794, Dropmore, Buckinghamshire, England. 1792–1795, Somerley, Hampshire, England. 1792–1796, Trinity House; 1794–1796, 4 Cleveland Row; London. 1794–1805, Ramsgate Harbour, England. 1800–1805, Sundridge Park, Kent, England. 1801–1806, 40 Grosvenor Square, London. 1803, Hurts Hall, Suffolk, England. 1806, Flamborough Head Lighthouse, England. 1806, Trinity Almshouses, London. 1806–1807, Panshanger, Hertfordshire, England. 1807, Digswell House, Hampshire, England.

BIBLIOGRAPHY

ROBINSON, JOHN MARTIN 1973a "A Great Architectural Family." *Country Life* 13:2098–2101.
ROBINSON, JOHN MARTIN 1973b "Samuel Wyatt Architect." Unpublished Ph.D. dissertation, Oxford University.
ROBINSON, JOHN MARTIN 1979 *The Wyatts: An Architectural Dynasty.* London: Oxford University Press.
SKEMPTON, A. W. 1971–1972 "Early Members of the Smeatonian Society of Civil Engineers." *Transactions of the Newcomen Society* 44:23–47.

WYATT, THOMAS HENRY, and WYATT, MATTHEW DIGBY

Thomas Henry Wyatt (1807–1880) and Matthew Digby Wyatt (1820–1877), sons of Matthew Wyatt, an Irish lawyer and land agent, had extensive practices in London. Thomas Henry trained in PHILIP HARDWICK's office, and from 1838 to 1851 he was in partnership with DAVID BRANDON, though he was personally responsible for Saint Mary and Saint Nicholas, Wilton, Wiltshire (1840–1845). Thomas Henry's output was second only to that of GEORGE GILBERT SCOTT in quantity, and he had a large country house practice, mainly Tudor in style. Matthew Digby entered from 1844 to 1846. He became preoccupied with historic styles of architecture and decoration, writing several books. He was involved in the construction of JOSEPH PAXTON's Great Exhibition building (1851) and its subsequent reerection at Sydenham; and he collaborated with ISAMBERT KINGSOM BRUNEL at Paddington Station, London (1850–1855), and with George Gilbert Scott on the India Office, London (1868). Thomas Henry was president of the Royal Institute of British Architects from 1870 to 1873, and both received the Gold Medal.

DEREK LINSTRUM

WORKS

THOMAS HENRY WYATT

1835, Assize Court, Devizes; 1840–1845, Saint Mary and Saint Nicholas, Wilton; Wiltshire, England. 1841, Saint Andrew (with David Brandon), London. 1847, Fonthill House (with Brandon), Wiltshire, England. 1849, Saint Mary (with Brandon), Atherstone, Warwickshire, England. 1851, Roundway Hospital (with Brandon), Devizes, Wiltshire, England. 1854–1856, Saint Aidan's Theological College (with HENRY COLE), Birkenhead, England. 1858, Adelphi Theatre, London. 1862–1863, Garrison Church of Saint George (with Matthew Digby Wyatt), Woolwich, England. 1863–1867, Exchange Buildings, Liverpool, England. 1866, Holy Trinity, Fonthill Gifford, Wiltshire, England. 1868, Saint Lawrence, Weston Patrick, Hampshire, England. 1872–1874, Saint Peter, Wimblington, Cambridgeshire, England. 1877, Holy Cross, Whorlton-in-Cleveland, Yorkshire, England. 1878–1879, Knightsbridge Barracks; 1879–1882, Brompton Hospital; London.

MATTHEW DIGBY WYATT

1846–1850, Aldingham Hall, Lancashire, England. 1850–1855, Paddington Station (with Isambard K. Brunel and OWEN JONES), London. 1857–1862, East India Company Barracks Chapel, Little Warley, Essex, England. 1862–1863, Garrison Church of Saint George (with Thomas Henry Wyatt), Woolwich, England.

1863, Addenbroke's Hospital, Cambridge. 1865–1868, Temple Meads Station, Bristol, England. 1866, Rothschild Mausoleum, West Ham, Essex, England. 1866–1868, Possingworth Manor, Sussex, England. 1868, India Office (with George Gilbert Scott), London. 1869, Old Lands, near Uckfield, Sussex, England.

WYATVILLE, JEFFRY

Jeffry Wyatt (1766–1840), second son of Joseph, mason and architect of Burton-on-Trent, Staffordshire, became a pupil and assistant of his uncles in London, first SAMUEL WYATT and then JAMES WYATT. He then set up in practice in Brook Street, London, on his own account and also entered into partnership with John Armstrong, a carpentry contractor. Most of Wyatt's work, for which he often acted also as contractor and/or supplier, consisted of improvements to country houses, and he built up an impressive list of titled patrons. He designed large additions and alterations to Chatsworth House, Derbyshire (1818–1841), a skillful pastiche in early eighteenth-century classical style with fine neoclassical interiors. He was appointed architect by George IV (who authorized the change of surname to Wyatville in that year and knighted him in 1828) for the restoration and remodeling of Windsor Castle (1824–1840). The present familiar appearance of the building and its romantic silhouette are the result of this commission, which was executed with the thoroughness and professional integrity that distinguished all Wyatville's work. He provided rich interiors for the private apartments while making the necessary alterations to turn the historic but inconvenient castle into a comfortable early nineteenth-century royal palace. In his work, his aim was "to restore in the character of the place he improved," and he disclaimed "any vain notions of destroying the existing parts merely for the purpose of shewing a presumed ability to make better, but in such few changes as are to be made to have in view the original character of its construction." Although his country house designs never achieved the virtuosity of the best of his uncles' Wyatville modeled his styles on those he had learned in their offices. He also added to his repertoire relatively pioneering essays in Elizabethan (Longleat, Wiltshire [1806–1813]; Wollaton, Nottinghamshire [1801–1823]), Tudor (Banner Cross, Yorkshire [1817–1821]; Golden Grove, Carmarthen [1826–1837]; Lilleshall, Shropshire [1826–1830]), and *cottage orné* styles (Endsleigh, Devon [1810–1816?]).

DEREK LINSTRUM

WORKS

c.1799, Woolley Park, Berkshire, England. c.1801–1823, Wollaton Hall, Nottinghamshire, England. 1802–1806, Nonsuch Park, Surrey, England. 1806–1807, Hyde Hall, Hertfordshire, England. 1806–1813, Longleat House, Wiltshire, England. 1810–1816?, Endsleigh, Devon, England. c.1814–1817, Ashridge Park, Hertfordshire, England. 1814–1817, Dinton House, Wiltshire, England. c.1815, Bretton Hall; 1817–1821, Banner Cross; Yorkshire, England. 1818–1841, Chatsworth House (additions and alterations), Derbyshire, England. 1824–1840, Windsor Castle (restoration and remodeling), Berkshire, England. 1826–1830, Lilleshall Hall, Shropshire, England. 1826–1837, Golden Grove, Carmarthen, Wales. 1828–1829, Fort Belvedere, Berkshire, England.

BIBLIOGRAPHY

LINSTRUM, DEREK 1972 *Sir Jeffry Wyatville: Architect to the King.* Oxford: Clarendon Press.
ROBINSON, JOHN MARTIN 1979 *The Wyatts: An Architectural Dynasty.* Oxford University Press.

WYETH, MARION SIMS

Marion Sims Wyeth (1889–1982) was born in New York City to a family of distinguished physicians. After receiving his B.A. degree at Princeton University in 1910, he entered the Ecole des Beaux-Arts in Paris, where he studied in the HENRI DEGLANE atelier (1910–1914).

Wyeth worked briefly for BERTRAM G. GOODHUE (1915) and for CARRÈRE AND HASTINGS (1916–1917). In 1919, responding to the Florida building boom, Wyeth established his own office in Palm Beach. He and other men his age, such as MAURICE FATIO, constituted a second generation of architects who developed the Spanish idiom introduced by ADDISON MIZNER. In 1932, Wyeth formed a partnership with Frederick Rhinelander King, with whom he opened a New York office; William Johnson became a partner in 1946. Wyeth retired in 1973. Wyeth's private homes designed in a number of fancifully eclectic styles almost always delighted his well-to-do and socially prominent clientèle.

VICTORIA NEWHOUSE

WORKS

1920, Mar-A-Lago (plan and interior courtyard); 1925, James F. Donahue House; Palm Beach, Fla. 1940, Church of the Epiphany (with Eugene W. Mason); New York. 1947, Governor's Mansion, Tallahassee, Fla.

BIBLIOGRAPHY

HAMLIN, TALBOT F. 1940 "Three Churches." *Pencil Points* 21:72–91.
HOFFSTOT, BARBARA D. (1974)1980 *Landmark Architecture of Palm Beach.* Rev. ed. Pittsburgh: Ober Park Associates.
NEWCOMB, REXFORD 1928 *Mediterranean Domestic Architecture in the U.S.* Cleveland, Ohio: Jansen.

YAMASAKI, MINORU

Minoru Yamasaki (1912–) is considered one of the United States' most successful and controversial contemporary architects. His success can be measured by the number of important commissions and awards that he has received, coupled with his dedication to a humanistic approach to architectural design, always sensitive to such fundamental human characteristics as serenity, beauty, love, and hope. He creates environments that strive to provide meaning to existence. He is considered controversial by those who find his work decorative and merely ornamental, self-indulgent forms. This criticism is generated primarily by his early work which was influenced by international travel and confrontation with historical buildings. Although Gothic reference is still prevalent in his work, his later work is less decorative and combines his respect for tradition and history, human need, and modern technology.

Born in Seattle, Washington, of Japanese parents, Yamasaki decided to pursue architecture as a career at an early age. He rose above his childhood of tenements and prejudice and completed architecture school in 1934 at the University of Washington by working summers in fish canneries in Alaska. After graduation, Yamasaki moved to New York and worked as a designer and draftsman for the firms of SHREVE, LAMB, AND HARMON; HARRISON AND ABRAMOVITZ; and Raymond Loewy Associates. In 1945, he was hired as chief architectural designer for Smith, Hirschman, and Grylls in Detroit, Michigan, leaving them in 1949 to form his first partnership with George Hellmuth and Joseph Leinweber. One of their first major commissions, the Lambert-St. Louis Airport (1956) won several awards and established their international reputation. In 1955, Hellmuth withdrew and the partnership continued as Yamasaki, Leinweber, and Associates until 1959. The present firm of Minoru Yamasaki and Associates is still in practice in Troy, Michigan.

Yamasaki has designed many important buildings but will perhaps be remembered most for his revival of interest in the skyscraper with his design for the World Trade Center (1962–1976), New York, and for his sincere philosophy of humanistic architecture.

JO ANNE PASCHALL

WORKS

1951–1956, Terminal Building, Lambert Airport, St. Louis, Mo. 1955–1958, McGregor Memorial Community Conference Center, Wayne State University, Detroit, Mich. 1955–1959, Reynolds Metals Regional Sales Office, Southfield, Mich. 1959, United States Pavilion, World Agricultural Fair, New Delhi. 1959–1961,

Dhahran Air Terminal, Dhahran, Saudi Arabia. 1959–1962, Federal Science Pavilion, Seattle World's Fair, Seattle, Wash. 1961–1964, Northwestern National Life Insurance Company, Minneapolis, Minn. 1961–1966, Century Plaza Hotel, Century City, Los Angeles. 1962–1976, World Trade Center, New York. 1968–1974, Temple Beth-El, Bloomfield Township, Mich. 1968–1975, Century Plaza Towers, Century City, Los Angeles. 1973–1976, Performing Arts Center, Tulsa, Okla. 1973–1982, Saudi Arabian Monetary Agency Head Office, Riyadh, Saudi Arabia. 1978–1983, Founders Hall, Shinji Shumeikai, Shiga Prefecture, Japan.

BIBLIOGRAPHY

"A Conversation with Minoru Yamasaki." 1959 *Architectural Forum* 111:110–118.

HEYER, PAUL (1966)1978 *Architects on Architecture: New Directions in America.* Enl. ed. New York: Walker.

HUXTABLE, ADA LOUISE 1962 "Minoru Yamasaki's Recent Buildings." *Art in America* 50, no. 4:48–55.

"Six New Projects by Yamasaki." 1961 *Architectural Record* 130:125–140.

VERONESI, GIULIA 1961 "Minoru Yamasaki and Edward D. Stone." *Zodiac* 8:128–131.

YAMASAKI, MINORU 1979 *A Life in Architecture.* New York: Weatherhill.

YEON, JOHN B.

John Yeon (1910–), born in Portland, Oregon, is largely self-trained. His first projects, c.1933, include designs for a lodge on Mount Hood and the coast highway at Neahkahnie Mountain. His design for the Watzek House (1937), Portland, was the first to integrate local forms and materials with the spatial quality of the International style. Here and in other designs his handling of the landscape is as important as the architecture. In the late 1930s he introduced the use of standard plywood panels for exterior siding, a material also used in the Visitors Information Center, Portland, 1948. Later work includes the installation of important art collections in Portland, San Francisco, and Kansas City.

MARION DEAN ROSS

WORKS

1937, Aubrey Watzek House; 1939, Victor Jorgensen House; Portland, Ore. 1941, Vietor House, Arcata, Calif. 1948, Visitors Information Center (with Clarence H. Wick, Albert W. Hilgers, and Gerald G. Scott); 1949, E. W. Van Buren House; 1950, Lawrence Shaw House; 1950, Kenneth Swan House; Portland, Ore. 1963, Nelson Gallery–Atkins Museum (galleries); 1976, Nelson Gallery–Atkins Museum (galleries); Kansas City, Mo.

BIBLIOGRAPHY

HITCHCOCK, H. R., and DREXLER, ARTHUR (editors)
1952 *Built in USA: Post-War Architecture.* New York: Museum of Modern Art.

John Yeon: Buildings and Landscapes. 1977 Oregon: Portland Art Museum. Exhibition catalogue.

MOCK, ELIZABETH (editor) 1945 *Built in USA since 1932.* New York: Museum of Modern Art.

VAUGHAN, THOMAS, and FERRIDAY, VIRGINIA (editors) 1974 *Space, Style and Structure.* 2 vols. Portland: Oregon Historical Society.

YORK and SAWYER

Edward Palmer York (1865–1927) was born in Wellsville, New York, and studied architecture from 1887 to 1889 at Cornell University, leaving to enter the firm of McKIM, MEAD, AND WHITE. Philip Sawyer (1868–1949) was born in New London, Connecticut, obtained a knowledge of engineering with the U.S. Geological Survey in New Mexico, and entered McKim, Mead, and White in 1891. He left the firm for a brief stay at Columbia College and then proceeded to the Ecole des Beaux-Arts in Paris, enrolling in the atelier of Redon. On his return to New York, he re-entered McKim, Mead, and White. In 1898, the two men left to form a partnership on obtaining their first commission, a building for Vassar College. The most outstanding of the later partners was LOUIS AYRES, who also joined McKim, Mead, and White in 1899 and was made a partner in 1910.

York and Sawyer was among the more prominent firms in New York in the American Renaissance, the firm tending to specialize in banks, colleges, and hospitals. York handled the business end, and design fell to Sawyer in large part and to Ayres and several other partners. The work was largely classical, a mixture of ancient Roman and Italian Renaissance. Sawyer was a master of rustication as can be seen in the Federal Reserve Bank of New York (1924) and the Central Savings Bank (1928), also in New York. The firm had an unusual grasp of the monumental and achieving a striking visual effect that became the firm's trademark. Sawyer was particularly fond of the Tuscan arch, but they also handled the Georgian Colonial beautifully, the best example being Louis Ayres's Brick Presbyterian Church (1938) in New York.

Outside their regular practice, members of the firm served as consultants to the Board of Water Supply of the City of New York from 1907 to 1913 and in 1931 and they left their imprint on dams and watergate buildings. While consultant to the United States Treasury from 1909 to 1913, the firm won the competition for the Department of Commerce Building in 1913; a variation of the design was being built in 1932 for the Department. Equally important, the firm was represented by Louis Ayres on the board that advised the Secretary of the Treasury on the planning and construction of the Federal Triangle, the most elaborate complex of federal buildings in Washington. The firm's Commerce Building design of 1913 set the height of the complex and mandated the use of tile roofing.

HENRY HOPE REED

WORKS

1898–1928, Vassar College, Poughkeepsie, N.Y. 1899, Franklin Savings Bank, New York. 1900–1928, Middlebury College, Vt. 1903, New-York Historical Society. 1904 and 1931, American Security and Trust Company, Washington. 1905, Corning Hospital, N.Y. 1908–1948, Rutgers University Buildings, New Brunswick, N.J. 1911, Hospital for Special Surgery and Guaranty Trust Company; 1913, 14 East 71 Street; New York. 1914, Brooklyn Trust Company (now Manufacturers Hanover), Montague Street, N.Y. 1914, Mountainside Hospital, Glen Ridge, N.J. 1915, Rhode Island Hospital Trust Company, Providence. 1918, United States Assay Office, New York. 1920, Saint Paul's Hospital, Manila, Philippine Islands. 1921, First National Bank of Boston. 1921, Flower Fifth Avenue Hospital, New York. 1921, Lancaster Trust Company, Pa. 1922, Greenwich Savings Bank, New York. 1922, Washington Trust Company, Westerly, R.I. 1923, Bowery Savings Bank, 42 Street, New York. 1922–1923, Law Quadrangle, University of Michigan, Ann Arbor. 1924, Federal Reserve Bank of New York. 1925, Children's Hospital, Pittsburgh. 1926, New York Academy of Medicine. 1927, 660 Park Avenue; 1927, Salmon Tower, 11 East 42 Street; New York. 1927, Wilmington General Hospital, Del. 1928, Royal Bank of Canada, Montreal. 1928, Central Savings Bank; 1929, Lenox Hill Hospital Main Building; New York. 1929, New York Athletic Club. 1932, World War I Memorial Chapel, Meuse-Argonne, France. 1935, Allegheny General Hospital, Pittsburgh. 1936, Einhorn Memorial Building, Lenox Hill Hospital; 1938, Brick Presbyterian Church; New York.

BIBLIOGRAPHY

Office of York and Sawyer Architects. 1948 New York.
SAWYER, PHILIP 1951 *Edward Palmer York.* With a biographical sketch by Royal Cortissoz. Stonington, Conn.: Privately printed.

YORKE, FRANCIS

Francis Reginald Stevens Yorke (1906–1962) was trained at the Birmingham University School of Architecture, England, where he also studied town planning. He practiced from 1930 onward as one of the few committed Modern architects of the 1930s, and was a partner of the Bauhaus refugee MARCEL BREUER to 1938. Yorke was a founder member of the MARS (Modern Architectural Research) Group in 1932 and worked in reinforced concrete from 1933 when the use of this material

was a testament of true modernism. His exhibition house at the Royal Show, Bristol (1936; with Marcel Breuer), anticipated the style of the 1950s with rough rubble walls. Before the war, Yorke was best known for his books on the modern house and the modern flat, which introduced the purest work of the Continental Modern movement to British readers. His town planning interest is shown in the "Civic Centre of the Future" project with Breuer and in his book, *A Key to Modern Architecture* (1939), written with Colin Penn.

During World War II, Yorke worked on buildings for wartime industries, putting the enforced austerity to good effect. In 1944, he formed a partnership with EUGENE ROSENBERG and C. Mardall (YRM) which became one of the leading offices for public commissions in the 1950s and 1960s. Their work, which includes hospitals, schools, housing, and industrial buildings, was typical of its period, but the Barclay Secondary School, Stevenage, Hertfordshire, and the Sigmund Pumps Factory at Gateshead, Durham, deserve special mention. The firm also demonstrated the role of the architect in coordinating transport services in the planning of Gatwick Airport, where the style was influenced by the constructional purity of LUDWIG MIES VAN DER ROHE. Like BERTHOLD LUBETKIN, Yorke took to farming and specialized in the breeding of Guernsey cattle.

Yorke's contribution to the YRM partnership is difficult to evaluate separately, but he was one of the few pioneers of the 1930s to practice on a large scale after the war. His work with Breuer is disappointing compared to the English work of WALTER GROPIUS or ERIC MENDELSOHN, but he will be remembered as a propagandist of modernism who had a substantial impact on the face of postwar Britain.

ALAN POWERS

WORKS

1936, Exhibition House (with Marcel Breuer), Royal Show; 1936, House (with Breuer), Clifton; Bristol, England. 1936, House, High Street, Iver, Buckinghamshire, England. 1937, Sea Lane House (with Breuer), East Preston, Sussex, England. 1939, Cottages (with F. W. B. Yorke), Stratford upon Avon, England. 1939–1944, Government Depots, Camps, and Factories (with William Holford), England. 1940, Flats (with Arthur Korn), Camberwell, London).

BIBLIOGRAPHY

The Architecture of Yorke, Rosenberg, Mardall. 1972 With an introduction by Reyner Banham. London: Lund Humphries; New York: Crane Russak.
YORKE, FRANCIS REGINALD STEVENS (1934)1951 *The Modern House.* 7th ed., rev. London: Architectural Press.
YORKE, FRANCIS REGINALD STEVENS (1937)1948

The Modern House in England. 3d ed. London: Architectural Press.
YORKE, FRANCIS REGINALD STEVENS (1937)1950 *The Modern Flat.* 3d ed. London: Architectural Press.
YORKE, FRANCIS REGINALD STEVENS 1943 "Modern Architecture in Czechoslovakia." *Review 43* 1, no. 3:104–106.
YORKE, FRANCIS REGINALD STEVENS, and FOWKES, C. ROY 1948 *Flooring Materials.* London: Faber & Faber.
YORKE, FRANCIS REGINALD STEVENS, and PENN, COLIN 1939 *A Key to Modern Architecture.* London: Blackie.
YORKE, FRANCIS REGINALD STEVENS, and WHITING, PENELOPE (1951)1954 *The New Small House.* 2d ed. London: Architectural Press.

YOSHIDA, ISOYA

Born in Tokyo, Japan, Isoya Yoshida (1894–1974) graduated from the Tokyo College of Arts in 1923. He traveled in Europe and the United States in 1925 and after his return to Japan began to work as an architectural designer mainly of houses. He taught in the department of architecture at his alma mater from 1941 to 1961. He was awarded the Japan Arts Academy Award in 1952 for his contribution to the modernization of Japanese architecture.

Yoshida's lifelong project was to adapt the tradition of Japanese architecture to modern architecture. The result of his efforts is the style called modern *sukiya* which has been successfully used for Japanese restaurants, temples, inns, and houses.

TAKASHI HASEGAWA

WORKS

*1936, Kineya Villa, Atami, Shizuoka Prefecture, Japan. *1939, Matsushima Park Hotel, Miyagi Prefecture, Japan. 1940, Shinkiraku Restaurant; 1952, Shinkiraku Restaurant; 1958, Japan Academy of Arts Center; Tokyo. 1960, Yamato-Bunka Hall, Nara, Japan. 1962, Shinkiraku Restaurant, Tokyo. 1968, Naritasan Shinshoji Temple, Narita, Chiba Prefecture, Japan. 1973, Royal Hotel, Osaka, Japan.

BIBLIOGRAPHY

Gendainihon Kenchikuka Zenshu. 1970 Volume 3. Tokyo.
YOSHIDA, ISOYA 1976 *Works.* Tokyo.

Yoshida.
Shinkiraku Restaurant.
Tokyo.
1962

YOSHIDA, TETSURŌ

Born in Fukuno, Toyama Prefecture, Japan, Tetsurō Yoshida (1894–1956) graduated from Tokyo University, after which he started to work for the Building Department, Ministry of Communications, in 1919. His early works show some signs of Expressionism. After he designed the Main Post Office in Tokyo in 1931, he tried to apply the Japanese structural system to a concrete structure, making every post and beam visible. This approach reached its peak in his Main Post Office in Osaka in 1939. It can be said that the Kagawa Prefectural Office which KENZŌ TANGE designed some twenty years later was in the same line.

He loved European architecture and was somehow influenced by AUGUSTE PERRET. He was good in German and helped BRUNO TAUT when he came to Japan in 1933. He wrote several books in German to introduce Japanese architecture and gardens to the German public.

After he retired, Yoshida was appointed a professor of architecture at Nihon University. His book, *Swedish Architects,* was his last work.

SAKA-E OHMI
Translated from Japanese by
Bunji Kobayashi

WORKS

1931, Main Post Office; 1937, Kiyohiko Baba Residence; Tokyo. 1939, Main Post Office, Osaka, Japan.

BIBLIOGRAPHY

YOSHIDA, TETSURŌ 1952 *Japanische Architektur.* Tübingen, Germany: Wasmuth.
YOSHIDA, TETSURŌ 1935(1969) *The Japanese House and Garden.* Rev. ed. New York: Praeger. Originally published in German as *Das Japanische Wohnhaus.*
YOSHIDA, TETSURŌ (1957)1963 *Gardens of Japan.* Translated from the German by M. Sims. New York: Praeger.

YOSHIMURA, JUNZŌ

Born in Tokyo, Japan, Junzō Yoshimura (1908–) was graduated from the Tokyo Art Institute in 1931. While he was a student, he was attracted by the works of ANTONIN RAYMOND and began to work in his office. He worked for Raymond for ten years and opened up his own office in 1941. He evidently learned from his master modern design techniques and acquired an international outlook. He became a professor of architecture at Tokyo College of Arts and now is a professor emeritus. In 1966, he made a preliminary design of the New Imperial Palace in Tokyo. He was awarded a prize from the Japan Art Academy for his Annex to the

Nara National Museum in 1975.

His works always include features of both modern rationalism and traditional architecture. His ingenuity in creating space as well as the exquisite details of his wooden structures have been highly praised.

HIROSHI YAMAGUCHI
Translated from Japanese by
Bunji Kobayashi

WORKS

1955, International House of Japan (with K. Maekawa and J. Sakakura), Tokyo. 1959, Hotel Kowaku-en, Hakone, Kanagawa Prefecture, Japan. 1962, Architect's Summer Lodge, Karuizawa Prefecture, Japan. 1962, National Cash Register, Tokyo. 1971, Japan House, New York. 1973, Nara National Museum (annex), Japan. 1974, Nelson A. Rockefeller House, Pocantico Hills, N.Y. 1965–1974, Aichi Prefecture College of Arts, Nagakute, Japan.

BIBLIOGRAPHY

Collection of Junzō Yoshimura's Works. 1978 Tokyo.

YOSHIZAKA, TAKAMASA

Born in Tokyo and graduated from Waseda University in 1941, Takamasa Yoshizaka (1917–1980) started teaching at Waseda University in 1950. In 1952, he went to Paris to study at the studio of LE CORBUSIER. After his return to Japan, his main concern in his concrete buildings was a peculiar composition of massive blocks. He developed his own theory called *Yūkei-gaku*, or building morphology, which was the result of his College Seminar House (1965). In his last years, he was president of the Institute of Human Living (*Seikatsu-gakkai*).

SAKA-E OHMI

WORKS

*1955, Japanese Pavilion, Venice Bienniale, Italy. 1957, Villa Coucou; 1962, Athénée Français; 1965, College Seminar House, Hachiōji; Tokyo.

BIBLIOGRAPHY

KURITA, ISAMU (editor) 1971 *Yoshizaka*. Volume 15 in *Gendainihon Kenchikuka Zanshū*. Tokyo: Sanichi Shobo.

YOSHIZAKA, TAKAMASA 1961 *Genshi-kyō kara Bunmei-kyō-e*. Tokyo: Sagami Shobo.

YOSHIZAKA, TAKAMASA 1965 *Jūkyo-gaku*. Tokyo: Sagami Shobo.

YOUNG, AMMI B.

Ammi Burnham Young (1798–1874), in a long career, worked to establish the highest standards for design and construction of public buildings in America. He was born in Lebanon, New Hampshire, the son of a carpenter and builder. At the age of fourteen, he took up his father's trade, but by 1830, he was advertising himself as an architect and civil engineer, probably self-taught. He received some instruction from the Boston architect ALEXANDER PARRIS, but probably not before the late 1830s.

Young's earliest work, in a simple Federal style, is in the vicinity of Lebanon. Typical are two brick buildings for Dartmouth, Wentworth and Thornton Halls (1827–1828). In 1830, he opened an office in Burlington, Vermont, and within two years had secured the commission for the State House in Montpelier (1833–1836). The plan was derived from the Massachusetts State House, but the exterior, combining a Greek Doric portico with a low dome, was fully modern. The Vermont Legislature voted their thanks to Young in 1838, and in 1839 the University of Vermont awarded him an honorary M.A. Gutted by fire in 1857, the State House was rebuilt by Thomas W. Silloway, who had studied with Young in 1849–1850.

Most of Young's buildings during the Burlington period are classical in style, but Saint Paul's Episcopal Church (1832, transepts added 1867) is Gothic Revival. Young's earlier style was brought up-to-date for simpler buildings by the addition of pilasters and roof pediments, as seen in several projects, such as Reed Hall at Dartmouth (1839). Young returned to Dartmouth to receive an honorary M.A. degree in 1841 and to design the simple brick Shattuck Observatory (1854) for his brother, Ira Young, professor of astronomy.

Young was selected as architect for a new Customhouse in Boston (1837–1847, tower added 1915) and opened an office there by 1838. Again, he used the domed Greek temple as his theme, but in a more severe style than at Montpelier and with engaged columns encircling the building. The taste for "modern Grecian edifices" was fading even before the building was finished, and in 1844, ARTHUR D. GILMAN published a vicious attack on Young's design. There were many other projects in

Young.
Customhouse and Post Office.
Windsor, Vermont.
1856–1858

the Boston area. Interesting, in view of the criticism of the Customhouse, are the Broomfield Street Methodist Church in Boston (1848–1849) and the Courthouse in Lowell, Massachusetts (1850), both in a Norman style.

Young was named the first supervising architect of the Office of Construction of the Treasury Department in 1852. Alexander H. Bowman, captain and later major, Corps of Engineers, was placed "in Charge of the Office of Construction." With as many as eighty buildings in progress at one time, the successful development of this office was a major accomplishment of these two men. Architectural design for nearly all federal building was now centralized in Washington in Young's hands, giving him the first practice truly national in scope. They pioneered in the use of rolled and cast iron for ornamental and structural purposes beginning in 1852, and they encouraged its use through an extensive series of lithographed construction drawings of their projects.

Most of Young's federal buildings are customhouses, post offices, and federal courts, in variations on Italianate themes. One of the best is the Customhouse and Post Office in Windsor, Vermont (1856–1858), which uses iron for exterior ornament as well as interior structure and ornament. Designs were often repeated. The Customhouse in Wheeling, the Independence Hall of West Virginia (1855–1860), three stories high with round arched windows, is one of at least four identical designs. The Customhouse in Providence, Rhode Island (1855–1857), is typical of a large group, all three stories high with façades five, seven, or nine bays wide. Smaller buildings were usually two-story, often very effective variations of the larger ones, such as the Customhouse and Post Office in Galena, Illinois (1856–1858), and its twin on Thirty-first Street in Washington. Young also designed at least fifteen marine hospitals, which depart little from the model set by ROBERT MILLS in the 1830s and 1840s.

In 1861, Bowman was recalled to active military duty. His successor, Spencer M. Clark, was incompetent as an engineer and probably dishonest as an administrator. Following an investigation, hastily done because of the war, Young's position was temporarily dissolved in 1862. Caught between Clark's activities and the testimony of rival architects, he was judged incompetent. In ill health, he retired. Any scandal was not remembered at the time of Young's death in Washington in 1874. His obituary in the Washington *Evening Star* called him "one of the most faithful and upright of public officers" whose work was "marked by ability and the strictest integrity."

OSMUND OVERBY

WORKS

1817, Congregational Church, Norwich, Vt. 1827–1828, Thornton Hall; 1827–1828, Wentworth Hall; Dartmouth College, Hanover, N.H. 1828, Congregational Church, Lebanon, N.H. 1832, Saint Paul's Episcopal Church, Burlington, Vt. 1833–1836, Vermont State House, Montpelier. 1834–1841, Shaker Great Family Dwelling House, Enfield, N.H. 1837–1847, Customhouse, Boston. 1839, Reed Hall, Dartmouth College, Hanover, N.H. 1840, Timothy Follett House, Burlington, Vt. 1848–1849, Broomfield Street Methodist Church, Boston. 1850, Courthouse, Lowell, Mass. 1852–1856, Customhouse and Post Office, Mobile, Ala. 1852–1859, Customhouse, Norfolk, Va. 1853–1858, Customhouse and Post Office, Bath, Maine. 1853–1858, Customhouse and Post Office, Richmond, Va. 1854, Shattuck Observatory, Dartmouth College, Hanover, N.H. 1855–1856, Customhouse, Providence, R.I. 1855–1857, Marine Hospital, Chelsea, Mass. 1855–1858, Customhouse and Post Office, Bristol, R.I. 1855–1860, Department of the Treasury (south wing), Washington. 1855–1860, Customhouse and Post Office, West Virginia Independence Hall, Wheeling. 1856–1858, Customhouse and Post Office, Galena, Ill. 1856–1858, Customhouse and Post Office, Windsor, Vt. 1856–1861, Customhouse and Post Office (now Courthouse and Federal Building), Galveston, Tex. 1857–1858, Customhouse and Post Office, Washington. 1857–1860, Customhouse and Post Office, Portsmouth, N.H.

BIBLIOGRAPHY

EMLEN, ROBERT P. 1979 "The Great Stone Dwelling of the Enfield, New Hampshire Shakers." *Old-Time New England* 69, nos. 3–4:69–85.

HAMLIN, TALBOT (1944)1964 *Greek Revival Architecture in America.* Reprint. New York: Dover.

LEHMAN, DONALD J. 1973 *Lucky Landmark: A Study of a Landmark and Its Survival, The Galveston Customhouse, Post Office, and Courthouse of 1861.* Washington: General Services Administration. Public Buildings Service, Historical Study 4.

MORAN, GEOFFREY P. 1967 "The Post Office and Custom House at Portsmouth, New Hampshire and Its Architect, Ammi Burnham Young." *Old-Time New England.* 57:85–102.

OVERBY, OSMUND 1960 "Ammi B. Young in the Connecticut Valley." *Journal of the Society of Architectural Historians* 19:119–123.

OVERBY, OSMUND 1962 "Ammi B. Young, an architectural sketch." *Antiques* 81:530–533.

TOLLES, BRYANT FRANKLIN, Jr. 1970 "Ammi Burnham Young and the Gilmanton Theological Seminary." *Old-Time New England* 61:47–56.

WODEHOUSE, LAWRENCE 1966 "Ammi Burnham Young: 1798–1874." *Journal of the Society of Architectural Historians* 25:268–280.

WODEHOUSE, LAWRENCE 1968 "Ammi Young's Architecture in Northern New England." *Vermont History* 36:55–60.

WODEHOUSE, LAWRENCE 1970 "Architectural Projects in the Greek Revival Style by Ammi Burnham Young." *Old-Time New England* 60:73–85.

ŽÁK, LADISLAV

Ladislav Žák (1900–1973) was born in Prague, Czechoslovakia. At the end of the 1920s, Žák designed a set of chairs made of bent steel tubes. His work peaked in the mid–1930s in a group of family houses built in Prague where, step by step, Žák developed a special type of one-family residence with longitudinal living room on the first floor and cabinlike bedrooms on the second floor. The dominating architectural elements of his buildings were uninterrupted strip windows and aerodynamic shapes of volumes and terraces. After the war, he devoted himself to the theory of landscape planning. In 1946, Žák was appointed assistant professor of landscape planning at the Academy of Fine Arts in Prague. He was a member of the Czechoslovak Werkbund, the Left Front, the Union of Socialist Architects, and of the avant-garde S. V. U. Mánes art association.

VLADIMÍR ŠLAPETA

WORKS

1932, Czechoslovak Werkbund Exhibition (three villas in residential estate), Baba District; 1932–1933, Hain Villa, Vysočany District; 1934–1935, Martin Frič House, Hodkovičky District; 1937, Lída Baarová House, Dejvice District; Prague.

BIBLIOGRAPHY

"Prague." 1938 *Architectural Record* 84, no. 4:64–72.
ŠLAPETA, VLADIMÍR 1975 "Architektonické dílo Ladislava Žáka." *Národní Technické Museum. Sborník.* 14:189–225.
ŽÁK, LADISLAV 1934 *Byt.* Prague.
ŽÁK, LADISLAV 1947 *Obytná krajina.* Prague: Mánes.
ŽÁK, LADISLAV; HERAIN, KAREL; and SUTNAR, LADISLAV 1932 *O bydlení.* Prague: Svaz československého díla.

ZAKHAROV, ADRIAN DMITRIEVICH

Originally trained at the Academy in St. Petersburg, Russia, Adrian Dmitrievich Zakharov (1761–1811) worked in Paris from 1782–1786 under JEAN FRANÇOIS CHALGRIN. After travel in Italy, he returned to Russia in 1794 where he worked until his death. Zakharov's fame rests on his superb and imaginative neoclassical rebuilding of the enormous Admiralty (1806–1823) in St. Petersburg which was originally erected in 1732 by I. Korobov. He enlivened the long landside by dividing it into distinct geometrical units with a heavy, simplified central pavilion with arched en-

Z

trance and simplified sculpture beneath a square colonnade which was crowned by the gold spire of the original. The river side was terminated by similar simplified cubic pavilions with impressive colonnades all deriving from CLAUDE NICOLAS LEDOUX.

THOMAS J. MCCORMICK

WORKS

1806–1808, Warehouses on the Neva, St. Petersburg, Russia. 1806–1811, Church of Saint Andrew, Kronstadt, Russia. 1806–1811, The Admiralty (not completed until 1823), St. Petersburg, Russia.

BIBLIOGRAPHY

ARKIN, D. E.   1953   *Zakharov, Voronikhin.* Moscow.
GRABAR, IGOR; LAZAREV, V. N.; and KEMENOV, V. S. (editors)   1963   Volume 8, part 1 in *Istoriya russkogo iskusstva.* Moscow: Knebel.
GRIMM, G. G.   1940   *Arkhitektor Andreyan Zakharov.* Moscow: Akademii Arkhitektury SSSR.
LANCERAY, N.   1911   "Adrien Zakharov et l'Amirauté à St. Pétersbourg." *Starye Gooy* 12:3–64.
MILNER-GUILLAND, ROBIN   1980   "Art and Architecture in the Petersburg Age; 1700–1860." In Robert Auty and Dimitri Oblensky (editors), *An Introduction to Russian Art and Architecture.* Cambridge University Press.

ZEIDLER, E. H.

Eberhard H. Zeidler (1926–) was born in Braunsdorf, Germany, and educated at the Bauhaus in Weimar and the Technische Hochschule in Karlsruhe. He was a designer for Eiermann and Lindner in Karlsruhe and Osnabrück (1949–1951) before moving to Canada in 1951, when he joined the firm of Blackwell and Craig, Toronto, as an associate in charge of design. He became a partner in Blackwell, Craig, and Zeidler in 1954 and has retained responsibility for design through the successor firms, now the Zeidler Roberts Partnership.

His churches during the 1950s and 1960s, and Beth Israel Synagogue (1963–1964) in Peterborough, Ontario, struck a progressive yet inviting posture, without the oppressive monumentality of much contemporary work. The Health Sciences Centre (1967–1972) at McMaster University, Hamilton, Ontario, stands out among the many health-care facilities of innovative plan that followed. In spite of their diversity of form, a consistent intellectual set is evident even in the smallest of these, such as the Doctor Joseph O. Ruddy Hospital (1965–1970) in Whitby, Ontario. At the other end of the scale are the Toronto megastructures with which the firm is usually identified: Ontario Place (1969–1971), a recreational facility

on the waterfront; the Eaton Centre (1973–1981), a commercial galleria with a festive air (with Bregman and Hamann); and Queen's Quay Terminal (in progress since 1979), a multiple-use complex including dance theater and offices within a renovated warehouse, topped by new residential construction.

The methodical approach displayed is based on systematic (and theoretically extendible) repetition of large modules in layers, coupling vertically as well as horizontally. Environmental factors are recognized appropriately and high technology is used inobtrusively. This approach is remarkably tolerant, as sympathetic to human emotions and responses as it is sensitive to urban and natural contexts. The result is not only amenable but also joyful, with sequences of discrete spaces that are linked in a polyvalent way to support the most varied activities.

Taking a position between the extremes of the old "functionalism" (with its narrow formal code) and recent tendencies to pluralistic formalism, Zeidler (1974, pp. 96–97) insists "we must recognize that architectural form is created through the resolution of the conflict between the practical (the Content issues of architecture) and the emotional (the Image issues of architecture). Only when both Content and Image are included do we achieve a Total Architecture"—one that produces the delight that VITRUVIUS speaks of, in addition to the commodity ad firmness, as the essence of "well building."

DOUGLAS RICHARDSON

WORKS

1963–1964, Beth Israel Synagogue, Peterborough, Ontario. 1965–1967, Physical Sciences Building, University of Guelph, Ontario. 1965–1970, Dr. Joseph O. Ruddy Hospital, Whitby, Ontario. 1967–1972, Health Sciences Centre, McMaster University, Hamilton, Ontario. 1969–1971, Ontario Place, Toronto. 1972–1979, Detroit General Hospital (now Detroit Receiving Hospital; with Kessler Associates and Giffels Associates), Detroit, Mich. 1973–1981, Eaton Centre (with Bregman and Hamann), Toronto. 1975–, Health Sciences Centre, University of Edmonton, Alberta. 1979–, Queen's Quay Terminal, Toronto. 1981–, Discovery Bay Hotel, Hong Kong.

BIBLIOGRAPHY

Building with Words: Canadian Architects on Architecture 1981   Compiled and with an introduction by William Bernstein and Ruth Cawker. Toronto: Coach House Press.
FULFORD, ROBERT   1980   "The Rise and Fall of Modern Architecture." *Saturday Night* 95, no. 10:23–26, 28–31.
JACKSON, ANTHONY   1980   "Eberhard Zeidler." Pages 921–922 in Muriel Emanuel (editor), *Contemporary*

Architects. New York: St. Martin's.

ZEIDLER, EBERHARD H. 1974 *Healing the Hospital—McMaster Health Science Centre: Its Conception and Evolution.* Toronto: Zeidler Partnership.

ZEIDLER, EBERHARD H. 1980 "Architecture: The Fine Art of Survival." *Canadian Architect* 25, no. 2:38–41, 44.

ZETTERVALL, HELGO

Helgo Zettervall (1831–1907) was the most influential Swedish architect in the 1870s and in the 1880s. He had a versatile and highly qualified architectural practice, but for the public at large he was—and still is—especially famous for his radical and much disputed restorations of Swedish medieval cathedrals.

After being educated at the Royal Academy of Arts in Stockholm (1854–1860), Zettervall became architect of the cathedral in Lund (Scania), and during his twenty-one years there he became the outstanding architect of the southern provinces of Sweden, designing all kinds of buildings. From 1882 to 1897, he was chief of the National Board of Public Building in Stockholm. Zettervall's architecture, belonging to the last creative phase of nineteenth-century eclecticism, is sculptural, powerful, and often recognized by proportions out of the ordinary. As a true eclecticist, he used different styles, but always in his own way, being much more an architect than a specialist in styles.

When the reaction against nineteenth-century architecture arose, Zettervall became its main Swedish target, though mostly because of his restorations. His ambition to idealize medieval architecture in an artistic way was the opposite of the more antiquarian view of the twentieth century. Anyhow, his restoration of the exterior of the Cathedral of Lund (1868–1880) is an outstanding example, even in a European context. In Uppsala, however, he was less successful as far as the exterior is concerned, believing too firmly in concrete as a technically acceptable substitute for limestone.

ANDERS ÅMAN

WORKS

1868, Hospital; 1868–1880, Cathedral of Lund (restoration); Lund, Sweden. 1871, High School, Skara, Sweden. 1871, Helgo Zettervall House, Lund, Sweden. 1877, Bolinder House; 1880, High School (Norra Latin); Stockholm. 1882, University Building, Lund, Sweden. 1885–1893, Cathedral of Uppsala (restoration), Sweden. 1886, Palme House, Stockholm. 1886–1894, Cathedral of Skara (restoration), Sweden. 1891, All Saints, Lund, Sweden. 1892, Saint Matthew's, Norrköping, Sweden. 1893, Oscar Fredrik Church, Göteborg, Sweden.

BIBLIOGRAPHY

A rich collection of Zettervall's drawings is in the Swedish Museum of Architecture, Stockholm.

ÅMAN, ANDERS 1966 *Helgo Zettervall: 1831–1907.* Stockholm: Swedish Museum of Architecture. Exhibition catalogue.

LINDAHL, GÖRAN 1955 *Högkyrkligt, lågkyrkligt, frikyrkligt i svensk arkitektur 1800–1950.* Stockholm: Svenska Kyrkans Diakonistyrelses Bokförlag.

ZEVI, BRUNO

To make modern architecture a synonym for democratic habitat, free from authoritarian precepts, and history an instrument for enriching the contemporary language against all kinds of academic historicism are the main aims of the work of Bruno Zevi (1918–).

Born in Rome of an old Jewish family, Zevi struggled against Fascism from an early age. He left Italy in 1939 and took his M.A. (1941) at the Harvard Graduate School of Architecture. Early in 1943, he returned to Europe to fight in the Italian underground movement.

His first book, *Towards an Organic Architecture* ([1941]1950), was like a peaceful bomb upon the dictatorial rhetoric and monumentalism. *Architecture as Space* ([1948]1974) applied the space-time concept to the whole of architectural history. *The Modern Language of Architecture* ([1973a]1977) codified the creative principles of the past and the present in opposition to those of the classical language.

All his other books, the magazines he has edited, *Metron-Archittectura* (1945–1955) and *L'architettura-Cronache estoria* (1955–), the weekly column written for *L'Espresso* since 1954, and his courses in architectural history at Venice and Rome Universities (1948–1979) are inspired by the same purpose to stimulate a modern, organic, popular idiom against the International style, post-Modernism, neo-academism, and neo-eclecticism.

LISA RONCHI

BIBLIOGRAPHY

ZEVI, BRUNO (1945)1950 *Toward an Organic Architecture.* London: Faber. Originally published with the title *Verso un'architettura organica.*

ZEVI, BRUNO (1948)1980 *Architecture as Space: How to Look at Architecture.* New York: Horizon. Originally published with the title *Saper vedere l'architettura.*

ZEVI, BRUNO (1950)1975 *Storia dell'architettura moderna.* 5th ed., rev. Torino, Italy: Einaudi.

ZEVI, BRUNO (1960)1972 *Architectura in nuce.* 2d ed. Florence: Sansoni.

ZEVI, BRUNO (editor) 1964 *Michelangiolo architetto.* Torino, Italy: Einaudi.

ZEVI, BRUNO 1970 *Erich Mendelsohn: Opera completa.* Milan: Etas/Kompass.

ZEVI, BRUNO (1971)1973 *Saper verdere l'urbanistica: Ferrara di Biagio Rossetti, la prima città moderna europea.* Rev. ed. Torino, Italy: Einaudi.

ZEVI, BRUNO (1973a)1978 *The Modern Language of Architecture.* Seattle: University of Washington Press. Originally published with the title *Il linguaggio moderno dell'architettura.*

ZEVI, BRUNO (1973b)1977 *Spazi dell'architettura moderna.* Rev. ed. Torino, Italy: Einaudi.

ZEVI, BRUNO (1974a)1978 *Architettura e storiografia.* 2d ed. Torino, Italy: Einaudi.

ZEVI, BRUNO (1974b)1976 *Poetica dell'architettura neoplastica.* 2d ed. Torino, Italy: Einaudi.

ZEVI, BRUNO 1977 *Zevi su Zevi.* Milan: Editrice Magma.

ZEVI, BRUNO 1979 *Frank Lloyd Wright.* Bologna, Italy: Zanichelli.

ZHOLTOVSKY, IVAN V.

Ivan Vladislavovich Zholtovsky (1867–1959), a Belorussian by birth, studied at the St. Petersburg Academy of Art (1887–1898) and practiced in Moscow from 1900 on. He expanded his education by working for architectural firms and by traveling abroad. As an educator, he stressed practical experience and he employed many of his students—among them, NIKOLAI A. LADOVSKY and KONSTANTIN MELNIKOV—after their graduation.

Zholtovsky was an ardent student and devoted scholar of classic architecture, determined to uncover the eternal principles of beauty and to define corresponding methods of architectural design. He found inspiration and guidelines for his own work in the experimental spirit of the baroque and in the rational methods of ANDREA PALLADIO, whose *Four Books on Architecture* he translated in 1936. His concerns for quality of building materials and construction methods are evident in all his projects: from his Equestrian Society headquarters (1905) influenced by Russian classicism, through his Culture-Education Department Pavilion and Entrance Gate at the First All-Russian Exhibition for Agriculture and Home Industries (1923), to his model of Socialist Realism—the housing complex on Bolshoi Kaluzhkoi Street (1940–1949).

Though bestowed the Stalin award (1950) for the latter and favored with privileges for his consequent contributions to Socialist Realism, Zholtovsky, at the end of his life, saw his work criticized and discredited when Socialist Realism was refuted after Stalin's death.

MILKA T. BLIZNAKOV

WORKS

1905, Equestrian Society Headquarters; 1910, Tarasov's Mansion (now the Polish Embassy); *1922–1923, Master Plan, Entrance Gate, and Pavilion of Culture (with V. Koronin and N. Kolli), First All-Russian Exhibition for Agriculture and Home Industries; Moscow. 1926–1928, House of the Soviets of Dagestan ASSR, Makhach-Kala, Russia. 1927–1929, State Bank; 1927–1930, Termal Station (MOGES); 1933–1934, Housing Complex (now Inturist), Mokhovaya (now Marx) Street; Moscow. 1934–1937, Dom VTsIK (now the Town Hall), Sochi, Russia. 1940–1949, Housing Complex, Bolshoi Kaluzhskoi (now Lenin Prospect); 1952–1953, Housing Complex, Smolensk Square, Moscow.

BIBLIOGRAPHY

BARKIN, M. G. (editor) 1975 *Mastera sovetskoĭ arkhitektury ob arkhitekture.* Moscow: Iskusstvo.

KOPP, ANATOLE 1978 *L'architecture de la période Stalinienne.* Grenoble, France: Presses Universitaires.

KORNFELD, YA. A. 1953 *Laureaty Stalinskikh premiĭ v arkhitekture: 1941–1950.* Moscow: Izd. lit. po stroitelstvu i arkhitekture.

LEBEDEV, G., and SUKOYAN, N. 1953 "Vydaiushchiiisia sovetskii zodchii." *Arkhitektura SSSR* 1:17–26.

LIZON, PETER 1971 "The Palace of the Soviets: Change in Direction of Soviet Architecture." Unpublished Ph.D. dissertation, University of Pennsylvania, Philadelphia.

OSHCHEPKOV, GRIGORI D. 1955 *I. V. Zholtovskii: Proekty i postroiki.* Moscow: Izd. lit. po stroitelstvu i arkhitekture.

ZHOLTOVSKII, I. V. 1933 "Printsip zodchestva." *Arkhitektura SSSR* 5:28–29.

ZHOLTOVSKII, I. V. 1934 "Ploshchad Sverdlova." *Arkhitektura SSSR* 2:14–15.

ZHOLTOVSKII, I. V. 1951 "O Rabote arkhitektora na stroitelstve." *Sovetskaia arkhitektura* 1:43–48.

ZHOLTOVSKII, I. V. 1953 "Arkhitektura krupnopanelnykh zdanii." *Arkhitektura SSSR* 7:4–6.

ZIEBLAND, GEORG FRIEDRICH

Georg Friedrich Ziebland (1800–1878) was born in Regensburg and trained under KARL VON FISCHER in Munich. Much influenced in his interest in medieval architecture by the romantic paintings of Domenico Quaglio—whose castellated Schloss Hohenschwangau (1839–1850) he completed—and by his fellow pupil FRIEDRICH VON GÄRTNER, Ziebland was sent by King Ludwig I to Rome in 1826 to study early Christian basilicas as models for a new Munich church. The Saint Boniface Basilica (1834–1850), a brick and terra-cotta synthesis of Roman and Ravennate models, was a pioneer in the revival of interest in early Christian forms in German religious architecture. Incongruously attached to the Monastery of Saint Boniface is Ziebland's stone neoclassical Exhibition Building (1838–1848), the lackluster Corinthian component of LEO VON KLENZE's Königsplatz. After failure in the 1850 competition for the Maximillianstrasse, Ziebland contented himself with sundry designs for Hohenschwangau and teaching duties at the Royal Academy in Munich.

BARRY BERGDOLL

WORKS

*1829–1831, Villa Malta (interior decoration), Rome. 1830, Steuerkataster Kommission, Munich. 1833–1835, Theresien Monument, Bad-Aibling, Germany. 1834–1850, Saint Boniface Basilica and Monastery; 1838–1848, Exhibition Building, Königsplatz; Munich. 1839–1850, Schloss Hohenschwangau (interior decorations and stables), Upper Bavaria, Germany. 1843, Mariahilfkirche in der Au (completion; begun by D. Ohlmüller), Munich.

BIBLIOGRAPHY

KARNAPP, BIRGIT-VERENA 1971 "Georg Friedrich Ziebland; Studien zu seinem Leben und Werk." Unpublished Ph.D. dissertation, University of Innsbruck, Austria.
REIDELBACH, HANS 1888 *König Ludwig I. von Bayern und seine Kunstschöpfungen.* Munich: Roth.
STUBENVOLL, BEDA 1875 *Die Basilika und das Benedictinerstift St. Bonifax in München.* Munich: Ernst Stahl.
WÖRNER, HANS JAKOB 1974 "Zieblands Basilika in München und Hardeggers Liebfrauenkirche in Zürich." *Das Münster* 27:50–67.

ZIMMERMANN BROTHERS

Although the Zimmermann brothers, Dominikus Zimmermann (1685–1766) and Johann Baptist Zimmermann (1680–1758), often worked independently, when they collaborated on such churches as Steinhausen and Die Wies, they significantly contributed to the *Gesamtkunstwerk* concept of architecture, whereby building, stucco work, sculpture, frescoes, and other ornament were designed from the outset as a consistent entity. Although the first great work of the ASAM BROTHERS, at Weltenburg (begun in 1716), precedes the Zimmermanns' major achievements in this respect, Johann Baptist's frescoes and stuccoes in the parish church of Schliersee (1714) already demonstrate a new sense of relationship, through color, between these elements.

Both brothers were born at Gaispoint near Wessobrunn, in southwestern Bavaria, and both were trained as stuccoists at the abbey of Wessobrunn. This center was so pre-eminent that its workers were welcomed as far afield as Franconia, Berlin, Poland, Austria, and Switzerland. Dominikus, however, developed primarily as an architect, whereas Johann Baptist became a leading stuccoist and fresco painter. It is not clear to what extent the latter practiced architecture, but the complete renovation of the Andechs abbey church seems to have been under his control, and it is likely that when he worked with Dominikus he participated in the overall design.

Dominikus Zimmermann was born at the end of June 1685 and died on November 16, 1766, in the house he built opposite his pilgrimage church of Die Wies, not far from the abbey of Steingaden. The father, Elias, was a mason and modest stucco worker; the mother, widowed as early as 1695, remarried another stuccoist, Christoph Schäffler. More important is the probability that in his early teens Dominikus was trained under Johann Schmuzer, the leading Wessobrunn stuccoist and architect. He could hardly have failed to have known Schmuzer's ornate pilgrimage church at Vilgertshofen (1686–1692), only a dozen miles northwest of Wessobrunn, although he was much too young to have participated in the execution of what was to become a model for the choir of his final masterpiece at Die Wies.

Johann Baptist Zimmermann, born at Gaispoint on March 1, 1680, presumably also trained under Johann Schmuzer, and—being five years older than his brother—may have been a very young assistant at Vilgertshofen. In later life (1734), he returned there to execute the choir fresco. His career as stuccoist and fresco painter was distinguished; and on his death in Munich he was buried in the important church of Saint Peter.

Dominikus Zimmermann's early activity was limited to stucco work and *scagliola* (polished stucco inlay), but since he is known to have married Therese Zöpf (daughter of his stuccoist godfather) at Füssen in 1708, he may have worked there under the architect Johann Jakob Herkomer and learned from him the technique of building plaster vaults as well as becoming acquainted with elements of French Régence ornament—differing greatly from Schmuzer's heavily baroque designs—that had begun to make their way into Germany from Paris and Versailles. Dominikus's first securely documented work is a series of five *scagliola* altars (1708) at Fischingen, in northeastern Switzerland. In 1709–1712, he provided altars and stucco ornament for the Carthusian monastery at Buxheim, near Memmingen in Bavarian Swabia. His brother also executed a fresco there. After completing altars for churches at Biberach and Wemding, Dominikus settled in 1716 at Landsberg, on the Bavarian-Swabian border. Here in

1718–1720, he stuccoed the façade and interiors of the Rathaus. By 1734, he was a member of the town council, and in 1749 he became one of Landsberg's four mayors.

As for Johann Baptist, his range of activity was by no means limited to western Bavaria and Swabia proper; on all accounts, his career was much more cosmopolitan. Modest beginnings, however, preceded a challenging turn of events in 1720. From 1714, following his work at Schliersee, to 1719, he was engaged in stucco and *scagliola* commissions for the great Benedictine abbey of Ottobeuren, including its library, refectory, chapter house, and cloister galleries. In 1716, he ornamented the cloister of the Cathedral of Freising, where he had become a citizen six years earlier. In 1719 and 1722, he signed frescoes in his brother's first important architectural commission, the Dominican nunnery church of Mödingen, just north of the Danube at Dillingen.

After 1720, Johann Baptist's career centered in Munich and prospered under the patronage of the Bavarian electors Max Emanuel and Carl Albrecht. Presumably, it was his fine stuccoes at Ottobeuren (often visited by Max Emanuel) and Freising that led to his being called in 1720 to stucco JOSEPH EFFNER's stairhall and *Festsaal* in the huge Neues Schloss at Schleissheim, north of Munich itself. Other important decorative commissions of the 1720s include apartments (destroyed) in Schloss Nymphenburg; the interior of Effner's Palais Preysing in Munich (1724–1725); the library and refectory, respectively, of the Benedictine monasteries of Benediktbeuren and Tegernsee; and stuccoes in Effner's Ahnengalerie in the Munich Residenz (1728–1730).

Meanwhile, Dominikus Zimmermann had built the Dominican convent church at Mödingen (1716–1721), the Dominican monastic church at Schwäbisch-Gmund (1724–1725), the parish church at Buxheim (c.1726–1727), and another Dominican convent church at Siessen (1726–

1733). In 1732, however, his two proposed plans for the great abbey church of Ottobeuren were rejected—one of them with a vast central rotunda awkwardly sandwiched between unbalanced nave and choir extensions. Clearly, his genius lay in small-scale projects. Construction began in 1728 on his first masterwork, the pilgrimage church of Steinhausen, some 35 miles southwest of Ulm. Here, in the main vault, Johann Baptist executed *his* first masterpiece in fresco (1731). He then returned to Benediktbeuren to decorate the Festsaal, and to Munich to stucco the Schatzkammer and the Reiche Zimmer of the Residenz (1733–1737) and both the exterior and interior of FRANÇOIS DE CUVILLIÉS's Amalienburg in the gardens of the Nymphenburg Palace (1734–1739).

The work of both brothers, then, was relatively hesitant until shortly before 1730. Mödingen differs little from a small Gothic church except for its ornament, window shapes, and flattened ceiling. The Buxheim parish church, likewise with an aisleless rectangular nave and extended narrower choir, has more elegant proportions and sturdier piers and entablatures. The upper tier of side windows has a tentative form of the so-called "elephant ears" soon to become further developed at Steinhausen and later at Die Wies. At Siessen, however, the flanking members of these triple lights are curiously inverted, as later at Günzburg. Structurally, Siessen is a one-time experiment in vaulting by a series of four circular cupolas on pendentives extending longitudinally to a narrower choir. This treatment results in a broken-up effect not unlike that in the Romanesque Aquitanian churches of southern France.

In decoration, these early interiors have a lacework elegance and an intimacy of scale far removed from the aggressive baroque interiors of the Asam brothers. White dominates, then gold, shell pink, and muted blues and greens. In the stuccoes, the promise of a lilting rococo rhythm already stirs. Paintings are usually small and isolated in circular, oval, or irregularly shaped medallions. Stucco runs to clearly defined bands, often featuring small circles or squares, and to Régence fillers of gentle tendrils and geometric grillwork. On a basis of quality the stuccoing of Johann Baptist is noticeably finer than Dominikus's; after 1720, when Johann Baptist worked under such Paris-trained designers as Joseph Effner and François Cuvilliés, the gap widened.

We turn now to the pilgrimage church of Steinhausen, a dependency of the nearby Premonstratensian abbey of Schussenried. Planned in 1727, begun in the next year, and dedicated in 1733, the design, in which Johann Baptist may have participated, marks an unbelievable leap forward in the art of both brothers. Dominikus signed himself, in Latin, under the organ gallery, as ARCHIT.E.STUCKADOR. Johann Baptist was paid only for the frescoes—further evidence that we must attribute the stuccoing to Dominikus. The marvel of Steinhausen as a whole is that its design came only a year after the construction of Siessen got under way. Both churches were completed for dedication in the same year. We know that the abbess of Siessen recommended Dominikus to the abbot of Schussenried, and that the latter had acquired a number of plans from CASPAR MOOS-BRUGGER, chief architect of the important Swiss Benedictine abbey of Einsiedeln. Based upon or influenced by publications of the work of SEBASTI-ANO SERLIO, these plans included proposals for an oval plan with free-standing supports. Thus, Dominikus's plan, for which there was no precedent in his earlier work and little in Germany besides Cosmas Damian Asam's plan for Weltenburg, was much indebted to Moosbrugger and to Abbot Didacus Ströbele of Schussenried. It is true that oval plans were much in vogue in the churches and palaces of JOHANN BERNHARD FISCHER VON ERLACH and LUKAS VON HILDE-BRANDT in Vienna and Salzburg, but it is doubtful that Dominikus knew of them. Tall and elegant, almost Gothic in its proportions, Steinhausen is fronted by a single high tower—the exterior effect has been compared to that of Strasbourg Cathedral. The oval plan is defined without by curved sections between the slightly projecting high-gabled side walls and the balancing vestibule and choir areas. Although the choir itself is a transverse oval, it ends in a gabled flat wall, similar to the façade below the tower. Ten free-standing pilastered piers shape the main oval within and provide support for the vault, here of stone. Since for structural reasons these piers are relatively close together, the light entering between them is more muted than at Die Wies, which has a plaster vault. Exterior windows are tall and narrow, with scalloped tops, and over each one is an elephant-eared triplet light.

Above the nave arcade, stucco ornament explodes in Régence profusion—there is no specifically rococo detail as yet—to form a magical transition to Johann Baptist's brilliant and all-encompassing fresco glorifying the Virgin as savior after the Fall from Eden. Above the florid pier capitals and entablatures are ten seated Apostles whose rather crude execution clearly indicates that Dominikus was their author. Over the upper windows of the aisle are multicolored garlands inhabited by insects and birds—spiders and hoopoes are especially memorable. Such fascination with and close observation of nature, which

has no parallel in French ornament of the time, is strictly German; and it has been pointed out that naturalistic stops like the Kuckuck and the Waldflöte were being introduced in church organs of the day. In similar spirit, Johann Baptist's fresco is filled with landscape elements, a major innovation in fresco design of the time.

Bernard Rupprecht, in *Die Bayerische Rokoko-kirche* (1959), has argued convincingly that Steinhausen is the first truly rococo church, despite the absence of rocaille forms in its ornament. His argument turns on structure, lighting, and the illusionary effect of stucco-cum-fresco in the main vault. Here, there is a striking departure from earlier practice of clearly demarcated beginnings and endings. The stucco zone, with its array of niched apostles, balustrades, floral urns, and undulating cornices, now becomes a major element in uniting the whole design. It is at once a transition between structure below and magical illusion above, and by its own character a transformation of structure into illusion. Johann Baptist's painted world is indeed an unworldly vision.

Dominikus's next major work was the parish church of Günzburg, on the Danube east of Ulm (1736–1744), but here his brother did not participate and the miracle of Steinhausen was not equaled. Existing monastic buildings precluded a normal façade and the long side wall acts in lieu of one. The entrance is off center near the western end, and a single tower is placed at the junction of the nave and the extended rectangular choir. The church is aisleless, for here the vault is of wood; as a result, the lighting is direct and plentiful. A roughly oval shape is effected within the major exterior rectangle by deep corner niches; but the irregular oval itself is not unlike that of JOHANN MICHAEL FISCHER's Sankt Anna am Lehel (1727). Most adventurous, however, is the large choir with its galleried ambulatory opening between paired square piers. The high altar occupies two superposed levels—as in Johann Schmuzer's Vilgert-shofen and again in Dominikus's final and still more elaborate solution at the pilgrimage church of Die Wies.

Set in a meadow with a view south to the Bavarian Alps, Die Wies (1746–1754) echoes their silhouette in its roof lines: an entrance pavilion, a raised nave, a choir at the lower level of the entrance mass, and finally a still lower extension to provide L-shaped quarters for the resident clergy. A single tower rises centrally between this extension and the choir, and low passages flanking it provide connection with the church. From the small parabola-shaped vestibule we enter the spacious, but somewhat squatly proportioned nave, a Steinhausen oval expanded laterally into a "fat" shape. Johann Baptist's great fresco deceptively gives it a breath-taking feeling of height, but in fact the vault is nearly flat, being coved only at its base. Because the vault is of plaster, suspended

Zimmermann Brothers.
Pilgrimage Church.
Die Wies, Germany.
1746–1754

Zimmermann Brothers.
Pilgrimage Church
(interior).
Die Wies, Germany.
1746–1754

Zimmermann Brothers.
Pilgrimage Church (altar).
Die Wies, Germany.
1747–1754

from the rafters, and not of stone as at Steinhausen, the latter's ten supporting piers are here reduced to eight. But at Die Wies the piers are coupled columns beneath a single high entablature block. Each column has four tiny arrises, unnoticed at first, that continue upward the corner angles of the supporting base. This subtle variation catches the light in such a way as to counteract the horizontality of the interior proportions. The wide interstices between the piers allow a more generous passage of light than at Steinhausen, and correspondingly the exterior windows are enlarged. The main lights are paired, as at Siessen, with an elaborate elephant-eared triplet above, but only over the main side altars in the slightly projecting "transept" arms of the nave. Elsewhere, these upper openings are of a single irregular oval shape.

The lighting of Die Wies, then, is of the most advanced rococo sort. Rococo too is the rocaille-dominated stuccoing, here in wildest profusion, even including balustraded niches cut into the base of the nave vault. Altogether rococo is Johann Baptist's aerial fresco, like a great hole opened to the heavens and with only small figures—not massive baroque ones—whirling about in a cloud-flecked blue sky. There are other penetrations as well, cut through the aisle vault supports behind the main piers, not only horizontally above the small transverse arches but also vertically as we look directly overhead up into a minute circular fresco (a small heaven). Still more extreme is the extended choir, an elaborate version of that at Günzburg, and again suggesting Schmuzer's choir of Vilgertshofen as its ultimate source. A pilgrim's ambulatory flanks it and continues behind the lower story of the high altar. Above, a passage of equal width forms a gallery, brilliantly lighted, with bluish gray *Stuckmarmor* columns—not square piers—supporting what can no longer be called an arcade, but rather a drooping swag under scalloped openings that penetrate the base of the choir vault itself. As at Günzburg, the high altar is at two levels, the upper one set back to allow a continuation of the gallery passage across its front.

We have emphasized the rococo extremes of Dominikus's solution at Die Wies, yet the very profusion of ornament—stuccoes, altars, pulpit and abbot's chair balancing it across axis, the choir gallery, and a range of increasingly strong color as we proceed from very white nave to heavily laden high altar with its reddish enframing columns—all these suggest something of a return to the Bavarian baroque spirit of interiors by the Asam brothers. Columns, not flat pilasters, are emphasized throughout, not only in the nave, choir gallery, and high altar, but also on the impressive bowed façade. If indeed this façade reminds us of Johann

Michael Fischer's at Zwiefalten (erected 1750), we should remember that Fischer's subsequent architecture moved away from grandiose baroque effects to a final pilaster-dominated neoclassicism. Dominikus Zimmermann's architecture at the end moved in the opposite direction. In contrast with Die Wies, Steinhausen has a kind of pre-Mozartian purity. If his signature there, under the organ loft, is in Latin and announces him as both architect and stuccoist, that at Die Wies, in the same position, is in provincial German and claims its author only as architect. (This does not preclude his having designed the rather heavy stuccoes, however, and they are usually attributed to him.)

The dates of Die Wies are 1746–1754, and the patrons were Hyazinth Gassner and Marianus Mayr, abbots of Steingaden. Dominikus built a marvelous shell, but it is clear that his stuccoes and Johann Baptist's frescoes share equally in the creation of a masterful *Gesamtkunstwerk*.

Other late works of Dominikus include the highly inventive little Johanniskirche at Landsberg (1741, executed a decade later) and his nearby pilgrimage chapel at Pöring (1739), from which it seems to have evolved. His wood model for rebuilding the abbey of Schüssenried (1748), still preserved there, was realized only with many modifications in the 1750s and 1760s by Jakob Emele.

Just before Die Wies, Johann Baptist impressively decorated Johann Michael Fischer's church at Berg-am-Lain and the Augustinian abbey church of Dietramszell (both c.1743–1744). A drawing of 1745 for the choir gallery of Die Wies itself demonstrates that the execution of the stuccoes was less elegant than what he proposed, as Christina Thon (1977) has pointed out. In 1751-1753 he redecorated, and perhaps reconstructed, the Benedictine abbey church of Andechs, on the Ammersee. His last works were purely decorative, but very fine: stuccoes and frescoes in the abbey of Schäftlarn and the Neustift at Freising (both interiors by Fischer); and in the *Neuer Festsaal* in the main block of the Nymphenburg palace, "under the direction"—as the documents tell us—of François Cuvilliés. These projects were completed in the four years before his death in Munich in 1758.

S. LANE FAISON, JR.

WORKS

JOHANN BAPTIST ZIMMERMANN

1709–1712, Carthusian Monastery Church (frescoes), Buxheim, near Memmingen, Germany. 1714, Parish Church (stucco, frescoes), Schliersee, Germany. 1714-1719, Benedictine Abbey (stucco), Ottobeuren, Germany. 1716, Cathedral and Cloister of Freising (stucco and frescoes), Germany. 1719–1722, Dominican Nunnery Church (frescoes), Mödingen, Germany. 1720-1725, Neues Schloss (stucco), Schleissheim, Germany. 1726–1733, Dominican Nunnery Church (frescoes), Siessen, Germany. 1728-1730, Ahnengalerie, Residenz (stucco), Munich. 1728–1733, Pilgrimage Church (frescoes), Steinhausen, Germany. 1733–1737, Schatzkammer and Reiche Zimmer, Residenz (stucco), Munich. 1734–1739, Nymphenburg, Amalienburg (stucco), Germany. 1743–1744, Saint Michael's Church (stucco, frescoes), Berg-am-Lain, Munich, Germany. 1743–1744, Augustinian Abbey Church (stucco, frescoes), Dietramszell, Germany. 1746–1754, Pilgrimage Church (frescoes), Die Wies, Germany. 1751–1755, Benedictine Abbey Church (design?, stucco, frescoes), Andechs, Germany. 1754–1756, Premonstratensian Abbey Church (stucco and frescoes), Schäftlarn, Germany. 1756, Neustift (stucco and frescoes), Freising, Germany. 1755–1757, Neuer Festsaal (stucco and fresco), Nymphenburg, Munich.

DOMINIKUS ZIMMERMANN

1708, Iddakapelle, Benedictine Abbey (five altars), Fischingen, Switzerland. 1709–1712, Carthusian Monastery Church (stucco and altars), Buxheim, Germany. 1715, Parish Church (high altar), Birkland, Germany. 1716–1721, Dominican Nunnery Church (design, stucco), Mödingen, Germany. 1718–1720, Rathaus (façade and interiors); 1721, Parish Church (altar), Landsberg-am-Lech, Germany. 1724–1725, Dominican Monastery Church, Schwäbisch-Gmünd, Germany. 1726?–1727, Parish Church (architect, stucco), Buxheim, Germany. 1726–1733, Dominican Nunnery Church (design, stucco), Siessen, Germany. 1728–1733, Pilgrimage Church (design, stucco), Steinhausen, Germany. 1733–1739, Cloister (including Annakapelle), Carthusian Monastery, Buxheim, Germany. 1736–1741, Parish Church, Günzburg, Germany. 1739, Pilgrimage Chapel, Pöring, Germany. 1741, Johanniskirche (not built until 1751), Landsberg-am-Lech, Germany. 1746–1754, Pilgrimage Church (design, stucco), Die Wies, Germany. 1756–1757, Parish Church, Eresing, Germany.

BIBLIOGRAPHY

FEULNER, ADOLF 1923 *Bayerisches Rokoko*. Munich: Wolff.

HAGER, LUISA 1955 *Nymphenburg*. Munich: Hirmer.

HITCHCOCK, H. R. 1968 *German Rococo: The Zimmermann Brothers*. Baltimore: Penguin.

KASPER, ALFONS, and STRACHE, WOLF 1957 *Steinhausen, ein Juwel unter den Dorfkirchen*. Stuttgart, Germany: Strache.

LAMB, CARL (1948)1964 *Die Wies*. Munich: Süddeutscher.

LAMPL, SIXTUS 1979 *Johann Baptist Zimmermanns Schlierseer Anfänge*. Schliersee, Germany: The author.

RUPPRECHT, BERNHARD 1959 *Die Bayerische Rokokokirche*. Kallmünz, Germany: Lassleben.

SCHNELL, HUGO (1934)1981 *Die Wies*. 21st ed., rev. Munich: Schnell & Steiner.

THON, CHRISTINA 1977 *Johann Baptist Zimmermann als Stukkator*. Munich: Schnell & Steiner.

ZUAZO UGALDE, SECUNDINO

Born in Bilbao, Spain, Secundino Zuazo Ugalde (1887–1971), studied at the schools of architecture in Barcelona and Madrid and graduated in 1913. At first, he collaborated with the architects Joaquín Otamendi and Antonio Palacios and his style was eclectic and a little baroque. However, he soon dedicated himself to the study of urban problems and designed such distinguished plans as that for the interior reform of Bilbao, the urbanization plan for Seville, and the district plan of Madrid including the extension of the Avenue of the Castellana. From historical studies around the monastery of the Escorial he learned about classical ironwork architecture which he then employed, simplified, in his own work.

For a commission from the Ministry of Public Works he moved to Saragossa where he collaborated with the Saragossan Society of Urbanization and built the Convent of the Carmelites.

In 1924, he was commissioned by the government to build post offices for Madrid, Santander, and Bilbao (1927). Between 1924 and 1926, he designed the Palacio de la Música in Madrid in a pseudo-Renaissance style that contrasts sharply with the Post Office in Bilbao, which was clearly influenced by the Viennese school. His most avant-garde work was the Casa de Flores (1930–1932) in Madrid. In the Canary Islands, he built numerous works in a style that attempted to be typical of the region; an example is the Insurance Bank of Las Palmas on Grand Canary. Between 1930 and 1937, he was occupied by the great urban plans of the New Ministries of Madrid begun under the dictatorship (1923–1930), in a style soberly classicist similar to contemporary works in Italy and Germany. After the Spanish Civil War, he continued working until his death in 1971. In 1947, he designed the house for the bullfighter Domingo Ortega, and in 1952, he built the office building of the Petroleum Monopoly in Madrid, both in a very classical style.

JUAN BASSEGODA NONELL
Translated from Spanish by
Judith E. Meighan

WORKS

A complete list of Zuazo's works is contained in volume 146 of Arquitectura *(1971).*
1924–1926, Palacio de la Música de Madrid. 1927, Post Office, Bilbao, Spain. 1928, Residencia S. Miranda; 1930–1932, Casa de las Flores; 1946–1947, Casa Domingo Ortega; Madrid. 1957, Secundino Zuazo Ugalde House, Zuazo-Enea, Zarauz, Spain. n.d., Convent of the Carmelites, Saragossa, Spain. n.d., Las Palmas Insurance, Canary Islands. n.d., Post Office, Madrid. n.d., Post Office, Santander, Spain.

BIBLIOGRAPHY

"La Casa de las Flores." 1959 *Arquitectura* 1, no. 12:33–39.
FLORES LOPEZ, CARLOS 1961 *Arquitectura española contemporánea.* Madrid: Aguilar.
TAFURI, M. 1976 *Arquitectura Contemporánea.* Madrid: Electa.

ZUCCALLI FAMILY

The Zuccalli, a family of builder-architects from Roveredo in the Italian-Swiss canton of the Grisons, were active in Bavaria in the second half of the seventeenth century. The first member of the family whose name has survived was Giovanni (?–1678). Little is known about his life. He worked as a stuccoist in the Grisons in the 1640s and 1650s; in 1675, his presence is recorded at Altötting, where he was employed as a foreman under his son Enrico. The work of the next generation is better documented. Dominikus Christophorus (?–1702) and Kaspar (1629?–1678), Giovanni's son and son-in-law respectively, appeared in Bavaria around 1650. Working at first together (until around 1666) and then separately, they were involved in the design and construction of numerous churches and conventual buildings, particularly in the Inn valley. In 1668, Kaspar obtained the post of master mason to the court in Munich. The following year, he traveled to Roveredo and brought back his family and brother-in-law Enrico (c.1642–1724). Enrico, who had apparently studied building under Kaspar, was introduced at court and quickly rose to prominence. In 1673, he was appointed court architect. During the early reign of Elector Max Emanuel (1679–1704), who gave him unconditional support, he was unquestionably the leading architect in the Bavarian capital. Enrico figured as an important transmitter of the architectural vocabulary of the Italian baroque to Bavaria. His success lay in his ability to adapt this to local conventions and, in palace design, to absorb ideas from France and Austria. In the 1670s, Enrico's major commissions were two large-scale religious projects. For the Heilige Kapelle at Altötting, a popular pilgrimage site, he designed a votive church (1672–1679) in the form of a domed, galleried rotunda. This was abandoned in 1679 with no more than the foundations in place. At the Theatinerkirche Sankt Cajetan (1674–1692) in Munich, where he took over direction of the work from Agostino Barelli in 1674, Enrico contributed the twin front towers, the design of the façade (executed 1765–1768 by FRANÇOIS CUVILLIÉS, who altered it somewhat), the design of the dome, and the interior decoration. His finest work was Schloss Schleissheim near Munich. This project, which grew in scope with the elector's political ambitions, occupied most of his attention from 1684 to 1704. In 1684–1685, Enrico was sent to Paris to study French palace design, and in the 1690s, during Max Emanuel's tenure as governor of the Spanish Netherlands (1692–1701), made several trips to Brussels and Holland, where he inspected Dutch palaces. Development at the Schleissheim site began with a small *maison de plaisance,* Lustheim (1684–1689), set within a vast layout of gardens and canals. In 1693, a sizable new palace, for which Lustheim would serve as a *point de vue,* was projected. The planning went through a complicated succession of stages. Early designs, perhaps inspired by JOHANN BERNHARD FISCHER VON ERLACH, showed an oval central hall connecting quadrangular tracts. Later, incorporating suggestions from Schloss Schönbrunn in Vienna and GIOVANNI LORENZO BERNINI's Louvre projects, Enrico experimented with variations on a layout of either three or four wings surrounding an arcaded courtyard. Only the *corps-de-logis* (east wing) was erected (1701–1704). During Max Emanuel's exile in France (1704–1714), Zuccalli lost his official position to his archrival Giovanni Antonio Viscardi, although he continued to receive private commissions. His last important work was the renovation of the abbey church at Ettal (1709–1726), for which he designed the impressive, undulating façade reaching out to widely spaced corner towers. Zuccalli was reinstated as court architect when Max Emanuel returned to Munich in 1714, but he relinquished artistic leadership to JOSEPH EFFNER, who, with his Parisian training, was better equipped to satisfy the elector's demands for interiors in the latest French manner. The last member of the family to practice architecture was Johann Kaspar (1667?–1717), son of Dominikus Christophorus. He studied with Enrico and in 1685 settled in Salzburg, where his principal works were the Theatinerkirche Sankt Cajetan (1691–1711) and the Pfarrkirche Sankt Erhard (1685–1689) in the suburb Nonnthal.

SAMUEL J. KLINGENSMITH

WORKS

KASPAR AND DOMINIKUS CHRISTOPHORUS ZUCCALLI

1657–1665, Monastery Buildings; 1661–1690, Church; Kloster Gars, Germany.

KASPAR ZUCCALLI

1666–?, Pfarrkirche Sankt Stephan, Hilgertshausen, Germany. 1675–1696, Pfarrkirche, Sankt Oswald, Traunstein, Germany.

DOMINIKUS CHRISTOPHORUS ZUCCALLI

1686–1688, Monastery Buildings, Kloster Au am Inn, Germany. 1696–1697, Pfarrkirche Sankt Andreas, Feldkirchen bei Mattighofen, Austria.

ENRICO ZUCCALLI

*After 1670, Palais Wahl, Munich. 1672–1684, Heilige Kapelle (administrative buildings), Altötting, Germany. 1674–1692, Theatinerkirche Sankt Cajetan; 1674–1704, Schloss Nymphenburg (enlargement); *after 1678, Palais Au; *1679–1701, Residenz (Kaiserzimmer, Alexanderzimmer, Sommerzimmer); 1684–1689, Schloss Lustheim; *1691–1695, Kloster der Englischen Fräulein; *after 1692, Palais Törring-Seefeld; 1693–1694, Palais Fugger-Portia; 1693–1704, Schloss Schleissheim; Munich. 1695–?, Palais des princes-évêques (renovation), Liège, Belgium. 1695–1703, Residenz, Bonn. 1709–1726, Kloster Ettal (renovation), Germany.

JOHANN KASPAR ZUCCALLI

1685–1689, Pfarrkirche Sankt Erhard, Vorstadt Nonnthal; 1685–1700, Theatinerkirche Sankt Cajetan; Salzburg, Austria. 1691–1711, Schloss Aurolzmunster, Austria.

BIBLIOGRAPHY

EBHARDT, MANFRED 1975 *Die Salzburger Barockkirchen im 17. Jahrhundert: Beschreibung und kunstgeschichtliche Einordnung.* Baden-Baden, Germany: Koerner.

HAGER, LUISA 1955 *Nymphenburg: Schloss, Park and Burgen.* Munich: Hirmer.

HAGER, LUISA, and HOJER, GERHARD (1965)1976 *Schleissheim: Neues Schloss und Garten.* 4th ed., rev. Munich: Bayerische Verwaltung der Staatlichen Schlösser, Gärten und Seen.

HAUTTMANN, MAX 1921 *Geschichte der Kirchlichen Baukunst in Bayern, Schwaben und Franken, 1550–1780.* Munich: Schmidt.

HEMPEL, EBERHARD (1965)1977 *Baroque Art and Architecture in Central Europe.* 2d ed. New York: Viking.

HUBALA, ERICH 1957a "Schleissheim und Schönbrunn." *Kunstchronik* 10:349–353.

HUBALA, ERICH 1957b "Das Schloss Austerlitz in Südmähren." *Adalbert-Stifter-Jahrbuch* 5:174–200.

HUBALA, ERICH 1966 "Henrico Zuccallis Schlossbau in Schleissheim: Planung und Baugeschichte, 1700–1704." *Münchner Jahrbuch der bildenden Kunst* Series 3 17:161–200.

LIEB, NORBERT 1941 *Münchener Barockbaumeister: Leben und Schaffen in Stadt und Land.* Munich: Schnell & Steiner.

LIEB, NORBERT (1953)1976 *Barockkirchen zwischen Donau und Alpen.* 4th ed., rev. Munich: Hirmer.

PAULUS, RICHARD 1912 *Der Baumeister Henrico Zuccalli am kurbayerischen Hofe zu München: Ein kunstgeschichtlicher Beitrag zur Entwicklung des Münchener Barock und beginnenden Rokoko.* Strasbourg, France: Heitz.

PETZET, MICHAEL 1971 "Unbekannte Entwürfe

Zuccallis für die Schleissheimer Schlossbauten." *Münchner Jahrbuch der bildenden Kunst* Series 3 22:179–204.

RIEDL, DORITH 1977 *Henrico Zuccalli: Planung und Bau des Neuen Schlosses Schlessheim.* Munich: The author.

ZENDRALLI, ARNOLDO 1930 *Graubündner Baumeister und Stukkatoren in deutschen Landen zur Barock- und Rokokozeit.* Zurich: Fretz & Wasmuth.

ZUCKER, ALFRED

Alfred Zucker (1852–?) was born in Freiburg, Prussian Silesia, and received his architectural training in Germany. He went to New York in 1873 and worked in Washington, as a draftsman in the Office of the Supervising Architect of the Treasury. Between 1876 and 1882, Zucker practiced in the South, where he served as architect for public buildings in Mississippi and as consulting architect for the Vicksburg & Meridian Railroad. He returned to New York in 1883. As the successor to HENRY FERNBACH, Zucker maintained a successful practice until 1904, specializing in tall commercial buildings of eclectic and ornate design. Among his partners were John Moser (1877–1879), John R. Hinchman (1884–1888), and J. RIELEY GORDON (1902–1904).

JOY M. KESTENBAUM

WORKS

*1879–1880, State Agricultural and Mechanical College (with John Moser), Starkville, Miss. 1889–1890, Rouss Building, 555 Broadway; 1890–1891, 484–490 Broome Street; 1890–1891, Charles Wise Building, 3–5 Washington Place; 1891, Durst Building, 409–411 Lafayette Street; 1894–1895, New York University Main Building; *1896–1897, Commodore Eldridge T. Gerry Law Library; 1899–1901, Harlem Casino, 2081 Seventh Avenue; New York. 1900, Ricks Memorial Library, Yazoo City, Miss.

BIBLIOGRAPHY

Drawings and photographs of buildings by Alfred Zucker are in the Architectural Drawings Collection, The General Libraries, University of Texas at Austin.

FRANCIS, DENNIS STEADMAN 1980 *Architects in Practice, New York City, 1840–1900.* New York: Committee for the Preservation of Architectural Records.

A History of Architecture and the Building Trades of Greater New York. 1899 2 vols. New York: Union History Company.

A History of Real Estate, Building and Architecture in New York City During the Last Quarter of a Century. (1898)1967 Reprint. New York: Arno.

Leslie's History of the Greater New York. 1878 Volume 3 in Daniel VanPelt, *Encyclopedia of New York's Biography and Genealogy.* New York: Arkell.

NEW YORK LANDMARKS PRESERVATION COMMISSION 1973 *Soho Cast-iron Historic District, Designation Report.* New York: The commission.

SPRAGUE, JOHN F. 1891 Part 1 in *New York, the Metropolis: Its Noted Business and Professional Men.* New York Recorder.

STROH, MARY KATHRYN 1973 "The Commercial Architecture of Alfred Zucker in Manhattan." Unpublished M.A. thesis, Pennsylvania State University, University Park.

ZUCKER, ALFRED 1894 *Architectural Sketches Photographed from Designs for Buildings and from Buildings Erected by Alfred Zucker, Architect.* New York: National Chemograph.

ZUCKER, PAUL

Better known as an architectural historian and theoretician, Paul Zucker (1888–1971) was also an architect, practicing in his native Berlin during the 1920s and 1930s until he emigrated to America in 1937 in the face of Nazi repression and anti-Semitism. Graduating from the Technische Hochschule in Berlin in 1911, Zucker received an architectural education a generation removed from the one he described in his 1942 article, "Architectural Education in Nineteenth Century Germany." His doctoral degree, granted in 1913, was awarded upon presentation of his dissertation concerning the representation of space in architectural scenes by Florentine painters of the first half of the Quattrocento.

His preoccupation with space and space-time in architecture was influential in his own limited architectural oeuvre, but of greater importance is the role it played in his architectural theory. In *Ideas of Space in German Architectural Theory, 1850–1930,* part three of *Space in Architecture,* Cornelis van de Ven groups Zucker with Leo Adler, Dagobert Frey, Otto Höver, Hans Jantzen, Otto Karow, and Paul Klopfer in a chapter entitled "The third generation of architectural theorists, 1920–30."

Associated with the *Novembergruppe* and the *Arbeitsrat für Kunst,* Zucker was deeply involved in the cultural and intellectual milieu of 1920s Berlin, where he taught at the Lessing Hochschule (ultimately becoming dean of the faculty of fine arts), the Reimann Schule, and the Staatliche Hochschule für Bildende Kunst. In New York, Zucker's primary teaching associations were with the Cooper Union and the New School for Social Research.

Zucker's publications, which span the years 1910 to 1970, include fourteen monographs, a number of coauthored works, and approximately four hundred book reviews and articles. In his last major book, *Town and Square* (1959), he continues his discussion of space and space-time in a city-planning rather than purely architectural context. His interest in city planning was of long standing; in 1925, he received the *Wasmuths Monatshefte* city planning award for his competition project for a reorganization of the plaza adjacent to the State Opera House in Berlin. At the time of his death in New York in 1971, Zucker was working on an aesthetic investigation of steps and stairways.

A designer of numerous villas, mostly in the fashionable western districts of Berlin, Zucker also designed the auditorium for the Lessing Hochschule (1928), office buildings, headquarters for a medical association (1928), elegant shops for two retail lingerie chains (1928), a major Berlin retail shoe shop (1927), and a one-room studio-boathouse (1930) which still stands on the banks of the Kleiner Wannsee.

ARNOLD L. MARKOWITZ

WORKS

1921–1922, Etam Hosiery Shops; 1924, Bankhaus Lewinsky, Retzlaff and Company, 23 Taubenstrasse (now combined with a later building); 1924, House, 36 Bayernallee (later altered), Charlottenburg; 1927, Henkel House, 30 Hagenstrasse, Grunewald; 1927, House, 2 Winklerstrasse, Grunewald; 1927, Leiser Schuhgeschäft, 20 Tauentzienstrasse, Charlottenburg; *1928, Ärztekammer und Ärzteverband der Provinz Brandenburg, 22 Hubertusallee, Grunewald; 1928, Festa Lingerie Shops; *1928, Lessing Hochschule Auditorium, 11 Keithstrasse, Charlottenburg; 1929, Britan House, 6 Am Birkenhügel, Wannsee; 1930, Posnansky Boathouse, Kleiner Wannsee; Berlin.

BIBLIOGRAPHY

MARKOWITZ, ARNOLD L. 1977 "Paul Zucker, Architect/Art Historian, 1888/1971: A Bibliography." *Papers of the American Association of Architectural Bibliographers* 12:53–145.

VEN, CORNELIS VAN DE (1978)1980 *Space in Architecture: The Evolution of a New Idea in the Theory and History of the Modern Movements*. Assen, Netherlands: Van Gorcum.

ZUCKER, PAUL 1919–1920 "Architektur-Aesthetik." *Wasmuths Monatshefte für Baukunst* 4:83–86.

ZUCKER, PAUL 1924 "Der Begriff der Zeit in der Architektur." *Repertorium für Kunstwissenschaft* 44:237–245.

ZUCKER, PAUL 1942 "Architectural Education in Nineteenth Century Germany." *Journal of the Society of Architectural Historians* 2, no. 3:6–13.

ZUCKER, PAUL 1945 "The Aesthetics of Space in Architecture, Sculpture and City Planning." *Journal of Aesthetics and Art Criticism* 4, no. 1:12–19.

ZUCKER, PAUL 1951 "The Paradox of Architectural Theories at the Beginning of the 'Modern Movement'." *Journal of the Society of Architectural Historians* 10, no. 3:8–14.

ZUCKER, PAUL 1959 *Town and Square: From the Agora to the Village Green*. New York: Columbia University Press.

ZWIRNER, ERNST FRIEDRICH

The career of Ernst Friedrich Zwirner (1802–1861), begun in the architecture schools of Breslau and Berlin, was determined in 1833 when KARL FRIEDRICH SCHINKEL recommended him for the post of *Dombaumeister* (cathedral architect) at Cologne, a post he held for life. Much influenced by the chorus of voices, led by Sulpiz Boisserée, praising the cathedral as a German and Christian monument, he prepared designs for its completion and organized the *Dombauhütte* (cathedral workshop) long before the 1842 decision to resume construction. Contrary to Schinkel's proposals, Zwirner insisted upon faithful adherence to High Gothic details. He trained a whole school of Gothic Revivalists, including Vincenz Statz and Friedrich von Schmidt; yet he was no dogmatist. Whereas the Apollinariskirche (1839–1843), set dramatically above the Rhine at Remagen, bears witness to Schinkel's neo-Gothic in its symmetrical composition and brittle applied detail, Zwirner's smaller churches reflect the local preference for Rhineland Romanesque sources handled with considerable freedom and simplicity.

BARRY BERGDOLL

WORKS

1833–1880, Cologne Cathedral (north and south transcepts); *1838, Houses, Trankgasse; Cologne, Germany. 1839–1843, Apollinariskirche, near Remagen, Germany. 1840, Saint George, Cologne, Germany. 1846–1847, Church, Heimerzheim, near Euskirchen, Germany. 1848–1852, Schloss (remodeling), Herdringen, Westphalia, Germany. 1849–1855, Westerholl Schloss, Argenfels near Hönningen, Germany. 1850, Agricultural Institute, Bonn. 1852–1854, Catholic Church, Antweiker, Germany. 1852–1858, Reformed Church, Elberfeld, Germany. 1854, Church, Donsbrüggen, Germany. 1855, Chapel, Schloss Schwerin, Germany. 1857, Saint Audomar, Frechen, Germany. 1857, Monument, Burg Drachenfels, Germany. *1857–1864, Liebfrauenkirche (tower and nave walls survive), Mülheim an der Ruhr, Germany. *1859–1861, Synagogue; 1860, Cologne Cathedral (sacristy); Cologne, Germany. *1862–1865, Catholic Church, Elsdorf, Germany.

BIBLIOGRAPHY

BORGER, HUGO (editor) 1980 *Der Kölner Dom im Jahrhundert seiner Vollendung*, 2 vols. Cologne, Germany: Museen der Stadt Köln. Exhibition catalogue.

GERMANN, GEORG 1972 *Gothic Revival in Europe and Britain: Sources, Influences and Ideas*. Translated by Gerald Onn. London: Lund Humphries.

MANN, ALBRECHT 1966 *Die Neuromanik*. Cologne, Germany: Greven.

RODE, HERBERT 1961–1962 "Ernst Friedrich Zwirners Planentwicklung für den Ausbau des Kölner Domes

1833–1844." *Kölner Domblatt* 20:45–98.

RODE, HERBERT 1973 "Dombaumeister Ernst Friedrich Zwirner über den Kunstwert der norfranzösischen Kathedralen." In Joseph Hoster and Albrecht Mann (editors), *Vom Bauen, Bilden, und Bewahren: Festschrift für Willy Weyres.* Cologne, Germany: Greven.

Verbeek, Albert 1954 *Rheinischer Kirchenbau im 19. Jahrhundert.* Cologne, Germany: Wienand.

WEYRES, WILLY 1968 "Ernst Friedrich Zwirner, 1802–1861," *Rheinische Lebensbilder* 3:173–189.

WEYRES, WILLY 1974 "Rheinischer Sakralbau im 19. Jahrhundert." In Ludwig Grote (editor), *Die deutsche Stadt im 19. Jahrhundert.* Munich: Prestel.

WEYRES, WILLY 1976 "Die Kölner Dombauhütte und die Neugotik in Rheinland." *Kölner Domblatt* 41:195–214.

WEYRES, WILLY, and MANN, ALBRECHT 1968 *Handbuch zur rheinischen Baukunst des 19. Jahrhunderts.* Cologne, Germany: Greven.

ZWIRNER, E. F. 1842 *Vergangenheit und Zukunft des Dombaues.* Cologne, Germany.

For an approximate idea of the sequence and distribution of the architects treated in the encyclopedia, the following table is provided. The list is organized by the birth or death date of each architect and the inclusive dates of architectural firms or families' activities.

Chronological Table of Contents

The titles presented below could have been cited throughout the bibliographies to the biographies in the *Macmillan Encyclopedia of Architects*. This list was therefore compiled to refer the reader to the basic biographical sources in architecture as well as to a few standard books on architectural history.

General Bibliography

Avery Index to Architectural Periodicals. (1963)1973 2d ed., rev. & enl. Boston: Hall.

Avery Obituary Index of Architects. 1980 2d ed. Boston: Hall.

BANCHAL, CHARLES 1887 *Nouveau dictionnaire biographique et critique des architectes français.* Paris: André, Daly.

BENEVOLO, LEONARDO (1971)1977 *History of Modern Architecture.* 2 vols. Cambridge, Mass.: M.I.T. Press.

BRIGGS, MARTIN S. (1927)1974 *The Architect in History.* Reprint. New York: Da Capo.

Catalogue of the Avery Memorial Architectural Library. 1968- 2d ed., enl. Boston: Hall. Includes four supplements to date.

COLVIN, H. C. (1954)1978 *A Biographical Dictionary of British Architects: 1600–1840.* Reprint. London: J. Murray.

EMANUEL, MURIEL (editor) 1980 *Contemporary Architects.* New York: St. Martin's.

FLETCHER, BANISTER (1896)1975 *A History of Architecture.* 18th ed. London: Scribners.

HAMLIN, TALBOT F. (1940)1953 *Architecture Through the Ages.* New York: Putnam.

HAUTECOEUR, LOUIS 1943–1965 *Histoire de l'architecture classique en France.* 7 vols. Paris: Picard.

JORDY, WILLIAM H., and PIERSON, WILLIAM H., JR. 1970–1973 *American Buildings and Their Architects.* 4 vols. Garden City, N.Y.: Doubleday. A fifth volume is in preparation.

MAYER, LEO A. 1956 *Islamic Architects and Their Works.* Geneva: Kundig.

Pelican History of Art series:

BLUNT, ANTHONY (1953)1973 *Art and Architecture in France: 1500–1700.*

GERSON, H., and TER KUILE, E. H. 1960 *Art and Architecture in Belgium: 1600–1800.*

HAMILTON, G. H. (1954)1976 *Art and Architecture of Russia.* 2d ed.

HEMPEL, EBERHARD 1965 *Baroque Art and Architecture in Central Europe.*

HEYDENREICH, LUDWIG H., and LOTZ, WOLFGANG (1967)1974 *Architecture in Italy: 1400–1600.*

HITCHCOCK, H. R. (1958)1977 *Architecture: Nineteenth and Twentieth Centuries.*

KALNEIN, WEND G., and LEVEY, MICHAEL (1972)1973 *Art and Architecture of the Eighteenth Century in France.*

KUBLER, GEORGE (1959)1976 *The Art and Architecture of Ancient America.* 2d ed.

ROSENBERG, SLIVE, and TER KUILE, E. H. 1966 *Dutch Art and Architecture: 1600–1800.*

SUMMERSON, JOHN (1953)1971 *Architecture in Britain: 1530–1830.* Rev. ed.

WITTKOWER, RUDOLF (1958)1973 *Art and Architecture in Italy: 1600–1750.* Rev. ed.

PEVSNER, NIKOLAUS (1943)1974 *Outline of European Architecture.* 7th ed. London: Allen Lane.

PEVSNER, NIKOLAUS et al. 1976 *Dictionary of Architecture.* Rev. & enl. ed. New York: Overlook Press.

PORTOGHESI, PAOLO (editor) 1969 *Dizionario Enciclopedico di architettura e urbanistica.* 6 vols. Rome: Istituto Editoriale.

RICHARDS, J. M. (editor) 1977 *Who's Who in Architecture From 1400 to the Present.* London: Weidenfeld & Nicolson.

THIEME, ULRICH, and BECKER, FELIX L. (1907–1950) 1934–1964 *Künstlerlexikon: Allgemeines Lexikon der bildenden Künstler von der Antike bis zur Gegenwart.* 37 vols. Leipzig, Germany: Engelmann.

TORRE, SUSANNA (editor) 1977 *Women in American Architecture: A Historic and Contemporary Perspective.* New York: Watson-Guptill.

VASARI, GIORGIO (1568)1973 *Le opere di Giorgio Vasari, con nuove annotazioni e commenti.* 9 vols. Edited by G. Milanesi. Reprint. Florence: Sansoni. Originally published with the title *Le vite de piv eccelenti architetti.* There are many English translations and selections from Vasari's *Lives,* the standard one by G. du C. de Vere was published in ten volumes in London by the Medici Society in 1912–1915.

VOLLMER, HANS 1953–1962 *Künstlerlexikon: Allgemeines Lexikon der bildenden Künstler des 20. Jahrhunderts.* 6 vols. Leipzig, Germany: Seemann.

WITHEY, HENRY F., and WITHEY, ELSIE RATHBURN (1956)1970 *Biographical Dictionary of American Architects (Deceased).* Reprint. Los Angeles: Hennessey & Ingalls.

Fondation Le Corbusier
Foscari
Foto:gta-Archive
Frantz, Alison
Free Library of Philadelphia
French Government Tourist Office
Frykenstedt, Holger
Gabinetto Fotografico Soprintendenza, Uffizi
Gamble House
Garmey, Stephen S.
Gautherot, Marcel
Gayle, Margot
Gebhard, David
Gemeentelijke Archiefdienst van Amsterdam
German Information Center
Greek National Tourist Office
Ghirardo, Diane
Giraudon
Hager, Hellmut
Hancock (John) Mutual Life Insurance Company
Harris, John
Hedrich-Blessing Studio
Hefferman, James
Heinz, Thomas
Hermitage
Hirsch, David
Historic American Building Survey, Library of Congress
Historical Society of Pennsylvania
Howarth, Thomas
Illinois Department of Conservation, Division of Historic Sites
Irish Tourist Board
Jackson-Stops, Gervase
Japan Architect
Japan National Tourist Organization
Kaufmann, Edgar jr.
Kelder, Diane M.
Keller, Fritz-Eugen
Kidder-Smith, G. E.
Kirby, John B. Jr.
Kuban, Doğan
Lehmann, Phyllis Williams
Lewis, Douglas
Library of Congress
Lichtbildwerkstätte "Alpenland"
Little, Christopher
MacDonald, William L.
Mainfrankisches Museum
Man and His World

Marder, Tod A.
Martinez í Matamala, Adolf
Maryland Historical Society
Massachusetts Institute of Technology
Massar, Phyllis Dearborn
McAslan, John
McCormick, Thoms J.
McGraw-Hill
Mellon (Andrew) Library
Metropolitan Museum of Art
Metropolitan Opera Association
Mexican National Tourist Council
Millon, Henry A.
Moncalvo, Riccardo
Moneo, José Rafael
Monuments Historiques
Museo Civico
Museum of the City of New York
Museum of Finnish Architecture
Museum of Modern Art, Collection
Museum of Modern Art, Mies van der Rohe Archive
National Monuments Record
National Park Service
Neuman, Robert
New York Convention and Visitors Bureau
New-York Historical Society
New York Life Insurance Company
New York Stock Exchange
Norberg-Schulz, Christian
Northwest Architectural Archives, University of Minnesota
Oechslin, Werner
Overby, Osmund
Pedretti, Carlo
Pedrini
Perceval, Alain
Photographie Bulloz
Photothèque Française
The Plaza
Phillips Petroleum Company
Pierson, William H. Jr.
Pinto, John
Posener, Julius
Rand, Marvin
Réunion des Musées Nationaux
Richards, J. M.
Rijksdienst voor de Monumentenzorg
Roberto, M.
Roth, Leland M.
Royal Commission on the Ancient and Historical Monuments of Scotland

Royal Institute of British Architects, British Architectural Library
Saint Augustine's
Sandak, Incorporated
Saskia, Limited
Schmidt-Glassner, Helga
Scully, Arthur Jr.
Shulman, Julius
Simmon Architects Associates
Singelenberg, Pieter
Smithsonian Institution
Soane's (Sir John) Museum, Trustees
Society for the Preservation of New England Antiquities
Sopaintendenza dei Monumenti del Piemonte
Sprague, Paul E.
Stanton, Phoebe B.
Staatliche Museen Preussischer Kulturbesitz, Kunstbibliothek
Statni Ustav Pamatkove Pece a Ochravy Prirody
Stillman, Damie
Stroud, Dorothy
Summerson, John
Svenska Institutet
Swiss National Tourist Office
The Architects Collaborative, Incorporated
Tadgell, Christopher
Tarán, Marina E. L.
Tatum, George B.
Teitelman, Edward
Topple, Edward C.
Tucci, Douglass Shand
University of Illinois Archives
Venturi, Rauch, and Scott Brown
Verwaltung der Staatlichen Schlösser und Gärten
Victoria and Albert Museum
Vsesojuznoje Agentstvo Po Avtorskim Pravam
Waisman, Marina
Watson, Norman S.
Whiffen, Marcus
Wilton-Ely, John
Woolworth (F.W.) and Company
Wright (Frank Lloyd) Memorial Foundation
Württembergische Landesbibliothek
Yale University Art Gallery, Stokes Collection

The purpose of this glossary is to provide definitions for architectural terms mentioned in the biographical entries. Terms applying solely to fine arts topics, historical periods or events, the work of one architect, and military structures have been excluded. In the case of multiple meanings, the words commonly used in architectural literature are defined and irrelevant meanings are ignored.

Readers are encouraged to use several excellent dictionaries and glossaries as a supplement to this glossary, particularly to locate diagrams of the more technical terms. Recommended titles include:

ARCHITECTURAL PUBLICATION SOCIETY 1852–1892 *The Dictionary of Architecture.* 8 vols. London: Richards.

FLETCHER, BANISTER 1975 *A History of Architecture.* 18th ed. New York: Scribner.

HARRIS, CYRIL, M. (editor) 1975 *Dictionary of Architecture and Construction.* New York: McGraw-Hill.

HARRIS, CYRIL M. (editor) 1977 *Historic Architecture Sourcebook.* New York: McGraw-Hill.

OSBORNE, HAROLD (editor) 1970 *The Oxford Companion to Art.* Oxford: Clarendon.

PEVSNER, NIKOLAUS ET AL. 1976 *A Dictionary of Architecture.* Rev. & enl. ed. Woodstock, N.Y.: Overlook Press.

abutment. The masonry structure that absorbs the lateral thrust coming from an arch.

academicism. A philosophy, particularly widespread during the nineteenth century, favoring the formal teachings of schools like the Ecole des Beaux-Arts in Paris over independent architectural ideas.

acanthus. An ornamental motif, used on Corinthian and Composite capitals or in a scroll design, with the shape of the leaf of the acanthus plant which is common in the Mediterranean area.

acroterion. A rectangular base or plinth positioned on a roof at its peak or corners to support an ornament or sculpture. The term is now used to refer to both the base and what stands on it.

aedicula. A structure to frame a window, niche, or similar opening and consisting of flanking columns, pilasters, or colonnettes, with a gable or canopy above. Strictly speaking, an aedicula is a shrine recessed in a temple wall and crowned by an entablature and pediment.

agora. An ancient Greek open-air assembly place or meetingplace located in the heart of a city and, like the Roman forum, usually surrounded by a colonnade.

***all'antica* style.** In the ancient mode, meaning the Roman style.

ambulatory. The aisle space surrounding the sides and back of an apse and usually separated from it by

Glossary
BY KATHE CHIPMAN

511

an arcade. Less commonly, the covered passage around a cloister is called an ambulatory.

Amsterdam school. A group of Dutch architects with Expressionist tendencies, active from c.1915 to the early 1920s. Their work was influenced by H. P. Berlage and Eduard Cuypers, and by German Expressionism. Members included Michel de Klerk and P. L. Kramer; they were responsible for the design of many large-scale housing projects in Amsterdam.

annular vault. A circular barrel vault without interruption, creating a ring around a core usually separated by an arcade.

antechoir. The space created by the front and back of the passageway or gates of a choir screen.

antechurch. The part of a church directly west of the nave; it is like a narthex except that it is usually divided into nave and aisle sections.

anthemion. An ornamental motif depicting a honeysucklelike plant. It was used in Greek friezes, with alternating flowers and leaves.

antis, in   *see* in antis

apse. The space, usually at the east end of a church, where the altar is located. Apses normally are semicircular or polygonal and have a dome or round vault. The apse form is based on the space that terminated a Roman basilica.

arabesque. A flat or low-relief decoration consisting of an over-all pattern of plant motifs, sometimes stylized or geometrically arranged and characterized by flowing lines.

Arbeitsrat für Kunst. A radical German group (Workers' Council for Art) organized in Berlin late in 1918 and later combined with the Novembergruppe.

Archaic architecture. The period of Greek architecture from the late eighth through early fifth centuries B.C., when many forms, such as the Doric and Ionic orders, were developed.

architectonic. Relating to the architecture or design of a structure. The noun "architectonics" refers to architecture as a science.

architrave. Either the beam that forms the bottom layer of an entablature or the frame that serves as a molding around a doorway or comparable opening.

archivolt. The curved molding, band of moldings, or ornamental architrave that surrounds the opening of an arch.

arcuated. Having arches as the main structural component, as opposed to trabeated construction.

Art Deco style. Primarily an American style, Art Deco was popular in the 1920s and 1930s and is characterized by the use of straight and angular lines and a sleekness of design. The term originated with the 1925 Paris Exposition Internationale des Arts Décoratifs et Industriels.

articulation. The exterior organization of structure or surface into its parts and elements.

Art Nouveau. A style of architecture and decoration popularized in France and Belgium in the 1890s. Characteristics include the use of glass and metal, organic and undulating lines, and a nonhistorical and often whimsical mood. It was sometimes called "style nouveau" after the name of a Paris shop that opened in 1895. Counterparts of Art Nouveau in other countries are *Jugendstil* (Germany), *Secession* (Austria), *Stile Liberty* (Italy), and *Modernismo* (Spain).

Arts and Crafts movement. A late nineteenth-century English decorative arts movement made famous by William Morris and emphasizing quality of design and the use of handcrafted products. The term originated with the Arts and Crafts Exhibition Society, founded in 1888, and is sometimes referred to as the "craftsman" style.

ashlar. Building blocks cut in rectangular shapes and laid horizontally.

astylar. Lacking columns or pilasters; applies particularly to façades.

atelier concept. A system of architectural education, originated in late nineteenth-century France, based on placing students for training in the studios of faculty members who were successful practicing architects.

atlas. A sculpture of a man used in the place of a column, with the entablature resting on the figure's raised arms, head, or shoulders. The plural is atlantes and an alternate term is telamon (telamones).

atrium. Either an inner hall in an ancient Roman domestic building or the forecourt to a Christian basilica. In both cases the center was likely to be roofless or partly open and the space surrounded by columns. In recent architecture, the term applies to any building's central court or interior space, sometimes glass covered.

attic. In classic architecture, the story of a building or triumphal arch above the wall cornice or entablature, sometimes concealing a structure behind it.

Attic base. A common Greek column base which consists of two convex sections (tori) separated by a concave one (scotia).

Attic style. Architecture in the ancient Greek state of Attica, including Athens.

aula. A large room or hall that serves as an assembly place for students.

avant-corps. That section of a building which stands out from the rest—the fore part.

azotea. A Spanish term for the flat roof or platform on a house.

baldachin or *baldacchino.* A canopy with a support, sometimes a complex and ornate structure, over an altar, throne, tomb, or niche opening. One type, a ciborium, houses a high altar and consists of a dome on four columns.

balloon frame.   A timber construction method introduced in the United States in the nineteenth century, using closely spaced, full height studs. The rest of the structure is rapidly nailed to this frame.

balustrade.   A series of posts or short pillars connected by a horizontal rail across the tops, and sometimes by a bottom rail.

banding.   A decoration consisting of a flat, convex, or low-relief horizontal strip or molding, sometimes used to separate the areas of a wall surface.

baptistery.   A building used for performing baptismal rites, usually separate from a church and having a circular or polygonal plan with the font at the center.

bargeboard.   Wood used to cover the projecting edges (verges) of a gable roof. Also called gableboard or vergeboard and often decoratively carved.

baroque architecture.   The period of European architecture which started in Italy at the beginning of the seventeenth century and was practiced in areas of Germany and Austria into the eighteenth century. It is based on Renaissance and Mannerist forms and is characterized by a spatial complexity, curved surfaces, and an exuberance in the use of color and sculpture. Baroque buildings in England and France are more restrained. An individual building which falls outside the baroque period can also be described as "baroque" in its characteristics.

baroque revival   *see* neobaroque architecture

barrel vault.   A vault having an uninterrupted semicircular cross section and resting on arcades or walls. Also called a tunnel vault or wagon vault.

bartizan.   A small round turret with corbels, like a *tourelle,* frequently used in Scottish buildings.

bar tracery.   Tracery formed by the lines or bars of moldings which create a quatrefoil or circular pattern at the top of a Gothic window. Bar tracery was first used in the thirteenth century and is sometimes called geometric tracery.

base.   Generally speaking, the bottommost visible level of a structure; specifically, the lower section of a column, beneath and wider than the shaft and placed on a square plinth. (*see also* Attic base; Ephesian base)

basilica.   A type of plan used in ancient Rome for a court or hall of justice. The oblong shape, with side aisles, a clearstory, and often one or more apses, evolved in the early Christian period into a longitudinal church plan with a nave.

bas-relief.   Low relief or shallow carving.

Bauhaus.   A German school, founded by Walter Gropius, which brought together a large number of talented designers, craftsmen, and architects between 1919 and 1933. The fame of the Bauhaus is due to its methodology and to the development of a widely accepted functional aesthetic.

bay.   A unit of division of the vertical plan of a building, such as a roof or aisle by beams or ribs, or of an exterior or interior wall by columniation or fenestration.

beading.   Of several meanings, the most common is a type of molding with carving in the shape of beads.

Beaux-Arts style.   An architecture of grand scale based on the historical and eclectic ideas taught during the nineteenth century at the Ecole des Beaux-Arts in Paris. The influence of Beaux-Arts design was particularly great in North America in the early twentieth century.

belfry.   Either that portion of a tower or the framework of a steeple which contains bells, or an entire bell tower whether free-standing or attached to a larger building.

belt course.   An alternate term for a stringcourse; also, a simpler, flat wood board that creates a horizontal line on a building.

belvedere.   An open and ornamented lookout tower built on a rooftop or as a separate structure at a prominent site in a garden.

béton brut.   Raw concrete, left with the marks from the formwork showing instead of being bush-hammered. (*see also* Brutalism)

bevel angle.   An angle made in masonry or construction when two surfaces do not meet at a right angle.

Biedermeier.   A style of German and Austrian decoration and painting enjoyed by the middle class during the first half of the nineteenth century for its utilitarian classicism.

bifora.   An Italian term, after the Latin "biforis," for a two-part window with a vertical division.

blind arch.   An arch closed by a wall on the back side.

board and batten.   An exterior wall covering for frame buildings, in which the joints between the boards are covered by narrow strips of wood called battens.

bolection molding.   A molding used to cover and decorate a joint created when two surfaces meet at different levels, projecting farther than either surface.

bosket.   A grove or thicket created by a small group of trees. In French, a *bosquet.*

boss.   A decorative knoblike projection carved at the intersection of ceiling ribs or at the ends of moldings. Motifs usually are plant forms, less often a human figure or heraldic theme.

bracketed style.   A style, popular in the United States during the mid-nineteenth century, that made extensive use of carved decorative brackets under overhanging eaves.

brise-soleil.   A screenlike arrangement of fins or louvers on the sunny side of a building, used since the mid-twentieth century in warm climates to prevent the sun's rays from hitting the building or a window. Also called a sun-break.

broken flight stair   *see* dogleg stair

Brutalism.   A style of the 1950s emphasizing the use of raw forms of concrete, often heavy and/or dark. The term derives from *béton brut* (naked concrete) and is known alternately as New Brutalism.

bugnato.   A boss or large stone projecting from the edge of a wall or opening.

bungalow.   A one-story frame dwelling or cottage, often having a veranda, first used in India and popular in England and the United States in the twentieth century. One type, associated with the Arts and Crafts movement, is called the Craftsman bungalow.

bush-hammering.   Or *bouchardage,* a technique for treating raw concrete (*béton brut*) that removes the uneven surface which resulted from the formwork. First used in the middle third of the twentieth century.

butterfly roof.   A roof with a low valley in the center flanked by two winglike, rising roof surfaces. The form appears in twentieth-century construction.

buttery.   Either a room for storing food or wine, or—particularly in Great Britain—a building for purchasing provisions as at a college or university.

buttress.   A masonry or brick construction attached to an exterior wall, the purpose of which is to absorb the lateral thrust of weight from a roof and to strengthen that wall. (*see also* flying buttress)

Byzantine architecture.   Architecture of the Byzantine empire, spanning approximately ten centuries beginning in the fourth century and reaching a peak in the sixth century with the Hagia Sophia in Istanbul. Characteristics include the use of early Christian forms, large domes, and an increasing richness with colorful painted and mosaic decoration. Byzantine influence in the West is particularly evident in buildings in Ravenna and Venice, Italy.

caisson.   Either a concrete well-like space built to facilitate construction below the water table, or, a recessed ceiling panel such as a coffer.

campanile.   A bell tower, usually a separate structure near a church. The earliest examples are early Medieval Italian.

canalis.   A groove or channel, which can be either a small detail as on a capital or a large gutterlike passage between buildings.

canopy.   A hoodlike structure which functions as a decorative roof over a pulpit, niche, or choir stall. Canopies are often carved in miniature tracery patterns.

cantilever.   A horizontal structural element, such as a beam or girder, which projects farther than the wall. In classical architecture, a cantilever is a bracket extending out beneath a cornice or a balcony.

capital.   The top section of a column, located above the shaft and usually supporting a horizontal or arched structure. Capitals are often highly decorated.

capomaestro.   The Italian term, widely used in the late Middle Ages, for a chief builder or architect.

capriccio.   A view of a town or architectural subject that is inventive and sometimes fantastic.

capstone.   A stone or block from the masonry on the top row of a wall, chimney, or similar structure.

caravansary.   A large Middle Eastern structure which serves as an inn for caravans, with separate spaces for travelers and animals. Built along trade routes and also in cities, it is usually rectangular with a large central courtyard. Also spelled "caravanserai."

Carolingian architecture.   Early medieval French and German architecture associated with the rise of the Carolingian empire in the eighth and ninth centuries. It reflects Charlemagne's interest in Roman and early Christian architectural forms, as seen in the Palace Chapel (Cathedral) at Aachen.

cartouche.   A framelike panel with curled or scrolled edges, often elaborately decorated or having an inscription in the center.

caryatid.   A sculpture of a draped female figure used in place of a column as a support for the entablature above.

casement.   Either the part of a hinged window that opens along a vertical line, or, a concave molding.

casino.   A clubhouse. Historically, a pavilion, lodge, or summerhouse (a type common in the Italian Renaissance), or a place for dancing (especially in the eighteenth century). In the twentieth century, a gambling hall.

castellated.   Having exterior structures like those of a fortification. The "castle style" became popular in the second half of the eighteenth century and early nineteenth century.

cast iron.   Iron with a high carbon content, which makes it easy to cast into molds but too brittle to be worked by hammering or rolling. It was little used before the sixteenth century and was most common in the nineteenth and early twentieth centuries.

Catalan school.   A movement in Catalonia, Spain, from the late 1880s through the early 1900s focusing on the revival of regional art—the *Renaixensa Catalán*—and the absorption of the new Art Nouveau style, locally called *Modernismo.*

catenary vault.   A vault with the shape of the inversion of the curve formed by a rope hanging between two points.

cathedra.   The chair or throne of a bishop, first used at the rear of the apse in early Christian churches.

cavetto.   A concave molding the size of approximately a quarter of a circle, often used in cornices.

cella. The central portion of a Greek or Roman temple where the cult statue was located.

cenotaph. A monument located away from the burial site of the person honored by it.

chaitya hall. An Indian Buddhist prayer hall constructed out of a cave, using a basilica plan with aisles.

chamfer. The surface created by cutting or beveling the edge of a block or board at an angle (usually 45 degrees) to adjacent sides.

chancel. That part of a church which is east of the crossing and is used by clergy and choir. The term derives from the Latin word for the lattice or screen that separates this area from the main church space.

channeling. A succession of decorative grooves (channels).

charnel house. A structure, sometimes a separate building, for storing the bones of the dead.

château. A French castle or prominent country house.

château style. A mid-nineteenth- and early twentieth-century imitation of old French château design. Also called "Châteauesque."

chevet. The east end of a church with a circular or polygonal apse surrounded by an ambulatory. It is most appropriately used for French Gothic churches with radiating chapels.

Chicago school. A movement in the mid-1880s and 1890s characterized by its nonhistoricism, the use of steel framing, and the dominance of vertical and horizontal lines. Louis Sullivan was its most prominent architect.

Chicago window. A window so named after its first use in Chicago in the 1890s and consisting of a fixed broad central pane flanked by two movable narrow windows.

chimneypiece. A decorative structure or carved frame over or around a fireplace.

Chinoiserie. Western European architecture and decorative art which used Chinese structures and designs. This imitative style was most fashionable in the eighteenth century.

choir. The section of a church, between the apse and the nave, where singers participate in the service.

choir screen. A railing or wall-like division between the nave and the choir sections of a church, often elaborately carved.

choir stall. A church chair used by choir members or clergy, having arms and a high back and sometimes a canopy. A carving underneath the seat is called a misericord.

CIAM. The Congrès Internationaux d'Architecture Moderne, an association of architects which first met in 1928 in Switzerland and disbanded in 1956. CIAM had representatives in west European countries and was committed to functionalist aesthetics.

ciborium. A domed or vaulted canopy supported by four columns and constructed to house a high altar.

Cinquecento architecture. Italian architecture during the sixteenth century.

circus. Either an ancient Roman oblong or oval roofless structure for contests or athletic exercises, with seating in tiers, or, in modern times, an open circular arrangement of buildings.

Cistercian architecture. Medieval church architecture in western Europe associated with the Cistercian order during the twelfth and thirteenth centuries. The reforms of Cistercians such as Saint Bernard of Clairvaux are reflected in their relatively simple and austere church plans.

City Beautiful movement. An American movement of the early 1900s inspired by examples of planning at world fairs and favoring a greater use of parks and attractive boulevards and waterfronts in town planning.

classical architecture. The architecture of ancient Greece and Rome—recognized by elements such as the orders—which became a model for subsequent styles, particularly during the Italian Renaissance and the baroque and neoclassical periods.

classical revival. A movement in the early nineteenth century, particularly in England and the United States, based on ancient Greek and Roman models. Specific forms are identified as Greek Revival, Federal architecture, or Roman Revival.

classicism. The practice of the principles of ancient Greek and Roman architecture at periods during Western civilization. It can also include the application of an Italian Renaissance interpretation of classical modes in subsequent periods.

clearstory or clerestory. An upper level of windows that looks out over a lower roof, thereby bringing light into a tall space, as in the nave of a church.

clinker brick. A brick subjected to extreme heat and thus misshapen.

cloister. A roofed, arcaded passageway surrounding a quadrangular courtyard and connecting various monastic buildings.

cloistered vault. A vault rising from a square or polygonal base and having four curved surfaces separated by groins. Also called a coved vault or domical vault.

clustered column. A column formed by the placement of several shafts together around a central core. Pilasters can also be clustered on a wall surface.

coffer. A panel recessed in a ceiling or similar space, usually square or polygonal and in any of several materials, including stucco and stone. The whole decorative surface is called "coffering."

Collegiate Gothic. A secular form of Gothic Revival architecture popular in North America for several decades beginning in the 1890s and based on the

English Gothic style of Oxford and Cambridge collegiate buildings. Also known as the Academic Gothic style.

Colonial architecture. Architecture of the western hemisphere which was introduced from Europe during the seventeenth and eighteenth centuries. In the context of Latin America and the southwestern United States, this means Spanish and Portuguese styles, while in the eastern part of North America Colonial architecture is either Dutch Colonial, Georgian, or in the New England style.

Colonial Revival. Also called the neo-Colonial style, this usually is used in reference to the revival of North American Colonial architecture during the late nineteenth century. (*see also* Spanish Colonial Revival)

colonnade. Columns placed in a row, separated by regular intervals and carrying the weight of an entablature.

colonnette. A small column, sometimes thin and usually decorative.

colorism. The use of color.

colossal order. Columns of any order that are higher than one story. Also called "giant order."

colossus. An overly large statue, a type used in ancient temples.

column. A circular, vertical element. Although it can stand alone as a monument, a column in classical architecture has a base, shaft, and capital and functions as a support. (*see also* detached column; engaged column)

columniation. The way in which columns and the orders are used.

Commissioners era. The two decades after 1818 during which more than two hundred Greek and Gothic Revival churches were built in England under the supervision of the Commissioners appointed by Parliament.

Composite order. A column, first used by the Romans, with Ionic and Corinthian elements combined. The capital displays volutes above acanthus leaves.

compound pier. A pier formed by grouping several colonnettes or columns together.

confessio. In the early medieval period, a subterranean space containing a relic or tomb over which a church has been constructed with the altar over this space.

Congrès Internationaux d'Architecture Moderne *see* CIAM

conservatory. A structure or room, with extensive glass, used for growing and displaying plants.

console. A decorated bracket, usually curved and ending in a scroll shape, used for the support of a cornice or shelf.

Constructivism. A Russian movement in the 1920s, particularly influential in the design field, emphasizing the use of geometric shapes and industrial materials.

corbel. A stone, often elaborately carved, or masonry projecting from a wall in order to support an overhanging feature. Construction involving a series of corbels is used to create a "corbel vault."

Corinthian order. The most elaborate of the three Greek orders, the Corinthian is characterized by an acanthus leaf pattern in its bell-shaped capital.

cornice. The uppermost section of a classical entablature, or, more generally, the projecting ("crowning") molding at the top of a wall or building.

corps-de-logis. The main section of a large building, excluding wings, best seen in seventeenth- and eighteenth-century French domestic architecture.

cortile. The Italian term for an inner, arcaded courtyard in a palace or residence.

Cosmati work. A type of decorative stonework particularly common in Italian Romanesque buildings, consisting of colored stones, mosaics, and glass inlaid in marble.

cottage orné. A type of cottage popular in the late eighteenth and early nineteenth centuries in England. Based on rustic models, the *cottage orné* made conscious use of vernacular details and appealed to the middle class and sometimes to the upper class when used in a Picturesque setting.

cottage style. A style of domestic architecture, often used in a Picturesque manner, popular in the nineteenth century, first in England where it was based on traditional houses and then in the United States where it was adopted by A. J. Downing and A. J. Davis.

counterfort. A masonry pier used to support a wall or foundation from the inside, that is the side from which the thrust comes.

country house. Aside from the general meaning—a house in the country—this is a large or prominent country home of the type popular in Great Britain in the eighteenth century.

courbe Davilerte. A type of flattened arch which was made popular by Charles Daviler, a seventeenth-century French architect.

cour d'honneur. The French term for a building's forecourt.

course. A horizontal masonry row or a continuous layer of tiles or other roofing material. (*see also* belt course; stringcourse)

Court style. The sophisticated style of Gothic art and architecture in Paris during the reign of Louis IX (Saint Louis) from 1226 to 1270.

cove. A concave area, often used as a transition space or ornate molding between a wall and ceiling. Coving is also used for the arched surfaces of a cloistered vault.

creep. Deformation of a material as a result of long-term stress within or upon the structure.

crenellation. The use of masonry alternating with open spaces (crenels), normally in battlements but also as a way of decorating a roofline or wall top.

crepidoma. In Greek temple architecture, the stepped layer which serves as a base for the building. The uppermost level holds columns and is called a stylobate.

cresting. A decorative feature continuing along the top of a wall or screen and having a light, open pattern. Made of metal or stone, a crest can also be called a finial.

crocket. A Gothic ornament carved with foliage, used to decorate the angled or sloping lines of gables, pinnacles, and canopies.

crossing. The space in a cross-plan church where nave, transepts, and chancel meet.

crown. The top part of an architectural feature such as an arch, vault, or molding.

crypt. The space beneath the main floor of a church, usually under the apse. (*see also* confessio)

cryptoporticus. A portico or gallery enclosed except for windows. The term derives from Roman subterranean passages.

cupola. A dome, most often of small size.

curtain wall. In medieval architecture, the wall of a fortification connecting tower structures or surrounding a courtyard. In twentieth-century architecture, a nonsupporting wall, usually constructed of light materials and glass, fronting a building.

cusped arch. An arch with decorative tracery points (cusps) along its curve.

cut brick. Brick shaped roughly by chipping with a tool.

cyma. A molding with a double, or ogee, curve. Also spelled "sima."

cyma recta. A molding with a double curve in which the concave part forms the outer (upper) section and the convex part forms the inner (lower) section.

cyma reversa. A molding with a double curve in which the convex part forms the outer (upper) section and the concave part forms the inner (lower) section.

dado. Either the middle section of a pedestal supporting a column in classical architecture (also called a die), or, the paneling below waist height on an interior wall.

deambulatory. A covered walkway used for exercise, as in a cloister.

decastyle. In classical architecture, a portico with ten columns or rows with ten columns.

Decorated style. English Gothic architecture during the late thirteenth century and first half of the fourteenth century, known for its richness of decoration, extensive ribbing, and use of ogee curves in tracery and arches. The Decorated style followed the early English style, preceded the Perpendicular

style, and itself has two phases, the Geometric and the Curvilinear. It was revived in Great Britain in the nineteenth century.

dentil. One of a series of toothlike, square blocks used to create a decorative row (dentilation) on an Ionic, Corinthian, or Doric entablature.

De Stijl   *see* Stijl, De

detached column. A column not attached or built into a wall (engaged). A detached column is called free-standing if it is not supporting an entablature or roof.

Deutscher Werkbund   *see* Werkbund

diaconia. A hospice-type building attached to a church for use by the sick or the poor.

diapering or **diaper work.** Low-relief carving or decoration in an all-over diamond (diaper) or lozenge pattern, especially as seen on a wall.

diaphragm arch. A stone arch across a wooden roof, also called a transverse arch, the purpose of which is to segment the roof.

dipteral. Having two rows of columns on all four sides, as in ancient Greek temples.

distyle. In classical architecture, a portico with two columns between antae at either end, described as "distyle in antis."

dodecastyle. In classical architecture, a portico with twelve columns.

dogleg stair. A flight of stairs lacking a wellhole and making a half-circle turn on a landing. Also called a broken flight stair.

dome. A curved or hemispherical roof or vault on a circular or polygonal base. The term derives from the Italian word for cathedral ("duomo"). (*see also* geodesic dome; melon dome; onion dome; saucer dome; semidome)

domestic revival. The revival of interest in the design of detached single-family housing in Great Britain in the early twentieth century, when the garden city movement and town planning were primary influences.

doorcase. The framing for a doorway.

Doric order. The simplest and heaviest of the three Greek orders, the Doric is characterized by the plain circular shape of its capital and by triglyphs and metopes in the entablature.

dormer. A vertical structure built into a sloping roof, having a gable roof of its own and a window.

dovecot or **dovecote.** A small building or structure used for raising pigeons, with numerous exterior openings and roosting spaces on the inside.

dressing. The use of masonry in a decorative way, by applying a finer or carved stone to a molding or edge of a wall; also, the treatment of stone by smoothing its surface. "Dressings" are the actual moldings or bricks.

drip mold. A molding projecting from an exterior cornice for the purpose of acting as a rainspout.

dripstone. A stone molding over a door or window, which disperses rainwater. Also called a hood molding.

drum. Either the cylindrical or polygonal wall beneath a dome, or, the individual stone cylinders which constitute the shaft of a column.

Dutch Colonial architecture. The style associated with buildings built by Dutch settlers in the United States during the seventeenth century and continuing into the eighteenth century. Traditional aspects are overhanging eaves and a gambrel roof.

early Christian architecture. Architecture in western Europe and the Middle East in the centuries following the rule of Constantine the Great. The early fourth century through the sixth century saw the development of Christian architectural forms, such as the basilical church, and the beginnings of Byzantine architecture.

eaves. The bottom section of a sloping roof that extends beyond the line of intersection with the wall.

Ecclesiological movement. A mid-nineteenth-century movement in Great Britain focusing on the study of church decoration and architecture and deriving its popularity from a periodical published by the Ecclesiological Society. It is one aspect of the Gothic Revival and an influence on the "parish church revival."

eclecticism. A theory of incorporating elements from a variety of architectural styles or periods in a new building design. This practice was especially popular in Europe and the United States during the second half of the nineteenth century.

Edwardian architecture. British architecture named for Edward VII in the first decade and a half of the twentieth century, including Arts and Crafts influences, the English Free style, and a renewed interest in the baroque.

egg and dart. A motif used to decorate convex moldings, consisting of alternating, vertically placed eggs and darts.

Egyptian architecture. The architecture of ancient Egypt from c.3000 B.C. to the first century A.D. Characteristic monuments are temples, pyramids, and massive decorated columns. Periods usually are identified by kingdom or dynasty, except for the latest, the Ptolemaic period.

Egyptian Revival. A lesser aspect of the revivalism of the first half of the nineteenth century, influenced by archeological interest in ancient Egypt.

elevation. A drawing or diagram of the vertical plan of any side of a building, or, more simply, the height of a building above the ground.

Elizabethan architecture. Architecture in the second half of the sixteenth century, representing the beginning of Renaissance architecture in England. Named for Queen Elizabeth I, it exhibits ornamentation such as strapwork and mullion decoration.

Empire style. The style of neoclassical decoration popular in France from the 1790s to c.1830; so named for the First Empire (1804–1815).

enceinte. Either the walls or fortifications surrounding a town or castle, or, the area enclosed by these walls.

enfilade. The arrangement in one line of a series of doors to a group or suite of rooms.

engaged column. A column attached to or apparently partially built into a wall.

English Free style. Progressive English architecture at the beginning of the twentieth century, characterized by an informal use of nineteenth-century styles and an emphasis on vernacular traditions.

English landscape garden *see* garden style

entablature. The horizontal area of an order above the columns, composed, from top to bottom, of a cornice, frieze, and architrave.

entasis. The use of a slight convex curve on the shaft of a column to compensate for an optical illusion of concavity.

Ephesian base. A column base decorated with low-relief carving, so named after the introduction in the fourth century B.C. of this type of base at the Later Temple of Artemis, in Ephesus.

equestrian statue. A statue of a horse with a rider—of architectural interest when it is lifesize or larger and used as a monument in a public setting.

escutcheon. One of two kinds of ornament: a shield depicting a coat of arms, or, a metal plate around a door.

esquisse. A rough sketch done at the beginning of a project, comparable to a written outline for a literary work.

Etruscan architecture. Eighth through third centuries B.C. architecture in what is now Tuscany and Umbria, Italy, under the Etruscans. The few remaining monuments include tombs, temples, fortifications, and arches.

eustyle. A system of intercolumniation in which the space between columns is two and one quarter times their diameter.

exedra. A semicircular or rectangular wall recess containing a bench. First used by the Greeks, later adopted for the extension of an apse, and now applicable to any such alcove with seating.

Expressionist architecture. An architectural counterpart to Expressionism in painting and literature. The angular and sometimes sensational forms of Expressionist designs appeared in the late 1910s and early 1920s, particularly in Germany.

extrados. The outer (upper) curve of an arch.

fabbrica (pl. *fabbriche*). The Italian term for the office responsible for the construction of a building.

façade. The face or front of a building or an exterior side serving as a front by virtue of its decoration or architectural emphasis.

fan vault.   A vault composed of four conelike sections expanding toward the apex of the vault and having a pattern in which the ribs resemble the divisions of a fan.

fascia.   An undecorated horizontal band projecting slightly from a wall surface. The term is used for the architrave section of an entablature and for the board at the top of an exterior wall just under the eaves.

Federal architecture.   An American style popular from c.1790 to 1830 and characterized by classical details. Also called "Federalist architecture."

Federal Revival.   The revival in the United States, during the first decades of the twentieth century, of the Federal-style architectural forms used a century earlier.

fenestration.   The system or arrangement of windows in the wall of a building.

ferrocemento.   A type of reinforced concrete invented and used by P. L. Nervi.

ferroconcrete   *see* reinforced concrete

festoon.   A festive swag of flowers, leaves, and/or fruit tied with ribbons and hung loosely between two points. Also, a carving of this decoration.

fictive architecture.   Painting depicting architectural features so realistically that they look three-dimensional. This form of illusionism was popular in the sixteenth and seventeenth centuries, particularly in Italy.

finial.   A carved ornament at the top of a pointed architectural feature, such as a gable or spire.

Flamboyant style.   Fifteenth-century, or late Gothic, French architecture; so called because of the use of flowing or flamelike tracery.

flier.   A tread in a straight flight of stairs, where all treads have a uniform width.

flitch plate.   A steel plate used in bolting two timbers to make a larger beam (flitch beam).

floreale.   The Italian term for floral, used in reference to Art Nouveau.

fluting.   The use of decorative grooves (flutes) on the shaft of a column, usually in a vertical arrangement.

flying buttress.   A buttress consisting of a masonry arch extending out from a wall and down to a pier which absorbs the thrust.

foam concrete.   A light concrete that is produced by adding foam or a gas to the mixture before hardening occurs. The resulting material is best suited for stiffening or insulating, not supporting, uses. Also called aerated concrete, cellular concrete, or foamed concrete.

foliation.   One of two types of decoration: leaflike carvings, or, a foil pattern of cusps or circular curves as used in tracery.

Fontainebleau school   *see* school of Fontainebleau

forecourt.   A plazalike court in front of an entrance to a building or a complex of buildings.

forum.   A Roman open-air assembly and market place, comparable to the Greek agora and surrounded by colonnades and civic buildings.

François I style (Francis I style).   French architecture of the first half of the sixteenth century, best represented in the châteaux built for King Francis I in the Loire Valley and at Fontainebleau. The style was heavily influenced by Italian early Renaissance architecture.

French window.   A window which reaches to the floor and has two sections that open like doors. Also called a French door.

fret.   A repeating pattern created by straight lines intersecting at right angles, best seen in classical buildings. A single band of frets is called a key pattern.

frieze.   Either the middle section of an entablature, whether plain or carved with dentils, foliage, or human figures, or, a decorative horizontal band beneath the cornice of an interior wall.

frontispiece.   A building's façade or the section of the façade used as an entrance.

fronton.   A small ornamental pediment over a door or niche.

frosted work.   The carving of large masonry blocks with a pattern resembling icicles.

Functionalism.   An architectural philosophy emphasizing the uses (function) of a building and its parts and revealing its structure and materials. Functionalism emerged in the twentieth century and was a major principle of the International style.

Futurism.   Primarily a fine arts style, Futurism was a major movement in the 1910s in Italy and displays in its architecture an enthusiasm for modern technology and industry.

gable.   The wall space between the two sides of a sloping roof. It is triangular unless the roof is stepped or gambrel.

gallery.   A long room or passageway, inside or outside, often above the ground floor. In an auditorium a gallery contains seating; in a church it is above an aisle and opens to the nave. The term also describes a long hall for displaying art, and, in Italy, a building with shops.

gambrel roof.   A roof with a double slope on two sides. In Britain, the gambrel roof has small gables at either end.

garden city movement.   A movement in the first decade of the twentieth century, particularly in England and later Germany, to build suburban communities in which civic buildings, residences, parks, and agricultural areas are planned.

garden style.   An eighteenth- and nineteenth-century landscaping style emphasizing an informal, picturesque quality, sometimes referred to as "gardenesque" and widely known as the "English landscape garden" (*le jardin anglais, der englische Garten, il giardino inglese*). It is in direct contrast to the highly planned French formal garden.

gargoyle. A carved stone waterspout in the shape of an animal or distorted human, used to throw rainwater from the roof edge of a building. Gargoyles were first used in medieval buildings and were used decoratively in the nineteenth century.

garland. A wreath, swag, or festoon of flowers, leaves, and/or fruit draped in an ornamental manner. Also, a carving of this decoration.

gatehouse. A structure surrounding or adjacent to the gate or entrance to the grounds of a castle or estate.

gazebo. A small summerhouse or open garden structure, traditionally placed on a site with a view. If it is located on a roof or is used as a lookout tower, it is called a belvedere. If it is grand in scale or heavily decorated, it is described as a pavilion.

genre pittoresque. An aspect of eighteenth-century French rococo taste, characterized by asymmetry and organic design and showing both Italian and Oriental influences.

geodesic dome. A more or less hemispherical structure with a framework of straight, lightweight materials—widely used in the mid-twentieth century.

Georgian architecture. The dominant style of British and American architecture during the eighteenth century. It uses classical forms from the Renaissance and baroque periods and is named after the reigns of kings George I, II, and III.

Georgian Revival. The revival, in the 1890s to 1910s, of eighteenth-century British and American architecture.

Gesamtkunstwerk. A concept, formulated in the nineteenth century in Germany, expressing the potential for achieving a unity or totality of all the arts.

giant order   *see* colossal order

girandole. A support with branches for multiple candles or lights, either to place on a table or to attach to a wall.

girder. A wood or steel beam used as a principal horizontal support.

Gläserne Kette, Die. A German movement of 1919 and 1920 focusing on the shared creative writings of Bruno Taut, Walter Gropius, and twelve others who explored the role of the unconscious in architecture.

Glass Chain   *see* Gläserne Kette, Die

glazing. The use of glass in window openings.

Gothic architecture. A major development in the history of western European medieval architecture, the Gothic style followed the Romanesque, beginning in France in the twelfth century and lasting there through the fifteenth century. It is distin-

guished by the use of pointed arches, flying buttresses, window tracery, and an increasing amount of stained glass. In distant areas of Europe, Gothic architecture survived into even the eighteenth century. It was widely appreciated in the nineteenth century with the neo-Gothic or Gothic Revival.

Gothick. An eighteenth-century term for Gothic Revival.

Gothic Revival. A late eighteenth- and nineteenth-century movement in Europe and North America, continuing into the twentieth century in church and collegiate architecture. It was used for public and domestic buildings and was widely discussed from both a spiritual and an archeological point of view.

Grecian architecture   *see* Greek Revival

Greco-Roman architecture. The architecture of ancient Greece and the Roman Empire.

Greek architecture. The architecture of ancient Greece, from the seventh through first centuries B.C., characterized by the use of the orders. (*see also* Archaic architecture; Hellenistic architecture)

Greek-cross plan. A church plan consisting of a cross with four equal arms.

Greek Revival. The major form of classical revival architecture, first practiced in the late eighteenth century and at a peak of popularity c.1830.

greenbelt. In town planning, a band of parks or open land which has been protected from development.

grillage. A construction technique used especially where the ground is weak: steel, concrete, or wood beams are crossed to create a horizontal network to disperse the load over a wide area.

groin vault. A vault formed by the intersection of two equal-size barrel vaults at a right angle. The resulting curved ridges or edges within the vault are called groins.

grotesque or *grottesca*. A painted or sculpted decoration using human or animal shapes in an imaginative or distorting manner, often with foliage and sometimes creating an arabesque pattern.

grotto. A decorative cave with fountains or waterfalls, using rocks or shells for ornamentation. Often designed as part of an over-all landscape plan.

ground plan. A building plan showing the ground level.

guilloche. A pattern created by interlacing (braiding) two or three long narrow bands and leaving small round spaces between the bands.

gutta. One of a large number of cone-shaped or cylindrical ornaments (guttae) used beneath the mutules and triglyphs of a Doric entablature.

ha-ha. A sunken area like a ditch serving as an invisible fence to restrict the movement of animals, without interfering with the view. Also spelled "haw-haw."

half-timbering. A method of framing in which the wood frame supporting a building is filled in with brick or plaster.

hall church. A church with nave and aisles of the same height, and consequently without a clearstory. This plan creates an openness. It was used in the late Middle Ages.

hammerbeam roof. A roof constructed with hammer beams, which are short horizontal beams placed beneath the roof in place of tie beams for the purpose of decreasing the area to be spanned by arched braces.

Hathoric column. An Egyptian column having the face of the goddess Hathor carved on all four sides of its capital.

Hellenistic architecture. The late period of ancient Greek architecture, covering the late fourth through first centuries B.C., the time from the death of Alexander the Great to the dominance of the Romans.

hemicycle. A semicircular room or space.

herm. A rectangular post serving as a body supporting a head of Hermes. This was an ancient Greek boundary marker, used decoratively on buildings during later periods.

hermitage. A building used as a retreat or a secluded dwelling place.

hexastyle. In classical architecture, a portico with six columns.

high tech. A late twentieth-century term for a design or interior with shapes, materials, and surfaces reflecting the latest developments in technology.

hippodrome. A structure used by the Greeks for horse and chariot races, similar to but larger than the Roman circus.

hip roof. A roof with its ends sloped instead of vertical, thereby creating slopes on all four sides. Also called a hipped roof.

historiated. Having human or animal figures as decoration.

historicism. A philosophy of using past historical styles and architectural features. Since the decline of the Beaux-Arts style and the beginning of the Modern movement, there has been little expression of historicism.

hood. A protective cover over a window or door frame or above a fireplace opening.

hôtel. A French term for a large town house of the type built in Paris in the sixteenth through the eighteenth centuries.

hôtel particulier. A private town house.

housewright. A house builder.

hypostyle. A hall or large space with columns supporting a flat roof, as in ancient Egyptian temples.

ideal city. A concept, much discussed in Italian architectural treatises of the fifteenth and sixteenth centuries, of planning cities, most having radial plans and few actually realized. The philosophy re-emerged c.1900 with the garden city, the City Beautiful, and the new-town movements.

Ilkhanid period. Persian architecture in the late thirteenth and early fourteenth centuries under the Ilkhan Mongols, who continued the Islamic tradition of building mosques and mausoleums.

illusionism. The creation of an illusion of something by means of decorative or artistic techniques such as perspective. (*see also* fictive architecture; *quadratura; trompe l'oeil*)

imperial style. A style associated with the rule of an empire. Most commonly used with reference to the Roman Empire and its large-scale buildings, arches and vaulting systems of the first century B.C. through the third century A.D.

impost. A square or carved molding on which an arch rests and receiving the weight of the arch.

in antis. The position of columns on a portico of an ancient Greek temple, meaning between antae (walls) at either end.

incrustation. A decorative facing achieved by applying a thick or rich material on top of a simple base material.

inglenook. An area beside a fireplace, usually having a built-in bench for seating, like a chimney corner.

intarsia. A method of wood inlay, made popular in fifteenth- and sixteenth-century Italy, in which patterns and scenes are composed with woods of different color.

intercolumniation. The method of spacing columns, usually according to a system using multiples of the diameters of the columns.

interlace. A decoration composed of interweaving or intersecting bands.

International style. A style, first identified by this term in the 1930s, that was functional, nontraditional, and nonregional. The International style was widely recognized at the time of the 1932 International Exhibition of Modern Architecture in New York and was practiced worldwide in the 1930s, 1940s, and 1950s.

International Union of Architects *see* CIAM

Ionic order. One of the three Greek orders, the Ionic is characterized by the volutes or scroll shapes in its capital.

Isabelline Gothic style. Late Gothic architecture in Spain under Queen Isabella (1474–1504).

Islamic architecture. Architecture in the Middle East, the Mediterranean area, and parts of southern Asia under the Muslims, from the seventh through the seventeenth centuries. Characteristic building types include caravansaries, minarets, mosques, and madrasahs, and decoration is rich, with patterns of mosaic and tile.

Italianate architecture. Architecture outside of Italy, particularly in the mid-nineteenth century, emphasizing characteristics found in palazzos or villas.

Italian Movement for Rational Architecture *see* Rationalist movement

Italian villa style *see* villa style

jack arch. An arch that is horizontal or nearly so. Also called a flat arch.

Jacobean architecture. English architecture during the first half of the seventeenth century, named for James I (1603–1625). It is characterized by the use of Renaissance details and ornament in conjunction with Elizabethan forms and was revived in the mid-nineteenth century.

Jacobethan architecture. A combination of Elizabethan and Jacobean styles.

jalousie. A blind or shutter with adjustable horizontal slats, allowing for ventilation at the same time as giving privacy.

jamb. A post or vertical section forming either side of the frame for a window. The visible outer surface of the jamb is the reveal.

joist. One of several parallel horizontal beams placed from wall to wall to support floor boards and itself sometimes supported by girders.

Jugendstil. A German movement of the late 1890s and first decade of the twentieth century which corresponds to the Art Nouveau style of architecture and applied art popular elsewhere in Europe. The term means "youth style" and comes from the journal *Jugend.*

keystone. The stone in the center (apex) of an arch, often distinguished from the rest of the voussoirs by elaborate carving or greater size.

kiosk. A small open pavilion, with pillars and a balustrade, based on the Turkish *köşk* and constructed in a garden or as a newsstand or bandstand.

lamella roof. An arched roof built of numerous sections (lamellae) made of wood, concrete, or metal and intersecting at angles.

lancet or **lancet window.** A tall narrow window with a pointed arch, common in English architecture c.1200 and so named because it is shaped like the tip of a spear.

lantern. A small decorative structure with windows, built atop a roof or dome.

Latin-cross plan. A church plan consisting of three short arms and one long arm, the latter corresponding to the nave.

lattice truss. A truss with its upper and lower beams horizontal, and its braces crossing diagonally.

latticework. A decoration or surface consisting of narrow strips (laths) crossing in a diagonal pattern and leaving open spaces in between.

lazaretto. A building or hospital used to quarantine persons with contagious diseases.

lesene. A wall element consisting of a slightly projecting pilaster without a capital or base, often used in the Middle Ages in a series, possibly to strengthen the masonry. Also called a pilaster strip.

Liberty style *see* Stile Liberty

light court. A recessed area with windows in an exterior wall of a building.

lintel. A horizontal stone or beam placed over an opening, such as an architrave.

lisene *see* lesene

lodge. An association or guild of builders or craftsmen—common in the late Middle Ages—organized to regulate work and provide training.

loggia. A long colonnaded or arcaded space like a gallery, open on one or more sides.

Lombard architecture. Seventh- and eighth-century north Italian architecture, named after the Lombard kingdom and not confined to the present-day region of Lombardy.

London School Board style. A style made popular by Edward Robert Robson and John James Stevenson with their designs for school buildings in the 1870s.

Louis Quatorze style (Louis XIV style). The style of French architecture during the reign of Louis XIV (1643–1715), a period of classicism best represented in the buildings and decorations at the Palace of Versailles.

Louis Quinze style (Louis XV style). The rococo style of French architecture and decoration popular during the reign of Louis XV (1715–1774).

Louis Seize style (Louis XVI style). The period of French architecture associated with the reign of Louis XVI (1774–1792), a late rococo style emphasizing simplicity and volume in classical designs.

lunette. A semicircular wall area created by the curve of an arch or vault, which can be open, glazed, or decorated, as with a tympanum.

lych-gate. A churchyard gate with a wooden roof and open sides, used as a resting place for a coffin before continuing to the grave. Also spelled "lich gate."

madrasah. An Islamic building for students of law and theology, comparable to a seminary, having small rooms around a courtyard, and sometimes associated with a number of other buildings.

maison de plaisance. A building located on the grounds of an estate and used for pleasure, as a weekend or summer house. Also called a "plaisance" or "Lusthaus."

majestas. A representation of Christ giving the Benediction or surrounded by symbols of the four evangelists, a type often seen in an apse or tympanum.

Mannerism. A style in the architecture of Italy in the second half of the sixteenth century and to a lesser extent elsewhere in Europe. Mannerism falls between the Renaissance and baroque periods and uses classical elements in an unconventional manner.

mansard roof. A roof with a double slope on all sides, the lower section being steeper than the upper. (In Britain, the double slope is only on two sides.) So named after François Mansart.

MARS group *see* Modern Architecture Research Group

martyrium. A crypt or building to house a relic of a martyr or to mark a martyr's grave.

masjid. A Muslim building for prayer, often used synonymously with mosque.

mastaba. A type of tomb, common in Egypt in the third millennium B.C., having a rectangular shape and sloping walls, with a passage to an underground burial chamber. The term derives from the Arab for bench.

master builder. An accomplished builder who has a good knowledge of architecture and may be placed in charge of building for a civic or religious body.

mausoleum. A large tomb or a building serving as a monument to house a tomb.

Maximilianstil. Named for King Maximilian II of Bavaria, this refers to the revival of English and German late Gothic architecture encouraged by Maximilian, as seen in the façades along the Maximilianstrasse in Munich. Characteristics include the use of brick and terra cotta.

medieval architecture. The architecture of Europe from the fifth through the fifteenth centuries, including the Byzantine, Carolingian, Ottonian, pre-Romanesque, Romanesque, and Gothic styles.

meetinghouse. A place of worship, used particularly in the case of Quakers.

melon dome. A circular dome with equidistant ribs projecting down from its center. Also called a parachute, pumpkin, or umbrella dome.

mensa. The top part of an altar.

Metabolism. A style associated with a group formed in Tokyo in 1960, emphasizing the organic relationship between individual buildings and between different parts of an urban area.

metope. One of a series of squares alternating with triglyphs in the frieze of a Doric entablature.

MIAR *see* Rationalist movement

mihrab. A masonry niche or recess in a mosque, often domed and usually highly decorated, placed as a focal point on the side toward Mecca.

minaret. A tall, thin tower on or attached to a mosque, having one or more balconies used to call Muslims to prayer.

minster. A church affiliated with a monastery. The term has been retained for cathedrals that once had monastic connections.

Mir Iskusstva *see* World of Art movement

mission. A church or monastery building in Mexico or California dating from the Spanish presence in the eighteenth century.

Mission Revival. The revival, particularly in California in the 1890s and the twentieth century, of eighteenth-century Spanish religious architectural forms and materials, such as low arcades and stucco.

Modern Architecture Research Group (MARS). A group of progressive British architects and designers organized in 1932 and 1933 to represent Britain at CIAM meetings, to promote modern architectural ideas, and to conduct research.

modernism *see* Modern movement

Modernismo. A Spanish movement and variation of Art Nouveau that was centered in Barcelona in the early 1900s. Also called "Modernista" and sometimes identified as the "Catalan school."

Modern movement. With beginnings in Europe c.1900, "modern" architecture is that which is functional, rational, and nonhistorical. A second phase of modernism occurred in the 1930s, also the time when the Modern movement gained acceptance in the United States with the onset of the International style (sometimes used interchangeably with "International Modern"). In the 1960s and 1970s, a turning away from these values has been identified as Postmodernism.

modillion. One of a series of brackets used to support a cornice by projecting horizontally. It can be either a plain stone (block modillion) or carved in the shape of a scroll (like a console).

Mogul architecture. Islamic architecture in India during the two centuries after 1526. The palaces, mosques, and tombs are characterized by a mixture of Persian and Hindu construction and decoration.

molding. A linear decoration used to add a rectilinear or curved contour to a surface or an edge. Also spelled "moulding."

monitor roof. A roof with a raised section, usually at the ridge, with windows or louvers for ventilation.

Moorish architecture. Architecture in Islamic-ruled North Africa and Spain during the Middle Ages, characterized by extensive use of geometrical decoration. The Moorish style was revived in Europe during the nineteenth century.

mosque. A prayer hall for Muslims. A large one (jami) is intended to hold an entire congregation, while the smaller (masjid) is used daily and is more common. (*see also* masjid)

mudejar architecture. Architecture of the Moors in Spain during the thirteenth through fifteenth centuries, showing a mixture of Islamic and western elements.

Mughal architecture *see* Mogul architecture

mullion. The post, often structural, between vertical windows or doors.

muqarnas **vault.** A vault with a honeycomb structure created by numerous surfaces or corbels and common in Islamic buildings.

mutule.   A low inclined block projecting above the frieze in a Doric entablature and having guttae on the underside.

naiskos.   A Greek term for a small shrine.

naos.   The central area (cella) of a Greek temple, where a statue was located. Also used to describe the sanctuary of a Byzantine church with a central plan.

narthex.   The vestibule, often arcaded, across the front of a church.

National Romanticism.   A Scandinavian movement of the first decades of the twentieth century, particularly strong in Sweden, which showed a taste for the informal and the vernacular.

nave.   The hall-like center aisle of a church. Sometimes used to describe the entire area west of the crossing and east of the narthex.

necking.   A narrow band or molding on a Doric, Tuscan, or Roman Doric column beneath the capital and above the sinking or astragal at the top of the shaft.

neobaroque architecture.   The revival of baroque architecture.

neo-Byzantine style.   The revival of Byzantine architecture.

neoclassical architecture.   A style of European architecture of the late eighteenth and nineteenth centuries, showing a formal or correct use of elements and an over-all severity of form, somewhat as a reaction against the more expressive rococo style of the eighteenth century.

neo-Colonial architecture   *see* Colonial Revival

neo-Federal architecture   *see* Federal Revival

neo-Georgian architecture   *see* Georgian Revival

neo-Gothic architecture   *see* Gothic Revival

néo-grec.   A French form of the Greek Revival, developed in the 1840s and characterized by the use of brick and cast iron.

neo-Greek architecture   *see* Greek Revival

neo-Hispanic style   *see* Spanish Colonial Revival

neo-Norman architecture.   The revival of Norman architecture.

neo-Palladian architecture   *see* Palladianism

neo-Renaissance architecture   *see* Renaissance Revival

neorococo architecture.   The revival of rococo architecture.

neo-Romanesque architecture   *see* Romanesque architecture

neo-Tudor architecture.   The revival of Tudor architecture.

net vault.   A vault in which numerous ribs create a diamondlike pattern.

Neue Sachlichkeit.   A German movement, lasting from c.1923 to 1933, emphasizing a "new objectivity" in architecture. Functionalism and nonsenti-mentality in design were combined with an increase in social values.

New Brutalism   *see* Brutalism

New Empiricism.   A name for the new movement in Scandinavian architecture of the late 1940s.

New Objectivity   *see* Neue Sachlichkeit

New Tendencies   *see* Nuove Tendenze

niche.   A recess in a wall, usually used to display a statue and often highly decorated.

nogging.   Brickwork used to fill the spaces between timber framing or studs.

Norman architecture.   English architecture from the mid-eleventh century to the late twelfth century, corresponding to the Romanesque style then current in France and Germany. The name derives from the Norman Conquest of England in 1066, not from a direct use of the Normandy Romanesque style.

Novecento architecture.   Italian architecture of the twentieth century.

Novembergruppe.   A group of leftist German artists who organized in Berlin c.1919 and disbanded in the mid-1920s. Members included Expressionists, who themselves were influential later in the Bauhaus.

Nuove Tendenze **(New Tendencies).**   An Italian group organized in 1912 and holding its first exhibition in 1914.

nymphaeum.   In Roman architecture, a building containing statues of nymphs and a fountain. Generally speaking, a room with plants, fountains, and sculpture used for pleasure.

obelisk.   A tall pillar with four sloping sides and a pyramidal top, originally erected by the ancient Egyptians and decorated with hieroglyphs.

octastyle.   In classical architecture, a portico with eight columns.

oculus.   A round window.

ogee.   An s-shape or double-curve line, as in a vault or molding with a combination of concave and convex lines.

ogive.   A pointed arch, or, a diagonal rib in a vault. Used in the nineteenth century as an adjective to describe French Gothic architecture.

Old English style.   A revival in mid-nineteenth century English domestic architecture of vernacular forms such as half-timbering and local materials used in the sixteenth and seventeenth centuries.

onion dome.   A bulb-shaped dome ending in a point, common in Russian churches and in Muslim buildings.

Opbouw.   A group of Dutch architects who organized in 1920, represented CIAM functionalism for three decades, and were particularly active in Rotterdam.

orangery.   A building used for growing trees such as

oranges and thus with extensive windows on the south side.

oratory. A small private chapel, used for prayer.

order. One of the five styles in classical architecture identified by characteristics of a column and entablature. (*see also* Doric order; Ionic order; Corinthian order; Tuscan order; Composite order)

organic architecture. Architecture with shapes and structure based on natural forms and usually blending with the landscape. Theoretical interest in organic design began in the nineteenth century and is best demonstrated in twentieth-century buildings, above all by Frank Lloyd Wright.

oriel. A bay window usually above the ground floor and projecting out from the wall with corbels for support.

Oriental style. A style characterized by the use of Near Eastern and/or Asian elements or styles.

ornament. A general term for all types of architectural decoration and embellishment.

orthostat. In ancient architecture, one stone in a section of large stones at the base of a masonry wall.

Osiride pillar. An Egyptian pillar so named because a statue of the goddess Osiris is carved into or against its front.

Ottoman architecture. Architecture of the Turkish Empire for five centuries beginning in the fourteenth century, following the Seljuk period.

Ottonian architecture. Tenth- and early eleventh-century German medieval architecture, named after the Holy Roman Emperors Otto I and Otto II. It followed the Carolingian period and preceded the Romanesque style.

overdoor. A decorative section over a door, either painted or carved and having a similar frame. Also known by the Italian term *sopraporta.*

overmantel. Ornamental cabinetwork above a mantel, sometimes incorporating a mirror.

ovolo. A convex molding, usually having the shape of one quarter of a circle.

pagoda. A tall Buddhist temple having several stories with elaborate projecting roofs. Imitated in the West for garden structures.

palazzo. The Italian word for palace, used to describe a public or private building of substantial size and importance.

Palladianism. A revival style based on the buildings and publications of the sixteenth-century architect Andrea Palladio marked by ancient Roman architectural forms. It was most popular in eighteenth-century England, partially because of the publications of Lord Burlington, and is sometimes called Palladian classicism.

Palladian window *see serliana*

parapet. A low wall used at a roof edge or bordering a terrace or bridge to prevent an abrupt drop. It can be solid or elaborately carved with openings.

parterre. Either the seating area behind the orchestra in a theater, or, a low area of formal garden next to a house.

parti. The over-all concept for an architectural project.

patera. A flat or low-relief circle used in an ornamental row in a classical frieze, often depicting leaves or petals in a radial composition.

pattern book. A book of designs or plans circulated or published to enable widespread copying, a common practice in eighteenth-century England and nineteenth-century America.

pavilion. A structure, often open and ornamental, either projecting from a larger building or located in a garden and used for leisure activities.

pedestal. The structure supporting a column, statue, or monument. It consists of a plinth (base), a dado (die), and a cornice (cap molding).

pediment. The triangular gable line above an entablature and beneath a low sloping roof, or a similar decorative treatment above a window or door, sometimes having curved sides. A pediment is described as broken or split if the top (apex) or bottom (bed) is not continuous. (*see also* fronton)

pendant. An ornamental carved projection hanging from a Gothic vault or roof, particularly from a rib or molding. Also spelled "pendent."

pendentive. One of a series of concave triangles built beneath a dome to provide a structural transition to the square or polygonal area on which the dome rests.

per angolo. An angle view; applies to the use of asymmetrical and complex perspective, first used in theaters during the seventeenth century.

pergola. A garden walkway having pillars on either side, an open roof created by joists, and climbing plants trained as a cover. Also spelled "pergula."

peripteral. In classical architecture, having one row of columns on all four sides.

peristyle. A colonnade or row of columns surrounding a building or the space defined by these columns, as in a courtyard.

Perpendicular style. The third and last phase of English Gothic architecture, covering the mid-fourteenth to mid-sixteenth centuries, the last seventy years also described as "Tudor style." The Perpendicular style is characterized by a dominance of vertical elements and the development of the fan vault.

phalanstery. The buildings or the entire utopian community of followers of the French socialist Charles Fourier. Used loosely to refer to the dwellings of any socialist community.

piano nobile. The main living and reception area of a formal residence, usually above the ground floor and of greater height than the floors above. The type was developed in Italian Renaissance palazzos.

piazza.   An open square surrounded by buildings.

Picturesque movement.   A philosophy of landscape architecture in England in the late eighteenth and early nineteenth centuries characterized by the use of buildings of various styles—often asymmetrical—as focal points. Picturesque taste is based upon the informal, sometimes rugged, and "sublime" scenes depicted in French paintings.

pier.   A thick pillar or a distinct projecting section of a masonry wall built to support a heavy load. Also, a wall section between windows or doors. (*see also* compound pier)

pietra serena.   A sandstone with a bluish tint.

pilaster.   A pillar which is attached to a wall and projects only slightly. It may be a simple rectangular shape or highly decorated, with a capital and base.

pilaster strip   *see* lesene

pilastrade.   A row of pilasters.

pillar.   A pier or column, whether free-standing or supporting a structure.

pilotis.   The French term for piles extending above ground (stilts) used to support a structure, thereby creating open space at the ground level.

pinnacle.   A decorative termination to exterior building parts such as buttresses and spires, as in Gothic buildings. Usually consists of a conical or pyramidal top on a richly ornamented shaft.

plasticity.   A sculpturelike quality.

Plateresque style.   A sixteenth-century Spanish, early Renaissance style characterized by a richness of decoration and so named because it is "silversmithlike." The first phase of the Plateresque is known as the Isabelline period.

plate tracery.   Tracery with the appearance of having its openings cut through a thin layer of stone.

plaza.   In the historical sense, an open area in a city that serves as a public square.

plinth.   A thin block, usually square, serving as the bottom layer of the base of a column. Also applies to the base section of a pedestal.

Pointed architecture.   A term no longer used for Gothic architecture but popular in the mid-nineteenth century.

polychromy.   The use of a number of colors. Constructional polychromy is the application of different color building materials to create a "polychromatic" surface.

portal.   An imposing and/or decorated entrance or door.

porte cochère.   A projecting section of a porch, large enough to allow a carriage to pass through.

portico.   A roofed, colonnaded entrance to a temple or other building.

Postmodernism.   A trend, appearing in the 1960s, away from the functional aesthetic of the International style and the severity of Brutalism, and favoring a return to historical references and individualized and emotionally satisfying solutions in architectural design.

Prairie school.   A movement in the American Midwest during the early 1900s which focused on the work of Frank Lloyd Wright, and is so named for his "Prairie House" plans.

prefabricated.   Having been constructed before arrival at a building site. May apply to sections that are standardized and mass-manufactured, to be assembled quickly on site.

presbytery.   The area at the east end of a church which is behind the choir and containing the high altar.

prestressed concrete.   Concrete that has had its internal strength increased by means of tensioning steel cables (tendons) before or after casting the concrete.

priory.   A monastic community led by a prior or prioress.

pronaos.   The area in a classical temple which is behind the portico columns and in front of the naos or cella.

propylaeum.   A monumental portal or entrance to a temple, so named after the Propylaea in Athens.

propylon.   A monumental free-standing gateway with sloping sides marking the area before the pylon (entrance) to an Egyptian temple.

proscenium arch.   The broad arch over the opening to the stage, between the orchestra and the curtain, in a modern theater.

prostyle.   Having a row of free-standing columns on a portico.

pseudodipteral.   Having the appearance of two rows of columns on four sides, but with the inside row used only in the front.

pseudoperipteral.   Having the appearance of a row of columns on four sides but only the front—and sometimes rear—ones are free-standing; columns on the other sides are placed against the wall.

pulpit.   A wood or stone stand, usually raised and highly decorated and sometimes having a canopy, situated near the front of a church for use by a preacher or reader.

pumpkin vault.   A circular vault with ribs projecting out from the center. Also called an umbrella or melon vault.

Purism.   A comprehensive design concept developed in 1918 by Amédée Ozenfant and Le Corbusier in reaction to Cubism, favoring simplicity and a machine aesthetic.

pylon.   The large entrance structure of an Egyptian temple, characterized by slanting rectangular walls on either side. In modern usage, a monumental gateway.

qiblah.   The orientation toward Mecca, necessary for

Muslims during prayer (also called a kiblah or keblah). The *qiblah* wall of a mosque contains a niche called a *mihrab.*

quadratura. Ceiling or wall painting that creates an illusion, a technique commonly practiced in the baroque period by artists called *quadraturisti.*

quadrature. The division of an area, such as a vault, into four parts.

Quattrocento architecture. Italian architecture in the fifteenth century.

Queen Anne style. A style of domestic architecture popular from the 1870s through the 1890s in England and the United States. Strictly speaking, the Queen Anne was a revival of the simple vernacular architectural forms used in England in the early eighteenth century. The term is also used for houses based on Elizabethan and Tudor models, particularly in the United States.

quoin. One of a series of stones laid, usually in an alternating pattern, at the corner of an exterior wall. Quoins in theory strengthen the angle, but they may be used just for decoration. The entire vertical line of the corner may also be called a quoin.

raking. Having an inclination, as in the case of a cornice or molding that follows the slant of a roof.

rationalism. A philosophy in the eighteenth and nineteenth centuries, especially in France, favoring solutions in architectural design based on reason rather than tradition.

Rationalist movement. An Italian branch of the Modern movement of the 1920s and 1930s, known in Italy as the Movimento Italiano per l'Architecttura Razionale, or MIAR.

Rayonnant style. French Middle Gothic architecture of the thirteenth and fourteenth centuries, so named because of its round windows with radiating tracery.

reeding. The use of two or more parallel, adjacent convex moldings (reeds) for decoration; the opposite of fluting.

refectory. The dining hall in an institution such as a monastery or college.

Régence style. The elegant rococo style of decoration in France in the early eighteenth century under Philip of Orleans, regent for Louis XV from 1715 to 1723.

Regency architecture. Neoclassical architecture in England during the 1810s and 1820s, named for George IV who acted as regent for his father, George III.

regionalism. A philosophy of emphasizing the architectural characteristics of a particular region by either using local forms and/or materials or designing in a manner that develops the potential of the regional style.

reinforced concrete. The addition of steel rods to concrete in order to improve its strength, a technique perfected in the late nineteenth century. Also called ferroconcrete. (*see also ferrocemento*)

relieving arch. An arch built into the masonry to disperse weight from above a door, window, or other opening. Also called a discharging arch.

Renaissance architecture. The architecture of Italy during the fifteenth century and first half of the sixteenth century and elsewhere in Europe from the mid-sixteenth century through the early seventeenth century. The term refers to the rebirth (*rinascimento*) of classical taste. Renaissance architecture shows a return to ancient Roman orders and architectural elements. It followed the Gothic style and evolved into Mannerism in Italy and eventually into the baroque style.

Renaissance Revival. Also called neo-Renaissance, a reuse of the forms of fifteenth- and sixteenth-century Italian architecture. It was one aspect of the revivalism of the nineteenth century and became popular after the 1820s with the wide use of the palazzo and the villa styles.

Renaixensa Catalán see Catalan school

reredos. The wall-like screen, sometimes of elaborately carved wood or stone, which is placed behind an altar.

ressant. An architectural member projecting beyond another, particularly in the case of moldings. Also spelled "ressaut" or "ressault."

retable. An ornamental structure located behind an altar and decorated with reliefs, mosaics, or paintings. This sometimes includes movable wings and an elaborate architectural framework.

retrochoir. The space behind the high altar in a large church.

reveal. The vertical side of the wall facing (perpendicular to) a window or door opening, or the thickness of the wall at the opening if it lacks a door or window frame.

revivalism. A philosophy, popular in the late eighteenth and nineteenth centuries, of using earlier styles in the design of new buildings. Major types of revival architecture are the Greek and the Gothic, while a combining of styles was often used to create eclectic designs. Revival styles are often designated by the use of the prefix "neo" with a previous historical style, such as "neo-Tudor" or "neo-Futurist."

rez-de-chaussée. The ground floor.

rib. A band or molding projecting from a ceiling or vault and usually separating sections.

rib vault. A vault in which support is provided by a framework of curved ribs. Also called a ribbed vault.

ridge. The horizontal line along which the top edges of two sloping roof surfaces meet.

rilievo schiacciato. A type of very low relief used in fifteenth-century Italy. Also spelled "stiacciato."

rinceau. A decorative band, first used in classical architecture, consisting of a flowing scroll-like line with foliage.

Ring, Der. A group of radical German architects which organized in 1924 and included members from the *Novembergruppe.*

rocaille. A decorative scroll motif imitating rockwork, curving plants and shells, typical of rococo art of the mid-eighteenth century. The term was previously used as the name for the rococo style.

rock-temple. A temple built into solid rock or a cave, as in India and Egypt, using little or no masonry.

rococo architecture. An eighteenth-century style which originated and developed most fully in France. It has extensive, rich architectural decoration, usually light and elegant and employing natural motifs in the ornamentation of rooms.

Roman arch. The arch characteristic of Roman building, having a semicircular shape.

Roman architecture. The architecture of ancient Rome, from the third century B.C. to the fourth century A.D., characterized by the extensive use of arches and vaulting. (*see also* imperial style)

Romanesque architecture. The style of medieval architecture practiced in western Europe in the eleventh and twelfth centuries and characterized by the use of round arches and various large-scale vaulting systems. It followed the Ottonian period and led to the Gothic style. The Romanesque period is so called because of its use of Roman wall articulation.

Romanesque Revival. Also called neo-Romanesque, this style is the return to Romanesque forms, particularly the round arch, that occurred in the second half of the nineteenth century. In Germany, an eclectic movement called the *Rundbogenstil* used round arches. In the United States the Romanesque Revival was led in the 1870s by H. H. Richardson, whose buildings popularized a style referred to as the "Richardsonian Romanesque."

Roman Revival. The revival in the nineteenth century, especially in England and the United States, of ancient Roman architectural forms.

romanticism. A philosophy favoring a romantic interpretation of styles, popular especially in Germany in the nineteenth century. The major romantic movement, Romantic classicism, was established by the late eighteenth century and continued to c.1850. (*see also* National Romanticism)

rood screen. A wall-like screen supporting the rood (large cross) at the entrance to the chancel in the east end of a church. It can include elaborate stone or wood carvings, sculptures, and architectural features.

rose window. A circular window with a radiating tracery pattern. Also called a wheel window.

rotunda. A circular building or room, usually with a dome.

roundel. A small, circular decorative area or window, such as an oculus.

rowhouse. One house in a row of attached residences.

rubble masonry. Masonry consisting of rough stones (rubble) laid in an irregular (uncoursed) manner, as in walls or paving. Also called rubble-work.

Rundbogenstil. A mid-nineteenth century German style which employed round arches and combined Romanesque and Renaissance elements in an eclectic manner.

rustication. The use of heavy stone blocks that have been shaped to emphasize deep joints and have beveled or chamfered edges or a particular surface finish. Rusticated masonry was widely used in Renaissance Italy.

Sachlichkeit   see Neue Sachlichkeit

sacristy. A room in a church used for storing vestments and altar vessels.

Safavi architecture. Sixteenth- and seventeenth-century Iranian architecture during the Safavid dynasty, characterized by the extensive use of ceramic tile and mosaic.

sahn. In Islamic architecture, the courtyard of a mosque.

sail vault. A vault constructed over a square but without pendentives, using the four corners like fixed points for an air-filled sail.

Salomonic column. A spiral column. Also called a Solomonic column, barley-sugar column, or *salomónica.*

salon. A room, such as a fashionable drawing room, used for receiving visitors, or a hall for exhibiting art.

sanctuary. In the general sense, a sacred place; in church architecture, the area around the altar, such as a presbytery or chancel.

Saracenic architecture. A European term, meaning eastern, for Muslim architecture in general. More specifically, it refers to the Arab style of Muslim architecture. Revived in the nineteenth century.

sarcophagus. A coffin for a prominent person, usually highly decorated and often including an inscription.

saucer dome. A shallow dome, having a radius greater than its height and lacking a drum.

scaena frons. The front of the *scaena,* the structure at the rear of an ancient theater used by actors for changing costumes.

scagliola. A plaster which has pigmented marble chips or dust, such as gypsum, added to produce a mottled coloring, in imitation of marble or other stone.

scenae frons   see scaena frons

school of Fontainebleau. A group of Italian architects, stuccoists, and mural painters who were invited by King Francis I of France to decorate his palace at Fontainebleau in the 1530s. The richness of their work made the Fontainebleau school a major influence in Renaissance architectural decoration elsewhere in Europe. Sometimes called the "First school" to distinguish it from a later group.

sconce. An ornamental light designed like a bracketed candleholder to mount on a wall. In military architecture, an earthwork for defense.

Scottish Baronial style. A style practiced in Scotland in the mid-nineteenth century favoring large and romantic designs based on earlier Scottish buildings.

screen. A partition to separate areas of activity, as with choir screens or rood screens.

Secession. An Austrian movement of the 1890s which was a version of the Art Nouveau then popular in France and Belgium. The name *Sezession* derives from the decision of its adherents to secede from the Academy of Art in Vienna.

Second Empire style. An eclectic style popularized in France under Napoleon III in the 1850s and 1860s by the large-scale development and building in Paris. Second Empire architecture is characterized by the use of mansard roofs and pavilions.

Seicento architecture. Italian architecture in the seventeenth century.

semidome. Half a dome, used as a roof for an apse or other semicircular space.

serliana. A window with three vertical sections separated by pilasters or columns, named for Sebastiano Serlio. The middle section is wider and is usually topped by an arch. This motif also is used for nonwindow openings and can be called a Palladian motif or Venetian motif.

Sezession *see* Secession

sgraffito. A technique for creating patterns in plasterwork in which the exterior layer is incised or scratched to reveal a different color layer.

shaft. The tall, central section of a column, also called a trunk, located between the base and capital and usually having a cylindrical shape.

shell construction. Construction consisting of curved sections assembled like a membrane around a space which remains unfilled.

Shingle style. An American style of domestic architecture first used in the late 1870s and popular on both coasts and in the Midwest during the 1880s. It is characterized by the use of shingles on both roofs and walls and an informality and fluidity in exterior wall surfaces. Influences were American Colonial buildings and the work of English architects such as R. Norman Shaw and Philip Webb.

Shoin style. Japanese architecture incorporating a writing area into the main room of a residence, a plan established in the sixteenth century.

sima *see* cyma

skeleton construction. Construction in which the weight is borne by the framework and not by the walls.

Socialist Realism. The official style of art and architecture in the U.S.S.R. since the 1930s.

socle. A low, plain pedestal or plinth base.

soffit. The visible underside of any raised part of a building, such as a lintel or cornice. When speaking of the inner curve of an arch, the soffit is also called an intrados.

spandrel. A triangular area adjacent to an arch and created by the horizontal line from the crown (apex), the vertical line from the springer, and the curve of the extrados, or by the space between two arches in an arcade.

Spanish Colonial Revival. A style, practiced particularly in California during the 1910s and 1920s, that reuses the Colonial styles that were introduced by Spanish settlers to Latin America and the southwestern United States during the seventeenth and eighteenth centuries. This is sometimes referred to as the Spanish Revival or Spanish style.

spire. The tall, pointed top of a tower or roof, usually having an octagonal shape.

split pediment *see* pediment

springer. The lowest stone on either side of an arch and resting on an impost, from which the arch appears to spring. The height or line of the springer is called a springing line.

squinch. An arch, or system of arches, built across an upper corner of a square space to aid in supporting a polygonal or circular structure.

stanchion. A vertical post used for support of a roof or other building part.

standing seam. A method of overlapping two pieces of metal on a roof.

stave. One of several thin strips of wood used to construct a curved surface, such as the side of a barrel.

steeple. The tall structure on a church, a combination of a tower and a spire.

stele. A vertical stone, carved and usually having an inscription, used as a tombstone or a memorial.

Stick style. An American style of Victorian domestic architecture that emphasizes the frame of a wood building, its flat vertical boards (called "stickwork"), and details such as verandas. First used in the 1860s, the Stick style derived from the English Picturesque style and was popular in the East and Midwest through the early 1870s. It is sometimes referred to as the Eastlake style.

Stijl, De. A Dutch group of artists and designers who came together in 1917. Architecture associated with the movement shows a nonsubjective, geometrical style emphasizing space and using primary colors.

Stile Liberty. An Italian movement of the 1890s to 1910s corresponding to the French Art Nouveau. The name derives from the Liberty and Company department store in London. It is sometimes identified as the *Stile Floreale.*

stoa.   The Greek term for a detached colonnade comparable to a portico.

strapwork.   An ornament made by an interlace pattern of bands resembling leather straps.

stringcourse.   A horizontal layer of masonry, on the exterior of a building, which may project or have different dimensions and/or distinctive carving.

strip window.   One window in a horizontal band of windows; also called a ribbon window.

strut.   In framing, a brace placed in any direction to resist thrust; the opposite of a tie.

style Louis XV, le   *see* Louis Quinze style

style moderne, le   *see* Art Nouveau

stylobate.   The top layer of the stepped base of a Greek temple, or, loosely, any surface supporting columns.

Sublime.   An aesthetic concept applied to literature and art popular in England and France during the eighteenth century. Sublimity was discussed along with Beauty and was an ideal in landscape design and the use of nature.

sukiya.   A style of Japanese architecture showing the influence of the traditional teahouse, including the use of unfinished materials to create a natural effect.

Suleiman architecture.   Turkish architecture under Suleiman the Magnificent in the sixteenth century, a period of great building.

sun-break   *see* brise-soleil

superposition.   The use of the different classical orders in different stories, with one over the other, usually beginning with Doric and up to Ionic and Corinthian. Also called supercolumniation.

surround.   A border or enclosure functioning like a frame.

tabernacle.   A niche with much carving and usually having a canopy, or an ornamental shelter on an altar.

tabularium.   A building to house public archives, as in ancient Rome. Also called an archivium.

tambour.   A drum shape, as under a cupola or within a Corinthian or Composite capital.

Team 10.   An international group of architects who organized in the mid-1950s, introducing new ideas to CIAM at its 1956 meeting, and consequently influencing the breakup of the congress.

tectonic.   Relating to construction or building.

tempietto.   A small temple, particularly one that is circular and/or ornamental, as was popular in Renaissance Italy.

template.   In masonry construction, a stone placed horizontally at the top of a wall to receive and distribute weight from joists.

temple.   A building for purposes of worship or in recognition of a deity. (*see also* rock-temple)

tepidarium.   A heated room in Roman thermae.

term.   Either a "terminal figure"—a head or a bust sculpted onto a downward tapering pedestal—or a "terminus"—a bust or top half of a body that merges with a block, bracket, or other decorative feature.

tessera.   One of the numerous small cubes of colored stone, glass, or tile used in a mosaic.

tetrastyle.   In classical architecture, a portico with a row or rows of four columns.

thermae.   Thermae—the Latin word for "baths"—are a major type of public building in the Roman period, having a number of rooms for exercising and bathing at different temperatures, with the two sexes separate.

tholos.   A round domed building, as found in early Greek tombs, or the dome itself.

thrust.   The force exerted upon a load-bearing structure, such as a wall bearing the weight of an arch.

tiburio.   A polygonal structure crowned by a roof over a flat dome, a type common in early Christian and Byzantine church architecture and adapted as a crossing tower in the fifteenth and sixteenth centuries.

tie.   In construction, a lateral connection between two points, such as a tie in framing.

tie beam.   A beam used in roofing to span the distance between opposite points beneath rafters, thus strengthening the entire roof.

timber framing.   The wood skeletal structure of a building, including roofing, flooring, walls, and partitions, before it is filled in.

tondo.   A circular painting or carving.

torus.   A convex, circular molding which is the bottom part of the base of a column and sits on a plinth.

tourelle   *see* turret

town house.   A city residence, often attached to the buildings on either side.

trabeated.   Having post and lintel construction, as opposed to arcuated construction.

tracery.   A pattern made by the stonework and openings in a window, panel, vault, or screen for the purpose of decoration. Increasingly complex patterns were used in Gothic buildings over three centuries. (*see also* bar tracery; plate tracery)

transept.   In a church with a cross plan, one of two arms that intersect the nave and choir axis, thereby creating a square area called a crossing.

transverse section.   A vertical plan of the inside of a building, taken at a right angle to the longitudinal axis. Also called a cross section.

Trecento architecture.   Italian architecture during the fourteenth century.

tribunal.   A raised place of honor or judge's seat at the end of a Roman basilica, often having a semicircular wall.

tribune.   A raised platform used by a speaker, or, in

church architecture, an apse. Less commonly used for the gallery of a church.

triconch. A room or building having conchlike niches with half-domes on three sides.

triforium. A narrow hall in a church above the aisle and beneath the clearstory, like a gallery but having an arcade—usually with three sections—opening to the nave area. Also called a blind story because it lacks windows.

triglyph. One of a series of blocks, carved with three vertical channels, alternating with metopes in the frieze of a Doric entablature.

tripartite. Having three sections.

triumphal arch. An arch built by the Romans to commemorate a victory and hence usually erected along a processional route. The type often had extensive relief sculpture and has been imitated during later periods.

trompe l'oeil. A visual illusion achieved artistically, particularly in painting. Fictive architecture and *quadratura* are two such techniques used in architecture.

truss. In framing, a wood or steel structure, usually triangular with inner triangular sections, used for spanning openings where heavy loads exist. (*see also* lattice truss; Warren truss)

Tudor architecture. English late Gothic architecture during the reigns of Henry VII and Henry VIII (1485–1547), a final phase of the Perpendicular style and predecessor of the Elizabethan style. Revived in the nineteenth century, sometimes in a "Tudor-Gothic" style.

tunnel vault   *see* barrel vault

turret. A small tower, often built at a corner and sometimes containing stairs or projecting slightly from the rest of the wall with corbels. In the latter case, the turret is identified by the French term *tourelle.*

Tuscan order. One of the classical orders, the Tuscan is a simplified version of the Doric and the Roman Doric, with a base and an unfluted shaft.

Tuscan villa style   *see* villa style

tympanum. The triangular space formed by a pediment, or, in medieval architecture, the semicircular space formed by an arch and the lintel of the door beneath it.

urbanism. Interest in and study of urban life and development.

Usonian house. A design for a modest-size house introduced by Frank Lloyd Wright in the 1930s and based on his "Prairie House" plans.

valley. The diagonal line along which the lower edges of two sloping roof surfaces intersect. It functions as a trough to discharge water.

vault. A masonry roof built up by an arch or arches. (*see also* annular vault; barrel vault; cloistered vault; fan vault; groin vault; *muqarnas* vault; net vault;

pumpkin vault; rib vault; sail vault)

veduta. A type of topographical view developed in seventeenth- and eighteenth-century Italy, depicting buildings and landscapes with great accuracy. Painters of such views are called *vedutisti.*

veduta per angolo   *see per angolo*

velarium. A large awning over the seating area of a Roman amphitheater or theater, supported by masts and beams.

Venetian window   *see serliana*

veranda. A long, roofed porch or balcony, sometimes partially enclosed.

vergeboard   *see* bargeboard

vernacular architecture. Architecture representative of local or regional types and using traditional materials. "Vernacular revival" architecture became particularly popular in England in the nineteenth century.

Victorian architecture. Architecture in Great Britain and the United States from c.1830 to c.1901, named after Queen Victoria. Revival and eclectic philosophies, particularly the Gothic Revival, were a major force in the Victorian period.

villa style. A nineteenth-century style used for prominent country houses in Britain and the United States, based on rural Italian models, particularly those in Tuscany. Characteristics include a low roof, rounded windows, and an informal plan with wings.

volute. A spiral scroll used decoratively as in an Ionic capital.

Vorarlberg school. A seventeenth-century regional Austrian school of builder-architects famous for its monastery church plan (*Vorarlberger Münsterschema*) in which free-standing pillars assume a wall-like character and emphasize the longitudinal space.

votive church. A church erected for purposes of prayer and services dedicated to vows.

voussoir. A masonry block that is wedge-shaped to fit into the curve of an arch.

Warren truss. A truss with parallel upper and lower beams, with a triangular pattern created by the connecting braces.

wattlework. Construction by interlacing twigs and branches, as in wickerwork; used especially for fences.

Werkbund. A movement of designers and craftsmen that originated in 1907 with the formation of the Deutscher Werkbund in Munich. Its major activity was exhibitions and its goals were similar to those of the English Arts and Crafts artists. Similar associations appeared in Austria and Switzerland about five years later. After over a decade of inactivity due to the war, the Deutscher Werkbund organized again in the late 1940s.

Werkstätte   *see* Wiener Werkstätte

Wiener Werkstätte. A society of craftsmen founded

in 1903 in Vienna to promote quality in design and decoration.

winder.   A stair tread which is wider at one edge than the other for the purpose of changing the direction of a staircase.

World of Art movement.   A Russian avant-garde movement founded in the 1890s and coinciding with the Art Nouveau style popular elsewhere in Europe. So named for the journal *Mir Iskusstva*.

wrought iron.   Iron with a low carbon content, which is sufficiently soft to be easily worked and less subject to rusting than is cast iron or steel. It was a common material for ornamental ironwork through the eighteenth century and was largely replaced for this purpose in the early nineteenth century by mass-produced cast iron.

Index of Names

In the name index, CAPITAL LETTERS indicate the subjects of biographies in the encyclopedia; **boldface** indicates volume numbers.

This index is alphabetized letter by letter (e.g. Newport before New York). The buildings, structures, monuments, or projects are listed by their most commonly known name. Since, however, they do not always have proper names, the reader should also consult the location, such as Beverley Minster, and the generic type, such as courthouse, cathedral, and church. In the case of the latter, the listing may appear under the name of the Saint to whom the church is dedicated.

Index of Works